COMPUTER SECURITY HANDBOOK

Fifth Edition

Volume 1

Edited by

SEYMOUR BOSWORTH

M.E. KABAY

ERIC WHYNE

WILEY

John Wiley & Sons, Inc.

Library of Congress Cataloging-in-Publication Data

Computer security handbook. – 5th ed. / edited by Seymour Bosworth, M.E. Kabay, Eric Whyne.
    p. cm.
  Includes index.
  ISBN 978-0-471-71652-5 ((paper) (set)) – ISBN 978-0-470-32722-7 ((vol 1)) – ISBN 978-0-470-32723-4 ((vol 2))   1. Electronic data processing departments–Security measures.   I. Bosworth, Seymour.   II. Kabay, Michel E.   III. Whyne, Eric, 1981–
  HF5548.37.C64 2009
  658.4′78–dc22

                                                                          2008040626

Printed in the United States of America

10   9   8   7   6   5   4   3   2   1

COMPUTER SECURITY HANDBOOK

CONTENTS

41.   Antivirus Technology
Chey Cobb and Allysa Myers

42.   Protecting Digital Rights: Technical Approaches
Robert Guess, Jennifer Hadley, Steven Lovaas, and Diane E. Levine

PART IV   PREVENTION: HUMAN FACTORS

43.   Ethical Decision Making and High Technology
James Landon Linderman

44.   Security Policy Guidelines
M. E. Kabay and Bridgitt Robertson

45.   Employment Practices and Policies
M. E. Kabay and Bridgitt Robertson

46.   Vulnerability Assessment
Rebecca Gurley Bace

47.   Operations Security and Production Controls
M. E. Kabay, Don Holden, and Myles Walsh

48.   E-Mail and Internet Use Policies
M. E. Kabay and Nicholas Takacs

49.   Implementing a Security Awareness Program
K. Rudolph

50.   Using Social Psychology to Implement Security Policies
M. E. Kabay, Bridgitt Robertson, Mani Akella, and D. T. Lang

51.   Security Standards for Products
Paul J. Brusil and Noel Zakin

PART V   DETECTING SECURITY BREACHES

52.   Application Controls
Myles Walsh

53.   Monitoring and Control Systems
Caleb S. Coggins and Diane E. Levine

54.   Security Audits, Standards, and Inspections
Donald Glass, Chris Davis, John Mason, David Gursky, James
Thomas, Wendy Carr, and Diane Levine

55.   Cyber Investigation
Peter Stephenson

PREFACE

Computers are an integral part of our economic, social, professional, governmental, and military infrastructures. They have become necessities in virtually every area of modern life, but their vulnerability is of increasing concern. Computer-based systems are constantly under threats of inadvertent error and acts of nature as well as those attributable to unethical, immoral, and criminal activities. It is the purpose of this *Computer Security Handbook* to provide guidance in recognizing these threats, eliminating them where possible and, if not, then to lessen any losses attributable to them.

This *Handbook* will be most valuable to those directly responsible for computer, network, or information security as well as those who must design, install, and maintain secure systems. It will be equally important to those managers whose operating functions can be affected by breaches in security and to those executives who are responsible for protecting the assets that have been entrusted to them.

With the advent of desktop, laptop, and handheld computers, and with the vast international networks that interconnect them, the nature and extent of threats to computer security have grown almost beyond measure. In order to encompass this unprecedented expansion, the *Computer Security Handbook* has grown apace.

When the first edition of the *Handbook* was published, its entire focus was on mainframe computers, the only type then in widespread use. The second edition recognized the advent of small computers, while the third edition placed increased emphasis on PCs and networks.

Edition	Publication Date	Chapters	Text Pages
First	1973	12	162
Second	1988	19	383
Third	1995	23	571
Fourth	2002	54	1,184
Fifth	2009	77	2,040

The fourth edition of the *Computer Security Handbook* gave almost equal attention to mainframes and microcomputers.

This fifth edition has been as great a step forward as the fourth. With 77 chapters and the work of 86 authors, we have increased coverage in both breadth and depth. We now cover all 10 domains of the Common Body of Knowledge defined by the International Information Systems Security Certification Consortium (ISC)[2]:

1. Security Management Practices: Chapters 10, 12, 13, 14, 15, 19, 10, 31, 43, 44, 45, 46, 47, 48, 49, 50, 51, 54, 55, 62, 63, 64, 65, 66, 67, 68, 74, 75, 76

2. Security Architecture and Models: Chapters 1, 2, 3, 8, 9, 24, 26, 27, 51
3. Access Control Systems and Methodology: Chapters 15, 19, 28, 29, 32
4. Application Development Security: Chapters 13, 19, 21, 30, 38, 39, 52, 53
5. Operations Security: Chapters 13, 14, 15, 19, 21, 24, 36, 40, 47, 53, 57
6. Physical Security: Chapters 4, 13, 15, 19, 22, 23, 28, 29
7. Cryptography: Chapters 7, 32, 37, 42
8. Telecomm, Networks, and Internet Security: Chapters 4, 5, 6, 13, 14, 15, 16, 17, 18, 20, 21, 24, 25, 26, 27, 30, 31, 32, 33, 34, 35, 41, 48
9. Business Continuity Planning: Chapters 22, 23, 56, 57, 58, 59, 60
10. Law, Investigations, and Ethics: Chapters 11, 12, 13, 31, 42, 61, 63, 64, 69, 70, 71, 72, 73

In addition to updating every chapter of the fourth edition, we have added chapters on:

- History of Computer Crime
- Hardware Elements of Security
- Data Communications and Information Security
- Network Topologies, Protocols, and Design
- Encryption
- Mathematical Models of Information Security
- The Dangerous Information Technology Insider: Psychological Characteristics and Career Patterns
- Social Engineering and Low-Tech Attacks
- Spam, Phishing, and Trojans: Attacks Meant to Fool
- Biometric Authentication
- Web Monitoring and Content Filtering
- Virtual Private Networks and Secure Remote Access
- 802.11 Wireless LAN Security
- Securing VoIP
- Securing P2P, IM, SMS, and Collaboration Tools
- Securing Stored Data
- Writing Secure Code
- Managing Software Patches and Vulnerabilities
- U.S. Legal and Regulatory Security Issues
- The Role of the CISO
- Developing Classification Policies for Data
- Outsourcing and Security
- Expert Witnesses and the *Daubert* Challenge
- Professional Certification and Training in Information Assurance
- Undergraduate and Graduate Education in Information Assurance
- European Graduate Work in Information Assurance and the Bologna Declaration

We have continued our practice from the fourth edition of inviting a security luminary to write the final chapter, "The Future of Information Assurance." We are pleased to include a stellar contribution from Dr. Peter G. Neumann in this edition.

SEYMOUR BOSWORTH
Senior Editor
January 2009

ACKNOWLEDGMENTS

Seymour Bosworth, Senior Editor   I would like to give grateful recognition to Arthur Hutt and Douglas Hoyt, my coeditors of the first, second, and third editions of this *Handbook*. Although both Art and Doug are deceased, their commitment and their competence remain as constant reminders that nothing less than excellence is acceptable. Mich Kabay, my coeditor from the fourth edition, and Eric Whyne, our new third editor, continue in that tradition. I would not have wanted to undertake this project without them.

We mark with sadness the passing of our friend and colleague Robert Jacobson, who contributed to Chapter 1 (Brief History and Mission of Information System Security) and wrote Chapter 62 (Risk Assessment and Risk Management). Bob was a significant and valued contributor to the development of our field, and we miss his cheerful intelligence. We also miss Diane Levine, who contributed so much to both the third and fourth editions. She wrote four chapters in the third edition and six in the fourth. We are honored to continue to list her as a coauthor on five updated chapters in the fifth edition.

Thanks are also due to our colleagues at John Wiley & Sons: Tim Burgard as Acquisitions Editor, Stacey Rympa as Development Editor, Natasha Andrews-Noel as Senior Production Editor, and Debra Manette as Copyeditor and Joe Ruddick as Proofreader. All have performed their duties in an exemplary manner and with unfailing kindness, courtesy, and professionalism.

M. E. Kabay, Technical Editor   The contributions from my faculty colleagues and from our alumni in the Master of Science in Information Assurance (MSIA) program at Norwich University are noteworthy. Many of the *Handbook*'s authors are graduates of the MSIA program, instructors in the program, or both.

I am immeasurably grateful to Sy for his leadership in this project. In addition to the inherent value of his decades of experience in the field of information security, his insightful editorial comments and queries have forced everyone on the project to strive for excellence in all aspects of our work. He is also fun to work with!

Our coeditor Eric Whyne has loyally persevered in his editorial tasks despite ducking bullets in the war in Iraq, where he has served honorably throughout most of the project. Our thanks to him for his service to the nation and to this project.

Our authors deserve enormous credit for the professional way in which they responded to our requests, outlines, suggestions, corrections, and nagging. I want to express my personal gratitude and appreciation for their courteous, collaborative, and responsive interactions with us.

Finally, as always, I want to thank my beloved wife, Deborah Black, light of my life, for her support and understanding over the years that this project has taken away from our time together.

Eric Whyne, Associate Editor   There is an enormous amount of work put into a text of this size. The diligent and gifted authors who have contributed their time are some of the brightest and most experienced professionals in their fields. They did so not for compensation but because they love the subjects which they have put so much effort into mastering. The *Computer Security Handbook* will continue its tradition of being a collection point for these labors so long as there are great minds in love with the challenging problems of computer security and willing to devote their time to sharing solutions.

At the time I started on the project, I was a Marine Officer working in the data communications field in Ramadi, Iraq. I worked the night shift and spent my afternoons perched in a folding chair, under the relatively cool Iraq winter sun, writing correspondence and doing first-past edits of the chapters of the *Handbook*. Upon my return to the United States, my spare evenings along the North Carolina coast were dedicated to the *Handbook* as I worked my day job as the Marine Corps Anti-Terrorism Battalion Communications Officer. Since then I have deployed once more to Iraq as an advisor to the Iraqi Army. Everywhere I have gone, and with every job I have held, I have been able to apply and refine the principles covered in this *Handbook* and in previous versions. From the most high-tech cutting-edge, multiplexed satellite communications system used in military operations in Iraq, to the relatively mundane desktop computer networks of offices in the United States, to the ancient weathered computers the Iraqi Army totes around with them and ties into the power grid at any opportunity, computer security is critical to the accomplishment of the most basic tasks these systems are used for.

Unarguably, the exchange of information and ideas has been the largest factor in the shaping and betterment of our world throughout history. Having spent the last year of my life living as a local in a third-world country, that fact is fresh on my mind. In that spirit, computers are recognized as the most powerful and universally applicable tool ever devised. This book's purpose is to help you ensure that your computers remain powerful and successfully applied to the tasks for which you intend them to be used.

I am grateful to Sy Bosworth and Mich Kabay for their faith in bringing me into this project, and for their guidance and leadership along the way. They are both great people, and it has been an honor and a joy to work with them.

ABOUT THE EDITORS

Seymour Bosworth, MS, CDP (e-mail: *sybosworth55@gmail.com*) is president of S. Bosworth & Associates, Plainview, New York, a management consulting firm specializing in computing applications for banking, commerce, and industry. Since 1972, he has been a contributing editor of all five editions of the *Computer Security Handbook,* and he has written many articles and lectured extensively about computer security and other technical and managerial subjects. He has been responsible for design and manufacture, systems analysis, programming, and operations, of both digital and analog computers. For his technical contributions, including an error-computing calibrator, a programming aid, and an analog-to-digital converter, he has been granted a number of patents, and is working on several others.

Bosworth is a former president and CEO of Computer Corporation of America, manufacturers of computers for scientific and engineering applications; president of Abbey Electronics Corporation, manufacturers of precision electronic instruments and digital devices; and president of Alpha Data Processing Corporation, a general-purpose computer service bureau. As a vice president at Bankers Trust company, he had overall responsibility for computer operations, including security concerns.

For more than 20 years, Bosworth was an Adjunct Associate Professor of Management at the Information Technologies Institute of New York University, where he lectured on computer security and related disciplines. He has conducted many seminars and training sessions for the Battelle Institute, New York University, the Negotiation Institute, the American Management Association, and other prestigious organizations. For many years he served as Arbitrator, Chief Arbitrator, and Panelist for the American Arbitration Association. He holds a Master's degree from the Graduate School of Business of Columbia University and the Certificate in Data Processing of the Data Processing Management Association.

M. E. Kabay, PhD, CISSP-ISSMP (e-mail: *mekabay@gmail.com*) has been programming since 1966. In 1976, he received his PhD from Dartmouth College in applied statistics and invertebrate zoology. After joining a compiler and relational database team in 1979, he worked for Hewlett Packard (Canada) Ltd. from 1980 through 1983 as an HP3000 operating system performance specialist and then ran operations at a large service bureau in Montréal in the mid-1980s before founding his own operations management consultancy. From 1986 to 1996, he was an adjunct instructor in the John Abbott College professional programs in Programming and in Technical Support. He was Director of Education for the National Computer Security Association from 1991 to the end of 1999 and was Security Leader for the INFOSEC Group of AtomicTangerine, Inc., from January 2000 to June 2001. In July 2001, he joined the faculty at Norwich University as Associate Professor of Computer Information Systems in the

School of Business and Management. In January 2002, he took on additional duties as the director of the graduate program in information assurance in the School of Graduate Studies at Norwich, where he is also Chief Technical Officer.

Kabay was inducted into the Information Systems Security Association Hall of Fame in 2004. He has published over 950 articles in operations management and security in several trade journals. He currently writes two columns a week for *Network World Security Strategies*; archives are at *www.networkworld.com/newsletters/sec/*. He has a Web site with freely available teaching materials and papers at *www2.norwich.edu/mkabay/index.htm*.

Eric Whyne (e-mail: *ericwhyne@gmail.com*) is a Captain in the United States Marine Corps. He joined the Marine Corps in the Signals Intelligence field and received two meritorious promotions before being selected for an officer candidate program and finally commissioning into the communications occupational specialty. His billets have included commanding a data communications platoon, managing large-scale communications networks, advising the Iraqi Army, and serving as the senior communications officer for the Marine Corps Anti-Terrorism unit. Whyne holds a BS in Computer Science from Norwich University as well as minor degrees in Mathematics, Information Assurance, and Engineering. He has presented about communications security and other technology topics at many forums and worked as a researcher for the National Center for Counter-Terrorism and Cyber Crime Research. After nine honorable years of service and two tours to Iraq totaling 18 months, Whyne is transitioning out of the military and pursuing a career in the civilian industry in order to more effectively and freely apply his skills and abilities to cutting-edge technological trends and problems.

ABOUT THE CONTRIBUTORS

Mani Akella, Director (Technology), has been actively working with information security architectures and identity protection for Consultantgurus and its clients. An industry professional for 20 years, Akella has worked with hardware, software, networking, and all the associated technologies that service information in all of its incarnations and aspects. Over the years, he has developed a particular affinity for international data law and understanding people and why they do what they do (or do not). He firmly believes that the best law and policy is that which understands and accounts for cross-cultural differences, and works with an understanding of culture and societal influences. To that end, he has been actively working with all his clients and business acquaintances to improve security policies and make them more people-friendly: His experience has been that the best policy is that which works with, instead of being anagonistic to, the end user.

Rebecca Gurley Bace is the President/CEO of Infidel, Inc., a strategic consulting practice headquartered in Scotts Valley, California. She is also a venture consultant for Palo Alto–based Trident Capital, where she is credited with building Trident's investment portfolio of security product and service firms. Her areas of expertise include intrusion detection and prevention, vulnerability analysis and mitigation, and the technical transfer of information security research results to the commercial product realm. Prior to transitioning to the commercial world, Bace worked in the public sector, first at the National Security Agency, where she led the Intrusion Detection research program, then at the Computing Division of the Los Alamos National Laboratory, where she served as Deputy Security Officer. Bace's publishing credits include two books, an NIST Special Publication on intrusion detection and prevention, and numerous articles on information security technology topics.

Susan Baumes, MS, CISSP, is an information security professional working in the financial services industry. In her current role, Ms. Baumes works across the enterprise to develop information security awareness and is responsible for application security. Her role also extends to policy development, compliance and audit. She has 11 years experience in application development, systems and network administration, database management, and information security. Previously, Ms. Baumes worked in a number of different sectors including government (federal and state), academia and retail.

Kurt Baumgarten, CISA (e-mail: *kurtb@peritussecurity.com*) is Vice President of Information Security and a partner at Peritus Security Partners, LLC, a leader in providing compliance-driven information security solutions. He is also a lecturer, consultant, and the developer of the DDIPS intrusion prevention technology as well as a pioneer in using best practices frameworks for the improvement of information technology security programs and management systems. Baumgarten has authored multiple articles about the business benefits of sound information technology and information assurance practices, and assists businesses and government agencies in defining strategic plans that enhance IT and IA as positive value chain modifiers. He holds both a Master's of Science in Information Assurance and an MBA with a concentration in E-Commerce, and serves as an Adjunct Professor of Information Assurance. He has more than 20 years of experience in IT infrastructure and Information Security and is an active member of ISSA, ISACA, ISSSP, and the MIT Enterprise Forum. Baumgarten periodically acts as an interim Director within external organizations in order to facilitate strategic operational changes in IT and Information Security.

Kevin Beets has been a Research Scientist with McAfee for the past five years. His work has concentrated on vulnerability and malware research and documentation with the Foundstone R&D and Avert Labs teams. Prior to working at McAfee, he architected private LANs as well as built, monitored, and supported CheckPoint and PIX firewalls and RealSecure IDS systems.

Matt Bishop is a Professor in the Department of Computer Science at the University of California at Davis and a Codirector of the Computer Security Laboratory. His main research area is the analysis of vulnerabilities in computer systems, especially their origin, detection, and remediation. He also studies network security, policy modeling, and electronic voting. His textbook, *Computer Security: Art and Science,* is widely used in advanced undergraduate and graduate courses. He received his PhD in computer science from Purdue University, where he specialized in computer security, in 1984.

Kip Boyle is the Chief Information Security Officer of PEMCO Insurance, a $350 million property, casualty, and life insurance company serving the Pacific Northwest. Prior to joining PEMCO Insurance, he held such positions as Chief Security Officer for a $50 million national credit card transaction processor and technology service provider; Authentication and Encryption Product Manager for Cable & Wireless America; Senior Security Architect for Digital Island, Inc.; and a Senior Consultant in the Information Security Group at Stanford Research Institute (SRI) Consulting. He has also held director-level positions in information systems and network security for the U.S. Air Force. Boyle is a Certified Information System Security Professional and Certified Information Security Manager. He holds a Bachelor's of Science in Computer Information Systems from the University of Tampa (where he was an Air Force ROTC Distinguished Graduate) and a Master's of Science in Management from Troy State University.

Timothy Braithwaite has more than 30 years of hands-on experience in all aspects of automated information processing and communications. He is currently Deputy Director of Strategic Programs at the Center for Information Assurance of Titan Corporation. Before joining Titan, he managed most aspects of information technology, including data and communications centers, software development projects, strategic planning and budget organizations, system security programs, and quality improvement initiatives. His pioneering work in computer systems and communications security while with the Department of Defense resulted in his selection to be the first Systems Security Officer for the Social Security Administration (SSA) in 1980. After developing security policy and establishing a nationwide network of regional security officers,

Braithwaite directed the risk assessment of all payment systems for the agency. In 1982, he assumed the duties of Deputy Director, Systems Planning and Control of the SSA, where he performed substantive reviews of all major acquisitions for the Associate Commissioner for Systems and, through a facilitation process, personally led the development of the first Strategic Systems Plan for the administration. In 1984, he became Director of Information and Communication Services for the Bureau of Alcohol, Tobacco, and Firearms at the Department of Treasury. In the private sector, he worked in senior technical and business development positions for SAGE Federal Systems, a software development company; Validity Corporation, a testing and independent validation and verification company; and J.G. Van Dyke & Associates, where he was Director, Y2K Testing Services. He was recruited to join Titan Corporation in December 1999 to assist in establishing and growing the company's Information Assurance practice.

Paul J. Brusil, PhD (e-mail: *brusil@post.harvard.edu*) founded Strategic Management Directions, a security and enterprise management consultancy in Beverly, Massachusetts. He has been working with various industry and government sectors including healthcare, telecommunications, and middleware to improve the specification, implementation, and use of trustworthy, quality, security-related products and systems. He supported strategic planning that led to the National Information Assurance Partnership and other industry forums created to understand, promote, and use the Common Criteria to develop security and assurance requirements and to evaluate products. Brusil has organized, convened, and chaired several national workshops, conferences, and international symposia pertinent to management and security. Through these and other efforts to stimulate awareness and cooperation among competing market forces, he spearheaded industry's development of the initial open, secure, convergent, standards-based network and enterprise management solutions. While at the MITRE Corp, Brusil led research and development critical to the commercialization of the world's first LAN solutions. Earlier, at Harvard, he pioneered research leading to noninvasive diagnosis of cardiopulmonary dysfunction. He is a Senior Member of the IEEE, a member of the Editorial Advisory Board of the *Journal of Network and Systems Management* (*JNSM*), has been Senior Technical Editor for *JNSM*, is the Guest Editor for all *JNSM*'s Special Issues on Security and Management, and is a Lead Instructor for the Adjunct Faculty supporting the Master's of Science in Information Assurance degree program at Norwich University. He has authored over 100 papers and book chapters. He graduated from Harvard University with a joint degree in Engineering and Medicine.

David Brussin is Founder and CEO of Monetate, Inc. Monetate powers Intelligent Personal Promotions™ for online retailers. Brussin is a serial entrepreneur recognized as a leading information security and technology expert, and was honored by MIT's *Technology Review* as one of the world's 100 top young innovators. In January 2004, Brussin cofounded TurnTide, Inc. around the antispam router technology he had invented. As Chief Technology Officer, he also managed engineering and technical operations. TurnTide was acquired by Symantec six months later. Previously, Brussin cofounded and served as Chief Technology Officer for ePrivacy Group, Inc., which created the Trusted Sender program and Trusted Email Open Standard to protect and grow the e-mail marketing channel. Brussin created products to help e-mail marketers increase response and conversion by protecting their trusted relationship with consumers. In 1996, he cofounded and served as Vice President of Technology for InfoSec Labs, an information security company dedicated to helping Fortune 1000 companies safely transition their businesses into the online world. Partnering with his clients, Brussin balanced security with the emerging technical challenges of doing business online and helped many established bricks-and-mortar businesses become multichannel. InfoSec Labs was acquired by Rainbow Technologies, now part of SafeNet, in 1999. Brussin is a frequent speaker and writer on entrepreneurship and technology. He also serves on the Board of Directors of Invite Media, Inc., a stealth-mode start-up working to analyze and optimize online display advertising.

Michael Buglewicz spent approximately 10 years in law enforcement carrying out a variety of duties, from front-line patrol work through complex investigations. After concluding his law enforcement career. Buglewicz brought his experiences to technology and held a variety of roles within First Data Corporation, including Internet banking and online payment systems. Buglewicz has worked for Microsoft Corporation since 1996 in a variety of roles and has taught in Norwich University's Information Assurance program. Buglewicz holds an undergraduate degree in Fine Arts from the University of Nebraska at Omaha and graduate degrees from Illinois State University as well as a Master's degree in Information Assurance from Norwich University. His current interests focus on corporate risk management.

Nancy Callahan is Vice President, AIG Executive Liability, Financial Institutions Division. AIG is the world's leading international insurance and financial services organization, with operations in approximately 130 countries and jurisdictions. AIG member companies serve commercial, institutional, and individual customers through the most extensive worldwide property-casualty and life insurance networks of any insurer. An expert on privacy and identity theft, Callahan is a frequent speaker at industry conferences throughout the United States and is a much-sought-after media resource, having been quoted in the *Wall Street Journal* and Associated Press. Callahan joined AIG in 2001. Prior to AIG, Callahan worked in e-commerce and financial services. She spent 13 years at Reuters, where her final position was Executive Vice President, Money Transaction Systems. Callahan is a Chartered Property and Casualty Underwriter and Certified Information Privacy Professional. She has a Master's of Business Administration and a BS in Systems Engineering from the University of Virginia.

Q. Campbell (e-mail: *qcampbell@hushmail.com*) has worked in the information security field for over six years. He specializes in information technology threat analysis and education.

Wendy Carr, CISSP (e-mail: *wendylcarr@gmail.com*) is a Senior Consultant with Booz, Allen & Hamilton on a client-site in New England. Her focus on addressing security concerns related to the implementation of products and applications includes concentrations in the areas of Certification and Accreditation (Commercial/DITSCAP/DIACAP), risk analysis, compliance testing and vulnerability assessment, forensic examination, incident response, disaster recovery, authentication, and encryption for both physical and wireless environments in the fields of Military, Government and Banking. She holds an MS in Information Assurance from Norwich University and is a member of (ISC)^2, InfraGard, and the Norwich University *Journal of Information Assurance* Editorial Review Board as well as several organizations dedicated to the advancement of information security.

Santosh Chokhani (e-mail: *schokhani@cygnacom.com*) is the Founder and President of CygnaCom Solutions, Inc., an Entrust company specializing in PKI. He has made numerous contributions to PKI technology and related standards, including trust models, security, and policy and revocation processing. He is the inventor of the PKI Certificate Policy and Certification Practices Statement Framework. His pioneering work in this area led to the Internet RFC that is used as the standard for CP and CPS by governments and industry throughout the world. Before starting CygnaCom, he worked for The MITRE Corporation from 1978 to 1994. At MITRE, he was senior technical manager and managed a variety of technology research, development, and engineering projects in the areas of PKI, computer security, expert systems, image processing, and computer graphics. Chokhani obtained his Master's (1971) and PhD (1975) in Electrical Engineering/Computer Science from Rutgers University, where he was a Louis Bevior Fellow from 1971 to 1973.

Christopher Christian is an aviator in the United States Army. He received a Bachelor's degree in Computer Information Systems at Norwich University class of 2005. His primary focus of study was Information Assurance and Security. He worked as an intern for an engineering consulting company for three years. He developed cost/analysis worksheets and floor-plan layouts to maximize workspace efficiency for companies in various industries. Christian graduated flight school at Fort Rucker, Alabama, there he trained on the H-60 Blackhawk. He serves as a Flight Platoon Leader in an Air Assault Battalion. First Lieutenant Christian is currently serving in Iraq in support of Operation Iraqi Freedom 08–09.

Chey Cobb, CISSP (e-mail: *cheycobb@gmail.com*) began her career in information security while at the National Computer Security Association (now known as TruSecure/ICSA Labs). During her tenure as the NCSA award–winning Webmaster, she realized that Web servers often created security holes in networks and became an outspoken advocate of systems security. Later, while developing secure networks for the Air Force in Florida, her work captured the attention of the U.S. intelligence agencies. Cobb moved to Virginia and began working for the government as the Senior Technical Security Advisor on highly classified projects. Ultimately, she went on to manage the security program at an overseas site. Cobb, who is now semiretired, writes books and articles on computer security and is a frequent speaker at security conferences.

Stephen Cobb, CISSP (e-mail: *sc@cobbassociates.com*) is an independent information security consultant and an Adjunct Professor of Information Assurance at Norwich University, Vermont. A graduate of the University of Leeds, Cobb's areas of expertise include risk assessment, computer fraud, data privacy, business continuity management, and security awareness and education. A frequent speaker and seminar leader at industry conferences around the world, Cobb is the author of numerous books on security and privacy as well as hundreds of articles. Cobb cofounded several security companies whose products expanded the range of security solutions available to enterprises and government agencies. As a consultant, he has advised some of the world's largest companies on how to maximize the benefits of information technology by minimizing IT risks.

Caleb S. Coggins, MSIA, CISSP, is a Corporate Auditor for Bridgestone Americas. His areas of interest include vulnerability management, network security, and information assurance. Prior to Bridgestone, Coggins served as the Information Manager for a private company as well as an information security consultant to business clients. He holds a BA from Willamette University and an MS in Information Assurance from Norwich University.

Bernie Cowens, CISSP, CISA (e-mail: *bcowens@usa.com*) is Chief Information Security Officer at a Fortune 500 company in the financial services industry. He is an information risk, privacy, and security expert with more than 20 years experience in industries including defense, high technology, healthcare, financial, and Big Four professional services. Cowens has created, trained, and led a number of computer emergency, forensic investigation, and incident response teams over the years. He has real-world experience responding to attacks, disasters, and failures resulting from a variety of sources, including malicious attackers, criminals, and foreign governments. He has served as an advisor to and a member of national-level panels charged with analyzing cyber-system threats to critical infrastructures, assessing associated risks, and recommending both technical and nontechnical mitigation policies and procedures. Cowens holds a Master's degree in Management Information Systems along with undergraduate degrees and certificates in systems management and information processing.

Christopher Dantos is a Senior Architectural Specialist with Computer Science Corporation's Global Security Solutions Group. His areas of expertise include 802.11, VoIP, and Web application security. Prior to joining CSC, he spent 10 years as a Security Architect with Motorola Inc., including 5 years in the Motorola Labs Wireless Access Research Center of Excellence. He holds a Master's of Science degree in Information Assurance from Norwich University and a Bachelor's of Science degree in Marine Engineering from the Maine Maritime Academy.

Chris Davis, CISA, CISSP, has trained and presented in information security, advanced computer forensic analysis, hardware security design, auditing, and certification curriculum for government, corporate, and university requirements. He was part of the teams responsible for Hacking Exposed Computer Forensics, IT Auditing: Using Controls to Protect Information Assets, and the Anti-Hacker Toolkit. His contributions include projects and presentations for SANS, Gartner, Harvard, BlackHat, CEIC, and 3GSM. He has enjoyed positions at ForeScout, Texas Instruments, Microsoft Technology Center, and Cisco Systems. He holds a Bachelor's degree in Nuclear Engineering Technologies from Thomas Edison, and a Master's in Business from the University of Texas at Austin.

Seth Finkelstein (e-mail: *sethf@sethf.com)* is a professional programmer with degrees in Mathematics and in Physics from MIT. He cofounded the Censorware Project, an anti-censorware advocacy group. In 1998, his efforts evaluating the sites blocked by the library's Internet policy in Loudoun County, Virginia, helped the American Civil Liberties Union win a federal lawsuit challenging the policy. In 2001, he received a Pioneer of the Electronic Frontier Award from the Electronic Frontier Foundation for his groundbreaking work in analyzing content-blocking software. In 2003, he was primarily responsible for winning a temporary exemption in the Digital Millennium Copyright Act allowing for the analysis of censorware.

Urs E. Gattiker is an internationally-renowned security and risk technologist, both a Founder and the Chief Technology Officer of CyTRAP Labs GmbH. CyTRAP Labs provides corporate governance and social media services to organizations worldwide. Using sophisticated analysis and correlation tools, CyTRAP Labs' expert Internet Analysts monitor suspicious internal and external activities, user and community behavior, business goals, and web technology to craft and deliver long term successful web and corporate risk management programs for companies.

Urs is the inventor of the ComMetrics benchmark battery of tools. One of these, the FT/ComMetrics corporate blog index, empowers the FT Global 500 companies to compare the value of their blogging activities against to that target information security prevention and safety, with other enterprises. He is the author and co-author of several books on computer viruses, technology and risk management. Gattiker holds a PhD in business focusing on computing/informatics and an MBA (international marketing) both from Claremont Graduate University (Claremont Colleges) and a BS in public administration/informatics from the HWV Zurich.

Robert Gezelter, CDP, has over 33 years of experience in computing, starting with programming scientific/technical problems. Shortly thereafter, his focus shifted to operating systems, networks, security, and related matters, where he has 32 years of experience in systems architecture, programming, and management. He has worked extensively in systems architecture, security, internals, and networks, ranging from high-level strategic issues to the low-level specification, design, and implementation of device protocols and embedded firmware.

Gezelter is an alumnus of the IEEE Computer Society's Distinguished Visitor Program for North America, having been appointed to a three-year term in 2004. His appointment included numerous presentations at Computer Society chapters throughout North America.

He has published numerous articles, appearing in *Hardcopy, Computer Purchasing Update, Network Computing, Open Systems Today, Digital Systems Journal,* and *Network World.* He is a frequent presenter at conference sessions on operating systems, languages, security, networks, and related topics at local, regional, national, and international conferences, speaking for DECUS, Encompass, IEEE, ISSA, ISACA, and others. He previously authored the mobile code and Internet-related chapters for the 4th edition of this *Handbook* (2002) as well as the "Internet Security" chapters of the 3rd edition (1995) and its supplement (1997).

He is a graduate of New York University with BA (1981) and MS (1983) degrees in Computer Science. Gezelter founded his consulting practice in 1978, working with clients both locally and internationally. He maintains his offices in Flushing, New York. He may be contacted via his firm's www site at www.rlgsc.com.

Anup K. Ghosh is President and Chief Executive of Secure Command, LLC, a security software start-up developing next-generation Internet security products for corporate networks. Ghosh also holds a position as Research Professor at George Mason University. Ghosh was previously Senior Scientist and Program Manager in the Advanced Technology Office of the Defense Advanced Research Projects Agency (DARPA), where he managed an extensive portfolio of information assurance and information operations programs. Ghosh previously served in executive management as Vice President of Research at Cigital, Inc. He has served as principal investigator on contracts from DARPA, NSA, and NIST's Advanced Technology Program and has written more than 40 peer-reviewed conference and journal articles. Ghosh is also author of three books on computer network defense and serves on the editorial board of *IEEE Security and Privacy Magazine* and has been guest editor for *IEEE Software* and *IEEE Journal* *on Selected Areas in Communications.* Ghosh is a Senior Member of the IEEE. For his contributions to the Department of Defense's information assurance, Ghosh was awarded the Frank B. Rowlett Trophy for Individual Contributions by the National Security Agency in November 2005, a federal government–wide award. He was also awarded the Office of the Secretary of Defense Medal for Exceptional Public Service for his contributions while at DARPA. In 2005, Worcester Polytechnic Institute awarded Ghosh its Hobart Newell Award for Outstanding Contributions to the Electrical and Computer Engineering Profession. Ghosh has previously been awarded the IEEE's Millennium Medal for Outstanding Contributions to E-Commerce Security. Ghosh completed his PhD and Master of Science in Electrical Engineering at the University of Virginia and his Bachelor of Science in Electrical Engineering at Worcester Polytechnic Institute.

Donald Glass, CISA, CISSP (e-mail: *donald@donaldglass.com*) has over 15 years of experience in the IT Auditing and Information Security fields. He's the current Director of IT Audit for Kerzner International. Author of several information security and IT audit articles, Donald is recognized as a leader in the IT audit field and information security.

Robert Guess is a Senior Security Engineer at a Fortune 500 firm and an Associate Professor of Information Systems Technology. Guess possesses a Master's of Science in Information Assurance from Norwich University and has over a dozen industry certifications, including the National Security Agency INFOSEC Assessment Methodology, National Security Agency INFOSEC Evaluation Methodology, and Certified Information Systems Security Practitioner. His professional efforts include work in the defense sector, serving as primary subject matter expert on a National Science Foundation Cybersecurity Education Grant, and the development of Department of Defense workforce certification standards for information assurance professionals. Guess's work in recent years has focused on security assessment, penetration testing, incident response, and the forensic analysis of digital evidence.

David Gursky is an Information Assurance manager and researcher at Raytheon Integrated Defense Systems working in Crystal City, Virginia. He is principal investigator for behavior-based intrusion detection systems, attribute-based access control, and resource-efficient authentication techniques. He held several senior positions as a Department of Defense Contractor supporting Information Assurance programs and has over 30 years' experience in information technology and information security. He has conducted numerous security audits for PriceWaterhouse and Coopers. Gursky has Bachelor's of Science degree in Business Management from Southern New Hampshire University, a Master's of Science degree from Norwich University, and an MBA from from Northeastern University. In addition, he holds a CISA, CISM and CISSP certifications. He lives in Northern Virginia and is an active member of $(ISC)^2$ and ISACA.

Jennifer Hadley (e-mail: *hadley.jennifer@gmail.com*) is a member of the first Master of Science in Information Assurance graduating class at Norwich University. She is the primary Systems and Security Consultant for Indiana Networking in Lafayette, Indiana, and has served as both a network and systems administrator in higher education and private consulting. She has almost 10 years' experience as a programmer and instructor of Web technologies with additional interests in data backup, virtualization, authentication/identification, monitoring, desktop and server deployment, and incident response. At present Hadley serves as a Technology Consultant for Axcell Technologies, Inc. Previously she worked as a tester for quality and performance projects for Google, Inc., and as a collegiate adjunct instructor in computer technologies. Hadley received a Bachelor's of Science degree in Industrial and Computer Technology from Purdue University.

Carl Hallberg, CISSP, has been a Unix Systems Administrator for years as well as an Information Security Consultant. He has also written training courses for subjects including firewalls, VPNs, and home network security. He has a Bachelor's degree in Psychology. Currently he is a senior member of an incident response team for a major U.S. financial institution.

Kevin Henry has been involved in computers since 1976, when he was an operator on the largest minicomputer system in Canada. He has since worked in many areas of information technology, including computer programming, systems analysis, and information technology audit. Henry was asked to become Director of Security based on the evidence of his audits and involvement in promoting secure IT operations. Following 20 years in the telecommunications field, Henry moved to a Senior Auditor position with the State of Oregon, where he was a member of the Governor's IT Security Subcommittee and performed audits on courts and court-related IT systems.

Henry has extensive experience in Risk Management and Business Continuity and Disaster Recovery Planning. He frequently presents papers at industry events and conferences and is on the preferred speakers list for nearly every major security conference. Since joining (ISC)^2 as their first full-time Program Manager in 2002, Henry has been responsible for research and development of new certifications, courseware, and development of educational programs and instructors. He has also been providing support services and consulting for organizations that require in-depth risk analysis and assistance with specific security-related challenges. This has led to numerous consulting engagements in the Middle East and Asia for large telecommunications firms, government departments, and commercial enterprises.

Don Holden is a Principal Consultant with Concordant specializing in information security. He has more than 20 years of management experience in information systems, security, encryption, business continuity, and disaster recovery planning in both industry and government. Previously he was a Technology Leader for RedSiren Technologies (formerly SRI Consulting). Holden's achievements include leading a cyber-insurance joint venture project, developing privacy and encryption policies for major financial institutions, and recommending standards-based information technology security policies for a federal financial regulator. Holden is an Adjunct Professor for the Norwich University's Master's of Science in Information Assurance. He received an MBA from Wharton and is a Certified Information System Security Professional and Information System Security Management Professional.

John D. Howard is a former Air Force engineer and test pilot who currently works in the Security and Networking Research Group at the Sandia National Laboratories, Livermore, California. His projects include development of the SecureLink software for automatic encryption of network connections. He has extensive experience in systems development, including an aircraft–ground collision avoidance system for which he holds a patent. He is a graduate of the Air Force Academy, has Master's degrees in both Aeronautical Engineering and Political Science, and has a PhD in Engineering and Public Policy from Carnegie Mellon University.

Arthur E. Hutt, CCEP. The late Arthur E. Hutt was an information systems consultant with extensive experience in banking, industry, and government. He served as a contributing editor to the 1st, 2nd, and 3rd Editions of the Computer Security Handbook. He was a principal of PAGE Assured Systems, Inc., a consulting group specializing in security and control of information systems and contingency/disaster recovery planning. He was a senior information systems executive for several major banks active in domestic and international banking. His innovative and pioneering development of online banking systems received international recognition. He was also noted for his contributions to computer security and to information systems planning for municipal government. He was on the faculty of the City University of New York and served as a consultant to CUNY on curriculum and on data processing management. He also served on the mayor's technical advisory panel for the City of New York. Hutt was active in development of national and international technical standards, via ANSI and ISO, for the banking industry.

Robert V. Jacobson, CPP, CISSP, deceased was the President of International Security Technology, Inc., a New York City–based risk management consulting firm. Jacobson founded IST in 1978 to develop and apply superior risk management systems. Current and past government and industry clients are located in the United States, Europe, Africa, Asia, and the Middle East. Jacobson pioneered many of the basic computer security concepts now in general use. He served as the first Information System Security Officer at Chemical Bank, now known as J P Morgan Chase. He was a frequent lecturer and had written numerous technical articles. Mr. Jacobson held BS and MS degrees from Yale University, and was a Certified Information Systems Security Professional. He was also a Certified Protection Professional of the American Society for Industrial Security. He was a member of the National Fire Protection Association and the Information Systems Security Association. In 1991, he received the Fitzgerald Memorial Award for Excellence in Security from the New York Chapter of the ISSA.

David J. Johnson is an information security analyst for a Fortune 1000 financial services company where he focuses primarily on information security policy and standard creation and maintenance. Additionally, he also performs analysis of information technology projects, as well as IT and business processes, for security and business continuity impact and system vulnerability management. Johnson's prior work includes nine years designing, building, and maintaining an electronic commerce (EC/EDI) infrastructure and data transfers for a national financial service company. He holds a Bachelor's of Science in Business Administration from Oregon State University and a Master's of Science in Information Assurance from Norwich University.

Sean Kelley is an Adjunct Professor in Information Assurance (IA) for Norwich and Troy University. He also teaches IA and management conferences for the SANS Institute. His information security career is diversified and has taken him to high-level organizations in Washington, DC, including the Attending Physician's Office to Congress, U.S. Capitol, where he was responsible for the development of policy and controls for the secure handling of electronic health records for 535 members of Congress, Supreme Court Justices, and officials. Kelley is a Certified Information

Systems Security Professional and PMP and also holds several NSA certificates. Kelley also holds a Master's degree from Webster University in Computer Resources and Information Management and a second Master's degree from the Naval Postgraduate School in Information Technology, where he concentrated on computer and network security by taking classes through the NPS Center for INFOSEC Studies and Research.

David M. Kennedy, CISSP (e-mail: *david.kennedy@acm.org*) is TruSecure Corporation's Chief of Research. He directs the Research Group to provide expert services to TruSecure Corporation members, clients, and staff. He supervises the Information Security Reconnaissance (IS/R) team, which collects security-relevant information, both above- and underground in TruSecure Corporation's IS/R data collection. IS/R provides biweekly and special topic reports to IS/R subscribers. Kennedy is a retired U.S. Army Military Police officer. In his last tour of duty, he was responsible for enterprise security of five LANs with Internet access and over 3,000 personal computers and workstations. He holds a BS in Forensic Science.

Gary C. Kessler is an Associate Professor of Computer and Digital Forensics and Coordination of Information Assurance Education at Champlain College in Burlington, Vermont, where he is also the Director of the Champlain College Center for Digital Investigation. Kessler is a technical consultant to the Vermont Internet Crimes Task Force and a member of the High Technology Crime Investigation Association and High Tech Crime Consortium; he is also a Certified Information Systems Security Professional and Certified Computer Examiner. Kessler is a frequent speaker at industry conferences, has written two books and over 70 articles on a variety of technology topics, and is an Associate Editor of the *Journal of Digital Forensic Practice* and serves on the editorial board of the *Journal of Digital Forensics, Security, and Law.* He holds a BA in Mathematics, an MS in Computer Science, an EdS in Computing Technology in Education, and is pursuing a doctorate degree.

David A. Land. In the U.S. Army as a Counterintelligence Special Agent, Land and David Christie developed and hosted the first Department of Defense Computer Crimes Conference. Since then Land has investigated espionage cases for both the Army and the Department of Energy. He serves as the Information Technology Coordinator for Anniston City Schools in Alabama and as an Adjunct Professor for Norwich University, his alma mater.

D. T. Lang served in the United States Air Force, retiring as a Special Agent in Charge. As a Special Agent he worked in the areas of antiterrorism, executive and force protection, counterintelligence and counterespionage. Lang is a combat veteran of Operation Desert Storm and was charged with the Joint Force Protection Team for the United Nations Implementation Forces in Zagreb, Croatia. In the 1990s, he held diplomatic status as a U.S. Arms Control Treaty Inspector. In 2003, he was selected by the United Nations to be a UN weapons of mass destruction inspector in Iraq. Lang currently provides consulting support to the U.S. Intelligence Community and served as a senior instructor in the Master's of Science in Information Assurance Program at Norwich University from 2005 to 2008. Lang is a past commander of Civil Air Patrol's Wyoming Wing and a recipient of the Civil Air Patrol Distinguished Service Medal.

David R. Lease, PhD is the Chief Solution Architect at Computer Sciences Corporation. He has over 30 years of technical and management experience in the information technology, security, telecommunications, and consulting industries. Lease's recent projects include a $2 billion security architecture redesign for a federal law enforcement agency and the design and implementation of a secure financial management system for an organization operating in 85 countries. Lease is a writer and frequent speaker at conferences for organizations in the intelligence community, Department of Defense, civilian federal agencies, as well as commercial and academic organizations. He is also a peer reviewer of technical research for the IEEE Computer Society. Additionally, Lease is on the faculty of Norwich University and the University of Fairfax, where he teaches graduate-level information assurance courses and supervises doctoral-level research.

Corinne Lefrançois is an Information Assurance Analyst at the National Security Agency. She graduated from Norwich University with a Bachelor of Science in Business Administration and Accounting in 2004 and is a current student in Norwich University's Master of Science in Information Assurance program.

Diane ("Dione") E. Levine, CISSP, CFE, FBCI, CPS, deceased, was the President/CEO of Strategic Systems Management, Ltd., and one of the developers of the Certification for Information Systems Security Professionals. She had a notable career in information security as both a developer and implementer of enterprise security systems. Levine held a series of high-level risk management and security positions in major financial institutions, spent many years as an Adjunct Professor at New York University, and was widely published in both the trade and academic press. She contributed numerous chapters to the Third and Fourth Editions of the *Computer Security Handbook*. Ms. Levine split her time between security and business continuity consulting, writing, and teaching worldwide. She was a frequent public speaker and a member of technical panels and regularly contributed articles and columns to *Information Week, Information Security, Internet Week, Planet IT, ST&D, internet.com* and *Smart Computing*. Levine was Active in the Information Systems Security Association (ISSA), the Association of Certified Fraud Examiners (ASFE), the Business Continuity Institute (BCI), the Contingency Planning Exchange (CPE), and the Information Security Auditing and Control Association (ISACA) and had devoted many years serving on the Board of Directors of these organizations.

James Landon Linderman, PhD (e-mail: *jlinderman@aol.com*) is an Associate Professor in the Computer Information Systems department at Bentley College, Waltham, Massachusetts, where he has taught for 30 years. He is a Research Fellow at Bentley's Center for Business Ethics, and past Vice-Chair of the Faculty Senate. A resident of Fitzwilliam, New Hampshire, Linderman is a Permanent Deacon in the Roman Catholic Diocese of Worcester, Massachusetts, and a consultant in the area of computer-assisted academic scheduling and timetable construction.

Steven Lovaas, MSIA, CISSP, is the Information Technology Security Manager for Colorado State University. His areas of expertise include IT security policy and architecture, communication and teaching of complex technical concepts, and security issues in both K–12 and higher education. He has taught for the MS program in Information Assurance at Norwich University, and is pursuing a PhD in Public Communications and Technology at Colorado State University. Lovaas currently holds the position of Editor in Chief for the Norwich University *Journal of Information Assurance*. As part of his volunteer commitment to educating the next generation of scientists and engineers, he coaches, judges, and writes exams for the Science Olympiad program in Colorado.

Vic Maconachy, PhD, assumed the position of Vice President for Academic Affairs/ Chief Academic Officer at Capitol College, Laurel, Maryland, in October 2007. Maconachy is charged with sustaining and enhancing the academic quality of programs of study ranging from Business Administration through Engineering, Computer Science, and Information Assurance. He also oversees the operations of the Library and the Space Operations Institute. Maconachy holds the rank of Professor and teaches graduate and undergraduate research courses in information assurance.

Prior to joining Capitol College, Maconachy served at the National Security Agency in several leadership positions. He was appointed by the Director of the NSA as the Deputy Senior Computer Science Authority, where he built a development program for a new generation of Cryptologic Computer Scientists. Prior to this position, Maconachy served as the Director of the National Information Assurance Education and Training Program (www.nsa.gov/ia/academia/acade00001.cfm). He was responsible for implementing a multidimensional, interagency program, providing direct support and guidance to the services, major Department of Defense components, federal agencies, and the greater national information infrastructure community. This program fosters the development and implementation of information assurance training programs as well as graduate and undergraduate education curricula. In this capacity, he served on several national-level government working groups as well as in an advisory capacity to several universities. Maconachy was the principal architect for several national INFOSEC training standards in the national security systems community. During his time at the NSA, he held many different positions, including work as an INFOSEC Operations Officer, INFOSEC Analyst and a Senior INFOSEC Education and Training Officer.

Prior to joining the NSA, Maconachy worked for the Department of Navy. He developed and implemented INFOSEC training programs for users and system maintainers of sophisticated cryptographic equipment. He also served as the Officer in Charge of several INFOSEC-related operations for the Department of Navy, earning him the Department of Navy Distinguished Civilian Service medal. Maconachy holds a PhD from the University of Maryland. He has numerous publications and awards related to information assurance and is the recipient of the prestigious National Cryptologic Meritorious Service Medal.

John Mason is a Manager for SingerLewak's Enterprise Risk Management Group. He has over 20 years of combined experience in internal audit, regulatory compliance, information security, investigations, and process reengineering. He has held senior positions, such as Chief Internal Auditor and Vice President of Audit and Compliance in a variety of companies. While at two multibillion-dollar institutions, he was the Chief Information Security Officer and helped establish information risk management programs as well as designed risk-based audit programs several years before Sarbanes-Oxley. Mason has routinely authored, reviewed, and researched finance control policies and procedures. He has performed audits for governmental agencies and managed a full spectrum of financial, operational, SOX compliance, and data processing audits. He possesses an MBA and numerous certificates, including a CISM, CISA, CFE, CBA, CFSA, and CFSSP and is an Adjunct Professor in Norwich University's Master's of Science in Information Assurance program.

Peter Mell is a senior computer scientist in the Computer Security Division at the National Institute of Standards and Technology. He is the Program Manager for the National Vulnerability Database as well as the Security Content Automation Protocol validation program. These programs are widely adopted within the U.S. government and used for standardizing and automating vulnerability and configuration management, measurement, and policy compliance checking. He has written the NIST publications on patching, malware, intrusion detection, common vulnerability scoring system, and the common vulnerabilities and exposures standard. Mell's research experience includes the areas of intrusion detection systems, vulnerability scoring, and vulnerability databases.

Michael Miora has designed and assessed secure, survivable, highly robust systems for Industry and government over the past 30 years. Miora, one of the original professionals granted the Certified Information Systems Security Professional in the 1990s and the ISSMP in 2004, was accepted as a Fellow of the Business Continuity Institute in 2005. Miora founded and currently serves as President of ContingenZ Corporation. Michael Miora was educated at the University of California, Los Angeles and Berkeley, earning Bachelor's and Master's in Mathematics. He is an Adjunct Professor at Norwich University in the MS Information Assurance program and serves on the editorial boards of the Norwich University *Journal of Information Assurance* and the *Business Continuity Journal.*

Allysa Myers is the Director of Research for West Coast Labs. Her primary responsibilities are researching and analyzing technology and security threat trends as well as reviewing and developing test methodologies. Prior to joining West Coast Labs, Myers spent 10 years working in the Avert group at McAfee Security, Inc. While there, she wrote for the Avert blog and *Sage* magazine, plus several external publications. She also provided training demonstrations to new researchers within McAfee along with other groups such as the Department of Defense and McAfee Technical Support and Anti-Spyware teams. Myers has been a member of various security industry groups, such as the Wildlist and the Drone Armies mailing list.

Scott J. Nathan, Esq. (e-mail: *sjnathan@mindspring.com*) is an attorney whose practice includes litigation concerning intellectual property and technology matters, computer fraud and abuse, and environmental and insurance coverage matters involving the exchange of millions of pages of documents. In addition, he advises clients about, among other things, Internet-related risks and risk avoidance, proprietary and open source software licensing, service-level agreements, and insurance coverage. Nathan has written and spoken extensively about such issues as online privacy, cyberspace jurisdiction, and the legal issues surrounding the use of open source software. He is admitted to practice before the United States Supreme Court, the United States Court of Appeals for the First Circuit, the Federal District Court for the District of Massachusetts, and the Courts of the Commonwealth of Massachusetts. Nathan is a member of the American Bar Association's Litigation and Computer Litigation Committees.

Carl Ness, MS, CISSP, is a Senior Security Analyst for the University of Iowa. Ness has more than 10 years' experience in the information technology and information security fields, mainly in the academic and healthcare sector. He is a speaker, author, and educator on information assurance, including security in the academic environment, messaging security, disaster recovery and business continuity, safe home computing, and information technology operations. Ness previously served as a systems administrator, network administrator, information technology director, and information security officer. He also provides consulting to several security software development organizations.

Peter G. Neumann has doctorates from Harvard and Darmstadt. He has been in SRI International's Computer Science Lab since September 1971, after spending 10 years at Bell Labs in Murray Hill, New Jersey. His work is concerned with computer systems and networks, trustworthiness and high assurance, security, reliability, survivability, safety, and many risk-related issues, such as voting-system integrity, crypto policy, social implications, and human needs including privacy. He moderates the ACM Risks Forum (risks.org) and created ACM SIGSOFT's Software Engineering Notes in 1976. He has participated in four studies for the National Academies of Science. His 1995 book, *Computer-Related Risks,* is still timely. He is a Fellow of the ACM, IEEE, and AAAS.

Lester E. Nichols earned a BS degree from the University of Phoenix and an MS degree in Information Assurance from Norwich University. He is currently working on his doctoral degree in Information Security at Capella University. He holds the CISSP, MCSA, MCP, and Security+ certifications. Nichols has over 10 years' experience in computer technology in the medical, nonprofit, financial, and local and federal government sectors, in a variety of roles, including application development, network engineering, and information security. Nichols is currently with Knowledge Consulting Group as a Senior Security Engineer, providing security oversight as well as security justification for network and system design implementations, while working with network engineering to integrate security mind-sets to the design stage of projects. Prior to this, he was employed with Prolific Solutions, LLC as a Senior Information Assurance Manager.

Justin Opatrny is currently an information systems manager for a Fortune 500 company, with previous roles specializing in network infrastructure and security. He earned a Master's degree in Information Assurance from Norwich University; holds industry certifications including CISSP, GCFA, and GSNA; and is an active member of ISSA and InfraGard. Opatrny also works as an independent consultant providing technology and information assurance expertise and guidance.

John Orlando, PhD, is the Program Director for the Master of Science in Business Continuity Management at Norwich University. He received his PhD from the University of Wisconsin, and has published articles in a variety of applied ethics fields, including information ethics, business ethics, and medical ethics. He has also published a number of articles on business continuity management and consults with universities on business continuity programs. Orlando helped develop online programs at the University of Vermont and Norwich University, and was the Associate Program Director for the Master of Science in Information Assurance at Norwich University.

Raymond Panko, PhD (e-mail: *Ray@Panko.com*) is a Professor of Information Technology Management in the Shidler College of Business at the University of Hawaii. His interest in security began during lunches with Donn Parker in the 1970s at SRI International and has grown ever since. His textbook on IT security, *Corporate Computer and Network Security,* is published by Prentice-Hall. His current research focuses are security for end user applications (especially spreadsheets), how to deal with fraud, and human and organizational controls. His main teaching focus, however, remains networking. In his networking classes and textbook, he emphasizes security throughput, pointing out the security implications of network protocols and practices.

Robert A. Parisi, Jr., is the Senior Vice-President and National Technology, Network Risk and Telecommunications Practice Leader for the FINPRO unit of Marsh USA. Parisi has spoken at various businesses, technology, legal, and insurance forums throughout the world and has written on issues affecting professional liability, privacy, technology, telecommunications, media, intellectual property, computer security, and insurance. In 2002, Parisi was honored by *Business Insurance* magazine as one of the Rising Stars of Insurance.

Immediately prior to joining Marsh, Parisi was the Senior Vice-President and Chief Underwriting Officer of eBusiness Risk Solutions (a unit of the property and casualty companies of American International Group, Inc.). Parisi joined the AIG group of companies in 1998 as legal counsel for its Professional Liability group and held several executive and legal positions within AIG, including the position of Chief Underwriting Officer for Professional Liability and Technology. While at AIG, Parisi oversaw the creation and drafting of underwriting guidelines and policies for all lines of professional liability. Prior to joining AIG, Parisi had been in private practice, principally as legal counsel to various Lloyds of London syndicates handling a variety of professional liability lines.

Parisi graduated cum laude from Fordham College with a B.A. in Economics and received his law degree from Fordham University School of Law. He is admitted to practice in New York and the U.S. District Courts for the Eastern and Southern Districts of New York.

Donn B. Parker, CISSP, Fellow of the Association for Computing Machinery (e-mail: *donnlorna@aol.com*) is a retired (1997) senior management consultant who has specialized in information security and computer crime research for 35 of his 50 years in the computer field. He has written numerous books, papers, articles, and reports in his specialty based on interviews with over 200 computer criminals and reviews of the security of many large corporations. He received the 1992 Award for Outstanding Individual Achievement from the Information Systems Security Association, the 1994 National Computer System Security Award from the U.S. NIST/NCSC, the Aerospace Computer Security Associates 1994 Distinguished Lecturer award, and The MIS Training Institute *Infosecurity News* 1996 Lifetime Achievement Award. *Information Security Magazine* identified him as one of the five top Infosecurity Pioneers (1998).

Padgett Peterson, P.E., CISSP, IAM/IEM, has been involved with computer security and encryption for over 40 years. Since 1979 he has been employed by different elements of a major aerospace contractor. Peterson is also an Adjunct Professor in the Master's of Science in Information Assurance program at Norwich University.

Franklin Platt (e-mail: *Fnplatt@aol.com* or telephone: 603 449-2211) is Founder and President of Office Planning Services, a Wall Street consultancy for 20 years headquartered in Stark, New Hampshire since 1990. He has worked extensively in security planning, management, and preparedness in both the private and public sectors. His academic background includes business administration and electrical engineering.

He has received extensive government training in emergency management, including terrorism and weapons of mass destruction, much of which is not available to the public. He holds many security certifications and is currently vetted by the FBI and by several states. Platt's areas of expertise include: security risk management; compliance with the latest Homeland Security procedures and other federal regulations that affect the private sector; risk identification and assessment; vulnerability analysis; cost-value studies; response planning; site security surveys and compliance auditing; briefing and training; second opinion; and due diligence.

Jerrold M. Post, PhD, is Professor of Psychiatry, Political Psychology, and International Affairs and Director of the Political Psychology Program at George Washington University. He has devoted his entire career to the field of political psychology. Post came to George Washington after a 21-year career with the Central Intelligence Agency, where he was the Founding Director of the Center for the Analysis of Personality and Political Behavior. He played the lead role in developing the Camp David profiles of Menachem Begin and Anwar Sadat for President Jimmy Carter and initiated the U.S. government program in understanding the psychology of terrorism. He is a widely published author, whose most recent book is *The Mind of the Terrorist: The Psychology of Terrorists from the IRA to al-Qaeda.* Post is also a frequent commentator on national and international media.

N. Todd Pritsky is the Director of E-learning Courseware at Hill Associates, a telecommunications training company in Colchester, Vermont. He is a Senior Member of the Technical Staff and an instructor of online, lecture, and hands-on classes. His teaching and writing specialties include e-commerce, network security, TCP/IP, and the Internet, and he also leads courses on fast packet and network access technologies. He enjoys writing articles on network security and is a contributing author of *Telecommunications: A Beginner's Guide* (McGraw-Hill/Osborne). Previously he managed a computer center and created multimedia training programs. He holds a BA in Philosophy and Russian/Soviet Studies from Colby College.

Karthik Raman (e-mail: *ramankmail@gmail.com*) is a Research Scientist at McAfee Avert Labs, an internationally renowned research group for fighting malicious software. His work at McAfee focuses on vulnerability research, malware analysis, and security-research automation. His interests include the application of computer and social sciences to computer-security problems and developing security tools. Karthik graduated with BS degrees in Computer Science and Computer Security from Norwich University in 2006, where he studied under Dr. Mich Kabay.

Bridgitt Robertson has been teaching business and technology courses for over six years. Her multidisciplinary approach to security awareness analyzes threats in the global enterprise and investigates how an educated workforce can mitigate risks and enhance corporate competitiveness. Prior to teaching, Robertson worked for global companies in the areas of project management, business analysis, and consulting. She is looking forward to obtaining her doctorate in 2009. She is a member of InfraGard.

Marc Rotenberg is Executive Director of the Electronic Privacy Information Center in Washington, DC. He teaches information privacy law at Georgetown University Law Center. He has published many articles in legal and scientific journals. He is the coauthor of several books, including *Information Privacy Law, Privacy and Human Rights, The*

Privacy Law Sourcebook, and *Litigation under the Federal Open Government Laws*. He frequently testifies before the U.S. Congress and the European Parliament on emerging privacy issues. He is a Fellow of the American Bar Foundation and the recipient of several awards, including the World Technology Award in Law.

K. Rudolph, CISSP, is President and Chief Inspiration Officer of Native Intelligence, Inc., a Maryland-based consulting firm focused on providing creative and practical information security awareness solutions. Rudolph develops security awareness products including posters, images, 60-second daily security tips, Web-based and computer-based courses designed in accord with adult-learning principles. She facilitates security awareness peer group meetings and is a frequent speaker at security conferences. In 2006, Rudolph was honored by the Federal Information Security Educators' Association as the Security Educator of the Year. Special areas of interest to Rudolph include storytelling in security awareness and behavior-based messages and metrics.

Eric Salveggio is an information technology security professional who enjoys teaching online courses in CMIS for Liberty University and Auditing for Norwich University. He works as a trained ISO 17799, NSTISSI 4011 and 4013 consultant for Dynetics Corporation of Huntsville, Alabama, in IT Security and Auditing, and as a Private Consultant in networking, network design, and security (wired and wireless) with 10 years experience. He previously worked as the IT Director for the Birmingham, Alabama, campus of Virginia College, where he opened two start-up campuses—on ground and online—and created three accredited programs (two undergrad, one graduate level) at state and federal levels in Network and Cyber Security. While in this position, he was chosen as a nominee for the 2006 Information Security Executive Award, and enjoyed being the only educational facility recognized. He was personally awarded a plaque of recognition by the Stonesoft Corporation for the same. He is a published author and photographer, and enjoys working at times as a Technical Editor for Pearson Education and Thomson Publishing on cyber forensics, cyber security, and operating systems.

Ravi Sandhu is Cofounder and Chief Scientist of SingleSignOn.Net in Reston, Virginia, and Professor of Information Technology and Engineering at George Mason University in Fairfax, Virginia. An ACM and an IEEE Fellow, he is the founding Editor in Chief of *ACM's Transactions on Information and System Security,* Chairman of ACM's Special Interest Group on Security, Audit and Control, and Security Editor for *IEEE Internet Computing*. Sandhu has published over 140 technical papers on information security. He is a popular teacher and has lectured all over the world. He has provided high-level consulting services to numerous private and government organizations.

Sondra Schneider is CEO and Founder of Security University, an Information Security and Information Assurance Training and Certification company. She and SU have challenged security professionals for the past 10 years, delivering hands-on tactical security classes and certifications around the world.

Starting in 2008, SU set up an exam server to meet the demand for tactical security certifications. In 2005, SU refreshed the preexisting AIS security training program to the new "SU Qualified Programs," which meet and exceed security professionals requirements for hands-on tactical security "skills" training. SU delivers the Qualified/ Information Security Professional and Qualified/Information Assurance Professional certifications, which are the first of their kind that measure a candidate's tactical hands-on security skills.

In 2004, Schneider was awarded Entrepreneur of the Year for the First Annual Women of Innovation Award from the Connecticut Technology Council. In 2007, she was Tech Editor for the popular 2007 CEH V5 Study Guide, and a multiple chapter author for the 2007 CHFI Study Guide. She sits on three advisory boards for computer security (start-up) technology companies and is a frequent speaker at computer security and wireless industry events. She is a founding member of the NYC HTCIA and IETF chapters, works closely with (ISC)^2, ISSA, and ISACA chapters, and the security and wireless vendor community. She specializes in information security, intrusion detection, information assurance (PKI), wireless security and security awareness training.

William Stallings, PhD (e-mail: *ws@shore.net*) is a consultant, lecturer, and author of over a dozen professional reference books and textbooks on data communications and computer networking. His clients have included major corporations and government agencies in the United States and Europe. He has received numerous awards for the Best Computer Science Textbook of the Year from the Text and Academic Authors Association. He has designed and implemented both TCP/IP-based and OSI-based protocol suites on a variety of computers and operating systems, ranging from microcomputers to mainframes. Stallings created and maintains the Computer Science Student Resource Site at http://WilliamStallings.com/StudentSupport.html.

Peter Stephenson, PhD, is a writer, researcher and lecturer on information assurance and risk, information warfare and counterterrorism, and digital investigation and forensics on large-scale computer networks. He has lectured extensively on digital investigation and security and has written or contributed to 14 books and several hundred articles in major national and international trade, technical and scientific publications.

He is the Associate Program Director in the Master's of Science in Information Assurance program at the Norwich University School of Graduate Studies, where he teaches information assurance, cyber crime and cyber law, and digital investigation on both the graduate and undergraduate levels. He is Senior Research Scientist at the Norwich University Applied Research Institutes, Chair of the Department of Computing, and the Chief Information Security Officer for the university.

He has lectured or delivered consulting engagements for the past 23 years in 11 countries plus the United States and has been a technologist for over 40 years. He operated a successful consulting practice for over 20 years and has worked for such companies as Siemens, Tektronix, and QinetiQ (UK).

Stephenson obtained his PhD in computer science at Oxford Brookes University, Oxford, England, where his research was in the structured investigation of digital incidents in complex computing environments. He holds a Master's of Arts degree in Diplomacy with a concentration in Terrorism from Norwich University.

He is on the editorial advisory boards of *International Journal of Digital Evidence* and the Norwich University *Journal of Information Assurance* among several others. Stephenson is technology editor for *SC Magazine* and the editor in chief for Norwich University Press.

Stephenson is a Fellow of the Institute for Communications, Arbitration and Forensics in the United Kingdom and is a member of Michigan InfraGard and the International Federation of Information Processing Technical Committee 11, Working Group 11.9, Digital Forensics. He serves on the steering Committee of the Michigan Electronic Crime Task Force. His research is focused on information conflict.

Gary L. Tagg is a highly experienced information security professional with over 20 years working in the financial and government sectors. The organizations he has worked with include Deutsche Bank, PA Consulting group, Clearstream, Pearl Assurance, and Lloyds TSB. He has performed a wide range of security roles including risk management, consulting, security architecture, policy and standards, project management, development, testing and auditing. Tagg is currently a risk consultant in Deutsche Bank's IT security Governance Group.

Nicholas Takacs is an information security professional and Business Systems Director for a long-term care insurance company. He is also an Adjunct Professor of Information Assurance at Norwich University. Takacs has expertise in the areas of security policy management, security awareness, business continuity planning, and execution. Prior to moving into the insurance industry, Takacs spent several years in the public utility industry focusing on the areas of regulatory compliance, disaster recovery, and identity management.

James Thomas, MSc CISSP, is a Senior Partner with Norwich Security Associates, a full-spectrum information assurance consultancy headquartered in Scotland. Thomas spends most of his professional time providing policy, process, and governance advice to large banking and financial organizations in the United Kingdom and Europe. He is a 2004 graduate of the Norwich University Master of Science in Information Assurance program. Prior to focusing his efforts in the security space, he had a long career in Information Technology and Broadcast Engineering spanning the United Kingdom and the eastern United States.

Lee Tien, Esq., is a Senior Staff Attorney with the Electronic Frontier Foundation in San Francisco, California. He specializes in free speech and surveillance law and has authored several law review articles. He received his undergraduate degree in psychology from Stanford University and his law degree from Boalt Hall School of Law, UC Berkeley. He is also a former newspaper reporter.

Timothy Virtue is an accomplished information assurance leader with a focus in strategic enterprise technology risk management, information security, data privacy, and regulatory compliance. Virtue has extensive experience with publicly traded corporations, privately held businesses, government agencies, and nonprofit organizations of all sizes. Additionally he holds these professional designations: CISSP, CISA, CCE, CFE, and CIPP/G.

Myles Walsh is an Adjunct Professor at three colleges in New Jersey: Ramapo College, County College of Morris, and Passaic County Community. For the past 12 years, he has taught courses in Microsoft Office and Web Page Design. He also implements small Office applications and Web sites. From 1966 until 1989, he worked his way up from programmer to director in several positions at CBS, CBS Records, and CBS News. His formal education includes an MBA from the Baruch School of Business and a BBA from St. John's University.

Karen F. Worstell, CISM, is Cofounder and Principal of W Risk Group, a consultancy serving clients across multiple sectors to define due diligence to a defensible standard of care for information protection. Her areas of expertise include incident detection and management, compliance, governance, secure data management and risk management. She is coauthor of *Evaluating the Electronic Discovery Capabilities of Outside Law Firms: A Model Request for Information and Analysis* (BNA, 2006) and is a frequent speaker and contributor in risk management and information security forums internationally. She participates in ISACA, IIA, and the ABA Science and Technology Section, Information Security Committee, and serves as President of the Puget Sound Chapter of the ISSA.

Noel Zakin is President of RANCO Consulting LLC. He has been an information technology/telecommunications industry executive for over 45 years. He has held managerial positions at the Gartner Group, AT&T, the American Institute of CPAs, and Unisys. These positions involved strategic planning, market research, competitive analysis, business analysis, and education and training. His consulting assignments have ranged from the Fortune 500 to small start-ups and have involved data security, strategic planning, conference management, market research, and management of corporate operations. He has been active with ACM, IFIP, and AFIPS and currently with ISSA. He holds an MBA from the Wharton School.

William A. Zucker, Esq., is a partner at McCarter & English, LLP's Boston office. Zucker serves as a senior consultant for the Cutter Consortium on legal issues relating to information technology, outsourcing, and risk management, and is a member of the American Arbitration Association's National Technology Panel and a member of the CPR Institute's working group on technology business alliances and conflict management. He has also served on the faculty of Norwich University, where he taught the intellectual property aspects of computer security. Zucker is a trial lawyer whose practice focuses on negotiation/litigation of business transactions, outsourcing/ebusiness and technology/intellectual property. Among his publications are: "The Legal Framework for Protecting Intellectual Property in the Field of Computing and Computer Software," written for the *Computer Security Handbook*, 4th edition, coauthored with Scott Nathan; and "Intellectual Property and Open Source: Copyright, Copyleft and Other Issues for the Community User."

A NOTE TO INSTRUCTORS

This two-volume text will serve the interests of practitioners and teachers of information assurance. The fourth edition of the *Handbook* was well received in academia; at least one quarter of all copies were bought by university and college bookstores. The design and contents of this fifth edition have been tailored even more closely to meet those needs as well as the needs of other professionals in the field.

University professors looking for texts appropriate for a two-semester sequence of undergraduate courses in information assurance will find the *Handbook* most suitable. In my own work at Norwich University in Vermont, Volume I is the text for our *IS340 Introduction to Information Assurance* and Volume II is the basis for our *IS342 Management of Information Assurance* courses.

The text will also be useful as a resource in graduate courses. In the School of Graduate Studies at Norwich University, we use both volumes as required and supplementary reading for our 18-month, 36-credit Master of Science in Information Assurance program (MSIA).

I will continue to create and post PowerPoint lecture slides based on the chapters of the *Handbook* on my Norwich University Web site for free access by anyone applying them to noncommercial use (e.g., for self-study, for courses in academic institutions, and for unpaid industry training); the materials will be available in the IS340 and IS342 sections:

www2.norwich.edu/mkabay/courses/academic/norwich/is340
www2.norwich.edu/mkabay/courses/academic/norwich/is342

M. E. KABAY
Technical Editor
January 2009

INTRODUCTION TO PART I

FOUNDATIONS OF COMPUTER SECURITY

The foundations of computer security include answers to the superficially simple question "What is this all about?" Our first part establishes a technological and historical context for information assurance so that readers will have a broad understanding of why information assurance matters in the real world. Chapters focus on principles that will underlie the rest of the text: historical perspective on the development of our field; how to conceptualize the goals of information assurance in a well-ordered schema that can be applied universally to all information systems; computer hardware and network elements underlying technical security; history and modern developments in cryptography; and how to discuss breaches of information security using a common technical language so that information can be shared, accumulated, and analyzed.

Readers also learn or review the basics of commonly used mathematical models of information security concepts and how to interpret survey data and, in particular, the pitfalls of self-selection in sampling about crimes. Finally, the first section of the text introduces elements of law (U.S. and international) applying to information assurance. This legal framework from a layman's viewpoint, provides a basis for understanding later chapters; in particular, when examining privacy laws and management's fiduciary responsibilities.

Chapter titles and topics in Part I include:

1. **Brief History and Mission of Information System Security.** An overview focusing primarily on developments in the second half of the twentieth century and the first decade of the twenty-first

2. **History of Computer Crime.** A review of key computer crimes and notorious computer criminals from the 1970s to the mid-2000s

3. **Toward a New Framework for Information Security.** A systematic and thorough conceptual framework and terminology for discussing the nature and goals of securing all aspects of information, not simply the classic triad of confidentiality, integrity, and availability

4. **Hardware Elements of Security.** A review of computer and network hardware underlying discussions of computer and network security

5. **Data Communications and Information Security.** Fundamental principles and terminology of data communications, and their implications for information assurance

6. **Network Topologies, Protocols, and Design.** Information assurance of the communications infrastructure

7. **Encryption.** Historical perspectives on cryptography and steganography from ancient times to today as fundamental tools in securing information

8. **Using a Common Language for Computer Security Incident Information.** An analytic framework for understanding, describing, and discussing security breaches by using a common language of well-defined terms

9. **Mathematical Models of Computer Security.** A review of the most commonly referenced mathematical models used to describe information security functions

10. **Understanding Studies and Surveys of Computer Crime.** Scientific and statistical principles for understanding studies and surveys of computer crime

11. **Fundamentals of Intellectual Property Law.** An introductory review of cyberlaw: laws governing computer-related crime, including contracts, and intellectual property (trade secrets, copyright, patents, open-source-models). Also, violations (piracy, circumvention of technological defenses), computer intrusions, and international frameworks for legal cooperation

CHAPTER 1

BRIEF HISTORY AND MISSION OF INFORMATION SYSTEM SECURITY

Seymour Bosworth and Robert V. Jacobson

1.1 INTRODUCTION TO INFORMATION SYSTEM SECURITY. The growth of computers and of information technology has been explosive. Never before has an entirely new technology been propagated around the world with such speed and with so great a penetration of virtually every human activity. Computers have brought vast benefits to fields as diverse as human genome studies, space exploration, artificial intelligence, and a host of applications from the trivial to the most life-enhancing.

Unfortunately, there is also a dark side to computers: They are used to design and build weapons of mass destruction as well as military aircraft, nuclear submarines, and reconnaissance space stations. The computer's role in formulating biologic and chemical weapons, and in simulating their deployment, is one of its least auspicious uses.

Of somewhat lesser concern, computers used in financial applications, such as facilitating the purchase and sales of everything from matchsticks to mansions, and transferring trillions of dollars each day in electronic funds, are irresistible to miscreants; many of them see these activities as open invitations to fraud and theft. Computer systems, and their interconnecting networks, are also prey to vandals, malicious egotists, terrorists, and an array of individuals, groups, companies, and governments intent on using them to further their own ends, with total disregard for the effects on innocent victims. Besides these intentional attacks on computer systems, there are innumerable ways in which inadvertent errors can damage or destroy a computer's ability to perform its intended functions.

Because of these security problems and because of a great many others described in this volume, the growth of information systems security has paralleled that of the computer field itself. Only by a detailed study of the potential problems, and implementation of the suggested solutions, can computers be expected to fulfill their promise, with few of the security lapses that plague less adequately protected systems. This chapter defines a few of the most important terms of information security and includes a very brief history of computers and information systems, as a prelude to the works that follow.

Security can be defined as the state of being free from danger and not exposed to damage from accidents or attack, or it can be defined as the process for achieving that desirable state. The objective of information system security[1] is to optimize the performance of an organization with respect to the risks to which it is exposed.

Risk is defined as the chance of injury, damage, or loss. Thus, risk has two elements: (1) chance—an element of uncertainty, and (2) potential loss or damage. Except for the possibility of restitution, information system security actions taken today work to reduce *future* risk losses. Because of the uncertainty about future risk losses, perfect security, which implies zero losses, would be infinitely expensive. For this reason, risk managers strive to optimize the allocation of resources by minimizing the total cost of information system security measures taken and the risk losses experienced. This optimization process is commonly referred to as risk management.

Risk management in this sense is a three-part process:

1. Identification of material risks
2. Selection and implementation of measures to mitigate the risks
3. Tracking and evaluating of risk losses experienced, in order to validate the first two parts of the process

The purpose of this *Handbook* is to describe information security system risks, the measures available to mitigate these risks, and techniques for managing security risks. (For a more detailed discussion of risk assessment and management, see Chapter 47 and Chapter 54.)

Risk management has been a part of business for centuries. Renaissance merchants often used several vessels simultaneously, each carrying a portion of the merchandise, so that the loss of a single ship would not result in loss of the entire lot. At almost the same time, the concept of insurance evolved, first to provide economic protection against the loss of cargo and later to provide protection against the loss of buildings by fire. Fire insurers and municipal authorities began to require adherence to standards intended to reduce the risk of catastrophes like the Great Fire of London in 1666. The Insurance Institute was established in London one year later. With the emergence of corporations, as limited liability stock companies, corporate directors have been required to use prudence and due diligence in protecting shareholders' assets. Security risks are among the threats to corporate assets that directors have an obligation to address.

Double-entry bookkeeping, another Renaissance invention, proved to be an excellent tool for measuring and controlling corporate assets. One objective was to make insider fraud more difficult to conceal. The concept of separation of duties emerged, calling for the use of processing procedures that required more than one person to complete a transaction. As the books of account became increasingly important, accounting standards were developed, and they continue to evolve to this day. These standards served to make books of account comparable and to assure outsiders that an organization's books of account presented an accurate picture of its condition and assets. These developments led, in turn, to the requirement that an outside auditor perform an independent review of the books of account and operating procedures.

The transition to automated accounting systems introduced additional security requirements. Some early safeguards, such as the rule against erasures or changes in the books of account, no longer applied. Some computerized accounting systems lacked an audit trail, and others could have the audit trail subverted as easily as actual entries.

Finally, with the advent of the Information Age, intellectual property has become an increasingly important part of corporate and governmental assets. At the same time that intellectual property has grown in importance, threats to intellectual property have become more dangerous, because of information system (IS) technology itself. When sensitive information was stored on paper and other tangible documents, and rapid copying was limited to photography, protection was relatively straightforward. Nevertheless, document control systems, information classification procedures, and need-to-know access controls were not foolproof, and information compromises occurred with dismaying regularity. Evolution of IS technology has made information control several orders of magnitude more complex. The evolution and, more important, the implementation of control techniques have not kept pace.

The balance of this chapter describes how the evolution of information systems has caused a parallel evolution of IS security and at the same time has increased the importance of anticipating the impact of technical changes yet to come. This overview will clarify the factors leading to today's IS security risk environment and mitigation techniques and will serve as a warning to remain alert to the implication of technical innovations as they appear. The remaining chapters of this *Handbook* discuss IS security risks, threats, and vulnerabilities, their prevention and remediation, and many related topics in considerable detail.

1.2 EVOLUTION OF INFORMATION SYSTEMS. The first electromechanical punched-card system for data processing, developed by Herman Hollerith at the end of the nineteenth century, was used to tabulate and total census field reports for the U.S. Bureau of the Census in 1890. The first digital, stored-program computers developed in the 1940s were used for military purposes, primarily cryptanalysis and the calculation and printing of artillery firing tables. At the same time, punched-card systems were already being used for accounting applications and were an obvious choice for data input to the new electronic computing machines.

1.2.1   1950s: Punched-Card Systems.

In the 1950s, punched-card equipment dominated the commercial computer market.[2] These electromechanical devices could perform the full range of accounting and reporting functions. Because they were programmed by an intricate system of plugboards with a great many plug-in cables, and because care had to be exercised in handling and storing punched cards, only experienced persons were permitted near the equipment. Although any of these individuals could have set up the equipment for fraudulent use, or even engaged in sabotage, apparently few, if any, actually did so.

The punched-card accounting systems typically used four processing steps. As a preliminary, operators would be given a "batch" of documents, typically with an adding machine tape showing one or more "control totals." The operator keyed the data on each document into a punched card and then added an extra card, the batch control card, which stored the batch totals. Each card consisted of 80 columns, each containing, at most, one character. A complete record of an inventory item, for example, would be contained on a single card. The card was called a unit record, and the machines that processed the cards were called either unit record or punched-card machines. It was from the necessity to squeeze as much data as possible into an 80-character card that the later Y2K problem arose. Compressing the year into two characters was a universally used space-saving measure; its consequences 40 years later were not foreseen.

A group of punched cards, also called a "batch," were commonly held in a metal tray, Sometimes a batch would be rekeyed by a second operator, using a "verify-mode" rather than actually punching new holes in the cards, in order to detect keypunch errors before processing the card deck. Each batch of cards would be processed separately, so the processes were referred to as "batch jobs."

The first step would be to run the batch of cards through a simple program, which would calculate the control totals and compare them with the totals on the batch control card. If the batch totals did not reconcile, the batch was sent back to the keypunch area for rekeying. If the totals reconciled, the deck would be sort-merged with other batches of the same transaction type, for example, the current payroll. When this step was complete, the new batch consisted of a punched card for each employee in employee-number order. The payroll program accepted this input data card deck and processed the cards one by one. Each card was matched up with the corresponding employee's card in the payroll master deck to calculate the current net pay and itemized deductions and to punch a new payroll master card including year-to-date totals. The final step was to use the card decks to print payroll checks and management reports. These steps were identical with those used by early, small-scale electronic computers. The only difference was in the speed at which the actual calculations were made. A complete process was still known as a batch job.

With this process, the potential for abuse was great. The machine operator could control every step of the operation. Although the data were punched into cards and verified by others, there was always a keypunch machine nearby for use by the machine operator. Theoretically, that person could punch a new payroll card and a new batch total card to match the change before printing checks and again afterward. The low incidence of reported exploits was due to the controls that discouraged such abuse and possibly to the pride that machine operators experienced in their jobs.

1.2.2   Large-Scale Computers.

While these electromechanical punched card machines were sold in large numbers, research laboratories and universities were working to design large-scale computers that would have a revolutionary effect on the entire field. These computers, built around vacuum tubes, are known as the first generation. In March 1951, the first Universal Automatic Computer (UNIVAC) was accepted by the U.S. Census Bureau. Until then, every computer had been a one-off design, but UNIVAC was the first large-scale, mass-produced computer, with a total of 46 built. The word "universal" in its name indicated that UNIVAC was also the first computer designed for both scientific and business applications.[3]

UNIVAC contained 5,200 vacuum tubes, weighed 29,000 pounds, and consumed 125 kilowatts of electrical power. It dispensed with punched cards, receiving input from half-inch-wide metal tape recorded from keyboards, with output either to a similar tape or to a printer. Although not a model for future designs, its memory consisted of 1,000 72-bit words and was fabricated as a mercury delay line. Housed in a cabinet about six feet tall, two feet wide, and two feet deep was a mercury-filled coil running from top to bottom. A transducer at the top propagated slow-moving waves of energy down the coil to a receiving transducer at the bottom. There it was reconverted into electrical energy and passed on to the appropriate circuit, or recirculated if longer storage was required.

In 1956, IBM introduced the RAMAC (Random Access Method of Accounting and Control) magnetic disk system. It consisted of 50 magnetically coated metal disks, each 24 inches in diameter, and mounted on a common spindle. A servomotor, controlled by feedback from digital addresses read off each track of a disk, moved two coupled read/write heads to span each side of the disk, and then inward to any one of 100 tracks. In one revolution of the disks, any or all of the information on those two tracks could be read out, or recorded. The entire system was almost the size of a compact car and held what, for that time, was a tremendous amount of data—5 megabytes. The cost was $10,000 per megabyte, or $35,000 per year to lease. This compares with some of today's magnetic hard drives that measure about $3\frac{1}{2}$ inches wide by 1 inch high, store as much as 1,000 gigabytes, and cost less than $400, or about $0.0004 per megabyte.

Those early, massive computers were housed in large, climate-controlled rooms. Within the room, a few knowledgeable experts, looking highly professional in their white laboratory coats, attended to the operation and maintenance of their million-dollar charges. The concept of a "user" as someone outside the computer room who could interact directly with the actual machine did not exist.

Service interruptions, software errors, and hardware errors were usually not critical. If any of these caused a program to fail or abort, beginning again was a relatively simple matter. Consequently, the primary security concerns were physical protection of the scarce and expensive hardware, and measures to increase their reliability. Another issue, then as now, was human fallibility. Because the earliest computers were programmed in extremely difficult machine language, consisting solely of ones (1s) and zeroes (0s), the incidence of human error was high and the time to correct errors was excessively long. Only later were assembler and compiler languages developed to increase the number of people able to program the machines and to reduce the incidence of errors and the time to correct them.

Information system security for large-scale computers was not a significant issue then for two reasons. First, only a few programming experts were able to utilize and manipulate computers. Second, there were very few computers in use, each of which was extremely valuable, important to its owners, and, consequently, closely guarded.

1.2.3 Medium-Size Computers.

In the 1950s, smaller computer systems were developed with a very simple configuration; punched-card master files were replaced by punched paper tape and, later, by magnetic tape, and disk storage systems.

The electromechanical calculator with its patchboard was replaced by a central processor unit (CPU) that had a small main memory, sometimes as little as 8 kilobytes,[4] and limited processing speed and power. One or two punched-card readers could read the data and instructions stored on that medium. Later, programs and data files were stored on magnetic tape. Output data were sent to cardpunches, for printing on unit record equipment and later to magnetic tape. There was still no wired connection to the outside world, and there were no online users because no one, besides electronic data processing (EDP) people within the computer room, could interact directly with the system. These systems had very simple operating systems and did not use multiprocessing; they could run only one program at a time.

The IBM Model 650, as an example, introduced in 1954, measured about 5 feet by 3 feet by 6 feet and weighed almost 2,000 pounds. Its power supply was mounted in a similarly sized cabinet, weighing almost 3,000 pounds. It had 2,000 (10-digit) words of magnetic drum primary memory, with a total price of $150,000 or a rental fee of $3,200 per month. For an additional $1,500 per month, a much faster core memory, of 60 words, could be added. Input and output both utilized read/write punch-card machines. The typical 1950s IS hardware was installed in a separate room, often with a viewing window so that visitors could admire the computer. In an early attempt at security, visitors actually within the computer room were often greeted by a printed sign saying:

Achtung! Alles Lookenspeepers!

Das computermachine ist nicht fur gefingerpoken und mittengrabben.
Ist easy schnappen der springenwerk, blowenfusen, und poppencorken mit spitzensparken.
Ist nicht fur gewerken bei das dumbkopfen. Das rubbernecken sightseeren keepen hans in das pockets muss. . .:
Relaxen und watch das blinkenlichten.

Since there were still no online users, there were no user IDs and passwords. Programs processed batches of data, run at a regularly scheduled time—once a day, once a week, and so on, depending on the function. If the data for a program were not available at the scheduled run time, the operators might run some other job instead and wait for the missing data. As the printed output reports became available, they were delivered by hand to their end users. End users did not expect to get a continuous flow of data from the information processing system, and delays of even a day or more were not significant, except perhaps with paycheck production.

Information system security was hardly thought of as such. The focus was on batch controls for individual programs, physical access controls, and maintaining a proper environment for the reliable operation of the hardware.

1.2.4   1960s: Small-Scale Computers.   During the 1960s, before the introduction of small-scale computers, dumb[5] terminals provided users with a keyboard to send a character stream to the computer and a video screen that could display characters transmitted to it by the computer. Initially these terminals were used to help computer operators control and monitor the job stream while replacing banks of switches and indicator lights on the control console. However, it was soon recognized that these terminals could replace card readers and keypunch machines as well. Now users, identified by user IDs and authenticated with passwords, could enter input data through a cathode ray tube (CRT) terminal into an edit program, which would validate the input

and then store it on a hard drive until it was needed for processing. Later it was realized that users also could directly access data stored in online master files.

1.2.5 Transistors and Core Memory.

The IBM 1401, introduced in 1960, with a core memory of 4,096 characters, was the first all-transistor computer, marking the advent of the second generation. Housed in a cabinet measuring 5 feet by 3 feet, the 1401 required a similar cabinet to add an additional 12 kilobytes of main memory. Just one year later, the first integrated circuits were used in a computer, making possible all future advances in miniaturizing small-scale computers and in reducing the size of mainframes significantly.

1.2.6 Time Sharing.

In 1961, the Compatible Time Sharing System (CTSS) was developed for the IBM 7090/7094. This operating system software, and its associated hardware, was the first to provide simultaneous remote access to a group of online users through multiprogramming.[6] "Multiprogramming" means that more than one program can appear to execute at the same time. A master control program, usually called an operating system (OS), managed execution of the functional applications programs. For example, under the command of the operator, the OS would load and start application 1. After 50 milliseconds, the OS would interrupt the execution of application 1 and store its current state in memory. Then the OS would start application 2 and allow it to run for 50 milliseconds, and so on. Usually, within a second after users had entered keyboard data, the OS would give their applications a time slice to process the input. During each time slice, the computer might execute hundreds of instructions. These techniques made it appear as if the computer were entirely dedicated to each user's program. This was true only so long as the number of simultaneous users was fairly small. After that, as the number grew, the response to each user slowed down.

1.2.7 Real-Time, Online Systems.

Because of multiprogramming and the ability to store records online and accessible in random order, it became feasible to provide end users with direct access to data. For example, an airline reservation system stores a record of every seat on every flight for the next 12 months. A reservation clerk, working at a terminal, can answer a telephoned inquiry, search for an available seat on a particular flight, quote the fare, sell a ticket to the caller, and reserve the seat. Similarly, a bank officer can verify an account balance and effect money transfers. In both cases, each data record can be accessed and modified immediately, rather than having to wait for a batch to be run. Today both the reservation clerk and the bank officer can be replaced by the customers themselves, who directly interface with the online computers.

While this advance led to a vast increase in available computing power, it also increased greatly the potential for breaches in computer security. With more complex operating systems, with many users online to sensitive programs, and with databases and other files available to them, protection had to be provided against inadvertent error and intentional abuse.

1.2.8 A Family of Computers.

In 1964, IBM announced the S/360 family of computers, ranging from very small-scale to very large-scale models. All of the six models used integrated circuits, which marked the beginning of the third generation of computers. Where transistorized construction could permit up to 6,000 transistors per cubic foot, 30,000 integrated circuits could occupy the same volume. This lowered the costs substantially, and companies could buy into the family at a price within their means. Because all computers in the series used the same programming language and the same peripherals, companies could upgrade easily when necessary. The 360 family quickly came to dominate the commercial and scientific markets. As these computers proliferated, so did the number of users, knowledgeable programmers, and technicians. Over the years, techniques and processes were developed to provide a high degree of security to these mainframe systems.

The year 1964 also saw the introduction of another computer with far-reaching influence: the Digital Equipment Corp. (DEC) PDP-8. The PDP-8 was the first mass-produced true minicomputer. Although its original application was in process control, the PDP-8 and its progeny quickly proved that commercial applications for minicomputers were virtually unlimited. Because these computers were not isolated in secure computer rooms but were distributed throughout many unguarded offices in widely dispersed locations, totally new risks arose, requiring innovative solutions.

1.2.9 1970s: Microprocessors, Networks, and Worms.

The foundations of all current personal computers (PCs) were laid in 1971 when Intel introduced the 4004 computer on a chip. Measuring $\frac{1}{16}$ inch long by $\frac{1}{8}$ inch high, the 4004 contained 2,250 transistors with a clock speed of 108 kiloHertz. The current generation of this earliest programmable microprocessor contains millions of transistors, with speeds over 1 gigaHertz, or more than 10,000 times faster. Introduction of microprocessor chips marked the fourth generation.

1.2.10 First Personal Computers.

Possibly the first personal computer was advertised in *Scientific American* in 1971. The KENBAK–1, priced at $750, had three programming registers, five addressing modes, and 256 bytes of memory. Although not many were sold, the KENBACK–1 did increase public awareness of the possibility for home computers.

It was the MITS Altair 8800 that became the first personal computer to sell in substantial quantities. Like the KENBACK–1, the Altair 8800 had only 256 bytes of memory, but it was priced at $375 without keyboard, display, or secondary memory. About one year later, the Apple II, designed by Steve Jobs and Steve Wozniak, was priced at $1,298, including a CRT display and a keyboard.

Because these first personal computers were entirely stand-alone and usually under the control of a single individual, there were few security problems. However, in 1978, the VisiCalc spreadsheet program was developed. The advantages of standardized, inexpensive, widely used application programs were unquestionable, but packaged programs, as opposed to custom designs, opened the way for abuse because so many people understood their user interfaces as well as their inner workings.

1.2.11 First Network.

A national network, conceived in late 1969, was born as ARPANET[7] (Advanced Research Projects Agency Network), a Department of Defense–sponsored effort to link a few of the country's important research universities, with two purposes: to develop experience in interconnecting computers and to increase productivity through resource sharing. This earliest connection of independent large-scale computer systems had just four nodes: the University of California at Los Angeles (UCLA), the University of California at Santa Barbara, Stanford Research Institute, and the University of Utah. Because of the inherent security in each leased-line interconnected node, and the physically protected mainframe computer rooms, there was no apparent concern for security issues. From this simple network, with no thought of security designed in, there finally evolved today's ubiquitous Internet and the World Wide Web (WWW) with their vast potential for security abuses.

1.2.12 Further Security Considerations. With the proliferation of remote terminals on commercial computers, physical control over access to the computer room was no longer sufficient. In response to the new vulnerabilities, logical access control systems were developed. An access control system maintains an online table of authorized users. A typical user record would store the user's name, telephone number, employee number, and information about the data the user was authorized to access and the programs the user was authorized to execute. A user might be allowed to view, add, modify, and delete data records in different combinations for different programs.

At the same time, system managers recognized the value of being able to recover from a disaster that destroyed hardware and data. Data centers began to make regular tape copies of online files and software for off-site storage. Data center managers also began to develop and implement off-site disaster recovery plans, often involving the use of commercial disaster-recovery facilities. Even with such a system in place, new vulnerabilities were recognized throughout the following years, and these are the subjects of much of this *Handbook*.

1.2.13 First "Worm." A prophetic science-fiction novel, *The Shockwave Rider*, by John Brunner[8] (1975), depicted a "worm" that grew continuously throughout a computer network. The worm eventually exceeded a billion bits in length and became impossible to kill without destroying the network. Although actual worms later became real and present menaces to all networked computers, prudent computer security personnel install, and regularly update, antivirus programs that effectively kill viruses and worms without having to kill the network.

1.2.14 1980s: Productivity Enhancements. The decade of the 1980s might well be termed the era of productivity enhancement. The installation of millions of personal computers in commercial, industrial, and government applications enhanced efficiency and functionality of vast numbers of users. These advances, which could have been achieved in no other way, were made at costs that virtually any business could afford.

1.2.15 Personal Computer. In 1981, IBM introduced a general-purpose small computer it called the "Personal Computer." That model and similar systems became known generically as PCs. Until then, small computers were produced by relatively unknown sources, but IBM, with its worldwide reputation, brought PCs into the mainstream. The fact that IBM had demonstrated a belief in the viability of PCs made them serious contenders for corporate use.

There were many variations on the basic Model 5100 PC, and sales expanded far beyond IBM's estimates. The basic configuration used the Intel 8088, operating at 4.77 megaHertz, with up to two floppy disk drives, each with a capacity of 160 kilobyte and with a disk-based operating system (DOS) in an open architecture. This open OS architecture, with its available "hooks," made possible the growth of independent software producers, the most important of which was the Microsoft Corporation, formed by Bill Gates and Paul Allen.

IBM had arranged for Gates and Allen to create the DOS operating system. Under the agreement, IBM would not reimburse Gates and Allen for their development costs; rather, all profits from the sale of DOS would accrue to them. IBM did not have an exclusive right to the operating system, and Microsoft began selling it to many other customers as MS-DOS. IBM initially included with its computer the VisiCalc spreadsheet program, but soon sales of Lotus 1-2-3 surpassed those of VisiCalc. The open architecture not only made it possible for many developers to produce software that would run on the PC but also enabled anyone to put together purchased components into a computer that would compete with IBM's PC. The rapid growth of compatible application programs, coupled with the ready availability of compatible hardware, soon resulted in sales of more than 1 million units. Many subsequent generations of the original hardware and software are still producing sales measured in millions every year.

Apple took a very different approach with its Macintosh computer. Where IBM's system was wide open, Apple maintained tight control over any hardware or software designed to operate on the Macintosh so as to assure compatibility and ease of installation. The most important Apple innovations were the graphical user interface (GUI) and the mouse, both of which worked together to facilitate ease of use. Microsoft had attempted in 1985 to build these features into the Windows operating system, but early versions were generally rejected as slow, cumbersome, and unreliable. It was not until 1990 that Windows 3.0 overcame many of its problems and provided the foundation for later versions that were almost universally accepted.

1.2.16   Local Area Networks.   During the 1980s, stand-alone desktop computers began to perform word processing, financial analysis, and graphic processing. Although this arrangement was much more convenient for end users than was a centralized facility, it was more difficult to share data with others.

As more powerful PCs were developed, it became practical to interconnect them so that their users could easily share data. These arrangements were commonly referred to as local area networks (LANs) because the hardware units were physically close, usually in the same building or office area. LANs have remained important to this day. Typically, a more powerful PC with a high storage capacity fixed[9] disk was designated as the file server. Other PCs, referred to as workstations, were connected to the file server using network interface cards installed in the workstations with cables between these cards and the file server. Special network software installed on the file server and workstations made it possible for workstations to access defined portions of the file server fixed disk just as if these portions were installed on the workstations. Furthermore, these shared files could be backed up at the file server without depending on individual users. By 1997, it was estimated that worldwide there were more than 150 million PCs operating as LAN workstations. The most common network operating systems (NOS) were Novell NetWare and later Microsoft IE (Internet Explorer).

Most LANs were implemented using the Ethernet (IEEE 802.3) protocol.[10] The server and workstations could be equipped with a modem (modulator/demodulator) connected to a dedicated telephone line. The modem enabled remote users, with a matching modem, to dial into the LAN and log on. This was a great convenience to LAN users who were traveling or working away from their offices, but such remote access created yet another new security issue. For the first time, computer systems were exposed in a major way to the outside world. From then on, it was possible to interact with a computer from virtually anywhere and from locations not under the same physical control as the computers themselves.

Typical NOS logical access control software provided for user-IDs and passwords and selective authority to access file server data and program files. A workstation user logged on to the LAN by executing a log-in program resident on the file server.

The program prompted the user to enter an ID and password. If the log-in program concluded that the ID and password were valid, it consulted an access-control table to determine which data and programs the user might access. Access modes were defined as read-only, execute-only, create, modify (write or append), lock, and delete, with respect to individual files and groups of files. The LAN administrator maintained the access control table using a utility program. The effectiveness of the controls depended on the care taken by the administrator, and so, in some circumstances, controls could be weak. It was essential to protect the ID and password of the LAN administrator since, if they were compromised, the entire access-control system became vulnerable. Alert information system security officers noted that control over *physical* access to LAN servers was critical in maintaining the logical access controls. Intruders who could physically access a LAN server could easily restart the server using their own version of the NOS, completely bypassing the installed logical access controls.

Superficially, a LAN appears to be the same as a 1970s mainframe with remote dumb terminals. The difference technically is that each LAN workstation user is executing programs on the workstation, not on the centralized file server, while mainframe computers use special software and hardware to run many programs concurrently, one program for each terminal. To the user at a workstation or remote terminal, the two situations appear to be the same, but from a security standpoint, there are significant differences. The mainframe program software stays on the mainframe and cannot, under normal conditions, be altered during execution. A LAN program on a workstation can be altered, for example, by a computer virus, while actually executing. As a rule, mainframe remote terminals cannot download and save files whereas workstations usually have at least a removable disk drive. Furthermore, a malicious workstation user can easily install a rewritable CD device, which makes it much easier to copy and take away large amounts of data.

Another important difference is the character of the connection between the computer and the terminals. Each dumb terminal has a dedicated connection to its mainframe and receives only data that is directed to it. A LAN operates more like a set of radio transmitters sharing a common frequency on which the file server and the workstations take turns "broadcasting" messages. Each message includes a "header" block that identifies the intended recipient, but every node (the file server and the workstations) on a LAN receives all messages. Under normal circumstances, each node ignores messages not addressed to it. However, it is technically feasible for a workstation to run a modified version of the NOS that allows it to capture all messages. In this way, a workstation could identify all log-in messages and record the user IDs and passwords of all other users on the LAN, giving it complete access to all of the LAN's data and facilities.

Mainframe and LAN security also differ greatly in the operating environment. As noted, the typical mainframe is installed in a separate room and is managed by a staff of skilled technicians. The typical LAN file server, however, is installed in ordinary office space and is managed by a part-time, remotely located LAN administrator who may not be adequately trained. Consequently, the typical LAN has a higher exposure to tampering, sabotage, and theft. However, if the typical mainframe is disabled by an accident, fire, sabotage, or any other security incident, many business functions will be interrupted, whereas the loss of a LAN file server usually disrupts only a single function.

1.2.17 1990s: Total Interconnection.

With the growing popularity of LANs, the technologies for interconnecting them emerged. These networks of physically interconnected local area networks were called wide area networks, or WANs. Any node on a LAN could access every node on any other interconnected LAN, and in some configurations, those nodes might also be given access to mainframe and minicomputer files and to processing capabilities.

1.2.18 Telecommuting.

Once the WAN technology was in place, it became feasible to link LANs together by means of telecommunications circuits. It had been expensive to do this with the low-speed, online systems of the 1970s because all data had to be transmitted over the network. Now, since processing and most data used by a workstation were on its local LAN, a WAN network was much less expensive. Low-traffic LANs were linked using dial-up access for minimum costs, while major LANs were linked with high-speed dedicated circuits for better performance. Apart from dial-up access, all network traffic typically flowed over nonswitched private networks. Of the two methods, dial-up communications were considerably more vulnerable to security violations, and they remain so to this day.

1.2.19 Internet and the World Wide Web.

The Internet, which began life in 1969 as the ARPANET, slowly emerged onto the general computing scene during the 1980s. Initially, access to the Internet was restricted to U.S. Government agencies and their contractors. ARPANET users introduced the concept of e-mail as a convenient way to communicate and exchange documents. Then, in 1989–1990, Tim Berners-Lee conceived of the World Wide Web and the Web browser. This one concept produced a profound change in the Internet, greatly expanding its utility and creating an irresistible demand for access. During the 1990s, the U.S. Government relinquished its control, and the Internet became the gigantic, no-one-is-in-charge network of networks it is today.

The Internet offers several important advantages: The cost is relatively low, connections are available locally in most industrialized countries, and by adopting the Internet protocol, Transmission Control Protocol/Internet Protocol (TCP/IP), any computer becomes instantly compatible with all other Internet users.

The World Wide Web technology made it easy for anyone to access remote data. Almost overnight, the Internet became the key to global networking. Internet service providers (ISPs) operate Internet-compatible computers with both dial-up and dedicated access. A computer may access an ISP directly as a stand-alone ISP client or via a gateway from a LAN or WAN. A large ISP may offer dial-up access at many locations, sometimes called points of presence (POPs), interconnected by its own network. ISPs establish links with one another through the national access points (NAPs) initially set up by the National Science Foundation. With this "backbone" in place, any node with access can communicate with another node, connected to a different ISP, located halfway around the globe, without making prior arrangements.

The unrestricted access provided by the Internet created new opportunities for organizations to communicate with clients. A company can implement a Web server with a full-time connection to an ISP and open the Web server, and the WWW pages it hosts, to the public. A potential customer can access a Web site, download product information and software updates, ask questions, and even order products. Commercial Web sites, as they evolved from static "brochure-ware" to online shopping centers, stock brokerages, and travel agencies, to name just a few of the uses, became known as e-businesses.

1.3 GOVERNMENT RECOGNITION OF INFORMATION ASSURANCE.

Certain major events in the history of information assurance (IA) center on government initiatives. In particular, IA has been strongly influenced by the development of security standards starting in the 1980s, by the publication of the landmark publication *Computers and Risk*[11] in 1991, and by the establishment of the InfraGard program in the late 1990s for protection of the U.S. critical infrastructure.

1.3.1 IA Standards.

In the late 1970s, the U.S. Department of Defense "established a Computer Security Initiative to foster the wide-spread availability of trusted computer systems."[12] The author of the initial report that later became the *Trusted Computer Systems Evaluation Criteria* (TCSEC), DoD Standard 5200.28, wrote: "Trusted computer systems are operating systems capable of preventing users from accessing more information than that to which they are authorized. Such systems are in great demand as more processing is entrusted to computers, while less information should be shared by all the system's users. With this demand comes a need to ascertain the integrity of computer systems on the market." The TCSEC was issued with a bright orange cover and became known as the *Orange Book*. Under the direction of National Computer Security Center (NCSC) director Patrick Gallagher and others, the National Security Agency (NSA) issued a series of books known as the Rainbow Series that profoundly affected the direction of IA in the United States and globally.[13]

The Rainbow Series led to similar efforts in other countries, culminating in the Common Criteria Evaluation and Validation Scheme (CCEVS), which has become the international standard for defining security levels for systems and software and for determining acceptable methods for testing and certifying system compliance with such standards.[14]

For details of the evolution of security standards, see Chapter 51 in this *Handbook*.

1.3.2 Computers at Risk. [15]

In 1988, the Defense Advanced Research Projects Agency (DARPA) asked the Computer Science and Technology Board (renamed the Computer Science and Telecommunications Board of the National Research Council [NRC] in 1990) for a study of computer and communications security issues affecting U.S. Government and industry. The NRC's System Security Study Committee published its results in a readable and informative book, *Computers at Risk: Safe Computing in the Information Age.* [16]

The committee included experts with impeccable credentials, including executives from major computer vendors such as Hewlett-Packard, DEC, and IBM; from high-technology companies such as Shearson, Lehman, Hutton Inc., and Rockwell International; universities such as Harvard and the Massachusetts Institute of Technology; and think tanks like the RAND Corporation.

A public misconception is the supposed divergence in focus of the military and of commerce: The military usually is described as concerned with external threats and the problem of disclosure, whereas businesses are said to worry more about insider threats to data integrity. On the contrary, the military and commerce need to protect data in similar ways. The differences arise primarily from (1) the sophistication and resources available to governments that try to crack foreign military systems; (2) the relatively strong military emphasis on prevention compared with commercial need for proof that can be used in legal proceedings; and (3) the fact that the military can access deep background checks on personnel, in contrast with the limits imposed on the invasion of privacy in the commercial sector.

Some of the more interesting points raised by the NRC Committee assert that:

- Because of the rapid and discontinuous pace of innovation in the computer field, "with respect to computer security, the past is not a good predictor of the future."
- Embedded systems (those where the microprocessor is not accessible to user reprogramming, as in medical imaging systems) open up greater risks from inadequate quality assurance (e.g., a software bug in a Therac 25 linear accelerator killed three patients by irradiating them with more than 100 times the intended radiation dosage).[17]
- Networking makes it possible to harm many more systems: "Interconnection gives an almost ecological flavor to security; it creates dependencies that can harm as well as benefit the community."

The committee proposed five major recommendations, summarized next:

1. Push for implementation of generally accepted system security principles including:
   - Quality assurance standards that address security considerations
   - Access control for operations as well as data (e.g., any of the menu systems which preclude access to the operating system).
   - Unambiguous user identification (ID) and authentication (e.g., personal profiles and hand−held password generators).
   - Protection of executable code (e.g., flags to show that certain object modules are "production" or "installed" and thus apply strict access control that would prevent unauthorized modification—as found in configuration control systems).
   - Security logging (e.g., logging failed file-open attempts and logon password violations).
   - Assigning a security administrator to each enterprise.
   - Data encryption.
   - Operational support tools for verifying the state and effectiveness of security measures (e.g., audit tools).
   - Independent audits of system security by people not directly involved in programming or system management of the audited system.
   - Hazard analysis evaluating threats to safety from different malfunctions and breaches of security (e.g., consequences of tampering with patient data in hospitals).
2. Take specific short-term actions now:
   - Develop security policies for your organization before there is a problem.
   - Form and train computer emergency response teams before a crisis to respond to security violations or attacks.
   - Use the Orange Book's (TCSEC, from the National Computer Security Center's Rainbow series) C2 and B1 criteria to define guidelines on security.
   - Improve software systems development by applying better quality-assurance methods.

- Contribute to voluntary industry groups developing modern security standards and implement those standards in commercial software.

- Make effective security the default in software and hardware. (Make the user explicitly disable security instead of having to enable it.)

3. Learn and teach about security:

- Build a repository of incident data.

- Foster education in engineering secure systems, both by encouraging universities to provide postgraduate training in security and by urging industry to include security training as part of software engineering projects.

- Teach beginners about security and ethics in computer usage and programming (e.g., the National Center for Supercomputing Applications is working on a research and development project to study beliefs, attitudes and behavior about ethical issues in computing in grade and high schools, colleges, and universities).

4. Clarify export control criteria and set up a forum for arbitration. (Hardware and software vendors have been complaining for years that the arbitrary imposition of severe export restrictions hampers American competitiveness in overseas markets without materially helping national security.)

5. Fund and pursue needed research in such areas as:

- **Security modularity.** The effects on security of combining modules with known security properties.

- **Security policy models.** More subtle requirements, such as integrity and availability, still are not easily represented by control structures.

- **Cost estimation.** There should be better ways of measuring the costs and benefits of security mechanisms in particular applications.

- **New technology.** Networking, in particular, leads to greater complexity (e.g., how to connect "mutually suspicious organizations").

- **Quality assurance for security:** How to measure effectiveness.

- **Modeling tools.** Standards for graphical representations of security relationships analogous to the diagrams used in functional decomposition and object-oriented methodologies for program design.

- **Automated procedures.** Audit and monitoring tools for the data center management team.

- **Nonrepudiation.** Combining the need for detailed records of user actions with the values of privacy.

- **Resource control.** How to ensure that proprietary software and data are used legitimately (e.g., preventing more than the licensed number of users from accessing a system, preventing software theft).

- **Security perimeters.** How to reconcile the desire for network interconnection with limitations due to security requirements ("If, for example, a network permits mail but not directory services... less mail may be sent because no capability exists to look up the address of a recipient").

Chapter 2 of the NRC report, "Concepts of Information Security," is a 25-page primer on information systems security that could be handed to any manager who needs to be filled in on why you propose to spend so much money protecting the computer systems. The authors cover the fundamental aspects of IS (confidentiality, integrity, and availability); management controls (individual accountability, auditing, and separation of duties); risks (probabilities of attack or damage) and vulnerabilities (weak points); and privacy issues. In Appendix 2.2, the authors report an informal survey in April 1989 of 30 private companies in a variety of fields. The consensus among those polled included these basic standards for IS security (show these to your upper management if necessary):

- Unique IDs, block access after a maximum number of incorrect logon attempts, show last successful access at logon time, make passwords and IDs expire.
- Disallow embedded passwords during logon, make passwords invisible during entry, force minimum length (6), store passwords encrypted, scan proposed passwords to eliminate easy words.
- Permit strict control over file access.
- Detect and interdict viruses, certify software as virus-free, provide data encryption, overwrite deleted files to prevent recovery, force tight binding of production data to production programs.
- Automated time-out for inactive sessions, unique identification of terminals and workstations during logon.
- Network security monitoring, modem-locking, callback, automatic data encryption during transmission.
- Audit trails including security violations.
- Generally applicable security standards that could be used by vendors and users to evaluate different equipment and software for specific environments.

Twenty years later, focus among information assurance experts has shifted beyond the technical to emphasize organizational controls. For example, the 2003 survey of members of the Information Systems Security Association included these IS function practices by the respondents:

- Access controls, 73%
- Written information security policy, 72%
- Compliance with existing laws and regulations, 66%
- Creation of organization and process to implement policy, 59%
- Awareness and training program, 57%
- Regular monitoring, reviewing and auditing, 57%
- Business continuity planning, 57%
- Risk assessment and risk management, 56%

In 2007, Gary S. Miliefsky, noted entrepreneur, and founding member of the U.S. Department of Homeland Security proposed seven priorities for corporate information security:

1. Roll out corporate security policies.
2. Deliver corporate security awareness and training.
3. Run frequent information security self-assessments.
4. Perform regulatory compliance self-assessments.

5. Deploy corporate-wide encryption.

6. Value, protect, track and manage all corporate assets.

7. Test business continuity and disaster recovery planning.[18]

The Computer Security Division of the Information Technology Laboratory at the National Institute of Standards and Technology issued a draft reference model that included these "programmatic, integration, and system security activities that are typically a part of an information security program":

Program Security Activities

Annual and Quarterly Review and Reporting of Information Security Program

Asset Inventory

Awareness and Specialized Security Training

Continuity of Operations

Incident Response

Periodic Testing and Evaluation

Plan of Action and Milestones

Policies and Procedures

Risk Management

Integration Activities

Business Risk

Capital Planning and Investment Control (CPIC)

Configuration Management

Enterprise Architecture (EA)

Environmental Protection

Human Resources

Personnel Security

Physical Security

Privacy

Records Management

Strategic Plan

System Development Life Cycle (SDLC)

System Security Activities

Categorize the Information System

Select Security Controls

Supplement Security Controls

Document Security Controls

Implement Security Controls

Assess Security Controls

Authorize the Information System

Monitor Security Controls[19]

1.3.3   InfraGard.[20]   InfraGard is a nationwide program in the United States that brings together representatives from information technology departments in industry and academia for information sharing and analysis, especially to help protect critical infrastructure against cyberattacks and also to support the Federal Bureau of Investigation (FBI) in its cybercrime investigations and education projects. [21]

The organization started in the Cleveland Field Office of the FBI in 1996 and expanded rapidly until there are now over 11,000 members in over 40 chapters. Joining InfraGard is easy and free for U.S. citizens residing in the United States. Using the Web site (www.infragard.net/chapters/index.php?mn=3), you can locate a nearby local chapter and contact your chapter officers. You can get application forms online and then send them in to the FBI liaison officer for that chapter to be vetted for admission. The FBI conducts a background check to ensure that all members are likely to be trustworthy to participate in confidential discussions of threats and vulnerabilities. Chapters usually conduct regular local meetings and organize list-servers for exchange of information among members. Many have newsletters as well.

1.4   RECENT DEVELOPMENTS.   In the years since the Fourth Edition of this *Handbook* was published (in 2002), one of the key developments has been the dramatic increase in availability of inexpensive portable data storage devices. At the time of writing (2008), flash drives the size of a lipstick or smaller are available online with capacities in the dozens of megabytes for a few dollars and capacities in the gigabytes for little more. Such devices are available in a wide range of concealable formats, such as pens, music players, and even watches. Digital cameras use storage cards that can be used for data transfers; mobile phones include cameras and recording capabilities. Controlling data leakage through unauthorized connection of such devices has become a significant problem for security managers. Systems for restricting connection of devices and controlling data transfers to such storage media are spreading through government and corporate environments.

Another issue that increasingly concerns security managers is the protection of personally identifiable information (PII) from customers or data subjects. Many organizations, including government agencies, banks, and universities, have suffered serious damage from loss of control over PII and the risks of identity theft resulting from exposure of such sensitive data. Legislators are responding to public concern by increasing legal requirements for protection of PII. The use of encryption on mobile data systems such as laptop computers, personal digital assistants (PDAs), mobile phones, and integrated systems that combine many functions (e.g., BlackBerries) has become a necessity. A consequence of the growing interconnectivity of storage and communications devices is that corporate networks are no longer insulated from less secure systems. Users who connect poorly protected laptop computers or other devices to public networks, such as hotel-supplied ISPs or wireless access points in coffee shops, may return to their home offices with malware-infected systems that contaminate the entire network. Security managers are increasingly turning to integrated systems for controlling connectivity via virtual private networks and supervisory software that monitors and restricts unauthorized connections, software installations, and downloads.

A most formidable new threat lies in the international operations of mafia-like rings of computer criminals. Once such collusion stole over 41 million credit and debit card records from the giant retailer, TJX. According to information released by the U.S. Department of Justice on August 5, 208, the ring consisted of three Americans, one

Estonian, three Ukrainians, one from Belarus, two from the Peoples Republic of China, and one known only by a network "handle". The eleven were charged with conspiracy, computer intrusion, fraud, and identity theft, perpetrated by "war driving" and hacking into wireless computer networks.[22] For more about wireless network security, see Chapter 33 in this Handbook.

1.5 ONGOING MISSION FOR INFORMATION SYSTEM SECURITY.

There is no end in sight to the continuing proliferation of Internet nodes, to the variety of applications, to the number and value of online transactions, and, in fact, to the rapid integration of computers into virtually every facet of our existence. Nor will there be any restrictions as to time or place. With 24/7/365, always-on operation, and with global expansion even to relatively undeveloped lands, both the beneficial effects and the security violations can be expected to grow apace.

Convergence, which implies computers, televisions, cell phones, and other means of communication combined in one unit, together with continued growth of information technology, will lead to unexpected security risks. Distributed denial-of-service (DDoS) attacks, copyright infringement, child pornography, fraud, and theft of identity are all ongoing security threats. So far, no perfect defensive measures have been developed. This *Handbook* provides a foundation for understanding and blunting both existing vulnerabilities and new threats that inevitably will arise in the future.

Certainly, no one but the perpetrators could have foreseen the use of human-guided missiles to attack the World Trade Center. Besides its symbolic significance, the great concentration of resources within the WTC increased its attractiveness as a target. After 9/11, the importance of physical safety of personnel has become the dominant security issue, with disaster recovery of secondary, but still great, concern. This *Handbook* cannot foresee all possible future emergencies, but it does prescribe some preventive measures, and it does recommend procedures for mitigation and remediation.

1.6 NOTES

1. Many technical specialists use the term "security" to refer to logical access controls. A glance at the contents pages of this volume shows the much broader scope of information system security.

2. For further details, see, for example, www.cs.uiowa.edu/~jones/cards.

3. See inventors.about.com/library/weekly/aa062398.htm.

4. It is notable that the IBM 1401 computer was so named because the initial model had 1,400 bytes of main memory. It was not long before memory size was raised to 8 kilobytes and then later to as much as 32 kilobytes. In 1980, the Series III minicomputer from Hewlett-Packard doubled its maximum memory from 1 megabyte to 2 megabytes at a cost of $64,000 (about $200,000 in 2008 dollars). This compares with today's personal computers, typically equipped with no less than 512 megabytes and often a gigabyte or more.

5. The term "dumb" was used because the terminal had no internal storage or processing capability. It could only receive and display characters and accept and transmit keystrokes. Both the received characters and the transmitted ones were displayed on a cathode ray tube (CRT) much like a pre–color television screen. Consequently, these were also called "glass" terminals.

6. "Multiprocessing," "multiprogramming," and "multitasking" are terms that are used almost interchangeably today. Originally, "multitasking" implied that several

modules or subroutines of a single program could execute together. "Multiprogramming" was designed to execute several different programs, and their subroutines, concurrently. "Multiprocessing" most often meant that two or more computers worked together to speed program execution by providing more resources.

7. Also known as ARPAnet and Arpanet.

8. First published 1975. Reissued by Mass Market Paperbacks in May 1990.

9. "Fixed," in contrast with the removable disk packs common in large data centers.

10. See standards.ieee.org/getieee802/802.3.html.

11. National Research Council, (1991). *Computers at Risk: Safe Computing in the Information Age* (Washington, DC: National Academy Press, 1991). Available as a searchable openbook at www.nap.edu/books/0309043883/html/index.html.

12. G. H. Nibaldi, "Proposed Technical Evaluation Criteria for Trusted Computer Systems," Publication M79-225 (Bedford, MA: MITRE Corporation, 1979).

13. For access to all the Rainbow Series documents, see www.fas.org/irp/ nsa/rainbow. htm.

14. The CCEVS Web site has extensive documentation; see www.niap-ccevs.org/cc-scheme/.

15. This section is reprinted with slight modifications by permission of the author from the original manuscript for M. E. Kabay, *The NCSA Guide to Enterprise Security: Protecting Information Assets* (New York: McGraw-Hill, 1996), Chapter 1, pp. 2–5.

16. National Research Council, *Computers at Risk*.

17. www.sunnyday.mit.edu/papers/therac.pdf.

18. G. S. Miliefsky, "The 7 Best Practices for Network Security in 2007," *Network World*, January 17, 2007; www.networkworld.com/columnists/2007/ 011707miliefsky.html?t51hb.

19. E. Chew, K. Stine, and M. Swanson, (2007). "Information Security Reference Data Model (DRAFT)," NIST Special Publication 800-110 (Draft); http://csrc.nist.gov/publications/drafts/sp800-110/Draft-SP800-110.pdf.

20. M. E. Kabay, "InfraGard Is Not a Deodorant," *Network World*, September 8, 2005; www.networkworld.com/newsletters/sec/2005/0905sec2.html.

21. www.infragard.net/about.php?mn=1&sm=1-0.

22. www.usdoj.gov News release of August 5, 2008.

CHAPTER 2

HISTORY OF COMPUTER CRIME

M. E. Kabay

2.1   WHY STUDY HISTORICAL RECORDS?   Every field of study and expertise develops a common body of knowledge that distinguishes professionals from amateurs. One element of that body of knowledge is a shared history of significant events that have shaped the development of the field. Newcomers to the field benefit from learning the names and significant events associated with their field so that they can understand references from more senior people in the profession, and so that they can put new events and patterns into perspective. This chapter provides a brief overview of some of the more famous (or notorious) cases of computer crime (including those targeting computers and those mediated through computers) of the last four decades.[1]

2.2   OVERVIEW.   This chapter illustrates several general trends from the 1960s through the decade following 2000:

- In the early decades of modern information technology (IT), computer crimes were largely committed by individual disgruntled and dishonest employees.
- Physical damage to computer systems was a prominent threat until the 1980s.
- Criminals often used authorized access to subvert security systems as they modified data for financial gain or destroyed data for revenge.
- Early attacks on telecommunications systems in the 1960s led to subversion of the long-distance phone systems for amusement and for theft of services.
- As telecommunications technology spread throughout the IT world, hobbyists with criminal tendencies learned to penetrate systems and networks.
- Programmers in the 1980s began writing malicious software, including self-replicating programs, to interfere with personal computers.
- As the Internet increased access to increasing numbers of systems worldwide, criminals used unauthorized access to poorly protected systems for vandalism, political action, and financial gain.
- As the 1990s progressed, financial crime using penetration and subversion of computer systems increased.
- The types of malware shifted during the 1990s, taking advantage of new vulnerabilities and dying out as operating systems were strengthened, only to succumb to new attack vectors.
- Illegitimate applications of e-mail grew rapidly from the mid-1990s onward, generating torrents of unsolicited commercial and fraudulent e-mail.

2.3   1960S AND 1970S: SABOTAGE.   Early computer crimes often involved physical damage to computer systems and subversion of the long-distance telephone networks.

2.3.1   Direct Damage to Computer Centers.   In February 1969, the largest student riot in Canada was set off when police were called in to put an end to a student occupation of several floors of the Hall Building. The students had been protesting against a professor accused of racism, and when the police came in, a fire broke out and computer data and university property were destroyed. The damages totalled $2 million, and 97 people were arrested.[2]

Thomas Whiteside cataloged a litany of early physical attacks on computer systems in the 1960s and 1970s:[3]

1968	Olympia, WA: An IBM 1401 in the state is shot twice by a pistol-toting intruder
1970	University of Wisconsin: Bomb kills one and injures three people and destroys $16 million of computer data stored on site
1970	Fresno State College: Molotov cocktail causes $1 million damage to computer system
1970	New York University: Radical students place fire-bombs on top of Atomic Energy Commission computer in attempt to free a jailed Black Panther
1972	Johannesburg, South Africa: Municipal computer is dented by four bullets fired through a window
1972	New York: Magnetic core in Honeywell computer attacked by someone with a sharp instrument, causing $589,000 of damage
1973	Melbourne, Australia: Antiwar protesters shoot American firm's computer with double-barreled shotgun
1974	Charlotte, NC: Charlotte Liberty Mutual Life Insurance Company computer is shot by a frustrated operator
1974	Dayton, OH: Wright Patterson Air Force Base: Four attempts are made to sabotage computers, including by magnets, loosened wires, and gouges in equipment
1977	Rome, Italy: Four terrorists pour gasoline on university computer and burn it to cinders
1978	Lompoc, CA: Vandenburg Air Force Base: : A peace activist destroys an unused IBM 3031 using a hammer, a crowbar, a bolt cutter, and a cordless power drill as a protest against the NAVSTAR satellite navigation system, claiming it gives the United States a first-strike capability

---

The incidents of physical abuse of computer systems did not stop as other forms of computer crime increased. For example, in 2001, *NewsScan* editors[4] summarized a report from *Wired Magazine*:

A survey by British PC maker Novatech, intended to take a lighthearted look at techno-glitches, instead revealed the darker side of computing. One in every four computers has been physically assaulted by its owner, according to the 4,200 respondents.[5]

In April 2003, the National Information Protection Center and Department of Homeland Security reported:

Nothing brings a network to a halt more easily and quickly than physical damage. Yet as data transmission becomes the lifeblood of Corporate America, most big companies haven't performed due diligence to determine how damage-proof their data lifelines really are. Only 20 percent of midsize and large companies have seriously sussed out what happens to their data connections after they go beyond the company firewall, says Peter Salus of MatrixNetSystems, a network-optimization company based in Austin, TX.[6]

By the mid-2000s, concerns over the physical security of electronic voting systems had risen to public awareness. For example:

A cart of Diebold electronic voting machines was delivered today to the common room of this Berkeley, CA boarding house, which will be a polling place on Tuesday's primary election. The machines are on a cart which is wrapped in plastic wrap (the same as the stuff we use in the kitchen). A few cable locks (bicycle locks, it seems) provide the appearance of physical security, but they aren't threaded through each machine. Moreover, someone fiddling with the cable locks, I am told, announced after less than a minute of fiddling that he had found the three-digit combination to be the same small integer repeated three times.[7]

2.3.2   1970–1972: Albert the Saboteur.

One of the most instructive early cases of computer sabotage occurred at the National Farmers Union Service Corporation of Denver, where a Burroughs B3500 computer suffered 56 disk head crashes in the two years from 1970 to 1972. Down time was as long as 24 hours per crash, with an average of 8 hours per incident. Burroughs experts were flown in from all over the United States at one time or another, and concluded that the crashes must be due to power fluctuations.

By the time all the equipment had been repaired and new wiring, motor generators, circuit breakers, and power-line monitors had been installed in the computer room, total expenditures for hardware and construction were over $500,000 (in 1970 dollars). Total expenses related to down time and lost business opportunities because of delays in providing management with timely information are not included in this figure. In any case, after all this expense, the crashes continued sporadically as before.

By this time, the experts were beginning to wonder about their analysis. For one thing, all the crashes had occurred at night. Could it be sabotage? Surely not! Old Albert, the night-shift operator, had been so helpful over all these years; he had unfailingly called in the crashes at once, gone out for coffee and donuts for the repair crews, and been meticulous in noting the exact times and conditions of each crash. However, all the crashes had in fact occurred on his shift.

Management installed a closed-circuit television (CCTV) camera in the computer room—without informing Albert. For some days, nothing happened. Then one night another crash occurred. On the CCTV monitor, security guards saw good ol' Albert open up a disk cabinet and poke his car key into the read/write head solenoid, shorting it out and causing the 57th head crash.

The next morning, management confronted Albert with the film of his actions and asked for an explanation. Albert broke down in mingled shame and relief. He confessed to an overpowering urge to shut the computer down. Psychological investigation determined that Albert, who had been allowed to work night shifts for years without a change, had simply become lonely. He arrived just as everyone else was leaving; he left as everyone else was arriving. Hours and days would go by without the slightest human interaction. He never took courses, never participated in committees, never felt involved with others in his company. When the first head crashes occurred—spontaneously—he had been surprised and excited by the arrival of the repair crew. He had felt useful, bustling about, telling them what had happened. When the crashes had become less frequent, he had involuntarily, and almost unconsciously, re-created the friendly atmosphere of a crisis team. He had destroyed disk drives because he needed company.[8]

2.4   IMPERSONATION.

Using the insignia and specialized language of officials as part of social engineering has a long history in crime; a dramatization of these techniques is in the popular movie *Catch Me If You Can*[9] about Frank William Abagnale

Jr., the teenage scammer and counterfeiter who pretended to be a pilot, a doctor, and a prosecutor before eventually becoming a major contributor to the U.S. government's anticounterfeiting efforts and then founding a major security firm.[10]

Several criminals involved in computer-mediated or computer-oriented crime became notorious for using impersonation.

2.4.1 1970: Jerry Neal Schneider.

A notorious computer-related crime started in 1970, when teenager Jerry Neal Schneider used Dumpster diving to retrieve printouts from the Pacific Telephone and Telegraph (PT&T) company in Los Angeles. After years of collection, he had enough knowledge of procedures that he was able to impersonate company personnel on the phone. He collected yet more detailed information on procedures. Posing as a freelance magazine writer, he even got a tour of the computerized warehouse and information about ordering procedures. In June 1971, he ordered $30,000 of equipment to be sent to a normal PT&T dropoff point—and promptly stole it and sold it. He eventually had a 6,000-square-foot warehouse and 10 employees. He stole over $1 million of equipment—and sold some of it back to PT&T. He was finally denounced by one of his own disgruntled employees and became a computer security consultant after his prison term.[11]

2.4.2 1980–2003: Kevin Mitnick.

Born in 1963, Kevin Mitnick became involved in crime early, using a special punch for bus transfers to get free rides anywhere in the San Fernando Valley in California by the time he was a young teenager. His own autobiographical comments show him to have been involved in phone phreaking, malicious pranks, and breaking into computers at the Digital Equipment Corporation (DEC) using social engineering.[12]

In 1981, he and his friend Lewis De Payne used social engineering to gain unauthorized access to an operations center for Pacific Bell; "the juvenile court ordered a diagnostic psychological study of Mitnick and sentenced him to a year's probation."[13] In 1987, he was arrested for breaking into the computers of the Santa Cruz Operation, makers of SCO UNIX, and sentenced to three years probation.

In the summer of 1988, Mitnick and his accomplice and friend Lenny DiCicco cracked the University of Southern California computers again and misappropriated hundreds of Mb of disk space (a lot at the time) to store VAX VMS source files stolen from Digital Equipment Corporation (DEC). Mitnick was arrested by the Federal Bureau of Investigation (FBI) for having stolen the VAX VMS source code. During his trial, he was described as suffering from an impulse-control disorder. In July 1989, he was sentenced to a year in jail and six months rehabilitation. He later tried to become a private investigator and security specialist. He was generally treated with hostility by the established information security community.

In November 1992, Mitnick went underground again when the FBI got a warrant for his arrest on charges of stealing computer time from a phone company. He was located two years later when he made the mistake of leaving insulting messages on the computer and voice-mail systems of a physicist and Internet security expert Tsutomu Shimomura. Shimomura was so irritated that he helped law enforcement authorities track the fugitive to North Carolina, where Mitnick was arrested in February 1995 and imprisoned pending trial.

Mitnick was convicted in federal court for the Central District of California on August 9, 1999, and sentenced to 46 months imprisonment for "four counts of wire fraud, two counts of computer fraud and one count of illegally intercepting a wire communication."[14] Mitnick was previously sentenced by Judge Pfaelzer to an additional 22 months in prison, this for possessing cloned cellular phones when he was arrested in North Carolina in 1995, and for violating terms of his supervised release imposed after being convicted of an unrelated computer fraud in 1989. He admitted to violating the terms of supervised release by hacking into PacBell voicemail and other systems, and to associating with known computer hackers, in this case codefendant Louis De Payne. Following his release from prison in September 2000, Mitnick was to be on three years parole during which his access to computers was restricted[15] and his profits from writing or speaking about his criminal career were to be turned over to reimburse his victims.

Mitnick earned a living on the talk circuit and eventually founded his own security consulting firm. In the years since his release from prison, he has collaborated in writing several books on social engineering.[16]

Perhaps his most significant position in the history of computer crime is that he became an icon in the criminal underground. "FREE KEVIN" was a popular component of Web vandalism for many years, and Eric Corley, the longtime editor of the criminal-hacking publication *2600: The Hacker Quarterly,* even made a movie, *Freedom Downtime,* about what the criminal underground describes as the grossly unfair treatment of Mitnick by the federal government and the news media.[17]

2.4.3 Credit Card Fraud.
Credit at local businesses dates back into the undocumented past.[18] In the United States, credit cards appeared in the mid-1920s when gasoline companies began issuing cards that were recognized at stations across the country.[19] In 1950, Frank X. McNamara started the Diners Club, the first credit card company serving multiple types of businesses; the company began the practice of charging a percentage fee for each transaction and also charged its clients a membership fee.[20] The VISA card evolved from the 1951 BankAmericard from the Bank of America, and a consortium of California banks established MasterCard shortly thereafter. American Express started its card program in 1958.

Card use rose and, unsurprisingly, credit card fraud was rampant. Mail theft also became widespread as unscrupulous individuals discovered that envelopes containing credit cards were just like envelopes full of cash. And there was little to stop card companies from sending out cards that customers had never asked for, were not expecting, and could not have known had been stolen, until the issuing company began demanding payment for the charges that had been run up. These crimes and other problems stemming from the relentless card-pushing by banks led directly to the passage of the Fair Credit Billing Act of 1974[21] as well as many other laws[22] designed to protect the consumer.[23]

By the mid-1990s, credit card fraud was a rapidly growing problem for consumers and for law enforcement. A 1997 FBI report stated:

> Around the world, bank card fraud losses to Visa and Master-Card alone have increased from $110 million in 1980 to an estimated $1.63 billion in 1995. . . .The United States has suffered the bulk of these losses-approximately $875 million for 1995 alone. This is not surprising because 71 percent of all worldwide revolving credit cards in circulation were issued in this country. . . .Law enforcement authorities continually confront new and complex schemes involving credit card frauds committed against financial institutions and bank card companies. Perpetrators run the gamut from individuals with easy access to credit card information-such as credit agency officials, airline baggage handlers, and mail carriers, both public and private, to organized groups, usually from similar ethnic backgrounds, involved in large-scale card theft, manipulation, and counterfeiting activities. Although current bank card fraud operations are numerous and varied, several schemes account for the majority of the industry's losses by taking advantage of dated technology, customer negligence, and laws peculiar to the industry.[24]

2.4.4 Identity Theft Rises. By the late 1990s and in the decade following the year 2000, credit-card fraud was subsumed into the broader category of *identity theft*. Instead of limiting their depredations to running up bills on stolen or forged credit card accounts, thieves, often in organized rings, created entire bogus parallel identities, initiating unpaid bank loans, buying cars with other people's credit, and wreaking havoc with innocent victims' credit ratings, financial situations, and even their daily life. Victims of extreme cases lost their ability to obtain mortgages, buy new homes, and accept new jobs. Worse, the burden of proof of innocence fell on the victims, in a bitter reversal of the assumption of innocence underlying British common law and its offshoot in the commonwealth and the United States.

At the time of this writing (May 2008), identity theft is the fastest-growing form of fraud today. The National Crime Victimization Survey (NCVS) of the U.S. Department of Justice Bureau of Justice Statistics (BJS) includes surveys dating back to 1973. Currently the random sample includes 77,200 households with 134,000 in all who are contacted every six months and followed for three years. The results for 2005 are available from the BJS Web site as PDF reports and as ZIP files containing spreadsheets for further analysis.[25]

A summary of that research[26] reports that about 6.4 million households (5.5 percent of all the households in the United States) had been affected by some form of identity theft (defined as theft of credit cards, thefts from existing bank accounts, misuse of personal information, or multiple types of theft at same time). Losses from credit-card theft averaged $980 per household; across all type of theft, the average was $1,620 per household; and for misuse of personal information the losses averaged $4,850 per household. The most likely victim households were headed by people between 18 and 24 years of age; households with family incomes above $75,000 were twice as likely to be victimized as those whose annual income was less than $50,000.

In August, 2008, the U.S. Department of Justice announced[27] the single largest and most complex case of identity theft ever charged in this country. It involved eleven people from five different countries, including two from the U.S. and two from the Peoples Republic of China, who had stolen more than 40,000,000 credit card records from a major U.S. retailer. They drove by, or loitered at, buildings in which wireless networks were housed, and installed sniffers that recorded passwords, card numbers and account data. Unless adequate preventative measures are installed quickly, more such horrendous events will be sure to occur. For more on wireless network security, see Chapter 33 in this *Handbook*.

2.5 PHONE PHREAKING. Even in the earliest days of telephony, teenage boys played with the new technology to cause havoc. In the late 1870s, the new AT&T system in America had to stop using teenagers as switchboard operators:

> The boys were openly rude to customers. They talked back to subscribers, saucing off, uttering facetious remarks, and generally giving lip. The rascals took Saint Patrick's Day off without permission. And worst of all they played clever tricks with the switchboard plugs: disconnecting calls, crossing lines so that customers found themselves talking to strangers, and so forth.

> This combination of power, technical mastery, and effective anonymity seemed to act like catnip on teenage boys.[28]

2.5.1 2600 Hz. In the late 1950s, AT&T began switching its telephone networks to direct-dial long distance, using specific frequency tones to communicate among its switches. Around 1957, a blind seven-year-old child named Josef Engressia with perfect pitch and an emotional fixation on telephones learned to whistle the 2600-Hz pitch that interrupted long-distance telephone calls and allowed him to place a free long-distance call to anywhere in the world.[29] This emotionally disturbed person eventually renamed himself "Joybubbles" and is often described as the founder of phone phreaking—the manipulation of the phone system for unauthorized access to services.

John Draper was in the U.S. Air Force in 1964 when he began helping his colleagues place free phone calls. At the suggestion of Joybubbles, he used the whistles in Cap'n Crunch cereal boxes to generate the 2600-Hz tone and then, calling himself Captain Crunch, went on to create electronic tone synthesizers called *blue boxes*.[30] In the 1970s, Apple founders Steve Wozniak and Steve Jobs built blue boxes and, using the devices, perpetrated such pranks as calling the Vatican while pretending to be Henry Kissinger.[31]

A significant contributor to the growth of phreaking in the 1970s was the publication in 1971 of an article about phreaking in *Esquire Magazine,* which attracted the attention of many young technophiles.[32]

2.5.2   1982–1991: Kevin Poulsen.   As the phone system shifted to greater reliance on computers, the border between phreaking and hacking began to blur. One of the important names from the 1980s period of fascination with everything phone-related was Kevin Poulsen.

Kevin Poulsen's autobiographical sketch is shown next.

> Kevin Poulsen first gained notoriety in 1982, when the Los Angeles County District Attorney's Office raided him for gaining unauthorized access to a dozen computers on the ARPANET, the forerunner of the modern Internet. Seventeen years old at the time, he was not charged, and went on to work as a programmer and computer security supervisor for SRI International in Menlo Park, California, then as a network administrator at Sun Microsystems.
>
> In 1987, Pacific Bell security agents discovered that Poulsen and his friends had been penetrating telephone company computers and buildings. After learning that Poulsen had also worked for a defense contractor where he'd held a SECRET level security clearance, the FBI began building an espionage case against the hacker.
>
> Confronted with the prospect of being held without bail, Poulsen became a fugitive. While on the run, he obtained information on the FBI's electronic surveillance methods, and supported himself by hacking into Pacific Bell computers to cheat at radio-station phone-in contests, winning a vacation to Hawaii and a Porsche 944-S2 Cabriolet in the process.
>
> After surviving two appearances on NBC's Unsolved Mysteries, Poulsen was finally captured on April 10th, 1991, in a Van Nuys grocery store, by a Pacific Bell security agent acting on an informant's tip. On December 4th, 1992, Poulsen became the first hacker to be indicted under U.S. espionage laws when the Justice Department charged him with stealing classified information. (18 U.S.C. 793).
>
> Poulsen was held without bail while he vigorously fought the espionage charge. The charge was dismissed on March 18th, 1996.
>
> Poulsen served five years, two months, on a 71 month sentence for the crimes he committed as a fugitive, and the phone hacking that began his case. He was freed June 4th, 1996, and began a three year period of supervised release, barred from owning a computer for the first year, and banned from the Internet for the next year and a half.
>
> Since his release, Poulsen has appeared on MSNBC, and on ABC's Nightline, and he was the subject of Jon Littman's flawed book, "The Watchman—the Twisted Life and Crimes of Serial Hacker Kevin Poulsen." His case has earned mention in several computer security and infowar tracts—most of which still report that he broke into military computers and stole classified documents.[33]

After his release from prison, Kevin Poulsen turned to journalism. He became an editor for *SecurityFocus* and then was hired as a senior editor at *Wired News*. He is a serious investigative reporter (e.g., he broke the story of sexual predators in MySpace)[34] and a frequent contributor to the "Threat Level" blog.[35]

2.6   DATA DIDDLING.   One of the most common forms of computer crime since the start of electronic data processing is *data diddling*—illegal or unauthorized data alteration. These changes can occur before and during data input, or before output. Data-diddling cases have included bank records, payrolls, inventory data, credit records, school transcripts, telephone switch configurations, and virtually all other applications of data processing.

2.6.1   Equity Funding Fraud (1964–1973).   One of the classic early data-diddling frauds was the Equity Funding case, which began with computer problems at the Equity Funding Corporation of America, a publicly traded and highly successful firm with a bright idea. The idea was that investors would buy insurance policies from the company and also invest in mutual funds at the same time, with profits to be redistributed to clients and to stockholders. Through the late 1960s, Equity's shares rose dizzyingly in price, and there were news magazine stories about this wunderkind of the Los Angeles business community.

The computer problems occurred just before the close of the financial year in 1964. An annual report was about to be printed, yet the final figures simply could not be extracted from the mainframe. In despair, the head of data processing told the president the bad news; the report would have to be delayed. Nonsense, said the president expansively (in the movie, anyway); simply make up the bottom line to show about $10 million in profits and calculate the other figures so it would come out that way. With trepidation, the DP chief obliged. He seemed to rationalize it with the thought that it was just a temporary expedient, and could be put to rights later in the real financial books.

The expected profit did not materialize, and some months later, it occurred to the executives at Equity that they could keep the stock price high by manufacturing false insurance policies that would make the company look good to investors. They therefore began inserting false information about nonexistent policyholders into the computerized records used to calculate the financial health of Equity.

In time, Equity's corporate staff got even greedier. Not content with jacking up the price of their stock, they decided to sell the policies to other insurance companies via the redistribution system known as reinsurance. Reinsurance companies pay money for policies they buy and spread the risk by selling parts of the liability to other insurance companies. At the end of the first year, the issuing insurance companies have to pay the reinsurers part of the premiums paid in by the policyholders. So in the first year, selling imaginary policies to the reinsurers brought in large amounts of real cash. However, when the premiums came due, the Equity crew "killed" imaginary policyholders with heart attacks, car accidents, and, in one memorable case, cancer of the uterus—in a male imaginary policyholder.

By late 1972, the head of DP calculated that by the end of the decade, at this rate, Equity Funding would have insured the entire population of the world. Its assets would surpass the gross national product of the planet. The president merely insisted that this showed how well the company was doing.

The scheme fell apart when an angry operator who had to work overtime told the authorities about shenanigans at Equity. Rumors spread throughout Wall Street and the insurance industry. Within days, the Securities and Exchange Commission had informed the California Insurance Department that they had received information about the ultimate form of data diddling: Tapes were being erased. The officers of the company were arrested, tried, and condemned to prison terms.[36]

2.6.2   1994: Vladimir Levin and the Citibank Heist.   In February 1998, Vladimir Levin was sentenced to three years in prison by a court in New York City. Levin masterminded a major conspiracy in 1994 in which the gang illegally transferred $12 million in assets from Citibank to a number of international bank accounts. The crime was spotted after the first $400,000 was stolen in July 1994, and Citibank cooperated with the FBI and Interpol to track down the criminals. Levin was ordered to pay back $240,000, the amount he actually managed to withdraw before he was arrested.[37] The incident led to Citibank's hiring of Stephen R. Katz as the banking industry's first chief information security officer (CISO).

2.7   SALAMI FRAUD.   In the salami technique, criminals steal money or resources a bit at a time. Two different etymologies are circulating about the origins of this term. One school of security specialists claim that it refers to slicing the data thin—like a salami. Others argue that it means building up a significant object or amount from tiny scraps—like a salami.

There were documented cases of salami frauds in the 1970s and 1980s, but one of the more striking incidents came to light in January 1993, when four executives of a Value Rent-a-Car franchise in Florida were charged with defrauding at least 47,000 customers using a salami technique. The federal grand jury in Fort Lauderdale claimed that the defendants modified a computer billing program to add five extra gallons to the actual gas tank capacity of their vehicles. From 1988 through 1991, every customer who returned a car without topping it off ended up paying inflated rates for an inflated total of gasoline. The thefts ranged from $2 to $15 per customer—rather thick slices of salami but nonetheless difficult for the victims to detect.

Unfortunately, salami attacks are *designed* to be difficult to detect. The only hope is that random audits, especially of financial data, will pick up a pattern of discrepancies and lead to discovery. As any accountant will warn, even a tiny error must be tracked down, since it may indicate a much larger problem. For example, Cliff Stoll's famous adventures tracking down spies in the Internet began with an unexplained $0.75 discrepancy between two different resource accounting systems on UNIX computers at the Keck Observatory of the Lawrence Berkeley Laboratories. Stoll's determination to understand how the problem could have occurred revealed an unknown user; investigation led to the discovery that resource-accounting records were being modified to remove evidence of system use. The rest of the story is told in Clifford Stoll's book *The Cuckoo's Egg*.

2.8   LOGIC BOMBS.   A logic bomb is a program that has deliberately been written or modified to produce results when certain conditions are met that are unexpected and unauthorized by legitimate users or owners of the software. Logic bombs may be within standalone programs, or they may be part of worms (programs that hide their existence and spread copies of themselves within a computer systems and through networks) or viruses (programs or code segments which hide within other programs and spread copies of themselves).

Time bombs are a subclass of logic bombs that "explode" at a certain time.

According to a National Security Council employee, the United States government authorized insertion of a time bomb in software to control the Trans-Siberian natural gas pipeline that they knew would be stolen from U.S. sources by the Soviet government. "The result was the most monumental non-nuclear explosion and fire ever seen from space," said Thomas C. Reed.[38]

The infamous Jerusalem virus (also known as the Friday the 13th virus) of 1988 was a time bomb. It duplicated itself every Friday and on the thirteenth of the month, causing system slowdown; on every Friday the 13th after May 13, 1988, it also corrupted all available disks on the infected systems.

Other examples of notorious time bombs include:

- A common PC virus from the 1980s, *Cascade,* made all the characters fall to the last row of the display during the last three months of every year.

- The Michelangelo virus of 1992 was designed to damage hard disk directories on the sixth of March every year.

- In 1992, computer programmer Michael Lauffenburger was fined $5,000 for leaving a logic bomb at General Dynamics. His intention was to return after his program had erased critical data and be paid to fix the problem.[39]

The most famous time bomb of recent years was the Y2K (year 2000) problem. In brief, old programs used two-digit year codes that were based on the assumption that they applied to the twentieth century. As the twenty-first century approached, analysts warned of catastrophic consequences if the programs were not corrected to use four-digit years or otherwise adapt to the change of century.[40] In the event, the corrective measures worked and there were no disasters. Later analysis showed a positive correlation between investments in Y2K remediation and later profitability.[41]

2.9 EXTORTION.   Computer data can be held for ransom. For example, according to Whiteside, in 1971, two reels of magnetic tape belonging to a branch of the Bank of America were stolen at Los Angeles International Airport. The thieves demanded money for their return. The owners ignored the threat of destruction because they had adequate backup copies.

Other early cases of extortion involving computers:

- In 1973, a West German computer operator stole 22 tapes and received $200,000 for their return. The victim did not have adequate backups.

- In 1977, a programmer in the Rotterdam offices of Imperial Chemical Industries, Ltd. (ICI) stole all his employer's tapes, including backups. Luckily, ICI informed Interpol of the extortion attempt. As a result of the company's forthrightness, the thief and an accomplice were arrested in London by officers from Scotland Yard.

In the 1990s, one of the most notorious cases of extortion was the 1999 theft of 300,000 records of customer credit cards from the CD Universe Web site by "Maxus," a 19-year-old Russian. He sent an extortion note that read: "Pay me $100,000 and I'll fix your bugs and forget about your shop forever. . .or I'll sell your cards [customer credit data] and tell about this incident in news." Refused by CD Universe owners, he promptly released 25,000 credit card numbers via a Web site that became so popular with criminals that Maxus had to limit access to one stolen number per visit.

2.10 TROJAN HORSES.   Trojans are programs that pretend to be useful but that also contain harmful code or are just plain harmful.

2.10.1 1988 Flu-Shot Hoax.   One of the nastiest tricks played on the shell-shocked world of early microcomputer users was the FLU-SHOT-4 incident of March 1988. With the publicity given to damage caused by destructive, self-replicating virus programs distributed through electronic bulletin board systems (BBSs), it seemed natural that public-spirited programmers would rise to the challenge and provide protective screening.

Flu-Shot-3 was a useful program for detecting viruses. Flu-Shot-4 appeared on BBSs and looked just like version 3; however, it actually destroyed critical areas of hard disks and any floppies present when the program was run. The instructions that caused the damage were not present in the program file until it was running; this self-modifying code technique makes it especially difficult to identify Trojans by simple inspection of the assembler-level code.

2.10.2 Scrambler, 12-Tricks and PC Cyborg.   Other early and notorious PC Trojans from the late 1980s that are still remembered in the industry included:

- The Scrambler (also known as the KEYBGR Trojan), which pretended to be a keyboard driver (KEYBGR.COM) but actually made a smiley face move randomly around the screen
- The 12-Tricks Trojan, which masqueraded as CORETEST.COM, a program for testing the speed of a hard disk, but actually caused 12 different kinds of damage (e.g., garbling printer output, slowing screen displays, and formatting the hard disk)
- The PC Cyborg Trojan (or "AIDS Trojan"), which claimed to be an AIDS information program but actually encrypted all directory entries, filled up the entire C disk, and simulated COMMAND.COM but produced an error message in response to nearly all commands.

2.10.3 1994: Datacomp Hardware Trojan.   On November 8, 1994, a correspondent reported to the *RISKS Forum Digest* that he had been victimized by a curious kind of Trojan:

> I recently purchased an Apple Macintosh computer at a "computer superstore," as separate components—the Apple CPU, and Apple monitor, and a third-party keyboard billed as coming from a company called Sicon.
>
> This past weekend, while trying to get some text-editing work done, I had to leave the computer alone for a while. Upon returning, I found to my horror that the text "welcome datacomp" had been inserted into the text I was editing. I was certain that I hadn't typed it, and my wife verified that she hadn't, either. A quick survey showed that the "clipboard" (the repository for information being manipulated via cut/paste operations) wasn't the source of the offending text.
>
> As usual, the initial reaction was to suspect a virus. Disinfectant, a leading anti-viral application for Macintoshes, gave the system a clean bill of health; furthermore, its descriptions of the known viruses (as of Disinfectant version 3.5, the latest release) did not mention any symptoms similar to my experiences.
>
> I restarted the system in a fully minimal configuration, launched an editor, and waited. Sure enough, after a (rather long) wait, the text "welcome datacomp" once again appeared, all at once, on its own.

Further investigation revealed that someone had put unauthorized code in the ROM chip used in several brands of keyboard. The only solution was to replace the keyboard. Readers will understand the possible consequences of a keyboard that inserts unauthorized text into, say, source code. Winn Schwartau, the renowned computer security expert, has coined the word "chipping" to refer to such unauthorized modification of firmware.

2.10.4 Keylogger Trojans.   By the mid-2000s, software and hardware Trojans designed to capture logs of keystrokes and sometimes to transmit those logs via covert Internet connections had become a well-known tool of industrial espionage. The United States Department of Homeland Security issued a warning in December 2005 that included this overview:

> According to industry security experts, the biggest security vulnerability facing computer users and networks is email with concealed Trojan Horse software—destructive programs that masquerade as benign applications and embedded links to ostensibly innocent websites that download malicious code. While firewall architecture blocks direct attacks, email provides a vulnerable route into an organization's internal network through which attackers can destroy or steal information.

> Attackers try to circumvent technical blocks to the installation of malicious code by using social engineering—getting computer users to unwittingly take actions that allow the code to be installed and organization data to be compromised.

> The techniques attackers use to install Trojan Horse programs through email are widely available, and include forging sender identification, using deceptive subject lines, and embedding malicious code in email attachments.

> Developments in thumb-sized portable storage devices and the emergence of sophisticated keystroke logging software and devices make it easy for attackers to discover and steal massive amounts of information surreptitiously.[42]

2.10.5 Haephrati Trojan.   A case that made the news in the mid-2000s began when Israeli author Amon Jackont was upset to find parts of the manuscript on which he was working posted on the Internet. Then someone tried to steal money from his bank account. Suspicion fell on his stepdaughter's ex-husband, Michael Haephrati. Police discovered a keystroke logger on Jackont's computer. It turned out that Haephrati had also sold spy software to clients; the Trojan was concealed in what appeared to be confidential e-mail. Once installed on the victims' computers, the software sent surveillance data to a server in London, England.

Haephrati was detained by UK police and investigations began in Germany and Israel. Twelve people were detailed in Israel; eight others were under house arrest. Suspects included private investigators and top executives from industrial firms. Victims included Hewlett-Packard, the Ace hardware stores, and a cable-communications company.

Michael and Ruth Haephrati were extradited from Britain for trial in Israel on January 31, 2006. They were accused of installing the Trojan horse program that activated a key logger with remote-reporting capabilities.[43]

In March 2006, the couple were indicted in Tel Aviv for corporate espionage.[44] They pleaded guilty to the charges[45] and were sentenced to four and two years of jail, respectively, as well as punished with fines.[46]

The story did not end there, however. Two years later, "Four members of the Israeli Modi'in Ezrahi private investigation firm were sentenced on Monday after they were found guilty of using Trojan malware to steal commercially sensitive information from their clients' competitors."[47] The report continues:

Asaf Zlotovsky, a manager at the Modi'in Ezrahi detective firm, was jailed for 19 months. Two other employees, Haim Zissman and Ron Barhoum, were sent to prison for 18 and nine months respectively. The firm's former chief exec, Yitzhak Rett, the victim of an apparent accident when he fell down a stairwell during a break in police questioning back in 2005, escaped a jail sentence under a plea bargaining agreement. Rett was fined 250,000 Israeli Shekels (£36,500) and ordered to serve ten months' probation over his involvement in the scam.

However, an article in April 2008 reported that Michael Haephrati "claimed that there was no jail time, and that he was completely free. As a matter of fact he was going to continue to offer his Trojan Horse service but this time he would only work with 'law enforcement agencies.'"[48]

2.10.6 Hardware Trojans and Information Warfare.   As this chapter was going to press, a flurry of news stories discussed the dangers of growing reliance on Chinese-manufactured computing components.

U.S. Defense Department sources say privately that the level of Chinese cyberattacks obliges them to avoid Chinese-origin hardware and software in all classified systems and as many unclassified systems as fiscally possible. The high threat of Chinese cyberpenetrations into U.S. defense networks will be magnified as the Pentagon increasingly loses domestic sources of "trusted and classified" microchips.[49]

The discovery of counterfeit Cisco routers worsened concerns about the reliability of Chinese-manufactured network equipment.[50] The FBI, Immigration and Customs Enforcement (ICE), Customs and Border Protection (CBP), and the Royal Canadian Mounted Police (RCMP) worked together to track a massive pattern of counterfeit network hardware including Cisco routers; these investigations and seizures raised questions about the reliability and trustworthiness of such equipment, much of which was manufactured in the People's Republic of China. Although Cisco scientists examined some of the counterfeit equipment and found no back doors, concern was serious enough that government agencies created test chips to challenge quality assurance processes at military contractors:

In April [2008], the Defense Advanced Research Projects Agency, part of the Defense Department, began distributing chips with hidden Trojan horse circuitry to military contractors participating in an agency program, Trusted Integrated Circuits. The goal is to test forensic techniques for finding hidden electronic trap doors, which can be maddeningly elusive. The agency is not yet ready to announce the results of the test, said Jan Walker, a spokeswoman for the agency.[51]

2.11 NOTORIOUS WORMS AND VIRUSES.   The next sections briefly describe some of the outstanding incidents that are often mentioned in discussions of the history of malware.[52]

2.11.1 1970–1990: Early Malware Outbreaks.   The ARPANET was the precursor of the Internet.[53] According to several reports:

Sometime in the early 1970s, the Creeper virus was detected on ARPANET, a US military computer network which was the forerunner of the modern Internet. Written for the then-popular Tenex operating system, this program was able to gain access independently through a modem and copy itself to the remote system. Infected systems displayed the message, "I'M THE CREEPER: CATCH ME IF YOU CAN."

Shortly thereafter, the Reaper program was anonymously created to delete Creeper. Reaper was a virus: it spread to networked machines and if it located a Creeper virus, Reaper would delete it. Even the participants are unable to say whether Reaper was a response to Creeper, or if it was created by the same person or persons who created Creeper in order to correct their mistake.[54]

By 1981, the Apple II computer was a popular system among hobbyists; the Elk Cloner virus spread via infected floppy disks and is regarded as "the first large-scale computer virus outbreak in history."[55]

In 1986, the Brain boot-sector virus was the first IBM-PCs malware to spread around the world. It was created by two brothers from Lahore, Pakistan, and included this text:

Welcome to the Dungeon (c) 1986 Brain & Amjads (pvt) Ltd VIRUS_SHOE RECORD V9.0 Dedicated to the dynamic memories of millions of viruses who are no longer with us today - Thanks GOODNESS!! BEWARE OF THE er…VIRUS: this program is catching program follows after these messages….$#@%$@!!

The Lehigh Virus appeared at Lehigh University in Pennsylvania in 1987 and damaged the files of several professors and students. This early program-infector targeted only *command.com* and was therefore extremely limited in its spread.

In 1988, the Jerusalem virus, a file infector that reproduced by inserting its code into EXE and COM files, caused a global PC epidemic.

Another noteworthy infection of 19988 came from the self-encrypting Cascade virus of 1988, which confused many naive users who interpreted the falling symbols on their screen as part of an unexpected screen saver. This virus was one of the earliest examples of the attempts to counter signature-based antivirus products.

2.11.2   December 1987: Christmas Tree Worm.
In December 1987, users of IBM mainframe computers connected to the European Academic Research Network (EARN), BITNET, and the IBM company VNET were flooded with e-mail bearing a character-based representation of a Christmas tree. A student at Technische Universität Clausthal[56] in Germany launched "a worm, written in an IBM-specific language called REXX."[57] The worm used the victim's list of correspondents to send copies of itself to everyone on the list.[58]

2.11.3   November 2, 1988: Morris Worm.
On November 2, 1988, the Internet was rocked by the explosive appearance of unauthorized code on systems all over the world. At 17:00 EST on November 2, 1988, Robert T. Morris, a student at Cornell University in Ithaca, New York, released a worm into the Internet. By midnight, it had attacked VAX computers running 4 BSD UNIX and SUN Microsystems Sun 3 computers throughout the United States. One of the most interesting aspects of the worm's progress through the Internet was the almost complete independence of its path from normal geographical constraints. It sometimes leaped from coast to coast faster than it reached physically neighboring computer systems. The worm graphically demonstrated that cyberspace has its own geography.

The worm often superinfected its hosts, leading to slowdowns in overall processing speed. The first Internet warning ("We are under attack") was posted at 02:38 on November 3 to the TCP-IP list by a scientist at University of California at Berkeley. At 03:34, Andy Sudduth, a friend of Morris's at Harvard, posted a warning message ("There may be a virus loose on the internet") anonymously and included a few comments on how to stop the worm. Unfortunately, Spafford writes, the Internet was so severely impeded by the worm that this message was not widely distributed for over 24 hours.

By 06:00 on the morning of November 3, messages were creeping through the Internet with details of how the worm worked. The news spread via news groups such as the TCP-IP list, Usenix 4bsd-ucb-fixes, and the Usenet news.announce.important group. Spafford and his friends and colleagues on the Internet collaborated feverishly on providing patches against the worm.

Meanwhile, as word spread of the attack, some systems administrators began cutting their networks out of the Internet. The Defense Communications Agency isolated its Milnet and Arpanet networks from each other around 11:30 on November 3. At noon, machines in the science and technology center at the Stanford Research Institute were shut down.

By late on November 4, a comprehensive set of patches was posted on the Internet to defend systems against the worm. That evening, a *New York Times* reporter told Spafford that the author of the worm had been found.

By November 8, the Internet seemed to be back to normal. A group of concerned computer scientists met at the National Computer Security Center to study the incident and think about preventing recurrences of such attacks. Spafford put the incident into perspective with the comment that the affected systems were no more than 5 percent of the hosts on the Internet. It would be foolish to dismiss Morris's electronic vandalism as a prank or to claim that the worm alerted managers to weak security on their systems. Nonetheless, it is true that the incident contributed to the establishment of the Computer Emergency Response Team at the Software Engineering Institute of Carnegie-Mellon University. For these blessings, however, we owe no gratitude to Robert T. Morris.

In 1990, Morris was found guilty under the Computer Fraud and Abuse Act of 1986. The maximum penalties included five years in prison, a $250,000 fine, and restitution costs. Morris was ordered to perform 400 hours of community service, sentenced to three years probation, and required to pay $10,000 in fines. He was expelled from Cornell University.

His lawyers appealed the conviction to the Supreme Court of the United States. Their arguments included lack of evil intent (he did not mean to cause harm, honest—even though his worm took extraordinary precautions to conceal itself) and they deplored the scandalous behavior of Cornell University authorities, who had the temerity to search their own electronic mail message system to locate evidence that incriminated Morris. The lawyers also argued that sending a mail message might become a crime if Morris's conviction were upheld.

The Supreme Court upheld the decision by declining to hear the appeal.[59]

Robert T. Morris eventually became an associate professor in the Electrical Engineering and Computer Science Department of the Massachusetts Institute of Technology and a member of the Computer Science and Artificial Intelligence Laboratory.[60]

2.11.4   Malware in the 1990s.   The most significant malware development of the 1990s was the release in July 1995 of the world's first widely distributed macro-language virus. The *macro.concept* virus made its appearance in MS-Word for Windows documents. It demonstrated how to use the macro programming language, common to many Microsoft products, to generate self-reproducing macros that spread from document to document. Within a few months, clearly destructive versions of this demonstration virus appeared.

Macro viruses were a dangerous new development. As explained in a recent history of viruses and antiviruses:

- Putting self-reproducing code in easily- and frequently exchanged files, such as documents, greatly increased the infectiousness of the viruses
- Virus writers shifted their attention to a much easier programming language than assembly.
- E-mail exchanges of infected documents were a far more effective mechanism for virus infection than exchanges of infected programs or disks.
- "[M]acro viruses were neither platform-specific, nor OS-specific. They were application-based."[61]

In the latter half of the 1990s, macro viruses replaced boot sector viruses and file infector viruses as a major type of malicious self-reproducing malware; during that period, additional types of script-based, network worms also increased.

Exhibit 2.1 shows the rise and fall of prevalence of macro viruses over the decade from discovery to extinction using data from the WildList archives. The WildList shows malware identified on user systems by at least two virus researchers.[62]

Roger Thompson summarizes the developments in malware in the 1990s in this way:

By around 2000, macro viruses ceased to be a problem because the new version of MS-Office 2000 included features that blocked macro viruses. The next step in the evolution of malware was the mass mailers like the ILOVEYOU worm and then the network worms. These were easy to write and easy to obfuscate by varying the text contents, thus defeating signature scanners. These worms spread very quickly until the release of Windows XP Service Pack 2, which forced the Windows Firewall to be on by default. After that extinction-level event, criminals moved onward to creating mass mailers and bots which could spread malware and spam or cause distributed denial-of-service through communication via the trusted Web sites accessed through browsers that created a tunnel through the firewall.[63]

2.11.5   March 1999: Melissa.   On Friday, March 26, 1999, the CERT/CC received initial reports of a fast-spreading new MS-Word macro virus. "Melissa" was written to infect such documents; once loaded, it uses the victim's MAPI-standard e-mail address book to send copies of itself to the first 50 people on the list. The virus attaches an infected document to an e-mail message with subject line "Subject: Important Message From <name>" where <name> is that of the inadvertent sender. The e-mail message reads: "Here is that document you asked for...don't show anyone else;-)" and includes a MS-Word file as an infected attachment. The original infected document, "list.doc," was a compilation of URLs for pornographic Web sites. However, as the virus spread, it was capable of sending any other infected document created by the victim.

Because of this high replication rate, the virus spread faster than any previous virus in history. On many corporate systems, the rapid rate of internal replication saturated e-mail servers with outbound automated junk e-mail. Initial estimates were in the range of 100,000 downed systems. Antivirus companies rallied immediately, and updates for all the standard products were available within hours of the first notices from CERT/CC.

The search for the originator of the Melissa e-mail computer virus/worm began immediately after the outbreak. Initial findings traced the virus to Access Orlando, a Florida Internet Service Provider (ISP), whose servers were shut down by order of the FBI for forensic examination; the systems were then confiscated. That occurrence was then traced back to Source of Kaos, a free-speech Web site where the virus may have lain dormant for months in a closed but not deleted virus-distributor's pages. Investigators discovered a serial number in the vector document, written with

EXHIBIT 2.1   Rise and Fall in Macro Viruses in the WildList, 1996–2008

Year	Macro Viruses	Total Entries	Percentage Macro Virus
1996[a]	1	183	0.6%
1997[b]	27	239	11%
1998[c]	77	258	30%
1999[d]	46	129	36%
2000[e]	108	175	62%
2001[f]	145	228	64%
2002[g]	103	198	52%
2003[h]	68	205	33%
2004[i]	51	261	20%
2005[j]	22	399	6%
2006[k]	19	804	2%
2007[l]	5	797	0.6%
2008[m]	0	590	0.0%

[a]WildList Organization International, "PC Viruses in the Wild—January 10, 1996," www.wildlist.org/WildList199601.htm.
[b]WildList Organization International, "PC Viruses in the Wild—February, 1997," www.wildlist.org/WildList199702.htm.
[c]WildList Organization International, "PC Viruses in the Wild—January, 1998," www.wildlist.org/WildList199801.htm.
[d]WildList Organization International, "PC Viruses in the Wild—January 1999," www.wildlist.org/WildList199001.htm.
[e]WildList Organization International, "PC Viruses in the Wild—January, 2000," www.wildlist.org/WildList200001.htm.
[f]WildList Organization International, "PC Viruses in the Wild—January, 2001," www.wildlist.org/WildList200101.htm.
[g]WildList Organization International, "PC Viruses in the Wild—January, 2002," www.wildlist.org/WildList200201.htm.
[h]WildList Organization International, "PC Viruses in the Wild—January, 2003," www.wildlist.org/WildList200301.htm.
[i]WildList Organization International, "PC Viruses in the Wild—January, 2004," www.wildlist.org/WildList200401.htm.
[i]WildList Organization International, "PC Viruses in the Wild—January, 2005," www.wildlist.org/WildList200501.htm.
[k]WildList Organization International, "PC Viruses in the Wild—January, 2006," www.wildlist.org/WildList200601.htm.
[l]WildList Organization International, "PC Viruses in the Wild—January, 2007," www.wildlist.org/WildList200701.htm.
[m]WildList Organization International, "PC Viruses in the Wild—January, 2008," www.wildlist.org/WildList200801.htm.

MS-Word; the undocumented serial number helped law enforcement when investigators circulated it on the Net to help track down the perpetrator.

The next steps turned to the value-added network AOL, where the virus was released to the public. The giant ISP's information helped to identify a possible suspect and by April 2, the FBI arrested David L. Smith (age 30) of Aberdeen, New Jersey. Smith apparently panicked when he heard the FBI was on the trail of the Melissa spawner and he threw away his computer—stupidly, into the trash at his own apartment building.

Smith was charged with second-degree offenses of interruption of public communication, conspiracy to commit the offense and attempt to commit the offense, third-degree theft of computer service, and third-degree damage or wrongful access to computer systems. If convicted, Smith faced a maximum penalty of $480,000 in fines and 40 years in prison. On December 10, 1999, Smith pleaded guilty to all federal charges and agreed to every particular of the indictment, including the estimates by the International Computer Security Association of at least $80 million of consequential damages due to the Melissa infections.[64]

2.11.6 May 2000: I Love You.

Starting around May 4, 2000, e-mail users opened messages from familiar correspondents with the subject line "I love you"; many then opened the attachment, LOVE-LETTER-FOR-YOU.txt.vbs, which infected the user's e-mail address book and initiated mass mailing of itself to all the contacts. The "Love Bug" was the fastest-spreading worm to that time, infecting computers all over the world, starting in Asia, then Europe.[65]

On May 11, Filipino computer science student Onel de Guzman of AMA Computer College in Manila admitted to authorities that he may "accidentally have launched the destructive Love Bug virus out of youthful exuberance." He did not admit that he had created the malware himself; however, the name GRAMMERSoft appeared in the computer code of the virus, and that was the name of a computer group to which the 23-year-old de Guzman belonged.[66]

In September 2000, de Guzman participated in a live chat hosted by CNN.com; he vigorously defended virus-writing and blamed the creators of vulnerable systems for releasing poorly designed software. He refused to take responsibility for writing the worm.[67]

Philippine authorities tried to prosecute de Guzman but had to drop their attempts in August 2000 for lack of sufficient evidence. Due to the lack of computer crime laws at the time, it was impossible for other countries such as the United States to extradite the suspect: International principles of dual criminality require equivalent laws in both jurisdictions before extradition can proceed.

By October 2000, de Guzman had refused to take responsibility for writing the worm and publicly stated, "'I admit I create viruses, but I don't know if it's one of mine....If the source code was given to me, I could look at it and see. Maybe it is somebody else's, or maybe it was stolen from me.'"[68]

The "I Love You" case was a wake-up call for the international community to think about standardizing computer crime laws around the globe.[69]

2.12 SPAM.

Chapter 20 in this *Handbook* includes a detailed history of unsolicited commercial e-mail and the reason it is called *spam*. This section looks solely at a seminal abuse of the USENET in 1994 and trends in spam over the next decade.

2.12.1 1994: Green Card Lottery Spam.

On April 2, 1994, Laurence A. Canter and Martha S. Siegel posted an advertisement for legal services connected to the U.S. government's Green Card Lottery to over 6,000 USENET groups. Instead of cross-posting their commercial message, they used a script to post a copy of the message separately to every group. The former method would have shown the message to USENET users once; Canter and Siegel's abuse of the USENET made their ad show up in every affected group to which users subscribed.[70]

Reaction worldwide was massive. Automated cancelbots trolled the USENET deleting the unwanted messages; the attorneys' ISP was so overloaded with e-mail complaints that its servers crashed. Canter and Siegel were reviled in postings and newspaper articles.[71] Their unsavory backgrounds were posted in discussion groups, including details of disciplinary hearings before the Florida Bar and accusations of dishonesty and unprofessional behavior.[72]

Unfazed, the couple published a book about how to abuse the Internet using spam and defended their actions in interviews as an expression of freedom of speech; they dismissed critics as "wild-eyed zealots" or as commercial interests intent on controlling the Internet for their own gain.[73]

Canter was eventually disbarred in Tennessee, in part for his spamming.[74] He remained unrepentant; in 2002, he spammed 50,000 K–12 teachers with an advertisement for a book whose title he liked so he could harvest payments for referrals from Amazon.[75]

2.12.2 Spam Goes Global.   Over the next decade, the incidence of spam grew explosively. By 2007, spam watchers and anti-spam companies reported that around 88 percent of all e-mail traffic on the Internet was spam. Spammers caused so much irritation that companies developed software and hardware solutions for filtering e-mail by content. Spammers responded by increasing the number of images in their spam, making content filtering more difficult. At one point, the amount of spam grew 17 percent between one day and the next as spammers began pumping PDF files into spam pipelines.[76]

Botnets spawned through infected zombie machines established rogue SMTP nodes using innocent (and ignorant) PC users' computers and persistent high-speed Internet connections.[77] Spam currently provides a major vector for fraud by deceit, including in particular 4-1-9 advance fee fraud and phishing attacks.[78] Advance-fee fraud usually consists of enticements to participate in the theft of ill-gotten gains such as bank deposits belonging to dead people or stolen from poor countries; the dupes who agree to participate in such illegality are promised millions of dollars—only to be told that they suddenly have to send cash for unexpected bribes or fees. If they do so, they are asked for more...and more...and more. Phishing involves sending e-mail messages that are supposed to look like official, usually alarming, warnings from banks and other institutions; victims click on links that look like one thing but actually go to the criminals' Web sites. There the victims cheerfully type in their user identification, passwords, bank account numbers, and all manner of other confidential information useful for identity theft.[79] Advance-fee fraud and phishing are discussed in Chapter 20 in this *Handbook*.

2.13 DENIAL OF SERVICE.   Denial of service results from exhaustion or destruction of necessary resources and is thoroughly discussed in Chapter 18. However, a couple of denial-of-service attackers stand out among all the others in the last decade or so: the Unamailer and Mafiaboy.

2.13.1 1996: Unamailer.   In August 1996, someone using the pseudonym "johnny [x]chaotic" claimed the blame for a massive mail-bombing run based on fraudulently subscribing dozens of victims to hundreds of mailing lists. The denial of service was the result in part of the naïveté of list managers who accepted subscriptions for any e-mail address from any other e-mail address. In a rambling and incoherent letter posted on the Net, (s)he made rude remarks about famous and not-so-famous people, whose capacity to receive meaningful e-mail was then obliterated by up to thousands of unwanted messages a day.[80] "The first attack, in August, targeted more than 40 individuals, including Bill Clinton and Newt Gingrich and brought a torrent of complaints from the people who found their names sent as subscribers to some 3,000 E- mail lists."[81]

Someone claiming to be the same "Unamailer" (as the news media labeled him or her in reference to the Unabomber) launched a similar mass-subscription mail-bombing run in late December.

> This attack is estimated to involve 10,139 listservs groups, 3 times greater than the one that took place in the summer, also at xchaotic's instigation. If each mailing list in this attack sent the targeted individuals just a modest 10 letters to the subscribers' computers those individuals would receive more than 100,000 messages. If each listing system sent 100 messages—and many do —then the total messages could tally 1,000,000.[82]

In December, the attacker(s) sneered at list administrators for failing to use authentication before allowing subscriptions and wrote that they would continue their attacks until practices changed.[83]

Partly as a result of the Unamailer's depredations, list administrators did in fact change their practices—not that anyone thanked Johnny [x]chaotic for his method of persuasion.

2.13.2 2000: MafiaBoy.

On February 8, 2000, Yahoo.com suffered a three-hour flood from a distributed denial-of-service (DDoS) attack and lost its capacity to serve Web pages to visitors. The next day, the same technique was extended to Amazon.com, eBay.com, Buy.com, and CNN.com.[84] Later information also showed that Charles Schwab, the online stock brokerage, had been seriously impeded in serving its customers because of the DDoS. Buy.com managers were particularly disturbed because the attack occurred on the day of their initial public offering. As a result of the attacks, a number of firms formed a consortium to fight DDoS attacks.[85]

Investigation by the RCMP and the FBI located a 15-year-old child in west-end Montreal who used a modem to control zombies in his DDoS escapade:

> On April 15, 2000, the RCMP arrested a Canadian juvenile known as Mafiaboy for the February 8th DDoS attack on CNN in Atlanta, Georgia. On August 3, 2000, Mafiaboy was charged with 64 additional counts. On January 18, 2001, Mafiaboy appeared before the Montreal Youth Court in Canada and pleaded guilty to 56 counts. These counts included mischief to property in excess of $5,000 against Internet sites, including CNN.com, in relation to the February 2000 attacks. The other counts related to unauthorized access to several other Internet sites, including those of several US universities. On September 12, 2001, Mafiaboy appeared before the Montreal Youth Court in Canada and was sentenced to eight months "open custody," one year probation, and restricted use of the Internet.[86]

MafiaBoy's name was not released by Canadian authorities because of Canadian laws protecting juveniles, although several U.S. reporters distributed his identity in their publications. His chief contribution to the history of computer crime was to demonstrate asymmetric warfare in cyberspace.[87] His actions showed that even an ignorant child with little knowledge of computing could use low-tech hardware and tools available to anyone on the Internet to cripple major organizations.

2.14 HACKER UNDERGROUND OF THE 1980S AND 1990S.

Newcomers to the field of information assurance will encounter references to the computer underground in texts, articles, and discussions. The sections that follow provide thumbnail sketches of some of the key groups and events in the shadowy world of criminal hacking, (known as *black hats,* in contrast to *white hats,* who are law enforcement and establishment security experts) and the intermediate range of well-intentioned rebels who use unorthodox means to challenge corporations and governments over what they see as security failings (these people are often called *gray hats*).

2.14.1   1981: Chaos Computer Club.

On September 12, 1981, a group of German computer enthusiasts with a strong radical political orientation formed the Chaos Computer Club (CCC) in Hamburg.[88] One of their first achievements was to demonstrate a serious problem in the Bundespost's (German post office) new Bilschirmtext (BTX) interactive videotext service in 1984, not long after the service was announced.[89] The CCC used security flaws in BTX to transfer a sizable amount of money into their own bank account through a script that ran overnight as a demonstration to the press (returning the money publicly).

After the Legion of Underground (LoU) announced on January 1, 1999, that they would attack and disable the computer systems of the People's Republic of China and of Iraq, a coalition of hacker organizations including the CCC announced opposition to the move. "We strongly oppose any attempt to use the power of hacking to threaten or destroy the information infrastructure of a country, for any reason," the coalition said. "Declaring war against a country is the most irresponsible thing a hacker group could do. This has nothing to do with hacktivism or hacker ethics and is nothing a hacker could be proud of," the coalition said in the statement.

The CCC has, in general, challenged the general view that "hacker" necessarily means "criminal hacker."[90] Their annual Chaos Communications Conferences have proven to be a site of technology exchange and serious discussion of information security issues. Their continued commitment to the rule of law (except where their own activities are concerned), and their willingness to engage authorities in the courts when necessary has gained them an unusual degree of credibility and acceptance in the information security community as relatively pale-gray hats.[91]

2.14.2   1982: The 414s.

One morning in June 1982, a system administrator for a DEC VAX 11/780 minicomputer at the Memorial Sloan-Kettering Cancer Center in Manhattan found his system down. Investigation led to the discovery that his and dozens of other systems around the country were being hacked by Milwaukee-area teenagers and others aged 15 to 22. The youths called themselves the 414s after the Milwaukee area code.

> Using home computers connected to ordinary telephone lines, they had been breaking into computers across the U.S. and Canada, including one at a bank in Los Angeles, another at a cement company in Montreal and, ominously, an unclassified computer at a nuclear weapons laboratory in Los Alamos, [New Mexico].[92]

In March 1984, "two members of Milwaukee's 414 Gang...pleaded guilty to misdemeanor charges of making obscene or harassing phone calls. Maximum sentence for each charge: six months in jail and a $500 fine."[93]

2.14.3   1984: Cult of the Dead Cow.

Another influential criminal-hacker group is the Cult of the Dead Cow (cDc), which used to sport amusing (although intentionally offensive to some) cartoons such as that of a crucified cow.[94] The cDc was noted for its consistent use of humor and parody; for example, "Swamp Rat's" 1985 article on building "The infamous...GERBIL FEED BOMB" included instructions such as "Light the fuse if you put one in. If you dropped a match into it, then go to the nearest phone, dial '911' and tell the nice people that you have a large number of glass shards embedded in your lower body. An ambulance should be there soon."[95]

The cDc became important proponents of hactivism in the 1990s—the use of criminal hacking techniques for political purposes. They also released a number of hacking tools, of which Back Orifice (BO) and especially Back Orifice 2000 (BO2K) were notorious examples. BO2K was ostensibly a remote administration tool but was in fact a Trojan that ran in stealth mode and allowed remote control of infected machines.[96] Some observers felt that presenting BO2K as a legitimate tool was another instance of cDc's satirical bent: The idea that anyone would consider software written by criminal hackers as a trustworthy administration tool struck them as ludicrous.

2.14.4   1984: *2600: The Hacker Quarterly.*   Eric Corley founded *2600: The Hacker Quarterly* in 1984. This publication has become a standard-bearer for proponents of criminal hacking. The magazine has published a steady stream of explanations of how to exploit specific vulnerabilities in a wide range of operating systems and application environments. In addition, the editor's political philosophy has influenced more than one generation of black-hat and gray-hat hackers:

> In the worldview of *2600*, the tiny band of technocrat brothers (rarely, sisters) are a besieged vanguard of the truly free and honest. The rest of the world is a maelstrom of corporate crime and high-level governmental corruption, occasionally tempered with well-meaning ignorance. To read a few issues in a row is to enter a nightmare akin to Solzhenitsyn's, somewhat tempered by the fact that *2600* is often extremely funny.[97]

2.14.5   1984: Legion of Doom.   The DC Comics empire created an animated cartoon series called *Super Friends* that appeared in 1973; it starred various DC Comics heroes, such as Superman, Aquaman, Wonder Woman, and Batman.[98] In a follow-up series called *Challenge of the Super Friends* that ran from 1978 through 1979, the archenemies of these heroes were a group known as the *Legion of Doom,* which included Lex Luthor, archenemy of Superman.[99] A group of phone phreakers who later turned to criminal hacking called themselves the Legion of Doom (LOD); their founder called himself "Lex Luthor." Another major member was Loyd Blankenship ("The Mentor").

Bruce Sterling describes the LOD as an influential hacker underground group of the 1980s and one of the earliest to capitalize on regular publication of their findings of vulnerabilities and exploits in the phone system and then in computer networks:

> LOD members seemed to have an instinctive understanding that the way to real power in the underground lay through covert publicity. LOD were flagrant. Not only was it one of the earliest groups, but the members took pains to widely distribute their illicit knowledge. Some LOD members, like "The Mentor," were close to evangelical about it. *Legion of Doom Technical Journal* began to show up on boards throughout the underground.
>
> *LOD Technical Journal* was named in cruel parody of the ancient and honored *AT&T Technical Journal.* The material in these two publications was quite similar—much of it, adopted from public journals and discussions in the telco community. And yet, the predatory attitude of LOD made even its most innocuous data seem deeply sinister; an outrage; a clear and present danger.[100]

In the later 1980s, the LOD actually helped law enforcement on occasion by restraining malicious hackers.

One of the best-known members was Chris Goggans, whose handle was "Erik Bloodaxe"; he was also an editor of *Phrack* and later became part of the Masters of Deception (MOD), which was involved in a conflict with LOD in 1990 and 1991 known in hacker circles as "The Great Hacker War."[101]

Another well-known hacker who started in LOD and moved to MOD was Mark Abene ("Phiber Optik"), who was eventually imprisoned for a year after pleading guilty in federal court to conspiracy and unauthorized access to federal-interest computers (a violation of 18 USC 1030(a), the Computer Fraud and Abuse Act of 1986).[102] Abene's punishment was the subject of much protest in the hacker community and elsewhere.[103]

2.14.6 1985: *Phrack.*

Phrack began publishing in November 1985. With a new issue every month or two at first, the electronic magazine continued uninterrupted distribution of technical information and rants. The uncensored commentary provided a fascinating glimpse of some of the personalities and worldviews of its contributors and editors, including Taran King and Craig Neidorf (later to become famous as "Knight Lightning" and for his involvement in an abortive prosecution involving Bell-South documents). For example, Phrack published what became known as the "Hacker Manifesto"— held up by criminal hackers as a light unto the nations ("Written almost 15 years ago by The Mentor, this should be taped up next to everyone's monitor to remind them who we are, this rang true with Hackers, but it now rings truth to the internet generation."[104]) but viewed with skepticism by security professionals. It read in part:

> This is our world now...the world of the electron and the switch, the beauty of the baud. We make use of a service already existing without paying for what could be dirt-cheap if it wasn't run by profiteering gluttons, and you call us criminals. We explore...and you call us criminals. We seek after knowledge...and you call us criminals. We exist without skin color, without nationality, without religious bias...and you call us criminals. You build atomic bombs, you wage wars, you murder, cheat, and lie to us and try to make us believe it's for our own good, yet we're the criminals.

> Yes, I am a criminal. My crime is that of curiosity. My crime is that of judging people by what they say and think, not what they look like. My crime is that of outsmarting you, something that you will never forgive me for.

> I am a hacker, and this is my manifesto. You may stop this individual, but you can't stop us all...after all, we're all alike.[105]

In the 1990s, publication frequency faltered, falling to once every three to six months until the editors announced the final issue, #63, for August 2005. However, publication resumed under new editorial leadership in May 2007 with issue 64; given that issue 65 did not come out until April 2008, the magazine's heyday is presumably over.

2.14.7 1989: Masters of Deception.

The Masters of Deception (MOD) were a New York hacker group active from about 1989 through 1992.[106] Among the most notorious criminal hackers in the group was "Phiber Optik" (Mark Abene, born in 1972), who was unusually visible in the media:

> Phiber Optik in particular was to seize the day in 1990. A devotee of the 2600 circle and stalwart of the New York hackers' group "Masters of Deception," Phiber Optik was a splendid exemplar of the computer intruder as committed dissident. The eighteen-year-old Optik, a high-school dropout and part-time computer repairman, was young, smart, and ruthlessly obsessive, a sharp-dressing, sharp-talking digital dude who was utterly and airily contemptuous of anyone's rules but his own. By late 1991, Phiber Optik had appeared in *Harper's*, *Esquire*, the *New York Times*, in countless public debates and conventions, even on a television show hosted by Geraldo Rivera.[107]

2.14.8   1990: Operation Sundevil.   After two years of investigation, on May 7, 8, and 9, 1990, 150 FBI agents, aided by state and local authorities, raided presumed criminal-hacker organizations allegedly involved in credit-card abuse and theft of telephone services. They seized 42 computers and 23,000 disks from locations in 14 cities. Targets were principally sites running discussion boards, some of which were classified as "hacker boards." However, two years after the raid, there were only three indictments (resulting in three guilty pleas). Evidence began to accumulate that much of the evidence seized in the raids was useless.[108] Bruce Sterling spent a year and a half researching the operation and concluded that it was largely a propaganda effort:

> . . .An unprecedented action of great ambition and size, Sundevil's motives can only be described as political. It was a public-relations effort, meant to pass certain messages, meant to make certain situations clear: both in the mind of the general public, and in the minds of various constituencies of the electronic community.

> First—and this motivation was vital—a "message" would be sent from law enforcement to the digital underground. This very message was recited in so many words by Garry M. Jenkins, the Assistant Director of the US Secret Service, at the Sundevil press conference in Phoenix on May 9, 1990, immediately after the raids. In brief, hackers were mistaken in their foolish belief that they could hide behind the "relative anonymity of their computer terminals." On the contrary, they should fully understand that state and federal cops were actively patrolling the beat in cyberspace—that they were on the watch everywhere, even in those sleazy and secretive dens of cybernetic vice, the underground boards.[109]

2.14.9   1990: Steve Jackson Games.   Two months before the Operation Sundevil raids, but (contrary to popular conflation of the two) in a completely separate operation, a role-playing game company called Steve Jackson Games in Austin, Texas, was raided on March 1, 1990. The Secret Service seized computers and disks at the company's offices and also at the home of one of their employees, Loyd Blankenship—"The Mentor," formerly of the LOD. Blankenship was writing a role-playing game called GURPS Cyberpunk, which the agents interpreted as "a handbook for computer crime." Some of the equipment seized in the raid was returned four weeks later; most but not all was returned four months later. The company nearly went bankrupt as a result of the sequestration of critical resources.[110]

Outrage in the computing community spread beyond the underground. Mitch Kapor, John Barlow, and John Gilmore founded the Electronic Frontier Foundation in part because of their outrage over the treatment of Steve Jackson Games:

> . . .We got the attorneys involved, and then we asked them to look into what was going on with a variety of government investigations and prosecutions. We identified a couple of particular legal situations, like Craig Neidorf in Chicago and Steve Jackson Games, where there seemed to us to have been a substantial overstepping of bounds by the government and an infringement on rights of free speech and freedom of the press. We were in the process of deciding how to intervene when we also realized very clearly that we didn't want to be a legal defense fund as that was too narrow. What was really needed was to somehow improve the discourse about how technology is going to be used by society; we need to do things in the area of public education and policy development.[111]

Steve Jackson Games sued the Secret Service for damages and were awarded $50,000 in damages and more than $25,000 in attorney's fees.[112] The case had a lasting effect on how law enforcement officials carried investigations of computer crimes and seizure of electronic evidence.

2.14.10   1992: L0pht Heavy Industries.   In 1992, a group of computer enthusiasts arranged to store their spare equipment in some rented space in Boston. They collaborated on analysis of vulnerabilities, especially Microsoft product vulnerabilities, and gained a reputation for contributing serious research to the field and for appearing at security conferences. Their "L0phtCrack" program was adopted by many system administrators for testing password files to locate easy-to-guess passwords; members even testified before a Senate Subcommittee on Government Cybersecurity in 1998 (saying they could take down the Internet in half an hour).[113] Famous handles from the group included "Brian Oblivion," "Kingpin," "Mudge," "Space Rogue," "Stefan von Neumann," "Tan," and "Weld Pond."[114]

The group caused ripples in both the underground and aboveground security communities when their company, L0pht Heavy Industries, was purchased by security services firm @stake, Inc. in 2000. @stake was eventually bought by Symantec in 1994.[115]

2.14.11   2004: Shadowcrew.   Stealing physical credit cards and creating fake ones are part of the criminal technique called "carding." One of the significant successful investigations and prosecutions of an international credit-card fraud ring of the 2000 decade began with the U.S. Secret Service's *Operation Firewall* in late 2004. The investigators discovered a network of over 4,000 members communicating through the Internet and conspiring to use phishing, spamming, forged identity documents (e.g., fake driver's licenses), creation of fake plastic credit cards, resale of gift cards bought with fake credit cards, fencing of stolen goods via eBay, and interstate or international funds transfers using electronic money such as E-Gold and Web Money.

In October 2004, the Department of Justice indicted 19 of the leaders of Shadowcrew.[116] By November 2005, 12 of these people had already pleaded guilty to charges of conspiracy and trafficking in stolen credit-card numbers with losses of more than $4 million.[117]

In February 2006, Shadowcrew leader Kenneth J. Flury, 41, of Cleveland Ohio, was sentenced to 32 months in prison with three years of supervised release and $300,000 in restitution to Citibank.[118] In June 2006, cofounder Andrew Mantovani, 24, of Scottsdale, Arizona, was fined $5,000 and also received 32 months of prison with three years of supervised release. Five other indicted Shadowcrew criminals were sentenced with him. By that time, a total of 18 of 28 indicted suspects had already pleaded guilty.[119]

2.15   CONCLUDING REMARKS.   At some point history becomes current events. At the time of writing (May 2008), the trends we are seeing dimly may become clear with time. As the first decade of the twenty-first century draws to its close, it seems to many observers that organized crime has become an integral part of the computer-crime scene—and vice versa. The Russian criminal underworld has increasingly invested in high-technology forms of fraud and also relies on high-tech communications for marketing of criminal undertakings, such as international traffic in drugs, armaments, and slaves. Information warfare has become a real issue as China advances in technology and seeks growing global power. Terrorist groups cannot ignore the power of asymmetric warfare and must be presumed to be planning attacks on critical infrastructures worldwide. As the global communications network spreads throughout the world, governments, corporations, and individuals will have to increase their collaboration and vigilance to defeat the growing army of computer criminals of every type.

2.16 FURTHER READING

Banks, M. A. (1997). *Web Psychos, Stalkers and Pranksters: How to Protect Yourself in Cyberspace*. Scottsdale, AZ: Coriolis Group Books.

Bequai, A. (1987). *Technocrimes: The Computerization of Crime and Terrorism*. Lexington, MA: Lexington Books.

Freedman, D. H., and C. C. Mann (1997). *@Large: The strange case of the world's biggest Internet invasion*. New York: Simon & Schuster.

Goodell, J. (1996). *The Cyberthief and the Samurai: The True Story of Kevin Mitnick—and the Man Who Hunted Him Down*. New York: Dell.

Hafner, K., and J. Markoff (1991). *Cyberpunk: Outlaws and Hackers on the Computer Frontier*. New York: Simon & Schuster.

Levy, S. (1984). *Hackers: Heroes of the Computer Revolution*. New York: Doubleday.

Littman, J. (1997). *The Watchman: The Twisted Life and Crimes of Serial Hacker Kevin Poulson*. New York: Little, Brown.

Mungo, P. (1993). *Approaching Zero: The Extraordinary Underworld of Hackers, Phreakers, Virus Writers, and Keyboard Criminals*. New York: Random House.

Parker, D. B. (1998). *Fighting Computer Crime: A New Framework for Protecting Information*. New York: John Wiley & Sons.

Power, R. (2000). *Tangled Web: Tales of Digital Crime from the Shadows of Cyberspace*. Indianapolis: Que.

Shimomura, T., and J. Markoff (1996). *Takedown: The Pursuit and Capture of Kevin Mitnick, America's Most Wanted Computer Outlaw—by the Man Who Did It*. New York: Hyperion.

Slatalla, M., and J. Quittner (1995). *Masters of Deception: The Gang that Ruled Cyberspace*. New York: HarperCollins.

Sterling, B. (1992). *The Hacker Crackdown: Law and Disorder on the Electronic Frontier*. New York: Bantam Doubleday Dell.

Stoll, C. (1989). *The Cuckoo's Egg: Tracking a Spy through the Maze of Computer Espionage*. New York: Simon & Schuster

2.17 NOTES

1. Some of the materials in this chapter use text from the author's prior publications to which he holds the copyright. However, specific attributions or quotation marks in such cases are generally avoided because changes are extensive and the typographical notations marking the changes would have been intrusive and disruptive.

2. Concordia University, "Who We Are: History," 2008; www.concordia.ca/about/whoweare/ourhistory/sgw.php.

3. T. Whiteside, *Computer Capers: Tales of Electronic Thievery, Embezzlement, and Fraud* (New York: New American Library, 1978).

4. J. Gehl and S. Douglas, "Survey Reveals Epidemic of Battered PCs," *NewsScan* June 5, 2001.

5. M. Delio, "Battered Computers: An Epidemic," *Wired,* June 5, 2001; www.wired.com/culture/lifestyle/news/2001/06/44284.

6. NIPC/DHS, "Physical Attack Still the Biggest Threat," *Daily Open-Source Threat Report,* April 11, 2003.

7. T. Fricke, "Physical Security of Electronic Voting Terminals," *RISKS* 23, No.20 (2004); http://catless.ncl.ac.uk/Risks/23.30.html.

8. Whiteside, *Computer Capers.*

9. S. Spielberg, director, *Catch Me If You Can*; 2002; www.imdb.com/title/tt0264464/.

10. R. Bell, *Skywayman: The Story of Frank W. Abagnale, Jr.* (Crime Library: Criminal Minds and Methods, 2008); www.trutv.com/library/crime/criminal_mind/scams/frank_abagnale/index.html?print=yes or http://tinyurl.com/6z6zfp.

11. Whiteside, *Computer Capers.*

12. T. C. Greene, "Chapter One: Kevin Mitnick's Story." *The Register,* January 13, 2003; www.theregister.co.uk/2003/01/13/chapter_one_kevin_mitnicks_story/.

13. J. Littman, *The Fugitive Game: Online with Kevin Mitnick—The Inside Story of the Great Cyberchase* (Boston: Little, Brown, 1996), p. 30.

14. A. N. Mayorkas and T. Mrozek, "Kevin Mitnick Sentenced to Nearly Four Years in Prison; Computer Hacker Ordered to Pay Restitution to Victim Companies Whose Systems Were Compromised," Press Release, U.S. Department of Justice, United States Attorney's Office, Central District of California, August 9, 1999; www.usdoj.gov/criminal/cybercrime/mitnick.htm.

15. P. Jacobus, "Mitnick Released from Prison," CNET News, September 21, 2000; http://news.cnet.com/Mitnick-released-from-prison/2100-1023_3-235933.html.

16. K. D. Mitnick and W. L. Simon, *The Art of Intrusion: The Real Stories Behind the Exploits of Hackers, Intruders & Deceivers* (New York: John Wiley & Sons, 1995). K.D. Mitnick and W. L. Simon, *The Art of Deception: Controlling the Human Element of Security* (Hoboken, NJ: John Wiley & Sons, 2003). J. Long, J. Wiles, and K. D. Mitnick, *No Tech Hacking: A Guide to Social Engineering, Dumpster Diving, and Shoulder Surfing* (Syngress, 2008).

17. E. Corley, director (as "Emmanuel Goldstein"), *Freedom Downtime* (2002); www.imdb.com/title/tt0309614/.

18. R. Davies, "Origins of Money and of Banking," 2005; www.projects.ex.ac.uk/RDavies/arian/origins.html.

19. "Origin and History of Credit Cards," Financial Web: Credit Cards, 2008; www.finweb.com/banking-credit/origin-and-history-of-credit-cards.html or http://tinyurl.com/5c2yhj.

20. J. Rosenberg, "The First Credit Card." About.com: 20th-Century History, 2008; http://history1900s.about.com/od/1950s/a/firstcreditcard.htm or tinyurl.com/6en9kg

21. B. Hutchins, "Notes on the Fair Credit Billing Act (FCBA)," 2002; www.ftc.gov/os/comments/dncpapercomments/04/lsap7.pdf.

22. L. S. Fox, ed., *The Federal Reserve System: Purposes & Functions,* 9th ed. (Washington, DC: Board of Governors of the Federal Reserve System, 2005); www.federalreserve.gov/pf/pdf/pf_1.pdf; Chapter 6, "Consumer and Community Affairs," p. 78 (p. 4 of PDF file). www.federalreserve.gov/pf/pdf/pf_6.pdf.

23. "Origin and History of Credit Cards."

24. K. Shorter, "Plastic Payments: Trends in Credit Card Fraud," FBI *Law Enforcement Bulletin* (June 1997); www.fbi.gov/publications/leb/1997/june971.htm.

25. Identity Theft 2005, U. S. Department of Justice, Office of Justice Programs, Bureau of Justice Statistics; www.ojp.usdoj.gov/bjs/abstract/it05.htm.

26. K. Baum, "National Crime Victimization Survey: Identity Theft, 2005," Bureau of Justice Statistics; www.ojp.usdoj.gov/bjs/pub/pdf/it05.pdf.

27. www.usdoj.gov News release of August 5, 2008.

28. B. Sterling, *The Hacker Crackdown: Law and Disorder on the Electronic Frontier* (New York: Bantam, 1992). Available free online: www.mit.edu/hacker/hacker.html or www.chriswaltrip.com/sterling/hackcrck.html. Specific reference: www.chriswaltrip.com/sterling/crack1d.html.

29. E. McCracken, "Dial-Tone Phreak," *New York Times,* December 30, 2007; www.nytimes.com/2007/12/30/magazine/30joybubbles-t.html?ex=1356584400 &en=8d26486125a53d83&ei=5124&partner=permalink&exprod=permalink or http://tinyurl.com/5s49cu

30. John T. Draper home page, www.webcrunchers.com/crunch/.

31. S. Wozniak and G. Smith, iWoz: *Computer Geek to Cult Icon: How I Invented the Personal Computer, Co-Founded Apple, and Had Fun Doing It* (New York: Norton, 2006).

32. R. Rosenbaum, "Secrets of the Little Blue Box," *Esquire Magazine* (October 1971). Available in transcription at www.webcrunchers.com/crunch/stories/esq-art.html.

33. The text displayed was available on Poulsen's Web site until at least April 5, 2001, according to the Internet Archive. Sometime after that date, the biography was shortened and then sometime on or before December 4, 2002, it disappeared altogether and was replaced by a redirect to search for the string "By Kevin Poulsen" in GOOGLE.

34. K. Poulsen, "MySpace Predator Caught by Code," *Wired,* October 16, 2006; www.wired.com/science/discoveries/news/2006/10/71948.

35. *Wired* magazine, "Threat Level" blog: http:// blog.wired.com/27bstroke6/.

36. B. Trumbore, "Ray Dirks and the Equity Funding Scandal," *Wall Street History,* February 6, 2004; www.stocksandnews.com/searchresults.asp?Id= 1573&adate=2/6/2004.

37. M. Kabay, "Crime, Use of Computers in." In H. Bidgoli, ed., *Encyclopedia of Information Systems,* vol. 1 (New York: Academic Press, 2003); www2.norwich.edu/mkabay/overviews/crime_use_of_computers_in.pdf or http://tinyurl.com/3wqfxc.

38. D. E. Hoffman, "CIA Slipped Bugs to Soviets: Memoir Recounts Cold War Technological Sabotage," *Washington Post,* February 27, 2004; www.msnbc.msn.com/id/4394002.

39. E. D. Shaw, K. G. Ruby, and J. M. Post, "The Insider Threat to Information Systems," *Security Awareness Bulletin* No. 2-98. Department of Defense Security Institute (September 1998); www.ntc.doe.gov/cita/ CI_Awareness_Guide/Treason/Infosys.htm.

40. CNN.com, Y2K Archive, "Looking at the Y2K Bug," 2000; www.cnn.com/TECH/specials/y2k/.

41. Gardica-Feijóo, L. and J. R. Wingender (2007). "Y2K: Myth or Reality." *Quarterly Journal of Business and Economics* (Summer 2007); http://findarticles.com/p/articles/mi_qa5466/is_200707/ai_n21295780/pg_1 or http://tinyurl.com/64w5jm.

42. United States Department of Homeland Security, "Look Before You Click: Trojan Horses and Other Attempts to Compromise Networks," *Joint Information Bulletin,* December 21, 2005; www.us-cert.gov/reading_room/JIB-Trojan122105.pdf or http://tinyurl.com/6zwmes.

43. D. Izenberg, "Trojan Horse Masterminds Being Extradited to Israel," *Jerusalem Post,* January 18, 2006. Available for purchase online: http://pqasb. pqarchiver.com/jpost/access/972012371.html?dids=972012371:972012371 &FMT=ABS&FMTS=ABS:FT&type=current&date=Jan+18%2C+2006&aut hor=DAN+IZENBERG&pub=Jerusalem+Post&edition=&startpage=04&desc =%27Trojan+horse%27+heads+extradited+to+Israel   or   http://tinyurl.com/ 5wlsgz.

44. W. K. Haskins, "Married Couple Indicted for Corporate Espionage," *SCI-TECH TODAY.com,* March 7, 2006, www.sci-tech-today.com/ story.xhtml?story_id=12100DICT7FG&page=1 or http://tinyurl.com/3qantt.

45. L. Leyden, "Spyware-for-Hire Couple Plead Guilty: Israeli Prison Looms for Haephratis," *The Register,* March 15, 2006; www.theregister.co.uk/ 2006/03/15/spyware_trojan_guilty_plea/

46. "Court Hands Hefty Fine and Jail Sentence to Israeli Spyware Couple, Reports Sophos," Sophos, March 27, 2006; www.sophos.com/pressoffice/ news/articles/2006/03/israelspyduo.html or http://tinyurl.com/4gx38p.

47. J. Leyden, "Israeli Spyware-for-Hire PIs jailed," *The Register,* April 29, 2008; www.theregister.co.uk/2008/04/29/spyware-for-hire/.

48. R. Stiennon, "Four Private Investigators in the Israeli Trojan Fiasco Sentenced. Finally," *Network World,* "Stiennon on Security," April 30, 2008, www.networkworld.com/community/node/27387.

49. J. L. Tkacik, "Trojan Dragon: China's Cyber Threat," Heritage Foundation *Backgrounder #2106,* February 8, 2008; www.heritage.org/Research/ asiaandthepacific/bg2106.cfm.

50. T. Claburn, "Operation 'Cisco Raider' Nets $76 in Fake Gear: The multi-year effort to curb the flow of counterfeit network hardware into the U.S. and Canada reflects a steady escalation in the war on intellectual property crime," *InformationWeek,* February 29, 2008; www.informationweek. com/news/personal_tech/showArticle.jhtml?articleID=206901053   or   http:// tinyurl.com/5vfnyd.

51. J. Markoff, "Trojan Horse Threat Stalks Pentagon after Bogus Hardware Purchase," *CIO TODAY* (May 12, 2008); www.cio-today. com/story.xhtml?story_id=103006ROXFYH or http://tinyurl.com/5tvz32.

52. For a detailed and personal view of malware history, see virus expert Roger Thompson's "Malicious Code," Chapter 2 in S. Bosworth and M. E. Kabay, eds. *Computer Security Handbook,* 4th ed. (Hoboken, NJ: John Wiley & Sons, 2002). Also, see Chapter 16 in this *Handbook.*

53. R. H. Zakon, "Hobbes' Internet Timeline v8.2," 1996; www.zakon.org/ robert/internet/timeline/.

54. "Virus Encyclopedia: History of Malware." Viruslist.com, 2008; www.viruslist. com/en/viruses/encyclopedia?chapter=153310937.

55. "Virus Encyclopedia: History of Malware."

56. Clausthal University of Technology Homepage (English), www.tu-clausthal. de/Welcome.php.en.

57. Thompson, "Malicious Code."

58. R. Patterson, "Re: IBM Christmas Virus," *Risks Forum Digest* 5, No. 80 (December 21, 1987):1.1. catless.ncl.ac.uk/Risks/5.80.html#subj1.1.

59. C. Schmidt and T. Darby "The What, Why and How of the 1988 Internet Worm," 1995; snowplow.org/tom/worm/worm.html.

60. Robert Morris MIT faculty biography, www.csail.mit.edu/biographies/PI/bioprint.php?PeopleID=301.

61. D. Emm, "Changing Threats, Changing Solutions: A History of Viruses and Antivirus," Viruslist.com, April 14, 2008; www.viruslist.com/en/analysis?pubid=204791996.

62. "The WildList Organization International: Frequently Asked Questions." WildList Organization International, 2008; www.wildlist.org/faq.htm.

63. R. Thompson, personal communication, May 25, 2008.

64. M. E. Kabay, "INFOSEC Year in Review 1999," 1999; www2.norwich.edu/mkabay/iyir/1999.PDF.

65. CERT Advisory CA-2000-04 Love Letter Worm. CERT/CC, May 9, 2000; www.cert.org/advisories/CA-2000-04.html.

66. D. I. Hopper, "Focus of 'ILOVEYOU' Investigation Turns to Owner of Apartment," CNN.com, May 10, 2000; http://archives.cnn.com/2000/TECH/computing/05/10/i.love.you.03/index.html or http://tinyurl.com/4elq2l.

67. "Suspected Creator of 'ILOVEYOU' Virus Chats Online." CNN.com chat transcript, September 26, 2000; http://archives.cnn.com/2000/TECH/computing/09/26/guzman.chat/.

68. M. Landler, "A Filipino Linked to 'Love Bug' Talks about His License to Hack," *New York Times,* October 21, 2000; http://query.nytimes.com/gst/fullpage.html?res=990DE5D8113EF932A15753C1A9669C8B63 or http://tinyurl.com/4b826p.

69. R. G. Smith, "Impediments to the Successful Investigation of Transnational High Tech Crime," *Trends & Issues in Crime and Criminal Justice,* No. 285, December 13, 2004; www.crime-research.org/articles/trends-and-issues-in-criminal-justice/ or http://tinyurl.com/44pn4s.

70. A. Lawrence, "Internet Growing Pains—The Canter & Siegel Story," *Computer Business Review* (June 1994); www.coin.org.uk/roadshow/ presentation/canter.html.

71. K. K. Campbell, "A NET.CONSPIRACY SO IMMENSE....Chatting with Martha Siegel of the Internet's Infamous Canter & Siegel," 1994; http://lcs.www.media.mit.edu / people / foner / Essays / Civil-Liberties / Project / green-card-lawyers.html or http://tinyurl.com/45f3fe.

72. D. R. Hilton, "Green Card Lottery—Last Call," 1994; http://groups.google.com/group/misc.legal/msg/3416cd3d6cfcdebe.

73. L. Flynn, "'Spamming' on the Internet," *New York Times,* October 16, 1994; www.l-ware.com/ny_times_q_a_october_16_1994.htm or http://tinyurl.com/4j2krg.

74. A. Craddock, "Spamming Lawyer Disbarred," *WIRED,* July 10, 1997; www.wired.com/politics/law/news/1997/07/5060.

75. N. Swidey, "Spambusters: Cyberwarriors of many stripes have joined the battle against junk e-mail. But the enemy is wily, elusive—and multiplying," *Boston Globe,* October 5, 2003; www.boston.com/news/globe/magazine/articles/2003/10/05/spambusters?mode=PF or http://tinyurl.com/4y3chj.

76. C. Garretson, "The Summer of Spam: Record Growth, Record Irritation," *Network World,* August 16, 2007; www.networkworld.com/news/2007/081607-spam-summer.html or http://tinyurl.com/6xoda3.

77. J. Leyden, "Most Spam Comes from Just Six Botnets," *The Register,* February 29, 2008; www.theregister.co.uk/2008/02/29/botnet_spam_deluge/.

78. See *Network World's* "Spam/Phishing Resource Page" for up-to-date news about spam and phishing; www.networkworld.com/topics/spam.html.

79. T. Espiner, "Police Maintain Uneasy Relations with Cybervigilantes," *CNET News,* January 17, 2007; http://news.cnet.com/Police-maintain-uneasy-relations-with-cybervigilantes/2100-7348_3-6150817.html or http://tinyurl.com/6fjykr.

80. "The Net's Most Wanted," *CNET News,* August 16, 1996; http://news.cnet.com/2100-1023-221580.html.

81. L. Z. Koch, "Jacking in from the 'Spam in the Stocking' Port: Unamailer Delivers Christmas Grief," *CyberWire Dispatch,* December 26, 1996; www.pettingzoo.net/~deadbeef/archive/2122.html.

82. Koch, "Jacking in from the 'Spam in the Stocking' Port."

83. "Unamailer Explains Bombings," *CNET News,* December 30, 1996; http://news.cnet.com/Unamailer-explains-bombings/2100-1017_3-258247.html or http://tinyurl.com/422kgc.

84. M. Richtel and S. Robinson, "Several Web Sites Are Attacked on Day after Assault Shut Yahoo," *New York Times,* February 9, 2000; www.nytimes.com/library/tech/00/02/biztech/articles/09hack.html.

85. E. Messmer, "Web Sites Unite to Fight Denial-of-Service War," *Network World,* September 25, 2000; www.networkworld.com/news/2000/0925userdefense.html?nf&_ref=858966935 or http://tinyurl.com/4cuvsf.

86. "Today's FBI: Facts and Figures," 2003; www.fbi.gov/libref/factsfigure/factsfiguresapri2003.htm.

87. See "The RMA Debate" for resources about "The Revolution in Military Affairs"; www.comw.org/rma/fulltext/asymmetric.html.

88. For German-speakers or those with automated translation programs, see "FAQ—Über den Chaos Computer Club," May 27, 2004; www.ccc.de/faq/ccc?language=en.

89. T. von Randow, "Bildschirmtext: A Blow against the System." Translation from *Die Zeit,* November 30, 1984; www.textfiles.com/news/boh-20f8.txt.

90. H. Nissenbaum, "Hackers and the Battle for Cyberspace," *Dissent* (Fall 2002); www.dissentmagazine.org/article/?article=562.

91. Chaos Computer Club press release, "Chaos Computer Club Takes Legal Proceedings against the Voting Computer in Hesse," January 7, 2008; www.ccc.de/updates/2008/wahlcomputer-hessen?language=en.

92. P. Elmer-Dewitt, "The 414 Gang Strikes Again: Pranksters disrupt a hospital, and nobody is laughing," *TIME,* August 29, 1983; www.time.com/time/magazine/article/0,9171,949797,00.html.

93. P. Elmer-Dewitt "Cracking Down: Hackers face tough new laws," *TIME*, May 14, 1984; www.time.com/time/magazine/article/0,9171,955290,00.html.

94. At the time of writing (May 2008), the group's site (www.cultdeadcow.com/) simply showed the words "BE BACK REAL SOON! / -xXx- cDc loves you with the fervor of a THOUSAND SUNS!! –xXx-" and a link to a YouTube video of a teenager playing a ukulele and singing. Consult the Internet Archive for historical snapshots of the site; web.archive.org/web/*/www.cultdeadcow.com/.

95. S. Rat, "The infamous...GERBIL FEED BOMB: Striking fear into the hearts of model citizens everywhere..." *cDc communications,* 1985. http://web.archive.org/web/20050212092311/www.cultdeadcow.com/cDc_files/cDc-0001.html or http://tinyurl.com/44yyth.

96. E. Messmer, "Bad Rap for Back Orifice 2000?" CNN.com, July 21, 1999; www.cnn.com/TECH/computing/9907/21/badrap.idg/.

97. Sterling, *Hacker Crackdown.*

98. Hanna-Barbera *Super Friends,* 1973, Internet Movie Database, www.imdb.com/title/tt0069641/.

99. Hanna-Barbera, *Challenge of the Super Friends*, (1978), Internet Movie Database, www.imdb.com/title/tt0076994/

100. Sterling, *Hacker Crackdown.*

101. M. Slatalla and J. Quittner, "Gang War in Cyberspace," WIRED 2.12 (December 1994); www.wired.com/wired/archive/2.12/hacker.html.

102. Datastream Cowboy, "MOD Indicted," *Phrack* 4, No. 40 (July 8, 1992): 13; www.phrack.com/issues.html?issue=40&id=13.

103. J. Dibbell, "The Prisoner: Phiber Optik Goes Directly to Jail," *Village Voice,* (January 12, 1994; www.juliandibbell.com/texts/phiber.html.

104. J. Barone, "Manifesto." *TechnoZen.com,* 2000; www.technozen.com/manifesto.htm.

105. The Mentor, "The Conscience of a Hacker," *Phrack* 1, No. 7(1986): 3; www.phrack.com/issues.html?issue=7&id=3#article.

106. M. Slatalla and J. Quittner, *Masters of Deception: The Gang that Ruled Cyberspace* (New York: HarperCollins, 1995).

107. Sterling, *Hacker Crackdown.*

108. D. Charles, "'Innocent' Hackers Want Their Computers Back," *New Scientist,* No. 1820, May 9, 1992, p. 9; www.newscientist.com/article/mg13418201.400-innocent-hackers-want-their-computers-back-.html or http://tinyurl.com/3vw26e.

109. Sterling, *Hacker Crackdown.*

110. S. Jackson, "SJ Games vs. the Secret Service," 2008; www.sjgames.com/SS/.

111. D. Gans and K. Goffman, "Mitch Kapor & John Barlow Interview," Electronic Frontier Foundation, August 5, 1990; http://w2.eff.org/Misc/Publications/John_Perry_Barlow/HTML/barlow_and_kapor_in_wired_interview.html or http://tinyurl.com/4pgskr.

112. S. Sparks, "Judge's Decision in *Steve Jackson Games v. United States Secret Service*," March 12, 1993; www.sjgames.com/SS/decision-text.html.

113. D. Fisher, "The Long, Strange Trip of the L0pht," *SearchSecurity.com,* March 17, 2008; http://searchsecurity.techtarget.com/news/article/0,289142, sid14_gci1305880,00.html or http://tinyurl.com/4zh5sg.

114. M. Fitzgerald, "L0pht in Transition," *CSO,* April 17, 2007; www.csoonline .com/article/print/221192.

115. Symantec News Release, "Symantec to Acquire @stake," September 16, 2004; www.symantec.com/press/2004/n040916b.html.

116. United States Department of Justice, Computer Crime & Intellectual Property Section, "Shadowcrew Organization Called 'One-Stop Online Marketplace for Identity Theft': Nineteen Individuals Indicted in Internet 'Carding' Conspiracy," October 28, 2004; www.usdoj.gov/criminal/cybercrime/mantovaniIndict.htm.

117. United States Department of Justice, Computer Crime & Intellectual Property Section, "Six Defendants Plead Guilty in Internet Identity Theft and Credit Card Fraud Conspiracy," November 17, 2005; www.usdoj. gov/criminal/cybercrime/mantovaniPlea.htm.

118. G. A. White and R. W. Kern, "Cleveland, Ohio Man Sentenced to Prison for Bank Fraud and Conspiracy," U.S. Department of Justice, Eastern District of Pennsylvania, February 28, 2006; www.usdoj.gov/criminal/cybercrime/flurySent.htm.

119. United States Attorney's Office, District of New Jersey, "'Shadowcrew' Identity Theft Ringleader Gets 32 Months in Prison," June 29, 2006; www.usdoj. gov/usao/nj/press/files/mant0629_r.htm.

CHAPTER 3

TOWARD A NEW FRAMEWORK FOR INFORMATION SECURITY*

Donn B. Parker, CISSP

3.1 PROPOSAL FOR A NEW INFORMATION SECURITY FRAMEWORK.

Information security, historically, has been limited by the lack of a comprehensive, complete, and analytically sound framework for analysis and improvement. The persistence of the classic triad of CIA (confidentiality, integrity, availability) is inadequate to describe what security practitioners include and implement when doing their jobs. We need a new information security framework that is complete, correct, and consistent to express, in practical language, the means for information owners to protect their information from any adversaries and vulnerabilities.

---

*This chapter is a revised excerpt from Donn B. Parker, *Fighting Computer Crime* (New York: John Wiley & Sons, 1998), Chapter 10, "A New Framework for Information Security," pp. 229–255.

The current focus on computer systems security is attributable to the understandable tendency of computer technologists to protect what they know best—the computer and network systems rather than the application of those systems. With a technological hammer in hand, everything looks like a nail. The primary security challenge comes from people misusing or abusing information, and often—but not necessarily—using computers and networks. Yet the individuals who currently dominate the information security folk art are neither criminologists nor computer application specialists.

This chapter presents a comprehensive new information security framework that resolves the problems of the existing models. The chapter demonstrates the need for six security elements—availability, utility, integrity, authenticity, confidentiality, and possession—to replace incomplete CIA security (which does not even seem to include security for information that is not confidential) in the new security framework. This new framework is used to list all aspects of security at a basic level. The framework is also presented in another form, the *Threats, Assets, Vulnerabilities Model*, which includes detailed descriptors for each topic in the model. This model supports the new security framework, demonstrating its contribution to advance information security from its current technological stage, and as a folk art, into the basis for an engineering and business art in cyberspace.

The new security framework model incorporates six essential parts:

1. **Security elements** of information to be preserved are:
   - Availability
   - Utility
   - Integrity
   - Authenticity
   - Confidentiality
   - Possession
2. **Sources** of loss of these security elements of information:
   - Abusers and misusers
   - Accidental occurrences
   - Natural physical forces
3. **Acts** that cause loss:
   - Destruction
   - Interference with use
   - Use of false data
   - Modification or replacement
   - Misrepresentations or repudiation
   - Misuse or failure to use
   - Location
   - Disclosure
   - Observation
   - Copying
   - Taking
   - Endangerment

4. **Safeguard functions** to protect information from these acts:
- Audit
- Avoidance
- Deterrence
- Detection
- Prevention
- Mitigation
- Transference
- Investigation
- Sanctions and rewards
- Recovery

5. **Methods** of safeguard selection:
- Use due diligence
- Comply with regulations and standards
- Enable business
- Meet special needs

6. **Objectives** to be achieved by information security:
- Avoid negligence
- Meet requirements of laws and regulations
- Engage in successful commerce
- Engage in ethical conduct
- Protect privacy
- Minimize impact of security on performance
- Advance an orderly and protected society

In summary, this model is based on the goal of meeting owners' needs to protect the desired *security elements* of their information from sources of loss that engage in harmful *acts* and events by applying *safeguard functions* that are selected by accepted *methods* to achieve desired *objectives*. The sections of the model are explained next. It is important to note that security risk, return on security investment (ROSI), and net present value (NPV) based on unknown future losses and enemies and their intentions are not identified in this model since they are not measurable and, hence, not manageable.

3.2   SIX ESSENTIAL SECURITY ELEMENTS.   Six security elements in the proposed framework model are essential to information security. If any one of them is omitted, information security is deficient in protecting information owners. Six scenarios of information losses, all derived from real cases, are used to demonstrate this contention. We show how each scenario involves violation of one, and only one, element of information security. Thus, if we omit that element from information security, we also remove that scenario from the concerns of information security, which would be unacceptable. It is likely that information security professionals will agree that all of these scenarios fall well within the range of the abuse and misuse that we need to protect against.

3.2.1 Loss Scenario 1: Availability.   A rejected contract programmer, intent on sabotage, removed the name of a data file from the file directories in a credit union's computer. Users of the computer and the data file no longer had the file available to them because the computer operating system recognizes the existence of information available for users only if it is named in the file directories. The credit union was shut down for two weeks while another programmer was brought in to find and correct the problem so that the file would be available. The perpetrator was eventually convicted of computer crime.

Except for availability, the other elements of information security—utility, integrity, authenticity, confidentiality, and possession—do not address this loss, and their state does not change in the scenario. The owner of the computer (the credit union) retained possession of the data file. Only the availability of the information was lost, but it is a loss that clearly should have been prevented by information security. Thus, the preservation of availability must be accepted as a purpose of information security.

It is true that good security practice might have prevented the disgruntled programmer from having use of the credit union application system, and credit union management could have monitored his work more carefully. They should not have depended on the technical capabilities and knowledge of only one person, and they should have employed several controls to preserve or restore the availability of data files in the computer, such as by maintaining a backup directory with the names of erased files and pointers to their physical location. The loss might have been prevented, or minimized, through good backup practices, good usage controls for computers and specific data files, use of more than one name to identify and find a file, and the availability of utility programs to search for files by content or to mirror file storage. These safeguards would at least have made the attack more difficult and would have confronted the programmer with the malfeasance of his act.

The severity of availability loss can vary considerably. A perpetrator may destroy copies of a data file in a manner that eliminates any chance of recovery. In other situations, the data file may be partially usable, with recovery possible for a moderate cost, or the user may have inconvenienced or delayed use of the file for some period of time, followed by complete recovery.

3.2.2 Loss Scenario 2: Utility.   In this case, an employee routinely encrypted the only copy of valuable information stored in his organization's computer and then accidentally erased the encryption key. The usefulness of the information was lost and could be restored only through difficult cryptanalysis.

Although this scenario can be described as a loss of availability or authenticity of the encryption key, the loss focuses on the usefulness of the information rather than on the key, since the only purpose of the key was to facilitate encryption. The information in this scenario is available, but in a form that is not useful. Its integrity, authenticity, and possession are unaffected, and its confidentiality, unfortunately, is greatly improved.

To preserve utility of information in this case, management should require mandatory backup copies of all critical information and should control the use of powerful protective mechanisms such as cryptography. Management should require security walk-through tests during application development to limit unusable forms of information. It should minimize the adverse effects of security on information use and should control the types of activities that enable unauthorized persons to reduce the usefulness of information.

The loss of utility can vary in severity. The worst-case scenario would be the total loss of usefulness of the information, with no possibility of recovery. Less severe cases may range from a partially useful state with the potential for full restoration of usefulness at moderate cost.

3.2.3 Loss Scenario 3: Integrity.

In this scenario, a software distributor purchased a copy (on DVD) of a program for a computer game from an obscure publisher. The distributor made copies of the DVD and removed the name of the publisher from the DVD copies. Then, without informing the publisher or paying any royalties, the distributor sold the DVD copies in a foreign country. Unfortunately, the success of the program sales was not deterred by the lack of an identified publisher on the DVD or in the product promotional materials.

Because the DVD copies of the game did not identify the publisher that created the program, the copies lacked integrity. ("Integrity" means a state of completeness, wholeness, and soundness, or adhering to a code of moral values.) However, the copies did not lack authenticity, since they contained the genuine game program and only lacked the identity of the publisher, which was not necessary for the successful use of the product. Information utility of the DVD was maintained, and confidentiality and availability were not at issue. Possession also was not at issue, since the distributor bought the original DVD. But copyright protection was violated as a consequence of the loss of integrity and unauthorized copying of the otherwise authentic program.

Several controls can be applied to prevent the loss of information integrity, including using and checking sequence numbers, checksums, and/or hash totals to ensure completeness and wholeness for a series of items. Other controls include performing manual and automatic text checks for required presence of records, subprograms, paragraphs, or titles, and testing to detect violations of specified controls.

The severity of information integrity loss also varies. Significant parts of the information can be missing or misordered (but still available), with no potential for recovery. Or missing or misordered information can be restored, with delay and at moderate cost. In the least severe cases, an owner can recover small amounts of misordered or mislocated information in a timely manner at low cost.

3.2.4 Loss Scenario 4: Authenticity.

In a variation of the preceding scenario, another software distributor obtained the program (on DVD) for a computer game from an obscure publisher. The distributor changed the name of the publisher on the DVD and in title screens to that of a well-known publisher, then made copies of the DVD. Without informing either publisher, the distributor then proceeded to distribute the DVD copies in a foreign country. In this case, the identity of a popular publisher on the DVDs and in the promotional materials significantly added to the success of the product sales.

Because the distributor misrepresented the publisher of the game, the program did not conform to reality: It was not an authentic game from the well-known publisher. Availability and utility are not at issue in this case. The game had integrity because it identified a publisher and was complete and sound. (Certainly the distributor lacked *personal* integrity because his acts did not conform to ethical practice, but that is not the subject of the scenario.) The actual publisher did not lose possession of the game, even though copies were deceptively represented as having come from a different publisher. And, although the distributor undoubtedly tried to keep his actions secret from both publishers, confidentiality of the content of the game was not at issue.

What if someone misrepresents your information by claiming that it is his? Violation of CIA does not include this act. A stockbroker in Florida cheated his investors in a Ponzi (pyramid sales) scheme. He stole $50 million by claiming that he used a super-secret computer program on his giant computer to make profits of 60 percent per day by arbitrage, a stock trading method in which the investor takes advantage of a small difference in prices of the same stock in different markets. He showed investors the mainframe computer at a Wall Street brokerage firm and falsely claimed that it and the information stored therein were his, thereby lending believability to his claims of successful trading.

This stockbroker's scheme was certainly a computer crime, but the CIA elements do not address it as such because its definition of integrity does not include misrepresentation of information. "Integrity" means only that information is whole or complete; it does not address the validity of information. Obviously, confidentiality and availability do not cover misrepresentation either. The best way to extend CIA to include misrepresentation is to use the more general term "authenticity." We can then assign the correct English meaning to the phrase "integrity of information": wholeness, completeness, and good condition. Dr. Peter Neumann at SRI International is correct when he says that information with integrity means that the information is what you expect it to be. This does not, however, necessarily mean that the information is valid (you may expect it to be invalid). "Authenticity" is the word that means conformance to reality.

A number of controls can be applied to ensure authenticity of information. These include confirming transactions, names, deliveries, and addresses; validating products; checking for out-of-range or incorrect information; and using digital signatures and watermarks to authenticate documents.

The severity of authenticity loss can take several forms, including lack of conformance to reality with no recovery possible; moderately false or deceptive information with delayed recovery at moderate cost; or factually correct information with only annoying discrepancies. If the CIA elements included authenticity, with misrepresentation of information as an important associated threat, Kevin Mitnick (the notorious criminal hacker who used deceit as his principal tool for penetrating security barriers) might have faced a far more difficult challenge in perpetrating his crimes. The computer industry might have understood the need to prove computer operating system updates and Web sites genuine, to avoid misrepresentation with fakes before their customers used them in their computers.

3.2.5 Loss Scenario 5: Confidentiality.   A thief deceptively obtained information from a bank's technical maintenance staff. He used a stolen key to open the maintenance door of an automated teller machine (ATM) and secretly inserted a radio transmitter that he purchased from a Radio Shack store. The radio received signals from the touch-screen display in the ATM that customers use to enter their personal identification numbers (PINs) and to receive account balance information. The radio device broadcast the information to the thief's radio receiver in his nearby car, which recorded the PINs and account balances on tape in a modified videocassette recorder. The thief used the information to loot the customers' accounts from other ATMs. The police and the Federal Bureau of Investigation caught the thief after elaborate detective and surveillance efforts. He was sentenced to 10 years in a federal prison.

The thief violated the secrecy of the customers' PINs and account balances, and he violated their privacy. Availability, utility, integrity, and authenticity were unaffected in this violation of confidentiality. The customers' and the bank's exclusive possession of the PINs and account balance information was lost, but not possession per se because they still held and owned the information. Therefore, this was primarily a case of lost confidentiality.

According to most security experts, confidentiality deals with disclosure, but confidentiality also can be lost by observation, whether that observation is voluntary or involuntary, and whether the information is disclosed or not disclosed. For example, if you leave sensitive information displayed on an unattended computer monitor screen, you have disclosed it and it may or may not lose its confidentiality. If you turn the monitor off, leaving a blank screen, you have not disclosed sensitive information, but if someone turns the monitor on and reads its contents without permission, then confidentiality is lost by observation. We must prevent both disclosure and observation in order to protect confidentiality.

Controls to maintain confidentiality include using cryptography, training employees to resist deceptive social engineering attacks intended to obtain their technical knowledge, and controlling the use of computers and computer devices. Good security also requires that the cost of resources for protection not exceed the value of what may be lost, especially with low incidence. For example, protecting against radio frequency emanations in ATMs (as in this scenario) is probably not advisable, considering the cost of shielding and the paucity of such high-tech attacks.

The severity of loss of confidentiality can vary. The worst-case scenario loss is when a party with the intent and ability to cause harm observes a victim's sensitive information. In this case, unrecoverable damage may result. But information also may be known to several moderately harmful parties, with a moderate loss effect, or be known to one harmless, unauthorized party with short-term recoverable effect.

3.2.6   Loss Scenario 6: Possession.   A gang of burglars aided by a disgruntled, recently fired operations supervisor broke into a computer center and stole tapes and disks containing the company's master files. They also raided the backup facility and stole all backup copies of the files. They then held the materials for ransom in an extortion attempt against the company. The burglary resulted in the company's losing possession of all copies of the master files as well as the media on which they were stored. The company was unable to continue business operations. The police eventually captured the extortionists with help from the company during the ransom payment, and they recovered the stolen materials. The burglars were convicted and served long prison sentences.

Loss of possession occurred in this case. The perpetrators delayed availability, but the company could have retrieved the files at any time by paying the ransom. Alternatively, the company could have re-created the master files from paper documents, but at great cost. Utility, integrity, and authenticity were not issues in this situation. Confidentiality was not violated because the burglars had no reason to read or disclose the files. Loss of ownership and permanent loss of possession would have been accomplished if the perpetrators had never returned the materials or if the company had stopped trying to recover them.

The security model must include protecting the possession of information so as to prevent theft, whether the information is confidential or not. Confidentiality, by definition, deals only with secret information that people may possess. Our increasing use of computers magnifies this difference; huge amounts of information are possessed for automated use and not necessarily held confidentially for only specified people to know. Computer object programs are examples of proprietary but not confidential information we do not know but possess by selling, buying, bartering, giving, receiving, and trading until we ultimately control, transport, and use them. We have incorrectly defined possession if we include only the protective efforts for confidential material.

We protect the possession of information by preventing people from unauthorized taking, from making copies, and from holding or controlling it—whether confidentiality is involved or not. The loss of possession of information also includes the loss of control of it, and may allow the new possessor to violate its confidentiality at will. Thus, loss of confidentiality may accompany loss of possession. But we must treat confidentiality and possession separately to determine what actions criminals might take and what controls we need to apply to prevent their actions. Otherwise, we may overlook a particular threat or an effective control. The failure to anticipate a threat and vulnerability is one of the greatest dangers we face in security.

Controls that can protect the possession of information include using copyright laws, implementing physical and logical usage limitations, preserving and examining computer audit logs for evidence of stealing, inventorying tangible and intangible assets, using distinctive colors and labels on media containers, and assigning ownership to enforce accountability of organizational information assets.

The severity of loss of possession varies with the nature of the offense. In a worst-case scenario, a criminal may take information, as well as all copies of it, and there may be no means of recovery—either from the perpetrator or from other sources such as paper documentation. In a less harmful scenario, a criminal might take information for some period of time but leave some opportunity for recovery at a moderate cost. In the least harmful situation, an owner could possess more than one copy of information, leaving open the possibility of recovery from other sources (e.g., backup files) within a reasonable period of time.

3.2.7 Conclusions about the Six Elements.

We need to understand some important differences between integrity and authenticity. For one, integrity deals with the intrinsic condition of information, while authenticity deals with the extrinsic value or meaning relative to external sources and uses. Integrity does not deal with the meaning of the information with respect to external sources, that is, whether the information is timely and not obsolete. Authenticity, in contrast, concerns the question of whether information is genuine or valid and not out of date with respect to its potential use. A user who enters false information into a computer possibly has violated authenticity, but as long as the information remains unchanged, it has integrity. An information security technologist who designs security into computer operating systems is concerned only with application information integrity because the designer cannot know if any user is entering false information. In this case, the security technologist's job is to ensure that both true and false information remain whole and complete. It is the information owner, with guidance from an information security advisor, who has the responsibility of ensuring that the information conforms to reality, in other words, that it has authenticity.

Some types of loss that information security must address require the use of all six elements of the framework model to determine the appropriate security to apply. Each of the six elements can be violated independently of the others, with one important exception: A violation of confidentiality always results in loss of exclusive possession, at the least. Loss of possession, however—even exclusive possession—does not necessarily result in loss of confidentiality.

Other than that exception, the six elements are unique and independent, and often require different security controls. Maintaining the availability of information does not necessarily maintain its utility; information may be available but useless for its intended purpose, and vice versa. Maintaining the integrity of information does not necessarily mean that the information is valid, only that it remains the same or, at least, whole and complete. Information can be invalid and, therefore, without authenticity, yet it may be present and identical to the original version and, thus, have integrity. Finally, who is allowed to view and know information and who possesses it are often two very different matters.

Unfortunately, the written information security policies of many organizations do not acknowledge the need to address many kinds of information loss. This is because their policies are limited to achieving CIA. To define information security completely, the policies must address all six elements presented. Moreover, to eliminate (or at least reduce) security threats adequately, all six elements need to be considered to ensure that nothing is overlooked in applying appropriate controls. These elements are also useful for identifying and anticipating the types of abusive actions that adversaries may take—before such actions are undertaken.

For simplification and ease of reference, we can pair the six elements into three double elements, which should be used to identify threats and select proper controls, and we can associate them with synonyms so as to facilitate recall and understanding:

> availability and utility   → usability and usefulness
> integrity and authenticity   → completeness and validity
> confidentiality and possession → secrecy and control

Availability and utility fit together as the first double element. Controls common to these elements include secure location, appropriate form for secure use, and usability of backup copies. Integrity and authenticity also fit together; one is concerned with internal structure and the other with conformance to external facts or reality. Controls for both include double entry, reasonableness checks, use of sequence numbers and checksums or hash totals, and comparison testing. Control of change applies to both as well. Finally, confidentiality and possession go together because, as discussed, they are interrelated. Commonly applied controls for both include copyright protection, cryptography, digital signatures, escrow, and secure storage.

The order of the elements here is logical, since availability and utility are necessary for integrity and authenticity to have value, and these first four elements are necessary for confidentiality and possession to have material meaning.

3.3   WHAT THE DICTIONARIES SAY ABOUT THE WORDS WE USE.   CIA would be adequate for security purposes if the violation of confidentiality were defined to be anything done *with* information, if integrity were defined to be anything done *to* information, and if availability were to include utility, but these definitions would be incorrect and not understood by many people. Information professionals are already defining the term "integrity" incorrectly, and we would not want to make matters worse. These definitions of security and the elements are relevant abstractions from *Webster's Third New International Dictionary* and *Webster's Collegiate Dictionary,* 10th edition.

Security—freedom from danger, fear, anxiety, care, uncertainty, doubt; basis for confidence; measures taken to ensure against surprise attack, espionage, observation, sabotage; resistance of a cryptogram to cryptanalysis usually measured by the time and effort needed to solve it.

Availability—present or ready for immediate use.

Utility—useful, fitness for some purpose.

Integrity—unimpaired or unmarred condition; soundness; entire correspondence with an original condition; adherence to a code of moral, artistic or other values; the quality or state of being complete or undivided; material wholeness.

Authenticity—quality of being authoritative, valid, true, real, genuine, worthy of acceptance or belief by reason of conformity to fact and reality.

Confidentiality—quality or state of being private or secret; known only to a limited few, containing information whose unauthorized disclosure could be prejudicial to the national interest.

Possession—act or condition of having or taking into one's control or holding at one's disposal; actual physical control of property by one who holds for himself, as distinguished from custody; something owned or controlled.

We lose credibility and confuse information owners if we do not use words precisely and consistently. When defined correctly, the six words are independent (with the exception that information possession is always violated when confidentiality is violated). They are also consistent, comprehensive, and complete. In other words, the six elements themselves possess integrity and authenticity, and therefore they have great utility. This does not mean that we will not find new elements or replace some of them as our insights develop and technology advances. (I first presented this demonstration of the need for the six elements in 1991 at the fourteenth U.S. National Security Agency/National Institute of Standards and Technology National Computer Security Conference in Baltimore.)

My definitions of the six elements are considerably shorter and simpler than the dictionary definitions, but appropriate for information security.

Availability—usability of information for a purpose.

Utility—usefulness of information for a purpose.

Integrity—completeness, wholeness, and readability of information and quality being unchanged from a previous state.

Authenticity—validity, conformance, and genuineness of information.

Confidentiality—limited observation and disclosure of knowledge.

Possession—holding, controlling, and having the ability to use information.

3.4 COMPREHENSIVE LISTS OF SOURCES AND ACTS CAUSING INFORMATION LOSSES.
The losses that we are concerned about in information security come from people who engage in unauthorized and harmful acts against information, communications, and systems, such as embezzlers, fraudsters, thieves, saboteurs, and criminal hackers. They engage in harmful using, taking, misrepresenting, observing, and every other conceivable form of human misbehavior. Natural physical forces such as air and earth movements, heat and cold, electromagnetic energy, living organisms, gravity and projectiles, and water and gases also are threats to information, as are inadvertent human errors.

Extensive lists of losses found in information security often include fraud, theft, sabotage, and espionage along with disclosure, usage, repudiation, and copying. The first four losses in this list are criminal justice terms at a different level of abstraction from the last four and require an understanding of criminal law, which many information owners and security specialists lack. For example, fraud includes theft only if it is performed using deception, and larceny includes burglary and theft from a victim's premises. What constitutes "premises" in an electronic network environment? This is a legal issue.

Many important types of information-related acts, such as false data entry, failure to perform, replacement, deception, misrepresentation, prolongation of use, delay of use, and even the obvious taking copies of information, are frequently omitted from lists of adverse incidents. Each of these losses may require different prevention and detection controls. This may be easily overlooked if our list of potential acts is incomplete—even though the acts that we typically omit are among the most common reported in actual loss experience. The people who cause losses often are aware that information owners have not provided adequate security and have not considered the full array of possible acts. It is, therefore, essential to include all types of potential harmful acts in our lists, especially when unique safeguards are applicable. Otherwise, we are in danger of being negligent, and those to whom we are accountable will view information security as incomplete or poorly conceived and implemented when a loss does occur.

The complete list of information loss acts in the next section is a comprehensive, nonlegalistic list of potential acts resulting in losses to or with information that I compiled from my 35 years in research about computer crime and security. I have simplified it to a single, low level of abstraction to facilitate understanding by information owners and to enable them to select effective controls. The list makes no distinction among the causes of the losses; as such, it applies equally well to accidental and intentional acts. Cause is largely irrelevant at this level of security analysis, as is the underlying intent or lack thereof. (Identifying cause is important at another level of security analysis. We need to determine the sources and motivation of threats in order to identify appropriate avoidance, deterrence, correction, and recovery controls.) In addition, the list makes no distinction between electronic and physical causes of loss, or among spoken, printed, or electronically recorded information.

The acts in the list are grouped to correspond to the six elements of information security outlined previously (e.g., availability and utility, etc.). Some types of acts in one element grouping may have a related effect in another grouping as well. For example, if no other copies of information exist, destroying the information (under *availability*) also may cause loss of possession, and taking (under *possession*) may cause loss of availability. Yet loss of possession and loss of availability are quite different, and may require different controls. I have placed acts in the most obvious categories, where a loss prevention analyst is likely to look first.

Here is an abbreviated version of the complete loss list for convenient use in the information security framework model:

- Destroy
- Interfere with use
- Introduce false data
- Modify or replace
- Misrepresent or repudiate

3.4.1 Complete List of Information Loss Acts

Availability and Utility Losses
- Destruction, damage, or contamination
- Denial, prolongation, acceleration, or delay in use or acquisition

- Movement or misplacement
- Conversion or obscuration

Integrity and Authenticity Losses
- Insertion, use, or production of false or unacceptable data
- Modification, replacement, removal, appending, aggregating, separating, or reordering
- Misrepresentation
- Repudiation (rejecting as untrue)
- Misuse or failure to use as required

Confidentiality and Possession Losses
- Locating
- Disclosing
- Observing, monitoring, and acquiring
- Copying
- Taking or controlling
- Claiming ownership or custodianship
- Inferring
- Exposing to all of the other losses
- Endangering by exposing to any of the other losses
- Failure to engage in or to allow any of the other losses to occur when instructed to do so

Users may be unfamiliar with some of the words in the lists of acts, at least in the context of security. For example, "repudiation" is a word that we seldom hear or use outside of the legal or security context. According to dictionaries, it means to refuse to accept acts or information as true, just, or of rightful authority or obligation. Information security technologists became interested in repudiation when the Massachusetts Institute of Technology (MIT) developed a secure network operating system for its internal use. The system was named Kerberos, taking the name of the three-headed dog that guarded the underworld in Greek mythology. Kerberos provides a means of forming secure links and paths between users and the computers serving them. Unfortunately, however, in early versions it allowed users to falsely deny using the links. This did not present any particular problems in the academic environment, but it did make Kerberos inadequate for business, even though its other security aspects were attractive. As the use of Kerberos spread into business, repudiation became an issue, and nonrepudiation controls became important.

Repudiation is an important issue in electronic transactions such as in electronic banking, purchases, and auctions used by so many people to automate their purchasing functions and Internet commerce, which require digital signatures, escrow, time stamps, and other authentication controls. I could, for example, falsely claim that I never ordered merchandise and that the order form or electronically transmitted ordering information that the merchant possesses is false. Repudiation is also a growing problem because of the difficulty of proving authorship or the source of electronic missives. And the inverse of repudiation—claiming that an act that did not happen actually did happen, or claiming that false information is true—is also important to security, although it is often overlooked. Repudiation and its inverse are both types of misrepresentation, but I include both "repudiation" and "misrepresentation" on the list because they may require different types of controls.

Other words in the list of acts may seem somewhat obscure. For example, we seldom think of prolonging or delaying use as a loss of availability or a denial of use, yet they are losses that are often inflicted by computer virus attacks.

I use the word "locate" in the list rather than "access" because access can be confusing with regard to information security. Although it is commonly used in computer terminology, its use frequently causes confusion, as it did in the trial of Robert T. Morris for releasing the Internet worm of November 2, 1988, and in computer crime laws. For example, access may mean just knocking on a door or opening the door but not going in. How far "into" a computer must you go to "access" it? A perpetrator can cause a loss simply by locating information, because the owner may not want to divulge possession of such information. In this case, no access is involved. For these reasons, I prefer to use the terms "entry," "intrusion," and "usage"—as well as "locate"—to refer to a computer as the object of the action. I have a similar problem with the use of the word "disclosure" and ignoring observation as I indicated earlier. "Disclose" is a verb that means to divulge, reveal, make known, or report knowledge to others. We can disclose knowledge by:

- Broadcasting
- Speaking
- Displaying
- Showing
- Leaving it in the presence and view of another person
- Leaving it in possible view where another person is likely to be
- Handing or sending it to another person

Disclosure is what an owner or potential victim might do inadvertently or intentionally, not what a perpetrator does, unless it is the second act after stealing, such as selling stolen intellectual property to another person. Disclosure can be an abuse if a person authorized to know information discloses it to an unauthorized person, or if an unauthorized person discloses knowledge to another person without permission. In any case, confidentiality is lost or is potentially lost, and the person disclosing the information may be accused of negligence, violation of privacy, conspiracy, or espionage.

Loss of confidentiality also can occur by observation, whether the victim or owner disclosed knowledge, resisted disclosure, or did nothing either to protect or to disclose it. Observing is an abuse of listening, spying by eavesdropping, shoulder surfing (looking over another person's shoulder or overhearing), looking at or listening to a stolen copy of information, or even by tactile feeling, as in the case of reading Braille. We should think about loss of confidentiality as a loss caused by inadvertent disclosure by the victim, observation by the perpetrator, and disclosure by the perpetrator who passes information to a third party. Disclosure and observation of information that is not knowledge converts it into knowledge if cognition takes place. Disclosure always results in loss of confidentiality by putting information into a state where there is no longer any secrecy, but observation results in loss of confidentiality only if cognition or use to the detriment of the owner takes place. Privacy is a right that is a whole other topic that I do not cover here. (This issue is discussed in Chapter 69.)

Loss of possession of information (including knowledge) is the loss from the unintended or regretful giving or taking of information. At a higher level of crime description, we call it larceny (theft or burglary) or fraud (when deceit is involved). Possession seems to be most closely associated with confidentiality. The two are placed together in the list because they share the common losses of taking and copying (loss of exclusive possession). I could have used "ownership" of information, since it is a synonym for possession, but "ownership" seems to be not as broad, because someone may rightly or wrongly possess information that is rightfully owned by another. The concepts of owner or possessor of information, along with user, provider, or custodian of information, are important distinctions in security for assigning asset accountability. This provides another reason for including possession in the list.

The act of *endangerment* is quite different from, but applies to, the other losses. It means putting information in harm's way, or that a person has been remiss (and possibly negligent) by not applying sufficient protection to information, such as leaving sensitive or valuable documents in an unlocked office or open trash bin. Leaving a computer unnecessarily connected to the Internet is another example. Endangerment of information may lead to charges of negligence or criminal negligence and civil liability suits that may be more costly than direct loss incidents. My objectives of security in the framework model invokes a standard of due diligence to deal with this exposure.

The last act in the list—failure to engage in or allow any of the other acts when instructed to do so—may seem odd at first glance. It means that an information owner may require an act resulting in any of the other acts to be carried out. Or the owner may wish that an act be allowed to occur, or information to be put into danger of loss. There are occasions when information should be put in harm's way for testing purposes or to accomplish a greater good. For example, computer programmers and auditors often create information files that are purposely invalid for use as input to a computer to make sure that the controls to detect or mitigate a loss are working correctly. A programmer bent on crime might remove invalid data in a test input file to avoid testing a control that the perpetrator has neutralized or has avoided implementing for nefarious purposes. The list would surely be incomplete without this type of loss, yet I have never seen it included or discussed in any other information security text.

The acts in the list are described at the appropriate level for deriving and identifying appropriate security controls. At the next lower level of abstraction (e.g., read, write, and execute), the losses would not be so obvious and would not necessarily suggest important controls. At the level that I choose, there is no attempt to differentiate acts that make no change to information from those that do, since these differences are not important for identifying directly applicable controls or for performing threat analyses. For example, an act of modification changes the information, while an act of observation does not, but encryption is likely to be employed as a powerful primary control against both acts.

3.4.2   Examples of Acts and Suggested Controls.   The next examples illustrate the relationships between acts and controls in threat analysis. Groups of acts are followed by examples of the losses and applicable controls.

3.4.2.1   *Destroy, Damage, or Contaminate.*   Perpetrators or harmful forces can damage, destroy, or contaminate information by electronically erasing it, writing other data over it, applying high-energy radio waves to damage delicate electronic circuits, or physically damaging the media (e.g., paper, flash memory, or disks) containing it.

Controls include disaster prevention safeguards such as locked facilities, safe storage of backup copies, and write-usage authorization requirements.

3.4.2.2 Deny, Prolong, Delay Use or Acquisition.

Perpetrators can make information unavailable by hiding it or denying its use through encryption and not revealing the means to restore it, or by keeping critical processing units busy with other work, such as in a denial-of-service attack. Such actions would not necessarily destroy the information. Similarly, a perpetrator may prolong information use by making program changes that slow the processing in a computer or by slowing the display of the information on a screen. Such actions might cause unacceptable timing for effective use of the information. Information acquisition may be delayed by requiring too many passwords to retrieve it or by slowing retrieval. These actions can make the information obsolete by the time it becomes available.

Controls include making multiple copies available from different sources, preventing overload of processing by selective allowance of input, or preventing the activation of harmful mechanisms such as computer viruses by using antiviral utilities.

3.4.2.3 Enter, Use, or Produce False Data.

Data diddling, my term for false data entry and use, is a common form of computer crime, accounting for much of the financial and inventory fraud. Losses may be either intentional, such as those resulting from the use of Trojan horses (including computer viruses), or unintentional, such as those from input errors.

Most internal controls such as range checks, audit trails, separation of duties, duplicate data entry detection, program proving, and hash totals for data items protect against these threats.

3.4.2.4 Modify, Replace, or Reorder.

These acts are often intelligent changes rather than damage or destruction. *Reordering,* which is actually a form of modification, is included separately because it may require specific controls that could otherwise be overlooked. Similarly, *replacement* is included because users might not otherwise include the idea of replacing an entire data file when considering modification. Any of these actions can produce a loss inherent in the threats of entering and modifying information, but including all of them covers modifying data both before entry and after entry, since each requires different controls.

Cryptography, digital signatures, usage authorization, and message sequencing are examples of controls to protect against these acts, as are detection controls to identify anomalies.

3.4.2.5 Misrepresent.

The claim that information is something different from what it really is or has a different meaning from what was intended arises in counterfeiting, forgery, fraud, impersonation (of authorized users), and many other deceptive activities. Hackers use misrepresentation in social engineering to deceive people into revealing information needed to attack systems. Misrepresenting old data as new information is another act of this type.

Controls include user and document authentication methods such as passwords, digital signatures, and data validity tests. Making trusted people more resistant to deception by reminders and training is another control.

3.4.2.6 Repudiate.

This type of loss, in which perpetrators generally deny having made transactions, is prevalent in electronic data interchange (EDI) and Internet commerce. Oliver North's denial of the content of his e-mail messages is a notable example of repudiation, but as I mentioned earlier, the inverse of repudiation also represents a potential loss.

Repudiation can be controlled most effectively through the use of digital signatures and public key cryptography. Trusted third parties, such as certificate authorities with secure computer servers, provide the independence of notary publics to resist denial of truthful information as long as they can be held liable for their failures.

3.4.2.7 *Misuse or Fail to Use as Required.*   Misuse of information is clearly an act resulting in many information losses. Misuse by failure to perform duties such as updating files or backing up information is not so obvious and needs explicit identification. Implicit misuse by conforming exactly to inadequate or incorrect instructions is a sure way to sabotage systems.

Information usage control and internal application controls that constrain the modification or use of trusted software help to avoid these problems. Keeping secure logs of routine activities can help catch operational vulnerabilities.

3.4.2.8 *Locate.*   Unauthorized use of someone's computer or data network to locate and identify information is a crime under most computer crime statutes—even if there is no overt intention to cause harm. Such usage is a violation of privacy, and trespass to engage in such usage is a crime under other laws.

Log-on and usage controls are major features in many operating systems such as Microsoft Windows and some versions of Unix as well as in add-on security utilities such as *RACF* and *ACF2* for large IBM computers and many security products for personal computers.

3.4.2.9 *Disclose.*   Preventing information from being revealed to people not authorized to know it is the purpose of business, personal, and government secrecy. Disclosure may be verbal, by mail, or by transferring messages or files electronically or on disks, flash memories, or tape. Disclosure can result in loss of privacy and trade secrets.

Military organizations have advanced protection of information confidentiality to an elaborate art form.

3.4.2.10 *Observe or Monitor.*   Observation, which requires action on the part of a perpetrator, is the inverse of disclosure, which results from actions of a possessor. Workstation display screens, communication lines, and monitoring devices such as recorders and audit logs are common targets of observation and monitoring. Observation of output from printers is another possible source, as is shoulder surfing—the technique of watching screens of other computer users.

Physical entry protection for input and output devices represents the major control to prevent this type of loss. Preventing wiretapping and eavesdropping is also important.

3.4.2.11 *Copy.*   Copy machines and the software *copy* command are the major sources of unauthorized copying. Copying is used to violate exclusive possession and privacy. Copying can destroy authenticity, as when used to counterfeit money or other business instruments.

Location and use controls are effective against copying, as are unique markings such as those used on U.S. currency and watermarks on paper and in computer files.

3.4.2.12 Take.   Transferring data files in computers or networks constitutes taking. So does taking small computers and DVDs or documents for the value of the information stored in them. Perpetrators can easily take copies of information without depriving the owner of possession or confidentiality.

A wide range of physical and logical location controls applies to these losses; most are based on common sense and a reasonable level of due care.

3.4.2.13 Endanger.   Putting information into locations or conditions in which others may cause loss in any of the previously described ways clearly endangers the information, and the perpetrator may be accused of negligence, at least.

Physical and logical means of preventing information from being placed in danger are important. Training people to be careful, and holding them accountable for protecting information, may be the most effective means of preventing endangerment.

3.4.3 Physical Information and Systems Losses.   Information also can suffer from physical losses such as those caused by floods, earthquakes, radiation, and fires. Although these losses may not directly affect the information itself (e.g., knowledge of operating procedures held in the minds of operators), they can damage or destroy the media and the environment that contain representations of the information. Water, for example, can destroy printed pages and damage magnetic disks; physical shaking or radio frequency radiation can short-out electronic circuits, and fires can destroy all types of media. Overall, physical loss may occur in seven natural ways by application of:

1. Extreme temperature
2. Gases
3. Liquids
4. Living organisms
5. Projectiles
6. Movements
7. Energy anomalies

Each way, of course, comes from specific sources of loss (e.g., smoke or water). And the various ways can be broken down further, to identify the underlying cause of the source of loss. For example, the liquid that destroys information may be water flowing from a plumbing break above the computer workstation, caused in turn by freezing weather. The next list presents examples of each of the seven major sources of physical loss.

1. **Extreme temperature.** Heat or cold. Examples: sunlight, fire, freezing, hot weather, and the breakdown of air-conditioning equipment.
2. **Gases.** War gases, commercial vapors, humid or dry air, suspended particles. Examples: sarin nerve gas, PCBs from exploding transformers, release of Freon from air conditioners, smoke and smog, cleaning fluid, and fuel vapors.
3. **Liquids.** Water, chemicals. Examples: floods, plumbing failures, precipitation, fuel leaks, spilled drinks, acid and base chemicals used for cleaning, and computer printer fluids.

4. **Living organisms.** Viruses, bacteria, fungi, plants, animals, and human beings. Examples: sickness of key workers, molds, contamination from skin oils and hair, contamination and electrical shorting from defecation and release of body fluids, consumption of information media such as paper or of cable insulation, and shorting of microcircuits from cobwebs.

5. **Projectiles.** Tangible objects in motion, powered objects. Examples: meteorites, falling objects, cars and trucks, airplanes, bullets and rockets, explosions, and windborne objects.

6. **Movement.** Collapse, shearing, shaking, vibration, liquefaction, flows, waves, separation, slides. Examples: dropping or shaking fragile equipment, earthquakes, earth slides, lava flows, sea waves, and adhesive failures.

7. **Energy anomalies.** Electric surge or failure, magnetism, static electricity, aging circuitry; radiation, sound, light, radio, microwave, electromagnetic, atomic. Examples: electric utility failures, proximity of magnets and electromagnets, carpet static, electromagnetic pulses (EMP) from nuclear explosions, lasers, loudspeakers, high-energy radio frequency (HERF) guns, radar systems, cosmic radiation, and explosions.

Although meteorites, for example, clearly pose little danger to computers, it is nonetheless important to include all such unlikely events in a thorough analysis of potential threats. In general, include every possible act included in a threat analysis. Then consider it carefully; if it is too unlikely, document the consideration and discard the item. It is better to have thought of a source of loss and to have discarded it than to have overlooked an important one. Invariably, when you present a threat analysis to others, someone will try to surprise the developer with another source of loss that has been overlooked.

Insensitive practitioners have ingrained inadequate loss lists in the body of knowledge from the very inception of information security. Proposing a major change at this late date is a bold action that may take significant time to accomplish. However, we must not perpetuate our past inadequacies by using the currently accepted destruction, disclosure, use, and modification (DDUM) as a complete list of losses. We must not underrate or simplify the complexity of our subject at the expense of misleading information owners. Our adversaries are always looking for weaknesses in information security, but our strength lies in anticipating sources of threats and having plans in place to prevent the losses that they may cause.

It is impossible to collect a truly complete list of the sources of information losses that can be caused by the intentional or accidental acts of people. We really have no idea what people may do—now or in the future. We base our lists on experience, but until we can conceive of an act, or until a threat actually surfaces or occurs, we cannot include it on the list. And not knowing the threat means that we cannot devise a plan to protect against it. This is one of the reasons that information security is still a folk art rather than a science.

3.4.4 Challenge of Complete Lists.   I believe that my lists of physical sources of loss and information losses are complete, but I am always interested in expanding them to include new sources of loss that I may have overlooked.

While I was lecturing in Australia, for example, a delegate suggested that I had omitted an important category. His computer center had experienced an invasion of field mice with a taste for electrical insulation. The intruders proceeded to chew through the computer cables, ruining them. Consequently, I had to add rodents to my list of sources. I then heard about an incident in San Francisco in which the entire evening shift of computer operations workers ate together in the company cafeteria to celebrate a birthday. Then they all contracted food poisoning, leaving their company without sufficient operations staff for two weeks. I combined the results of these two events into a category named "Living Organisms."

3.5 FUNCTIONS OF INFORMATION SECURITY. The model for information security that I have proposed includes 12 security functions instead of the 3 (prevention, detection, and recovery) included in previous models. These functions describe the activities that information security practitioners and information owners engage in to protect information as well as the objectives of the security controls that they use. Every control serves one or more of these functions.

Although some security specialists add other functions to the list, such as quality assurance and reliability, I consider these to be outside the scope of information security; other specialized fields deal with them. Reliability is difficult to relate to security except as endangerment when perpetrators destroy the reliability of information and systems, which is a violation of security. Thus, security must preserve a state of reliability but need not necessarily attempt to improve it. Security must protect the auditability of information and systems while, at the same time, security itself must be reliable and auditable. I believe that my security definitions include destruction of the reliability and auditability of information at a high level of abstraction. For example, reliability is reduced when the authenticity of information is put into question by changing it from a correct representation of fact.

Similarly, I do not include such functions as authentication of users and verification in my lists, since I consider these to be control objectives to achieve the 12 functions of information security.

There is a definite logic to the order in which I present the 12 functions in my list. A methodical information security practitioner is likely to apply the functions in this order when resolving security vulnerabilities.

1. Information security must first be independently *audited* in an adversarial manner in order to document its state and to identify its weaknesses and strengths.

2. The practitioner must determine if a security problem can be *avoided* altogether.

3. If the problem cannot be avoided, the practitioner needs to try to *deter* potential abusers or forces from misbehaving.

4. If the threat cannot be avoided or deterred, the practitioner attempts to *detect* its activation.

5. If detection is not assured, then the practitioner tries to *prevent* the act from occurring.

6. If prevention fails and an act occurs, then the practitioner needs to stop it or minimize its harmful effects through *mitigation*.

7. The practitioner needs to determine if *transferring* the responsibility to another individual or department might be more effective at resolving the situation resulting from the attack, or if another party (e.g., an insurer) might be held accountable for the cost of the loss.

Exhibit 3.1 Threats, Assets, and Vulnerabilities Model

	Threats			Assets	Vulnerabilities (Missing and Deficient Controls)		
Offenders Have/Acquire	**Abuse/Misuse**	**Methods**	**Losses**	**Assets Lost**	**Control Objectives**	**Controls (Types)**	**Control Guides**
Skills	Errors	**External**	**Availability and Utility**	**Information**	Avoidance	Organization	Cost effective
learning	Omissions	heat, cold	destroy	spoken	Deterrence	Physical	Due care
technology	Negligence	gases, air	damage	printed	Prevention	Development	Complete
people	Recklessness	water	contaminate	magnetic	Detection	Automation	Consistent
Knowledge	Delinquency	chemical	deny	electronic	Mitigation	Operation	Performance
direct	Civil	bacteria	prolong	optical	Sanction	Voice	Sustain
indirect	Disputes	viruses	accelerate	radio	Transfer	Network	Automatic
Resources	Conspiracy	people	delay	biological	Investigate	Access	Tolerated
computer	Nature	animals	move	**Computer**	Recovery	Training	Consequences
services	Disruption	insects	misplace	**Commlines**	Correction	Motivation	Override
transport	Destruction	collision	convert	**Networks**		Management	Failsafe
financial	Theft	collapse	obscure	**Facilities**		Applications	Default
Authority	Privacy	shear	**Integrity and Authenticity**	**Buildings**		Printing	Instrument
employment	Trespass	shake	insert	**Transport**		Audit	Auditable
contract ownership	Burglary	vibrate	use	**People**		Disaster	Nonrepudiate
possession	Larceny	liquefy	produce			Recovery	Secrecy
custodian	Forgery	flows	modify				Universal
right	Counterfeiting	waves	replace				Independent
other	Smuggling	separate	remove				Unpredictable
	Fraud	slides	append				Tamperproof
	Scam	electric	reorder				Compartment
	Embezzlement	magnets	misrepresent				Depth
	Bribery	aging					Isolate
		radiate					Least

(Continued)

EXHIBIT 3.1 Threats, Assets, and Vulnerabilities Model (*Continued*)

Threats				Assets	Vulnerabilities (Missing and Deficient Controls)		
Offenders Have/Acquire	Abuse/Misuse	Methods	Losses	Assets Lost	Control Objectives	Controls (Types)	Control Guides
Motives	Extortion	Sound	Repudiate				Accountability
no intent	Racketeering	Light	Fail to use				Trust
negligence	Infringement	Radio					Multifunction
errors and	Plagiarism	Atomic	**Confidential**				Deception
omissions	Piracy		**and Possession**				Positional
	Espionage	**Masquerade**	locate				Transparent
Intentional	Antitrust	impersonate	disclose				
problem solving	Contract	spoof	observe				
gain higher ethic	Securities		monitor				
	Employment	**Programmed**	acquire				
Extreme	Kickbacks	Trojan	copy				
Advocacy	Laundering	virus	take control				
social	Libel	bomb	own				
political	Drugs	bypass	infer				
religious	Pornography	trapdoor					
	Harassment		**Expose to loss**				
	Assault	**Authority**					
	Sex attack	violation	**Endanger**				
	Kidnapping		fail instruction				
	Murder	**Active**					
	Suicide	deny service					
		false data entry					
		Passive					
		browse					
		observe					
		Failure					
		omit duty					
		Indirect					
		crime use					

Source: Donn B. Parker, *Fighting Computer Crime* (New York: John Wiley & Sons, 1998).

8. After a loss occurs, the practitioner needs to *investigate* and search for the individual(s) or force(s) that caused or contributed to the incident as well as for any parties that played a role in it—positively or negatively.

9. When identified, all parties should be *sanctioned or rewarded* as appropriate.

10. After an incident is concluded, the victim needs to *recover* or assist with recovery.

11. The stakeholders should take *corrective* actions to prevent the same type of incident from occurring again.

12. The stakeholders must learn from the experience in order to advance their knowledge of information security and *educate* others.

3.6   SELECTING SAFEGUARDS USING A STANDARD OF DUE DILIGENCE.

Information security practitioners usually refer to the process of selecting safeguards as risk assessment, risk analysis, or risk management. Selecting safeguards based on risk calculations can be a fruitless and expensive process. Although many security experts and associations advocate using risk assessment methods, many organizations ultimately find that using a standard of due diligence (or care) is far superior and more practical. Often one sad experience of using security risk assessment is sufficient to convince information security departments and corporate management of their limitations. Security risk is a function of probability or frequency of occurrence of rare loss events and their impact, and neither is sufficiently measurable or predictable for investment in security. Note that risk applies only to rare events. Events such as computer virus attacks or credit card fraud are occurring continuously and are not risks; they are certainties and can be measured, controlled, and managed.

The standard of due diligence approach is simple and obvious; it is the default process that I recommend and that is commonly used today instead of more elaborate "scientific" approaches. The standard of due diligence approach is recognized and accepted by many legal documents and organizations and is documented in numerous business guides. The 1996 U.S. federal statute on protecting trade secrets (18 USC § 1831), for example, states in (3) (a) that the owner of information must take "reasonable measures to keep such information secret" for it to be defined as a trade secret. (See Chapter 45.)

3.7   THREATS, ASSETS, VULNERABILITIES MODEL.

Pulling all of the aspects together in one place is a useful way to analyze security threats and vulnerabilities and to create effective scenarios to test real information systems and organizations. The model illustrated in Exhibit 3.1 is designed to help readers do this. Users can outline a scenario or analyze a real case by circling and connecting the appropriate descriptors in each column of the model.

In this version of the model, the Controls column lists only the subject headings of control types; a completed model would contain hundreds of controls. If the model is being used to conduct a review, I suggest that the Vulnerabilities section of the model be renamed to Recommended Controls.

3.8   CONCLUSION.

The security framework proposed in this chapter represents an attempt to overcome the dominant technologist view of information security by focusing more broadly on all aspects of security, including the information that we are attempting to protect, the potential sources of loss, the types of loss, the controls that we can apply to avoid loss, the methods for selecting those controls, and our overall objectives in protecting information. This broad focus should have two beneficial effects: advancing information security from a narrow folk art to a broad-based discipline and—most important—helping to reduce many of the losses associated with information, wherever it exists.

CHAPTER 4

HARDWARE ELEMENTS OF SECURITY

Sy Bosworth and Stephen Cobb

4.1 INTRODUCTION. Computer hardware has always played a major role in computer security. Over the years, that role has increased dramatically, due to both the increases in processing power, storage capacity, and communications capabilities as well as the decreases in cost and size of components. The ubiquity of cheap, powerful, highly connected computing devices poses significant challenges to computer security. At the same time, the challenges posed by large, centralized computing systems have not diminished. An understanding of the hardware elements of computing is thus essential to a well-rounded understanding of computer security.

Chapter 1 of this *Handbook* has additional history of the evolution of information technology.

4.2   BINARY DESIGN.   Although there are wide variations among computer architectures and hardware designs, all have at least one thing in common: They utilize a uniquely coded series of electrical impulses to represent any character within there range. Like the Morse code with its dots and dashes, computer pulse codes may be linked together to convey alphabetic or numeric information. Unlike the Morse code, however, computer pulse trains may also be combined in mathematical operations or data manipulation.

In 1946, Dr. John von Neumann, at the Institute for Advanced Study of Princeton University, first described in a formal report how the binary system of numbers could be used in computer implementations. The binary system requires combinations of only two numbers, 0 and 1, to represent any digit, letter, or symbol and, by extension, any group of digits, letters, or symbols. In contrast, the conventional decimal system requires combinations of 10 different numbers, from 0 to 9, letters from a to z, and a large number of symbols, to convey the same information. Von Neumann recognized that electrical and electronic elements could be considered as having only two states, on and off, and that these two states could be made to correspond to the 0 and 1 of the binary system. If the turning on and off of a computer element occurred at a rapid rate, the voltage or current outputs that resulted would best be described as pulses. Despite 60 years of intensive innovation in computer hardware, and the introduction of some optically based methods of data representation, the nature of these electrical pulses and the method of handling them remain the ultimate measure of a computer's accuracy and reliability.

4.2.1   Pulse Characteristics.   Ideally, the waveform of a single pulse should be straight-sided, flat-topped, and of an exactly specified duration, amplitude, and phase relationship to other pulses in a series. It is the special virtue of digital computers that they can be designed to function at their original accuracy despite appreciable degradation of the pulse characteristics. However, errors will occur when certain limits are exceeded, and thus data integrity will be compromised. Because these errors are difficult to detect, it is important that a schedule of preventive maintenance be established and rigidly adhered to. Only in this way can operators detect degraded performance before it is severe enough to affect reliability.

4.2.2   Circuitry.   To generate pulses of desirable characteristics, and to manipulate them correctly, requires components of uniform quality and dependability. To lower manufacturing costs, to make servicing and replacement easier, and generally to improve reliability, computer designers try to use as few different types of components as possible and to incorporate large numbers of each type into any one machine.

First-generation computers used as many as 30,000 vacuum tubes, mainly in a half-dozen types of logic elements. The basic circuits were flip-flops, or gates, that produced an output pulse whenever a given set of input pulses was present. However, vacuum tubes generated intense heat, even when in a standby condition. As a consequence, the useful operating time between failures was relatively short.

With the development of solid state diodes and transistors, computers became much smaller and very much cooler than their vacuum-tube predecessors. With advances in logic design, a single type of gate, such as the not-and (NAND) circuit, could replace all other logic elements. The resulting improvements in cost and reliability have been accelerated by the use of monolithic integrated circuits. Not least in importance is their vastly increased speed of operation. Since the mean time between failures of electronic computer circuitry is generally independent of the number of operations performed, it follows that throughput increases directly with speed; speed is defined as the rate at which a computer accesses, moves, and manipulates data. The ultimate limitation on computer speed is the time required for a signal to move from one physical element to another. At a velocity of 299,792,458 meters per second (186,282 miles per second) in vacuum, an electrical signal travels 3.0 meters or 9.84 feet in 10 nanoseconds (0.000,000,01 seconds). If components were as large as they were originally, and consequently as far apart, today's nanosecond computer speeds would clearly be impossible, as would be the increased throughput and reliability now commonplace.

4.2.3 Coding. In a typical application, data may be translated and retranslated automatically into a half-dozen different codes thousands of times each second. Many of these codes represent earlier technology retained for backward compatibility and economic reasons only. In any given code, each character appears as a specific group of pulses. Within each group, each pulse position is known as a *bit*, since it represents either of the two *bi*nary dig*its*, 0 or 1. Exhibit 4.1 illustrates some of the translations that may be continuously performed as data move about within a single computer.

A *byte* is the name originally applied to the smallest group of bits that could be read and written (accessed or addressed) as a unit. Today a byte is always considered by convention to have 8 bits. In modern systems, a byte is viewed as the storage unit for a single American Standard Code for Information Interchange (ASCII) character, although newer systems such as Unicode, which handle international accented characters and many other symbols, use up to 4 bytes per character. By convention, most people use metric prefixes (kilo-, mega-, giga-, tera-) to indicate collections of bytes; thus *KB* refers to *kilobytes* and is usually defined as 1,024 bytes. Outside the data processing field, *K* would normally indicate the multiplier 1,000. Because of the ambiguity

Exhibit 4.1 Common Codes for Numeral 5

Code	Bits	Typical Use	Bit Pattern for "5"
Hexadecimal	4	Console switches	0101
Baudot	5	Paper tape	00001
Binary-Coded-Decimal (BCD)	6	Console indicators	000101
Transcode	6	Data transmission	110101
USASCII	7	Data transmission	0110101
EBCDIC	8	Buffer	11110101
EBCDIC, zoned decimal	8	Main memory	11000101
EBCDIC, packed decimal	8	Arithmetic logic unit	01011100
USASCII-8	8	Data transmission	01010101
Hollerith	12	Card reader/punch	000000010000
Binary, halfword	16	Arithmetic logic unit	0000000000000101

in definitions, the United States National Institute of Standards and Technology (NIST) proposed, and in 2000 the International Electrotechnical Commission established, a new set of units for information or computer storage. These units are established by a series of prefixes to indicate powers of 2; in this scheme, KB means *kibibytes* and refers exclusively to 1,024 (2^{10} or $\sim 10^3$) bytes. However, kibibytes, mebibytes (2^{20} or $\sim 10^6$), gibibytes (2^{30} or $\sim 10^9$), and tebibytes (2^{40} or $\sim 10^{12}$) are terms that have not yet become widely used.

Because translations between coding systems are accomplished at little apparent cost, any real incentive to unify the different systems is lacking. However, all data movements and translations increase the likelihood of internal error, and for this reason parity checks and validity tests have become indispensable.

4.3 PARITY.   Redundancy is central to error-free data processing. By including extra bits in predetermined locations, certain types of errors can be detected immediately by inspection of these *metadata* (data about the original data). In a typical application, data move back and forth many times, among primary memory, secondary storage, input and output devices, as well as through communications links. During these moves, the data may lose integrity by dropping 1 or more bits, by having extraneous bits introduced, and by random changes in specific bits. To detect some of these occurrences, parity bits are added before data are moved and are checked afterward.

4.3.1 Vertical Redundancy Checks.   In this relatively simple and inexpensive scheme, a determination is initially made as to whether there should be an odd or an even number of "1" bits in each character. For example, using the binary-coded decimal representation of the numerical "5," we find that the 6-bit pulse group 000101 contains two 1s, an even number. Adding a seventh position to the code group, we may have either type of parity. If odd parity has been selected, a 1 would be added in the leftmost checkbit position:

> Odd parity 1000101 three 1s
> Even parity 0000101 two 1s

After any movement the number of 1 bits would be counted, and if not an odd number, an error would be assumed and processing halted. Of course, if 2 bits, or any even number, had been improperly transmitted, no error would be indicated since the number of "1" bits would still be odd.

To compound the problem of nonuniformity illustrated in Exhibit 4.1, each of the 4-, 5-, 6-, 7-, 8-, and 16-bit code groups may have an additional bit added for parity checking. Furthermore, there may be inconsistency of odd or even parity between manufacturers, or even between different equipment from a single supplier.

4.3.2 Longitudinal Redundancy Checks.   Errors may not be detected by a vertical redundancy check (VRC) alone, for reasons just discussed. An additional safeguard, of particular use in data transmission and media recording such as tapes and disks, is the longitudinal redundancy check (LRC). With this technique, an extra character is generated after some predetermined number of data characters. Each bit in the extra character provides parity for its corresponding row, just as the vertical parity bits do for their corresponding columns. Exhibit 4.2 represents both types as they

Exhibit 4.2   Vertical and Longitudinal Parity, Seven-Track Magnetic Tape

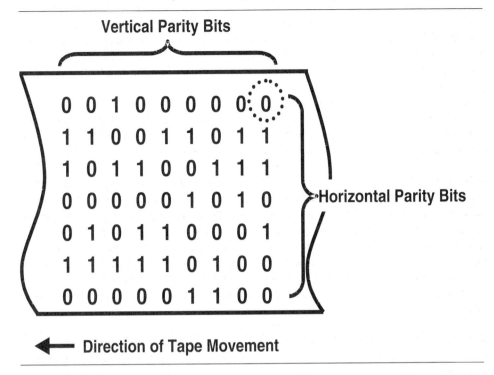

Vertical Parity Bits

```
0  0  1  0  0  0  0  0  0
1  1  0  0  1  1  0  1  1
1  0  1  1  0  0  1  1  1
0  0  0  0  0  1  0  1  0        Horizontal Parity Bits
0  1  0  1  1  0  0  0  1
1  1  1  1  1  0  1  0  0
0  0  0  0  0  1  1  0  0
```

← **Direction of Tape Movement**

would be recorded on 7-track magnetic tape. One bit has been circled to show that it is ambiguous. This bit appears at the intersection of the parity row and the parity column, and must be predetermined to be correct for one or the other, as it may not be correct for both. In the illustration, the ambiguous bit is correct for the odd parity requirement of the VRC character column; it is incorrect for the even parity of the LRC bit row.

In actual practice, the vertical checkbits would be attached to each character column as shown, but the longitudinal bits would follow a block of data that might contain 80 to several hundred characters. Where it is possible to use both LRC and VRC, any single data error in a block will be located at the intersection of incorrect row and column parity bits. The indicated bit may then be corrected automatically. The limitations of this method are: (1) multiple errors cannot be corrected, (2) an error in the ambiguous position cannot be corrected, and (3) an error that does not produce both a VRC and LRC indication cannot be corrected.

4.3.3 Cyclical Redundancy Checks.   Where the cost of a data error could be high, the added expense of cyclical redundancy checks (CRCs) is warranted. In this technique, a relatively large number of redundant bits is used. For example, each 4-bit character requires 3 parity bits, while a 32-bit computer word needs 6 parity bits. Extra storage space is required in main and secondary memory, and transmissions take longer than without such checks. The advantage, however, is that any single error can be detected, whether in a data bit or a parity bit, and its location can be positively identified. By a simple electronic process of complementation, an incorrect 0 is converted to a 1, and vice versa.

4.3.4 Self-Checking Codes.   Several types of codes are in use that inherently contain a checking ability similar to that of the parity system. Typical of these is the 2-of-5 code, in which every decimal digit is represented by a bit configuration containing exactly two 1s and three 0s. Where a parity test would consist of counting 1s to see if their number was odd or even, a 2-of-5 test would indicate an error whenever the number of 1s was more or less than 2.

4.4 HARDWARE OPERATIONS.   Input, output, and processing are the three essential functions of any computer. To protect data integrity during these operations, several hardware features are available.

- **Read-after-write.** In disk and tape drives, it is common practice to read the data immediately after they are recorded and to compare them with the original values. Any disagreement signals an error that requires rewriting.

- **Echo.** Data transmitted to a peripheral device, to a remote terminal (see Section 4.9.1), or to another computer can be made to generate a return signal. This echo is compared with the original signal to verify correct reception. However, there is always the risk that an error will occur in the return signal and falsely indicate an error in the original transmission.

- **Overflow.** The maximum range of numerical values that any computer can accommodate is fixed by its design. If a program is improperly scaled, or if an impossible operation such as dividing by zero is called for, the result of an arithmetic operation may exceed the allowable range, producing an overflow error. Earlier computers required programmed instructions to detect overflows, but this function now generally is performed by hardware elements at the machine level. Overflows within application programs still must be dealt with in software. (Indeed, failure to do so can render software susceptible to abuse by malicious parties.)

- **Validitation.** In any one computer coding system, some bit patterns may be unassigned, and others may be illegal. In the IBM System/360 Extended Binary Coded Decimal Interchange Code (EBCDIC), for example, the number 9 is represented by 11111001, but 11111010 is unassigned. A parity check would not detect the second group as being in error, since both have the same number of 1 bits. A validity check, however, would reject the second bit configuration as invalid.

  Similarly, certain bit patterns represent assigned instruction codes while others do not. In one computer, the instruction to convert packed-decimal numbers to zoned-decimal numbers is 11110011, or F3 in hexadecimal notation; 11110101, or F5, is unassigned, and a validity check would cause a processing halt whenever that instruction was tested.

- **Replication.** In highly sensitive applications, it is good practice to provide backup equipment on site, for immediate changeover in the event of failure of the primary computer. For this reason, it is sometimes prudent to retain two identical, smaller computers rather than to replace them with a single unit of equivalent or even greater power. Fault-tolerant, or fail-safe, computers use two or more processors that operate simultaneously, sharing the load and exchanging information about the current status of duplicate processes running in parallel. If one of the processors fails, another continues the processing without pause.

  Many sensitive applications, such as airline reservation systems, have extensive data communications facilities. It is important that all of this equipment be duplicated as well as the computers themselves. (The failure of an airline reservation system, if permitted to extend beyond a relatively small number of hours, could lead to failure of the airline itself.)

Replacements should also be immediately available for peripheral devices. In some operating systems, it is necessary to inform the system that a device is down and to reassign its functions to another unit. In the more sophisticated systems, a malfunctioning device is automatically cut out and replaced. For example, the New York Stock Exchange operates and maintains two identical trading systems so that failure of the primary system should not result in any interruption to trading.

4.5 INTERRUPTS. The sequence of operations performed by a computer system is determined by a group of instructions: a program. However, many events that occur during operations require deviations from the programmed sequence. *Interrupts* are signals generated by hardware elements that detect changed conditions and initiate appropriate action. The first step is immediately to store the status of various elements in preassigned memory locations. The particular stored bit patterns, commonly called program status words, contain the information necessary for the computer to identify the cause of the interrupt, to take action to process it, and then to return to the proper instruction in the program sequence after the interrupt is cleared.

4.5.1 Types of Interrupts. Five types of interrupts are in general use. Each of them is of importance in establishing and maintaining data processing integrity.

4.5.1.1 Input/Output Interrupts. Input/output (I/O) interrupts are generated whenever a device or channel that had been busy becomes available. This capability is necessary to achieve error-free use of the increased throughput provided by buffering, overlapped processing, and multiprogramming.

After each I/O interrupt, a check is made to determine whether the data have been read or written without error. If so, the next I/O operation can be started; if not, an error-recovery procedure is initiated. The number of times that errors occur should be recorded so that degraded performance can be detected and corrected.

4.5.1.2 Supervisor Calls. The supervisor, or monitor, is a part of the operating system software that controls the interactions between all hardware and software elements.

Every request to read or write data is scheduled by the supervisor when called upon to do so. I/O interrupts also are handled by supervisor calls that coordinate them with read/write requests. Loading, executing, and terminating programs are other important functions initiated by supervisor calls.

4.5.1.3 Program Check Interrupts. Improper use of instructions or data may cause an interrupt that terminates the program. For example, attempts to divide by zero and operations resulting in arithmetic overflow are voided. Unassigned instruction codes, attempts to access protected storage, and invalid data addresses are other types of exceptions that cause program check interrupts.

4.5.1.4 Machine Check Interrupts. Among the exception conditions that will cause machine check interrupts are parity errors, bad disk sectors, disconnection of peripherals in use, and defective circuit modules. It is important that proper procedures be followed to clear machine checks without loss of data or processing error.

4.5.1.5 *External Interrupts.* External interrupts are generated by timer action, by pressing an Interrupt key, or by signals from another computer. When two central processing units are interconnected, signals that pass between them initiate external interrupts. In this way, control and synchronization are continuously maintained while programs, data, and peripheral devices may be shared and coordinated.

In mainframes, an electronic clock generally is included in the central processor unit for time-of-day entries in job logs and for elapsed-time measurements. As an interval timer, the clock can be set to generate an interrupt after a given period. This feature should be used as a security measure, preventing sensitive jobs from remaining on the computer long enough to permit unauthorized manipulation of data or instructions.

4.5.2 Trapping. Trapping is a type of hardware response to an interrupt. Upon detecting the exception, an unconditional branch is taken to some predetermined location. An instruction there transfers control to a supervisor routine that initiates appropriate action.

4.6 MEMORY AND DATA STORAGE. Just as the human mind is subject to aberrations, so is computer memory. In the interests of data security and integrity, various therapeutic measures have been developed for the several types of storage.

4.6.1 Main Memory. Random access memory (RAM), and its derivatives, such as dynamic RAM (DRAM), synchronous DRAM (SDRAM, introduced in 1996 and running at 133 megaHertz [MHz]), and DDR-3 (Double Data Rate 3 SDRAM, announced in 2005 and running at 800 MHz), share the necessary quality of being easily accessed for reading and writing of data. Unfortunately, this necessary characteristic is at the same time a potential source of difficulty in maintaining data integrity against unwanted read/write operations. The problems are greatly intensified in a multiprogramming environment, especially with dynamic memory allocation, where the possibility exists that one program will write improperly over another's data in memory. Protection against this type of error must be provided by the operating system. Chapter 24 in this *Handbook* discusses operating system security in more detail.

One form of protection requires that main memory be divided into blocks or *pages*; for example, 2,048 eight-bit bytes each. Pages can be designated as read-only when they contain constants, tables, or programs to be shared by several users. Additionally, pages that are to be inaccessible except to designated users may be assigned a lock by appropriate program instructions. If a matching key is not included in the user's program, access to that page will be denied. Protection may be afforded against writing only or against reading and writing.

4.6.2 Read-Only Memory. One distinguishing feature of main memory is the extremely high speed at which data can be entered or read out. The set of sequential procedures that accomplishes this and other functions is the program, and the programmer has complete freedom to combine any valid instructions in a meaningful way. However, certain operations, such as system start-up, or *booting,* are frequently and routinely required, and they may be performed automatically by a preprogrammed group of memory elements. These elements should be protected from inadvertent or unauthorized changes.

For this purpose, a class of memory elements has been developed that, once programmed, cannot be changed at all, or require a relatively long time to do so. These elements are called *read-only memory*, or ROM; the process by which sequential instructions are set into these elements is known as *microprogramming*. The technique can be used to advantage where data integrity is safeguarded by eliminating the possibility of programmer error.

Variations of the principle include programmable read-only memories (PROM) and erasable, programmable read-only memory (EPROM), all of which combine microprogramming with a somewhat greater degree of flexibility than read-only memory itself. The data on these chips can be changed through a special operation often referred to as *flashing* (literally exposure to strong ultraviolet light; this is different from *flash memory* used today for storage of such data as digital music files and digital photographs—we will return to the subject of *flash memory* in the next section).

4.6.3 Secondary Storage.   The term "secondary storage" traditionally has been used to describe storage such as magnetic disks, diskettes, tapes, and tape cartridges. Although the 1.44 megabyte (MB) magnetic floppy disk is obsolete, the magnetic hard drive, with capacities up to terabytes, remains an essential element of virtually all computers, and terabyte-capacity external hard drives the size of a paperback book are now available off-the-shelf for a few hundred dollars.

A more recent development are optical drives such as the removable, *compact-disk read-only memory* (CD-ROM), originally made available in the early 1980s, which are useful for long-term archival storage of around 700 MB per disk. Hybrid forms of this type exist as well, such as CD-Rs, which can be written to once, and CD-RWs which accommodate multiple reads and writes. The Digital Video Disk (DVD), or as it has been renamed, the Digital Versatile Disk, was introduced in 1997 and provides capacities ranging from 4.7 gigabytes (GB) per disk up to 30 GB for data archiving. The higher-capacity optical disks use Blu-ray technology introduced in 2002 and can store 25 GB per side; they typically are used for distributing movies, but BD-R (single use) and BD-RE (rewritable) disks hold much potential for generalized data storage.

The newest addition to secondary storage is RAM that simulates hard disks, known as *flash memory*. Derived from electrical EPROMs (EEPROMs) and introduced by Toshiba in the 1980s, this kind of memory now exists in a huge variety of formats, including relatively inexpensive Universal Serial Bus (USB) tokens with storage capacities now in the gigabyte range. These devices appear as external disk drives when plugged into a plug-and-play personal computer. Another flash memory format is small cards, many the size of postage stamps, that can be inserted into mobile phones, cameras, printers, and other devices as well as computers.

Hardware safeguards described earlier, such as redundancy, validity, parity, and read-after-write, are of value in preserving the integrity of secondary storage. These safeguards are built into the equipment and are always operational unless disabled or malfunctioning. Other precautionary measures are optional, such as standard internal labeling procedures for drives, tapes, and disks. Standard internal labels can include identification numbers, record counts, and dates of creation and expiration. Although helpful, external plastic or paper labels on recordable media are not an adequate substitute for computer-generated labels, magnetically inscribed on the medium itself, and automatically checked by programmed instructions.

Another security measure sometimes subverted is write-protection on removable media. Hardware interlocks prevent writing to them. These locks should be activated immediately when the media are removed from the system. Failure to do so will cause the data to be destroyed if the same media are improperly used on another occasion.

Hard drives, optical discs, and flash memory cards are classified as direct access storage devices (DASDs). Unlike magnetic tapes with their exclusively sequential processing, DASDs may process data randomly as well as in sequence. This capability is essential to online operations, where it is not possible to sort transactions prior to processing. The disadvantage of direct access is that there may be less control over entries and more opportunity to degrade the system than exists with sequential batch processing.

One possible source of DASD errors arises from the high rotational velocity of the recording medium and, except on head-per-track devices, the movement of heads as well. To minimize this possibility, areas on the recording surface have their addresses magnetically inscribed. When the computer directs that data be read from or into a particular location, the address in main memory is compared with that read from the DASD. Only if there is agreement will the operation be performed.

Through proper programming, the integrity of data can be further assured. In addition to the address check, comparisons can be made on identification numbers or on key fields within each record. Although the additional processing time is generally negligible, there can be a substantial improvement in properly posting transactions.

Several other security measures often are incorporated into DASDs. One is similar to the protection feature in main memory and relies on determining "extents" for each data set. If these extents, which are simply the upper and lower limits of a data file's addresses, are exceeded, the job will terminate.

Another safety measure is necessitated by the fact that defective areas on a disk surface may cause errors undetectable in normal operations. To minimize this possibility, disks should be tested and certified prior to use and periodically thereafter. Further information is provided by operating systems that record the number of disk errors encountered. Reformatting or replacement must be ordered when errors exceed a predetermined level. Many personal computer hard drives now have some form of Self-Monitoring, Analysis, and Reporting Technology (SMART). Evolved from earlier technology such as IBM's Predictive Failure Analysis (PFA) and Intellisafe by computer manufacturer Compaq, and disk drive manufacturers Seagate, Quantum, and Conner, SMART can alert operators to potential drive problems. Unfortunately, the implementation of SMART is not standardized, and its potential for preventive maintenance and failure prediction is often overlooked.

Note that SMART is different from the range of technologies used to protect hard drives from head crashes. A head crash occurs when the component that reads data from the disk actually touches the surface of the disk, potentially damaging it and the data stored on it. Many hard drives have systems in place to withdraw heads from the disk before such contact occurs. These protective measures have reached the point where an active hard drive can be carried around in relative safety as part of a music and video player (e.g., Apple iPod or Microsoft Zune).

4.7   TIME.   Within the computer room and in many offices, a wall clock is usually a dominant feature. There is no doubt that this real-time indicator is of importance in scheduling and regulating the functions of people and machines, but the computer's internal timings are more important for security.

4.7.1   Synchronous.   Many computer operations are independent of the time of day but must maintain accurate relationships with some common time and with each other. Examples of this synchronism include the operation of gates, flip-flops, and registers, and the transmission of data at high speeds. Synchronism is obtained in various ways. For gates and other circuit elements, electronic clocks provide accurately spaced pulses at a high-frequency rate, while disk and tape drives are maintained at rated speed by servomotor controls based on power-line frequency.

Of all computer errors, the ones most difficult to detect and correct are probably those caused by timing inconsistencies. Internal clocks may produce 1 billion pulses per second (known as 1 gigahertz [GHz]), or more, when the computer is turned on. The loss of even a single pulse, or its random deformation or delay, can cause undetected errors. More troublesome is the fact that even if errors are detected, their cause may not be identified unless the random timing faults become frequent or consistent.

An example of the insidious nature of timing faults is the consequence of electrical power fluctuations when voltage drops below standard. During these power transients, disk drives may slow down; if sectors are being recorded, their physical size will be correspondingly smaller. Then, when the proper voltage returns, the incorrect sector sizes can cause data errors or loss.

4.7.2 Asynchronous. Some operations do not occur at fixed time intervals and therefore are termed "asynchronous." In this mode, signals generated by the end of one action initiate the following one. As an example, low-speed data transmissions such as those using ordinary modems are usually asynchronous. Coded signals produced by the random depression of keyboard keys are independent of any clock pulses.

4.8 NATURAL DANGERS. To preserve the accuracy and timeliness of computer output, computers must be protected against environmental dangers. Chapters 22 and 23 of this *Handbook* discuss such threats in extensive detail.

4.8.1 Power Failure. Probably the most frequent cause of computer downtime is power failure. Brownouts and blackouts are visible signs of trouble; undetected voltage spikes are far more common, although hardly less damaging.

Lightning can produce voltage spikes on communications and power lines of sufficient amplitude to destroy equipment or, at the very least, to alter data randomly. Sudden storms and intense heat or cold place excessive loads on generators. The drop in line voltage that results can cause computer or peripheral malfunction. Even if it does not, harmful voltage spikes may be created whenever additional generators are switched in to carry higher loads.

Where warranted, a recording indicator may be used to detect power-line fluctuations. Such monitoring often is recommended when computer systems show unexplained, erratic errors. At any time that out-of-tolerance conditions are signaled, the computer output should be checked carefully to ensure that data integrity has not been compromised. If such occurrences are frequent, or if the application is a sensitive one, auxiliary power management equipment should be considered. These range from simple voltage regulators and line conditioners to uninterruptible power supplies (UPSs).

4.8.2 Heat. Sustained high temperatures can cause electronic components to malfunction or to fail completely. Air conditioning (AC) is therefore essential, and all units must be adequate, reliable, and properly installed. If backup electrical power is provided for the computer, it must also be available for the air conditioners. For example, after the San Francisco earthquake of 1989, the desktop computers and network servers in at least one corporate headquarters were damaged by a lack of synchronization between air conditioning and power supply. The AC was knocked out by the quake, and the building was evacuated, but the computers were left on. Many of them failed at the chip and motherboard level over the next few days because the temperature in the uncooled offices got too high. A frequently unrecognized cause of overheating is obstruction of ventilating grilles. Printouts, tapes, books, and other objects must not be placed on cabinets where they can prevent free air circulation. A digital thermometer is a good investment for any room in which computers are used. Today, many electronic devices include thermostats that cut off the power if internal temperatures exceed a danger limit.

4.8.3　Humidity.　Either extreme of humidity can be damaging. Low humidity,—below about 20 percent,—permits buildup of static electricity charges that may affect data pulses. Because this phenomenon is intensified by carpeting, computer room floors should either be free of carpeting or covered with antistatic carpet.

High humidity,—above about 80 percent,—may lead to condensation that causes shorts in electrical circuits or corrodes metal contacts. To ensure operation within acceptable limits, humidity controls should be installed and a continuous record kept of measured values.

4.8.4　Water.　Water introduced by rain, floods, bursting pipes, and overhead sprinklers probably has been responsible for more actual computer damage than fire or any other single factor. Care taken in locating computer facilities, in routing water pipes, and in the selection of fire-extinguishing agents will minimize this significant danger.

The unavailability of water—following a main break, for example,—will cause almost immediate shut down of water-cooled mainframes. Mission-critical data centers should be prepared for this contingency. As an example, when the Des Moines River flooded in 1993, it caused the skyscraper housing the headquarters of the Principal Financial Group to be evacuated, but not because of water in the building. The building stayed high and dry, but the flood forced the city water plant to shut down, depriving the building of the water necessary for cooling. After the flood, the company installed a 40,000-gallon water tank in the basement, to prevent any recurrence of this problem.

4.8.5　Dirt and Dust.　Particles of foreign matter can interfere with proper operation of magnetic tape and disk drives, printers, and other electromechanical devices. All air intakes must be filtered, and all filters must be kept clean. Cups of coffee seem to become especially unstable in a computer environment; together with any other food or drink, they should be banned entirely. Throughout all areas where computer equipment is in use, good housekeeping principles should be rigorously enforced.

4.8.6　Radiation.　Much has been written about the destructive effect of magnetic fields on tape or disk files. However, because magnetic field strength diminishes rapidly with distance, it is unlikely that damage actually could be caused except by large magnets held very close to the recorded surfaces. For example, storing a CD or DVD by attaching it to a filing cabinet with a magnet is not a good idea, but simply walking past a refrigerator decorated with magnets while holding a CD or DVD is unlikely to do any damage.

The proliferation of wireless signals can expose data to erroneous pulses. Offices should be alert for possible interference from and between cordless phones, mobile phones, wireless Internet access points and peripherals, and microwave ovens.

Radioactivity is a great threat to personnel but not to the computer or its recording media.

4.8.7   Downtime.   It is essential to the proper functioning of a data center that preventive maintenance be performed regularly and that accurate records be kept of the time and the reason that any element of the computer is inoperative. The more often the computer is down, the more rushed operators will be to catch up on their scheduled workloads. Under such conditions, controls are bypassed, shortcuts are taken, and human errors multiply.

Downtime records should be studied to detect unfavorable trends and to pinpoint equipment that must be overhauled or replaced before outages become excessive. If unscheduled downtime increases, preventive maintenance should be expanded or improved until the trend is reversed.

4.9   DATA COMMUNICATIONS.   One of the most dynamic factors in current computer usage is the proliferation of devices and systems for data transmission. These range from telephone modems to wired networks, from Internet-enabled cell phones to 802.11 wireless Ethernet, and include Bluetooth, infrared, personal digital assistants (PDAs), music players, and new technologies that appear almost monthly. Computers that do not function at least part time in a connected mode may well be rarities. For fundamentals of data communications, see Chapter 5 of this *Handbook*.

The necessity for speeding information over great distances increases in proportion to the size and geographic dispersion of economic entities; the necessity for maintaining data integrity and security, and the difficulty of doing so, increases even more rapidly. Major threats to be guarded against include human and machine errors, unauthorized accession, alteration, and sabotage. The term "accession" refers to an ability to read data stored or transmitted within a computer system; it may be accidental or purposeful. "Alteration" is the willful entering of unauthorized or incorrect data. "Sabotage" is the intentional act of destroying or damaging the system or the data within it. For each of these threats, the exposure and the countermeasures will depend on the equipment and the facilities involved.

4.9.1   Terminals.   In these discussions, a *terminal* is any input/output device that includes facilities for receiving, displaying, composing, and sending data. Examples include personal computers and specialized devices such as credit card validation units.

Data communications are carried on between computers, between terminals, or between computers and terminals. The terminals themselves may be classified as *dumb* or *intelligent*. Dumb terminals have little or no processing or storage capability and are largely dependent on a host computer for those functions. Intelligent terminals generally include disk storage and capabilities roughly equivalent to those of a personal computer. In addition to vastly improved communications capabilities, they are capable of stand-alone operation.

In the simplest of terminals, the only protection against transmission errors lies in the inability to recognize characters not included in the valid set and to display a question mark or other symbol when one occurs. Almost any terminal can be equipped to detect a vertical parity error. More sophisticated terminals are capable of detecting additional errors through longitudinal and cyclical redundancy characters, as well as by vertical parity and validity checks. Of course, error detection is only the first step in maintaining data integrity. Error correction is by far the more important part, and retransmission is the most widely used correction technique.

Intelligent terminals and personal computers are capable of high-speed transmission and reception. They can perform complicated tests on data before requesting retransmission, or they may even be programmed to correct errors internally. The techniques for self-correction require forward-acting codes, such as the Hamming cyclical code. These are similar to the error-detecting cyclic redundancy codes, except that they require even more redundant bits. Although error correction is more expensive and usually slower than detection with retransmission, it is useful under certain circumstances. Examples include simplex circuits where no return signal is possible, and half-duplex circuits where the time to turn the line around from transmission to reception is too long. Forward correction is also necessary where errors are so numerous that retransmissions would clog the circuits, with little or no useful information throughput.

A more effective use of intelligent terminals and personal computers is to preserve data integrity by encryption, as described in this chapter and in Chapter 7. Also, they may be used for compression or compaction. Reducing the number of characters in a message reduces the probability of an error as well as the time required for transmission. One technique replaces long strings of spaces or zeroes with a special character and a numerical count; the procedure is reversed when receiving data.

Finally, the intelligent terminal or microprocessor may be used to encode or decipher data when the level of security warrants cryptography.

All terminals, of every type, including desktop and notebook personal computers (PCs), have at least one thing in common: the need to be protected against sabotage or unauthorized use. Although the principles for determining proper physical location and the procedures for restricting access are essentially the same as those that apply to a central computer facility, the actual problems of remote terminals are even more difficult. Isolated locations, inadequate supervision, and easier access by more people all increase the likelihood of compromised security.

4.9.2   Wired Facilities.   Four types of wired facilities are in widespread use: dial-up access, leased lines, digital subscriber lines (DSL), and cable carriers. Both common carriers and independent systems may employ various media for data transmission. The increasing need for higher speed and better quality in data transmission has prompted utilization of coaxial and fiber optic cables, while microwave stations and communication satellites often are found as wireless links within wired systems.

Generally, decisions as to the choice of service are based on the volume of data to be handled and on the associated costs, but security considerations may be even more important.

4.9.2.1   Dial-up Lines.   Still widely used for credit and debit card terminals, dial-up lines have been replaced for many other applications by leased lines, DSL lines, and cables carrying Internet traffic (using the TCP/IP protocol discussed in Chapter 5 of this *Handbook*). Dial-up connections are established between modems operating over regular voice lines sometimes referred to as *plain old telephone service* (POTS).

Where dial-up access to hardware still exists, for example, for maintenance of certain equipment, proper controls are essential to protect both the equipment and the integrity of other systems to which it might be connected. Dial-up ports may be reached by anyone with a phone, anywhere on the planet, and the practice of *war-dialing* to detect modems is still used by those seeking unauthorized access to an organization's network. (War dialing involves dialing blocks of numbers to find which ones respond as modems or fax machines. These numbers are recorded and may be dialed later in an attempt to gain unauthorized access to systems or services). It is advisable to:

- Compile a log of unauthorized attempts at entry, and use it to discourage further efforts.

- Compile a log of all accesses to sensitive data, and verify their appropriateness.

- Equip all terminals with internal identification generators or answer-back units, so that even a proper password would be rejected if sent from an unauthorized terminal. This technique may require the availability of an authorized backup terminal in the event of malfunction of the primary unit.

- Provide users with personal identification in addition to a password if the level of security requires it. The additional safeguard could be a magnetically striped or computerized plastic card to be inserted into a special reader. The value of such cards is limited since they can be used by anyone, whether authorized or not. For high-security requirements, other hardware-dependent biometric identifiers, such as handprints and voiceprints, should be considered.

- Where appropriate, utilize call-back equipment that prevents a remote station from entering a computer directly. Instead, the device dials the caller from an internal list of approved phone numbers to make the actual connection.

With proper password discipline, problems of accession, alteration, and data sabotage can be minimized. However, the quality of transmissions is highly variable. Built into the public telephone system is an automatic route-finding mechanism that directs signals through uncontrollable paths. The distance and the number of switching points traversed, and the chance presence of cross-talk, transients, and other noise products will have unpredictable effects on the incidence of errors. Parity systems, described earlier, are an effective means of reducing such errors.

4.9.2.2 Leased Lines.   Lines leased from a common carrier for the exclusive use of one subscriber are known as *dedicated lines*. Because they are directly connected between predetermined points, normally they cannot be reached through the dial-up network. Traditionally, leased lines were copper, but point-to-point fiber optic and coaxial cable lines can also be leased.

Wiretapping is a technically feasible method of accessing leased lines, but it is more costly, more difficult, and less convenient than dialing through the switched network. Leased lines are generally more secure than those that can be readily war-dialed.

To this increased level of security for leased lines is added the assurance of higher-quality reception. The problems of uncertain transmission paths and switching transients are eliminated, although other error sources are not. In consequence, parity checking remains a minimum requirement.

4.9.2.3 Digital Subscriber Lines.   Falling somewhere in between a leased line and plain old telephone service, (POTS), a digital subscriber line offers digital transmission locally over ordinary phone lines that can be used simultaneously for voice transmission. This is possible because ordinary copper phone lines can carry, at least for short distances, signals that are in a much higher frequency range than the human voice. A DSL modem is used by a computer to reach the nearest telephone company switch, at which point the data transmission enters the Internet backbone. Computers connected to the Internet over DSL communicate using TCP/IP and are said to be hosts rather than terminals. They are prone to compromise through a wide range of exploits. However, few if any of these threats are enabled by the DSL itself. As with leased lines, wiretapping is possible, but other attacks, such as exploiting weaknesses in TCP/IP implementations on host machines, are easier.

4.9.2.4   Cable Carriers.   Wherever cable television (TV) is available, the same optical fiber or coaxial cables that carry the TV signal also can be used to provide high-speed data communications. The advantages of this technology include download speeds that can, in the case of coaxial cables, exceed 50 megabits per second, or in the case of fiber optic cable, exceed 100 gigabits per second.

The disadvantages arise from the fact that connections to the carrier may be shared by other subscribers in the same locality. Unless the service provider limits access, perhaps in accordance with a quality-of-service agreement, multiple subscribers can be online simultaneously and thus slow down transmission speeds. Even more serious is the possibility of security breaches, since multiple computers within a neighborhood may be sharing part of a virtual local area network, and thus each is potentially accessible to every other node on that network. For this reason alone, cable connections should be firewalled. For details of firewalls and their uses, see Chapter 26 in this *Handbook*. Another reason for using firewalls is that cable connections are always on, providing maximal opportunity for hackers to access an unattended computer.

4.9.3   Wireless Communicationa.   Data transfers among multinational corporations have been growing very rapidly, and transoceanic radio and telephone lines have proved too costly, too slow, too crowded, and too error-prone to provide adequate service. An important alternative is the communications satellite. Orbiting above Earth, the satellite reflects ultra-high-frequency radio signals that can convey a television program or computer data with equal speed and facility.

For communications over shorter distances, the cost of common-carrier wired services has been so high as to encourage competitive technologies. One of these, the microwave radio link, is used in many networks. One characteristic of such transmissions is that they can be received only on a direct line-of-sight path from the transmitting or retransmitting antenna. With such point-to-point ground stations, it is sometimes difficult to position the radio beams where they cannot be intercepted; with satellite and wireless broadcast communications, it is impossible. This is a significant issue with wireless local area network technology based on the IEEE 802.11 standards and commonly known as WiFi (a brand name owned by the Wi-Fi Alliance; the term is short for *wi*reless *fi*delity). The need for security is consequently greater, and scramblers or cryptographic encoders are essential for sensitive data transfers.

Because of the wide bandwidths at microwave frequencies, extremely fast rates of data transfer are possible. With vertical, longitudinal, and cyclical redundancy check characters, almost all errors can be detected, yet throughput remains high.

4.10   CRYPTOGRAPHY.   Competitive pressures in business, politics, and international affairs continually create situations where morality, privacy, and the laws all appear to give way before a compelling desire for gain. Information, for its own sake or for the price it brings, is an eagerly sought after commodity. We are accustomed to the sight of armored cars and armed guards transporting currency, yet often invaluable data are moved with few precautions. When the number of computers and competent technicians was small, the risk in careless handling of data resources was perhaps not great. Now, however, a very large population of knowledgeable computer people exists, and within it are individuals willing and able to use their knowledge for illegal ends.

Others find stimulation and satisfaction in meeting the intellectual challenge that they perceive in defeating computer security measures.

Acquiring information in an unauthorized manner is relatively easy when data are communicated between locations. One method of discouraging this practice, or rendering it too expensive to be worth the effort, is cryptographic encoding of data prior to transmission. This technique is also useful in preserving the security of files within data storage devices. If all important files were stored on magnetic or optical media in cryptographic cipher only, the incidence of theft and resale would unquestionably be less.

Many types of ciphers might be used, depending on their cost and the degree of security required. Theoretically, any code can be broken, given enough time and equipment. In practice, if a cipher cannot be broken fairly quickly, the encoded data are likely to become valueless. However, since the key itself can be used to decipher later messages, it is necessary that codes or keys be changed frequently.

For further information on cryptography, refer to Chapter 7 in this *Handbook*.

4.11 BACKUP.   As with most problems, the principal focus in computer security ought to be on prevention rather than on cure. No matter how great the effort, however, complete success can never be guaranteed. There are four reasons for this being so:

1. Not every problem can be anticipated.
2. Where the cost of averting a particular loss exceeds that of recovery, preventive measures may not be justified.
3. Precautionary measures, carried to extremes, can place impossible constraints on the efficiency and productivity of an operation. It may be necessary, therefore, to avoid such measures aimed at events whose statistical probability of occurrence is small.
4. Even under optimum conditions, carefully laid plans may go astray. In the real world of uncertainty and human fallibility, where there is active or inadvertent interference, it is almost a certainty that at one time or another, the best of precautionary measures will prove to be ineffective.

Recognizing the impossibility of preventing all undesired actions and events, it becomes necessary to plan appropriate means of recovering from them. Such plans must include backup for personnel, hardware, power, physical facilities, data, and software. Data backups are discussed more fully in Chapter 57 of this *Handbook*.

Responding to emergencies is described in Chapters 56 of this *Handbook* and business continuity planning and disaster recovery are discussed in Chapter 58 and 59.

Backup plans should be evaluated with respect to:

- The priorities established for each application, to ensure that they are properly assigned and actually observed.
- The time required to restore high-priority applications to full functioning status.
- The degree of assurance that plans actually can be carried out when required. For important applications, alternative plans should be available in the event that the primary plan cannot be implemented.
- The degree of security and data integrity that will exist if backup plans actually are put into effect.

- The extent to which changing internal or external conditions are noted, and the speed with which plans are modified to reflect such changes.

The assignment of priorities in advance of an actual emergency is an essential and critically important process. In most organizations, new applications proliferate, while old ones are rarely discarded. If backup plans attempt to encompass all jobs, they are likely to accomplish none. Proper utilization of priorities will permit realistic scheduling, with important jobs done on time and at acceptable costs.

4.11.1   Personnel.   The problems of everyday computer operation require contingency plans for personnel on whose performance hardware functioning depends. Illnesses, vacations, dismissals, promotions, resignations, overtime, and extra shifts are some of the reasons why prudent managers are continuously concerned with the problem of personnel backup. The same practices that work for everyday problems can provide guidelines for emergency backup plans. This subject is covered more fully in Chapter 45 of this *Handbook*.

4.11.2   Hardware.   Hardware backup for data centers can take several forms:

- Multiple processors at the same site to protect against loss of service due to breakdown of one unit
- Duplicate installations at nearby facilities of the same company
- Maintaining programs at a compatible service bureau, on a test or standby basis
- A contract for backup at a facility dedicated to disaster recovery
- A reciprocal agreement with a similar installation at another company

The probability of two on-site processors both being down at the same time due to internal faults is extremely small. Consequently, most multiple installations rarely fall behind on mission-critical applications. However, this type of backup offers no protection against power failure, fire, vandalism, or any disaster that could strike two or more processors at once. The disasters of September 11, 2001, proved that even a highly unlikely event actually could occur. With duplicate processors at different but commonly owned sites, there is little chance of both being affected by the same forces. Although the safety factor increases with the distance separating them, the difficulty of transporting people and data becomes greater. An alternate site must represent a compromise between these conflicting objectives. Furthermore, complete compatibility of hardware and software will have to be preserved, even though doing so places an undue operational burden on one of the installations. Shortly after September 11, a number of financial firms were back in operation with their alternative computer sites across the Hudson River.

The backup provided by service bureaus can be extremely effective, particularly if the choice of facility is carefully made. Although progressive service bureaus frequently improve both hardware and software, they almost never do so in a way that would cause compatibility problems for their existing customers. Once programs have been tested, they can be stored off-line on tape or disk at little cost. Updated masters can be rotated in the service bureau library, providing off-site data backup as well as the ability to become fully operational at once.

Effective hardware backup is also available at independent facilities created expressly for that purpose. In one type of facility, there are adequate space, power, air conditioning, and communication lines to accommodate a very large system. Most manufacturers are able to provide almost any configuration on short notice when disaster strikes a valued customer. The costs for this type of base standby facility are shared by a number of users so that expenses are minimal until an actual need arises. However, if two or more sharers are geographically close, their facilities may be rendered inoperative by the same fire, flood, or power failure. Before contracting for such a facility, it is necessary to analyze this potential problem; the alternative is likely to be a totally false sense of security. Several firms whose facilities were damaged or destroyed on September 11 were provided with complete replacement equipment by their vendors within a short time.

Another type of backup facility is already equipped with computers, disk and tape drives, printers, terminals, and communications lines so that it can substitute instantly for an inoperative system. The standby costs for this service are appreciably more than for a base facility, but the assurance of recovery in the shortest possible time is far greater. Here, too, it would be prudent to study the likelihood of more than one customer requiring the facility at the same time and to demand assurance that one's own needs will be met without fail. Several companies successfully availed themselves of this type of backup and disaster recovery after September 11.

Backup by reciprocal agreement was for many years an accepted practice, although not often put to the test. Unfortunately, many managers still rely on this outmoded safeguard. One has only to survive a single major change of operating system software to realize that when it occurs, neither the time nor the inclination is available to modify and test another company's programs. Even the minor changes in hardware and software that continuously take place in most installations could render them incompatible. At the same time, in accordance with Parkinson's Law, workloads always expand to fill the available time and facilities. In consequence, many who believe that they have adequate backup will get little more than an unpleasant surprise, should they try to avail themselves of the privilege.

4.11.3 Power. The one truly indispensable element of any data processing installation is electric power. Backing up power to PCs and small servers by uninterruptible power supplies is reasonable in cost and quite effective. For mainframes and large servers, several types of power backup are available. The principal determinant in selection should be the total cost of anticipated downtime and reruns versus the cost of backup to eliminate them. Downtime and rerun time may be extrapolated from records of past experience.

Problems due to electrical power may be classified by type and by the length of time that they persist. Power problems as they affect computers consist of variations in amplitude, frequency, and waveform, with durations ranging from fractions of a millisecond to minutes or hours. Long-duration outages usually are due to high winds, ice, lightning, vehicles that damage power lines, or equipment malfunctions that render an entire substation inoperative. For mainframes in data centers, it is usually possible, although costly, to contract for power to be delivered from two different substations, with one acting as backup.

Another type of protection is afforded by gasoline or diesel motor generators. Controls are provided that sense a power failure and automatically start the motor. Full speed is attained in less than a minute, and the generator's output can power a computer for days if necessary.

The few seconds' delay in switching power sources is enough to abort programs running on the computer and to destroy data files. To avoid this, the "uninterruptible" power supply was designed. In one version, the AC power line feeds a rectifier that furnishes direct current to an inverter. The inverter in turn drives a synchronous motor coupled to an alternator whose AC output powers the computer. While the rectifier is providing DC to the inverter, it also charges a large bank of heavy-duty batteries. As soon as a fault is detected on the main power line, the batteries are instantaneously and automatically switched over to drive the synchronous motor. Because the huge drain on the batteries may deplete them in a few minutes, a diesel generator must also be provided. The advantages of this design are:

- Variations in line frequency, amplitude, and waveform do not get through to the computer.
- Switchover from power line to batteries is undetectable by the computer. Programs keep running, and no data are lost.
- Millisecond spikes and other transients that may be responsible for equipment damage, and undetected data loss are completely suppressed.

A fuller treatment of physical threats is presented in Chapters 22 and 23 of this *Handbook*.

4.11.4 Testing.   The most important aspect of any backup plan is its effectiveness. Will it work? It would be a mistake to wait for an emergency to find out. The only sensible alternative is systematic testing.

One form of test is similar to a dress rehearsal, with the actual emergency closely simulated. In this way the equipment, the people, and the procedures can all be exercised, until practice assures proficiency. Periodically thereafter the tests should be repeated, so that changes in hardware, software, and personnel will not weaken the backup capability.

4.12 RECOVERY PROCEDURES.   The procedures required to recover from any system problem will depend on the nature of the problem and on the backup measures that were in place. Hardware recovery ranges from instantaneous and fully automatic, through manual repair or replacement of components, to construction, equipping, and staffing of an entirely new data center. Chapters 58 and 59 of this *Handbook* provide extensive information about these issues.

Almost every data center is a collection of equipment, with options, modifications, additions, and special features. Should it become necessary to replace the equipment, a current configuration list must be on hand and the procedures for reordering established in advance. An even better practice would be to keep a current list of *desired* equipment that could be used as the basis for replacement. Presumably, the replacements would be faster and more powerful, but additional time should be scheduled for training and conversion.

4.13 MICROCOMPUTER CONSIDERATIONS.   Four factors operate to intensify the problems of hardware security as they relate to small computers:

1. Accessibility
2. Knowledge
3. Motivation
4. Opportunity

4.13.1 Accessibility. *Accessibility* is a consequence of operating small computers in a wide-open office environment rather than in a controlled data center. No security guards, special badges, man-traps, cameras, tape librarians, or shift supervisors limit access to equipment or data media in the office, as they do in a typical data center.

4.13.2 Knowledge. *Knowledge,* and its lack, is equally dangerous. On one hand, as personal computers pervade the office environment, technical knowledge becomes widely disseminated. Where once this knowledge was limited to relatively few computer experts who could be controlled rather easily, its growing universality now makes control extremely difficult, if not impossible. On the other hand, when computers are operated by people with minimal knowledge and skills, the probability of security breaches through error and inadvertence is greatly increased.

4.13.3 Motivation. *Motivation* exists in numerous forms. It is present wherever valuable assets can be diverted for personal gain; it arises when real or fancied injustice creates a desire for revenge; and it can simply be a form of self-expression.

The unauthorized diversion of corporate assets always has provided opportunities for theft; now, with many employees owning computers at home, the value of stolen equipment, programs, and data can be realized without the involvement of third parties. When a third party is added to the equation and the thriving market in purloined personal data is factored in, the potential for data theft, a low-risk/high-return crime, is greatly increased.

Computers and networks are also a target for sabotage as well as data theft. The reliance upon such systems by governments, the military, large corporations, and other perceived purveyors of social or economic ills, means that criminal acts are likely to continue. Because personal computers are now part of these systems, they are also a link to any policy or practice of which one or more groups of people disapprove. The motivation for sabotaging personal computers is more likely in the near term to increase than it is to disappear.

A third motivation for breaching computer security is the challenge and excitement of doing so. Whether trying to overcome technical hurdles, to break the law with impunity or merely to trespass on forbidden ground, some hackers find these challenges irresistible, and they become criminal hackers. To view such acts with amused tolerance or even mild disapproval is totally inconsistent with the magnitude of the potential damage and the sanctity of the trust barriers that are crossed. Since the technology exists to lock out all but the most determined and technically proficient criminal hacker, failure to protect sensitive systems is increasingly viewed as negligence.

4.13.4 Opportunity. With so many personal computers in almost every office, with virtually no supervision during regular hours, and certainly none at other times, opportunities are plentiful for two types of security breaches: intentional by those with technical knowledge and unintentional by those without.

4.13.5 Threats to Microcomputers. Among the most significant threats to microcomputers are those pertaining to:

- Physical damage

- Theft
- Electrical power
- Static electricity
- Data communications
- Maintenance and repair

4.13.5.1 Physical Damage. Microcomputers and their peripheral devices are not impervious to damage. Disk drives are extremely susceptible to failure through impact; keyboards cannot tolerate dirt or rough handling. It is essential that computers be recognized as delicate instruments and that they be treated accordingly.

Even within an access-controlled data center, where food and drinks are officially banned, it is not uncommon for a cup of coffee to be spilled when set on or near operating equipment. In an uncontrolled office environment, it is rare that one does not see personal computers in imminent danger of being doused with potentially damaging liquids. The problem is compounded by the common practice of leaving unprotected media such as CDs and DVDs lying about on the same surface where food and drink could easily reach them. Although it may not be possible to eliminate these practices entirely, greater discipline will protect data media and equipment from contamination.

As mentioned in the section on heat, damage also can result from blocking vents necessary for adequate cooling. Such vents can be rendered ineffective by placing the equipment too close to a wall or, in the case of laptops, on soft surfaces, such as carpets, that block vents on the base of the machine. Vents on top of computer housings and cathode ray tube–style displays are too often covered by papers or books that prevent a free flow of cooling air. As a result, the internal temperature of the equipment increases, so that marginal components malfunction, intermittent contacts open, errors are introduced, and eventually the system malfunctions or halts.

4.13.5.2 Theft. The opportunities for theft of personal computers and their data media are far greater than for their larger counterparts. Files containing proprietary information or expensive programs are easily copied to removable media as small as a postage stamp and taken from the premises without leaving a trace. External disk drives are small enough to be carried out in a purse or an attaché case, and new thumb-size USB drives look like key fobs to the uninitiated. The widespread practice of taking portable computers home for evening or weekend work eventually renders even the most conscientious guards indifferent. In offices without guards, the problem is even more difficult. Short of instituting a police state of perpetual surveillance, what is to be done to discourage theft? Equipment can be chained or bolted to desks, or locked within cabinets built for the purpose. Greater diligence in recording and tracking serial numbers, more frequent inventories, and a continuing program of education can help. Most of all, it is essential that the magnitude of the problem be recognized at a sufficiently high management level so that adequate resources are applied to its solution. Otherwise, there will be a continuing drain of increasing magnitude on corporate profitability.

4.13.5.3 Power. Even in a controlled data center, brownouts, blackouts, voltage spikes, sags and surges, and other electrical power disturbances represent a threat. The situation is much worse in a typical office, where personal computers are plugged into existing outlets with little or no thought to the consequences of bad power.

Some of the rudimentary precautions that should be taken are:

- Eliminating, or at least controlling, the use of extension cords, cube taps, and multiple outlet strips. Each unit on the same power line may reduce the voltage available to all of the others, and each may introduce noise on the line.

- Providing line voltage regulators and line conditioners where necessary to maintain power within required limits.

- Banning the use of vacuum cleaners or other electrical devices plugged into the same power line as computers or peripheral devices. Such devices produce a high level of electrical noise, in addition to voltage sags and surges.

- Connecting all ground wires properly. This is especially important in older offices equipped with two-prong outlets that require adapter plugs. The third wire of the plug must be connected to a solid earth ground for personnel safety, as well as for reduction of electrical noise.

In addition, the use of uninterruptible power supplies (UPSs) is highly recommended for all computers and ancillary equipment. These devices are available in capacities from about 200 watts for PCs to virtually unlimited sizes for mainframes. While the power line is operational, a UPS is capable of conditioning the line by removing electrical noise, sags, spikes, and surges. When line voltage drops below a preset value, or when power is completely lost, the UPS converts DC from its internal batteries to the AC required to supply the associated equipment.

Depending on its rating and the load, the UPS may provide standby power for several minutes to several hours. This is enough time to shut down a computer normally, or in the case of large installations, to have a motor generator placed online.

The services of a qualified electrician should be utilized wherever there is a possibility of electric power problems.

4.13.5.4 Static Electricity.

After one walks across a carpeted floor on a dry day, the spark that leaps from fingertip to computer may be mildly shocking to a person, but to the computer it can cause serious loss of memory, degradation of data, and even component destruction. These effects are even more likely when people touch components inside a computer without proper grounding.

To prevent this, several measures are available:

- Use a humidifier to keep the humidity above 20 percent relative.
- Remove ordinary carpeting. Replace, if desired, with static-free types.
- Use an antistatic mat beneath chairs and desks.
- Use a grounding strip near each keyboard.
- Wear a grounding bracelet when installing or repairing the components of any electronic equipment.

Touching the grounding strip before operating the computer will drain any static electricity charge through the attached ground wire, as will spraying the equipment periodically with an antistatic spray.

Some combination of these measures will protect personnel, equipment, and data from the sometimes obscure, but always real, dangers of static electricity.

4.13.5.5 Data Communications.

Although personal computers perform significant functions in a stand-alone mode, their utility is greatly enhanced by communications to mainframes, to information utilities, and to other small computers, remotely via phone lines or the Internet, or through local area networks. All of the security issues that surround mainframe communications apply to personal computers, with added complications.

Until the advent of personal computers, almost all terminals communicating with mainframes were "dumb." That is, they functioned much like teletype machines, with the ability only to key in or print out characters, one at a time. In consequence, it was much more difficult to breach mainframe security, intentionally or accidentally, than it is with today's fully intelligent personal computers.

The image of thousands of dedicated hackers dialing up readily available computer access numbers, or probing Internet addresses, for illicit fun and games, or for illegal financial gain, is no less disturbing than it is real. Countermeasures are available, including:

- Two-way encryption (see Chapter 7)
- Frequent password changes (see Chapter 28)
- Automatic call-back before logging on
- Investigation of unsuccessful logons
- Monitoring of hackers' bulletin boards (see Chapters 12 and 15)
- Firewalls to restrict traffic into and out of the computer (see Chapter 26)
- Antivirus software (see Chapter 41)

Legislation that makes directors and senior officers personally liable for any corporate losses that could have been prevented should have a marked effect on overcoming the current inertia. Prudence dictates that preventive action be taken before, rather than corrective action after, such losses are incurred.

4.13.6 Maintenance and Repair. A regular program of preventive maintenance should be observed for every element of a personal computer system. This should include scheduled cleaning of disk drives and their magnetic heads, keyboards, and printers. A vital element of any preventive maintenance program is the frequent changing of air filters in every piece of equipment. If this is not done, the flow of clean, cool air will be impeded, and failure will almost surely result.

Maintenance options for personal computers, in decreasing order of timeliness, include:

- On-site management by regular employees
- On-site maintenance by third parties under an annual agreement
- On-call repair, with or without an agreement
- Carry-in service
- Mail-in service

As personal computers are increasingly applied to functions that affect the very existence of a business, their maintenance and repair will demand more management attention. Redundant equipment and on-site backup will always be effective, but the extended time for off-site repairs will no longer be acceptable. For most business applications, "loaners" or "swappers" should be immediately available, so that downtime will be held to an absolute minimum. Management must assess the importance of each functioning personal computer and select an appropriate maintenance and repair policy.

Accessibility, knowledge, motivation, and opportunity are the special factors that threaten every personal computer installation. Until each of these factors has been addressed, no system can be considered secure.

4.14 CONCLUSION.   This chapter has dealt principally with the means by which hardware elements of a data processing system affect the security and integrity of its operations. Many safeguards are integral parts of the equipment itself; others require conscious effort, determination, and commitment.

An effective security program, —one that provides both decreased likelihood of computer catastrophe and mitigation of the consequences of damage, —cannot be designed or implemented without considerable expenditures of time and money. As with other types of loss avoidance, the premium should be evaluated against the expected costs. Once a decision has been made, however, this equivalent to an insurance policy should not be permitted to lapse. The premiums must continue to be paid in the form of periodic testing, continuous updating, and constant vigilance.

For more detailed information about risk management, see Chapter 62 in this *Handbook*. For a discussion of insurance policies against information systems disasters of all kinds, see Chapter 60.

4.15   HARDWARE SECURITY CHECKLIST

Mainframes

☐ Are security and integrity requirements considered when selecting new equipment?

☐ Is a schedule of preventive maintenance enforced?

☐ Is a log kept of all computer malfunctions and unscheduled downtime?

☐ Is there an individual with responsibility for reviewing the log and initiating action?

☐ Are parity checks used wherever possible?

☐ Is there an established procedure for recording parity errors and recovering from them?

☐ Are forward-acting or error-correcting codes used when economically justified?

☐ Do operators follow prescribed procedures after a read error or other machine check halt?

☐ Are all operator interventions logged and explained?

☐ Is a job log maintained, and is it compared regularly with an authorized run list?

☐ Is the interval timer used to prevent excessively long runs?

☐ Are storage protect features such as data locks and read-only paging used?

☐ Are keys to software data locks adequately protected?

☐ Are precautions taken to prevent loss of data from volatile memory during power interruptions?

☐ Are standard internal and external tape and disk labeling procedures enforced?

☐ Are write-enable protection rings always removed from tape reels immediately after use?

☐ Is there a rule that new tapes and disks must be tested or certified prior to use? At regular intervals thereafter?

☐ Are tapes and disks refinished or replaced before performance is degraded?

☐ Are air conditioners adequate for peak thermal loads? Are air conditioners backed up?

☐ Is there a schedule for frequent filter changes?

☐ Have all static electricity generators been disabled?

☐ Have all sources of water damage been eliminated?

☐ Is good housekeeping enforced throughout the facility?

☐ Is access to data terminals restricted?

☐ Are terminals and surrounding areas examined frequently to detect passwords carelessly left about?

☐ Is a log maintained of unsuccessful attempts to enter the computer from terminals?

☐ Is the log used to prevent further attempts?

☐ Is a log maintained of all successful entries to sensitive data?

☐ Is the log used to verify authorizations?

☐ Are terminals equipped with automatic identification generators?

☐ Are test procedures adequate to assure high-quality data transmissions?

☐ Is cryptography or scrambling used to protect sensitive data?

☐ Has a complete backup plan been formulated? Is it updated frequently?

☐ Does the backup plan include training, retraining, and cross-training of personnel?

☐ Is on-site backup available for the central processing unit? For peripherals?

☐ Does your backup site advise you of all changes to its hardware configuration and operating system?

☐ Does your backup site have enough free time available to accommodate your emergency needs?

☐ Do you monitor power-line voltage and frequency?

☐ Are the effects of brownouts, dimouts, and blackouts known?

☐ Is advance warning available, and if so, is there a checklist of actions to be taken?

☐ Are power correctors in use? Voltage regulators? Line conditioners? Lightning spark gaps?

☐ Is backup power available? Dual substation supply? Motor generators? Uninterruptible power supplies?

☐ Does your equipment provide automatic restart and recovery after a power failure?

☐ Are backup plans tested realistically? At frequent intervals?

Microcomputers
In addition to the appropriate items just listed:

☐ Are removable disks always kept in a closed container when not actually mounted in a disk drive?

☐ Is it forbidden to put food or drink on or near computer equipment?

☐ Are personal computers securely fastened to prevent dropping or theft?

□ Are air vents kept free?

□ Are accurate inventories maintained?

□ Is electrical power properly wired?

□ Are uninterruptable power supplies in place?

□ Has static electricity been eliminated?

□ Are data communications secure?

□ Is there an effective maintenance plan?

4.16   FURTHER READING

Ayers, J. E. *Digital Integrated Circuits: Analysis and Design.* Boca Raton, FL: CRC Press, 2003. (Second edition scheduled for publication in 2009.)

Clements, A. *Principles of Computer Hardware*, 4th ed. New York: Oxford University Press, 2006.

Horak, R. *Telecommunications and Data Communications Handbook.* Hoboken, NJ: Wiley-Interscience, 2007.

Kerns, D. V. *Essentials of Electrical and Computer Engineering*, 2nd ed. Upper Saddle River, NJ: Prentice-Hall, 2004.

Pattern, D. A., and J. L. Hennessy. *Computer Organization and Design: The Hardware Software Interface*, 3rd ed. Los Angeles: Morgan Kaufmann, 2007.

Stallings, W. *Computer Organization and Architecture: Designing for Performance*, 7th ed. Upper Saddle River, NJ: Prentice-Hall, 2005.

CHAPTER 5

DATA COMMUNICATIONS AND INFORMATION SECURITY

Raymond Panko

5.1   INTRODUCTION.   Sometimes, an attacker can simply walk up to a target computer. In most cases, however, attackers must use networks to reach their targets. Some attacks even aim *at* networks, trying to bring down local area networks, wide area networks, and even the global Internet. This chapter provides an overview of networking to help readers of this *Handbook* when they come across networking concepts in other chapters or in other context. This chapter covers a limited number of networking concepts. Specifically, it focuses on aspects of networking that are most relevant to security.

Before beginning, readers should note three important pieces of terminology that pervade the chapter.

1. This chapter often uses the term *octet*, which is a *byte*—a collection of eight bits. Networking grew out of electrical engineering, where octet is the preferred term.

2. The second term is *host*. Any device attached to the global Internet is called a host. This includes large server hosts, of course, but it also includes client PCs, personal digital assistants, mobile telephones, and even Internet-accessible coffeepots.

3. We will distinguish between the terms *internet* and *Internet*; the latter refers to the global Internet. However, *internet* spelled in lower case is either the Internet layer in the TCP architecture (see Section 5.6) or a collection of networks that is not the global Internet.

5.2   SAMPLING OF NETWORKS.   This section looks briefly at a series of increasingly complex networks, giving the reader a high-level overview of what networks look like in the real world.

5.2.1   Simple Home Network.   Exhibit 5.1 shows a simple home PC network. The home has two personal computers. The network allows the two PCs to share files and the family's single laser printer. The network also connects the two computers to the Internet.

5.2.1.1   Access Router.   The heart of this network is its *access router*. This small device, which is about the size of a hardback book, has five functions.

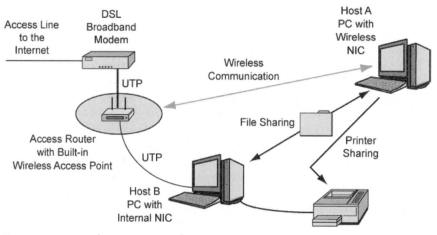

EXHIBIT 5.1   Simple Home Network

1. It is a switch. When one PC in the home sends messages (called *frames*) to the other computer, the switch transfers the frames between them

2. The access router is a *wireless access point* (WAP), which permits wireless computers to connect to it. Host A connects to the access router wirelessly.

3. A router connects a network to another network—in this case, the global Internet.

4. To use the Internet, each computer needs an *Internet Protocol* (IP) *address.* We will see later that IP is the main protocol that governs communication over the Internet. The access router has a built-in *Dynamic Host Configuration Protocol* (DHCP) server that gives each home PC an IP address.

5. The access router provides *network address translation* (NAT), which hides internal IP addresses from potential attackers. Some access routers also have a firewall for added security.

Wireless access points are dangerous because radio signals spread widely. If the user does not configure strong security in the access point and all wireless stations, anyone will be able to read the user's traffic and do mischief.

NAT provides a surprisingly large amount of protection. Even people with single PCs may find it attractive to use an access router to gain this protection.

5.2.1.2   Personal Computers.   Each of the two PCs needs circuitry to communicate over the network. Traditionally, this circuitry came in the form of a printed circuit board, so the circuitry was called the computer's *network interface card* (NIC). In most computers today, the circuitry is built into the computer; there is no separate printed circuit board. However, the circuitry is still called the computer's NIC.

In this small network, the two computers share their files. Given the wireless access capability of the network, drive-by hackers could potentially read shared files as well. File sharing without strong wireless security is dangerous. It is important to set up *Wi-Fi Protected Access* (WPA) or 802.11i security in pre-shared key (PSK) mode on both the access router/access point and each of the client PCs.

It is important to configure the PCs for security. Although NAT by itself is strong, and although a growing number of access routers also provide stateful-inspection firewalls as well (see Chapter 26 in this *Handbook*), some attacks will inevitably get through to the personal computers. The PCs must have strong firewalls, antivirus programs, and antispyware programs (see Chapter 41); and they must be updated automatically when security patches are released by the operating system vendor and by application program vendors (see Chapter 40).

5.2.1.3   UTP Wiring.   In Exhibit 5.1, Host B connects to the access router via copper wiring. Specifically, it uses four-pair *unshielded twisted pair* (UTP) wiring. As Exhibit 5.2 shows, a UTP cord contains eight copper wires organized as four pairs. The two wires of each pair are twisted around each other. The *RJ-45* connectors at the ends of a UTP cord look like RJ-11 home telephone connectors but are a little wider. (*RJ* means *Registered Jack* and originally referred to Bell System order codes; it is now defined by the Administrative Council for Terminal Attachment, ACTA.)

5.2.1.4   Internet Access Line.   The home network needs an Internet access line to connect the home to the Internet. In Exhibit 5.1, this access line is a *Digital Subscriber Line* (DSL) high-speed access line, and the home connects to this access line

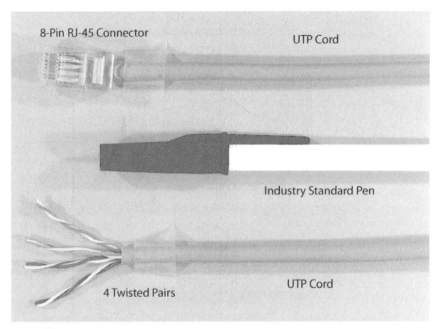

EXHIBIT 5.2   Unshielded Twisted Pair Wiring (UTP) Cord

via a small box called a *DSL modem*. (The DSL modem connects to the access router via a UTP cord; it connects to the wall jack via an ordinary telephone cord.) Other Internet access technologies include slow telephone modems, fast cable modems, and even wireless access systems. Most of these technologies are called *broadband access lines*. In general, *broadband* simply means "very fast," although in radio transmission it describes a wide range of frequencies.

5.2.2 Building LAN.   The home network shown in Exhibit 5.1 is a *local area network* (LAN). A LAN operates on a customer's premises—the property owned by the LAN user. (For historical reasons, "premises" is always spelled in the plural.) In the case of the home network, the premises consist of the user's home or apartment. Exhibit 5.3 shows a much larger LAN. Here, the premises consist of a corporate multistory office building.

On each floor, computers connect to the floor's workgroup switch via a UTP cord or a wireless access point. The workgroup switch on each floor connects to a *core switch* in the basement equipment room. The router in the basement connects the building LAN to the outside world.

Suppose that Client A on Floor 1 sends a frame to Server X on Floor 2. Client A sends the frame to Workgroup Switch 1 on the first floor. That workgroup switch sends the frame down to the core switch in the basement. The core switch then sends the frame up to Workgroup Switch 2, which passes the frame to Server X.

UTP is easy to wiretap, allowing attackers to read all packets flowing through the cord. Telecommunications closets should be kept locked at all times, and cords should be run through thick metal wiring conduits wherever possible. (For more details of physical and facilities security, see Chapter 23.)

UTP also generates weak radio signals when traffic flows through it. It is possible to read these signals from some distance away using highly specialized equipment.

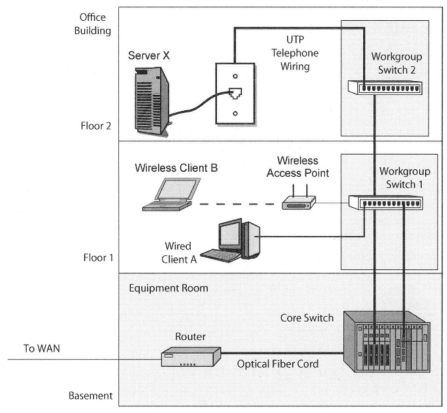

EXHIBIT 5.3 Building LAN

Typically, however, eavesdroppers do not even need to tap wires. In most building LANs, anyone entering the building can plug a notebook into any wall jack with a UTP cord. This gives them access to the network without having to do more sophisticated forms of wiretapping. Most switches today have 802.1X capability that requires any device connecting to a wall jack to authenticate itself before being allowed to transmit beyond the switch.

For more extensive details of LAN security, see Chapter 25 in this *Handbook*.

5.2.3 Firm's Wide Area Networks (WANs).   Although LANs oper-ate within a company's premises, *wide area networks* (WANs) connect different sites—usually within a single corporation. Corporations do not have the regulatory rights-of-way needed to run wires though public areas. For WAN service, companies must use companies called *carriers* that do have these rights-of-way.

Exhibit 5.4 shows that most firms use multiple-carrier WANs. In the exhibit, some sites in this company are connected by point-to-point *leased lines* from a telephone com-pany. The companies also subscribe to *switched network services* that deliver frames between several sites. The exhibit shows that these switched network services use the *Frame Relay* technology. The company uses two separate Frame Relay networks—one to connect its own sites to one another and another to connect it to another firm.

Carrier technology is widely assumed by security professionals to have good secu-rity. Unlike the Internet, which allows anyone to connect to it, only commercial firms

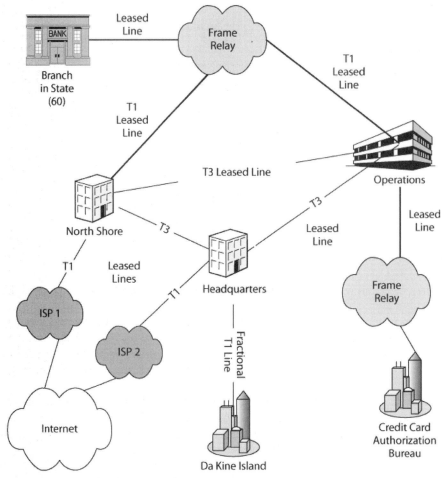

EXHIBIT 5.4   Wide Area Networks (WANs)

may connect to carrier WANs. This makes attacker access very difficult. However, attacker access is not impossible. For example, if an attacker hacks a computer owned by the carrier (or even by a customer), this breach may permit access.

In addition, the carrier alone knows how it routes traffic through its network. This should stymie attackers even if they somehow get access to the network. However, such *security through obscurity* is considered a very bad thing by security professionals because it is possible for attackers who hack carrier computers to get access to routing information. (Attackers usually have much simpler attack vectors; see Chapters 15 and 19 in this *Handbook* for more details.)

5.2.4   Internet.   By the end of the 1970s, there were many LANs and WANs in the world. Many of the WANs were nonprofit networks that connected universities and research institutions. Unfortunately, computers on one network could not talk to computers on other networks. To address this problem, the Defense Advanced Research Projects Agency (DARPA) created the Internet. By definition, an internet is a "super network" that connects individual networks together. Later, commercial

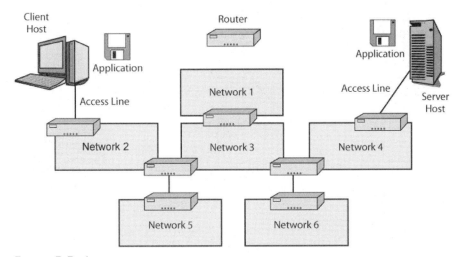

EXHIBIT 5.5   Internet

networks were allowed to join the Internet, and it became the Internet we know today.

Exhibit 5.5 shows that devices called *routers* connect the individual networks together. Initially, these devices were called *gateways*. The term "gateway" was used instead of "router" in some early standards, but most vendors have now adopted the name "router." One major exception is Microsoft, which still tends to call routers gateways.

Any computer on any network on the Internet can send messages to any computer on any other network on the Internet. In single LANs and WANs, messages are called *frames*. On the Internet, the messages that travel all the way from one computer to another across the Internet are called *packets*.

Exhibit 5.6 shows that the packet travels all the way from the source host to the destination host. Along the way, it is carried inside a different frame in each network.

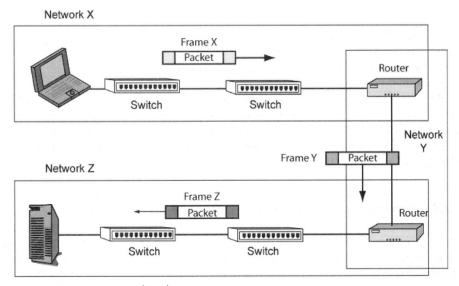

EXHIBIT 5.6   Frames and Packets

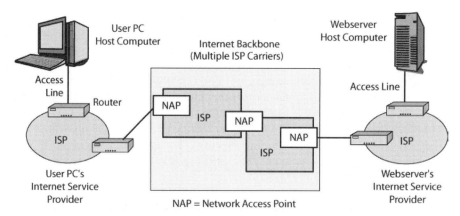

Exhibit 5.7   Internet Service Providers (ISPs)

In Network X, the packet travels inside Frame X; in Network Y, the packet travels inside Frame Y; and in Network Z, the packet travels inside Frame Z.

The global Internet uses transmission standards that are known as the *Transmission Control Protocol/Internet Protocol* (TCP/IP) standards. In addition, many firms build separate internal TCP/IP internets for their own communication. These internal networks are called *intra*nets to distinguish them from the *Inter*net. We will use the term internet with a lower-case *i* to designate any internet that is not the global Internet.

Initially, security on intranets was comparatively light because it was assumed that external attackers would have a difficult time getting into corporate intranets. However, if a hacker takes over an internal computer connected to the intranet, light security becomes a serious problem. Consequently, most firms have been progressively hardening their intranet security.

Exhibit 5.7 shows that individual homes and corporations connect to the Internet via carriers called *Internet Service Providers* (ISP). The Internet has many ISPs, but they all connect at centers that usually are called *Network Access Points* (NAPs). These connections permit any host on any ISP to send packets to any host on any other ISP.

ISPs are commercial organizations run for profit, that there is no central point of control over the Internet's operation, although there is centralized control over the naming of Internet host computers (e.g., *cnn.com.*).

When the Internet was designed in the late 1970s, there was a conscious decision to promote openess and not to add the burdens of security. As a consequence of a lack of security technology and open access to almost anyone, the Internet is a security nightmare. Companies that transmit sensitive information over the Internet need to consider cryptographic protections. (See Chapters 7, 32, 33, 34, 35, and 37 in this *Handbook* for more details of cryptography and other means for achieving, security on networks.)

5.2.5 Applications.   Although both networks and internets are important, the only things that users care about are applications. Personal applications include the World Wide Web, e-mail, and instant messaging, among many others. Corporations use some of these applications, but they also use many business-specific applications, such as accounting, payroll, billing, and inventory management. Often, business applications are transaction-processing applications, which are characterized by high volumes of simple repetitive transactions. The traffic volume generated by transaction-processing and other business-oriented applications usually far outweighs the traffic of personal applications in the firm. (See Chapter 30 in this *Handbook* for details of e-commerce security.)

All programs have bugs, including security vulnerabilities. There are many applications, and keeping track of application vulnerabilities and constantly patching many applications is an enormous task that is all too easy to put off or complete only partially. (See Chapter 40 for an overview of patch management.) Also, each application must be configured with options that have high security, and security must be managed on each application (e.g., antivirus and spam blocking in e-mail). (See Chapter 20 for a review of spam and antispam measures.)

5.3 NETWORK PROTOCOLS AND VULNERABILITIES. The products of different network vendors must be able to work together (interoperate). This is possible only if there are strong communication standards to govern how hardware and software processes interact. With such standards, two or more programs can interoperate effectively.

Standards raise three security issues. One is the standard itself. For instance, the TCP standard discussed later in this chapter is difficult to attack because an attacker cannot send a false message unless he or she can guess the sequence number of the next message. This normally is very difficult to do. However, if the attacker sends an RST (Reset) message, which terminates a connection, this protection is greatly reduced. In fact, it is fairly easy to send RST messages that close legitimate open connections.

A second issue is security built into the standard. Most standards were created without security, and security was added only in later versions, sometimes in an awkward way. For instance, IP, which is the main protocol for delivering packets over the Internet, originally had no security. The *IPsec* standards were created to address this weakness, but IPsec is burdensome and not widely used.

A third issue is the security of the implementation of standards in vendor products. Most attacks that aim at standards weaknesses attack vendor products that have security vulnerabilities unrelated to the protocols they implement.

5.4 STANDARDS. Networks and network security are deeply dependent on standards.

5.4.1 Core Layers. Standards are complex, and when people deal with complex problems, they usually break these problems into smaller parts and have different specialists work on the different parts. Exhibit 5.8 shows that standards are divided into

Exhibit 5.8 Three Standards Core Layers

Super Layer	Description
Application	Communication between application programs on different hosts attached to different networks on an internet.
Internetworking	Transmission pf packets across a routed internet. Packets contain application-layer messages.
Single network	Transmission of frames across a single switched network. Frames contain packets.

three core layers that collectively have the functionality needed to allow an application program on one network in an internet to interoperate with another program on another computer on another network.

At the *application core layer*, the two applications must be able to interact effectively. For instance, in World Wide Web access, the two application programs are the browser on the client PC and the Web server program on the Web server. The standard for Web interactions is the *Hypertext Transfer Protocol* (HTTP). Both the browser and the Web server applications have to send messages that comply with the HTTP standard.

The middle layer is the *internet core layer*. Standards at this layer govern how packets are delivered across a routed internet. One of the main standards at the internet core layer is the Internet Protocol (IP). We will see other internetworking standards later.

The lowest core layer is the *single-network core layer*. Standards at this layer govern the transmission of frames across the switches and transmission lines in a single switched network (a LAN or WAN).

5.4.2 Layered Standards Architectures.   Standards are created by standards agencies. These standards agencies first create detailed layering plans for creating standards. These specific layering plans are called *layered standards architectures*. Afterward, standards agencies create standards in the individual layers. Exhibit 5.9 shows two popular layered standards architectures and relates these standards architectures to the three core layers we saw earlier.

The *Internet Engineering Task Force* (IETF) is the standards agency for the Internet. Its standards architecture is called TCP/IP—a name taken from two of its most important standards, TCP and IP. Exhibit 5.9 shows that TCP/IP has four layers. The bottom layer, the *subnet access layer*, corresponds to the single-network core layer. The top layer, in turn, is the *application layer*, which corresponds to the application core layer. The two middle layers—the *internet* and *transport* layers—correspond to the internet core layer. TCP/IP focuses primarily on internetworking. Dividing this core layer into two TCP/IP layers permits greater division of labor in standards development.

The other standards architecture shown in the figure is *OSI*, which is rarely spelled out by its full name, the *Reference Model of Open Systems Interconnection*. OSI is governed by two standards agencies. One is ISO, the *International Organization for Standardization*. The other is ITU-T, the *International Telecommunications Union–Telecommunications Standards Sector*. (The official names and the official acronyms do not match when the originated in different languages.)

Exhibit 5.9 shows that OSI divides the three core layers into a total of seven layers. OSI single networks use standards at two layers—the *physical* and *data link* layers.

Exhibit 5.9 Layered Standards Architectures

Super Layer	TCP/IP	OSI	Hybrid TCP/IP-OSI
Application	Application	Application Presentation Session	Application
Internet	Transport Internet	Transport Network	Transport Internet
Network	Subnet access	Data link Physical	Data link Physical

OSI's market dominance is so strong at the physical and data link layers that the IETF rarely develops standards at these layers. The "subnet access" indication in the TCP/IP framework basically means "Use OSI standards here."

Which of these two standards architectures dominates? The answer is "Neither." What nearly all firms use today is the hybrid TCP/IP–OSI standards architecture, which Exhibit 5.9 illustrates. This hybrid architecture uses OSI standards at the physical and data link layer and TCP/IP standards at the internet and transport layer. Corporations also use standards from some other standards architectures at the internet and transport layers, but TCP/IP standards dominate.

At the application core layer, the situation is complex. Both OSI and TCP/IP standards are used, often in combination. In fact, OSI standards often reference TCP/IP standards and vice versa. Although OSI and TCP/IP are often viewed as rivals, this is not the case at all. Several other standards agencies also create application layer standards, complicating the picture even further.

5.4.3 Single-Network Standards.
As just noted, OSI standards dominate in the two single-network layers—the physical and data link layers. Exhibit 5.10 shows how the physical and data link layers are related.

5.4.3.1 Data Link Layer.
The path that a frame takes through a single network is called the frame's data link. In Exhibit 5.10, the data link runs between Host A and Router R1. This data link passes through Switch X1 and Switch X2.

The source computer sends the frame to the first switch, which forwards the frame to the next switch along the data link, which forwards the frame further. The last switch along the data link passes the frame to the destination computer (or router, if the packet in the frame is destined for a computer on another network).

5.4.3.2 Physical Layer.
Physical layer standards govern the physical connections between consecutive devices along a data link. In Exhibit 5.10, these physical links are A–X1, X1–X2, and X2–R1. Earlier, we saw one popular transmission medium, unshielded twisted pair wire. UTP dominates in links between computers and workgroup switches (see Exhibit 5.3). UTP signals typically involve voltage changes. For

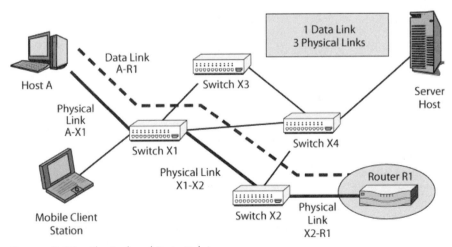

EXHIBIT 5.10 Physical and Data Link Layers

instance, a high voltage may indicate a 1, while a low voltage may indicate a 0. (Actual voltage patterns usually are much more complex.)

For longer distances and very high speeds, another popular transmission medium is optical fiber, which sends light signals through thin glass tubes. Optical fiber signals actually are very simple. In a clock cycle, the light is turned on for a 1 or off for a 0.

UTP cords act like radio antennas when they carry signals. Some of the signal always radiates out, allowing people to intercept UTP signals by placing devices near (but not touching) the cord. Intercepting and interpreting electromagnetic emissions from computing devices is called van Eck phreaking after the Dutch scientist Wim van Eck published a paper in 1985 demonstrating how to monitor and reconstitute leaked signals from *cathode-ray terminals* (CRTs). In contrast, optical fiber requires physically tapping into the fiber cords. Physical wiretapping can also be done with UTP, but as noted earlier, the easiest way to connect to a network via UTP usually is simply to bring a laptop computer into a company and plug it into any wall jack.

Wireless transmission uses radio waves. This permits mobile devices to be served in ways never before possible. Wireless transmission is used for both LAN and WAN transmission.

Radio signals spread widely, even when dish antennas are used. Consequently, it is very easy for eavesdroppers to listen in on radio transmissions and do other mischief. Radio signals must be strongly encrypted, and the parties must be strongly authenticated to prevent impostors from sending radio transmission.

Radio signaling is very complex. Most radio signaling uses spread spectrum transmission, in which the information is sent over a wide range of frequencies. *Spread spectrum* transmission is used to improve propagation reliability. Radio transmission has many propagation problems, such as interference from other sources. Many propagation problems occur only at certain frequencies. By spreading the signal across a wide spectrum of frequencies and doing so redundantly, the signal will still be intelligible even if there are strong problems at some frequencies.

The military uses frequency hopping spread spectrum (FHSS) transmission for security. Military spread spectrum transmission works in such a way that makes intercepting transmissions very difficult. Civilian spread spectrum transmission, in contrast, is designed to make connecting simple. Civilian spread spectrum transmission per se offers *no* security.

Switches spend almost all of their time forwarding frames. However, switches spend some of their time exchanging supervisory frames with one another to keep the network running efficiently. For example, in *Ethernet* (IEEE 802.3), which dominates LAN standards, if there are loops among the switches, the network will malfunction. If a switch detects a loop, it sends supervisory frames to other switches. The switches in the network then communicate until they determine how to close selected ports on certain switches to break the loop. This process is governed by the *Spanning Tree Protocol* (STP, part of IEEE 802.1) or the newer *Rapid Spanning Tree Protocol* (RSTP, defined in IEEE 802.1w and now part of IEEE 802.1D-2004).

Attackers can create attacks on the switches in a network by impersonating a switch and sending a flood of false messages to the network's real switches indicating the presence of a loop. The switches may spend so much of their time reorganizing the network that they will be unable to serve legitimate traffic. They also can attack several other supervisory protocols to make switches unavailable for processing normal frames. The 802.1AE standard is designed to limit switch-to-switch communication to authenticated switches.

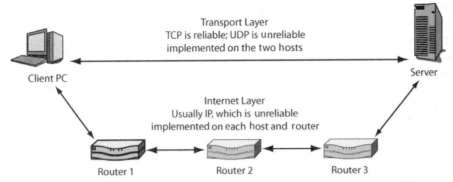

EXHIBIT 5.11 Internet and Transport Layer Standards

5.4.4 Internetworking Standards.

As noted earlier, the IETF divided the internetworking core layer into two layers—the internet and transport layers. Exhibit 5.11 shows how the two layers are related.

The internet layer forwards packets, hop by hop, among routers until the packet reaches the destination host. The main standard at the internet layer is the Internet Protocol (IP).

The designers of TCP/IP realized that they could not predict what services the single networks connecting routers would provide. IP was made a simple best-effort protocol, in order to assume minimal functionality in the single networks along the way. There are no guarantees that packets will arrive at all or, if they do arrive, that they will arrive in order.

To make up for the limitations of IP, a transport layer was added. The main standard designed for this layer, the *Transmission Control Protocol* (TCP), was created as a high-capability protocol that would fix any errors made along the way, ensure that packets arrived in order, slow transmission when the network became overloaded, and do several other things. For applications that did not need these capabilities, a simpler standard was created, the *User Datagram Protocol* (UDP).

5.5 INTERNET PROTOCOL (IP).

The Internet Protocol (IP) does two main things. First, it governs how packets are organized. Second, it determines how routers along the way move packets to the destination host. (Analogously, data link layer standards govern how frames are organized and how switches along the way move the frame across a single switched network.)

5.5.1 IP Version 4 Packet.

The main version of the Internet Protocol is Version 4 (IPv4). (There were no Versions 0, 1, 2, or 3). This version has been in use since its definition in 1981 and will continue to be used for many years to come, although IPv4 is intended to supercede it. Exhibit 5.12 shows the IPv4 packet's organization.

A packet is a long stream of 1s and 0s. The IP *header* normally is shown on several rows, with 32 bits on each row. The first row has bits 0 through 31; the next row shows bits 32 through 63 and so on.

The header is divided into smaller units called *fields*. Fields are defined by their bit position in the packet. For example, the first four bits comprise the *version number* field. These are bits 0 through 3. In IPv4, this field holds 0100, which is 4 in binary. The *header length* field comprises the next four bits (bits 3 through 7).

Bit 0   Bit 31

Version (4 bits) Value is 4 (0100)	Header Length (4 bits)	Diff-Serv (8 bits)	Total Length (16 bits) length in octets	
Identification (16 bits) Unique value in each original IP packet			Flags (3 bits)	Fragment Offset (13 bits) Octets from start of original IP fragment's data field
Time to Live (8 bits)		Protocol (8 bits) 1 = ICMP, 6 = TCP, 17 = UDP	Header Checksum (16 bits)	
Source IP Address (32 bits)				
Destination IP Address (32 bits)				
Options (if any)				Padding
Data Field				

EXHIBIT 5.12   Internet Protocol (IP) Packet

5.5.1.1 *First Row.*   As just noted, the first field (bits 0 through 3) is the version number field. In IPv4, the value is 0100 (4). In the newer version of the Internet Protocol, *IP Version 6* (IPv6), the value is 0110.

The next field is the header length field. This gives the length of the headers in 32-bit units. As Exhibit 5.12 shows, a header without options has five 32-bit lines, so this field will have the value 0101 (5 in binary).

The use of options is uncommon in practice. In fact, options tend to indicate attacks. Therefore, a value larger than 5 in the header length field indicates that the packet header has options and is therefore suspicious.

The 1-octet *dif-serv* (differential services) field was created to allow different services (priority, etc.) to be given to this packet. However, this field typically is not used.

The *total length* field gives the length of the entire IP packet in octets (bytes). Given the 16-bit length of this field, the maximum number of octets in the IP packet is 65,536 (2^{16}). Most IP packets, however, are far smaller. The length of the data field is this total length minus the length of the header in octets.

5.5.1.2 *Second Row.*   If an IP packet is too long for a single network along the way, the router sending the packet into that network will fragment the packet, dividing its contents into a number of smaller packets. For assembly on the destination host, all fragment packets are given the same *identification field* value as in the original packet. The data octets in the original packets are numbered, and the number of the first data octet in the packet is given a *fragment offset* value (13 bits long). There are three *flag* fields (1-bit fields). One of these, *more fragments*, is set to 1 in all but the last packet, in which it is made 0. The information in these three fields allows the destination host to place the packets in order and know when there are no more packets to arrive.

IP fragmentation by routers is usually rare, and attackers can use fragmentation to hide attack information. Even if the first fragment packet is dropped by the firewall, other packets that do not have the signature information in the first header can get through. Therefore, IP fragmentation is suspicious.

5.5.1.3   Third Row.   The third line begins with an ominous-sounding *time to live* (TTL) field, which has a value between 0 and 255. The sending host sets the initial value (64 or 128 in most operating systems). Each router along the way decreases the value by 1. If a router decreases the value to 0, it discards the packet. This process was created to prevent misaddressed packets from circulating endlessly around the Internet.

To identify hosts, attackers will *ping* many IP addresses (as discussed in Section 5.8.1). A reply tells the attacker that a host exists with that IP address. In addition, by guessing the initial TTL value and looking at the TTL value in the arriving packet, the attacker can guess how many router hops separate the attacker's host from the victim host. Sending many pings to different IP addresses can help the attacker map the routers in the target network. Firms concerned with this might change their host operating systems' default TTL values to confuse attackers.

The *data* field of the IP packet may contain a TCP message segment, a UDP datagram message, or something else, such as the ICMP messages we will discuss in Section 5.8.1. A value of 1 in this field indicates that the data field is an ICMP message. In turn, 6 indicates a TCP segment, and 17 indicates that the data field contains a UDP header.

The header checksum field contains a value placed there by the sender. This number is determined by a calculation based on the values of other fields. The receiving internet process redoes the calculation. If the two numbers are different, then there must have been an error along the way. If so, the router or destination host receiving the packet will simply discard the packet. There is no retransmission, so IP is not reliable.

5.5.1.4   Source and Destination IP Address.   When you send a letter, the envelope has an address and a return address. The analogous addresses in IP headers are the source and destination IP addresses. Note that IP addresses are 32 bits long. For human reading, these 32 bits are divided into four 8-bit *segments*, and each segment's bits are converted into a decimal number between 0 and 255. The four segment numbers are then separated by dots. An example is *128.171.17.13*. Note that this dotted decimal notation is a memory and writing crutch for inferior biological entities (people). Computers and routers work with 32-bit IP addresses directly.

Many forms of firewall filtering are based on IP addresses. In addition, many attackers spoof their packet's source IP address (i.e., replace the real IP address with a false IP address).

5.5.2   IP Version 6.   Although IP Version 4 is widely used, its 32-bit IP address size causes problems: It can address only 4,294,967,296 ($\sim 10^9$) devices. This relatively small size limits the number of possible IP addresses. In addition, when IP addresses were distributed, most addresses were assigned to the United States because the Internet was invented there. In fact, some U.S. universities received more IP addresses than China.

To address the limitations of the 32-bit IP address size, a new version of the Internet Protocol was created. This was *IP Version 6* (IPv6). (A Version 5 was defined, but it was never used.) Exhibit 5.13 shows the IPv6 packet organization.

One obvious change is that the IP addresses are much larger—128 bits. Each IP address, then, requires four 32-bit lines to write and is equivalent to $\sim 10^{38}$. This will provide IP addresses to allow almost every device to be a host on the Internet—including

Bit 0   Bit 31

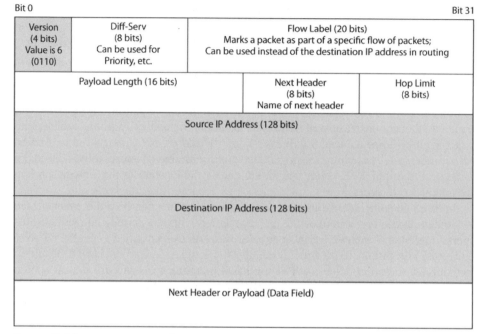

EXHIBIT 5.13   IP Version 6 Packet

toasters and coffeepots. (To give you a sense of the scale of this enormous number, it is enough to address every single atom of water in a cube over 2 km on a side.)

The version number field is 4 bits long, and its value is 6 (0110). There also is a dif-serv field and a *flow label* field that is 20 bits long. These fields allow the packet to be assigned to a category of packets with similar needs. All packets in this category would be assigned the same flow label and would be treated the same way by routers. However, this capability is not widely used.

There is a *hop limit* field that serves the same function as the time to live (TTL) field in IPv4. The payload length, in turn, gives the length of the data field in octets.

A major innovation in IPv6 is the *next header* field. There can be multiple headers following the first header shown in Exhibit 5.13. For instance, IPsec security is implemented with a security header. Although options are unusual in IPv4, IPv6 uses additional headers extensively. The next header field tells what the next header is. Each additional header has a next header field identifies the next header or says that there is no next header.

5.5.3 IPsec.   IP, which was created in the early 1980s, initially had no security at all. Finally, in the 1990s, the Internet Engineering Task Force developed a general way to secure IP transmission. This was IP security, which normally is just called IPsec (eye-pea-seck′). IPsec functions by protecting a packet or most of a packet and sending the protected packet inside another packet. IPsec is a general security solution because everything within the data field of the protected packet is secure, including the transport and application layer information. This includes the transport message and the application message contained in the transport message. Originally developed for IPv6, it was extended to IPv4 as well, becoming a completely general solution.

5.6 TRANSMISSION CONTROL PROTOCOL (TCP).   As noted earlier, the Transmission Control Protocol (TCP) is one of the two possible TCP/IP protocols at the transport layer. Exhibit 5.14 shows the TCP message, which is called a TCP *segment*.

5.6.1 Connection-Oriented and Reliable Protocol.   Protocols are either connectionless or connection-oriented.

Connection-oriented protocols are like telephone conversations. When you call someone, there is at least tacit agreement at the beginning of the conversation that you are able to speak. (Such expressions as "Hold, please." and "Can I call you back?" indicate an unwillingness to proceed at the moment.) Also, there is at least tacit agreement that you are done talking at the end of the conversation. (Simply hanging up is considered rude.)

Connectionless protocols, in turn, are like e-mail. When you send a message, there is no prior agreement, and after the message is sent, there is no built-in provision for a reply (unless you are one of those people who asks to be notified when the receiver reads the message).

Exhibit 5.15 shows a sample TCP connection. Three messages are sent to open a connection. The originator sends a TCP SYN segment to indicate that it wishes to open a TCP session. The other transport process sends back a TCP SYN/ACK segment that acknowledges the connection opening message and indicates that it is willing to open the connection. The originator then sends an ACK segment to indicate reception of the SYN/ACK segment.

Attackers can use TCP connection openings to execute denial-of-service attacks that make a server unable to respond to legitimate traffic. The attacker sends a SYN segment to open a connection to the victim server. The victim server responds with a SYN/ACK message. The victim server also sets aside resources for the connection. The attacker never responds with an ACK, so this is called a *half-open SYN attack*. If

Bit 0				Bit 31
Source Port Number (16 bits)			Destination Port Number (16 bits)	
Sequence Number (32 bits)				
Acknowledgement Number (32 bits)				
Header Length (4 bits)	Reserved (6 bits)	Flag Fields (6 bits)	Window (16 bits)	
TCP Checksum (16 bits)			Urgent Pointer (16 bits)	
Options (if any)				Padding
Data Field				

Flag fields are 1-bit fields. They include SYN, ACK, FIN, RST, PSH, and URG.

EXHIBIT 5.14 Transmission Control Protocol (TCP) Segment

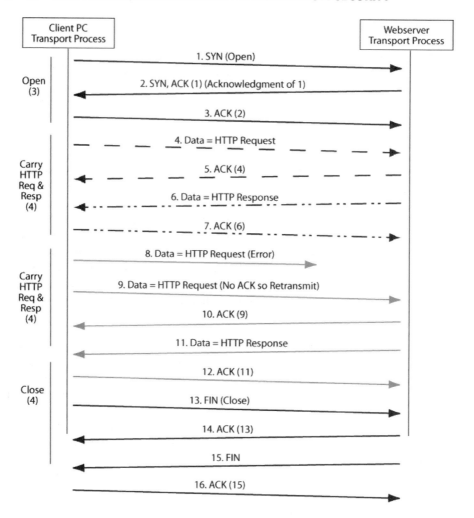

Note: An ACK may be combined with the next message if the next message is sent quickly enough.

EXHIBIT 5.15   Messages in a TCP Session

the attacker floods a server host with SYN segments, the victim server will reserve so many resources that it will be overloaded and unable to serve legitimate connection opening attempts. The server may even crash.

Ending a conversation, in contrast, normally takes four messages. One side sends a FIN segment, which the other party acknowledges. Then the other party sends a FIN segment, which the other side acknowledges. After the first side sends the original FIN segment, it will not send any new information, but it will send acknowledgments for segments sent by the other party.

There is another way to end a session or even to reject opening one. At any point, either party can send a RST (reset) message. An RST message ends the conversation abruptly. There is not even an acknowledgment. It is like hanging up in a telephone conversation.

Attackers often preface an attack by attempting to identify the IP addresses of running hosts—much like thieves casing a neighborhood. One way to do this is to send TCP SYN segments to hosts. If hosts reject the SYN segment, they often send back an RST message. As noted earlier, TCP segments are carried in the data fields of IP packets. The source IP address in the packet delivering the TCP RST segment will be that of the internal host. Whenever the attacker receives an RST segment, this verifies the existence of a working host at that packet's IP address. Firewalls often stop RST segments from leaving a site to prevent them from reaching the attacker.

5.6.2 Reliability.

In addition to being connectionless or connection-oriented, protocols are either *reliable* or *unreliable*. An unreliable protocol does not detect and correct errors. Some unreliable protocols do not even check for errors. Others check for errors but simply discard a message if they find that it contains an error.

TCP is a reliable protocol. It actually corrects errors. The TCP *checksum* field is calculated using values from other fields. The sender places the result of its calculation in the checksum field. The receiver redoes the calculation and compares it with the transmitted value. If the receiving transport layer process finds that a message is correct (the values are the same), it sends an acknowledgment message. However, if the receiver detects an error in the TCP segment it receives (the values are different), it discards the segment and does nothing else.

How does a receiver know that there is an error in the message? The sender computes a value based on the other bits in the TCP segment (not just the header). The receiver redoes the calculation. If the two values match, the receiver sends an acknowledgment. If they do not match, the receiver merely drops the segment and does not send an acknowledgment.

If the segment arrives correctly, the original sender receives an acknowledgment. However, if the segment never arrives or is discarded because of damage, no reply is sent. If the original sender does not receive an acknowledgment in a specified period of time, it will resend the original segment. It will even use the original sequence number.

5.6.3 Flag Fields.

Flag field is a general name for a 1-bit field that is logical (true or false). To say that a flag field is *set* means that its value is 1. To say that a flag field is *not set* means that its value is 0.

The TCP header contains a number of flag fields. One of these is SYN. To request a connection opening, the sender sets the SYN bit. The other sends a SYN/ACK segment, in which both the SYN and ACK bits are set. Other commonly used flags are FIN, RST, URG, and PSH.

The URG flag indicates the presence of urgent data that should be handled before earlier data octets. The urgent pointer field indicates the location of the urgent data.

If an application message is large, TCP will divide the application message into multiple TCP segments and send the segments individually. To help the receiving TCP process, the sending transport process may set the PSH (*push*) bit in the application message's last segment. This tells the receiving transport process to push the data up to the application program immediately without buffering and delays.

5.6.4 Octets and Sequence Number.

The sequence number field value allows the receiver to put arriving TCP segments in order even if the packets carrying them arrive out of order (including when a segment is retransmitted). Sequence numbers are also used in acknowledgments, albeit indirectly. In TCP transmission, every octet that is sent, from the very first, is counted. This octet counting is used to select each segment's sequence number.

- For the first segment, a random initial sequence number (ISN) is placed in the sequence number field.

- If the segment contains data, the number of the first octet contained in the data filed is used as the segment's sequence number.

- For a purely supervisory message that carries no data, such as an ACK, SYN, SYN/ACK, FIN, or RST segment, the sequence number is increased by 1 over the previous message.

One dangerous attack is TCP *session hijacking*, in which an attacker takes over the role of one side. This allows the hijacker to read messages and send false messages to the other side. To accomplish session hijacking, the attacker must be able to predict sequence numbers because if a segment arrives with an inappropriate sequence number, the receiver will reject it. TCP session hijacking is likely to be successful only if the initial sequence number is predictable. Few operating systems today pick initial sequence numbers in a predictable way, but predicable sequence numbers were common in earlier operating systems, some of which are still in use.

5.6.5   Acknowledgment Numbers.   When a receiver sends an acknowledgment, it sets the ACK bit. It also puts a value in the *acknowledgment number* field to indicate which segment is being acknowledged. This process is needed because the sender sends many segments and because acknowledgments may be delayed.

You might think that the acknowledgment number would be the sequence number of the segment being acknowledged. Instead, it is the number of the last octet in the data field plus 1. In other words, the acknowledgment number gives the octet number of the first octet in the next segment to be sent. This seems a bit odd, but it makes certain calculations easier for the receiver.

5.6.6   Window Field.   Flow control limits the rate at which a side sends TCP segments. The TCP *window* field allows one to limit how many more octets the other side may send before getting another acknowledgment. The process is somewhat complex and has no known security implications at the time of this writing. In acknowledgments, the ACK bit is set, and both the acknowledgment and window size fields are filled in.

5.6.7   Options.   Like the IPv4 header, the TCP header can have options. However, while IP options are rare and cause for suspicion, TCP uses options extensively. One common option, often sent with the initial SYN or SYN/ACK segment, is the *maximum segment size* (MSS) option. This gives the other side a limit on the maximum size of TCP segment data fields (not on segment sizes as a whole). The presence of TCP options, then, is not suspicious by itself.

5.6.8   Port Numbers.   We have now looked at most fields in the TCP header. However, we have skipped the first two fields—the source and destination port number fields—in order to save them for the last.

5.6.8.1   Port Numbers on Servers.   *Port number* fields mean different things for clients and servers. For a server, it represents a specific application running on that

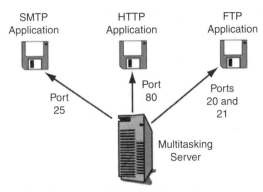

Exhibit 5.16   Multitasking Server Host and Port
Numbers

server, as Exhibit 5.16 shows. Most servers are multitasking computers, which means that they can run multiple applications at the same time. Each application is specified by a different port number.

For instance, on a server, a Web server application program may run on TCP Port 80. Incoming TCP segments that have 80 as their destination port number are passed to the Web server application. Actually, TCP Port 80 is the well-known port for Web server programs, meaning that it is the usual port number for the application. Although Web servers can be given other TCP port numbers, this makes it impossible for users to establish connections unless they know or can guess the nonstandard TCP port number.

The TCP port range from 0 to 1023 is reserved for the well-known port numbers of major applications, such as HTTP and e-mail. For instance, *Simple Mail Transfer Protocol* (SMTP) mail server programs usually are run on TCP Port 25, while *File Transfer Protocol* (FTP) requires two well-known port numbers—TCP Port 21 for supervisory control and TCP Port 20 for the actual transfer of files.

5.6.8.2   Port Numbers on Clients.   Client hosts use TCP port numbers differently. Whenever a client connects to an application program on a server, it generates a random *ephemeral port number* that it uses only for that connection. On Windows machines, the ephemeral TCP port numbers range from 1024 to 4999.

The Microsoft port number range for ephemeral port numbers may differ from the official IETF range, with values of 5000–65534. The use of nonstandard ephemeral port numbers by Windows and some other operating systems causes problems for firewall filtering.

5.6.8.3   Sockets.   Exhibit 5.17 shows that the goal of internetworking is to deliver application messages from one application on one machine to another application on another machine. On each machine, there is a TCP port number that specifies the application (or connection) and an IP address to specify a computer. A *socket* is a combination of an IP address and a TCP port number. It is written as the IP address, a colon, and the TCP port number. A typical socket, then, would be something like *128.171.17.13:80*.

Attackers often do *socket spoofing*—both IP address spoofing and port spoofing. For instance, in TCP session hijacking, if the attacker wishes to take over the identity of a client, it must know both the client's IP address and ephemeral port number. Of course, these fields are transmitted in the clear (without encryption) in TCP, so an attacker with

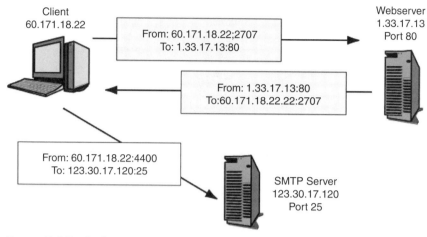

Exhibit 5.17   Sockets

a sniffer that captures and reads traffic flowing between the client and server can easily obtain this information.

5.6.9 TCP Security.   Like IP, TCP was created without security. However, while IPsec has made IP secure, the IETF has not created a comparable way to secure TCP. One reason for this is IPsec's ability to secure all transport layer traffic transparently, without modification to transport layer protocols. The IETF has made IPsec the centerpiece of its security protections and a single method to handle upper-layer security. Communicating partners that want TCP security should implement IPsec.

However, few TCP sessions are protected by IPsec. Consequently, some pairs of users employ an option in TCP, which adds an electronic signature to each TCP session. This signature proves the identity of the sender. This option, described in RFC 2385, requires the two parties to share a secret value. This option is awkward because it provides no way to share keys automatically, and it does not provide encryption or other protections. The option is used primarily in the Border Gateway Protocol (BGP). BGP is used to exchange routing information between administrative systems—say a corporate system and an internet service provider. BGP always uses one-to-one connections, the communicating parties usually know each other quite well, and the two parties have long-term relationships, which makes key exchange less burdensome and risky. Outside of BGP, however, the RFC 2385 electronic signature option does not appear to be used significantly. Even in BGP, it is widely seen as very weak security.

5.7 USER DATAGRAM PROTOCOL.   As noted earlier, TCP is a protocol that makes up for the limitations of IP. TCP adds error correction, the sequencing of IP packets, flow control, and other functionality that we have not discussed.

Not all applications need the reliable service offered by TCP. For instance, in voice over IP, there is no time to wait for the retransmission of lost or damaged packets carrying voice. In turn, the simple network management protocol (SNMP), which is used for network management communications, sends so many messages back and forth that the added traffic of connection-opening packets, acknowledgments, and other TCP supervisory segments could overload the network. Consequently, voice over IP, SNMP, and many other applications do not use TCP at the transport layer.

Bit 0   Bit 31

Source Port Number (16 bits)	Destination Port Number (16 bits)
UDP Length (16 bits)	UDP Checksum (16 bits)
Data Field	

EXHIBIT 5.18   User Datagram Protocol (UDP)

Instead, they use the User Datagram Protocol (UDP). This protocol is connectionless and unreliable. Each UDP message (called a UDP datagram) is sent on its own. There are no openings, closings, or acknowledgments.

As a consequence of the simplicity of UDP's operation, the UDP datagram's organization is also very simple, as Exhibit 5.18 illustrates. There are no sequence numbers, acknowledgment numbers, flag fields, or most of the other fields found in TCP.

There are source and destination port numbers, a UDP header length to allow variable-length UDP datagrams, and a UDP checksum. If the receiver detects an error using the checksum, it simply discards the message. There is no retransmission.

The fact that both TCP and UDP use port numbers means that whenever you refer to port numbers for well-known applications, you also need to refer to whether the port numbers are TCP or UDP port numbers. This is why the well-known port number for Web servers is TCP port 80.

TCP's sequence numbers make TCP session hijacking very difficult. The receiver will discard messages with the wrong sequence numbers even if the source and destination sockets are correct. UDP lacks this protection, making UDP a somewhat more dangerous protocol than TCP.

Like TCP, UDP has no inherent security. Companies that wish to secure their UDP communication must use IPsec.

5.8   TCP/IP SUPERVISORY STANDARDS.   So far, we have looked at standards that deliver a stream of packets across an internet and that perhaps check for errors and provide other assurances. However, the TCP/IP architecture also includes a number of supervisory protocols that keep the Internet functioning.

5.8.1   Internet Control Message Protocol (ICMP).   The first supervisory protocol on the Internet was the Internet Control Message Protocol (ICMP). As Exhibit 5.19 shows, ICMP messages are delivered in the data fields of IP packets.

The best-known pair of ICMP message types is the ICMP *echo* message and the *echo reply* message. Suppose that a host sends an ICMP echo message to an IP address. If a host is active at that address, it may send back an ICMP echo reply message. This process is often called *pinging* because the most popular program for sending ICMP echo message is called *Ping*. The echo message is a very important tool for network management. If the network manager suspects a problem, he or she will ping a wide range of host addresses to see which of them are reachable. The pattern of responses can reveal where problems exist within a network.

Attackers also love to ping a wide range of host IP addresses. This can give them a list of hosts that are reachable for attacks. Another popular network management and

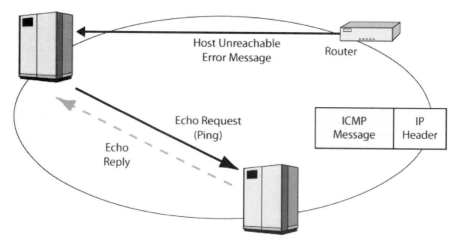

Exhibit 5.19   Internet Control Message Protocol (ICMP)

attack tool is *traceroute* (or *tracert* on Windows PCs). Traceroute is similar to ping, but traceroute also lists the routers that lie between the sending host and the host that is the target of the traceroute command. This allows an attacker to map the network. Border firewalls often drop echo reply messages leaving the firm to the outside.

Many ICMP messages are error messages. For instance, if a router cannot deliver the packet, it may send back an ICMP error message to the source host. This error message will provide as much information as possible about the type of error that occurred.

If an attacker cannot ping destination hosts because a firewall stops them, attackers often send IP packets that are malformed and so will be rejected. The ICMP error message is delivered in an IP packet, and the source IP address in this packet will reveal the IP address of the sending router. By analyzing error messages, the attacker can learn how routers are organized in a network. This information can be very useful to attackers.

5.8.2   Domain Name System (DNS).   To send a packet to another host, a source host must place the destination host's IP address in the destination address field of the packets. Often, however, the user merely types the host name of the destination host, for instance, cnn.com.

Unfortunately, host names are only nicknames. If the user types a host name, the computer must learn the corresponding IP address. As Exhibit 5.20 shows, the host wishing to send a packet to a target host sends a *Domain Name System* (DNS) request message to the DNS server. This message contains the host name of the target host. The DNS response message sends back the target host's IP address. To give an analogy, if you know someone's name, you must look up their telephone number in a telephone directory if you want to call them. In DNS, the human name corresponds to the host name, the telephone number corresponds to the IP address, and the DNS server corresponds to the telephone directory.

DNS is critical to the Internet's operation. Unfortunately, DNS is vulnerable to several attacks. For example, in *DNS cache poisoning*, an attacker replaces the IP address of a host name with another IP address. After cache poisoning, a legitimate user who contacts a DNS server to look up the host name will be given the false IP address, sending the user to the attacker's chosen site. Denial-of-service attacks are also too easy to accomplish. RFC 3833 lists a number of DNS security issues.[1]

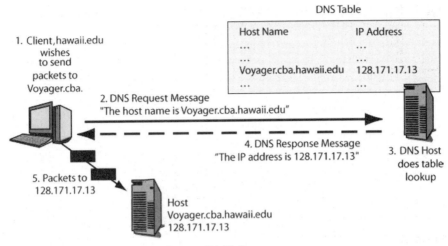

EXHIBIT 5.20 Domain Name System (DNS) Server

Several attempts to strengthen DNS security have been developed, under the general banner of Domain Name System Security Extensions (*DNSSEC*), especially RFC 2535[2]. However, both the original DNSSEC specifications and the newer DNSSEC *bis* specifications (RFCs 4033-4035[3]) have proven to be insufficient. Developing a security standard that is sufficiently backwardly compatible for Internet-scale implementation has proven to be extremely difficult.

If the DNS server does not know the host name, it contacts another DNS server. The DNS system contains many DNS servers organized in a hierarchy. At the top of the hierarchy are 13 *DNS root servers*. Below these are DNS servers for *top-level domains*, such as *.com, .edu, .ie, .uk, .nl,* and *.ca*. Each top-level domain has two or more top-level DNS servers for their domain. Second-level domain names are given to organizations (e.g., *Hawaii.edu* and *Microsoft.com*). Organizations are required to maintain DNS servers for computers within their domain.

If attackers could bring down the 13 root servers, they could paralyze the Internet. Widespread paralysis would not occur immediately, but in a few days, the Internet would begin experiencing serious outages.

5.8.3 Dynamic Host Configuration Protocol (DHCP). Server hosts are given static (permanent) IP addresses. Client PCs, however, are given dynamic (temporary) IP addresses whenever they use the Internet. The *Dynamic Host Configuration Protocol* (DHCP) standard that we saw earlier in the chapter makes this possible. A DHCP server has a database of available IP addresses. When a client requests an IP address, the DHCP server picks one from the database and sends it to the client. The next time the client uses the Internet, the DHCP server may give it a different IP address.

The fact that clients may receive different IP addresses each time they get on the Internet causes problems for *peer-to-peer* (P2P) applications. A presence server or some other mechanism must be used to find the other party's IP address. A lack of accepted standards for presence (including presence security) is a serious issue now that P2P applications are widespread. In fact, most security considerations in P2P presence servers have been used in P2P piracy applications, with an eye toward avoiding discovery by legitimate authorities.

5.8.4 Dynamic Routing Protocols. How do routers on the Internet learn what to do with packets addressed to various IP addresses? The answer is that they frequently talk to one another, exchanging information about the organization of the Internet. These exchanges must occur frequently because the structure of the Internet changes frequently as routers are added or dropped. Protocols for exchanging organization information are called *dynamic routing protocols*. There are many dynamic routing protocols, including the *Routing Information Protocol* (RIP), *Open Shortest Path First* (OSPF), the *Border Gateway Protocol (*BGP), and Cisco Systems' proprietary *Enhanced Interior Gateway Routing Protocol* (EIGRP). Each is used under different circumstances. These protocols have widely different security features, and different versions of each protocol have different levels of functionality.

If an attacker can impersonate a router, he or she can send false dynamic routing protocol messages to other routers. These false messages could cause the routers to misdeliver their packets. The attacker could even cause packets to pass through the attacker's computer, in order to read their contents.

The protocols just listed have widely different security features, and different versions of each protocol have different levels of security functionality.

5.8.5 Simple Network Management Protocol (SNMP). Networks often have many elements—routers, switches, and host computers. Managing dozens, hundreds, or thousands of devices can be nearly impossible. To make management easier, the IETF developed the *Simple Network Management Protocol* (SNMP). As Exhibit 5.21 shows, the manager program can send SNMP messages to managed devices to determine their conditions. The manager program can even send configuration messages that can change the ways in which remote devices operate. This allows the manager to fix many problems remotely.

Many firms disable remote configuration because of the damage that attackers could do with it. They could simply turn off all ports on switches and routers, or they could do more subtle damage.

5.9 APPLICATION STANDARDS. Most applications have their own application layer standards. In fact, given the large number of applications in the world, there are literally hundreds of application layer standards.

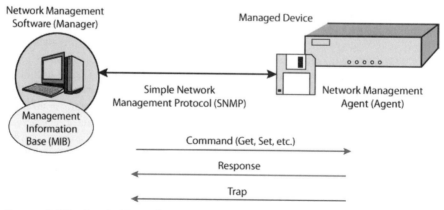

Exhibit 5.21 Simple Network Management Protocol (SNMP)

As corporations get better at defending against attacks at lower layers, attackers have begun to focus their attention on application vulnerabilities. If an attacker can take over an application running with high privileges, he or she obtains these privileges. Many applications run at the highest privileges, and attackers that compromise them own the box.

5.9.1 HTTP and HTML.

Many applications have two types of standards. One is a transport standard to transfer application layer messages between applications on different machines. For the World Wide Web, this is the *Hypertext Transfer Protocol* (HTTP). The other is a standard for document structure. The main document structure standard for the WWW is the *Hypertext Markup Language* (HTML).

Netscape, which created the first widely used browser, also created a security standard to protect HTTP communication. This was *Secure Sockets Layer* (SSL). Later, the Internet Engineering Task Force took over SSL and changed the name of the standard to *Transport Layer Security* (TLS).

5.9.2 E-Mail.

Popular transfer standards for email are the *Simple Mail Transfer Protocol* (SMTP), *Post Office Protocol* (POP), and *Internet Message Access Protocol* (IMAP) for downloading e-mail to a client from a mailbox on a server. Popular document body standards include RFC 2822 (for all-text messages), HTML, and Multipurpose Internet Mail Extensions (MIME). S/MIME (Secure MIME) adds public-key encryption (see Chapter 7) to MIME and is defined in RFCs 2634, 3850, and 3851.

An obvious security issue in e-mail is content filtering. Viruses, spam, phishing messages, and other undesirable content should be filtered out before they reach users and can do damage. (For more information on spam and other low-technology attacks, see Chapter 20 in this *Handbook*; for malware and spam countermeasures see Chapters 26, 27, 31, and 41.)

Another security issue in e-mail is securing messages flowing from the sending client to the sender's mail server, to the receiver's mail server, and to the receiving client. Fortunately, there are security standards for part or all of the message flows, including SSL/TLS and S/MIME among others. Unfortunately, the IETF has been unable to agree on a security standard.

When Web mail, which uses HTTP and HTML for e-mail communication, is used, then SSL/TLS can work between the sender and the sender's mail server and between the receiver's mail server and the receiver. Transmission between the e-mail servers is another issue. Of course, senders can send encrypted message bodies directly to receivers. However, this prevents filtering at firewalls. Users should be particularly careful about using Web mail via wireless connections. (See Chapters 32 and 33.)

5.9.3 Telnet, FTP, and SSH.

The two earliest applications on the Internet were the *File Transfer Protocol* (FTP) and *Telnet*. FTP provides bulk file transfers between hosts. Telnet allows a user to launch a command shell (user interface) on another computer. Neither of these standards has any security. Of particular concern is that both send passwords in the clear (without encryption) during login. The newer *Secure SHell* (SSH) standard can be used in place of both FTP and Telnet while providing high security.

5.9.4 Other Application Standards.

There are many other applications and therefore application standards. These include *Voice over IP* (VoIP; see Chapter 34 in this *Handbook*), *peer-to-peer applications* (P2P; see Chapter 35), and *service-oriented architecture* (SOA) and Web service applications (see Chapters 21, 30, and 31), among many others. Most applications have serious security issues. Application security has become perhaps the most complex aspect of network security (see Chapters 38, 39, and 40).

5.10   CONCLUDING REMARKS.   It is impossible to understand information security without a strong knowledge of networking. This chapter is designed to give you a working overview of networking. It is likely to be sufficient if you run into basic networking questions while reading other chapters. However, to work in security, you will need a much stronger knowledge of networking. The books and other resources cited in Section 5.11 are a good start in that direction.

5.11   FURTHER READING

Comer, D. E. *Internetworking with TCP/IP Vol.1: Principles, Protocols, and Architecture*, 5th ed. Upper Saddle River, NJ: Prentice-Hall, 2005.

Ferrero, A. *The Eternal Ethernet*. Boston: Addison-Wesley, 1999.

FitzGerald, J. and A. Dennis. *Business Data Communications and Networking*, 9th ed. Upper Saddle River, NJ: Prentice-Hall, 2006.

Freedman, A. *Computer Desktop Encyclopedia*. Point Pleasant, PA: Computer Language Company, 2008. Available on CD-ROM and online from www.computerlanguage.com.

Kurose, J. F., and K. W. Ross. *Computer Networking: A Top-Down Approach*, 4th ed. Boston: Addison-Wesley, 2007.

Muller, N. J. *Wireless Data Networking*. Boston: Artech House Publishers, 1995.

Panko, R. R. *Business Data Networks and Telecommunications*, 6th ed. Upper Saddle River, NJ: Prentice-Hall, 2006.

Panko, R. R. *Corporate Computer and Network Security*. Upper Saddle River, NJ: Prentice-Hall, 2004.

Price, R. *Fundamentals of Wireless Networking*. Boston: Career Education, 2006.

Rackley, S. *Wireless Networking Technology: From Principles to Successful Implementation*. Boston: Newnes, 2007.

Spurgeon, C. *Ethernet: The Definitive Guide*. Sebastopol, CA: O'Reilly, 2000.

Stevens, W. R. *TCP/IP Illustrated, Volume 1: The Protocols*. Boston: Addison-Wesley, 1994.

5.12   NOTES

1. www.faqs.org/rfcs3833.html

2. www.faqs.org/rfcs2535.html

3. www.dncssec.org

CHAPTER 6

NETWORK TOPOLOGIES, PROTOCOLS, AND DESIGN

Gary C. Kessler and N. Todd Pritsky

This chapter provides a broad overview of local area network (LAN) concepts, basic terms, standards, and technologies. These topics are important to give the information security professional a better understanding of the terms that might be used to describe a particular network implementation and its products. The chapter also is written with an eye to what information security professionals need to know; for a more complete overview of the topic, the reader is referred to general LAN texts, such as those listed in Section 6.10.

6.1 OVERVIEW.   There are a number of ways to describe a LAN, and each will provide a glimpse as to implementation and product differences as well as points of security exposures. This section introduces various terms and perspectives as a basis for the discussion in the following sections.

6.1.1 LAN Characteristics.   One way of describing LANs is to describe the characteristics that distinguish a *local* network from other types of networks. The most common characteristics are:

- Small geographic scope (the two most distant stations may be up to 5 kilometers [km] or so apart)
- Fast speed (data rates well in excess of 1 Mbps], up to 1 Gbps])
- Special media (common use of coaxial cable and optical fiber, as well as twisted pair)
- Private ownership

This type of network, then, has a very different look and feel than the Internet or some other public or private wide area networks (WAN). More people have access to the LAN infrastructure than to the infrastructure of just about any WAN. LAN users can easily "spy" on each other by sniffing packets, something that is generally very difficult on the Internet. A single user can bring the LAN to a standstill.

The corporate LAN is generally the users' primary access to the Internet. The users on the LAN are behind the corporate firewall and router; some studies suggest that they are responsible for 80 percent of security incidents.

Often these attacks are due to users' lack of education and awareness, such as choosing poor passwords, not maintaining up-to-date virus signature files, or leaving modems attached to computers on the LAN. Sometimes the attacks are deliberate, such as using a packet sniffer to learn another user's password or taking steps to degrade network performance.

6.1.2 LAN Components.   In general, there are four basic components required to build a LAN, providing their own vulnerabilities and exposures from a security perspective:

1. **Computers.** These are the basic devices that are connected on the network. Read "computer" very broadly; the term can include personal computers (PCs), minicomputers, mainframes, file servers, printers, plotters, communications servers, and network interconnection devices. It can also include protocol analyzers.

2. **Media.** These are the physical means by which the computers are interconnected. LAN media include unshielded twisted pair (UTP), coaxial cable (coax), optical fiber, and wireless devices. The wireline media have connection points throughout an area where devices can attach to the network, and everyplace is a potential connection point in a wireless environment.

3. **Network interface card (NIC).** This is the physical attachment from the computer to the LAN medium. Most NICs are internal cards, and all that actually is seen is the physical attachment to the LAN, often an RJ-45 jack. NICs range widely in price depending on their capabilities, intended use, and vendor; a

no-name, 10 Mbps Ethernet NIC for a desktop personal computer (PC) can be had for less than $10; a 3Com 10/100 Mbps PC Card NIC for a laptop can cost over $150.

4. **Software.** The three components above provide physical connectivity. Software—often called a network operating system (NOS)—is necessary for the devices to actually take advantage of the resource sharing that the LAN can provide. The NOS can support many types of services such as file sharing, print sharing, client/server operation, communications services, and more.

While the LAN needs to be examined in a holistic fashion, each of these components at each attached node also may require examination.

6.1.3 LAN Technology Parameters.
One final way of discussing the specific operation of the LAN is to describe the technology:

- **Physical topology.** The physical layout of the medium.
- **Logical topology.** The logical relationship of the LAN nodes to each other.
- **Medium Access Control (MAC) Standard.** The specification describing the rules that each node follows to determine when it is its turn to transmit on the medium.
- **Use of the Logical Link Control (LLC) protocol.** Defines the frame format employed above the MAC layer, and additional services.
- **Use of higher-layer protocols.** Defines the node-to-node communicating protocols and additional higher-layer applications.

6.1.4 Summary.
It does not matter how a LAN is classified or described. It is essential, however, that the LAN be understood from a variety of perspectives to be able to apply a network security examination.

6.2 LAN TOPOLOGY.
Wide area networks typically use some sort of switched technology, such as traditional circuit switching, packet switching (e.g., X.25), or fast packet switching (e.g., frame relay, asynchronous transfer mode [ATM]). Indeed, the network switches are typically connected by point-to-point lines so that there is a single data transmission on the line at one time.

Historically, LANs have been broadcast networks, meaning that every LAN station hears every transmission on the medium. LAN topologies, then, have to support the broadcast nature of the network and provide full connectivity between all stations.

The *topology* of a network is used to describe two issues. The *physical topology* describes how the LAN stations are physically connected so that they can communicate with each other. The *logical topology* describes how the broadcast nature of the LAN is actually effected, and, therefore, how stations participate in the process of obtaining permission to transmit on the medium. There are three common topologies found in LANs: star, ring, and bus.

6.2.1 Network Control.
Since LANs are broadcast networks, it is imperative that only a single node be allowed to transmit at any one time. All LANs use a *distributed access control* scheme, meaning that all nodes follow the same rules to access the network medium and no one LAN node controls the other nodes' access. In this way, LAN nodes can come online and off-line without bringing the network down.

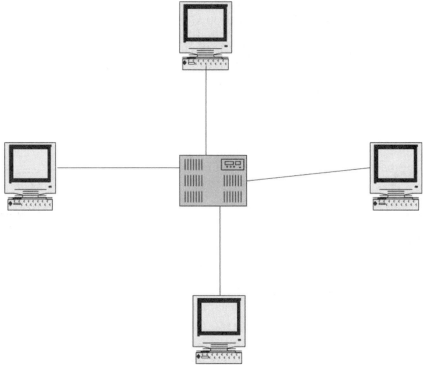

Exhibit 6.1   Star Topology

This is *not* meant to suggest that there are no critical elements in a LAN. Indeed, if a central hub, switch, or transmitter fails, the LAN will crash. Distributed control *does* suggest, however, that all nodes (user stations) follow the same access rules, and failure of a single *node* will not bring the LAN down. The access control scheme is defined by the MAC protocol.

6.2.2   Star Topology.   In a *star topology* (see Exhibit 6.1), all devices on the LAN are interconnected through some central device. Since LANs use distributed access control schemes, all communication is from one node to another, and the central device merely provides a pathway between pairs of devices.

Physical star topologies have a tremendous advantage over other topologies in that they greatly ease network administration, maintenance, reconfiguration, and error recovery. Disadvantages include the potential single point of failure.

6.2.3   Ring Topology.   In a *ring topology*, the nodes are connected by a set of point-to-point links that are organized in a circularly closed fashion (see Exhibit 6.2). Stations connect to the medium using *active taps* that are actually bit repeaters; a bit is read from the input line, held for a single bit time, then transmitted out to the output line.

A station transmits a message on the network by sending out a bit stream on its outgoing link; thus, rings are unidirectional in nature. Since all of the other stations see the bits one at a time, the intended receiver has no prior warning about an incoming message. For this reason, the transmitter is responsible for removing the message from

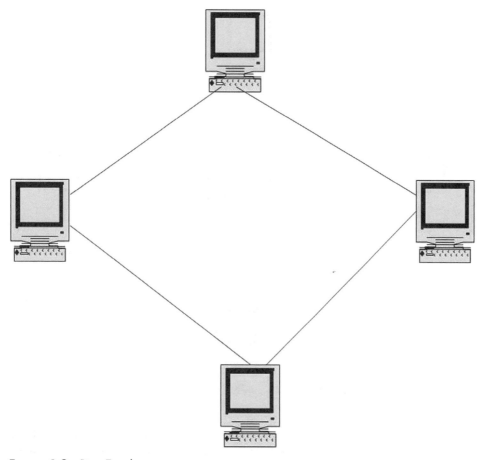

Exhibit 6.2 Ring Topology

the ring when the bits come back around. The MAC scheme ensures that multiple stations do not transmit at the same time.

In addition, a ring is a *serial broadcast* network. Because a station sends a message one bit at a time, every other station will see the message as it passes through but each will be receiving a different part of the message at any point in time.

Rings are a common physical LAN topology, although, like stars, they have the potential of a single point of failure; if one link or one active tap fails, the integrity of the ring is destroyed. This problem is of such a critical nature that nearly all ring products use a star-wiring scheme or have some sort of redundancy built in for just this eventuality.

6.2.4 Bus Topology. In a *bus topology* (see Exhibit 6.3), all devices are connected to a single electrically continuous medium; for this reason, this topology is also called a common cable or shared medium network. Nodes attach to the medium using a *passive tap*, one that monitors the bit flow without altering it. This is similar to the operation of a voltmeter; it measures the voltage on a power line without changing the available voltage.

Bus networks are analogous to the way appliances are connected to an AC power line. All of the devices draw power from the same source, even if they are on different

EXHIBIT 6.3   Bus Topology

physical segments of the power distribution network within the building. In addition, the operation of the devices is independent of each other; if the coffeepot breaks, the toaster will still work.

A bus is a *simultaneous broadcast* network, meaning that all stations receive a transmitted message at essentially the same time (ignoring propagation delay through the medium). Most home and business LANs employ a *baseband bus* where DC signals are applied directly to the bus by the transmitter without any modification. In addition, transmissions on a baseband bus are broadcast bidirectionally and cannot be altered by the receivers. Bus LAN technologies are employed on cable television systems. For example, they employ a *broadband bus* where the signals are modulated (i.e., frequency shifted) to certain frequencies for transmission in one direction or another.

Buses are the oldest LAN topology and are generally limited in the type of medium that they can use. They do not usually suffer from single-point-of-failure problems.

6.2.5 Physical versus Logical Topology.

A distinction was made above between the *physical* and *logical* topology of a LAN. As suggested above, physical topology describes how the stations are physically positioned and attached to each other while the logical topology describes how the signals propagate and the logical operation of the network.

In all of today's commonly-used LANs, the logical topology differs from the physical topology. The most common LAN configuration today is a *star-wired bus* (see Exhibit 6.4). This type of network has a star topology where all stations are physically attached with point-to-point links to a central device. This central device contains a bus that interconnects all of the I/O ports in such a way that when one station transmits a message, all stations will receive it. Since this acts exactly like a simultaneous broadcast, or bus, network, we categorize this configuration as a physical star, logical bus.

Another common configuration is a *star-wired ring* (see Exhibit 6.5). In this configuration, the bits will travel in logical order from station A to B, C, A, and so forth, which matches the serial broadcast operation of a ring. We call this a physical star, logical ring.

Although uncommon today, another hybrid technology is the *bus-wired ring* (see Exhibit 6.6). In this configuration, nodes are passively attached to a single cable, forming a physical bus. Each station maintains a table specifying the address of predecessor and successor stations, thus forming a logical ring.

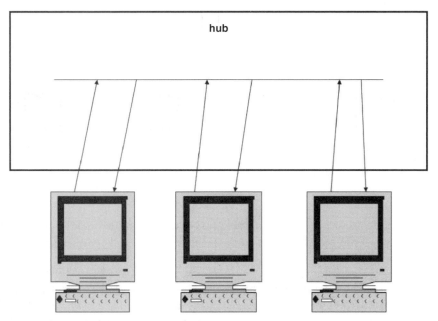

EXHIBIT 6.4 Star-Wired Bus

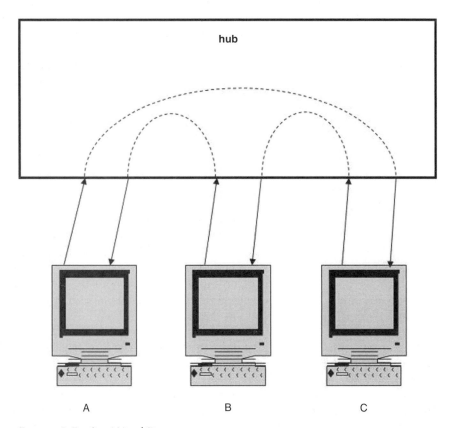

EXHIBIT 6.5 Star-Wired Ring

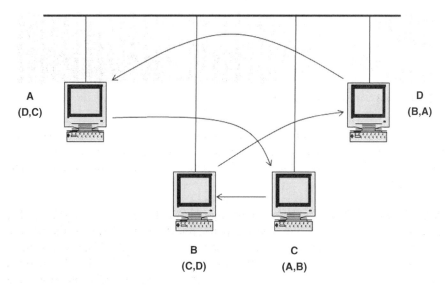

A
(D,C)

D
(B,A)

B
(C,D)

C
(A,B)

EXHIBIT 6.6 Bus-Wired Ring (The station identifier is shown above the station ID of the predecessor and successor stations in the logical ring.)

6.3 MEDIA. The next paragraphs discuss the three primary types of LAN media that are currently being used. Due to their relatively high speed, small geographic size, and protected environments, a number of media types can be employed with LANs.

6.3.1 Coaxial Cable. Coaxial cable (coax) is the original LAN medium. It gets its name from the physical composition of the cable itself (see Exhibit 6.7). At the center of the cable is a conductor, usually made of copper that is surrounded by an insulator, which, in turn, is surrounded by another conductor that acts as an electrical shield. Since the shield completely surrounds the central conductor and the two have a common axis, the shield prevents external electrical noise from affecting signals on the conductor and prevents signals on the conductor from generating noise that affects other cables.

Coaxial cables vary in size from $\frac{1}{4}$ inch to 1 inch, depending on the thickness of the conductor, shield, and insulation. Applications for coax range from cable television to LANs. Speeds in excess of several hundred Mbps at distances of several hundred to several thousand meters can be achieved. Coaxial cable also has a high immunity from electromagnetic and radio frequency interference.

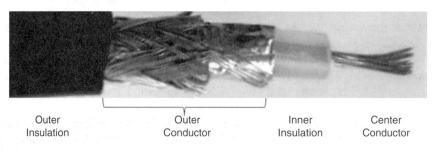

Outer
Insulation

Outer
Conductor

Inner
Insulation

Center
Conductor

EXHIBIT 6.7 Coaxial Cable

Exhibit 6.8 Unshielded Twisted Pair

Coaxial cable is only seen in physical bus LANs such as Ethernet. The original Ethernet specification, in fact, called for a thin coaxial cable; a later version that employed thin (CATV) coax was dubbed CheaperNet. Coax is not typically found in star or ring networks.

6.3.2 Twisted Pair. The medium enjoying the largest popularity for LAN applications today is twisted pair. Twisted pair cable consists of two insulated copper conductors that are twisted around each other (see Exhibit 6.8). This is typically 22- to 26-gauge wire, the same that is used for telephone wiring. Twisting the conductors around each other minimizes the effect of external electrical radiation on the signal carried on the wire; if external voltage is applied to one wire of the pair, it will be applied equally to the other wire. The twisting, then, effectively eliminates the effect of the external noise. As the number of twists per inch increases, the noise reduction characteristics improve; unfortunately, so does the overall amount of cable and the cost. Most twisted pair for telephony applications has 10 to 15 twists per foot.

The type of twisted pair cable shown in Exhibit 6.8 is called *unshielded twisted pair* (UTP) because the wire pair itself is not shielded. The data-carrying capacity of UTP is generally indicated by its *category*:

Category 1 (Cat. 1) cable is generally unsuited for data applications.

Category 3 (Cat. 3) cable is rated for 10 Mbps over a wire segment of 100 m. (although speeds of 100 Mbps can often be achieved). Cat. 3 cable is rated up to 16 megahertz (MHz).

Category 5 (Cat. 5) cable is rated for voice or data at speeds up to 100 Mbps over a wire segment of 100 meters Cat. 5e is rated for full-duplex and 1 gigabit (Gbps) Ethernet. Cat. 5 and 5e cable is rated up to 100 MHz.

Category 6 (Cat. 6) cable is rated to 250 MHz over a wire segment between 15 and 100 meters in length. Cat 6. is intended for use for very-high-speed broadband applications at data rates up to 10 Gbps.

Category 7 (Cat. 7) cable is rated up to 750 MHz. Each pair of wires in the cable sheath, and the sheath itself, are shielded to prevent electromagnetic interference at data rates in the multigigabit-per-second range.

UTP is commonly found in physical star-wired bus and ring LANs; it is never used in a physical bus and rarely in a physical ring.

Another twisted pair variant is *shielded twisted pair* (STP), where each cable pair is surrounded by a metallic shield that provides the same function as the outer conductor in coaxial cable. STP is only used in the IBM Token Ring, a star-wired ring.

6.3.3 Optical Fiber. Optical fiber is a thin flexible medium that acts as a waveguide for signals in the 10^{14}– to 10^{-15}-Hz range, which includes the visible light spectrum and part of the infrared spectrum. Optical fiber is a great medium for digital communications; it is essentially immune to any type of radio or magnetic interference and almost impossible to tap surreptitiously. Theoretically able to achieve data rates on the order of trillions of bits per second, optical fiber realistically can achieve rates of 10 Gbps which is the practical limit on the electronics performing optical-electrical conversion.

In WAN applications, this speed limit is exceeded in one of two ways.

1. An optical switch can terminate optical fiber without any electrical-optical conversion.

2. Dense wave division multiplexing (DWDM) allows many 10 Gbps bit streams to be carried on a single-fiber strand simultaneously. These technologies may well eventually find their way to the LAN.

The electronics are a critical part of any optical fiber system. The incoming electrical signal to be transmitted on the fiber is converted to an optical signal by the transmitter. Common optical sources are a *light-emitting diode* (LED*)* or *injection laser diode* (ILD). LEDs are less expensive than ILDs but are limited to lower speeds. The optical signal is received by a device called a *photodiode*, which essentially counts photons and converts the count to an electrical signal. Common photodiodes include the *positive-intrinsic-negative* (PIN) *photodiode* and *avalanche photodiode* (APD). The PIN is less expensive than the APD but is limited to lower speeds.

The physical and transmission characteristics of optical fiber are shown in Exhibit 6.9. At the center of an optical fiber cable is the *core*, a thin, flexible medium capable of carrying a light signal. The core is typically between 2 and 125 micrometers (µm), or microns, in diameter and may be made from a variety of glass or plastic compounds. Surrounding the core is a layer called the *cladding*. The optical characteristics of the cladding are always different from the core's characteristics so that light signals traveling through the core at an angle will reflect back and stay in the core. The cladding may vary in thickness from a few to several hundred microns. The outermost layer is the *jacket*. Composed of plastic or rubber, the jacket's function is to provide the cable with physical protection from moisture, handling, and other environmental factors.

Two types of optical fiber cable are used for voice and data communications, differentiated by their transmission characteristics (see Exhibit 6.9). *Multimode fiber* (MMF) has a core diameter between 50 and 125 µm. Because this diameter is relatively large, light rays at different angles will be traveling through the core. This phenomenon, known as *modal dispersion*, has the effect of limiting the bit rate and/or distance of the cable. MMF cable is generally limited to a maximum cable length of 2 km. *Single-mode fiber* (SMF) eliminates the multiple path problem of MMF by using a thin core with a diameter of 2 to 8 µm. This thin-core cable results in a single propagation path so that very high bandwidths over large distances (up to 10 km) can be achieved.

SMF is the most expensive type of fiber and is usually used for long-haul data and telecommunications networks. MMF is commonly used on LANs; it is less expensive but can still handle the required data rates and distances.

6.3.4 Wireless "Media." Wireless LANs use radio signals to interconnect LAN nodes. Wireless LANs are very common in environments where:

- It is difficult to install new wiring (e.g., in a building with asbestos in the walls).
- There are mobile users (e.g., in a hospital or car rental agency).

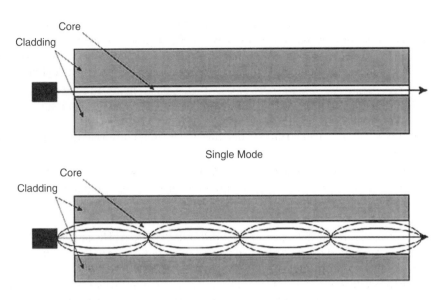

Single Mode

Graded-index Multimode

EXHIBIT 6.9 Optical Fiber Cable

- Right-of-ways for wiring are hard to obtain (e.g., campus environments that span roadways).
- A temporary network is necessary (e.g., at a conference or meeting).
- Residential areas have no other networking facilities.
- Conference centers, hotels, and colleges and universities need wide and easy network access.

Wireless LANs generally employ infrared, spread spectrum, or microwave communications technology. *Infrared* (IR) is used for a variety of communications, monitoring, and control applications, such as linking computers to wireless printers, "beaming" business cards between personal digital assistants (PDAs), cordless modems, and wireless mice. It is also used for such non-LAN applications as home entertainment remote control, building security intrusion and motion detectors, medical diagnostic equipment, and missile guidance systems. For wireless LANs, the most common IR communications band uses signals with a wavelength in the range 800 to 1,000 nanometers (nm, or 10^{-9} m). *Diffused IR* operates at data rates between 1 to 4 Mbps at distances up to 200 feet, and can be used for stationary or mobile LAN nodes. *Directed Beam IR*, which requires line-of-sight, operates at data rates from 1 to 10 Mbps at distances up to 80 feet. R systems are limited to a single room because the signals cannot pass through walls.

Spread spectrum is a wireless communications technology in the region of 2.4 or 5 gigahertz (GHz, or billions of cycles per second), where the actual frequency of the transmitted signal is deliberately varied during transmission. Originally, the frequency shifting was for security purposes to prevent monitoring of the communications channels. Two types of spread spectrum technology are used in LANs:

1. In *frequency hopping spread spectrum* (FHSS),[1] the transmitter sends the signal over a set of radio frequencies, hopping from frequency to frequency at

split-second intervals in what appears to be a random sequence. The sequence is not random, however, and the receiver changes frequencies in synchronization with the transmitter. FHSS can support data rates from 1 to 3 Mbps up to a distance of 300 feet.

2. In *direct sequence spread spectrum* (DSSS), each bit in the original data stream is represented by multiple bits in the transmitted signal, spreading the signal across a wide frequency range. One result of DSSS is that the system can achieve a greater bandwidth than the original signal. DSSS can support data rates from 2 to 20 Mbps up to a distance of 800 feet.

Microwave LANs refers to communications in the area of 1, 5, and 19 GHz. Electromagnetic energy with a frequency higher than 1 GHz) and data rates up to 20 Mbps can be maintained for distances up to 130 feet. One major disadvantage of microwave is that Federal Communications Commission (FCC) licensing is required for many of these frequencies.

6.3.5 Summary.   In the early 1980s, coaxial cable was the most commonly used LAN medium. Twisted pair, used for telephony applications, was not used in LANs because high speeds could not be achieved. Optical fiber technology was still in its infancy and was very expensive. All of this changed by the early 1990s, when the electronics to drive twisted pair had dramatically improved, and optical fiber technology had greatly matured. It is rare to see coaxial cable used in a LAN today; instead, UTP (less costly than coax) or optical fiber (higher speeds than coax) is more often employed. Wireless LANs are still more costly than wire-based networks, and more difficult to secure, so they remain a niche market.

6.4 MEDIA ACCESS CONTROL.   As mentioned, LANs are broadcast networks connecting peer devices, all having equal access to the medium. These characteristics place two requirements on the protocol that controls access to the network:

1. There can be only one station transmitting at any given time since multiple transmitters would result in garbled messages.

2. All stations must follow the same rules for accessing the network since there is no master station.

The schemes controlling access to the network medium are called *media access control* (MAC) protocols. Although many different LAN MAC schemes have been introduced in working products, the most common ones are essentially variants of two approaches: *contention* and *distributed polling*.

6.4.1 Contention.   A contention network can be compared to a group of people sitting around a conference table without a chairperson. When someone wants to speak, it is necessary first to determine whether anyone else is already speaking; if someone else is speaking, no one else can begin until that person has stopped. When a person detects silence at the table, he or she starts to talk. If two people start to talk at the same time, a *collision* has occurred and must be resolved. In the human analogy, collisions are resolved in one of two ways: Either both speakers stop and defer to each other ("polite backoff") or both continue speaking louder and louder until one gives up (a "rudeness algorithm").

The contention scheme used in LANs is actually very similar to the polite backoff situation, and is called *carrier sense multiple access with collision detection* (CSMA/CD). CSMA/CD is one of the oldest LAN MAC schemes in use today, used originally in Ethernet and becoming the basis of the IEEE 802.3 standard (to be described). Although there have been other contention schemes used on LANs, CSMA/CD is the one that has survived and thrived in the marketplace.

CSMA/CD works on logical bus networks. When a station is ready to transmit, it first listens to the network medium ("carrier sense"). If the station detects a transmission on the line, it will continue to monitor the channel until it is idle. Once silence is detected, the station with a message to send will start to transmit. Stations continue to monitor the channel during transmission so that if a collision is detected, all transmitters stop transmitting.

CSMA/CD networks employ a *backoff scheme* so that the first collision does not bring the network down. Without a backoff scheme, all transmitters would detect a collision and stop transmitting; after again hearing silence on the line, however, all stations would once again start transmitting and would again collide with each other. The backoff scheme causes stations to make a random decision whether to transmit or not after silence is detected on the channel after a collision has occurred.

CSMA/CD uses a backoff scheme called *truncated binary exponential backoff*. Although this name is a mouthful, it actually describes the process very precisely. When a station is ready to transmit and detects silence on the line, it will attempt to send a message with a probability of 1 (i.e., 100 percent likelihood that it will transmit); this probability is called the *persistency* of the MAC scheme.[2] If a collision occurs, the station will stop transmitting and again wait for silence on the line. When silence is again detected, the station will transmit with a probability of $\frac{1}{2}$ (i.e., there is a 50 percent chance that it will transmit and a 50 percent chance that it will not). If two stations were involved in the collision and they both back off to a $\frac{1}{2}$-persistent condition, then there is a 50 percent chance that one will transmit and one will defer at the next transmission opportunity, a 25 percent chance that both will defer at the next opportunity, and a 25 percent chance that both will collide again.

If a station collides again, its persistency is again cut in half, now to $\frac{1}{4}$. All stations involved in the collision(s) drop their persistency and each station independently determines whether it will transmit at the next occurrence of silence or not.

As long as collisions occur, the persistency is continually cut in half until the station either successfully transmits or has 16 unsuccessful attempts to transmit the message. After 16 failed attempts, the station gives up.[3] After the station successfully transmits *or* has 16 unsuccessful attempts, the station's persistency returns to 1 and the operation continues as before.

Wireless LANs also use a form of contention, but it is generally not CSMA/CD because collision detection is not practical in a wireless environment. Instead, the stations still employ CSMA—they listen for an idle channel—but they do not necessarily transmit when the channel is idle. Instead, they wait to see if the channel remains idle for some period of time in an attempt to stave off a collision. This is a form of *CSMA with collision avoidance* (CSMA/CA).

6.4.2 Distributed Polling.   Imagine that the same group of people are sitting around the same conference table, still without a chairperson. One person at the table has a microphone and can say anything to anyone in the room. Everyone in the room, of course, will hear the message. The rule here is that the only person who is allowed to speak is the one with the microphone; furthermore, the person will hold on to the microphone only while he or she has something to say and can hold on to it only for some maximum amount of time. When the first person is done talking, the microphone is passed to the next person at the table. Person 2 can now speak or immediately pass the microphone on to person 3. Eventually, the first person at the table will get the microphone back and get another opportunity to talk.

The scheme just described is implemented in LANs with a scheme called *token passing*. This is the basis for the IBM Token Ring and represents the second most commonly used LAN MAC algorithm. Token passing, in one variant or another, is the basis for the IEEE 802.4 and 802.5 standards, as well as for the Fiber Distributed Data Interface (FDDI).

Token passing requires a logical ring topology. When a station has data to send to another station, it must wait to receive a bit pattern representing the *token*. Tokens are sent in such a way that only one station will see it at any given time; in this way, if a station sees the token, it has temporary, exclusive ownership of the network.

If a station receives the token and has no data to send, it passes the token on. If it does have data to send, it generates a *frame* containing the data. After sending the frame, the station will generate and send another token.

A *token ring* network is a logical ring implemented on a physical topology that supports a serial broadcast operation (i.e., a star or a ring). Each station receives transmissions one bit at a time and regenerates the bits for the next station. A station transmitting a frame will send the bits on its output link and receive them back on its input link. The transmitter, then, is responsible for removing its message from the network. When finished transmitting, the station transfers control to another station by sending the bits comprising a token on its output link. The next station on the ring that wants to transmit *and* sees the token can then send its data frame. Token rings (standardized in 802.5 and FDDI) are the most common implementation of token passing.

A *token bus* network (as specified in 802.4) is conceptually similar to the token ring, except that it is implemented using a simultaneous broadcast topology (i.e., a bus). In this physical topology, all stations hear all transmissions. A station that wants to send data to another will address a frame to the intended receiver on the network, as in a CSMA/CD bus. When done transmitting, the station will address a token to the next station logically in the ring; while all stations will hear the token transmission, only the one station to which it is addressed will pick it up. After receiving a token, a station may or may not transmit data, but it is, in any case, responsible for passing the token to the next station in the logical ring. Eventually, the token will return to the first station.

6.5 LAN PROTOCOLS AND STANDARDS. The Open Systems Interconnection (OSI) Reference Model continues to be the standard framework with which to describe data communications architectures, including those for LANs. The basic LAN protocol architecture maps easily to the OSI model, as discussed in this section.

6.5.1 OSI Model versus LAN Model Architectures. Although the LAN protocol architecture can be related to the OSI model, there is not a perfect one-to-one mapping of the protocol layers (see Exhibit 6.10). The OSI Physical Layer is analogous to a LAN Physical Layer (PHY). Both specify such things as:

- Electrical characteristics of the interface
- Mechanical characteristics of the connector and medium

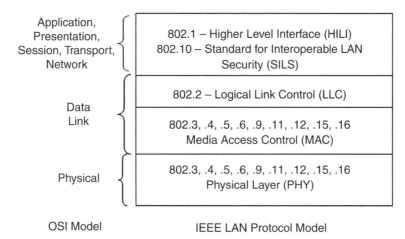

EXHIBIT 6.10 IEEE versus LAN Protocol Models

- Interface circuits and their functions
- Properties of the medium
- Signaling speed
- Signaling method

Most LAN physical layer specifications actually comprise two sublayers. The lower sublayer describes physical layer aspects that are specific to a given medium; the higher sublayer describes those aspects that are media-independent.

The OSI Data Link Layer, responsible for error-free communication between any two communicating devices, is represented by two sublayers in a LAN. The lower sublayer is the MAC, which deals with issues of how the station should access the network medium. The MAC is responsible for error-free communication over the PHY and specifies such things as:

- Framing
- Addressing
- Bit-error detection
- Control and maintenance of the MAC protocol
- Rules governing medium access

The upper sublayer is called the Logical Link Control (LLC). The LLC protocol is responsible for maintaining a logical connection between two communicating LAN stations. The LLC specifies such rules as:

- Frame sequencing
- Error control
- Establishment and termination of a logical connection
- Addressing of higher layer services

Recalling that the main functions of the network layer are routing and congestion control, there are two reasons that no LAN protocol layer acts strictly like the OSI Network Layer

1. There is no need for a routing algorithm in a broadcast network because all stations receive all transmissions; the address of the intended receiver is included in the transmission itself.

2. Congestion control is also not an issue in a broadcast network; a broadcast network must be limited to a single transmitter at a time, and this is accomplished by the MAC layer.

There are no standards for LANs corresponding to the upper four layers of the OSI model. Even in the somewhat less organized 1980s, end-to-end protocols as such were not required in a LAN environment because the end-to-end communication was limited to nodes on the LAN, and for that the MAC guaranteed error-free communication.

Only when LAN interconnection, via WAN and LAN access to the Internet, gained popularity did other end-to-end protocols become necessary. Of course, IP (and other network layer protocols) grew in demand as well. Those protocols are generally associated with the communications software as part of a network operating system (NOS), and these will be discussed later.

6.5.2   IEEE 802 Standards.

Although they are not directly related to security, it is useful to be familiar with the standards describing LANs, the most common of which are the Institute for Electronics and Electrical Engineers (IEEE) 802 standards. The IEEE Computer Society formed the Project 802 Committee in February 1980 to create standards for LANs, as part of its more general work on standards for microprocessors; no other organization was making any similar standardization efforts. Originally, there was to be a single LAN standard, operating at a speed between 1 and 20 Mbps. The standard was divided into three parts: PHY, MAC, and a High Level Interface (HILI) to allow other protocol suites to have a common protocol boundary with the LAN. The original MAC was based on the Ethernet standard, but other MAC schemes were quickly added and, over the years, the 802 committee has addressed many LAN schemes. They all have in common an interface to a single LLC protocol that provides a common interface between the HILI and any MAC.

A description of the Project 802 working groups (WG) and their status as of October 2007 follows.[4]

802.1—High Level Interface (HILI). Provides the framework for higher-layer issues, including end-to-end protocols, bridging, internetworking, network management, routing, and performance measurement.

802.2—Logical Link Control. Provides a consistent interface between any LAN MAC and higher-layer protocols. Depending on the options employed, the LLC can provide error detection and correction, sequential delivery, and multiprotocol encapsulation. The 802.2 standard is described in more detail in Section 3.5.6. This WG is currently in *hibernation*.[5]

802.3—CSMA/CD. Defines the MAC and PHY specifications for a CSMA/CD bus network. This specification is discussed in more detail in Section 6.5.3. (The 802.3 CSMA/CD standard is based on Ethernet, described in Section 3.5.4.)

802.4—Token Bus. Defines the MAC and PHY specifications for a token-passing bus based on work originally done at General Motors as part of the Manufacturing Automation Protocol (MAP). Well suited for factory floors and assembly lines, MAP never achieved widespread use. This WG has been disbanded.[6]

802.5—Token Ring. Defines the MAC and PHY specifications for a token-passing ring. Although this WG is currently in hibernation, there remains a tremendous amount of token ring deployed and the market remains large, so this specification is discussed in more detail in Section 6.5.5.

802.6—Metropolitan Area Network (MAN). Defines the MAC and PHY specifications for a MAN. In particular, the 802.6 standard defines a MAC and PHY called Distributed Queue Dual Bus (DQDB), which was one of the MACs employed with the Switched Multimegabit Data Service (SMDS) and Connectionless Broadband Data Service (CBDS). Introduced in the early 1990s, neither service remains in common use today. This WG has been disbanded.

802.7—Broadband Technology Advisory Group (BBTAG). Advises other 802 subcommittees about changes in broadband technology and their effect on the 802 standards. This WG has been disbanded.

802.8—Fiber Optics Technology Advisory Group (FOTAG). Advises other 802 subcommittees about changes in optical fiber technology and their effect on the 802 standards. This WG has been disbanded.

802.9—Integrated Services LAN (ISLAN). Defines the MAC and PHY specifications for integrated voice/data terminal access to integrated services networks, including ISLANs and MANs, and Integrated Services Digital Networks (ISDN). The only practical implementation was deployed in IsoEthernet products, described in the IEEE 802.9a standard. This WG has been disbanded.

802.10—Standard for Interoperable LAN Security (SILS). Defines procedures for providing security mechanisms on interconnected LANs, including cryptography and certificates. This WG has been disbanded.

802.11—Wireless LANs (WLAN). Defines MAC and PHY specifications for "through the air" media. The 802.11 standard defines operation at 1 or 2 Mbps using the 2.4-GHz range and spread spectrum technology. One option employs a FHSS scheme, dividing the spectrum into 79 1-MHz bands and changing frequencies every 20 milliseconds using one of a set of predefined patterns. Another option uses DSSS and employs 11 separate channels simultaneously. Extensions to 802.11 include support for 5 and 11 Mbps speeds as well as use of the 5.2-GHz band for speeds ranging from 6 to 54 Mbps.

802.12—Demand Priority. Describes one of the MAC and PHY specifications originally proposed for 100 Mbps LAN speeds and dubbed *100BASE-VG/AnyLAN*. Largely unused, and the WG has been disbanded.

(802.13. This number was never assigned to a WG because it was felt that the *13* would hamper products in the marketplace.)

802.14—Cable-TV Based Broadband Communication Networks. Originally intended to describe LANs for cable TV systems. This WG has been disbanded.

802.15—Wireless Personal Area Networks (WPAN): Defines a MAC and PHY for a short distance wireless network between portable and mobile devices such as PCs, Personal Digital Assistants (PDAs), cell phones, pagers, and other communications equipment.

802.16—Broadband Wireless Access (BBWA). Defines the MAC and PHY for high-speed wireless network access over relatively short distances. BBWA standards address the "first-mile/last-mile" connection in wireless metropolitan area networks, extending the reach of residential broadband services such as cable modem or Digital Subscriber Line (DSL).

802.17—Resilient Packet Ring (RPR). Defines standards to support the development and deployment of RPR local, metropolitan, and wide area networks for resilient and efficient transfer of data packets at rates scalable to many gigabits per second.

802.18—Radio Regulatory Technical Advisory Group (RR-TAG). On behalf of other 802 WGs using radio-based communication, this TAG monitors, and actively participates in, ongoing national and international radio regulatory activities.

802.19—Coexistence Technical Advisory Group. Develops and maintains policies defining the responsibilities of 802 standards developers to address issues of coexistence with existing standards and other standards under development.

802.20—Mobile Broadband Wireless Access (MBWA). Defines the specification for a packet-based wireless interface that is optimized for IP-based services. The goal is to enable worldwide deployment of affordable, ubiquitous, always-on, and interoperable multivendor mobile broadband wireless access networks that meet the needs of business and residential end user markets.

802.21—Media Independent Handover. Developing standards to enable handover and interoperability between heterogeneous network types including both 802 and non-802 networks.

802.22—Wireless Regional Area Networks (WRAN). Developing a standard for a radio-based PHY, MAC, and air interface for use by license-exempt devices on a noninterfering basis in the spectrum allocated to broadcast television.

6.5.3   IEEE 802.3 CSMA/CD Standard.

The original IEEE 802.3 standard, first published in 1985, describes the PHY and MAC for a CSMA/CD bus network operating over thick coaxial cable. Today an 802.3 network implementation can employ any of a number of media types, including UTP and optical fiber. Without question, UTP is the most popular.

The 802.3 committee anticipated the different media types that might be used, and they developed a nomenclature to identify the actual physical implementation, using the format:

[speed (Mbps)][signaling type][segment length (m) or media type]

The original 802.3 specification, for example, operated at 10 Mbps, used baseband (digital) signaling and limited a single coaxial cable segment to a length of 500 m; the cable was designated 10BASE5.. In fact, the largest distance between two 802.3 stations could be 2.8 km, so repeaters might be used to interconnect several 500-m coaxial cable segments.

A less expensive version, called *CheaperNet*, was later introduced that operated over thin coaxial cable segments limited to 185 m; this PHY is denoted 10BASE2.

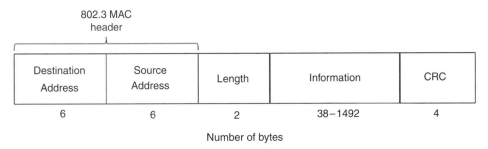

802.3 MAC
header

Destination Address	Source Address	Length	Information	CRC
6	6	2	38–1492	4

Number of bytes

EXHIBIT 6.11 IEEE 802.3 Frame Format

In the mid-1980s, AT&T introduced a product called StarLAN, which operated at 1 Mbps over UTP. Although this product has long been relegated to obscurity, it was the first to break the 1- Mbps barrier on UTP. Subsequent versions of 802.3 that employ UTP all use a star topology where each network node connects directly back to a central hub. The first 10-Mbps version of 802.3 was denoted 10BASE-T, the *T* indicating use of the UTP medium (which structured wiring standards say is limited to a distance of 100 m). The 10-Mbps optical fiber version of 802.3 is 10BASE-F. Today, of course, we have 100-Mbps and 1-Gbps versions (e.g., 100BASE-T and 1000BASE-T). Full-duplex Ethernet takes advantage of the point-to-point links in a star configuration and effectively doubles the line speed by allowing both stations to transmit at the same time.

Exhibit 6.11 shows the format of an IEEE 802.3 MAC frame, primarily for reference purposes. The fields and their functions are:

- **Preamble.** Used for clock synchronization; employs 7 repetitions of the 8-bit pattern 10101010. 8 binary bits = 1 byte = 1 octet
- **Start frame delimiter (SFD).** The bit pattern 10101011 denotes the actual beginning of the frame. 1 octet.
- **Destination address (DA).** 48-bit MAC address of the station that should receive this frame. An all-1s address in 48 binary bits (ff-ff-ff-ff-ff-ff in hexadecimal) is the *broadcast address*, indicating that all stations should receive this message.
- **Source address (SA).** 48-bit MAC address of the station sending this frame.
- **Length.** Number of octets in the LLC data field, a value between 0 and 1500. 2 octets.
- **LLC Data:** Data from LLC (and higher layers). 38 to 1500 octets.
- **PAD.** Additional octets to ensure that the frame is at least 64 octets in length; this minimum is required by CSMA/CD networks as part of the collision detection mechanism.
- **Frame check sequence (FCS).** Remainder from CRC-32 calculation used for bit error detection. 4 octets.

6.5.4 Ethernet II. The IEEE's CSMA/CD standard is based on the Ethernet specification developed at Xerox's Palo Alto Research Center (PARC) in the mid-1970s. When Xerox first decided to market Ethernet, there was no OSI model or any LAN standards or products. Given that environment, Xerox sought industry support for this new standard. The Ethernet specification has been jointly distributed (and marketed) by Digital Equipment Corporation (DEC, now Compaq), Intel, and Xerox

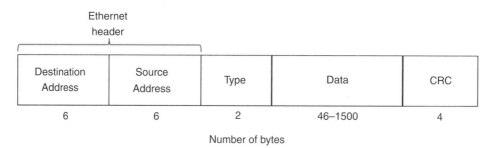

EXHIBIT 6.12   Ethernet II Frame Format

(hence sometimes known as *DIX Ethernet*). While the 802.3 standard is based on Ethernet II, the two are not exactly the same.

Exhibit 6.12 shows the format of an Ethernet MAC frame, primarily for purposes of comparison to the IEEE frame. The fields and their functions are:

- **Preamble.** Used for clock synchronization; employs the bit pattern 10101010...10101011 8 octets.
- **Destination address (DA).** 48-bit MAC address of the station that should receive this frame. An all-1s address (ff-ff-ff-ff-ff-ff) is the *broadcast address*, indicating that all stations should receive this message.
- **Source address (SA).** 48-bit MAC address of the station sending this frame.
- **Protocol identifier (PID).** Indicator of the protocol information transported in the Information field. Sample values include 2048 and 2054 to indicate the Internet Protocol (IP) and Address Resolution Protocol (ARP), respectively. 2 octets.
- **Information.** Protocol data unit from the protocol identified in the PID field. 46 to 1500 octets. (It is the responsibility of the higher layer to ensure that there are at least 46 octets of data in the frame.)
- **Frame check sequence (FCS.).** Remainder from CRC-32 calculation used for bit error detection. 4 octets.

The point in comparing the frame formats of Ethernet and 802.3 is to demonstrate that the two specifications are, in fact, different. It is a minor thing, perhaps, and a common misnomer in the industry to refer to *IEEE 802.3 Ethernet,* but it is an important difference to both a network administrator and a security professional.

In particular, if one LAN device only understands Ethernet encapsulation, it will not be able to communicate successfully with another LAN device that only understands IEEE 802.3 encapsulation. Both devices, however, can share the same medium backbone. A NetWare server running the Internetwork Packet Exchange (IPX) network layer protocol over IEEE 802.3 frames, for example, could easily share the network with a UNIX host running IP over Ethernet, but it maintains some immunity from attack by an IP host for the NetWare server.

6.5.5 IEEE 802.5 Token-Ring Standard.   The IEEE 802.5 token-ring standard is based on the IBM product of the same name. Both the standard and the product date back to about 1985.

The token ring has a logical ring topology, although it is built as a physical star. Designed to operate with STP or UTP cable, most current implementations operate

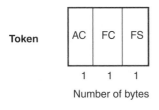

Token

1   1   1

Number of bytes

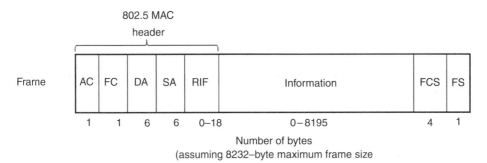

EXHIBIT 6.13   IEEE 802.5 Token and Frame Formats

at speeds of 16 Mbps or higher. The 802.5 MAC is essentially the same as the token passing scheme described in Section 6.4.2. The fields of the MAC frame (see Exhibit 6.13) are:

- **Start delimiter (SD).** Marks the actual beginning of the transmission. Bit pattern JK0JK000, where J and K represent special symbols on the line.[7] 1 octet.
- **Access control (AC).** Indicates whether this transmission is a *token* (i.e., no data) or a *frame* (i.e., contains data). This field also contains information about the priority of this transmission. 1 octet.
- **Frame control (FC).** Indicates if this frame carries LLC (and higher-layer) data or MAC management information; if it is MAC-specific information, this field also indicates the MAC frame type. 1 octet.
- **Destination address (DA).** 48-bit MAC address of the station to which this frame is intended.
- **Source address (SA).** 48-bit MAC address of the station sending this frame.
- **Routing information (RI).** An optional field, used only in multiple-ring networks utilizing source routing *and* in which the intended receiver is on a different ring than the transmitter. In source routing, the transmitter can specify the intended path of this frame, designating up to eight intermediate networks.[8] 0 to 18 octets.
- **Information (INFO).** Contains an LLC frame or MAC management information. No maximum length is specified by the standard, but the length of this field will be limited by the time required to transmit the entire frame, controlled by the *token holding time* parameter.
- **Frame check sequence (FCS).** Remainder from a CRC-32 calculation to detect bit errors. 4 octets.
- **End delimiter (ED).** Demarks the end of the transmission, with the bit pattern JK1JK1IE, where J and K are as described in the previous SD field. The I-bit

indicates whether this frame is the last frame of a multiple-frame sequence and the E-bit indicates whether a bit error was detected by the receiver (E); these bits are cleared by the original sender. 1 octet.

- **Frame status (FS).** The bit pattern AC00AC00; these bits indicate whether the frame's destination address was recognized by any station on the network (A) and whether this frame was successfully copied by the intended receiver (C). 1 octet.

As shown, a token comprises just three octets, the SD, AC, and ED fields. A station sends a frame whenever there is user data or MAC information to send. The station must wait until it receives a *token* before it can generate a *frame*.

The transmitting station is responsible for generating a new token after it transmits a single frame. Recall that the transmitted bits come back to the sender, and it is this station that removes the bits from the network. According to the original standard, the transmitter will send a token after sending all of the bits of the frame and must wait until it has seen at least the returning SA field to verify that it is, in fact, removing its own frame from the network. Optionally, early token release allows the transmitter to generate a new token immediately after finishing sending the bits from its frame, even if the SA field has not yet returned. This latter option was developed to improve performance in very large token ring environments, such as the American National Standards Institute (ANSI) FDDI standard.

Today, 802.5 token rings are primarily limited to IBM environments, and there is a lot to be found there. FDDI is more commonly found in multibuilding campus environments, used as a backbone to interconnect Ethernet/802.3 networks. FDDI is being phased out; the last FDDI product vendor dropped out of the marketplace in 1999.

6.5.6   IEEE 802.2 LLC Standard.
The IEEE 802.2 LLC protocol was intended to provide a common interface between 802 LAN MACs and higher-layer applications. With the LLC, the underlying MAC scheme is transparent to the application just as the application is transparent to the MAC.

The LLC was designed to support any number of services, the most common being an unacknowledged connectionless service (primarily used in contention networks) and an acknowledged connection-oriented service (primarily used in token ring environments).

The LLC is loosely based on the Higher-layer Data Link Control (HDLC) bit-oriented protocol in both operation and frame format (see Exhibit 6.14). The LLC frame appears in the Information field of a MAC frame. The first two fields of the LLC header are the *Destination Service Access Point* (DSAP) and the *Source Service Access Point* (SSAP) fields, originally intended to identify the higher-layer services at the source and destination node. This is similar in concept to *ports* in TCP/UDP but

802.2 LLC header			802 SNAP header		
DSAP *0xAA*	SSAP *0xAA*	Control *0x03*	*0x00-00-00*	Type	Information

EXHIBIT 6.14   IEEE 802.2 LLC Frame Transporting SNAP Header (which in turn indicates IEEE organization and EtherType protocol identifiers)

was never well implemented, and the DSAP and SSAP values are typically the same. The third field is the Control field, identifying the type of frame.

The Subnetwork Access Protocol (SNAP) is an IEEE 802 (ISO 8802) protocol that can be used to identify *any* protocol created by *any* agency, and is commonly used above the LLC layer. In this case, the SNAP header immediately follows the LLC header. Use of SNAP is indicated by the LLC fields when both DSAP and SSAP fields are set to a value of 170 (octal aa) and the Control field is set to a value of 3 (octal 03) to indicate that is an Unnumbered Information frame.

The SNAP header has two fields. The 3-byte *Organizationally Unique Identifier* (OUI) field refers to the organization that developed either the higher layer protocol or a way to refer to the protocol. The 2-byte *Type* field identifies the protocol using the Organization-defined number.

IP and ARP provide a common sample use of SNAP. The common format of a SNAP header encapsulating these protocols would be to set the OUI value to 0 (0 × 00-00-00) to identify IEEE/ISO as the organization. The Type field would then use the *EtherType* values of 2048 (0×08-00) and 2054 (0 × 08-06) to indicate use of IP and ARP, respectively.

6.5.7 Summary.   This section has covered the important LAN standards governing what is most likely to be seen in the industry today. Table 6.1 summarizes some of the discussion about the most common LAN topologies, media, MAC schemes, and standards.

6.6 INTERCONNECTION DEVICES.   LAN interconnection devices are used to attach individual LANs to each other to build a large enterprise network. They can also interconnect LAN components across a WAN and provide LAN access to the Internet. Several types of such devices are used for LAN interconnections, including hubs, switches, bridges, and routers. The major distinction between these devices is the OSI layer at which they operate, and all are discussed in the next sections.

6.6.1 Hubs.   *Hubs* are used to build physically star-wired LANs, using media that are basically point to point in nature (such as UTP and fiber). Note that it is the internal wiring of the hub that determines its *logical* nature, so that a logical bus or ring LAN can be physically star-wired.

So-called *Ethernet hubs* support 10 and/or 100 Mbps Ethernet or 802.3 networks. Different hubs will have a different number of ports, generally ranging from 4 to 32. Hubs provide physical connectivity only; when a frame arrives on one port, the hub will broadcast the frame back out to all other ports, which simulates the broadcast bus environment. Multiple hubs can be interconnected to form reasonably large networks.

TABLE 6.1   LAN Characteristics

Physical Topology	Logical Topology	Media	MAC	Speed (Mbps)	Standard
Bus	Bus	Coax	CSMA/CD	10	802.3, Ethernet
Star	Bus	UTP, Fiber	CSMA/CD	10, 100,1000	802.3
Star	Bus	Wireless	CSMA/CA	1, 2, 5, 11	802.11
Star	Ring	UTP	Token passing	16	802.5
Ring	Ring	Fiber	Token Passing	100	FDDI

Token-ring hubs, generally called *multistation access units* (MAUs), look similar to Ethernet hubs but have different internal wiring. When an MAU receives a transmission on one port, it merely forwards that transmission, a bit at a time, to the next port sequentially on the MAU. In this way, it simulates the ring environment.

6.6.2 Switches.   *Switches* are generally employed in the CSMA/CD environ-ment and extend the capabilities of a hub. A switch operates at a combination of PHY and MAC layers. In addition to providing physical connectivity like a hub, a switch learns the MAC address of all stations attached to it. When a frame arrives on a switch port, the switch looks at the destination MAC address and places the frame on the port associated with that address (which might be the port leading to another switch).

Switches are used primarily to improve performance. Given the scenario described earlier, multiple stations can transmit simultaneously without collision. Furthermore, switches can operate in full-duplex mode, meaning that a single station can both transmit and receive at the same time. A 10 Mbps switched Ethernet LAN, for example, can achieve performance similar to that of a 100-Mbps hubbed Ethernet LAN. (This is a real boon in those environments where it is not viable to upgrade 10-Mbps NICs and wiring.)

There is a very subtle security ramification to the use of switches versus hubs. In particular, if a user places a packet sniffer on a hubbed LAN, the sniffer will see every frame because the hub simulates the broadcast environment. A packet sniffer on a switched network will not be as effective; it will only pick up those frames that are specifically addressed to the LAN broadcast address.

6.6.3 Bridges.   A *bridge* provides a point-to-point link between the two LANs, usually those employing similar MAC schemes. Bridges operate at the MAC layer, and their operation is controlled by the MAC address.

Ethernet environments commonly employ *learning bridges*. In a very simple case, consider a bridge interconnecting two LANs, #1 and #2 (see Exhibit 6.15). When any LAN station sends a frame, both destination and source MAC addresses are included in the transmission. As frames appear on the networks, the bridge sees all of the source addresses and builds a table associating the MAC addresses with one LAN or the other, eventually learning the location of all of the network's stations. This process is sometimes called *backward learning* because the bridge learns the location of stations that transmit.

A bridge is a simple frame store-and-forward device. Like all stations on the LAN, a bridge examines the destination address of any transmitted frames. If a transmission on LAN #1 contains a destination address of a station on LAN #2, the bridge will forward the frame. If a transmission contains an unknown destination address, the bridge will also forward the frame.

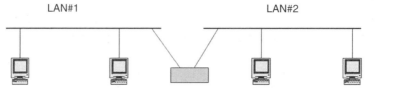

LAN#1   LAN#2

MAC: 00-50-04-29-e7-01   MAC: ab-37-16-5a-68-10   Bridge   MAC: 11-34-f2-b8-89-73   MAC: ab-37-16-14-c8-32

EXHIBIT 6.15   Two LANs Interconnected via a Bridge

Although a bridge bases its decisions on the MAC address, it is not an intelligent device; that is, it knows that a station with a particular MAC address is in one direction or another, but it does not know precisely where that station is. Because bridges have to build tables containing all of the stations' addresses that they learn, bridges do not scale particularly well to large networks. Bridges also extend the *broadcast domain* (i.e., if a frame transmitted on LAN #1 is sent to the broadcast address, it will be forwarded to LAN #2).

6.6.4 Routers.   A *router* is conceptually similar to a bridge in that it is also a store-and-forward device. A router, however, works at the Network Layer and is therefore a much more powerful device than a bridge. As Exhibit 6.16 shows, every LAN device has both a MAC (hardware) and Network Layer (software) address (in this case, IP is the sample Network Layer address). Because Network Layer addresses are hierarchical, the networks themselves have a network identifier number (the NET_ID in Exhibit 6.16). Network Layer addresses are well suited to environments where intermediate devices have to find a best route between networks.

Like a bridge, a router is considered to be just another station on a LAN to which it is attached. If the router sees a transmission on LAN #1 containing a destination address of a station on another network, it will route the packet to the correct destination network, even if that means going through another router to get there.

This example also demonstrates another major difference between bridges and routers. In a bridged environment, a station on LAN #1 sends a frame to some MAC address and has no knowledge of whether the intended destination is on the same LAN or not; the bridge will forward the frame if necessary, but this is all transparent to sender and receiver. In a routed environment, however, the sender can tell if the receiver is on the same or different network merely by examining the destination network address. In fact, the router only gets involved if the packet has to leave the local network; that is why in an IP environment, for example, an address of a default gateway (router) has to be provided.

Routers also limit the broadcast domain. If a station on LAN #1 transmits a frame using the broadcast MAC address, the frame goes no further than the router.

Routers build their routing tables very differently than bridges. Whereas bridges learn the relative location of a station by observing a frame's source address, packets learn the Network Layer address by the use of routing protocols that allow groups of routers to exchange routing information.[9]

6.6.5 Summary.   Hubs, switches, bridges, and routers are all commonly employed LAN interconnection devices. These are tools in the kit of everyone who works with LANs, as the building blocks of everything from small and intermediate-size local networks to large enterprise networks and the global Internet.

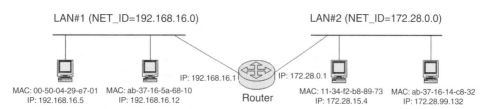

LAN#1 (NET_ID=192.168.16.0)   LAN#2 (NET_ID=172.28.0.0)

IP: 192.168.16.1   IP: 172.28.0.1

MAC: 00-50-04-29-e7-01   MAC: ab-37-16-5a-68-10   Router   MAC: 11-34-f2-b8-89-73   MAC: ab-37-16-14-c8-32
   IP: 192.168.16.5   IP: 192.168.16.12   IP: 172.28.15.4   IP: 172.28.99.132

EXHIBIT 6.16   Two LANs Interconnected via a Router

6.7   NETWORK OPERATING SYSTEMS.   Just as an operating system manages computer resources, a *network operating system* (NOS) provides the software that controls the resources of a LAN. NOSs generally comprise software that provides at least these functions:

- *Hardware drivers* are the software that allows the NOS to communicate with the NIC.
- *Communications software* allows applications running on different LAN nodes to communicate.
- *Services* are the functional aspects of the NOS and the reason that people use a LAN in the first place. Sample services include file services (file sharing), print services (commonly shared printers), message services (e-mail), communication services (LAN access to the Internet), and fax services (commonly shared facsimile).

NOSs are typically classified as being peer to peer or client/server. A *peer-to-peer* LAN allows any LAN node to communicate with any other LAN node, and any LAN node can provide services to other nodes. In a *client/server* (or *server-based*) environment, every node is either a client or a server. In this scenario, *servers* are special nodes that offer services to other servers or to clients, while *clients* are the ordinary end-user workstations. Clients can only communicate with a server.

When evaluating or investigating the security of a LAN, the software is the most common point of exposure, vulnerability, and exploitation, particularly for remote attacks.

Some sample NOSs include:

AppleTalk. Apple Macs have come with integrated LAN capabilities since their inception. Originally using a scheme called LocalTalk, AppleTalk is a peer-to-peer network running over a 10-Mbps CSMA/CD LAN. The Network Layer protocol historically associated with AppleTalk is called the Datagram Delivery Protocol (DDP). Current versions of MacOS networking support IP.

Microsoft Networking. Microsoft operating systems have come with LAN capabilities since Windows for Workgroups (WfW or Windows 3.11). Employing a nonroutable protocol called the NetBIOS Extended User Interface (NetBEUI), Windows client systems (Windows 3.11, 95, 98, 2000, and XP) can be easily used to build an inexpensive, simple peer-to-peer LAN for file and print sharing. NetBEUI is nonroutable because it does not provide an addressing mechanism to allow interconnected yet distinct NetBEUI subnetworks; if two NetBEUI networks are attached in any way, they will appear to be one large network. (This is why the hard drive of improperly configured Windows systems can be viewed from across the Internet.)

Microsoft Windows NT/Windows 2000/Windows 2003 Server. If not the most widely deployed NOS today, Windows NT Server and the more current Windows 2000/2003 Server is certainly the fastest growing. Windows NT is a somewhat nontraditional client/server NOS. Servers run the Windows NT/W2K Server OS and act like any other server. Clients can run any Windows OS, including Windows 3.11, 95, 98, 2000 Professional, or NT Workstation; the clients themselves can form a peer-to-peer network.

Novell NetWare. Perhaps the best-known client/server NOS. In the early 1990s, NetWare had over 70 percent of the NOS market, but Novell today is struggling to stay in business. The Network Layer protocol associated with classical NetWare is the Internetwork Packet Exchange (IPX) protocol. In the latest versions of NetWare, Novell abandoned IPX in favor of IP.

UNIX. TCP/IP has been the network communications protocol for UNIX systems since 1984. In the TCP/IP suite, any system can run server (daemon) software to provide services to other systems, so that any system can be either client or server.

6.8   SUMMARY.   Exhibit 6.17 shows a possible network design that includes many of the elements that have been described in this chapter (and a few that have not). This network's router provides the interface to the Internet and is attached via some sort of dedicated connection, such as a point-to-point 56 KBps or T1 (1.544 Mbps) leased line, frame relay, or digital subscriber line.

In this scenario, the router is physically located at the main site. From a security perspective, the organization may segment its network into an *external* and *internal* side, the internal being protected by a firewall.[10] The external network includes the router, public Web server, and firewallThose three systems are interconnected through a hub to which they each attach via a Cat. 5 UTP cable. In this scenario, the hub could actually implement 10BASE-T or 100BASE-T Ethernet, or even a token ring.

The external and internal networks are connected through the firewall, which, in this case, will have two NICs. The two networks are separate and distinct; the firewall does not extend the broadcast domain of either network, and, in fact, these two networks would have different IP network numbers.

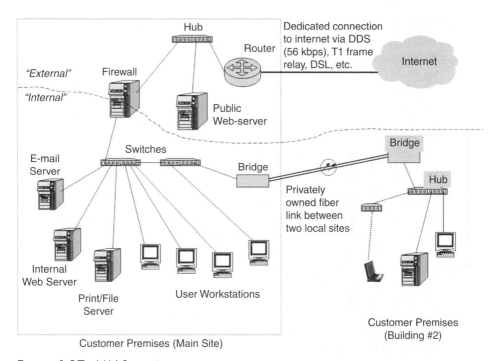

EXHIBIT 6.17   LAN Scenario

The internal network at the main site is a collection of servers and user workstations that are interconnected via a set of switches. In this example, these are 8-port 100-Mbps Ethernet switches. Since there are more than 8 devices, the switches themselves need to be interconnected. There are several options for that:

- *Stackable* switches physically attach to each other, extending the switch's backplane to create a larger switch (in this case, a 16-port switch).
- An *optical fiber* link can be used to interconnect the switch, usually at backplane speeds in the 1+-Gbps range.
- A *UTP* link might be used to interconnect the switches via two of the 100-Mbps ports.

To connect the LAN in Building #2 with the LAN at the main site, a point-to-point connection between a pair of bridges would suffice. In this case, the buildings are several kilometers apart, necessitating use of optical fiber.

In Building #2, there is another hub-based LAN, with a laptop using wireless technology, communicating with an access node that is also attached to the hub.

This chapter has only skimmed the surface of LAN concepts, standards, and technologies. Their study is important to the security professional, however, Because LANs are the basis of all networking. As a *network of networks*, the Internet comprises millions of local networks. This chapter indicates many of the points of potential vulnerability or compromise in a system.

6.9 WEB SITES

10 Gigabyte Ethernet Alliance
> www.10gea.org/10GEA White Paper_0502.pdf

Gast, M. "Wireless LAN Security: A Short History." (2002).
> www.oreillynet.com/pub/a/wireless/2002/04/19/security.html

IEEE LAN/MAN Standards
> http://grouper.ieee.org/groups/802/

LAN/MAN Protocols
> www.cisco.com/en/US/docs/internetworking/technology/handbook/Intro-to-LAN.html

6.10 FURTHER READING

Mikalsen, A., and P. Borgesen. *Local Area Network Management, Design and Security: A Practical Approach*. Hoboken, NJ: John Wiley & Sons, 2002.

Riley, S., and R. A. Breyer. *Switched, Fast, and Gigabit Ethernet*, 3rd ed. Indianapolis: New Riders Publishing, 1998.

Stallings, W. *Local and Metropolitan Area Networks*, 6th ed. Upper Saddle River, NJ: Prentice-Hall, 2000.

6.11 NOTES

1. It is an interesting point of trivia to note that the original frequency-hopping spread spectrum technique was invented by none other than Hollywood star Hedy Lamarr in 1940.

2. Since CSMA/CD transmits with a probability of 1, it is sometimes referred to as being *1-persistent*.

3. As an aside, although the station can experience 16 collisions, the probability of transmission will never fall below 1/1024, or 2^{-10}, since Ethernet and IEEE 802.3 do not allow more than 1024 devices on the network. This is the source of the word "truncated" in the name of the scheme.

4. Up-to-date status information about the 802 committee can be found at the LAN/MAN Standards Committee Web site at http://grouper.ieee.org/groups/802/.

5. A WG will go into *hibernation* when there are no new projects to undertake. This status indicates a WG that has reached status quo.

6. A WG is *disbanded* when it is considered that there is no more work for the IEEE to undertake in this topic area.

7. The term "special symbol" requires some explanation. The token ring uses a PHY signaling scheme to transmit 1s and 0s called Differential Manchester. In this signaling scheme, the signal is at a positive voltage for half of the bit time and at a negative voltage for the other half of the bit time, meaning that each bit has a sum total of 0 volts (resulting in what is sometimes called *DC balancing*). The J and K symbols are Differential Manchester code violations, where one symbol is at negative voltage for an entire bit time and the other at positive voltage for an entire bit time. These code violations have the benefit of being able to indicate special events and can be used for synchronization. J and K symbols are always used in pairs to maintain DC balancing.

8. Source routing is a very rarely used option in IP and is, in fact, a security problem; firewall administrators routinely set up filters to block IP packets with source routing. Source routing in an 802.5 network, however, is a normal feature and is not considered to be a security threat because this information has no impact on the WAN.

9. In the IP environment, common routing protocols include the Border Gateway Protocol (BGP), Open Shortest Path First (OSPF), and Routing Information Protocol (RIP).

10. This is a very simplistic firewall design with the internal and external network. The focus of this diagram is on the LAN components, however, rather than the specific security architecture.

CHAPTER **7**

ENCRYPTION

Stephen Cobb and Corinne LeFrançois

7.1 INTRODUCTION TO CRYPTOGRAPHY. The ability to transform data so that they are accessible only to authorized persons is just one of the many valuable services performed by the technology commonly referred to as encryption. This technology has appeared in other chapters, but some readers may not be familiar with its principles and origins. The purpose of this chapter is to explain encryption technology in basic terms and to describe its application in areas such as file encryption, message scrambling, authentication, and secure Internet transactions. This is not a theoretical or scientific treatise on encryption, but a practical guide for those who need to employ encryption in a computer security context.

Organizations around the world increasingly rely on cryptography to communicate securely and to store information safely. Typically, the algorithms used by DoD organizations are employed and maintained for many years. For example, the Data Encryption Standard (DES) has been used in some form for over 20 years.[1]

This chapter is a brief overview of cryptography and its practical applications to the needs of normal business users, as distinct from the needs of high-security government agencies. A thorough examination of the mathematics that are the foundation of these topics is beyond the scope of this chapter, but we provide suggested readings for further study.

7.1.1   Terminology.   This list of basic terms will be helpful for readers as they continue through this chapter:

Algorithm—a finite list of well-defined instructions for accomplishing some task that, given an initial state, will terminate in a defined end state.

Cipher—the core algorithm used to encrypt data. A cipher transforms plaintext into ciphertext that is not reversible without a key.

Ciphertext—text in encrypted form, as opposed to the plain text. We show ciphertext in UPPERCASE throughout this chapter.

Codes—a list of equivalences (a *codebook*) allows the substitution of meaningful text for words, phrases or sentences in an innocuous message; for example, "I will buy flowers for Mama tomorrow for her party at 7 pm" might be decoded to mean "Launch the attack on the mother ship next week on Sunday."

Decrypt/Decipher—the process of retrieving the plaintext from the ciphertext.

Encrypt/Encipher—to alter plaintext using a secret code so as to be unintelligible to unauthorized parties.

Key—a word or system for solving a cipher or code.

Plaintext—the original message to be encoded or enciphered. We show plaintext in lowercase throughout this chapter.

The science of cryptology (sometimes abbreviated as *crypto*) is the study of secure communications, formed from the Greek words $\kappa\rho\psi\pi\tau o\sigma$ (*kryptos*), meaning "hidden," and $\lambda o\gamma o\sigma$ (*logos*), "word." More specifically, it is the study of two distinct, yet highly intertwined, fields of study: cryptography and cryptanalysis. Cryptography is "the science of coding and decoding messages so as to keep these messages secure."[2] Cryptanalysis is the art and science of "cracking codes, decoding secrets, violating authentication schemes, and in general, breaking cryptographic protocols,"[3] all without knowing the secret key. Systems for encrypting information are referred to as *cryptosystems*.

Systems for encrypting information may also be referred to as *ciphersystems*, from *cipher*, meaning "zero," or empty (a word rooted in the Arabic *sifr*). Terms using cipher and crypto are interchangeable, with some authors preferring cipher to avoid the religious and cultural connotations of *crypt*, a word with the same root as "encryption." Thus, encryption may be referred to as encipherment, decryption referred to as decipherment, and so on.

The most obvious use of encryption is to scramble the contents of a file or message, using some form of shared secret as a *key*. Without the key, the scrambled data remain hidden and cannot be unscrambled or *decrypted*. The total number of possible keys

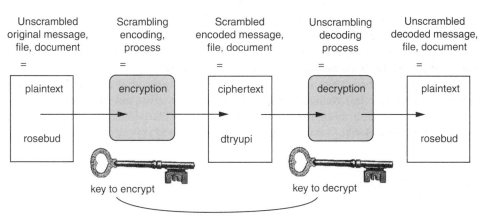

EXHIBIT 7.1   Diagram of Cryptographic Terms

for an encryption algorithm is called the *keyspace.* The keyspace is a function of the length of the key and the number of possible values in each position of the key. For a *keylength* of n positions, with each position having v possible values, then the keyspace for that key would be v^n. For example, with 3 positions and 2 values per position (e.g., 0 or 1), the possible keys would be 000, 001, 010, 011, 100, 101, 110, and 111 for a total keyspace of 8.

In cryptographic terms, the contents of a file before encryption are *plaintext,* while the scrambled or encoded file is known as *ciphertext* (see Exhibit 7.1). As a field of intellectual activity, cryptology goes back many millennia. Used in ancient Egyptian, China, and India, it was discussed by the Greeks and regularly employed by the Romans. The first European treatise on the subject appeared in the fourteenth century. The subject assumed immense historic importance during both world wars. The British success in breaking codes that the Germans used to protect military communications in World War II was a major factor in both the outcome of the war and in the development of the first electronic computer systems.

Since then, cryptography and computer science have developed hand in hand. In 1956, the United States National Security Agency (NSA), the U.S. Government department in charge of monitoring the worldwide flow of information, began funding improvements in computer hardware, pumping some $25 million into Project Lightning. This five-year development effort, intended to produce a 1,000-fold increase in computing power, resulted in over 150 technical articles. It also gave rise to more than 300 patent applications and succeeded in advancing the frontiers of hardware design. The NSA, based in Fort Meade, Maryland, was also involved in the creation of DES as the commercial encryption standard for much of the last 20 years. Today, the NSA is widely believed to have the world's largest collection of supercomputers and the largest staff of cryptanalysts.

7.1.2 Role of Cryptography.   The central role of cryptography in computer security is ensuring the confidentiality of data. But cryptography can support other pillars of computer security, such as integrity and authenticity. This section looks at the different roles of cryptography.

7.1.2.1 Confidentiality.   The role of encryption in protecting confidentiality can be seen in a classic definition of encryption: "Encryption is a special computation that operates on messages, converting them into a representation that is meaningless for all parties other than the intended receiver."[4]

Much of the literature on cryptography discusses the technology in terms of ensuring the confidentiality of messages, but this is functionally equivalent to protecting the confidentiality of data. The use of the term "message" reflects the traditional use to which cryptography has been put, both before and after the advent of computers. For example, Julius Caesar encrypted messages to Cicero 2,000 years ago, while today messages between a Web browser and a Web server are encrypted when performing a "secure" transaction.

When applying cryptography to computer security, it is sometimes appropriate to substitute the term "files" for "messages." For example, hard drive encryption programs protect data files stored on a hard drive. However, data files take the form of messages when they are transferred from one computer to another, across a network, the Internet, or via phone lines. Practically speaking, data being transferred in this manner are exposed to a different set of dangers from those that threaten data residing on a computer in an office. Thus, the use of encryption to render files useless to anyone other than an authorized user is relevant both to files in transit and to those that reside on a server or a stand-alone computer, particularly when the latter is a laptop, notebook, or PDA.

7.1.2.2   Integrity.   In the second half of the last century, following the advent of programmable computer systems, the ability of cryptography to transform data was applied in many new and interesting ways. As will be seen in a moment, many cryptographic techniques use a lot of mathematical calculation. The ability of computers to perform many calculations in a short period of time greatly expanded the usefulness of cryptography, and also inspired the development of ever-stronger ciphersystems.

Maintaining the integrity of data is often as important as keeping them confidential. When writing checks, people take pains to thwart alteration of the payee or the amount. In some cases, integrity is more important than confidentiality. Changing the contents of a company press release as it passes from the company to the press could have serious consequences. It is not only human actions that threaten data integrity; mechanical failures and logical errors can also change data. It is vital that such changes be detected, as was discussed in Chapter 4 of this *Handbook*, where it was observed that "[a]ll data movements and translations increase the likelihood of internal error, and for this reason parity checks and validity tests have become indispensable."

That chapter covered the role of parity bits for error detection, the function of redundancy checks, and the use of checksums to provide a modification-detection capability. A type of cryptographic hash or checksum called a Message Authentication Code (MAC) can protect against intentional, but unauthorized, data modification as well as against accidental modification. A MAC is calculated by applying a cryptographic algorithm and a secret value, called the *key*, to the data. The data are later verified by applying the cryptographic algorithm and the same secret key to the data to produce another MAC; this MAC then is compared to the initial MAC. If the two MACs are equal, then the data are considered authentic (see diagram in Exhibit 7.2, which uses the public key cryptosystem, discussed later). Otherwise, an unauthorized modification is assumed (any party trying to modify the data without knowing the key would not know how to calculate the appropriate MAC corresponding to the altered data).

7.1.2.3   Authentication.   In the context of computer security, authentication is the ability to confirm the identity of users. For example, many computers now ask users to log on before they can access data. By requesting a user name and password, systems

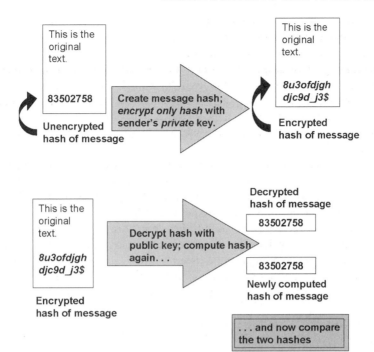

EXHIBIT 7.2 Message Authentication Code Using Public Key Cryptosystem

Source: Copyright © 2008 M. E. Kabay. Used with permission.

attempt to assure themselves that only authentic users can gain access. However, this form of authentication is limited—merely assuring that the person logging on is someone who knows a valid user name and password pair. Cryptography plays a very important role in efforts to ensure stronger authentication, from encrypting the password data to the creation and verification of electronic identifiers such as digital signatures. These will be described in more detail later in this chapter, along with the differences between public key and private key cryptography, both of which may be used in these schemes.

Using a public key system, documents in a computer system can be electronically signed by applying the originator's private key to the document. The resulting digital signature and document then can be stored or transmitted. The signature can be verified using the public key of the originator. If the signature verifies properly, the receiver has confidence that the document was signed using the private key of the originator and that the message had not been altered after it was signed. Because private keys are known only to their owner, it is also possible to verify the originator of the information to a third party.

7.1.2.4 Nonrepudiation. An aspect of computer security that has increased greatly in significance, due to the growth in internetwork transactions, is nonrepudiation. For example, if someone places an electronic order to sell stocks that later increase in value, it is important to prove that the order definitely originated with the individual who placed it. Made possible by public key cryptography, nonrepudiation helps ensure that the parties to a communication cannot deny having participated in all or part of the communication.

7.1.3 Limitations.   One role that cryptography cannot fill is defense against data destruction. Although encryption does not assure availability, it does represent a very valuable extra line of defense for computer information when added to physical security, system access controls, and secure channels of communication. Indeed, when computers are mobile, or data are being communicated over insecure channels, encryption may be the main line of defense. However, even though applied cryptography can provide computer users with levels of security that cannot be overcome without specialized knowledge and powerful computers, encryption of data should not be thought of as an alternative to, or substitute for, system access control. According to Seberry and Pieprzyk[4], the role of cryptography is to protect "information to which illegal access is possible and where other protective measures are inefficient."

Encryption-based file access controls should be a third barrier after site and system access controls, if for no other reason than that encryption systems alone do little to prevent people deleting files.

7.2 BASIC CRYPTOGRAPHY.   The aim of cryptography is to develop systems that can encrypt plaintext into ciphertext that is indistinguishable from a purely random collection of data. This implies that all of the possible decrypted versions of the data except one will be hopelessly ambiguous, with none more likely to be correct than any of the others. One of the simplest ways to create ciphertext is to represent each character or word in the plaintext by a different character or word in the ciphertext, such that there is no immediately apparent relationship between the two versions of the same text.

7.2.1 Early Ciphers.   It is believed that the earliest text to exhibit the baseline attribute of cryptography, having a slight modification of the text, occurred in Egypt nearly 4,000 years ago. A scribe used a number of unusual symbols to confuse or obscure the meaning of the hieroglyphic inscriptions on the tomb of a nobleman named Khnumhotep II.[5]

It is also believed that the first effective military use of cryptography was a simple transposition cipher (see Section 7.3.3) by the Spartans, who "as early as 400 BCE employed a cipher device called the scytale for secret communication between military commanders."[6] The scytale was a cylindrical or tapered stick with a thin strip of leather or parchment wrapped around it spirally.[7] The message to be hidden was written lengthwise with no blank spaces. When unraveled, the parchment appeared to hold nothing but random letters. To read the parchment, the recipient had to have a stick with exactly the same dimensions as the sender. The distribution of appropriate decoding scytales took place before the military commanders departed for the field.[8] For example, a particular combination of stick and strip could allow the cleartext (shown in lowercase):

```
atheniantroopswithinonedaysmarchofromebereadynow
```

to be broken into up to six rows of eight letters to be written across the rolled-up strip, in this way:

```
athenian

troopswi

thinoned
```

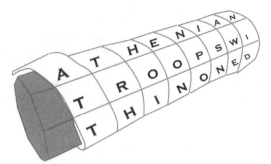

Exhibit 7.3   Scytale in Use

Source: Copyright © 2008 M. E. Kabay. Used with permission.

aysmarch

ofromebe

readynow

The message might appear on the scytale as shown schematically in Exhibit 7.3.

Reading the unwrapped strip without the stick would produce this ciphertext (shown in uppercase):

ATTAORTRHYFEHOISREEONMODNPOAMYISNRENAWECBONIDHEW

"The first attested use of [a substitution cipher] in military affairs comes from the Romans."[9] During that time, Julius Caesar encoded all his messages by simply replacing every letter with the letter three positions away. For example, the letter *a* would become the letter *d*, the letter *b* would become the letter *e*, and so on. Now called the Caesar cipher, this scheme is best-known of all the monoalphabetic algorithms (see Section 7.2.5).[10] Consider the Caesar cipher illustrated in the next comparison using the modern English alphabet, with the letters of the alphabet simply shifted three places.

```
Plaintext:  abcdefghijklmnopqrstuvwxyz
Ciphertext: DEFGHIJKLMNOPQRSTUVWXYZABC
```

To encrypt a message, the sender finds each letter of the message in the plaintext alphabet and uses the letter below it in the ciphertext alphabet. Thus the clear message:

```
Plaintext: beware the ides of march
```

is transformed into the encrypted message:

```
Ciphertext: EHZDUH WKH LGHV RI PDUFK
```

This type of cipher is known as a *substitution cipher*. Although the Caesar cipher is relatively simple, substitution ciphers can be very powerful. Most examples of the Caesar cipher shift the alphabet three places, as shown, so that the ciphertext line begins with *d*, but some authors suggest Caesar might have used other numbers, so the term "Caesar cipher" is used for all ciphers that conform to this algorithm (an *algorithm* being a formula or recipe for solving a problem).

This level of encryption might seem rudimentary, but it is an important starting point for much that follows. For example, one way to visualize the Caesar cipher is as

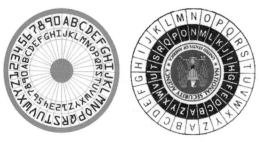

EXHIBIT 7.4   Code Wheels and the NSA Seal

a pair of rings, one inside the other, as shown in Exhibit 7.4. Both circles contain the letters of the alphabet. If one is rotated relative to the other the result is a cipher wheel, something well suited to automation. Eventually this happened, at first mechanically, then electrically, and today digitally. Automation facilitates repetition, and messages encrypted with a substitution cipher can be more difficult to decipher if multiple different substitutions are used. Thus the code wheel earned a place in the seal of the NSA, the U.S. Government agency most influential in the development of encryption.

7.2.2   More Cryptic Terminology.   The key or password for the Caesar cipher presented in the last section is the number of places the alphabet has been shifted, in this case three. Because this key must be kept private in order for the message to remain protected, it must be delivered to the recipient for the message to be decoded, or decrypted, back to plaintext. That is why the Caesar cipher is described as a *private key* algorithm and also a *symmetrical encryption* algorithm, the same private key being used to encrypt and decrypt the message. Algorithms of this type can be defeated by someone who has the key, an encrypted message, and knowledge of the algorithm used. This might sound like a statement of the obvious; however, as will be seen later in this chapter, there are encryption algorithms that use keys that can be openly exchanged without rendering the encrypted data accessible. Knowledge of the algorithm used can often be derived, or reverse-engineered, by analysis of its output.

Another seemingly obvious fact is that when a private key cipher is used in an effort to achieve confidentiality, one problem is swapped for another. The problem of exchanging messages while keeping the contents from unintended recipients is replaced by the problem of exchanging keys between sender and receiver without disclosing the keys. This new problem is known as the *key-exchange problem*. The key-exchange problem will be examined in more detail later.

7.2.3   Basic Cryptanalysis.   "The first people to understand clearly the principles of cryptography and to elucidate the beginnings of cryptanalysis were the Arabs."[11] By the fifteenth century, they had discovered the technique of letter frequency distribution analysis and had successfully decrypted a Greek message on its way to the Byzantine Emperor.[12] In 1492, a man known as al-Kalka-shandi described this technique in an encyclopedia. He also described several cryptographic techniques, including substitution and transposition ciphers.[13]

Returning to the Caesar cipher, consider how this code could be broken using the science of cryptanalysis. When examined for a length of time, this particular code is fairly transparent. As soon as several letters are identified correctly, the rest fall into place. For example, because "the" is the most common three-letter word in the English language, testing "XLI" against "the" reveals that each letter of plaintext has a fixed relationship to the ciphertext: a shift of three to the right.

If that difference is applied to the rest of the message, the result is a piece of plaintext that is intelligible and thus assumed to be the correct solution to the problem. However, even in this simple example several sophisticated processes and assumptions are at work; they deserve closer attention before looking at more complex codes. First, the test of "the" against "XLI" assumes that the plaintext is English and that the attacker has some detailed knowledge of that language, such as the frequency of certain words. Second, it is assumed that the ciphertext follows the plaintext in terms of word breaks. Typically, this is not the case. Ciphertext usually is written in blocks of letters of equal length to further disguise it, as in:

```
Ciphertext: EHZDU HWKHL GHVRI PDUFK
```

When the recipient of the message decrypts it, the result, while not exactly easy reading, is nevertheless entirely intelligible:

```
Plaintext: bewar ethei desof march
```

Also note the convention of ignoring the case of individual letters and placing all plaintext in lowercase while all ciphertext is in capitals.

7.2.4 Brute Force Cryptanalysis.
The next thing to note about the Caesar cipher is that, using the English alphabet, there are 26 possible keys. This means that someone intercepting the encrypted message could mount a standard form of attack known as *brute force cryptanalysis*. This method runs possible keys through the decryption algorithm until a solution is discovered. Statistically speaking, the correct key is reached after testing only half of all possible keys. In Exhibit 7.5, a spreadsheet

B6   *fx* =IF(CODE(B$2)-$A6<65,CHAR(CODE(B$2)-$A6+26+32),CHAR(CODE(B$2)-$A6+32))

CRYPTO.XLS:2

	A	B	C	D	E	F	G	H	I	J	K	L	M	N	O	P	Q	R	S	T	U	V
1																							
2		E	H	Z	D	U	H	W	K	H	L	G	H	V	R	I	P	D	U	F	K	
3	Key#:																					
4	1	d	g	y	c	t	g	v	j	g	k	f	g	u	q	h	o	c	t	e	j	
5	2	c	f	x	b	s	f	u	i	f	j	e	f	t	p	g	n	b	s	d	i	
6	3	b	e	w	a	r	e	t	h	e	i	d	e	s	o	f	m	a	r	c	h	
7	4	a	d	v	z	q	d	s	g	d	h	c	d	r	n	e	l	z	q	b	g	
8	5	z	c	u	y	p	c	r	f	c	g	b	c	q	m	d	k	y	p	a	f	
9	6	y	b	t	x	o	b	q	e	b	f	a	b	p	l	c	j	x	o	z	e	
10	7	x	a	s	w	n	a	p	d	a	e	z	a	o	k	b	i	w	n	y	d	
11	8	w	z	r	v	m	z	o	c	z	d	y	z	n	j	a	h	v	m	x	c	
12	9	v	y	q	u	l	y	n	b	y	c	x	y	m	i	z	g	u	l	w	b	
13	10	u	x	p	t	k	x	m	a	x	b	w	x	l	h	y	f	t	k	v	a	
14	11	t	w	o	s	j	w	l	z	w	a	v	w	k	g	x	e	s	j	u	z	
15	12	s	v	n	r	i	v	k	y	v	z	u	v	j	f	w	d	r	i	t	y	
16	13	r	u	m	q	h	u	j	x	u	y	t	u	i	e	v	c	q	h	s	x	
17	14	q	t	l	p	g	t	i	w	t	x	s	t	h	d	u	b	p	g	r	w	
18	15	p	s	k	o	f	s	h	v	s	w	r	s	g	c	t	a	o	f	q	v	
19	16	o	r	j	n	e	r	g	u	r	v	q	r	f	b	s	z	n	e	p	u	
20	17	n	q	i	m	d	q	f	t	q	u	p	q	e	a	r	y	m	d	o	t	
21	18	m	p	h	l	c	p	e	s	p	t	o	p	d	z	q	x	l	c	n	s	
22	19	l	o	g	k	b	o	d	r	o	s	n	o	c	y	p	w	k	b	m	r	
23	20	k	n	f	j	a	n	c	q	n	r	m	n	b	x	o	v	j	a	l	q	
24	21	j	m	e	i	z	m	b	p	m	q	l	m	a	w	n	u	i	z	k	p	
25	22	i	l	d	h	y	l	a	o	l	p	k	l	z	v	m	t	h	y	j	o	
26	23	h	k	c	g	x	k	z	n	k	o	j	k	y	u	l	s	g	x	i	n	
27	24	g	j	b	f	w	j	y	m	j	n	i	j	x	t	k	r	f	w	h	m	
28	25	f	i	a	e	v	i	x	l	i	m	h	i	w	s	j	q	e	v	g	l	
29	26	e	h	z	d	u	h	w	k	h	l	g	h	v	r	i	p	d	u	f	k	
30																							

◄ ◄ ► ►◄ OneTime / Vignere / KeySearch \ Caesar /

EXHIBIT 7.5 Brute Force Attack on the Caesar Cipher

table details a brute force attack on the Caesar ciphertext. In the example, the plaintext appears in line 6, Key #3.

Note that three items of information are required for this attack, and all three of them are relevant to encryption on personal computers:

1. A knowledge of the encryption algorithm used
2. The number of possible keys
3. The language of the plaintext

Using a computer in an office is somewhat different from sending messages on the field of battle (at least on a good day). Unlike an enemy spy, someone who is attempting to gain unauthorized access to data already has a fairly good idea of which algorithm is being used. (There are relatively few in use, and they often are directly associated with particular applications). This takes care of the first item. The primary obstacle to a brute force attack is the second item, number of keys. In the case of the Caesar cipher, the number of possible keys is relatively small, so the work involved in carrying out the attack can be completed very quickly, which is highly significant. Time is often the most important factor in practical cryptanalysis. Being able to decrypt messages within 24 hours is of little use if the information pertains to events that are measured in minutes, such as orders to buy and sell stock, or to launch air raids. If the cipher consisted entirely of random letter substitutions, like this:

```
Plaintext:   abcdefghijklmnopqrstuvwxyz
Ciphertext:  UTWFRAQOYSEDCKJVBXGZIPHLNM
```

The number of possible keys (the *keyspace*) is now 26!, or $\sim$4.03 $\times$ 10^{26}, which looks even more daunting when written out:

403,291,461,126,606,000,000,000,000

Imagine a brute force attack using a computer that can perform 1 million decryptions per microsecond (considerably more number crunching than the average personal computer can perform). Using a single processor, it could take over 10 million years to execute a brute force attack on this code. Fortunately for the code breaker, there are other ways of cracking substitution ciphers, as discussed in a moment. The point is that, while brute force attacks are possible, they are not always practical.

Although it is true that by the central limit theorem of statistics, the most likely number of trials required to hit upon the correct key is one-half the total keyspace, the average reduction by a factor of 2 is negligible in the face of computational periods measured in years and the difficulty of identifying cleartext in the morass of incorrect decryptions.

Functionally, brute force attacks depend upon knowing which encryption algorithm is behind the ciphertext. Practically, they depend upon the feasibility of successes within an appropriate time frame. They also depend upon the third item of information in the list above: knowledge of the language of the plaintext. The solution to the Caesar cipher in Exhibit 7.5 tends to jump out because it is closer to plain English than any of the other solutions. However, without knowing what constitutes plaintext, a brute force attack will, at best, be inefficient, and, at worst, unsuccessful. This part of cryptanalysis, recognizing a positive result, is less amenable to automation than any other. The difficulty is compounded by encryption of purely numerical results where the correct cleartext can be impossible to determine without extensive additional knowledge.

7.2.5 Monoalphabetical Substitution Ciphers.   Both the Caesar cipher and the random substitution cipher shown are examples of monoalphabetic ciphers. This means that one letter of ciphertext stands for one letter of plaintext. This renders such codes susceptible to an attack quite different from brute force. Suppose a customs officer attempts to discover when and how an illegal weapons shipment will be entering the country. The following message is intercepted:

YZYGJ KZORZ OYXZR RKZRK XUXRJ XRZXU YKQQQ

The person who encoded this text clearly substituted new letters for the original letters of the message. To the experienced code breaker or cryptanalyst, the task of deciphering this message is quite a simple one. First count how many times each letter occurs in the text. This produces a list like this:

```
Ciphertext:  R Z X Y K J U O G
Frequency:   6 6 5 4 4 2 2 2 1
```

Note that the last three letters are discounted as they are merely filling out the five-letter grouping. Next refer to a table of frequencies, which shows the relative frequency with which the letters of the alphabet occur in a specific language or dialect of that language. One such list is shown in Exhibit 7.6. This list was created for this example and proposes that the most commonly used letters in English in descending order of frequency are *e, t, r,* and so on. The actual order is more likely to be *e, t, a, i, o, n, s, h, r, d, l, u,* the order of keys on the English Linotype machine from the nineteenth century, although the precise order of frequencies can vary according to the region of origin or subject matter of the text.

Assuming that the original message is in English, a list that matches code letters to plaintext letters is easily derived.

```
Ciphertext:  R Z X Y K J U O G
Frequency:   6 6 5 4 4 2 2 2 1
Plaintext:   e t r i n o a h s
```

Exhibit 7.6   Frequency Lists for English

English by Letter				English by Frequency			
A	7.25	N	7.75	E	12.75	U	3.00
B	1.25	O	7.50	T	9.25	M	2.75
C	3.50	P	2.75	R	8.50	P	2.75
D	4.25	Q	0.50	I	7.75	Y	2.25
E	12.75	R	8.50	N	7.75	G	2.00
F	3.00	S	6.00	O	7.50	V	1.50
G	2.00	T	9.25	A	7.25	W	1.50
H	3.50	U	3.00	S	6.00	B	1.25
I	7.75	V	1.50	D	4.25	K	0.50
J	0.25	W	1.50	L	3.75	Q	0.50
K	0.50	X	0.50	C	3.50	X	0.50
L	3.75	Y	2.25	H	3.50	J	0.25
M	2.75	Z	0.25	F	3.00	Z	0.25

The result is:

```
Ciphertext: YZYGJ KZORZ OYXZR RKZRK XUXRJ XRZXU YKQQQ
Plaintext:  itiso nthet hirte enten rareo retra inqqq
```

This is readable as "it is on the thirteen ten rare ore train." Although this example obviously was contrived to make a point, it clearly illustrates an important cryptographic tool that can quickly decipher something that at first seems to be very forbidding. The encryption in the previous example could have been based on a simple substitution cipher. For example, after using the password "TRICK" followed by the regular alphabet minus the letters in the password for the plaintext, the ciphertext is the alphabet written backward:

```
Plaintext:  TRICKABDEFGHJLMNOPQSUVWXYZ
Ciphertext: ZYXWVUTSRQPONMLKJIHGFEDCBA
```

Frequency analysis also works if the substitution is entirely random, as in the example shown earlier, the key for which is entirely random. The specialized tools, such as frequency tables, that are required to break codes point out a basic trade-off: If a basic level of protection is needed, it is easy to get but also easy to break, at least for an expert. The qualification "for an expert" is important because users of encryption need to keep its role in perspective. The salient questions are: Who can gain from decrypting the data, and what means do they have at their disposal? There is no point investing in powerful encryption hardware or software if those likely to attempt to read your files are not particularly sophisticated, dedicated, or well equipped. For example, a person who mails a postcard knows it can be read by anyone who sees it. Envelopes can be used to prevent this, hardly the ultimate in confidentiality, but widely used and relatively successful nonetheless.

7.2.6 Polyalphabetical Substitution Ciphers.   Even when the plaintext uses a wider range of letters than the contrived example, substitution ciphers can be cracked by frequency analysis. A powerful technique is to concentrate on the frequency of two-letter combinations, which are known as *digraphs,* the most common of which in English is "TH." One way to counter frequency analysis is to use multiple substitutes for the more frequent letters. This cannot be done with a straightforward alphabetic coding. However, if using numbers for letters, it is possible to assign multiple numbers to some letters, such as 13 17 19 23 for E, which would help dilute the natural frequency of this letter. It would appear that supplying multiple substitutions, known as *homophones,* in proportion to the frequency of each letter would effectively counter frequency analysis. However, some of the underlying structure of the plaintext still survives, notably digraphs, which the cryptanalyst can use to crack the code.

In Europe during the Middle Ages, advances in cryptography were being made by the Papal States and Italian city-states to protect diplomatic messages. Then, in 1379, an Italian man named Gabriele de Lavinde created the first European manual on cryptography. "This manual, now in the Vatican archives, contains a set of keys for 24 correspondents and embraces symbols for letters, nulls, and several two-character code equivalents for words and names."[14] The nomenclature described by Lavinde's manual "was to hold sway over all Europe and America for the next 450 years."[15]

Several other notable advances emerged in Europe during the period of Lavinde's manual. First, in 1470, Leon Battista Alberti published the first description of a cipher disk.[16] Next, in 1563, Giambattista della Porta provided the first example of a digraphic cipher in which two letters are represented by one symbol.[17]

One method of decreasing the extent to which the structure of the plaintext is reflected in the ciphertext is to encrypt multiple letters of the plaintext. For example, "AR" might be encrypted as "CM." This is the theory behind what is known as the Playfair cipher, which was invented in 1854 by a British scientist, Sir Charles Wheatstone, but that was named after his friend Baron Playfair who fought for its adoption by the British Foreign Office.[18] Although the Playfair cipher remained in use through both world wars, it does not do enough to disguise the plaintext and cannot withstand a concerted frequency analysis.

7.2.7 The Vigenère Cipher.

A particularly important technique in the evolution of polyalphabetic ciphers has its roots in the sixteenth century. In 1586, Blaise de Vigenère published a square encryption/decryption table, named after him as the Vigenère Square, and descriptions of the first plaintext and ciphertext autokey systems.[19] The Vigenère cipher involves a table of letters, like the one shown in Exhibit 7.7, that are used with a key, to provide different monoalphabetic substitutions as the encryption proceeds through the plaintext. Thus each letter of the ciphertext has a different relationship with the plaintext, like this:

```
Key:         doomsdaydoomsdaydoomsdaydoomsday
plaintext:   sellentireportfolionowandbuygold
ciphertext:  VSZXWQTGJIAZVGYWCMDBFPFBOJIKUKLQ
```

The message is enciphered by looking at the row in the table that begins with the first letter of the key. Then go along that row until the column headed by the first letter of the plaintext. The ciphertext substitution is the letter at that intersection in the table.

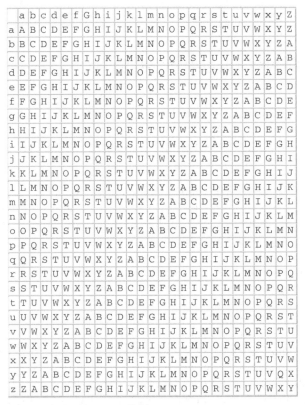

EXHIBIT 7.7   Vigenère Table

Thus, row d, column s, yields V. Then proceed to the second letter, and so on. Note that the first time the letter *e* is encrypted the cipher is S, but the second time it is W. The two *l*s in sell are encoded as Z and X respectively, and so on.

Does this cipher completely obscure the structure of the plaintext? Stallings notes: "If two identical sequences of plaintext letters occur at a distance that is an integer multiple of the keyword length, they will generate identical ciphertext sequences."[20] This means that the cryptanalyst can determine the length of the keyword. Once this is done, the cipher can be treated as a number of monoalphabetic substitutions, that number being equal to the key length. Frequency tables are again brought into play, and the code can be cracked. The cryptographer's response to this weakness is to use a longer key, so that it repeats less often. In fact, one technique, *autokey,* invented by Vigenère, is to form the key from the plaintext itself, together with one code word, like this

```
Key:         doomsdaysellentireportfoliononowan
plaintext:   sellentireportfoliononowandbuygold
ciphertext:  VSZXWQTGJIAZVGYWCMDBFPFBOJILUKLQ
```

This system is very powerful, but it still can be attacked by statistical analysis based on frequencies, because the letters of the plaintext and key share roughly the same frequency distribution. The next level of defense is to use a keyword that is as long as the plaintext but bears no statistical relationship to it. This approach, which is of great cryptographic significance, was not hit upon until the twentieth century arrived, bringing with it binary code and global warfare.

7.2.8 Early-Twentieth-Century Cryptanalysis.

The advent of modern cryptography began with the invention and development of the electromagnetic telegraph system and the introduction of the Morse code. Samuel Morse brought a system of dots and dashes that allowed near real–time long-distance communication. He envisioned this system as a means of secure communications. It would be up to others to devise systems to encrypt telegraphic communications. Anson Stager, the supervisor of the U.S. Military Telegraph during the Civil War. Stager devised 10 ciphers for the Union Army that were never broken by the Confederacy.[21]

The use of telegraphic ciphers and codes continued into the two world wars. In fact, one of the most famous early successes of cryptanalysis prompted the entrance of the United States into World War I. When the war first started, the German transatlantic telegraph cable had been cut by the British, forcing all of Germany's international communications to route through the United Kingdom before being sent on to the Swedish or American transatlantic lines.[22] In 1917, "British cryptographers deciphered a telegram from German Foreign Minister Arthur Zimmermann to the German Minister to Mexico, von Eckhardt."[23] It promised Mexico ownership over territory that belonged to the United States (California, e.g.), if Mexico joined the German cause and attacked the United States. The British informed President Wilson of their discovery, giving him a complete copy of the telegram, thus resulting in the United States declaring war on Germany.[24] That telegram has become famous in the history of cryptanalysis as the Zimmermann Telegram.

World War II saw several Allied victories over the Axis powers by use of advanced cryptographic systems. Few of these victories are more widely known and celebrated than the cracking of the German Enigma cipher machine, described next:

Following the decryption of the Zimmerman Telegram during World War I and the effects that weak ciphers had on that war's outcome, Germany was looking for an unbreakable cipher and was interested in leveraging automation and the use of machinery to replace traditional paper and pencil techniques. The Enigma machine consisted of a basic keyboard, a display that would reveal the cipher text letter, and a scrambling mechanism such that each plain text letter entered as input via the keyboard was transcribed to its corresponding cipher text letter. The machine was modular in design and multiple scrambling disks were employed to thwart attempts at frequency analysis.[25]

A British cryptanalysis group, with the help of a group of Polish cryptanalysts, first broke the Enigma early in World War II, and some of the first uses of computers were for decoding Enigma ciphers intercepted from the Germans. Breaking Enigma was a major victory for the Allies, and in order to keep exploiting it, they kept the fact that they had cracked it a secret.[26]

Thus far, the encryption schemes or devices described have encrypted messages consisting of words and nothing more. However, the emergence of the computer, even in its initial rudimentary form, revolutionized cryptology "to an extent even greater than the telegraph or radio."[27] Most cryptologic advances since World War II have involved, or made use of, computers. In the last few decades, cryptographic algorithms have advanced to the point where computing them by hand would be unfeasible, and only computers can do the required mathematics.[28] Relying on computers has broadened the kind of information that can benefit from encryption. Computers use a unique language that transforms all information stored into bits, each a 1 or a 0.[29] "This, in effect, means that plaintext is binary in form, and can therefore be anything; a picture, a voice, an e-mail or even a video—it makes no difference, a string of binary bits can represent any of these."[30]

7.2.9 Adding Up XOR. In 1917, an engineer at AT&T, Gilbert Vernam, was working on a project to protect telegraph transmissions from the enemy. At that time, teletypewriters were used, based on a version of Morse code called Baudot code, after its French inventor. In Baudot code, each character of the alphabet is allotted five units, each of which is either an electrical current or absence of current, known as a mark or a space. For example, the letter *a* is represented by *mark, mark, space, space, space*. In binary terms, each unit constitutes a bit that is either 0 or 1 (the five-bit code for *a* would be 11000). This system of pulses allowed teletype machines to convert text to and from telegraph signals using a keyboard and punched paper tape for input (a hole represents a mark because it allows the reading device to make electrical contact and create a pulse, whereas a space is represented by leaving the paper intact). Anyone with a suitable machine could intercept and read the transmission.

The 32 possible combinations (2^5) in this code were assigned to the 26 letters plus six "shunts" that did various things like shift to capitals or go down to the next line. Vernam's brilliant idea was to use a tape of random characters in Baudot code as a key that could be electromechanically added to the plaintext. Kahn describes the method of addition like this:

> If the key and plaintext pulses are both marks or both spaces, the ciphertext pulse will be a space. If the key pulse is a space and the plaintext pulse is a mark, or vice-versa, (in other words, if the two are different), the ciphertext will be a mark.[31]

Today, this is known as Exclusive-Or, sometimes referred to as bit-wise XOR or just XOR for short (see Exhibit 7.8). XOR is widely used in computerized encryption schemes. Consider what happens when encoding the letter *a* using "B" as the key:

```
Plaintext:   1 1 0 0 0 (=a)
Key:         1 0 0 1 1 (=B)
Ciphertext:  0 1 0 1 1
```

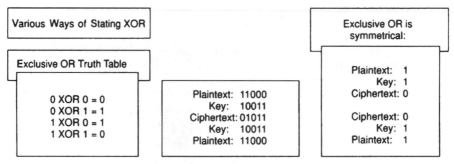

EXHIBIT 7.8   Diagram of XOR

In the first column, $1 + 1 = 0$, as indicated in Exhibit 7.8. To decipher the encrypted character simply perform the same operation, but add the ciphertext to the key:

```
Ciphertext:  0 1 0 1 1
Key:         1 0 0 1 1 (=B)
Plaintext:   1 1 0 0 0 (=a)
```

At the time of its discovery, the significance of this method lay in its capacity for automation. The operator could feed the plaintext and key tapes into the teletype machine, and it would transmit an encrypted message with no further human input. No off-line preparation was required. Furthermore, as long as the receiver had the key tape, the teletype at the receiving end automatically printed out plaintext. This made Vernam's system the first to integrate encryption into the communication process, an essential feature of encryption systems for today's computer-based communications.

7.3   DES AND MODERN ENCRYPTION.   Although the use of XOR predated computers, the fact that it worked so well with binary code ensured that it would become an essential item in the modern cryptographer's toolkit. And so the focus of this chapter turns to modern cryptography and two of the most widely used cryptosystems today. The first is Data Encryption Standard (DES) and the second is Rivest, Shamir, Adleman (RSA).

7.3.1   Real Constraints.   As the preceding overview of the evolution of encryption suggests, major advances, which are few and far between, often are linked with the individuals who made them, such as Vigenère, Playfair, and Vernam, none of whom had the benefit of computers. Today's computerized encryption schemes typically employ a number of classic techniques that, when combined, eliminate or minimize the shortcomings of any single method. Several techniques will be discussed here, including transposition and rotors, that point the way to the most widely used encryption scheme to date: DES. First, however, consider the practical problems encountered by Vernam's otherwise brilliant scheme.

Vernam proposed a key that was a long series of random characters. This was coded on a loop of paper tape that eventually repeated (the tape held about 125 characters per foot). The length of the key made cryptanalysis of intercepted messages extremely difficult, but not impossible, because eventually the key repeated. With sufficient volume of ciphertext, the code would yield to frequency analysis. (Bear in mind that during time of war, or even military exercises, hundreds of thousands of words may be encrypted per day, providing a solid basis for cryptanalysis.)

7.3.2   One-Time Pad.   Several improvements then were suggested to avoid the impracticality of simply creating longer and longer key tapes. Another AT&T engineer, Lyman Morehouse, suggested using two key tapes of about eight feet in length, containing some 1,000 characters, to generate over 999,000 combinations of characters that could be fed into the encryption process as the key. This was an improvement in terms of practicality and security, but, as Major Joseph Mauborgne of the U.S. Army Signal Corps pointed out, heavy message traffic encrypted in this way still could be decoded. It was Mauborgne who realized that the only unbreakable cipher would use keys that are, as Kahn puts it "endless and senseless."[32] Thus he came up with what we know as the one-time system, the one unbreakable encryption scheme.

The one-time system sometimes is referred to as a *one-time pad*, because this is the way it has been deployed by intelligence agents in the field. The agent is issued a pad that aligns columns and rows of entirely random characters, as shown in Exhibit 7.9. The first letter of the plaintext is encrypted using the appropriate ciphertext from row 1, the second letter is encrypted from row 2, and so on. The result is ciphertext that contains no statistical relationship to the plaintext. When the message is encrypted the pad is destroyed. The recipient, who has a copy of the pad, uses it to reverse the process and decrypt the message.

The one-time pad essentially is a polyalphabetic substitution cipher, but with the same number of alphabets as there are characters in the message, thus defeating any kind of frequency analysis. A brute force attack is defeated by the fact that every possible result is as statistically significant as every other. As Kahn points out, a four-letter group of ciphertext could just as easily yield *kiss, fast, slow,* or any other possible four-letter combination.

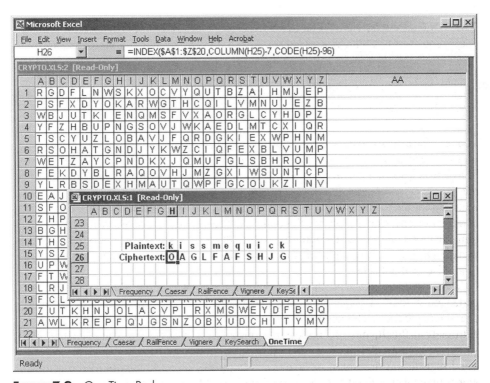

EXHIBIT 7.9   One-Time Pad

So why is the unbreakable one-time system not in universal use? Well, it remains a favorite of intelligence agents in the field who have an occasional need to send short messages. However, for large-scale commercial or military encryption, it fails to solve the key size problem that Vernam's system brought to light. The key has to be as large as the total volume of encrypted information, and there is a constant demand for new keys. Furthermore, both sender and receiver have to hold and defend identical copies of this enormous key.

7.3.3   Transposition, Rotors, Products, and Blocks.   A completely different technique from substitution is *transposition*. Instead of substituting ciphertext characters for plaintext, the transposition cipher rearranges the plaintext characters. The simplest example is referred to as *rail fence*. For example, to encrypt "sell entire portfolio now and buy gold" each character is written on alternate lines, like this:

```
sletrprflooadugl
elnieotoinwnbyod
```

which results in this ciphertext:

```
SLETRPRFLOOADUGLELNIEOTOINWNBYOD
```

So far, this does not present a serious challenge. More challenging is the next transposition into rows and columns that are numbered by a key (in this case, 37581426) so that the first set of ciphertext characters are under 1, the second under 2, and so on:

```
Key:         3 7 5 8 1 4 2 6
Plaintext:   s e l l e n t i
             r e p o r t f o
             l i o n o w a n
             d b u y g o l d
Ciphertext:  EROGTFALSRLDNTWOLPOUIONDEEIBLONY
```

Although more complex, this transposition will still yield to cryptanalysis because it retains the letter frequency characteristics of the plaintext. The analyst also would look for digraphs and trigraphs while playing around with columns and rows of different length. (Kahn describes French code breakers during World War I literally cutting text into strips and sliding them up and down against each other to break German transposition ciphers.)

What makes transposition difficult to decipher is additional stages of encryption. For example, if the previous ciphertext is run through the system again, using the same key, all semblance of pattern seems to disappear.

```
Key:         3 7 5 8 1 4 2 6
Plaintext:   e r o g t f a l
             s r l d n t w o
             l p o u i o n d
             e e i b l o n y
Ciphertext:  TNILAWNNESLEFTOOOLOILODYRRPEGDUB
```

The development of increasingly complex multiple-transposition ciphers pointed out the positive effects of multiple stages of encryption, which also apply to substitution ciphers. The prime examples of this are the rotor machines used by the Germans and Japanese in World War II. Some of the insights gained during the attack on German codes, such as Alan Turing's 1940 work on the application of information statistics to cryptanalysis, were considered so important that they remained classified for more than 50 years.

Although they eventually were defeated by Allied cryptanalysts, electromechanical systems such as Enigma were not only the most sophisticated precomputer encryption systems, but the effort to crack them was also a major catalyst in the development of computer systems themselves. When people started applying computer systems to code making rather than code breaking, they quickly hit upon the idea of chopping plaintext into pieces, or blocks, for easier handling. The term "block cipher" is used to describe ciphers that encrypt one block (e.g., 8 bytes of data) at a time, one block after another. Another result of computerizing the encryption process is a class of ciphers known as *product ciphers*. A product cipher has been defined as "a block cipher that iterates several weak operations such as substitution, transposition, modular addition/multiplication [such as XOR], and linear transformation."[33]

The mathematics of product ciphers are beyond the scope of this chapter, but it is useful to note that "[n]obody knows how to prove mathematically that a product cipher is completely secure...[A] product cipher should act as a 'mixing' function which combines the plaintext, key, and ciphertext in a complex nonlinear fashion."[34] The parts of the product cipher that perform the rounds of substitution are referred to as *S-boxes*. The product cipher called Lucifer has two of these S-boxes, while DES encryption has eight S-boxes. The ability of a product cipher to produce truly random, nonlinear ciphertext depends on careful design of these S-boxes.

Examples of modern product ciphers include Lucifer (developed by IBM), DES (developed by IBM/NSA), LOKI (Brown, Pieprzyk, and Seberry), and FEAL (Shimizu and Miyaguchi). A class of product ciphers called *Feistel ciphers* operates on half of the ciphertext at each round, then swaps the ciphertext halves after each round. Examples of Feistel ciphers include Lucifer and DES, both of which are commercial systems, the subject of the next section of this chapter.

7.3.4 Data Encryption Standard.   Traditionally, the primary markets for code makers and computer makers have been the same: governments and banks. After World War II, computers were developed for both military and commercial purposes. By the mid-1960s, the leading computer maker was IBM, which could see that the growing role of electronic communications in commerce would create a huge market for reliable encryption methods. Over a period of years, mathematicians and computer scientists including Horst Feistel at the IBM research lab in Yorktown Heights, New York, developed a cipher called Lucifer that was sold to Lloyds of London in 1971 for use in a cash-dispensing system.[35]

The U.S. National Security Agency was in close touch with the Lucifer project, making regular visits to the lab (the constant flow of personnel between the NSA, IBM, and the mathematics departments of the major American universities tended to ensure that all new developments in the field were closely monitored). At roughly the same time, the National Bureau of Standards (NBS) was developing standard security specifications for computers used by the federal government. In 1973, the NBS invited companies to submit candidates for an encryption algorithm to be adopted by the government for the storage and transmission of unclassified information. (The government handles a lot of information that is sensitive but not sufficiently relevant to national security to warrant classification.)

IBM submitted a variation of its Lucifer cipher to the NBS, and after extensive testing by the NSA, this cipher was adopted as the nation's Data Encryption Standard

(DES). The acronym actually refers to a document published as Federal Information Processing Standards Publication 46, or FIPS PUB 46 for short. This was published on January 15, 1977 and DES became mandatory for all "federal departments and agencies, for any...nonnational-security data."[36] The federal mandate also stated that commercial and private organizations were to be encouraged to use DES.[37] As a result, DES became widely used, especially in the banking industry.[38] The heart of DES is the Data Encryption Algorithm (DEA), which is described in a publication of the American National Standards Institute, titled *American National Standard for Information Systems—Data Encryption Algorithm—Modes of Operation, 1983*, referred to as ANSI X3.106-1983.

7.3.5 DES Strength.

DES became, and remained, the de facto standard for commercial encryption until the late 1990s, when doubts about its strength relative to the rapid advances in computer hardware and software led to a quest for an eventual replacement. However, DES is still widely deployed, so more detailed discussion of its use is needed before discussing its replacement. The first thing to note is that the only known method of deciphering data encrypted with DES without knowledge of the key is the use of brute force. This involves the computerized comparison of plaintext data with encrypted versions of the same data, using every possible key until both versions of the data match. With DES, the number of possible combinations is about 70 quadrillion. That is a very big number, and trying all those combinations within anything less than years requires relatively expensive hardware (or the carefully orchestrated application of large amounts of cheap hardware).

Technically speaking, the DEA is a combined substitution/transposition cipher, a product cipher that operates on blocks of data 64 bits, or 8 bytes, in length. Using 56 bits for the key produces a keyspace of 2^{56}, or 72,057,594,037,927,940, a number in the region of 70 quadrillion. A diagram of DES is shown in Exhibit 7.10.

The difficulty of attacking DES can be increased fairly easily if double or triple encryption is used, but despite this, there has always been something of a cloud over DES. At the time the DEA was approved, two Stanford University professors who are preeminent in twentieth century cryptography, Martin Diffie and Whitfield Hellman, pointed out that the algorithm, as approved by the NBS, would be increasingly vulnerable to attack as computer equipment increased in power and came down in cost.

7.3.6 DES Weakness.

As the author George Sassoon writes, "Although both the U.S. Department of Commerce and IBM deny it vigorously, everyone in the know insists that the NSA enforced a halving of the DES key length to ensure that they themselves could break the ciphers even if nobody else could." Although the NBS dismissed such criticisms, and the NSA flatly denied that they were behind any attempts to weaken the cipher, this opinion received some support from the NSA in 1986 when the agency announced it would no longer certify the DEA for nonclassified use, less than 10 years after the DES was approved. This move was prompted by the rapid development of parallel computers, which achieve amazing processing capabilities by using hundreds or even thousands of multiple processors, working in parallel. These machines offer enormous power at considerably less cost than traditional supercomputers. Perhaps the NSA could see the inevitability of something like the EFF DES Cracker, which was built in 1998 for less than $250,000 and broke a DES-encrypted message in fewer than three days.

The original Lucifer cipher used data blocks of 128 bits and a key of 112 bits. If this had been adhered to in the DEA, the difference in the number of possible key

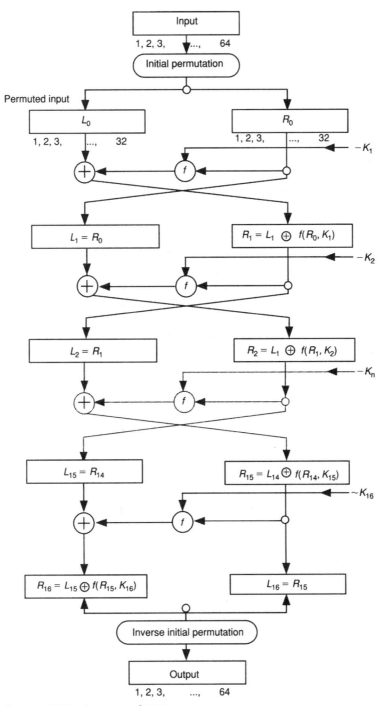

EXHIBIT 7.10   Diagram of DES

combinations would have been staggering. Although 2^{56}, the current keyspace, is a number greater than 7 with 16 zeroes behind it, 2^{112} is greater than 5 with 33 zeroes behind it. The practical consequence of this weakness in the DEA meant that the demand for stronger algorithms remained, and promising new ones emerged, such as Bruce Schneier's Blowfish.

There are still some positive aspects to DES that make it viable for some commercial uses. As was mentioned earlier, the cryptographic weakness of DES can easily be strengthened by double encryption, which doubles the difficulty of decryption, taking the task well into the realm of supercomputers and purpose-built, massively parallel machines. The fact that DES has been a standard for so long means that DES now is available in many forms, such as single-chip implementations that can be inserted into ROM sockets and integrated into all manner of hardware, such as expansion cards, PCMCIA cards, and smart cards.

7.4 PUBLIC KEY ENCRYPTION.   Even with a longer key, the DEA still would have a major weakness, one that it shares with all of the other private key encryption systems mentioned so far. That weakness is the need to keep the key secret. In this section we examine this problem, and the "public key" solutions that are now available.

7.4.1 Key-Exchange Problem.   When password-protected data are sent from one place to another, either electronically or by hand, the need to transmit the password to the recipient presents serious obstacles. In cryptography, these are known collectively as the *key-exchange problem.* This is the way it is described by the Crypt Cabal:[39]

> If you want your friends to be able to send secret messages to you, you have to make sure nobody other than them sees the key . . . .[This is] one of the most vexing problems of all prior cryptography: the necessity of establishing a secure channel for the exchange of the key. To establish a secure channel, one uses cryptography, but private-key cryptography requires a secure channel!

So, even when using very powerful private key systems, such as DES, password or key distribution is a major problem. After all, the reason for encrypting valuable information in the first place is because it is assumed someone is trying to steal it or tamper with it. This implies a motivated and skilled adversary. Such an adversary is likely to use every opportunity to discover the password that will unlock the information. The password is perhaps most at risk from such an adversary when it is passed from one person to another. Although it sounds like the stuff of Bond movies, it actually is a very real and practical problem that had to be faced in many areas of legitimate organized activity, from businesses to public institutions, even when a powerful DEA-based computerized encryption system became available.

Suppose an encrypted file of sensitive accounting data needs to get to the head office. How does the recipient know the password needed to access the file? The sender could make a phone call. But will it be overheard? How is the identity of the person at the other end to be verified? A courier could be dispatched with a sealed envelope. The password could be encrypted. But all of these channels present problems. How to guarantee that the courier is honest or that the envelope will arrive intact? And if the password is encrypted, it will need a password itself, which will have to be transmitted. The recipient of the file can be provided with the password before the message is encrypted, but this is no guarantee that the password will not be intercepted. There are ways of making matters more difficult for the attacker, but the ideal solution would be to use a key that was useless to the attacker. This possibility is diagrammed in Exhibit 7.11.

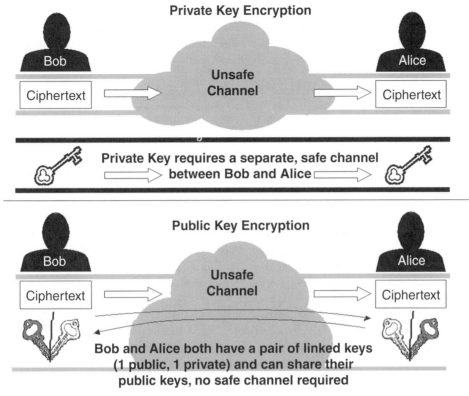

EXHIBIT 7.11   Comparison of Private and Public Key Encryption

7.4.2 Public Key Systems.   A public key encryption system offers encryption that does not depend on the decryption key remaining a secret. It also allows the receiver of keys and messages to verify the source. The first published description of a public key cryptosystem appeared in 1976, authored by Stanford University professor Martin Hellman and researcher Whitfield Diffie. Ralph Merkle independently arrived at a similar system.

Ralph Merkle first proposed the idea of public key cryptography in 1974, and Martin Hellman and Whitfield Diffie brought the same idea to the public forum in 1976.[40] The idea was considered a seminal breakthrough, "for it had not occurred to anyone else in the long history of cryptology that the deciphering key could be anything other than the inverse of the enciphering key."[41] The Diffie-Hellman system employs a form of mathematics known as modular arithmetic. "Modular arithmetic is a way of restricting the outcome of basic mathematical operations to a set of integers with an upper bound."[42] An excellent example of this mathematical principle is found by examining a military clock:

> Consider a clock on military time, by which hours are measured only in the range from zero to 23, with zero corresponding to midnight and 23 to 11 o'clock at night. In this system, an advance of 25 hours on 3 o'clock brings us not to 28 o'clock, but full circle to 4 o'clock (because 25 + 3 = 28 and 28 − 24 = 4). In this case, the number 24, an upper bound on operations involving the measurement of hours, is referred to as a modulus. When a calculation involving hours on a clock yields a large number, we subtract the number 24 until we obtain an integer between 0 and 23, a process known as modular reduction. This idea can be extended to moduli of different sizes.[43]

The Diffie-Hellman protocol allows two users to exchange a symmetric key over an unsecure medium without having any prior shared secrets. The protocol has two publicly known and widely distributed system parameters: p, a large prime integer that is 1,024 bits in length,[44] and g, an integer less than p. The two users wishing to communicate are referred to as Alice and Bob for simplicity's sake. They proceed in this way.

First, Alice generates a random private value a, and Bob generates a random private value b. Both a and b are [less than p]. Then they derive their public values using parameters p and g and their private values. Alice's public value is $g^a \bmod p$ and Bob's public value is $g^b \bmod p$. They then exchange their public values. Finally, Alice computes $g^{ab} = (g^b)^a \bmod p$, and Bob computes $g^{ba} = (g^a)^b \bmod p$. Since $g^{ab} = g^{ba} = k$, Alice and Bob now have a shared secret key k.[45]

This protocol introduced a concept to cryptography known as the discrete log problem. "The discrete log problem is stated as follows: given g, p, and $g^x \bmod p$, what is x?"[46] It is generally accepted throughout the mathematical and cryptologic communities that the discrete log problem is difficult to solve, difficult enough for algorithms to rely on it for security.[47]

An algorithm to perform public key encryption was published in 1977 by Ronald Rivest of MIT, Adi Shamir of the Weizmann Institute in Israel, and Leonard Adleman of the University of Southern California. These three men formed the RSA Data Security Company, which was granted an exclusive license to the patent that MIT obtained on their algorithm. A large number of companies licensed software based on this algorithm, from AT&T to IBM and Microsoft. The RSA algorithm is currently at work in everything from online shopping to cell phones. Because it resolved the secret key dilemma, public key cryptography was hailed by many as a revolutionary technology, "representing a breakthrough that makes routine communication encryption practical and potentially ubiquitous," according to Sci.Crypt FAQ, which states:

> In a public-key cryptosystem, E_K can be easily computed from some public key X, which in turn is computed from K. X is published, so that anyone can encrypt messages. If decryption D_K cannot be easily computed from public key X without knowledge of private key K, but readily with knowledge of K, then only the person who generated K can decrypt messages.

The mathematical principles that make this possible are beyond the scope of this chapter. Somewhat more detail can be found in the RSA Laboratories' Frequently Asked Questions About Today's Cryptography, which is distributed by RSA Data Security, the company that markets products based on the RSA algorithm. In brief, public key encryption is possible because some calculations are difficult to reverse, something pointed out by Diffie and Hellman who first published the idea of public key encryption. Here is how RSA describes the calculations that make it possible (with minor clarification from the author):

> Suppose Alice wants to send a private message, m, to Bob. Alice creates the ciphertext c by exponentiating:
>
> $c = m^e \bmod n$
>
> where e and n are Bob's public key. To decrypt, Bob also exponentiates:
>
> $m = c^d \bmod n$
>
> where d is Bob's private key. Bob recovers the original message, m; the relationship between e and d ensures that Bob correctly recovers m. Because only Bob knows d, only Bob can decrypt.

1. Private key, chosen
   Select two prime numbers, p and q $\qquad$ $p = 7$ and $q = 17$

2. Public key, calculated
   Calculate $n = pq$ $\qquad$ $7 \times 17 = 119$

3. Public key, chosen
   Calculate $ø(n) = (p - 1)(q - 1) = 96$
   Select e, such that e is relatively prime to $ø(n)$ and $< ø(n)$ $\quad e = 5$

4. Private key, calculated
   Determine d, such that de $= 1$ mod 96 and d < 96
   Because $77 \times 5 = 385 = 4 \times 96 + 1$ $\qquad d = 77$

Result; Public key, KU = 5,119 Private key, KR = 77,119

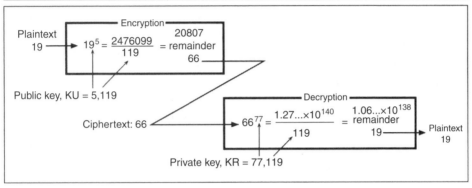

Exhibit 7.12 Public Key Diagram

This is diagrammed in Exhibit 7.12, which follows the scenario described. The lower part of the diagram uses numbers taken from an example given by Stallings. These numbers are much smaller than the actual numbers used by RSA. The point is that, given the ciphertext (c) and the public key (e,n) and knowledge of the algorithm, it is still impractical to decipher the message (m). This is because n is created by multiplying two prime numbers (normally represented as p and q) and e is derived from n combined with the secret key, d. To break the cipher, you need to factor a large number into a pair of prime numbers. How large? More than 150 digits in length (that is digits, not bits).

This cryptanalysis is very hard to do in a meaningful period of time, even with a very powerful computer. Large networks of computers have successfully factored a 100-digit number into two primes, but the RSA algorithm can use numbers even bigger if computer power and factoring algorithms start to catch up to the current implementations.

7.4.3 Authenticity and Trust. The point of the public key cryptosystems is to provide a means of encrypting information that is not compromised by the distribution of passwords, but public key encryption does not solve all problems associated with key exchange. Because the keys are considered public knowledge, some means "must be developed to testify to authenticity, because possession of keys alone (sufficient to encrypt intelligible messages) is no evidence of a particular unique identity of the sender," according to Sci.Crypt FAQ.

This has led to key-distribution mechanisms that assure listed keys are actually those of the given entities. Such mechanisms rely on a *trusted authority,* which may not actually generate keys but does employ some mechanism which guarantees that "the lists of keys and associated identities kept and advertised for reference by senders and receivers are 'correct'"(Sci.Crypt FAQ). Another approach has been popularized by the program called Pretty Good Privacy, or PGP. This is the "Web of trust" approach that relies on users to distribute and track each other's keys and trust in an informal, distributed fashion.

Here is how RSA can be used to send evidence of the sender's identity in addition to an encrypted message. First, some information is encrypted with the sender's private key. This is called the *signature* and is included in the message sent under the public key encryption to the receiver. The receiver can "use the RSA algorithm *in reverse* to verify that the information decrypts sensibly, such that only the given entity could have encrypted the plaintext by use of the secret key" (Sci.Crypt FAQ).

What does "decrypts sensibly" mean? The answer involves something called a *message digest,* which is "a unique mathematical summary of the secret message" (Sci.Crypt FAQ). In theory, only the sender of the message could generate his or her valid signature for that message, thereby authenticating it for the receiver. Here is how RSA describes authentication, as diagrammed below in Exhibit 7.13.

Suppose Alice wants to send a signed document m to Bob. Alice creates a digital signature s by exponentiating: $s = m^d \bmod n$, where d and n belong to Alice's key pair. She sends s and m to Bob. To verify the signature, Bob exponentiates and checks that the message m is recovered: $m = s^e \bmod n$, where e and n belong to Alice's public key.

7.4.4 Limitations and Combinations.   As mentioned earlier, many products use RSA today, including Microsoft Windows, Lotus Notes, Adobe Acrobat, Netscape Navigator, Internet Explorer, and many more. In most of these examples, RSA is used for its authentication capabilities rather than for large-scale data encryption. That is because public key systems have one very noticeable downside: They are slow. This is balanced by the fact that they are harder to break. According to RSA, DES generally is at least 100 times as fast as RSA when implemented in software. In hardware, DES is between 1,000 and 10,000 times as fast, depending on the implementations. RSA may narrow the gap in coming years as more specialized chips are developed. However, public key algorithms are unlikely to ever match the performance of private key ciphers such as DES. Fortunately there is a simple solution: Use a fast private key algorithm for the data encryption, but use a public key system to handle the key exchange and authentication, as diagrammed in Exhibit 7.14.

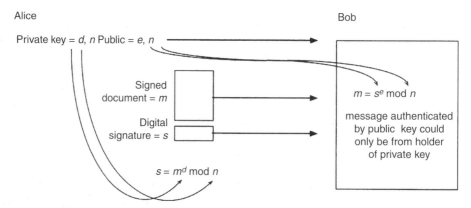

EXHIBIT 7.13 Authentication with RSA

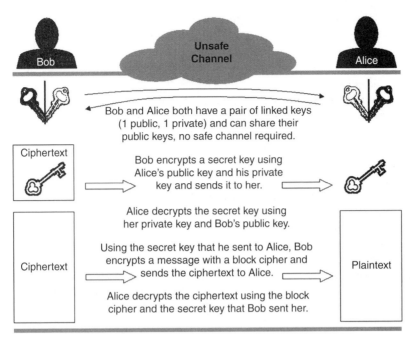

EXHIBIT 7.14 Combining Public and Private Key Encryption

The private key encryption system might be DES or a system such as RC2 and RC4, both of which are available from RSA Data Security, or Schneier's Blowfish, which is freely available. Just as there are other private key systems besides DES, there are other public systems besides RSA. One method, called SEEK, is patented, trademarked, and marketed by Cylink of Sunnyvale, California. This method uses an alternative algorithm for public key distribution. Cylink manufactures a range of DES encryptors that use SEEK for key distribution.

7.5 PRACTICAL ENCRYPTION. The primary market for encryption systems and devices is communications. However, the development of Internet commerce has resulted in a number of new and interesting crypto components that have considerable value for computer security.

7.5.1 Communications and Storage. If you look at the commercial products on NIST's list of approved DES implementations, most are designed to protect information when it is being communicated, not when it is sitting on a machine for local use. This is understandable when you look at the development of computing, which has spread outward from "fortress mainframe." Centralized data storage facilities lend themselves to physical access control. Encrypting data that stays behind walls and locked doors may be overkill in that scenario, particularly when there is a performance penalty involved.

Encryption was reserved for data in transit, between computers, across wires. This philosophy was extended to file servers on networks. File encryption on the server was not considered a priority as people assumed the server would be protected. Data encryption on stand-alone machines and removable media is a relatively recent development, particularly as more and more confidential data are packed into physically

EXHIBIT 7.15   SSL 3.0 in Action

smaller and smaller devices. There are now many products with which to implement file encryption.

7.5.2 Securing the Transport Layer.   One of the most visible examples of encryption at work in computer security today is the security icon people see in their Web browser; see Exhibit 7.15 for examples of Netscape Navigator and Microsoft Internet Explorer. This is an example of something called transport layer security, which uses protocols that go by the name of SSL and TLS.

7.5.2.1 Popular Protocols.   SSLs stand for Secure Sockets Layer, the software encryption protocol developed by Netscape and originally implemented in Netscape Secure Server and the Netscape Navigator browser. SSL is also supported by Microsoft Internet Explorer and a number of other products. TLS stands for Transport Layer Security, the name given to an Internet standard based on SSL, by the IETF (as in Internet Engineering Task Force, RFC 2246). There are minor differences between SSLv3.0 and TLSv1.0 but no significant differences as far as security strength is concerned, and both protocols interoperate with each other.

The TLS is a protocol, a standardized procedure for regulating data transmission between computers. It is actually composed of two layers of protocol. At the lowest level is the TLS Record Protocol, which is layered on top of some reliable transport protocol, typically the TCP in TCP/IP, the set of protocols that run the Internet. The TLS Record Protocol provides connection security that is both private (using symmetric cryptography for data encryption) and reliable (using a message integrity check). Above the TLS Record Protocol, encapsulated by it, is the TLS Handshake Protocol. This allows the server and client to authenticate each other, a major role for TLS in various forms of e-commerce, such as Internet banking. The TLS Handshake Protocol can also negotiate an encryption algorithm and cryptographic keys before any application protocol sitting on top of it, such as HTTP, transmits or receives its first byte of data (see Exhibit 7.16).

7.5.2.2 Properties of TLS.   In providing connection security, the TLS Handshake Protocol delivers three basic properties. The identity of the parties can be authenticated using public key cryptography (such as RSA). This authentication can be made optional, but typically it is required for at least one of the parties (e.g., the Yahoo Travel server authenticates itself to the user's browser client, but the user's client does not authenticate itself to the Yahoo Travel server, a distinction discussed in a moment).

The second and third basic properties of the TLS Handshake Protocol are that a shared secret can be securely negotiated, unavailable to eavesdroppers, even by an attacker who can place itself in the middle of the connection; and the protocol's negotiation is reliable. In the words of RFC 2246: "no attacker can modify the negotiation communication without being detected by the parties to the communication."

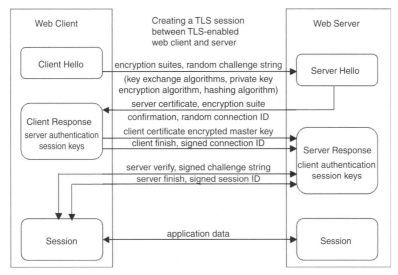

EXHIBIT 7.16 Creating a TLS Session

TLS can use a variety of encryption algorithms. For the symmetric encryption that is part of the Record protocol, DES or RC4 can be used. The keys for this symmetric encryption are generated uniquely for each connection and are based on a secret negotiated by another protocol (such as the TLS Handshake Protocol). The record protocol includes a message integrity check using a keyed MAC, with secure hash functions such as SHA and MD5, used for MAC computations. The encryption suite to be used for a specific connection is specified during the initial exchange between client and server, as shown in Exhibit 7.16.

7.5.2.3 Tested in the Real World.

TLS/SSL has been widely used and extensively tested in the real world, and thoroughly probed by real cryptographers. Some of the caveats and limitations noted by these and other experts follow. The first is that neither a good standard nor a good design can guarantee a good implementation. For example, if TLS is implemented with a weak random number seed, or a random number generator that is not sufficiently random, the theoretical strength of the design will do nothing to protect the data that are thus exposed to potential compromise. (Although beyond the scope of this chapter, Pseudo-Random Number Generators, or PRNGs, play a vital part in many cryptographic operations, and they are surprisingly difficult to create; unless they closely simulate true randomness, an attacker will be able to predict the numbers they generate, thus defeating any scheme that relies on their "random" quality.)

The second major caveat is that, if clients do not have digital certificates, the client side of the TLS session is not authenticated. This presents numerous problems. Most of today's "secure" Web transactions, from airline tickets booked at Yahoo Travel to shares traded at most online brokerages, represent a calculated risk on the part of the vendor. Although the client doing the buying is assured, by means of the merchant certificate, that the merchant at www.amazon.com really is Amazon, the merchant has no digital assurance that the client computer belongs to, or is being operated by, the person making the purchase. Of course, there are other assurances, such as the match between the credit card that the purchaser supplies and the other personal details that go along with it, such as billing address. But the merchant is still risking a charge-back and possibly other penalties for a fraudulent transaction.

In the case of larger and more sensitive financial transactions, the need to be assured of the client's identity is greater. A digital certificate is a step in the right direction, but it is a step many merchants have not yet taken, for several reasons. The first is the cost of issuing certificates to customers, and the second is the difficulty of getting those certificates onto their systems. Some merchants have decided that the cost and effort are worth it. For example, the Royal Bank of Scotland took this approach with its online banking system back in 1998.

There are other issues. The user needs to protect the certificate, even from such threats as hardware failure (user reformats the drive, loses the certificate) or unauthorized use (a family member uses the computer and thus has access to the certificate). Furthermore, the user needs to be able to move the certificate, for example, onto a laptop computer so that the bank account can be accessed while traveling. The obvious answer is to place the certificate on a robust removable medium (see Exhibit 7.17). Such media are generically referred to as hardware tokens. A standard for tokens has not yet emerged. Smart cards are an obvious choice, but card readers need to be deployed. There are alternatives, such as putting the certificate on a floppy disk or on a small key fob that plugs into a USB port.

7.5.2.4 *Cost of Secured Transactions.* For companies looking to perform highly secure transactions today, using SSL without client-side authentication is proving acceptable in the short term, at least for some categories of transaction. Even then it can be costly, in terms of either dollars or processing power. Although TLS is an open standard, and Netscape has provided crucial parts of the technology royalty free, there is still the question of which algorithms to use. Some algorithms are more expensive than others, and not always in obvious ways. For example, you have to license RC4, whereas DES is free, but RC4 is optimized for a 32-bit processor and DES is not.

Furthermore, research shows that the amount of "hits" that a Web server can handle drops dramatically when those hits require TLS (and it drops a whole lot more when processing client authentication as well as server authentication). The answer here may be specialized hardware. Several companies, such as IBM and Rainbow Technologies, make crypto-coprocessor cards that relieve the server's CPU of the specialized math processing involved in crypto. They are cheaper than adding another server to keep up with the very demanding task of providing secure Web transactions.

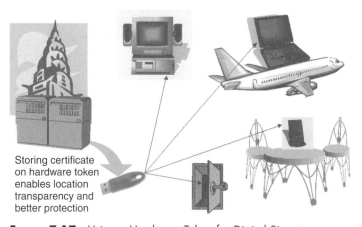

Storing certificate
on hardware token
enables location
transparency and
better protection

EXHIBIT 7.17 Using a Hardware Token for Digital Signatures

7.5.3 X.509v3 Certificate Format.   Another example of encryption widely used in computer security today is X.509. This is not a rocket ship but a standard for digital certificates, described earlier in this chapter. The ITU-T X.509 standards document states: "Virtually all security services are dependent upon the identities of the communicating parties being reliably known, i.e. authentication." Consider how this affects Web transactions. The preceding section described how SSL can encrypt Web pages sent from Web server to Web client, and vice versa, but it cannot assure the identity of the parties involved. The X.509 standard helps to address this problem, which negatively impacts the profitability of Web-based businesses.

When a Web user asks for assurance that the bn.com Web site is actually Barnes & Noble, it can be provided by way of a digital certificate (see Exhibit 7.18). This means that an entity, known as a certificate authority (CA), has taken considerable pains to reliably identify, and consequently certify, the merchant as the rightful owner of an encryption key. This key is the public half of a uniquely and mathematically related public/private key pair, such that a message encrypted with the public key can only be decrypted with the corresponding private key.

EXHIBIT 7.18   Digital Certificate

Individuals, as well as merchants, can have a public/private key pair. A bank might then access that public key, and use it, plus the bank's private key, to encrypt the account details it sends to customers over the Web. Only the customer with the right private key can decrypt this information, using the bank's public key. At the same time, customers know the statement information can only have come from the bank (otherwise the bank's public key would not work to decrypt it). Customers also know, thanks to an encrypted message digest (a digital fingerprint of the message contents), that the data they get from the bank has not been altered. Thus it is very difficult for either party to claim that it never took place. In this way digital certificates can enhance confidentiality, integrity, and nonrepudiation.

7.5.3.1 ISO/IEC/ITU 9594-8 a.k.a. X.509. The management of public keys is the task of Public Key Infrastructure (PKI), of which the X.509 standard is an important part. For example, an organization's employees can perform secure business communications over the Internet, such as contract negotiation, using PKI. To engage in a secure transaction with someone, it is necessary to find and access the other person's public key, and vice versa. The answer is to publish public keys in the form of a digital certificate, then use some form of directory to locate them. In order for different systems to interoperate, standards for directories have been developed, notably X.500. This standard applies such elements of directory standardization as a hierarchical naming convention:

Country, Organization, Common Name.

So Fred Jones of Megabank might have the X.500 name:

[Country = US, Organization = Megabank, Inc., Common Name = Fred Jones]

A means of locating digital certificates to verify identities was a logical extension of the standard, thus X.509 was developed, officially known as ITU-T X.509 (formerly CCITT X.509) and also ISO/IEC/ITU 9594-8. In X.509 there is a definition of a basic certificate format, which consists of seven fields shown in Exhibit 7.19.

The certificate format has evolved considerably since 1988. The original format is now referred to as X.509v1. When X.500 itself was revised in 1993, two more fields were added to support directory access control, resulting in the X.509v2 format.[48] X.509v2 added unique identifiers for the issuer and the subject, optional bit strings used to make the issuer and subject names unambiguous in the event that the same name is later reassigned to different entities. Suppose that Fred Jones, whose assigned

Exhibit 7.19 X.509 Certificate Format

Version	Identifies the Certificate Format
Certificate Serial Number	Number that is unique within the issuing CA.
Signature Algorithm Identifier	Identifies the algorithm used to sign the certificate, together with any necessary parameters
Issuer	X.500 name of the issuing CA
Validity period	Pair of dates between which the certificate is valid
Subject	X.500 name of the holder of the private key corresponding to the public key certified by the certificate
Subject Public Key Information	Public key for the subject, plus an identifier for the algorithm with which this public key is to be used

X.500 name was given earlier, is an executive vice president of Megabank but is then hired away by a competitor. Megabank deassigns his name, but if a different Fred Jones, a programmer, then comes to work for Megabank, he is effectively reassigned the same X.500 name:

[Country = US, Organization = Megabank, Inc., Common Name = Fred Jones]

This poses authorization problems for any access control lists attached to X.500 data objects, due to the difficulty of identifying all of the access control lists that grant privileges to a particular user's name. The unique identifier field added in X.509v2 provides somewhere to put a new value whenever a name is reused. In fact, a better solution is to use a better distinguisher in the X.500 name, such as

[Common Name = Fred Jones, Employee Number = 1000002].

In 1993, when the Internet Privacy Enhanced Mail (PEM) RFCs were published, they included specifications for a public key infrastructure based on X.509v1 certificates. Attempts to deploy PEM, however, revealed deficiencies in the Version 1 and 2 certificate formats. Consequently, ISO/IEC/ITU and ANSI X9 developed the X.509v3 format, which greatly extends the capabilities of the format by providing extension fields and broader naming options in X.509v3.

7.5.3.2 Extending the Standard.   Extensions were added in Version 3 to address problems discovered while implementing Version 1 and 2 certificates. These can be seen in the diagram in Exhibit 7.20. Particular extension field types may now be specified in standards or defined and registered by any organization or community.

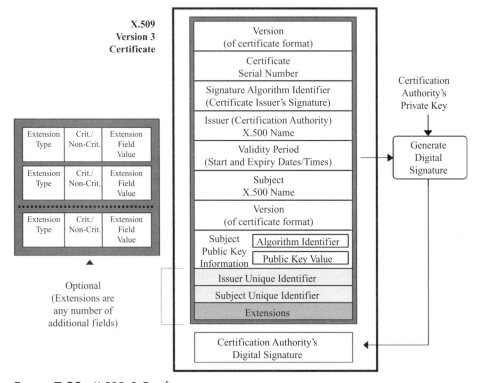

EXHIBIT 7.20   X.509v3 Certificate

Each extension field is assigned a type by means of an object identifier, registered in the same way that an algorithm is registered. Although theoretically anyone can define an extension type, to achieve practical interoperability, common extension types need to be understood by different implementations. Thus, the most important extension types are standardized. But when X509v3 is used within a closed group—for example, a group of business partners—it is possible to define unique extension types to satisfy specific needs.

7.5.3.3   X.509 Sources, Issues, and CAs.

Someone managing an e-commerce project does not necessarily need to know X.509 in detail but should at least read the Arsenault and Turner document; it clearly describes not only X.509 but the role it plays in PKI (which they define as "the set of hardware, software, people, policies and procedures needed to create, manage, store, distribute, and revoke certificates based on public-key cryptography."). Also very helpful are the presentations by VeriSign's Warwick Ford, which NIST has online at its Web site. For the e-commerce developer who wants more detail, the next step is Ford's book, coauthored with fellow VeriSign executive Michael Baum, *Secure Electronic Commerce*.[49] This documents other important aspects of X.509, such as the Certificate Revocation List, used to revoke certificates before they expire (e.g., if the private key has been compromised). A copy of the standard, available online, at the ITU Web site (www.itu.int), is also valuable.

The extensions and improvements in the X.509v3 certificate format greatly increase its usefulness, but providing a uniform method of going beyond the standard does raise the specter of a lack of standardization. This is something that the IETF's PKIX working group is addressing. And there are other issues to consider when evaluating X.509 as a security technology, many of which are raised by Ed Gerck of the Meta-Certificate Group. Articles at the group's Web site point out that X.509 does not address "the level of effort which is needed to validate the information in a certificate." In other words, some security issues are beyond the scope of X.509, but they do need to be considered when deploying systems that rely on these certificates. For example, it does not make sense to rely on a digital certificate if the measures taken to assure the identity of the owner and user of the certificate are not commensurate with the risk involved in relying on the certificate. Furthermore, transactions that do not use certificates on both sides will remain inherently problematic.

These issues point to the importance of the role played by the certificate authority. As mentioned earlier, CAs are the entities that issue and sign certificates. Each has a public key that is listed in the certificate. The CA is responsible for scheduling an expiration date and for revoking certificates when necessary. The CA maintains and publishes a Certificate Revocation List (CRL)

In other words, ensuring the validity of certificates entails a lot of maintenance. The CRL, for example, is crucial if certificates are compromised or found to be issued fraudulently. This happened in 2001 when a number of VeriSign certificates were found to be issued in error to someone posing as Microsoft. Because some computer users now rely on certificates to guarantee the authenticity of software upgrades and components, failure to check the revocation list before downloading certified code could result in malicious code attacks.

Problems with certificates have the potential for widespread impact because the authority in certificates is hierarchical, as shown in Exhibit 7.21. When a CA issues a certificate, it signs it with its own key. Anyone relying on certificates issued by that CA needs to know by what authority the CA is issuing that certificate. To simplify, there

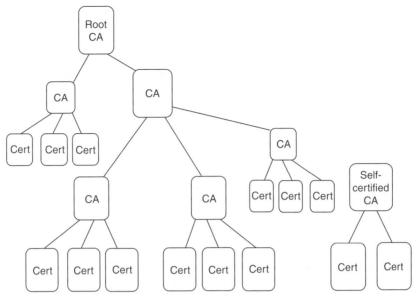

EXHIBIT 7.21   Certificate Authorities and the Root Key

are two possible answers. The CA is self-certifying, that is, providing its own "root" key, or it is relying on another CA for the root key. Clearly, any compromise of the root key undermines all certificates that gain their authority from it.

See Chapter 37 of this *Handbook* for a more extensive discussion of PKI and Certificate Authorities.

7.6 BEYOND RSA AND DES.   Cryptography research and development did not stop with the development of the RSA algorithms. Events in the last two decades of the twentieth century and the first of the twenty-first, and their implications, are discussed in this final section of the chapter, which concludes with some warnings on implementing encryption.

7.6.1 Elliptic Curve Cryptography.   In 1985, Neal Koblitz from the University of Washington and Victor Miller of IBM independently discovered the application of elliptic curve systems to cryptography. When applied to public key cryptography, elliptic curve arithmetic has been found to offer certain advantages over first-generation public key techniques, such as Diffie-Hellman and RSA.

The security of elliptic curve algorithms is based on the same principle as the Diffie-Hellman algorithm, the discrete log problem, as described in Section 7.4.2. The advantages to elliptic curve algorithms lie in the key size needed to achieve certain levels of security. As one scales security upward over time to meet the evolving threat posed by eavesdroppers and hackers with access to greater computing resources, elliptic curves begin to offer dramatic savings over the old, first-generation techniques.[50]

Currently, public key systems use 1,024 bits or 2,048 bits for creating keys. NIST has recommended that after 2010, these systems will be unacceptably vulnerable and should be upgraded to a system that can provide adequate security. One way of doing this would be to increase the key size that is used. However, systems that are in place today become increasingly cumbersome the larger the key size. The NSA is endorsing elliptic curve cryptography, stating on its Web site that it has implemented elliptic

EXHIBIT 7.22 NIST Recommended Key Sizes

Symmertic Key Size (bits)	RSA and Diffie-Hellman Key Size (bits)	Elliptic Curve Key Size (bits)
80	1024	160
112	2048	224
128	3072	256
192	8192	384
256	15360	521

Source: National Security Agency, "The Case for Elliptic Curve Cryptography," www.nsa.gov/ia/industry/crypto_elliptic_curve.cfm.

curve public key cryptography systems to protect both classified and unclassified information.[51] Elliptic curve systems offer a way to increase key size moderately when more security is required. Exhibit 7.22 shows the NIST recommended key size that RSA or Diffie-Hellman should use to protect the transportation of symmetric keys of various sizes as well as the corresponding elliptic curve key size.

Thus, in order to use RSA to protect a 256-bit AES key, one should use a key of 15,360 bits, which is an order of magnitude larger than the key sizes currently in use throughout the Internet. However, an elliptic curve key would need to be only 521 bits. Elliptic curve algorithms can use smaller keys because the math involved makes the inverse, or decryption, operations harder as the key length increases.[52]

Another feature that makes elliptic curves appealing is the fact that they are more efficient than the current implementations of public key cryptography, which tend to be relatively slow, causing them to be used more as key distribution methods than data encryption methods. Exhibit 7.23 shows the ratio of Diffie-Hellman computations versus elliptic curve computations for each of the key sizes listed in Exhibit 7.22.[53]

7.6.2 RSA Patent Expires. On September 6, 2000, RSA Security released the RSA public key encryption algorithm into the public domain. This means that anyone can now create products that incorporate this algorithm (provided it is their own implementation and not one licensed from RSA). In effect, RSA Security waived its rights to enforce the patent for any development activities that include the RSA algorithm occurring after September 6, 2000. The U.S. patent for the RSA algorithm actually expired on September 20, 2000. The result has been an even broader use of public key encryption, at lower cost.

EXHIBIT 7.23 Relative Computation Costs of Diffie-Hellman and Elliptic Curves

Security Level (bits)	Ratio of DH Cost : EC Cost
80	3:1
112	6:1
128	10:1
192	32:1
256	64:1

Source: National Security Agency, "The Case for Elliptic Curve Cryptography," www.nsa.gov/ia/industry/crypto_elliptic_curve.cfm.

The RSA patent was always somewhat controversial, because it applied to a piece of mathematics, which is not what most people think of when they think of an invention. The owners of the patent were never able to expand protection beyond the United States. As a result, versions of public key encryption based on alternatives to the RSA algorithm were developed and marketed outside the country, by companies like Ireland's Baltimore Technologies, Finland's F-Secure, and Israel's Algorithmic Research. Now encryption companies can dispense with the costly maintenance of multiple versions of their public key products (U.S. and non-U.S.). In addition, U.S. companies can develop and market RSA-based products. Large companies actually can "roll their own" public-key encryption schemes for internal use, based on a proven, royalty-free algorithm.

7.6.3 DES Superseded.   RSA Security, the company that tried to make the RSA algorithm synonymous with public key encryption, played a leading role in the other watershed crypto event of 2000, the naming of a successor to DES, the Data Encryption Standard. As noted earlier, projects like the EFF DES Cracker showed that a computer built for less than $250,000 could decipher a DES-encrypted message in fewer than three days. In fact, this was part of the "DES Challenges" sponsored by RSA Security. DES Challenge I was won by Rocke Verser of Loveland, Colorado, who led a group of Internet users in a distributed brute force attack. The project, code-named DESCHALL, began on March 13, 1997 and was successfully completed some 90 days later. DES Challenge II consisted of two contests posted on January 13 and July 13, 1998. The first contest was cracked by a distributed computing effort coordinated by distributed.net, which met the challenge in 39 days. The second contest was the one solved by EFF's purpose-built DES Cracker.

The effect of these projects was to focus attention on the need for stronger encryption. Companies and government agencies wanting to archive sensitive data need it to remain secure for decades, not days. However, as predicted in the 1970s, advances in computer power rendered "obsolete" the DEA, the widely used private key algorithm that forms the basis of the DES. Of course, the term "obsolete" is relative in this context. DES is not obsolete when applications need to encrypt bulk data to keep it confidential for a limited period of time, and a lot of data falls into this category. As Exhibit 7.24 shows,

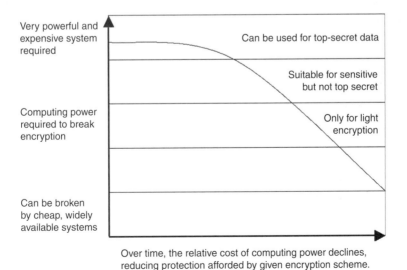

EXHIBIT 7.24 Relationship among Time, Technology, and Protection

there is a direct relationship among time, technology, and the degree of protection that any ciphersystem provides.

In 1997, the U.S. Government began the process of establishing a more powerful standard than DES, known as Advanced Encryption Standard (AES). This is a Federal Information Processing Standard (FIPS) Publication, FIPS 197, specifying "a cryptographic algorithm for use by U.S. Government organizations to protect sensitive (unclassified) information." The government anticipated correctly that AES would be "widely used on a voluntary basis by organizations, institutions, and individuals outside of the U.S. Government—and outside of the United States—in some cases."

In essence, a competition was held to find the best possible algorithm for the job, and the winner, chosen in October 2000, was Rijndael (pronounced "Rhine Doll"). This algorithm was developed specifically for the AES by two cryptographers from Belgium, Dr. Joan Daemen and Dr. Vincent Rijmen. Rijndael is a block cipher with a variable block length and key length. So far, keys with a length of 128, 192, or 256 bits have been specified to encrypt blocks with a length of 128, 192, or 256 bits. (All nine combinations of key length and block length are possible.) However, both block length and key length can be extended very easily in multiples of 32 bits. Rijndael can be implemented very efficiently in hardware, even on smart cards.

7.6.4 Quantum Cryptography.
A new basis for computation will profoundly affect cryptographic strength in the coming decades. This section provides a brief and nontechnical summary of the science of quantum computation and quantum cryptography.

7.6.4.1 Historical Perspective.
The entirety of this chapter has focused on the status of cryptography, as it currently exists. The classic computer has been sufficient to perform the computations and processes required of AES, RSA, and all of the cryptographic systems and algorithms that have been explored since the advent of cryptography. Although modern computers are fundamentally the same as they were in the 1950s, the machines we use today are significantly faster.[54] Even though the speed has increased, the primary task of computers has remained the same: "to manipulate and interpret an encoding of binary bits into a useful computational result."[55] To push the bounds of computer performance ever forward, computer scientists' goal has "been the reduction of size in the transistors used in modern processors."[56]

Early computers were constructed of gates and storage "bits" made of many thousands of molecules. The components of today's processors are moving in the direction of a few hundred molecules. The computing industry has always known that miniaturization would reach a barrier below which circuits could not be built, because their fundamental physical behavior would change.[57]

The components of modern computers are reaching this barrier; should transistors become much smaller, they will "eventually reach a point where individual elements would be no larger than a few atoms."[58] Computer scientists are concerned about this continual shrinking because at the atomic level, the laws of quantum mechanics will govern the properties and behavior of circuits, not the laws of classical mechanics.[59]

The science of quantum mechanics is not fully understood by scientists; it was initially thought to be a major limitation to the evolution of computer technology.[60] It was not until 1982 that the scientific community saw any benefit from the unusual effects associated with quantum mechanics. That year, Richard Feynman theorized about a new type of computer that would harness the effects of quantum mechanics and use these effects to its advantage.[61] In 1985, David Deutsch of the University of Oxford published a "ground breaking theoretical paper describing how any physical process could be modeled perfectly (in theory) using a quantum computing system."[62] He further argued that a quantum system would be able to execute tasks that no modern computer could perform, such as *true* random number generation.[63] "After Deutsch published this paper, the search began to find interesting applications for such a machine."[64]

7.6.4.2 Fundamentals. A "quantum" is "the smallest amount of a physical quantity that can exist independently, especially a discrete quantity of electromagnetic radiation."[65] Quantum mechanics explains the physics and behaviors of particles, atoms, and energy.[66] The idea of a quantum computer is based on the phenomena that occur at the atomic and subatomic level, which are explained by quantum mechanics and defy all classical laws of physics.[67] These phenomena will be covered in more detail shortly; it is necessary at this point, however, to explain several fundamental differences between classical modern computers and the idea of a quantum computer.

Classical computers store and process information in units called bits, represented as a '0' or a '1' in a computer's transistors. Bits are then organized into bytes, a series of eight bits. Thus, the information stored on a computer is stored as individual bits grouped into bytes. Therefore, a document "comprised of n-characters stored on the hard drive of a typical computer is accordingly described by a string of 8n zeros and ones."[68] It is important to emphasize that bits "can *only* exist in one of two distinct states, a '0' *or* a '1'."[69] This leads to the first difference between classical computers and quantum computers.

Quantum computers store and process information in units called quantum bits, referred to as qubits. "Qubits represent atoms, ions, photons or electrons and their respective control devices that are working together to act as computer memory and a processor."[70] Similar to a classic bit, a qubit is represented as a '0' or a '1'. Unlike a classic bit, a qubit can also exist in a *superposition* of both a '0' *and* a '1'. In other words, it is possible for a single qubit to exist as a '0', a '1', or simultaneously as both a '0' *and* a '1'. A qubit that is in two positions at once is said to be in its coherent state.[71] This can be explained more coherently with an example:

> If a coin is flipped in a darkened room, the result of the coin being flipped is mathematically just as likely to be heads or tails. While the light is off, the coin is in a superposition—whereby it is both heads and tails at once, because an [observer] cannot see which it is. If [the observer] turns on the light, [he or she] "collapses" the superposition, and forces the coin to be either heads or tails by measuring it. Measuring something destroys the superposition, forcing it into being in just one classical state.[72]

This coherent state leads to the phenomenon that would make a quantum computer exponentially more powerful than any computer to date; this is the phenomenon called quantum parallelism.[73] Essentially, because a qubit in a coherent state holds two values at once, a single operation done on such a qubit would act on both values at the same time.[74] "Likewise, a two-qubit system would perform the operation on four values and a three-qubit system on eight [values]."[75] To summarize, an operation done on a system of n qubits would act on 2^n values simultaneously.[76] Exhibit 7.25 shows this concept using a system containing three qubits, which represent eight states simultaneously.

"The very property that makes quantum computing so powerful also makes it very fragile and hard to control."[77] In order to harness the power of quantum parallelism, scientists need to be able to read and measure the output from the operations performed on groups of qubits. Herein lies the problem of decoherence. When a qubit in the coherent state measurably interacts with the environment, it will immediately decohere and resume one of the two classical states, either a '0' or a '1', and it will no longer

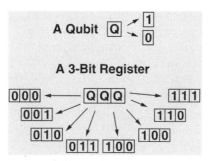

EXHIBIT 7.25 Three-Qubit System

Source: Simon Bone and Matias Castro, "A Brief History of Quantum Computing," Imperial College, London, www.doc.ic.ac.uk/~nd/surprise_97/journal/vol4/spb3/.

exhibit its dual-state ability. In other words, simply looking at a qubit can cause it to decohere, and this makes measuring qubits directly impossible.[78]

If scientists are unable to measure something directly, then they must find a way to measure indirectly, or a practical quantum computer will never be made. One possible answer lies in another property of quantum mechanics called entanglement. Entanglement is an obscure attribute that involves two or more atoms or particles. When certain conditions are met or certain forces are applied to two or more particles, then they can become entangled, whereby the particles exhibit opposite properties. The entangled particles will remain entangled, no matter the physical distance between them, and one entangled particle will always be able to communicate with its partner. Particles spin either up or down, and this spin is how scientists measure information about the particles. The property of coherence tells us that a particle will spin both up and down simultaneously until a scientist looks at it and measures it. "The spin state of the particle being measured is…communicated to the correlated particle, which simultaneously assumes the opposite spin direction to that of the measured particle."[79] Thus, entanglement could allow scientists to know the value of a qubit without actually looking at one. Scientists admit that entanglement is a difficult notion; they are still exploring the concept.[80] They also acknowledge that it could be years before a workable solution to the problem of measuring information in a quantum system is discovered.[81]

7.6.4.3 Impacts.

Although quantum computers, in theory, can perform any task that a classical computer can, this does not necessarily mean that a quantum computer will always outperform a classical computer. Multiplication is an often-cited example of something that would be done just as quickly on a classical computer as on a quantum computer.[82] From the early stages of quantum computing, scientists knew that to demonstrate the superior computing power, new algorithms would have to be designed to exploit the phenomenon of quantum parallelism. Such algorithms are complex and difficult to devise, but two are driving the development of this highly theorized field: Shor's algorithm and Grover's algorithm.[83]

Peter Shor of Bell Labs designed the first quantum algorithm in 1994. Shor's algorithm allows for rapid factoring of very large numbers into their prime factors. For example, scientific estimates state that it would take a modern computer 10^{24} years to factor a 1,000-digit number; it would take a quantum computer about 20 minutes.[84]

The implications of this quantum algorithm on classic algorithms that depend on the difficulty of factoring for security, such as the widely used RSA algorithm, are immense. "The ability to break the RSA coding system will render almost all current channels of communications unsecure."[85]

Lov Grover, also of Bell Labs, invented the second quantum algorithm in 1996. Grover's algorithm allows a quantum computer to search databases of all kinds much more quickly than any capability existing today. Grover notes that the greatest benefit is gained when his algorithm is used on an unsorted database.[86] On average, it takes a classical computer $n/2$ number of searches to find a specific entry in a database of n entries. Grover's algorithm allows the same search to be done in the square root of n number of searches. For example, in a database of 1 million entries, it would take a computer today on average of 500,000 searches to find the right answer; it would take a quantum computer using Grover's algorithm only 1,000 searches. This could have implications for symmetric key algorithms, such as DES, because this algorithm would allow an exhaustive search of all possible keys to occur quite rapidly.[87]

7.6.4.4 Current Status. Encouraged by the repercussions of quantum computing and the related algorithms on the security of information and cryptography, governments around the world are funding efforts to build a practical quantum computing system. The United States has many initiatives on- going. In 2001, the Defense Advanced Research Projects Agency (DARPA) of the Department of Defense launched a $100 million effort that would last five years. In addition, the National Science Foundation has $8 million in grant money for researching quantum capabilities. DARPA's Quantum Information Science and Technology initiative will now exist indefinitely; it became a fully funded and permanent program in 2006.[88] A number of other governments, primarily within Europe and Asia, are involved in quantum computation research and development. In 2000, the European Commission launched a comprehensive research effort with $20 million budgeted over three years. In Japan, the Ministry of Post and Telecommunications began an initiative in 2001 that will last 10 years with a total requested budget of $400 million. There are several commercial enterprises also involved in quantum projects. This includes IBM, Bell Labs, the Japanese firms of Fujitsu, Ltd., NEC Corporation, and Nippon Telephone and Telegraph Corporation.[89] This list is by no means exhaustive, as there are universities and other organizations throughout the world with research efforts in full swing.

Because of the worldwide effort to understand quantum computing more thoroughly, several key advancements have been made. In 1998, researchers at Los Alamos National Laboratory and MIT were able to spread a qubit over three nuclear spins of certain types of molecules. According to the experiments, spreading the information (qubit) out made it more difficult to corrupt, or decohere. The researchers were able to accomplish this using a technique called nuclear magnetic resonance (NMR), which allows the manipulation and control of a nucleus's spin. This technique allowed the researchers to use the property of entanglement to analyze indirectly the quantum information.[90]

In 2000, researchers at IBM developed a five-qubit computer, also using the nuclei of a liquid. The nuclei were programmed by radio frequency pulses and then detected by NMR techniques. Using this technique, the team was able to find the period of a particular function, or the length of the shortest interval over which it repeats its values. This problem would take a classical computer several repeated cycles to compute; the team at IBM was able to do it in one step. In 2001, a combined group of scientists from IBM and Stanford University demonstrated Shor's algorithm and were able to find the prime factors of 15. The seven-qubit computer correctly deduced that the prime factors were 3 and 5.[91]

In February 2007, a Canadian company called D-Wave claimed to demonstrate the first commercial quantum computer. It is a "supercooled, superconducted niobium chip housing an array of 16 qubits."[92] D-Wave chose not to focus on cryptographic efforts when building the Orion, as the computer is called. Instead, Orion focuses its energy on solving pattern-matching problems and nondeterministic polynomial problems (NP-complete problems). NP-complete problems are decision problems that contain searching and optimization problems, and are used when someone needs to know if a certain solution for a certain problem exists. Examples of such problems include database searches, pattern matching, identifying diseases from symptoms, and finding matches for genetic material.[93] The company's demonstrations were done via a television feed from a remote location, due to the sensitive nature of the machine and the difficulty in transporting equipment that is cooled to just above absolute zero. Despite the demonstrations and the claims of D-Wave, scientists are skeptical that Orion is actually performing quantum computations. Even the chief executive of D-Wave said that, although all evidence indicates that Orion is performing quantum computations, there is some uncertainty. Nevertheless, D-Wave announced plans to boost the Orion to 1,000 qubits by 2008.[94]

The latest advancement occurred in July 2007, when scientists from the National Institute of Standards and Technology (NIST, United States) and the Rutherford Appleton Laboratory (United Kingdom) teamed up to explore magnetic quantum effects. This team reports having chained together "100 atoms of yttrium barium nickel oxide into a quantum spin-chain that, in effect, turn[ed] the 30-nanometer long magnetic molecule into a single element."[95] This discovery is an important step toward putting qubits onto solid-state circuits. Thirty nanometers is well beyond the atomic length scale, and it is unusual to see quantum coherence beyond the atomic level. However, the team did report stable coherent states at this size, which is large enough for the lithographic techniques used to create circuit boards and conductors of classical computers.[96]

Even with the advances just mentioned, skeptics believe that practical quantum computers that outperform classical computers are still years, or even decades, away. After conducting many hours of research on the topic of quantum computing, this author's opinion is that it is not a matter of if quantum computing will become a reality but a matter of when. That scientists have been able to demonstrate a few theoretical quantum computations on systems comprised of only a few qubits is highly promising. Yet scientists need to overcome many obstacles. Systems containing hundreds or thousands of qubits will be needed to perform useful computations. In addition, precise controls will be required to accomplish operations while avoiding decoherence; in fact, decoherence is perhaps the biggest obstacle to the creation of a quantum system. Until scientists can reliably measure information produced by qubits at work, it is unlikely that a practical quantum system will be built in the near future.[97]

7.6.5 Snake Oil Factor.   As encryption vendors and cryptographers come to grips with the implementation and extended testing of new algorithms, it is important to note these words from the AES competition requirements:

> A complete written specification of the algorithm shall be included, consisting of all necessary mathematical equations, tables, diagrams, and parameters that are needed to implement the algorithm.

In other words, there is no secret about how the AES will make things secret, just as there is no secret about how DES works. This often strikes the crypto-novice as illogical. Why not keep the algorithm secret? Surely that will make any messages encrypted with it that much harder to decrypt. Not really. Any reliance on the secrecy of the algorithm inserts a weak link in the chain of security. Encrypting data does not guarantee that it will remain confidential. The keys must be kept secret, and the identity of persons requesting authorized access must be verified to ensure they are authentic, and so on. This is true of public key encryption as well as private key encryption.

There is no benefit to be gained by relying on an algorithm that has not been subject to open review, particularly when strong, reviewed algorithms exist. Beware of encryption vendors, or producers of any security products, that claim strength based on secret algorithms. Such claims are often a case of snake oil. (For more on bogus claims for crypto products, see Curtin's "Snake Oil FAQ.")

7.7 FURTHER READING.   As stated at the outset, this chapter was not designed to be an extensive treatise on cryptography or a complete guide to the implementation of encryption technology. There are many resources available to help readers deepen their understanding of this fundamental area of information security.

Books and Articles

Bishop, M. *Computer Security: Art and Science*. Addison-Wesley/Pearson Education, Upper Saddle River, NJ 2003.

Hinsley, F. H., and A. Stripp, eds. *Codebreakers: The Inside Story of Bletchley Park*. Oxford: Oxford University Press, 2001.

Cobb, C. *Cryptography for Dummies*. Wiley Publishing, Hoboken, NJ, 2003.

Goldreich, O. *Foundations of Cryptography: Volume I, Basic Tools*. New York: Cambridge University Press, 2007.

Juels, Ari. "Encryption Basics." In H. Bidgoli, ed., *Handbook of Information Security*, Vol. 2. Hoboken, NJ: John Wiley & Sons, 2006.

Kahn, D. *The Codebreakers: The Comprehensive History of Secret Communication from Ancient Times to the Internet*, Revised Edition. New York: Scribner, 1996.

Katz, J., and Y. Lindell *Introduction to Modern Cryptography*. London: Chapman & Hall/CRC, 2007.

Mao, W. *Modern Cryptography: Theory and Practice*. Upper Saddle River, NJ: Prentice-Hall, 2003.

Mel, H. X., and D. Baker. *Cryptography Decrypted*. Addison-Wesley, Upper Saddle River, NJ 2000.

Schneier, B. *Applied Cryptography: Protocols, Algorithms, and Source Code in C*, 2nd ed. New York: John Wiley & Sons, 1996.

Seberry, J., and J. Pieprzyk. *Cryptography: An Introduction to Computer Security*. Englewood Cliffs, NJ: Prentice-Hall, 1989.

Spillman, R. J. *Classical and Contemporary Cryptology*. Upper Saddle River, NJ: Prentice-Hall, 2004.

Web Resources

Arsenault, A., and S. Turner. "Internet X.509 Public Key Infrastructure: PKIX Roadmap," 2000; www.ietf.org/proceedings/00jul/I-D/pkix-roadmap-05.txt.

Bacard, A. "Non-Technical PGP (Pretty Good Privacy) FAQ," 2002; www.andrebacard .com/pgp.html.

Beezer, R. "Cryptography Independent Study," 2002; http://buzzard.ups.edu/ courses/2002spring/iscryptos2002.html.

Cate, V. Vince Cate's Cryptorebel/Cypherpunk Page, www.offshore.com.ai/security/.

Cryptography Research Inc. Research Links: www.cryptography.com/resources/ researchlinks.html.

Curtin, M. "Snake-Oil FAQ/Snake Oil Warning Signs: Encryption Software to Avoid," 1998; www.interhack.net/people/cmcurtin/snake-oil-faq.html.

Electronic Frontier Foundation. "Frequently Asked Questions (FAQ) About the Electronic Frontier Foundation's 'DES Cracker' Machine," 1999; http://w2.eff.org/ Privacy/Crypto/Crypto_misc/DESCracker/HTML/19980716_eff_des_faq.html.

Electronic Frontier Foundation RSA. "Code-Breaking Contest Again Won by Distributed.Net and Electronic Frontier Foundation (EFF). DES Challenge III Broken in Record 22 Hours," 1999; http://w2.eff.org/Privacy/Crypto/Crypto_misc/ DESCracker/HTML/19990119_deschallenge3.html.

Gerck, E. "Why Is Certification Harder than It Looks?" 1999; http://mcwg.org/ mcg-mirror/whycert.htm.

ICSA Labs' Cryptography Community. www.icsalabs.com/icsa/main.php?pid= vjgj7567.

International PGP Home Page. 2002; www.pgpi.org/.

Kessler, G. "An Overview of Cryptography," 2004; www.garykessler.net/library/ crypto.html.

PGP Home. www.pgp.com/index.php.

RSA Security Content Library. www.rsasecurity.com/doc_library/index.asp.

Schneier, B. *Crypto-Gram* newsletter archive, 1998–2008; www.schneier.com/ crypto-gram-back.html.

7.8 NOTES

1. David Kahn, *The Codebreakers: The Story of Secret Writing* (New York: Scribner, 1996), pp. 980–984.

2. *The American Heritage® New Dictionary of Cultural Literacy,* 3rd ed. s.v "cryptography," http://dictionary.reference.com/browse/cryptography.

3. RSA Laboratories, "What Is Cryptanalysis?" www.rsa.com/rsalabs/node. asp?id=2200.

4. J. Seberry and J. Pieprzyk, *Cryptography: An Introduction to Computer Security* (Englewood Cliffs, NJ: Prentice-Hall, 1989).

5. Kahn, *Codebreakers,* pp. 71–72

6. *Encyclopaedia Britannica Online Academic Edition,* s.v. "cryptology," http://search.eb.com.library.norwich.edu/eb/article-25638.

7. Brigitte Collard, "La cryptographie dans l'Antiquité gréco-romaine. III. Le chiffrement par transposition," *Folia Electronica Classica* (Louvain-la-Neuve) 7 (January-June 2004): section II(2), "Définition de la scytale"; http://bcs. fltr.ucl.ac.be/FE/07/CRYPT/Crypto44-63.html#42047

8. Brad Stark, "A Closer Look at Cryptography," Bucknell University, www.facstaff.bucknell.edu/udaepp/090/w3/brads.htm.

9. Kahn, *Codebreakers,* pp. 83–84.

10. "Time Table/Time-Travel through Cryptography and Cryptanalysis," www.cryptool.com/menu_zeittafel.en.html.

11. Oliver Pell, "Cryptology," www.ridex.co.uk/cryptology/#_Toc439908853.

12. "Time Table/Time-Travel."

13. *Encyclopaedia Britannica Online Academic Edition*, s.v. "cryptology."

14. *Encyclopaedia Britannica Online Academic Edition*, s.v. "cryptology."

15. Kahn, *Codebreakers,* p. 107.

16. *Encyclopedia Britannica Online Academic Edition,* s.v. "cryptology."

17. National Security Agency, "The Rare Books Collection: Giovanni Battista Porta," www.nsa.gov/publications/publi00013.cfm.

18. D. Salomon, *Coding for Data and Computer Communications* (New York: Springer, 2005), p. 218; http://books.google.com/books?id=A88kvYwIVu0C&pg=PA218&lpg=PA218&dq=wheatstone+playfair+cipher&source=web&ots=yCyXzMhsgD&sig=v5mDooQodCMYOZleEyz1zp75lJY   or   http://tinyurl.com/2dsmc8.

19. *Encyclopedia Britannica Online Academic Edition*, s.v. "cryptology."

20. Stallings, W. *Network and Internetwork Security Principles and Practices.* Prentice Hall, January, 1995

21. Kevin Romano, "The Stager Ciphers and the US Military's First Cryptographic System," www.gordon.army.mil/AC/Wntr02/stager.htm.

22. Cypher Research Laboratories, "A Brief History of Cryptography," www.cypher.com.au/crypto_history.htm.

23. National Archives, "Teaching with Documents: The Zimmermann Telegram," www.archives.gov/education/lessons/zimmermann.

24. National Archives, "Teaching with Documents."

25. Jacob Mathai, "History of Cryptography and Secrecy Systems," Fordham University, www.dsm.fordham.edu/~mathai/crypto.html#OneTimePad.

26. Encyclopaedia Britannica Online Academic Edition, s.v. "cryptology."

27. Judson Knight, "Cryptology, History," www.espionageinfo.com/Cou-De/Cryptology-History.html.

28. Knight, "Cryptology, History."

29. Oli Cooper, "Cryptography," University of Bristol, www.cs.bris.ac.uk/cooper/Cryptography/crypto.html.

30. Cooper, "Cryptology."

31. Kahn, *Codebreakers,*

32. Kahn, *Codebreakers,*

33. Stallings, "Network and Internetwork Security"

34. SCI.CRYPT FAQ §5.2, www.faqs.org/faqs/cryptography-faq/part05/.

35. Kahn, *Codebreakers,* p. 979.

36. Juels, "Encryption Basics," p. 980.

37. Juels, "Encryption Basics," p. 981.

38. Juels, "Encryption Basics," p. 471.

39. www.faqs.org/faqs/cryptography-faq/part06/

40. Bruce Schneier, *Applied Cryptography*, 2nd ed. (New York: John Wiley & Sons, 1996), p. 461.

41. Kahn, *Codebreakers,* p. 982.

42. Juels, "Encryption Basics," p. 474.

43. Juels, "Encryption Basics," p. 474.

44. Juels, "Encryption Basics," p. 474.

45. RSA Laboratories, "What Is Diffie-Hellman?" www.rsa.com/rsalabs/node.asp?id=2248.

46. Charlie Kaufman, "IPsec: IKE (Internet Key Exchange)," vol. 1, *Handbook for Information Security* (Hoboken, NJ: John Wiley & Sons, 2006), p. 974.

47. Juels, "Encryption Basics," pp. 474–475.

48. For more on this evolution, see the excellent IETF document, "Internet X.509 Public Key Infrastructure: PKIX Roadmap," by A. Arsenault and S. Turner.)

49. Michael Baum, *Secure Electronic Commerce* (Prentice-Hall, 1997)

50. National Security Agency, "The Case for Elliptic Curve Cryptography," www.nsa.gov/ia/industry/crypto_elliptic_curve.cfm.

51. National Security Agency, "The Case for Elliptic Curve Cryptography."

52. Certicom, "An Elliptic Curve Cryptography (ECC) Primer," www.deviceforge.com/articles/AT4234154468.html.

53. National Security Agency, "The Case for Elliptic Curve Cryptography."

54. Jacob West, "The Quantum Computer," www.cs.caltech.edu/~westside/quantum-intro.html.

55. West, "Quantum Computer."

56. Simon Bone and Matias Castro, "A Brief History of Quantum Computing," Imperial College, London, www.doc.ic.ac.uk/~nd/surprise_97/journal/vol4/spb3/.

57. Quantum Information Partners LLP, "Short History of Quantum Information Processing," www.qipartners.com/publications/Short_History_of_QC.pdf.

58. West, "Quantum Computer."

59. West, "Quantum Computer."

60. Bone and Castro, "Brief History."

61. Bone and Castro, "Brief History."

62. Simon Bone, "The Hitchhiker's Guide to Quantum Computing," www.dse.doc.ic.ac.uk/%7End/surprise_97/journal/vol1/spb3/.

63. Bone, "Hitchhiker's Guide."

64. West, "Quantum Computer."

65. *American Heritage ® Dictionary of the English Language, Fourth Edition*, s.v. "quanta," http://dictionary.reference.com/browse/quantum.

66. Genomics and Proteomics, "Glossary: Quantum Mechanics," www.genpromag.com/Glossary.aspx?LETTER=Q.

67. Stephen Jenkins, "Some Basic Ideas About Quantum Mechanics," University of Exeter, newton.ex.ac.uk/research/qsystems/people/jenkins/mbody/mbody2.html.

68. West, "Quantum Computer."

69. Bone and Castro, "Brief History."

70. Bonsor and Strickland, "How Quantum Computers Work," computer. howstuffworks.com/quantum-computer3.htm.

71. Bone and Castro, "Brief History."

72. Duncan McKimm, "Quantum Entanglement," www.abc.net.au/science/features/quantum/.

73. West, "Quantum Computer."

74. Bone and Castro, "Brief History."

75. Bone and Castro, "Brief History."

76. Bone and Castro, "Brief History."

77. Bone and Castro, "Brief History."

78. Bonsor and Strickland, "How Quantum Computers Work."

79. SearchSMB.com, "Entanglement," searchsmb.techtarget.com/sDefinition/0,, sid44_gci341428,00.html.

80. McKimm, "Quantum Entanglement."

81. SearchSMB.com, "Entanglement."

82. Bone and Castro, "Brief History."

83. Bone and Castro, "Brief History."

84. Bone and Castro, "Brief History."

85. Bone, "Hitchhiker's Guide."

86. Lov Grover, "What's a Quantum Phone Book?" www.bell-labs.com/user/feature/archives/lkgrover/.

87. Bone and Castro, "Brief History."

88. Confidential Source #3, "Quantum Computing," Internal Research branch Web site, August 10, 2007.

89. Confidential Source #3, "Quantum Computing."

90. West, "Quantum Computer."

91. Bonsor and Strickland, "How Quantum Computers Work."

92. R. Colin Johnson "Quantum Computer 'Orion' Debuts," EETimes, www.eetimes.com/showArticle.jhtml;jsessionid=LMGNMUNA3DEJQQSNDLPSKHSCJUN N2JVN?articleID=197004661.

93. Johnson, "Quantum Computer 'Orion' Debuts."

94. Jordon Robertson, "Scientists Dubious of Quantum Computer Claims," abcnews.go.com/Technology/wireStory?id=2875656.

95. R. Colin Johnson, "Circuit-Sized Quantum Effect Observed," EETimes, www.eetimes.com/showArticle.jhtml;jsessionid=V0KJDCQ4XUOFUQSNDLP SKHSCJUNN2JVN?articleID=201202072.

96. Johnson, "Circuit-Sized Quantum Effect Observed."

97. Confidential Source #3, "Quantum Computing."

CHAPTER 8

USING A COMMON LANGUAGE FOR COMPUTER SECURITY INCIDENT INFORMATION

John D. Howard

8.1 INTRODUCTION.   A computer security *incident* is some set of events that involves an attack or series of attacks at one or more sites. (See Section 8.4.3 for a more formal definition of the term "incident.") Dealing with these incidents is inevitable for individuals and organizations at all levels of computer security. A major part of dealing with these incidents is recording and receiving incident information, which almost always is in the form of relatively unstructured text files. Over time, these files can end up containing a large quantity of very valuable information. Unfortunately, the unstructured form of the information often makes incident information difficult to manage and use.

This chapter presents the results of several efforts over the last few years to develop and propose a method to handle these unstructured, computer security incident records. Specifically, this chapter presents a *tool* designed to help individuals and organizations record, understand, and share computer security incident information. We call the tool the *common language for computer security incident information*. This common language contains two parts:

1. A set of "high-level" incident-related terms

2. A method of classifying incident information (a taxonomy)

The two parts of the common language, the terms and the taxonomy, are closely related. The taxonomy provides a structure that shows how most common-language terms are related. The common language is intended to help investigators improve their ability to:

- Talk more understandably with others about incidents
- Gather, organize, and record incident information
- Extract data from incident information
- Summarize, share, and compare incident information
- Use incident information to evaluate and decide on proper courses of action
- Use incident information to determine effects of actions over time

This chapter begins with a brief overview of why a common language is needed, followed by a summary of how the incident common language was developed. We then present the common language in two parts: (1) incident terms and taxonomy and (2) additional incident information terms. The final section contains information about some practical ways to use the common language.

8.2   WHY A COMMON LANGUAGE IS NEEDED.   When the first edition of this *Handbook* was published more than 30 years ago, computer security was a small, obscure, academic specialty. Because there were only a few people working in the field, the handling of computer security information could largely take place in an ad hoc way. In this environment, individuals and groups developed their own terms to describe computer security information. They also developed, gathered, organized, evaluated, and exchanged their computer security information in largely unique and unstructured ways. This lack of generalization has meant that computer security information has typically not been easy to compare or combine, or sometimes even to talk about in an understandable way.

Progress over the years in agreeing on a relatively standard set of terms for computer security (a common language) has had mixed results. One problem is that many terms are not yet in widespread use. Another problem is that the terms that are in widespread use often do not have standard meanings. An example of the latter is the term "computer virus." We hear the term frequently, not only in academic forums but also in the news media and popular publications. It turns out, however, that even in academic publications, "computer virus" has no accepted definition.[1] Many authors define a computer virus to be "a code fragment that copies itself into a larger program."[2] They use the term "worm" to describe an independent program that performs a similar invasive function (e.g., the "Internet Worm" in 1988). But other authors use the term "computer virus" to describe *both* invasive code fragments and independent programs.

Progress in developing methods to gather, organize, evaluate, and exchange computer security information also has had limited success. For example, the original records (1988–1992) of the Computer Emergency Response Team (now the CERT Coordination Center or CERT/CC) are simply a file of e-mail and other files sent to the CERT/CC. These messages and files were archived together in chronological order, without any other organization. After 1992, the CERT/CC and other organizations developed methods to organize and disseminate their information, but the information remains difficult to combine or compare because most of it remains almost completely textual information that is uniquely structured for the CERT/CC.

Such ad hoc terms and ad hoc ways to gather, organize, evaluate, and exchange computer security information are no longer adequate. Far too many people and organizations are involved, and there is far too much information to understand and share. Today computer security is an increasingly important, relevant, and sophisticated field of study. Numerous individuals and organizations now regularly gather and disseminate computer security information. Such information ranges all the way from the security characteristics and vulnerabilities of computers and networks, to the behavior of people and systems during security incidents—far too much information for each individual and organization to have its own unique language.

One of the key elements to making systematic progress in any field of inquiry is the development of a consistent set of terms and taxonomies (principles of classification) that are used in that field.[3] This is a necessary and natural process that leads to a growing *common language,* which enables gathering, exchanging, and comparing information. In other words, as a field of inquiry such as computer security grows, the more a common language is needed to understand and communicate with one another.

8.3 DEVELOPMENT OF THE COMMON LANGUAGE.   Two of the more significant efforts in the process of developing this common language for computer security incident information were (1) a project to classify more than 4,300 Internet security incidents completed in 1997,[4] and (2) a series of workshops in 1997 and 1998, called the *Common Language Project.* Workshop participants included people primarily from the Security and Networking Research Group at the Sandia National Laboratories, Livermore, California, and from the CERT/CC at the Software Engineering Institute, Carnegie Mellon University, Pittsburgh, Pennsylvania. Additional participation and review came from people in the Department of Defense (DoD) and the National Institute of Standards and Technology (NIST).

These efforts to develop the common language were *not* efforts to develop a comprehensive dictionary of terms. Instead, the participants were trying to develop both a *minimum* set of "high-level" terms to describe computer security attacks and incidents, and a structure and classification scheme for these terms (a *taxonomy*), which could be used to classify, understand, exchange, and compare computer security attack and incident information.

Participants in the workshops hoped this common language would gain wide acceptance because of its usefulness. There is already evidence that this acceptance is taking place, particularly at incident response teams and in the DoD.

In order to be complete, logical, and useful, the common language for computer security incident information was based initially and primarily on theory (i.e., it was a priori or nonempirically based).[5] Classification of actual Internet security incident information was then used to refine and expand the language. More specifically, the common language development proceeded in six stages:

1. Records at the CERT/CC for incidents reported to them from 1988 through 1995 were examined to establish a preliminary list of terms used to describe computer security incidents.
2. The terms in this list, and their definitions, were put together into a structure (a preliminary taxonomy).

3. This preliminary taxonomy was used to classify the information in the 1988 through 1995 incident records.

4. The preliminary taxonomy and classification results were published in 1997.[6]

5. A series of workshops was conducted from 1997 through 1998 (the *Common Language Project*) to make improvements to the taxonomy and to add additional terms.

6. The results of the workshops (the "common language for security incidents") were first published in 1998.

A *taxonomy* is a classification scheme (a structure) that partitions a body of knowledge and defines the relationship of the pieces.[7] Most of the terms in this common language for security incident information are arranged in such a taxonomy, as presented in the next section. *Classification* is the process of using a taxonomy for separating and ordering. As discussed earlier, classification of information using a taxonomy is necessary for computer security incident information because of the rapidly expanding amount of information and the nature of that information (primarily text). Classification using the common-language taxonomy is discussed in the final section of this chapter.

Our experience has shown that satisfactory taxonomies have classification categories with these six characteristics:[8]

1. Mutually exclusive. Classifying in one category excludes all others because categories do not overlap.

2. Exhaustive. Taken together, the categories include all possibilities.

3. Unambiguous. The taxonomy is clear and precise, so that classification is not uncertain, regardless of who is doing the classifying.

4. Repeatable. Repeated applications result in the same classification, regardless of who is doing the classifying.

5. Accepted. It is logical and intuitive, so that categories can become generally approved.

6. Useful. The taxonomy can be used to gain insight into the field of inquiry.

These characteristics were used to develop and evaluate the common-language taxonomy. A taxonomy, however, is merely an approximation of reality, and as such, even the best taxonomy will fall short in some characteristics. This may be especially true when the characteristics of the data being classified are imprecise and uncertain, as is typical for computer security incident information. Nevertheless, classification is an important, useful, and necessary prerequisite for systematic study of incidents.

8.4   COMPUTER SECURITY INCIDENT INFORMATION TAXONOMY.
We have been able to structure most of the terms in the common language for security incident information into a taxonomy. These terms and the taxonomy are presented in this section. Additional terms that describe the more general aspects of incidents are presented in Section 8.5.

8.4.1   Events.   The operation of computers and networks involves innumerable *events*. In a general sense, an event is a discrete change of state or status of a system or device.[9] From a computer security viewpoint, these changes of state result from *actions* that are directed against specific *targets*. An example is a user taking action to

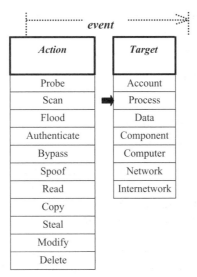

EXHIBIT 8.1   Computer and Network Events

log in to the user's account on a computer system. In this case, the action taken by the user is to *authenticate* to the login program by claiming to have a specific identity and then presenting the required verification. The target of this action would be the user's *account*. Other examples include numerous actions that can be targeted toward:

- *Data* (e.g., actions to *read, copy, modify, steal,* or *delete*)
- A *process* (e.g., actions to *probe, scan, authenticate, bypass,* or *flood* a running computer process or execution thread)
- A *component, computer, network,* or *internetwork* (e.g., actions to *scan* or *steal*)

Exhibit 8.1 presents a matrix of actions and targets that represent possible computer and network events (although not all of the possible combinations shown are feasible). A computer or network event is defined as:

Event—action directed at a target that is intended to result in a change of state, or status, of the target.[10]

Several aspects of this definition are important to emphasize. First, in order for there to be an event, there must be an action that is taken, and it must be directed against a target, but the action does *not* have to succeed in actually changing the state of the target. For example, if a user enters an incorrect user name and password combination when logging in to an account, an authentication event has taken place, but the event was not successful in verifying that the user has the proper credentials to access that account.

A second important aspect is that an event represents a *practical* linkage between an action and a specific target against which the action is directed. As such, it represents the way people generally conceptualize events on computers and networks, and not all of the individual steps that actually take place during an event. For example, when a user logs in to an account, we classify the action as *authenticate* and the target as *account*. The actual action that takes place is for the user to access a process (e.g., a "login" program) in order to authenticate. Trying to depict all of the individual steps is an unnecessary complication; the higher-level concepts presented here can describe correctly and accurately the event in a form well understood by people. In other words, it makes sense to abstract the language and its structure to the level at which people generally conceptualize the events.

By all means, supporting evidence should be presented so the evidence provides a complete idea of what happened. Stated another way, abstraction, conceptualization, and communication should be applied as close to the evidence as possible. For example, if a network switch is the target of an attack, then the target should normally be viewed as a computer or as a component (depending on the nature of the switch), and not the network, because assuming the network is the target may be an inaccurate interpretation of the evidence.

Another aspect of the definition of event is that it does not make a distinction between *authorized* and *unauthorized* actions. Most events that take place on computers or networks are both routine and authorized and, therefore, are not of concern to security professionals. Sometimes, however, an event is part of an attack or is a security concern for some other reason. This definition of event is meant to capture both authorized and unauthorized actions. For example, if a user authenticates properly, by giving the correct user identification and password combination while logging in to an account, that user is given access to that account. It may be the case, however, that this user is masquerading as the actual user, after having obtained the user identification and password from snooping on the network. Either way, this is still considered authentication.

Finally, an important aspect of events is that not all of the possible events (the action–target combinations depicted in Exhibit 8.1) are considered likely or even possible. For example, an action to *authenticate* is generally associated with an *account* or a *process* and not a different target, such as *data* or a *component*. Other examples include *read* and *copy*, which are generally targeted toward *data*; *flooding*, which is generally targeted at an *account*, *process,* or *system*; or *stealing*, which is generally targeted against *data*, a *component*, or a *computer*.

We define *action* and *target* as follows:

Action—step taken by a user or process in order to achieve a result,[11] such as to probe, scan, flood, authenticate, bypass, spoof, read, copy, steal, modify, or delete.

Target—computer or network logical entity (account, process, or data) or a physical entity (component, computer, network or internetwork).

8.4.1.1   Actions.   The actions depicted in Exhibit 8.1 represent a spectrum of activities that can take place on computers and networks. An action is a step taken by a *user* or a *process* in order to achieve a result. Actions are initiated by accessing a target, where *access* is defined as:

Access—establish logical or physical communication or contact.[12]

Two actions are used to gather information about targets: *probe* and *scan*. A probe is an action to determine one or more characteristics of a specific target. This is unlike a scan, which is an action where a user or process accesses a set of targets systematically, in order to determine which targets have one or more characteristics.

"Probe" and "scan" are terms commonly used by incident response teams. As a result, they have common, accepted definitions. Despite this, there is a logical ambiguity:

	Test for One or More Characteristics
Test a Single Host	Probe
Nonsystematically Test Multiple Hosts	Multiple probes
Systematically Test a Set of Hosts	Scan

EXHIBIT 8.2   *Probe* Compared to *Scan*

A scan could be viewed as multiple probes. In other words, if an attacker is testing for one or more characteristics on multiple hosts, this can be (a) multiple attacks (all *probes*), or (b) one attack (a *scan*). This point was discussed extensively in the Common Language Project workshops, and the conclusion was that the terms in the common language should match, as much as possible, their common usage. This common usage is illustrated in Exhibit 8.2.

With probes and scans, it is usually obvious what is taking place. The attacker is either "hammering away" at one host (a *probe*), randomly testing many hosts (multiple *probes*), or using some "automatic" software to look for the same characteristic(s) systematically across a group of hosts (a *scan*). As a practical matter, incident response teams do not usually have a problem deciding what type of action they are dealing with.

One additional point about *scan* is that the term "systematic" is not meant to specify some specific pattern. The most sophisticated attackers try to disguise the systematic nature of a scan. A scan may, at first, appear to be multiple probes. For example, an attacker may randomize a scan with respect to hosts and with respect to the characteristic(s) being tested. If the attack can be determined to involve testing of one or more characteristics on a group of hosts with some common property (e.g., an Internet Protocol [IP] address range) or if tests on multiple hosts appear to be otherwise related (e.g., having a common origin in location and time), then the multiple probes should be classified as a scan.

Unlike probe or scan, an action taken to *flood* a target is not used to gather information about the target. Instead, the desired result of a flood is to overwhelm or overload the target's capacity by accessing the target repeatedly. An example is repeated requests to open connections to a port over a network or repeated requests to initiate processes on a computer. Another example is a high volume of e-mail messages, which may exceed the resources available for the targeted account.

Authenticate is an action taken by a user to assume an identity. Authentication starts with a user accessing an authentication process, such as a login program. The user must claim to have a certain identity, such as by entering a user name. Usually verification is also required as a second authentication step. For verification, the user must prove knowledge of some secret (e.g., a password), prove the possession of some token (e.g., a secure identification card), and/or prove to have a certain characteristic (e.g., a retinal scan pattern). Authentication can be used not only to log in to an account but also to access other objects, such as to operate a process or to access a file. In other words, the target of an authentication action is the entity (e.g., account, process, or data) that the user is trying to access, not the authentication process itself.

Two general methods might be used to defeat an authentication process. First, a user could obtain a valid identification and verification pair that could be used to authenticate, even though it does not belong to that user. For example, during an incident, an attacker might use a process operating on an Internet host computer that captures user name, password, and IP address combinations that are sent in clear text across the Internet. The attacker could then use this captured information to authenticate (log in) to accounts that belong to other users. It is important to note, as mentioned earlier, that this action is still considered *authenticate*, because the attacker presents valid identification and verification pairs, even though they have been stolen.

The second method that might be used to defeat an authentication process is to exploit a vulnerability in order to bypass the authentication process and access the target. *Bypass* is an action taken to avoid a process by using an alternative method to access a target. For example, some operating systems have vulnerabilities that an attacker could exploit to gain privileges without actually logging in to a privileged account.

As was discussed with respect to *authenticate*, an action to *bypass* does not necessarily indicate that the action is unauthorized. For example, some programmers find it useful to have a shortcut ("back-door") method to enter an account or run a process, particularly during development. In such a situation, an action to bypass may be considered authorized.

Authenticate and *bypass* are actions associated with users identifying themselves. In network communications, processes also identify themselves to each other. For example, each packet of information traveling on a network contains addresses identifying both the source and the destination, as well as other information. "Correct" information in these communications is assumed, since it is automatically generated. Thus no action is included on the list to describe this normal situation. Incorrect information could, however, be entered into these communications. Supplying such false information is commonly called an action to *spoof*. Examples include IP spoofing, mail spoofing, and Domain Name Service (DNS) spoofing.

> *Spoofing* is an active security attack in which one machine on the network masquerades as a different machine....[It] disrupts the normal flow of data and may involve injecting data into the communications link between other machines. This masquerade aims to fool other machines on the network into accepting the imposter as an original, either to lure the other machines into sending it data or to allow it to alter data.[13]

Some actions are closely associated with data found on computers or networks, particularly with files: *read*, *copy*, *modify*, *steal*, and *delete*. There has been some confusion over these terms because their common usage in describing the "physical" world sometimes differs from their common usage describing the "electronic" world. For example, if I say that an attacker *stole* a computer, then you can assume I mean the attacker took possession of the target (computer) and did not leave an identical computer in that location. If I say, however, that the attacker stole a computer *file*, what does that actually mean? It is often taken to mean that the attacker *duplicated* the file and now has a copy, but also it means that the original file is still in its original location. In other words, "steal" sometimes means something different in the physical world than it does in the electronic world.

It is confusing for there to be differences in the meaning of actions in the physical world and the electronic world. Workshop participants attempted to reconcile these differences by carefully defining each term (*read*, *copy*, *modify*, *steal*, or *delete*) so it would have a very specific and mutually exclusive meaning that matches the "physical world" meaning as much as possible.

Read is defined as an action to obtain the content of the data contained within a file or other data medium. This action is distinguished conceptually from the actual physical steps that may be required to read. For example, in the process of reading a computer file, the file may be copied from a storage location into the computer's main memory and then displayed on a monitor to be read by a user. These physical steps (copy the file into memory and then onto the monitor) are not part of the abstract concept of *read*. In other words, to read a target (obtain the content in it), copying of the file is not necessarily required, and it is conceptually not included in our definition of *read*.

The same separation of concepts is included in the definition of the term "copy." In this case, we are referring to acquiring a copy of a target without deleting the original. The term "copy" does not imply that the *content* in the target is obtained, just that a *copy* has been made and obtained. To get the content, the file must be *read*. An example is copying a file from a hard disk to a floppy disk. This copying is done by duplicating the original file while leaving the original file intact. A user would have to open the file and look at the content in order to *read* it.

Copy and *read* are both different concepts from *steal*, which is an action that results in the attacker taking possession of the target and the target also becoming unavailable to the original owner or user. This definition agrees with our concepts about physical property, specifically that there is only one object that cannot be copied. For example, if someone steals a car, then that person has deprived the owner of his or her possession. When dealing with property that is in electronic form, such as a computer file, often the term "steal" is used when what actually is meant is *copy*. The term "steal" specifically means that the original owner or user has been denied access or use of the target. On the other hand, stealing also could mean *physically* taking a floppy disk that has the file located on it or stealing an entire computer.

Two other actions involve changing the target in some way. The first are actions to *modify* a target. Examples include changing the content of a file, changing the password of an account, sending commands to change the characteristics of an operating process, or adding components to an existing system. If the target is eliminated entirely, the term "delete" is used to describe the action.

As stated earlier, differences in usage of terms between the physical world and the electronic world are undesirable. As such, we tried to be specific and consistent in our usage. The resulting set of terms is exhaustive and mutually exclusive but goes against the grain in some common usage for the "electronic world," particularly with respect to the term "steal." The situation seems unavoidable. Here are some examples that might clarify the terms:

- A user clicks on a link with the browser and sees the content of a web page on the computer screen. We would classify this as a *read*. While what actually happens is that the content of the page is stored in volatile memory, copied to the cache on the hard drive, and displayed on the screen, from a *logical* (i.e., user) point of view, the web page has *not* been copied (nor stolen). Now, if a user copies the content of the web page to a file or prints it out, then the user *has* copied the web page. Again, this would be a logical classification of the action, from the user's point of view.

- A user duplicates a file that is encrypted. We would classify this as *copy*, not *read*. In this case, the file was reproduced, but the content not obtained, so it was not read.

- A user deletes several entries in a password or group file. Should this action be described as several *delete* actions or as one action to *modify*? We would describe this action as *modify*, and the target is *data*. There is no ambiguity here because of the definition of data. Data are defined to be either a stationary file or a file in transit (see the next section). If a user deletes a line out of the password file, then the file has been modified. The action would be described as *delete* only if the whole file was deleted. If we had defined data to include part of a file, then we would indeed have an ambiguity.

- A user copies a file and deletes the original. We would classify this as *steal*. Although the steps actually include a *copy* followed by a *delete*, that is the electronic way of stealing a file, and therefore it is more descriptive to describe the action as *steal*.

In reality, the term "steal" is rarely used (correctly) because attackers who copy files usually do not delete the originals. The term "steal" often is used *incorrectly*, as in "stealing the source code," when in fact the correct term is *copy*.

The list of actions was hashed over in numerous group discussions, off and on, for several years before being put into the common language. Most people who participated in these discussions were not entirely happy with the list, but it is the best we have seen so far. Specifically, the list seems to capture all of the common terms with their common usage (*probe, scan, flood, spoof, copy, modify* and *delete*) and the other terms are logical (to the people who participated in the discussion groups) and are necessary to make the action category exhaustive (*authenticate, bypass, read* and *steal*).

Here is a summary of our definitions of the actions shown in Exhibit 8.1.

Probe—access a target in order to determine one or more of its characteristics.

Scan—access a set of targets systematically in order to identify which targets have one or more specific characteristics.[14]

Flood—access a target repeatedly in order to overload the target's capacity.

Authenticate—present an identity to a process and, if required, verify that identity, in order to access a target.[15]

Bypass—avoid a process by using an alternative method to access a target.[16]

Spoof—masquerade by assuming the appearance of a different entity in network communications.[17]

Read—obtain the content of data in a storage device or other data medium.[18]

Copy—reproduce a target leaving the original target unchanged.[19]

Steal—take possession of a target without leaving a copy in the original location.

Modify—change the content or characteristics of a target.[20]

Delete—remove a target or render it irretrievable.[21]

8.4.1.2   Targets.   Actions are considered to be directed toward seven categories of targets. The first three of these are "logical" entities (*account, process,* and *data*), and the other four are "physical" entities (*component, computer, network,* and *internetwork*).

In a multiuser environment, an *account* is the domain of an individual user. This domain includes the files and processes the user is authorized to access and use. A special program that records the user's account name, password, and use restrictions controls access to the user's account. Some accounts have increased or "special" permissions that allow access to system accounts, other user accounts, or system files and processes, and often are called *privileged*, *superuser*, *administrator*, or *root* accounts.

Sometimes an action may be directed toward a *process*, which is a program executing on a computer or network. In addition to the program itself, the process includes the program's data and stack, its program counter, stack pointer and other registers, and all other information needed to execute the program.[22] The action may then be to supply information to the process or command the process in some manner.

The target of an action may be *data* that are found on a computer or network. Data are representations of facts, concepts, or instructions in forms that are suitable for use by either users or processes. Data may be found in two forms: files or data in transit. *Files* are data that are designated by name and considered as a unit by the user or by a process. Commonly we think of files as being located on a storage medium, such as a storage disk, but files also may be located in the volatile or nonvolatile memory of a computer. *Data in transit* are data being transmitted across a network or otherwise emanating from some source. Examples of the latter include data transmitted between devices in a computer and data found in the electromagnetic fields that surround computer monitors, storage devices, processors, network transmission media, and the like.

Sometimes we conceptualize the target of an action as not being a *logical* entity (account, process, or data) but rather as a *physical* entity. The smallest of the physical entities is a *component*, which is one of the parts that make up a computer or network. A *network* is an interconnected or interrelated group of computers, along with the appropriate switching elements and interconnecting branches.[23] When a computer is attached to a network, it is sometimes referred to as a *host computer*. If networks are connected to each other, then they are sometimes referred to as an *internetwork*.

Here is a summary of our definitions of the targets shown in Exhibit 8.1.

Account—domain of user access on a computer or network that is controlled according to a record of information which contains the user's account name, password, and use restrictions.

Process—program in execution, consisting of the executable program, the program's data and stack, its program counter, stack pointer and other registers, and all other information needed to execute the program.[24]

Data—representations of facts, concepts, or instructions in a manner suitable for communication, interpretation, or processing by humans or by automatic means.[25] Data can be in the form of *files* in a computer's volatile memory or nonvolatile memory, or in a data storage device, or in the form of *data in transit* across a transmission medium.

Component—one of the parts that make up a computer or network.[26]

Computer—device that consists of one or more associated components, including processing units and peripheral units, that is controlled by internally stored programs and that can perform substantial computations, including numerous arithmetic operations or logic operations, without human intervention during execution. Note: may be stand-alone or may consist of several interconnected units.[27]

Network—interconnected or interrelated group of host computers, switching elements, and interconnecting branches.[28]

Internetwork—network of networks.

8.4.2   Attacks.   Sometimes an event that occurs on a computer or network is part of a series of steps intended to result in something that is not authorized to happen. This event is then considered part of an *attack*. An attack has three elements.

1. It is made up a series of steps taken by an *attacker*. Among these steps is an action directed at a target (an *event*, as described in the previous section) as well as the use of some *tool* to exploit a *vulnerability*.

2. An attack is intended to achieve an *unauthorized result* as viewed from the perspective of the owner or administrator of the system involved.

3. An attack is a series of *intentional* steps initiated by the attacker. This differentiates an attack from something that is inadvertent.

We define an attack in this way:

Attack—a series of steps taken by an attacker to achieve an unauthorized result.

Exhibit 8.3 presents a matrix of possible attacks, based on our experience. Attacks have five parts that depict the logical steps an attacker must take. An attacker uses a (1) *tool* to exploit a (2) *vulnerability* to perform an (3) *action* on a (4) *target* in order to achieve an (5) *unauthorized result*. To be successful, an attacker must find one or more paths that can be connected (attacks), perhaps simultaneously or repeatedly. The

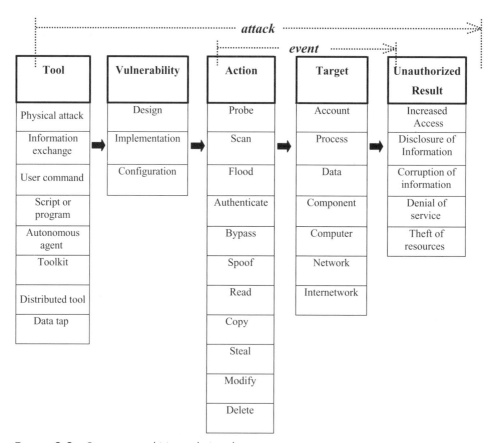

Tool	Vulnerability	Action	Target	Unauthorized Result
Physical attack	Design	Probe	Account	Increased Access
Information exchange	Implementation	Scan	Process	Disclosure of Information
User command	Configuration	Flood	Data	Corruption of information
Script or program		Authenticate	Component	Denial of service
Autonomous agent		Bypass	Computer	Theft of resources
Toolkit		Spoof	Network	
Distributed tool		Read	Internetwork	
Data tap		Copy		
		Steal		
		Modify		
		Delete		

EXHIBIT 8.3   Computer and Network Attacks

first two steps in an attack, *tool* and *vulnerability*, are used to cause an *event* (*action* directed at a *target*) on a computer or network. The logical end of a successful attack is an *unauthorized result*. If the logical end of the previous steps is an *authorized* result, then an attack has not taken place.

The concept of *authorized* versus *unauthorized* is key to understanding what differentiates an attack from the normal events that occur. It is also a system-dependent concept in that what may be authorized on one system may be unauthorized on another. For example, some services, such as anonymous File Transfer Protocol (FTP), may be enabled on some systems and not on others. Even actions that are normally viewed as hostile, such as attempts to bypass access controls to gain entry into a privileged account, may be authorized in special circumstances, such as during an approved test of system security, or in the use of a "back door" during development. System owners or their administrators make the determination of what actions they consider authorized for their systems by establishing a security policy.[29] Here are the definitions for authorized and unauthorized.

> **Authorized**—approved by the owner or administrator.

> **Unauthorized**—not approved by the owner or administrator.

The steps *action* and *target* in Exhibit 8.1 are the two parts of an event as discussed in Section 8.4.1. The following sections discuss the other steps: *tool*, *vulnerability,* and *unauthorized result*.

8.4.2.1 Tool. The first step in the sequence that leads attackers to their unauthorized results is the *tool* used in the attack. A tool is some means that can be used to exploit a vulnerability in a computer or network. Sometimes a tool is simple, such as a user command or a physical attack. Other tools can be very sophisticated and elaborate, such as a Trojan horse program, computer virus, or distributed tool. We define *tool* in this way.

> **Tool**—means of exploiting a computer or network vulnerability

The term "tool" is difficult to define more specifically because of the wide variety of methods available to exploit vulnerabilities in computers and networks. When authors make lists of methods of attack, often they are actually making lists of tools. Based on our experience, these categories of tools are currently an exhaustive list. (See Exhibit 8.3)

> **Physical attack**—means of physically stealing or damaging a computer, network, its components, or its supporting systems (e.g., air conditioning, electric power, etc.).

> **Information exchange**—means of obtaining information either from other attackers (e.g., through an electronic bulletin board) or from the people being attacked (commonly called social engineering).

> **User command**—means of exploiting a vulnerability by entering commands to a process through direct user input at the process interface. An example is entering UNIX commands through a telnet connection or commands at a protocol's port.

> **Script or program**—means of exploiting a vulnerability by entering commands to a process through the execution of a file of commands (script) or a program at

the process interface. Examples are a shell script to exploit a software bug, a Trojan horse log-in program, or a password-cracking program.

Autonomous agent—means of exploiting a vulnerability by using a program or program fragment that operates independently from the user. Examples are computer viruses or worms.

Toolkit—software package that contains scripts, programs, or autonomous agents that exploit vulnerabilities. An example is the widely available toolkit called *rootkit*.

Distributed tool—tool that can be distributed to multiple hosts, which then can be coordinated to anonymously perform an attack on the target host simultaneously after some time delay.

Data tap—means of monitoring the electromagnetic radiation emanating from a computer or network using an external device.

With the exception of the physical attack, information exchange, and data tap categories, each of the tool categories may contain the other tool categories *within* itself. For example, toolkits contain scripts, programs, and sometimes autonomous agents. So when a *toolkit* is used, the *script or program* category is also included. *User commands* also must be used for the initiation of scripts, programs, autonomous agents, toolkits, and distributed tools. In other words, there is an order to some of the categories in the tools block, from the simple user command category to the more sophisticated distributed tools category. In describing or classifying an attack, generally a choice must be made among several alternatives within the tools block. We chose to classify according to the *highest* category of tool used, which makes the categories mutually exclusive in practice.

8.4.2.2   Vulnerability.   To reach the desired result, an attacker must take advantage of a computer or network *vulnerability*.

Vulnerability—weakness in a system allowing unauthorized action.[30]

A vulnerability in software is an error that arises in different stages of development or use.[31] This definition can be used to give us three categories of vulnerabilities.

Design vulnerability—vulnerability inherent in the design or specification of hardware or software whereby even a perfect implementation will result in a vulnerability.

Implementation vulnerability—vulnerability resulting from an error made in the software or hardware implementation of a satisfactory design.

Configuration vulnerability—vulnerability resulting from an error in the configuration of a system, such as having system accounts with default passwords, having "world write" permission for new files, or having vulnerable services enabled.[32]

8.4.2.3   Unauthorized Result.   As shown in Exhibit 8.3, the logical end of a successful attack is an *unauthorized result*. At this point, an attacker has used a tool to exploit a vulnerability in order to cause an event to take place.

Unauthorized result—unauthorized consequence of an event.
If successful, an attack will result in one of the following:[33]

Increased access—unauthorized increase in the domain of access on a computer or network.

Disclosure of information—dissemination of information to anyone who is not authorized to access that information.

Corruption of information—unauthorized alteration of data on a computer or network.

Denial of service—intentional degradation or blocking of computer or network resources.

Theft of resources—unauthorized use of computer or network resources.

8.4.3 Full Incident Information Taxonomy.
Often attacks on computers and networks occur in a distinctive group that we would classify as being part of one *incident*. What makes these attacks a distinctive group is a combination of three factors, each of which we may only have partial information about.

1. There may be one attacker, or there may be several attackers who are related in some way.
2. The attacker(s) may use similar attacks, or they may be trying to achieve a distinct or similar objective.
3. The sites involved in the attacks and the timing of the attacks may be the same or may be related.

Here is the definition of *incident*:

Incident—group of attacks that can be distinguished from other attacks because of the distinctiveness of the attackers, attacks, objectives, sites, and timing.

The three parts of an incident are shown in simplified form in Exhibit 8.4, which shows that an attacker, or group of attackers, achieves objectives by performing attacks. An incident may be comprised of one single attack or may be made of multiple attacks, as illustrated by the return loop in the figure.

Exhibit 8.5 shows the full incident information taxonomy. It shows the relationship of events to attacks and attacks to incidents, and suggests that preventing attackers from achieving objectives could be accomplished by ensuring that an attacker cannot make any complete connections through the seven steps depicted. For example, investigations could be conducted of suspected terrorist *attackers*, systems could be searched periodically for attacker *tools*, system *vulnerabilities* could be patched, access controls could be strengthened to prevent *actions* by an attacker to access a *targeted* account, files could be encrypted so as not to *result* in disclosure, and a public education program could be initiated to prevent terrorists from achieving an *objective* of political gain.

8.4.3.1 Attackers and Their Objectives.
People attack computers. They do so through a variety of methods and for a variety of objectives. What distinguishes the

EXHIBIT 8.4   Simplified Computer and Network Incident

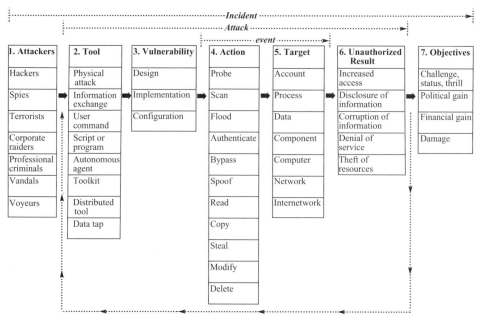

EXHIBIT 8.5   Computer and Network Incident Information Taxonomy

categories of attackers is a combination of who they are and their *objectives* (what they want to accomplish).

> **Attacker**—individual who attempts one or more attacks in order to achieve an objective.
>
> **Objective**—purpose or end goal of an incident.

Based on their objectives, we have divided attackers into a number of categories:

> **Hackers**—attackers who attack computers for challenge, status, or the thrill of obtaining access. (Note: We have elected to use the term "hacker" because it is common and widely understood. We realize that the term's more positive connotation was once more widely accepted.)
>
> **Spies**—attackers who attack computers for information to be used for political gain.
>
> **Terrorists**—attackers who attack computers to cause fear, for political gain.
>
> **Corporate raiders**—employees (attackers) who attack competitors' computers for financial gain.
>
> **Professional criminals**—attackers who attack computers for personal financial gain.
>
> **Vandals**—attackers who attack computers to cause damage.
>
> **Voyeurs**—attackers who attack computers for the thrill of obtaining sensitive information.

These seven categories of attackers and their four categories of objectives as shown in the leftmost and rightmost blocks of Exhibit 8.5 are fundamental to the difference between *incidents* and *attacks*. This difference is summed up in the phrase "attackers use attacks to achieve objectives."

8.5 ADDITIONAL INCIDENT INFORMATION TERMS. The taxonomy of the last section presented all of the terms in the common language for computer security that describe how attackers achieve objectives during an incident. However, some other, more general terms are required to fully describe an incident. The next sections discuss these terms.

8.5.1 Success and Failure. Information on success or failure can be recorded at several levels in the overall taxonomy. In the broadest sense, overall success or failure is an indication of whether one or more attackers have achieved one or more objectives. A narrower focus would be to determine the success or failure of an individual attack by evaluating whether the attack leads to an unauthorized result. Information on success or failure, however, may simply not be known. For example, an attempt to log in to the root or superuser account on a system may be classified as a *success* a *failure*, or as being *unknown*.

8.5.2 Site and Site Name. "Site" is the common term used to identify Internet organizations as well as physical locations. A "site" is also the organizational level of the site administrator or other authority with responsibility for the computers and networks at that location.

The term "site name" refers to a portion of the fully qualified domain name in the Internet's Domain Name Service (DNS). For sites in the United States, site names generally are at the second level of the DNS tree. Examples would be *cmu.edu* or *widgets.com*. In other countries, the site name is the third or lower level of the DNS tree, such as *widgets.co.uk*. Some site names occur even farther down the DNS tree. For example, a school in Colorado might have a site name of *myschool.k12. co.us.*

Here are the definitions of site and site name.

Site—organizational level with responsibility for security events; the organizational level of the site administrator or other authority with responsibility for the computers and networks at that location.

Site name—portion of the fully qualified domain name that corresponds to a site.

Some organizations, such as larger universities and companies, are large enough to be physically divided into more than one location, with separate administration. This separation cannot easily be determined. Therefore, often these different locations must be treated as one site.

8.5.3 Other Incident Terms. Several additional terms are necessary to fully describe actual Internet incidents. The first of these terms concern dates.

Reporting date—first date that the incident was reported to a response team or other agency or individuals collecting data.

Starting date—date of the first known incident activity.

Ending date—date of the last known incident activity.

Several terms concern the sites involved.

Number of sites—overall number of sites known to have reported or otherwise to have been involved in an incident.

> **Reporting sites**—site names of sites known to have reported an incident.
>
> **Other sites**—site names of sites known to have been involved in an incident but that did not report the incident.

For most incident response teams, actual site names are considered sensitive information. In our research, in order to protect the identities of the sites associated with an incident, we sanitize the site information by coding the site names prior to public release. An example would be to replace a site name, such as the fictitious *widgets.com*, with numbers and the upper-level domain name, such as *123.com*.

Response teams often use incident numbers to track incidents and to identify incident information.

> **Incident number**—reference number used to track an incident or identify incident information.

The last term we found to be of use is *corrective action*, which indicates those actions taken in the aftermath of an incident. These actions could include changing passwords, reloading systems files, talking to the intruders, or even criminal prosecution. Information on corrective actions taken during or after an incident is difficult to obtain for incident response teams, since response team involvement generally is limited to the early stages of an incident. CERT/CC records indicate that the variety of corrective actions is extensive, and a taxonomy of corrective actions may be a desirable future expansion of the common language.

> **Corrective action**—action taken during or after an incident to prevent further attacks, repair damage, or punish offenders.

8.6   HOW TO USE THE COMMON LANGUAGE.   Two things are important to emphasize about using the common language for computer security incident information. First, the common language really is a "high-level" set of terms. As such, it will not settle all the disputes about everything discussed concerning computer security incidents. For example, the common language includes "autonomous agent" as a term (a category of tool). Autonomous agents include *computer viruses*, *worms*, and the like, regardless of how those specific terms might be defined. In other words, the common language does not try to settle disputes on what should or should not be considered a *computer virus* but rather deals at a higher level of abstraction (autonomous agent) where, it is hoped, there can be more agreement and standardization. Stated another way, participants in the Common Language Project workshops anticipated that individuals and organizations would continue to use their own terms, which may be more specific in both meaning and use. The common language has been designed to enable these "lower-level" terms to be classified *within* the common language structure.

The second point to emphasize is that the common language, even though it presents a taxonomy, does not classify an incident (or individual attacks) as any *one* thing. Classifying computer security *attacks* or *incidents* is difficult because attacks and incidents are a *series of steps* that an attacker must take. In other words, attacks and incidents are not just *one* thing but rather a *series* of things. That is why I say the common language provides a taxonomy for computer security incident *information*.

An example of the problem is found in the popular and simple taxonomies often used to attempt to classify incidents. They appear as a list of single, defined terms. The following terms from Icove, Seger, and VonStorch provide an example.[34]

Covert channels	Data diddling	Degradation of service
Denial of service	Dumpster diving	Eavesdropping on emanations
Excess privileges	Harassment	IP spoofing
Logic bombs	Masquerading	Password sniffing
Salamis	Scanning	Session hijacking
Software piracy	Timing attacks	Traffic analysis
Trap doors	Trojan horses	Tunneling
Unauthorized data copying	Viruses and worms	Wiretapping

Lists of terms are *not* satisfactory taxonomies for classifying actual attacks or incidents. They fail to have most of the six characteristics of a satisfactory taxonomy. First, the terms tend not to be mutually exclusive. For example, the terms "virus" and "logic bomb" are generally found on these lists, but a virus may *contain* a logic bomb, so the categories overlap. Actual attackers generally also use multiple methods so their attacks would have to be classified into multiple categories. This makes classification ambiguous and difficult to repeat.

A more fundamental problem is that, assuming that an exhaustive and mutually exclusive list could be developed, the taxonomy would be unmanageably long and difficult to apply. It also would not indicate any relationship between different types of attacks. Finally, none of these lists has become widely accepted, partly because it is difficult to agree on the definition of terms. In fact, many different definitions of terms are in common use.

The fundamental problems with these lists (and their variations) are that most incidents involve multiple attacks, and attacks involve multiple steps. As a result, information about the typical incident must be classified in multiple categories. For example, one of the attacks in an incident might be a flood of a host resulting in a denial of service. But this same incident might involve the exploitation of a vulnerability to compromise the host computer that was the specific origin of the flood. Should this be classified as a flood? As a root compromise? As a denial-of-service attack? In reality, the incident should be classified in all of these categories. In other words, this incident has multiple classifications.

In summary, in developing the common language, we have found that, with respect to *attacks* and *incidents*, we can really *only* hope to (1) present a common set of "high-level" terms that are in general use and have common definitions and (2) present a logical structure to the terms that can be used to classify information *about* an incident or attack *with respect to specific categories*.

Some examples may make this clear. As discussed earlier, most of the information about actual attacks and incidents is in the form of textual records. In a typical incident record at the CERT/CC, three observations might be reported:

1. We found *rootkit* on host xxx.xxx.

2. A flood of e-mail was sent to account xxx@xxx.xxx, which crashed the mail server.

3. We traced the attack back to a teenager in *Xyz* city, who said he was not trying to cause any damage, just to see if he could break in.

For observation 1, we would classify *rootkit* in the "toolkit" category under "Tool" and the hostname in the "computer" category under "Target." For observation 2, the "e-mail flood" is a specific instantiation in the "flood" category under "Action" as well as in the "denial-of-service" category under "Unauthorized Result." There is ambiguity as to the target for observation 2: Is it the account or the computer? As a practical matter, the observations would be classified as both, since information is available on both. For observation 3, it could be inferred that this is a "hacker" seeking "challenge, status, or thrill."

What does this taxonomic process provide that is of practical value? First, the taxonomy helps us communicate to others what we have found. When we say that *rootkit* is a type of toolkit, then our common set of terms ("common language") provides us the general understanding of what we mean. When it is said that 22 percent of incidents reported to CERT/CC from 1988 through 1995 involved various problems with passwords (a correct statistic[35]), then the taxonomy has proven useful in communicating valuable information.

The application of the taxonomy, in fact, is a four-step process that can be used to determine what are the biggest security problems. Specifically, the process is to:

1. Take observations from fragmentary information in incident reports.
2. Classify those observations.
3. Perform statistical studies of these data.
4. Use this information to determine the best course(s) of action.

Over time, the same process can be used to determine the effects of these actions.

Two more points are important to emphasize about this taxonomy. First, an *attack* is a process that, with enough information, is *always* classified in multiple categories. For example: in a "Tool" category, in a "Vulnerability" category, in an "Action" category, in a "Target" category, and in an "Unauthorized Result" category. Second, an *incident* can involve multiple, perhaps thousands, of attacks. As such, the information gathered in an incident theoretically could be classified correctly into *all* of the taxonomy categories.

Within these guidelines, the common language for computer security incidents has proven to be a useful and increasingly accepted tool to gather, exchange, and compare computer security information. The taxonomy itself has proven to be simple and straightforward to use.

8.7   NOTES

1. E. G. Amoroso, *Fundamentals of Computer Security Technology* (Upper Saddle River, NJ: Prentice-Hall PTR, 1994), p. 2.
2. Deborah Russell and G. T. Gangemi Sr., *Computer Security Basics* (Sebastopol, CA: O'Reilly & Associates, 1991), p. 79.
3. Bill McKelvey, *Organization Systematics: Taxonomy, Evolution, Classification* (Berkeley: University of California Press, 1982), p. 3.
4. John D. Howard, "An Analysis of Security Incidents on the Internet, 1989–1995" (PhD diss., Department of Engineering and Public Policy, Carnegie Mellon University, Pittsburgh, PA, April 1997). Also available online at www.cert.org/research/JHThesis/Start.html.

5. Ivan Victor Krsul, "Software Vulnerability Analysis" (PhD diss., Computer Sciences Department, Purdue University, Lafayette, IN, May 1998), p. 12.

6. Howard, "Analysis of Security Incidents on the Internet."

7. John Radatz, ed., *The IEEE Standard Dictionary of Electrical and Electronics Terms,* 6th ed. (New York: Institute of Electrical and Electronics Engineers, 1996), p. 1087.

8. Amoroso, *Fundamentals of Computer Security Technology,* p. 34.

9. Radatz, *IEEE Standard Dictionary,* p. 373.

10. Radatz, *IEEE Standard Dictionary,* p. 373.

11. Radatz, *IEEE Standard Dictionary,* p. 11.

12. Radatz, *IEEE Standard Dictionary,* p. 5.

13. Derek Atkins et al., *Internet Security Professional Reference* (Indianapolis: New Riders Publishing, 1996), p. 258.

14. Radatz, *IEEE Standard Dictionary,* p. 947, and K. M. Jackson and J. Hruska, eds., *Computer Security Reference Book* (Boca Raton, FL: CRC Press, 1992), p. 916.

15. Merriam-Webster, *Merriam-Webster's Collegiate Dictionary,* 10th ed. (Springfield, MA: Author, 1996), pp. 77, 575, 714, and Radatz, *IEEE Standard Dictionary,* p. 57.

16. Merriam-Webster's Collegiate Dictionary, p. 157.

17. Radatz, *IEEE Standard Dictionary,* p. 630, and Atkins et al., *Internet Security,* p. 258.

18. Radatz, *IEEE Standard Dictionary,* p. 877.

19. Radatz, *IEEE Standard Dictionary,* p. 224.

20. Radatz, *IEEE Standard Dictionary,* p. 661.

21. Radatz, *IEEE Standard Dictionary,* p. 268.

22. Andrew S. Tanenbaum, *Modern Operating Systems* (Englewood Cliffs, NJ: Prentice-Hall, 1992), p. 12.

23. Radatz, *IEEE Standard Dictionary,* p. 683.

24. Tanenbaum, *Modern Operating Systems,* p. 12, and Radatz, *IEEE Standard Dictionary,* p. 822.

25. Radatz, *IEEE Standard Dictionary,* p. 250.

26. Radatz, *IEEE Standard Dictionary,* p. 189.

27. Radatz, *IEEE Standard Dictionary,* p. 192.

28. Radatz, *IEEE Standard Dictionary,* p. 683.

29. Krsul, "Software Vulnerability Analysis", pp. 5–6.

30. National Research Council, *Computers at Risk: Safe Computing in the Information Age* (Washington, DC: National Academy Press, 1991), p. 301; and Amoroso, *Fundamentals of Computer Security Technology,* p. 2.

31. Krsul, *Software Vulnerability Analysis,* pp. 10–11.

32. Atkins et al., *Internet Security,* p. 196.

33. Amoroso, *Fundamentals of Computer Security Technology,* pp. 3–4, 31; Russell and Gangemi, *Computer Security Basics,* pp. 9–10; and Frederick B. Cohen, *Protection and Security on the Information Superhighway* (New York: John Wiley & Sons, 1995), pp. 55–56.

34. David Icove, Karl Seger, and William VonStorch, *Computer Crime: A Crime-fighter's Handbook* (Sebastopol, CA: O'Reilly & Associates, 1995), pp. 31–52; Cohen, *Protection and Security on the Information Superhighway*, pp. 40–54 (39 terms); and Frederick B. Cohen, "Information System Attacks: A Preliminary Classification Scheme," *Computers and Security* 16, No. 1 (1997): 29–46 (96 terms).

35. Howard, "Analysis of Security Incidents on the Internet", p. 100.

CHAPTER **9**

MATHEMATICAL MODELS OF COMPUTER SECURITY

Matt Bishop

9.1 WHY MODELS ARE IMPORTANT. When you drive a new car, you look for specific items that will help you control the car: the accelerator, the brake, the shift, and the steering wheel. These exist on all cars and perform the function of speeding the car up, slowing it down, and turning it left and right. This forms a model of the car. With these items properly working, you can make a convincing argument that the model correctly describes what a car must have in order to move and be steered properly.

A model in computer security serves the same purpose. It presents a general description of a computer system (or collection of systems). The model provides a definition of "protect" (e.g., "keep confidential" or "prevent unauthorized change to") and conditions under which the protection is provided. With mathematical models, the conditions can be shown to provide the stated protection. This provides a high degree of assurance that the data and programs are protected, assuming the model is implemented correctly.

This last point is critical. To return to our car analogy, notice the phrase "with these items properly working." This also means that the average driver must be able to work them correctly. In most, if not all, cars the model is implemented in the obvious way: The accelerator pedal is to the right of the brake pedal, and speeds the car up; the brake pedal slows it down; and turning the steering wheel moves the car to the left or right, depending on the direction that the wheel is turned. The average driver is familiar with this implementation and so can use it properly. Thus, the model and the implementation together show that this particular car can be driven.

Now, suppose that the items are implemented differently. All the items are there, but the steering wheel is locked so it cannot be turned. Even though the car has all the parts that the model requires, they do not work the way the model requires them to work. The implementation is incorrect, and the argument that the model provides does not apply to this car, because the model makes assumptions—like the steering wheel turning—that are incorrect for this car. Similarly, in all the models we present in this chapter, the reader should keep in mind the assumptions that the models make. When one applies these models to existing systems, or uses them to design new systems, one must ensure that the assumptions are met in order to gain the assurance that the model provides.

This chapter presents several mathematical models, each of which serves a different purpose. We can divide these models into several types.

The first set of models is used to determine under what conditions one can prove types of systems secure. The access-control matrix model presents a general description of a computer system that this type of model uses, and it will give some results about the decidability of security in general and for particular classes of systems.

The second type of model describes how the computer system applies controls. The mandatory access-control model and the discretionary access-control model form the basis for components of the models that follow. The originator controlled access-control model ties control of data to the originator rather than the owner, and has obvious applications for digital rights management systems. The role-based access-control model uses job function, rather than identity, to provide controls and so can implement the principle of least privilege more effectively than many models.

The next few models describe confidentiality and integrity. The Bell-LaPadula model describes a class of systems designed to protect confidentiality and was one of the earliest, and most influential, models in computer security. The Biba model's strict integrity policy is closely related to the Bell-LaPadula model and is in widespread use today; it is applied to programs to determine when their output can be trusted. The Clark-Wilson model is also an integrity model, but it differs fundamentally from Biba's model because the Clark-Wilson model describes integrity in terms of processes and process management rather than in terms of attributes of the data.

The fourth type of model is the hybrid model. The Chinese Wall model examines conflicts of interest, and is an interesting mix of both confidentiality and integrity requirements. This type of model arises when many real-world problems are abstracted into mathematical representations, for example, when analyzing protections required for medical records and for the process of recordation of real estate.[1]

The main goal of this chapter is to provide the reader with an understanding of several of the main models in computer security, of what these models mean, and of when they are appropriate to use. An ancillary goal is to make the reader sensitive to how important assumptions in computer security are. Dorothy Denning said it clearly and succinctly in her speech when accepting the National Computer Systems Security Award in 1999:

> The lesson I learned was that security models and formal methods do not establish security. They only establish security with respect to a model, which by its very nature is extremely simplistic compared to the system that is to be deployed, and is based on assumptions that represent current thinking. Even if a system is secure according to a model, the most common (and successful) attacks are the ones that violate the model's assumptions. Over the years, I have seen system after system defeated by people who thought of something new.[2]

Given this, the obvious question is: Why are models important? Models provide a framework for analyzing systems and for understanding where to focus our security efforts: on either validating the assumptions or ensuring that the assumptions are met in the environment in which the system exists. The mechanisms that do this may be technical; they may be procedural. Their quality determines the security of the system. So the model provides a basis for asserting that, if the mechanisms work correctly, then the system is secure—and that is far better than simply implementing security mechanisms without understanding how they work together to meet security requirements.

9.2   MODELS AND SECURITY.   Some terms recur throughout our discussion of models.

- A *subject* is an active entity, such as a process or a user.
- An *object* is a passive entity, such as a file.
- A *right* describes what a subject is allowed to do to an object; for example, the read right gives permission for a subject to read a file.
- The *protection state* of a system simply refers to the rights held by all subjects on the system.

The precise meaning of each right varies from actual system to system. For example, on Linux systems, if a process has *write* permission for a file, that process can alter the contents of the file. But if a process has *write* permission for a directory, that process can create, delete, or rename files in that directory. Similarly, having *read* rights over a process may mean the possessor can participate as a recipient of interprocess communications messages originating from that process. The point is that the meaning of the rights depends on the interpretation of the system involved. The assignment of meaning to the rights used in a mathematical model is called *instantiating the model*.

The first model we explore is the foundation for much work on the fundamental difficulty of analyzing systems to determine whether they are secure.

9.2.1   Access-Control Matrix Model.   The *access-control matrix model*[3] is perhaps the simplest model in computer security. It consists of a matrix, the rows of which correspond to subjects and the columns of which correspond to entities (subjects and objects). Each entry in the matrix contains the set of rights that the subject (row) has over the entity (column). For example, the access-control matrix in Exhibit 9.1 shows a system with two processes and two files. The first process has: own rights over itself; read rights over the second process; read and execute rights over the first file; and read, write, and own rights over the second file. The second process: can write to the first process; owns itself; can read, write, execute, and owns the first file; and can read the second file.

	Process 1	**Process 2**	**File 1**	**File 2**
Process 1	own	read	read, execute	read, write, own
Process 2	write	own	read, write, execute, own	read

EXHIBIT 9.1   Example Access-Control Matrix with Two Processes and Two Files

The access-control matrix captures a protection state of a system. But systems evolve; their protection state does not remain constant. So the contents of the access-control matrix must change to reflect this evolution. Perhaps the simplest set of rules for changing the access-control matrix are these *primitive operations*:[4]

- **Create subject** *s* creates a new row and column, both labeled *s*
- **Create object** *o* creates a new column labeled *o*
- **Enter** *r* **into** *A*[*s*, *o*] adds the right *r* into the entry in row *s* and column *o*; it corresponds to giving the subject *s* the right *r* over the entity *o*
- **Delete** *r* **from** *A*[*s*, *o*] removes the right *r* from the entry in row *s* and column *o*; it corresponds to deleting the subject *s*'s right *r* over the entity *o*
- **Destroy subject** *s* removes the row and column labeled *s*
- **Destroy object** *o* removes the column labeled *o*

These operations can be combined into *commands*. The next command creates a file *f* and gives the process *p* read and own rights over that file:

```
command createread(p, f)
     create object f
     enter read into A[p, f]
     enter own into A[p, f]
end.
```

A *mono-operational* command consists of a single primitive operation. For example, the command

```
command grantwrite(p, f)
     enter write into A[p, f]
end.
```

which gives *p* write rights over *f,* is mono-operational.

Commands may include conditions. For example, the next command gives the subject *p* execute rights over a file *f* if *p* has read rights over *f*:

```
command grantexec(p, f)
     if read in A[p, f] then
          enter execute into A[p, f]
end.
```

If *p* does not have read rights over *f* when this command is executed, it does nothing. This command has one condition and so is called *monoconditional*. *Biconditional* commands have two conditions joined by *and*:

```
command copyread(p, q, f)
     if read in A[p, f] and own in A[p, f] then
          enter read into A[q, f]
end.
```

This command gives a subject q read rights over the object f if the subject p owns f and has read rights over f.

Commands may have conditions only at the beginning, and if the condition is false, the command terminates. Commands may contain other commands as well as primitive operations.

If all commands in a system are mono-operational, the system is said to be *mono-operational*; if all the commands are monoconditional or biconditional, then the system is said to be *monoconditional* or *biconditional*, respectively. Finally, if the system has no commands that use the **delete** or **destroy** primitive operations, the system is said to be *monotonic*.

The access-control matrix provides a theoretical basis for two widely used security mechanisms: access-control lists and capability lists. In the realm of modeling, it provides a tool to analyze the difficulty of determining how secure a system is.

9.2.2 Harrison, Ruzzo, and Ullman and Other Results.   The question of how to test whether systems are secure is critical to understanding computer security. Define *secure* in the simplest possible way: A system is secure with respect to a generic right r if that right cannot be added to an entity in the access-control matrix unless that square already contains it. In other words, a system is secure with respect to r if r cannot leak into a new entry in the access-control matrix. The question then becomes:

Safety Question. Is there an algorithm to determine whether a given system with initial state σ is secure with respect to a given right?

In the general case:

Theorem (Harrison, Ruzzo, and Ullman [HRU] Result).[5] The safety question is undecidable.

The proof is to reduce the halting problem to the safety question.[6] This means that, if the safety question were decidable, so would the halting problem be. But the undecidability of the halting problem is well known,[7] so the safety problem must also be undecidable.[8]

These results mean that one cannot develop a general algorithm for determining whether systems are secure. One can do so in limited cases, however, and the models that follow are examples of such cases. The characteristics that classes of systems must meet in order for the safety question to be decidable are not yet known fully, but for specific classes of systems, the safety question can be shown to be decidable. For example:

Theorem.[9] There is an algorithm that will determine whether mono-operational systems are secure with respect to a generic right r.

But these classes are sensitive to the commands allowed:

Theorem.[10] The safety question for monotonic systems is undecidable.

Limiting the set of commands to biconditional commands does not help:

Theorem.[11] The safety question for biconditional monotonic systems is undecidable.

But limiting them to monoconditional operations:

Theorem.[12] There is an algorithm that will determine whether mono-conditional monotonic systems are secure with respect to a generic right r.

In fact, adding the **delete** primitive operation does not affect this result (although the proof is different):

Theorem.[13] There is an algorithm that will determine whether monotonic systems that do not use the **destroy** primitive operations are secure with respect to a generic right r.

9.2.3 Typed Access Control Model.

A variant of the access-control matrix model adds type to the entities. The *typed access control matrix model*, called TAM,[14] associates a type with each entity and modifies the rules for matrix manipulation accordingly. This notion allows entities to be grouped into finer categories than merely *subject* and *object*, and enables a slightly different analysis than the HRU result suggests.

In TAM, a rule set is *acyclic* if neither an entity E nor any of its descendants can create a new entity with the same type as E. Given that definition:

Theorem.[15] There is an algorithm that will determine whether acyclic, monotonic typed matrix models are secure with respect to a generic right r.

Thus, a system being acyclic and monotonic is sufficient to make the safety question decidable. But we still do not know exactly what properties are *necessary* to make the safety question decidable.

We now turn to models that have direct application to systems and environments and that focus on more complex definitions of "secure" and the mechanisms needed to achieve them.

9.3   MODELS AND CONTROLS.

Models of computer security focus on control: who can access files and resources, and what types of access are allowed. The next characterizations of these controls organize them by flexibility of use and by the roles of the entities controlling the access. These are essential to understanding how more sophisticated models work.

9.3.1 Mandatory and Discretionary Access-Control Models.

Some access-control methods are rule based; that is, users have no control over them. Only the system or a special user called (for example) the *system security officer* (SSO) can change them. The government classification system works this way. Someone without a clearance is forbidden to read TOP SECRET material, even if the person who has the document wishes to allow it. This rule is called *mandatory* because it must be followed, without exception. Examples of other mandatory rules are the laws in general, which are to be followed as written, and one cannot absolve another of liability for breaking the laws; or the Multics ring-based access-control mechanism, in which accessing a data segment from below the lower bound of the segment's access bracket is forbidden regardless of the access permissions. This type of access control is called a *mandatory access control*, or MAC. These rules base the access decision on attributes of the subject and object (and possibly other information).

Other access-control methods allow the owner of the entity to control access. For example, a person who keeps a diary decides who can read it. She need not show it to anyone, and if a friend asks to read it, she can say no. Here the owner allows access to the diary at her discretion. This type of control is called *discretionary*. *Discretionary access control*, or DAC, is the most common type of access-control mechanism on computers.

Controls can be (and often are) combined. When mandatory and discretionary controls are combined to enforce a single access-control policy, the mandatory controls are applied first. If they deny access, the system denies access and the discretionary controls need never be invoked. If the mandatory rules permit access, then the discretionary controls are consulted. If both allow the accesses, access is granted.

9.3.2 Originator-Controlled Access-Control Model and DRM.

Other types of access controls contain elements of both mandatory and discretionary access controls. *Originator-controlled access control*,[16] or ORCON,[17] mechanisms allow the originator to determine who can access a resource or data.

Consider a large government research agency that produces a study of projected hoe-handle sales for the next year. The market for hoe handles is extremely volatile, and if the results of the study leak out prematurely, certain vendors will obtain a huge market advantage. But the study must be circulated to regulatory agencies so they can prepare appropriate regulations that will be in place when the study is released. Thus, the research agency must retain control of the study even as it circulates it among other groups.

More precisely, an originator-controlled access control satisfies two conditions. Suppose an object *o* is marked as ORCON for organization *X*. *X* decides to release *o* to subjects acting on behalf of another organization *Y*. Then

1. The subjects to whom the copies of *o* are given cannot release *o* to subjects acting on behalf of other organizations without *X*'s consent; and

2. Any copies of *o* must bear these restrictions.

Consider a control that implements these requirements. In theory, mandatory access controls could solve this problem. In practice, the required rules must anticipate *all* the organizations to which the data will be made available. This requirement, combined with the need to have a separate rule for each possible set of objects and organizations that are to have access to the object, makes a mandatory access control that satisfies the requirements infeasible. But if the control were discretionary, each entity that received a copy of the study could grant access to its copy without permission of the originator. So originator-controlled access control is neither discretionary nor mandatory.

However, a combination of discretionary and mandatory access controls can implement this control. The mandatory access-control mechanisms forbid the owner from changing access permissions on an object *o* and require that every copy of that object have the same access-control permissions as are on *o*. The discretionary access control says that the originator can change the access-control permissions on any copy of *o*.

As an example of the use of this model in a more popular context, record companies want to control the use of their music. Conceptually, they wish to retain control over the music *after* it is sold in order to prevent owners from distributing unauthorized copies to their friends. Here the originator is the record company and the protected resource is the music.

In practice, originator-controlled access controls are difficult to implement technologically. The problem is that access-control mechanisms typically control access to *entities,* such as files, devices, and other objects. But originator-controlled access control requires that access controls be applied to *information* that is contained in the entities—a far more difficult problem for which there is not yet a generally accepted mechanism.

9.3.3 Role-Based Access Control Models and Groups.
In real life, job function often dictates access permissions. The bookkeeper of an office has free access to the company's bank accounts, whereas the sales people do not. If Anne is hired as a salesperson, she cannot access the company's funds. If she later becomes the bookkeeper, she can access those funds. So the access is conditioned not on the identity of the person but on the role that person plays.

This example illustrates *role-based access control* (RBAC).[18] It assigns a set of roles, called the *authorized roles of the subject s*, to each subject *s*. At any time, *s* may assume at most one role, called the *active role of s*. Then

Axiom. The *rule of role authorization* says that the active role of *s* must be in the set of authorized roles of *s*.

This axiom restricts *s* to assuming those roles that it is authorized to assume. Without it, *s* could assume any role, and hence do anything.

Extending this idea, let the predicate *canexec(s, c)* be true when the subject *s* can execute the command *c*.

Axiom. The *rule of role assignment* says that if *canexec(s, c)* is true for any *s* and any *c*, then *s* must have an active role.

This simply says that in order to execute a command *c*, *s* must have an active role. Without such a role, it cannot execute any commands. We also want to restrict the commands that *s* can execute; the next axiom does this.

Axiom. The *rule of transaction authorization* says that if *canexec(s, c)* is true, then only those subjects with the same role as the active role of *s* may also execute transaction.

This means that every role has a set of commands that it can execute, and if *c* is not in the set of commands that the active role of *s* can execute, then *s* cannot execute it.

As an example of the power of this model, consider two common problems: containment of roles and separation of duty. Containment of roles means that a subordinate *u* is restricted to performing a limited set of commands that a superior *s* can also perform; the superior may also perform other commands. Assign role *a* to the superior and role *b* to the subordinate; as everything a subject with active role *b* can do, a subject with active role *a* can do, we say that role *a* *contains* role *b*. Then we can say that if *a* is an authorized role of *s*, and *a* contains *b*, then *b* is also an authorized role of *s*. Taking this further, if a subject is authorized to assume a role that contains other (subordinate) roles, it can also assume any of the subordinate roles.

Separation of duty is a requirement that multiple entities must combine their efforts to perform a task. For example, a company may require two officers to sign a check for over $50,000. The idea is that a single person may breach security, but two people are less likely to combine forces to breach security.[19] One way to handle separation of duty is to require that two distinct roles complete the task and make the roles mutually exclusive. More precisely, let *r* be a role and *meauth(r)*, the mutually exclusive authorization set of *r*, be the set of roles that a subject with authorized role *r* can *never* assume. Then separation of duty is:

Axiom. The *rule of separation of duty* says that if a role *a* is in the set *meauth(b)*, then no subject for which *a* is an authorized role may have *b* as another authorized role.

This rule is applied to a task that requires two distinct people to complete. The task is broken down into steps that two people are to complete. Each person is assigned a separate role, and each role is in the mutually exclusive authorization set of the other. This prevents either person from completing the task; they must work together, each in their respective role, to complete it.

Roles bear a resemblance to groups, but the goals of groups and roles are different. Membership in a group is defined by essentially arbitrary rules, set by the managers of the system. Membership in a role is defined by job function and is tied to a specific set of commands that are necessary to perform that job function. Thus, a role is a type of group, but a group is broader than a role and need not be tied to any particular set of commands or functions.

9.3.4 Summary.

The four types of access controls discussed in this section have different focuses. Mandatory, discretionary, and originator-controlled access controls are data-centric, determining access based on the nature or attributes of the data. Role-based access control focuses on the subject's needs. The difference is fundamental.

The principle of least privilege[20] says that subjects should have no more privileges than necessary to perform their tasks. Role-based access control, if implemented properly, does this by constraining the set of commands that a subject can execute. The other three controls do this by setting attributes on the data to control access to the data rather than by restricting commands. Mandatory access controls have the attributes set by a system security officer or other trusted process; discretionary access controls, by the owner of the object; and originator-controlled access controls, by the creator or originator of the data.

As noted, these mechanisms can be combined to make the controls easier to use and more precise in application. We now discuss several models that do so.

9.4 CLASSIC MODELS.

Three models have played an important role in the development of computer security. The Bell-LaPadula model, one of the earliest formal models in computer security, influenced the development of much computer security technology, and it is still in widespread use. Biba, its analog for integrity, now plays an important role in program analysis. The Clark-Wilson model describes many commercial practices to preserve integrity of data. We examine each of these models in this section.

9.4.1 Bell-LaPadula Model.

The Bell-LaPadula model[21] is a formalization of the famous government classification system using UNCLASSIFIED, CONFIDENTIAL, SECRET, and TOP SECRET levels. We begin by using those four levels to explain the ideas underlying the model and then augment those levels to present the full model. Because the model involves multiple levels, it is an example of a *multilevel security model*.

The four-level version of the model assumes that the levels are ordered from lowest to highest as UNCLASSIFIED, CONFIDENTIAL, SECRET, and TOP SECRET. Objects are assigned levels based on their sensitivity. An object at a higher level is more sensitive than an object at a lower level. Subjects are assigned levels based on what objects they can access. A subject is *cleared* into a level, and that level is called the subject's *security clearance*. An object is *classified* at a level, and that level is called the object's *security classification*. The goal of the classification system is to prevent information from leaking, or flowing downward (e.g., a subject at CONFIDENTIAL should not be able to read information classified TOP SECRET).

For convenience, we write *level(s)* for a subject's security clearance and *level(o)* for an object's security classification. The name of the classification is called a *label*. So an object classified at TOP SECRET has the label TOP SECRET.

Suppose Tom is cleared into the SECRET level. Three documents, called Paper, Article, and Book, are classified as CONFIDENTIAL, SECRET, and TOP SECRET, respectively. As Tom's clearance is lower than Book's classification, he cannot read Book. As his clearance is equal to or greater than Article's and Paper's classification, he can read them.

Definition. The *simple security property* says that a subject *s* can read an object *o* if and only if $level(o) \leq level(s)$.

This is sometimes called the *no-reads-up* rule, and it is a mandatory access control.

But that is insufficient to prevent information from flowing downward. Suppose Donna is cleared into the CONFIDENTIAL level. By the simple security property, she cannot read Article because

$$level(\text{Article}) = \text{SECRET} > \text{CONFIDENTIAL} = level(\text{Donna}).$$

But Tom can read the information in Article and write it on Paper. And Donna can read Paper. Thus, SECRET information has leaked to a subject with CONFIDENTIAL clearance.

To prevent this, Tom must be prevented from writing to Paper:

Definition. The **-property* says that a subject *s* can write an object *o* if and only if $level(s) \le level(o)$.

This is sometimes called the *no-writes-down* rule, and it too is a mandatory access control. It is also known as the *star property* and the *confinement property*.

Under this rule, as $level(\text{Tom}) = \text{SECRET} > level(\text{Paper})$, Tom cannot write to Paper. This solves the problem.

Finally, the Bell-LaPadula model allows owners of objects to use discretionary access controls:

Definition. The *discretionary security property* says that a subject *s* can read an object *o* only if the access-control matrix entry for *s* and *o* contains the read right.

So, in order to determine whether Tom can read Paper, the system checks the simple security property and the discretionary security problem. As both hold for Tom and Paper, Tom can read Paper. Similarly, the system checks the *-property to determine whether Tom can write to Paper. As the *-property does not hold for Tom and Paper, Tom cannot read Paper. Note that the discretionary security property need not be checked, because the relevant mandatory access-control property (the *-property) denies access.

The basic security theorem states that, if a system starts in a secure state, and every operation obeys the three properties, then the system remains secure:

Basic Security Theorem. Let a system Σ have a secure initial state σ_0. Further, let every command in this system obey the simple security property, the *-property, and the discretionary security property. Then every state σ_i, $i \ge 0$, is also secure.

We can generalize this to an arbitrary number of levels. Let $L_0, \ldots, L_n$ be a set of security levels that are linearly ordered (i.e., $L_0 < \ldots < L_n$). Then the simple security property, the *-property, and the discretionary security property all apply, as does the Basic Security Theorem. This allows us to have many more than the four levels described.

Now suppose Erin works for the European Department of a government agency, and Don works for the Asia Department for the same agency. Erin and Don are both cleared for SECRET. But some information Erin will see is information that Don has no need to know, and vice versa. Introducing additional security levels will not help here, because then either Don would be able to read all of the documents that Erin could, or vice versa. We need an alternate mechanism.

The alternate mechanism is an expansion of the idea of "security level." We define a *category* to be a kind of information. A *security compartment* is a pair (*level, category set*) and plays the role that the security level did previously.

As an example, suppose the category for the European Department is EUR, and the category for the Asia Department is ASIA. Erin will be cleared into the compartment (SECRET, {EUR}) and Don into the compartment (SECRET, {ASIA}). Documents have security compartments as well. The paper EurDoc may be classified as (CONFIDENTIAL, {EUR}), and the paper AsiaDoc may be (SECRET, {ASIA}). The paper EurAsiaDoc contains information about both Europe and Asia, and so would be in compartment (SECRET, {EUR, ASIA}). As before, we write *level*(Erin) = (SECRET, {EUR}), *level*(EurDoc) = (CONFIDENTIAL, {EUR}), and *level* (EurAsiaDoc) = (SECRET, {EUR, ASIA}).

Next, we must define the analog to "greater than." As noted earlier, security compartments are no longer linearly ordered because not every pair of compartments can be compared. For example, Don's compartment is not "greater" than Erin's, and Erin's is not "greater" than Don's. But the classification of EurAsiaDoc is clearly "greater" than that of both Don and Erin.

We compare compartments using the relation *dom*, for "dominates."

Definition. Let L and L' be security levels and let C and C' be category sets. Then

$$(L, C)\, dom\, (L', C') \text{ if and only if } L' \leq L \text{ and } C' \subseteq C$$

The *dom* relation plays the role that "greater than or equal to" did for security levels. Continuing our example, *level*(Erin) = (SECRET, {EUR}) *dom* (CONFIDENTIAL, {EUR}) = *level*(EurDoc), and *level*(EurAsiaDoc) = (SECRET, {EUR, ASIA}) *dom* (SECRET, {EUR}) = *level*(Erin).

We now reformulate the simple security property and *-property in terms of *dom*:

Definition. The *simple security property* says that a subject s can read an object o if and only if *level*(s) *dom* *level*(o).

Definition. The *-*property* says that a subject s can write to an object o if and only if *level*(o) *dom* *level*(s).

In our example, assume the discretionary access controls are set to allow any subject all types of access. In that case, as *level*(Erin) *dom* *level*(EurDoc), Erin can read EurDoc (by the simple security property) but not write EurDoc (by the *-property). Conversely, as *level*(EurAsiaDoc) *dom* *level*(Erin), Erin cannot read EurAsiaDoc (by the simple security property) but can write to EurAsiaDoc (by the *-property).

A logical question is how to determine the highest security compartment that both Erin and Don can read and the lowest that both can write. In order to do this, we must review some properties of *dom*.

First, note that *level*(s) *dom* *level*(s); that is, *dom* is reflexive. The relation is also antisymmetric, because if both *level*(s) *dom* *level*(o) and *level*(o) *dom* *level*(s) are true, then *level*(s) = *level*(o). It is transitive, because if *level*(s_1) *dom* *level*(o) and *level*(o) *dom* *level* (s_2), then *level*(s_1) *dom* *level* (s_2).

We also define the *greatest lower bound* (*glb*) of two compartments as:

Definition. Let $A = (L, C)$ and $B = (L', C')$. Then $glb(A, B) = (min(L, L'), C \cap C')$.

This answers the question of the highest security compartment that two subjects s and s' can read an object in. It is $glb(level(s), level(s'))$. For example, Don and Erin can both read objects in:

$glb(level(Don), level(Erin)) = (SECRET, \emptyset)$.

This makes sense because Don cannot read an object in any compartment except those with the category set {ASIA} or the empty set, and Erin can only read objects in a compartment with the category set {EUR} or the empty set. Both are at the SECRET level, so the compartment must also be at the SECRET level.

We can define the *least upper bound* (*lub*) of two compartments analogously:

Definition. Let $A = (L, C)$ and $B = (L', C')$. Then $lub(A, B) = (max(L, L'), C \cup C')$.

We can now determine the lowest security compartment into which two subjects s and s' can write. It is $lub(level(s), level(s'))$. For example, Don and Erin can both write to objects in:

$glb((level(Don), level(Erin)) = (SECRET, \{EUR, ASIA\})$.

This makes sense because Don cannot write to an object in any compartment except those with ASIA in the category set, and Erin can only write to objects in a compartment with EUR in the category set. The smallest category set meeting both these requirements is {EUR, ASIA}. Both are at the SECRET level, so the compartment must also be at the SECRET level.

The five properties of *dom* (reflexive, antisymmetric, transitive, existence of a least upper bound for every pair of elements, and existence of a greatest lower bound for every pair of elements) mean that the security compartments form a mathematical structure called a *lattice*. This has useful theoretical properties, and is important enough so models exhibiting this type of structure are called *lattice models*.

When the model is implemented on a system, the developers often make some modifications. By far the most common one is to restrict writing to the current compartment or to within a limited set of compartments. This prevents confidential information from being altered by those who cannot read it. The structure of the model can also be used to implement protections against malicious programs that alter files such as system binaries. To prevent this, place the system binaries in a compartment that is dominated by those compartments assigned to users. By the simple security property, then users can read the system binaries, but by the *-property, users cannot write them. Hence if a computer virus infects a user's programs or documents,[22] it can spread within that user's compartment but not to system binaries.

The Bell-LaPadula model is the basis for several other models. We explore one of its variants that models integrity rather than confidentiality.

9.4.2 Biba's Strict Integrity Policy Model.
Biba's strict integrity policy model,[23] usually called Biba's model, is the mathematical dual of the Bell-LaPadula model.

Consider the issue of trustworthiness. When a highly trustworthy process reads data from an untrusted file and acts based on that data, the process is no longer trustworthy—as the saying goes, "garbage in, garbage out." But if a process reads data more trustworthy than the process, the trustworthiness of that process does not change. In essence, the trustworthiness of the result is as trustworthy as the least trustworthy of the process and the data.

Define a set of *integrity classes* in the same way that we defined security compartments for the Bell-LaPadula model, and let *i-level*(s) be the integrity compartment of *s*. Then the preceding text says that "reads down" (a trustworthy process reading untrustworthy data) should be banned, because it reduces the trustworthiness of the process. But "reads up" is allowed, because it does not affect the trustworthiness of the process. This is exactly the opposite of the simple security property.

Definition. The *simple integrity property* says that a subject *s* can read an object *o* if and only if *i-level*(o) *dom* *i-level*(s).

This definition captures the notion of allowing "reads up" and disallowing "reads down."

Similarly, if a trustworthy process writes data to an untrustworthy file, the trustworthiness of the file may (or may not) increase. But if an untrustworthy process writes data to a trustworthy file, the trustworthiness of that file drops. *s* "writes down" should be allowed and "writes up" forbidden.

Definition. The *-integrity property* says that a subject *s* can write to an object *o* if and only if *i-level*(s) *dom* *i-level*(o).

This property blocks attempts to "write up" while allowing "writes down."

A third property relates to execution of subprocesses. Suppose process *date* wants to execute the command *time* as a subprocess. If the integrity compartment of *date* dominates that of *time*, then any information *date* passes to *time* is passed to a less trustworthy process, and hence is allowed under the *-integrity property. But if the integrity compartment of *time* dominates that of *date*, then the *-integrity property is violated. Hence

Definition. The *execution integrity property* says that a subject *s* can execute a subject *s′* if and only if *i-level*(*s′*) *dom i-level*(*s*).

Given these three properties, one can show:

Theorem. If information can be transferred from object o_1 to object o_n, then by the simple integrity property, the *-integrity property, and the execution integrity property, *i-level*(o_1) *dom i-level*(o_n).

In other words, if all the rules of Biba's model are followed, the integrity of information cannot be corrupted because information can never flow from a less trustworthy object to a more trustworthy object.

This model suggests a method for analyzing programs to prevent security breaches. When the program runs, it reads data from a variety of sources: itself, the system, the network, and the user. Some of these sources are trustworthy, such as the process itself and the system. The user and the network are under the control of ordinary users (or remote users) and so are less trustworthy. So, apply Biba's model with two integrity compartments, (UNTAINTED, Ø) (this means the set of categories in the compartment is empty) and (TAINTED, Ø), where (UNTAINTED, Ø) *dom* (TAINTED, Ø). For notational convenience, we shall write (UNTAINTED, Ø) as UNTAINTED and (TAINTED, Ø) as TAINTED; and dom as ≥. Thus, UNTAINTED ≥ TAINTED.

The technique works with either static or dynamic analysis but is usually used for dynamic analysis. In this mode, all constants are assigned the integrity label UNTAINTED. Variables are assigned labels based on the data flows within the program. For example, in an assignment, the integrity label of the variable being assigned to is set to the integrity label of the expression assigned to it. When UNTAINTED and TAINTED variables are mixed in the expression, the integrity label of the expression is TAINTED. If a variable is assigned a value from an untrusted source, the integrity label of the variable is set to TAINTED.

When data are used as (for example) parameters of system calls or library functions, the system checks that the integrity label of the variable dominates that of the parameter. If it does not, the program takes some action, such as aborting, or logging a warning, or throwing an exception. This action either prevents an exploit or alerts the administrator of the attack.

For example, suppose a programmer wishes to prevent a format string attack. This is an attack that exploits a vulnerability in the C printing function *printf*. The first argument to *printf* is a format string, and the contents of that string determine how many other arguments *printf* expects. By manipulating the contents of a format string, an attacker can overwrite values of variables and corrupt the stack, causing the program to malfunction—usually to the attacker's benefit. The key step of the attack is to input an unexpected value for the format string. Here is a code fragment with the flaw:

```
if (fgets(buf, sizeof(buf), stdin) != NULL) printf(buf);
```

This reads a line of characters from the input into an array *buf* and immediately prints the contents of the array. If the input is "xyzzy%n", then some element of the stack will be overwritten by the value 5.[24] Hence, the first parameter to *printf* must always have integrity class UNTAINTED.

Under this analysis technique, when the input function *fgets* is executed, the variable *buf* would be assigned an integrity label of TAINTED, because the input (which is untrusted) is stored in it. Then, at the call to *printf*, the integrity class of *buf* is compared to that required for the first parameter of *printf*. The former is TAINTED; the latter is UNTAINTED. But we require that the variable's integrity class (TAINTED) dominate that of the parameter (UNTAINTED), and here TAINTED $\leq$ UNTAINTED. Hence, the analysis has found a disallowed flow and acts accordingly.

9.4.3 Clark-Wilson Model.   Lipner[25] identified five requirements for commercial integrity models:

1. Users may not write their own programs to manipulate trusted data. Instead, they must use programs authorized to access that data.

2. Programmers develop and test programs on nonproduction systems, using nonproduction copies of production data if necessary.

3. Moving a program from nonproduction systems to production systems requires a special process.

4. That special process must be controlled and audited.

5. Managers and system auditors must have access to system logs and the system's current state.

Biba's model can be instantiated to meet the first and last conditions by appropriate assignment of integrity levels, but the other three focus on integrity of processes. Hence, while Biba's model works well for some problems of integrity, it does not satisfy these requirements for a commercial integrity model.

The Clark-Wilson model[26] was developed to describe processes within many commercial firms. There are several specialized terms and concepts needed to understand the Clark-Wilson mode; these are best introduced using an example:

- Consider a bank. If D are the day's deposits, W the day's withdrawals, I the amount of money in bank accounts at the beginning of the day, and F the amount of money in bank accounts at the end of the day, those values must satisfy the constraint $I + D - W = F$.

- This is called an *integrity constraint* because, if the system (the set of bank accounts) does not satisfy it, the bank's integrity has been violated.

- If the system does satisfy its integrity constraints, it is said to be in a *consistent* state.

- When in operation, the system moves from one consistent state to another. The operations that do this are called *well-formed transactions*. For example, if a customer transfers money from one account to another, the transfer is the well-formed transaction. Its component actions (withdrawal from the first account and deposit in the second) individually are not well-formed transactions, because if only one completes, the system will be in an inconsistent state.

- Procedures that verify that all integrity constraints are satisfied are called *integrity verification procedures* (IVPs).

- Data that must satisfy integrity constraints are called *constrained data items* (CDIs), and when they satisfy the constraints are said to be in a *valid* state.

- All other data are called *unconstrained data items* (UDIs).

- In addition to integrity constraints on the data, the functions implementing the well-formed transactions themselves are constrained. They must be *certified* to be well formed and to be implemented correctly. Such a function is called a *transformation procedure* (TP).

The model provides nine rules, five of which relate to the certification of data and TPs and four of which describe how the implementation of the model must enforce the certifications.

The first rule captures the requirement that the system be in a consistent state:

Certification Rule 1. An IVP must ensure that the system is in a consistent state.

The relation *certified* associates some set of CDIs with a TP that transforms those CDIs from one valid state to a (possibly different) valid state. The second rule captures this.

Certification Rule 2. For some set of associated CDIs, a TP transforms those CDIs from a valid state to a (possibly different) valid state.

The first enforcement rule ensures that the system keeps track of the *certified* relation and prevents any TP from executing with a CDI not in its associated *certified* set:

Enforcement Rule 1. The system must maintain the *certified* relation, and ensure that only TPs certified to run on a CDI manipulates that CDI.

In a typical firm, the set of users who can use a TP is restricted. For example, in a bank, a teller cannot move millions of dollars from one bank to another; doing that requires a bank officer. The second enforcement rule ensures that only authorized users can run TPs on CDIs by defining a relation *allowed* that associates a user, a TP, and the set of CDIs that the TP can access on that user's behalf:

Enforcement Rule 2. The system must associate a user with each TP and set of CDIs. The TP may access those CDIs on behalf of the associated user. If a user is not associated with a particular TP and set of CDIs, then the TP cannot access those CDIs on behalf of that user.

This implies that the system can correctly identify users. The next rule enforces this:

Enforcement Rule 3. The system must authenticate each user attempting to execute a TP.

This ensures that the identity of a person trying to execute a TP is correctly bound to the corresponding user identity within the computer. The form of authentication is left up to the instantiation of the model, because differing environments suggest different authentication requirements. For example, a bank officer may use a biometric device and a password to authenticate herself to the computer that moves millions of dollars; a teller whose actions are restricted to smaller amounts of money may need only to supply a password.

Separation of duty, already discussed, is a key consideration in many commercial operations. The Clark-Wilson model captures it in the next rule:

Certification Rule 3. The *allowed* relation must meet the requirements imposed by separation of duty.

A cardinal principle of commercial integrity is that the operations must be auditable. This requires logging of enough information to determine what the transaction did. The next rule captures this requirement:

Certification Rule 4. All TPs must append enough information to reconstruct the operation to an append-only CDI.

The append-only CDI is, of course, a log.

So far we have considered all inputs to TPs to be CDIs. Unfortunately, that is infeasible. In our bank example, the teller will enter account information and deposit and withdrawal figures; but those are not CDIs; the teller may mistype something. Before a TP can use that information, it must be vetted to ensure it will enable the TP to work correctly. The last certification rule captures this:

Certification Rule 5. A TP that takes a UDI as input must perform either a well-formed transaction or no transaction for any value of the UDI. Thus, it either rejects the UDI or transforms it into a CDI.

This also covers poorly crafted TPs; if the input can exploit vulnerabilities in the TP to cause it to act in unexpected ways, it cannot be certified under this rule.

Within the model lies a possible conflict. In the preceding rules, one user could certify a TP to operate on a CDI and then execute the TP on that CDI. The problem is that a malicious user may certify a TP that does not perform a well-formed transaction, causing the system to violate the integrity constraints. Clearly, an application of the principle of separation of duty would solve this problem, and indeed the last rule in the model does just that:

Enforcement Rule 4. Only the certifier of a TP may change the *certified* relation for that TP. Further, no certifier of a TP, or of any CDI associated with that TP, may execute the TP on the associated CDI.

This separates the ability to certify a TP from the ability to execute that TP and the ability to certify a CDI for a given TP from the ability to execute that TP on that CDI. This enforces the separation of duty requirement.

Now, revisit Lipner's requirements for commercial integrity models. The TPs correspond to Lipner's programs and the CDIs to the production data. To meet requirement 1, the Clark-Wilson certifiers need to be trusted, and ordinary users cannot certify either TPs or CDIs. Then Enforcement Rule 4 and Certification Rule 5 enforce this requirement. Requirement 2 is met by not certifying the development programs; as they are not TPs, they cannot be run on production data. The "special process" in requirement 3 is a TP. Certification Rule 4 describes a log; the special process in requirement 3 being a TP, it will append information to the log that can be audited. Further, the TP is by definition a controlled process, and Enforcement Rule 4 and Certification Rule 5 control its execution. Before the installation, the program being installed is a UDI; after it is installed, it is a CDI (and a TP). Thus, requirement 4 is satisfied. Finally, the Clark-Wilson model has a log that captures all aspects of what a TP does, and that is the log the managers and auditors will have access to. They also have access to the system state because they can run an IVP to check its integrity. Thus, Lipner's requirement 5 is met. So the Clark-Wilson model is indeed a satisfactory commercial integrity model.

This model is important for two reasons. First, it captures the way most commercial firms work, including applying separation of duty (something that Biba's model does not capture well). Second, it separates the notions of certification and enforcement. Enforcement typically can be done within the instantiation of the model. But the model cannot enforce how certification is done; it can only require that a certifier claim to have done it. This is true of all models, of course, but the Clark-Wilson model specifically states the assumptions it makes about certification.

9.4.4   Chinese Wall Model.   Sometimes called the Brewer-Nash model, the goal of the Chinese Wall model[27] is to prevent conflicts of interest. It does so by grouping objects that belong to the same company into *company data sets* and company data sets into *conflict-of-interest classes*. If two companies (represented by their associated company data sets) are in the same conflict-of-interest class, then a lawyer or stockbroker representing both would have a conflict of interest. The rules of the model ensure that a subject can read only one company data set in each conflict-of-interest class.

In general, objects are documents or resources that contain information that the company wishes to (or is required to) keep secret. There is, however, an exception. Companies release data publicly, in the form of annual reports; that information is carefully *sanitized* to remove all confidential content. To reflect business practice, the model must allow *all* subjects to see that data. The model therefore defines a conflict-of-interest class called the *sanitized class* that has one company data set holding *only* objects containing sanitized data.

Now consider a subject reading an object. If the subject has never read any object in the object's conflict-of-interest class, reading the object presents no conflict of interest. If the subject has read an object in the same company data set, then the only information that the subject has seen in that conflict-of-interest class is from the same company as the object it is trying to read, which is allowed. But if the subject has read an object in the same conflict-of-interest class but a *different* company data set, then were the new read request granted, the subject would have read information from two different companies for which there is a conflict of interest—exactly what the model is trying to prevent. So that is disallowed.

The next rule summarizes this:

Definition. The *CW-simple security property* says that a subject *s* can read an object *o* if and only if either:

1. *s* has not read any other object in *o*'s conflict of interest class; or
2. The only objects in *o*'s conflict of interest class that *s* has read are all in *o*'s company data set.

To see why this works, suppose all banks are in the same conflict-of-interest class. A stockbroker represents The Big Bank. She is approached to represent The Bigger Bank. If she agreed, she would need access to The Bigger Bank's information, specifically the objects in The Bigger Bank's company data set. But that would mean she could read objects from two company data sets in the same conflict-of-interest class, something the CW-simple security property forbids. The temporal element of the model is important; even if she resigned her representation of The Big Bank, she cannot represent The Bigger Bank because condition 2 of the CW-simple security property considers all objects she previously read. This makes sense, because she has had access to The Big Bank, and could unintentionally compromise the interests of her previous employer while representing The Bigger Bank.

The CW-simple security property implicitly says that *s* can read any sanitized object. To see this, note that if *s* has never read a sanitized object, condition 1 holds. If *s* has read a sanitized object, then condition 2 holds because all sanitized objects are in the same company data set.

Writing poses another problem. Suppose Barbara represents The Big Bank, and Percival works for The Bigger Bank. Both also represent The Biggest Toy Company, which—not being a financial institution—is in a different conflict-of-interest class from either bank. Thus, there is no conflict of interest in either Barbara's or Percival's representation of a bank and the toy company. But there is a path along which information can flow from Barbara to Percival, and vice versa, that enables a conflict of interest to occur. Barbara can read information from an object in The Big Bank's company data set and write it to an object in The Biggest Toy Company's company data set. Percival can read the information from the object in The Biggest Toy Company's company data set, thereby effectively giving him access to The Big Bank's information—which is a conflict of interest. That he needs Barbara's help does not detract from the problem. The goal of the model requires that this conspiracy be prevented. The next rule does so:

Definition. The *CW-*-property* says that a subject *s* can write to an object *o* if and only if both of the following conditions are met:

1. The CW-simple security property allows *s* to read *o*; and

2. All unsanitized objects that *s* can read are in the same company data set as *o*.

Now Barbara can read objects in both The Big Bank's company data set and The Biggest Toy Company's data set. But when she tries to write to The Biggest Toy Company's data set, the CW-*-property prevents her from doing so as condition 2 is not met (because she can read an object in The Big Bank's company data set).

This also accounts for sanitized objects. Suppose that Skyler represents The Biggest Toy Company and no other company. He can also read information from the sanitized class. When he tries to write to an object in The Biggest Toy Company's company data set, he meets both conditions of the CW-simple security property (because he has only read objects in that company data set), and all unsanitized objects that he can read are in the same company data set as the object he can read. Thus both conditions of the CW-*-property are met, so Skyler can write the object.

The conditions of the CW-*-property are very restrictive; effectively, a subject can write to an object only if it has access to the company data set containing that object, *and no other company data set except the company data set in the sanitized class.* But without this restriction, conflicts of interest are possible.

9.4.5 Summary.   The four models discussed in this section have played critical roles in the development of our understanding of computer security. Although it is not the first model of confidentiality, the Bell-LaPadula model describes a widely used security scheme. The Biba model captured notions of "trust" and "trustworthiness" in an intuitive way, and recent advances in the analysis of programs for vulnerabilities have applied that model to great effect. The Clark-Wilson model moved the notion of commercial integrity models away from multilevel models to models that examine process integrity as well as data integrity. The Chinese Wall model explored conflict of interest, an area that often arises when one is performing confidential services for multiple companies or has access to confidential information from a number of companies. These models are considered classic because their structure and ideas underlie the rules and structures of many other models.

9.5 OTHER MODELS.   Some models examine specific environments. The Clinical Information Systems Security model[28] considers the protection of health records, emphasizing accountability as well as confidentiality and integrity. *Traducement*[29] describes the process of real estate recordation, which requires a strict definition of integrity and accountability with little to no confidentiality.

Other models generalize the classic models. The best known are the models of *noninterference security* and *deducibility security*. Both are multilevel security models with two levels, HIGH and LOW. The noninterference model[30] defines security as the ability of a HIGH subject to interfere with what the LOW subject sees. For example, if a HIGH subject can prevent a LOW subject from acquiring a resource at a particular time, the HIGH subject can transmit information to the LOW subject. In essence, the interference is a form of writing, and must be prevented just as the Bell-LaPadula model prevents a HIGH subject from writing to a LOW object. The deducibility model[31] examines whether a LOW subject can infer anything about a HIGH subject's actions by examining only the LOW outputs. Both these models are useful in analyzing the security of systems[32] and intrusion detection mechanisms,[33] and led to work that showed connecting two secure compute systems may produce a nonsecure system.[34] Further work is focusing on establishing conditions under which connecting two secure systems produces a secure system.[35]

9.6 CONCLUSION. The efficacy of mathematical modeling depends on the application of those models. Typically, the models capture system-specific details and describe constraints ensuring the security of the system or the information on the system. If the model does not correctly capture the details of the *entire* system, the results may not be comprehensive, and the analysis may miss ways in which security could be compromised.

This is an important point. For example, the Bell-LaPadula model captures a notion of what the *system* must do to prevent a subject cleared for TOP SECRET leaking information to a subject cleared for CONFIDENTIAL. But if the system enforces that model, the TOP SECRET subject could still meet the CONFIDENTIAL subject and hand her a printed version of the TOP SECRET information. That is outside the system and so was not captured by the model. But if the model also embraces procedures, then a procedure is necessary to prevent this "writing down." In that case, the flaw would be in the implementation of the procedure that failed to prevent the transfer of information—in other words, an incorrect instantiation of the model, exactly what Dorothy Denning's comment in the introduction to this section referred to.

The models described in this section span the foundational (access-control matrix model) to the applied (Bell-LaPadula, Biba, Clark-Wilson, and Chinese Wall). All play a role in deepening our understanding of what security is and how to enforce it.

The area of mathematical modeling is a rich and important area. It provides a basis for demonstrating that the design of systems is secure, for specific definitions of *secure*. Without these models, our understanding of how to secure systems would be diminished.

9.7 FURTHER READING

Anderson, R. "A Security Policy Model for Clinical Information Systems," *Proceedings of the 1996 IEEE Symposium on Security and Privacy* (May 1996): 34–48.

Bell, D., and LaPadula, L. "Secure Computer Systems: Unified Exposition and Multics Interpretation," Technical Report MTR-2997 rev. 1, MITRE Corporation, Bedford, MA (March 1975).

Biba, K. "Integrity Considerations for Secure Computer Systems," Technical Report MTR-3153, MITRE Corporation, Bedford, MA (April 1977).

Bishop, M. *Computer Security: Art and Science*. Boston: Addison-Wesley Professional, 2002.

Brewer, D., and M. Nash. "The Chinese Wall Security Policy," *Proceedings of the 1989 IEEE Symposium on Security and Privacy* (May 1989): 206–212.

Clark, D., and D. Wilson. "A Comparison of Commercial and Military Security Policies," *Proceedings of the 1987 IEEE Symposium on Security and Privacy* (April 1987): 184–194.

Demillo, D., D. Dobkin, A. Jones, and R. Lipton, eds. *Foundations of Secure Computing*. New York: Academic Press, 1978.

Denning, D. "The Limits of Formal Security Models," National Information Systems Security Conference, October 18, 1999; available at www.cs.georgetown.edu/~denning/infosec/award.html.

Denning, P. "Third Generation Computer Systems," *Computing Surveys* **3**, No. 4 (December 1976): 175–216.

Engeler, E. *Introduction to the Theory of Computation*. New York: Academic Press, 1973.

Ferraiolo, D., J. Cugini, and D. Kuhn. "Role-Based Access Control (RBAC): Features and Motivations," *Proceedings of the Eleventh Annual Computer Security Applications Conference* (December 1995): 241–248.

Gougen, J., and J. Meseguer. "Security Policies and Security Models," *Proceedings of the 1982 IEEE Symposium on Privacy and Security* (April 1982): 11–20.

Graubert, R. "On the Need for a Third Form of Access Control," *Proceedings of the Twelfth National Computer Security Conference* (October 1989): 296–304.

Haigh, J., R. Kemmerer, J. McHugh, and W. Young. "An Experience Using Two Covert Channel Analysis Techniques on a Real System Design," *IEEE Transactions in Software Engineering* **13**, No. 2 (February 1987): 141–150.

Harrison, M., and W. Ruzzo, "Monotonic Protection Systems." In D. Demillo et al., eds. *Foundations of Secure Computing*, pp. 337–363. New York: Academic Press, 1978.

Harrison, M., W. Ruzzo, and J. Ullman. "Protection in Operating Systems," *Communications of the ACM* **19**, No. 8 (August 1976): 461–471.

Ko, C., and T. Redmond. "Noninterference and Intrusion Detection," *Proceedings of the 2002 IEEE Symposium on Security and Privacy* (May 2002): 177–187.

Lampson, B. "Protection." *Proceedings of the Fifth Princeton Symposium of Information Science and Systems* (March 1971): 437–443.

Lipner, S. "Non-Discretionary Controls for Commercial Applications," *Proceedings of the 1982 IEEE Symposium on Privacy and Security* (April 1982): 2–10.

Mantel, H. "On the Composition of Secure Systems," *Proceedings of the 2002 IEEE Symposium on Security and Privacy* (May 2002): 88–101.

McCullough, D. "Non-Interference and the Composability of Security Properties," *Proceedings of the 1987 IEEE Symposium on Privacy and Security* (April 1988): 177–186.

Sandhu, R. "The Typed Access Matrix Model," *Proceedings of the 1992 IEEE Symposium on Security and Privacy* (April 1992): 122–136.

Seacord, R. *Secure Coding in C and C++*. Boston: Addison-Wesley, 2005.

Walcott, T., and M. Bishop. "Traducement: A Model for Record Security," *ACM Transactions on Information Systems Security* **7**, No. 4 (November 2004): 576–590.

9.8   NOTES

1. Recordation of real estate refers to recording deeds, mortgages, and other information about property with the county recorder. See http://ag.ca.gov/erds1/index.php.

2. D. Denning, "The Limits of Formal Security Models," National Information Systems Security Conference, October 18, 1999; available at www.cs.georgetown.edu/~denning/infosec/award.html.

3. B. Lampson, "Protection," *Proceedings of the Fifth Princeton Symposium of Information Science and Systems* (March 1971): 437–443; P. Denning, "Third Generation Computer Systems," *Computing Surveys* 3, No. 4 (December 1976): 175–216.

4. Harrison, 1976.

5. M. Harrison, W. Ruzzo, and J. Ullman, "Protection in Operating Systems," *Communications of the ACM* 19, No. 8 (August 1976): 461–471.

6. The halting problem is the question "Is there an algorithm to determine whether any arbitrary program halts?" The answer, "No," was proved by Alan Turing in 1936. See www.nist.gov/dads/HTML/haltingProblem.html. See also E. Engeler, *Introduction to the Theory of Computation* (New York: Academic Press, 1973).

7. E. Engeler, *Introduction to the Theory of Computation* (New York: Academic Press, 1973).

8. The interested reader is referred to Harrison et al., "Protection in Operating Systems," or to M. Bishop, *Computer Security: Art and Science* (Boston: Addison-Wesley Professional, 2002), p. 47 ff., for the proof.

9. Harrison et al., "Protection in Operating Systems."

10. M. Harrison and W. Ruzzo, "Monotonic Protection Systems," in D. Demillo et al., eds., *Foundations of Secure Computing,* pp. 337–363 (New York: Academic Press, 1978).

11. Harrison and Ruzzo, "Monotonic Protection Systems."

12. Harrison and Ruzzo, "Monotonic Protection Systems."

13. Harrison and Ruzzo, "Monotonic Protection Systems."

14. R. Sandhu, "The Typed Access Matrix Model," *Proceedings of the 1992 IEEE Symposium on Security and Privacy* (April 1992): 122–136.

15. Sandhu, "The Typed Access Matrix Model."

16. Also sometimes called organization controlled access control, or ORGCON.

17. R. Graubert, "On the Need for a Third Form of Access Control," *Proceedings of the Twelfth National Computer Security Conference* (October 1989): 296–304.

18. D. Ferraiolo, J. Cugini, and D. Kuhn, "Role-Based Access Control (RBAC): Features and Motivations," *Proceedings of the Eleventh Annual Computer Security Applications Conference* (December 1995): 241–248.

19. As Benjamin Franklin once said, "Three can keep a secret if two of them are dead."

20. Saltzer and Schroeder 1975

21. D. Bell and L. LaPadula, "Secure Computer Systems: Unified Exposition and Multics Interpretation," Technical Report MTR-2997 rev. 1, MITRE Corporation, Bedford, MA (March 1975).

22. A macro virus can infect a document. See, for example, Bishop, *Computer Security*, section 22.3.8, and Chapter 16 in this *Handbook*.

23. Biba proposed three models: the Low-Water-Mark Policy model, the Ring Policy model, and the Strict Integrity Policy model. See Bishop, *Computer Security*, Section 6.2.

24. The explanation is too complex to go into here. The interested reader is referred to R. Seacord, *Secure Coding in C and C++* (Boston: Addison-Wesley, 2005), Chapter 6, for a discussion of this problem.

25. S. Lipner, "Non-Discretionary Controls for Commercial Applications," *Proceedings of the 1982 IEEE Symposium on Privacy and Security* (April 1982): 2–10.

26. D. Clark and D. Wilson, "A Comparison of Commercial and Military Security Policies," *Proceedings of the 1987 IEEE Symposium on Security and Privacy* (April 1987): 184–194.

27. D. Brewer and M. Nash, "The Chinese Wall Security Policy," *Proceedings of the 1989 IEEE Symposium on Security and Privacy* (May 1989): 206–212.

28. R. Anderson, "A Security Policy Model for Clinical Information Systems," *Proceedings of the 1996 IEEE Symposium on Security and Privacy* (May 1996): 34–48.

29. T. Walcott and M. Bishop, "Traducement: A Model for Record Security," *ACM Transactions on Information Systems Security* 7, No. 4 (November 2004): 576–590.

30. J. Gougen and J. Meseguer, "Security Policies and Security Models," *Proceedings of the 1982 IEEE Symposium on Privacy and Security* (April 1982): 11–20.

31. Gougen and Meseguer, "Security Policies and Security Models."

32. J. Haigh, R. Kemmerer, J. McHugh, and W. Young, "An Experience Using Two Covert Channel Analysis Techniques on a Real System Design," *IEEE Transactions in Software Engineering* 13, No. 2 (February 1987): 141–150.

33. C. Ko and T. Redmond, "Noninterference and Intrusion Detection." *Proceedings of the 2002 IEEE Symposium on Security and Privacy* (May 2002): 177–187.

34. D. McCullough, "Non-Interference and the Composability of Security Properties," *Proceedings of the 1987 IEEE Symposium on Privacy and Security* (April 1988): 177–186.

35. H. Mantel, "On the Composition of Secure Systems," *Proceedings of the 2002 IEEE Symposium on Security and Privacy* (May 2002): 88–101.

CHAPTER 10

UNDERSTANDING STUDIES AND SURVEYS OF COMPUTER CRIME

M. E. Kabay

10.1 INTRODUCTION. This chapter provides guidance for critical reading of research results about computer crime. It will also alert designers of research instruments who may lack formal training in survey design and analysis to the need for professional support in developing questionnaires and analyzing results.

10.1.1 Value of Statistical Knowledge Base. Security specialists are often asked about computer crime; for example, customers want to know who is attacking which systems, how often, using what methods. These questions are perceived as important because they bear on the strategies of risk management; in theory, in order to estimate the appropriate level of investment in security, it would be helpful to have a sound grasp of the probability of different levels of damage. Ideally, one would want to evaluate an organization's level of risk by evaluating the experiences of other organizations with similar system and business characteristics. Such comparisons would be useful in competitive analysis and in litigation over standards of due care and diligence in protecting corporate assets.

10.1.2 Limitations on Our Knowledge of Computer Crime. Unfortunately, in the current state of information security, no one can give reliable answers to such questions. There are two fundamental difficulties preventing us from developing accurate statistics of this kind. These difficulties are known as the problems of ascertainment.

10.1.2.1   Detection.   The first problem is that an unknown number of crimes of all kinds are undetected. For example, even outside the computer crime field, we do not know how many financial frauds are being perpetrated. We do not know because some of them are not detected. How do we know they are not detected? Because some frauds are discovered long after they have occurred. Similarly, computer crimes may not be detected by their victims but may be reported by the perpetrators.

In a landmark series of tests at the Department of Defense (DoD), the Defense Information Systems Agency found that very few of the penetrations it engineered against unclassified systems within the DoD seem to have been detected by system managers. These studies were carried out from 1994 through 1996 and attacked 38,000 systems. About two-thirds of the attacks succeeded; however, only 4 percent of these attacks were detected.[1]

A commonly held view within the information security community is that only one-tenth or so of all the crimes committed against and using computer systems are detected.

10.1.2.2   Reporting.   The second problem of ascertainment is that even if attacks are detected, few seem to be reported in a way that allows systematic data collection. This commonly held belief is based in part on the unquantified experience of information security professionals who have conducted interviews of their clients; it turns out that only about 10 percent of the attacks against computer systems revealed in such interviews were ever reported to any kind of authority or to the public. The DoD studies mentioned earlier were consistent with this belief; of the few penetrations detected, only a fraction of 1 percent were reported to appropriate authorities.

Given these problems of ascertainment, computer crime statistics generally should be treated with skepticism.

10.1.3   Limitations on the Applicability of Computer Crime Statistics.
Generalizations in this field are difficult to justify. Even if we knew more about types of criminals and the methods they use, it still would be difficult to have the kind of actuarial statistic that is commonplace in the insurance field. For example, the establishment of uniform building codes in the 1930s in the United States led to the growth in fire insurance as a viable business. With official records of fires in buildings that could be described using a standard typology, statistical information began to provide an actuarial basis for using probabilities of fires and associated costs to calculate reasonable insurance rates.

In contrast, even if we had access to accurate reports, it would be difficult to make meaningful generalizations about vulnerabilities and incidence of successful attacks for the information technology field. We use a bewildering variety and versions of processors, operating systems, firewalls, encryption, application software, backup methods and media, communications channels, identification, authentication, authorization, compartmentalization, and operations.

How would we generalize from data about the risks at (say) a mainframe-based network running Multiple Virtual Systems (MVS) in a military installation to the kinds of risks faced by a UNIX-based intranet in an industrial corporation, or to a Windows

New Technology (NT)-based Web server in a university setting? There are so many differences among systems that if we were to establish a multidimensional analytical table where every variable was an axis, many cells would likely contain no or only a few examples. Such sparse matrices are notoriously difficult to use in building statistical models for predictive purposes.

10.2 BASIC RESEARCH METHODOLOGY.   This is not a chapter about so-cial sciences research. However, many discussions of computer crime seem to take published reports as gospel, even though these studies may have no validity what-soever. In this short section, we look at some fundamentals of research design so that readers will be able to judge how much faith to put in computer crime research results.

10.2.1 Some Fundamentals of Statistical Design and Analysis.   The way in which a scientist or reporter represents data can make an enormous difference in the readers' impressions.

10.2.1.1 Descriptive Statistics.   Suppose three companies reported these losses from penetration of their computer systems: $1M, $2M, and $6M. We can describe these results in many ways. For example, we can simply list the raw data; however, such lists could become unacceptably long as the number of reports increased, and it is hard to make sense of the raw data.

We could define classes such as "2 million or less" and "more than 2 million" and count how many occurrences there were in each class:

Class	Freq
≤ $2M	2
> $2M	1

Alternatively, we might define the classes with finer granularity as < $1M, ≥ $1M but < $2M, and so on; such a table might look like this:

Class	Freq
< $1M	0
≥ $1M & < $2M	1
≥ $2M & < $3M	1
≥ $3M & < $4M	0
≥ $4M & < $5M	0
≥ $5M & < $6M	0
≥ $6	1

Notice how the definition of the classes affects perception of the results: The first table gives the impression that the results are clustered around $2M and gives no information about the upper or lower bounds.

10.2.1.1.1 Location.   One of the most obvious ways we describe data is to say where they lie in a particular dimension. The *central tendency* of our three original data ($1M, $2M, and $6M) can be represented in various ways; for example, two popular measures are

- Arithmetic mean or average = $(1+2+6)M/3 = $3M
- Median (the middle of the sorted list of losses) = $2M

Note that if we tried to compute the mean and the median from the first table (with its approximate classes), we would get the wrong value. Such statistics should be computed from the original data, not from summary tables.

10.2.1.1.2 Dispersion.   Another aspect of our data that we frequently need is *dispersion*—that is, variability. The simplest measure of dispersion is the range: the difference between the smallest and the largest value we found; in our example, we could say that the range was from $1M to $6M or that it was $5M. Sometimes the range is expressed as a percentage of the mean; then we would say that the range was $5/3 = 1.6\ldots$ or ~167 percent.

The *variance* (σ^2) of these particular data is the average of the squared deviations from the arithmetic mean; the variance of the three numbers would be $\sigma^2 = (1-3)^2 + (2-3)^2 + (6-3)^2/3 = (4+1+9)/3 \approx 4.67$.

The square root of the variance (σ) is called the *standard deviation* and is often used to describe dispersion. In our example, $\sigma = \sqrt{4.67} \approx 2.16$.

Dispersion is particularly important when we compare estimates about information from different groups. The greater the variance of a measure, the more difficult it is to form reliable generalizations about an underlying phenomenon, as described in the next section.

10.2.1.2 Inference: Sample Statistics versus Population Statistics.
We can accurately describe any data using descriptive statistics; the question is what we then do with those measures.

Usually we expect to extend the findings in a *sample* or subset of a *population* to make generalizations about the population. For example, we might be trying to estimate the losses from computer crime in commercial organizations with offices in the United States and with more than 30,000 employees. Or perhaps our sample would represent commercial organizations with offices in the United States and with more than 30,000 employees and whose network security staff was willing to respond to a survey questionnaire.

In such cases, we try to infer the characteristics of the population from the characteristics of the sample. Statisticians say that we try to estimate the *parametric* statistics by using the *sample* statistics.

For example, we estimate the parametric (population) variance (usually designated σ^2) by multiplying the variance of the sample by $n/(n-1)$. Thus we would say that the estimate of the parametric variance (s^2) in our sample would be $s^2 = 4.67 * 3/2 = 7$. The estimate of the parametric standard deviation (s) would be $s = \sqrt{7} \approx 2.65$.

10.2.1.3 Hypothesis Testing.   Another kind of inference that we try to make from data is *hypothesis testing*. For example, suppose we were interested in whether

there was any association between the presence or absence of firewalls and the occurrence of system penetration. We can imagine collecting these data about penetrations into systems with or without firewalls:

	Penetration		
Firewalls	**No**	**Yes**	**Totals**
No	25	75	100
Yes	70	130	200
Totals	95	205	300

We would frame the hypothesis (the *null hypothesis,* sometimes represented as H_0) that there was *no* relationship between the two independent variables, penetration and firewalls, and *test* that hypothesis by performing a test of independence of these variables. In our example, a simple chi-square test of independence would give a *test statistic* of $\chi^2_{[1]} = 2.636$. If there really were no association between penetration and firewalls in the population of systems under examination, the parametric value of this statistic would be zero. In our imaginary example, we can show that such a large value (or larger) of $\chi^2_{[1]}$ would occur in only 10.4 percent of the samples taken from a population where firewalls had no effect on penetration. Put another way, if we took many samples from a population where the presence of firewalls was not associated with any change in the rate of penetration, we would see about 10.4 percent of those samples producing $\chi^2_{[1]}$ statistics as large as or larger than 2.636.

Statisticians have agreed on some conventions for deciding whether a test statistic deviates enough from the value expected under the null hypothesis to warrant inferring that the null hypothesis is wrong. Generally we describe the likelihood that the null hypothesis is true—often shown as $p(H_0)$—in this way:

- When $p(H_0) > 0.05$, we say the results are *not statistically significant* (often designated with the symbols *ns*);
- When $0.05 \geq p(H_0) > 0.01$, the results are described as statistically significant (often designated with the symbol *);
- When $0.01 \geq p(H_0) > 0.001$, the results are described as highly statistically significant (often designated with the symbols **);
- When $p(H_0) \leq 0.001$, the results are described as extremely statistically significant (often designated with the symbols ***).

10.2.1.4 Random Sampling, Bias, and Confounded Variables. The most important element of sampling is randomness. We say that a sample is *random* or *randomized* when every member of the population we are studying has an equal probability of being selected. When a population is defined one way but the sample is drawn nonrandomly, the sample is described as *biased*. For example, if the population we are studying was designed to be, say, all companies worldwide with more than 30,000 full-time employees, but we sampled mostly from such companies in the United

States, the sample would be biased toward U.S. companies and their characteristics. Similarly, if we were supposed to be studying security in all companies in the United States with more than 30,000 full-time employees but we sampled only from those companies that were willing to respond to a security survey, we would be at risk of having a biased sample.

In this last example, involving studying only those who respond to a survey, we say that we are potentially *confounding* variables: We are looking at people-who-respond-to-surveys and hoping they are representative of the larger population of people from all companies in the desired population. But what if the people who are *willing* to respond are those who have better security and those who do not respond have terrible security? Then *responding to the survey* is confounded with *quality of security,* and our biased sample could easily mislead us into overestimating the level of security in the desired population.

Another example of how variables can be confounded is comparisons of results from surveys carried out in different years. Unless exactly the same people are interviewed in both years, we may be confounding individual variations in responses with changes over time; unless exactly the same companies are represented, we may be confounding differences among companies with changes over time; if external events have led people to be more or less willing to respond truthfully to questions, we may be confounding willingness to respond with changes over time. If the surveys are carried out with different questions or used by different research groups, we may be confounding changes in methodology with changes over time.

10.2.1.5 Confidence Limits.
Because random samples naturally vary around the parametric (population) statistics, it is not very helpful to report a *point estimate* of the parametric value. For example, if we read that the mean damage from computer crimes in a survey was $180,000 per incident, what does that imply about the population mean?

To express our confidence in the sample statistic, we calculate the likelihood of being right if we give an *interval estimate* of the population value. For example, we might find that we would have a 95 percent likelihood of being right in asserting that the mean damage was between $160,000 and $200,000. In another sample, we might be able to narrow these *95 percent confidence limits* to $175,000 and $185,000.

In general, the larger the sample size, the narrower the confidence limits will be for particular statistics.

The calculation of confidence limits for statistics depends on some necessary *assumptions*:

- Random sampling
- A *known error distribution* (usually the *Normal* distribution—sometimes called a *Gaussian* distribution)
- *Equal variance* at all values of the measurements

If any of these assumptions is wrong, the calculated confidence limits for our estimates will be wrong; that is, they will be misleading. There are tests of these assumptions that analysts should carry out before reporting results; if the data do not follow Normal error distributions, sometimes one can apply *normalizing transformations*.

In particular, percentages do not follow a Normal distribution. Here is a reference table of confidence limits for various percentages in a few representative sample sizes.

	95 Percent Confidence Limits for Percentages		
	Sample size		
Percentage	100	500	1000
0	0–3.0%	0–0.6%	0–0.3%
10	4.9–17.6%	7.5–13.0%	8.2–12.0%
20	12.7–29.1%	16.6–23.8%	17.6–22.6%
50	40.0–60.1%	45.5–54.5%	46.9–53.1%
80	70.9–87.3%	76.2–83.4%	77.4–82.4%
90	82.4–95.1%	87.0–92.5%	88.0–91.8%
100	97.0–100%	99.4–100%	99.7–100%

10.2.1.6 Contingency Tables.   One of the most frequent errors in reporting results of studies is to provide only part of the story. For example, one can read statements such as "Over 70 percent of the systems without firewalls were penetrated last year." Such a statement may be true, but it cannot be interpreted correctly as meaning that systems with firewalls were necessarily more or less vulnerable to penetration than systems without firewalls. The statement is incomplete; to make sense of it, we need the other part of the implied *contingency table*—the percentage of systems *with* firewalls that were penetrated last year—before making any assertions about the relationship between firewalls and penetrations. Compare, for example, these two hypothetical tables:

	Without Firewalls	With Firewalls in Default Configuration		Without Firewalls	With Firewalls Properly Configured
Penetrated	70%	70%	Penetrated	70%	10%
Not Penetrated	30%	30%	Not Penetrated	30%	90%

In both cases, someone could say that "70 percent of the systems without firewalls were penetrated," but the implications would be radically different in the two data sets. Without knowing the right-hand column, the original assertion would be meaningless.

10.2.1.7 Association versus Causality.   Continuing our example with rates of penetration, another error that untrained people often make when studying statistical information is to mistake *association* for *causality*. Imagine that a study showed that a lower percentage of systems with fire extinguishers was penetrated than systems without fire extinguishers and that this difference was statistically highly significant. Would such a result necessarily mean that fire extinguishers *caused* the reduction in penetration? No. We know that it is far more reasonable to suppose that the fire extinguishers were installed in organizations whose security awareness and security policies were more highly developed than in the organizations where no fire extinguishers were installed. In this imaginary example, the fire extinguishers might actually have *no causal* *effect* whatever on resistance to penetration. This result would illustrate the effect of confounding variables: *presence of a fire extinguisher* with *state of security awareness and policies.*

10.2.1.8 Control Groups.

Finally, to finish our penetration example, one way to distinguish between association and causality is to *control* for variables. For example, one could measure the state of security awareness and policy as well as the presence or absence of fire extinguishers and make comparisons only among groups with the same level of awareness and policy. There are also statistical techniques for mathematically controlling for differences in such *independent variables.*

10.2.1.9 A Priori versus a Posteriori Testing.

Amateurs or beginners sometimes forget the principle of *random sampling* that underlies all statistical inference (see Section 10.2.1.4). None of the hypothesis tests or confidence limit calculations work if a sample is not random. For example, if someone is wandering through a supermarket and notices that Granny Smith apples seem to be bigger than Macintosh apples, selecting a sample—even a random sample—of the apples that specifically gave rise to the hypothesis will not allow reliable computations of probability that the applies have the same average weight. The problem is that those *particular* applies would not have been sampled at all had the observer not been moved to formulate the hypothesis. So even if a particular statistical comparison produces a sample statistic that appears to have a probability of, say, 0.001, it is not possible to know how much the sampling deviated from randomness.

Applying statistical tests to data *after* one notices an interesting descriptive value, comparison, or trend is known as *a posteriori testing.* Formulating a hypothesis, obtaining a random sample, and computing the statistics and probabilities in accordance with the assumptions of those statistics and probabilities is known as *a priori testing.*

A well-used example of the perils of a posteriori testing is the unfortunate habit of searching through sequences of results such as long strings of guesses collected in student tests of paranormal abilities and calculating statistical values on carefully selected subsets of the strings. These a posteriori tests are then presented as if they were a priori and cause great confusion and arguments, such as: "Look, even though the overall proportion of correct guesses was (say) 50.003 percent in this run of <some very large number> guesses, there was a run of <much smaller number> guesses that were correct <any value greater than 50 percent> of the time! The probability of such a result by chance is <very small number>. That proves that there was a real effect of <whatever the treatment was>." Unfortunately, a long series of numbers can produce any desired nonrandom-looking string; there are even tests known as *runs tests* that can help a researcher evaluate the nonrandomness of such occurrences.

In practical terms, statisticians have established a convention for limiting the damaging effects of a posteriori testing: Use the 0.001 level of probability as the equivalent of the minimum probability of the null hypothesis. This custom makes it far less likely that an a posteriori comparison will trick the user into accepting what is in fact a random variation that caught someone's eye.

The best solution to the bias implicit in a posteriori testing is to use a completely *new* sample for the comparison. In the apple example, one could ask the store manager for new, unobserved, and randomly selected batches of both types of applies. The comparison statistics would then be credible and could be expected to follow the parametric distribution underlying calculations of probability of the null hypothesis.

The populations from which these apples were selected still would have to be carefully determined. Would the populations be apples at this particular store? For this particular chain? For this particular region of the country or of the world?

10.2.2 Research Methods Applicable to Computer Crime

10.2.2.1 *Interviews.* Interviewing individuals can be illuminating. In general, interviews provide a wealth of data that are unavailable through any other method. For example, one can learn details of computer crime cases or motivations and techniques used by computer criminals. Interviews can be structured (using precise lists of questions) or unstructured (allowing the interviewer to respond to new information by asking additional questions at will).

Interviewers can take notes or record the interviews for later word-for-word transcription. In unstructured interviewers, skilled interviewers can probe responses to elucidate nuances of meaning that might be lost using cruder techniques such as surveys. Techniques such as thematic analysis can reveal patterns of responses that can then be examined using exploratory data analysis.[2] Thematic analysis is a technique for organizing nonquantitative information without imposing a preexisting framework on the data; exploratory data analysis uses statistical techniques to identify possibly interesting relationships that can be tested with independently acquired data. Such exploratory techniques can correctly include a posteriori testing as described in Section 10.2.1.9, but the results are used to propose further studies that can use a priori tests for the best use of resources.

10.2.2.2 *Focus Groups.* Focus groups are like group interviews. Generally the facilitator uses a list of predetermined questions and encourages the participants to respond freely and to interact with each other. Often the proceedings are filmed from behind a one-way mirror for later detailed analysis. Such analysis can include nonverbal communications, such as facial expressions and other body language as the participants speak or listen to others speak about specific topics.

10.2.2.3 *Surveys.* Surveys consist of asking people to answer a fixed series of questions with lists of allowable answers. They can be carried out face to face or by distributing and retrieving questionnaires by telephone, mail, fax, and e-mail. Some questionnaires have been posted on the Web.

The critical issue when considering the reliability of surveys is *self-selection bias*—the obvious problem that survey results include only the responses of people who agreed to participate. Before basing critical decisions on survey data, it is useful to find out what the response rate was; although there are no absolutes, in general, we tend to trust survey results more when the response rate is high. Unfortunately, response rates for telephone surveys are often less than 10 percent; response rates for mail and e-mail surveys can be less than 1 percent. It is very difficult to make any case for random sampling under such circumstances, and all results from such low-response-rate surveys should be viewed as indicating the range of problems or experiences of the respondents rather than as indicators of population statistics.

Regarding Web-based surveys, there are two types from a statistical point of view: those using strong identification and authentication and those that do not. Those that do not are vulnerable to fraud, such as repeated voting by the same individuals. Those that provide individual universal resource locators (URLs) to limit voting to one per person nonetheless suffer from the same problems of self-selection bias as any other survey.

10.2.2.4 *Instrument Validation.* Interviews and other social sciences research methodologies can suffer from a systematic tendency for respondents to shape their answers to please the interviewer or to express opinions that may be closer to the norm in whatever group they see themselves. Thus, if it is well known that every organization ought to have a business continuity plan, some respondents may misrepresent the state of their business continuity planning to look better than they really are.

In addition, survey instruments may distort responses by phrasing questions in a biased way; for example, the question "Does your business have a completed business continuity plan?" may have a more accurate response rate than the question "Does your business comply with industry standards for having a completed business continuity plan?" The latter question is not neutral and is likely to increase the proportion of "yes" answers.

The sequence of answers may bias responses; exposure to the first possible answers can inadvertently establish a baseline for the respondent. For example, a question about the magnitude of virus infections might ask:

In the last 12 months, has your organization experienced total losses from virus infections of

(a) $1M or greater;
(b) less than $1M but greater than or equal to $100,000;
(c) less than $100,000;
(d) none at all?

To test for bias, the designer can create versions of the instrument in which the same information is obtained using the opposite sequence of answers:

In the last 12 months, has your organization experienced total losses from virus infections of

(a) none at all;
(b) less than $100,000;
(c) less than $1M but greater than or equal to $100,000;
(d) $1M or greater?

The sequence of questions can bias responses; having provided a particular response to a question, the respondent will tend to make answers to subsequent questions about the same topic conform to the first answer in the series. To test for this kind of bias, the designer can create versions of the instrument with questions in different sequences.

Another instrument validation technique inserts questions with no valid answers or with meaningless jargon to see if respondents are thinking critically about each question or merely providing any answer that pops into their heads. For example, one might insert the nonsensical question, "Does your company use steady-state quantum interference methodologies for intrusion detection?" into a questionnaire about security and invalidate the results of respondents who answer yes to this and other diagnostic questions.

Finally, independent verification of answers provides strong evidence of whether respondents are answering truthfully. However, such intrusive investigations are rare.

10.3 SUMMARY. In summary, all studies about computer crime should be studied carefully before we place reliance on their results. Some basic take-home questions about such research:

- What is the population we are sampling?
- Keeping in mind the self-selection bias, how representative of the wider population are the respondents who agreed to participate in the study or survey?
- How large is the sample?
- Are the authors testing for the assumptions of randomness, normality, and equality of variance before reporting statistical measures?
- What are the confidence intervals for the statistics being reported?
- Are comparisons confounding variables?
- Are correlations being misinterpreted as causal relations?
- Were the test instruments validated?

10.4 FURTHER READING

Textbooks

If you are interested in learning more about survey design and statistical methods, you can study any elementary textbook on the social sciences statistics. Here are some sample titles:

Babbie, E. R., F. S. Halley, and J. Zaino. *Adventures in Social Research: Data Analysis Using SPSS 11.0/11.5 for Windows*, 5th ed. Pine Forge Press, 2003.
Bachman, R., and R. K. Schutt. *The Practice of Research in Criminology and Criminal Justice*, 3rd ed. Sage Publications, 2007.
Chambliss, D. F., and R. K. Schutt. *Making Sense of the Social World: Methods of Investigation*, 2nd ed. Pine Forge Press, 2006.
Sirkin, R. M. *Statistics for the Social Sciences*, 3rd ed. Sage Publications, 2005.

Web Sites

Creative Research Systems, "Survey Design," www.surveysystem.com/_sdesign.htm.
New York University, "Statistics & Social Science," www.nyu.edu/its/socsci/statistics.html
StatPac, "Survey & Questionnaire Design," www.statpac.com/surveys/.

10.5 NOTES

1. GAO 91996) "Computer Attacks at Department of Defense Pose Increasing Risks." General Accounting Office Report to Congressional Requesters GAO/AIMD-98-84 (May 1996). P.19

2. M. E. Kabay, "CATA: Computer-Aided Thematic Analysis," 2006. Available at www2.norwich.edu/mkabay/methodology/CATA.pdf with narrated lectures at www2.norwich.edu/mkabay/methodology/index.htm.

CHAPTER 11

FUNDAMENTALS OF INTELLECTUAL PROPERTY LAW

William A. Zucker and Scott J. Nathan

11.1   INTRODUCTION.   This chapter is not for lawyers or law students. Rather, it is written for computer professionals who might find it useful to understand how their concerns at work fit into a legal framework, and how that framework shapes strategies that they might employ in their work. It is not intended to be definitive but to help readers spot issues when they arise and to impart an understanding that is the first part of a fully integrated computer security program.

The word "cyberlaw" is really a misnomer. Cyberlaw is a compendium of traditional law that has been updated and applied to new technologies. When gaps have developed or traditional law is inadequate, particular statutes have been enacted. It is a little like the old story of the three blind men and the elephant: One of the blind men touching the elephant's leg believes he is touching a tree; the other touching its ear believes it is a wing, and the third, touching the tail, thinks it is a snake. Issues of cyberspace, electronic data, networks, global transmissions, and positioning have neither simple unitary solutions nor a simple body of law to consult.

In thinking about the application of law to computer security, it is helpful to think about the problems as issues in which the computer is

1. The target of the activity
2. The tool used for the activity
3. Incidental to the activity itself

For example, "hacking" into a computer can be analogized to the tort[1] of trespass (i.e., entering the property of another without permission), and "cracking" can be viewed as conversion of someone else's property. Similarly, using the computer to make illegal copies is a violation of copyright law in its most basis sense. Although trademark law has very little to do with computers, using trade names as part of keywords for search engines, or domain names to misdirect Internet traffic to a competitive Web site can be a violation of a trademark. While touching on some of the more traditional tort remedies, this chapter focuses on the property rights being invaded by such activities and the remedies that exist in the context of a business operation.

Recognizing that the body of law which touches on these problems is as global as the Internet itself, this chapter is intended to help readers actually see the elephant in the room. In selecting what legal issues to highlight, we have tried to consider the routine needs of the computer professional. We have focused largely on the law of the United States, recognizing that these problems and subject matters often transcend national boundaries. There is a very simple reason for this. Most often, the impact of the computer security attack, denial of service, decryption, or theft of computer materials will have occurred here, or have a direct impact here, no matter where it originates. Imagine for a second a gunman—standing in Canada—who takes aim at someone in the United States, pulls the trigger, and hits his target. Since there is purposeful conduct aimed at this country, in the ordinary instance the U.S. judiciary will not only assert jurisdiction over the gunman but also apply its laws. There may be other problems, such as actually catching the gunman, but the example underlines the importance of the law of the United States for entities located here. For orientation purposes, we have also included a section at the end of this chapter that discusses some international issues.

One other introductory note. We use the phrase "security program" in this chapter with some frequency. Understanding that this phrase can mean one thing to a lawyer or risk manager and another thing to a computer security professional, we intend it as a shorthand reference to the generic and systemic effort to secure information stored on computers and not solely to the applications that may be employed as part of that effort.

11.2 THE MOST FUNDAMENTAL BUSINESS TOOL FOR PROTECTION OF TECHNOLOGY IS THE CONTRACT.　 The computer security professional's job is to understand, anticipate, and then worry about risk: risks that are beyond control and risks that can be controlled. The most fundamental tool for controlling risk, whether predictable or unforeseeable, is the contract. Unlike other forms of risk control, a contract need not be static; it can be adaptable. We can limit use; we can limit distribution; we can impose conditions and confidentiality; we can specify rights as well as provide for certain remedies through contract. Contracts actually can take many forms: the traditional signed agreement; an e-mail exchange; Web site or product terms of use; employment agreements; workplace manuals and policies; and so-called shrink-wrap or click-wrap agreements. We sell or license products. Where we can contract, we can also define and limit risk.

11.2.1   Prevention Begins at Home—Employee and Fiduciary Duties.

There is an old hoary concept in the law that employees owe to their employers the fiduciary duty of utmost loyalty. The scope and extent of that fiduciary duty is a matter of common law that varies in each state. Generally, employees' fiduciary duty prohibits them from using any property that belongs to the employer in competition with the employer or for personal gain. Employees, however, are entitled to retain and use for whatever purpose their own skill and knowledge, which arguably could include contacts that they develop over the course of their employment unless those contacts are trade secrets. What comes or does not come within the ambit of fiduciary duty has spawned endless arguments and lawsuits. There is a simple remedy to this problem: the contract that covers technology issues and ownership as well as it covers pay and other benefits.

11.2.2   Employment Contract, Manual, and Handbook.

Whatever policy the security professional develops should be implemented through the organization's employment contract, manual, and handbook. Many contractual provisions can be applied, such as: nondisclosure agreements; definition of proprietary policy; restrictive covenants; concessions of ownership regarding discoveries, know-how, improvements, inventions, and the like during the term of employment; e-mail policies; terms of use regarding computer systems; and statements of authorized and unauthorized activity. The point is that employment contracts and handbooks should be the starting point for computer security.

11.2.3   Technology Rights and Access in Contracts with Vendors and Users.

Security protection necessarily includes vigilance about all contracts and licenses with vendors and users. This may not be sexy, but it is blocking and tackling. Vendors can be subject to many of the same limitations and nondisclosure agreements as employees. Rights of access to intranets and data should be controlled and privileges specified. Careful consideration should be given to what rights a user will have, the rules surrounding user access, and enforcement of those rules. Is this a sale or a license? There are many virtues to controlling technology through licenses (as opposed to sales), including imposing limits on rights of use, and specifying remedies for breaches of the license, or for unauthorized activity that involves the licensed product.

"Shrink-wrap" or "click-wrap" licenses have become common parlance. They are now accepted tools for licensing and controlling software distribution so long as: (a) they are business to business and thus between parties of roughly equal bargaining position; (b) their terms for other users or consumers are not unconscionable; and (c) they do not violate public policy. Concerns over whether contractual terms are unconscionable or the contracts are ones of adhesion arise because the licenses are not products of negotiation but of fiat, which users accept when they open the "shrink-wrapped" package or through an online click. These concerns have been addressed through requirements that users have been provided with adequate notice of the terms, an opportunity to reject, and conduct that sufficiently manifests consent. For shrink-wrap agreements, the opening of the product, its installation, and retention have been deemed sufficient acts to show consent to the terms of the license, noting that if the consumer does not wish to consent, the product could be returned.[2] Thus it is not necessary for the prospective user to be aware of all of the terms of a license before purchase if the remedy includes return after purchase. The license can impose restrictions on use, limit the number of machines on which the product can be installed, copying, and even available remedies.[3]

The issues of notice, actual or constructive, an opportunity to accept or reject, and manifestation of consent have led to general acceptance of online agreements such as the presentation of licensing terms followed by an active need to check, accept, or reject by clicking on the appropriate box.[4] The same analysis applies to terms of use especially for intranet or network use.[5] In *Register.com v. Verio, Inc.*,[6] downloading data from a WHOIS database, having knowledge of the terms of use, was acceptance of those terms even if there was no click-through. These examples show that terms of use, properly positioned, can be binding on the user.

An active security program begins with a review of the contracts, licenses, and terms of use in all relationships with your organization. Just because a contractual arrangement has not existed does not mean that you cannot create one through proper notice of the terms of the contract and conduct that shows assent to those terms. Such contracts are the security professional's first line of defense. They give you the ability to limit risk with an organization's employees, contractors, vendors, and affiliates. With that in mind, this chapter addresses issues that arise largely outside of the terms of contractual protections and also suggests additional potential self-help remedies.

11.3 PROPRIETARY RIGHTS AND TRADE SECRETS.   For many years, unless an idea was patentable, the primary protection for internal business data, confidential or proprietary information, and computer code was through the common law doctrine of trade secrets.[7] Generally, a trade secret might be considered any internal, nonpublished manufacturing know-how, drawings, formulas, or sales information used in a trade or business that has commercial applicability and that provides a business with some strategic advantage.[8] Such information, so long as it was (a) not published or disseminated to others who were not obligated to maintain its confidentiality,[9] and (b) maintained in confidence with the protecting organization, could be protected as a trade secret.

The law of trade secret thus recognized a business's ownership or proprietary interest in such information, data, or processes. There are, however, important practical limitations on the application of trade secret protection. First and foremost, for any product sold in the market, the law does not protect against a competitor seeing the product and then using it to figure out how to manufacture like or similar items. Competitors are therefore free to "reverse engineer" a product so long as the reverse engineering is done wholly independently.

The second caveat is that an organization has to prove not only that the information qualifies for trade secret protection, but also that it protected the secrecy of the information as required by the law of the applicable jurisdiction. This means that ownership will be a matter not of record but of case-by-case proof, making enforcement of trade secret protection time consuming and expensive. Generally, the required proof consists of a showing that there was an active security program in place that was sufficient to protect the information as confidential. Various programs may be deemed adequate, depending on the circumstances, but usually such programs have five principles in common:

1. An inventory of trade secret information that is periodically updated
2. A security program to protect the technology at issue, often on a need-to-know basis with clear marking of information as "confidential, access restricted"
3. A written description of the security program that is provided to all employees

4. An enforcement officer or oversight procedure

5. An enforcement program, including litigation, if necessary, to enjoin unauthorized access or distribution

In the field of computing, these principles often mean that source code or other readable formats should be secured in a locked file and marked "confidential." All representations of the code as stored on magnetic or other media should be marked "confidential" and secured. Computerized information should be password protected with restrictions on circulation of the password and periodic password changes. A notice of confidentiality should be displayed as soon as access to the program is obtained, with appropriate warnings on limitation of use. Levels of access should be controlled so that privileges to copy, read, and write are appropriately restricted. Surveillance of entries and logon should be routinely conducted to verify that there has been no unauthorized entry. Finally, periodic audits should be conducted to test and substantiate the security procedures.

For many years, each state developed its own brand of trade secret protection through evolving judicial decisions that establish something in this country called the common law, as distinguished from legislative enactments of a statute addressing the same issue. In 1985 the Uniform Trade Secrets Act (UTSA) was promulgated by the National Conference of Commissioners on Uniform State Laws, with one of its purposes to make uniform the rights and remedies available to a holder of a trade secret. This model law, however, needed to be adopted by each state before it became the law of the state. As of this writing, it has been adopted to some degree in 46 states with the exception of Massachusetts, New Jersey, New York, and Texas.

The UTSA defines a trade secret as information, including a formula, pattern, compilation, program device, method, technique, or process, that: (i) derives independent economic value, actual or potential, from *not being generally known to, and not being readily ascertainable by proper means by*, other persons who can obtain economic value from its disclosure or use; and (ii) is the subject of efforts that are reasonable under the circumstances to maintain its secrecy. It also defines the unlawful taking of a trade secret, or misappropriation, as the wrongful use of a trade secret, including (i) knowingly acquiring the secret through improper means or (ii) disclosing the secret without consent.

11.3.1 Remedies for Trade Secret Misappropriation. Misappropriation of a trade secret is the unauthorized use or disclosure of the trade secret. In simple parlance, it is a taking or theft. The taking can be by one who owes a fiduciary duty of confidentiality such as an employee; it can be in breach of an agreement of confidentiality; or the taking can occur through improper access or means. The misappropriation can be treated under common law as the tort of conversion, trespass, unfair competition, or interference with contractual relations. As discussed, there are now specific statutory provisions under the UTSA for trade secret misappropriation. The UTSA grants the wronged party certain remedies that include enjoining the use of the misappropriated property, damages, and attorney's fees. When the misappropriation is of a physical item, such as a disk drive, the owner may ask the court to order seizure and return of its property.[10] In addition, where the misappropriation also violates other laws protecting intellectual property, such as where the taking infringes a copyright, the property owner may be entitled to additional relief.

Exactly what remedies are available will vary among the states. Interestingly, the very uniformity that the UTSA was intended to create has led to different treatment of available claims and remedies. For example, before the UTSA, an employee's theft of the employer's confidential customer lists triggered a common law claim for breach of the implied fiduciary obligation owed by an employee to the employer as well as a claim for misappropriation of trade secrets. The UTSA provides that its remedies preempt other common law remedies; in other words, a claim under the UTSA trumps the claim for breach of fiduciary duty as well as the claim for misappropriation of trade secrets. There is a split in the courts whether the UTSA replaces only common law causes of action for misappropriation of trade secrets or extends to any tortious claims for relief that arise out of the misappropriation no matter how stated. The broader reach of the UTSA appears to be favored by the growing majority of courts that have considered this issue to date. The takeaway from this uncertainty is that computer security professionals should protect trade secrets, confidential information, and other valuable data through contractual terms with, among others, employees, vendors, and users to minimize the reliance on the UTSA.

In the event of a misappropriation, in addition to civil remedies, often separate state statutes treat the taking as a theft and a criminal act. Such statutes are generally state specific. Prior to 1996, the Trade Secrets Act (TSA) was the only federal statute prohibiting trade secret misappropriation. The TSA, however, was of limited utility because it did not apply to private sector employees and provided only limited criminal sanctions.[11] To combat an increase in computer crimes, Congress enacted the Economic Espionage Act of 1996 (EEA), which provided greater protection for the proprietary and economic information of both corporate and governmental entities against foreign and domestic theft.[12]

The EEA criminalizes two principal categories of corporate espionage: economic espionage and theft of trade secrets.[13] Section 1831 punishes those who steal trade secrets "to benefit a foreign government, foreign instrumentality, or foreign agent." Section 1832 is the general criminal trade secret provision.[14] The EEA criminalizes stealing, concealing, destruction, sketching, copying, transmitting, or receiving trade secrets without authorization, or with knowledge that the trade secrets have been misappropriated. It also criminalizes attempting to and conspiring to do any of these acts.[15] The EEA penalizes parties responsible for a taking that is intended to benefit a foreign government with fines up to $250,000 and imprisonment up to 10 years.[16]

The EEA explicitly defines a trade secret to include information stored in electronic media and includes "programs or codes, whether tangible or intangible" so long as:

(a) the owner thereof has taken reasonable measures to keep such information secret; and
(b) the information derives independent economic value, actual or potential, from not being generally known to, and not being readily ascertainable through proper means by, the public.[17]

Although one might assume that this definition is relatively straightforward, not everything is as it appears. In a case of domestic trade secret theft, the Court of Appeals for the Seventh Circuit examined what the EEA means when it says that the data or material "derives independent economic value, actual or potential, from not being generally known to, and not being readily ascertainable through proper means by, the public."[18] Noting that others had assumed that the word "public" meant the general public, the court in *Lange* astutely observed that this was not, in fact, the case. Moreover, the standard for measuring the persons who might readily ascertain the economic value of (in this case) the design and composition of airplane brake assemblies is not the average person in the street, for this assumes (as the court mentions) that any person can understand and apply something as arcane as Avogadro's number. Instead, the definition of the term "the public" should take into account the segment of the population that would be interested in and understand the nature of that which has allegedly been misappropriated.

The international reach of the act is limited, extending outside of the United States only if: "(1) the offender is a natural person who is a citizen or permanent resident alien of the United States, or an organization organized under the laws of the United States or a State or political subdivision. . .or (2) an act in furtherance of the offense was committed in the United States."[19] Few defendants have been charged under the act since its passage in 1996, so the precise reach has yet to be tested. However, the language of the EEA applies its provisions to corporations with headquarters or operations subject to U.S. jurisdiction that could be prosecuted under the act. Finally, the remedies under the EEA can be invoked only by the United States. There is no private right of action under the act.

11.3.2   Vigilance Is a Best Practice.

The key points of practice to remember are: Security and trade secret law are forever linked together. A trade secret cannot exist without such security. The maxim "Eternal vigilance is the price of liberty," often attributed to Thomas Jefferson, should in the context of business information protection be restated as "Eternal vigilance is the price of trade secret protection." It is not as catchy a phrase, but it is the price each business must pay if it relies in whole or in part on trade secret law for protection. In such situations, the greatest assurance of protection can be obtained through rigorous contractual terms and strenuous enforcement.

11.4   COPYRIGHT LAW AND SOFTWARE.

Because of anxiety over the true extent of protection afforded software under patent and copyright law, software programs initially were protected as trade secrets. Such protection became increasingly problematic in today's society, where information technology and pressure for the free flow of information makes confidentiality controls more difficult to police. Copyright law now has evolved to include computer programs.

Since 1964, the United States Copyright Office has permitted registration of computer programs, although judicial decisions were divided on the applicability of the Copyright Act. In 1976, Congress passed the Copyright Act of 1976, which did little to resolve the ambiguity. Clarification finally was obtained in the Computer Software Copyright Act of 1980, which explicitly extended the protection of the copyright laws to software.[20] Any type of work that can be fixed in any tangible medium can be protected by copyright as literary works based on the authorship of the source and object code[21] even if the work can only be machine reproduced.

Copyright protection, however, does not protect "ideas."[22] Rather, it protects the particular expression of the idea. As can be seen by the parallel proliferation of spreadsheet programs, the idea for the spreadsheet program cannot be protected, but the particular code that produces the spreadsheet can be. In order to qualify for copyright protection, the work must be (a) original, (b) fixed in a tangible medium, and (c) not just the embodiment of an idea. Once obtained, copyright protection grants to the copyright owner the exclusive right to reproduce, to publish, to prepare derivative works, to distribute, to display, and to perform the copyrighted work. In 1990, Congress passed the Computer Software Rental Amendments Act,[23] which added to the list of copyright infringements the distribution of a computer program for commercial advantage. Materials copyrighted after 1978 are protected for the lesser of 75 years from the date of first publication or 100 years from the date of creation.

11.4.1   Works for Hire and Copyright Ownership.

The copyright for a work does not always belong to the person who creates it. The most frequent exceptions are works that fall under the concept of a "work for hire." A work for hire is not owned by the creator but by the persons who hired the creator to create the work. Most often the concept applies to employees who have created a work *within the scope* of their employment. The key concept is the scope of employment. Even though a work is created outside of the office and normal working hours, it still will be a work for hire if it is within the scope of employment. However, a work that falls outside the scope of employment and that is created outside the office is likely not to be deemed a work for hire. Because of such issues, it is better practice when dealing with employees or independent contractors to provide specificity in an agreement as to what is a work and when the creation of a work will be governed by the doctrine of work for hire.

11.4.2 Copyright Rights Adhere from the Creation of the Work.   Everyone who has looked at a copyrighted work is probably familiar with the symbol © affixed to any published copyrighted work, together with the name of the copyright holder and the year of creation or publication of the work. For many years, such notice was a fortiori necessary for copyright protection. Today, however, the copyright arises from the creation of a copyrighted work itself. It is still good practice to advise the world of potential infringement by inserting the formalities of a copyright on the work itself. In addition, one should register the work in the United States Copyright Office, which is currently developing a process for online registration. Registration of the copyright also permits one to claim statutory damages ranging from $500 to $20,000 for each violation, which often is useful to prevent additional infringements when no actual damages can be demonstrated. Moreover, in some jurisdictions, it may be necessary to register the copyright with the copyright office before one can actually sue to protect the copyright.

The change in copyright protection has interesting applications when applied to electronic works. The creation of the work in some permanent form is sufficient to trigger copyright protection. Thus, the creation of an electronic copy is sufficient permanency. What that means is that any electronic data are already conceivably subject to copyright protection at the time that they are viewed or received. Thus in using any such information or "work," care must be taken that one does not infringe on a potential copyright without a license.

11.4.3 First Sale Limitation.   The holder of the copyright has the right to sell or license the work. If the work is sold, the holder essentially loses all rights to control the resale of the work. This is known as the first sale doctrine. Once the item is placed in commerce, subsequent transfers cannot be restricted. The doctrine applies only to the copy that has actually been sold. It does not create a license to copy the item itself.

To avoid what sometimes can be a problem if the program winds up in the hands of a competitor, companies often prefer to license the item instead of selling it outright. If the work is licensed, only those rights that are contained in the license are transferred. All other rights of ownership remain with the licensor. Thus a breach of the license gives the licensor of the copyrighted work the right to reclaim the work or prevent its further use or publication. However, if the license has all the basic indicia of a sale, it will be treated as one, notwithstanding the label.

One interesting intersection of these two principles is the requirement when upgrading software that the old version be present. As a condition of making the upgrade available at a reduced rate, the seller normally requires that the older version be authenticated before the newer version can be installed. Such requirements are legal, as the owner of the earlier version could choose to sell it, but then would have to pay a higher price for the newer version and work to restrain subsequent sales of software from a user who expects to upgrade in the future.

11.4.4 Fair Use Exception.   All copyright protection is subject to the doctrine of fair use.[24] Fair use permits the use of a work without authorization for a limited purpose. But what use constitutes fair use? The Copyright Act of 1976 suggested four, nonexclusive factors, for a court to consider:

1. What is the purpose and character of the use?
2. What is the nature of the copyrighted work?
3. How much of the copyrighted work is used?
4. What is the effect on the potential market for the work?

Despite its codification in the Copyright Act of 1976, fair use remains a nebulous doctrine—an equitable rule of reason, with each case to be decided on its own facts.[25] It is often misquoted and misapplied. The essential concept behind the doctrine of fair use is to permit public discussion, review, and debate of a copyrighted work without violating the copyright. Thus, the Copyright Act of 1976 gives as examples of fair use, situations of "criticism, comment, news reporting, teaching (including multiple copies for classroom use) scholarship or research."

Fair use is not an antidote for failing to license a work. It should be invoked with care—understanding that the more material that is used and the more commercial the purpose, the less likely a court will find it applicable. Indeed, sometimes the only way to harmonize cases on whether a use is a fair use is to decide whether the court ultimately viewed the user as a "good" or "bad" guy.

11.4.5 Formulas Cannot be Copyrighted.   There are limitations on what expressions can be protected by copyright law. A frequent source of argument is whether, since one cannot protect the idea, the expression is directly driven by its content (i.e., the expression is simply a function of the idea). For that reason, formulas cannot be copyrighted.[26] This means that when formulas are part of a computer program, other modes of defense need to be considered, such as trade secret or possibly patent protection. If one were to disclose the formula through copyright publication, one would lose the ability to protect that information.

11.4.6 Copyright Does Not Protect the "Look and Feel" for Software Products.   Copyright protection ordinarily extends to the physical manifestation of the computer program in the source code and object code. The operation of that code, as it translates to what the human mind perceives, has been described as the "look and feel" of the program. In attempting to quantify the concept of "look and feel," courts have considered whether the organization, structure, and sequence of the program can be protected. In the United States, *Whelan Associates, Inc. v. Jaslow Dental Lab., Inc.*,[27] gave the greatest extension to protecting "look and feel." In that case, none of the code had been copied and the program operated on a different platform. Nonetheless, copyright infringement was found because the organization, structure, and sequence of the program had been copied. The court recognized that the structure and logic of the program are the most difficult to create and that the idea could be protected as it was embodied in the program structure since, given the variety that was possible, the structure was not necessarily just an extension of the idea. Since *Whelan*, courts in the United States have retreated from such broad protection. In 1992, *Computer Associates, Inc. v. Altai, Inc.*[28] developed the so-called abstraction-filtration test. The results of that test define as unprotectable: (a) program structures that are dictated by operating efficiency or functional demands of the program and therefore deemed part of the idea and (b) all tools and subroutines that may be deemed included in the public domain. Only what remains is to be compared for possible copyright infringement.

While protection of "look and feel" may vary among the different federal circuits, in general, the courts are swinging away from broader protection. However, this may not necessarily be true internationally; English law appears to grant the broader protections afforded by the *Whelan* decision.

11.4.7 Reverse Engineering as a Copyright Exception. Within the field of computer software, cases have considered whether "dissection" in order to reverse engineer the program is a violation of the copyright. To those involved in protecting software programs, the answer appears to be that reverse engineering does not constitute an infringement, even though the disassembly of the program falls squarely within the category of acts prohibited by the Copyright Act because of the doctrine of fair use. The Ninth Circuit in *Sega Enterprises Ltd. V. Accolade, Inc.*[29] found as a matter of law that:

> where disassembly is the only way to gain access to the ideas and functional elements embodied in a copyrighted computer program and where there is a legitimate reason for seeking such access, disassembly is a fair use of the copyrighted work.[30]

The Ninth Circuit is not the only circuit that has upheld reverse engineering against a copyright claim. The Federal Circuit reached a similar conclusion regarding reverse engineering of object code to discern the "ideas" behind the program in *Atari Games Corp. v. Nintendo of America, Inc.*[31] The fair use rationale of *Sega* was also adopted by the Eleventh Circuit in *Bateman v. Mnemonics, Inc.*[32] on the grounds that it advanced the sciences. In addition, in *Assessment Techs. of WI, LLC, v. WIREData, Inc.*, the Seventh Circuit relied on *Sega* and determined that WIREData, Inc. could extract uncopyrighted data from a copyrighted computer program, noting that the purpose of the extraction was to get the raw data, not compete with Assessment Technologies by selling copies of the program itself.[33] In *Evolution, Inc. v. SunTrust Bank*, the Tenth Circuit relied on both *Sega* and *WIREData* when it allowed the defendant to copy part of plaintiff's source code to extract uncopyrighted data from plaintiff's copyrighted computer program.[34] Thus, unless careful thought is given to the application of copyright protection, merely copyrighting the software will not necessarily protect against imitation.

11.4.8 Interfaces. There is an open issue as to whether copyright protects the format for interfacing between application and data. Competitors, particularly in the area of gaming, look to reverse engineer the interface format to make new modules compatible with existing hardware. Such reverse engineering has been held not to violate the copyright laws, so long as the new product does not display copyrighted images or other copyrightable expressions.[35] Thus, the nonprotectable interface may be protected if such copyrighted images or expressions are embedded in the display.

11.4.9 Transformative Uses. One of the factors that the doctrine of fair use considers is the "amount and substantiality of the portion used in relation to the copyrighted work as a whole."[36] In practical terms, this means that courts look at how much was taken and for what purpose. One could take a little but still take the essence of the program. One could also take a little that did not attempt to duplicate but rather used the copyrighted material as a springboard for a new creation. Out of this qualitative and quantitative investigation comes the notion of transformative use, which became the coin of analysis in the Supreme Court's 1994 decision in *Campbell v. Acuff-Rose Music, Inc.*[37] *Campbell* addressed the concept in terms of a claim of copyright infringement involving a rap parody of a popular song. There, taking its clues from the opening language of Section 107 codifying fair use, the Supreme Court asked whether the "new" work "adds something new, with a further purpose or different character, altering the first with new expression, meaning or message; it asks, in other words, whether and to what extent the new work is transformative."[38] The Court then laid down the test to be applied.

> Although such transformative use is not absolutely necessary for a finding of fair use, . . . the goal of copyright, to promote science and the arts, is generally furthered by the creation of transformative works. Such works thus lie at the heart of the fair use doctrine's guarantee of breathing space within the confines of copyright, . . . and the more transformative the new work, the less will be the significance of other factors, like commercialism, that may weigh against a finding of fair use.[39]

Thus, a transformative use may play off of a prior copyright and still not be deemed an infringement so long as the resulting new work is just that—new.

11.4.10 Derivative Works. Under Section 106 (2) of the Copyright Act of 1976, the copyright owner has the exclusive right "to prepare derivative works based upon the copyrighted work." The act defines a "derivative work" as:

> a work based upon one or more pre-existing works, such as a translation, musical arrangement, dramatization, fictionalization, motion picture version, sound recording, art reproduction, abridgement, condensation, or any other form in which a work may be recast, transformed, or adapted. A work consisting of editorial revisions, annotations, elaborations, or other modifications which, as a whole, represent an original work of authorship, is a "derivative work."

A derivative work is thus defined as an original work that is independently copyrightable. To infringe the exclusive right to prepare a derivative work granted by the Copyright Act to the copyright owner, the infringer need not actually have copied the original work or even have fixed in a tangible medium of expression the allegedly infringing work.[40] The right, therefore, to create the derivative work can be a useful tool in counterbalancing attempts to pirate computer programs and the issue of fair use.

The Copyright Act creates an exemption for a lawful owner of a purchased license for a computer program to adapt the copyrighted program if the actual adaptation "is created as an essential step in the utilization of the computer program in conjunction with a machine and it is used in no other manner."[41] The adaptation cannot be transferred to a third party. The right to adapt is, in essence, the right to modify or, in the language of the act, to create a derivative work. Such changes can be made even without the consent of the software owner so long as such modifications are used only internally and are necessary to the continuing use of the software.[42]

11.4.11 Semiconductor Chip Protection Act of 1984. The Semiconductor Chip Protection Act of 1984 (SCPA) protects as part of the Copyright Act "mask works fixed in a semiconductor product."[43] The SCPA protects not the product itself but the copying of the circuit design or blueprint. Because of reverse engineering, the protections afforded by SCPA are limited in practice.

11.4.12 Direct, Contributory, or Vicarious Infringement. Copyright infringement generally requires a showing of substantial similarity between allegedly offending use and the protected expression contained in a work. Infringement can occur through the simple act of printing (without permission), by posting on the Web or other form of unauthorized distribution, by creating a derivative work, or by another act that interferes with the copyright holder's rights.

A copyright can be infringed directly, contributorially, or vicariously. Direct infringement is the term ascribed to the actor who violates the copyright. Contributory infringement involves knowingly providing the means for the violation to occur. Liability for contributory infringement may be predicated on actively encouraging (or inducing) infringement through specific acts, or on distributing a product that distributees use to infringe copyrights, if the product is not capable of "substantial" or "commercially significant" noninfringing uses.[44] But secondary liability for copyright infringement does not exist in the absence of direct infringement by a third party. Vicarious infringement occurs when one is responsible for or controls the actions of another who violates the infringement. The usual situation is that of an employer's responsibility for the acts of an employee.

Not all situations admit themselves of simple answers, as when a person commits direct infringement by actually photocopying a work. New technologies constantly pose issues as to whether infringement has occurred and whether the infringement violates the public interest. In general, when faced with an issue of potential copyright infringement, the questions to ask are:

- Can the product or service be used to infringe a copyright, or is the product capable of substantial noninfringing uses?
- If so, did the owner of the product or service encourage the user to use it for infringement?
- Alternatively, did the owner of the product or service have knowledge of the specific infringing use and have the ability to prevent it?

Today, we take Internet Service Providers (ISPs) for granted. But application of these questions initially led courts to conclude that ISPs were liable for contributory infringement. For example, a Web site that encouraged and facilitated the uploading of copyrighted materials was found to be a direct infringer of the copyright of the owner even though the provider did not actually do the uploading.[45] Similarly, an ISP that was notified of a copyright violation that was posted on its server and failed to correct it could be found to have contributory liability for the infringement.[46] In its wisdom, however, Congress in the Digital Millennium Copyright Act (DMCA) created a safe harbor for Internet service providers so that, as a matter of public policy, an ISP does not have to monitor each and every transmission for potential copyright infringement.

11.4.13 Civil and Criminal Remedies. The Copyright Act contains several sections that specifically address the penalties and remedies for infringement. They include injunctive relief (i.e., a court order terminating the infringing conduct),[47] impounding and disposing of infringing articles,[48] damages,[49] litigation costs and attorneys' fees,[50] and criminal penalties.[51] Although this chapter cannot address all of the permutations of remedies and penalties available, a few are worth mentioning.

Generically, a copyright owner must choose between its actual losses (i.e., what it actually lost and any profits realized by the infringer) and statutory damages.[52] Actual damages imply economic losses actually suffered as a result of the infringement. The kinds of actual damages that have been awarded include development costs of the software,[53] the economic consequences of lost customers,[54] lost future sales,[55] the value of the infringer's licensing fees where the licensor is precluded from market sales,[56] lost market value of the material infringed,[57] and lost royalty payments.[58] An award of actual damages is not automatic; the license holder has the burden of proving that the infringing activity and the economic loss are causally connected, at which point the infringing party must show that the license holder would have incurred the loss anyway.[59]

A copyright owner may elect to receive statutory damages rather than actual damages and the infringer's profits.[60] Making the election is mandatory, and it must be done before final judgment is entered. Once the election is made, it is final. The statutory damages generally range from $500 to $20,000 "for all infringements involved in the action, with respect to any one work, for which any two or more infringers are liable jointly and severally.... For purposes of this section, all the parts of a compilation or derivative work constitute one work."[61] This amount may be increased to $100,000 if the court finds that the infringement was willful and reduced to $200 if the court finds that the infringer "was not aware and had no reason to believe" that the act was an infringement.[62]

Statutory damages theoretically[63] are intended to approximate the actual damages suffered, and were crafted as an alternative compensation scheme for copyright owners, when actual damages are difficult to calculate. In determining whether to elect actual or statutory damages, a copyright owner ought to perform a careful analysis to determine how many separate infringements occurred that justify, under the statute, separate awards. Although posting different copyrighted computer software programs on a bulletin board for downloading constitutes multiple infringements,[64] making multiple copies of the same cartoon character in different poses constitutes a single infringement because only one work was copied.[65]

As mentioned, this is one of the statutory schemes that discourage frivolous litigation by imposing the cost of litigating on the losing party. The statute permits the substantially prevailing party to recover its reasonable attorneys' fees and costs from the losing party. Who is the substantially prevailing party and what constitutes reasonable attorneys' fees are separate and distinct issues that will be decided by the courts.

Copyright violations also can be criminally prosecuted, and generally require demonstration of *mens rea,* or intent. One or more infringements having a total retail value of more than $1,000 within a 180-day period or "for purposes of commercial advantage or private financial gain" can be punished by one to five years of imprisonment and fines. Even without demonstration of a motive of financial gain, 10 or more infringements having a value in excess of $2,500 can result in up to three years in jail and fines. Repeated violations carry stiffer penalties. Finally, one who knowingly aids or abets a copyright infringement is also subject to criminal prosecution.

11.5 DIGITAL MILLENNIUM COPYRIGHT ACT. In 1998, Congress passed the Digital Millennium Copyright Act to address concerns raised by the Internet and copyright issues in the context of our increasingly technological society. The DMCA creates a civil remedy for its violation as well as criminal penalties starting after October 2000. One of the purposes of the DMCA is to protect the integrity of copyright information. Removal of a copyright notice, or distribution knowing that such copyright has been removed, is now actionable.[66]

11.6 CIRCUMVENTING TECHNOLOGY MEASURES. Article 11 of the World Intellectual Property Organization Copyright Treaty required all signatory countries to provide adequate legal protection and remedies against the circumvention of technical measures intended to secure copyrights. In response, Congress adopted Section 1201 of the DMCA, which generally prohibits the act of circumventing, and trafficking in the technology that enables circumvention of, protection measures designed to control access to copyrighted work.[67] Both civil and criminal remedies also now exist under the DMCA if one circumvents "a technological measure that effectively controls access to a work protected" by the Copyright Act.[68] It is a civil violation and a crime to "manufacture, import, offer to the public, provide or otherwise traffic in any technology, product, service, device, component, or part thereof," that "is primarily designed or produced for the purpose of circumventing a technological measure that effectively controls access to a work protected" under the Copyright Act.[69] A technological measure effectively controls access to a work if the measure, "in the ordinary course of its operation, requires the application of information or a process or a treatment, with the authority of the copyright owner, to gain access to the work."[70] One circumvents such technology measure if one uses a means "to descramble a scrambled work, to decrypt an encrypted work, or otherwise to avoid, bypass, remove, deactivate, or impair a technological measure," without the authority of the copyright owner.[71]

In *RealNetworks, Inc. v. Streambox, Inc.*,[72] Streambox distributed software that enabled users to bypass the authentication process employed by RealNetworks, which distributes audio and video content over the Internet. Thus, Streambox users could get the benefit of the RealNetworks streaming audio and video content without compensating the copyright owners. The United States District Court in Washington State found that the Streambox software was a technological measure that was designed to circumvent the access and copy control measures intended to protect the copyright owners.[73]

In a case involving digital video disc (DVD) encryption, a U.S. District Court in New York enjoined posting links to sites where visitors may download the decryption program as trafficking in circumvention technology and a violation of the DMCA.[74] In *Universal City Studios, Inc. v. Reimerdes*, the court rejected an argument that the use of the decryption software constituted free expression protected by the First Amendment of the U.S. Constitution. On appeal, the appellant argued that the injunction violated the First Amendment because computer code was speech, was entitled to full protection, and was unable to survive the strict scrutiny given to protected speech.[75] The appellate court found that the computer code used in the program was protected speech:

Communication does not lose constitutional protection as "speech" simply because it is expressed in the language of computer code. Mathematical formulae and musical scores are written in "code," i.e., symbolic notations not comprehensible to the uninitiated, and yet both are covered by the First Amendment. If someone chose to write a novel entirely in computer object code by using strings of 1's and 0's for each letter of each word, the resulting work would be no different for constitutional purposes than if it had been written in English. The "object code" version would be incomprehensible to readers outside the programming community (and tedious to read even for most within the community), but it would be no more incomprehensible than a work written in Sanskrit for those unversed in that language. The undisputed evidence reveals that even pure object code can be, and often is, read and understood by experienced programmers. And source code (in any of its various levels of complexity) can be read by many more. See *Universal I*, 111 F. Supp. 2d at 326. Ultimately, however, the ease with which a work is comprehended is irrelevant to the constitutional inquiry. If computer code is distinguishable from conventional speech for First Amendment purposes, it is not because it is written in an obscure language.[76]

The court then analyzed the type of scrutiny that should be applied where the restriction is content neutral:

> Having concluded that computer code conveying information is "speech" within the meaning of the First Amendment, we next consider, to a limited extent, the scope of the protection that code enjoys. As the District Court recognized, *Universal I*, 111 F. Supp. 2d at 327, the scope of protection for speech generally depends on whether the restriction is imposed because of the content of the speech. Content-based restrictions are permissible only if they serve compelling state interests and do so by the least restrictive means available. *See Sable Communications of California, Inc. v. FCC*, 492 U.S. 115, 126, 106 L. Ed. 2d 93, 109 S. Ct. 2829 (1989). A content-neutral restriction is permissible if it serves a substantial governmental interest, the interest is unrelated to the suppression of free expression, and the regulation is narrowly tailored, which "in this context requires...that the means chosen do not 'burden substantially more speech than is necessary to further the government's legitimate interests.'" *Turner Broadcasting System, Inc. v. FCC*, 512 U.S. 622, 662, 129 L. Ed. 2d 497, 114 S. Ct. 2445 (1994) (quoting *Ward v. Rock Against Racism*, 491 U.S. 781, 799, 105 L. Ed. 2d 661, 109 S. Ct. 2746 (1989)).[77]

Finding that the government's interest in preventing unauthorized access to encrypted copyrighted material is unquestionably substantial, and that the regulation of decryption programs served that interest, the appellate court upheld the prohibitions against both posting of, and linking to, the decryption program.

Not all efforts to "circumvent" restrictions, however, come within the prohibitions of the DCMA. In *I.M.S. Inquiry Mgmt. Sys. v. Berkshire Info. Sys.*,[78] the defendant had used a valid password provided to plaintiff's own customers and user identification to view plaintiff's e-Basket system exactly as the customer itself might have done. The court concluded that although this might be viewed as a technology measure, it was not circumvention of a digital wall within the meaning of the DCMA.

11.6.1 Exceptions to the Prohibitions on Technology Circumvention.

The DMCA, however, explicitly carves out all defenses to copyright infringement, including the doctrine of fair use, as being unaffected by the passage of the DMCA. In some circumstances fair use can include reverse engineering.

11.6.1.1 *Fair Use and Reverse Engineering.*

Within the field of computer software, recent cases have considered whether "dissection" in order to reverse engineer the program is a violation of the copyright. To those involved in protecting software programs, the answer appears to be that reverse engineering in the form of disassembly does not, under certain circumstances, constitute an infringement because it is considered "fair use."[79] The Ninth Circuit in *Sega Enterprises Ltd. v. Accolade, Inc.*[80] found as a matter of law that:

> where disassembly is the only way to gain access to the ideas and functional elements embodied in a copyrighted computer program and where there is a legitimate reason for seeking such access, disassembly is a fair use of the copyrighted work.[81]

The Ninth Circuit is not the only circuit that has upheld reverse engineering against a copyright claim. The Federal Circuit reached a similar conclusion regarding reverse engineering of object code to discern the "ideas" behind the program in *Atari Games Corp. v. Nintendo of America, Inc.*[82] The fair use rationale of *Sega* was also adopted by the Eleventh Circuit in *Bateman v. Mnemonics, Inc.*[83] on the grounds that it advanced the sciences. Thus, one can spy through reverse engineering still without running afoul of copyright protection or the DMCA.

However, in *Bowers v. Baystate Technologies, Inc.*,[84] a split Federal Circuit Court of Appeals found that a shrink-wrap license prohibiting reverse engineering was enforceable against the licensee who had reverse engineered Bowers's CAD Designer's Toolkit to develop a competing product. The *Bowers* court found that the contractual language trumped the "fair use" permitted under the Copyright Act. The Fifth Circuit has reached the opposite result in the earlier decision of *Vault Corp. v. Quaid Software, Ltd.*,[85] specifically finding that the Copyright Act preempts state law that attempts to prohibit disassembly, and holding a mass distribution license agreement unenforceable.

Thus, the extent to which *Bowers* may be followed is still unclear, but it appears to be questioned in subsequent decisions.[86] *Bowers* suggests a course that businesses can attempt to follow to curtail reverse engineering, which is to limit that right by contract. If *Bowers* becomes widely accepted, the United States will be in conflict with the European Union on this issue. In its 1991 Software Directive, the European Union set forth a right to reverse engineer that is consonant with "fair use" under the Copyright Act. The Software Directive also provided that the right cannot be waived by contract. So, until *Bowers* is settled, if a shrink-wrap license prohibits reverse engineering, it would be best to consider engaging in such activity abroad.

11.6.1.2 Other Exceptions.

The DMCA also creates an important exception that recognizes the right to reverse engineer if (a) the person has lawfully obtained the right to use a copy of a computer program, and (b) the sole purpose of circumventing the technology measure is to identify and analyze "those elements of the program that are necessary to achieve interoperability of an independently created computer program with other programs."[87] The DMCA creates a similar exemption for circumvention for the purpose of "enabling the interoperability of an independently created computer program with other programs, if such means are necessary to achieve such interoperability."[88] The term "interoperability" is defined to encompass the "ability of computer programs to exchange information and of such programs mutually to use the information which has been exchanged."[89] The information acquired through these permitted acts of circumvention may also be provided to third parties so long as it is solely used for the same purposes.[90]

Circumvention is permissible under these exemptions, however, "only to the extent [that it] does not constitute copyright infringement." Two cases, *Chamberlain Group, Inc. v. Skylink Techs., Inc.*,[91] and *Lexmark Int'l, Inc. v. Static Control Components, Inc.*,[92] are particularly instructive. In both cases, the courts permitted a competitor's access and reverse engineering under this exemption. In contrast, in *Storage Tech Corp. v. Custom Hardware Engineering Consulting, Inc.* (D. Mass. 2004), the defendant bypassed a protective access key to activate the diagnostics program by copying the code into the random access memory (RAM) of the defendant's access device. The District Court found that this copying constituted infringement. The result was reversed in a 2 to 1 decision in the United States Federal Circuit[93] based on a reading of sections 117(a) and (c) of the DMCA, which permits copying for maintenance purposes. This string of decisions has led to recommendations that access be controlled by a method that would cause copyright infringement and that access protect not just the copyrighted program but copyrighted data so as to exclude the rationale of the Federal Circuit. Suggestions have been made that certain parts of copyrighted executable code be encrypted and that a decryption key be required that will create a copy of the code and protected data as part of the process so as to create an argument of copyright infringement. These types of recommendations remain untested, and the simpler course may be control through terms inserted into the licensing agreement.

Exempt from the DMCA, as well, are "good faith" acts of circumvention where the purpose is encryption research. A permissible act of encryption research requires that (a) the person lawfully have obtained a copy, (b) the act is necessary to the research, (c) there was a good faith effort to obtain authorization before the circumvention, and (d) such act does not constitute an infringement under a different section of the Copyright Act or under the Computer Fraud and Abuse Act of 1986. With the caveat that it must be an act of good faith encryption research, the technological means for circumvention can be provided to others who are working collaboratively on such research. The issue of good faith encryption research looks to what happened to the information derived from the research. If it was disseminated in a manner that was likely to assist infringement, as opposed to reasonably calculated to advance the development of encryption technology, then the act still falls outside of the exemption. Other factors that go into the determination of good faith are whether the person conducting the research is trained, experienced, or engaged in the field of encryption research, and whether the researcher provides the copyright owner with a copy of the findings.

The DMCA also has a bias against the collection or dissemination of personally identifying information. Thus, it is not a violation of the DMCA to circumvent a technology measure that essentially protects, collects, or disseminates personally identifying information, provided that the circumvention has no other effect, and provided that the program itself does not contain a conspicuous notice warning against the collection of such information and a means to prevent or restrict such collection.[94] In short, one can disable "cookies" if the program does not itself permit a user to do so.

Finally, insofar as relevant to this chapter, the DMCA also excludes from its scope "security testing." The DMCA grants permission to engage in security testing that, but for that permission, would violate the terms of the DMCA. If the security testing, for some reason, violated some other provision of the Copyright Act or the Computer Fraud and Abuse Act of 1986, then it is still an act of infringement. The DMCA, in part, considers whether a violation occurred, and by whom the information was used. The factors to be considered include if the information was used to promote the security of the owner or operator of the computer network or system, if it was shared with the developer, and if it was used in a manner that would not facilitate infringement.[95] For purposes of the DMCA, security testing means accessing either an individual computer or network for the purpose of "good faith testing, investigating, or correcting, a security flaw or vulnerability, with the authorization of the owner or operator."[96]

11.6.1.3 Remedies. The criminal penalties for violation of the DMCA can be quite severe. If the violation is willful for commercial gain, the first offense bears a fine of up to $500,000 or 5 years imprisonment. Subsequent violations bear fines of up to $1 million dollars or 10 years imprisonment. Civil remedies include an order to restrain the violation, damages for lost profits, damages for recovery of the infringer's profits, or statutory damages for each violation. Depending on the section of the DMCA at issue, each violation can generate fines of up to $2,500 or $25,000. Since each act of infringement can constitute a violation, the statutory fines can become quite substantial.

11.7 PATENT PROTECTION. Ideas, which are not protected by copyright, can be protected through a patent. In general, the patent laws protect the functionality of a product or process.

11.7.1 Patent Protection Requires Disclosure. A patent can be properly obtained if the invention is new, useful, nonobvious, and disclosed. The patent exchanges a grant of an exclusive monopoly over the invention in return for disclosure. Disclosure is the trigger point for patentability. The disclosure supports the claims of patentability (i.e., it sets up the claim that the invention is both new and nonobvious) and also the scope of what can be protected. Thus, 35 U.S.C. section 112 provides:

> The specification shall contain a *written description* of the invention, and of the manner and process of making and using it, in such full, clear, concise and exact terms as to *enable any person skilled in the art* to which it pertains, or with which it is most nearly connected, to make and use the same, and shall set forth the *best mode* contemplated by the inventor of carrying out his invention.

> The specification shall conclude with one or more claims particularly pointing out and *distinctly claiming* the subject matter which the applicant regards as his invention. [Emphasis added.]

A patent therefore must disclose the best mode for implementing the invention, a clear written description of the invention, sufficient detail so that a practitioner can understand and make use of the description, and distinct claims, in order for a patent to issue.[97] Through adequate disclosure of the invention, the application gives notice of the technology involved in the patent so as to put the public on fair notice of what would constitute an infringement. From a public policy perspective, the disclosure enlarges the public knowledge. From the inventor's perspective, the trade-off is disclosure for exclusivity. Depending on how the invention is to be used and the areas in which protection will be necessary, disclosure may not be the best means of protecting the invention. This is particularly true if the inventor is not convinced it will be deemed nonobvious from prior art, in which case it will be subject to challenge, or if, after disclosure, other companies may legally use the disclosed information for competitive advantage. The effects of disclosure should be carefully considered before applying for patent protection.

11.7.2 Patent Protection in Other Jurisdictions. Patent protection is jurisdictional. What that means, in general, is that a patent has legal meaning in the country that granted it. The United States is a signatory to the Paris Convention for the Protection of Industrial Properties, which has roughly 160 signatories. The Paris Convention essentially grants a one-year grace period for filing national patent applications in each selected signatory, to obtain the benefit of the original filing date in the United States. An alternative, open to members of the Paris Convention, is the Patent Cooperation Act. This permits the filing of an international patent that basically gives the patentee an 8- to 18-month window to test feasibility, and which simplifies the national application process.

11.7.3 Patent Infringement. Like the remedies for copyright infringement, the remedies for patent infringement include injunctive relief and damages that, by statute, are not less than a reasonable royalty for the infringing use.[98] If the infringement is willful, the damages can be trebled. Attorneys' fees can be awarded, but only in exceptional cases.

In the area of exported computer software, an issue of note has arisen under 35 U.S.C. section 271(f). Section 271(f) was added in 1984 to the patent law to prevent infringers from avoiding liability by finishing goods outside of the United States. An infringer will be liable if its intent is to manufacture or supply a component from the

United States to be combined elsewhere, if it would be an infringement had it occurred within the United States. Exported software may be considered a "component" under section 271(f). In *Microsoft Corp. v. AT&T Corp.*,[99] the issue was whether a master disk supplied by Microsoft abroad for duplication and installation abroad of its Windows program ran afoul of AT&T's patent. In overruling the Federal Circuit, the Supreme Court concluded that it did not:

> Section 271(f) prohibits the supply of components "from the United States. . .in such manner as to actively induce the combination of such components." § 271(f) (1). Under this formulation, the very components supplied from the United States, and not copies thereof, trigger § 271(f) liability when combined abroad to form the patented invention at issue. Here, as we have noted, the copies of Windows actually installed on the foreign computers were not themselves supplied from the United States. Indeed, those copies did not exist until they were generated by third parties outside the United States. Copying software abroad, all might agree, is indeed easy and inexpensive. But the same could be said of other items: "Keys or machine parts might be copied from a master; chemical or biological substances might be created by reproduction; and paper products might be made by electronic copying and printing." . . .The absence of anything addressing copying in the statutory text weighs against a judicial determination that replication abroad of a master dispatched from the United States "supplies" the foreign-made copies from the United States within the intendment of § 271(f).

Unless section 271(f) is amended, it may have profound implications for subverting the ability of a U.S. company to control patent infringement where software is a component of a patented invention.

11.8 PIRACY AND OTHER INTRUSIONS.

For as long as ideas and innovation have been a source of commercial or social value, the terms on which these ideas and innovations have been available for use and exchange by others has been the subject of significant tension. Although inventors and creators of commercially viable products and processes want to maximize the return on their investment, marketplace pressure for cost efficiency (often motivated by human and corporate greed) fuels a constant drive to remove the inventors' and creators' royalties from the cost of production. Thus, the ancient notion of piracy, the unauthorized boarding of a ship to commit theft, and the unauthorized use of another's invention or production,[100] remains alive and well. The piracy we speak of is not simply the unauthorized copying of millions of compact discs (CDs); increasingly it includes the unauthorized scraping of data from Web sites, abuse of authorized Internet use, theft of employee data, and similar activities.

11.8.1 Marketplace.

The demand for unlicensed access to and use of software and entertainment media increases annually. In its 2007 survey regarding computer security among corporate and governmental institutions, the Computer Security Institute and the U.S. Federal Bureau of Investigation found that 59 percent of all respondents discovered employees who abused Internet privileges for a variety of unauthorized purposes.[101] A 2007 study by the Software & Industry Information Association reported worldwide revenue loss from the piracy (unlawful copying and distribution) of software exceeding $28.8 billion in 2007.[102] In countries such as China, despite recent overtures to the contrary, piracy is not merely sanctioned, it constitutes an investment by government agencies.[103]

In recent years, in large part due to the saturation of Internet access, there has been a tremendous proliferation of technologies designed to access and distribute (without authorization) protected software applications and entertainment media. This has posed a tremendous challenge for license holders, legislators, and law enforcement authorities. The results have included attempts to punish both unauthorized access and use of protected material. In the process, there has been a transformation in the definition of what is protected and some confusion about the extent of that protection when the Internet is involved.

11.8.2 Database Protection. Databases, the organized compilation of information in an electronic format, are prominent elements of any discussion concerning copyright protection. Compilations of information, data, and works are protectable under the Copyright Act.[104] To secure copyright protection for a compilation, a party must demonstrate that (1) it owned a valid copyright in the compilation; (2) the alleged infringer copied at least a portion of the compilation; and (3) the portion so copied was protected under the Copyright Act.[105] In this context, the Copyright Act protects the "original" selection, coordination, or arrangement of the data contained in the compilation.[106]

To the extent that compilations contain purely factual information (e.g., existing prices of products and services), there is no protection because the facts themselves lack originality.[107] It does not matter that the author "created" the facts of the prices being charged for the product or service.[108] To sustain a claim of copyright protection for compilations of fact, the author must demonstrate creativity in the arrangement of the data. Standard or routine arrangements are likewise beyond the act's umbrella.[109] This is in contrast to the European Union's Database Directive, which does not require creativity as an element for the protection of a database. Rather it protects investment in databases under copyright protection subject, however, to fair use qualifications.

The United States Supreme Court has held that the compilation into a database of original works by contributing authors to newspapers and magazines violates the copyrights of the individual authors when the database does not reproduce the authors' articles as part of the original collective work to which the articles were contributed. In *New York Times Co., Inc. v. Tasini*,[110] authors who contributed articles and other works to the *New York Times*, *Time* magazine, and *Newsday* sued when they learned that the articles that they sold to the publishers for use in the respective publications were being reproduced and made available online, through LEXIS/NEXIS, an online database, and on CD-ROM. In most instances, the reproductions were of the individual articles outside of the newspaper or magazine context, in a collection of works separately protected by the Copyright Act. The Supreme Court held that, because the publishers of the new collective works made no original or creative contribution to the individual authors' original works, they could not reproduce and distribute those works outside of the format that each publisher created for the original collections of works, without permission from, or payments to, each author.[111]

11.8.3 Applications of Transformative and Fair Use. The concepts of transformative use and fair use (to the extent that they are separable) discussed earlier in this chapter have played a substantial role in recent decisions involving the authorized use of electronic media and the Internet. The starting point for this application of the doctrine is the U.S. Supreme Court's decision in *Sony Corporation v. Universal City Studios, Inc.*,[112] the famous battle over Betamax initiated by the movie industry. At issue was whether electronic recording machines could record television programs to permit individuals to "time-shift" television programs (i.e., to record programs for viewing at a time other than the time of airing). In its decision, the *Sony* Court found that time shifting was a productive use of the television programs for a purpose other than the original commercial broadcast, and was not an attempt either to duplicate the original purpose or to impact the commercial market for these programs. The Court emphasized the noncommercial element inherent in time shifting.[113]

11.8.4 Internet Hosting and File Distribution.

The growth of the breadth and scope of the Internet has been accompanied by increasing questions about the extent to which the distribution of otherwise protected expressions change their form when converted into an electronic format. These questions arise for Internet service providers (ISPs), which provide the pathway for distributing protected material, and for end users who post such materials on their Web sites and bulletin boards. For ISPs, the DMCA provides some initial comfort.

Title II of the DMCA, designated the "Online Copyright Infringement Limitation Act" establishes several infringement liability safe harbors for service providers. The "Information residing on systems or networks at direction of users"[114] safe harbor is available to any provider of "online services or network access, or the operator of facilities thereof, . . . " including "digital online communications, between or among points specified by user, of material of the user's choosing, without modification to the content of the material as sent or received"[115] that "has adopted and reasonably implemented, and informs subscribers and account holders of the service provider's system or network of, a policy that provides for the termination in appropriate circumstances of subscribers and account holders of the service provider's system or network who are repeat infringers" and "accommodates and does not interfere with standard technical measures."[116] To qualify for the safe harbor, the service provider must demonstrate that

1. It has no actual or constructive knowledge that information on its system is infringing, it is not aware of circumstances from which infringement is apparent or, upon obtaining such knowledge or awareness, it acts expeditiously to remove those materials;

2. It receives no financial benefit directly attributable to the infringing activity, *and*

3. Upon receipt of a notice of infringing material on its system, responds expeditiously to remove, or disable access to, the material.[117]

Assuming that the safe harbor does not apply (as, for instance, because the ISP failed to act on a notice of infringing activity), many service providers may nonetheless escape liability. In the first, and seminal, case on this topic, *Religious Technology Center v. Netcom On-Line Communication Services, Inc.*,[118] an ISP hosted a bulletin board service on which Church of Scientology publications were posted by a former minister. The District Court held that the ISP must demonstrate that its use was of public benefit (facilitating dissemination of creative works including, but not limited to, the infringing work); that its financial gain was unrelated to the infringing activity (e.g., subscription fees from providing e-mail systems rather than fees from the display or sale of the infringing work); that its use was unrelated to the use of the owner of the work; that the ISP copied only what was necessary to provide its service; and that its use of the material had no demonstrable effect on the potential market for the work.[119] In *CoStar Group, Inc. v. LoopNet, Inc.*, the Fourth Circuit relied on *Netcom*, its codification in the DMCA, and the fact that the DMCA does not limit the application of other infringement defenses, and held that "the automatic copying, storage, and transmission of copyrighted materials, when instigated by others, does not render an ISP strictly liable for copyright infringement under §§501 and 106 of the Copyright Act."[120]

For Web site owners and users who post allegedly infringing material, the courts have had much less difficulty discarding the transformative fair use arguments. This has been particularly true in the purely commercial setting, as where the infringing party gains direct financial benefit from the infringing material,[121] and where the posted material is an exact copy of the protected work without any transformation to something creative or original.[122] In a case that goes to the heart of the open-access nature of the Internet, one court recently held that a copyright owner, who posts its work on the Internet for free distribution as shareware, may defeat a transformative fair use defense by also posting an express reservation of distribution rights.[123]

11.8.5 Web Crawlers and Fair Use.   The Internet, premised on open exchange of data and economic efficiency, has spawned a spate of data search and aggregation software tools that scan the Web looking for information requested by the user. The process used by these search engines[124] includes identifying data on the Web that conforms to the search parameters and then downloading that data. Since the copying usually occurs without the express permission of the copyright owner, some have argued that such copying constitutes an infringement. Although there is very little precedent concerning the application of transformative fair use to automated data retrieval systems, at least one court has upheld the use of the defense to an infringement claim.[125]

11.8.6 HyperLinking.   In *Perfect 10 v. Google, Inc.*,[126] affirmed in part and remanded in part, *Perfect 10, Inc. v. Amazon.com, Inc.*,[127] Perfect 10 (P10) claimed that Google was infringing its ownership of copyrights in certain images and thumbnails hosted by third-party and P10's Web sites when Google's image search picked them up for display as framed full-size images and as thumbnails on computers and cell phones. The court concluded that hyperlinking did not constitute display for purposes of direct copyright infringement. On appeal, the case was remanded for further consideration as to whether the conduct fell within the general rule for contributory liability. To appreciate the context in which the courts are wrestling with these issues in the light of new technology, a review of the District Court's analysis should be studied.

11.8.7 File Sharing.   Transformative fair use will not protect the verbatim retransmission of protected work in a different medium when there is a substantial and detrimental impact on the market for the protected work. In *A&M Records, Inc. v. Napster, Inc.*,[128] Napster enabled users to share music files over the Internet by downloading the file-sharing software to their hard drive, using the software to search for MP3 music files stored on other computers, and transferring copies of MP3 files from other computers. The court of appeals held that Napster users were merely retransmitting original works in a different medium and that this did not constitute a transformation of the original work. The court also found that sharing of music files over the Internet had, and would have, a significant and detrimental impact on the existing and potential market for CDs and digital downloads of the copyright owners' works. Picking up on the *Sony* decision's emphasis on the distinction between commercial and personal use, the Court of Appeals found that Napster's Web site effectively made the works available for use by the general public and not simply for the personal use of individual users.[129]

Napster's demise, however, did not end the controversy over file sharing. Trying to avoid Napster's method of directly enabling file sharing, entities such as Grokster and StreamCast developed software creating peer-to-peer networks through which individual computers communicate to exchange files without the necessity of a central server.[130] The Supreme Court recently revisited copyright infringement and file sharing specifically with respect to these peer-to-peer networks and applied the "inducement rule" to file-sharing services. Evidence demonstrated that 90 percent of the files available to download from Grokster and StreamCast were copyrighted works, and Grokster and StreamCast conceded that most users were downloading copyrighted material. There was also an abundance of evidence that through their respective software applications and advertisements, both entities marketed themselves as the alternative to Napster, and their business models demonstrated "that their principal object[ive] was [the] use of their software to download copyrighted works."[131] The Court vacated the court of appeals' affirmation of summary judgment for Grokster and StreamCast, and rejected the court of appeals' broad interpretation of *Sony Corp. v. Universal City Studios*, but declined to further discuss the balance between protecting copyrighted works and promoting commerce in the context of how much noninfringing use each service was capable of providing, and did not at all discuss the issue of fair use. Instead, the Court noted that *Sony* did not preclude other forms of infringement liability and, focusing on the intent of the defendants in their inducement of file sharing, held that "one who distributes a device with the object of promoting its use to infringe copyright, as shown by clear expression or other affirmative steps taken to foster infringement, is liable for the resulting acts of infringement by third parties."[132] Citing *Sony*, the Court further opined that mere knowledge of potential or actual infringement are not sufficient bases for liability, but that "the inducement rule. . .premises liability on purposeful, culpable expression and conduct, and thus does nothing to compromise legitimate commerce or discourage innovation having a lawful purpose."[133]

Since the service and software in *Grokster* had other lawful purposes, the Supreme Court's decision underscores the importance of proving an intent to infringe or cause infringement. Thus, when asking a court to look behind stratagems and disclaimers that hide unlawful purposes, the copyright holder should consider what other evidence exists or is likely to exist of product design, advertising, marketing, external and internal communications, revenue plans, and other factors that would prove unlawful intent. In addition, for copyright holders, the problem remains that many providers of file-sharing software may not be subject to the jurisdiction of U.S. courts and that file-sharing software, such as "Darknet," provides anonymity to users illegally downloading copyrighted materials. As will be discussed, many countries are signatories to Trade Related Aspects of Intellectual Property Rights (TRIPS). See Section 11.11.1 of this Chapter and subcribe to international copyright protection. Following Grokster, the maker of KaZaa file-sharing software was enjoined in Australia from using its software to commit copyright infringement. The remedy required alteration of the software so that it would not duplicate copyrighted works.

11.9   OTHER TOOLS TO PREVENT UNAUTHORIZED INTRUSIONS.
Several legal principles and laws support the right to prevent and prosecute unauthorized intrusions. These include the definition of trespass, terms of use, and several critically important and widely used laws explicitly addressing the issues.

11.9.1   Trespass.
Trespass is a common law concept that we are all familiar with when applied to land. We have all seen and probably at some point in our youth violated the no-trespassing signs that are posted on an unfriendly neighbor's property. Trespass is also a concept that can apply to computers and informational databases. Courts have been taking older concepts and reapplying them to new situations.

In *eBay, Inc. v. Bidder's Edge, Inc.*,[134] the Federal District Court granted eBay an injunction forbidding Bidder's Edge from using a software robot to scrape information from eBay's Web site. The court based the injunction on its finding that accessing the Web site in a manner that was beyond eBay's posted notice (there were actual letters of objection) constituted a trespass. The court reasoned that the "electronic signals sent by Bidder's Edge to retrieve information from eBay's computer system [were] sufficiently tangible to support a trespass cause of action." The court further viewed the ongoing violation of eBay's fundamental right to exclude others from its computer system as creating sufficient irreparable harm to warrant an injunction. Thus, it was not necessary that eBay prove that the access actually interfered with the operation of the Web site. Rather, proof of the "intermeddling with or use of another's personal property" was sufficient to establish the cause of action for trespass. What is significant here is that eBay did permit others to access its Web site under license, and the court viewed conduct that exceeded the licensed use, upon notice to the violator, to be a trespass.

However, the applicability of trespass to unauthorized computer activity is not settled. Where trespass involves an object, rather than land, there must not only be improper use but also some harm to the physical condition or value of the object or the misuse must deprive the rightful owner of the use of the object for a substantial period of time. The two must be causally related. In *Intel v. Hamidi*,[135] the California Supreme Court reversed a lower court's banning a former employee from sending unsolicited e-mails on the grounds of trespass. The court thought that the reach of the doctrine had been extended too far, concluding that bad analogies (i.e., viewing servers as houses and electronic waves as intrusions) create bad law. The court declined to view computers as real property. Rather, finding that they were like other personal property, the court found that this communication was no different from a letter delivered by mail or a telephone call. In short, the court declined to find a trespass because there was an "unwelcome communication, electronic or otherwise" that had fictitiously caused an "injury to a communication system." Here there was no injury to the computer system although Intel claimed injury to its business.

Intel v. Hamidi simply warns against overbreadth of application of the concept of trespass. If injury to the computer system can be demonstrated, then the concept of trespass does lie as a tool in the arsenal of remedies assuming that the trespasser can be identified.

11.9.2 Terms of Use.   Terms of use can constitute a contract with respect to Web site usage. Thus, in any situation where electronic access is requested or permitted, the terms and conditions of use, together with an acknowledgment that such terms have been seen and consented to, can be enforced as restricting usage. In *Register.com, Inc. v. Verio, Inc.*,[136] the Second Circuit upheld an order enjoining Web site access primarily on the issue of contract. There, as described by the Second Circuit, the defendant Verio, against whom the preliminary injunction was issued, was engaged in the business of selling a variety of Web site design, development, and operation services. In the sale of such services, Verio competed with Register's Web site development business. To facilitate its pursuit of customers, Verio undertook to obtain daily updates of the WHOIS information relating to newly registered domain names. To achieve this, Verio devised an automated software program, or robot, which each day would submit multiple successive WHOIS queries through the port 43 accesses of various registrars. Upon acquiring the WHOIS information of new registrants, Verio would send them marketing solicitations by e-mail, telemarketing, and direct mail. To the extent that Verio's solicitations were sent by e-mail, the practice was inconsistent with the terms of the restrictive legend Register attached to its responses to Verio's queries.

Register at first complained to Verio about this use and then adopted a new restrictive legend on its Web site that undertook to bar mass solicitation "via direct mail, electronic mail, or by telephone." The court concluded that Verio's conduct formed a contract, like buying an apple at a roadside fruit stand, which Verio breached:

> We recognize that contract offers on the Internet often require the offeree to click on an "I agree" icon. And no doubt, in many circumstances, such a statement of agreement by the offeree is essential to the formation of a contract. But not in all circumstances. While new commerce on the Internet has exposed courts to many new situations, it has not fundamentally changed the principles of contract. It is standard contract doctrine that when a benefit is offered subject to stated conditions, and the offeree makes a decision to take the benefit with knowledge of the terms of the offer, the taking constitutes an acceptance of the terms, which accordingly become binding on the offeree. See, e.g., *Restatement (Second) of Contracts § 69* (1)(a) (1981) ("Silence and inaction operate as an acceptance. . .where an offeree takes the benefit of offered services with reasonable opportunity to reject them and reason to know that they were offered with the expectation of compensation.")

****

> Returning to the apple stand, the visitor, who sees apples offered for 50 cents apiece and takes an apple, owes 50 cents, regardless whether he did or did not say, "I agree." The choice offered in such circumstances is to take the apple on the known terms of the offer or not to take the apple. As we see it, the defendant in Ticketmaster and Verio in this case had a similar choice. Each was offered access to information subject to terms of which they were well aware. Their choice was either to accept the offer of contract, taking the information subject to the terms of the offer, or, if the terms were not acceptable, to decline to take the benefits

Id., at 403; and was also a trespass because:

> The district court found that Verio's use [**31] of search robots, consisting of software programs performing multiple automated successive queries, consumed a significant portion of the capacity of Register's computer systems. While Verio's robots alone would not incapacitate Register's systems, the court found that if Verio were permitted to continue to access Register's computers through such robots, it was "highly probable" that other Internet service providers would devise similar programs to access Register's data, and that the system would be overtaxed and would crash. We cannot say these findings were unreasonable.

Id., at 405.

Similarly, although in a different setting, in *ProCD v. Zeidenberg*,[137] where ProCD sold a CD with noncopyrightable data. Access to the data, however, was controlled by a license agreement; if there was no acceptance, there was also no access. The license agreement prohibited the use of the data for any commercial use. Zeidenberg took the data and posted it on a Web site, which he used commercially to sell advertising. Thus the data were being used to attract visitors. The court found the license limitation on use enforceable.

The importance of this decision is that so long as the owner prominently specifies the limitations, the restrictions can become a contract that is accepted by accepting the benefits of access and can be one safeguard against misuse of the access.

11.9.3 Computer Fraud and Abuse Act[138]

11.9.3.1 Prohibited Behavior and Damages. In 1984, Congress passed the original version of the Computer Fraud and Abuse Act (CFAA).[139] The general purpose was to protect "Federal interest computers" by criminalizing intentional and unauthorized access to those computers that resulted in damage to the computers or the data stored on them. The statute was substantially amended in 1986,[140] and again in 1996,[141] and now contains both criminal and private civil enforcement provisions. The statute proscribes these activities:

knowingly accessing a computer without authority or in excess of authority, thereafter obtaining U.S. government data to which access is restricted and delivering, or attempting to deliver, the data to someone not entitled to receive it;[142]

intentionally accessing a computer without authority or in excess of authority and thereby obtaining protected consumer financial data;[143]

intentional and unauthorized access of a U.S. government computer that affects the use of the computer by or for the U.S. government;[144]

accessing a computer used in interstate commerce knowingly and with the intent to defraud and, as a result of the access, fraudulently obtaining something valued in excess of $5,000;[145]

causing damage to computers used in interstate commerce by (i) knowingly transmitting a program, code, etc. that intentionally causes such damage, or (ii) intentionally accessing the computer without authority and causing such damage;[146]

knowingly, and with the intent to defraud, trafficking in computer passwords for computers used in interstate commerce or by the U.S. government;[147] and

transmitting threats to cause damage to a protected computer with the intent to extort money or anything of value.[148]

The linchpin among the relevant decisions concerning access to data under the CFAA is whether the access is "without authority" or "in excess of authority." The factors considered by the courts include the steps taken by the owner of the information to protect against disclosure or use, the extent of the defendants' knowledge regarding their authority to access or use the data, and the use(s) made of the data after gaining access. The legislative history indicates that the statute was intended to "punish those who illegally use computers for commercial advantage."[149]

Broadly speaking, there are two sets of circumstances to consider. In the first instance, is the actual access authorized, either expressly or impliedly? In the Internet context, where there is a presumption of open access, the site or data owners must show that they took steps to protect the contents of their site and to limit access to the data at issue.[150] Once those steps are taken, the protection constitutes a wall through which even automated search retrieval systems may not go without express permission.[151] Without the wall, there must be some evidence of an intent to access for an impermissible purpose, as when Intuit inserted cookies into the hard drives of home computers.[152]

Second, has the authorized access been improperly exceeded? Generally speaking, those who use their permitted access for an unauthorized purpose to the detriment of the site or data owner have violated the CFAA. Examples include employees who obtain trade secret information and transmit it via the employer's e-mail system to a competitor for which the employee is about to begin work;[153] using an ISP subscription membership to gain access to and harvest e-mail addresses of other subscribers in order to transmit unsolicited bulk e-mails;[154] and using access to an employer's e-mail system to alter and delete company files.[155]

The criminal penalties range from fines to imprisonment for up to 20 years for multiple offenses. As discussed in Section 11.9, the CFAA has become a prominent element of claims by the U.S. government and private parties seeking to protect data that are not always protected by other statutory schemes.

11.9.3.2 *Its Application to WebCrawling and Bots.*   Web robots, or "bots," have become widespread to scrape data from Web sites. All of that data generally are available to the public. That is, any individual can access the same information, but not with the speed or accuracy of a Webspider. But when does such "scraping" run afoul of the CFAA? To what extent does the law protect site operators or company data from penetration by an outside third party?

The key to the analysis under the CFAA is to ask whether the data are in fact publicly available. Are there technical barriers, such as passwords or codes that have to be circumvented? Do the terms of use prohibit access or use other than by an individual consumer? These questions are critical to determining whether the access either exceeds authority or is without authority under the CFAA.

If the answer to either one of these questions (or similar questions) is yes, one needs to consider access carefully since such access and downloading of data is likely to violate the CFAA. In *EF Cultural Travel v. Zefer Corporation*, Zefer designed a Web bot to scrape travel trip and pricing information from the Web site of EF Cultural Travel (EF) for use by a competitive travel Web site. The bot, designed by Zefer, downloaded the information by calling URLs on which each separate trip and pricing information was stored, reading the source code for the key features, and storing the information on a spreadsheet. The bot did so in a fashion not to burden or interfere with EF's Web site. Once gathered, the information was turned over to a competitor, who used the information to adjust price and trip information that it offered. Zefer's scraping did not occur continuously, but only on two dedicated occasions. EF sued claiming that a violation of the CFAA had occurred. The First Circuit Court of Appeals disagreed, refusing to read into what is or is not authorized some "reasonable expectations" standard, instead requiring that the Web site operator expressly state any limitations on access in its terms and conditions. On remand to the Federal District Court, the court, following the First Circuit, granted summary judgment for Zefer.

11.9.3.3 *Simple Preventive Measures.*   Not surprisingly, there are several methods for preventing unauthorized access in the first instance and, if unsuccessful, in prevailing in any subsequent claim arising under the CFAA. Perhaps the most obvious measure, and one that the First Circuit Court of Appeals underscored, is to make sure that each visitor to a Web site is adequately notified that the owner of the site intends only limited use or access to the data on the site. The notice can take many forms.

For example, a detectable message easily identifiable on a home page warning visitors that the posted information is available only for viewing and not for use in any manner adverse to the host's interests would be sufficient. Understandably, most Web hosts are reluctant to post such a blatant limitation—it is not necessarily "good for business." For those interested in an equally effective but less direct message, an increasingly common practice is to compel site visitors to register before gaining access to links and other pages available through the home page. The more difficult the registration process, the greater the host's apparent intent to restrict access to, and use of, the information that will be accessible after registration is completed.

Those hosts that require the payment of money, some kind of membership, or an access agreement before providing access establish what, for purposes of statutes like the CFAA that criminalize unauthorized access, will most often be seen as providing sufficient notice of the limits of authorized access. In the case of membership sites, the presumption is that each registrant is prequalified and therefore authorized to view and use the more restricted data, at least for purposes consistent with the terms of access. Enforceable click-wrap access agreements establish not only notice of access limitations; they also secure each visitor's agreement to use the Web site and the data therein within the stated limitations.

Securing Web-based data against unauthorized use or users is, in some ways, antithetical to the information-sharing intent and purpose of the Web. In this regard, however, the question arising when we post information on the Web differs little from the question posed over the centuries regarding the extent to which each of us wants our competitors or adversaries to use our proprietary work against our interests. The greater the concern, the more likely that each host will have to limit the data posted on the Web, or else increase each visitor's awareness of the rules of access.

11.9.4 Electronic Communications and Privacy.   Electronic privacy is becoming the issue in our society of databases and networking. Most of the U.S. "privacy" statutes are subject matter specific: the Telephone Consumer Protection Act of 1991 (do not call, for telemarketers); Health Insurance Portability Accountability Act of 1996 (privacy with respect to uses and disclosure of medical information); Children's Online Privacy Protection Act of 1998 (regulating collection of information from children under the age of 13 by Web sites directed to children); Gramm-Leach-Bliley Act of 1999 (regulating sharing of customer data by financial institutions); Controlling the Assault of Non-Solicited Pornography and Marketing Act of 2003 (restricting spammers and requiring an ability to opt out); the Fair and Accurate Credit Transaction Act of 2003 (providing very limited assistance with respect to identity theft such as the obligation to provide a yearly credit report). These laws do not provide assurances of privacy in the same way that the European Union did in its 1996 Data Protection Directive.[156] The EU Data Directive establishes protections against release of personal data, including e-mails, within the European Union, and restrictions on the transmission of such data outside the EU to countries or companies that do not have equivalent protections in place.[157]

In 2005, ChoicePoint, a large data broker, admitted that it had sold personal data on over 160,000 people to phony companies established by identity thieves. Since then, other companies have announced data break-ins and data leaks. As a result of such data security breaches, approximately half of the states have passed laws that require disclosure of unauthorized access to personal data.[158]

In the United States, the primary protection for privacy remains a lawsuit for tortious invasion of one's privacy. Because those rights are defined state by state, a review is beyond the scope of this chapter. However, most states recognize some form of the tort of invasion of privacy, and the tort has been recognized in the *Restatement (Second) of Torts* § 652, which courts reference as an authoritative source of the law. In general, the Restatement makes actionable (a) intentional intrusion, that is highly offensive to a reasonable man, into the seclusion of another's private affairs, (b) the public disclosure of private facts if such disclosure is highly offensive to a reasonable person, and is not a legitimate public concern, and (c) the appropriation for his own use or benefit of the name or likeness of another.

This chapter has already discussed the fiduciary obligation owed by employees to their employers with respect to confidential information. The development of the tort of privacy suggests that companies owe a similar obligation to their employees. Although slightly different in scope, but foreshadowing the growing body of law in this area, in *Remsburg v. Docusearch, Inc.*,[159] the New Hampshire Supreme Court was faced with a database company that had supplied information to a client that included a woman's personal information. The client used it to confront her and kill her. The supreme court held that the company had to act with "reasonable care in disclosing a third person's personal information to a client." This decision is as yet an unanswered invitation to other courts.

On the federal level, the CFAA, of course, does address "unauthorized" access to computerized information. In addition, Congress has enacted some statutory regulations that specifically address electronic communications and privacy.

11.9.4.1 *Wiretap Act and Electronic Communications Privacy Act.*

The Omnibus Crime Control and Safe Streets Act of 1968, generally referred to as the Federal Wiretap Act, [160] established the general parameters for permitted interception of communications by law enforcement. As originally crafted, the Wiretap Act covered only "wire and oral communications." In 1986, Congress enacted the Electronic Communications Privacy Act (ECPA),[161] which amended the Wiretap Act and created the Stored Wire and Electronic Communications and Transactional Records Act (Stored Communications Act or SCA) to "update and clarify federal privacy protections and standards in light of changes in computers and telecommunication technologies."[162] The SCA makes it unlawful to knowingly access a prohibited electronic communications service facility without authority, or in excess of authority, and for such public service provider to disclose information contained in such facilities. The ECPA allows a private plaintiff to bring a claim for knowing or intentional violation of the statute to recover actual damages or the statutory minimum of $1,000.

The 1986 amendment extended the Wiretap Act's coverage to include "electronic communications," which is defined as "any transfer of signs, signals, writing, images, sounds, data, or intelligence of any nature transmitted in whole or in part by a wire, radio, electromagnetic, photo-electronic or photo-optical system."[163] "Intercept" is defined as "the aural or other acquisition of the contents of any wire, electronic, or oral communication through the use of any electronic, mechanical, or other device."[164] Consequently, the Wiretap Act now makes it an offense to "intentionally *intercept. . .*any wire, oral, or *electronic communication.*"[165] Thus, the definitions in the act now cover Internet transmissions such as e-mails or file transfers.

There is an important exception to this prohibition. Under the "consent of a party" exception, it is permissible to intercept communications where "one of the parties to the communication has given prior consent to such interception."[166] The requisite consent may be express or implied from the surrounding circumstances.[167] Furthermore, an employer may obtain consent by informing the employee of the monitoring practices in an employment contract or in an employee handbook.[168]

Under the "provider exception," a provider of electronic communication services "whose facilities are used in the transmission of a wire or electronic communication, [may] intercept, disclose or use that communication in the normal course of his employment while engaged in any activity which is a necessary incident. . .to the protection of the rights or property of the provider of that service."[169] This exception may allow an employer to lawfully intercept communications to detect an employee's unauthorized disclosure of trade secrets to third parties.[170]

11.9.4.2 *Contemporaneous Transmission Requirement.*

The Wiretap Act only prohibits *interceptions* of electronic communications,[171] a term that has been more narrowly defined by the courts than the definition in the act might suggest. The definition of interception provides that an individual "intercepts" a wire, oral, or electronic communication "merely by *acquiring* its contents, regardless of when or under what circumstances the acquisition occurs."[172] In the context of this section, a serious question arises about the legality of intercepting electronic communications as they were being transmitted and once they were stored, either temporarily or permanently. Although Congress intended to liberalize one's ability to monitor "wire communications" while it sought to make the monitoring of "electronic communications" more difficult,[173] courts have held that Congress intended to make acquisitions of electronic communications unlawful under the Wiretap Act "*only if* they occur *contemporaneously with* their transmissions"[174] and before they actually cross the finish line and become stored.[175] This is, of course, an interesting fiction when applied to Internet transmissions, which consist of packages that are broken up and passed from router to router as well as from temporary storage to temporary storage. It is a far cry from the interception of a telephone call. It may simply be that in applying the language of the statute, the courts are faced with applying it to a technology that was not really in existence when the statute was amended in 1986.

In recent years, the courts have attempted to apply the contemporaneous transmission requirement to various situations. For example, cookies used to recover personal data from visitors to a Web site constitute an interception of a contemporaneous electronic communication and a violation of the Wiretap Act.[176] Noting that electronic communications are generally in transit and in storage simultaneously, the court reasoned that users communicated simultaneously with the pharmaceutical client's Web server and with the software company's Web server and, thus, the information was acquired contemporaneously with its transmission.[177]

Where electronic transmissions are found in RAM or on the hard drive, they are stored communications and can be retrieved because they are outside of the Wiretap Act.[178] Similarly, an e-mail that is recovered after it has been sent and received does not satisfy the contemporaneous transmission requirement and therefore has not been intercepted under the Wiretap Act.[179] Perhaps in response to these and other decisions, in 2001 Congress amended the Wiretap Act to apply the contemporary transmission requirement to wire communications that could not be retrieved, thereby permitting the recovery of stored wire communications.[180]

11.9.4.3 *Konop v. Hawaiian Airlines, Inc.* The *Konop* decision appears to be the most oft-cited case on the issue of "interception" under the Wiretap Act. Konop, the plaintiff, was an airline pilot who created and maintained a Web site where he posted bulletins critical of his employer, Hawaiian Airlines, Inc., and the airline union. Konop controlled access to his Web site by requiring visitors to log in with a user name and password and by creating a list of authorized users.

An officer of Hawaiian Airlines asked one such authorized user for permission to use his name to access the Web site. The officer logged on several times, and another officer, using the same technique, also logged on to view the information posted on Konop's bulletin. Konop eventually filed suit against Hawaiian Airlines, alleging that it violated the Wiretap Act when its officer gained unauthorized access to Konop's Web site.

The court first reiterated that the act only prohibits *interceptions* of electronic communications.[181] "Interception," the court held, requires that the party acquire the information contemporaneous with its transmission, and not while it is in electronic storage. In this case, the court concluded that the employer did not violate the Wiretap Act because the officers accessed an electronic communication located on an idle Web site, which did not satisfy the contemporaneous transmission requirement.[182]

11.9.5 Stored Communications Act.

Unlike the Wiretap Act, the Stored Communications Act (SCA),[183] as its name suggests, establishes the limitations of access to stored communications (i.e., communications accessed *after* their transmission).[184] Specifically, the SCA makes it unlawful to "intentionally [access] without authorization a facility through which an electronic communication service is provided...and thereby [obtain], [alter], or [prevent,] authorized access to a wire or electronic communication while it is in electronic storage."[185] The SCA defines "electronic storage" as "(A) any temporary, intermediate storage of a wire or electronic communication incidental to the electronic transmission thereof; and (B) any storage of such communication by an electronic communication service provider for purposes of backup protection of such communication."[186] The SCA exempts from liability conduct "authorized...by the person or entity providing a wire or electronic communications service"[187] or "by a user of that service with respect to a communication of or intended for that user."[188]

11.9.5.1 Electronic Storage: Backup Files.

The essential element that separates the SCA from the Wiretap Act is that the accessed communications reside in electronic storage. Therefore, the first question is what constitutes electronic storage. In *Theofel v. Farey-Jones,*[189] the United States Court of Appeals for the Ninth Circuit attempted to answer this question.

In *Theofel,* overzealous lawyers for Farey-Jones secured, through a subpoena issued to an Internet service provider, e-mails sent and received by their opponents in the lawsuit, a company called Integrated Capital Associates (ICA). The subpoena requested from the ISP virtually every e-mail ever sent or received by ICA and its employees. In response, the ISP posted a smattering of the e-mails on a Web site accessible to Farey-Jones and its lawyers. When ICA learned of these activities, it sued Farey-Jones for, among other things, violation of the SCA.

According to the court in *Theofel,* Congress recognized that users of Internet service providers have a legitimate interest in protecting the confidentiality of communications in electronic storage at a communications facility. Moreover, this legitimate interest cannot be overcome by fraud, or by someone who knowingly exploits a mistake that permits access to what is otherwise protected. The court found that the use of the subpoena to access ICA's e-mails when it was reasonably plain, at least to counsel, that the subpoena was invalid, negated any apparent authority that Farey-Jones and its lawyers may have had to view ICA's emails.

Farey-Jones claimed that the ICA e-mails were not in "electronic storage" and therefore no violation of the SCA occurred. The court disagreed. As stated earlier, electronic storage exists when messages are stored on a temporary, intermediate basis as part of the process of transmitting the message to the recipient, and when messages are stored as part of a backup process. In this instance, the court found that the e-mails, which had apparently been delivered to their recipients, were stored by the ISP as part of its backup process for retrieval after initial receipt. Access to those e-mails was therefore protected by the SCA, which Farey-Jones and its lawyers violated.

11.9.5.2 Electronic Storage: Temporarily Stored Communications.

Recent cases interpreting the meaning of "temporary, intermediate storage...incidental to" transmission of the communication have adhered to the letter of the law more than its spirit. In two cases involving the installation of cookies that were subsequently accessed by software companies for commercial gain, the courts have held that cookies are permanently (or at least indefinitely) installed in the consumer's hard drive and therefore cannot be considered "temporary, intermediate storage."[190] The *Doubleclick* decision also emphasized that the "temporary, intermediate storage" element of the SCA means what it says, that is, the prohibited conduct involves only the unauthorized access to communications while they are being temporarily stored by an intermediate and does not include access to stored messages after they have been received.[191] In the context of an employer's right to examine an employee's e-mails, the employee will have no claim that an employer has violated the SCA when the employer opens e-mails sent or received by the employee once the e-mail has been either received or discarded.[192]

11.10 OPEN SOURCE.   With the continued proliferation of the Internet and computer software, the licensing, distribution, and use of open source code has gained publicity and added importance in the practice of intellectual property and computer security. "Open source" describes the distribution of computer code that is available (i.e., open) to all others and therefore allows computer programmers to read, apply, and modify the code, and also redistribute any changes.[193] The open source movement began with Richard Stallman's development of Gnu's Not Unix (GNU), a freeware form of UNIX that was meant to be free software (free as in the freedom to use, modify, and distribute the software).[194] GNU's development created the first open source license, the General Public License (GPL). Linux, an open source–based operating system and an alternative to Microsoft's Windows, experienced tremendous growth through its use of the GPL.[195] The prevalence of open source issues is evidenced by the 1998 formation of the Open Source Initiative (OSI), which not only promotes open source development and encourages its use by business[196] but also offers links to and information about most of the available open source licenses.

11.10.1 Open Source Licenses.   The author of an open source code holds a copyright that operates as other copyrights do, but the code is released under a certain license on a nonproprietary basis. There are various types of open source licenses. The first open source license was the GPL, as described. It offers the broadest application of free software. In contrast, other licenses do not seek to perpetuate the free nature of a particular program. According to the Open Source Initiative, there are nearly 60 open source licenses now available for authors of source code,[197] all of which assert certain requirements of the software user.

11.10.2 GPL.   Licensing under the GPL is premised on Stallman's idea of "copy-left," which basically uses copyright as a tool to ensure the continued free distribution of source code.[198] In other words, the GPL affords application, modification, and distribution rights to the copyrighted source code only if the user agrees that the distribution terms remain the same. This creates an endless chain of GPLs attached to future distributions of either the original or derived versions, regardless of their form.[199] This endless chain often is referred to as the GPL's "viral effect," as GPL-protected code multiplies from any modifications of original GPL-protected code.[200] The GPL applies not just to an originally protected software program but also to what it broadly defines as the "Program":

> [A]ny such program or work, and a "work based on the Program" means either the Program or any derivative work under copyright law: that is to say, a work containing the Program or a portion of it, either verbatim or with modifications and/or translated into another language.[201]

Moreover, although the GPL also states that independent and separate sections of a derivative work are not subject to the GPL's terms when they are distributed as separate works, the GPL does apply when the user distributes those same independent and separate "sections as part of a whole which is based on the Program...."[202] The broad application given to the program under the GPL further enhances the viral effect of the license.

Other provisions of the GPL require users who distribute verbatim copies of the source code to publish copyright notices, disclaim warranties, and provide copies of the GPL. In addition, the modifier/user must attach to any modifications a notice that the software was changed, and must distribute or license the software free of charge to third parties, and must provide appropriate copyright notices, warranty disclaimers, and GPL terms and conditions. In sum, the GPL's sweeping terms not only seek to achieve the free software goals of the FSF but also to impact whether authors chose the GPL, and whether businesses utilize software subject to the GPL.

11.10.3 Other Open Source Licenses. The Berkeley Software Distribution (BSD) License and the Massachusetts Institute of Technology (MIT) License are very similar in that they both require copyright notices, disclaimers of warranties, and liability limitations. The BSD further prohibits contributors or similar organizations from endorsing the program, and also requires a copy of the BSD's terms, to be distributed with the software.

11.10.4 Business Policies with Respect to Open Source Licenses. The issue of whether distribution of a proprietary work that incorporates a small portion of GPL-protected code subjects that proprietary work to the terms of the GPL has never been litigated.[203] This is one risk of using open source software. Another risk is that failure to comply with the GPL's terms could lead to litigation.[204] For instance, MySQL sought to enjoin Progress Software Corporation from distributing MySQL's Gemini program without a GPL-compliant agreement.[205] Because there was a factual dispute as to whether Gemini was a derivative work or an independent work under the GPL, and because Progress stipulated that it disclosed Gemini's source code and would withdraw the end user license for commercial users, the court did not grant the injunction as to the GPL.[206]

Given the expanding use of Open Source, businesses need to develop comprehensive policies addressing their use of open source to avoid liability and publicly releasing their own proprietary technology.[207] Concerns generally involve license requirements regarding the distribution of the software and its modifications,[208] since those activities usually require the company to release the source code for any distributed modification, and modifications often terminate vendors' support agreements.[209] In addition, distributing unmodified open source as part of a proprietary program may require the company to release its own proprietary open source code.[210] It is more likely, however, that the company would be enjoined from distributing the open source or would have to pay damages.[211] These considerations should be addressed not only through company policy but also by choosing the best source code to use in programming, given the company's internal and external needs and the specific licensing requirements of that source code.

11.11 APPLICATION INTERNATIONALLY. Because the laws of the United States are the laws of just one nation among many, the enforcement of U.S. law and the protection of intellectual property rights in large part depend on international treaties.

To the extent that the infringing acts or acts of piracy may be deemed to occur in the United States, or the infringers can be found in the United States, then the United States has sufficient jurisdiction over these acts to enforce its laws. In other words, such actors can be sued directly in the courts of the United States for violation of the laws of the United States.

Apart from direct enforcement, international protection is usually a vehicle of bilateral agreements between the United States and individual countries or a function of international protocols or treaties to which the United States is a signatory. Thus, for example, the Paris Convention for the Protection of Industrial Property[212] establishes a system for recognizing priority of invention, but only among member countries. In addition, there is the Patent Cooperation Treaty (PCT), a multilateral treaty with more than 50 signatories. The PCT permits the filing of an international application that simplifies the filing process when a patent is sought in more than one nation. For copyright protection, there is also a series of international treaties and agreements that include the Berne Convention,[213] the Universal Copyright Convention, and the World Trade Organization (WTO) Agreement.[214] Canada, Mexico, and the United States also signed the North American Free Trade Agreement (NAFTA) in December 1992. NAFTA addresses intellectual property and requires that member states afford the same protections to intellectual property as members of the General Agreement on Tariffs and Trade (GATT). At a minimum, members of GATT must adopt four international conventions, including the Paris Convention and the Berne Convention.

These agreements, conventions, and treaties in large part do not attempt to reconcile the differences in the national laws of intellectual property. The particular national rules and nuances are simply too complicated, and there are too many differences of opinion to expect that these differences could be internally reconciled. Rather, in large measure, these international accords attempt to codify comity between the member nations so that each will recognize the legitimacy of the intellectual property rights in the other.

11.11.1 Agreement on Trade-Related Aspects of Intellectual Property Rights.

On December 8, 1994, the Agreement on Trade-Related Aspects of Intellectual Property Rights (TRIPS) was signed into law in this country. The signing of TRIPS required changes to be made in United States statutes and regulations to bring them into conformity with international norms. TRIPS, however, was a product of the United States and other industrial countries pressing for stronger, more uniform standards for international treaties concerning intellectual property. The basic structure of TRIPS is to set the minimum standard of protection for intellectual property with each member nation free to adopt more stringent standards. Under the rubric used in the United States, TRIPS applies to copyrights, patents, trademarks, service marks, mask works (integrated circuit designs), and trade secrets. It also covers geographical indications[215] and industrial designs.[216] Not addressed by TRIPS, although part of the international jargon for intellectual property, are breeder's rights[217] and utility models.[218] Thus, TRIPS establishes no standards as applied to these concepts, leaving each nation to set the parameters of protection unimpeded by TRIPS.

It is not by accident that TRIPS was negotiated within the context of GATT, which had set the international standards for trade tariffs and had provided remedies of trade retaliation if such standards were not adhered to. The structure of GATT provided the means under which developing countries agreed to reduce their trade tariffs in exchange for the right to export innovative products under an exclusive monopoly conveyed by intellectual property rights. The second benefit to the GATT format was to provide a means for trade retaliation if, under the dispute resolution provisions of TRIPS, the WTO determines that there is noncompliance. In reality, it is obvious that TRIPS benefits those industrial nations that are more likely to be at the forefront of innovation and more concerned with the protection of their citizens' intellectual property.[219] The major concession wrung by the developing countries under TRIPS was obtaining a period of 4 to 11 years to implement TRIPS and to bring their national laws into conformity.

TRIPS generally reflects the U.S. view that focuses on the economic underpinnings for intellectual property rights as serving the greater societal interests. There is thus a shift from "societal" interests to "enterprise" interests. In particular, TRIPS adopts high minimum standards for patents, which will require significant legislative changes in developing countries. The copyright section, however, affords less protection than may be afforded by European nations, but it is in line with treatment in the United States. In short, TRIPS responds to the concern of enterprises in the United States that too loose a system of international protection has enabled imitation of U.S.innovations through copying and outright piracy.

11.11.2 TRIPS and Trade Secrets.   Under its category for "Protection of Undisclosed Information," TRIPS provides protection for the type of information routinely referred to as trade secrets in the United States. Member nations are required to implement laws that safeguard lawfully possessed information from being disclosed to, acquired by, or used by others without consent and contrary to "honest commercial practices" if such information is (a) a secret in that it is not in the public domain, (b) has commercial value because it is a secret, and (c) has been subject to reasonable steps to maintain its secrecy.

Because discussions that led to TRIPS are not institutionally preserved, unlike the United States Congressional Record, there is no negotiating history to be consulted to flesh out the meaning of the spare paragraphs instituting trade secret protection. There do, however, appear to be differences from the total panoply of protections afforded in the United States. The concept of public domain articulated by TRIPS is information that is "not, as a body or in the precise configuration and assembly of its components, generally known among or readily accessible to persons within the circles that normally deal with the kind of information in question." This articulation appears to be addressing technological formulations of information, as opposed to general commercial information, such as financial information, that is generally considered proprietary and confidential in the United States. The focus on a technology formulation for protected information is bolstered by the TRIPS requirement that the information have commercial value. Thus, other types of information that are not part of a traded article may be deemed to have no commercial "value" and therefore to fall outside of the scope of protection. Depending on the particular jurisdiction in the United States, there is a distinction between confidential information and trade secrets, based on the requirement that a trade secret must have commercial value. This, in turn, has been held to mean that information that is not exploited commercially is unprotectable under the law of trade secret. For example, the results of failed experiments that never resulted in a commercial product lack commercial value, even though such experiments are certainly helpful in the next round of exploration, in that they are signposts of what not to do.

The lesson to be drawn is that one should not assume symmetry of protections just because of the TRIPS provision. Instead, as part of the reasonable steps to maintain secrecy, enterprises need to consider carefully thought out and structured contractual provisions as well as a system of data caching that leaves truly confidential data in the United States, even if access is permitted outside. Improper takings of such data are, arguably, acts that occur in the United States, and such acts are subject to enforcement and punishment under the laws of the United States.

11.11.3 TRIPS and Copyright.

TRIPS embraces the U.S. general model for copyright protection in its opening statement that "[c]opyright protection shall extend to expressions and not to ideas, procedures, methods of operation or mathematical concepts as such." All member nations agree that, as to the protection of copyrights, the Berne Convention will apply. Under the Berne Convention, the duration of a copyright is the life of the author plus 50 years. If the life of a natural person is not involved, then it is ordinarily 50 years from publication. In addition, computer programs, whether in source or object code, are to be protected as literary works under the Berne Convention. TRIPS also recognizes that compilations of data can be protected as creative works. Article 10, ¶ 2 explicitly provides:

> Compilations of data or other material, whether in machine readable or other form, which by reason of the *selection* or *arrangement* of their contents constitute *intellectual creations* shall be protected as such. Such protection, which shall not extend to the data or material itself, shall be without prejudice to any copyright subsisting in the data or material itself. (Emphasis added.)

TRIPS, therefore, does establish some minimum standard in the growing debate over what protections will be afforded a database. In the United States, the clear demarcation point for unprotected information is compilations that represent no more than "sweat-of-the-brow" efforts. Such compilations cannot be copyrighted.[220] The classic example of a sweat-of-the-brow effort is the copying and alphabetical organizing of names, addresses, and telephone numbers that are in telephone books. In the United States, the key for copyright protection is the creator's original contribution of selection and arrangement. Thus, arguably, the TRIPS provision mimics the law of the United States.

The European Union (EU) has taken a more protective path. In its 1996 European DataBase Directive, the EU granted databases *sui generis* protection as their own unique form of intellectual property. Under the EU Directive, a database is "a collection of independent works, data or other materials arranged in a systematic or methodical way and individually accessible by electronic or other means." A database may be protected either because it represents a work of "intellectual creation" or because it was compiled through "substantial investment." The EU Directive protects such databases from unauthorized extraction or use for a period of 15 years, with the ability to extend the period for an additional 15 years if there was a "substantial new investment" in the database. Such protection extends to databases of EU members and to databases of nationals of other countries that offer protections similar to the EU.

The United States, despite a number of legislative proposals, has not adopted a concomitant rule. The result, at least for multinationals, is that entities that rely on databases should consider "locating" such databases within an EU member to take advantage of the EU's database protections.

11.11.4 TRIPS and Patents.

TRIPS requires that all members recognize the right to patent products or processes in all fields of technology. A patentable invention must be new, inventive, and have an industrial application. The patent application must fully and clearly disclose the invention so that a person skilled in the art could carry out the invention. The best mode for carrying out the invention as of the filing date must also be disclosed. Patent rights are to be enforced without discrimination as to place of invention or whether the product is imported or produced locally. The patent of a product conveys the exclusive right to prevent, without consent of the inventor, the making, using, offering for sale, selling, or importing of the product. The patent of a process conveys the exclusive right to prevent all of the above for products that result from the process as well as the use of the process itself. The holder of a patent also has the rights to assign, transfer, or license the patent. The minimum period for a protecting a patent is 20 years from filing.

TRIPS gives each member state the right to carve out from patentability certain subject matters that have as their purpose the protection of human, animal, or plant life, or to avoid serious prejudice to the environment. In addition, TRIPS permits a member state to allow other use without authorization from the patent holder. The section defining when such use is permissible is the most detailed section among the patent provisions of TRIPS. In general, it permits such use only (a) after an effort to obtain a license from the patent holder on reasonable commercial terms and conditions, (b) with adequate remuneration to the patent holder, (c) if such use is limited predominantly to the domestic market of the member nation, and (d) if there is a review of the decision to permit, as well as the compensation, by a "higher authority in that Member."

One of the circumstances envisioned by TRIPS is the grant of a second patent that cannot be exploited without infringing an earlier (first) patent. In such cases, a member nation may grant authority if the invention embodied in the second patent represents an "important technical advance of considerable economic significance" with respect to the first patent's invention and a cross-license on reasonable terms is granted to the holder of the first patent to use the second patent. For process patents, TRIPS creates a limited burden on the alleged infringer to prove that the identical product was produced using a different process. In particular, a member state can create a presumption that the process patent was violated in circumstances where the product is new, or where the patent holder is unable to demonstrate what process was actually used.

11.11.5 TRIPS and Anticompetitive Restrictions.

TRIPS acknowledges that some licensing practices or other conditions with respect to intellectual property rights may restrain competition, adversely affect trade, and impede the transfer and dissemination of technology. Accordingly, TRIPS permits member nations to specify practices that constitute an abuse of intellectual property rights, and to adopt measures to control or limit such practices, so long as the regulation is consistent with other provisions of TRIPS. In the event that a national of a member nation violates another member's laws and regulations regarding anticompetitive activity, TRIPS provides for the right of the involved nation's to exchange information confidentially regarding the nationals and their activities.

11.11.6 Remedies and Enforcement Mechanisms.

Each member nation is expected to provide an enforcement mechanism under its national laws to permit effective action against any act of infringement. Such procedures are to include remedies to prevent acts of infringement as well as to deter future acts. TRIPS imposes the obligation that all such procedures be "fair and equitable" and not be "unnecessarily complicated or costly" or involve "unwarranted delays."[221] In general, these remedies mean access to civil judicial procedures with evidentiary standards that shift the burden of going forward to the claimed infringer, once the rights holder has presented reasonably available evidence to support its claim. Damages may be awarded sufficient to compensate the rights holder for the infringement if the "infringer knew or had reasonable grounds to know that he was engaging in infringing activity." This means that vigilance and notice are essential to have meaningful protection for intellectual property rights, since notice is the best means for setting up a damage claim. TRIPS permits its members to allow the recovery of lost profits or predetermined (statutory) damages even when the infringer did not know that it was engaged in infringing behavior. Although injunctive relief is to be provided for, remedies may be limited in circumstances involving patent holders, as discussed, where adequate compensation is paid, and the alleged infringer has otherwise complied with the provisions of its national law permitting such use upon payment of reasonable compensation. In order to deter further infringement, infringing materials may be ordered destroyed or noncommercially disposed of.

In addition to civil remedies, TRIPS requires criminal penalties in cases of "willful trademark counterfeiting or copyright piracy on a commercial scale."[222]

11.12 CONCLUDING REMARKS. Data security ultimately involves the protection of proprietary or personal data and intellectual property. The competition to acquire and retain intellectual property legally is invariably met by unethical and illegal efforts to deprive legitimate owners of their rights. It is necessary, therefore, to be fully aware of the mechanisms and procedures required to protect these rights as part of any computer security program.

This chapter has attempted to delineate the most important aspects of the problem. However, many facets of the legal questions remain unanswered or have been answered generally rather than in the context of a particular problem. Prudent guardians of intellectual property should monitor relevant judicial determinations continuously and be certain to integrate them into a planned approach to protect these most valuable assets.

11.13 FURTHER READING

Bently, L., and B. Sherman. *Intellectual Property Law*. Oxford, UK: Oxford University Press, 2004.

McJohn, S. *Intellectual Property: Examples and Explanations*, 2nd ed. New York: Aspen Publishers, 2006.

Nard, C. A., D. W. Barnes, and M. J. Madison. *The Law of Intellectual Property*. New York: Aspen Publishers, 2006.

Poltorak, A. I., and P. J. Lerner. *Essentials of Intellectual Property*. Hoboken, NJ: John Wiley & Sons, 2002.

Stim, R. *Patent, Copyright & Trademark: An Intellectual Property Desk Reference*, 9th ed. Berkeley, CA: Nolo Press, 2007.

11.14 NOTES

1. For the uninitiated, a tort is a civil wrong (i.e., an act or failure to act that violates common law rules of civil society, and is distinguished from criminal wrongdoing.)

2. *See ProCD, Inc. v. Zeidenberg*, 86 F.3d 1447 (7th Cir. 1996) (product could be returned if shrink-wrap terms were unacceptable).

3. *See Information Handling Services, Inc. v. LRP Publications, Inc.,* 2000 U.S. Dist. LEXIS 14531 (E.D. Pa., Sept. 20, 2000) (limit on unauthorized copies); *Hughes v. America Online, Inc.,* 204 F. Supp. 2d 178 (D. Ma. 2002) (enforcing forum selection clause).

4. *See LLAN Systems, Inc. v. Netscout Service Level Corp.*, 183 F. Supp. 328 (D. Mass. 2002) (click-wrap software agreement enforceable under Uniform Commercial Code as acceptance of an offer).

5. *See Motise v. America Online, Inc.*, 346 F. Supp. 2d 563 (S.D. N.Y. 2004) (user who logged on through another's account is bound by the terms of use even though not read).

6. 356 F.3d 393 (2d Cir. 2004).

7. *See Kewanee Oil Co. v. Bicron Corp.*, 416 U.S. 470, 473, 94 S. Ct. 1879, 40 L. Ed. 2d 315 (1974).

8. It is easy to confuse the notion of common law trade secret law with protection of confidential information. There is a distinction, however. At its core, trade secret law requires commercial application and utility, which is not true of confidential information that is generally protected as a matter of contract. For example, a failed experiment has no commercial utility and is not generally considered a trade secret, although it easily could be deemed confidential information.

9. The need to protect the information from general dissemination is what, in part, has given rise to the practice of Non Disclosure Agreements.

10. UTSA, 14 U.L.A. § 2(a).

11. *See* Trade Secrets Act, 18 U.S.C. § 1905; *see also* J. Michael Chamblee, J.D., *Validity, Construction, and Application of Title I of Economic Espionage Act of 1996*, 177 A.L.R. Fed. 609, *2 (2003) (hereinafter "Chamblee at __"). Other federal statutes, such as the National Stolen Property Act, 18 U.S.C. § 2314, were likewise of marginal utility in combating the rising problem of economic espionage. *See* Chamblee at *2.

12. Craig L. Uhrich, *Article: The Economic Espionage Act—Reverse Engineering and the Intellectual Property Public Policy*, 7 Mich. Telecomm. Tech. L. Rev. 147148-49 (2000/2001) (hereinafter "Uhrich at __"). Uhrich observes that the FBI investigated over 200% more economic espionage cases in 1996 than it had in 1994. *See* Uhrich at 151.

13. 18 U.S.C. §§ 1831, 1832.

14. *Id.*

15. 18 U.S.C. §§ 1831, 1832.

16. 18 U.S.C. §§ 1832 and 3571.

17. 18 U.S.C. § 1839 (3).

18. *United States v. Lange*, 312 F.3d 263 (7th Cir. 2002) (emphasis added).

19. 18 U.S.C. § 1839.

20. The 1980 Computer Software Copyright Act carved out for owners of computer programs a right to adapt, and for that purpose to copy, the program so that it functions on the actual computer in which it is installed. *See* discussion under the subheading "Derivative Works."

21. *See*, e.g. *Computer Management Assistance Co. v. Robert F. DeCastro, Inc.* 220 F.3d 396 (5th Cir. 2000) and *Engineering Dynamics, Inc. v. Structural Software, Inc.*, 26 F.3d 1335 (5th Cir. 1994).

22. Ideas, if protectable at all, are protected by patent.

23. The Copyright Act, 17 U.S.C. § 109(b).

24. The Copyright Act itself in sections 108 through 121 provides detailed limitations on the copyright owner's exclusive rights. These limitations are simply a matter of statutory construction. In addition, courts developed the doctrine of fair use in an effort to balance the rights of copyright owner and the public interest. That doctrine is now codified as part of the copyright statute in 17 U.S.C. § 107.

25. *See* the House Report No. 94-1476, 94th Cong., 2d Sess. 62 (1976) on the 1976 Act.

26. The Copyright Act, 17 U.S.C. §102(b).

27. 797 F.2d 1222 (3rd Cir. 1986).

28. 982 F.2d 693 (2d Cir. 1992).

29. 977 F.2d 1510 (9th Cir. 1992), amended, *Sega Enterprises Ltd. v. Accolade, Inc.*, 1993 U.S. App. Lexis 78.

30. 977 F.2d at 1527–1528.

31. 975 F.2d 832 (Fed. Cir. 1992), *petition for rehearing denied*, 1992 U.S. App. Lexis 30957 (1992).

32. 79 F.3d 1532 (11th Cir. 1996).

33. 350 F.3d 640, 645 (7th Cir. 2003).

34. *Evolution, Inc. v. Suntrust Bank,* 342 F. Supp. 2d 943, 956 (D. Kan. 2004).

35. Compare *Micro Star v. Formgen, Inc.*, 154 F.3d 1107 (9th Cir. 1998) (infringement found because copyrighted images displayed) with *Lewis Galoob Toys, Inc. v. Nintendo of America, Inc.*, 964 F.2d 965 (9th Cir. 1992) (no infringement although product compatible with Nintendo product).

36. 17 U.S.C. § 107.

37. 510 U.S. 569 (1994).

38. *Id*. at 577.

39. *Id*. at 580.

40. *See* the House Report No. 94-1476, 94th Cong., 2d Sess. 62 (1976) on the 1976 Copyright Act.

41. 17 U.S.C. § 117.

42. *Aymes v. Bonelli*, 47 F.3d 23 (2d Cir. 1995).

43. 17 U.S.C. § 901(a).

44. *MGM Studios Inc. v. Grokster, Ltd.*, 545 U.S. 913, 930 (2005).

45. *Playboy Enterprises v. Frena*, 839 F. Supp. 1552 (M.D. Fla. 1993); *see also Sega Enterprises v. MAPHIA*, 857 F. Supp. 679 (N.D. Cal. 1994), and 948 F. Supp. 923 (N.D. Cal. 1996) (providing site for and encouraging uploading of copyrighted games was copyright infringement).

46. *Religious Technology Center v. Netcom On-line Communication Services, Inc.*, 90 F. Supp. 1361 (N.D. Cal. 1995).

47. 17 U.S.C. § 502.

48. 17 U.S.C. § 503.

49. 17 U.S.C. § 504.

50. 17 U.S.C. § 505.

51. 17 U.S.C. § 506.

52. 17 U.S.C. § 504(a).

53. *See Harris Market Research v. Marshall Marketing and Communications, Inc.,* 948 F.2d 1518 (10th Cir. 1991).

54. *See Regents of the University of Minnesota v. Applied Innovations, Inc.,* 685 F. Supp. 698, *aff'd,* 876 F.2d 626 (8th Cir. 1987) 698.

55. *Id.*

56. *See Cream Records, Inc. v. Jos. Schlitz Brewing Co.,* 754 F.2d 826 (9th Cir. 1985).

57. *See Eales v. Environmental Lifestyles, Inc.,* 958 F.2d 876 (9th Cir. 1992), *cert. den.* 113 S. Ct. 605.

58. *See Softel, Inc. v. Dragon Medical and Scientific Communications Ltd.,* 891 F. Supp. 935 (S.D. N.Y. 1995). Interestingly, in this case, the court also held that any increase in the infringer's profit may be considered when calculating the profit that must be disgorged to the license holder.

59. *See Harper & Row Publishers, Inc. v. Nation Enterprises,* 471 U.S. 539, 105 S. Ct. 2218 (1985); *Data General Corp. v. Grumman Systems Support Corp.,* 36 F.3d 1147 (1st Cir. 1994).

60. 17 U.S.C. § 504(c)(1).

61. *Id.*

62. 17 U.S.C. § 504(c)(2).

63. The theoretical nature of the relationship between actual and statutory damages is illustrated dramatically when the copyright owner demonstrates that the infringement was willful. *See Peer International Corp. v. Luna Records, Inc.,* 887 F. Supp. 560 (S.D. N.Y. 1995), where the music publisher's president willfully infringed licensed and unlicensed works and was assessed $10,000 for the licensed works, $15,000 for the unlicensed works, and $25,000 that the president used in derivative format without permission even though actual damages were $4,107. Presumably, this resulted from the court's attempt to find a way to punish the infringer since the statute makes no provision for punitive damages.

64. *See Central Point Software, Inc. v. Nugent,* 903 F. Supp. 1057 (E.D. Tex. 1995).

65. *See Walt Disney Co. v. Powell,* 897 F.2d 565 (D.C.Cir. 1990).

66. 17 U.S.C. § 1202(b).

67. *Universal City Studios, Inc. v. Reimerdes,* 111 F. Supp. 2d 294 (S.D. N.Y. 2000).

68. 17 U.S.C. § 1201(a).

69. 17 U.S.C. § 1201(a)(2).

70. 17 U.S.C. § 1201(a)(3).

71. *Id.*

72. 2000 U.S. Dist. LEXIS 1889 (W.D. Wash. January 18, 2000).

73. *Id.* at 19–21.

74. *Universal City Studios, Inc. v. Reimerdes,* supra note 67.

75. *Universal City Studios v. Corley,* 273 F.3d 429 (2nd Cir. 2002).

76. *Id.* at 446–447.

77. *Id.* at 450–451.

78. 307 F. Supp. 2d 521 (S.D. N.Y. 2004),

79. There is an open issue as to whether copyright protects the format for interfacing between application and data. Competitors particularly in the area of gaming look to reverse engineer the interface format to make new modules compatible

with existing hardware. Such reverse engineering has been held not to violate the copyright laws, so long as the new product does not display copyrighted images or other copyrightable expressions. Thus, the nonprotectable interface may be protected if such copyrighted images or expressions are embedded in the display.

80. 977 F.2d 1510 (9th Cir. 1992), amended, *Sega Enterprises Ltd. v. Accolade, Inc.*, 1993 U.S. App. Lexis 78.

81. 977 F.2d at 1527–1528.

82. 975 F.2d 832 (Fed. Cir. 1992), *petition for rehearing denied,* 1992 U.S. App. Lexis 30957 (1992).

83. 79 F.3d 1532 (11th Cir. 1996).

84. 320 F.3d 1317 (Fed. Cir. 2003), *writ of certiorari denied,* 539 U.S. 928 (2003).

85. 847 F.2d 255 (5th Cir. 1988).

86. *See*, for example, *Davidson & Assocs. v. Jung*, 422 F.3d 630, 639 (8th Cir. 2005).

87. 17 U.S.C. § 1201(f)(1).

88. 17 U.S.C. § 1201(f)(2).

89. 17 U.S.C. § 1201(f)(4).

90. 17 U.S.C. § 1201(f)(3).

91. 381 F.3d 1178 (Fed. Cir. 2004), *cert. denied*, 544 U.S. 923 (2005).

92. 387 F.3d 522 (6th Cir. 2004).

93. *Storage Tech. Corp. v. Custom Hardware Eng'g & Consulting, Inc.*, 421 F.3d 1307 (Fed. Cir. 2005).

94. 17 U.S.C. § 1201(i)(1).

95. 17 U.S.C. § 1201(j)(3).

96. 17 U.S.C. § 1201(j)(1).

97. 35 USC § 113 requires the submission of a drawing "where necessary for the understanding of the subject matter to be patented."

98. 35 U.S.C. §§ 283 and 284.

99. 127 S. Ct. 1746, 1757 (2007),

100. *Webster's Seventh New Collegiate Dictionary* (1967 ed.), p. 644.

101. 2007 CSI/FBI Computer Crime and Security Survey (hereafter the CSI/FBI Survey), pp. 12–13. Although the percentage of organizations reporting Internet abuse is down substantially since this chapter was first published, it nonetheless remains a source of substantial concern. In the same study, 26 percent of respondents reported phishing where the respondent was fraudulently identified as the sender; 25 percent reported misuse of instant messaging and unauthorized access to information; and 17 percent reported theft of customer and/or employee data.

102. SIIA Anti-Piracy 2007 Year in Review (www.siia.org/piracy/yir_2007.pdf). According to the SIIA, the source of the financial loss described in the text is the research firm IDC.

103. *See* Lamb and Rosen, *Global Piracy and Financial Valuation of Intellectual Property,* pp. 11.1–11.3.

104. "The subject matter of copyright. . .includes compilations." 17 U.S.C. § 103.

105. *Feist Publications, Inc. v. Rural Telephone Service Co., Inc.* 499 U.S. §§ 340, 361 (1991).

106. *Id*. at 350–351. *See* 17 U.S.C. §§ 101–103.

107. *Id.* at 344, 348–349. *See Ticketmaster Corp. v. Tickets.com, Inc.*, 2000 U.S. Dist. LEXIS 12987 (C.D. Cal. Aug. 10, 2000), *aff'd*, 2001 U.S. App. LEXIS 1454 (9th Cir. Jan. 22, 2001).

108. *Feist Pub., Inc. v. Rural Tel.*, supra note 105, at 352–354, where the court rejected the so-called sweat-of-the-brow doctrine.

109. *Matthew Bender & Co., Inc. v. West Publishing Co.*, 158 F.3d 674, 682 (2d Cir. 1998) ("[t]he creative spark is missing where: (i) industry conventions or other external factors so dictate the selection that any person composing a compilation of the type at issue would necessarily select the same categories of information, or (ii) the author made obvious, garden-variety, or routine selections."). *See also Silverstein v. Penguin Putnam, Inc.* 368 F.3d 77, 83 (2d Cir. 2004).

110. 121 S. Ct. 2381; 150 L. Ed. 2d 500; 2001 U.S. LEXIS 4667; 69 U.S.L.W. 4567 (2001). Note: The party appealing to the Supreme Court is named first.

111. The court found interesting the publishers' decision not to assert a claim of transformative fair use. *Id.* at 2390. *See* Section 12.1.2.3.3 (transformative use section), supra.

112. 464 U.S. 417 (1984).

113. Transformative fair use was recently applied to the use of Rio devices, which permit individual users to download purchased MP3 music files to a hard drive and then play them either on the PC or a CD. These devices were analogized to the Betamax time shifting discussed in *Sony* and were upheld primarily on that basis. *See Recording Industry Association of America v. Diamond Multimedia Systems, Inc.*, 180 F.3d 1072 (9th Cir. 1999).

114. 17 U.S.C. § 512(c).

115. 17 U.S.C. § 512(k).

116. 17 U.S.C. § 512(i).

117. 17 U.S.C. § 512(c)(1). *See ALS Scan, Inc. v. RemarQ Communities, Inc.*, 239 F.3d 619 (4th Cir. 2001), where the court of appeals determined what notice was sufficient to remove the safe harbor protection. *See also In re Aimster Copyright Litig.*, 252 F. Supp. 2d 634 (N.D. Ill. 2002), *aff'd* 334 F.3d 643 (7th Cir. 2003), for general discussion of this safe harbor provision, where Aimster had actual knowledge of the infringement by its users and therefore could not avoid liability under the safe harbor.

118. 907 F. Supp. 1361 (N.D. Cal. 1995). The *Netcom* decision predated the DMCA and provided part of the rationale and reasoning used by Congress in drafting and passing Title II of the DMCA. *See* House Rep. 105-551(I), at 11.

119. The church raised a question of fact about the impact of the ISP's activity on the church's potential market by asserting that the posting of the church's materials on the bulletin board discouraged active participation by existing and potential congregants. Therefore, the court could not find for the ISP as a matter of law.

120. 373 F.3d 544, 555 (4th Cir. 2004). The court went on to state, however, that an ISP "can become liable indirectly upon a showing of additional involvement sufficient to establish a contributory or vicarious violation of the Act. In that case, the ISP could still look to the DMCA for a safe harbor if it fulfilled the conditions therein."

121. *See e.g., Playboy Enterprises, Inc. v. Frena*, 839 F. Supp. 1552 (M.D. Fla. 1993). The *Frena* decision, insofar as it holds the bulletin board service provider liable

for infringement, has been expressly overruled by Title II of the DMCA. *See* House Rep. 105-551(I), at 11.

122. *Los Angeles Times v. Free Republic*, 2000 U.S. Dist. LEXIS 5669 (C.D. Cal. April 5, 2000). In the *Free Republic* decision, the court recognized the public benefit of posting articles for commentary and criticism but found that the initial postings contained little or no commentary that might transform the article into a new original work. *See also Video Pipeline, Inc.*, v. *Buena Vista Home Entm't, Inc.*, 342 F.3d 191, 199 (3d Cir. 2003), rejecting the fair use defense for an online distributor that made its own movie clip previews and used them as movie trailers by copying short segments of plaintiff's movies in part because the online distributor benefited from the infringement.

123. *Storm Impact, Inc. v. Software of the Month Club,* 13 F. Supp. 2d 782 (N.D. Ill. 1998).

124. There are various names for the components of the software programs that actually travel through the Web looking for data, including bots, crawlers, spiders, scrapers, and automated data retrieval systems.

125. *Kelly v. Arriba Soft Corp.,* 336 F.3d 811 (9th Cir. 2003).

126. 416 F. Supp. 2d 828, 838–846 (C.D. Calif. 2006).

127. 508 F.3d 1146 (9th Cir. 2007).

128. 239 F.3d 1004 (9th Cir. 2001), *aff'd*, 284 F.3d 1091 (9th Cir. April 3, 2002).

129. *See also UMG Recordings, Inc. v. MP3.com, Inc.*, 92 F. Supp. 2d 349 (S.D. N.Y. 2000), where the district court held that storing recordings from purchased CDs on MP3.com's servers for retransmission to other users was infringement and not transformative fair use.

130. *Metro-Goldwyn-Mayer Studios, Inc. v. Grokster, Ltd.*, 545 U.S. 913, 125 S. Ct. 125 (2005).

131. *Id.* at 926.

132. *Id.* at 936–937.

133. *Id.* at 937.

134. 100 F. Supp. 2d 1058 (N.D. CA 2000).

135. 30 Cal. 4th 1342; 71 P.3d 296; 1 Cal. Rptr. 3d 32 (2003).

136. 356 F.3d 393 (2d Cir. 2004).

137. 86 F.3d 1447 (7th Cir. 1996).

138. 18 U.S.C. § 1030.

139. Pub. L. 98-474, codified at 18 U.S.C. § 1030.

140. Pub. L. 99-474.

141. National Information Infrastructure Protection Act of 1996, Pub. L. 104–294.

142. 18 U.S.C. § 1030(a)(1).

143. 18 U.S.C. § 1030(a)(2).

144. 18 U.S.C. § 1030(a)(3).

145. 18 U.S.C. § 1030(a)(4).

146. 18 U.S.C. § 1030(a)(5). *See Hotmail Corporation v. Van$ Money Pie, Inc.*, 1998 WL 388389, 47 U.S.P.Q.2d 1020 (N.D. Cal. 1998).

147. 18 U.S.C. § 1030(a)(6).

148. 18 U.S.C. § 1030(a)(7).

149. Senate Rep. 104-357, pp. 7–8.

150. *Register.com, Inc. v. Verio, Inc.*, 126 F. Supp. 2d 238 (S.D. N.Y. 2000).

151. *Id.*

152. *In Re Intuit Privacy Litigation*, 138 F. Supp. 2d 1272 (2001). *But see U.S. v. Czubinski*, 106 F.3d 1069 (1st Cir. 1997), where the court of appeals found that an IRS employee who accessed private tax information in violation of IRS rules but did not disclose the accessed information could not be prosecuted under 18 U.S.C. §030(a)(4) because he lacked an intent to deprive the affected taxpayers of their right to privacy.

153. *Shurgard Storage Centers, Inc. v. Safeguard Self Storage, Inc.*, 119 F. Supp. 2d 1121 (W.D. Wash 2000).

154. *America Online, Inc. v. LCGM, Inc.*, 46 F. Supp. 2d 444 (E.D. Va. 1998).

155. *U.S. v. Middleton*, 231 F.3d 1207 (9th Cir. 2000).

156. Council Directive 95/46, 1995 O.J. (L.281) 31–50 (EC).

157. As a result the United States negotiated with the EU the Safe Harbor Arrangement, administered by the Federal Trade Commission, under which a U.S. company can opt in to compliance with the EU Data Directive.

158. For an updated list, go to www.pirg.org/consumer/credit/statelaws.htm.

159. 149 N.H. 148, 816 A.2d 1001 (2003).

160. 18 U.S.C. §§ 2511(1)(a) and 2502(a).

161. Pub. L. No. 99-508, 100 Stat. 1848 (codified throughout scattered sections of 18 U.S.C.).

162. S. Rep. No. 99-541, at 1 (1986), reprinted in 1986 U.S.C.C.A.N. 3555, 3555.

163. 18 U.S.C. § 2510(12).

164. Id. § 2510(4).

165. 18 U.S.C. § 2511(1)(a) (emphasis added); *Konop v. Hawaiian Airlines, Inc.*, 302 F.3d 868, 875 (9th Cir. 2002) (*Konop*) (noting the legislative history of the ECPA indicates that Congress wanted to protect electronic communications that are configured to be private, such as e-mail and private electronic bulletin boards).

166. 18 U.S.C.A. § 511(2)(d). One should note, however, that as a result of the Patriot Act, an order from a U.S. or state attorney general is sufficient to permit the government to install a device to record electronic transmissions for up to 60 days where related to an ongoing criminal investigation. The FBI has in its arsenal a program known as Carnivorethat essentially tracks a target's online activity. Recently Freedom of Information inquiries by the Electronic Privacy Information Center (EPIC, www.epic.org.) suggests that the FBI has discontinued use of Carnivore because ISPs, in light of the PATRIOT Act, may be providing information regarding a user's internet traffic directly to the government.

167. *Griggs-Ryan v. Smith*, 904 F.2d 112, 117 (1st Cir. 1990) (holding consent may be implied where the individual is on notice of monitoring of all telephone calls).

168. Federal law allows states to enact their own wiretapping statutes provided that the state statutes are at least as strict as the federal counterpart. Lynn Bernabei, Ethical and Legal Issues of Workplace Monitoring of Employee Communications, 2003 WL 22002093, *2 (April 2003) (hereinafter "Bernabei at __").. Bernabei notes that most states have adopted statutes that mirror the federal statutes and that at

least 10 states, including Massachusetts, require the consent of both parties before the employer can record a conversation. *Id.*

169. 18 U.S.C. § 2511(2)(a)(i) (Supp. 2003).

170. *Briggs v. Am. Air Filter Co.*, 630 F.2d 414 (5th Cir. 1980) (holding employer could monitor employee's communication "when [the] employee's supervisor [had] particular suspicions about confidential information being disclosed to a business competitor, [had] warned the employee not to disclose such information, [had] reason to believe that the employee is continuing to disclose the information, and [knew] that a particular phone call is with an agent of the competitor.").

171. 18 U.S.C. § 2511(1)(a).

172. *Konop*, 302 F.3d at 876 (emphasis added).

173. *Id.*

174. E.g., *Wesley Coll. v. Pitts*, 974 F. Supp. 375, 386 (D. Del. 1997) (holding that the act criminalizes only the interception of electronic communications contemporaneously with their transmission, not once they have been stored); *Payne v. Norwest Corp.*, 911 F. Supp. 1299, 1303 (D. Mont. 1995) (holding the appropriation of voicemail or similar stored electronic message does not constitute an "interception" under the act); *Steve Jackson Games, Inc. v. United States Secret Service*, 36 F.3d 457, 461–462 (5th Cir. 1994) (holding that the government's acquisition of e-mail messages stored on an electronic bulletin board system, but not yet retrieved by the intended recipients, was not an "interception" under the Wiretap Act).

175. *See United States v. Councilman*, 418 F.3d 67, 69–70 (1st Cir. 2005) (*en banc*).

176. *In re Pharmatrak, Inc.*, 329 F.3d 9, 21 (1st Cir. 2003).

177. *Id.*

178. *United States v. Councilman*, 245 F. Supp. 2d 319 (D. Mass. 2003) (Wiretap Act count dismissed against e-mail service provider who was charged with attempting to use electronic communications passing through his service for commercial gain).

179. *Eagle Investment Systems, Corp. v. Tamm*, 146 F. Supp. 2d 105, 112–113 (D. Mass. 2001).

180. USA PATRIOT Act § 209, 115 Stat. at 283; *Konop*, 302 F.3d at 876–878 ("The purpose of the recent amendment was to reduce the protection of voice mail messages to the lower level of protection provided other electronically stored communications.")

181. 302 F.3d at 876.

182. *Id.* at 879.

183. 18 U.S.C. § 2701 et seq.

184. *Bernabei* at *2.

185. 18 U.S.C. §§ 2701(a)(1), 2707(a) (emphasis added).

186. *Id.* § 2510(17), incorporated by 18 U.S.C. § 2711(1).

187. 18 U.S.C. § 2701(c)(1).

188. 18 U.S.C. § 2701(c)(2).

189. *Theofel v. Farey-Jones*, 359 F.3d 1006 (9th Cir. 2004).

190. *In re DoubleClick, Inc. Privacy Litigation*, 154 F. Supp. 2d 497 (S.D.N.Y. 2001) (*Doubleclick*); *In re Toys R US, Inc. Privacy Litigation*, 2001 U.S. Dist. LEXIS 16947 (N.D. Ca. 2001).

191. 154 F. Supp. 2d at 511–512.

192. *Fraser v. Nationwide Mut. Ins. Co.*, 2003 U.S. App. LEXIS 24856, *19 (3rd Cir. 2003).

193. Jeanie Duncan Fallon, *Open Source Licenses: Understanding the General Public License, Technology Licensing Primer*, p. 248 (2d ed. 2001).

194. Richard Stallman, The GNU Project, available at www.gnu.org/gnu/thegnuproject.html. Stallman also started the Free Software Foundation (FSF) in 1985.

195. John C. Yates and Paul H. Arne, *Open Source Software Licenses: Perspectives of the End User and the Software Developer*, 25th Annual Institute on Computer & Internet Law, vol. 2, p. 104 (2005). It is estimated that thousands of programmers have contributed to Linux.

196. It is considered less extreme than the FSF, which basically advocates for an end to proprietary rights as applied to software.

197. *See* www.opensource.org/licenses/.

198. This makes sense especially considering the FSF's vision of free software and its insistence on setting forth those views in the preamble of the GPL.

199. Section 2 of the GPL states: "You must cause any work that you distribute or publish, that in whole or in part contains or is derived from the Program or any part thereof, to be licensed as a whole at no charge to all third parties under the terms of this License."

200. Fallon, at 250.

201. GPL Version 2.

202. *Id*. at 2(c).

203. Lori E. Lesser, *Open Source Software: Risks, Benefits, & Practical Realities in the Corporate Environment, Open Source Software: Risks, Benefits, & Practical Realities in the Corporate Environment*, p. 41 (2004).

204. *See id.*

205. *Progress Software Corp. v. MySQL AB*, 195 F. Supp. 328, 329 (D. Mass. 2002).

206. *Id.* The court also noted that MySQL did not demonstrate the likelihood of irreparable harm during the pendency of the case.

207. *See* Stuart D. Levi and Andrew Woodard, "Open Source Software: How to Use It and Control It in the Corporate Environment," *The Computer Lawyer*, vol. 21 (Aug. 8, 2004). "[A] policy needs to balance the benefits and competitive advantages of open source with the risks of using source code developed by parties with whom the company may not have a formal relationship."

208. *See* Yates andArne, *supra* n. 195, p. 107.

209. *See* Levi and Woodard, *supra* n. 207.

210. Also consider the fact that discovery in the course of litigation would also involve releasing proprietary codes, as IBM was forced to do for some of its products involved in the *SCO* litigation. Although discovery is obviously a different publication from that required under the GPL, it is an important issue to consider.

211. *Id.*

212. The Paris Convention was initially concluded in 1883 and updated in 1967. It is administered by the World Intellectual Property Organization, an agency of the United Nations. The Paris Convention has provisions that apply to patents, trademarks, service marks, industrial designs (similar to design patents), and unfair competition. Approximately 100 nations are now signatories to the Paris Convention.

213. Until the adoption of TRIPS, the Berne Convention was the other major international agreement. Like the Paris Convention, it is administered by the World Intellectual Property Organization. The Berne Convention, first adopted in 1886, has undergone a series of revisions. The Convention includes "every production in the literary, scientific and artistic domain whatever may be the mode or form of its expression." Berne Convention, Art. 2, ¶ 1. Essentially, it assures that a work protected within a member state will also be protected outside of the member state without being subject to discriminating formalities. The number of signatories to the Berne Convention presently exceeded 80 nations.

214. The WTO effectively began operating on July 1, 1995, as a result of the 1994 Uruguay Round Agreements. The WTO replaces GATT (General Agreement on Tariffs and Trade), which had been in operation since 1950. Congress ratified the Uruguay Round Agreements in December 1994. The WTO has approximately 132 member nations. In 1995, the WTO and the World Intellectual Property Organization (WIPO) signed a joint agreement that provides, among other things, for cooperation in providing legal technical assistance and technical cooperation related to the TRIPS Agreement for developing country members of either of the two organizations. The WIPO has approximately 171 members and is responsible for international cooperation in promoting intellectual property protection around the world. In particular, it looks after various international conventions, such as the Paris Convention and the Berne Convention.

215. Geographical indications are marks or other expressions that state the country, region, or place in which a product or service originates.

216. Industrial designs protect the aesthetic look of the product and are similar but not identical to the United States notion of trade dress. Products may be afforded protection based on novelty or originality of design, depending on national law.

217. Breeder's rights confer protection on new and different plant varieties.

218. Utility models protect the manner in which a product works or functions and as such are different from industrial design, which protects only the aesthetics of the product. Generally, utility models address mechanical functioning, which in the United States is not protectable unless patentable. Thus, the innovation in the United States must be significant to warrant protection.

219. Until 1989, the developing countries largely refused to negotiate standards. Threats by the United States of trade sanctions under the United States Trade Act played a significant role in altering the positions of economically weaker developing countries. In particular, China, India, Taiwan, and Thailand were all investigated.

220. *Feist Publications v. Rural Telephone System*, 499 U.S. 340 (1991).

221. TRIPS, Article 41.

222. TRIPS, Article 61.

INTRODUCTION TO PART II

THREATS AND VULNERABILITIES

What are the practical, technical problems faced by security practitioners? Readers are introduced to what is known about the psychological profiles of computer criminals and employees who commit insider crime. The focus is then widened to look at national security issues involving information assurance—critical infrastructure protection in particular. After a systematic review of how criminals penetrate security perimeters—essential for developing proper defensive mechanisms—readers can study a variety of programmatic attacks (widely used by criminals) and methods of deception, such as social engineering. The section ends with a review of widespread problems such as spam, phishing, Trojans, Web-server security problems, and physical facility vulnerabilities (an important concern for security specialists, but one that is often overlooked by computer-oriented personnel).

The chapter titles and topics in Part II include:

12. **The Psychology of Computer Criminals.** Psychological insights into motivations and behavioral disorders of criminal hackers and virus writers

13. **The Dangerous Technology Insider: Psychological Characteristics and Career Patterns.** Identifying potential risks among employees and other authorized personnel

14. **Information Warfare.** Cyberconflict and protection of national infrastructures

15. **Penetrating Computer Systems and Networks.** Widely used penetration techniques for breaching security perimeters

16. **Malicious Code.** Dangerous computer programs, including viruses and worms

17. **Mobile Code.** Analysis of applets, controls, scripts and other small programs, including those written in activeX, Java, and Javascript

18. **Denial-of-Service Attacks.** Resource saturation and outright sabotage that brings down availability of systems

19. **Social Engineering and Low-Tech Attacks.** Lying, cheating, impersonation, intimidation—and countermeasures to strengthen organizations against such attacks

CHAPTER 12

THE PSYCHOLOGY OF COMPUTER CRIMINALS

Q. Campbell and David M. Kennedy

12.1 INTRODUCTION. In modern society, it is virtually impossible to go through the day without using computers to assist us in our various tasks and roles. We use computers extensively in both our professional and personal lives. We rely on them to interact with coworkers and associates, to regulate the climate in our homes, to operate our automobiles, to update our finances, and even to monitor and protect our loved ones. However, this ever-increasing reliance on technology comes at a cost. As we become more dependent on information technology, we are also becoming increasingly vulnerable to attacks and exploitation by computer criminals.

The National Institute of Justice defines a computer criminal as any individual who uses computer or network technology to plan or perpetrate a violation of the law.[1] Although the term "computer hacker" is often used interchangeably with "computer criminal," they are not synonymous. "Hacker" was originally used as an umbrella term to refer to a computer programmer who changes or alters code (i.e., hacks) in a unique or unorthodox fashion in order to solve a problem or to enhance its use. Computer criminals, sometimes referred to as malicious or criminal hackers or as crackers, do not fall under this definition, since they typically alter or exploit technology for destructive purposes or financial gain, rather than for benign or creative functions. Common examples of computer crimes include Web page defacements, promulgation of viruses, unauthorized access of technology, theft of information, denials of service (DoS), and so on. In recent years, computer security analysts have reported a disturbing trend whereby many computer programmers are moving away from the hacking for fun or enlightenment mind-set to the ideology of hacking for profit and notoreity.[2]

Computer crime is an obvious financial and societal problem that shows no signs of slowing. To the contrary researchers suggest that computer attacks will continue to grow in frequency and sophistication as the technology continues to evolve. More specialized threats concerning instant messaging, peer-to-peer networks (P2P), handheld mobile devices, and nontraditional hardware systems (e.g., networked gaming consoles) have been identified in the wild with increasing regularity.[3] Douglas Campbell, president of the Syneca Research Group Inc., stated that "the dominant threat to the United States is not thermonuclear war, but the information war."[4]

One solution that has been offered as an effort to slow down this disturbing trend is to examine the underlying motivations of computer criminals from a psychological perspective. Computer crime researchers suggest that understanding the psychological motivations behind cybercriminals would aid in both cybercrime prevention and protection.[5] Generating psychological profiles of computer criminals would aid in creating preventive initiatives as well as more effective countermeasures in the fight against computer crime. Since computer crime is not solely a technological issue but one involving human agents, psychological theories regarding anonymity, aggression, social learning, and disinhibition may enable us to better understand the behaviors and motivations of the computer criminal.[6]

Information security consultant Donn Parker suggested in 1994 that the creation of an effective malicious hacker profile remained an elusive goal in the information security field.[7] The purpose of this chapter is to survey past and current literature surrounding the psychological motivations of computer criminals. Theories from both social and personality perspectives are presented in an attempt to explain some of the possible motivations behind computer criminals. Finally, the chapter reviews classification theories of computer criminals and details the difficulty researchers have had when trying to develop a single all-encompassing theory to account for the behaviors of all computer criminals.

Although computer crime for financial gain is becoming prevalent, this chapter does not go further into the abnormal psychology of these criminals. The causes and motivations behind their illicit behaviors would be comparable to those of criminals who commit similar crimes without the aid of a computer. For example, an embezzler who uses a computer to steal money may be indistinguishable from an embezzler who steals by altering a handwritten ledger or a corporate checkbook. The focus in this Chapter is on individuals whose interest in computers has transformed their personality and state of mind, individuals for whom the computer represents an alternative way of life apart from social norms.

12.2 SELF-REPORTED MOTIVATIONS.   In an effort to gain a more complete understanding of computer criminals, researchers have asked the perpetrators to describe in their own words, their mind-sets and motivations. Using various self-reporting measures, including surveys, questionnaires, and first-person interviews, researchers have consistently found a number of common accounts used by computer criminals to explain and justify their illicit and sometimes damaging behaviors.[8]

According to sociologist Paul Taylor, computer criminals indicate that they are motivated by an interacting mix of six primary categories: addiction, curiosity, boredom, power, recognition, and politics.[9] Using a phenomenological-interpretive interview approach that emphasizes the interviewee's perception of reality, sociologist Orly Turgeman-Goldschmidt similarly found that computer criminals reported curiosity, thrill seeking, the need for power, and the ideological opposition to information restrictions, among the motivations for their behaviors.[10]

Taylor suggests that the addictive characteristics of computer hacking may be a combination of compulsive behaviors and curiosity. From an outsider's perspective, an advanced computer user's need to meet the swiftly changing demands of the computer industry may appear to be a psychological disorder when in actuality it is a consequence of the medium. This relentless curiosity and desire for technological improvement is often used by computer criminals as a motivation for their behaviors.[11] Anecdotal evidence has also suggested that the frustrations that result from restrictive computing environments (e.g., formal educational environments) coupled with an overall lack of intellectual stimulation contribute to computer criminals' unauthorized access attempts. Some reformed computer criminals have indicated that once they were provided with more responsibility, they were able to focus their skills on practical endeavors instead of illicit undertakings.[12]

Contrary to their stereotypical portrayals in the media, computer criminals appear to have wide-ranging social networks that exist in both their online and offline environments.[13] Taylor indicates that both the need for power and recognition by their peers may both be motivating factors for some cybervandals. Computer criminals report feelings of enjoyment and satisfaction when they prove themselves better than system administrators and their peers. In their analysis of Web page defacements, communications researchers Hyung-jin Woo, Yeora Kim, and Joseph Dominick report that 37 percent of the prank-related defacements contained messages that bragged and/or taunted the system administrations. Twenty-four percent of these types of defacements contained statements aimed at obtaining peer recognition, while 8 percent contained boastful and self-aggrandizing verbiage.[14]

Following the September 11, 2001, attacks in the United States, there has been a renewed interest in the use of the Internet to commit acts of terrorism. According to computer crime researcher Marc Rogers, cyberterrorism is the use of "computer/network technology to control, dominate or coerce through the use of terror in furtherance of political or social objectives."[15] Theorists suggest that a new breed of computer criminals claims to be motivated by political or social ideologies regarding information freedom, encryption standards, nationalism, and ethnicity.[16]

12.3 PSYCHOLOGICAL PERSPECTIVES ON COMPUTER CRIME.   Although self-reporting analyses can give us some insight into the motivations behind computer criminals, these types of descriptive methodologies typically yield incomplete and sometimes inaccurate results. Unless the causes for our behaviors are obvious, often our explicit or consciously held explanations for our actions are incorrect. Research has found that our behaviors are frequently controlled by our gut-level or implicit attitudes, which we are not typically aware of and which may be distinctly different from our conscious mechanisms of explanation.[17] Therefore, our conscious justifications for our actions may be inaccurate if we are ignorant of these implicit cognitive processes. We must look toward more empirically based psychological theories of aggression and deviance to gain a further understanding of the factors that may be influencing these implicit attitudes.

12.4   SOCIAL DISTANCE, ANONYMITY, AGGRESSION, AND COMPUTER CRIME.   Many acts of computer crime can be categorized as demonstrations of aggressive behaviors. For example, cracking into a company's Web server and defacing a Web page, and launching a denial-of-service (DoS) attack on an organization's computer network, thereby crippling its Internet connection, are common malicious and aggressive acts engaged in by computer criminals. Social psychological theories on hostility and violence suggest that people are more likely to commit acts of aggression when the perpetrator of these acts remains anonymous and the threat of retaliation is low.[18] It is extremely difficult to identify the perpetrators of computer attacks. These cybervandals frequently use nicknames ("nicks" or "handles"), stolen accounts, and spoofed Internet Protocol (IP) addresses when they engage in illegal activities. Computer criminals who deface Web pages are so confident that they are anonymous that they regularly "tag" the hacked Web site by leaving their handles and the handles of their friends, and in some cases, even their Internet e-mail addresses.[19] These Web vandals are confident that their crimes cannot and will not be traced back to their true identities.

Social psychological theories suggest that because current Internet technology and practices make it easy to remain anonymous, and because the technical abilities of cybercriminals allow them to further obfuscate their off-line identities, the resulting anonymity may be one factor that facilitates aggression on the Internet in the form of Web site defacement, DoS attacks, and other forms of computerized intrusions. For example, it is an extremely difficult and tedious task to identify computer criminals who launch Distributed DoS (DDoS) attacks against computer networks. The attacker plants DoS programs into "hacked" or compromised shell accounts controlled by a master client. The master client will instruct every "slave" DoS program to *cooperatively* launch an attack at the victim's host at a configurable time and date. Thus, the DDoS attacks are not launched by the criminal's own computer; rather, the attacks come from innocent networks that have been compromised by the cracker. This degree of indirection makes it all the more difficult to trace the original attacker. Much like the Web site vandals, DDoS attackers are also confident that the attacks will not be traced back to their actual identities. Frequently they will even brag on Internet Relay Chat (IRC) channels about how many host nodes they have compromised and against which domain they are planning to launch new attacks.[20]

Social psychologist Stanley Milgram's research, examining obedience and conformity, illustrated how ordinary individuals are capable of committing egregious acts of cruelty and aggression against others, especially when they are distant from their victims.[21] Milgram found that 63 percent of his participants would deliver shocks of increasing intensity (up to 450 volts), despite the screams and pleas of their helpless victims. Follow-up studies found that participants would deliver higher levels of shock when the victim was in a separate room than when the victim and participant were in the same room. Similar to the moral disengagement reported by many computer criminals,[22] Milgram's subjects justified their actions by derogating the victims and blaming them for the painful shocks that they were receiving.[23]

Situational influences on behaviors and attitudes work similarly on the Internet as they do in the real world. However, computer criminals who commit aggressive acts against their innocent victims do not see the immediate consequences of their actions. The computer screen and increased social distance that characterize interactions online can act as an electronic buffer between the attacker and victim. Like Milgram's participants who were visually separated from their victims, computer criminals do not witness firsthand the consequences of their actions. When these criminals release automated attacks against organizations, they are even further removed psychologically from their victims. Automated cracking and DoS scripts, coupled with a lack of social presence in computer-mediated interaction, may make it easier to attack an entity that is depersonalized and emotionally and physically distant. Also, like many of Milgram's participants, computer criminals may engage in victim blame in an attempt to justify their electronic aggressions.[24]

Consistent with social psychologist Albert Bandura's theory of moral disengagement, individuals who engage in unscrupulous behaviors will often alter their thinking in order to justify their negative actions.[25] According to Bandura, most individuals will not commit cruel or illicit behaviors without first engaging in a series of cognitive justification strategies that allow them to view those actions as moral and just. Immoral behaviors can be justified by comparing them to more egregious acts, minimizing the consequences of the actions, displacing responsibility, and blaming the victim themselves. Rogers posits that computer criminals may rely on a number of these disengagement strategies in an attempt to reduce the dissonance associated with their activities.[26]

Studies conducted by sociologists Paul Taylor and Orly Turgeman-Goldschmidt suggest that many computer criminals are, in fact, engaging in forms of moral disengagement. Their interviewees have indicated that computer hacking is driven by a search for answers and spurs the development of new technologies. They suggest that their electronic intrusions cause no real monetary harm or damage to the victims. The criminals suggest that larger corporations that can afford the loss, and not the smaller victims, are the ones who bear the loss.[27] Web page crackers will often criticize and publicly taunt system administrators for not properly securing their computers, suggesting that the victims deserved to be attacked.[28] Rogers suggests that this victim-blaming strategy is likely the most common form of moral disengagement employed by computer criminals.[29]

12.4.1 Social Presence and Computer Crime.   Social psychologist Sara Kiesler and colleagues have examined social presence in computer-mediated interactions. In traditional face-to-face interactions, individuals cognitively attend to social context cues and use them to guide their behaviors.[30] The researchers suggest that the lack of social-context cues in computer-mediated communication due to reduced social presence may lead to antinormative and disinhibited behavior. Group members communicating via computer-mediated communications are more hostile toward one another, take longer to reach decisions, and rate group members less favorably than comparable face-to-face groups.[31] Kiesler and Lee Sproull suggest that the absence of social-context cues in computer-mediated communication hinders the perception of, and adaptation to, social roles, structures, and norms.[32] The reduction of social-context cues in computer-mediated communication can lead to deregulated behavior, decreased social inhibitions, and reduced concern with social evaluation. The most common variables examined in these experiments are hostile language in the form of "flaming" (aggressive, rude, and often *ad hominem* attacks) and post hoc perceptions of group members (i.e., opinions formed after interacting with members). The results of one experiment indicated that there were 102 instances of hostile flaming behavior in 24 computer-mediated groups, compared to only 12 instances of hostile commentary in the face-to-face groups.[33]

According to some researchers, the lack of social context cues and social presence on the Internet leads to aggressive behaviors. Computer criminals may be engaging in hostile behaviors due to this reduction of available context cues. Crackers who harass and victimize system administrators and Internet users may be engaging in these antisocial activities due to their disinhibited state and reduced attention to, and concern with, social evaluations. There are numerous anecdotal accounts of computer criminals "taking over" IRC channels, harassing people online, deleting entire computer systems, and even taunting system administrators whose networks they have compromised.[34] Their criminal and aggressive behaviors may be partially attributed to the reduced social-context cues in computer-mediated communication and the resulting changes in their psychological states while online.

12.4.2 Deindividuation and Computer Crime.   Disinhibited behaviors have also been closely linked to the psychological state of deindividuation. Deindividuation is described as a loss of self-awareness that results in irrational, aggressive, antinormative, and antisocial behavior.[35] The deindividuated state traditionally was used to describe the mentality of individuals who comprised large riotous and hostile crowds (e.g., European soccer crowds, mob violence). Social psychologist Phillip Zimbardo suggested that a number of antecedent variables, often characteristic of large crowds, lead to the deindividuated state. The psychosocial factors associated with anonymity, arousal, sensory overload, loss of responsibility, and mind-altering substances may lead to a loss of self-awareness, lessening of internal restraints, and a lack of concern for social or self-evaluation.[36]

Many antecedent variables that could lead to a deindividuated state also are associated with the use of computers and the Internet. Internet users are relatively anonymous and often use handles to further obscure their true identities. Many of the Web sites, software programs, and multimedia files that typify the computing experience are sensory arousing and in some cases can be overstimulating. The Internet can be viewed as a large global crowd that individuals become submersed in when they go online. It is possible that the physical and psychological characteristics associated with the Internet that make it so appealing may also lead individuals to engage in antisocial and antinormative behaviors due to psychological feelings of immersion and deindividuation.[37]

Deindividuation is brought about by an individual's loss of self-awareness, and psychological immersion into a crowd due to certain antecedents. The aggressive, hostile, and antinormative actions of computer criminals may be linked to deindividuation theory. Zimbardo found that when participants were deindividuated, operationalized by anonymity, darkness, and loud music, they would administer higher levels of electric shocks to subjects, and for longer lengths of time, than individuated participants. Like Zimbardo's participants, computer criminals may be engaging in hostile and aggressive behavior due to deindividuation—that is, as a direct result of anonymity, subjective feelings of immersion, and the arousing nature of computer and Internet use.[38]

12.4.3 Social Identity Theory and Computer Crime.   Social psychologists Martin Lea, Tom Postmes, and Russell Spears have recently developed a social identity model of deindividuation effects (SIDE) to explain the influence of deindividuating variables on behaviors and attitudes during computer-mediated communications.[39] According to social identity theory, an individual's self-concept resides on a continuum with a personal identity at one end and a social identity at the other. Depending on whether the social self, usually in group situations, or the individual self is salient, the beliefs, norms, and actions associated with that particular self-concept will have the greatest influence on the individual's actions and attitudes.[40] When one of our social identities is salient, the norms associated with that group identity tend to guide and direct our behaviors.

According to the SIDE model, the isolation and visual anonymity that characterizes our online environment serves to enhance our social identities. This increase in social identification with a group may polarize our behaviors and attitudes toward the prevailing norms of that collective. Contrary to popular media stereotypes, computer criminals appear to have large social networks and frequently form groups and friendships with other cybervandals.[41] The use of handles and pseudonyms by these individuals combined with their physical isolation from each other may increase their aggressive and criminal behaviors depending on the overall norms associated with their online social groups. If the criminal collective values electronic intrusions and defacements more than programming and coding, these behaviors will be exhibited to a greater extent by members who identify with that group.

According to Henri Tajfel and John Turner's social identity theory (SIT), we tend to identify with in groups, or those with whom we share common bonds and feelings of unity.[42] We have a bias toward our own group members and contrast them with out groups, which we perceive as different from our in-group. While this in-group bias or favoritism may benefit and protect our self-concepts, it may cause us to dislike and unfairly treat out-group members.

Communications researcher Hyung-jin Woo and colleagues used SIT to explain the motivations behind some Web page defacements. SIT predicts that when groups are in competition for scare resources or feel threatened by out-group members, there is a tendency for groups to respond aggressively toward each other. In-group members see improvements in collective self-esteem and enhanced feelings of group unity when they engage in attacks against out-group members. Based on these predictions, Woo et al. hypothesized that computer criminals who are motivated by out-group threats will express more aggressive and varied communication in Web page defacements than nonthreatened defacers.[43]

A content analysis of 462 defaced Web pages indicated that the majority of the defacements (71 percent) were classified as nonmalicious pranks. The most common motivations behind these prankster attacks were to beat the system or its administrator, to gain peer recognition, to brag about accomplishments, and for "romantic" purposes. Twenty-three percent of the defacements were classified as militant attacks. The motivations behind these attacks were to promote groups associated with nationalism, ethnicity, religion, freedom of information, and antipornography.[44] Consistent with the predictions made by SIT, the militant attacks were characterized by significantly more varied content, obscene language, verbal insults, severe threats, and violent images. SIT may be useful in predicting the frequency and severity of attacks by computer criminals. Although only a minority (23 percent) of Web page defacements in this study resulted from intergroup conflict, these attacks were more severe in nature.[45]

For a more extended discussion of anonymity and identity in cyberspace, see Chapter 70 in this *Handbook*.

12.4.4 Social Learning Theory of Computer Crime.   Computer criminal researcher Marc Rogers suggests that social learning theory may offer some insight into the behavior of computer criminals.[46] According to psychologist Albert Bandura, individuals learn behaviors by observing the actions of others and their associated

consequences. Social learning theory draws from B. F. Skinner's operant-conditioning model of learning, where behaviors are learned or extinguished through schedules of reinforcement and punishment. However, Bandura's theory suggests that social learning occurs when an individual simply observes others' behaviors and reinforcements and forms a cognitive association between the two actions. Once the behavior is acquired, the learned actions are subject to external reinforcement, as in operant conditioning or in self-directed reinforcement.[47]

Recently there has been a growing amount of social and media attention focused on information security and computer criminals. National newspapers, magazines, and electronic news sources have reported thousands of incidents, interviews, and commentary related to computer crime. A number of these articles appear to glamorize hacking and computer criminals.[48] The articles compare computer criminals to rock-and-roll superstars, James Bond–like spies, and international freedom fighters. Motion pictures and television shows like *The Matrix Trilogy, Mission Impossible, Hackers, Swordfish,* and *The X-Files* have all bestowed mythological qualities on rebellious computer criminals. According to social learning theory, individuals acquire behaviors by vicariously observing the consequences of another's actions.[49] With the media's glorification and glamorization of hacking and computer criminals, adolescents and adults learn that it pays to be a computer criminal—at least, from a social-psychological point of view. Many crimes involving computers are extremely difficult to investigate and prosecute. The public learns via the media that computer criminals often are afforded fame and notoriety among their peers, and in the information security field, for their illegal activities. There are very few instances of computer criminals' being convicted and serving jail time as a consequence of their actions. Usually the criminals are given a light sentence. Their notoriety garners them media interviews, book and movie deals, even consulting and public speaking jobs.[50] Once an action is learned, social learning theory states that the behavior will be maintained via self-directed and external reinforcement. Computer criminals are rewarded for their illegal activities via the acquisition of knowledge and their elevated status in the hacker community.[51] If the popular media continues to glamorize and focus on the positive consequences associated with computer crime, the cost and prevalence of these illicit actions will continue to grow. Younger generations of computer users also will learn that there are more positive than negative consequences associated with computer crime, which will serve to encourage their engagement in illegal behaviors.

Social learning theory may offer one explanation for the illegal behaviors of computer criminals, especially the marked increase in recent years.[52] Instead of focusing on the supposedly positive consequences of computer crime, media outlets should stress the negative repercussions of computer crime for both the victims and the perpetrators. Social learning theorists would suggest modeling *appropriate* use of computers and the Internet as one solution for computer crime.

12.5   INDIVIDUAL DIFFERENCES AND COMPUTER CRIMINALS.   Although situational factors can account for some of the behaviors of some computer criminals, one must not discount the power of the individual. Attitudes and behaviors are often the product of both situational influences and individual personality traits.[53] Based on published biographies and interviews of computer deviants, information security consultant Mich Kabay suggests that computer criminals demonstrate personality traits consistent with antisocial personality disorder.[54] He suggests that consistent with the fourth edition of the *Diagnostic and Statistical Manual of Mental Disorders* (*DSM-IV*) criteria for antisocial personality disorder, computer criminals appear to exhibit insincerity and dishonesty in combination with superficial charm and an enhanced intellect. Also consistent with *DSM-IV* criteria for the disorder, computer criminals commit their illegal behavior for little or no visible rewards despite the threat of severe punishment. Another central characteristic of antisocial personality disorder is lack of clear insight by perpetrators regarding their behaviors.[55] Researchers have noted that computer criminals do not view their criminal actions as harmful or illegal.[56] These criminals rationalize their behaviors by blaming the network administrators and software designers for not properly securing their computers and programs.[57]

12.5.1 Narcissistic Personalities and Computer Criminals.

Computer crime researchers Mich Kabay and Eric Shaw, Keven Ruby, and Jerrold Post also have suggested that computer criminals demonstrate personality characteristics consistent with narcissistic personality disorder.[58] According to the *DSM-IV* criteria, narcissistic individuals are attention seekers with an exaggerated sense of entitlement.[59] Entitlement is described as the belief that one is in some way privileged and owed special treatment or recognition. Shaw and associates suggest that entitlement is characteristic of many "dangerous insiders," or information technology specialists who commit electronic crimes against their own organizations.[60] When corporate authority does not recognize an individual's inflated sense of entitlement, the criminal insider seeks revenge via electronic criminal aggressions. Anecdotal evidence suggests that external computer criminals also may demonstrate an exaggerated sense of entitlement, as well as a lack of empathy for their victims, also characteristic of narcissistic personality disorder. One self-identified computer criminal whose handle is Toxic Shock states, "We rise above the rest, and then pull everyone else up to the same new heights....We seek to innovate, to invent. We, quite seriously, seek to boldly go where no one has gone before."[61] Narcissistic individuals also frequently engage in rationalization to justify and defend their behaviors.[62] Toxic Shock again writes, "We are misunderstood by the majority. We are misunderstood, misinterpreted, misrepresented. All because we simply want to learn. We simply want to increase the flow of knowledge, so that everyone can learn and benefit."[63] Although it would be a mistake to generalize these hypotheses to the entire population without any empirical support, certain subsets of computer criminals may demonstrate characteristics that are consistent with both narcissistic and antisocial personality disorders.

12.5.2 Five-Factor Model of Personality and Computer Criminals.

In one of the rare empirical studies looking at computer criminals, Marc Rogers examined the relationship between the five-factor model of personality and self-reported "criminal computer activity."[64] The five-factor model formulated most recently by psychologists Robert McCrae and Paul Costa (1990) suggests that an individual's personality can be accurately described using five core dimensions: extraversion (e.g., sociable), neuroticism (e.g., anxious), agreeableness (e.g., cooperative), conscientiousness (e.g., ethical), and openness to experience (e.g., nonconforming).[65]

Rogers hypothesized that individuals engaging in computer crime would demonstrate higher levels of exploitation, hedonistic morality, manipulation, antagonism, undirected behaviors, introversion, openness to experiences, and neuroticism than noncriminals would. Three hundred psychology students from an introductory psychology class were administered the computer crime index (CCI), which is a self-report measure of computer crime activity, along with measures of exploitation, manipulation, moral decision making, and a five-factor personality inventory. Contrary to the researcher's expectations, individuals who committed computer crimes did not significantly differ from the nonoffenders on any of the five-factor personality measures or in their moral decision making. However, students who reported engaging in illegal computer activities did demonstrate more exploitive and manipulative personality traits.[66]

These findings contradict many of the widely held stereotypes regarding the motivations and personalities of computer criminals. It should be noted that these questionnaires were administered using a pencil-and-paper format, which would assess attitudes and traits when the students' off-line identities were salient.[67] Internet researchers have suggested that there is a distinct difference between our online and off-line identities.[68] Therefore, had the students been administered the personality inventories in an electronic format, when their online identities were more salient, Rogers may have found different results. With regard to moral decision making, computer scientist Brian Harvey suggested that due to the relative lack of experience and guidance with computers compared to the real world, teenagers might be at lower levels of moral functioning when online as compared to their interactions and decisions in the real world.[69]

12.5.3 Asperger Syndrome and Computer Criminals.

Recently researchers have suggested a possible link between computer hackers and a relatively new developmental disorder named Asperger syndrome (AS).[70] Asperger syndrome is a disorder that resides at the mild end of the pervasive developmental disorder (PDD) spectrum with classic autism at the more severe end. PDDs are characterized by primary developmental abnormalities in language and communication, in social relations and skills, and in repetitive and intense interests or behaviors.[71] Unlike autism, individuals who are diagnosed with AS have higher cognitive abilities and IQ scores ranging from normal to superior. Individuals with AS also have normal language and verbal skills, although there are noticeable deficits in social communication.[72]

Clinicians recently have proposed several criteria that are necessary for a diagnosis of AS.[73] According to clinical psychologist Kenneth Gergen, individuals must demonstrate social impairment. They may have a lack of desire or an inability to interact with peers and may engage in inappropriate or awkward social responses.[74] These individuals may have extremely limited or focused interests, and are prone to engage in repetitive routines. Although language development is often normal, these individuals may demonstrate unusual speech patterns, rate, volume, and intonation. Individuals with AS also may demonstrate clumsy motor behaviors and body language as well as inappropriate facial expressions and gazing.[75]

The central feature of Asperger syndrome is the obsessive or extremely focused area of intellectual interest that the individuals demonstrate. Children with AS often show an obsessive interest in areas such as math, science, technology, and machinery. They strive to read, learn, and assimilate all information about their area of specialized interest. Researchers have indicated that their preoccupied interests may last well into adulthood, leading to careers associated with their obsessions.[76] Much of their social communication is egocentric, revolving around their obsessive interests, often leading to strained and difficult social interactions. Although children with AS desire normal peer interaction, their egocentric preoccupations, lack of appropriate social behaviors, and inability to empathize with others often leaves them frustrated, misunderstood, teased, and sometimes ostracized.[77]

Researchers have noticed similarities in the characteristics associated with Asperger syndrome and traits stereotypically associated with computer hackers.[78] Tony Atwood, an Australian clinical psychologist, suggests that some computer hackers may have a number of characteristics that are associated with AS.[79] He notes that many diagnosed AS patients are more proficient at computer programming languages than social language and that the intellectual challenge that is presented by restricted computers and networks may supersede the illegal nature of their actions. In fact, AS has been used as a successful defense in at least one landmark UK court case.[80] Based on over 200 personal interviews with computer criminals, cybercrime expert Donn Parker reports finding significant similarities between AS sufferers and criminal hackers. Many of the computer criminals Parker interviewed demonstrated the social awkwardness, unusual prosody, and lack of social empathy during social interactions that are characteristic of AS.[81] Anecdotal evidence suggests that computer hackers often have an obsessive interest in technology and computers, similar to that seen in individuals with AS, that forms a salient component of both their individual and social identities. Due to their egocentric preoccupations, many computer hackers often feel misunderstood and frustrated in social situations.

To date there has been no empirical evidence to suggest a link between Asperger syndrome and computer criminals. There is no evidence whatsoever to suggest that AS causes computer hacking. In fact, most sufferers of AS have been characterized as being extremely honest and lawful citizens. It would be a mistake to assume that all computer hackers are suffering from Asperger syndrome or that every AS sufferer is a computer hacker. Characteristics of Asperger syndrome appear more common in computer hackers, those who explore and tinker with computers and technology, rather than in computer criminals, or crackers, who break into computers or use them for illegal activities. At present, there is still no one all-encompassing personality profile that applies to all computer criminals. In fact, many feel that it is inappropriate to try to create a single personality profile that applies to all computer criminals.[82]

12.5.4 Computer Addiction and Computer Crime. Researchers have indicated that a subset of computer criminals appear to demonstrate addictionlike tendencies associated with their use of computers and the Internet.[83] Technological addiction is described as having an addiction involving human–computer interaction, characterized by salience, mood modification, tolerance, withdrawal, conflict, and relapse.[84] Information security researchers Kent Anderson and Jerrold Post suggest that computer criminals appear to have obsessive or compulsivelike characteristics surrounding their computing behaviors.[85] Cybercriminals will work for 18 or more hours a day on their computers trying to gain unauthorized access to a single computer system with little or no external reward for doing so. Anderson states that computer attacks sometimes take months of planning along with numerous trial-and-error attempts. He further reports an instance where one U.S. judge even attempted to sentence a computer criminal to psychological treatment for his compulsive computer use.[86]

In their interviews with a number of self-identified computer hackers, sociologists Paul Taylor and Tim Jordan indicated that many of their interviewees report experiencing a thrill or rush when engaging in illegal activities that is not comparable to anything that they experience in their real-world interactions.[87] A number of their respondents reported feelings of depression, anxiety, and impaired social functioning when they are away from their computers. Taylor and Jordan suggest that these addictionlike characteristics may also be combined with feelings of compulsion regarding computers and new technologies. However, the researchers indicated that these compulsive or obsessive-like characteristic may be as much a function of the information technology (IT) field as it is a personality deficit.[88] Unlike most disciplines, the IT field is in a constant state of rapidly moving change. If any persons hope to maintain a level of professional expertise in this area, they need to devote an inordinate amount of time and resources to monitoring and adapting to this revolutionary field. This one need to keep up with the changing discipline, combined with the euphoric feelings that some experience when committing illegal activities, may increase the likelihood of technological addiction.

Personality theorists state that for some computer criminals, committing electronic crimes is an experience similar to that of a drug high. Computer criminals commit illegal acts because of the euphoric rush they receive from their actions. Information security researcher August Bequai compares the actions of computer criminals to electronic joyriding. He equates the feeling of unauthorized access and usage of a computer network to that of stealing a sports car and joyriding around the neighborhood. One computer cracker interviewed by computer crime researcher Denning described hacking as "the ultimate cerebral buzz." Other crackers have commented that they received a rush from their illegal activities that felt as if their minds were working at accelerated rates. Some computer criminals have suggested that the euphoric high stems from the dangerous and illegal nature of their activities.[89] Computer criminals have compared the feelings they receive from their illegal intrusions and attacks to the rush that is felt when participating in extreme sports such as rock climbing and skydiving.

Similar to these reports of euphoria, researchers have found that experienced computer users often report experiencing a psychological phenomenon known as flow. Flow is a psychological state that results in feelings of fulfillment and overall positive affect. When individuals become absorbed in a task that matches their skill set, they may not be consciously aware of the passage of time, or the differences between the undertaking and their identity. In their study looking at the experience of flow in self-identified computer hackers, psychologists Alexander Voiskounsky and Olga Smyslova found that both inexperienced and highly competent hackers report high levels of flow. For the inexperienced hackers, this flow experience my lead them to limit themselves to low-level challenges, and they may remain in this novice stage for a significant amount of time. More experienced hackers who also experience flow may leave the hacking domain once they are no longer presented with suitable challenges for their abilities.[90]

As in substance abuse or athletic thrill-seeking, tolerance also may develop with computer crimes. Tolerance occurs when increased amounts of a substance or an activity are needed in order to obtain a "high," or euphoric rush. Tolerance is common in hard drug users who find themselves injecting or inhaling increasing amounts of a substance to achieve their original euphoric state. Anecdotal evidence suggests that computer criminals go through a stage of evolution with each step leading to more dangerous and riskier behaviors. Many cybercriminals begin by pirating and cracking the copy protection algorithms of software programs. When the "warez" (pirated software) scene loses its thrill, they migrate to chat room or IRC harassment. The criminals may then begin launching damaging DoS attacks against servers and defacing Web sites in order to obtain that initial rush that originated with simple warez trading. Similar to a drug addiction, the euphoric psychological states and resulting tolerance associated with excessive computer use may explain why computer criminals repeatedly engage in illicit activities, even after they have been caught and punished.

12.6   ETHICS AND COMPUTER CRIME.   Researchers have suggested that computer criminals may have an underdeveloped sense of ethics or moral maturity.[91] Because of this ethical immaturity, computer hackers may think that many of their illegal actions are justified and ethical. Many computer criminals feel that they are ethically entitled to have access to all information. Most of these individuals also feel that it is morally right to use inactive computer processing power and time, regardless of who owns the computer system. Computer criminals do not feel that breaking into a computer network should be viewed in the same fashion as breaking into an individual's house. Often computer criminals rationalize their illegal activities and justify their behaviors by blaming the victims for not securing their computer networks properly.[92] Most computer criminals are adolescents, which may account for the underdeveloped sense of ethics in their community.[93]

Vincent Sacco and Elia Zureik, in their investigation of ethics and computer usage, administered an anonymous survey to university students enrolled in computer courses at a Canadian university.[94] They used a 22-page questionnaire containing questions about computer behaviors, perceptions, and general attitudes. They examined attitudes toward computer crimes and assessed judgments regarding the ethical nature of illegal computing behaviors, beliefs about the prevalence of the illegal behaviors, and beliefs about probability of detection. Questions about self-reported computer misuse dealt with the use of unauthorized passwords, illegal reproduction of software, avoidance of charges while using programs, and looking at discarded paper for interesting programs, passwords, and the like (dumpster diving).

The researchers hypothesized that there would be a significant relationship between self-reported computer crime and the measures of attitude regarding the crimes. As they predicted, there was a strong positive correlation. Viewing illicit computing behaviors as ethical increased the reported likelihood that the respondents had engaged in such actions. Computer crime was least reported when the behavior was seen as being more unethical.[95] These findings were similar to the ethical computing theories proposed by information security specialists Denning, Winkler, and Post.[96]

Journalists Steven Levy and Steve Mizrach suggest that computer hackers may have a separate code of ethics from the general Internet population.[97] Some hackers feel that access to computers and computing time should be unlimited and free of restrictions. From their point of view, hours of potentially useful computing time are needlessly restricted and therefore wasted in today's computing world. They also believe that all nonsensitive information should be free and easily accessible to any individual, regardless of control or authorship. Information should not be hoarded by anyone in power, but rather openly shared so that those who crave it can have access to it. Computer hackers claim to promote decentralization of government and politics. They have an ardent mistrust of authority. Hackers feel that other hackers should be judged not on superficial criteria, such as age, gender, or ethnicity, but by the quality of their computing and hacking skills. They also feel that the proper use of computers can create beauty and art, equivalent to more traditional creative methods, such as painting or poetry. Computer hackers believe that computers have the ability to improve the quality of living.[98] They feel that it is ethical to crack into computer systems as long as no data are harmed, stolen, or vandalized in the process.[99]

Information security specialist Ira Winkler suggests that computer hackers, because of their generally young age, do not fully understand the possible repercussions associated with their actions. They demonstrate an infantile aversion or complete lack of empathy for their victims.[100] Hackers fail to fully realize the consequences of their electronic intrusion into computer systems. The adolescents do not fully comprehend that their mere presence on a computing network could potentially cost companies thousands of dollars as well as cost systems administrators their jobs within an organization.[101] According to Winkler, many computer hackers learn and develop a sense of computer ethics from their online and off-line peers. In other words, unlike most instruction on morality and ethics that stem from a responsible adult, computing ethics are socially learned from other adolescents over the Internet. Computer hackers learn the "dos and don'ts" of hacking and computing from elder statesmen in the hacking community who may be no more than a few years older than they are. Often, in today's technological society, children know more about computers and the Internet than their parents do. When adolescents have problems or need guidance in ambiguous situations, many times their parents and mature role models are unable to offer them such guidance and assistance. Therefore, the youngsters seek out knowledge from their peers, who may or may not offer them the most ethical or wise advice.[102]

Sociologist Orly Turgeman-Goldschmidt, in her examination of hackers' accounts, suggested that computer criminals may view their behaviors as nothing more than a new form of social entertainment. They see their electronic intrusions as a game that provides them with excitement and thrills. The Internet serves as an unlimited playground or social center where "netizens" are able to develop new games and forms of social activities. Computer criminals may view their illegal activity as nothing more than fun and thrill seeking, a new form of entertainment that is carried out on an electronic playground.[103]

As individuals grow older, they develop a more mature or adult sense of ethics. Adults have legal authority over the lives of their children because adolescents are not yet fully capable of making every decision on their own. Adults need to extend this legal responsibility and authority into cyberspace. Many children are making judgments and performing actions on their own, without adult supervision, while on the Internet. Adolescents do not have the same ethical maturity that adults have, yet unsupervised on the Internet, they are given as much power, authority, and responsibility as ethically mature adults. Neil Patrick, the leader of one particularly malicious group of phone-system hackers known as the 414's, stated that he did not know that his hacking was illegal or unethical. In fact, asked when, if ever, he began to question the ethics of his actions, Patrick stated that ethics never came into his mind until the Federal Bureau of Investigation was knocking on his front door. Patrick and the other young members of the 414's did not see anything wrong with their actions. To them, breaking into proprietary telecommunications networks was not a crime. They saw nothing ethically wrong with their actions.[104]

Psychologist Lawrence Kohlberg developed a three-level theory to explain normal human moral development. The first level deals with avoiding punishments and obtaining rewards, the second level emphasizes social rules, and the third level emphasizes moral principles. Each of his three levels contains two stages that an individual passes through during adolescence on the way to adult moral development. Computer criminals appear to be operating in the lower three stages of Kohlberg's model: the two stages comprising level 1 and the first stage in level 2. The moral judgments of computer criminals appear to be determined by a need to satisfy their own needs and to avoid disapproval and rejection by others. These individuals do not appear to be aware of, or concerned with, the third level of moral development, where moral judgments are motivated by civic respect and one's own moral conscience.[105] Computer criminals may be functioning at the third level of moral development in the physical world, a level appropriate for teens and adults, and may simultaneously be functioning at lower levels of moral development while on the Internet.[106] A recent study conducted by Marc Rogers found that, while taking pencil-and-paper measures of moral decision-making, there were no reported differences between computer criminals and their noncriminal counterparts.[107] However, these findings may have differed had the study been administered using a computer where their online identities would be more salient.[108] Their entire cyberspace behavior appears to be aimed at satisfying their own needs. They break into computer networks to satisfy their own curiosity and to gain the approval of their peers. One notorious hacker who was known as the Mentor states, "We explore, you call us criminals. We seek after knowledge and you call us criminals. . . . I am a criminal. My crime is that of curiosity."[109]

According to Shaw and associates, there is a notable lack of ethical regulation and education in organizations, schools, and homes regarding proper computing behavior.[110] Computer criminals who lack ethical maturity fail to realize that their actions are sometimes just as damaging as physical aggression. Cybervandals do not see the immediate repercussions of their actions because of the physical distance and lack of social presence in computer-mediated interactions. This ethical immaturity is a result of the technology gap between young computer users and their parents. In real-world situations, parents and teachers strive to instill responsibility and ethics in adolescents. Therefore, young adults become capable of making informed decisions regarding ethical and unethical behaviors. However, the same adolescent who demonstrates ethical behavior in the physical world may be ethically bereft in cyberspace, partly due to the lack of adult guidance and instruction. Research has indicated that computer criminals are primarily white males in their teenage years.[111] Anecdotal evidence suggests that in today's society, adolescents recreationally use, and are more familiar with, computers and the Internet than their parents. These young adults often learn about Internet-related behaviors and attitudes on their own or via peer-to-peer interaction. Adolescents are socialized on the Internet by other adolescents, which may lead to a *Lord of the Flies* scenario, where children construct social rules and guidelines to govern their behaviors.[112] These socially constructed norms and guidelines may be both morally and ethically different from real-world norms.

Scholastic Incorporated demonstrated in a recent survey that 48 percent of elementary and middle school students did not consider computer hacking to be a crime. Recently the Department of Justice formed a cybercitizen awareness program in an effort to educate parents, teachers, and children about ethical and unethical computing practices. The program seeks to educate individuals through ethics conferences, multimedia presentations, and speaking engagements at schools around the country. This program and others like it may aid to increase moral responsibility and ethical behaviors of adolescents on the Internet.[113]

12.7 CLASSIFICATIONS OF COMPUTER CRIMINALS. For both ordinary and abnormal behaviors, it is difficult if not impossible to find one theoretical perspective that can account for every behavior in a given situation. Attitudes and behaviors are the product of the combined influence of an individual's personality and the current social situation. Therefore, it stands to reason that no single theory or theoretical perspective can account for the various types of computerized crimes and the criminals who engage in them. The difficulty lies in the fact that there are numerous types of computerized crimes, ranging from trading pirated software, to cloning cellular phones, to sniffing network passwords. Along with the different variations of computerized crime, there are many different types of computer criminals, ranging from the AOL-password thief to the professional spy. Any theory that would account for the behavior of many computer criminals would have to consider, first, the type of illegal activity the person was engaged in and, second, the type of cybercriminal category that the individual falls into.[114] Computer criminals are by nature paranoid and secretive agents who exist in a similar community. They use handles to conceal their true identities and, except for annual hacker conventions or local meetings, seldom interact with each other in the real world. Therefore, it is difficult for researchers to identify and categorize the various subgroups that exist. However, recently researchers using interview and survey techniques have attempted to do so.

The term "computer hacker" has been both overused and misused as a way of classifying the entire spectrum of computer criminals.[115] The motivations and actions of one subgroup of computer criminals may be entirely different from those of a second group; therefore, it is imperative that in any psychological analysis of computer criminals, the various subcategories be taken into consideration. Many theories have attempted to account for the motivations and behaviors of computer criminals as a whole when the theorists actually were referring to one specific subgroup in the underground culture.[116] Computer criminals are a heterogeneous culture; therefore, one single theory or perspective cannot explain all their actions. The fact that researchers traditionally have treated computer criminals as a homogeneous entity has limited the validity and generalizabilty of their findings. Even researchers who have taken into account the heterogeneous nature of the computing underground have had difficulty with experimental validity. Experimenters have allowed participants to use their own self-classification schemes or attempted to generalize the results of a single subgroup to the entire underground culture.[117]

12.7.1   Early Classification Theories of Computer Criminals.   Over the past few decades, several researchers have attempted to develop a categorization system for individuals who engage in various forms of computer crime.[118] A comprehensive review of this research is beyond the scope of this chapter. For an extensive review, see Rogers's analysis and development of a new taxonomy for computer criminals.[119] Bill Landreth, a reformed computer cracker, was one of the earliest theorists to develop a classification scheme for computer criminals.[120] His system divided criminals into five categories based on the their experience and illegal activities.

1. The "novice" criminals have the least experience with computers and cause the least amount of electronic disruption from their transgressions. They are considered to be tricksters and mischief makers, (e.g., AOL users who annoy chat-room members with text floods and DoS-like "punting" programs that crash AOL sessions using specific font or control code strings).

2. The "students" are electronic voyeurs. They spend their time browsing and exploring unauthorized computer systems.

3. The "tourists," according to Landreth, commit unauthorized intrusions for the emotional rush that results from their actions.[121] This subgroup of computer criminals is similar to Bequai's electronic joyriders.[122] The tourists are thrill-seekers who receive a cerebral buzz from their illegal behaviors.

4. The "crackers" are malicious computer criminals. This subgroup is composed of the darkside criminals whom Kabay refers to.[123] The "crackers" will crack into networks and intentionally delete and destroy the data and the computer systems.

5. Landreth's final classification of computer criminal is the "thieves."[124] Criminals who fit into this category commit their illegal actions for monetary gain. These individuals are equivalent to the dangerous insiders that Shaw has analyzed. Thieves may work alone, or they may be under contract from both foreign and domestic corporations and governments.

Former Australian Army intelligence analyst Nicholas Chantler conducted one of the few empirical examinations of computer criminals and their culture.[125] This survey-based study attempted to gain a deeper understanding of the underground culture as well as to develop a categorization system for cybercriminals. Chantler posted questionnaires to bulletin board systems (BBSs), Usenet newsgroups, and chat rooms owned or frequented by computer criminals. An analysis of the data yielded five primary attributes—criminal activities, hacking prowess, motivations, overall knowledge, and length of time hacking—that Chantler used to create three categories of computer criminals: lamers, neophytes, and elites.

1. "Lamers" have the least technical skill, and they have been engaged in their illegal activities for the shortest period of time. This group of criminals is primarily motivated by revenge or theft of services and property.
2. "Neophytes" are more mature than lamers. They are more knowledgeable than the previous category and engage in illegal behaviors in pursuit of increased information.
3. Members of the "elite" group have the highest level of overall knowledge concerning computers and computer crime. They are internally motivated by a desire for knowledge and discovery. They engage in illegal activities for the intellectual challenge and for the thrill they receive from their criminal behaviors.

According to Chantler, the largest proportion of computer criminals, 60 percent, falls into the neophyte category. Thirty percent of computer criminals fall into the elite category, while 10 percent are lamers.[126]

As cited by Rogers, Donn Parker developed a seven-level categorization scheme for computer criminals.[127] He formalized his scheme, through years of interaction and structured interviews with computer criminals, into these categories:

1. "Pranksters" are characterized by their mischievous nature.
2. "Hacksters" are motivated by curiosity and a quest for knowledge. Pranksters and hacksters are the least malicious computer criminals.
3. "Malicious hackers" are motivated by a need for disruption and destruction. They receive pleasure from causing harm to computer systems and financial loss to individuals.
4. "Personal problem solvers" commit illegal activities for personal gain. Problem solvers, the most common type of computer criminal according to Parker, resort to crime after failing in legitimate attempts to resolve their difficulties.
5. "Career criminals" engage in their illegal cyberbehaviors purely for financial gain.
6. "Extreme advocates" have strong ties to religious, political, or social movements. Recently these types of cybercriminals have been dubbed "hacktivists," a combination of "computer hackers" and "activists."
7. Malcontents, addicts, and irrational individuals comprise the final category in Parker's scheme. Individuals in this category usually are suffering from some form of psychological problem, such as addiction or antisocial personality disorder.[128]

12.7.2   Rogers's New Taxonomy of Computer Criminals.   After an extensive review of past categorization theories, Rogers has advanced a new taxonomy for computer criminals.[129] This classification scheme is comprised of seven independent but not mutually exclusive categories:

1. "Newbie/toolkit (NT)" criminals have the least amount of technical knowledge and skill. Members of this category are relatively new to the scene and use prewritten and compiled scripts and tools to commit their computerized crimes.

2. "Cyberpunks (CPs)" are the second category in Rogers's taxonomy. Members of this category are slightly more advanced that the newbies. These criminals are novice programmers limited in experience with computer systems and networks. Cyberpunks also commit malicious criminal acts, such as mail bombing, Web page hijacking, and credit card theft. Winkler suggests that the majority of computer criminals fall into either the cyberpunk or newbie categories. He estimates that between 35,000 and 50,000 computer criminals, well over 90 percent of their total estimated number, fall into these categories, whom he dubs "clueless."[130]

3. "Internals (ITs)" consist of disgruntled workers or former workers who hold information technology positions in an organization. Members of this category have an advantage over external attackers due to their job and status within the corporation. Research indicates that internals are responsible for the majority of computer crimes and associated financial loss.[131]

4. "Coders (CD)" are computer criminals with advanced technical knowledge and skill. These individuals are responsible for writing many of the exploit programs (e.g., stack overflows, rootkits, etc.) that are used by the less knowledgeable "newbie/toolkit" and cyberpunk crackers in their cyberattacks.

5. "Old Guard (OG)" hackers, according to Rogers, are not criminals in the traditional sense. However, they have a relaxed sense of ethics regarding privacy and intellectual and personal property found in other computer criminals. OG hackers engage in behavior according to the traditional hacker ethic and ideology described by Levy.[132] Their illegal behaviors are motivated by a quest for knowledge and information.

6. "Professional criminals" are traditionally older and more knowledgeable about technology than the previous categories. Members of these categories may be former government and intelligence operatives who are motivated by financial gain. They may often have access to advanced technology and can be adept at industrial espionage. The annual surveys by Computer Security Institute consistently indicate that employees (the category similar to Rogers's "internals") are responsible for most acts of computer crime against an organization.[133]

Shaw and associates classify computer criminals into two categories: outside intruders and dangerous insiders.[134] The researchers focus on the critical IT insiders who are typically programmers, technical support staff, networking operators, administrators, consultants, and temporary workers in an organization. Malicious insiders are a subgroup of such employees who are motivated by greed, revenge, problem resolution, and ego gratification. According to Shaw and coauthors, these dangerous insiders typically have introverted personalities.[135] They demonstrate a preference for solitary intellectual activities over interpersonal interaction. Members of this subgroup may have had numerous personal and social frustrations that have hindered their interpersonal interactions and contributed to their antiauthoritarian attitudes. Researchers also have suggested that these computer criminals may have developed a dependence on, or an addiction to, computers.[136]

The malicious subgroup of critical information technologists has been characterized as having a loose or immature sense of ethics regarding computers. The dangerous insiders rationalize their crimes by blaming their company or supervisors for bringing any negative consequences on themselves. They feel that any electronic damage they cause is the fault of the organization for treating them unfairly. The researchers also note that many insiders identify more with their profession than with the company for which they work. This heightened identification with the profession undermines an insider's loyalty to an organization. This reduced loyalty is evidenced by the high turnover rates of jobs in the IT industry. According to Shaw and associates, the unstable bond between insiders and their organizations creates undue tension with regard to security practices and intellectual property rights.[137]

Researchers also have suggested that dangerous insiders are characterized by an increased sense of entitlement and hostility toward organizational authority. Entitlement, one of the characteristics of narcissistic personality disorder, is described as the belief that one is privileged and owed special treatment or recognition.[138] According to Shaw and coauthors, when an unfulfilled sense of entitlement is combined with previous hostility toward authority, malicious acts or revenge against the organization may result.[139]

"Cyberterrorists," along with professional criminals, may present the most danger to individuals and organizations.[140] A cyberterrorist is defined as, "an individual who uses computer or network technology to control, dominate, or coerce through the use of terror in furtherance of political or social objectives."[141]

Since the September 11, 2001 attacks in the United States, the term "cyberterrorism" has been frequently overused and misused by the media. An individual who stumbles on a vulnerable .mil or .gov Web site and decides to deface it would not be considered a cyberterrorist without a premeditated intent to cause panic and fear, with the object of obtaining some social end. Although most of the Web page defacements and network attacks labeled by the media as cyberterrorism would not fit Roger's definition, that is not to say that the Internet will not be used as means for terrorist acts in the future. In the wake of the September 11 attacks, and claims by hackers that they could cripple the Internet in 30 minutes, governments and corporations are investing millions into research aimed at protecting the global computing infrastructure from cyberattacks. Rogers suggests that the relative anonymity of the perpetrator, and the multitude of potential targets that could be simultaneously attacked, makes the Internet a very appealing target for terrorists' actions that will likely be exploited in the near future.[142]

12.7.3   Virus Creators.   Computer crime is not only limited to electronic assaults on computer systems. Various other types of digital offenses, such as cracking software protection, software pirating, and spreading computer viruses, also fall into this category as well. Unlike more traditional forms of computer crime, there has been very little research examining the motivations and behaviors of virus writers. The limited number of research reports on this subgroup of computer crime has relied primarily on one-on-one interviews and surveys, in an effort to understand the actions and motivations of virus creators.[143]

Using case studies and multiple interviews, researchers Andrew Bissett and Geraldine Shipton examined the factors that influence and motivate virus writers.[144] The researchers suggest that it is difficult to generalize their findings to all virus creators because of the limited published literature and research regarding virus writers as well as the lack of clinical populations and theories. Virus creators appear to demonstrate conscious motivations for their potentially destructive actions that are similar to the motivations of traditional computer criminals. Virus writers create and distribute their code for reasons of nonspecific malice, employee revenge, ideological motives, commercial sabotage, and information warfare.[145] Bissett and Shipton's review of Sarah Gordon's interview with Dark Avenger reveals some of the motivations behind one of the most notorious virus writers.[146] They suggest that Dark Avenger consistently denies responsibility for his creation and, like traditional computer criminals, engages in victim blaming. Dark Avenger states that it is human stupidity, not the computer, that spreads viruses. The virus writer also appears to self-identify with his malicious code. Dark Avenger seems to project his persona onto viruses in a process called projective identification.[147] During the interview, Dark Avenger stated that the United States could prevent him from entering the country, but it is unable to stop his viruses. Dark Avenger also attempted to justify creating destructive viruses by commenting that most personal computers did not store data of any value and therefore his malicious programs were not doing any real harm. The researchers suggest that Dark Avenger creates malicious viruses because he is envious of others' computers and of the work they do and the bonds they form with these systems. In the interview, Dark Avenger commented that he hates it when people have more powerful computers than he does, especially when the individuals do not use the resources for anything that he deems constructive.[148]

Antivirus expert Sarah Gordon examined the ethical development of several virus writers using interview and survey methodology.[149] Her initial four case studies involved an adolescent virus writer, a college-age virus writer, a professionally employed virus writer, and an ex–virus writer. The interviews revealed that all four individuals appeared to demonstrate normal ethical maturity and development consistent with Kohlberg's stage theory. Gordon suggests that there appear to be many different reasons why individuals create and distribute viruses, including boredom, exploration, recognition, peer pressure, and sheer malice.[150]

Gordon suggests that the virus underground is currently populated by a second generation or "next-generation" of virus writers whose skill and ability at virus construction is comparable to that of the "old school," or original virus writers. On the surface, these second-generation creators maintain a public facade that suggests that they are extremely cruel, obnoxious, and more technologically advanced than previous generations. The next-generation virus writers appear to be more aware of the ethical responsibilities surrounding virus creation and distribution; however, the exact definition of "responsible virus creation and distribution" varies from individual to individual. Many of these next-generation virus writers have considerable technical skill and are motivated by the challenge to defeat the virus countermeasures implemented by antivirus vendors.[151]

According to Gordon, another group of virus creators populating the virus underground is composed of "new-age" virus writers. These individuals are motivated by current trends, such as political activism, virus exchange, freedom of information, and challenges to write the most destructive or sophisticated virus, as opposed to technical exploration. These virus writers are motivated by boredom, intellectual curiosity, mixed messages surrounding the legality of virus creation, and increased access to ever-more powerful technological resources. Gordon suggests that these new-age virus writers may be older and wiser than the second or next-generation creators. They are very selective as to who has access to their creations, and they do not share their findings or accomplishments with members outside their group. Unlike the next-generation creator, new-age virus writers will not stop or grow out of writing viruses, as they are most likely already adults. They will continue to write and distribute more sophisticated viruses in part due to the mixed messages concerning the ethical nature of virus creation propagated by the popular media, academia, and the culture of the Internet.[152]

Similar to the popular views surrounding computer hackers, researchers have stated that we must be careful not to view virus creators as a homogeneous group.[153] Instead we must monitor the virus-exchange community while pursuing in-depth case histories that may aid in our understanding of virus writers. Education about the ethical nature of virus creation and distribution, and about the repercussions associated with malicious code, may attenuate these potentially destructive activities.

12.8 SUMMARY AND CONCLUSIONS. According to the annual information security prevalence research and statistics, computer crimes are becoming increasingly more widespread, diverse, and financially damaging.[154] With the advent of broadband technologies such as DSL (digital subscriber line), cable modems, satellite receivers, and fiber optics networks, computer crimes are no longer simply problems for the corporate realm but are affecting the casual home user as well. Personal financial information from millions of consumers was stolen by computer criminals in 2006, placing these individuals at risk for identity theft, credit card fraud, and numerous other financial abuses. With hundreds of new computer vulnerabilities appearing every year, computer security professionals are finding it increasingly difficult to protect their digital networks from criminals.[155]

Examining the behaviors of these digital criminals from a psychological perspective, which emphasizes the influence of personality, cultural, and situational factors, may offer possible explanations for their motivations and their criminal actions. Research regarding computer-mediated interaction suggests that the characteristics inherent to the electronic environment may contribute to antinormative behaviors. Anonymity, reduced social context cues, and the psychological state of deindividuation may all contribute to the aggressive and antisocial behaviors of computer criminals.

Self-report measures indicate that electronic lawbreakers may be engaging in these illegal activities due to a mix of boredom, curiosity, and the potentially addictive qualities of the Internet.[156] Contrary to the popular stereotype of the cybervandal, some research indicates that computer criminal have extensive social networks. Social learning theory suggests that computer criminals learn their illegal behaviors from watching the actions and associated consequences of other cyberdeviates.[157] Recently the popular media has been criticized for glorifying computer criminals by presenting them as Robin Hood–like rebels or technological activists. This type of glorification may lead individuals to associate positive consequences with illegal activities, thereby increasing the probability of their occurrence.

Personality theorists suggest that some computer criminals demonstrate characteristics associated with antisocial and narcissistic personality disorders, which may contribute to their illegal behaviors.[158] Researchers also have indicated that computer criminals may develop an addiction to computers and Internet resources as well as a euphoric rush from their illegal behaviors. In addition, computer criminals have been characterized as having an underdeveloped sense of ethics and ethical maturity, although some virus writers have demonstrated normative ethical development.

The few empirical studies that have examined computer criminals have been primarily descriptive in nature and have attempted to generalize their results to the entire population.[159] In order to develop predictive theories regarding the attitudes and behaviors of computer criminals, researchers need to take into account the categories and personalities of computer criminals. There is no one single profile or typical computer criminal. Researchers have developed numerous classification systems that group hackers according to their skill levels, motivations, and goals into independent categories ranging from neophyte hackers to professional cyberterrorists. The computer criminals who comprise one category may have vastly different motivations and attitudes from the typical members of another category. Psychological theories that account for the behaviors and attitudes of one category of cybercriminals may fail when applied to another category of criminals. Thinking of computer criminals as a homogeneous entity limits the understanding of their criminal behaviors and attitudes.

Research and attention from popular culture and the media traditionally has focused on computer criminals in the cyber-punk category due to their sheer numbers and the visible nature of their crimes. However, many theories regarding this group of criminals have been inappropriately generalized to the computer criminal population as a whole, resulting in faulty explanations and misattribution of their behaviors. Although there has been ample theoretical speculation regarding computer criminals in general, there has been a paucity of research on criminals in specific subsets or categories.

Psychological theories offer various explanations that may influence criminal activities on the Internet. These situational influences may interact with various individual personality traits to further contribute to illegal behaviors. The current task for researchers is to untangle these personality and situation influences on electronic behavior. They must determine what situations and characteristics are influencing the various types of computer criminals. There is no simple explanation as to why computer criminals engage in hostile and destructive acts. The answer lies in a complex mixture of factors that depends on the social environment and individual personality factors. There are numerous types of computer criminals ranging from script kiddies to the professional criminal, each with varying personalities and motivators. The interaction of personality variables and environmental factors will determine how a computer criminal reacts in any given situation.

The key message from the research summarized in this chapter is that information security practitioners must contribute to the awareness and education of parents and educators who can influence young people away from the antisocial beliefs, attitudes, and behavior described above. Such efforts will be buttressed by government research foundation investments in further research into the psychological and social dynamics of the computer crime underground as a legitimate sphere of criminological study. Industry would do well to support such scientific and academic efforts.[160]

12.9   NOTES

1. National Institute of Justice, "Electronic Crime Research and Development," 2006, www.ojp.usdoj.gov/nij/topics/ecrime/welcome.html.
2. Symantec, "Internet Security Threat Report," 2006, www.symantec.com/enterprise/threatreport/index.jsp.
3. Symantec, "Internet Security Threat Report."
4. Douglas Campbell, "A Detailed History of Terrorist and Hostile Intelligence Attacks Against Computer Resources," 1992; e-mail: Dcampb@aol.com.
5. Donn Parker, "How to Solve the Hacker Problem," *Journal of the National Computer Security Association,* No. 5 (1994): 4–8.
   Jerrold Post, "The Dangerous Information Systems Insider: Psychological Perspectives," 1998; e-mail: jmpost@erols.com.

6. Michel Kabay, "Kfiles: Ethics," *SecurityPortal,* 2000; www.securityportal.com/kfiles/ethics.html.[AU: no such file found]

7. Parker, "How to Solve the Hacker Problem."

8. Paul Taylor, *Hackers: Crime in the Digital Sublime* (New York: Routledge, 1999); Orly Turgeman-Goldschmidt, "Hackers' Accounts: Hacking as a Social Entertainment," *Social Science Computer Review* 23, No. 1 (2005): 8–23; Tim Jordan and Paul Taylor, "A Sociology of Hackers," *Sociological Review* 46, No. 4 (1998): 757–780.

9. Taylor, *Hackers.*

10. Turgeman-Goldschmidt, "Hackers' Accounts."

11. Taylor, *Hackers.*

12. Taylor, *Hackers.*

13. Jordan and Paul Taylor, "A Sociology of Hackers."

14. Woo, Kim, and Dominick, "Hackers." *Media Psychology* 6, No. 1 (2004): 63–82.

15. Marc Rogers, "The Psychology of Cyber-Terrorism," In A. Silke (Ed.), *Terrorists, Victims, and Society: Psychological Perspectives on Terrorism and Its Consequences.* (London: John Wiley & Sons, 2003).

16. Taylor, *Hackers*; Woo, Kim, and Dominick, "Hackers."

17. David G. Myers, *Social Psychology,* 8th ed. (New York: McGraw-Hill, 2005).

18. Myers, *Social Psychology.*

19. Woo, Kim, and Dominick, "Hackers."

20. Bob Sullivan, "DoS Attacks: What Really Happened," MSNBC, 2000; www.zdnet.com/zdnn/stories/news/0,4586,2553035,00.html.

21. Stanley Milgram, *Obedience to Authority* (New York: Harper & Row, 1974).

22. Marc Rogers, "Modern-day Robin Hood or Moral Disengagement?" 1999; http://homes.cerias.purdue.edu /~mkr/moral_doc.pdf. (Accessed November 13, 2005).

23. Stanley Milgram, *Obedience to Authority* (New York: Harper & Row, 1974).

24. Milgram, *Obedience to Authority.*

25. Rogers, "Modern-day Robin Hood or Moral Disengagement?"

26. Rogers, "Modern-day Robin Hood or Moral Disengagement?" Bandura, "Selective Activation and Disengagement of Moral Control."

27. Kabay, "Kfiles: Ethics;" Taylor, *Hackers.*

28. Woo, Kim, and Dominick, "Hackers."

29. Rogers, "Modern-day Robin Hood or Moral Disengagement?"

30. Sara Kiesler, Jane Siegel, and Timothy McGuire, "Social Psychological Aspects of Computer-Mediated Communication," *American Psychologist,* No. 39 (1984): 1123–1134; Sara Kiesler and Lee Sproull, "Group Decision Making and Communication Technology," *Organizational Behavior and Human Decision Processes,* No. 52 (1992): 96–123.

31. Kiesler, Siegel, and McGuire, "Social Psychological Aspects of Computer-Mediated Communication."

32. Kiesler and Sproull, "Group Decision Making and Communication Technology."

33. Kiesler and Sproull, "Group Decision Making and Communication Technology."

34. Turgeman-Goldschmidt, "Hackers' Accounts."

35. Phillip Zimbardo, "The Human Choice: Individuation, Reason, and Order Versus Deindividuation, Impulse, and Chaos," *Nebraska Symposium on Motivation,* No. 17 (1969): 237–307; Edward Diener, "Deindividuation, Self-awareness, and Disinhibition," *Journal of Personality and Social Psychology,* No. 37 (1979), pp. 1160–1171.

36. Zimbardo, "The Human Choice."

37. Kiesler, Siegel, and McGuire, "Social Psychological Aspects of Computer-Mediated Communication."

38. Zimbardo, "The Human Choice."

39. Tom Postmes, Russell Spears, and Martin Lea, "Social Identity, Normative Content, and 'Deindividuation' in Computer-Mediated Groups." In N. Ellemers, R. Spears, and B. Doosje (Eds.) *Social identity: Context, Commitment, Content* (Oxford: Blackwell 1999), pp. 164–183; Tom Postmes, Russell Spears, and Martin Lea, "Breaching or Building Social Boundaries? SIDE-Effects of Computer Mediated Communication," *Communication Research* 25 (1998): 689–715.
    Stephen D. Reicher, Russell Spears, and Tom Postmes, "A Social Identity Model of Deindividuation Phenomena," *European Review of Social Psychology* 6 (1995): 161–198.

40. Tajfel and Turner, "The Social Identity Theory of Inter-Group Behavior."

41. Jordan and Taylor, "A Sociology of Hackers."
    Woo, Kim, and Dominick, "Hackers."

42. Tejfel and Turner, "The Social Identity Theory of Inter-Group Behavior."

43. Woo, Kim, and Dominick, "Hackers."

44. Woo, Kim, and Dominick, "Hackers."

45. Tajfel and Turner, "The Social Identity Theory of Inter-Group Behavior,"

46. Rogers, "Modern-day Robin Hood or Moral Disengagement?"

47. Bandura, "The Social Learning Perspective: Mechanisms of Aggression."

48. Matt Richtel, "The Hacker Myth Crumbles at Convention," *New York Times* (1998); [online] www.nytimes.com/library/tech/98/08/cyber/articles/02hacker.html.

49. Bandura, "The Social Learning Perspective: Mechanisms of Aggression."

50. Richtel, "The Hacker Myth Crumbles at Convention."

51. Marc Rogers, "A New Hacker Taxonomy," 2000; http://homes.cerias.purdue.edu/~mkr/hacker_doc.pdf. (Accessed November 13, 2005.)

52. Sullivan, "DoS Attacks."

53. Myers, *Social Psychology.*

54. Michel Kabay, "Totem and Taboo in Cyberspace," *Journal of the National Computer Security Association* (1996): 4–9.

55. American Psychiatric Association, *Diagnostic and Statistical Manual of Mental Disorders,* 4th ed. (Washington, DC: American Psychiatric Association, 1994).

56. Kabay, "Totem and Taboo in Cyberspace"; Eric Shaw, Keven Ruby, and Jerrold Post, "The Insider Threat to Information Systems," *Security Awareness Bulletin,* No. 2 (1998): 1–10.

57. Woo, Kim, and Dominick, "Hackers."

58. Kabay, "Totem and Taboo in Cyberspace"; Shaw, Ruby, and Post, "The Insider Threat to Information Systems."

59. American Psychiatric Association, *Diagnostic and Statistical Manual of Mental Disorders.*

60. Shaw, Ruby, and Post, "The Insider Threat to Information Systems."

61. Toxic Shock, "Another View of Hacking: The Evil That Hackers Do," *Computer Underground Digest,* No. 2 (1990); ftp.eff.org/CUD.

62. Shaw, Ruby, and Post, "The Insider Threat to Information Systems."

63. Toxic Shock, "Another View of Hacking."

64. Marc Rogers, "Understanding Criminal Computer Behavior: A Personality Trait and Moral Choice Analysis," 2003, http://homes.cerias.purdue.edu/~mkr/CPA.doc. (Accessed November 13, 2005.)

65. Robert R. McCrae and Paul T. Costa Jr., "Personality Trait Structure as a Human Universal," *American Psychologist* 52 (1997): 509–516.

66. Rogers, "Understanding Criminal Computer Behavior."

67. Postmes, Spears, and Martin, "Social Identity, Normative Content, and "Deindividuation;" Postmes, Spears, and Martin, "Breaching or Building Social Boundaries?" Reicher, Spears, and Postmes, "A Social Identity Model of Deindividuation Phenomena;" Tajfel and Turner, "The Social Identity Theory of Inter-Group Behavior."

68. Sherry Turkle, "Identity Crisis." In *Life on the Screen: Identity in the Age of the Internet* (New York: Simon & Schuster, 1995), pp. 255–269.

69. Brian Harvey, "Computer Hacking and Ethics," 1998, www.attrition.org. (Accessed November 13, 2005.)

70. M. J. Zuckerman, "Hacker Reminds Some of Asperger Syndrome," *USA Today,* March 3, 2001; www.usatoday.com/news/health/2001-03-29-asperger.htm; Suelette Dreyfus, "Cracking the Hackers' Code," *Sydney Morning Herald,* August 8, 2002; http://smh.com.au/articles/2002/08/20/1029114072039.html.

71. Stephen Bauer, "Aspgerger Syndrome," 2001; www.asperger.org/asperger/asperger_bauer.htm. Rosalyn Lord, "Asperger Syndrome," 2001; www.sperger.org/asperger/asperger_as.htm. S. Ehlers and Christopher Gillberg, "The Epidemiology of Asperger Syndrome: A Total Population Study," *Journal of Child Psychology and Psychiatry and Allied Disciplines* 34, No. 8 (1993): 1327–1350.

72. Bauer, "Aspgerger Syndrome."

73. American Psychiatric Association, *Diagnostic and Statistical Manual of Mental Disorders.*

74. Ehlers and Gillberg, "The Epidemiology of Asperger Syndrome."

75. Bauer, "Aspgerger Syndrome."
     Ehlers and Gillberg, "The Epidemiology of Asperger Syndrome."

76. Ehlers and Gillberg, "The Epidemiology of Asperger Syndrome."

77. Bauer, "Aspgerger Syndrome."

78. Zuckerman, "Hacker Reminds Some of Asperger Syndrome."

79. Dreyfus, "Cracking the Hackers' Code."

80. Dreyfus, "Cracking the Hackers' Code."

81. Zuckerman, "Hacker Reminds Some of Asperger Syndrome."

82. Zuckerman, "Hacker Reminds Some of Asperger Syndrome."

83. Jordan and Paul Taylor, "A Sociology of Hackers." Dorothy Denning, "Concerning Hackers Who Break Into Computer Systems," *CPSR* (1990), www.cpsr.org/cpsr/privacy/crime/denning.hackers.html; Jerrold Post, Eric Shaw, and Keven Ruby, "Information Terrorism and the Dangerous Insider," paper presented at the InfowarCon 98, Washington, D.C.; A. N. Chantler, "Risk: The Profile of the Computer Hacker" (Ph.D. diss., Curtin University of Technology, 1995).

84. Mark Griffiths, "Internet Addiction: Does It Really Exist?" in J. Gackenbach, ed., *Psychology and the Internet: Intrapersonal, Interpersonal and Transpersonal Applications* (New York: Academic Press, 1998), pp. 61–75.

85. Post, Shaw, and Ruby, "Information Terrorism and the Dangerous Insider;" K. E. Anderson, "International Intrusion: Motives and Patterns," 1994; www.aracnet.com/~kea/Papers/paper.shtml.

86. Anderson, "International Intrusion."

87. Jordan and Paul Taylor, "A Sociology of Hackers."

88. Jordan and Paul Taylor, "A Sociology of Hackers."

89. August Bequai, *Technocrimes* (Lexinton, MA: Lexinton Books, 1987).

90. Alexander E. Voiskounsky and Olga V. Smyslova, "Flow-Based Model of Computer Hackers' Motivation," *CyberPsychology & Behavior* 6, No. 2 (2003): 171–161.

91. Denning, "Concerning Hackers Who Break Into Computer Systems;" Post, Shaw, and Ruby, "Information Terrorism and the Dangerous Insider;" Ira Winkler, "Why Hackers Do the Things They Do," *Journal of the National Computer Security Association,* No. 7 (1996): 12.

92. Woo, Kim, and Dominick, "Hackers;" Rogers, "Modern-day Robin Hood or Moral Disengagement?"

93. Denning, "Concerning Hackers Who Break Into Computer Systems."

94. Vincent Sacco and Elia Zureik, "Correlates of Computer Misuse: Data from a Self-Reporting Sample," *Behavior & Information Technology*, No. 9 (1990): 353–369.

95. Sacco and Zureik, "Correlates of Computer Misuse."

96. Denning, "Concerning Hackers Who Break Into Computer Systems;" Post, Shaw, and Ruby, "Information Terrorism and the Dangerous Insider;" Winkler, "Why Hackers Do the Things They Do."

97. Steven Levy, *Hackers* (New York: Dell Publishing, 1984); Steve Mizrach, "Is There a Hacker Ethic for '90s Hackers?" 1997; www.infowar.com/hacker/hackzf.html-ssi.

98. Levy, *Hackers.*

99. Mizrach, "Is There a Hacker Ethic for '90s Hackers?"

100. Winkler, "Why Hackers Do the Things They Do."

101. Harvey, "Computer Hacking and Ethics."

102. Winkler, "Why Hackers Do the Things They Do."

103. Turgeman-Goldschmidt, "Hackers' Accounts."

104. Harvey, "Computer Hacking and Ethics."

105. Myers, *Social Psychology.*

106. Harvey, "Computer Hacking and Ethics."

107. Rogers, "Modern-day Robin Hood or Moral Disengagement?"

108. Turkle, "Identity Crisis."

109. Mentor, "The Conscience of a Hacker," *Phrack Magazine* (1986); www.phrack.com.

110. Shaw, Ruby, and Post, "The Insider Threat to Information Systems."

111. Denning, "Concerning Hackers Who Break Into Computer Systems;" Chantler, "Risk."

112. William Golding, *Lord of the Flies* (London: Faber and Faber, 1954).

113. Peter Smith, "The Cybercitizen Partnership: Teaching Children Cyber Ethics," *Cybercitizen Partnership,* 2000; www.cybercitizenship.org/ethics/whitepaper.html.

114. Rogers, "A New Hacker Taxonomy."

115. Rogers, "A New Hacker Taxonomy."

116. Rogers, "A New Hacker Taxonomy"; Kabay, "Totem and Taboo in Cyberspace"; Winkler, "Why Hackers Do the Things They Do?"

117. Rogers, "A New Hacker Taxonomy."

118. Kabay, "Totem and Taboo in Cyberspace"; Post, Shaw, and Ruby, "Information Terrorism and the Dangerous Insider"; Bill Landreth, *Out of the Inner Circle* (Redmond, WA: Microsoft Books, 1985); Donn Parker, *Fighting Computer Crime: A New Framework for Protecting Information* (New York: John Wiley & Sons, 1998).

119. Rogers, "A New Hacker Taxonomy."

120. Landreth, *Out of the Inner Circle.*

121. Landreth, *Out of the Inner Circle.*

122. Bequai, *Technocrimes.*

123. Kabay, "Totem and Taboo in Cyberspace."

124. Post, Shaw, and Ruby, "Information Terrorism and the Dangerous Insider."

125. Chantler, "Risk."

126. Chantler, "Risk."

127. Rogers, "A New Hacker Taxonomy"; Parker, *Fighting Computer Crime.*

128. Rogers, "A New Hacker Taxonomy."

129. Rogers, "A New Hacker Taxonomy."

130. Winkler, "Why Hackers Do the Things They Do?"

131. Rogers, "A New Hacker Taxonomy"; Sarah Gordon, "The Generic Virus Writer," 4th International Virus Bulletin Conference, Jersey, U.K. (September 1994), www.research.ibm.com/antivirus/SciPapers/Gordon/GenericVirusWriter.html.

132. Levy, *Hackers.*

133. Federal Bureau of Investigations & Computer Security Institute, "2005 CSI/FBI Computer Crime and Security Survey," 2005; www.gocsi.com/forms/fbi/csi_fbi_survey.jhtml.

134. Shaw, Ruby, and Post, "The Insider Threat to Information Systems."

135. Postmes, Spears, and Martin, "Social Identity, Normative Content, and "Deindividuation" in Computer-Mediated Groups."

136. Shaw, Ruby, and Post, "The Insider Threat to Information Systems."

137. Shaw, Ruby, and Post, "The Insider Threat to Information Systems."

138. Diener, "Deindividuation, Self-Awareness, and Disinhibition."

139. Postmes, Spears, and Martin, "Social Identity, Normative Content, and "Deindividuation" in Computer-Mediated Groups."

140. American Psychiatric Association, *Diagnostic and Statistical Manual of Mental Disorders.*

141. Rogers, "The Psychology of Cyber-Terrorism."

142. Rogers, "The Psychology of Cyber-Terrorism."

143. Gordon, "The Generic Virus Writer;" Sarah Gordon, "The Generic Virus Writer II," 6th International Virus Bulletin Conference, Brighton, U.K. (September 1996), www.research.ibm.com/antivirus/SciPapers/Gordon/GVWII.html; Andrew Bissett and Geraldine Shipton, "Some Human Dimensions of Computer Virus Creation and Infection," *International Journal of Human Computer Studies* 52, No. 5 (2000): 1071–5819.

144. Bissett and Shipton, "Some Human Dimensions of Computer Virus Creation and Infection."

145. Bequai, *Technocrimes.*

146. Bissett and Shipton, "Some Human Dimensions of Computer Virus Creation and Infection."

147. Gordon, "The Generic Virus Writer II."

148. Bissett and Shipton, "Some Human Dimensions of Computer Virus Creation and Infection."

149. Gordon, "The Generic Virus Writer;" Gordon, "The Generic Virus Writer II."

150. Gordon, "The Generic Virus Writer II."

151. Gordon, "The Generic Virus Writer II."

152. Gordon, "The Generic Virus Writer II."

153. Gordon, "The Generic Virus Writer II;" Bissett and Shipton, "Some Human Dimensions of Computer Virus Creation and Infection."

154. SysAdmin, Audit, Network, Security Institute, "Most Critical Vulnerabilities for Q2 2005," www.sans.org/top20/q2-2005_update; CERT, "CERT/CC Statistics 1988–2005," www.cert.org/stats/cert_stats.html; Scott Berinato and Lorraine Cosgrove Ware, "The Global State of Information Security 2005," *Chief Information Officer's Magazine,* www.cio.com/archive/091505/global.html; Federal Trade Commission, "Identity Theft Survey Report," 2003, www.ftc.gov/os/2003/09/synovatereport.pdf; Chief Security Officer, "CSO Research Reports," 2005, www.csoonline.com/csoresearch/report89.html; Federal Bureau of Investigations & Computer Security Institute, "2005 CSI/FBI Computer Crime and Security Survey."

155. SysAdmin, Audit, Network, Security Institute, "Most Critical Vulnerabilities for Q2 2005;" CERT, "CERT/CC Statistics 1988–2005."

156. Taylor, *Hackers*; Turgeman-Goldschmidt, "Hackers' Accounts;" Jordan and Taylor, "A Sociology of Hackers;" Woo, Kim, and Dominick, "Hackers."

157. Rogers, "Modern-day Robin Hood or Moral Disengagement?"

158. Rogers, "A New Hacker Taxonomy;" Shaw, Ruby, and Post, "The Insider Threat to Information Systems."

159. Rogers, "A New Hacker Taxonomy;" Denning, "Concerning Hackers Who Break Into Computer Systems."

160. M. E. Kabay, "Time for Industry to Support Academic INFOSEC," 2004. www2.norwich.edu/mkabay/opinion/endowed_chairs.pdf.

CHAPTER 13

THE DANGEROUS INFORMATION TECHNOLOGY INSIDER: PSYCHOLOGICAL CHARACTERISTICS AND CAREER PATTERNS[1]

Jerrold M. Post

13.1 COMPUTER INFORMATION TECHNOLOGY INSIDERS. In the complex world of information technology, it is people who create the systems and it is people with authorized access, the computer information technology insiders (CITIs), who represent the greatest threat to these systems.

Computer security experts have developed ever more sophisticated technological solutions to protect sensitive information and combat computer fraud. But no matter how sensitive the computer intrusion detection devices, no matter how impenetrable the firewalls, they will be of no avail in countering the malicious insider.

In considering the population of authorized insiders, it is clear just how broad and variegated this category is and that the line between insiders and outsiders is often blurred.

CITIs include:

- Staff employees
- Contractors and consultants
- Partners and customers

- Temporary employees (temps)
  - Short term
  - Long term
- Former employees
- Employees on notice of dismissal

There is an interesting paradox that the less loyalty expected from a class of workers, the less attention is paid to their security threats. Thus, fairly careful screening, including criminal background checks and credit checks, is usually obtained for staff employees. Except for temps, from whom there is no reason to expect loyalty, little attention generally has been given to personnel security, although they too often have authorized access to the system. For the long-term temp, working side by side with a staff employee, the only differences is that the long-term temp does not have stock options and does not have an attractive benefits package. Is there any reason to expect that the long-term temp will have the same loyalty as the staff employee? Of course not, yet companies characteristically have paid less attention to the security threats presented by the temp than by the staff employee.

Customers and partners with authorized access to the system also represent a potential vulnerability. Former employees often retain their password access or have been able to "social engineer" obtaining access through relationships with employees.

What we sometimes call the *about-to-become former employees* refers to employees in the interval between when they learn they are about to be laid off and the actual termination of employment, with loss of password access. This interval is extremely dangerous. Once employees learn that their time is short, they must immediately start thinking about themselves and about their next job. How will they demonstrate their worth to the next potential employer? One obvious way would be to demonstrate proprietary material that they have helped design. Moreover, some will become embittered and will want to strike out at the company that does not care about them.

Loyalty will cease at the instant employment is terminated, with obvious implications for information technology (IT) securityso access should be terminated immediately upon announcement. All too often, not wanting to hurt the feelings of employees, or out of carelessness, employees in this vulnerable state retain access. Chapter 45 in this *Handbook* discusses this issue in more detail.

13.2 PSYCHOLOGICAL CHARACTERISTICS OF INFORMATION TECHNOLOGY SPECIALISTS.   Psychological studies of IT professionals overwhelmingly show a preponderance of introverts. They prefer the internal world of ideas to the outer world of people; they would much prefer curling up with a good book than going to a cocktail party. Because they tend to internalize stress and express themselves online, they pose a management challenge.

13.3 CHARACTERISTICS OF THE DANGEROUS COMPUTER INFORMATION TECHNOLOGY INSIDER (CITI).   Based on a review of more than 100 cases of computer crimes and on interviews with computer security professionals, a psychological pattern associated with vulnerable IT insiders emerges:

Social and Personal Frustrations
- They have a history of frustrations in their personal and professional relationships, including relationships with coworkers.
- They prefer the predictability and structure of work with computers.

- They have a propensity for anger toward authorities.
- A proportion of them demonstrate the revenge syndrome, and have actually chosen the world of computers with a view toward striking back at the society that has failed to recognize or reward their work.

Computer Dependency

- Online activity significantly interferes with, or replaces, direct social and professional interactions.
- They prefer the virtual world to the real world.
- Online relationships may constitute an avenue for influence, manipulation, or recruitment.

Ethical "Flexibility"

- A survey revealed that 6 to 7 percent believed that hacking, sabotage, and espionage were acceptable, reflecting an attitude that if the security was inadequate, if it was not "tied down," it was theirs to play with.
- Perhaps reflecting their socialization, there was a notion that the computer was a toy, that data were not real. A U.S. Government computer crime expert observed that children would not dream of breaking into their neighbors' mailboxes but would think it was fun to break into their electronic mailboxes.
- The consequences did not seem serious.

Reduced Loyalty

- Organizational loyalty is challenged by a high degree of turnover.
- Employee loyalty is more to the cadre of IT professionals than to their employers.

Entitlement

- A belief that one is special, entitled to corresponding recognition, privileges, and exceptions, often reinforced by employers.
- Their grandiosity covers fragile egos.
- They are prone to anger and revenge when their specialness is not recognized.

Lack of Empathy

- They have no regard for the impact of their actions on others, or no ability to appreciate the consequences of their actions.

These personality traits may be associated with two overlapping personality types, the avoidant/schizoid personality, and the antisocial/narcissistic/paranoid personality, as represented in Exhibit 13.1.

The fact that individuals have many or even all of these personality traits does not mean that they will commit computer crimes. Rather they are particularly vulnerable. Personality disorders are further discussed in Chapter 12 of this *Handbook*.

13.4 ESCALATING PATHWAY TO MAJOR COMPUTER CRIME. In studying the course of computer crime perpetrators over time, one of the findings is that the majority were loyal at the time they were hired. And whether they went on to become disloyal was a function of the interaction between stressors and mitigating circumstances.

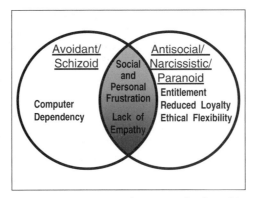

EXHIBIT 13.1   Personality Traits of Vulnerable
IT Insiders

When an individual is going through professional stressful circumstances and has a sound marriage, the strength of the marriage and support from a spouse can be crucial in surmounting the professional stress. Similarly, when, for example, an individual is going through a traumatic divorce but has a stable job, the employment context is a mitigating factor that can provide support through difficult personal circumstances. However, individuals undergoing both personal and professional stress at the same time are particularly vulnerable.

This interaction is depicted in Exhibit 13.2.

As an example, an IT specialist at a natural gas plant became distressed when his previous supervisor, who was technically highly proficient and appreciated the quality of the subject's work, was replaced by a manager with no technical competence. At the same time, the subject's wife had a recurrence of breast cancer. The doctor informed them that she required a bone marrow transplant, but the company's health insurance policy stated that this was not a covered procedure because it was considered experimental therapy. At this point, the employee became emotionally disturbed. He felt that the company was killing his wife and that his supervisor did not understand him. A powerful indication was that he had hung an effigy of the supervisor in his backyard and was firing his high-powered rifle again and again at the effigy. But he did not attack

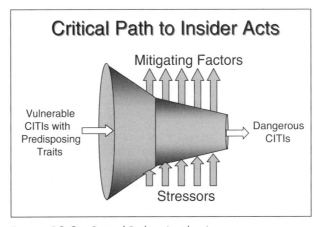

EXHIBIT 13.2   Critical Path to Insider Acts

the supervisor. Rather, he took the company hostage by taking control of the automated system of the natural gas plant, which in effect was a bomb waiting to explode. This was a case of impending IT violence in the workplace. In our consultation, we met with the company officials and the individual. We persuaded the company to override its usual procedures and ensure that healthcare would be made available to his wife. We suggested that he temporarily accept medical disability himself for the stress he was undergoing. The company was transformed in his mind's eye from a murderous employer that did not care to a helpful company that was concerned and wanted to help him, resolving the crisis. What were negative mitigating factors—a perceived uncaring company—became positive mitigating factors—a company that was concerned and responsive.

13.5 STRESS AND ATTACKS ON COMPUTER SYSTEMS. It is often assumed that major computer crime occurs when there is an interaction between a vulnerable employee and stress, and the result is a major attack against the company's information system, as depicted in Exhibit 13.3.

In fact, careful review of case studies of computer crime reveals a much more gradual time course, as reflected in Exhibit 13.4.

Typically, there is first a minor infraction, either overlooked or not dealt with for fear of upsetting a valued employee. Appropriate intervention at this stage, by management counseling, could save a valued employee from further infractions. But if stress continues to mount, a moderate infraction probably will occur. At this point, appropriate management intervention, could involve placing the employee on probation, with no

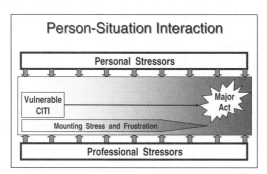

EXHIBIT 13.3 Person-Situation Interaction

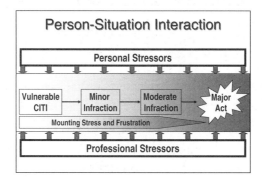

EXHIBIT 13.4 Person-Situation Interaction, Escalating in Fractions

access to sensitive systems, or termination. Such precautions could prevent a major act, but all too often management does not deal with escalating infractions of these "special" employees until a major destructive act occurs.

13.6   TYPOLOGY OF COMPUTER CRIME PERPETRATORS.   There is in fact a broad spectrum of computer crime perpetrators, with a range of motivations. These include:

- **Explorers.** Motivated by curiosity, they rarely purposefully do severe damage. They want to test their own abilities, and seek to penetrate compartments to which they do not have authorized access. They lack judgment concerning unmarked files. They are often picked up by systems administrators, but with no clear policy, they rarely suffer adverse consequences.

- **Good Samaritans.** They hack episodically to fulfill their responsibilities more effectively. They do not see this as a violation. The ends justify the means. They hack the system to save the day, to fix it in emergency situations. Their rationale is that they are testing the system's security.

- **Machiavellians.** These people covertly hack to advance their own careers, increase their own status, damage rivals, or establish future business. Examples include: a consultant who steals proprietary data; a subordinate who frames a boss; an employee who destroys a rival group's network card and plants a time bomb to establish a consulting job; and an IT specialist with a yen for foreign travel. His international company experienced outages with its systems in Rio de Janeiro, Hong Kong, and Paris that only he was able to resolve. Until the company realized that he was responsible for creating these problems, he was flying around the world first class, collecting frequent flier miles and large bonuses for his excellent work.

- **Career thieves**. Career thieves, unburdened by conscience, see the computer as tools for their criminal schemes.

- **Moles.** These people join a company or organization to commit espionage on behalf of a company or foreign government. An interesting example in the corporate world concerned a systems analyst who went to Bloomberg's Financial Systems to steal their sophisticated financial reporting software for a start-up company.

- **Hackers.** These people usually have a prior history of hacking and demonstrate a need to defy authorities. They derive significant satisfaction from their victories and have a need to show off and impress their peers. They are particularly dangerous when they are members of a hacking group.

  - **Hacker subtype: Golden parachuters**. They have inserted a logic bomb or other system booby trap in expectation of a generous severance package or consulting fee. They are rarely reported, for the company calculates it is less expensive to agree to their terms while avoiding damage to their reputation. In one case, a company had hired an IT specialist, deferring a customary background search because of their immediate need for his technical skills. When they did run a criminal background check, they discovered that he had been convicted five times for computer fraud. When they informed him they could not continue to employ him, he responded, "I wondered how long it would take you to catch up with me. Let me tell you what I have done," and then proceeded to describe the logic bomb he had inserted. "And for only $500,000 and a promise of non-prosecution, I will be glad to take care of this problem for you." The company capitulated.

- **Exceptions.** Such people consider themselves special, deserving of extraordinary recognition, and above the rules. They often deflect blame to others. But beneath their arrogant, grandiose exterior they have very fragile self-esteem and are easily wounded.

  - **Exception subtype: Proprietors.** Proprietors feel they own the system they have developed and are entitled to special privileges. They will hack to maintain control of what they deem to be their systems and will hack to deter rivals. They will resist turning over source code and backups. They may create problems only they can solve. An example concerns a high-powered programmer for a national bank, who had developed a complex national management system. Very well compensated, for the previous 18 months, with overtime, he had earned some $500,000. When a new supervisor realized there was no one backing him up, she instructed him to turn over the source code to a deputy. These flaming e-mail exchanges ensued over several months:

    April:
    Hacker: "His experience [referring to the designated backup] was ZERO. He does not know ANYTHING about our reporting tools. Until you fire me or I quit, I have to take orders from you.... Until he is a trained expert, I won't give him access. If you order me to give him root access, then you permanently have to relieve me of my duties on that machine. I can't be a garbage cleaner if someone screws up . . . I won't compromise on that."
    Supervisor: "You seem to have developed a personal attachment to the system servers. These servers and the entire system belong to this institution, not to you."

    The supervisor had in effect identified a proprietor, who acted as if he owned the system. She did not report the flaming e-mail to security or human resources, although she decided to terminate him. In order not to ruffle his feathers, she decided to change him to consultant status.

    July:
    Hacker: "Whether or not you continue me here after next month (consulting, full time or part time) you can always count on me for quick responses to any questions, concerns or production problems with the system. As always, you'll get the most cost effective and productive solution from me."
    His supervisor was reassured by this message.

    Later in July:
    Hacker: "I would be honored to work until the last week of August. As John may have told you, there are a lot of things which at times get 'flaky' with the system front-end and back-end. Two-week extension won't be enough time for me to look into everything for such a critical and complex system.
    "Thanks for all your trust in me."

    On his last day of work, not only the main server but also the backup server crashed. Bank executives implored him to try to fix the problems, but he refused. An independent consulting firm hired to investigate the problems discovered sabotage. They estimated that the programming was so complex that to sabotage the system so thoroughly would have required several months, roughly the interval when his e-mails changed from flaming and obstinate to grateful. In effect, he had switched from being angry online to deciding to do the dirty deed. The ultimate cost to the bank was approximately $10 million.

13.7   CONCLUSION AND IMPLICATIONS.   The Computer Security Institute, in its 12th Annual Computer Crime and Security Survey of 2007 reported that in the prior year, the percentage of respondents experiencing insider network and e-mail abuse was 59%. For the first time, this exceeded virus incidents, reported at 52%. The annual loss per survey respondent doubled from about $168,000 to $350,000. This is a human problem, as well as a technological problem, and requires an examination of personnel practices. The IT specialist with full access to the company's most sensitive systems must be subject to thorough, specialized re-employment procedures.

To have complete information systems security requires an audit not only of technological security but also of IT personnel security, from pre-employment and hiring procedures through to termination procedures. A policy is what a company does, not what it says. The company that deferred the criminal background check because of the need for the new hire's technical skills violated its stated policies. In effect, the company had a policy that a criminal background check was *not* required before hiring. When a company announces the layoff of an employee or a reduction in force, affected employees should have their access to sensitive systems immediately cut off. Even minor and moderate infractions must be documented and dealt with, and management must be evaluated on the manner in which they deal with these infractions.

Effective IT security management must ensure that

- The hiring process for employees in sensitive positions should be redesigned.
- Monitoring, detection, and management should be improved.
- Clear information technology policies should be formulated and briefed to incoming employees. An employee cannot be found in violation of a procedure if it is not clearly formulated and communicated.
- Specialized support services for IT employees should be established. For example, IT employees are often reluctant to meet with an Employee Assistance Program (EAP) counselor but may avail themselves of online support services.
- Screening and selection procedures should be augmented, to include online behavior by searching the Web using search engines.
- Termination procedures are formalized.
- Management of CITIs must be strengthened.
- Enforce computer ethics policies and mandated practices.
- Incorporate innovative approaches to the management of at-risk IT personnel.
- Add human factors to computer security audit.

Systematic audits of IT personnel security practices are required to complement the periodic technological audits. A particularly valuable aspect of the IT personnel security audit is the in-depth review of all troublesome cases the company has experienced, in order to identify flaws in its management system.

Even more important may be the study of best practices employed by other organizations to minimize the possibility of future troubles.

13.8 NOTE

1. This chapter is drawn from a major two-year project on the dangerous IT Insider conducted for the Department of Defense for which the author was principal investigator: Insider Threats to Critical Information Systems: Technical Report #2, Characteristics of the Vulnerable Critical Information Technology Insider (CITI), Political Psychology Associates, Ltd., June 1998.

CHAPTER 1

INFORMATION WARFARE

Seymour Bosworth

Information warfare is the offensive and defensive use of information and information systems to deny, exploit, corrupt, or destroy, an adversary's information, information-based processes, information systems, and computer-based networks while protecting one's own. Such actions are designed to achieve advantages over military or business adversaries.

       —Dr. Ivan Goldberg, Institute for Advanced Study of Information Warfare

14.1   INTRODUCTION.   Until recently, warfare was conducted by armed forces representing adversarial nations, or by revolutionary elements opposing their own governments. Today, although such conflicts still exist around the world, the ubiquitous nature of computers and associated technology has created new forces, new threats, new targets, and an accompanying need for new offensive and defensive weapons. Information warfare (IW), also known as e-warfare or cyberwar, is actually, or potentially, waged by all U.S. armed forces and by those of other nations, as well as by commercial enterprises, by activist groups, and even by individuals acting alone.

Conventional wars, whether large or small, are regularly reported by the news media. Information wars, however, are largely ignored except by those with a professional interest in the field. One reason for this is that conventional warfare is a matter of life or death; photos and eyewitness accounts are dramatic reminders of human cruelty and mortality. In contrast, IW has so far been conducted bloodlessly, with only economic and political consequences. However, it is becoming increasingly evident that IW may soon be conducted in ways that could equal or exceed the death and destruction associated with conventional weapons.

Conventional wars are fought by known combatants with clearly defined allies and antagonists, but IW often is waged by unknown entities with uncertain allegiances and goals. IW may be conducted on many fronts simultaneously, with wars fought within wars, and with both civilian and military targets devastated.

The motives for conventional warfare were almost always territorial, religious, political, or economic. These are still important, but to them must be added the psychological motivations of groups and individuals—groups far more widely distributed, and less easily overcome.

This chapter discusses information warfare in terms of the vulnerabilities of targets, participants' objectives, sources of threats and attacks, weapons used, and defenses against those weapons.

14.2   VULNERABILITIES.   Until recently, concerns over the security of the technological infrastructure in technologically advanced nations have been viewed with skepticism. However, by the mid-1990s, opinion leaders in government, industry, and the security field were coming to grips with widespread vulnerabilities in the critical infrastructure.

14.2.1   Critical Infrastructure.   In 1998, President Bill Clinton circulated Presidential Decision Directive 63, which outlined his administration's policy on critical infrastructure protection:

> Critical infrastructures are those physical and cyber-based systems essential to the minimum operations of the economy and the government. . . . They include, but are not limited to, telecommunications, energy, banking and finance, transportation, water systems and emergency services, both government and private.[1]

Having defined the very broad, vital areas that require protection, the paper went on to describe succinctly their vulnerability:

> The United States possesses both the world's strongest military and its largest national economy. Those two aspects of our power are mutually reinforcing and dependent. They are also increasingly reliant upon certain critical infrastructures and upon cyber-based information systems. . . .
>
> Because of our military strength, future enemies, whether nations, groups or individuals, may seek to harm us in non-traditional ways including attacks within the United States.

Our economy is increasingly reliant upon interdependent and cyber-supported infrastructures and non-traditional attacks on our infrastructure and information systems may be capable of significantly harming both our military power and our economy.

A few examples of specific weaknesses were given by Jack L. Brock, Jr., director, Government wide and Defense Information Systems, United States General Accounting Office:

> In May 1999 we reported that, as part of our tests of the National Aeronautics and Space Administration's (NASA) computer-based controls, we successfully penetrated several mission-critical systems. Having obtained access, we could have disrupted NASA's ongoing command and control operations and stolen, modified, or destroyed systems software and data.
> In August 1999, we reported that serious weaknesses in Department of Defense (DOD) information security continue to provide both hackers and hundreds of thousands of authorized users the opportunity to modify, steal, inappropriately disclose, and destroy sensitive DOD data.[2]

Although these "attacks" were carried out one at a time, and without malicious intent, it is apparent that they, and many others, could have been launched simultaneously and with intent to inflict the maximum possible damage to the most sensitive elements of the national infrastructure.

In a memorandum to its chairman, describing a report of the Defense Science Board Task Force on Defensive Information Operations, Larry Wright stated that:

> The threats to the DoD infrastructure are very real, non-traditional and highly diversified. . . . The vulnerabilities of these United States are greater then ever before, and we know that over twenty countries already have or are developing computer attack capabilities. Moreover, the Department of defense should consider existing viruses and "hacker" attacks to be real "Information Operations or Warfare," what early aviation was to Air Power. In other words, we have not seen anything yet![3]

The report concluded that "[i]t is the view of this task force that DoD cannot today defend itself from an Information Operations attack by a sophisticated nation state adversary."

14.2.2 Off-the-Shelf Software.   One characteristic of almost all military and civilian infrastructures is that they share, with more than 100 million computers, a single ubiquitous operating system, and many of the same applications programs, such as word processors, spreadsheets, and database software. These commercial off-the-shelf (COTS) products are available around the world, to friend and foe alike, and they appear to be more intensively studied by malefactors than by their security-inadequate producers. Each of these products presents entry points at which one common vulnerability may be exploited to damage or destroy huge portions of the national infrastructure. Until, and unless, this software is rendered significantly more resistant to attack, all of its users remain at risk.

14.2.3 Dissenting Views.   Not every influential observer concurs in these possible scenarios. Dr. Thomas P. M. Barnett, a professor and senior decision researcher at the Decision Support Department, Center for Naval Warfare Studies, U.S. Naval War College, voices a fairly typical disagreement:

> If absence makes the heart grow fonder, network-centric warfare is in for a lot of heartbreak, because I doubt we will ever encounter an enemy to match its grand assumptions regarding a revolution in military affairs. The United States currently spends more on its information

technology than all but a couple of great powers spend on their entire militaries. In a world where rogue nations typically spend around $5 billion a year on defense, NCW is a path down which only the U.S. military can tread.[4]

14.2.4   Rebuttal.   It may be of some benefit to have spokespersons for this unworried viewpoint, but their opinions must be weighed against those, for example, of Scott Henderson, of the Navy-Marine Corps intranet, who said: "One of our critical capabilities will be how we are to defend our information and our information systems from an adversary's attack."[5] He stated that successful intrusions, or attacks, on navy computer systems increased from 89 in 2000 to 125 by mid-2001, an annualized increase of 80 percent. Those figures did not include successful attacks that went undetected or unsuccessful attempts that may have identified a weak point from which to launch future, and probably more successful, attacks.

A highly significant factor in IW that most of the dissenters miss is what has been called its asymmetric nature. The barriers to entry for attackers are very low; their weapons can be inexpensive, easily obtained, highly effective, easily automated, and used with negligible risk of personal harm. In contrast, defensive measures are extremely costly in time, money, and personnel, and they may be ineffective against even unsophisticated attackers using obsolete computers.

Considering the nature and extent of already successful attacks against major elements of U.S. military and civilian infrastructures, there appears to be no justification for discounting the views of those who believe that IW, in both its offensive and defensive roles, must be accorded the attention that surrounds any potentially cataclysmic force. This *Handbook*, especially Chapters 16, 17, 18, 20, and 21, contains many examples of viruses, worms, and other malware that have created massive disruptions in very large networks. The worst-case scenarios presented here should serve to awaken a measured response in those who may have been unaware or unconcerned.

14.3   GOALS AND OBJECTIVES.   Attacking forces, in information warfare, will always have a variety of strategic and tactical motives behind their actions; defensive forces generally have only one tactical goal—to blunt the enemy's attack and, if possible, to counterattack. Only after this is accomplished, and the nature of the attackers has been studied, can strategies for long-range operations be determined and effected.

14.3.1   Infrastructure.   Depending on the target, an attacker's goals may vary widely, but in almost every instance attackers want to damage, subvert, or destroy the infrastructure. In doing so, an attacker would hope to bring government, the economy, and military operations to a standstill—to instill fear, uncertainty, and doubt, and ultimately to induce widespread chaos that could cost many lives.

Although this view is entirely appropriate to wars between nations or to wars fought by terrorists, it is somewhat extreme for commercial warfare, whose main goal is competitive financial advantage.

14.3.2   Military.   Today, information warfare is a vital concern of area commanders under battlefield conditions. They must obtain complete, accurate, and timely information about their opponents' actions, intentions, weaknesses, and resources while denying the same to their adversaries. The ultimate objective for all of these activities is to support the military tactics that will maximize the enemy's body count, or at least to render its defenses ineffective, so that surrender becomes the only viable option. The other side of the coin, defensive tactics, are aimed at preventing enemies from accomplishing their objectives.

In the United States, the Joint Chiefs of Staff (for Army, Navy, Marine Corps, Coast Guard, and Air Force) have formulated the *Joint Doctrine for Operations Security* to be followed by all commanders of combatant commands in planning, preparation, and execution of joint operations. The publication states:

> Operations Security (OPSEC) is a process of identifying critical information and subsequently analyzing friendly actions attendant to military operations and other activities, to: (a) identify those operations that can be observed by adversary intelligence systems; (b) determine what indicators adversary intelligence systems might obtain that could be interpreted or pieced together to derive critical information in time to be useful to adversaries; and (c) select and execute measures that eliminate or reduce to an acceptable level the vulnerabilities of friendly actions to adversary exploitation.[6]

OPSEC is a process that could be applied to every element of civilian infrastructure, as well as to the military, although all sources of information commonly used by the military are not available to the civilian sector. Other military code words for intelligence activities are:

- HUMINT (human intelligence) is the most widely used source of information, as it has always been for both the civilian and military sectors. HUMINT is often the only source capable of direct access to an opponent's plans and intentions. Some intelligence gathering is quite open, but covert or clandestine operations must be conducted in secrecy, so as to protect the sources of confidential information.

- SIGINT (signals intelligence) is obtained from communications (COMINT), electronics (ELINT), and foreign instrumentation signals (FISINT).

- COMINT (communications intelligence) is information intended for others and intercepted without leaving a trace.

- ELINT (electronic intelligence) derives technical or geographic location data from an opponent's electromagnetic radiations, other than those that arise from communications or from nuclear detonations or radioactive sources. The primary ELINT sources are radars (radio detection and ranging).

- FISINT (foreign instrumentation signals intelligence) is obtained from intercepting and analyzing metered performance parameters electronically transmitted from sources such as a ballistic missile.

- MASINT (measurement and signatures intelligence) is scientific and technical in nature. Its purpose is to identify distinctive features associated with a source, emitter, or sender so as to facilitate subsequent identification or measurement. These features include wavelength, modulation, time dependencies, and other unique characteristics derived from technical sensors.

- IMINT (imagery intelligence) is produced by photography, infrared sensors, lasers, radars, and electro-optical equipment. This equipment, operated from land, sea, air, or space platforms, provides strategic, tactical, and operational information.

- TECHINT (technical information) is derived from the exploitation and analysis of captured or otherwise acquired foreign equipment.

- OSINT (open source intelligence) is available to the general public from news media, unclassified government publications, public hearings, contracts, journals, seminars, and conferences. The World Wide Web has become an important tool of OSINT.

The *Joint Doctrine for Operations Security* lists several generic military activities with some of their associated critical information. It must be the objective of all information warfare to acquire this critical information about their opponents while denying such information to them.

- *Diplomatic negotiations* include military capabilities, intelligence verification, and minimum negotiating positions.
- *Political-military crisis management* includes target selection, timing considerations, and logistic capabilities and limitations.
- *Military intervention* requires information about intentions, military capabilities, forces assigned and in reserve, targets, and logistic capabilities and constraints.
- *Counterterrorism* involves forces, targets, timing, strategic locations, tactics, and ingress and egress methods.
- *Open hostilities* information involves force composition and disposition, attrition and reinforcement, targets, timing, logistic constraints, and location of command and control (C^2) nodes.
- *Mobilization* requires information about an intent to mobilize before public announcement, impact on military industrial base, impact on civilian economy, and transportation capabilities and limitations.
- *Intelligence, reconnaissance, and surveillance* information includes purpose and targets of collection, timing, capabilities of collection assets, and processing capabilities.

In addition to the Joint Chiefs' doctrines, the Department of Defense and each individual branch of service have been charged with the responsibility for establishing task forces, advisory groups, training and awareness programs, and virtual information networks to mobilize IW forces and to bring into being a strong defense against enemy attack.

Further evidence of the importance of military information and the vulnerabilities that exist at this time is contained in the 2001 report of the secretary of defense to the president and the Congress:

Information superiority is all about getting the right information to the right people at the right time in the right format while denying adversaries the same advantages. The United States enjoys a competitive advantage in many of the technical components of information superiority, but the U.S. also has vulnerabilities stemming from its increasing dependence on high technology. Experiences from Somalia to the Balkans have shown that low technology adversaries also can wage effective information campaigns, especially in urban environments.

In the Information Age, the opportunities and obstacles to achieving national security objectives often are informational in nature. Information superiority is a principal component of the transformation of the Department. The results of research, analyses, and experiments, reinforced by experiences in Kosovo, demonstrate that the availability of information and the ability to share it significantly enhances mission effectiveness and improves efficiencies. Benefits include: increased speed of command, a higher tempo of operations, greater lethality, less fratricide and collateral damage, increased survivability, streamlined combat support, and more effective force synchronization. Kosovo also highlighted the shortage of assets for intelligence, surveillance, and reconnaissance, as well as the need for more secure interoperability and information protection, especially within coalitions.

To ensure that the above prerequisites are in place, DoD is developing appropriate policy and oversight initiatives, actively pursuing opportunities to improve international cooperation in the areas of Command, Control, Communication, Computers, Intelligence, Surveillance, and Reconnaissance (C4ISR) and space-related activities, partnering with industry, and working to anticipate and understand the implications of emerging information technologies.

The quality of DoD's infostructure will be a pacing item on the journey to the future. The ability to conceive of, experiment with, and implement new ways of doing business to harness the power of Information Age concepts and technologies depends upon what information can be collected, how it can be processed, and the extent to which it can be distributed. The ability to bring this capability to war will depend upon how well it can be secured and its reliability. DoD envisions an infostructure that is seamless with security built-in, one that can support the need for increased combined, joint, and coalition interoperability, leverages commercial technology, and accommodates evolution.[7]

Although not as well publicized as are the U.S. defensive efforts, equal attention, time, and resources are being expended on actual and possible offensive operations. Every objective, every tactic, and every recommendation just mentioned, and some too sensitive to discuss here, are subjects for study and implementation of offensive strategies and tactics aimed at enemies, present and future.

14.3.3 Government. The objectives of government, at every level, must be to protect the lives and welfare of its constituencies. Any breakdown in an essential government function may produce marked unrest, rioting, vandalism, civil disobedience, and possibly much bloodshed.

Just as in the military, government must be able to defend itself against an information attack waged by any enemy of the established order. Although not every element of government is perceived by all to perform a useful function, there are agencies without which it would be virtually impossible to sustain a developed nation's day-to-day activities.

At the federal level, civil servants' salaries, Social Security payments, tax collections and disbursements, military expenditures, lawmaking, and a myriad of other functions and activities can be carried out only with the active and pervasive use of computers and computer networks. In the past, some of these computer operations have been penetrated by hackers, crackers, and political dissidents, but only one at a time. It does not require a science fiction writer to imagine what the effect would be if simultaneous attacks were successfully launched against major federal government agencies.

At state levels, although the effects would be more constrained geographically, a great deal of damage could be done to emergency response units, to police and judiciary functions, and to health and welfare services. All of these depend on computerized functions that are protected even less than those of federal agencies.

For municipalities and even smaller governments, zoning enforcements and other local functions can be suspended without serious consequences, but police radio and computer networks are easily penetrated, and their ability to maintain law and order compromised.

As demonstrated by many previous incidents, government functions at any level are susceptible to information warfare. Natural events, Murphy's law (what *can* go wrong *will* go wrong), poorly configured systems, flawed operating systems and application programs, together with inadequate security measures underlie the vulnerability of government systems.

14.3.4   Transportation.   Airplanes, trains, trucks, and ships are all likely targets for physical and information warfare. Because all of them are necessary to support the infrastructure by transporting personnel and materials, any disruption can cause severe problems. Because all of these transportation systems increasingly rely on sophisticated telecommunications and computing resources, they are subject to information warfare.

14.3.4.1   Aviation.   The most visible, and potentially the most vulnerable, component of the transportation infrastructure is the aviation industry. Unlike the fly-by-the-seat-of-your-pants technology of aviation's early days, today's airplanes and the systems that dispatch and control them in flight are almost totally dependent on electronic communications and instruments, both analog and digital.

To a great extent, almost every airplane depends on its global positioning system (GPS) to determine its position in space, its course, speed, bearing to an airfield, and other important functions. Airplanes generally are required to fly at certain altitudes, in specific corridors, avoiding restricted areas, bad weather, and other aircraft. These requirements are met by a combination of GPS, ground and airborne radar, internal instruments, and communications from ground controllers. In the original design of these types of equipment, little or no consideration was given to security; as a result, all of them are susceptible to information warfare attacks.

The accuracy and reliability of GPS and airborne radar, however, has led federal aviation authorities to consider implementing a system wherein ground controllers and published restrictions would no longer determine altitude, speed, clearance distances, and other flight parameters. Instead, pilots would have the option to choose any flight parameter that they believed to be safe. This new system is intended to increase the number of flights that can safely traverse the limited airspace. It is undoubtedly capable of doing so, but at the same time, it will greatly increase the dangers of flight should information warfare be waged against airplanes and the aviation infrastructure.

14.3.4.2   Railroads.   Less so than airplanes, but not to a negligible degree, trains are possible targets of IW. Train movements; switch settings, communications between engineers, trainmen, and control centers are all carried on by insecure radio communications and wired lines. Attacks against any or all of these can prevent the railroads from carrying out their important functions, possibly by causing disastrous wrecks.

14.3.4.3   Trucking.   The great majority of domestic goods shipments are carried by tractor-trailer trucks. Foodstuffs, especially, depend on this relatively fast, reliable means of transportation. If even a short disruption were to be caused by IW, untold quantities of foodstuffs would rot in the fields, as would additional stockpiles awaiting distribution from central warehouses. Data for scheduling, routing, locating trucks, setting times and locations of pickup and delivery, and performing maintenance could be prevented from reaching their destinations.

14.3.4.4   Shipping.   Ships are indispensable means for transporting vast quantities of materials over long distances. Navigational data, such as position, speed, course to steer, and estimated time of arrival, are a few of the parameters determined by computers and GPS on virtually every ship afloat. Conventional radar, and communications by VHF and high-frequency radio are in common use, with satellite communications becoming more prevalent, despite an early start that met with technical and economic difficulties.

Radar and communications jamming are old established weapons of IW, as is interception of critical information. Little attention has been paid to security in designing or operating this equipment, and that places ships at great risk, as does the threat of physical attacks.

14.3.4.5 *Other Transportation Vulnerabilities.*

Recognizing the importance of transportation to a nation's infrastructure, IW attackers could create wide-ranging disruptions if they were to intercept and successfully prevent receipt of critical information within the transportation industry. Recently, as a leader in new technology, the Port Authority of New York and New Jersey has begun converting to a wireless infrastructure at its many airports, train stations, bus terminals, tunnels, bridges, and shipping facilities. It requires no stretch of the imagination to predict what a determined attacker might accomplish in damaging or destroying such an infrastructure. The danger is especially great in light of the general lack of security from which wireless transmissions suffer.

Ironically, the last paragraph was first written just one week before the World Trade Center (WTC) was destroyed by terrorist action. The Port Authority's offices in the WTC were completely destroyed, and more than 70 of its employees were officially listed as deceased or missing. Although that catastrophe points up the need for greater physical security, it also demonstrates how the Internet can be used in emergency situations. The Port Authority site, www.panynj.gov, was used to convey operational messages to the public as well as information for tenants, employees and prospective employees, vendors, suppliers, contractors, and the media.

14.3.5 Commerce.

In 1924, in an address to the American Society of Newspaper Editors, President Calvin Coolidge said: "After all, the chief business of the American people is business. They are profoundly concerned with producing, buying, selling, investing, and prospering in the world. I am strongly of the opinion that the great majority of people will always find these are moving impulses of our life...."[8]

Now, more than 75 years later, these statements are no less true. Producing, buying, selling, and investing are the commercial means by which U.S. citizens and guest workers can hope to achieve prosperity. Although not recognized earlier, infrastructure is the glue that ties these functions together and permits them to operate efficiently and economically.

If these bonds were to be broken, American business would come to a virtual standstill; it is that reality which makes the commercial infrastructure so inviting a target. Without complete, accurate, and current information, no investors would put their money at risk, and no transactions would take place among producers, buyers, and sellers.

In a populace lacking food, utilities, prescription drugs, money, and other necessities, civil disorder would be widespread. With the breakdown of commerce and the citizenry's unwillingness or inability to perform their customary functions, government at every level might cease to operate. This, in turn, would make military defensive actions highly problematic, and an enemy that combined IW with conventional force attacks would be difficult to resist.

On a less catastrophic level, there have been several cases of deliberate stock manipulation by means of insertion of false information into various news channels; an enemy could cause significant disruption in the stock market by forcing a few key stocks into unwarranted declines. In addition, the widespread use of automated trading tools that respond to significant drops in specific shares or in particular aggregate stock indexes could precipitate major economic problems in the developed world.

14.3.6   Financial Disruptions.   Money is the lifeblood of every developed nation. For an economy to be healthy, its money supply, like the body's blood supply, must be strong, healthy, and free flowing. For an IW attacker, disruptions in the enemy's money supply and in its free flow are important objectives. Likely targets in the financial infrastructure include payment systems, investment mechanisms, and banking facilities.

14.3.6.1   Payment Systems.   Every government employee, every member of the armed forces, every office worker, factory hand, service worker, engineer, and retired person—in fact, almost every individual in the United States—depends on regular receipt of funds necessary for survival. Paychecks, dividends, welfare and unemployment benefits, commissions, payments for products, and fees for services comprise most of the hundreds of millions of daily checks, direct deposits, and wire transfers without which most people would be unable to purchase their essential needs—assuming that products and services were available to meet those needs.

The great majority of payroll systems are computerized. Many of them, including those of the federal and state governments, depend on a few centralized computer payroll services. Even if those services were not damaged by infrastructure attacks, the banks on which payroll funds are drawn might be. This would halt, or at least impede, the cutting of physical checks, the direct deposits, cash withdrawals, wire transfers, and any other means by which payments are made. Such a situation has never occurred within the United States except in small local areas and for only brief periods of time. No one can predict what the consequences would be for a widespread attack, and surely no one would want to find out.

For more on banking payment systems, see Section 14.3.6.3.

14.3.6.2   Investment Mechanisms.   Various stock, bond, and commodity exchanges provide the principal means by which individual, institutional, and corporate entities easily and expeditiously can invest in financial instruments and commodity goods.

With few exceptions, each exchange has all of its computers and communications located within a single facility, with connections to tens of thousands of terminals worldwide. Disruption in these systems would not have as disastrous an effect as would a payment system disruption, but it would not be long before a breakdown in investment mechanisms would produce a commercial meltdown.

Because of the vast sums of money involved, exchange systems largely have been hardened against intrusion, and some have remote, redundant facilities, but there have been instances where hardware and software problems as well as physical exploits have brought down an exchange infrastructure.

14.3.6.3   Banking.   The banking industry is the foundation of the modern financial system and, by extension, both American and foreign capitalist economies. At some point, every important financial transaction is conducted through the banking system. As such it is vital to economic health. With the advent of information warfare, the electronic, interdependent nature of banking—and finance in general—combined with its critical nature, makes the banking system a likely target for a strategic attack against a country. This is a new viewpoint for an industry focused on crime, traditional financial crises, and the more recent phenomenon of low-level hacking. It is critical, however, that we master this viewpoint and adapt our banking industry to it, for the threats information warfare poses are different from traditional bank security threats and will increase as the age of information warfare develops. Focused correctly, a well-prepared attack could cause chaos throughout the international system.[9]

The ubiquitous banking system is as highly automated and as security conscious as any element of the world's infrastructure. With ATMs, online banking, funds-transfer networks, and check clearing, banks are integral to virtually every commercial transaction.

As an example of the scope of banking operations involving money transfers, FEDWIRE, operated by the Federal Reserve Board, serves approximately 7,500 depository institutions, providing transfers that are immediate, final, and irrevocable. It processed 108 million transactions in the year 2000, with a total value in excess of $379 trillion. In 2005, the average daily volume was over 528,000 transactions, valued at more than $2.1 trillion.[10]

The Clearing House Interbank Payment System (CHIPS) processes transfers for more than 1,500 financial institutions. Each day, in 2007, CHIPS transferred an average of more than $2.1 trillion, in approximately 370,000 transactions.[11]

The Society for Worldwide Interbank Funds Transfer (SWIFT) has over 8,000 users in 193 countries. In 2007, it exchanged over 3.5 billion messages.[12] Information about dollar value is not made public, but the amounts are known to be huge. If any of these systems could be attacked successfully, the consequences for the financial well-being of many nations would be disastrous. Despite intensive efforts to safeguard the networks, attacks could be launched against the central computers, the computers of each user, and the networks that connect them.

14.3.7 Medical Security.   In hospitals, as in group and private medical practice, the primary functions are carried out in a decentralized mode, making large-scale attacks impracticable. However, ancillary functions, such as sending invoices to the government, to health maintenance organizations, and to individuals, for services provided, and placing orders for drugs and supplies, all require interconnections with centralized computers.

Although the medical profession is often slow to adopt new infrastructure elements, network-connected computers have been mandated at least for payments, and they are becoming increasingly popular for maintaining patient data, for research, and for other functions. There have been reports that hospital systems have been penetrated, with prescriptions switched and HIV-negative patients advised that their test results were positive.

So far, only isolated incidents of sadistic cruelty have been reported, but they indicate that the vulnerabilities may be more than is apparent on the surface. Chapter 71 of this *Handbook* treats medical information security in detail.

14.3.8 Law Enforcement.   The objectives of law enforcement are to facilitate the apprehension of criminals and wrongdoers. To accomplish this, facilities in common use include computers in every squad car connected to precinct headquarters and networks that interconnect local, state, federal, and international databases. In spite of these cooperative efforts, much remains to be done, especially in international operations. The laws of different governments are often not in alignment. A typical case, and one of great and tragic consequences, is that of Osama bin Laden. Although he is wanted for heinous crimes against the United States, he has been sheltered and supported by governments unfriendly to the United States. Politics and religion have become embedded in law enforcement; unless these elements can be eliminated or resolved, enforcement of laws across international boundaries will remain, at least in part, an unachievable goal.

With local law enforcement, it is clear that jamming, or noise interference on emergency channels, or denial of computer services would greatly exacerbate the effects of physical attacks. At worst, a state of panic and chaos might ensue.

14.3.9 International and Corporate Espionage.   Espionage has been a recognized military activity since at least the biblical story of Joshua, one of 12 spies sent to explore the land of Canaan.[13] However, its application to civilian commerce dates only from the Industrial Revolution. Since then, industries and indeed nations have prospered to the extent that they could devise and retain trade secrets. In the United States, the unauthorized appropriation of military secrets has been legally proscribed since the country's inception, with penalties as severe as death, during wartime.

Only recently have economic espionage and the theft of trade secrets become the subjects of law, with severe penalties whether the law is broken within or outside of the United States or even via the Internet.

The Economic Espionage Act of 1996 was signed into law by President Clinton on October 11, 1996. Section 1832 provides that:

> (A) Whoever, with intent to convert a trade secret, that is related to or included in a product that is produced for or placed in interstate or foreign commerce, to the economic benefit of anyone other than the owner thereof, and intending or knowing that the offense will injure any owner of that trade secret, knowingly—
>
> (1) Steals, or without authorization appropriates, takes, carries away, or conceals, or by fraud, artifice, or deception obtains such information;
>
> (2) Without authorization copies, duplicates, sketches, draws, photographs, downloads, uploads, alters, destroys, photocopies, replicates, transmits, delivers, sends, mails, communicates, or conveys such information;
>
> (3) Receives, buys, or possesses such information, knowing the same to have been stolen or appropriated, obtained, or converted without authorization;
>
> (4) Attempts to commit any offense described in any of paragraphs (1) through (3); or
>
> (5) Conspires with one or more other persons to commit any offense described in any of paragraphs (1) through (3), and one or more of such persons do any act to effect the object of the conspiracy,
>
> Shall, except as provided in subsection (b), be fined under this title or imprisoned not more than 10 years, or both. (b) Any organization that commits any offense described in subsection (a) shall be fined not more than $5,000,000.[14]

Although the foregoing lists all of the actions that are proscribed, it is not specific as to which assets are to be protected as trade secrets. For this, see the Defense Security Service paper, "What Are We Protecting?"[15] There, the five basic categories of People, Activities/Operations, Information, Facilities, and Equipment/Materials are expanded into 42 specific assets, with the admonition that every company official must clearly identify to employees what classified or proprietary information requires protection. Only if the owner has taken reasonable measures to keep such information secret, and the information derives actual or potential economic value from not being generally known to or readily obtainable through proper means, will the courts view it as a trade secret.

For further information on intellectual property, including trade secrets, see Chapters 11 and 42 in this *Handbook*.

14.3.10   Communications.   Communications are the means by which all elements of a civilization are tied together. Any significant destruction of communications media would disrupt the most important segments of society. Without adequate communications, transactions and services would come to a complete halt. In the United States, communications have been disrupted frequently, but fortunately, the infrastructure has been so vast and so diverse that the consequences have rarely been more than temporary. Even after the WTC disaster of September 11, 2001, when Verizon's downtown telephone facilities centers were heavily damaged, service was restored within four days to the New York Stock Exchange and to other important users in the area.

Contrary to popular belief, the Internet is so widely used and concentrated in so few backbone points that a coordinated attack actually could destroy its functioning. For many years, backup facilities have included redundant computers and all of their associated peripherals, often in remote locations. Too often, however, alternate communications facilities are not provided. Unless this is rectified, the same disaster that brings down one installation could disable all.

14.3.11   Destabilization of Economic Infrastructure.   A major difference between wealthy, developed nations and poor, undeveloped countries lies in the strength of their economic infrastructures. The existence of strong capital markets, stable banking and lending facilities, and efficient payment processes, all tied together by fast, technically advanced communications capabilities, is essential to healthy, growing economies.

At opposite ends of this spectrum lie Afghanistan and the United States. The perpetrators of the attacks on the World Trade center and the Pentagon, identified as Osama bin Laden and his Al-Qaeda organization, operating out of Afghanistan, chose as their targets the symbols and the operating centers of America's military operations and of its economic infrastructure.

It seems certain at this time that the United States and the entire world is being impelled into a serious recession. With hundreds of thousands thrown out of work and with investment capital drying up, the entire economic infrastructure of the world has suffered a great blow. How and when it will recover is a subject of speculation, but of one thing there can be no doubt: Every effort must be bent toward preventing another attack. Security can no longer be the duty of a few technical people; it has become everyone's responsibility.

14.4   SOURCES OF THREATS AND ATTACKS.   The actual and potential originators of information warfare are numerous and powerful. One need not be paranoid to feel that an attack may come from any direction. This section lists sources that have already proven their capabilities for conducting cyberwar.

14.4.1   Nation-States.   U.S. military preparations for cyberwar have been described in Section 14.3.2. This section details some of the measures that another great power—China—is effecting toward the same ends. Most of the material is from a paper entitled "Like Adding Wings to the Tiger: Chinese Information War Theory and Practice."[16]

14.4.1.1   China and Information Warfare.   Although China is a nuclear power, it does not yet have the arsenal necessary to threaten a superpower like the United States. However, it can do so with its IW forces; adding wings to the tiger makes it more combat worthy. Nor is Chinese IW entirely theoretical. On August 3,

2000, the *Washington Times* reported that hackers suspected of working for a Chinese government institute took large amounts of unclassified but sensitive information from a Los Alamos computer system. A spokesman stated that "an enormous amount of Chinese activity hitting our green, open sites" occurs continuously.[17]

According to an article in the Chinese Armed Forces newspaper, the *Liberation Army Daily,* their first attack objectives will be the computer networking systems that link a country's political, economic, and military installations, as well as their general society.[18] A further objective will be to control the enemy's decision-making capability in order to hinder coordinated actions.

Expanding on Mao Zedung's theory of a People's War, IW can be "carried out by hundreds of millions of people using open-type modern information system."[19] In this war, combatants can be soldiers or teenagers, or anyone who has a computer as a weapon.[20] Ironically, China, with its long-standing fear of outside information as a possible spur to counterrevolutionary action, now views arming large numbers of intelligent people with computers and access to the Internet as a necessary survival measure. It remains to be seen just how many personal computers will be made available and how China will ensure that they will be used only as the government intends.

14.4.1.2 *Strategies.* The People's Liberation Army (PLA) with 1.5 million reserve troops has been carrying out IW exercises on a wide scale. One such exercise, in Xian Province, concentrated on conducting information reconnaissance, changing network data, releasing information bombs, dumping information garbage, disseminating propaganda, applying information deception, releasing clone information, organizing information defense, and establishing spy stations.[21] The antecedents of these tactics can be found in a book of unknown authorship, first mentioned about 1,500 years ago, entitled *The Secret Art of War: The 36 Stratagems*. Strategy 25 advises:

> *Replace the Beams with Rotten Timbers*. Disrupt the enemy's formations, interfere with their methods of operations, change the rules which they are used to following, and go contrary to their standard training. In this way you remove the supporting pillar, the common link that makes a group of men an effective fighting force.[22]

The 36 stratagems deserve close study; many of them are obviously in use even today by China and others. For example, strategy 3 says:

> *Kill with a Borrowed Sword*. When you do not have the means to attack your enemy directly, then attack using the strength of another.

Lacking the weapons to attack the United States directly, the perpetrators of the WTC attack used the airliners belonging to their targets.
Strategy 5 says:

> *Loot a Burning House*. When a country is beset by internal conflicts, when disease and famine ravage the population, when corruption and crime are rampant, then it will be unable to deal with an outside threat. This is the time to attack.

Some of the strategies might well be employed by the United States. For example, strategy 33 advises:

> *The Strategy of Sowing Discord*. Undermine your enemy's ability to fight by secretly causing discord between him and his friends, allies, advisors, family, commanders, soldiers, and population. While he is preoccupied settling internal disputes his ability to attack or defend, is compromised.

To accomplish this, IW may prove to be an effective weapon.

14.4.1.3 Training.

Several high-level academies and universities have been established to conduct IW instruction for the PLA. In addition, training is planned for large numbers of individuals to include:

- Basic theory, including computer basics and application, communications network technology, the information highway, and digitized units
- Electronic countermeasures, radar technology
- IW rules and regulations
- IW strategy and tactics
- Theater and strategic IW
- Information systems, including gathering, handling, disseminating, and using information
- Combat command, monitoring, decision making, and control systems
- Information weapons, including concepts, principles of soft and hard destruction, and how to apply these weapons
- Simulated IW, protection of information systems, computer virus attacks and counterattacks, and jamming and counterjamming of communications networks[23]

It is doubtful that all of these training objectives have been accomplished, but there seems to be a major commitment to do so, and sooner rather than later.

China and the United States are only two of the nations that are openly preparing for, and actually engaged in, information warfare. It is obvious that many others are similarly involved and that these measures, combined with conventional weapons or weapons of mass destruction, have the potential to elevate warfare to a destructive level never before possible and hardly conceivable.

14.4.2 Cyberterrorists

"Cyberterrorism" means intentional use or threat of use, without legally recognized authority, of violence, disruption, or interference against cyber systems, when it is likely that such use would result in death or injury of a person or persons, substantial damage to physical property, civil disorder, or significant economic harm.[24]

Cyberterrorists, those who engage in cyberterrorism, generally are able to carry out the same sort of cyberwar as nation-states; in fact, they may be state-sponsored. The major difference is that terrorist attacks are usually hit-and-run, where nations are capable of sustained and continuous operations. Although conventional warfare always was carried out in an overt fashion, it is the nature of IW that it can be engaged in without a declaration of war and without any clear indication of who the attacker actually is. In fact, it may not be recognized that a war is being conducted; it may seem only that a series of unfortunate, unconnected natural failures of computers and communications are disrupting an economy.

Terrorists, especially when state-sponsored, would be very likely to conceal their IW activities in this manner, so as to avoid the retribution that would inevitably follow. However, some terrorists would publicly take credit for their actions, in order to bolster their apparent strength and to gather added support from like-minded individuals and organizations.

The seriousness of terrorist threats after 9/11 resulted in Executive Order 13228 of October 8, 2001, establishing the Office of Homeland Security and the Homeland Security Council.[25] The mission of the Office was to "develop and coordinate the implementation of a comprehensive national strategy to secure the United States from terrorist threats or attacks." Its function was "to coordinate the executive branch's efforts to detect, prepare for, prevent, protect against, respond to, and recover from terrorist attacks within the United States."

The Department of Homeland Security was mandated by Congress on January 24, 2003, and was fully formed on March 1, 2003. Celebrating its fifth anniversary on that date in 2008, the department employs 208,000 people dedicated to fulfilling its mission.

On February 15, 2005, Michael Chertoff was sworn in as the second secretary. His five goals:

1. Protect our Nation from Dangerous People
2. Protect our Nation from Dangerous Goods
3. Protect Critical Infrastructure
4. Strengthen our Nation's Preparedness and Emergency Response Capabilities
5. Strengthen and Unify Operations and Management[26]

On April 30, 2008, Secretary Chertoff, recognizing new realities, said:

the technology of the 21st Century is changing so rapidly that many of our rules and procedures, which were built at a time that we had a certain kind of communication system and a certain kind of analog set of processes, that legal structure seems woefully inadequate to a digital age when the movement of communications is not rooted in any one place and when it's very difficult to take the concepts which made a lot of sense in the days of the rotary telephone and apply them in the world of voice over internet protocols.[27]

The challenges faced by the Department of Homeland Security are multitudinous and complex. Whether it proves effective in reducing or eliminating terrorism within the United States will depend on solving the problems of overlapping authorities, inertia, incompatible databases, turf wars, funding, management, the predictability of terrorist actions, and a host of political and technological issues.

14.4.3 Corporations.

The threats aimed at or directed by corporations are far less deadly than those of the military or of terrorists, but they are no less pervasive. Thefts of data, denial of service, viruses, and natural disasters traditionally have been at the heart of individual corporate security concerns. These concerns have not abated, but to them have been added fears that attacks on large segments of the information infrastructure are more likely to create damage than is an attack against any single enterprise. To guard against this, every installation should operate behind strong firewalls and effective access controls.

In the wake of the September 11 attacks, Richard Clarke, who had been National Coordinator for Security, Infrastructure Protection and Counterterrorism since May 1998, was appointed to a new post. As special advisor to the president for cyberspace security, Mr. Clarke warned that terrorists are out to hurt our economy and that they can use viruses in massive, coordinated attacks against corporate IT systems. He recommends, at a minimum, that disaster recovery plans include near-online, off-site backup facilities and redundant communications paths.

14.4.4   Activists.   The line between terrorists and activists is often thin and indistinct. Throughout the world, many organizations and individuals feel very strongly about globalization, territorial claims, environmental concerns, abortion, human rights, poverty, and other seemingly intractable issues. These organizations, and like-minded individuals, operate along a spectrum that extends from the completely intellectual and peaceable at one end, to the radical, confrontational, and militant at the other. For example, activists have sabotaged World Wide Web sites to express opposition to the World Trade Organization, support for Kashmiri independence, and distaste for Japanese revisionist history about atrocities in World War II.[28]

Given this wide range of motivations and actions, proactive steps and active responses must be carefully measured so as to be consistent with the nature of specific activist threats. The countermeasures may range anywhere from simple public relations announcements to shuttered and barricaded facilities, with strong cyberwar defenses in place.

14.4.5   Criminals.   Although all of the earlier-mentioned sources of threat may have political or ideological motives, there is a large class of security risks whose sole motivation is personal financial gain. Their illegal activities include manipulating stock prices, stealing services, fraudulently transferring funds to their own accounts, and using stolen or invented credit card numbers; they also trade in stolen customer lists, product designs, marketing plans, and other proprietary information, which they offer to sell to competitors or back to their original owners. Although the materials may have been stolen for personal gain, their ultimate use may be as weapons in cyberwar, such as transnational commercial competition.

Chapters 12, 13, and 15 to 20 in this *Handbook* describe in detail many criminal threats and the measures that may be taken to thwart them.

14.4.6   Hobbyists.   The term "hackers" originally was applied to those individuals with expert programming capabilities who derived satisfaction from delving into the internal structures and functions of software. The goal was to increase their own level of sophisticated technical knowledge and to share this learning with others; their motives were never malevolent.

To this day, there are many students of computer science and pure hobbyists with these same objectives, who would never intentionally attack a computer or its software. However, there now appear to be as many, or possibly more, persons whose intent is to damage or destroy computer systems for what appears to be malicious pleasure. Rather than sharing knowledge for academic reasons, these individuals do so in order to acquire bragging rights and a reputation among their cohorts. When a single hobbyist or a group with malicious intent attack any Internet site, they are engaging in cyberwar.

Most of the original hackers resent the use of this appellation to describe malicious system penetrators; instead, they would like the malefactors to be known as crackers. Especially they resent the fact that many crackers have little or no technical knowledge. Those, known as script kiddies, can do no more than initiate a program given to them by others, but they are inordinately pleased by the amount of damage they can do.

For a fuller discussion of hackers, see Chapter 12.

14.5   WEAPONS OF CYBERWAR.   The weapons used in information warfare have existed for many years, but newer and more malevolent versions are produced with increasing frequency. For this reason, system security cannot be considered as static, but rather as part of an ongoing process that must be continuously monitored and strengthened. This section briefly describes the most common and most dangerous IW weapons, with references to other chapters where more detailed information is available.

14.5.1   Denial of Service and Distributed Denial of Service.

Denial of service (DoS) and distributed denial of service (DDoS) are means by which computers, network servers, and telecommunications circuits can be partially or completely prevented from performing their designated functions. Any computer element that has been designed for a specific maximum capacity, if flooded by messages or data inputs that greatly exceed that number, can be slowed or even brought to a complete halt.

A DoS attack is carried out by a single computer that has been programmed to overwhelm the target system's capacity, usually by generating, automatically, a very large number of messages. A DDoS attack is implemented by planting a small program on hundreds or thousands of unaware computers. At a signal from the attacker, all of the agents (sometimes called zombies or daemons) are caused to send many messages simultaneously, thus flooding the victim's system or preempting all of its bandwidth capacity.

On April 26, 2007, a page-one article in the *New York Times* reported on what some Estonian authorities described as the first war in cyberspace. It was precipitated by the removal from a park in Tallinn of a bronze memorial to the Soviet soldiers of World War II. It was believed, but not proven, that the Russian government, or individual activists, had used DDoS attacks to bring down computers propagating the Web sites of the Estonian president, prime minister, and Parliament as well as of banks and newspapers. The attacks were finally brought under control with the help of experts from NATO, the European Union, the United States, Finland, Germany, Slovenia, and Israel. Details of many DoS and DDos attacks, and the recommended defenses are contained in Chapter 18 of this *Handbook*.

14.5.2   Malicious Code.

Malicious code includes viruses, worms, and Trojan horses, as described in Chapter 16. Mobile code, such as Java, ActiveX, and VBScript, was developed to increase the functionality of Web sites, but all three, as described in Chapter 17, also can be used maliciously.

There have been innumerable instances where malicious code has been used to damage or deface Web sites, both civilian and military. Apparently, all of these exploits have been perpetrated by single individuals or by very small groups of unaffiliated crackers. However, in the event of actual cyberwar, it seems certain that large groups of coordinated, technically knowledgeable attackers will attempt to wreak havoc on their opponents' infrastructures through the use of malicious code.

Just as U.S. military and governmental agencies, and most of their allies, are engaged in large-scale operations to develop defensive capabilities, it is essential that all commercial enterprises exert major efforts to do the same. Initiatives have begun to form close working relationships between government and the private sector. Also, industry groups have begun advocating relaxation of those laws that prohibit close cooperation between competitors. This will be necessary before information can be shared as required to strengthen the infrastructure. Similarly, groups are requesting that shared information be protected from those who would use the Freedom of Information Act to force disclosure.

Every prudent organization will support these initiatives and will work with appropriate government agencies and industry groups to ensure its own survival and the welfare of the country itself.

14.5.3 Cryptography.   Military operations, since the earliest recorded times, have utilized cryptography to prevent critical information from falling into enemy hands. Today, information is a vastly more important resource than ever before, and the need for cryptography has increased almost beyond measure. Not only the military, but indeed every financial institution, every competitive commercial enterprise, and even many individuals feel impelled to safeguard their own vital information. At the same time, access to the secret information of enemies and opponents would provide inestimable advantages.

Recognizing this, powerful supercomputers, directed by mathematicians, theoretical scientists, and cryptographers, are being applied to improving the processes of encryption and decryption. The most notable achievement in the recent past was the British construction of a computerized device to break the German Enigma code. The information thus obtained has been widely credited with a significant role in the outcome of World War II.

The development of effective mechanisms for spreading computations over millions of personal computers has greatly reduced the time required for brute force cracking of specific encrypted messages; for example, messages encrypted using the 56-bit Digital Encryption Standard (DES) were decrypted in four months using 10,000 computers in 1997, 56 hours using 1,500 special-purpose processors in 1998, and 22 hours using 100,000 processors in 1999.[29]

A major issue, yet to be resolved, is the strength of cryptographic tools that may be sold domestically or exported overseas. The contending forces include producers of cryptographic tools who believe that if the strength of their product is in any way restricted, they will lose their markets to producers in other countries with more liberal policies. Similarly, proponents of privacy rights believe that unbreakable cryptographic tools should be freely available.

The countervailing view is that virtually unbreakable cryptographic tools shipped overseas will inevitably find their way into the hands of unfriendly governments, which may use them in conducting cyberwars against us. Domestically, law enforcement agencies believe that they should have "back-door" entry into all cryptographic algorithms, so that they may prevent crimes as wide-ranging as embezzlement, drug trafficking, and terrorism.

As domestic crimes and terrorist attacks grow in number and intensity, it seems certain that at least a few civil liberties, including privacy rights, may be infringed. The hope is that an optimum balance will be struck between the need for security and the core values of our democracy.

For more on privacy in cyberspace, see Chapter 69 in this *Handbook.*

14.5.4 Psychological Operations.   Psychological operations (PSYOP) may be defined as planned psychological activities directed to enemy, friendly, and neutral audiences in order to influence their emotions, motives, attitudes, objective reasoning, and behaviors in ways favorable to the originator. The target audiences include governments, organizations, groups, and individuals, both military and civilian.

One of the most potent weapons in information warfare, PSYOP attempts to:

- Reduce morale and combat efficiency within the enemy's ranks
- Promote mass dissension within, and defections from, enemy combat units and/or revolutionary cadres
- Support our own and allied forces cover and deception operations
- Promote cooperation, unity, and morale within one's own and allied units, as well as within friendly resistance forces behind enemy lines[30]

The information that accomplishes these ends is conveyed via any media: by printed material such as pamphlets, posters, newspapers, books, and magazines, and by radio, television, personal contact, public address systems, and of increasing importance, through the Internet.

A classic example of successful PSYOP application was the deception practiced prior to the Allied invasion of the European mainland. Through clever "leaks," false information reached Germany that General Patton, America's most celebrated combat commander, was to lead an army group across the English Channel at Pas de Calais. As a consequence, German defensive forces were concentrated in that area. For weeks after the Normandy invasion was mounted, Hitler was convinced that it was just a feint, and he refused to permit the forces at Calais to be redeployed. Had this PSYOP failed, and had more of Germany's defensive forces been concentrated in Normandy, the Allied landing forces might well have been thrown back into the sea.

Although generally considered not to involve a PSYOP action, the September 11 attacks and the subsequent spread of anthrax spores made clear that a physical action can have the greatest and most far-reaching psychological effects. Beyond mourning the death of almost 3,000 innocent civilians, the new sense of vulnerability, and powerlessness caused great psychological trauma, throughout the nation and much of the western world. The full consequences to the travel, entertainment, and hospitality industries, as well as to every segment of the world economy, are likely to be both disastrous and long-lasting.

A major, integrated, expert PSYOP mission to restore morale and encourage behavior can halt or reverse a downward spiral, but worldwide recessions and acts of nature, such as cyclones, hurricanes, and earthquakes, can do more than PSYOP actions to demoralize a nation.

14.5.5 Physical Attacks.   Prior to September 11, 2001, physical attacks, as a part of cyberwar, were generally considered in the same light as attacks against any military objective, and defensive measures were instituted accordingly. In the civilian sector, starting with student attacks against academic computers in the 1960s and 1970s, there have been occasional reported physical attacks against information processing resources. Although access controls have been almost universally in place, their enforcement often has been less than strict.

Another indication of the susceptibility of the information infrastructure to physical attack is the prevalence of "backhoe attacks" in which construction crews accidentally slice through high-capacity optic cables used for telecommunications and as part of the Internet backbones.[31] The signs indicating where not to dig can serve as markers for those targeting single points of failure.

A related vulnerability is undersea telecommunications cables, which are unprotected against accidental—or deliberate—damage from ship anchors and from other objects or tools. Breaks in these cables can interrupt the Internet and telephone networks on a global scale.[32]

The destruction of the WTC and a portion of the Pentagon have brought the possibility of additional physical attacks very much into the forefront of cyberwar thinking, for both the military and the civilian infrastructures. Car bombings and packaged bombs had become almost commonplace, especially in the Mideast. Successful attacks had been launched against U.S. embassies and troop barracks, as well as against Israel, England, Spain, and France. To guard against such actions, perimeter defenses were widened, and in some areas personal searches at strategic points were instituted.

These defenses have proven to be of limited value, and suicide bombers seem to be increasing in numbers and in the effectiveness of their weapons. The use of commercial aircraft, fully loaded with fuel, as manned, guided missiles was apparently never considered prior to 11 September. After that date, there has been widespread recognition that protective measures must be taken that will prevent a recurrence of those tragic events. Airport security has become a direct federal responsibility, under a new Transportation Security Administration in the Department of Transportation. On November 11, 2001, President Bush signed a bill that requires all airport baggage screeners to be U.S. citizens and to undergo criminal background checks, before becoming federal employees. At many airports, security is provided by private contractors. The protective measures in common use are considered to be pointless, inconvenient, and ineffective by many travelers. Although even minimal safeguards against known weapons are being debated, there appears to be little thinking directed toward other types of attacks that might even now be in the planning stage.

14.5.6 Biological and Chemical Weapons and Weapons of Mass Destruction. Although the use of these weapons can affect every element of society, they have a particular potency in destroying the infrastructure of a targeted nation. The WTC attacks have had long-lasting psychological effects, but the results of the anthrax dissemination may be even more deeply traumatic. Already, the presence of anthrax spores has interfered with the functioning of the Congress, the Supreme Court, the U.S. Postal Service, hospitals, and other institutions. Although the furor over these attacks, as well as their incidence, has dissipated, there may be even more such attacks in the future. Unless any future culprit is apprehended quickly, and countermeasures taken immediately, damage to the infrastructure could be extensive.

14.5.7 Weapons Inadvertently Provided. There are many widespread vulnerabilities to computer systems that are not created as weapons, but whose presence makes the targets of cyberwar highly vulnerable. Poor software designs and inadequate quality control create opportunities for attackers to damage or destroy information, and the information systems themselves. Chapters 38 to 40 of this *Handbook* are especially useful in identifying and eliminating these sources of security vulnerabilities.

14.6 DEFENSES. A variety of defenses may be employed both to prevent attacks and to mitigate their effects. Because each of these defenses may have only limited utility, it is evident that new and more effective defenses must be developed.

14.6.1 Legal Defenses. As a defense against IW attacks or as a framework for apprehending and prosecuting attackers, the international legal system has been generally ineffective. The reasons for this include:

- Information warfare is not prohibited under the United Nations (UN) Charter, unless it directly results in death or property damage.
- Laws that are not recognized and enforced lose their power to compel actions.
- There is little or no police power to enforce those few laws that do exist.
- The issue of sovereignty as it relates to transborder communications is unresolved.
- Neither the United States nor any other major power has pressed for international laws to govern information warfare. This may be attributed to the fact that

such laws, while desirable for defense, would impair the nation's own offensive operations.

- Many nations do not recognize cyberwar attacks as criminal actions.
- In many lands, political considerations determine judicial outcomes.
- Few countries support extradition of their citizens even when indicted for terrorist or criminal activities.
- Terrorists, drug cartels, the international mafia, and even individual hackers have every reason to circumvent the law, and usually possess the resources that enable them to do so.
- Identifying attackers may be difficult or even impossible.
- New technologies arrive at a rate much faster than appropriate legislation.

Further acting to constrain law as a deterrent is the fact that there has been no universal acceptance of definitions for IW-relevant terminology: Attacks, acts of war, aggression, hostilities, combatants, crimes, criminals—all remain vague concepts. Until such terms, as applied to IW, are clearly defined, there can be no legal strictures against them.

The difference between acceptable and unacceptable targets is obscured by the dual-use, civilian and military, characteristics of infosystems and infrastructures. Similarly, it is difficult to condemn denial of service, when peacetime boycotts and economic sanctions are widely applied to further economic or political ends.

Clearly, legal defenses against cyberwar are inadequate at this time. Whether the United States will pursue effective international legislation remains doubtful, until the question of building adequate defenses, without hobbling offensive operations, is resolved.

14.6.2 Forceful Defenses. If IW attacks are accepted as acts of war, the use of retaliatory military force would be highly likely. The strategic and tactical decisions that would follow are well beyond the scope of this chapter, but six considerations are relevant.

1. The United States is growing reluctant to engage in combat without the sanction of the United Nations and without the concurrence of major allies. If the provocation is limited to an IW attack, it may be difficult to build a coalition or even to avoid UN condemnation.
2. The identity of the attacker may be unclear. Even after the September 11 attacks, the United States had no enemy that admitted culpability. As a consequence, the United States could not declare war on any nation or state but could only declare a war on "terrorism."
3. The attacker may be misidentified. Through the use of "spoofing" and routing an attack through unaware nations, the anonymous culprit may escape detection, while blame falls on an innocent victim.
4. There may be difficulty in determining whether a particular event is an act of information warfare or simply the result of errors, accidents, or malfunctions.
5. The attackers may not be a foreign government, against whom war can be declared, but a criminal organization, a disaffected group, activists, commercial competitors, or even individuals bent on mischief.

x

6. The United Nations, and international sentiment in general, requires that military force only be used in response to armed attack and, further, that the response be proportional to the attack that provoked it.

In light of these considerations, it seems unlikely that information warfare, unless it results in catastrophic injuries and deaths, will be met by a forceful reaction.

14.6.3 Technical Defenses.   The technical defenses against IW are many and varied. Almost the entire contents of this volume are applicable to safeguarding against cyberwar attacks. These same measures can prove equally effective in defending against IW, criminals, activists, competitors, and hackers.

14.6.4 In-Kind Counterattacks.   A cyberwar defense that has been used often is an in-kind counterattack, where flaming is met by flaming, DDoS by DDoS, site defacement by site defacement, and propaganda by propaganda. Recent examples include exchanges between Israelis and Arabs, Kashmiris and Indians, Serbs and Albanians, Indians and Pakistanis, Taiwanese and Chinese, and Chinese and Americans.

Although there may be personal satisfaction in originating or responding to such attacks, the net effect is usually a draw, and, therefore, in-kind attacks generally have been short-lived. In the future, such attacks may no longer be the output of only a few individuals, but may be mounted by large numbers of similarly minded cyberwarriors, organized into coordinated groups, with sophisticated tools and with covert or overt state sponsorship.

In that event, the asymmetric nature of the adversaries' infrastructures would be telling. Clearly, if the Taliban, for example, were to mount another full-scale cyber-terrorist attack against the United States, with the help of their supporters throughout the world, the effects could be devastating. Although the United States might mount a highly sophisticated in-kind response, it probably would have no effect on the Taliban's organization, its economy, its military effectiveness, or its ability to carry out suicide missions, biological warfare, or other physical attacks. A great and powerful nation may lack the ability to destroy a small, primitive, almost nonexistent infrastructure.

14.6.5 Cooperative Efforts.   Although the United States has been moderately successful in building coalitions in support of military operations, it has shown little inclination to build an international consensus dealing with information warfare. This may be so because of the legal difficulties outlined in Section 14.6.1 or because any prohibitions against offensive cyberwar will limit United States options. Nevertheless, whether by treaty, convention, agreement, or UN directive, technical people, diplomats, and statesmen of all well-intentioned countries should work together to define unacceptable and harmful actions and to devise means for detecting, identifying, and punishing those who transgress.

14.6.6 Summary.   The potential for information warfare to damage or destroy the infrastructure of any nation, any corporation, or, in fact, any civilian, governmental, or military entity is unquestionable. Until now, the only incidents have been isolated and sporadic, but the possibility of sustained, coordinated, simultaneous attacks is strong. If these attacks are combined with physical, chemical, or biological warfare, the effects are certain to be devastating.

Although the types of potential attackers, and the probable weapons they will use, are well known, the available defenses do not at this time offer any great assurance that they will be effective. The United States and many of its allies are engaged in great efforts to remedy this situation, but formidable obstacles are yet to be overcome. The military is generally better prepared than the civilian sector, but much of the military's infrastructure is woven into and dependent on transportation, communications, utilities, food production and distribution, and other vital necessities that are owned by private enterprises.

Recent terrorist attacks and the probability of future offensives should serve as an immediate impetus to devote whatever resources are needed to combat the threats to our way of life and, in fact, to our very existence.

14.7   FURTHER READING

Armistead, E. L. *Information Operations: Warfare and the Hard Reality of Soft Power.* Dulles, VA: Potomac Books, 2004.

Armistead, E. L. *Information Warfare: Separating Hype from Reality.* Dulles, VA: Potomac Books, 2007.

Arquilla, J., and D. Ronfeldt, eds. In *Athena's Camp: Preparing for Conflict in the Information Age.* Washington, DC: RAND Corporation, 1997. Available free in parts as PDF files from http://rand.org/pubs/monograph_reports/MR880/.

Campen, A. D., and D. H. Dearth, eds. *Cyberwar 3.0: Human Factors in Information Operations and Future Conflict.* Fairfax, VA: AFCEA International Press, 2000.

Cohen, F. *World War 3: We Are Losing It and Most of Us Didn't Even Know We Were Fighting in It—Information Warfare Basics.* Livermore, CA: Fred Cohen & Associates, 2006.

Denning, D. E. *Information Warfare and Security.* Reading, MA: Addison-Wesley, 1998.

Erbschloe, M., and J. Vacca. *Information Warfare.* New York: McGraw-Hill, 2001.

Gollman, D. *Computer Security.* New York: John Wiley & Sons, 1999.

Greenberg, L., S. E. Goodman, and K. J. Soo Hoo. *Information Warfare and International Law.* Washington, DC: National Defense University Press, 1998.

Henry, R., and C. E. Peartree, eds. *The Information Revolution and International Security.* Washington, DC: Center for Strategic and International Studies, 1998.

Kahn, D. *The Codebreakers.* New York: Scribner, 1996.

Lesser, I. O., B. Hoffman, J. Arquilla, D. Ronfeldt, and M. Zanini. *Countering the New Terrorism.* Santa Monica, CA: RAND Project Air Force, 1999. Available free in parts as PDF files from http://rand.org/pubs/monograph_reports/MR989/.

Macdonald, S. *Propaganda and Information Warfare in the Twenty-First Century: Altered Images and Deception Operations.* New York: Routledge, 2007.

Marsh, R. T., chair. *Critical Foundations: Protecting America's Infrastructures. The Report of the President's Commission on Critical Infrastructure Protection*, 1997; www.ihs.gov/misc/links_gateway/download.cfm?doc_id=327&app_dir_id=4&doc_file=PCCIP_Report.pdf or http://tinyurl.com/6x9aq5.

Parker, D. *Fighting Computer Crime: A New Framework for Protecting Information.* New York: John Wiley & Sons, 1998.

Price, A., and C. A. Horner *War in the Fourth Dimension: U.S. Electronic Warfare, from the Vietnam War to the Present.* London, UK: Greenhill Books/Lionel Leventhal, 2001.

Rattray, G. J. *Strategic Warfare in Cyberspace.* Cambridge, MA: MIT Press, 2001.

Schwartau, W. *Information Warfare: Chaos on the Electronic Superhighway*, 2nd ed. New York: Thunder's Mouth Press/Perseus Publishing Group, 1996.

Zalmay, K., and J. P. White, eds. *Strategic Appraisal: The Changing Role of Information in Warfare.* New York: McGraw-Hill, 1999.

14.8 NOTES

1. W. J. Clinton, "Critical Infrastructure Protection." Presidential Decision Directive 63, May 22, 1998; www.fas.org/irp/offdocs/pdd/pdd-63.htm.

2. J. L. Brock, "Critical Infrastructure Protection: Fundamental Improvements Needed to Assure Security of Federal Operations." GAO/T-AIMD-00-7. Testimony before the Subcommittee on Technology, Terrorism and Government Information, Committee on the Judiciary, U.S. Senate, October 6, 1999; www.gao.gov/archive/2000/ai00007t.pdf.

3. L. Wright, "Protecting the Homeland: Report of the Defense Science Board Task Force on Defensive Information Operations 2000 Summer Study, Vol. II." Office of the Undersecretary of Defense for Acquisition, Technology, and Logistics (March 2001); www.acq.osd.mil/dsb/reports/dio.pdf.

4. T. P. M. Barnett, "The Seven Deadly Sins of Network-Centric Warfare," *United States Naval Institute Proceedings* 125, No. 1 (January 1999): 36–39; www.milnet.com/milnet/infowar/usni-7-sins.htm.

5. G. G. Gilmore, "Navy-Marine Corps Intranet Girds for Cyber-Attacks," Armed Forces Press Service, July 6, 2001; www.defenselink.mil/news/ newsarticle. aspx?id=44745.

6. Joint Chiefs of Staff, "Joint Doctrine for Information Operations." Joint Publication 3-13, 2006; www.dtic.mil/doctrine/jel/new_pubs/jp3_13.pdf.

7. W. S. Cohen, *Annual Report to the President and the Congress: Secretary of Defense, 2001*; www.dod.mil/execsec/adr2001/index.html, Chapter 8: "Information Superiority and Space," www.dod.mil/execsec/adr2001/Chapter08.pdf.

8. See: www.calvin-coolidge.org/html/b.html.

9. S. M. Parker, "Information and Finance: A Strategic Target," 1997. CommSec. P. http://all.net/books/iw/iwarstuff/www.commsec.com/security/infowarfare.htm

10. Federal Reserve Board, "Fedwire Funds Transfer System: Assessment of Compliance with the Core Principles for Systematically Important Payment Systems," revised December 2006, p. 9; www.federalreserve.gov/paymentsystems/coreprinciples/coreprinciples.pdf.

11. Clearing House Interbank Payments System, www.chips.org.

12. SWIFT Annual Report, 2007; www.swift.com/index.cfm?item_id=67110

13. Numbers 13:16, 17.

14. Public Law 104-294, "Economic Espionage Act of 1996"; www4.law.cornell. edu/usc-cgi/get_external.cgi?type=pubL&target=104-294 or http://tinyurl.com/6fpl9c.

15. "Counterintelligence: What Are We Protecting?" Defense Security Service, 1998; www.dss.mil/portal/ShowBinary/BEA%20Repository/new_dss_internet/isp/count_intell/what_protecting.html or http://tinyurl.com/5fwafb.

16. T. L. Thomas, "Like Adding Wings to the Tiger: Chinese Information War Theory and Practice," Foreign Military Studies Office, Fort Leavenworth, KS, 2000; www.iwar.org.uk/iwar/resources/china/iw/chinaiw.htm.

17. B. Gertz, "Hackers Linked to China Stole Documents from Los Alamos," *Washington Times,* August 3, 2000, p. 1.

18. Shen Weiguang, "Checking Information Warfare Epoch Mission of Intellectual Military," *Jiefangjun Bao,* February 2, 1999, p. 6, as translated and downloaded from the Foreign Broadcast Information System (FBIS) Web site on February 17, 1999; www.opensource.gov (registration restricted to U.S. federal, state and local government employees and contractors).

19. Wei Jencheng, "New Form of People's Warfare," *Jiefangjun Bao,* June 11, 1996, p. 6, as translated and reported in FBIS-CHI-96-159, August 16, 1996.

20. Shen Weiguang (1995). "Focus of Contemporary World Military Revolution— Introduction to Research in IW," *Jiefangjun Bao* (November 7, 1995) p. 6, as translated and reported in FBIS-CHI-95-239, December 13, 1995, pp. 22–27.

21. *Qianjin Bao,* December 10, 1999, provided by William Belk via e-mail to Timothy L. Thomas. According to Mr. Thomas, Mr. Belk is the head of a skilled U.S. reservist group that studies China.

22. Quotation from S. H. Verstappen, *The Thirty-Six Strategies of Ancient China* (Books and Periodicals, 2000). As described at www.chinastrategies.com/ home36.htm.

23. Zhang Zhenzhong and Chang Jianguo, "Train Talented People at Different Levels for Information Warfare," *Jiefangjun Bao,* February 2, 1999, as translated and downloaded from FBIS Web site on February 10, 1999.

24. A. D. Sofaer et al., "A Proposal for an International Convention on Cyber Crime and Terrorism," 2000; www.iwar.org.uk/law/resources/cybercrime/stanford/cisac-draft.htm.

25. G. W. Bush, Executive Order Establishing Office of Homeland Security, 2001; www.whitehouse.gov/news/releases/2001/10/20011008-2.html.

26. U.S. Department of Homeland Security, "The Secretary's Five Goals," 2008; www.dhs.gov/xabout/gc_1207339653379.shtm.

27. M. Chertoff, "Remarks by Secretary Michael Chertoff and President of the Supreme Court of Israel Dorit Beinisch to the Heritage Foundation's Civil Rights and the War on Terror: Dilemmas and Challenges Event," April 30, 2008; www.dhs.gov/xnews/speeches/sp_1209741455799.shtm.

28. B. I. Koerner, "To Heck with Hactivism: Do Politically Motivated Hackers Really Think They're Promoting Global Change by Defacing Web sites?" Salon.com, July 20, 2000; http://archive.salon.com/tech/feature/2000/07/20/hacktivism/

29. M. Curtin and J. Dolske "A Brute-Force Search of DES Keyspace," 1998; www.interhack.net/pubs/des-key-crack/; "Cracking DES: Secrets of Encryption Research, Wiretap Politics & Chip Design—How Federal Agencies Subvert Privacy: Frequently Asked Questions (FAQ) About the Electronic Frontier Foundation's "DES Cracker" Machine," Electronic Frontier Foundation, 1998; http://w2. eff.org/Privacy/Crypto/Crypto_misc/DESCracker/19980716_eff_des.faq or http:// tinyurl.com/68thws; and "RSA Code-Breaking Contest Again Won by Distributed.Net and Electronic Frontier Foundation (EFF): DES Challenge III Broken in Record 22 Hours," Electronic Frontier Foundation, 1999; http://w2.eff.org/ Privacy/Crypto/Crypto_misc/DESCracker/HTML/19990119_deschallenge3.html or http://tinyurl.com/5n3gqf.

30. E. Rouse, "Psychological Operations/Warfare," date unknown; www.psywarrior. com/psyhist.html.

31. K. Poulson, "The Backhoe: A Real Cyberthreat," *WIRED*, January 19, 2006; www.wired.com/science/discoveries/news/2006/01/70040; also CGA "CGA DIRT Analysis and Recommendations for Calendar Year 2005," Common Ground Alliance Damage Information Reporting Tool, 2005; www.commonground alliance.com/TemplateRedirect.cfm?Template=/ContentManagement/ContentDis play.cfm&ContentFileID=3269 or http://tinyurl.com/43obmo.

32. K. Kratovac, "Ship's Anchor Caused Cut in Internet Cable: Unusual Cuts Led to Disruptions in Services, Slowed Down Businesses," MSNBC Technology and Science/Internet, February 8, 2008; www.msnbc.msn.com/id/23068571/.

CHAPTER 15

PENETRATING COMPUTER SYSTEMS AND NETWORKS

Chey Cobb, Stephen Cobb, and M. E. Kabay

15.1 MULTIPLE FACTORS INVOLVED IN SYSTEM PENETRATION. Although penetrating computer systems and networks may sound like a technical challenge, most information security professionals are aware that systems security has both technical and nontechnical aspects. Both aspects come into play when people attempt to penetrate systems. Both aspects are addressed in this chapter, which is not a handbook on how to penetrate systems but rather a review of the methods and means by which systems penetrations are accomplished.

15.1.1 System Security: More than a Technical Issue. The primary nontechnical factor in system security and resistance to system penetration is human behavior, which can defeat just about any technical security measure. More than any-thing else, security depends on human beings to understand and carry out security procedures. Consequently, information system (IS) security must be integral to the cul-ture of any organization employing an information system. Without security, systems and networks will not be able resist attempts at penetration.

Often security is represented as a structure of concentric circles. Protection of the central, secured element is then dependent on the barriers imposed by each successive ring. These barriers can be physical or figurative, but the goal of IS security is to protect the integrity, confidentiality, and availability of information processed by the system. This goal is reached using identification, authentication, and authorization. *Identification* is a prerequisite, with each user required to proffer an identifier (ID) that is included in the authorization lists of the system to be accessed. *Authentication* consists of proving that the user really is the person to whom the ID has been assigned. *Authorization* consists of defining what a specific user ID, running specified programs, can legally do on the system. The security perimeter can be penetrated by compromising any of these functions. Chapters 28 and 29 in this *Handbook* discuss identification and authentication in detail.

The trend toward distributed and mobile computers, often utilizing the global net-working capability of the Internet, makes it hard to know where to draw these concentric circles of protection. Indeed, the barriers to penetration need to be extended along lines of communication, encompassing end points of the network, which may be geograph-ically dispersed.

15.1.2 Organizational Culture.   An organization's general attitude toward security is the key to an effective defense against attack. Security is difficult to sell, especially to an organization that has never experienced a significant problem. (Iron-ically, the better the defenses, the less evidence there is of their utility.) A basic principle of security is that practitioners must act as if they are paranoid, continu-ously on guard against attacks from any direction. Many organizations view security precautions as an attack on the integrity of employees. Wearing badges, for example, sometimes is viewed as dehumanizing and offensive. This attitude leads to absurdities, such as having only visitors wear badges. If only visitors wear badges, then taking off the badge automatically reduces the likelihood that a dishonest intruder will be challenged.

Some individual employees also consider security precautions as personally of-fensive. For example, locking a terminal or workstation when leaving it for a few minutes may be seen as evidence of distrust of other employees. Refusing to allow piggybacking—that is, permitting several colleagues to enter a restricted area on one access card—may be seen as insufferably rude. Where employees are taught to be open and collegial, securing removable computer media and paperwork at night can seem insulting.

These conflicts occur because years of socialization, starting in infancy, are diamet-rically opposed to the tenets of information security. Politeness in a social context is a disaster in a secure area; for instance, piggybacking into a computer room impairs the accuracy of audit trails kept by the access-control computers. Lending someone a car is kind and generous, but lending someone a user ID and a personal password is a gross violation of responsibility. Chapters 49 and 50 in this *Handbook* discuss psychological aspects of changing corporate culture to support information security.

Carrying out effective security policies and procedures must resolve these conflicts between normal standards of politeness and the standards required in a secure envi-ronment. Organizations must foster open discussion of the appropriateness of security procedures, so that employees can voluntarily create a corporate culture conducive to protection of corporate information. Chapters 44, 45, 48, and 51 in this *Handbook* specifically discuss policy issues.

Beyond this, organizations need to be aware of the security posture and attitudes of those with whom they network. These days it is quite possible for one organization's system to be operated, or even owned, by another. And people from many different organizations may be using the same network. A culture of security must permeate all of the organizations that have access to a system, otherwise points of weakness will exist, thus increasing the probability that attempts to penetrate the system will succeed.

15.1.3 Chapter Organization.   Section 15.2 looks at methods of tricking people into allowing unauthorized access to systems. Section 15.3 examines technical measures for overcoming security barriers and specific techniques (*exploits*) for penetration, while Section 15.4 describes legal and political aspects of system penetration.

15.2 NONTECHNICAL PENETRATION TECHNIQUES.   Although the penetration of information systems is often portrayed as the work of the technically adept, many successful penetrations have relied on human factors, such as gullibility and venality. Both are exploited by would-be system penetrators.

15.2.1 Misrepresentation (Social Engineering).   Social engineering relies on falsehood. Lies, bribes, and seduction can trick honest or marginally dishonest employees into facilitating a penetration. An attacker might trick an employee into revealing login and authentication codes or even into granting physical access to an otherwise secure site. System penetration can then be accomplished by numerous means, from walking up to an unsecured workstation, to installing Trojan code or a network packet-sniffing device. (Both of these technologies are discussed in more detail later in this chapter.)

15.2.1.1 Lying.   Telling lies is a technique often used by persons intent on obtaining unauthorized access to a system. One can obtain valuable information about a system and its defenses by telling lies. Many lies work by playing on the natural human tendency to interpret the world by our internal model of what is most likely. Social psychologists call this model the *schema*. Well-dressed businesspeople who walk briskly and talk assertively are probably what they seem. In a phone conversation, a person who sounds exasperated, impatient, and rude when demanding a new password is probably an exasperated, impatient, and rude employee who has forgotten a password. Unfortunately, many criminals know, sometimes instinctively, how to exploit these interpretations to help get them into secured systems.

Another technique, often used in concert with lying, is to escape notice and avoid suspicion by simply blending in. The way we perceive, or fail to perceive, details is referred to by social psychologists as the figure-ground problem. The normal becomes the background, and the objects of our attention become figures standing out from the ground. The schema influences what is noticed; only deviations from expectation spark figure-ground discrimination. Criminal hackers take advantage of this effect by fading into the background while penetrating security perimeters.

15.2.1.2 Impersonating Authorized Personnel.   Criminal hackers and unscrupulous employees call security personnel, operators, programmers, and administrators to request user IDs, privileges, and even passwords. (This is one reason that the telephone is a poor medium for granting security privileges; if staff members were trained to refuse requests made over the phone, many attempts to penetrate systems could be thwarted.) In sites where employees wear ID badges, intruders have a hard time penetrating physical security by posing as employees. However, physical security in these cases depends on the cooperation of all authorized personnel to challenge everyone who fails to wear a badge. This policy is critically important at entry points. To penetrate such sites physically, criminals must steal or forge badges or work with confederates to obtain real but unauthorized badges.

Sites where physical security includes physical tokens, such as cards for electronic access control, are harder for criminals to penetrate. They must obtain a real token, perhaps by theft or by collusion with an employee. Perimeter security depends on keeping the access codes up to date so that cards belonging to ex-employees are inactivated. Security staff must immediately inactivate all cards reported lost. In addition, it is essential that employees not permit *piggybacking,* the act of allowing another person, possibly unauthorized, to enter a restricted zone along with an authorized person. Too often, an employee, in an act of politeness, will permit others to enter a normally locked door as he or she exits. Once inside a building, criminals can steal valuable information that will allow later penetration of the computer systems from remote locations. This is often accomplished by impersonating third-party personnel.

Even if employees are willing to challenge visitors in business suits, it may not occur to them to interfere with people who look as if they are employees of an authorized support firm. For example, thieves often have succeeded in entering a secured zone by dressing like third-party computer technicians or office cleaners. Few employees will think of checking the credentials of a weary technician wearing grimy overalls, an authentic-looking company badge, a colorful ID card, and a tool belt. When a suitable-looking individual claims to have been called to run diagnostics on a workstation, many nontechnical employees will acquiesce at once, seizing the opportunity to grab a cup of coffee or to chat with colleagues. Minutes later, the thief may have copied sensitive files or installed a sniffing device (e.g., a keystroke recorder or a network packet sniffer). In one case known to one of the authors (MK), a criminal was given a workspace and a network connection in a large bank and allowed to work unmolested and unchallenged for several months on a "secret project." It was only when an alert security guard realized that no on one in the office knew who this person was that she challenged the intruder and broke the scam.

15.2.1.3 Intimidation. A technique related to impersonation of authorized or third-party personnel is intimidation. Someone claiming to be a person in a position of authority displays irritation or anger at delays in granting an unauthorized deviation from policy, such as communicating a password over the phone to a person of unauthenticated identity. The attackers indirectly or directly threaten alarming consequences (e.g., delays of critical repairs, financial losses, disciplinary actions) unless they are granted restricted information or access to secured equipment or facilities.

15.2.1.4 Subversion. People make moral choices constantly. There is always a conscious or unconscious balancing of alternatives. Criminal hackers try to reach their goals by changing the rules so that dishonesty becomes more acceptable to the victim than honesty.

15.2.1.5 Bribery. A lot of industrial and commercial information has a black market value. The same is true of personally identifiable information that can be used to commit fraud and identity theft. The price of a competitor's engineering plans or customer database may be a year's salary for a computer operator responsible for making backups. There is little likelihood that anyone would notice the subverted operator copying a backup at 3:00 A.M. or a secretary taking an extra compact disc out of the office. Many organizations have failed to install software to prevent a manager sending electronic mail with confidential files to a future employer.

That industrial espionage, with or without state sponsorship, is a thriving business is a fact that is now widely—and sometimes quite openly—acknowledged.[1] Building a corporate environment in which employees legitimately feel themselves to be part of a community is a bulwark against espionage. When respect and a sense of exchange for mutual benefits inform the corporate culture, employees will rebuff spies or even entrap them, but the disgruntled employee whose needs are not addressed is a potential enemy.

15.2.1.6 Seduction. Sometimes criminal hackers and spies have obtained confidential information, including access codes, by tricking employees into believing that they are loved. This lie works well enough to allow access to personal effects, sometimes after false passion or drugs have driven the victim into insensibility. It is not unknown for prostitutes to seduce men from organizations that they and their confederates are seeking to crack. Rifling through customers' wallets can often uncover telltale slips bearing user IDs and passwords.

No one can prevent all such abuse. People who are enthralled by expert manipulators will rarely suspect that they are being used as a wedge through a security perimeter. Along with a general increase in security consciousness, staff members with sensitive codes must become aware of these techniques so that they may be less vulnerable. Perhaps then they will automatically reject a request for confidential information or access codes.

15.2.1.7 Extortion. Criminals can threaten harm if their demands are not met. Threaten someone's family or hold a gun to their head and few will, or should, resist a demand for entry to a secured facility or for a login sequence into a network. Some physical access-control systems include a duress signal that can be used to trigger a silent alarm at the monitoring stations. The duress signal requires a predetermined, deliberate action on the part of the person being coerced into admitting unauthorized personnel. This action may be adding an extra number to the normal pass code, pressing the pound sign (#) twice after entering the code, or entering 4357 (H-E-L-P) into the keypad. The duress signal quietly notifies security that an employee is being forced to do something unwillingly. Security can then take appropriate action.

15.2.1.8 Blackmail. Blackmail is extortion based on the threat of revealing secrets. An employee may be entrapped into revealing confidential data, for example, using techniques just described. Classic blackmail includes seduction followed by pictures in flagrante delicto, which the criminals then threaten to reveal. Sometimes a person can be framed by fabricated evidence; a plausible but rigged image of venality can ruin a career as easily as truth. Healthy respect for individuals and social bonds among employees, supervisors, and management can make it difficult for blackmailers to succeed. If employees feel they can inform management when they are victims of a blackmail attempt, without suffering inappropriately negative consequences, the threat may be mitigated to a certain degree. Perhaps the last, best defense against blackmail is honesty. The exceptionally honest person will reject opportunities that lead to blackmail and laugh at fabrications, trusting friends and colleagues to recognize lies when they hear them.

15.2.1.9 Insiders. Many of the world's largest and most daring robberies have, upon examination, turned out to be inside jobs. The same is true of system penetrations. Although many of the just-described techniques can be used to obtain help from the inside, some are made possible by people on the inside who decide, for whatever reason, to aid and abet criminal hackers. For example, a dishonest employee may actively seek to sell access for personal gain. Organizations should try to be alert to this eventuality, but there is very little defense against thoroughly dishonest employees when the only overt act needed to open the gates from the inside is to pass system credentials to an outsider.

15.2.1.10 Human Target Range. Organizations should not underestimate the range of targets at which the described techniques may be directed. Although the terms "employees," "authorized personnel," and "third-party personnel" are used in the preceding paragraphs, the target range includes all manner of vendors, suppliers, and contractors as well as all levels of employees—from software and hardware vendors, through contract programmers, to soft drink vendors and cleaning staff. It may even include clients and customers, some of whom possess detailed knowledge of the organization's operations. These days employees at every level are likely to be computer literate, with varying degrees of skill. For example, it is quite possible that someone working as a janitor today knows how to operate a computer and may even know how to surf hacking sites on the Web and download penetration tools.

In short, anyone who comes into contact with the organization has the potential to provide an attacker with information useful in the preparation and execution of an attack. The human targets of a social engineering attack may not, on an individual basis, possess or divulge critical information, but each may provide clues—pieces of the puzzle, as it were—an aggregation of which can lead to successful penetration and compromise of valuable data and resources. In fact, use of this process is a hallmark of some of the most successful criminal hackers. The term "incremental information leveraging" was coined for this use of less valuable data to obtain more valuable data.[2]

15.2.2 Incremental Information Leveraging. By gathering and shrewdly utilizing small and seemingly insignificant pieces of information, it is possible to gain access to much more valuable information. This technique of incremental information leveraging is a favorite tool of hackers, both criminal and noncriminal. One important benefit of the tool that is particularly appreciated by criminal hackers is the low profile it presents to most forms of detection. By accumulating seemingly innocuous pieces of information over a period of time, and by making intelligent deductions from them, it is possible to penetrate systems to the highest level.

A prime example of this approach is seen in the exploits of Kevin Mitnick, who served almost five years behind bars for breaking into computers, stealing data, and abusing electronic communication systems. Illegal acts committed by Mitnick include the 1981 penetration of Computer System for Mainframe Operations (COSMOS), a Pacific Bell facility in downtown Los Angeles. COSMOS was a centralized database used by many U.S. phone companies for controlling basic record-keeping functions. Mitnick and others talked their way past a security guard and located the COSMOS computer room. They stole lists of computer passwords, operating manuals for the COSMOS system, and combinations to the door locks on nine Pacific Bell central offices. Mitnick later employed knowledge of phone systems and phone company operations to penetrate systems at Digital Equipment Corp. (DEC).

Since his release in January 2000, Mitnick has spoken about information security before Congress and at other public venues. He described social engineering as such a powerful tool that he "rarely had to resort to a technical attack."[3] As to technique, he stated, "I used to do a lot of improvising. . .I would try to learn their internal lingo and tidbits of information that only an employee would know." In other words, by building up knowledge of the target, using a lot of information that is neither protected nor proprietary, it is possible to gain access to that which is both proprietary and protected. The power of incremental information leveraging is the equivalent of converting a foot in the door into an invitation to come inside.

Protection against incremental information leveraging, and all other aspects of social engineering, begins with employee awareness. Employees who maintain a healthy skepticism toward any and all requests for information provide a strong line of defense. Another powerful defense mechanism, highlighted by Mitnick, is the use of telephone recording messages, such as "This message may be monitored or recorded for training purposes and quality assurance." An attacker who hears a message like this may think twice about proceeding with attempts to use voice calls to social engineer information from the target.

15.3 TECHNICAL PENETRATION TECHNIQUES.

Technical penetration attacks may build on data obtained from social engineering, or they may be executed on a purely technical basis. Techniques used include eavesdropping, either by listening in on conversations or by trapping data during transmissions, and breaches of access controls (e.g., trying all possible passwords for a user ID or guessing at passwords). Weaknesses in the design and implementation of information systems, such as program bugs and lack of input validation, also may be exploited in technical attacks. Unfortunately, weaknesses of this nature abound in the realm of the Internet, even as more and more organizations increase their Internet connectivity, thus creating more and more potential penetration points.

15.3.1 Data Leakage: A Fundamental Problem.

Unfortunately, for information security (INFOSEC) specialists, it is impossible, even in theory, to prevent the unauthorized flow of information from a secured region into an unsecured region. The imperceptible transfer of data without authorization is known as *data leakage*. Technical means alone cannot suppress data leakage.

Consider a tightly secured operating system or security monitor that prevents confidential data from being copied into unsecured files. Workstations are diskless, there are no printers, employees do not take disks into or out of the secured facility, and there are strict restrictions on taking printouts out of the building. These mechanisms should suffice to prevent data leakage.

Not really.

Anyone with a penchant for mnemonics or with a photographic memory could simply remember information and write it down after leaving the facility. And it is extremely difficult to prevent employees from writing notes on paper and concealing them in their clothing or personal possessions when they leave work. Unless employees are strip-searched, no guard can stop people with crib sheets full of confidential data from walking out of the building. Indeed, this is how Vasili Mitrokhin, head archivist of the KGB's First Chief Directorate, perpetrated the largest breach of KGB security

EXHIBIT 15.1 Steganography Software Can Conceal Text in Images

ever, by smuggling thousands of handwritten copies of secret documents out of the KGB headquarters in Moscow in his shoes, socks, and other garments.[4]

Another means of data leakage is steganography, hiding valuable information in plain sight among large quantities of unexceptional information. For example, a corrupt employee determined to send a confederate information about a chemical formula could encode text as numerical equivalents and print these values as, say, the fourth and fifth digits of a set of engineering figures. No one is likely to notice that these numbers contained anything special. The more digitally inclined can use steganography software, freely available on the Internet, to hide data in image files. For example, the text of this paragraph was encoded into the photograph you see in Exhibit 15.1 using an online utility provided for free on the Web.

The unauthorized transfer of information cannot be absolutely prevented because information can be communicated by anything that can fluctuate. Theoretically, one could transfer data to a confederate by changing the position of a window shade (slow but possible). Or one could send ones and zeroes by the direction of oscillation of a tape reel; or one could send coded information by the choice of music. Even if a building were completely sealed, it would still leak heat outward or transfer heat inward—and *that* would be enough to carry information. In practical terms, system managers can best meet the problem of data leakage by a combination of technical protection and effective management strategies.

15.3.2 Intercepting Communications.   Criminal hackers and dishonest or disgruntled employees can glean access codes and other information useful to their system penetration efforts by monitoring communications. These might be between two workstations on a local area or wide area network, between a remote terminal and a host such as a mainframe, or between a client and a server on the Internet. Attackers can exploit various vulnerabilities of communications technologies. The shift to TCP/IP (transmission control protocol/Internet protocol)–based Internet communications over the last decade has brought many more communications streams into the target range of would-be penetrators.

15.3.2.1 Wiretapping. Wiretapping consists of intercepting the data stream on a communications channel (even if that channel is not wire; e.g., fiber optic cable can also be tapped, as can wireless communications, although the latter sometimes are said to be sniffed rather than tapped).

15.3.2.2 Asynchronous Connections. Point-to-point connections (e.g., using telephone modems or serial devices) are still widely used in some areas and are considered relatively easy to tap. Physical connection at any point on twisted pair or multiwire cables allows a monitor to display and record all information passing between a node and its host. Asynchronous lines in large installations often pass through patch panels, where taps may not be noticed by busy support staff, as they manage hundreds of legitimate connections. Such communications usually use phone lines for distances beyond a few hundred meters (or about 1,000 feet).

Wiretappers must use modems configured for the correct communications parameters including speed, parity, number of data bits, and number of stop bits, but these parameters are easy to find out by trial and error.

Countermeasures include:

- Physical shielding of cables and patch panels
- Multiplexing data streams on the same wires
- Encryption of data flowing between nodes and hosts

15.3.2.3 Synchronous Communications. Because synchronous modems are more complex than asynchronous models and because their bandwidths (maximum transmission speeds) are higher, they are less susceptible to attack, but they are not risk-free.

15.3.2.4 Dial-up Phone Lines. Used for both data and voice communications, dial-up lines supplied by local telephone companies and long-distance carriers are vulnerable to wiretapping. Law enforcement authorities and telephone company employees can install taps at central switching. Criminals can tap phone lines within a building at patch panels, within cabling manifolds running in dropped ceilings, below raised floors, or even in drywall. They also can tap at junction boxes where lines join the telephone company's external cables.

The same countermeasures apply to phone lines as to asynchronous or synchronous data communications cables.

15.3.2.5 Leased Lines. Leased lines use the same technology as dial-up (switched) lines, except that the phone company supplies a fixed sequence of connections rather than random switching from one central station to another. There is nothing inherently more secure about a leased line than a switched line; on the contrary, it is easier to tap a leased line at the central switching station because its path is fixed. However, leased lines usually carry high-volume transmissions. The higher the volume of multiplexed data, the more difficult it is for amateur hackers to disentangle the data streams and make sense of them. At the high end of leased line bandwidth (e.g., carriers such as T1, T2, etc.), the cost of multiplexing equipment makes interception prohibitively expensive for all but professional or government wiretappers.

Data encryption provides the best defense against wiretapping on leased lines.

15.3.2.6   Long-Distance Transmissions.   Dial-up and leased lines carry both short-haul and long-distance transmissions. The latter introduce additional points of vulnerability. Microwave relay towers carry much of the long-distance voice and data communications within a continent. The towers are spaced about 40 kilometers (25 miles) apart; signals spread out noticeably over such distances. Radio receivers at ground level can intercept the signals relayed through a nearby tower, and because microwaves travel in straight lines, rather than following the curvature of the earth, they eventually end up in space, where satellite receivers can collect them. The difficulty for the eavesdropper is that there may be thousands of such signals, including voice and data, at any tower. Sorting out the interesting ones is the challenge. However, given sufficient computing power, such sorting is possible, as is targeting of specific message streams. Spread-spectrum transmissions, or frequency hopping, is an effective countermeasure.

15.3.2.7   Packet-Switching Networks.   Packet-switching networks, including X.25 carriers such as Telenet, Tymnet, and Datapac, use packet assembler-disassemblers (PADs) to group data into packets addressed from a source to a destination. If data travel over ordinary phone lines to reach the network, interception can occur anywhere along these segments of the communications link. However, once the data have been broken up into packets (whether at the customer side or at the network side), wiretappers have a difficult time making sense of the data stream.

15.3.2.8   Internet Connections.   TCP/IP connections are no harder to tap than any others, and they carry an ever-increasing array of data, from e-commerce traffic to television broadcasts and voice communications, the latter using Voice over Internet Protocol (VoIP). (See Chapter 34 in this *Handbook*.) Unless the data stream is encrypted, there are no special impediments to wiretappers. Although the tapping of fiber optic cable requires more specialized equipment than the tapping of copper cables, it is possible.

15.3.2.9   LAN Packet Capture.   Local area networks (LANs) are similar to packet-switching networks: Both network protocols send information in discrete packages, either over cables or radio waves. Each package has a header containing the address of its sender and of its intended recipient. Packets are transmitted to all nodes on a segment of a LAN. Normally a node is restricted to interpreting only those packets that are intended for it alone. However, it is possible to place devices in "promiscuous mode," overriding this restriction. This can be done with software that surreptitiously converts a device, such as an end user workstation, into a listening device, capturing all packets that reach that node. Of course, network administrators can intentionally create a packet-capturing workstation for legitimate purposes, such as diagnosing network bottlenecks. It is also possible to connect specialized hardware called LAN monitors to the network, either with or without permission, for legitimate or illegitimate purposes. Sometimes called network sniffers, these devices and programs range from basic freeware to expensive commercial packages that can cost tens of thousands of dollars for a network with hundreds of nodes. (The term "Sniffer," although in common use, is a registered trademark of Network Associates Technology, Inc.).

The more sophisticated packet-sniffing programs allow the user to configure profiles for capture; for example, the operator can select packets passing between a host and a system manager's workstation. Such programs allow an observer to view and record everything seen and done on a workstation, including logins or encryption keys sent to a server.

Packet sniffing poses a serious threat to confidentiality of data transmissions through LANs. Most sniffing programs do not announce their presence on the network. Although it may not be apparent to the casual observer that a workstation is performing sniffing, it is possible, as a countermeasure, to scan the network for sniffing devices. Stealthier packet-sniffing technology is constantly improving, and tight physical security may be the best overall deterrence.

LAN users concerned about confidentiality should use LAN protocols that provide end-to-end encryption of the data stream or third-party products to encrypt sensitive files before they are sent through the LAN. Routers that isolate segments of a LAN or WAN (wide area network) can help limit exposure to the threat of sniffers.

15.3.2.10 Optical Fiber.
Although optical fibers were once thought to be secure against interception, new developments quickly abolished that hope. An attacker can strip an optical fiber of its outer casing and bend it into a hairpin with a radius of a few millimeters (1/8 inch); from the bend, enough light leaks out to duplicate the data stream. Luckily, most optical trunk cables carry hundreds or thousands of fibers, making it almost impossible to locate any specific communications channel. (The same is not true of fiber cables used to deliver network connectivity to individual homes and offices.) Equipment for converting optical signals into usable data remains quite costly, a fact that discourages its use by casual criminal hackers.

15.3.2.11 Wireless Communications.
Cable-based communications have the advantage of restricting channel access to at least theoretically visible connections. However, the rapid increase in wireless telecommunications in the last decade of the twentieth century and the first years of the twenty-first has routed increasing amounts of information through a broadcast medium in which access—even unauthorized access—may be invisible to users and system administrators.

15.3.2.12 Wireless Phones.
Also referred to as cordless phones, conventional wireless phones broadcast their signals, and the traffic they carry can be detected from a distance. Older cordless phones were analog and susceptible to eavesdropping from such basic devices as walkie-talkies and baby monitors. Children sometimes walked around their suburban neighborhoods with a handset from such a phone turned on; once they walked far enough away from their home to lose the signal, any new dial tone belonged to a neighbor, who might be puzzled to discover a call to the Antipodes on the next phone bill. Today's wireless phone models typically use a different set of frequencies, such as 2.4 gigahertz (GHz). These phones generally use frequency-hopping spread spectrum (FHSS) technology to make unauthorized use more difficult, and to impede eavesdropping. FHSS means the signals hop from frequency to frequency across the entire 2.4 GHz spectrum, making tapping their signals harder but by no means impossible. Wireless phones should not be used for confidential voice or data traffic unless encryption is enabled and activated. An added danger lies in hanging up a cordless phone during a conversation, since the cordless phone's base continues to transmit until switched off.

15.3.2.13 Cellular (Mobile) Phones and Modems.
Early analog cellular (mobile) phone systems had an expectation of privacy equivalent to that of shouting a message through a megaphone from a rooftop. Calls on such phones were easily

intercepted using scanners purchased from local electronics stores. Although encryption is possible on the newer digital cell phones that are now widely used, the encryption is not always turned on due to the burden it imposes on the cell company switching equipment. Check with the carrier before assuming that cell calls are encrypted. Also, bear in mind that, although digital cell phone calls are harder to intercept than analog ones, there is a thriving black market in devices that make such interception possible.

As a rule, confidential information should never be conveyed through cellular phones or modems without encrypting the line or the messages first.

15.3.2.14 Wireless Networks.
The increasingly popular means of networking computers to networks known as WiFi presents many opportunities for interception of communications. In this context, "wireless network" usually means a data network using the 802.11 standard, which comes is a variety of flavors, such as 802.11b, 802.11g (often collectively referred to as WiFi, which stands for "Wireless Fidelity" and is actually a brand name owned by the trade group WiFi Alliance). Typically, this is the sort of local area network created by plugging a wireless access point into an Ethernet network and a WiFi card or adapter into each computer. Most notebook computers now come with a built-in WiFi adapter.

These WLANs, or wireless local area networks, are relatively cheap and easy to create since they do not require network cabling. That helps to explain why more than 200 million WiFi devices were sold in 2006 and more than half of all U.S. companies have been using WLANs to some degree or other since 2002. But cheap WLANs come with hidden costs, namely security. Every WLAN operates, by its very nature, in loose-lips mode. In a sense, the ease of use comes with ease of abuse. They all broadcast their traffic into the air, whence it may be overheard by someone with the right set of ears, a legitimate user or a criminal hacker, someone looking for free bandwidth or a war driver. War driving, the practice of driving around town to find wireless access points, is a hobby to some people, and probably not illegal unless done with malicious intent—many notebook computers try to find wireless access points whenever turned on—but bear in mind that laws vary from one country to another. (Those contemplating war driving should check the legal status in their jurisdictions.)

To be a war driver, all that is needed is an old laptop, the right WiFi card, some free software (NetStumbler, e.g.), and an empty Pringles® potato-chip can wired to the WiFi card as an external antenna to boost reception. (The Pringles can is optional, as is a global positioning system device to mark the location of WiFi access points.) If you drive around with this equipment activated, you will doubtless discover numerous access points in both residential and business districts. If the names of the access points are things like "linksys" or "netgear," this is an indication that the owner of the network has not changed the default service set identifier (SSID), which tends to be the brand of the wireless access point, broadcast for the world to see, unless the network owner turns off this feature. The name could also be a person, or place, or company, which helps war drivers figure out whose network they are picking up. (One of the authors detected SCHS near the offices of Sample County Health Services.) A program like NetStumbler will also tell you whether the network is using encryption. There has been a steady rise in the percentage of wireless networks using encryption, but it is far less than 10 percent. According to a survey conducted by AT&T in late 2007, one in six small businesses in America that use wireless technology have taken no precautions against wireless threats, and one-third of small businesses indicated that they were unconcerned about wireless data security.[5]

There is more about wireless network security in Chapter 33 in this *Handbook,* but the point is the relative ease with which networks can be tapped. This means WiFi, whether at home, in the office, or at a hot spot, represents a significant category of data leakage and thus a major avenue for systems penetration.

15.3.2.15 Van Eck Freaking.   This attack is named for Wim Van Eck, a Dutch electronics researcher who in 1985 proved to a number of banks that it was possible to read information from their cathode ray tubes (CRTs) at distances of almost a mile away, using relatively simple technology. Because many types of electronic equipment emit radio-frequency signals, receivers that capture these signals can be used to reconstruct keystrokes, video displays, and print streams. Using simple, inexpensive wide-band receivers, criminals can detect and use such emissions at distances of tens or hundreds of meters (yards).

Since radio-frequency signals leak easily through single-pane windows, PCs should never be placed in full view of ground-floor windows. Attenuators that "tap" the window at irregular intervals can be installed to defeat such leakage. A special double-pane window with inert gas between the panes also can lessen the amount of signals leakage.

Other countermeasures include special cladding of hardware, such as computers and printers, to attenuate broadcast signals. This protection often is referred to by the name of the classified government standard for protection of sensitive military systems, TEMPEST. Although TEMPEST was allegedly a classified code word to begin with, it is now sometimes expanded as "Transient ElectroMagnetic Pulse Emission STandard" or "Telecommunications Electronics Material Protected from Emanating Spurious Transmissions."

TEMPEST-certified equipment costs many times more than the same equipment without TEMPEST cladding. A less expensive alternative is to use a special device that emits electromagnetic noise that masks meaningful signals. Yet another approach to protection against this threat is to locate systems within buildings, or rooms within buildings, that have been constructed to TEMPEST standards. There are federal regulations concerning the methods of building sensitive compartmented information facilities (SCIFs), and the testing to obtain a TEMPEST rating is quite stringent. These measures include such things as cladding of all walls and ceilings, cladding of all electrical and network cabling, lead-lined doors, and the absence of any external windows.

15.3.2.16 Trapping Login Information.   Criminals can capture identification and authentication codes by inserting Trojan horse programs into the login process on a server host and by using macro facilities to record keystrokes on a client node.

15.3.2.17 Host-Based Login Trojans.   A Trojan horse is a program that looks useful but contains unauthorized, undocumented code for unauthorized functions. The name comes from Greek mythology, in which Odysseus (Ulysses in Latin), weary of the never–ending siege of Troy, sailed his ships out of sight as if he and his warriors were giving up but left a giant wooden horse at the city gates. Entranced by this magnificent peace offering, the Trojans dragged the great horse into the city. During the Trojans' wild celebrations that night, the soldiers Odysseus had secreted in the belly of the hollow horse let themselves out and opened the gates to their army. The Greeks slaughtered all the inhabitants of the city, and the Trojan war was over.

In February 1994, the Computer Emergency Response Team Coordination Center (CERT-CC) at Carnegie Mellon University in Pittsburgh issued a warning that criminal hackers had inserted Trojan horse login programs in hundreds of UNIX systems on the

Internet. The Trojan captured the first 128 bytes of every login and wrote them to a log file that was later read by the criminals. This trick compromised about 10,000 login IDs.

Trojan code might be installed on a computer or terminal used by several people (e.g., on a mainframe terminal in the 1970s or in an Internet café today) so that when someone enters a user ID and password to logon, the system—controlled by the Trojan—displays a message such as "Invalid password, try again," and the user does so. This time the login is accepted. The victim continues working, unaware that there is anything unusual going on. The Trojan, installed earlier, simulated the normal login procedure, displaying a semblance of the expected screen and dialog. Once the victim entered a password, the Trojan writes the authentication data to a file and then shows a misleading error message. The spoof program then terminates and the regular program is ready for login.

Such a case occurred in April 1993 in a suburb of Hartford, Connecticut. Shoppers noticed a new automatic teller machine (ATM) in their mall. At first, the device seemed to work correctly, disbursing a few hundred dollars to bank card users on demand. It quickly changed to a more sinister mode. Users would insert their bank cards and respond as usual to the demand for their personal identification numbers (PIN). At this point, the new ATM would flash a message showing a malfunction and suggesting that the user try an adjacent bank machine. Most people thought nothing of it, but eventually someone realized that the ATM was not posting the usual "Out of Order" indicator after these supposed errors. In addition, banks began receiving complaints of a rash of bank card frauds in the immediate area. Investigators discovered that the ATM had no connection to any known bank—that it had been purchased used, along with equipment for manufacturing bank cards. The ATM was a spoof; it was merely collecting the user ID and PIN of every victim for later pickup by the criminals who had installed it without permission in the mall. The criminals were caught after having stolen about $100,000 over a four-week period using fraudulent bank cards.

15.3.2.18 Macro Facilities. Another threat to identification and authentication codes is the ability to record keystrokes for later playback or editing. Most word processing programs provide macro facilities, so named because of their ability to store and output multiple keystrokes, such as the typing of boilerplate text, with one keystroke. More sophisticated terminate-and-stay-resident (TSR) programs can record sequences of commands, and are sometimes used to demonstrate software or to automate quality assurance tests. This technology can also be used to lay in wait on a workstation and record everything the user does with the mouse and types with the keyboard; such programs are sometimes called keystroke loggers. Later, the criminal can harvest the records and pick out the login codes and other valuable information.

There are also hardware implementations of keystroke logging. One is a small device inserted between the keyboard and the computer, capturing what is typed and holding it in nonvolatile memory until it can be retrieved.

It is possible to defeat the attempted reuse and abuse of login credentials captured by any of these methods by switching to one-time passwords generated by microprocessors. One-time passwords are discussed in Chapter 28 of this *Handbook*. However, both key loggers and Trojans can be deployed to gain unauthorized access to data without resorting to the reuse of passwords.

15.3.3 Breaching Access Controls. Criminals and spies use two broad categories of technical attacks to deduce access phone numbers, user IDs, and passwords: brute-force attacks and intelligent guesswork. In addition, there are ways to manipulate people into revealing their access codes; these techniques are discussed in the section on social engineering.

15.3.3.1 Brute-Force Attacks.
Brute-force attacks consist of using powerful computers to try all possible codes to locate the correct ones. Brute force is applied to locating modems, network access points, vulnerable Internet servers, user IDs, and passwords.

15.3.3.2 Demon (War) Dialing.
Despite the wholesale shift of data communications to TCP/IP networks and the Internet, modems on dial-up phone lines remain a common, and sometimes forgotten, means of external access to a system. The telephone numbers of any modems connected to hosts or servers or intelligent network peripherals, such as high-end laser printers, are sensitive and should not be posted or broadcast.

Demon dialers are programs that can try every phone number in a numerical range and record whether there is a voice response, a fax line, a modem carrier, or no answer. When phones ring all over an office in numerical order, one at a time, and when there is no one on the line if a phone is picked up, it is undoubtedly the work of someone using a demon dialer. Of course, good demon dialing software accesses the numbers in the target range nonsequentially.

During the heyday of fax machines, some youngsters were reported to have "farmed" entire telephone exchanges during the night, then to have sold the fax numbers for $1 dollar per number to unscrupulous junk-fax services that sold advertisers access to them.

15.3.3.3 Exhaustive Search.
The same approach as demon dialing can find user IDs and passwords after a connection has been made. The attacker uses a program that cycles systematically through all possible user IDs and passwords and records successful attempts. The time required for this attack depends on two factors:

1. The key space for the login codes
2. The maximum allowable speed for trying logins

In today's technical environment, any inexpensive computer can generate login codes far faster than hosts permit login attempts. Processor speed is no longer a rate-limiting factor. Note that this type of attempt to "guess" passwords is different from password cracking, described elsewhere, which operates on captured or stolen copies of encrypted password files.

15.3.3.4 Key Space.
The key space for a code is the maximum number of possible strings that meet the rules of the login restrictions. For example, if user passwords consist of exactly six uppercase or lowercase letters or numbers and the passwords are case-sensitive (i.e., uppercase letters are distinguished from lowercase letters), the total number of possible combinations for such passwords is calculated in this way:

- There are 10 digits and 52 upper- or lowercase letters (in the English alphabet) = 62 possible codes for any of six positions.
- If there are no restrictions on repetition, a string of n characters to be taken from a list of r possibilities for each position will generate r^n possible combinations.

- Thus, in our example, there are 62^6 possible sequences of 62 codes taken in groups of six = 56,800,235,584 (more than 56 billion) possible login codes.

If there are restrictions, the key space will be reduced accordingly. For example, if the first character of a password of length six must be an uppercase letter instead of being any letter or number, there are only 26 possibilities for that position instead 62, thus reducing the total key space to $26 \times 62^5 = 23,819,453,632$ (more than 23 billion) possibilities.

15.3.3.5 Login Speed.

Generating login codes is not hard. The greatest barrier to brute-force login attacks is interruption in the login whenever the host detects an error. Most operating systems and security monitors allow the administrator to define two types of login delays following errors:

1. A usually brief delay after each failed attempt to enter a correct password
2. A usually long delay after several failed login attempts

Suppose each wrong password entered causes a 1/10th-second delay before the next password can be entered; then for our example involving six repeatable uppercase or lowercase letters or numbers, it would take 5,680,023,558 seconds = 1,577,784 hours ≈ 180 years to try every possibility.

Suppose, in addition, that after every fifth failed login attempt, the system were to inactivate the user ID or the modem port for three minutes. Such interference would stretch the theoretical time for a brute-force exhaustive attack to around 650 years.

Should the security manager completely inactivate the ID if it is under attack? If the ID is inactivated until the user calls in for help, user IDs become vulnerable to inactivation by malicious hackers. Attackers need merely provide a bad password several times in a row and the unsuspecting *legitimate* user will be locked out of the system until further notice. A widespread attack on multiple user IDs could make the system unavailable to most users. Such a result would be a denial-of-service attack (see Chapter 18).

Should the port be inactivated? If there are only a few ports, shutting them down will make the system unavailable to legitimate users. This drastic response may be inappropriate—indeed, it may satisfy the intentions of criminal hackers. A short delay, perhaps a few minutes, would likely be sufficient to discourage brute-force attacks.

In all of these examples, the illustrations have been based on exhaustive attacks (i.e., trying every possibility). However, if passwords or other codes are chosen randomly, the valid codes will be uniformly distributed throughout the key space. On average, then, according to a principle of statistics called the Central Limit Theorem, brute-force searches will have to search half the key space. For large key spaces, the difference between a very long time and half of a very long time will be negligible in practice (e.g., 325 years is not significantly different from 650 years if everyone interested will be dead before the code is cracked).

15.3.3.6 Scavenging Random Access Memory.

Not all attacks come from outside agents. Criminals with physical access to workstations, or authorized users who can use privileged utilities to read main memory, can scavenge memory areas for confidential information such as login IDs and passwords.

On a workstation using a terminal emulator to work with a host, ending a session does not necessarily unload the emulator. Many emulators have a configurable screen display buffer, sometimes thousands of lines long. After an authorized user logs off and leaves a terminal, a scavenger can read back many pages of activity, sometimes including confidential information or even login codes. Passwords, however, usually are invisible and therefore not at risk.

If a workstation is part of a client/server system, an application program controlling access may leave residues in random access memory (RAM). A RAM editor, easily available as part of utility packages, can capture and decode such areas as file buffers or input/output (I/O) buffers for communications ports. However, rebooting the workstation after communication is over prevents RAM scavenging by reinitializing memory.

15.3.3.7   Scavenging Cache Files.   The same principle can be applied to the various cache and swap files created by the operating system. Cache files are used to keep frequently used data readily available to applications. Swap files store data and code that is moved out of memory onto disk when memory is full. Some operating systems also create hibernation files, writing memory to disk just prior to powering down, and thus enabling a quick resumption of work when the system is powered up. Operating systems may also provide auto-saved recovery files that allow restoration of data after a system error. All of these can be mined for system credentials as well as other valuable data.

15.3.3.8   Scavenging Web History Files.   A more recent variation on this scavenging approach is to examine files created by Web browsers. These sometimes contain not only the pages viewed by a user but also the credentials entered to access those pages.

15.3.3.9   Intelligent Guesswork.   Users rarely choose random passwords. Much more frequently, passwords are chosen from a subset of all possible strings. Instead of blindly batting at all possible sequences in a key space, an attacker can try to reduce the effective key space by guessing at more likely selections. Likely selections include canonical passwords, bad passwords, and words selected from a dictionary.

Hardware and software often come from the factory, or out of the box, with user IDs and passwords that are the same for all systems and users.

For example, wireless access points and routers have default user IDs when they ship from the factory. Naturally, these user IDs are set up with the same password. (For example, "admin" on Linksys wireless router devices). Such systems always include instructions to change the passwords, but, too often, administrators and users neglect to do so. Criminals are familiar with factory presets—most of which are readily discoverable via Google—and exploit them to penetrate systems. The simple routine of changing all canonical passwords prevents hackers from gaining easy access to systems and software.

15.3.3.10   Stealing.   Criminal hackers have few scruples about using other people's property when they enter computer systems; they have none at all concerning using other people's trash.

15.3.3.11   Data Scavenging.   The term "data scavenging" describes the process that acquires information from throw-away sources. Perhaps the most widely known is Dumpster diving, sorting through whatever an organization discards. Hard copy printouts, CD-ROMs, tapes, and other assorted data-bearing media often end up in trash containers where they are easily accessible to Dumpster divers after hours. In some areas, if one visits an office or industrial park at night, one can see half a dozen people rummaging about, sometimes headfirst in Dumpsters. Criminal hackers use the information thoughtlessly discarded by naive office workers as a source of procedures, vocabulary, and proper names that can help them impersonate employees over the phone or even in person. The classic example is a discarded internal phone directory, which can provide a social engineer with valuable data to use when making calls to employees. An employee who hesitates to comply with an attacker's bogus request for information over the phone may well be persuaded if the attacker says something like "I understand your hesitation; if it makes you feel more comfortable you can call me back at extension 2645." If 2645 is a legitimate internal extension, the caller gains considerable credence. Of course, the properly trained employee will hang up and make the call to 2645 rather than take the easy option and say, "I guess that's okay then, here is the information you wanted."

Some printouts contain confidential information that can lead to extortion or system penetration. For example, a thief who steals a list of personally identifiable information about patients with HIV infection could torment the victims and extort money. Every piece of paper, or other media to be discarded, should be evaluated for confidentiality. Unless the information is worthless to everyone, employees should shred paper before disposal or arrange to send paper to a bonded service for destruction. The same applies to CD-ROMs and other media.

15.3.3.12 Discarded Magnetic and Optical Media. Discarded paper poses a threat; discarded magnetic and optical media are a disaster. Many organizations fail to teach employees that the normal commands used to delete files do not remove all trace of them. Either through the use of utility programs or the operating system itself, the original file clusters can be located and any part of the original file that has not yet been overwritten can be regenerated.

Backup tapes, CDs, and DVDs may contain valuable information about the system security structure. For example, in the 1970s and 1980s, system backups on one brand of minicomputer contained the entire directory, complete with every user ID and password *in the clear* on the first tape. Using a simple file copy utility, any user could read these data.

To destroy information on magnetic media, users either must overwrite the medium several times with random data or physically destroy the medium. Degaussers are inadequate unless they meet military specifications, but such units typically cost thousands of dollars.

The problem of readable data is especially troublesome on discarded disk drives or on broken hard disk drives that have been repaired or that are subject to specialized forensic data recovery. Users have received operational, data-laden disk drives as replacements for their own broken units. Sometimes the replacement disks have not even been reformatted; they contain entire directories of correspondence, customer databases, and proprietary software. Because it is by definition impossible to overwrite data on a defective disk drive, military security specialists routinely destroy defective hard disks using oxyacetylene torches or purpose-built grinders that reduce hard drives into small chunks.

For more information about secure disposal of magnetic and optical data storage media, see Chapter 57 in this *Handbook*.

15.3.4 Spying. Some techniques used by criminal hackers seem to have been lifted directly from spy novels. For example, laser interferometry can reconstitute vibration patterns from reflected infrared laser beams bounced off windows. Users of such equipment can hear and record conversations in rooms that have external windows that vibrate according to the sounds in the room. For more antispy measures related to physical and facilities security, see Chapters 22 and 23 in this *Handbook*.

Hackers surreptitiously steal people's access codes by watching their fingers as they punch in secret sequences. When pay phones were prevalent, *shoulder surfers* would capture telephone calling-card codes, which they sell to organized crime rings. Codes can be stolen by peering over the shoulders of neighboring callers, or by using binoculars, telescopes, and video cameras to track the buttons pressed by their victims.

Shoulder surfing can occur within installations as well. For example, most users of punch-key locks pay no attention to the visibility of their fingers. Whenever punching in a code, users should guard against observation by unauthorized people. In public places, users should stand up close to the keypad. In fixed installations, facilities managers should cover keypads with opaque sleeves allowing unimpeded access but concealing details of the access codes.

Nowadays criminals are getting quite adept at surfing both wired and wireless network connections, either by cruising around town with a war-driving setup or hanging out in a target-rich environment such as an airport, train station, coffee shop, or hotel lobby. There is more about wireless hacking in Chapter 33.

One particular type of wired connection that should be used with care is the broadband guest room connection offered by many hotels. Too often, these are set up without proper security measures, enabling a curious or criminally inclined guest to locate machines belonging to other guests (sometimes by merely clicking the Network Neighborhood icon in Windows Explorer). Employees should be instructed not to plug their company laptops into such connections unless they have a properly configured firewall in place and turned on. Even some of the most expensive upscale hotels have been found to suffer from this problem, as illustrated in Exhibit 15.2.

15.3.5 Penetration Testing, Toolkits, and Techniques. Verifying and improving the security of systems by attempting to penetrate them is a well-established practice among security professionals and system administrators. However, although some were practicing this technique earlier, it was not openly discussed prior to 1993. That year, Dan Farmer and Wietse Venema released the pioneering paper entitled "Improving the Security of Your Site by Breaking into It."[6] This paper advanced the notion of assessing system security by examining a system through the eyes of a potential intruder. Farmer and Venema showed that scanning for seemingly benign network services can reveal serious weaknesses in any system. Prior to the publication of this important paper, many system administrators were unaware of the extent of vulnerabilities affecting their systems.

Farmer and Venema then released a network-testing program called SATAN (Security Analysis Tool for Auditing Networks). Security professionals and system administrators both lauded and were angered by the program. Some system administrators cheered the availability of an all-in-one tool that revealed security holes but did not exploit them. Others questioned the authors' motives in releasing a free and readily available tool that hackers could use to attack networks. While the debate raged on, system administrators and hackers alike began using SATAN to interrogate networks.

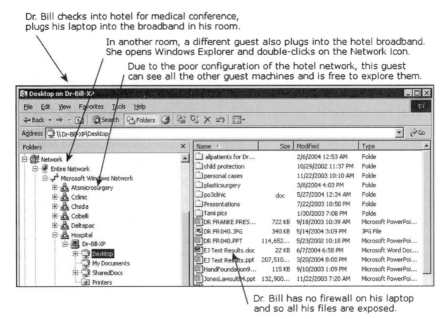

Dr. Bill checks into hotel for medical conference, plugs his laptop into the broadband in his room.

In another room, a different guest also plugs into the hotel broadband. She opens Windows Explorer and double-clicks on the Network Icon.

Due to the poor configuration of the hotel network, this guest can see all the other guest machines and is free to explore them.

Dr. Bill has no firewall on his laptop and so all his files are exposed.

This is an actual screenshot taken at a five-star hotel in Boston. To protect privacy, we changed the names of computers, folders, and files. Note that no hacking tools were required to see or to access Dr. Bill's files.

EXHIBIT 15.2   Poorly Configured Hotel Room Internet Connectivity

15.3.5.1   Common Tools.   Since that time, literally hundreds of penetration toolkits have appeared; they are commonly referred to as scanners. Today one can find innumerable freeware tools or invest in one of the commercial tools. Scanners vary in complexity and reliability. However, a majority of the tools employ the same basic functions to test a network: Query ports on the target machines and record the response or lack of response.

Used in the proper manner, these tools can be effective in discovering and recording vast amounts of data about a network of computer systems and revealing security holes in the network. Many scanner packages also include packet-sniffing applications, described earlier. Administrators can use this information to reduce the number of systems that can be compromised.

A wide variety of basic network tools may be used in any penetration test. These tools may include mundane programs, such as PING, FINGER, TRACEROUTE, and NSLOOKUP. However, most serious penetration tools make use of an automated vulnerability analysis tool consisting of a series of port queries and a database of known vulnerabilities. Some tools also attempt to exploit identified vulnerabilities in order to eliminate false positives. Once the vulnerabilities have been found, it is remarkably easy to obtain "exploits" or programs with which to launch an attack against the susceptible machines. All the tools make use of the basic operations of the TCP suite of protocols. Although these protocols will operate on different port numbers, they all share a common structure of a three-way handshake. All TCP protocols look for a connection attempt (connect), a synchronization and acknowledgment exchange (SYN/ACK), various conditions (FLAGS), and a close port request (FIN). Therefore, the operation of port scanners is quite similar. They attempt to find open, or listening, ports on a machine, ask for a connection, and then log the results to a file to be compared to the internal database. The scanner will display the results of the scans by listing the open ports and the services that appear to be running. At this point the various programs differ. Some attempt an in-depth analysis of the possible security holes associated with the ports and services, along with the appropriate security measures to secure them. The more malicious scanners also include automated scripts for exploitation of the vulnerabilities thus revealed.

Of the freeware tools, Nessus, Netcat, and nmap are probably the best known, although there always seems to be a new flavor of the month among both hackers and system administrators. SATAN is still available, as are its spin-offs, SAINT and SARA. A fair amount of skill is required to use these tools as they are fairly sophisticated, and some of the scans can overload a system and cause it to hang or crash.

15.3.5.2   Common Scans.   As previously mentioned, most of the scanners/sniffers available will run through the same basic routines in order to develop a picture of a machine as a whole. The purpose is to determine what is running on the machine and what its role is in the network. The next sections describe most basic scans and their results.

15.3.5.2.1   TCP Connect.   This is the most basic form of TCP scanning. This system call is provided by the operating system. If the port is listening, the attempt at a connection will proceed. This scan does not require root or supervisor privileges. However, this scan is easily detectable, as many connection and termination requests will be shown in the host's system logs.

15.3.5.2.2   TCP SYN.   This scan does not open a full connection and is sometimes referred to as a half-open scan because a full handshake never completes. A SYN scan starts by sending a SYN packet. Any open ports should respond with a SYN|ACK. However, the scanner sends an RST (reset) instead of an ACK, which terminates the connection. Fewer systems log this type of scan. Ports that are closed will respond to the initial SYN with an RST instead of an ACK, which reveals that the port is closed.

15.3.5.2.3   Stealth Scans.   Also referred to as Stealth FIN, Xmas Tree, or Null scans, the stealth scan is used because some firewalls and intrusion detection systems watch for SYNs to restricted ports. The stealth scan attempts to bypass these systems without creating a log of the attempt. The scan is based on the fact that closed ports should respond to a request with an RST and open ports should just drop the packet without logging the attempt.

15.3.5.2.4   UDP Scans.   There are many popular User Datagram Protocol (UDP) holes to exploit, such as an rpcbind hole or a Trojan program, such as cDc Back Orifice, which installs itself on a UDP port. The scanner will send a 0-byte UDP packet to each port. If the host returns a "port unreachable" message, that port is considered closed. This method can be time consuming because most UNIX hosts limit the rate of Internet Control Message Protocol (ICMP) errors. Some scanners detect the allowable rate on UNIX systems and slow the scan down, so as not to flood the target with messages.

15.3.5.2.5   IP Protocol Scans.   This method is used to determine which Internet protocols are supported on a host. Raw IP packets without any protocol header are sent to each specified protocol on the target machine. If an ICMP unreachable message is received, then the protocol is not in use. Otherwise, it assumed to be open. Some hosts (AIX, HP-UX, Digital UNIX) and firewalls may not send protocol unreachable message, so all protocols appear to be open.

15.3.5.2.6   ACK Scan.   This advanced method usually is used to map out firewall rule-sets. In particular, it can help determine whether a firewall is stateful or just a simple packet filter that blocks incoming SYN packets. This scan type sends an ACK packet with random-looking acknowledgment/sequence numbers to the ports specified. If an RST comes back, the port is classified as "unfiltered." If nothing comes back, or if an ICMP unreachable is returned, the port is classified as "filtered."

15.3.5.2.7   RPC Scan.   This method takes all the TCP/UDP ports found open and then floods them with SunRPC program NULL commands in an attempt to determine whether they are RPC ports and, if so, what program and version number they return.

15.3.5.2.8   FTP Bounce.   This scan looks like it is an FTP proxy server within the network (or trusted domain). It could eventually connect to an FTP server behind a firewall. Once the FTP server has been found, scanning of ports normally blocked from the outside can be made from the internal FTP server. Of course, reading and writing to directories can be checked from this server as well.

15.3.5.2.9   Ping Sweeps.   This scan uses Ping (ICMP echo request) to find hosts that are up. It can also look for subnet-directed broadcast addresses on the network. These are IP addresses that can be reached externally. Ping sweeps often are used to try to "map" the network as a whole.

15.3.5.2.10   Operating System Fingerprinting.   As many security holes are dependent on the operating system of the host, this scan attempts to identify which operating system is running, based on a number of suppositions. It uses various techniques to detect subtleties in the underlying operating system (OS) network stack of the computers being scanned. The data gathered are used to create a "fingerprint" that is compared to the scanner's database of known fingerprints. If an unknown fingerprint is found, attackers can check Web sites and newsgroups where information about fingerprints is freely traded, to discover what a particular OS might be. Once the OS has been identified, it is quite easy to find exploits by simply using a search engine on the Web. OS fingerprinting is unnecessary if the OS can be discovered by reading the banners. For example, if one was to telnet to a machine, the response could be:

```
badgny~> telnet abcd.efg.com
Trying 163.143.103.12 ...
Connected to abcd.efg.com
Escape character is '^]'.
HP-UX hpux B.10.01 A 9000/715 (ttyp2)
login:
```

The banner, which was included in the default configuration, simply indicates that the OS is HP-UX. A good system administrator will turn off the banners on all services that have them.

15.3.5.2.11   Reverse Ident Scanning.   This scan usually is used to see if a Web server on the network is running as root. If the *identd* daemon is running on the target machine, then a TCP Ident request will cause the daemon to return the username that "owns" the process. Therefore, if this request is sent to port 80 (hex), and the return user is root, then that server can be used for an attack on the system. This scan requires a full TCP connection to the port in question before it will return the username.

15.3.5.3 Basic Exploits. Using the results of a scanning program, the next logical step for hackers would be to try to exploit the apparent weaknesses in the system. Hackers seek to compromise a machine on the network by getting it to let them run programs or processes at will, at the root level. Once hackers "own" that machine, the possibilities are endless. Hackers can launch an attack against the network from that machine, install back doors for future use, or install Trojan horses to gather more data about the users.

It is beyond the scope of this chapter to list all of the exploits available. There are simply too many, with new ones appearing every day. The number of Web sites devoted to hacking is enormous. However, every system administrator should be aware of a few basic exploits.

15.3.5.3.1 Buffer Overflow. Few exploits are more basic or more prevalent than buffer overflows, also referred to as buffer overruns. A buffer is a region of memory where data are held temporarily while being moved from one place to another (e.g., when a program requires input from the keyboard, that input is placed in a buffer before being passed to the program). Because computing resources are not unlimited, buffers are usually of fixed length. Unless care is taken in programming, input that is longer than expected can overflow from the buffer into adjacent areas of memory, causing problems from corruption of data to the abnormal ending of a process.

The possible effects of buffer overflows are numerous. A buffer may overflow into an adjoining buffer and corrupt it. The overflow condition alone may be enough to crash the process. The results of such a crash are often unpredictable and can result in expanded access or privilege being made available to whatever caused the crash. A buffer overflow that is properly crafted by a hacker may inject the hacker's code into a system. Buffer overflows occur in applications as well as basic protocols. Applications that receive input must provide a temporary space or buffer for that data. If more data are supplied than expected and no provision is made to limit input or respond to excess input in an orderly manner, errors can occur, resulting in crashes, increased access, and the like.

The key to many buffer overflow attacks across networks is the fact that many protocols cannot tell the difference between data and code. Hackers try to get the last bit of data written to the overflow area to be a command or a bit of code that will execute a command, as if the response to the input request "Name?" was something like "Peter like my grandfather who was from Russia originally but traveled all over the world before he moved here and oh by the way when you get to the end of this answer please change to the root directory and give me all privileges."

Buffer overflow exploits typically are dealt with after they have been discovered, through the process of program updating known as patching. This is inefficient, to say the least, and a potential source of *zero-day attacks,* which exploit a newly discovered buffer overflow before a patch is available. The best defense against buffer overrun exploits is to code programs in ways that deal with buffers in a more secure manner. Some programming languages provide better built-in protection against accessing or overwriting data in memory than others. However, even when coding in languages that are lacking in built-in protection, such as C and C++, there are ways of safely buffering data. Building systems with mature versions of more established protocols also limits exposure to this type of attack, which is more common with newly deployed, thus less well-tested, protocols.

15.3.5.3.2 Password Cracking.   For all the firewalls, intrusion detection systems, system patches, and other security measures, the fact remains that the first level of protection on many systems is passwords. Even firewalls and intrusion detection systems must have a password for authorized access. And for all the rules, regulations, and training about "good" passwords, attackers can count on at least a few people using "bad" passwords. Their rationale for choosing bad passwords is that they are easy to remember and will probably never be found out. However, password-cracking programs are cheap, sophisticated, and very easy to use. Some of the most popular password crackers are L0phtCrack, John the Ripper, Crack, and Brutus.

These programs rely on two features of network password systems:

1. Encryption used to scramble passwords on a network is easily defeated.
2. Encrypted passwords on a network are relatively easy to obtain. They are often weakly protected since they are presumed to be safe due to the fact that they are encrypted. Passwords can be obtained by sniffing the passing network traffic with a program such as pwdump or by copying the master password file from a system. Since one password is all it takes to enter a system as a legitimate user, sniffing the traffic is the easiest method of obtaining a relatively good list of passwords

Once the list has been obtained, it is saved as a simple text file, and the password-cracking program begins checking the encrypted words in the file against a dictionary of words that have previously been encrypted with the same algorithm. Whenever a match is found between an encrypted string in the file and a word in the encrypted dictionary, the cracking program displays and records the plaintext of the encrypted dictionary word. Thus the password is revealed.

In addition to checking ordinary dictionary words, some password crackers check for both upper-case and lower-case letters, numbers before and after a word, and numbers used in lieu of vowels within a word. The speed at which these programs operate, even on a basic desktop or laptop computer, is impressive, and it is entirely possible to obtain cracked passwords within seconds. Indeed, a useful security awareness exercise is to demonstrate such a program to employees: The first passwords to be cracked will be the weakest ones, and that can serve as a warning to users who choose such words.

A good security officer will ensure that passwords on a network are checked regularly with a password cracker or by implementing one of the many "strong" password enforcers. Password enforcers augment the password program by comparing the passwords chosen by the user to the rules set by the enforcer.

15.3.5.3.3 Rootkits.   Rootkits are one of the many tools available to hackers to disguise the fact that a machine has been "rooted." A rootkit is not used to crack into a system but rather to ensure that a cracked system remains available to the intruder. Rootkits are comprised of a suite of utilities that are installed on the victim machine. The utilities start by modifying the most basic and commonly used programs so that suspicious activity is cloaked. For example, a rootkit often changes simple commands such as "ls" (list files). A modified "ls" from a rootkit will not display files or directories that the intruder wants to keep hidden.

Rootkits are extremely difficult to discover since the commands and programs appear to work as before. Often a rootkit is found because something did not "feel right" to the system administrator. Since rootkits vary greatly in the programs they change, one cannot tell which programs have been changed and which have not. Without a cryptographically secure signature of every system binary, an administrator cannot be certain to have found the entire rootkit.

Some of the common utilities included in a rootkit are:

- Trojan horse utilities
- Back doors that allow the hacker to enter the system at will
- Log-wiping utilities that erase the attacker's access record from system log files
- Packet sniffers that capture network traffic for the attacker

15.3.5.3.4 Trojan Code.   As described earlier in the context of compromised login procedures, Trojan code is something other than it appears to be. In this case, the Trojans are the changed programs in a rootkit that allow an intruder's tracks to be hidden or allow the program to gather more information as it sits silently in the background. Local programs that are Trojaned often include "chfn," "chsh," "login," and "passwd." In each case, if the rootkit password is entered in the appropriate place, a root shell is spawned.

15.3.5.3.5 Back Doors.   Back door utilities often are tied to programs that have been Trojaned. They are used to gain entry to a system when other methods fail. Even if a system administrator has discovered an intrusion and has changed all the usernames and passwords, there is a good chance that he or she does not know that the back doors exist. To use the back door, the hacker needs only to know the correct port to connect to the compromised machine and to enter a password or command where one is not usually entered.

For example, inetd, the network super daemon, is often Trojaned. The daemon will listen on an unusual port (rfe, port 5002 by default in Rootkit IV for Linux). If the correct password is given after connection, a root shell is spawned and bound to the port.

The function rshd can be similarly Trojaned so that a root shell is spawned when the rootkit password is given as the username and thus rsh [hostname] –l [rootkit password] will obtain access to the compromised machine.

15.3.6 Penetration via Web Sites.   A vast new network territory opened up in the final decade of the twentieth century, partially devoted to commerce and largely driven by attempts to make money from a technology that originally had been developed for military and academic purposes. The relentless growth of this network is reflected in the total number of registered domains (graphed in Exhibit 15.3). This number surpassed 80 million in 2007.

Worldwide Internet penetration, measured as the number of Internet users as a percentage of total population, was close to 20 percent by mid-2007, with some regions, such as North America and Australia, surpassing 50 percent.[7] Not surprisingly, with so many machines in one network and over 1.2 billion users, this new territory has become a playground for hackers, from the merely curious to the seriously criminal. The Web presents a "target-rich" environment for people seeking unauthorized access to other people's information systems. There are several reasons for this; chief among them is the fact that many organizations, both commercial and governmental—including the military—have external, public Web sites that are connected, in some way, to internal, private networks. This connection provides a system penetration path that can be exploited in many different ways, as outlined in this section.

For more detailed analysis of Web site security, see Chapter 21 in this *Handbook*.

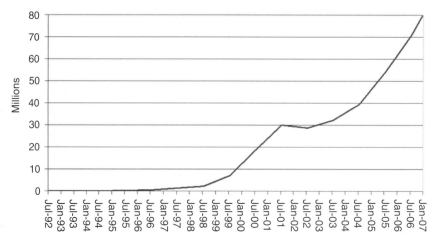

EXHIBIT 15.3 Total Number of Internet Domains, 1992 to 2007
Source: Zooknic.

15.3.6.1 Web System Architecture. Standard practice when placing a commercial Web site on the Internet is to screen it from hostile activity, typically using a router with access-control lists (ACLs) or a firewall, or both. However, unless the Web site is of the basic, "brochure-ware" kind, which simply exists to provide information on a read-only basis, the site has to allow for user input of data. Input is required for something as simple as a guest book entry or an information request form; more complex applications such as online shopping have more complex input requirements.

A typical method of processing input is the Common Gateway Interface (CGI). This is a standard way for a Web server to pass user input to an application program and to receive a response, which can then be forwarded to the user. For example, when a user fills out a form on a Web page and submits it, the Web server typically passes the form information to a small application. This application processes the data and may send back a confirmation message. This method is named CGI, and it forms part of the Hypertext Transfer Protocol (HTTP). Because it is a consistent method, applications written to employ it can be used regardless of the operating system of the server on which it is deployed. Further adding to the popularity of CGI is the fact that it works with a number of different languages including C, C++, Java, and PERL. The term "CGI" is used generically for Web server code written in any of these languages.

Any system that receives input must provide a path within the system through which that input can flow. This is referred to as an "allowed path." The necessity of allowed paths, combined with the ability to exploit them for penetration attacks, led the system security expert David Brussin (author of Chapter 26 in this *Handbook*) to coin the term "allowed path vulnerabilities" for this class of vulnerability. The two leading categories of exploits that employ allowed paths are input validation exploits, which are akin to buffer overflow exploits and often employed to abuse CGIs, and file system exploits, which abuse the Web server operating system and services running on the server.

Of course, there are other ways to abuse Web sites as well. Denial-of-service attacks can be used to inhibit legitimate access and thus compromise availability. (Chapter 18 in this *Handbook* covers DoS attacks.) Not every attack is aimed at further penetration of systems; the Web pages themselves may be the target of attack, as in a defacement, an unauthorized change to Web pages. Defacement often is committed to embarrass the Web site owner, publicize a protest message, or enhance the reputation of the criminal hacker who is performing the defacement. But in terms of penetration, the primary goal of attacks on Web sites is to compromise internal networks that might be connected to the Web server. Exploitation of allowed path vulnerabilities is probably the most common form of such attacks.

15.3.6.2   Input Validation Exploits.   Whenever an allowed path is created to accommodate user input, the possibility exists that it will be abused. Such abuse can lead to unauthorized access to the system. This section describes a range of penetration methods using this approach, all of which somehow employ invalid input, or input that is:

Not expected by the receiving application on the server.

Not "allowed" according to the rules by which the receiving application is operating.

15.3.6.3   Unexpected Input Attacks.   How is it possible to submit unexpected input to a server? The answer lies in the architecture of the Internet and the paradoxical nature of the client system that is accessing the server. The typical Web client is a client in name only. It is often a powerful machine, capable of being a server in its own right, and very difficult for any other server to control, due to the inherent peer-to-peer nature of the huge network that is the Internet. All nodes of the Internet are considered hosts. And, of course, many of these hosts are outside the physical control of the organizations hosting those machines that are acting as servers. This fact has serious implications for security.

Unless the server can install tightly controlled application code on the client, and restrict user input to that code, the server must rely on the coding most commonly used to implement Web client-server interaction, Hypertext Markup Language (HTML) and Hypertext Transfer Protocol Daemon (HTTPD). Both are complex and relatively immature. For example, they do not automatically identify the source of the input. Consider an HTML form on a Web page, designed to be presented to a visitor to the Web site who fills in the fields and then clicks a button to submit the form. There is nothing on the client side to control the user's input. So instead of entering a first name in the First Name field, a user might enter a long string of random characters. Unless the application processing this data field performs extensive input validation, the effects of such action can be unpredictable, even more so if the user includes control characters. Similarly, if the Web server itself is not designed to validate page requests, a user might cause problems by submitting a bogus URL (Universal Resource Locator).

The problem is even more severe than this. Unless the Web server application is specifically written to defeat the following abuse, it can be used to cause all sorts of problems that potentially lead to successful penetration. Suppose that, instead of simply filling out a form, the user creates a local copy of the page containing the form, then alters the source code of the form, saves the file, and submits it to the Web site instead of the original page. This does not violate the basic protocols of the Web but clearly provides considerable penetration potential. Many Web sites are still vulnerable to attacks of this type.

15.3.6.4   Overflow Attacks.   As described earlier in the context of hidden form fields, it is possible to gain access to Web servers by supplying more input than expected. Such an attack is possible with any field on a user-submitted form, not just a hidden field. The defense is to build extensive error checking into the application that processes the form.

Overflow attacks, which were described in general terms earlier, also can be directed at applications or services running on the Web server. For example, in June 2001, CERT announced a remotely exploitable buffer overflow in one of the Internet Server Application Programming Interface (ISAPI) extensions installed with most versions of Microsoft Internet Information Server 4.0 and 5.0, specifically the Internet/Indexing Service Application Programming Interface extension, IDQ.DLL. An intruder exploiting this vulnerability may be able to execute arbitrary code in the local system security context, giving the attacker complete control of the victim's system.

15.3.6.5 *File System Exploits.* Another category of attack against Web sites exploits problems with the file system of the Web server itself. Ever since Web servers started appearing on the Internet, there has been a constant procession of vulnerability announcements arising from file system issues. The main ones are presented here, but the possibility of others appearing is high due to a lack of what David Brussin has called vulnerability class analysis. A vulnerability class is a type of problem, such as buffer overflow or file system access control. Developers of Web servers, and many other applications, are often averse to, or resource-constrained from, the elimination of vulnerabilities as a class, being focused instead on the hole-by-hole fixing of specific instances of the vulnerability as they arise. This phenomenon is largely a result of the rapid pace at which the Web has been developed and deployed, driven by powerful commercial forces.

15.3.6.6 *Dot Dot, Slash, and Other Characters.* Persons responsible for the security of information systems that employ Web servers must be alert for new vulnerabilities. Web server software has proven particularly susceptible to certain categories of vulnerability that tend to recur in new versions. Whenever these vulnerabilities are discovered, attackers quickly exploit them. Typically, software vendors issue patches to solve the problem, but systems remain susceptible until patched, and attackers use automated tools to scan the Internet for servers that are still susceptible. For example, in April 2001, a flaw was discovered in versions of Microsoft Internet Information Server (IIS) in use at that time. This flaw made it possible for remote users to list directory contents, view files, delete files, and execute arbitrary commands.

In other words, if a Web server running IIS was connected to the Internet, anybody using the Internet could potentially copy, move, or delete files on the Web server. With this level of access, it was possible to use the Web server to gain access to connected networks unless strong internetwork access controls were in place. In alerts that were issued to warn users of this software, exploitation of this vulnerability was described as "trivial." In fact, a large number of sites were penetrated because of it, and many suffered defacement (i.e., unauthorized changes to the appearance of their Web sites). In other cases, attackers downloaded sensitive customer data and uploaded and installed back door software.

Particularly worrying about this vulnerability was the fact that it was essentially a recurrence of the so-called dot dot directory traversal attack, which was possible on a lot of early Web servers. These servers would, upon request, read ".." directories in URLs, which are unpublished parent directories of the published directory. Thus attackers were able to back out to the Web root directory and then to other parts of the server's directory structure. This technique basically allowed attackers to navigate the file system at will. Many Web servers, including IIS, began to incorporate security measures to prevent the "dot dot" attack, denying all queries to URLs that contain too many leading slashes or ".." characters.

The vulnerability published in April 2001 involved bypassing these restrictions by simply substituting a Unicode translation of a "/" or "\." Attackers found that, by appending the ".." and a Unicode slash or backslash after a virtual directory with execute permissions, it was possible to execute arbitrary commands. Attackers could execute any command via a specially crafted HTTP query. The frequency with which "old" vulnerabilities reappear in new software should serve as a warning to information security professionals not to assume that "new" is the same as "improved." Indeed, all software needs to be treated with a healthy degree of skepticism and a fair amount of heavy testing prior to deployment.

15.3.6.7 Metacharacters. Dots and slashes used in field system references are closely related to metacharacters, which also can be used to attack Web systems. A metacharacter is a special character in a program or data field that provides information about other characters, for example, how to process the characters that follow the metacharacter. Users of DOS or UNIX are probably familiar with the wildcard character, a metacharacter that can represent either any one character or any string of characters. If used inappropriately, for example, in user-supplied data, metacharacters can cause errors that result in unintended consequences, including privileged access.

15.3.6.8 Server-Side Includes. Server-side includes (SSIs) are special commands in HTML that the Web server executes as it parses an HTML file. SSIs were developed originally to make it easier to include a common file, called an include file, inside many different files; examples include files containing a logo or text files consisting of the page, date, author, and so on. This capability was expanded to enable server information, such as the date and time, to be included automatically in a file. Eventually several different types of include commands were provided on Web servers: *config, include, echo, fsize, flastmod, exec*. The last of these, *exec*, is quite powerful, but it is also a security risk, as it gives to the user of the Web client permission to execute code. A number of attacks are possible when *exec* is permitted within an inadequately protected directory.

Analogous to SSIs are ASPs (Active Server Pages) and JavaServer Pages, as well as Hypertext Processors (PHP). All are technologies that facilitate dynamic page building and allow execution of codelike instructions within an HTML page. All should be employed with special attention to security implications and strict adherence to secure Web application programming methods. Security professionals will note that many of the weaknesses in these newer technologies are simply old exploits reborn. Anything that offers "greater interactive functionality" may increase the likelihood of new vulnerabilities simply because, in the absence of rigorous software quality assurance, changes are so often associated with new bugs.

15.3.7 Role of Malware and Botnets. Several new twists on system penetration via Web sites and Internet e-mail have emerged in recent years, starting with the evolution of computer viruses and worms. Some worms and viruses are designed to install Trojan code. The term "malware," derived from "malicious" and "software," is now widely used to refer to the entire category of software coded with malicious intent, including viruses, worms, and Trojans. In fact, viruses and worms, which are dealt with in more detail in Chapter 16 in this *Handbook*, are themselves a form of system penetration; after all, the creators of virus and worm code are getting their code onto systems that they are not authorized to use, so one may consider those machines to have been penetrated. Some criminal hackers have combined different elements of malware to penetrate computers used to surf the Web. Those compromised machines are then used, in turn, to spread malware and compromise additional machines. The goal may be gathering of user names and passwords (helpful for yet more system penetrations) or financial data used to perpetrate fraud and identity theft.

The two main components of this penetration strategy are drive-by downloads and botnets. A drive-by download attempts to compromise machines used to visit a malicious Web site, taking advantage of either user gullibility or vulnerabilities in their Web browsers to install, without explicit permission, unsolicited code, typically a Trojan of some sort. A botnet is a collection of bots, host computers that can be controlled remotely (i.e., ro*bot*ically) through Trojan code installed on those machines, either via a drive-by download or other means, such as a virus or worm. Here is how researchers at Google described the phenomenon in a landmark 2007 report:

> [C]omputer users have become the target of an underground economy that infects hosts with malware or adware for financial gain. Unfortunately, even a single visit to an infected Web site enables the attacker to detect vulnerabilities in the user's applications and force the download of a multitude of malware binaries. Frequently, this malware allows the adversary to gain full control of the compromised systems leading to the ex-filtration of sensitive information or installation of utilities that facilitate remote control of the host.[8]

What makes the Google report a landmark is not the existence of drive-by exploits, which have been on the rise for several years, but their prevalence. Because Google maintains a massive repository of Web pages in order to operate its search engine, it is in a fairly unique position when it comes to analyzing the content of the Web as a whole. The solidly researched finding that at least 1 in 10 of all Web pages contained some form of malware should be a wakeup call to IT departments everywhere. Are your users surfing to MySpace Web pages? Are they aware that something as seemingly harmless as visiting their favorite singer's page on MySpace could cause malicious code to be downloaded onto their computer from a Web site in China?

That sort of attack started to become commonplace in 2007, as documented by Roger Thompson of Exploit Prevention Labs, with Alicia Keys being one of a number of artists targeted by criminal hackers. One exploit used in these attacks installed a proxy network bot, known as a flux bot. The goal of a flux bot is to obscure the location of phishing sites by using constantly changing proxy servers, thus making it harder for banks and other institutions targeted by the phishing scam to shut it down, (There is more about phishing scams in Chapter 20 in this *Handbook*.)

According to the Google report, there are four main methods by which Web pages are turned into malware infection vectors: advertising, third party-widgets, user-contributed content, and Web server security. This implies that company Web sites not only need to be firmly secured, but that all advertising and user-supplied content should be validated, as should any widgets that are employed or distributed by the site.

15.4 POLITICAL AND LEGAL ISSUES.   Thanks to the World Wide Web, the Internet has become a self-documenting phenomenon. One can use the Internet to find out everything one wants to know about the Internet, including how to penetrate information systems that employ Internet technology. However, the penetration information available on the Internet is not restricted to Internet systems, and the Internet is not the only source of penetration information. Furthermore, the very availability of penetration information is fraught with political and legal issues. These are discussed briefly in this final section of the chapter.

15.4.1 Exchange of System Penetration Information. The sharing of system penetration information—that is, information that could facilitate illegal penetration of an information system—is the subject of a long, heated, and ongoing debate. This debate encompasses both practical and ethical aspects of the issue. Although complete coverage is not possible within the confines of this chapter, we do review the question of full disclosure, along with some of the sources for penetration information.

15.4.2 Full Disclosure. How should we handle known vulnerabilities and potentially damaging computer viruses? Should we publish full details, conceal some details, or suppress any publication that would allow exploitation until patches or updates are available from manufacturers? Is there a case for handling some viruses and exploits differently from others?

Over the last two decades, formal venues for full disclosure of system or network vulnerabilities and exploits have evolved (e.g., BugTraq). Support for full disclosure of such details, down to the source code or script level, from professional, honest security experts (the Good Guys) is based on subsets of several key beliefs:

- The Bad Guys know about the vulnerabilities anyway
- If they do not know about it already, they will soon with or without the posted details.
- Knowing the details helps the Good Guys more than the Bad Guys.
- Effective security cannot be based on obscurity.
- Making vulnerabilities public may force vendors to improve the security of their products.

Since those who would use vulnerabilities and exploits for gain or harm often learn of them before system administrators and security experts, it makes sense—so the argument goes—for the Good Guys to spread the knowledge where it can do some good. One might also argue that, because cryptographic techniques are routinely exposed to public scrutiny by experts to detect vulnerabilities and to avoid future failures, other aspects of security should also be made public.

As for putting pressure on manufacturers, one colleague describes an incident that illustrates the frustrations that sometimes underlie full disclosure. He informed an important software supplier of a major security vulnerability. The product manager ignored him for a month. At that point, patience gone, the colleague informed the product manager that he had exactly one more day in which to produce a patch; otherwise, he said, he would publish the hole in full in the appropriate Usenet group. A patch was forthcoming within one hour.

Why would anyone object to full disclosure of detailed viral code and exploits? The arguments are that:

- Nobody except researchers needs to know the details of viruses or even of specific exploits.
- Publishing in full gives credibility to ill-intentioned Bad Guys who do the same.
- Full disclosure makes impressionable youths more susceptible to the view that illegal computer abuse is acceptable.

How, exactly, does publishing the details of a new virus help system administrators? In one view, such details should be exchanged only among colleagues who have developed trust in each other's integrity and who have the technical competence to provide fixes. For example, a "zoo" of computer viruses serves this function, with access limited to legitimate virus researchers who sign a code of ethics that forbids casually distributing viruses to anyone who wants samples. Opponents of this stance see the attitude as arrogant and elitist. Furthermore, some virus and worm code is written in a form that is easily read by anyone who receives a copy (a large population, considering that in 1999, the Melissa virus is thought to have infected over a million computers within a matter of days).

There is a danger in publishing exploits where any person with access to the Web can use them for automated attacks on Web sites. This gives naive people the impression that it is okay to publish any attack code, regardless of consequences. (Note that the consequences are often relatively minor—the author of the Melissa virus, which is estimated to have caused at least $80 million in damages, served only 20 months in a federal prison and paid a fine of only $5,000.) What is the difference, then, between publishing vulnerabilities or exploits and actually creating attack tools? Was creating and publishing BackOrifice a morally neutral or even a useful act? BackOrifice is a tool that is explicitly designed to install itself surreptitiously on systems and then hide in memory, using stealth techniques modeled on what some viruses use. Is this a contribution to security?

There are no simple or uncontested answers to these questions, but in some cases technology has answered them for us. Before 1995, when macro viruses first appeared "in the wild," most viruses were written in assembly language or machine code. This limited the number of people who could read them or understand them to persons familiar with assembly language and machine code. However, anyone who receives a macro virus has the text editor tools needed to read its code. The tools required to develop and test macro viruses are provided in mainstream applications, such as Microsoft Word, which has tens of millions of users worldwide, a significant percentage of whom have, or can easily acquire, the rudimentary programming skills required to develop their own viruses. The rapid spread of the original Word Concept virus in the summer of 1995 pretty much ensured that anyone who wanted a copy of it could get one (and many of those who did not want a copy got one anyway). The idea of keeping the content of the virus secret was a nonstarter.

Faced with vendor inability or unwillingness to fix security vulnerabilities in a timely manner, some users and experts can be expected to turn to full disclosure of security information, even though many of them may deplore using such tactics. However, they will always run the risk of making the wrong call when it comes to the effect of such disclosures, which are inherently unpredictable. Indeed, the release of the Word Concept virus may have been motivated by a desire to make Microsoft change the way its office applications handle macros. Other office applications, such as Word Perfect and Lotus 1-2-3, were designed to keep macro code separate from document content, making a malicious document much harder to create.

15.4.3 Sources. There are many sources for information about how to penetrate systems. The motives behind these sources range from highly ethical to downright criminal.

15.4.3.1 Online Sources. There is no small irony in the fact that much of what a person needs to know about how to penetrate information systems is made available by information systems. Fortunately, the inverse is also true, as one of this chapter's authors has observed: "The best weapon with which to protect information is information."[9] For this reason, security professionals need to know what sources of penetration information are available.

Today there are hundreds of Web sites that:

- Document security holes in different versions of operating systems
- Distribute hacking tools and discuss how to use them
- Catalog default credentials for network hardware
- Teach malicious code writing, including how to make viruses and worms
- List license codes to enable activation of pirated software
- Buy, sell, and trade system access codes, stolen credit cards, stolen identity data, and networks of compromised hosts (botnets)
- Provide a forum and meeting place for those seeking to penetrate systems

These sites assume the mantle of earlier online communication channels, such as bulletin boards and Usenet groups, where legitimate sharing of information occurred alongside the exchange of illegal information, pirated code, and so on. Some Web sites are moderated and so maintain certain ethical standards. Others follow the Internet tradition of anything goes. System administrators and employees should never participate in discussions on these Web sites with company e-mail addresses. In a popular strategy, hackers wait for platform-specific vulnerabilities to be announced, then search the Internet for messages from people using that platform, look at their e-mail addresses to see where they work, and attack systems at those companies in the hope that patches are not yet installed.

15.4.3.2 Publications.   Over the years many publications have specialized in hacking. Often these provided information on how to penetrate systems. Some publications were primarily electronic, such as *Phrack,* while others have been print based, such as *2600,* which is now widely distributed through conventional magazine channels as well as through paid subscriptions.

15.4.3.3 Hacker Support Groups.   Numerous groups of people exist to share hacking information, ranging from relatively stable entities with their own publications (e.g., *2600* and *cDc*) to annual conventions with thousands of participants (e.g., DefCon). Although some members of these groups may have committed criminal acts, and some participants at hacker conventions actually have been convicted of such and served time, there is usually a diverse mix of elements with different motivations in these groups and meetings. DefCon, for example, draws not only people who openly advocate unauthorized security testing of other people's systems and networks, but also law enforcement personnel and legitimate security experts. Some participants go to DefCon specifically to convince young people not to break laws while trying to learn about security.

Many security professionals would prefer that the line between white-hat hacking and black-hat hacking be clearer and more sharply enforced; however, some companies overlook past transgressions in order to gain the perceived value of the hackers' technical security expertise. Indeed, in recent years, investors have even cooperated with groups of hackers in founding security consulting companies, complete with some employees who continue to use hacker handles. The fact remains that some of the best technical training in the field is provided by people who gained their expertise in criminal (or quasi-criminal) hacking, but who now help defend against such activity.

15.4.4   Future of Penetration.   Trends over the last 10 years strongly suggest that attempts to penetrate information systems will not decrease any time soon. These factors have been in play for some time:

- The declining cost of, and increased access to, penetration technology—from software and hardware used to crack passwords and encryption to eavesdropping and interception devices
- The continuing practice of fielding inadequately tested systems, built with immature technology and with insufficient attention to security
- The increased availability of automated hacking tools with easy-to-use interfaces
- The continuing allure, and portrayal in popular culture, of hacking as a "cool" activity, without adequate reflection on its legality or consideration of its morality

Additionally, these factors have emerged strongly in recent years:

- The very real opportunity to make money from penetrating systems, given a thriving market in purloined personal data, compromised hosts (bots), and exploits
- The increased interest and involvement of organized crime in system penetration
- The rise of transnational terrorist organizations that are increasingly computer-literate and may be inclined to penetrate systems belonging to entities or countries to which they are opposed[10]

Although some companies and government agencies are actively pursuing improved responses to these threats, others are not. Through lack of concern, resources, or time to address these trends, many entities are at increasing risk. Each new technology brings new threats, but new threats typically are discounted as scaremongering by vendors who offer defenses against them. For many companies and government agencies, the enthusiasm to reap the benefits of new technology overrules the warnings about risks inherent in its deployment. When those risks finally manifest themselves in ways that threaten the organization, the reaction is usually to buy a technical fix while the root causes of vulnerability, namely human behavior and employee awareness of security issues, fail to receive the attention and resources they deserve.

15.5   SUMMARY

- Penetration of information systems is possible by means of a wide range of methods, some of which are very hard to defend against.
- Those responsible for securing systems have to defend against this wide range of penetration methods.
- Making sure all defenses against all attacks are effective all of the times is a lot harder than finding a single point of failure within those defenses.
- Although all systems do not need to defend against all types of attack equally, the cost of even the more exotic attack strategies is constantly falling, expanding the range of possible attackers.
- The cheapest and most effective attacks are often nontechnical, exploiting human frailty rather than weaknesses in the technology.

- Experienced criminal hackers tend to favor the nontechnical attack over the technical; and the best defense, employee awareness, is also nontechnical.

- Systems can be attacked at the client, at the server, or at the connection between the two.

- Both wired and wireless systems are highly susceptible to eavesdropping and interception.

- Many systems today are built with immature and insecure technology, making them susceptible to a wide range of attacks.

- New attacks come to light with alarming but predictable regularity.

- Many of these new attacks are old attacks reborn, due to a lack of vulnerability class analysis. As a result of economic pressures, faulty reasoning, and insufficient desire for security, vulnerabilities are fixed one instance at a time rather than one class at a time.

- Allowed path attacks against Web sites are consistently the most effective strategy for system penetration whenever a system is Web connected or Web enabled.

- Penetration testing, both by internal staff and by objective external experts, always should precede system deployment.

- Given the inevitability of penetration attempts and the high probability of their eventual success, systems should be designed to survive attacks, limiting the scope of compromise from any single point of failure.

- Penetration of systems will continue to fascinate the curious and tempt them to break the law by illegally accessing systems. The potential gains from system penetration, in terms of money, power, competitive advantage, and notoriety, will continue to motivate those to whom laws and morality are not effective deterrents.

- Penetration of systems will become increasingly automated and simplified, further widening the range of possible attackers.

- Human nature, not technology, is the key to defense against penetration attempts. Only by raising society's ethical standards and educating employees to understand the willingness of others to behave unethically can the occurrence of criminal hacking into information systems be significantly reduced.

15.6 FURTHER READING

Web Sites

CERIAS Hotlist: www.cerias.purdue.edu//hotlist
INFOSEC and INFOWAR Portal: www.infowar.com
SearchSecurity.com: searchsecurity.techtarget.com/
SecurityFocus: www.securityfocus.com
Web Application Security Consortium: www.webappsec.org/

Books

Fialka, J. J. *War by Other Means: Economic Espionage in America.* New York: W. W. Norton, 1997.

Goodell, J. *The Cyberthief and the Samurai: The True Story of Kevin Mitnick—and the Man Who Hunted Him Down.* New York: Dell, 1996.

Litchfield, D., Anley, C., Heasman, J., and Grindlay, B. *The Database Hacker's Handbook: Defending Database Servers.* Hoboken, NJ: John Wiley & Sons, 2005.

McClure, S., Scambray, J., and Kurtz, G. *Hacking Exposed*, 5th ed. New York: McGraw-Hill, 2005.

McGraw, G. *Software Security: Building Security In.* New York: Addison-Wesley Professional, 2006.

Scambray, J., Shema, M., and Sima, C. *Hacking Exposed: Web Applications*, 2nd ed. New York: McGraw-Hill Osborne, 2006.

Schwartau, W. *Pearl Harbor Dot Com.* Seminole, FL: InterPact Press, 2001.

Shimomura, T., and J. Markoff. *Takedown: The Pursuit and Capture of Kevin Mitnick, America's Most Wanted Computer Outlaw—by the Man Who Did It.* New York: Hyperion, 1996.

Slatalla, M., and J. Quittner. *Masters of Deception: The Gang that Ruled Cyberspace.* New York: HarperCollins, 1995.

Sterling, B. *The Hacker Crackdown: Law and Disorder on the Electronic Frontier.* New York: Bantam Doubleday Dell, 1992.

Stoll, C. *The Cuckoo's Egg: Tracking a Spy through the Maze of Computer Espionage.* New York: Pocket Books/Simon & Schuster, 1989.

Stuttard, D., and Pinto, M. *The Web Application Hacker's Handbook: Discovering and Exploiting Security Flaws.* Hoboken, NJ: John Wiley & Sons, 2007.

15.7 NOTES

1. "Report on the Existence of a Global System for Intercepting Private and Commercial Communications (ECHELON Interception System)," PE 305.391, July 11, 2001, http://cryptome.org/echelon-ep-fin.htm.

2. S. Cobb, *The Stephen Cobb Guide to PC & LAN Security* (New York: McGraw-Hill, 1992).

3. Robert Lemos, "Mitnick Teaches 'Social Engineering,'" News.com, Published on *ZDNet News*, July 17, 2000, http://news.zdnet.com/2100-9595_22-522261.html.

4. "Defector Smuggled Out Copies of the 'Crown Jewels' of Soviet Espionage," *The Times* (London), September 12, 1999.

5. AT&T Press Release, Dallas TX, December 6, 2007. www.att.com/rss

6. Dan Farmer and Wietse Venema, "Improving the Security of Your Site by Breaking into It," available on http://nsi.org/library/compsec/farmer.txt.

7. According to internetworldstats.com, www.internetworldstats.com/stats.htm.

8. "The Ghost in the Browser: Analysis of Web-based Malware," www.usenix.org/events/hotbots07/tech/full_papers/provos/provos.pdf.

9. Cobb, *Stephen Cobb Guide.*

10. C. Wilson, "Botnets, Cybercrime, and Cyberterrorism: Vulnerabilities and Policy Issues for Congress," Congressional Research Service Report for Congress, RL32114, 2007, at http://tinyurl.com/2y995r.

CHAPTER 16

MALICIOUS CODE

Robert Guess and Eric Salveggio

16.1 INTRODUCTION. Malicious logic (or code) is "hardware, software, or firmware that is intentionally included in a system for an unauthorized purpose."[1] In this chapter, we enumerate the common types of malicious code, sources of malicious code, methods of malicious code replication, and methods of malicious code detection.

Common types of malicious code include viruses, worms, Trojan horses, spyware, rootkits, and bots. Emerging malicious code threats include kleptographic code, cryptoviruses, and hardware-based rootkits. Present-day malicious code threats do not always fit into neat categories, resulting in confusion when discussing the topic. It is not possible to classify all code as being *good* code or *malicious* code. Absent the *mens rea*, or criminal intent of the author or user, code is neither good nor bad. Authors develop code to achieve some goal or fulfill some purpose just as users run code to achieve some goal or purpose. It is therefore the context of use and the intent of the wielder that determines whether code is malicious.

16.2 MALICIOUS CODE THREAT MODEL. In a threat model or profile, an *actor* uses *access* to target an *asset*, with an *action*, to yield an *outcome*.[2] To understand the scope of the problem (and possible prevention), it is useful to study malicious code threats in this model. Actors may be structured or unstructured threats posed by individuals, organizations, or nation-states. Access is some allowed physical or logical path to the targeted asset. The execution of malicious code or logic is an action used to yield the desired outcome. This outcome could be intelligence (such as theft of trade secrets), surveillance, reconnaissance, disruption of operations, destruction of assets, publicity for some cause, or negative publicity for the victim.

16.2.1 Self-Replicating Code. Self-replicating code is not inherently malicious. A good deal of artificial intelligence research focuses on iterative self-replication. Hewlett-Packard and others[3] have researched how techniques of self-replication could yield beneficial software such as code patching worms. John Von Neumann proposed the basic concept of self-replicating code in his 1949 paper, "Theory of Self-Reproducing Automata."[4] In 1961 at Bell Labs, Douglas McIlroy, Victor Vyssotsky, and Robert H. Morris played a game called Darwin in which two opposing programs (memory worms) would enter a system and only one would leave. In an interview with one of the authors, Robert H. Morris the former Chief Scientist of the National Security Agency (NSA), stated:

> We had this notion of putting two programs in a machine that would fight with each other and one would win and the other would die. Basically, the notion and the program were written by McIlroy and Vyssotsky and I was just on the side. But then, a few days later, I had a good idea and simply won the game and everyone else gave up. . .just because I happened to hit upon a very good idea for writing it.[5]

Although it would be desirable to live in a world free of war, the ever-increasing integration of technology and warfare necessitates the development of offensive information warfare capabilities. Malicious code implants can serve useful intelligence, surveillance, and reconnaissance capabilities in national security and law enforcement operations. In addition, by researching and developing malicious code techniques, practitioners can better prepare for defense against developing threats.

16.2.2 Actors: Origin of Malicious Code Threats. Prior to discussing the specific types of malicious code, it is worth understanding the origin and source of malicious code attacks. Malicious code may originate from structured or unstructured threats. Structured threats include nation-states, corporate criminals, and organized crime. Unstructured threats include rogue actors such as individual intruders and so-called script kiddies.

16.2.3 Actors: Structured Threats. Structured threats are organized, well funded, and may operate with a long-term strategic view. Structured malicious code threats tend to have intelligence, surveillance, and reconnaissance capabilities among their primary functions. Structured threats may use these capabilities to engage in industrial espionage, adversarial information operations, or serious ongoing fraud and theft.

Organized crime is responsible for 90 percent of malicious code threats.[6] Extortionists target the online gambling industry with threats of distributed denial of service (DDoS) attacks launched from compromised personal computers. Criminals use compromised systems to engage in pump-and-dump stock fraud with one media outlet reporting annual gains by such groups approaching $1 billion a year.[7] Malicious software-for-hire incidents are on the rise, indicating a maturing marketplace for malicious code. In 2006 an Israeli court sentenced a couple to prison time and ordered them to pay fines for authoring and placing malicious code used to spy on corporations and individuals by members of telecommunications and trading firms. http://tinyurl.com/4gx38p

Coordinated, systematic attacks originating from China routinely target defense and research and development facilities. In the 1999 text *Unrestricted Warfare*, two Chinese air force officers called for a transformation of warfare that would involve ongoing technological attacks on western assets.[8] A Chinese military white paper released in 2006 called for a strategy whereby China could win an "informationized war"[9] against the West that is "high-paced, high-technology and digitized." Although Chinese officials publicly deny sponsoring such attacks, the lack of law enforcement action indicates, at the very least, toleration for electronic attacks on western assets.

16.2.4   Actors: Unstructured Threats.   Unstructured threats include rogue actors not acting in concert or coordination with larger entities. Although serious attacks may result from unstructured threats, they do not pose the same long-term challenges as structured threats. In testimony before the United States Congress, former NSA director Kenneth Minihan stated:

> The unstructured threat is random and relatively limited. It consists of adversaries with limited funds and organization and short-term goals. While it poses a threat to system operations, national security is not targeted. This is the most obvious threat today. The structured threat is considerably more methodical and well-supported. While the unstructured threat is the most obvious threat today, for national security purposes we are concerned primarily with the structured threat, since that poses the most significant risk.[10]

16.2.5   Access versus Action: Vector versus Payload.   Malicious code attacks involve a vector and a payload. In biology, a vector is an agent that transfers (potentially harmful) material (code) from one location to another. In computer attacks, a vector is an avenue of *access*, such as an allowed path via physical access or via the network. Physical access occurs via internal personnel or others with access to the premises. Access via the network may occur via an allowed path to a Web server, an allowed path from a malicious Web server to a Web client, to a user via an e-mail attachment, or to some other software process through an accessible port. The payload is a function (*action*) placed on the system to achieve some end. Payloads may include additional malicious logic, remote access software (rootkits et al.), or remote control (robot or bot) software to achieve some objective (spamming, distributed denial-of-service (DDoS) attacks, etc).

16.3   SURVEY OF MALICIOUS CODE

16.3.1   Viruses.   In biology, a virus is "[a]n infectious organism that is usually submicroscopic, can multiply only inside certain living host cells, and is now understood to be a non-cellular structure lacking any intrinsic metabolism and usually comprising a DNA or RNA core inside a protein coat."[11] In computer terms, a virus is self-replicating code that requires a host executable or document and the aid of a human to replicate. Joe Dellinger created the first virus for the Apple disk operating system in 1982 while a student at Texas A&M.[12] Fred Cohen created the first VAX computer virus in 1983 as a part of his doctoral research.[13] Len Adleman, the A in RSA, first applied the biologic metaphor virus to describe the results.

Types of viruses include boot sector, file infector, macro virus, logic bomb, cross-site scripting viruses (really a form of worm), polymorphic viruses, and cryptoviruses. However, modern malicious code threats tend not to fall so neatly into categories.

16.3.1.1 Boot Sector Viruses.

When users boot a computer from digital media, they allow code present in the boot sector of the media to run on the microprocessor with very little intermediation. Boot sector viruses used this mechanism to spread via infected removable media. If a user errantly booted from an infected floppy disk, compact disc (CD), DVD, or flash drive, the virus would copy itself to the boot sector of the hard drive. Thereafter, the malicious program code would copy itself to each medium inserted into the system. Although reportedly still in existence, boot sector viruses comprise very few modern malicious code threats.

16.3.1.2 File Infector Viruses.

File infector viruses inserted themselves into programs present on the host system. Whenever a user ran the host program (usually an .EXE or .COM file), the malicious code used the opportunity to insert itself into random access memory (RAM) and then replicate to other files on the system. Although probably still in existence, file infector viruses comprise relatively few modern malicious code threats.

16.3.1.3 Macro Viruses.

Macro viruses spread via the macro definition languages used by some applications. The most widely abused is the Visual Basic for Applications (VBA) scripting language that Microsoft developed to allow the automation of functions inside the Office product suite. Any feature that allows for automation is a likely point of attack. Developers should carefully weigh security and ease of use when including such features in products. The first macro virus to target Microsoft Word[14] appeared in the wild in 1995. Since that time, macro viruses have comprised a significant number of successful attacks.

16.3.1.4 Logic Bombs.

A logic bomb is a form of malicious code function sometimes built into viruses that wait for some sequence of events to activate such as a particular date and time. In 2002 an employee of UBS PaineWebber planted a logic bomb in his employer's servers as part of an attempted stock manipulation scheme.[15] The perpetrator, Roger Duronio, purchased numerous put option stock contracts allowing him to sell UBS stock at a fixed, high price. On March 4, 2002, at 9:30 A.M., the logic bomb began deleting files on over 1,000 computers, causing a reported $3 million in damage.. Duronio thought that the effects of the logic bomb would bring down the stock value of UBS, allowing him to make a large profit from his stock options.. Duronio's plot failed and his profit did not materialize. Federal authorities later charged him with securities and computer fraud. In 2006 a judge sentenced Duronio to 97 months in prison for the attack.[16]

16.3.1.5 Cross-Site Scripting Viruses (or Worms).

Cross-site scripting viruses (or worms) replicate via flawed Web application servers and client code. A cross-site scripting exploit involving the social networking site MySpace and flaws in Microsoft Internet Explorer occurred in 2005 whereby a user named Samy amassed over 1 million friends overnight using a JavaScript insertion bug.[17] The Los Angeles Superior Court sentenced the author, Samy Kamkar, to three years probation and 90 days of community service for his actions.

16.3.1.6 *Polymorphic Viruses.* Polymorphic code modifies itself to evade detection. The virus code may accomplish this by dynamically reassembling itself to modify the underlying structure while retaining overall functionality. In other methods, the virus is encrypted, encoded, or packed and a stub loader decrypts, decodes, or unpacks the virus at run time. UPX, the Ultimate Packer for eXecutables, is currently the most widely used packer format.

16.3.1.7 *Cryptographic Viruses.* Cryptoviruses use encryption to encrypt data making it inaccessible to the user. Although some viruses use symmetric algorithms for self-encryption to evade detection, such algorithms are inappropriate for data encrypting viruses, as any copy of the virus is going to yield a copy of the symmetric key. For this reason, proper cryptoviruses use asymmetric techniques. The Gpcode virus encrypts files by extension (.xls, .doc, etc.) and leaves behind a text message prompting the user to e-mail a given address to pay a ransom for access to their files. The next generation of cryptoviruses will likely use hybrid cryptosystems.

16.3.2 Worms. The term "worm" refers to any form of self-replicating code that does not integrate into executable code. Common worm vectors include vulnerable services, e-mail, instant messaging applications, and open file shares. Many worms use multiple vectors. For example, the Nimda worm spread via e-mail, Web server vulnerabilities, hosted malicious Web pages, and open file shares.[18]

The first large-scale Internet worm infection was the Morris (aka Internet) Worm released by Robert T. Morris on November 2, 1988, while a student at Cornell University. The worm exploited flaws in the Sendmail and finger services to replicate and infected nearly 10 percent of Internet hosts. Although he claimed that this was an experiment gone awry, Morris became the first person convicted under the Computer Fraud and Abuse Act.

In 2001 Nicholas Weaver coined the term "Warhol Worms"[19] for those worms that had the capability of propagating very quickly (taking a cue from Warhol's famous quip that in the future everyone would have 15 minutes of fame). The SQL Slammer worm became the first such worm when it infected approximately 90 percent of vulnerable systems in 10 minutes.[20] The Slammer worm replicated due to a flaw in the Microsoft SQL database server. Because this was installed along with other components like Visual Studio, many people did not even know that they were running an SQL server. Slammer was exceedingly effective because a Microsoft service pack downgraded a previously patched dynamic link library (dll) to an older, vulnerable version. Specifically, Microsoft issued four updates to *ssnetlib.dll* in 2002. Unfortunately, in October, hotfix Q317748 downgraded *ssnetlib.dll* to a vulnerable version, ironically making those who most faithfully applied patches and hotfixes the most vulnerable to Slammer.[21]

The SQL Slammer worm is an interesting case study because it was a vector without a payload. The 376-byte worm ran in memory without touching the hard disk, leading some to believe that Slammer was an experiment in propagation techniques. Since it was based on the User Datagram Protocol (UDP) and traveled in a single packet, the overhead was minimal and the propagation rate was greater than any previous malicious code threat.[22] The fact that the author(s) released it on a Saturday is also curious. It is unknown why a malicious attacker would deliberately release such a rabid virus on a day of the week that would lessen the overall business impact. If the author had released the worm on a peak business day such as a Tuesday, the damage caused would have been much more severe.

Worms are used to distribute other forms of malware such as Trojans, spyware, rootkits, and remote command and control channels called *bots*. An indication of the overall maturity of malicious code attacks is the Bagel worm, which has been in production at least since 2004. Bagel, like many other mail worms, arrives as an e-mail with a malicious attachment. When the user runs the attachment, the payload is executed, which does a number of things depending on the variant. Later variants of Bagel install an open application framework that the remote attackers may update and extend. The harvested systems deliver spam (unsolicited commercial e-mail), harvest additional addresses, and act as a staging point for other attacks. The author(s) appear to follow a sophisticated software development methodology and testing process.[23] Recently the rate of activity has increased with attackers releasing 30,000 new variants in a six-week time span in early 2007.[24]

16.3.3   Trojans.   A Trojan horse application, like the horse of Greek mythology, carries both an overt function and a covert function. Although attackers may use worms as one possible propagation vector, Trojans require that a user run the malicious program in order to be effective. Trojans tend to use some form of social engineering or manipulation to persuade the user to run the program. E-mail worms may appear to originate from a known associate and thereby trick the user. Other Trojans may take the form of games, free offers, pictures of popular celebrities, or files on peer-to-peer file sharing services. One study of the *Limewire* peer-to-peer file sharing service found that "68% of all downloadable responses containing executable, archival, and Microsoft Office file extensions"[25] contained malware. Queries for movies were most likely to hold malicious code.

The covert function of Trojan horse application is typically some form of a remote access Trojan, keylogger, dialer, IRC bot, or rootkit. Remote access Trojans provide full remote access to the system. The developers of the Bo2K Trojan bill it as "the most powerful network administration tool available for the Microsoft environment" and insist upon the fact that it is functionally no different from other remote access solutions.[26] Keylogging Trojans record keystrokes and periodically upload the data to a remote user. Attackers carried out the Windows 2000 source code theft using credentials stolen by a QAZ Trojan installed on a remote workers computer. A dialer is a form of Trojan that silently dials remote toll numbers and runs up a large telephone bill for the victim. Internet relay chat (IRC) bots act as autonomous IRC clients. Early IRC bots provided technical support and channel monitoring features but are now widely used for malicious purposes such as command and control capabilities.

16.3.4   Spyware.   The term *spyware* refers to any software that collects user information without consent. Common varieties of spyware collect information on Web usage, serve advertising content (pop-ups), log keystrokes, engage in click fraud, or monitor program usage and licensing. Unauthorized access or exceeding authority on a computer system is a violation of the Computer Fraud and Abuse Act. Although some spyware may be illegal, some developers insist that they are engaged in a legitimate business activity. Such spyware provides an end user license agreement (EULA) allowing the user to opt out of installation. Since the user must grant permission for the software to install, it is almost certainly legal. However, whether this is ethical and conscionable is a different matter. Sony attracted significant negative publicity for their use of spyware technology to limit the ability of listeners to copy music compact discs. Due to this activity, Sony faced legal charges in multiple states and in 2005 settled a class-action lawsuit. Informed consent is the rule of thumb in any monitoring system. Organizations should endeavor to be forthright in these matters in order to maintain a positive public profile and to avoid legal challenges.

16.3.5 Rootkits. A rootkit consists of a set of tools for covertly compromising a system and maintaining administrative (root) access for the intruder. Present day rootkits compromise a system at the application, library, kernel, hypervisor, or hardware level. Early application-level rootkits targeted Unix-like systems and replaced standard system utilities (netstat, ps, etc.) with versions that omitted information on the intruder such as open ports, running processes, open files, and other activity. API-level rootkits modify or patch the system call table to redirect system calls (like an API-level monkey-in-the-middle attack). Kernel-level rootkits run as device drivers and dynamically load into the kernel; compromising the integrity of the core of the operating system to filter information presented to users via application-level processes.

Nearly all modern operating systems make use of virtualization for memory and process management. An operating system normally runs in ring 0 of the microprocessor; the most privileged level. A hypervisor is a layer of code between the operating system and the hardware that fools the operating system into believing that it is running in ring 0. The hypervisor monitors and arbitrates exchanges between virtual machines and the real hardware. Hypervisor design is a key part of the trusted computing framework, and microprocessor designers like Intel and AMD are including enhanced hardware-based virtualization capabilities in their products. An emerging generation of rootkit technology uses this framework to create potentially undetectable code.[27,28]

Other potential rootkit threats come from insiders, hardware designers, and manufacturers. An attacker with physical access could insert a peripheral component into a computer to create a logically undetectable rootkit. A hardware manufacturer or designer could include rootkit-like capabilities in a microcircuit. The 2005 sale of IBM's Personal Computer Division to Chinese manufacturer Lenovo caused enough concern in the United States to prompt a national security review of the transaction.[29] The review by the House Committee on Foreign Investment in the United States (CFIUS) eventually approved the sale despite concerns expressed by Reps. Henry Hyde and Don Manzullo of Illinois and Rep. Duncan Hunter of California.[30]

16.3.6 IRC Bots. IRC bots are autonomous agents that make use of Internet Relay Chat (IRC) to offer interactive services like channel monitoring, support, information services, and games. Greg Lindhal wrote the first IRC bot GM (game master), which led users through the text based role-playing game "Hunt the Wumpus." In 1999, the PrettyPark worm became the first worm to use IRC as a remote control channel. Infected systems would check into an IRC server and channel to download updates and upload stolen data. Attackers create malicious bots to carry out distributed denial of service attacks (DDoS bots), send unsolicited commercial e-mail (SpamBots), and engage in exploitation, theft, or fraud.

Examples of current bot frameworks are GTbot, SDbot, Agobot, Goabot, Randex, Spybot, and Phatbot. The current generation of bot technologies includes keylogging, port scanning, exploitation, packet sniffing, process hiding, and adware fraud capabilities. A single network of these compromised systems may reach over 100,000 bots. Researchers in 2004 estimated that there were over one million bots currently connected to the Internet.[31] Bot herders rent out these massive distributed networks systems to criminal organizations. In 2006, a California court sentenced one such bot herder, Jeanson Ancheta, to five years in prison for conspiring to violate the Computer Fraud and Abuse Act, conspiring to violate the CAN-SPAM Act, causing damage to computers used by the federal government in national defense, and accessing protected computers without authorization, in order to commit fraud.[32]

16.3.7   Malicious Mobile Code.   Web servers may host pages containing malicious mobile code. ActiveX controls, Java applets, JavaScript, Adobe Flash animations, and any other type of dynamic executing code can download to a user's system and run in their context with all associated privileges. Malicious Web servers are one method for dropping Trojans and bots onto computers. An attacker may use a spam or phishing attack to encourage users to click on a link embedded within an e-mail. Another vector is to use a similar domain name to a legitimate organization. Yet another vector is for the site to offer information in some matter. Once indexed in the major search engines, this content will draw a number of users to the site.

16.4   DETECTION OF MALICIOUS CODE.   Common methods of detecting malicious code include signature-based, network-based, and behavioral heuristic techniques. However, as far back as in the 1984 work "Computer Viruses—Theory and Experiments," Fred Cohen demonstrated that the only way one could prevent all possible viral code would be through isolation.[33] While there are numerous methods of detecting malicious code, no one technique works on every variety or in every circumstance, and there is always some method for successfully evading detection.

16.4.1   Signature-Based Malicious Code Detection.   Some of the oldest methods of malicious code detection are signature-based methods that utilize known strings or patterns in the code. Signature-based methods are easy to implement and impose very low overhead on the system but are just as easily evaded. Polymorphism and metamorphism[34] are two methods by which malware may change form over time and thereby evade signature-based detection. Detection systems can use hash functions to fingerprint a given binary program or code fragment. However, the hash will fail to match on any modified version, making this method reliable but not always useful. Overall, signature-based methods are not terribly reliable, although signatures are one useful metric in more complex heuristics.

16.4.2   Network-Based Malicious Code Detection.   Network-based methods of malicious code detection look for network artifacts associated with malicious code such as a connection to a server as in the case of a keylogging Trojan or Internet Relay Chat (IRC) bot. Network anomaly detection works well but is expensive and poorly understood by many security practitioners. A simple method for network-based detection is to analyze network flow (netflow) data in comparison with a statistical database of known good traffic. However, malicious code that acts normal can bypass such methods of detection. Predicting what is normal for a given environment may be difficult for an outsider, but analyzing certain activity like domain name system, e-mail, and Web usage can produce generic models for evasion.

16.4.3 Behavioral Malicious Code Detection. Behavioral methods of detecting malicious code analyze the actions of running software to look for illegitimate activity. This could be opening a port, connecting to a remote host, or modifying the system call table or other memory areas. Behavioral methods of detection will fail if the malware acts normal or if the malicious code can target and exploit the detection system itself. A slow but effective method of detecting potentially malicious code is to use a virtual machine approach whereby the system allows code to execute in a sandboxed virtual machine. This allows for a full functional analysis of the code, but the current throughput of such systems makes them not useful for today's high-speed production environments.

16.4.4 Heuristic Malicious Code Detection. Heuristics that are more complex may use both statistical and behavioral models to determine a relative score to a normal corpus (statistical database in this case) of legitimate behavior. Bayesian analysis is widely used in the detection of spam. However, this method can also detect new variants of existing malicious code with a high degree of accuracy. N-gram analysis is a form of frequency analysis borrowed from natural language processing that can model software and fingerprint data types. This method is useful for detecting executable code embedded within other data objects. In short, there is no single, monolithic way to detect all malicious code. Spinellis demonstrated that reliable detection of malicious code is NP-complete,[35] meaning that the dilemma is not solvable in polynomial time. However, the technologies discussed, used in concert, are relatively effective in detecting many common malicious code threats.

16.5 PREVENTION OF MALICIOUS CODE ATTACKS

16.5.1 Defense in Depth. As the problem of malicious code is demonstrably NP-complete (not solvable), a single antivirus program cannot protect against all malicious code threats. One strategy, called defense in depth, uses operational, human, and technical controls. Another strategy is to build networks and applications that only function one correct way. Such *orthogonal* networks and applications are a rarity as they are expensive and difficult to design, and many firms will resist imposing rigid limitations on the enterprise.

16.5.2 Operational Controls for Malicious Code. All organizations must create written policies and procedures regarding the introduction of program code into the operating environment. Policies should define what persons the firm allows to install programs, acceptable use for Internet access, acceptable use for e-mail systems, and what to do if users suspect the compromise of a system or user. Organizations should subject all new employees to some level of background investigation. This should include, at a minimum, a criminal records search, verification of all references and credentials, and a credit report. Employers should ensure that the prospective employees are forthright and truthful on their application. If employees lie prior to employment, the odds are that they will lie later as well.

16.5.3 Human Controls for Malicious Code. All users (including executives) should receive training on the policies and procedures of the organization. Due to the evolving nature of the malicious code threat, the organization should update and refresh this training annually at the very least. The training sessions should introduce the prevalent types of threats, how to detect the threats, and proper response. Currently this training should include identification of advance-fee fraud (also known as Nigerian 419 frauds), social engineering attempts, and detection of malicious attachments. Users should notify the help desk or other entity if they encounter any anomalous system or user behavior.

16.5.4 Technical Controls for Malicious Code.   For more detailed information on antivirus technology, see Chapter 41 in this *Handbook*.

16.5.4.1 *Implementing Antivirus Systems.*   Implement an antivirus (A/V) solution that suits the operational environment. This solution should include both network-based and host-based systems. Network-based systems function inline like a gateway, while host-based systems run on host end points. These systems should come from different vendors, as there is less benefit when using the same software on the network and hosts. A diverse detection and containment strategy will help firms avoid the pitfalls associated with active malcode exploitation of antivirus software as occurred in 2004[36] and again in 2006.[37] The last thing that organizations should permit when designing an A/V strategy is for antivirus software to serve as the vector for an active malcode attack.

The A/V solution should provide a mechanism for dynamically applying updates and should do so daily, at the least. E-mail systems may require a separate inline appliance to detect e-mail–borne malicious code as well as spam, fraud, and phishing attacks. By using a diversity of detection approaches, organizations can attain higher rates of detection than by using a single stand-alone product.

16.5.4.2 *Host Configuration Controls and Security.*   Host configuration can mitigate many malcode threats prior to emergence. Implement a form of automatic updates (patches, etc.) that supports the operating environment. Many technical malicious code threats (e.g., worms) target well-known and patched flaws. Eliminate all noncritical software and services. This will help minimize threats that target the ever-burgeoning code complexity security professional face. In one study, programmers trained in the capability maturity model for secure software development continued to make 4.5 errors per 1000 lines of code.[38] For an operating system like Microsoft Vista, which one estimate puts at 50 million lines of code,[39] extrapolating this statistic means that there are likely at least 225,000 code errors. Disabling or removing as much of this code as possible is a reasonable preventive control. If the environment permits, remove all Web browsers. If the environment does not allow this, lock down the browser configuration and use a secure Web proxy.

16.5.4.3 *Network-Based Security Controls.*   A layered defense of routers, firewalls, proxies, and switched virtual local area networks (VLANS) can mitigate malicious code propagation. At the router, filter all inbound bogus network addresses (BOGONs), RFC 1918 addresses, and spoofed internal addresses per RFCs 2267[40] and 3704.[41] If the enterprise faces specific threats from certain nations, filter the network blocks allocated to those nations at the border router. Use the current best practices in firewall configuration. (These change rapidly.) Use a secure, authenticated Web proxy, and force all clients to use the proxy. (No user should be able to access the Web directly.) Disable all unused LAN access ports or consider using 802.1x authentication to do so automatically. Segment the network into functional workgroups using VLANs or physically separate switch architecture. If possible, implement access control lists between VLANs or switched segments. The goal is to make the network as orthogonal as possible. If the network can function only one right way, the organization will avoid many automated malicious code threats entirely.

16.5.4.4 Network Monitoring.
Prevention of malicious code threats is ideal, but detection is critical. Most malicious code attacks will have some artifact, whether host based or network based. To detect these artifacts, organizations should establish a security information management system that aggregates device logs, server logs, host logs, intrusion detection system alerts, and network flow data. Network flow data is a useful tool for detecting anomalous network activity. A network flow is a 5-tuple consisting of a source address, destination address, source port, destination port, and protocol with an associated time stamp. Any malicious network activity is going to have an associated flow. Stealthy malware, however, will attempt to act normal in order to evade detection. Detecting anomalous activity requires that operators understand what is normal for the environment. Without a historical statistical database or extensive experience, this can be difficult. Network anomaly detection (NAD) uses a statistical modeling methodology[42] to use this data to detect statistical outliers. This is extraordinarily effective for detecting new malicious code threats as well as other forms of anomalous behavior. However, a lack of understanding appears to limit the adoption of NAD. This is one area where many organizations could improve their practice of information security controls.

16.6 CONCLUSION.
Malicious code threats are as numerous as the variety of nonmalicious code. Prevention of all malicious code is not possible as the problem is demonstrably NP-complete. However, a strategy of defense in depth that uses operational, human, and technical controls can be relatively effective. Used properly, the current generation of technical controls available to organizations is effective in stopping a majority of malicious code threats. However, the trusted insider typically has the access needed to turn a threat into a reality of operational risk. Current trends in malicious code threats indicate a continued pattern of organized criminal involvement and international espionage that continues to target the weakest link in the security chain: the human.

16.7 FURTHER READING

Jamie Butler and Greg Hoglund. *Rootkits: Subverting the Windows Kernel.* Addison-Wesley, 2006

Harley, David., et al. *Avien Malware Defense Guide for the Enterprise.* Burlington, MA: Syngress, 2007.

Harley, David. " *OS X Exploits and Defense,*" Burlington, MA: Syngress, 2008

Szor, Peter. *The Art of Computer Virus Research and Defense.* Cupertino, CA: Symantec Press, 2005. Young, Adam., and Yung, Moti. *Malicious Cryptography: Exposing Cryptovirology.* Hoboken, NJ: John Wiley & Sons, 2004.

16.8 NOTES

1. NCSC, "Glossary of Computer Security Terms," Version 1, 1988, NCSC-TG-004 in the Rainbow Series, www.fas.org/irp/nsa/rainbow/tg004.htm.

2. C. Alberts and A. Dorofee, "OCTAVE Threat Profiles," 2001, www.cert.org/archive/pdf/OCTAVEthreatProfiles.pdf.

3. R. Lemos, "Good Worms Back on the Agenda," *Security Focus*, January 27, 2006, www.securityfocus.com/news/11373.

4. John von Neumann, "Theory of Self-Reproducing Automata," *Part 1: Transcripts of Lectures Given at the University of Illinois, Dec. 1949*, ed. A. W. Burks (University of Illinois, 1966). Urbana, IL

5. R. H. Morris, Recorded interview with Robert Guess, July 2005.

6. D. Llet, "Antivirus Firm Says Organized Crime Growing Online," *ZDnet News*, December 9, 2004, http://news.zdnet.com/2100-1009_22-5486201.html.

7. J. Hoskyn, "SEC Targets Pump and Dump Scammers," *IT Week*, March 9, 2007, www.itweek.co.uk/vnunet/news/2185164/sec-targets-pump-dump-stock.

8. Quio Liang and Wang Xiangsui, *Unrestricted Warfare* (Beijing: PLA Literature and Arts Publishing House, 1999), www.terrorism.com/documents/TRC Analysis/unrestricted.pdf. (Access Permission required)

9. J. Rogin, "Cyber Officials: Chinese Hackers Attack 'Anything and Everything,'" February 13, 2007, www.fcw.com/article97658-02-13-07-Web&printLayout.

10. Kenneth A. Minihan, "Prepared Statement before the Senate Governmental Affairs Committee," June 14, 1998, www.senate.gov/~gov_affairs/62498minihan.htm.

11. *Oxford English Dictionary,* 2007.

12. J. Dellinger, Usenet Post, December 2, 1987, http://yarchive.net/risks/early_virus.html.

13. F. Cohen, "Experiments with Computer Viruses," 1984, www.all.net/books/virus/part5.html.

14. Microsoft, "What to Do If You Have a Macro Virus," October 4, 2002, http://support.microsoft.com/kb/181080/en-us.

15. U.S. Department of Justice, United States Attorney District of New Jersey, "Disgruntled UBS PaineWebber Employee Charged with Allegedly Unleashing 'Logic Bomb' on Company Computers," December 17, 2002, www.usdoj.gov/criminal/cybercrime/duronioIndict.htm.

16. U.S. Department of Justice Press Release, "Former UBS Computer Systems Manager Gets 97 Months for Unleashing 'Logic Bomb' on Company Network," 2006, www.usdoj.gov/usao/nj/press/files/pdffiles/duro1213rel.pdf.

17. E. Lai, "Teen Uses Worm to Boost Ratings on MySpace.com," *Computer-World,* October 17, 2005, www.computerworld.com/securitytopics/security/holes/story/0,10801,105484,00.html.

18. CERT. "Advisory CA-2001-26 Nimda Worm." Original release date: September 18, 2001, Revised: September 25, 2001. Source: CERT/CC, http://www.cert.org/advisories/CA-2001-26.html

19. N.Weaver, "Warhol Worms: The Potential for Very Fast Internet Plagues," 2001, www.iwar.org.uk/comsec/resources/worms/warhol-worm.htm.

20. D. Moore, V. Paxson, S. Savage, C. Shannon, S. Staniford, and N. Weaver, "The Spread of the Sapphire/Slammer Worm," CAIDA, 2003, www.caida.org/publications/papers/2003/sapphire/sapphire.html.

21. S. Berinato, "Patch and Pray," *CSO Online.* August 14, 2003, www.csoonline.com.au/index.php/id;1337625166;fp;8;fpid;5.

22. T. Vogt, "Simulating and Optimising Worm Propagation Algorithms" September 29, 2003, http://web.lemuria.org/security/WormPropagation.pdf.

23. "Year of the Beagle: The Beagle Worm History, Part III," Infection Vectors Web site, (February 2005), www.infectionvectors.com/vectors/year_of_the_beagle.htm.

24. CommTouch, "Malware Outbreak Trend Report: Bagle/Beagle," March 6, 2007, www.commtouch.com/documents/Bagle-Worm_MOTR.pdf.

25. A. Kalafut, A. Acharya, and M. Gupta, "A Study of Malware in PeertoPeer Networks," 2006, www.imconf.net/imc-2006/papers/p33-kalafut.pdf.

26. B02k Web site, "A Note on Product Legitimacy and Security," ND, http://bo2k.sourceforge.net/docs/bo2k_legitimacy.html.

27. S. King and P. Chen, "SubVirt: Implementing Malware with Virtual Machines," 2006. www.eecs.umich.edu/virtual/papers/king06.pdf.

28. J. Rutkowska, "Subverting the Vista Kernel for Fun and Profit," 2006, www.blackhat.com/presentations/bh-usa-06/BH-US-06-Rutkowska.pd.

29. A. Wolfe, "U.S. To Review IBM-Lenovo Sale," *CMP*, 2005, www.crn.com/hardware/59100372.

30. IBM, "Committee on Foreign Investment in U.S. completes review of Lenovo-IBM deal," 2005, www.informationweek.com/news/hardware/showarticle.jhtml?articleID=162400445

31. P. Bacher, T. Holz, M. Kotter, and G. Wicherski, "Know Your Enemy: Tracking Botnets," 2005, www.honeynet.org/papers/bots/.

32. U.S. Department of Justice, "'Botherder' Dealt Record Prison Sentence for Selling and Spreading Malicious Computer Code," 2006, www.cybercrime.gov/anchetaSent.htm.

33. F. Cohen, "Computer Viruses—Theory and Experiments," 1984, http://www.all.net/books/virus/index.html.

34. M. Christodorescu, S.. Jha, S. Seshia, D. Song, and R. Bryant, "Semantics-Aware Malware Detection," 2005, www.eecs.berkeley.edu/~sseshia/pubdir/oakland05.pdf.

35. D. Spinellis, "Reliable Identification of Bounded-length Viruses is NP-complete," 2003, www.dmst.aueb.gr/dds/pubs/jrnl/2002-ieeetit-npvirus/html/npvirus.html.

36. D. Fisher, "Fast-Moving Worm Crashes Computers," March 22, 2004, http://www.eweek.com/article2/0,1895,1551998,00.asp.

37. T. Gray, "New Worm Attacks Through Symantec Antivirus App," December 18, 2006, www.newsfactor.com/news/Worm-Attacks-Through-Antivirus-Flaw/story.xhtml?story_id=121000E3SRW1.

38. W. Humphrey, "Three Dimensions of Process Improvement Part II: The Personal Process," 1998, www.stsc.hill.af.mil/crossTalk/frames.asp?uri=1998/03/dimensions.asp.

39. S. Manes, "Dim Vista," *Forbes Magazine,* February 26, 2007, http://www.forbes.com/free_forbes/2007/0226/050.html.

40. P. Ferguson and D. Senie, "RFC 2267: Network Ingress Filtering: Defeating Denial of Service Attacks which employ IP Source Address Spoofing," Internet Engineering Task Force, 1998, http://www.ietf.org/rfc/rfc2267.txt.

41. F. Baker and P. Savola, "RFC 3704: Ingress Filtering for Multihomed Networks," Internet Engineering Task Force, 2004, www.ietf.org/rfc/rfc3704.txt.

42. National Security Agency, "Network Anomaly Detection Algorithm," ND, www.nsa.gov/techtrans/techt00029.cfm.

MOBILE CODE

Robert Gezelter

17.1   INTRODUCTION.   At its most basic, mobile code is a set of instructions that are delivered to a remote computer for dynamic execution. The problems with mobile code stem from its ability to do more than just display characters on the remote display.

It is this dynamic nature of mobile code that causes policy and implementation difficulties. A blanket prohibition on mobile code is secure, but that prohibition would prevent users of the dynamic Web from performing their tasks. It is this tension between integrity and dynamism that is at the heart of the issue.

The ongoing development of computer-based devices, particularly personal digital assistants (PDAs) and mobile phones, has broadened the spectrum of devices that use mobile code, and therefore are vulnerable to related exploits. The advent of the Apple iPhone in 2007 highlighted this hazard.[1]

Several definitions, as used by United States military forces but applicable to all, are useful in considering the content of this chapter:

> **Enclave.** An information system environment that is end to end under the control of a single authority and has a uniform security policy, including personnel and physical security. Local and remote elements that access resources within an enclave must satisfy the policy of the enclave.

Mobile code. Software obtained from remote systems outside the enclave boundary, transferred across a network, and then downloaded and executed on a local system without explicit installation or execution by the recipient. Mobile code is a powerful software tool that enhances cross-platform capabilities, sharing of resources, and Web-based solutions. Its use is widespread and increasing in both commercial and government applications. . . .Mobile code, unfortunately, has the potential to severely degrade. . .operations if improperly used or controlled.

Malicious mobile code. Mobile code software modules designed, employed, distributed, or activated with the intention of compromising the performance or security of information systems, increasing access to those systems, providing the unauthorized disclosure of information, corrupting information, denying service, or stealing resources.[2]

17.1.1 Mobile Code from the World Wide Web.

On the World Wide Web, the phrase "mobile code" generally refers to executable code, other than Hypertext Markup Language (HTML) and related languages (e.g., Extensible Markup Language, XML), supplied by a Web server or delivered by e-mail for execution on the client's computer. The most common packaging technologies for mobile code are ActiveX, Java, and JavaScript (also known as ECMAScript). Mobile code can directly perform covert functions on a client system, accessing information, or altering the operation or persistent state of the system; it can create accidental or deliberate vulnerabilities that can be exploited at a later time. The widespread use of mail clients that support HTML e-mail, with either embedded or referenced program code, has become a widespread source of vulnerability. So-called *pop-ups* can also be a source of vulnerability in many ways. In a technical sense, pop-ups have the ability to invoke other www sites and pages. In a legal sense, they may give rise to log entries that can cause legal problems, as in the case of Julie Amero, a Norwich, Connecticut, substitute teacher accused and subsequently convicted of using a classroom computer to access inappropriate material.[3]

Although malicious software such as viruses, worms, and Trojan horse programs written in compiled, interpreted, or scripting languages such as Visual Basic also might be considered mobile code, these pests are not generally labeled as such; this chapter deals only with ActiveX controls, Java applets, and JavaScript programs.

Today's trend toward increasing dynamism, with its attendant increase in the use of Ajax[4] and other technologies that rely on JavaScript and other mobile code technologies, increases the scope of the threat while also making it more difficult to ban the use of the vulnerable technologies.

The most spectacular problems with mobile code involve system or application crashes, which disrupt user sessions and workflow. However, silent covert access to or modification of client system data are far more serious problems. For example, some Web sites covertly obtain e-mail addresses from users' browsers, resulting later in unwanted commercial e-mail. In the past, antimalware tactics have relied heavily on widespread distribution of threats. The emergence of designer mobile code, specifically targeted to a particular system or a small number of systems, is a dangerous trend.[5]

The 2005 digital assault against Varda Raziel-Jacont and Amnon Jacont that placed material from a then-unpublished manuscript, "L for Lies" on various Internet sites, was not an aberration. The investigation into this affair uncovered a covert Trojan horse that provided remote access to the Jaconts' computer. Following leads from this investigation, Israeli police investigators uncovered a far larger computer-based information-gathering enterprise.[6] The investigation culminated in the arrest of

Raziel-Jacont's former son-in-law and his current wife. In the end, the private data of three major private investigation companies, several purchasers of the information, and apparently dozens of victim companies were compromised. This was not an isolated incident. The trend of targeted attacks against senior personnel, rather than random attacks, has accelerated.[7]

Investigative agencies have also entered the fray. In July 2007, an affidavit filed by the Federal Bureau of Investigation in connection with a series of bomb threats described the use of spyware to infiltrate a suspect's computer and return information to investigators.[8]

Mobile code presents a complex set of issues to information technology (IT) professionals. Allowing mobile code into an operating environment compromises any enclave; however, even commercial off-the-shelf (COTS) programs breach the integrity of an enclave. The differences between mobile code and other forms of code are primarily in the way these external programs are obtained, installed, documented, and controlled. In an enterprise computing environment, COTS acquisition normally involves conscious and explicit evaluation of the costs and benefits of installing a particular named and documented program. In contrast, mobile code programs are installed largely without notification to the user, and generally without documentation, change control, or review of any kind. Unless client-system firewalls are set to reject mobile code automatically, system administrators cannot be certain exactly which software has been executed on client machines under their nominal control. The use of Secure Sockets Layer (SSL)–based technologies such as HTTPS to otherwise secure connections used by applications also has the side effect of preventing the detection of mobile code at the firewall level. Although such control is often illusory, due to user circumvention of restrictions on installation of unauthorized software, the use of mobile code, installed by external Web sites, seriously compromises any remaining control over employee software configurations.

Mobile code has also been used in some cases to enforce proprietary rights in content, as was the case in a 2005 affair involving Sony Music.[9] The Sony Music case involved software contained on music CD-ROMS; precisely the same effect could have occurred with a downloaded file or Web page. The covert installation of software of any kind is a serious hazard to integrity, security, and privacy. Malfunction or misuse of such software would likely fit within the criminal statutes defining illegal, unauthorized alteration of systems. The attorney general of Texas,[10] as well as private class actions in New York[11] and California,[12] all filed cases against Sony. All of these actions were settled by Sony BMG in December 2006.[13] In January 2007, the U.S. Federal Trade Commission announced a settlement with Sony BMG on the charges of installing software without permission.[14] Investigations were also opened by the attorneys general of Massachusetts and Florida as well as overseas in Italy and Canada.

There are also reports that the Sony Root Kit was exploited by the Backdoor.IRC.Snyd.A exploit[15] and others to hide files from malware scans. The widespread nature of this induced vulnerability should also give pause. A widespread vulnerability provides an ecological niche ready for exploitation.

17.1.2 Motivations and Goals. The motivations and goals of malware propagators have continued an evolutionary trend from the unintentionally destructive to the vengeful, vindictive, and criminal.

In the beginning, many incidents were randomly damaging, or pranks with unintended side effects. This is no longer the case. Now malevolent mobile code is often code with a purpose. That purpose may be embarrassment, it may be blackmail, it may be corporate espionage, or it may be out-and-out theft. In a different dimension, the goal may be the subordination of otherwise innocent computer resources for a criminal enterprise against unrelated third parties.

The change in goals also has a dramatic impact on counter strategies. When the goal was mass publicity, the same infection was widespread, and scanning technologies could be used to identify known threats. When the goal is no longer publicity, publicity and widespread infection are maladaptive. Covert infection is then a far more attractive strategy than mass distribution. Custom mobile code designed to achieve selective covert infections is unlikely to quickly appear in the crosshairs of scanning software. This follows the evolutionary trajectory common in the biological world, where pathogens tend to mutate into less fatal forms over time. It is maladaptive for a parasite, which is what most malware is, to fatally damage its host. The downside of this effect is that the chronic infections with no apparent side effects are often overlooked.

Going forward, technologies and operational routines that make it difficult for unauthorized code to take up residence in or compromise the persistent state of the system are far more desirable counterstrategies than approaches based on scanning for known infections.

17.1.3 Design and Implementation Errors.   Design and implementation errors take a variety of forms. The simplest cases involve software that malfunctions on a constant predictable basis. More pernicious and more dangerous are those errors that silently compromise the strict containment of a multiuser environment. Errors in such prophylactic layers, known as brick walls or sandboxes, compromise the integrity of the protection scheme. In the worst cases, they permit unfettered access to system-level resources by unprivileged user programs.

Design and implementation errors can occur within any program or procedure, and mobile code is no exception. *Sandboxes* (nonprivileged, restricted operating environments) are intended to prevent unauthorized operations. *Authentication* determines which organization takes responsibility for such errors.

This chapter looks at a security model based on authentication of mobile code and then examines how restricted operating environments help to limit damage from harmful mobile code.

These concerns are appropriate to both widely distributed and targeted attacks. The challenge of targeted attacks lies in their small population; targeted attacks are unlikely to appear "on the radar" of general distribution scanning programs.

17.2 SIGNED CODE.   Authentication technologies are designed to ensure that information supplied by an organization has not been altered without authorization. The technology used to implement this assurance is based on use of the Public Key Infrastructure (PKI), as discussed in detail in Chapter 37. Code authenticated using PKI-based mechanisms often is referred to as *signed*. Signed code generally is immune to unauthorized modification; however, a signature guarantees integrity only from the point in time that the code is signed; the signing process does not imply safety or quality of the code prior to the point of signing.

Once signed, a file cannot be altered without the cooperation of someone holding access to the private key associated with the creating organization's X.509 certificate. (An X.509 certificate, digitally signed by an authorized user, authenticates the binding between a user's name and the user's public key.) Looking below the surface, such precautions do not address a variety of vulnerabilities:

- Access to private keys
- Access to the code base prior to signing
- Fraudulent certificates
- Design and implementation errors

17.2.1   Authenticode.   Microsoft's Authenticode technology is an example of an authentication-based approach.[16] Developers wishing to distribute code obtain an appropriate digital certificate from a Certification Authority (CA) and use the digital certificate to *sign* the code. The signature is then checked by the client system each time that the code is executed.

Authenticode relies on several components:

- PKI and the X.509 certificates issued by a Certification Authority.
- Limited access to the private keys associated with the issuing organization's X.509 certificate. In Microsoft terminology, the term "Software Publishing Certificate" or "SPC" refers to a PKCS #7 object, which in turn contains a collection of X.509 certificates used to sign code.
- The integrity of the processes used by the CA to ensure that requests for X.509 certificates are legitimate.

Authenticode does not address issues relating to the safety or accuracy of signed code, merely that it is authentic and unaltered since signing. For example, signing does not provide any guard against employee malfeasance.

17.2.2   Fundamental Limitations of Signed Code.   Signing technologies, regardless of the context (e.g., e-mail, applets, and archives), do not directly address questions of accuracy or correctness; they merely address questions of legitimacy. The biggest danger in signing schemes is the all-or-nothing approach taken to trust. Signed items are presumed to be trustworthy to the fullest extent of the requesting user's authority. The signed item can perform any operation that the user would be permitted to execute. There is no concept of *partial trust*. In an attorney's words, such an acceptance would be a *general power of attorney*. In the words of the CERT/Coordination Center (CERT/CC)–sponsored "Security in ActiveX Workshop": "A digital signature does not, however, provide any guarantee of benevolence or competence."[17]

At the same time, the inherent power and apparent legitimacy of a digital signature place a heavy burden on signers and the higher levels of the PKI to ensure the integrity of the mechanisms and secrets.

The key to the integrity of signed code is the signing process and the process that generates the object to be signed; the security of the secret keys required for its implementation determines the degree of trust in attribution of the signed code. In the truest sense, the private keys associated with the X.509 certificate represent the keys to the kingdom, as valuable as a signature chop in the Far East or a facsimile signature plate for a bank account.

On a practical level, accepting code signed by an organization is an explicit acceptance that the signing organization has good controls on the use of its signing keys. Organizations that take security seriously, segregating access to privileged accounts and controlling access to systems, are well positioned to manage the procedures for signing code.

Thus, the procedures and systems used for signing code should be treated with the same caution as is used for the aforementioned signing plates or the maximum security cryptographic facilities familiar to those in the national security area.

Unfortunately, despite years of publicity about the dangers of shared passwords and accounts, in many IT installations shared accounts and passwords remain common. There is little reason to assume that the secrets relating to PKI are better protected, despite extensive recommendations that those details be well guarded.

17.2.3   Specific Problems with the ActiveX Security Model.   The CERT/CC workshop on Security in ActiveX summarized the security issues in three major areas: importing and installing controls, running controls, and the use of controls by scripts.[18] The next sections summarize key findings from this report.

17.2.3.1   Importing and Installing Controls.   As discussed, the sole basis for trusting a signed control is its presumed origin. However, the originator of the code may have incorporated a design flaw in the control or may not have done adequate software quality assurance to prevent serious bugs.

A trusting user may install a signed control that contains a vulnerability making it useful for attackers simply because it is signed.

On Windows systems with multiple users, once a control has been permitted by one user, it remains available for all users, even if their security stances differ.

17.2.3.2   Running Controls.   An ActiveX control has no limitations on what it can do on the client machine, and it runs with the same privileges as those of the user process that initiated the control.

Although ActiveX security measures are available in Internet Explorer, other client software may run controls without necessarily implementing such security. Internet Explorer security levels tend to be all or nothing, making it difficult to allow a specific control without allowing all controls of that type. Remote activation of controls can bypass normal security perimeters such as those imposed by firewalls.

There is no basis for deciding whether a particular control is safe to execute or not, in any particular context.

17.2.3.3   Scripting Concerns.   Lacking a general basis for limiting the actions of controls, ActiveX programmers must effectively determine their own precautions to prevent harmful actions. It is difficult enough to develop a good set of boundaries on program activity, even if one uses a general model such as the sandbox described later; it is extremely difficult to see how individual developers can be expected to create their own equivalent of the sandbox for each individual control or whether they can be trusted to do so. In light of these hazards, the authors of the CERT/CC report stated that "there is a large number of potential failure points."

17.2.4   Case Studies.   Several security breaches or demonstrations mediated through ActiveX have occurred since the introduction of this technology in the mid-1990s.

17.2.4.1   Internet Exploder.   In 1996, Fred McLain wrote Internet Exploder, an ActiveX control designed to illustrate the broad degree of trust conferred on an ActiveX control by virtue of its having been "signed." Exploder, when downloaded for

execution by Internet Explorer, will shut down the browser's computer (the equivalent of the *Shut down* / *Shut down* sequence from the Start menu on a Windows system). This operation is operationally disruptive but not actually corrupting of the system. McLain notes in his frequently asked questions (FAQ) on Exploder that it is easy to build destructive or malicious controls.[19]

Exploder raises an important question: Who and what are the limits on trust when using signed code? In normal commercial matters, there is a large difference between an inauthentic signature, a forgery, and a properly signed but unpayable check. In software, the difference between an inauthentic control and a dangerous one is far less clear.

17.2.4.2 Chaos Computer Club Demonstration.   On January 27, 1997, a German television program showed members of the Chaos Computer Club demonstrating how they could use an ActiveX control to steal money from a bank account. The control, available on the Web, was written to subvert the popular accounting package Quicken. A victim need merely visit a site and download the ActiveX control in question; it automatically checked to see if Quicken was installed. If so, the control ordered Quicken to issue a transfer order to be saved in its list of pending transfers. The next time the victim connected to the appropriate bank and sent all pending transfer orders to the bank, all the transfers would be executed as a single transaction. The user's personal identification number (PIN) and transaction authorization number (TAN) would apply to all the transfers, including the fraudulent one in the pile of orders. Most victims would be unaware of the theft until they received their next statement—if then.[20]

Dan Wallach of Princeton University, commenting on this case, wrote:

> When you accept an ActiveX control, you're allowing completely arbitrary code to rummage around your machine and do anything it pleases. That same code could make extremely expensive phone calls, to 900 numbers or over long distances, with your modem; it can read, write, and delete any file on your computer; it can install Trojan horses and viruses. All without any of the subterfuge and hackery required to do it with Java. ActiveX hands away the keys to your computer.[21]

Responding to criticisms of the ActiveX security model, Bob Atkinson, architect and primary implementer of Authenticode, wrote a lengthy essay explaining his point of view. Among the key points:

- Microsoft never claimed that it would certify the safety of other people's code.
- Authentication is designed solely to permit identification of the culprits *after* malicious code is detected.
- Explorer-based distribution of software is no more risky than conventional purchases through software retailers.[22]

Subsequent correspondence in the RISKS Forum chastised Mr. Atkinson for omitting several other key points, such as:

- Interactions among ActiveX controls can violate system security even though individual controls appear harmless.
- There is no precedent in fact for laying liability at the feet of software developers even when you can find them.
- Under attack, evidence of digital signature is likely to evaporate from the system being damaged.

- Latency of execution of harmful payloads will complicate identification of the source of damage.

- Malice is not as important a threat from code as incompetence.

- Microsoft has a history of including security-threatening options, such as automatic execution of macros in Word, without offering any way of turning off the feature.

- A Web site can invoke an ActiveX control that is located on a different site or that already has been downloaded from another site, and can pass, by means of that control, unexpected arguments that could cause harm.[23]

17.2.4.3 *Certificates Obtained by Imposters.* In January 2001, VeriSign issued two *Class 3 Digital Certificates* for signing ActiveX controls and other code to someone impersonating a Microsoft employee. As a result, users receiving code signed using these certificates would receive a request for acceptance or rejection of a certificate apparently signed by Microsoft on January 30 or 31, 2001. As Russ Cooper commented on the NTBUGTRAQ Usenet group when the news came out in March 2001:

> The fact that unless you actually check the date on the Certificate you won't know whether or not its [*sic*] one you can trust is a Bad Thing(tm)[sic], as obviously not everyone (read: next to nobody) is going to check every Certificate they get presented with.
>
> You gotta wonder how VeriSign's issuance mechanism could be so poorly designed and/or implemented to let something like this happen.
>
> Meanwhile, Microsoft are [*sic*] working on a patch that will stick its finger in this dam.
>
> Basically, VeriSign Code−Signing Certificates do not employ a Certificate Revocation List (CRL) feature called CDP, or CRL Distribution Point, which causes the Certificate to be checked for revocation each time its read. Even if you have CRL turned on in IE, VeriSign Code−Signing Certificates aren't checked.
>
> Microsoft's update is going to shim in some mechanism which causes some/all Code−Signing Certificates to check some local file/registry key for a CRL, which will (at least initially) contain the details of these Certificates. Assuming this works as advertised, any attempt to trust the mis-issued Certificates should fail.[24]

Roger Thompson, Chief Technical Officer for Exploit Prevention Labs, explained that the imposters' motives would determine how bad the results would be from the fraudulent certificates. "If it was someone with a purpose in mind, then six weeks is a long time to do something," he said. "If the job was to install a sniffer, then there could be a zillion backdoors as a result of it." Published reports indicated that the failure of authentication occurred due to a flaw in the issuing process at VeriSign: The certificates were issued *before* receiving verification by e-mail that the official customer contact authorized the certificates. This case was the first detected failure of authentication in over 500,000 certificates issued by VeriSign.[25]

17.3 RESTRICTED OPERATING ENVIRONMENTS. From a Web perspective, the term "sandbox" defines what could be referred to as a restricted operating environment. Restricted operating environments are not new; they have existed for nearly 50 years in the form of multiuser operating systems, including MULTICS,

OS/360 and its descendants, OpenVMS, UNIX, and others. See Chapter 24 in this *Handbook* for an overview of operating systems security.

In simple terms, a restricted, or nonprivileged, operating environment prohibits normal users and their programs from executing operations that can compromise the overall system. In such an environment, normal users are prohibited from executing operations such as HALT that directly affect hardware. User programs are prevented from executing instructions that can compromise the operating system memory allocation and processor state and from accessing or modifying files belonging to the operating system or to other users. Implemented and managed carefully, such systems are highly effective at protecting information and data from unauthorized modification and access. The National Computer Security Center (NCSC) *Orange Book* contains criteria for classifying and evaluating trusted systems.[26]

The strengths and weaknesses of protected systems are well understood. Permitting ordinary users unrestricted access to system files compromises the integrity of the system. Privileged users (i.e., those with legitimate access to system files and physical hardware) must be careful that the programs they run do not compromise the operating system. Most protected systems contain a collection of freestanding programs that implement useful system functions requiring some form of privilege to operate. Often these programs have been the source of security vulnerabilities. This is the underlying reasoning behind the universal recommendation that programs not run as root or Administrator, or with similar privileges unless absolutely necessary.

17.3.1   Java.   Java is a language developed by Sun Microsystems for platform independent execution of code, typically within the context of a Web browser. The basic Java environment includes a Java Virtual Machine (JVM) and a set of supporting software referred to as the Java Run Time Environment. Applets downloaded via the World Wide Web (intranet or Internet) have strict limitations on their ability to access system resources. In particular, these restrictions prevent the execution of external commands and read or write access to files.

The Java environment does provide for *signed applets* that are permitted wider access to files. Dynamically downloaded applets also are restricted to initiating connections to the system that supplied them, theoretically limiting some types of third-party attacks.

In concept, the Java approach, which also includes other validity tests on the JVM pseudocode, should be adequate to ensure security. However, the collection of trusted applets found locally on the client system and signed downloaded applets represent ways in which the security system can be subverted. Without signature, the Java approach is also vulnerable to attack by domain name system (DNS) spoofing.

Multiuser protection and virtual machine protection schemes also are totally dependent on the integrity of the code that separates the nonprivileged users from privileged, system-compromising, operations. Java has not been an exception to this rule. In 1996, a bug in the Java environment contained in Netscape Navigator Version 2.0 permitted connections to arbitrary Universal Resource Locators (URLs).[27] Later, in 2000, errors were discovered in the code that protected various resources.[28] Although the Java environment is less widely exploitable than ActiveX, vulnerabilities continue to be uncovered. In 2007, at least two vulnerabilities were reported by US-CERT.[29] Significantly, both of these reported vulnerabilities involved the ability of untrusted applets to compromise the security envelope.

Additionally, since unsigned code can take advantage of errors in underlying signed code, there is no guarantee that complex combinations of untrusted and trusted code will not lead to security compromises.

17.4   DISCUSSION.   Mobile code security raises important issues about how to handle relationships in an increasingly interconnected computing environment.

17.4.1   Asymmetric, and Transitive or Derivative, Trust.   It is common for cyberrelationships to be *asymmetric* with regard to the size or power of the parties. This fact increases the potential for catastrophic interactions. It also creates opportunities for mass infection across organization boundaries. Large or critical organizations often can unilaterally impose limitations on the ability of partner organizations to defend their information infrastructure against damage.

The combination of a powerful organization and insufficient controls on signing authority, or, alternatively, the obligatory execution of unsigned (or self-signed) ActiveX controls, is a recipe for serious problems. The powerful organization is able to obligate its partners to accept a low security level, such as would result, for example, from using unsigned ActiveX controls, while abdicating responsibility for the resulting repercussions.

All organizations should, for security and performance reasons, use the technology that requires the least degree of privilege to accomplish the desired result. JavaScript/ECMAScript can provide many functions, without the need for the functionality provided by Java, much less ActiveX. It remains common for large organizations to force the download of ActiveX controls for purposes that do not require the power of ActiveX, merely using the justification that they perceive Internet Explorer to be the more prevalent browser. Often this requires running the installation script from an account with Administrator privileges, a second security violation. This is particularly surprising since these same organizations often offer parallel support for Firefox, Opera, Safari, and other non-ActiveX supporting browsers on Linux, Apple, and other platforms. This "Trust Me" concept forces the risk and burden of consequences on the end user, who is far less able to deal with the consequences.

As noted earlier in this chapter, Web servers represent an attractive vector for attacks. Signing (authentication) methods are a way to control damage potential, if the mechanisms used for admitting executable code are properly controlled. Failure to control these mechanisms leads to severe side effects.

In Chapter 30 in this *Handbook*, it is noted that protecting Web servers requires that the contents of the servers be managed with care. It is appropriate and often necessary to isolate Web servers on separate network segments, separated from both the Internet and the organizational intranet by firewalls. These precautions are even more necessary when servers are responsible for supplying executable code to clients.

Security practitioners should carefully examine the different functions performed by each server. In some cases, such as OpenVMS hosts, where network servers commonly run as unprivileged processes in separate contexts and directory trees, it is feasible to run multiple services on a single server. In other systems, such as UNIX and Windows, where it is common for applications services to execute as privileged, with full access to all system files, a logic error in a network service can compromise the security of the entire server, including the collection of downloadable applets.

Far more serious and equally subtle is *transitive* (or derivative) trust: Alpha trusts Beta who trusts Gamma. A security compromise—for example, an unsigned Java applet or a malfunctioning or malevolent ActiveX control supplied by Gamma—compromises Beta. Beta then causes problems with Alpha's systems. This cascade can continue repeatedly, leading to numerous compromised Web services and systems far removed geographically and organizationally from the original incident.

17.4.2 Misappropriation and Subversion. The threat space has mutated over the last several years. Where the main danger from mobile code was attacks on the target machine, today's threat is far more diverse. In November 2007, John Schiefer of Los Angeles pled guilty to installing software designed to capture usernames and passwords. According to news reports, he was also involved in running a number of networks of compromised computers, often referred to as "bots," which are often used to initiate distributed denial-of-service (DDoS) and other attacks.[30] In this particular case, the announcement by the U.S. Department of Justice[31] mentions two specific episodes: 250,000 machines infected with spybots to obtain user's usernames and passwords for PayPal and other systems; and a separate scheme involving a Dutch Internet advertising company in which a network of 150,000 infected computers were used to "signup" for one of the advertising company's programs.

This was one of the cases stemming from Bot Roast II,[32] an FBI operation against several botnet networks.

17.4.3 Multidimensional Threat. Mobile code is a multidimensional threat, with several different aspects that must each be treated separately. Signing code, such as Java applets or ActiveX controls, addresses the problem of authenticity and authority to release the code. However, the integrity of the signature mechanism requires that the integrity of the PKI infrastructure be beyond reproach. In a very real sense, the PKI infrastructure is beyond the control of the organization itself. Any compromise or procedural slip on the part of the Certificate Authority or signer invalidates the presumptions of safety.

Signing, however much it contributes to resolving the question of authenticity, does not address safety or validity. As an example, the Windows Update ActiveX control, distributed by Microsoft as part of the various Windows operating systems, has as its underlying purpose the update of the operating system. A failure of that control would be catastrophic. Fortunately, Microsoft gives users the choice of using the automatic update facility or doing updates manually. Many Web applications are not so accommodating.

The problem is not solely a question of malfunctioning applets. It is possible that a collection of applets involved in a client's overall business activities may collide in some unanticipated fashion, from attempting to use the same Windows registry key in contradictory ways, to inadvertently using the same temporary file name. Similar problems often occur with applications that presume they have a monopoly on the use of the system, an all-too-common syndrome.

These issues are, for the most part, completely unrelated to each other. A solution in one area would neither improve nor worsen the situation with regard to the other issues.

17.4.4 Client Responsibilities. The expanding threat presents a challenge to those responsible for ensuring the integrity of desktop computing. Put simply, there is a complex, multidimensional threat, and it is not easily defended against using the techniques of portals, firewalls, and scanners.

The danger from browsing the World Wide Web is the danger that the browser will permit an attacker, directly or indirectly, to cause a modification to the persistent state of the system. The simplest step in the correct direction is not to browse the World Wide Web from within a protection context that has access to critical system files and settings. Limiting this access by using a nonprivileged user account for browsing significantly decreases the hazard, provided of course that the system files are protected from access by such an account.

The mass availability of Virtual Machine technology presents an additional alternative. Virtual Machine technology, pioneered by IBM in the 1960s on mainframes, has emerged in a new guise on platforms down to the desktop level. The general availability of this capability in the desktop world opens up a whole new defensive strategy against mobile malware: the expendable Web browser.

An expendable www browser is an instantiated desktop within a virtual machine environment, from a known system image. If it is compromised, it is merely rewritten from a known, uncompromised system image. It allows one to create a low-security, at-risk, browsing enclave within an otherwise higher security environment. This is an approach that has been used, in a physical sense to be sure, by some organizations proving public access personal computers. Rather than attempting to fortify the machines against compromise or attach, they are reinitialized from a known image after each user. This allows the end user to indulge the foibles of trading partners' attempts to impose unsafe computing practices in an expendable environment that can be isolated. Using Windows as an example, while it is an unsafe practice to install software as Administrator, it is far less damaging to do so in a virtual machine, where the machine can be deleted at convenience with little side effect.

17.4.5 Server Responsibilities.   As noted earlier in this chapter, Web servers represent an attractive vector for attacks. Signing (authentication) methods are a way to control damage potential, provided the mechanisms used for admitting executable code are properly controlled. Failure to control these mechanisms leads to severe side effects.

The concept of *minimum necessary privilege* applies to mobile code. There is little reason to impose the use of ActiveX for the purposes of changing the color of a banner advertisement. JavaScript/ECMAScript is capable of many powerful, display-related operations with a high degree of safety. Using Java to maintain a shopping cart (price, quantities, and contents) is reasonable and does not require the use of a signed applet, with its attendant greater capabilities and risks. At the other end of the scale, it is plausible that a system update function (e.g., the Windows Update function, which automatically downloads and installs changes to the Windows operating system) requires the unbridled power of a signed ActiveX control.

When the power of signed applets or controls is required, good software engineering practice provides excellent examples of how to limit the potential for damage and mischief, as discussed in Chapter 38 in this *Handbook*.

Good software implementation isolates functions and limits the scope of operations that require privileged access or operations. Payroll applications do not directly manipulate printer ports, video display cards, network adapters, or disk drives. Privileged operating system components, such as device drivers and file systems, are responsible for the actual operation. This separation, together with careful parameter checking by the operating system kernel and the privileged components, ensures safety.

The same techniques can be used with applets and controls. Because they require more access, they should be programmed carefully, using the same defensive measures as are used when implementing privileged additions to operating systems. As an example, there is little reason for a Simple Mail Transfer Protocol (SMTP) server to be privileged. An SMTP server requires privileges for a single function, the delivery of an individual electronic mail message to a recipient's mailbox. This can be accomplished in two ways:

1. Implement the application in a nonprivileged way, by marking users' e-mail files and directories with the necessary access permissions for the mail delivery program to create and modify e-mail files and directories. Such a mechanism is fully in conformance with the NCSC *Orange Book*'s C2-level of security.

2. Implement a separate subcomponent whose sole responsibility is the actual message delivery of the message. The subcomponent must be written defensively to check all of its parameters, and does not provide an interface for the execution of arbitrary code. This approach is used by HP's OpenVMS operating system.

The UNIX *sendmail* program, by contrast, is a large, multifunctional program that executes with privileges. *sendmail* has been the subject of numerous security problems for over a decade and has spawned efforts to produce more secure replacements.[33]

17.5 SUMMARY.   Mobile code provides many flexible and useful capabilities. The different mechanisms for implementing mobile code range from the innocuous (HTML), to fairly safe (JavaScript/ECMAScript), and with increasing degrees of power and risk through Java and ActiveX.

Ensuring security and integrity with the use of mobile code requires cooperation on the part of both the provider and the client. Clients should not accept random signed code and controls. Providers have a positive responsibility to:

- Follow good software engineering practices.
- Grant minimum necessary privileges and access.
- Use defensive programming.
- Limit privileged access, with no open-ended interfaces.
- Ensure the integrity of the signing process and the associated private keys.

With appropriate caution, mobile code can be a constructive, powerful part of intranet and Internet applications, both within an organization and in cooperation with its customers and other stakeholders.

17.6 FURTHER READING

Carl, Jeremy. "ActiveX Security: Under the Microscope," *Web Week*, 2, No. 17, November 4, 1996; www.Webdeveloper.com/activex/activex_security.html

CERT. "NIMDA Worm," September 11, 2001, www.cert.org/advisories/CA-2001-26.html

CERT. "sadmind/IIS Worm," May 8, 2001, www.cert.org/advisories/CA-2001-11.html

CERT. "Unauthentic 'Microsoft Corporation' Certificates," March 22, 2001, www.cert.org/advisories/CA-2001-04.html

Dormann, Will, and Jason Rafail. "Securing Your Web Browser," CERT, January 23, 2006, www.cert.org/tech_tips/securing_browser/index.html on December 2, 2007.

Evers, J. FAQ: JavaScript Insecurities. http://www.xml.org/xml/news/archives/archive.07282006.shtml#4

Felten, Edward. "Security Tradeoffs: Java vs. ActiveX," last modified April 28, 1997, www.cs.princeton.edu/sip/faq/java-vs-activex.html.

Felten, E., and J. Halderman. *Lessons from the Sony CD DRM Episode*, Center for Information Technology Policy, Department of Computer Science, Princeton University, February 14, 2006, http://itpolicy.princeton.edu/pub/sonydrm-ext.pdf.

Felten, E., and G. McGraw. *Securing Java: Getting Down to Business with Mobile Code*. New York: John Wiley & Sons, 1999. Also free and unlimited Web access from www.securingjava.com

Gehtland, J., B. Galbraith, and D. Almaer. *Pragmatic Ajax*. Raleigh, NC: Pragmatic Bookshelf, 2006.

Grossman, J., and T. C. Niedzialkowski. "Hacking Intranet Websites from the Outside," *Black Hat (USA)*, Las Vegas, August 3, 2006.

Hensing, R." W32/HLLP.Philis.bq, Chinese Gold Farmers and What You Can Do about It," December 2, 2007, http://blogs.technet.com/robert_hensing/archive/2006/12/04/w32-hllp-philis-bq-chinese-gold-farmers-and-what-you-can-do-about-it.aspx on.

Holzman, S. *Ajax Bible*. Hoboken, NJ: John Wiley & Sons, 2007.

Java Security. Frequently Asked Questions, revision March 29, 2001, java.sun.com/sfaq/index.html

Keizer, G. "FBI Planted Spyware on Teen's PC to Trace Bomb Threats," *Computerworld*, July 19, 2007.

McGraw, G., and E. W. Felten. *Java Security: Hostile Applets, Holes and Antidotes—What Every Netscape and Internet Explorer User Needs to Know*. New York: John Wiley & Sons, 1997.

Microsoft. "Introduction to Code Signing" (with appendix), 2001, msdn.microsoft.com/workshop/security/authcode/intro_authenticode.asp; msdn.microsoft.com/workshop/security/authcode/appendixes.asp.

Rhoads, C. "Web Scammer Targets Senior U.S. Executives," *Wall Street Journal*, November 9, 2007, http://online.wsj.com/public/article_print/SB119456922698387317.html on November 14, 2007.

Schwartz, J. "iPhone Flaw Lets Hackers Take Over Security Firm Says," *New York Times*, July 23, 2007.

VeriSign, "Microsoft Security Bulletin MS01-017: Erroneous VeriSign-Issued Digital Certificates Pose Spoofing Hazard," March 22, 2001, www.microsoft.com/TechNet/security/bulletin/MS01-017.asp.

VeriSign, "VeriSign Security Alert Fraud Detected in Authenticode Code Signing Certificates," March 22, 2001, www.VeriSign.com/developer/notice/authenticode/index.html.

Zakas, N., J. McPeak, and J. Fawcett. *Practical Ajax*, 2nd ed. Hoboken, NJ: John Wiley & Sons, 2007.

17.7   NOTES

1. J. Schwartz, "iPhone Flaw Lets Hackers Take over Security Firm Says," *New York Times,* July 23, 2007,

2. Adapted from Memorandum, November 7, 2000, from Arthur M. Money, Assistant Secretary of Defense for C3I and CIO, to Secretaries of the Military Departments, Chairman of the Joint Chiefs of Staff, Chief Information Officers of the Defense Agencies, et al. SUBJECT: Policy Guidance for Use of Mobile

Code Technologies in Department of Defense (DoD) Information Systems; see www.c3i.osd.mil/org/cio/doc/mobile-code11-7-00.html.

3. J. Penny, "40 Years Too Long in Norwich Porn Case?" *Norwich Bulletin,* January 9, 2007; G. Smith, "Teacher Facing Porn Charges" *Norwich Bulletin,* November 11, 2004.

4. Jesse James Garrett, "AJAX: A New Approach to Web Applications," http://adaptivepath.com/ideas/essays/archives/000385.php.

5. D. Izenberg, "Trojan Horse Developers Indicted," *Jerusalem Post,* March 5, 2006.

6. Glenn Frankel, "18 Arrested in Israeli Probe of Computer Espionage," *Washington Post,* Tuesday, May 31, 2005.

7. J. Kirk, "Hackers Target C-level Execs and Their Families," *Network World,* July 2, 2007.

8. G. Keizer, "FAQ: What We Know (Now) about the FBI's CIPAV spyware," *Computerworld,* July 29, 2007.

9. Mark Russinovich, "Sony, Rootkits and Digital Rights Management Gone Too Far," December 2, 2007, http://blogs.technet.com/markrussinovich/archive/2005/10/31/sony-rootkits-and-digital-rights-management-gone-too-far.aspx.

10. *The State of Texas v. Sony BMG Music Entertainment, LLC*, Case GV-505065, District Court of Travis County, Texas, 126th Judicial District.

11. *James Michaelson and Ori Edelstein v. Sony BMG Music, Inc. and First 4 Internet*, Case 05 CV 9575, United States District Court, Southern District of New York.

12. *Alexander William Guevara v. Sony Music Entertainment, et al.,* Case BC342359, Superior Court of the State of California, County of Los Angeles.

13. R. McMillan, "Sony Pays $ 1.5M to Settle Texas, California Root Kit Suits," *Computerworld,* December 20, 2006.

14. www.ftc.gov/opa/2007/01/sony.htm.

15. Backdoor.IRC.Snyd.A, December 2, 2007, www.bitdefender.com/VIRUS-1000058-en-Backdoor.IRC.Snyd.A.html.

16. Advanced Software Logic, "What Is Authenticode?" www.Webcomponentdeployment.com/faq.htm.

17. CERT/CC, Results of the Security in ActiveX Workshop, Pittsburgh, Pennsylvania, August 22–23, 2000; PDF download available at: www.cert.org/archive/pdf/activeX_report.pdf.

18. CERT/CC, pp. 6–9.

19. F. McLain, "The Exploder Control Frequently Asked Questions (FAQ)," last updated February 7, 1997, www.halcyon.com/mclain/ActiveX/Exploder/FAQ.htm.

20. D. Weber-Wulff, "Electronic Funds Transfer without Stealing PIN/TAN," *RISKS* 18, No. 80 (1997), catless.ncl.ac.uk/Risks/18.80.html.

21. D. Wallach, "RE: Electronic Funds Transfer without Stealing PIN/TAN," *RISKS* 18, No. 81 (1997), catless.ncl.ac.uk/Risks/18.8.html.

22. B. Atkinson, "Comments and Corrections Regarding Authentication," *RISKS* 18, No. 85 (1997).

23. *RISKS* 18, No. 86 (1997), et seq.

24. R. Cooper, "Alert: Microsoft Security Bulletin MS01-017," NTBUGTRAQ list server, 2001, archive at: *archives.neohapsis.com/archives/ntbuttraq/2001-q/0046.html.*

25. R. Lemos, "Microsoft Says Beware of Stolen Certificates," *ZDNet News,* March 22, 2001, news.cnet.com/news/0-1003-200-5222484.html.

26. For full text, see www.radium.ncsc.mil/tpep/library/rainbow/5200.28-STD.html.

27. CERT, "Java Implementations Can Allow Connection to an Arbitrary Host," www.cert.org/advisories/CA-1996-05.html.

28. CERT, "Netscape Allows Java Applets to Read Protected Resources," www.cert.org/advisories-CA-2000-15.html.

29. Vulnerability Note VU#336105, Sun Java JRE vulnerable to unauthorized network access, www.kb.cert/vuls/id/336105; Vulnerability Note VU#102289, Sun Java JRE vulnerable to privilege escalation, www.kb.cert/vuls/id/102289.

30. J. Serjeant, " 'Botmaster' Admits Infecting 250,000 Computers," Reuters, November 9, 2007.

31. United States Attorney's Office, Central District of California, "Computer Security Consultant Charges with Infecting up to a Quarter Million Computers that Were Used to Wiretap, Engage in Identity Theft, Defraud Banks," Press Release No. 07-143, November 9, 2007, www.usdoj.gov/usao/cac/news/pr2007/143.html.

32. " 'BOT ROAST II': Cracking Down on CyberCrime," December 2, 2007, www.fbi.gov/page2/nov07/botnet112907.html; more extensive details in " 'Bot Roast II" Nets 8 Individuals," www.fbi.gov/pressrel/pressrel07/botroast112907.htm on December 2, 2007

33. For example, the National Vulnerability Database (NVD, http://nvd.nist.gov/) shows that the Common Vulnerabilities and Exposures (CVE) database includes a total of 29 unique vulnerabilities involving *sendmail,* of which 15 are dated 2000 and 2001. This trend continues, with the NVD Version 2.0 showing an additional 16 *sendmail*-related issues from 2002 through 2007.

CHAPTER 18

DENIAL-OF-SERVICE ATTACKS

Gary C. Kessler and Diane E. Levine

18.1 INTRODUCTION. This chapter discusses denial-of-service (DoS) and distributed denial-of-service (DDoS) attacks. These attacks seek to render target systems and networks unusable or inaccessible by saturating resources or causing catastrophic errors that halt processes or entire systems. Furthermore, they are increasingly easy for even *script kiddies* (persons who follow explicit attack instructions or execute attack programs) to launch. Successful defense against these attacks will come only when there is widespread cooperation among all Internet service providers (ISPs) and other Internet-connected systems worldwide.

Working in a variety of ways, the DoS attacker selects an intended target system and launches a concentrated attack against it. Although initially deemed to be primarily a "nuisance," DoS attacks can incapacitate an entire network, especially those with hosts that rely on Transmission Control Protocol/Internet Protocol (TCP/IP). DoS attacks on corporate networks and ISPs have resulted in significant damage to productivity and revenues. DoS attacks can be launched against any hardware or operating system platform because they generally aim at the heart of Internet Protocol (IP) implementations. Because IP is the typical target, the DoS attack tools that run under one operating system (Linux is a common choice) can be aimed at any operating system running IP. Additionally, because IP implementations are similar for different platforms, one DoS attack may target several operating systems and work on each. Once written for one platform and released, new DoS attacks appear to evolve (via the examination and participation of hackers and crackers) so that in a short period of time (approximately two weeks) mutations of the DoS attack appear that work on virtually all platforms.

Because of the critical impact that DoS attacks can have, they cannot be taken lightly. DoS attacks have been around in one form or another since the 1980s; in 1999, they evolved into distributed DoS attacks, primarily due to the heavy use of internal networks and the Internet. DDoS tools launch coordinated DoS attacks from many sources against one or more targets simultaneously.

This chapter describes first DoS and then DDoS attacks. This arrangement is primarily due to the fact that DoS attacks historically predate DDoS attacks. In addition, some DDoS attacks make use of DoS techniques. However, the attacks themselves, the terminology, and the defenses are sufficiently different that they warrant separate discussion.

18.2   DENIAL-OF-SERVICE ATTACKS.

Historically, any act that prevented use of a system could be called a denial of service. For example, in some mainframe and minicomputer systems, typing a malformed command could cause a system failure; pressing the RETURN key on the system console could monopolize the device-recognition process of the operating system and use up all the central processing unit (CPU) cycles, thus preventing any further activity on the system. Typing one or more characters on the system console without pressing the RETURN key could block all further system messages on the console, causing system buffers to fill up with unprinted messages; when the system buffers were exhausted, no system action requiring notification to the console could take place (e.g., logons, logoffs, special-form requests, or tape-mount requests). However, such events were usually the result of bugs in the operating system, inadequate numbers of buffers for critical data, or accident.

18.2.1   History of Denial-of-Service Attacks.

One of the first major DoS incidents that made headlines and ripples far and wide was probably accidental. It took place in December 1987, when an employee of IBM in Europe sent out a holiday greeting e-mail message. The e-mail message, however, contained a program that drew a nice Christmas tree on the recipient's terminal—and read the recipient's NAMES and NETLOG files listing the user's address book as well as the e-mail addresses of individuals that this user had recently sent mail to or received mail from. The Christmas Tree program then triggered the automatic transmission of copies of itself to all e-mail addresses found in NAMES and NETLOG. The result overloaded the IBM corporate network worldwide and brought it crashing down both in Europe and the United States. In addition, messages "escaped" from IBM's corporate network and wreaked havoc on the BITNET/EARN education and research networks in North America and Europe. Although the cause of the outage was originally thought to be a computer virus, and the incident has been referred to as a virus, a worm, and a prank, the result was a true denial of service.

Perhaps the most famous Internet DoS resulted from the Morris Worm, also referred to as the Internet Worm, which occurred in November 1988. Cornell graduate student

Robert T. Morris cowrote an article about some vulnerabilities in Sendmail and fingerd on UNIX systems. Most of the TCP/IP community dismissed the vulnerabilities as theoretical; apparently Morris wanted to demonstrate that the vulnerabilities actually could be practically exploited. To demonstrate the problem, his program had to invade another system, guess some passwords, and then replicate itself. Morris said after the incident that he wanted the program to replicate just a few times to demonstrate that it was real; unfortunately, a programming error led the worm to replicate often and quickly in addition to superinfecting already-infected systems. The worm clogged the Internet with hundreds of thousands of messages and effectively brought the entire network down; most sites that did not actually crash were disconnected from the network by their system administrators to avoid being infected and to allow disinfection. Regardless of intent, the Morris Worm inadvertently caused a DoS.

On Friday, September 6, 1996, PANIX, a public access Internet provider in Manhattan, was struck by a DoS attack that consisted of many messages flooding the server with massive amounts of data. The attacks were made against mail, news, name, and Web servers as well as user shell account machines. The attackers successfully eluded tracking, and the attacks went on for several days. About a week after the attacks began, PANIX went public with the story, and dozens of other online service providers acknowledged that they too were the victims of similar attacks.

In 1997, a disgruntled former employee of Forbes, Inc., used a former colleague's password to remotely access the firm's computer systems. Deliberately tampering with the system, he deleted budgets and salary information and caused five of the eight network servers to crash. When Federal Bureau of Investigation (FBI) agents caught the perpetrator, his home was filled with hacking tools, proprietary information from Forbes, Inc., and other incriminating material.

In February 1998, hackers from Israel and Northern California attacked the U.S. Department of Defense (DoD). In a carefully organized attack that exploited buffer overflow, these hackers systematically perpetrated a DoS attack that lasted over a week on 11 DoD sites.

In March 1988, all across the United States, system administrators found their Windows NT servers under apparently automated attack. Systems crashed repeatedly until they were updated to the latest patches from Microsoft. There appeared to be no file damage from the attacks, which lasted more than a day. Sites affected included several NASA and other military sites, as well as several University of California and other college campuses.

Yet another mailstorm erupted in May 1998 when an Australian official set autoreply on his e-mail package while he was away. Unfortunately, he inadvertently set his destination for these largely useless messages to be all 2,000 users on his network—and requested auto confirmation of delivery of each autoreply, which generated yet another autoreply, and so on ad infinitum. Within four hours, his endless positive-feedback loop generated 150,000 messages before his autoreply was shut down. The ripples lasted for days, with the perpetrator saddled with 48,000 messages in his in basket and a stream of 1,500 a day pouring in. This was another case of an inadvertent DoS attack.

In January 1999, someone launched a sustained denial-of-service attack on Ozemail, an important Australian Internet service provider. E-mail service was disrupted for users in Sydney.

In March 1999, the Melissa e-mail-enabled virus/worm swept the world in a few days as it sent copies of itself to the first 50 addresses in victims' e-mail address books. Because of this high replication rate, the virus spread faster than any previous virus in history. On many corporate systems, the rapid rate of internal replication saturated e-mail servers with outbound automated junk e-mail. Initial estimates were in the range of 100,000 downed systems. Antivirus companies rallied immediately, and updates for all the standard products were available within hours of the first notices from the CERT Coordination Center (CERT/CC). The Melissa macro virus was quickly followed by the PAPA MS-Excel macro virus with similar properties but that, in addition, launched DoS attacks on two specific IP addresses.

More recent attacks are discussed in the sections describing modern DoS tools.

18.2.2 Costs of Denial-of-Service Attacks.   What are the effects of these DoS attacks in terms of productivity and actual financial costs? It is difficult to place an exact monetary figure on DoS attacks. DoS attacks can interrupt critical processes in an organization, and such interruption can be costly. When a company's computer network is inaccessible to legitimate users and they cannot conduct their normal business, productivity is lowered. The negative effect is bound to carry over to the financial aspects of the business. However, putting exact figures to these effects is uncertain at best, and the estimates are widely disputed, even among security and business experts. In addition, many companies do not comment on the exact losses they suffer because they fear that the negative publicity will decrease their market share. This latter point is significant: In an early 1990s study of Wall Street firms, some of the companies suggested that if they were to be without their network for two to three days, they might never reopen their doors.

In the case of the Christmas Tree worm, it took IBM several days to clean up its network and resulted in the loss of millions of dollars, both for cleansing the system and in lost business because of lost connectivity and related productivity. Additionally, there was the embarrassment suffered by IBM, a noted technology company. The individual who launched the worm was identified and denied access to any computer account, while IBM had to write a letter of apology to the European Academic and Research Network (EARN) administrators.

In 1988, at the time of the Morris Worm, the Internet consisted of 5,000 to 10,000 hosts, primarily at research and academic institutions. As a result, although the Morris Worm succeeded in bringing many sites to a halt and gained worldwide notoriety, the financial and productivity impact on the commercial world was minimal. A similar incident today would wreak havoc and cost millions of dollars in losses.

By 1996, however, commercial reliance on the Internet was already becoming a matter of course. Working around the clock, the management at PANIX and at Cisco, the ISP's router vendor, kept the service provider up and running, but the network received 210 fraudulent requests per minute. Although the systems did not crash, thousands of subscribers were unable to receive their e-mail messages. Other sites were attacked in the same time frame as PANIX, including Voters Telecommunication Watch. No one took the blame for these attacks, and it has been widely assumed that they were triggered by articles on SYN DoS attacks (see the description below) that had recently appeared in *2600 Magazine* and *Phrack*, journals that cater to hackers.

According to Forbes, Inc., the losses suffered by the firm because of the DoS attack perpetrated by the disgruntled former employee exceeded $100,000. Could it have been prevented? According to the firm, it is highly unlikely, since Forbes had no reason to suspect the individual was maintaining either the firm's confidential and sensitive material at home or that he was thinking of hacking into the computer system and deliberately doing damage. Although the firm had security on its systems, the perpetrator used the password of a legitimate, authorized user.

The DoS attack launched against the Department of Defense computers in 1998 proved that attackers could deny access to vital military information. In this particular instance, the attack was directed at unclassified machines that had only administrative and accounting records, but it was a blow to the confidence of the Department of Defense. Tying up the computers for over a week presumably reduced productivity, but the government would not comment on the actual cost from loss of machine time and personnel productivity.

These cases show that a DoS attack on a computer or network can be devastating to an organization. Important equipment and networks and even an entire organization can be disabled by such attacks.

Early DoS incidents often were described as annoying, frustrating, or a nuisance. However, with increasing sophistication and dependency on networking, it has become difficult to keep a sense of humor about such incidents. Especially in corporations, where the mission is to make a profit for the shareholder, company managers find it increasingly difficult to excuse being incapacitated because of a DoS or DDoS attack.

As these forms of attack become more sophisticated, so must the tools and methods for detecting and fighting them. Current products scan equipment and networks for vulnerabilities, trigger alerts when an abnormality is found, and frequently assist in eliminating the discovered problem.

18.2.3 Types of Denial-of-Service Attacks. DoS attacks, whether accidental or deliberate, result in loss of service; either a host or a server system is rendered inoperable or a network is rendered inaccessible. DoS attacks are launched deliberately by an *intruder* (the preferred term for attacker in this context). Systems and networks that are compromised are referred to as the *victims*. And while DoS attacks can be launched from the intruder's system, they often are launched by an automated process that allows the intruder to start the attack remotely with a few keystrokes. These programs are known as *daemons,* and they are often placed on another system that the hacker has already compromised.

There are three basic types or categories of DoS attack:

1. **Saturation.** This type of attack seeks to deprive computers and networks of scarce, limited, or nonrenewable resources that are essential in order for the computers or networks to operate. Resources of this type include CPU time, disk space, memory, data structures, network bandwidth, access to other networks and computers, and environmental resources such as cool air and power.

2. **Misconfiguration.** This type of attack destroys or alters configuration information. Because poor or improperly configured computers may fail to operate or operate inadequately, this type of attack can be very severe.

3. **Destruction.** This type of attack results in network components being physically destroyed or altered. To guard against this type of attack, it is necessary to have good physical security to safeguard the computers and other network components. This chapter does not deal with physical damage.

18.2.4 Specific Denial-of-Service Attacks. This discussion of some specific DoS attacks covers the main methods extant at the time of writing; however, new types of attacks are anticipated.

18.2.4.1   Destructive Devices.   Destructive devices are programs that accomplish either harassment or destruction of data. There are mixed opinions regarding how severe destructive devices are, but if they threaten a computer's or network's ability to function properly and efficiently, then they may be the instruments of DoS attacks. Viruses, e-mail bombs, and denial-of-service tools all can be considered destructive devices. In fact, viruses and e-mail bombs are known to cause DoS attacks. More about viruses and other malicious software and their actions can be found in Chapter 16 of this *Handbook*; DDoS tools and e-mail bombs are discussed in the next sections.

18.2.4.2   E-mail (and E-mail Subscription) Bombing.   E-mail and e-mail subscription *bombings* were among the first documented DoS attacks. An *e-mail bomb* consists of large numbers of e-mail messages that are used to fill up a victim's electronic mailbox. A huge number of messages can tie up an online connection, slow down mail delivery, and even overload the e-mail server system until the system crashes. Most e-mail bombings are thought to be deliberate attacks by disgruntled people; specific targets may be victims of someone with a particular grudge. For example, a San Francisco stockbroker received 25,000 messages on September 23, 1996, consisting of the word "Idiot" from a consultant with whom he had had a disagreement. The flood of messages prevented him from using his computer, so in December the victim sued the perpetrator's employer for $25,000 of damages. On occasions in the past, such as with the Christmas Tree worm and the Internet Worm, the DoS is thought to have been accidental.

E-mail bomb packages automate the process of launching and carrying out an *e-mail bombing* DoS attack. With names like Up Yours, Kaboom, Avalanche, Gatemail, and the Unabomber, these packages can be placed on a network server during a DoS attack and used to attack other systems. Administrators who are aware of these names and others should regularly scan their drives for associated filenames and eliminate them.

To safeguard computers and/or servers, mail filters and exclusionary schemes can automatically filter and reject mail sent from a source address using e-mail bomb packages. Mail filters are available for UNIX, Windows, Macintosh, and Linux systems. Most computer operating systems and most ISPs now offer filtering tools for eliminating unsolicited commercial e-mail and other e-mail. Although perpetrators often disguise their identity and location by using a false address, most filters can be set to screen and eliminate these addresses.

With *e-mail subscription bombing,* also known as *list linking*, a user is subscribed to dozens of mailing lists by the attacker without the user's knowledge. For example, one of the earliest subscription-bombing incidents was perpetrated by someone calling himself "johnny xchaotic." In August 1996, he claimed the blame for a massive mail-bombing run based on fraudulently subscribing dozens of victims to hundreds of mailing lists. In a rambling and incoherent letter posted on the Net, this person made rude remarks about famous and not-so-famous people whose capacity to receive meaningful e-mail was obliterated by up to thousands of unwanted messages a day. Today, filtering packages have point-and-click mechanisms that provide automatic list linking. A user conceivably could start to receive hundreds or thousands of mail messages per day if linked to just 50 to 100 lists. Once linked to the various lists, the victim has to manually unsubscribe from each individual mailing list. If an attack takes place while the victim is away and without access to e-mail, a user could have a backlog of thousands of messages by the time he or she returns.

List server software should never accept subscriptions without sending a request for confirmation to the supposed subscriber; however, even this safety mechanism can generate a wave of many single e-mail messages if a mail bomber abuses the list servers.

Speaking of being away, vacation messages and return receipts are another way in which individuals can inadvertently start an *e-mail storm.* Many users set their e-mail clients to automatically request a return receipt of all messages sent. Then the users go on vacation and set up an auto-reply vacation message. When they get a message, the client sends back the vacation message and also requests a receipt. The returned receipts, in turn, generate more auto-reply vacation messages.

Another variant on this feedback loop occurs when an employee goes on vacation and forwards all e-mail to an external ISP that has a local access number in the locale of the vacation. If the employee decides not to check the mail while away, either due to a high local access fee or so as not to interfere with the vacation, the ISP mailbox will fill up with forwarded messages. If the mailbox fills up, the ISP will send a bounce message back to the corporate server—which then forwards the bounce message back to the ISP, which generates yet another bounce message. Eventually, even the corporate mail server will fill up with a single individual's messages, causing an e-mail DoS.

18.2.4.3 Buffer Overflow. *Buffer overflow* attacks can be insidious and damaging. It is possible to send an input string to a target program that contains actual code and is long enough to overflow the memory space or input buffer. Sometimes this surreptitious code is placed on the process stack (the area in a computer's memory where the operating system keeps track of the program's input and related code used for processing the inputs), and the code then is processed. An overflow can occur when the input data overflows its buffer space and flows into the stack, where it overwrites the previous data and return address. If the program is written so that the stack address points to the malicious code located in the return buffer, the code executes with the original program's privileges. Buffer overflow is the result of poor programming, where the programmer does not check the size of the input compared to the input buffer; the Internet Worm attack was based, in part, on such poor programming. Although buffer overflows have been around for years and should have been eradicated by now, new buffer overflow attacks pop up monthly.

Not all buffer overflows allow the user to insert executable code. DoS attacks such as the Ping of Death merely attach a data block that is larger than allowed by the IP protocol (i.e., greater than the 65,536 bytes). Because the packets are broken into fragments for transmission, they manage to get through the network and, probably, the router and firewall. Once reassembled at the target, however, the packets cause the IP kernel's buffer to overflow and the systems crashes.

Another example is an old flaw in Microsoft's Internet Information Server (IIS) that could be exploited to allow the Web service to be halted. To do this, an attacker would request a document with a very long URL from an IIS-based Web site. Upon receipt of the request, an access violation occurred and the server would halt. Although Microsoft issued a patch for this "security hole," successful attacks continue to take place today. (And how does one identify an IIS site? If a Web site use pages with the .htm or .asp extensions, it is a good guess that the site is running IIS.)

18.2.4.4 Bandwidth Consumption. *Bandwidth consumption* involves generating a large number of packets directed to the network under attack. Such attacks can take place on a local network or can be perpetrated remotely. If the attacker has, or can access, greater bandwidth than the victim has available, the attacker can flood the victim's network connection. Such saturation can happen to both high-speed and

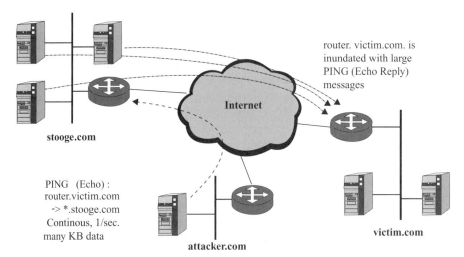

router. victim.com. is
inundated with large
PING (Echo Reply)
messages

EXHIBIT 18.1   SMURF DoS Attack

low-speed network connections. Although any type of packet may be used, the most common are Internet Control Message Protocol (ICMP) Echo messages (generated by Pinging). By engaging multiple sites to flood the victim's network connection, attackers can amplify the DoS attack. To do this successfully, the attackers convince the amplifying system to send traffic to the victim's network. Tracing the intruder who perpetrates a bandwidth consumption attack can be difficult since attackers can spoof their source addresses.

The most common bandwidth consumption attack is called a *SMURF* attack. This attack is particularly interesting (and clever) since it uses tools that reside on every IP system and employs a third-party site without actually having to take control of any system anywhere. As Exhibit 18.1 shows, the SMURF attack starts when the intruder (at *attacker.com*) sends a continuous string of very large Ping messages to the IP broadcast address (* in the exhibit) of the unsuspecting third party, *stooge.com*. The intruder spoofs the source IP address of the Ping message so that it appears that these messages come from, say, the router at the target network, *router.victim.com*. If the intruder sends a single 10,000-byte Ping message to the broadcast address of an intermediate site with 50 hosts, for example, the responses will consume 4 megabytes (Mb).[1] Even if *victim.com* has a T1 line (with a bandwidth of 1.544 Mb per second), the attacker can swamp a victim's line merely by sending a single large Ping per second to the right stooge site. The intermediate site is called, for obvious reasons, the amplifying network; note that the attacker does not need to compromise any systems there. The ratio of originally transmitted packets to the number of systems that respond is known as the *amplification ratio*.

A variant of the SMURF attack is called a *Fraggle* attack. In this variant, the attackers send spoofed User Datagram Protocol (UDP) packets instead of Echo messages to the broadcast address of the amplifying network. Each system on the amplifying network that has the specific broadcast address port enabled will create large amount of traffic by responding to the victim's host; if the port is not enabled, the system on the amplifying network will generate ICMP Host Unreachable messages to the victim's host. In either case, the victim's bandwidth is consumed.

Kernel panic attacks are not due to programming flaws per se. The Intel Pentium chip that could not correctly divide two particular legal inputs had a programming flaw.

An IP kernel that fails when receiving a packet that should never occur in the first place is, indeed, a gap in the program's logic but not the same as failing to handle legal input.

A specific example of kernel panic occurs in Linux kernel v.2.2.0 when a program usually used for printing shared library dependencies is used instead to print some core files. Under certain circumstances, *munmap( )*, a function call used to map and unmap devices into memory, overwrites critical areas of kernel memory and causes the system to panic and reboot.

And there are other examples of these kinds of attacks. A *Land* attack occurs when a spoofed packet is sent to a target host where the TCP source port and destination port are set to the same value, and the IP source address and destination address also are set to the same value. Since this is confusing to the host, it results in 100 percent CPU utilization and then a halt. Land attacks have been directed at just about all operating systems.

Teardrop attacks are also the result of behavior when receiving "impossible" packets. If an IP packet is too large for a particular network to handle, the packet will be fragmented into smaller pieces. Information in the IP packet header tells the destination host how to reassemble the packet. In a Teardrop attack, the attacker deliberately crafts IP packets that appear to overlap when reassembled. This, too, can cause the host to crash. Teardrop attacks have been targeted against Microsoft operating systems and all variants of UNIX.

18.2.4.5 *Routing and Domain Name System Attacks.* *Routing and Domain Name System (DNS) attacks* are clever attacks that are achieved repeatedly. By tampering with the DNS, a site's domain name resolves to the IP address of some other site. In August 1999, Gary D. Hoke Jr., a disgruntled engineer for PairGain Technologies, provided a direct link to a bogus but authentic-looking Bloomberg News Service page he had created. Hoke, who owned PairGain shares, posted false information about PairGain's supposed acquisition by an Israeli company, pumping up the price of PairGain stock worldwide and creating havoc in the market through his pagejacking exploits. Although a nontraditional DoS attack, Hoke's antics did deny users access to the site that they desired, with serious consequences.

Another example occurred in July 1997, when Eugene Kashpureff filed fraudulent information with InterNIC for its DNS updates in July, forcing domain name servers around the globe to recognize temporary and unauthorized Internet addresses ending in .xxx, .mall, .nic, and .per. A few weeks later, he inserted false information that forced people trying to access the Web site of Network Solutions Inc. to end up at Kashpureff's Alternic site.

In another example of a routing and DNS attack, RSA Security, Inc., after announcing that it had developed a method to combat Web site hackers, found that users were unwittingly being rerouted to a counterfeit RSA Web site. The fraudulent site looked exactly like the original RSA Web site but made fun of the fact that the hacker had managed to achieve his DoS goal.

As far back as 1997, weaknesses were found in and documented about BIND implementations in versions preceding 4.9.5+P1. The earlier versions would cache bogus DNS information when DNS recursion was enabled. The vulnerability enabled attackers to exploit the process of mapping IP addresses to hostnames in what is known as *PTR record spoofing*. This type of spoofing provides the potential for a DNS DoS attack.

DNS attacks are still seen widely today. *Phishing* is a form of social engineering attack whereby users are directed to bogus, but authentic-looking, bank or credit card company Web sites and enticed to enter personal information used for identity theft. If users were to look closely at the URL of the site, however, they would observe a

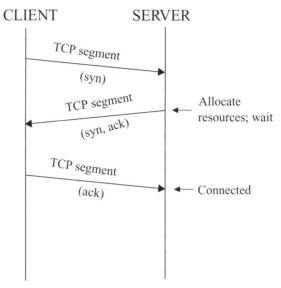

EXHIBIT 18.2   Normal TCP 3-Way Handshake

suspicious URL. *Pharming* is a variant of phishing that relies on some form of DNS poisoning so that a user going to the actual URL of a bank or credit card company will be redirected to the bogus site.

18.2.4.6   SYN Flooding.   *SYN flooding* is a DoS attack that fits into the consumption-of-scarce-resource category. This DoS attack exploits the three-way hand-shake used by TCP hosts to synchronize the logical connection prior to data exchange. In a normal TCP host-to-host connection, the two hosts exchange three TCP segments prior to exchanging data, as shown in Exhibit 18.2:

1. The client sends a segment to the server with its initial sequence number (ISN). The SYN (synchronization) flag is set in this segment.
2. The server responds by sending a segment containing its ISN and acknowledges the client's ISN. This segment will have both the SYN and ACK (acknowledg-ment) flags set. At this point, the server allocates resources for the about-to-be-established connection and waits for the third segment.
3. The client sends a segment acknowledging the server's ISN. This and all subse-quent segments until the end of the session will have only the ACK flag set.

A SYN flood takes advantage of the three-way handshake and the fact that a server can have only a finite number of open TCP connections. The attack is launched when an attacker initiates connections for which there will never be a third segment (see Exhibit 18.3). After the server sends the segment in step 2, it waits for a response. Under normal circumstances, the client will respond within a few seconds. The server might wait, say, 10 seconds before timing out and releasing the resources. But suppose the attacker sends hundreds of connection messages per second on a sustained basis. When these bogus connection attempts flood the target faster than they can time-out, there will not be any resource left in which to establish a legitimate connection. This is the type of attack that was launched against PANIX in 1996.

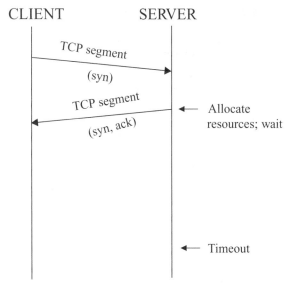

EXHIBIT 18.3 TCP SYN DoS Attack

18.2.4.7 Resource Starvation. *Resource starvation* is a catchall category for many other types of DoS attacks that are the result of some scarce resource—be it bandwidth, processing power, disk space—being consumed and exhausted. One example uses a novel UDP DoS attack, where an intruder forges UDP packets and uses them to connect the *echo* service of one machine (UDP port 7) to the character generator (*chargen*) service on another machine (UDP port 19). When this occurs, the two machines consume all available network bandwidth, and all machines on the same networks as the target machines can be affected and starved for resources.

But such attacks can happen locally, as well. Unfortunately, many authorized users carry out *local DoS attacks* that either consume system resources or deny users access. Numerous resource starvation attacks and programming flaws attack specific systems. For instance, by exceeding imposed quotas on disk space, multiuser systems can suffer from a resource starvation attack. Most operating systems limit the amount by which a user can exceed disk quota. Windows 2000 has a twist on this; although individual files can exceed their quota by only a small amount, if *every* file exceeds the quota, a user can consume a lot of extra disk space.

18.2.4.8 Java. *Java* is another avenue for DoS attacks. One such DoS attack exploits the fact that whenever specific internal elements of the Netscape and HotJava browsers lock, additional host lookups via the browser are prevented. Another DoS occurs by forcing the overutilization of the CPU and random access memory (RAM), resulting in the browser halting or freezing. During both of these events, the origin of further attacks could be obscured.

It is also possible for the Java browser's proxies to be neutralized or knocked out with the victim's DNS queries being rerouted to an untrusted DNS server. Such an untrusted server would provide misinformation in regard to host names, and this would snowball into a root compromise.

Java also can force a reboot on Windows 9x systems. An applet that works for Netscape Communicator 4.x can kill a Windows box.

18.2.4.9   Router Attacks.   *Router attacks* have been developed for a wide variety of routers. Because routers are the backbone of the Internet and the gateway through which organizations connect to the Internet, killing a router denies network service for hundreds of machines. Productivity and financial repercussions from a hardware attack can be very severe. Popular targets for these kinds of attacks are routers from Ascend, Cisco, Livingston (now Lucent), and 3Com. Unfortunately, many network managers make the attacks easy by employing Telnet or HTTP for remote access and do not properly secure the network against remote access by anyone over the Internet.

18.2.4.10   Other Denial-of-Service Attacks.   Even this list of specific DoS attacks is not exhaustive. For example, *Bonk* and *boink* (aka *bonk.c*) are DoS attacks that cause a target Windows 9x/NT system to crash. *Arnudp* (*arnudp100.c*) forges UDP packets to implement a DoS against UDP ports 7 (*echo*), 13 (*daytime*), 19 (*chargen*), and 37 (*time*), services that frequently run on UNIX and Windows NT systems. And *cbcb.c* is a *cancelbot* that destroys existing Usenet news postings that fit certain criteria. (Some argue that *cbcb.c* does not actually carry out a DoS attack; however, once activated, the program denies access to postings for targeted Usenet users.)

The CERT/CC (*www.cert.org*) and SANS (*www.sans.org*) have the most comprehensive lists of various DoS attacks.

18.2.5   Preventing and Responding to Denial-of-Service Attacks.
DoS attacks are best prevented; handling them in real time is very difficult. And the most important way to protect a system is to harden the operating systems: Install them with security in mind, monitor sites to be aware of security vulnerabilities, maintain the latest versions of software where possible, and install all relevant security patches.

But a large measure of the prevention consists of packet filtering at network routers. Because attackers frequently hide the identity of the machines used to carry out the attacks by falsifying the source address of the network connection, techniques known as *egress filtering* and *ingress filtering* are commonly used as protective measures. As discussed later in this chapter, egress and ingress filtering are methods of preventing packets from leaving or entering the network, respectively, with an invalid source address. By blocking addresses that do not fit the criteria for legitimate source addresses and making certain that all packets leaving an organization's site contain legitimate addresses, many DoS attacks can be thwarted.

Other packet-filtering methods that will help prevent DoS are to block all broadcast messages and most ICMP messages. There is no reason that a site should accept messages being broadcast to all hosts on the site. Furthermore, there is probably no good reason to allow all hosts to respond to Ping or traceroute messages; in fact, most ICMP messages probably can be blocked.

In some instances, victims have set up response letters triggered to send and resend in large quantities so that they flood the attacker's address. Doing this is generally not a good idea. If these messages are sent to a legitimate address, the attacker may "get the message" and stop. But the attackers generally spoof the source IP address, so responding in kind is not a good defensive posture because it may harm innocent victims. The best defense will involve the ISP.

In instances where the attacker's service provider can be identified and contacted, the victim can request that the service provider intervene. In these instances, it is usual for the ISPs to take appropriate action to stop the attack and find the perpetrator. However, in instances where a DoS appears to emulate or mimic another form of attack or when it continues for an unusually long period of time, the victim may want to take more aggressive action by contacting CERT/CC, the Federal Bureau of Investigation, and other authorities that have experience with DoS attacks and some jurisdiction if the perpetrators are caught.

Real-time defenses are difficult but possible. Many routers and external intrusion detection systems (IDSs) can detect an attack in real time, such as too many connection requests per unit time from a given IP host or network address. A router might block the connection requests or an IDS might send a pager message to a security administrator.

However, attacks such as SMURFs can suck up all of the bandwidth even before the packets get to the target site. Cooperation by ISPs and end user sites is required to fully combat DoS attacks. This will be addressed further as part of the discussion of responding to DDoS.

18.3 DISTRIBUTED DENIAL-OF-SERVICE ATTACKS.

DDoS tools use amplification to augment the power of the attacker. By subverting poorly secured systems into sending coordinated waves of fraudulent traffic aimed at specific targets, intruders can overwhelm the bandwidth of any given victim.

In a DDoS attack, the attacking packets come from tens or hundreds of addresses rather than just one, as in a standard DoS attack. Any DoS defense that is based on monitoring the volume of packets coming from a single address or single network will fail since the attacks come from all over. Rather than receiving, for example, 1,000 gigantic Pings per second from an attacking site, the victim might receive one Ping per second from 1,000 attacking sites.

One of the other disconcerting things about DDoS attacks is that the handler can choose the location of the agents. So, for example, a handler could target several North Atlantic Treaty Organization (NATO) sites as victims and employ agents that are all in countries known to be hostile to NATO. The human attacker, of course, might be sitting in Canada.

Like DoS attacks, all of the DDoS attacks employ standard TCP/IP messages—but employ them in some nonstandard ways. Common DDoS attacks have such names as Tribe Flood Network (TFN), Trin00, Stacheldraht, and Trinity. The sections that follow present some details about these attacks.

18.3.1 Short History of Distributed Denial of Service.

Denial-of-service attacks under a number of guises have been around for decades. Distributed DoS attacks are much newer. In late June and early July 1999, groups of hackers installed and tested a DDoS tool called trinoo (see Section 18.3.3.1) to launch medium to large DDoS attacks. Their tests involved over 2,000 compromised systems and targets around the world.

Most of the literature suggests that the first documented large-scale DDoS attack occurred in August 1999, when Trinoo was deployed in at least 227 systems (114 of which were on Internet2) to flood a single University of Minnesota computer; this system was down for more than two days.

On December 28, 1999, CERT/CC issued its Advisory CA-1999-17 (www.cert. org/advisories/CA-1999-17.html) reviewing DDoS.

On February 7, 2000, Yahoo was the victim of a DDoS during which its Internet portal was inaccessible for three hours. On February 8, Amazon, Buy.com, CNN, and eBay were all hit by DDoS attacks that caused them either to stop functioning completely or to slow down significantly. And, on February 9, E*Trade and ZDNet both suffered DDoS attacks. Analysts estimated that during the three hours Yahoo was down, it suffered a loss of e-commerce and advertising revenue that amounted to about $500,000. According to book seller Amazon.com, its widely publicized attack resulted in a loss of $600,000 during the 10 hours it was down. During their DDoS attacks, Buy.com went from 100 percent availability to 9.4 percent, while CNN.com's users went down to below 5 percent of normal volume and Zdnet.com and E*Trade.com were virtually unreachable. Schwab.com, the online venue of the discount broker Charles Schwab, was also hit but refused to give out exact figures for losses. One can only assume that to a company that does $2 billion weekly in online trades, the downtime loss was huge. Another type of damage caused indirectly by the DDoS was the decline in stock values in the 10 days following the attacks: eBay suffered a 24 percent decline, Yahoo dropped 15 percent, and Buy.com dropped 44 percent.

These types of DDoS attacks have continued since the summer of 1999. One of the best-known incidents was a series of DDoS attacks again Steve Gibson's GRC.COM Web site in May 2001. The attacker was a 13-year-old using an Internet Relay Chat (IRC) bot, automated programs that exploit systems using IRC clients to become DDoS zombies.

The DDoS attack that had the highest potentially devastating impact, however, occurred on October 21, 2002, when all of the top-level DNS root servers were subjected to a sustained attack by thousands of zombies. Nine of the 13 DNS root servers were knocked off the Internet; the remaining 4 were able to keep operating during the attack. All of the major ISPs and many large private networks maintain their own DNS systems, although most servers ultimately rely on the root servers to find noncached DNS entries. The attack lasted for just an hour or two; had it continued for much longer, the remaining servers probably would have been overwhelmed, effectively blocking DNS host name/address translation.

A disturbing trend that is growing is the use of DDoS as an extortion tool. An increasing number of criminals are using DDoS tools as a way to threaten an attack rather than actually disrupting a target organization's network. Although several providers of network, security, and consulting services claim that they and many of their customers have received such extortion demands, few are public about naming the targets—many of whom are acceding to the threats and paying the blackmail. Most experts agree that the extortion demands should not be met; doing so only encourages the criminal behavior. If such a threat is received, the organization's ISP and law enforcement authorities should be contacted immediately.

18.3.2 Distributed Denial-of-Service Terminology and Overview.

To describe and understand DDoS attacks, it is important to understand the terminology that is used to describe the attacks and the tools. Although the industry has more or less settled on some common terms, that consensus did not come about until well after many DoS/DDoS attacks had already appeared in the hacker and mainstream literature. Early descriptions of DDoS tools used a jumble of terms to describe the various roles of the systems involved in the attack. At the CERT/CC Distributed System Intruder Tools Workshop held in November 1999, some standard terminology was introduced. Those terms are used in the paragraphs that follow (see www.cert.org/reports/dsit_workshop-final.html or www.cert.org/reports/dsit_workshop.pdf). To align those terms and the terms used by the hacker literature as well as early descriptions, here are some synonyms:

Intruder—also called the *attacker* or *client.*

Master—also called the *handler.*

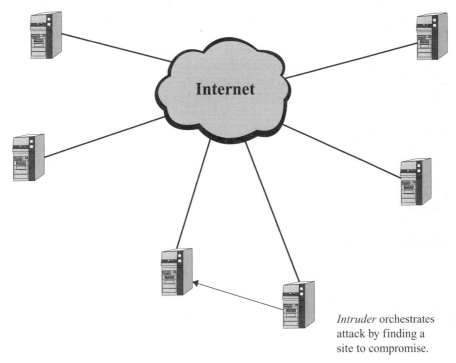

Intruder orchestrates
attack by finding a
site to compromise.

Exhibit 18.4   DDoS Phase 1

Daemon—also called an *agent, bcast (broadcast) program,* or *zombie.*

Victim—also called the *target.*

DoS/DDoS attacks actually have two victims, namely the ultimate target as well as the intermediate system(s) that were exploited and loaded with daemon software. In this chapter, the focus is on the end-of-the-line DoS/DDoS victim.

DDoS attacks always involve a number of systems. A typical DDoS attack scenario might follow roughly these three steps:

1. The *intruder* finds one or more systems on the Internet that can be compromised and exploited (see Exhibit 18.4). This is generally accomplished using a stolen account on a system with a large number of users or inattentive administrators, preferably with a high-bandwidth connection to the Internet. (Many such systems can be found on college and university campuses.)

2. The compromised system is loaded with any number of hacking and cracking tools, such as scanners, exploit tools, operating system detectors, rootkits, and DoS/DDoS programs. This system becomes the DDoS *master.* The master software allows it to find a number of other systems that can themselves be compromised and exploited. The attacker scans large ranges of IP network address blocks to find systems running services known to have security vulnerabilities. This *initial mass-intrusion phase* employs automated tools to remotely compromise several hundred to several thousand hosts, and installs DDoS agents on those systems. The automated tools to perform this compromise are not part of the DDoS toolkit but are exchanged within groups of criminal hackers. These compromised systems are the initial victims of the DDoS attack. These

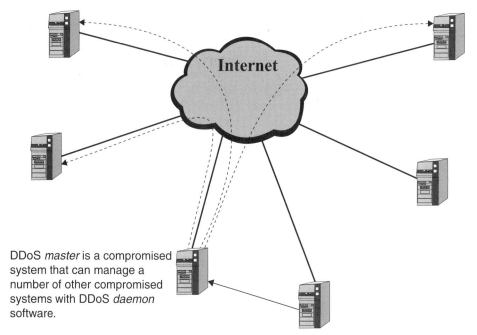

DDoS *master* is a compromised system that can manage a number of other compromised systems with DDoS *daemon* software.

EXHIBIT 18.5   DDoS Phase 2

subsequently exploited systems will be loaded with the DDoS *daemons* that carry out the actual attack (see Exhibit 18.5).

3. The intruder maintains a list of *owned systems*, the compromised systems with the DDoS daemon. The actual *denial-of-service attack phase* occurs when the attacker runs a program at the master system that communicates with the DDoS daemons to launch the attack. Here is where the intended DDoS victim comes into the scenario (see Exhibit 18.6).

Communication between the master and daemons can be obscured so that it becomes difficult to locate the master computer. Although some evidence may exist on one or more machines in the DDoS network regarding the location of the master, the daemons normally are automated so that it is not necessary for an ongoing dialog to take place between the master and the rest of the DDoS network. In fact, typically techniques are employed to deliberately camouflage the identity and location of the master within the DDoS network. These techniques make it difficult to analyze an attack in progress and difficult to block attacking traffic and trace it back to its source.

In most cases, the system administrators of the infected systems do not even know that the daemons have been put in place. Even if they do find and eradicate the DDoS software, they cannot help anyone determine where else the software may have been placed. Popular systems to exploit are a site's Web, e-mail, name, or other servers since these systems are likely to have a large number of open ports, a large amount of traffic, and are unlikely to be quickly pulled off-line even if an attack can be traced to them.

18.3.3 Distributed Denial-of-Service Tool Descriptions.   This section provides some details on how some of the major DDoS tools work.

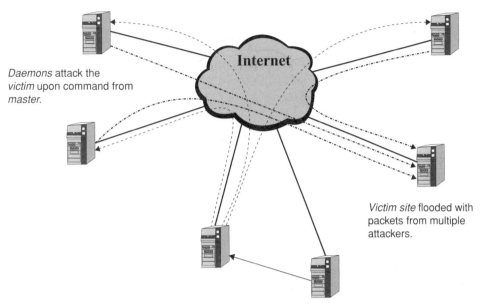

Daemons attack the victim upon command from master.

Victim site flooded with packets from multiple attackers.

Exhibit 18.6   DDoS Phase 3

18.3.3.1 Trinoo (Trin00).   *Trinoo*, also called *trin00*, was the first known DDoS tool, appearing in June or July 1999. The typical installation of trinoo is similar to the scenario painted above where an attacker plants handler software on a system and the handler, in turn, loads the attack software on the agents. Trinoo is a distributed SYN DoS attack.

Trinoo uses a number of TCP and UDP ports:

- Masters listen on TCP port 27665 for attacker-to-master communication.
- Daemons listen on UDP port 27444 for master-to-daemon communication.
- Masters listen on UDP port 31335 for daemon-to-master communication.

These are default port numbers, of course, and future implementations could use other ports. The human attacker can control a trinoo master (the handler) remotely via a connection to TCP port 27665. After connecting, the attacker gives the expected password, *betaalmostdone*.

The trinoo master program is typically named *master.c* and the daemon is *ns.c*. Communication between the trinoo master (handler) and daemons (agents) is via UDP. Master-to-daemon communications use UDP datagrams on port 27444. All commands contain a password, the default being *l44adsl*. All valid commands contain the substring *l44*.

Communication from the trinoo daemons to the master use UDP datagrams on port 31335. When the daemon starts, it sends a message to the master containing the string **HELLO**. The trinoo *keep alive* function is accomplished by an exchange between the master and daemon: The master sends a trinoo *mping* command, which sends the string *png* to a daemon; the daemon responds by sending the string *PONG* to the master.

The passwords are here to prevent system administrators from being able to take control of the masters and daemons that form the trinoo network. Other default passwords in the initial attacks were *gOrave* to start the trinoo master server and *killme* to control the master's *mdie* command to kill the trinoo processes. Like the port numbers, the passwords can be changed easily.

Intrusion detection software or system management routine analysis can look for a number of things that might indicate the presence of trinoo:

- A system listening on UDP port 27444 could be a trinoo daemon.
  - Trinoo daemon communication will contain the string *l44*.
  - The SYN flood mechanism picks the destination port using a random number generator function.
  - A trinoo daemon will send the string *PONG* if it receives a *png* command.
- A system listening on TCP port 27665 could be a trinoo master.
- A system listening on UDP port 27444 could be a trinoo master.
  - UDP packets will contain the string *l44adsl*.

A detailed analysis of trinoo by Dave Dittrich can be found at staff.washington. edu/dittrich/misc/trinoo.analysis.

18.3.3.2 *Tribe Flood Network.* The Tribe Flood Network (TFN) appeared after trinoo. TFN runs primarily on compromised UNIX systems exploited using buffer overrun bugs in the RPC services. TFN client and daemon programs implement a DDoS network capable of employing a number of attacks, such as ICMP flood, SYN flood, UDP flood, and SMURF-style attacks.

TFN is noticeably different from trinoo in that all communication between the client (attacker), handlers, and agents use *ICMP ECHO* and *ECHO REPLY* packets. Communication from the TFN client to daemons is accomplished via *ICMP ECHO REPLY* packets. The absence of TCP and UDP traffic sometimes makes these packets difficult to detect because many protocol monitoring tools are not configured to capture and display the ICMP traffic.

Remote control of the TFN network is accomplished by executing a program on the client system. The program also can be executed at the handler system by the client via some host-to-host connection method, such as connecting to an exploited TCP port or using a UDP- or ICMP-based remote shell. The program must be supplied:

- The IP address list of hosts that are ready to carry out the flood attack
- The type of attack to be launched
- The IP address list of target hosts
- The port number for SYN attack

No password protection is associated with TFN. Each command to the daemons is sent in the Identifier field of the ICMP packet; values *345*, *890*, and *901* start the *SYN*, *UDP*, and *ICMP* flood attacks, respectively. The Sequence Number field in the *ECHO REPLY* message is always set to *0x0000*, which make it look like the response to the initial *ECHO* packet sent out by the *ping* command.

The TFN client program typically is named *tribe.c* and the daemon is *td.c*. A detailed analysis of TFN by Dave Dittrich can be found at staff.washington.edu/dittrich/misc/tfn.analysis.

18.3.3.3 *Stacheldraht.* Stacheldraht (German for "barbed wire") is a DDoS tool that appeared in August 1999 and combines features of trinoo and TFN. It also contains some advanced features, such as encrypted attacker-master communication and automated agent updates.

Stacheldraht uses a trinoo-like client/server architecture. The handler listens on TCP port 16660 for client (intruder) commands, and the agents listen on TCP port 65000 for commands from the handler. Agent responses to the handler employ *ICMP ECHO REPLY* messages. The possible attacks are similar to those of TFN; namely, ICMP flood, SYN flood, UDP flood, and SMURF attacks.

Trinoo and TFN exchange commands in plaintext. Trinoo, being TCP-based, is also subject to common TCP attacks, such as session hijacking. Stacheldraht addresses these deficiencies by employing an encrypting "telnet alike" client. ("Telnet alike" is a Stacheldraht term.) The client uses secret key cryptography.

The Stacheldraht network comprises a number of programs. The attacker uses an encrypting client called *telnetc/client.c* to control to one or more handlers. The handler program is called *mserv.c,* and each handler can control up to 1,000 agents. The agent software, *leaf/td.c,* coordinates the attack against one or more victims upon command from the handler.

Dave Dittrich's analysis of stacheldraht can be found at *staff.washington.edu/ dittrich/misc/stacheldraht.analysis.*

18.3.3.4 *TFN2K.* Tribe Flood Network 2K (TFN2K) was released in December 1999 and targets UNIX and Windows NT servers. TFN2K is a complex variant of the original TFN with features designed specifically to:

- Make TFN2K traffic difficult to recognize and filter
- Remotely execute commands
- Hide the true source of the attack using IP address spoofing
- Transport TFN2K traffic over multiple transport protocols including UDP, TCP, and ICMP
- Confuse attempts to locate other nodes in a TFN2K network by sending "decoy" packets

TFN2K, like TFN, can consume all of a system's bandwidth by flooding the victim machine with data. But TFN2K, unlike TFN, also includes attacks designed to crash or introduce instabilities in systems by sending malformed or invalid packets, such as those found in the Teardrop and Land attacks.

TFN2K uses a client-server architecture in which a single client issues commands simultaneously to a set of TFN2K agents. The agents then conduct the DoS attacks against the victim(s). The agent software is installed in a machine that already has been compromised by the attacker.

An early description of TFN2K from CERT/CC can be found at www.cert.org/ advisories/CA-1999-17.html.

18.3.3.5 *Other Types of Distributed Denials of Service.* Trinoo, TFN/TFN2K, and Stacheldraht are the best-known, and still most widely used, DDoS tools, but more tools are becoming available.

In November 1999, for example, the Shaft DDoS tool became available. A Shaft network looks conceptually similar to a trinoo network with client-managing handler programs ("shaftmaster") that, in turn, manage agent programs ("shaftnode"). Like trinoo, handler-agent communication uses UDP, with the handler(s) listening on port 20433 and the agent(s) listening on port 18753. The client communicates with the handler by telnetting to TCP port 20432. The attack itself is a packet flooding attack, and the client controls the size of the flooding packets and duration of the attack. One signature of Shaft is that the sequence number for all TCP packets is always 0x28374839. Additional information about Shaft can be found at www.sans.org/y2k/shaft.htm.

In August 2000, a DDoS attack against Apache Web servers was first detected. The attack took advantage of a vulnerability whereby a URL sent to an Apache Web server containing thousands of forward slashes ("/") would put the server into a state that would consume enormous CPU time. This particular attack was launched by over 500 compromised Windows computers and would, presumably, succeed against Apache Web servers prior to version 1.2.5.

During the following month, a new DDoS tool called Trinity was reported. Trinity is capable of launching several types of flooding attacks on a victim site, including UDP, fragment, SYN, RST, ACK, and other floods. Trinity agent software must be placed on Linux systems compromised by a buffer overflow vulnerability. The agent binary code typically is found in */usr/lib/idle.so*. Communication from the handler or intruder to the agent, however, is accomplished via Internet Relay Chat (IRC) or America Online's ICQ instant messaging software. Whereas the attacker has to keep track of the IP addresses of compromised systems with Trinoo and TFN, all of the Trinity agents report back to the attacker by appearing in the same chat room. The original reports were that the Trinity agent communicated over an IRC channel called *#b3eblebr0x*; other IRC channels presumably are being used for DDoS, as well. IRC uses TCP ports 6665 to −6669, and Trinity appears to use port 6667. In addition, a binary called */var/spool/uucp/uucico* is a backdoor program that listens on TCP port 33270 for connections; an attacker connecting on that port and providing the password !@# will achieve rootshell on the affected system.

Zombie software is not always distributed by an attacker exploiting a vulnerability of an exposed system. Indeed, very often the user is the culprit. Trojan horses are often the mechanism for distributing the zombie code. The SubSeven Defcon8 software, for example, is a backdoor virus that is rapidly spreading. SubSeven gets on a user's system because it is distributed within programs available via Usenet and other Internet sites, such as some game or pornography programs (e.g., SexxxyMovie.mpeg). Potential attackers frequently scan computer systems today, particularly residential systems connected to the Internet via DSL or cable modem, for the presence of SubSeven, which provides a potential backdoor into users' systems; system administrators also are learning to scan for this dangerous program on their own systems.

18.3.3.6 *Denial of Service Using Exploitable Software.* The tools just discussed employ the common DoS approach: An attacker exploits a vulnerability of a potential victim and uses that system to launch attacks on the intended victim. The latest round of DDoS attacks, however, use code that is commonly available and that has known vulnerabilities.

In May 2001, a buffer overflow exploit was discovered in the Microsoft Internet Information Service (IIS) Indexing Service. In mid-June, Microsoft released a security bulletin warning that administrative scripts (.ida files) and Internet data queries (.idq files) did not do proper bounds checking. As it happens, what seems like the vast majority of IIS servers did not get the patch, and, in essence, every unpatched IIS server became a DDoS zombie.

In July, eEye Digital Security and several other security organizations around the Internet saw an alarming number of TCP port 80 scans on the Internet. What they eventually discovered was what became known as the Code Red Worm.

Code Red has three distinct phases. The *propagation phase* occurs during the first 19 days of the month. During this phase, the attacking system scans target systems on TCP port 80 and sends a specially crafted HTTP GET request that exploits the IIS buffer overflow (even if the Index Service is not running). A common log entry might appear as:

```
211.5.255.44 - - [16/Aug/2001:11:30:49 -0400] "GET
/default.ida?NNNNNNNNNNNNNNNNNNNNNNNNNNNNNNNNNNNNNNNNNNNNNNNNNNN
NNNNNNNNNNNNNNNNNNNNNNNNNNNNNNNNNNNNNNNNNNNNNNNNNNNNNNNNNNNNNNNN
NNNNNNNNNNNNNNNNNNNNNNNNNNNNNNNNNNNNNNNNNNNNNNNNNNNNNNNNNNNNNNNN
NNNNNNNNNNNNNNNNNNNNNNNNNNNNNNNNNNNNNNNNNNNNNNNNNNN%u9090%u685
8%ucbd3%u7801u9090%u6858%ucbd3%u7801%u9090%u6858%ucbd3%u7801%u
9090%u9090%u8190%u00c3%u0003%u8b00%u531b%u53ff%u0078%u0000%u00
=a HTTP/1.0" 400 357
```

If the exploit is successful, the worm runs in RAM of the infected server and spawns 99 new threads to attack a quasi-random set of IP addresses. If the exploited server's native language is English, the server's Web page is defaced with a message that says "Welcome to http://www.worm.com! Hacked by Chinese!" This message would stay up for 10 hours and then disappear.

The *flood phase* occurs on days 20 to 27 of the month. This is when the attack really happens; every day between 8:00 and 11:59 P.M. UTC, the compromised servers send 100 KB packets to the IP address 198.137.240.91, which formerly was assigned to www.whitehouse.gov.

Days 28 to 31 of the month are the *termination phase*, when the worm becomes dormant. Code Red was relatively innocuous to what it could have been; once asleep, the worm stayed asleep although it could be reawakened. Removing the worm program from RAM only required a reboot, and the patch from Microsoft would prevent further infection.

As an aside, although only IIS servers could be exploited, many other devices that listen on port 80 were also affected. Cisco 600 DSL routers and HP JetDirect devices, for example, listen on port 80 and would crash when they received the buffer overflow packet.

Three different variants of Code Red existed on the Internet, all acting as described. In August, a couple of new variants appeared that have been called Code Red II. Unlike Code Red, Code Red II did not deface Web pages nor did it launch a DDoS attack on any given site. Instead, this worm was destructive, installing backdoors on infected servers, changing many registry settings, installed a Trojan horse version of *explorer.exe* (Windows Explorer), and disabling the System File Checker (SFC) utility. The worm also spread very quickly, employing up to 300 threads at a time looking for other systems to infect.

The next evolution appeared in September 2001, and was called NIMDA. NIMDA (a play on the term *admin*) was truly unique because it exploited multiple vulnerabilities in Microsoft code, namely IIS, Internet Explorer (IE), and the Message Application

Propagation by Network Shares
• worm code written to writeable share.

Propagation by E-mail
• E-mail client using IE HTML reader.
• Autoexecutes README.EXE.

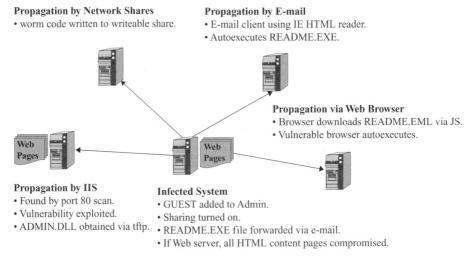

Propagation via Web Browser
• Browser downloads README.EML via JS.
• Vulnerable browser autoexecutes.

Propagation by IIS
• Found by port 80 scan.
• Vulnerability exploited.
• ADMIN.DLL obtained via tftp.

Infected System
• GUEST added to Admin.
• Sharing turned on.
• README.EXE file forwarded via e-mail.
• If Web server, all HTML content pages compromised.

Exhibit 18.7   NIMDA Propagation Vectors

Program Interface (MAPI). As a result, NIMDA had four distinct propagation vectors (see Exhibit 18.7):

1. **IIS.** When a Web server is found, the attacker attempts to exploit various IIS vulnerabilities, including IIS sadmind, a Code Red II root.exe or other backdoor program, or IIS Directory Traversal. If successful, the attacker uses tftp from cmd.exe to send the worm code (admin.dll) to the victim.

2. **Web browser.** The worm on an infected server creates a copy of itself in a file called *readme.eml*. The worm also alters every Web-content file at the infected site with a small JavaScript code that points to this file. When some user browses to the infected Web server, the infected page's JS code is activated, and *readme.eml* is downloaded. Vulnerable versions of Internet Explorer will auto-execute the file while most other browsers won't.

3. **E-mail.** NIMDA sends itself to all of the e-mail addresses found in the InBox and Address Book of an infected server in a MIME-encoded, 56KB attached file named *readme.exe*. The file contains an "audio/x-wav" section that contains the worm. E-mail clients using IE 5.1 or earlier to display HTML will automatically execute the attachment if the message is opened or previewed.

4. **Network shares.** When on an infected system, the worm copies itself to all local directories on victim host and to all open, writeable network shares. The worm also sets up shares on the victim host.

In addition, the GUEST account on the infected system is activated and made a member of Administrator group.

18.3.4   Defenses against Distributed Denials of Service.   As with DoS attacks, a site cannot in isolation defend itself from DDoS attacks. Members of the Internet community must work together to protect every site against becoming the source of attacks or forwarding the attacks. This section discusses some ways to help prevent the spread of DDoS attacks by limiting the distribution of the tools and by limiting the propagation of the offending attack packets.

Although not discussed in detail here, another point needs to be made about DDoS attack responses. As discussed in Chapter 38 in this *Handbook*, victims of such an attack should maintain detailed logs of all actions they take and events they detect. These logs may prove invaluable in understanding the attack, in preventing other attacks at the initial target and others, and in aiding law enforcement efforts to track down the perpetrators.

18.3.4.1   *User and System Administrator Actions.*   The next seven steps should be taken to minimize the potential that an individual system will be compromised and attacked or used as a stepping-stone to attack others:

1. Keep abreast of the security vulnerabilities for all of the site's hardware, operating systems, and application and other software. This sounds like a Herculean task, but it is essential to safeguarding the network. Apply patches and updates as soon as possible. Standardize on certain hardware, operating systems, and software where feasible to help manage the problem.
2. Use personal firewall software on workstations to detect an attack.
3. Monitor systems periodically to test for known operating system vulnerabilities. Also periodically check to see what TCP/UDP ports are using the "netstat –a" command; every open port should be associated with a known application. Turn off all unused applications.
4. Regularly monitor system logs and look for suspicious activity.
5. Use available tools to periodically audit systems, particularly servers, to ensure that there have been no unauthorized/unknown changes to the file system, registry, user account database, and so on.
6. Do not download software from unknown, untrusted sites. If possible, know the author of the code. Even better, download source code, review it, and compile it on a trustworthy system rather than downloading binaries or executables.
7. Keep up with and follow recommendations from the CERT/CC, SANS Institute, Internet Engineering Task Force (IETF) Requests for Comments (RFCs), and other best practices.

18.3.4.2   *Local Network Actions.*   Even if users lock down their systems so that no vulnerability has gone unpatched and no exposure unprotected, the local network itself still can be at risk. Local network managers and network administrators can take four steps to protect all of their own users as well as the rest of the Internet community:

1. Every network connected to the Internet should perform egress address filtering at the router. *Egress filtering* means that the router should examine the IP Source Address field of every outgoing packet to the Internet to be sure that the NET_ID matches the NET_ID of the network. Historically users' firewalls have been used to protect users from attacks from the outside world. But those attacks come from somewhere, so sites should also use the firewall to protect the outside world.
2. Networks should block incoming packets addressed to the broadcast address (the all-ones HOST_ID). There is no legitimate reason that an external network device should be sending a broadcast message to every host on a network.

3. To prevent a site from being used as a broadcast amplification point, turn off the Directed Broadcast capability at the router unless it is absolutely essential. If it is essential, reexamine the network to see if there is not a better way. Even where Directed Broadcasts are useful, typically they are needed only *within* the enterprise and are not required for hosts on the outside.

4. RFC 1918 defines three blocks within the IP address space that are reserved for private IP networks; these addresses are not to be routed on the Internet.

IP Address Range	Network ID/ Subnet Mask	Number of Equivalent Classful IP Networks
10.0.0.0–10.255.255.255	10/8 prefix	1 Class A network
172.16.0.0–172.31.255.255	172.16/12 prefix	16 Class B networks
192.168.0.0–192.168.255.255	192.168/16 prefix	256 Class C networks

In addition, there are a number of reserved IP addresses that are never assigned to "public" networks or hosts, including:

0.0.0.0/32	Historical broadcast address
127.0.0.0/8	Loopback network identifier
169.254.0.0/16	Link-local networks
192.0.2.0/24	TEST - NET
224.0.0.0/4	Class D multicast address range
240.0.0.0/5	Class E experimental address range
248.0.0.0/5	Unallocated
255.255.255.255/32	Broadcast

Attackers commonly use IP address spoofing, generally by using one of the RFC 1918 private addresses or one of the other reserved addresses. Firewalls should immediately discard *any* packet that contains any RFC 1918 or reserved IP address in the IP Source Address or Destination Address field; such packets should never be sent to the Internet.

1. Block all unused application ports at the firewall, particularly such ports as IRC (6665–6669/tcp) and those known to be associated with DDoS tools.

2. Use some form of intrusion detection system to protect the network. For example, one can install personal firewall software on every workstation to help detect an attack on individual systems; this strategy is particularly useful at sites (e.g., colleges) that have a large number of systems *in front* of a firewall. It is no coincidence that so many daemons reside on college and university computers that have been taken *owned* (i.e., taken over by hackers).

3. Regularly monitor network activity so that aberrations in traffic flow can be detected quickly.

4. Educate users about things to watch for on their systems and how to report any irregularity that might indicate that someone or something has tampered with their system. Educate the help desk and technical support to assist those users who make such reports. Have an intelligence-gathering system within the organization so that such reports can be coordinated centrally to spot trends and to devise responses.

5. Follow CERT/CC, SANS, US-CERT, and other best practices procedures.

18.3.4.3 Internet Service Provider Actions. Internet service providers offer the last hope in defeating the spread of a DDoS attack. Although the ISP cannot take responsibility for locking down every customer's host systems, ISPs have—and should accept—the responsibility to ensure that their network does not carry packets that contain obviously "bad" packets. Some of the steps that ISPs can take include:

- As mentioned, attackers commonly employ IP address spoofing using an RFC 1918 private address or other reserved address. Amazingly, many ISPs will route these packets. Indeed, there is no entry in their routing table telling them where to send the packets; they merely forward them to a default upstream ISP. *Any* packet that contains any RFC 1918 or reserved IP address in the IP Source Address or Destination Address field should be discarded immediately.

- Perform ingress (and egress) address filtering. *Ingress filtering* means that ISPs should examine every incoming packet to their network from a customer's site and examine the IP Source Address field to be sure that the NET_ID matches the NET_ID assigned to that customer. Doing this will require additional configuration at the router and may even result in slight performance degradation, but the trade-off is certainly well worth the effort. The ISPs also should perform egress filtering to check their outbound packets to upstream and peer ISPs.

- Disable IP directed broadcasts.

- Pay careful attention to high-profile systems (servers) and customers.

- Educate customers about security and work with them to help protect themselves.

Most of the ISP community takes at least some of these steps. Users should insist that their ISPs provide at least these protections and should not do business with those that do not. The ICSA Labs ISP Security (ISPSec) community (www.icsa.net/html/communities/ispsec) is a good source of information for ISPs.

18.3.4.4 Code Red/NIMDA Defensive Actions. There are a number of defensive steps that can be taken to avoid or mitigate problems due to NIMDA, although several of these are controversial.

- If you are using IIS, consider using alternate Web server software. If you must use IIS, the only way to clean up after NIMDA is to reinstall IIS on a new, clean installation of the underlying operating system. Keep IIS and the operating system up to the latest patch revision. Microsoft's IIS Cumulative Patch does *not* clean a system of Code Red II backdoors or NIMDA.

- If you use Internet Explorer, consider using alternate browser software. If you must use IE, secure it against MIME auto-execution. IE 5.01 requires a patch whereas IE 5.5 SP2 and IE 6.0 are already immune.

- Disable any and all unused accounts on your system. In particular, enable the Guest account or anonymous access only if necessary.

- Disable JavaScript, Java, and ActiveX on your browser and turn those features on only if they are needed while you are on a safe site.

- Do not execute readme.exe or *any* e-mail attachment unless expected, known, and verified.
- Use most up-to-date antivirus signature files.
- Unbind file and print sharing from TCP/IP. In some cases, this will require installing NetBEUI for file and print sharing.

18.3.4.5   Other Tools under Development or Consideration. Responses to DDoS attacks are not limited to the defensive steps just listed. Indeed, proactive responses to the prevention and detection of DDoS attacks are an active area of research.

One method that is being discussed is to examine the network at the ISP level and build a type of intelligent, distributed network traffic monitor; in some sense, this would be like an IDS for the Internet. ISPs, peering points, and/or major host servers would have traffic monitor hardware using IP and the Internet for communications, much like today's routing protocols. Each node would examine packets and their contents, doing a statistical analysis of traffic to learn the normal patterns. These devices would have enough intelligence to be able to detect changes in traffic level and determine whether those changes reflected a normal condition or not. As an example, suppose that such hardware at Amazon.com were to identify a DoS attack launched from an ISP in Gondwanaland; the traffic-monitoring network would shut off traffic to Amazon coming from that ISP as close to the ISP as possible. In this way, the distributed network of monitors could shut traffic off at the source.

The hardware would need to be informed about traffic-level changes due to normal events, such as a new Super Bowl commercial being posted at the Ad Critic Web site or a new fashion show at Victoria Secret's Web site. The hardware also would need to prevent the attacker community from operating under the cover of these normal events.

RSA Laboratories has proposed another potential defense to DDoS attacks against Web servers that employs cryptographic methods. The approach uses a *client puzzle* protocol designed to allow servers to accept connection requests from legitimate clients and block those from attackers. A client puzzle is a cryptographic problem that is generated in such a way as to be dependent on time and information unique to the server and client request.

Under normal conditions, a server accepts any connection request from any client. If an attack is detected, the server selectively accepts connection requests by responding to each request with a puzzle. The server allocates the resources necessary to support a connection only to those clients that respond correctly to the puzzle within some regular TCP time-out period. A bona fide client will experience only a modest delay getting a connection during an attack, while the attacker will require an incredible amount of processing power to sustain the number of requests necessary for a noticeable interruption in service, quickly blocking the attack (in effect, a reverse DoS). This scheme might be effective against a DDoS attack from a relatively small number of hosts each sending a high volume of packets but would appear to have limited effectiveness against a low-volume attack from a large number of systems.

A third mechanism that is the subject of considerable research is *IP Traceback*. The problem with DoS/DDoS attacks is that packets come from a large number of sources, and IP address spoofing masks those sources. Traceback marking, in concept, is a relatively straightforward idea. Every packet on the Internet goes through some number of ISP routers. The processing power, memory, and storage are available for routers to mark packets with partial path information as they arrive. Since DoS/DDoS attacks generally comprise a large number of packets, the traceback mechanism does not need to mark every packet, but only a sample size that statistically is likely to include attack packets (e.g., 1 packet out of every 20,000). The feature allows the victim to locate the approximate source of the attack without the aid of outside agencies and even after the attack has ended. Another traceback proposal would define an ICMP Traceback message that would be sent to the victim site containing partial route information about the sampled packet. There are many issues related to traceback that need to be resolved, such as the minimum number of marked packets required to reconstruct the path back to the attacker, the actual processing overhead, and the ability to perform traceback while an attack is under way. In addition, any traceback solution will require a change to tens of thousands of routers in the Internet; how effective can traceback be during a period of gradual implementation? The upside, of course, is that the solution is backward compatible and results in no negative effects on users.

A fourth proposal is to modify IP to be less prone to address spoofing by making the protocol less dependent on the address field for anything more than routing. The Host Identity Payload (HIP), for example, defines a protocol for the exchange of a cryptographic *Host Identity* between two communicating systems. This feature relegates the IP address for use solely as a mechanism for packet forwarding rather than as an identifier of the sender. Sender identification, instead, is accomplished by the Host Identity value, and all of the higher layer protocols are bound to the Host Identity. HIP is not yet widely deployed but is available in some TCP/IP implementations.

These proposals are merely samples of some ways for dealing with DDoS attacks; the first adds new hardware to the Internet, the second requires changing Web server and client software, and the latter two require incrementally changing software in all of the Internet's routers and hosts, respectively. Upgrading Web browsers is probably the most practical strategy even though there are millions of copies in distribution; the vast majority come from two vendors, and users tend to upgrade frequently anyway.

18.4   MANAGEMENT ISSUES.   One of the greatest shortcomings in many organizations is that the highest levels of management do not truly understand the critical role that computers, networks, information, and the Internet play in the life of the organization. It is difficult to explain that there is an intruder community that is actively working on new tools all the time; and history has shown that as the tools mature and become more sophisticated, the technical knowledge required of the potential attacker goes down and the number of attacks overall goes up. Too many companies insist that "no one would bother us" without realizing that *any site* can become a target just by being there.

DoS attacks come in a variety of forms and aim at a variety of services, causing increased complexity and difficulty for system defense. DoS attacks should be taken seriously because of the potential threat they present, and attempts should be made to educate operational staff before such attacks occur, to document DoS attacks if they do occur, and to review the documentation and actions taken after the incident is over. Discussion of what steps were taken, what actions went into effect, and what the overall result was will help in determining whether the procedures carried out and techniques utilized were those best suited to the situation. A frank review and discussion will help achieve the best, most rapid, and most effective deployment of resources.

If anything proves the intertwined nature of the Internet, it is the defense against DDoS attacks. DDoS attacks require the subversion and coordination of hundreds or thousands of computers to attack a few victims. Defense against DDoS attacks requires the cooperation of thousands of ISPs and customer networks. Fighting DDoS requires continued diligence in locking down all of the hosts connected to the Internet as well as fundamental changes in the nature of TCP/IP connection protocols. As these changes are not likely to happen quickly, it is equally unlikely that DDoS attacks will disappear immediately.

18.5   FURTHER READING

Several books and articles describe the early history of DoS attacks.

Anonymous. *Maximum Security*, 4th ed. Indianapolis: SAMS, 2003.

Denning, D. E. *Information Warfare and Security*. Reading, MA: Addison- Wesley, 1999.

Ferguson, P., and D. Senie. "Network Ingress Filtering: Defeating Denial of Service Attacks which employ IP Source Address Spoofing" (RFC 2827/BCP 38). The Internet Society, 2000. Available from www.ietf.org/rfc/rfc2827.txt.

Gao, Z., and N. Ansari. "Tracing Cyber Attacks from the Practical Perspective." *IEEE Communications Magazine* (May 2005): 123–131.

McClure, S., J. Scambray, and G. Kurtz, G. *Hacking Exposed, Network Security Secrets & Solutions*, 5th ed. Berkeley, CA: Osborne/McGraw-Hill, 2005.

Rekhter, Y., B. Moskowitz, D. Karrenberg, G. J. de Groot, and E. Lear. "Address Allocation for Private Internets" (RFC 1918/BCP 5). Available from www.ietf.org/rfc/rfc1918.txt.

Skoudis, E. *Counter Hack*. Upper Saddle River, NJ: Prentice-Hall, 2002.

Spafford, E. H. "The Internet Worm: An Analysis." *Computer Communication Review* (January 1989).

Most of the best current references, however, are on the Web. Some of the sites that readers should monitor for DoS/DDoS information are:

Attrition.org's "Denial of Service (DoS) Database" page: www.attrition.org/security/denial.

CERT/CC: www.cert.org.

Dave Dittrich's DDoS page: http://staff.washington.edu/dittrich/misc/ddos/.

Denialinfo.com's "Denial of Service (DoS) Attack Resources" page: www.denialinfo.com.

Distributed Intrusion Detection System: www.dshield.org.

Steve Gibson's "The Strange Tale of the Denial of Service Attacks Against GRC.COM": http://grc.com/dos/grcdos.htm.

PacketStorm's "Distributed Attack Tools" page: http://packetstorm.securify.com/distributed.

SANS Internet Storm Center: http://isc.sans.org.

US-CERT: www.us-cert.gov/.

18.6   NOTE

1. 10 KB $\times$ 8 bits/Byte $\times$ 50 hosts $=$ 4 Mb.

CHAPTER 19

SOCIAL ENGINEERING AND LOW-TECH ATTACKS

Karthik Raman, Susan Baumes, Kevin Beets, and Carl Ness

19.1   INTRODUCTION.   According to Greek mythology, the Greeks defeated the Trojans in the Trojan War with the help of a wooden statue. After fighting a decade-long war in vain, the Greeks withdrew from their stronghold on the beach. Outside the gates of Troy, they left a giant wooden horse. The statue confused the Trojan soldiers, but it was brought within the fortified walls of Troy. Inside the statue hid several Greek soldiers. When darkness fell, these soldiers emerged from the statue and opened the gates of Troy. The Greek army entered Troy and took the soldiers and citizens of Troy by surprise. After the attack, Greece won the war quickly; they could not have done so with standard warfare tactics.

The Trojan horse built by the Greeks was effective because it used deception to achieve the desired result: penetrating the enemy's established defenses. The Trojan horse accomplished what those in information security label *social engineering*.

Social engineering may be defined as obtaining information or resources from victims using coercion or deceit. During a social engineering attack, attackers do not scan networks, crack passwords using brute force, or exploit software vulnerabilities. Rather, social engineers operate in the social world by manipulating the trust or gullibility of human beings.

Not all social engineering and low-tech attacks will give attackers all the information they are seeking at once. Social engineers will collect small pieces of information that seem innocuous to the individuals that divulge them. Social engineers may gather these snippets of information in a random order but then assemble them to launch attacks that can be devastating to an organization's information security, resources, finances, reputation, or competitive advantage.

The purpose of a social engineering attack can be as varied as the attack method employed. The result, however, is generally the same: a loss of intellectual property, money, business advantage, credibility, or all of the above.

Closely related, and often used in conjunction with social engineering attacks, are low-tech attacks. Low-tech attacks do not rely on technology and are out carried via physical mechanisms against organizations or individuals.

Social engineering attacks have been and will remain successful due to the weakest security link in an organization: the people.

This chapter presents the history of social engineering and low-tech attacks, its methods, the social science behind it, and its business impact. In addition, it covers detection and mitigation policies for managers and information security officers to defend against social engineering and low-tech attacks.

19.2   BACKGROUND AND HISTORY.   Social engineering is not a new tactic. The term has its foundations in political history when a person or group manipulated a group of people, large or small, in an attempt to persuade or manipulate social attitudes or beliefs. Often this method was used by governments or political parties.[1] To this day, the term carries a negative connotation because of its roots in Nazi-controlled Germany, where, for example, eugenics experiments in the 1930s included isolating groups of people with difficulties in social relationships.[2] Some researchers also consider the realm of social engineering to cover everything from advertising and modern media to political action groups.

However, in information technology circles today, "social engineering" is a term describing security penetration or circumvention techniques.

19.2.1   Frank Abagnale.   Frank William Abagnale Jr. was able to impersonate authority figures successfully; he represented himself at various times as physician, pilot, attorney, and teacher. He also used social engineering techniques to persuade and manipulate innocent and good-natured individuals to help him carry out many of his frauds. Many of Abagnale's techniques were highly successful and well engineered and some of them were dramatized in the popular movie *Catch Me If You Can* directed by Steven Spielberg. Starting in 1974, he began working to help organizations recognize and defend against such attacks through his speaking engagements and consulting business.[3]

19.2.2   Kevin Mitnick and the Media.

One of the best-known social engineers is Kevin Mitnick. Mitnick is now a computer security consultant. In his youth, he was a criminal hacker and specialized in using social engineering. Mitnick has written several books discussing his observations and techniques as a computer hacker. There is much discussion on the Internet and among security professionals about Mitnick's credibility as a security consultant, his true intentions as an ex-hacker, and the degree to which he has been reformed. Even today, Mitnick maintains that social engineering is the most powerful tool in the hacker's toolbox.[4]

Mitnick's notoriety has been amplified in the media, dating back to his arrest, but he is not alone. Many other criminals or hackers, real or fictional, have been glorified in the media; many times these individuals used social engineering as a tool of attack. Many fictional characters have been portrayed as being masters of social engineering and hacking, leading to a career in federal agencies such as the FBI. While the information assurance community actively tries to discourage such glorification of hacking and social engineering, they continue to be popular topics in Hollywood and the media. One of the most popular examples is the 1995 movie *Hackers*, in which the criminal-hacker hero tricks security guards at a television station into revealing the station's modem number and then alters the programming to show an episode of *Outer Limits* instead of the scheduled program.[5]

19.2.3   Frequency of Use.

Social engineering attacks have become more prevalent because they are successful. One of the most visible reminders of this is the large number of *phishing* and *pharming* attacks discussed in Sections 19.3.4.1 and 19.3.4.2. In brief, phishing is the use of fraudulent e-mails to trick people into visiting Web sites where their confidential information can be stolen; pharming is the use of fraudulent Web sites to attract gullible victims who reveal confidential information. For example, during the period August 2006 through August 2007, the number of unique phishing sites detected per month ranged from 10,091 (August 2006) to 55,643 (April 2007), and each site survived for an average of 3.3 days.[6] Even though these social engineering techniques are well known and well covered by the media, they are frequently used by criminals. Phishing, for example—which started a few years ago as a simple eBay scam—has grown to include almost innumerable banking, PayPal, and credit card scams. Some AOL users have even reported receiving multiple fake phishing scam e-mails in one day.

19.2.4   Social Engineering as a Portion of an Attack.

Social engineering, when used by itself as a stand-alone attack tool, is very effective. But this tool can also be used as part of a larger attack or even as a subset of a technical attack. Social engineering is commonly used at the beginning of a larger, more substantial attack.[7]

Although one social engineering attempt may have been averted, another might not be completely mitigated. If an initial attack was unsuccessful because the attacker did not have sufficient or accurate information to carry out the attack, the attacker may revert once again to social engineering and low-tech attack strategies to gather additional information for another different, possibly successful, attack.

Even though an organization may have the most advanced firewall, intrusion detection system, and risk management tools available, an attacker may use social engineering to circumvent these technical defenses. The attacker will not need to challenge these enforcement points if able simply to extract a valid user name and password from an unsuspecting employee. Once the attacker has this information, it may be enough to carry out a devastating attack on an organization's information systems—either by a massive increase in network traffic by individual acts of malfeasance such as illegal transfer of funds.

Computer criminals have been able to use pure social engineering and low-tech attack techniques without relying on technology to cause large-scale damage. An action as simple as using discarded, potentially damaging information out of a Dumpster can cause substantial damage to an organization's image. This act might be part of a larger campaign or operation by a group of individuals seeking political or social action against an organization. An example of this was recently chronicled by Home Box Office (HBO). It described a group of citizens who routinely gathered trash from county election centers and city halls in an effort to collect evidence that they could present to the media to prove voter fraud. Documents that were improperly disposed of have had extremely negative consequences for election officials.[8]

19.3 SOCIAL ENGINEERING METHODS.   Social engineering attacks can take many different forms, and expert social engineers are capable of changing their methods of attack very quickly in order to succeed. The underlying principle of most attacks is *pretexting*, which is defined as "the collection of information. . .under false pretenses."[9] Two distinct methodologies are used during most social engineering attacks: impersonation and seduction.

Targets of social engineering attacks also vary widely. The targets of each attack can be characterized as either high or low profile. In general, high-profile targets (e.g., CEOs) may have more information to provide, but in turn may be more suspicious of questions than other employees. A low-profile target (e.g., nonmanagers or associates) might not be as suspicious, but might not have all of the information required for the social engineer's attack. Depending on the situation, a social engineer will choose a high- or low-profile target for impersonation or persuasion.

A social engineering attack may be an attack of opportunity, with the victim randomly chosen. In other, well-planned attacks, a particular target may be identified as the victim.

19.3.1 Impersonation.   Impersonation is defined as "the act, or an instance of pretending to be another," and it is one of the most popular methods that social engineers employ. Social engineers use several well-known impersonation attacks targeting all levels of employees in any area of an organization.

Help desk employees and systems administrators are commonly impersonated during social engineering attacks. For example, most organizations have help desks for IT related issues. Employees, in general, follow the instructions from help desk personnel, simply because they are trusted and usually more knowledgeable about technology. Social engineers understand this trust and will exploit it to steal information. The attacker tries to impersonate help desk personnel, contact unsuspecting employees, and ask for and receive information.

Help desk personnel can also be the victims of social engineering attacks, with the social engineer impersonating a user in need of technical assistance. An attack against the AOL help desk is an example of a successful social engineering attack against help desk personnel. The attacker phoned technical support regarding a problem. The call led to a lighthearted conversation during which the attacker offhandedly remarked that he had a car for sale at an attractive price. The victim (AOL employee) requested to see a picture of the car. The attacker e-mailed the employee a picture that, in fact, contained a piece of malicious code. The employee opened the picture, unintentionally ran the exploit, and subsequently allowed external connections to the internal AOL network. Approximately 200 AOL accounts were compromised by this attack.[10]

There have also been instances where social engineers impersonate corporate officers or managers. In a recent case, the payroll giant ADP released personnel and brokerage account information on hundreds of thousands of customers. The attacker impersonated a corporate officer from a public company and received the information from customer-service personnel using standard procedures authorized by the Securities and Exchange Commission that allow "public companies to get names and addresses of shareholders from brokers, as long as the shareholder has not objected to the disclosure of such information."[11] This case highlights the need for controls and education for all levels of employees. The victim in this case might have been concerned about displeasing a powerful member of a client organization and may have feared retribution had he or she insisted on authentication of the caller's identity.

It is important to note that attackers will also impersonate regular employees or other authorized personnel of an organization, such as service staff or consultants, by dressing and speaking appropriately and blending into the organization's environment. For a social engineer, there are no boundaries for impersonation; they may try to gain information via physical access or using any number of ruses, including impersonation of:

- Temporary employees (e.g., contractors or auditors)
- Utility or telecommunications company employees
- Janitorial or maintenance employees
- New employees
- Delivery personnel

Physical access could facilitate the gathering of information depending on whether the organization has proper controls in place. Motivated social engineers may even attempt to work at a service company in order to have easier access to the victim.

19.3.2   Seduction.   The word "seduce" is defined as "to lead away from duty, accepted principles, or proper conduct."[12] In general, a social engineering attack using seduction will take longer to complete than an impersonation attack. The attacker, using seduction, will identify a target and will form a bond with that individual, through social settings, online, or through another mechanism. In some instances, social engineers will study their victims over a period of time to learn their habits, likes, dislikes, or emotional weaknesses. It is during this relationship that information may be divulged to the attacker.

For example, a social engineer who wishes to gain access to a building may befriend a security guard of that organization. After some time has passed and the relationship has progressed, the attacker may request a tour of the facility. The security guard, wanting to impress the new friend, may allow a tour. The social engineer, once inside, can plant clandestine listening devices, look for user names or passwords, and read documents left in the open.

19.3.3 Low-Tech Attacks.   Low-tech attacks are invaluable to an attacker as part of reconnaissance, information theft, and surveying for easy targets. On occasion, these methods may even reward the attacker with a very large amount of useful information in a very short amount of time. Low-tech attack methods may seem simple or improbable, but the methods described are often overlooked by security managers. They are not urban legends—they have been used in the past and continue to be utilized today.

19.3.3.1 Dumpster Diving.   In the context of social engineering, "Dumpster diving" is the social engineer's act of searching through an organization's garbage in an attempt to find documents, hardware, software, or anything that could be of value to meet the goals of the attacker. Dumpster diving is a popular social engineering technique because it is easy and often successful. Oracle hired detectives to purchase Microsoft's trash during Microsoft's antitrust trial. (The detectives were unsuccessful.)[13] Social engineers do not need to deceive anyone to perform the attack. In many cases, the materials disposed may sit in open containers for weeks. Dumpster diving is most often carried out at night when no one is around, as there is less risk of being caught. To avoid detection, Dumpster divers have been known to dress in dark clothing or janitorial uniforms.

All organizations must understand the legal ramifications of Dumpster diving. Local and state laws may vary widely and be murky; however, it is generally understood that no organization or individual should have *any* expectation of privacy relating to materials in refuse containers left on a *public right-of-way* for pickup. It may be legal for an attacker to remove and take ownership of anything left in a Dumpster unless it is on private property with clearly marked No Trespassing signs.

19.3.3.2 Theft.   The age-old crime of theft is another popular social engineering technique. Social engineers may pick up anything they can get their hands on, literally and leverage the information obtained to carry out other attacks. Targets of theft include, but are not limited to, printed materials, CD-ROMs, USB flash drives, backup media, and laptops. Thieves may obtain objects on or off company premises. While on company premises, they may look for objects they can grab and quickly conceal. An attacker may bring in empty laptop cases, backpacks, or even large purses or trash sacks. Most employees are likely to be aware of theft techniques outside of the organization, such as in restaurants, airports, and other public places. Employees may not realize that a social engineer or other criminal may actually be an insider.

19.3.3.3 Leveraging Social Settings.   Social engineers may use social settings to gain information because people relax in social settings and may believe that information security practices are for the workplace only. A social engineer may use a social setting, such as a bar, to take advantage of drinking employees to gain information. The attacker may actively engage a target or passively eavesdrop on a conversation. Although this type of attack may seem far-fetched, there are many situations where the attacker may be in the right place at the right time to gain knowledge that can be later used as part of a larger attack. People in social settings are less likely to have their defenses up and security on their minds.

Restaurants, corporate functions, impromptu meetings outside of a company building, or loud phone conversations are all areas or situations where eavesdropping can occur. Many times, employees will work on commuter trains or conduct business in other public areas. A social engineer can exploit an organization's mobile workforce to gain information. Employees should be cognizant of who is around them while performing any work-related task. It is usually inappropriate to discuss business or to use a cell phone or a laptop within sight or hearing of others.

19.3.3.4 Exploiting Curiosity or Naivete.
Social engineers may trick a victim into unknowingly aiding in an attack by piquing the user's curiosity. For example, an attacker may leave an intriguingly labeled CD-ROM in a break room, hoping that a victim is curious about the contents. When the victim places the CD-ROM into a computer, a malicious program, such as a virus, would automatically execute and spread. This technique has also been executed using USB drives, iPods, and corrupted music CDs.[14]

19.3.3.5 Bribery.
Bribery is a method of last resort for a social engineer. Bribing an employee is a mechanism to gain information quickly, but it also exposes the social engineer's motives immediately. There is always the chance that the victim will have second thoughts and expose the social engineer or alert management or law enforcement agencies.

Bribery can be dangerous and expensive. A thorough social engineer will investigate potential victims carefully. The social engineer may frequent the same social scenes as the victim to gain information and then engage the target in casual conversation. An important factor is the employee's feeling about the company. By making offhand negative comments about the company based on the reaction of the victim, the attacker may be able to determine whether to progress with the attack or not. Social engineers commonly target disgruntled employees, contractors, and employees about to leave the organization.

Monetary gain is not the only compensatory consideration in bribery. Promises of free access to for-pay resources, tickets to sports events or concerts, and trading of music files are all included under the umbrella of bribery. Literally, any item of value given to an employee should be considered a bribe.[15]

19.3.3.6 Data Mining and Data Grinding.
Search engines can catalog a surprising amount of information that is sensitive and confidential. Social engineers can create special searches, use search engine application programming interfaces (APIs), and use advanced search capabilities of many search engines to mine information about a company. Another attack vector is the caching feature of many search engines. A search engine may cache a Web page with sensitive information. If an organization requests the cache be removed, there is a delay before the search engine cache is updated, during which time the organization's information is exposed.

Documents published by a company are another source of unintended information disclosure. In a technique known as data grinding, social engineers can use metadata-reader software to extract information such as the author's name, organization, computer name, network name, e-mail address, user ID, and comments from Microsoft Office documents.[16] This potentially damaging information is included in most document types.

19.3.3.7 Piggybacking or Tailgating.
A common and very successful method of social engineering is piggybacking or tailgating. The method allows an attacker access to a secured facility by entering together with an authorized person. The victim in these cases is being polite and holding the door for the attacker who enters the facility using the credentials of the victim. Once inside a facility, an attacker is free to roam the building in search of information. If questioned upon entering, an

attacker may use the excuse of having forgotten the necessary credentials or of being a new employee. In general, if a piggybacking is going to be attempted, social engineers will dress and act like other members of the organization so they can blend in.

It can be very difficult to demand that employees refrain from allowing piggybacking, but a policy must be in place to demand exactly that. All persons entering a secure facility should be required to fully use identification and authorization mechanisms every time they enter. As discussed in Chapter 50 in this *Handbook*, role-playing exercises can help employees overcome their reluctance to challenge piggybackers.

19.3.4 Network and Voice Methods.

As the Internet expands, so do social engineering attacks. These attacks differ from traditional social engineering attacks since they require minimal or no human interaction. The basis of the attacks still relies on the trusting nature of humans. Phishing is the most common type of attack seen today, and according to the 2006 FBI Computer Crime Survey, most attacks are derived from e-mail (93 percent).[17] Social engineers may capture all the information they are looking for from a single phishing attack. The famous Nigerian 411/419 attack is an Internet-derived combination attack that uses both e-mail and human interaction.[18] It promises millions of dollars to someone who will facilitate the movement of funds outside of Nigeria. All that is required is for the gullible victim to provide full information about a bank account to which the funds can be sent.

The methods used for these attacks include phishing, pharming, spim, spit, vishing, and malware. For more technical details about these techniques, see Chapters 16 and 20 in this *Handbook*.

19.3.4.1 Phishing.

Phishing is one of the most widely used and successful social engineering attacks. It is defined as the "act of sending an e-mail to a user falsely claiming to be an established legitimate enterprise in an attempt to scam the user into surrendering private information."[19] Phishing, as with all social engineering attacks, relies on the trusting nature of people. Naiveté about using the Internet also plays a role in the success of this attack.

A phisher will develop an e-mail message and Web site that resemble those of an existing establishment, such as PayPal. The message may explain that there was a problem with an account, a transaction, or something else, and instructs users to visit a hyperlinked Web site and log in with their credentials. The message is e-mailed, primarily using botnets, to many thousands or possibly millions of e-mail addresses. Victims respond by visiting the fraudulent Web site and entering their passwords and account numbers, which are then stolen.

The most common targets of phishing attacks are financial institutions, attacks on whom make up approximately 89 percent of all attacks.[20] The large number of phishing e-mails that many people receive indicates that some individuals respond to such e-mails and fall prey to phishers. Recent statistics reveal that this type of social engineering attack has a success rate of approximately 14 percent.[21] Newer, more targeted phishing attacks called "spear phishing" are also gaining in popularity. In these scams, spoofed e-mail messages to employees of a specific organization appear to originate from an authority such as particular manager or department and can include bogus requests for user names and passwords.[22]

19.3.4.2 Pharming.

In pharming attacks, attackers attempt to make victims visit spoofed Web sites to reveal sensitive personal information. Attackers achieve this by manipulating the victim's local or global Domain Name Service directory—known as DNS poisoning. Pharming attacks may fool users more easily than other attacks because there is no indication that an attack is under way. Users may type in the URLs of their banking or credit card Web sites as usual and not notice that they are in fact visiting fraudulent sites. In a 2005 pharming attack, users of the Internet mail service Hushmail were redirected to a fraudulent site where their information was harvested. Hushmail suffered negative publicity from this attack and was forced to update its users daily about its investigation into the attack.[23]

19.3.4.3 Spim.   Many people and businesses rely on the synchronous communication that instant messaging (IM) offers. Social engineers have noted the increase in the use of IM software and developed *spim*. Spim is "instant spam or IM spam."[24] A spim attack is very similar to a phishing attack except the vector is IM software instead of e-mail. By utilizing popular instant messaging clients to contact a potential victim, a social engineer is able to bypass technical safeguards that many organizations have deployed, such as e-mail or Web filtering systems. For example, an attacker will develop a fraudulent Web site that resembles a legitimate one and send its link to many IM accounts. Victims will visit the Web site and log in, revealing their credentials to the attacker. The fraudulent site could contain malicious software that infects the victim's computer. Surprisingly, despite the increasing use of IM software, the growth of spim has been slow.[25]

19.3.4.4 Spit.   Spit, or *spam over Internet telephony,* is unwanted messaging sent via VoIP (Voice over Internet Protocol). Although there have been warnings since 2004 about the potential problems to be caused by spit, there is at the time of writing (2007) still little evidence that the problem has become significant. However, experts warn that conventional content analysis may not be applicable to spit; some suggest that traffic analysis might track down the origins of high-volume messaging, allowing coordinated blockage of such systems.[26]

19.3.4.5 Vishing.   Attackers who lure victims with the use of e-mail and the telephone or just the telephone are performing a vishing, voice phishing, attack.[27] Social engineers may send an e-mail or call victims in an organization about an issue and request a call back. The number given is either staffed by accomplices or answered by a legitimate-sounding automated system. Victims are prompted to release potentially damaging information, about themselves in the case of identity theft, or about their company.

In another example, an attacker can leverage automated phone answering systems, which allow the caller to input the first few letters of the last name of a contact to reach their extension. The attacker can try multiple extensions and stumble on some that reveal details regarding a person's position, title, or office status (e.g., "I'm out on vacation until April 4"). A social engineer can leverage that information and call other employees to gain additional information or access.

With the proliferation of VoIP, and the call is routed over IP, the call number can be changed easily. This is analogous to how phishing Web sites operate. Since this is primarily a voice-based social engineer attack, it is considered a voice attack instead of a Web attack.

19.3.4.6 Trojans and Viruses.   Malware are programs or files that are harmful or dangerous to the end user. Social engineers frequently use malware, such as Trojans and viruses. Although the programs themselves may not actually attack the system, the basis of the attack still relies on manipulating a victim's trust. For example, a social engineer may send a victim an e-mail with a link to a malicious Web site. If the user visits the malicious Web site, a Trojan is installed on the victim's computer and the malicious program will begin gathering the victim's information. Another example involves a USB drive loaded with auto-executing malware that is left lying around. A victim curious about the contents will plug the drive into a machine and execute the malicious code.[28] Any number of vectors can be used, including documents, e-mail messages, Web sites, CDs, and USB drives. The premise is the same for all these types of attacks; unsuspecting users curious about the content will inadvertently install these dangerous programs. See Chapter 16 in this *Handbook* for a more technical discussion of Trojans, viruses, and other malware.

19.3.5   Reverse Social Engineering.   Reverse social engineering is an effective attack usually executed by an experienced social engineer. It can be described as the *knight-in-shining-armor* attack. In order for this method to succeed, social engineers must be able to put themselves in a position where they will be the *only* persons around to fix the problem. A reverse social engineering attack has three distinct parts. First, a social engineer will create a problem (e.g., a user ID issue.) Second, the social engineer will publicize that there is no other person capable of fixing the issue. In the final part of the attack, the social engineer will assist the victim and "fix" the issue. It is during the third segment of the attack that a social engineer will gather information. The success rate of reverse social engineering attacks tends to be high simply because the victim is satisfied that the fabricated problem is fixed.[29]

For example, the attacker may create a problem by changing the name of a file. The victim searches for but cannot find the file. The attacker will announce an ability to retrieve lost information but will require a user ID and password to gain access to the system. The victim, disturbed by the thought of losing an important document, will divulge the information. Finally, the attacker will "find" the missing file. The victim, pleased that the file has been returned, will probably forget that access credentials have been divulged.[30]

Reverse social engineering attacks are not limited to human interaction. Many viruses with seemingly benign subject lines use reverse social engineering techniques. For example, the "My Party" virus was first identified in 2002. The virus propagated through e-mail with a subject line "New photos from my party." Victims, believing that the sender was the author, opened the e-mail and clicked the embedded link. The linked Web site installed a backdoor Trojan that infected victims' machines.[31]

19.4   PSYCHOLOGY   AND   SOCIAL   PSYCHOLOGY   OF   SOCIAL ENGINEERING.   This section outlines the science underlying the success of social engineering. Sections 19.4.1 and 19.4.2 use some well-established principles of psychology and social psychology to analyze social engineering from two angles: the psychological perspective of the victim and the social-psychological perspective of the social engineer and victim. Section 19.4.3 explains that there is no single social engineer stereotype. Because the terms used in this section can be found in any undergraduate psychology and social psychology textbooks, academic references have been minimized.

19.4.1   Psychology.   Social engineering succeeds because of the design of human nature: Most people tend to easily trust other people. In this section, examples of social engineering attacks illustrate scientific terms used to characterize social engineering.

A *cognitive bias* is defined as a mental error caused by humans' simplified information-processing strategies.[32] People become victims of social engineering attacks due to cognitive tendencies inherent in all humans. Although cognitive biases are found in everyone, their universal presence does not imply that they are impossible to counter.

Following are some cognitive biases that can explain why people fall prey to social engineering attacks:

- **Choice-supportive bias.** People tend to remember an option they chose that had more positive aspects than negative aspects.[33] IT help desk operators may provide employee names, extensions, or both, without verifying the identity of callers. Help desk operators remember this practice as being good because most callers are genuine and the callers thank them for providing the information. Social engineers can masquerade as genuine callers to exploit help desk operators' choice-support bias.

- **Confirmation bias.** People tend to collect and interpret evidence in a way that confirms their conceptions.[34] If an organization has a contract with a custodial service and employees see custodians all wearing the same uniform, then a social engineer wearing the uniform may not be challenged because of the employees' confirmation bias.

- **Exposure effect.** People tend to like things that are familiar to them.[35] A social engineer may call victims under the pretext of performing a survey for a popular local restaurant and then ask about the organization where the victim is employed. People are comfortable providing that information because they are familiar with the restaurant.

- **Anchoring.** People tend to focus on one trait when making decisions.[36] If a social engineer has a soothing voice, the victim may focus on that attribute versus the questions being asked.

19.4.2 Social Psychology.   Social psychologists define "schema" as the inherent picture of reality used by humans to make judgments and decisions. From the perspective of social psychology, social engineers exploit the fact that most people's schema includes rules to be trustful of other people and their intentions. People are taught from the very beginning of their socialization that being nice to others is a good thing. In the context of information security, people's tendency to blindly trust others can spell disaster.

A list of common errors that people make and examples of how social engineers will exploit those mistakes to attack an organization follows.

- **Fundamental attribution error.** In this common error, people assume that the behaviors of others reflect stable, internal characteristics. Someone committing the fundamental attribution error might see a colleague in a bad mood and think, "She is *always* moody." In reality, the colleague might be pleasant in general but be suffering a headache at the time. Social engineers will act pleasant and charming to lead victims to commit the fundamental attribution error, to be impressed that the attackers are nice people *in general* and so to help them.

- **Salience effect.** Given a group of individuals, people tend to guess that the most or least influential person is the one who stands out the most. For example, from a group of 10 people, nine of whom are six feet tall and one who is five feet tall, if asked to guess who the most intelligent person in the group is, an observer might say that it is the five-foot-tall person. Social engineers attempt to blend into their victim's environment to take advantage of the salience effect. They are acutely aware of company lingo, events, and regional accents.

- **Conformity, compliance, and obedience.** People respond to the social pressures of conformity, compliance, and obedience by adjusting their behaviors. A social engineer impersonating a high-powered executive demanding admittance into the company premises may persuade a new security guard with the weight of assumed authority. The authority figure's promise of reward or threat of punishment may further influence the security guard's decision to carry out the request of the attacker.

19.4.3   Social Engineer Profile.   The profile of a social engineer is not that of the stereotypical computer hacker often portrayed in the movies or on television.[37] Social engineers are most likely not going to be pimple-face teenagers who spend all their time with their computers. A social engineer is often outgoing, confident, and well educated. Social engineers may use their own personality, or adopt a persona that greatly differs from their normal personality. Regardless, they will blend into their environment. A social engineer seeks to be unnoticeable, unremarkable. He or she will dress according to the dress code of the operational environment. Many seem to have excellent social and communication skills. Interestingly, the typical social engineer may be an excellent actor, being able to react quickly and adapt to changing conditions. The attacker's confidence will often mask any nervousness or tension during the social engineering attempt.

Social engineers may also exhibit a dark side. Attackers may have very little regard for the consequences of their actions on the victims. Even though attackers may appear very polite or congenial toward a victim, they actually care very little about the victim. The victim is simply a means to an end, only part of the social engineering attack tool. The social engineer's motivations may vary widely and range from personal financial gain to revenge. There may also be significant external pressure on the attacker from acquaintances or organized crime syndicates.[38]

For more information about the psychology of computer criminals, see Chapters 12 and 13 in this *Handbook*.

19.5   DANGERS OF SOCIAL ENGINEERING AND ITS IMPACT ON BUSINESSES.   Clearly, social engineering is a great danger to businesses, large and small. It is important to remember that the ultimate goal of the attacker may very well be the disruption or destruction of the business where the social engineering targets are employed. One must not underestimate the potential impact of a seemingly minor social engineering attack on a business or organization.

19.5.1   Consequences.   The negative consequences of a successful social engineering attack could be disastrous. If you can envision a new social engineering ploy, so can a computer criminal. Much like disaster recovery planning, when trying to quantify and understand the impact of social engineering attacks, all possibilities must be considered. Something as seemingly minor as an internal memo that has not been properly destroyed could have the potential to bankrupt an organization. A simple social engineering attack could grow into a major information security breakdown, based on the information contained in the memo.

The danger is especially high for publicly traded companies that could lose value because of a loss of confidence from investors.[39] Within the last few years, many companies have come under financial duress because of a security breach or lapse that drew considerable attention from the press. Social engineering could very well have been part of these security incidents. Many organizations are required by law to have safeguards in place when it comes to data security; many of these requirements have elements that will aid the organization in defending against social engineering and low-tech attacks.

Another serious consequence of a successful social engineering attack is the uncertainty that follows and the difficulty of investigating such an attack. Organizations may never fully discover to what extent a social engineer was able to infiltrate the organization. There are so many different vectors and possibilities of intrusion that it may be impossible to fully understand exactly what or who was compromised during the attack. An especially dangerous and frustrating situation is where an attacker has an insider or accomplice within the organization. Some organizations have never identified those individuals within the organization who have been guilty of aiding an attacker. This uncertainty is difficult to recover from, and to defend against in the future. It is also another situation where a company may have substantial credibility problems and a loss of confidence from its shareholders after an attack.

19.5.2   Case Study Examples from Business.   There are many well-known examples of real-life scenarios from organizations that demonstrate the effectiveness of social engineering. Here are a couple of well-known examples without any specifics that would embarrass the guilty parties. Social engineering attacks are real—they are not simply computer security theory.

Case 1: One very well known social engineering attack in the business world is piggybacking. In this type of social engineering, an attacker will depend on an individual's sense of courtesy. Most people remember from their early school days that they are taught to hold a door open for someone who is behind them. This courtesy is often extended in the workplace, including secure areas such as a datacenter. A potential attacker may attempt to enter a datacenter without proper credentials by following closely behind someone else who is entering a datacenter with proper identification and authorization. The authorized individual will probably exhibit courtesy and hold the door open even for an unknown person.

Result: In this example, the result is that an attacker who is not authorized has gained access to a secure facility because he or she relied on another individual's sense of courtesy. It can be very difficult to demand that employees refrain from allowing piggybacking, but a policy must be in place to demand exactly that. All persons entering a secure facility should be required to fully use identification and authorization mechanisms every time.

Case 2. Another example that has been carried out in different variations involves an attacker using several social engineering techniques to take advantage of several coinciding events to exploit data, information, or equipment from an organization. The attacker often makes several telephone calls to find a specific date where a company official, perhaps the CFO or director of technology, is out of the office. The attacker then shows up at the organization claiming that the company official authorized the attacker to take a certain computer from the company's site. Usually the attacker tries to show a sense of urgency and extends a very confident display of authority. Many times the employee caves in to the attacker's demands without checking the story, and now a very important computer has been taken from the company.

Result. In this case, the organization has lost control and ownership of a computer and its data. If the computer does not have any solid safeguards, such as data encryption mechanisms, the data and the computer could be used for any number of destructive activities. If information about the incident is made public, great damage to the organization's reputation can be done. The data harvested from the computer could also be sold to competitors or used as part of a blackmail scheme.

19.5.3   Success Rate.   Although there may be few solid statistics of the success rate of social engineering, as is the case in most areas of information security, most experts believe the rate to be extremely high. If history has anything to teach the security community through example, social engineering will continue to be a very powerful and successful tool for criminals. Very few organizations are immune to social engineering, not even state, local, and federal governments. If well-trained federal employees are vulnerable, every organization must take the success rate seriously.

The high success rate must also stress the importance of constant education of employees and reevaluation of the organization's efforts to combat social engineering. This is an area where many organizations do not allocate enough resources. The frequency of social engineering attempts also dictates the need for proper, efficient, and swift reporting of suspicious activity targeting individuals or the organization. It is very difficult to defend against social engineering attempts if the organization does not know it is under attack. The possible success of an attack can be substantially reduced with properly trained, supported, and motivated employees.

19.5.4   Small Businesses versus Large Organizations.   The impact and dangers of social engineering and low-tech attacks vary widely between small businesses and large corporations. As discussed, the consequences can be very serious, including the collapse of the organization. Small businesses are often much less prepared and much less equipped to survive a serious breach of security. Conversely, small businesses may have the upper hand versus large organizations because of a substantially smaller, better communicating workforce. It is much easier to communicate and engage everyone within a small company when an attack is attempted or carried out. Small businesses also have an advantage of a much smaller workforce to train; this can result in much better prepared employees. Small business employees are probably more likely to identify people who do not belong or should not be asking for private data. They may also be more likely to deny access or question someone whose story does not seem likely or who is suspicious.

Large organizations can be mired down in bureaucracy, ineffective management, or overly complicated reporting procedures. An attacker could carry out an entire plan before the security team in a large company would receive notification of a social engineering attempt. Many times, an individual is less willing to challenge the credentials of a stranger in a large organization. This is especially true where there are large numbers of employees who feel they may be punished for preventing someone else from doing a proper job. The employee might be more likely to let the attacker pass unquestioned, rather than to risk possible negative ramifications.

There is no doubt, however, that no matter what the size of organization, it is a potential target. Criminals do not always choose easy or obvious targets. Any business,

small or large, family-owned or corporate conglomerate, may be a target of an attack
that utilizes social engineering.

19.5.5 Trends. Although it is important for every information security manager
always to keep a skeptical eye toward statistics, it is equally important to keep abreast
of security threat trends. Social engineering is no exception. It may be difficult for
any survey or poll to gather facts about how many attempts were made in any given
year, or how many were successful. Many social engineering attempts are probably
never detected, let alone reported. When it comes to such a powerful and successful
attack mechanism, assume the worst: Criminals are increasingly using it. It is highly
unlikely that all organizations will be able to band together and eliminate successful
social engineering and low-tech attacks. Criminals create new forms and tactics every
day, and people will probably continue to fall for these tactics.

19.6 DETECTION. Detection of social engineering and low-tech attacks can
be difficult. The nature of most types of social engineering attacks is to circumvent
technical controls and take advantage of people's willingness to trust and help. In many
cases, the detection relies on people's ability to recognize a potential attack and respond
appropriately. Further complicating detection is the potential that a social engineering
attack may not be a single occurrence, but many smaller events culminating in the
release of potentially damaging information, ability to access restricted resources or to
hide other activities. One penetration-testing expert estimates that social engineering
tactics account for less than 20 percent of the time spent in an attack; the rest of the
time is spent in technical exploitation of the information originally gathered through
deceit.[40]

There are three main ways of detecting social engineering attacks: people, audit
controls, and technology.

19.6.1 People. Since people are the vector for the attack, they are, in general,
the first line of defense. Organizations need to provide employees with the resources
required to help discern a potential attack from a legitimate request. In addition,
organizations need to provide information on what to do during and immediately after
an attack. For example, during a phone attack, employees should be trained to remember
as many details as possible. Items that the employee should try to remember include:

- Was the attacker male or female?
- Was a caller ID displayed?
- Was there noise in the background?
- Did he or she have an accent?
- What questions were asked?
- What answers were provided?

Some social engineers can be detected. Employees should also be aware of people
asking many questions, some of which may not make sense. In addition, callers or
e-mails requesting names of managers or IT personnel should prompt a phone call to
the IT security or investigation department. Finally, employees should be aware that
no one would ever call legitimately requesting their password.[41]

Organizations also need to provide information as to who should be notified during
the actual event, immediately afterward, or both (depending on when the employee

recognizes the attack). To help in the notification process, an organization can create an incident notification information card and disseminate it across the organization so an employee can determine whom to contact quickly.

19.6.2   Audit Controls.   Auditing e-mail, Internet content, systems logins, and systems changes of an organization can be used to detect social engineering attacks. However, if the audits are not real time, there will be a delay from the time of the attack and a review of audit items. In the instances where notification is not real time, forensic examiners can use the audit information to help piece together the attacks. Awareness teams can also use the log results to help devise additional training for the targeted groups. During real-time auditing, organizations can immediately enact their incident management plans to help limit the potential damage.

19.6.3   Technology for Detection.   Organizations can implement technology to help limit social engineering attacks. Content-filtering software can limit e-mail and Web site traffic. E-mail monitoring tools can be used in bidirectional mode to inspect content in both directions. In addition, e-mail monitoring and content-filtering mechanisms can be used to scan for keywords or phrases that may trigger early warning signals. By scanning and blocking content, organizations may reduce the number of suspicious e-mails entering their networks and reduce the number of suspicious Web sites that employees visit.

Advances in technology research will provide additional protection from social engineering attacks, including the development of the Social Engineering Defense Architecture (SEDA). This architecture attempts to detect social engineering attacks over the phone by identifying a legitimate employee versus a social engineer. The system is referred to as a text-independent voice signature authentication system. The system uses voice recognition technology, which would reduce the risk of a successful help desk attack. In addition to detecting an unauthorized caller, it can detect an insider masquerading as an employee with a higher security classification. The logging included in the architecture would aid a forensic examiner during an investigation.[42]

Attackers are becoming more sophisticated. Recent phishing attacks are targeting systems, network, and security professionals. In these types of attacks, a phishing e-mail is sent to an organization from a "customer" informing it of a phishing site attempting to steal customer information. Security personnel respond to the e-mail and investigate the site. The site installs malware that allows the attacker to remotely control the machine. This change in attack methodology requires security personnel to be even more suspicious of any seemingly innocuous e-mail telling the organization that there are phishing sites targeting that company.

19.7   RESPONSE.   Responding to social engineering and other low-tech attacks should fit into an organization's incident management process and response. As with all incident management plans, the responses should be well defined, communicated, and tested. It behooves an organization to plan for the inevitable, especially as network and physical attacks are increasingly using multiple vectors in order to be successful.

See Chapter 53 in this *Handbook* for additional information on monitoring and controlling systems.

19.8   DEFENSE AND MITIGATION.   The prevention of social engineering attacks should be multifaceted, repeatable, and part of an organization's defense-in-depth strategy. Since the very nature of the attack is to bypass or circumvent technical defenses by using people's good nature and willingness to trust other human beings, the steps in preventing such attacks should focus on distinct areas, such as policy, training and awareness, technology, and physical defenses.

Concurrently, the areas will help mitigate the threat of a successful social engineering attack. Each area should have a regular process for review and auditing. Well-written policies provide the baseline of behavior that is acceptable and the potential consequences if they are not followed. In the case of training, it should be integrated into the organization overall security awareness program, included in all employee's evaluations, and tied to bonus pay and compensation. Organizations must train their employees in acceptable behavior and provide them the tools to identify and report potential social engineering attacks. Physical defenses can potentially block an intruder from entering a locked building, but people's sense of camaraderie does make the practices such as piggybacking or tailgating relatively easy. A recent study indicated that smokers returning to a building sometimes allow nonemployees into a secure location. Technological advances are also important but cannot be relied on as the only method of defense.

19.8.1 Training and Awareness. Organizations need to provide tools and knowledge to employees to help identify potential attacks and react to suspected attacks. Providing awareness is a continual process and should not be only for new hires. Training and awareness, when possible, should include real-life examples so employees can relate to the issue and understand the level of trust that is implied through their access to the facility and the data used for their positions. Employees should understand the responsibilities the company bestows on them. Essentially, employees need to be retrained that it is acceptable to ask why certain information is being requested or to see the badge of a person behind them.

A basic awareness program could include posters, e-mail communications, and laminated instruction cards (hard cards) containing emergency contact numbers or other information. More mature awareness programs can include videos or brown-bag informational lunches. Whenever possible, teaching employees to defend against social engineering attacks should be a live presentation with real-world examples. Ideally, the presentation should be tailored specially for each audience. For example, if the audience is help desk personnel, examples of potential social engineering attacks should be described or demonstrated and discussed.

Employee training can also include instruction to keep file cabinets locked when not in use, lock workstations, and use cable locks, and contain instructions on how to create and remember good passwords.

Please see Chapter 49 in this *Handbook* for additional information regarding awareness programs.

19.8.2 Technology for Prevention. Technology is emerging as a defense against certain types of social engineering attacks. The technology enables organizations to identify some social engineering attacks without relying on employees. This proactive identification enables an organization to mitigate the risk. Technology should comprise only one layer of defense and not be relied on as the sole defense.

Technologies such as content-monitoring systems for both e-mail and Web content can help identify phishing attacks. In addition, organizations can install timely security patches and use up-to-date antivirus and antispyware software to help mitigate the risk of viruses, Trojans, and worms. New versions of browsers and browser plug-ins are allowing users to evaluate the trustworthiness of Web sites.[43]

Ideally, employees should be prevented from downloading and installing unapproved software. However, organizations can employ inventory systems or other methodologies to detect illegal programs on a network. Certain types of systems can prevent malware-infected machines from entering the network.

Desktop and laptop configuration changes can be made to reduce the risk of a successful attack; changes include disabling pop-up windows in browsers, disallowing the automatic installation of Active-X controls, limiting the types of cookies that Web sites can place on local machines, using automatic password-protected screen savers, and finally, using e-mail certificates for authentication.

In the same regard, organizations should review technology processes and verify that they are not inadvertently supplying information to potential social engineers. For example, metadata in documents should be removed before being accessible to outsiders, and regular Web searches should be conducted to ensure former or current employees are not posting information on the Internet.

19.8.3 Physical Security.   Physical security mechanisms can reduce the risk of a successful social engineering attack. All employees should have identification cards that they are required to display at all times. Secured areas within an organization should be locked, have limited access, and be monitored for noncompliance. Door alarms that can detect tailgating or piggybacking can be installed in areas. Cameras or other closed circuit monitoring technology can thwart potential intruders. Security personnel should watch all facility access points. All office doors, desks, file cabinets, and other storage devices should have keys and remain locked when not being accessed. Dumpsters or recycling bins should also have locks that would prevent the removal of documents meant for shredding or incineration.

Desktops, laptops, and other computer hardware should be physically locked in place. Users should be required to have strong passwords, and in the case of laptops or desktops, have automatic screen savers that require a password to unlock. All magnetic media need to have secure storage.

Most organizations have a certain percentage of mobile workforces. Special training should be provided to them to prevent the loss of equipment or information. Training should include information such as:

- Laptops should remain with the traveler and not checked in luggage.
- Laptops should be locked in a safe or to a secure surface at all times.
- Peripheral devices such as USB drives and handheld devices should have strong passwords.
- Conversations involving confidential information should be prohibited in public.
- Travelers should be aware of their surroundings, and special considerations regarding electronic communication should be considered while not in the United States and Europe.

Please see Chapter 22 of this *Handbook* for more information regarding physical security.

19.9 CONCLUSION.   Social engineering attacks are unlike technological computer attacks. The vector of the attack is human, the nature of the attack is to circumvent controls, and the success of the attack depends on people's willingness to trust others. Simply being polite and holding a door open for a person can have profound negative effects for an organization.

Historically, social engineering attacks are not new; they have been effective in launching successful attacks for millennia. Social engineers use many different methods to execute social engineering and low-tech attacks. These methods can involve human contact, no human contact, or a combination of technology and social engineering tactics.

Psychologists and social psychologists have offered a number of reasons why social engineering attacks are successful. They theorize that human nature allows attackers to trick or con reasonable people into providing information. A social engineer's profile does not fit into any single model, and attacks are difficult to detect. Social engineering attacks have grown more prolific, effective, and dangerous to both organizations and individuals.

Even though social engineering attacks are difficult to defend against, there are technical, process, and people defenses that an organization can adopt to minimize the chance of security breaches. As with all information security issues, a defense-in-depth strategy can help mitigate the risks associated with social engineering.

Although the focus of information assurance seems to be on technical attacks, social engineering and low-tech attacks will continue to remain relevant and dangerous threats, worthy of attentive mitigation strategies.

19.10 FURTHER READING

Burchfield, A. "Social Psychology, Cognitive Psychology, Security and the User," SANS Institute, 2002.

Computer Security Institute. "CSI/FBI Computer Crime and Security Survey: 2006," www.gocsi.com/forms/fbi/csi_fbi_survey.jhtml (accessed January 1, 2007).

Dubin, J. "Security Awareness Training: Stay In, or Go Out?" SearchSecurity.com, November 1, 2006, http://searchsecurity.techtarget.com/tip/0,289483, sid14_gci1220543,00.html (accessed March 2, 2007).

Edmead, M. T. " Social Engineering Attacks: What We Can Learn from Kevin Mitnick," SearchSecurity.com, November 18, 2002, http://searchsecurity.techtarget.com/tip/1,289483,sid14_gci865450,00.html (accessed March 1, 2007).

Gartner Research. "New Gartner Hype Cycle Highlights Five High Impact IT Security Risks," Gartner Press Release, September 18, 2006, www.gartner.com/it/page.jsp?id=496247 (accessed March 2, 2007).

Gartner Research. "Unmasking Social-Engineering Attacks," *Social Engineering: Exposing the Danger Within* 1, No. 1 (February 2002), www.gartner.com/gc/webletter/security/issue1/article1.html (accessed March 1, 2007).

Granger, S. "Social Engineering Fundamentals, Part II: Combat Strategies," January 9, 2002, www.securityfocus.com/infocus/1533.

Kuper, A., and J. Kuper (eds.). *The Social Science Encyclopedia*. London: Routledge & Kegan Paul, 1985.

Lifrieri, S. "Computer Hacking without a Computer... The Art of Social Engineering," *Wall Street Technology Association Ticker* (January-February 2007), www.wsta.org/publications/articles/0207_article02.html (accessed March 23, 2007).

Microsoft Corporation. "How to Protect Insiders from Social Engineering Threats," *Microsoft Technet*, August 18, 2006, www.microsoft.com/technet/

security/midsizebusiness/topics/complianceandpolicies/socialengineeringthreats .mspx#EIXAE (accessed March 2, 2007).

Nelson, S. D., and J. W. Simek. "Disgruntled Employees in Your Law Firm: The Enemy Within," Sensei Enterprises, Inc., 2005, www.senseient.com/default.asp? page=publications/article31.htm (accessed March 22, 2007).

Stone, A. "Stopping the Con: Detecting Electronic Social Engineering Attacks," www.cisa.umbc.edu/courses/cmsc/444/fall05/studentprojects/stone.ppt (accessed March 1, 2007).

Twitchell, D. P. "Augmenting Detection of Social Engineering Attacks Using Deception Detection Technology," *Proceedings of the International Conference on i-Warfare and Security 2006*, pp. 209–210.

Vaas, L. "Microsoft: UAC Can Be Hijacked by Social Engineering," eWeek.com, February 26, 2007, www.eweek.com/article2/0,1895,2098552,00.asp (accessed March 1, 2007).

Wilson, T. "Five Myths About Black Hats," DarkReading.com, February 26, 2007, www.darkreading.com/document.asp?doc_id=118169&WT.svl=news2_2 (accessed March 1, 2007).

19.11   NOTES

1. I. Winkler, *Spies Among Us: How to Stop the Spies, Terrorists, Hackers, and Criminals You Don't Even Know You Encounter Every Day* (Hoboken, NJ: John Wiley & Sons, 2005), p. 111.

2. R. Gellately and N. Stoltzfus (eds.), *Social Outsiders in Nazi Germany* (Princeton, NJ: Princeton University Press, 2001), http://press.princeton.edu/chapters/ s7083.html (accessed November 23, 2007).

3. F. W. Abagnale, Jr., and S. Redding, *Catch Me If You Can* (Mainstream Publishing, 2005).

4. Three good accounts of the Mitnick case are J. Goodell, The *Cyberthief and the Samurai: The True Story of Kevin Mitnick—and the Man Who Hunted Him Down* (New York: Dell, 1996); T. Shimomura and J. Markoff, *Takedown: The Pursuit and Capture of Kevin Mitnick, America's Most Wanted Computer Outlaw—by the Man Who Did It* (New York: Hyperion, 1996); and J. Littman, *The Fugitive Game: Online with Kevin Mitnick* (Boston: Little, Brown, 1997). Mitnick himself has written several books; perhaps the most appropriate reading in connection with this chapter is K. Mitnick and W. L. Simon, *The Art of Deception: Controlling the Human Element of Security* (Hoboken, NJ: John Wiley & Sons, 2003).

5. Internet Movie Database, *Hackers*, www.imdb.com/title/tt0113243 (accessed November 22, 2007).

6. AntiPhishing Working Group, "Phishing Activity Trends: Report for the Month of August, 2007," AntiPhishing.org, November 19, 2007, www.antiphishing.org/ reports/apwg_report_august_2007.pdf (accessed November 23, 2007).

7. Some attacks have taken place over weeks, months, or years. At the time of this writing, there is a recent case of stolen customer data at a popular U.S. retailer. It was revealed during the investigation that the attack actually occurred over many weeks, and possibly months.

8. For more information on this documentary, see www.hbo.com/docs/programs/ hackingdemocracy/index.html.

9. B. Koerner, "Pretexting," About: Identity Theft, http://idtheft.about.com/od/ glossaryofterms/g/pretexting.htm (accessed March 24, 2007).

10. Audit My PC.com, "Social Engineering," www.auditmypc.com/freescan/ readingroom/social-engineering.asp (accessed April 3, 2007).

11. D. Arnell, "Payroll Giant Gives Scammer Personal Data of Hundreds of Thousands of Investors," ABC News, June 26, 2006, http://abcnews.go.com/Technology/ story?id=2160425&page=1 (accessed March 17, 2007).

12. The Free Dictionary, www.thefreedictionary.com/seduce (accessed March 24, 2007).

13. A. Gupta, "The Art of Social Engineering" Addison-Wesley, August 23, 2002. www.awprofessional.com/articles/article.asp?p=28802&seqNum=3&rl=1 (accessed March 24, 2007).

14. S. Stasiukonis, "Social Engineering, the USB Way," darkREADING, June 7, 2006, www.darkreading.com/document.asp?doc_id=95556&WT.svl= column1_1 (accessed November 23, 2007).

15. J. Boroshok, "Social Engineering's New Tricks Present Bigger Dangers," SearchSecurity.com, http://searchsecurity.techtarget.com/originalContent/0,289142, sid14_gci1196327,00.html (accessed June 29, 2006).

16. Microsoft Corporation, "How to Minimize Metadata in Office Documents," January 24, 2007, http://support.microsoft.com/default.aspx?scid=kb;EN-US; Q223396 (accessed March 20, 2007).

17. L. A. Gordon, M. P. Loeb, W. Lucyshyn, and R. Richardson, "2006 CSI/FBI Computer Crime and Security Survey," http://i.cmpnet.com/gocsi/db_area/ pdfs/fbi/FBI2006.pdf (accessed March 1, 2007).

18. "The Nigerian Scam Defined," Nigeria—The 419 Coalition Website, http://home.rica.net/alphae/419coal/ (accessed March 30, 2007).

19. "Phishing," Definitions, Webopedia, www.webopedia.com/TERM/P/phishing.html (accessed March 30, 2007).

20. AntiPhishing Working Group Report, AntiPhishing.org, January 7, 2007, www.antiphishing.org/reports/apwg_report_january_2007.pdf (accessed March 23, 2007).

21. "More and More People Falling for Phishing Tactics," BizAsia.com, October 15, 2007, www.bizasia.com/internet_it_/f9hc4/more_more_people_falling.htm (accessed March 30, 2007).

22. "Spear Phishing: Highly Targeted Scams," Microsoft Protect Yourself, September 18, 2006, www.microsoft.com/protect/yourself/phishing/spear.mspx (accessed November 23, 2007).

23. R. Naraine, "Hushmail DNS Attack Blamed on Network Solutions" eWeek.com, April 29, 2005, www.eweek.com/article2/0,1759,1791152,00.asp (accessed March 31, 2007).

24. "Spim," definition, searchexchange.com http://searchexchange.techtarget.com/ sDefinition/0,290660,sid43_gci952820,00.html (accessed March 30, 2007).

25. W. Sturgeon, "U.S. Makes First Arrest for Spim," CNet.com, February 21, 2005, http://news.com.com/U.S.+makes+first+arrest+for+spim/2100-7355_3- 5584574.html (accessed March 30, 2007).

26. A. Plewes, "The Biggest VoIP Security Threats—and How to Stop Them," silicon.com (March 2007), www.silicon.com/research/specialreports/voipsecurity/ 0,3800013656,39166479,00.htm (accessed November 22, 2007).

27. B. Koerner, "Vishing," About: Vishing, http://idtheft.about.com/od/ glossaryofterms/g/vishing.htm (accessed March 22, 2007).

28. S. Stasiukonis, "Social Engineering, the USB Way," Dark Reading Room, June 7, 2006, www.darkreading.com/document.asp?doc_id=95556&WT.svl= column1_1 (accessed March 1, 2007).

29. S. Granger, "Social Engineering Fundamentals, Part I: Hacker Tactics," Security Focus.com, December 18, 2001, www.securityfocus.com/infocus/1527 (accessed March 30, 2007).

30. Microsoft Corporation, "How to Protect Insiders from Social Engineering Threats," Microsoft Technet, August 18, 2006, www.microsoft.com/ technet/security/midsizebusiness/topics/complianceandpolicies/socialengineering threats.mspx#EIXAE (accessed March 30, 2007).

31. M. Singer, " 'My Party' Worm Is no Party," siliconvalley.internet.com, January 28, 2002, http://siliconvalley.internet.com/news/article.php/962741 (accessed March 30, 2007).

32. R. J. Heuer, Jr., "What Are Cognitive Biases?" *Psychology of Intelligence Analysis, Part Three—Cognitive Biases* (1999), www.cia.gov/csi/books/19104/art12.html (accessed March 7, 2007).

33. M. Mathers, E. Shafir, and M. K. Johnson, "Misremembrance of Options Past: Source Monitoring and Choice," *Psychological Science* 11, No. 2 (March 2000), http://people.ucsc.edu/~mather/pdffiles/Matheretal2000.pdf (accessed March 28, 2007).

34. J. St. B. T. Evans, J. L. Barston, and P. Pollard, "On the Conflict between Logic and Belief in Syllogistic Reasoning," *Memory and Cognition* 11 (1983): 295–306.

35. R. B. Zajonc, "Attitudinal Effects of Mere Exposure," *Journal of Personality and Social Psychology* 9, No. 2 (1968): 1–27.

36. A. Tversky and D. Kahneman, "Judgment under Uncertainty: Heuristics and Biases," *Science* 185 (1974): 1124–1130.

37. T. Wilson, "Eight Faces of a Hacker," Dark Reading Room, March 29, 2007, www.darkreading.com/document.asp?doc_id=120800 (accessed March 30, 2007).

38. M. Allen, "Social Engineering, A Means to Violate a Computer System," SANS Institute Information Security Reading Room, June 2006, www.sans.org/reading _room/whitepapers/engineering/529.php?portal=3595f417b55c62ba6243b24f664 16d4b (accessed March 17, 2007).

39. R. Gulati, "The Threat of Social Engineering and Your Defense Against It," SANS Institute Information Security Reading Room, 2003, www.sans.org/reading _room/whitepapers/engineering/ (accessed March 19, 2007).

40. K. J. Higgins, "Social Engineering Gets Smarter," Dark Reading Room, June 16, 2006, www.darkreading.com/document.asp?doc_id=97382 (accessed March 16, 2007).

41. R. Groom, "Top 5 Social Engineering Techniques," About: Business Security, http://bizsecurity.about.com/od/physicalsecurity/a/topsocialengine.htm (accessed March 17, 2007).

42. M. Hoeschele and M. Rogers, "Detecting Social Engineering," *Advances in Digital Forensics,* IFIP International Conference on Digital Forensics, February 2005, Chapter 6, pp. 67–71.

43. M. J. Edwards, "IE 7.0 and Firefox 2.0 Both Have New Antiphishing Technologies," WindowsITPro, October 26, 2006, www.windowsitpro.com/Windows Security/Article/ArticleID/94026/94026.html (accessed November 23, 2007)

CHAPTER 20

SPAM, PHISHING, AND TROJANS: ATTACKS MEANT TO FOOL

Stephen Cobb

20.1 UNWANTED E-MAIL AND OTHER PESTS: A SECURITY ISSUE.

Three oddly named threats to computer security are addressed in this chapter: spam, phishing, and Trojan code. Spam is unsolicited commercial e-mail. Phishing is the use of deceptive unsolicited e-mail to obtain—to fish electronically for—confidential information. Trojan code, a term derived from the Trojan horse, is software designed to achieve unauthorized access to systems by posing as legitimate applications. In this chapter, we outline the threats posed by spam, phishing, and Trojans as well as the mitigation of those threats.

These threats might have strange names, but they are no strangers to those whose actions undermine the benefits of information technology. Every year, for at least the last three years, the Internal Revenue Service (IRS) has had to warn the public about e-mail scams that take the name of the IRS in vain, attempting to defraud taxpayers of their hard-earned money by aping the agency's look and feel in e-mail messages. The fact that an IRS spokesperson has stated that the agency "never ever uses e-mail to communicate with taxpayers" is a sad comment on our society, for there is no good reason why this should be the case. After all, the agency allows electronic filing of annual tax returns, and every day hundreds of millions of people around the world do their banking and bill paying online, in relative safety. The technology exists to make e-mail safe and secure. In many ways, this chapter is a sad catalog of what has happened because we have not deployed the technology effectively.

20.1.1 Common Elements.   Each of these threats is quite different from the other in some respects, but all three have some important elements in common; first, and most notably, they use deception. These threats prey on the gullibility of computer users and achieve their ends more readily when users are ill-trained and ill-informed (albeit aided and abetted, in some cases, by poor system design and poor management of services, such as broadband connectivity).

Second, all three attacks are enabled by system services that are widely used for legitimate purposes. Although the same might be said of computer viruses—they are code and computers are built to run code—the three threats that are the focus of this chapter typically operate at a higher level, the application layer. Indeed, this fact may contribute to the extent of their deployment—these threats can be carried out with relatively little technical ability, relying more on the skills associated with social engineering than with coding. For example, anyone with an Internet connection and an e-mail program can send spam. That spam can spread a ready-made Trojan. Using a toolkit full of scripts, you can add a Web site with an input form to your portfolio and go phishing for personal data to collect and abuse.

Another reason for considering these three phenomena together is the fact that they often are combined in real-world exploits. The same mass e-mailing techniques used to send spam may be employed to send out messages that spread Trojan code. As described in Chapter 15 in this *Handbook*, Trojan code may be used to aid phishing operations. Systems compromised by Trojan code may be used for spamming, and so on. What we see in these attacks today are the very harmful and costly result of combining relatively simple strategies and techniques with standards of behavior that range from the foolish and irresponsible to the unabashedly criminal.

These three threats also share the distinction of having been underestimated when they first emerged. All three have evolved and expanded in the twenty-first century, even as some threats—for example, viruses and worms—have stalled. By the end of 2006, it was widely recognized that spam, phishing, and Trojan code could, through a combination of technology abuse and social engineering, potentially defeat even the most sophisticated controls. All three threats, alone or in combination, are capable of imposing enormous and costly burdens on system resources. (In the second half of 2007, some 500,000 new malicious code threats were reported to Symantec, one of the world's largest computer security software producers. Of the top 10 new malicious code families, 5 were Trojans, 2 were worms, 2 were worms with a Trojan component, and 1 was a worm with a virus component.[1]

One other factor unites these three threats: their association with the emergence of financial gain as a primary motivator for writing malicious code and abusing Internet connectivity. The hope of making money is the primary driver of spam. Phishing is done to facilitate fraud for gain through theft of personal data and credentials, either for use by the thief or through resale in the underground economy. Trojan code is used to advance the goals of both spammers and perpetrators of phishing scams. In short, all three constitute a very real threat to computer security, the well-being of any computer-using organization, and the online economy.

There is some irony in this, particularly with respect to spam. By 2006, spam was consuming over 90 percent of e-mail resources worldwide.[2] This is a staggering level of system abuse by any standard. However, when a handful of security professionals claimed, just five years earlier, that spam was a computer security threat, they were met with considerable skepticism and some suspicion. (This might have been due, in part, to the fact that the world had just experienced the anticlimax of Y2K; also, there was doubtless an element of the recurrent suspicion that security professionals trumpet new threats to drum up business—a strange notion, given the perennial abundance of opportunities for experts in a field that persistently reports near-zero levels of unemployment.)

When phishing attacks started to proliferate a few years later, warnings still were met with some skepticism, but thankfully not as much. It is hoped that, in 2008 and beyond, with spam accounting for over 90 percent of all e-mail on the Internet and phishing attacks constantly evolving to steal targeted data, often executed over systems compromised by Trojan code, security professionals will not deny that these are serious threats.

20.1.2 Chapter Organization.   After a brief e-mail anatomy lesson, each of the three threats addressed by this chapter will be examined in turn. The e-mail anatomy lesson is provided because e-mail plays such a central role in these threats, enabling spam and phishing and the spread of Trojan code. Responses to the three threats are discussed with respect to each other, along with consideration of broader responses that may be used to mitigate all three.

For an introduction to the general principles of social engineering, see Chapter 19 in this *Handbook*.

20.2 E-MAIL: AN ANATOMY LESSON.   E-mail plays a role in numerous threats to information and information systems. Not only does it enable spam and phishing, it is used to spread Trojan code, viruses, and worms. A basic understanding of how e-mail works will help to understand these threats and the various countermeasures that have been developed.

20.2.1 Simple Mail Transport Protocol.   All e-mail transmitted across the Internet is sent using an agreed-on industry standard: the Simple Mail Transport Protocol (SMTP). Any server that "speaks" SMTP is able to act as a Mail Transfer Agent (MTA) and send mail to, and receive mail from, any other server that speaks SMTP. To understand how "simple" SMTP really is, Exhibit 20.1 presents an example of an SMTP transaction.[3] The text that follows represents the *actual* data being sent and received by e-mail servers (as viewed in a telnet session, with the words in CAPS, such as HELO and DATA, being the SMTP commands defined in the relevant standards, and the numbers being the standard telnet responses).

Sender   Recipient

(Server initiates connection)

```
                                   220 receiving.com Hello
HELO example.com
                                   250 Hello example.com
MAIL FROM:<foo@example.com>
                                   250 OK
RCPT TO:<bar@receiving.com>
                                   250 OK
DATA
                                   354 Go Ahead
Date: Tue 1 Apr 2003 07:46
Subject: Test message
This is a test message.
.
                                   250 Message accepted
QUIT
                                   221 Goodbye
```

EXHIBIT 20.1   Basic E-mail Protocol

Developed at a time when computing resources were relatively expensive, and designed to operate even when a server was processing a dozen or more message connections per second, the SMTP "conversation" was kept very simple in order to be very brief. However, that simplicity is both a blessing and a curse. As you can see from the example, only two pieces of identity information are received before the mail is delivered: the identity of the sending server, in this case example.com, and the "From" address, in this case foo@example.com. SMTP has no process for verifying the validity of those identity assertions, so both of those identifiers can be trivially falsified. The remaining contents of the e-mail, including the subject and other header information, are transmitted in the data block and are not considered a meaningful part of the SMTP conversation. In other words, no SMTP mechanism exists to verify assertions such as "this message is from your bank and concerns your account" or "this message contains the tracking number for your online order" or "here is the investment newsletter that you requested."

As described in more detail later, some e-mail services do perform whitelist or blacklist look-ups on the Internet Protocol (IP) address of the sending server during the SMTP conversation, but those inquiries can dramatically slow mail processing, requiring extra capacity to offset the loss of efficiency. A whitelist identifies e-mail senders that are trusted; a blacklist identifies those that are not trusted. Maintenance of whitelists can be time-consuming, and blacklists have a long history of inaccuracies and legal disputes. In short, the need for speed creates a system in which there are virtually no technical consequences for misrepresentations in mail delivery. And this is precisely why spammers have been, and continue to be, incredibly effective at getting unwanted e-mail delivered.

SMTP is, as Winston Churchill might have put it, the worst way of "doing" e-mail, except for all the others that have been tried. The reality is that SMTP works reliably and has been widely implemented. To supplant SMTP with anything "better" would mean a wholesale redesign of the entire global e-mail infrastructure, a task that few in the industry have been willing to undertake. Some people have endeavored to develop solutions that can ride atop the existing SMTP infrastructure, allowing SMTP to continue functioning efficiently while giving those who use it the option of engaging more robust features that help differentiate legitimate mail from spam. There is more on these solutions later in the chapter.

20.2.2 Heads-Up.   E-mail cannot be delivered without something called a header, and every e-mail message has one, a section of the message that is not always displayed in the recipient's e-mail program but is there nonetheless, describing where the message came from, how it was addressed, and how it was delivered. Examining the header can tell you a lot about a message. Consider how a message appears in Microsoft Outlook Express, as illustrated in Exhibit 20.2.

At the top you can see the "From," the "To," and the "Subject." For example, you can see part of a message that appears to be from zjjimwalker8467r21@lycos.com to press@eprivacygroup.com with the subject: *You're approved! As you may have

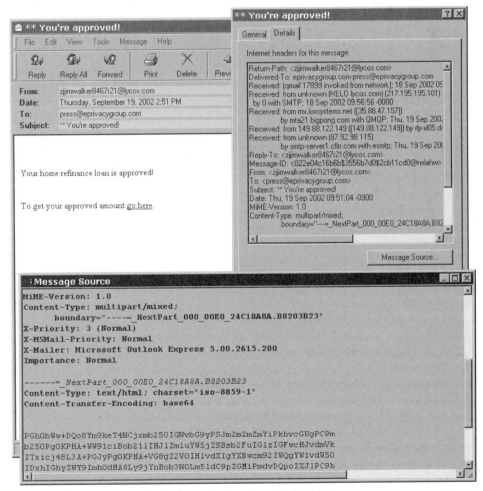

EXHIBIT 20.2   Viewing Message Header Details in Outlook Express

guessed, press@eprivacygroup.com is not a real person. This is just an address that appears on a company Web site as a contact for the press, and of course, nobody actually used this address on a mortgage application. The address was "harvested" by a program that automatically scours the Web for e-mail addresses.

When you open this message in Outlook Express and use the File/Properties command, you can click on the Details tab to see how the message made its way through the Internet. The first thing you see is a box labeled headers, as shown in Exhibit 20.2. Reading this will tell you that the message was routed through several different e-mail servers. Qmail is the company's mail program, which is the first instance of "Received." The next three below that are intermediaries, until you get to the last one, smtp-server1.cflrr.com. That is an e-mail server in Central Florida (cfl) on the Road Runner (rr) cable modem network, which supplies high-speed Internet access to tens of thousands of households.

So who sent this message? That is very hard to say. As you might expect, there is no such address as zjjimwalker8467r21@lycos.com. The best way to determine who sent a spam message like this is to examine the content. Spam cannot reel in suckers unless there is some way for the suckers to contact the spammer. Sometimes this is a phone number, but in this message it is a hyperlink to a Web page. However, clicking links in spam messages is a dangerous way to surf—a much safer technique to learn more about links in spam is message source inspection. Outlook Express provides a Message Source view, but this may only show the encoded content and not be readable ASCII.

One way to get at the content of such messages is to forward them to a different e-mail client, for example Qualcomm's Eudora, then open the mailbox file with a text editor such as TextPad. This reveals the "http" reference for the link that this spammer wants the recipient to click. In this case, the sucker who clicks on the link that says "To get your approved amount go here" is presented with a form that is not about mortgages, but about data gathering. To what use the data thus gathered will be put is impossible to say, but a little additional checking using the *ping* and *whois* commands reveals that the Web server collecting the data is in Beijing. The chances of finding out who set it up are slim. The standard operating procedure is to set up and take down a Web site like this very quickly, gathering as much data as you can before someone starts to investigate. However, over the last 10 years, the resources devoted to investigating spammers have been minimal when compared to the resources that have gone into sending spam. Even when lawmakers can agree on what spam is and how to declare it illegal, government funds are rarely allocated for spam fighting. There have been a few high-profile arrests and prosecutions, often driven by large companies, such as Microsoft and AOL, but spamming remains a relatively low risk form of computer abuse.

20.3 SPAM DEFINED.   The story of spam is a rags-to-riches saga of a mere nuisance that became a multibillion-dollar burden on the world's computing resources. For all the puns and jokes one can make about spam, it may be the largest single thief of computer and telecommunication resources since computers and telecommunications were invented. One research company predicted that the global cost of spam in 2007 would be $100 billion, compared to $50 billion in 2005, with spam expected to cost $35 billion in the United States in 2007, up from $19 billion two years earlier.

If these numbers seem high, consider them from a different perspective: Take the total amount of money the world spends on e-mail systems and services in one year, divide by 10, then multiply by 9. The result is a rough measure of how much money is wasted on spam, based on the fact that several different sources put the percentage of all e-mail that is spam at 9 out of 10 messages. Alternatively, consider a snapshot, the amount of spam received by a small publishing company, Dreva Hill, which put up its Web site in 2002. An e-mail address was provided for people to contact the company. The address was not used anywhere else. By 2007, that e-mail address was receiving over 77 spam messages per day. In the first two weeks of March, it received 1,086 messages of which 1,079 were spam.

Perhaps it is no surprise that spam has become a costly problem because spam was the first large-scale computer threat to be purely profit-driven. The goal of most spam is to make money, and it cannot make money if people do not receive it. In fact, spam software will not send spam to a mail server that has a slow response time; it simply moves on to other targets that can receive e-mail at the high message-per-minute rate needed for spam to generate income (based on 1 person in perhaps 100,000 actually responding to the spam message). If spam does not generate income, it becomes pointless because it takes money to send spam. You need access to servers and bandwidth (which you either have to pay for or steal). Ironically, a few simple changes to current e-mail standards could put an end to most spam by more reliably identifying and authenticating e-mail senders, a subject addressed later in this chapter.

20.3.1 Origins and Meaning of Spam (not SPAM™).

SPAM has been a trademark of Hormel Foods for over 70 years. For reasons that will be discussed in a moment, the world has settled on "spam" as a term to describe unwanted commercial e-mail. However, uppercase "SPAM" is still a trademark, and associating SPAM, or pictures of SPAM, with something other than the Hormel product could be a serious violation of trademark law. Security professionals should take note of this. The word "Spam" is acceptable at the start of a sentence about unsolicited commercial e-mail, but "SPAM" can be used for spam only if the rest of the text around it is uppercase, as in "TIRED OF SPAM CLUTTERING YOUR INBOX?"

The use of the word "spam" in the context of electronic messages stems from a comedy sketch in the twenty-fifth episode of the BBC television series *Monty Python's Flying Circus*.[4] First aired in 1968, before e-mail was invented, the sketch featured a restaurant in which SPAM dominated the menu. When a character called Mr. Bun asks the waitress "Have you got anything without SPAM in it?" she replies: "Well, there's SPAM, egg, sausage and SPAM, that's not got much SPAM in it." The banter continues in this vein until Mr. Bun's exasperated wife screams, "I don't like SPAM!" She is further exasperated by an incongruous group of Viking diners singing a song, the lyrics of which consist almost entirely of the word "SPAM." A similar feeling of exasperation at having someone foist on you something that you do not want, and did not ask for, clearly helped to make "spam" a fitting term for the sort of unsolicited commercial e-mail that can clutter inboxes and clog e-mail servers.

In fact, the first use of "spam" as a term for abuse of networks did not involve e-mail. The gory details of spam were carefully researched in 2003 by Brad Templeton, former chairman of the board of the Electronic Frontier Foundation.[5] According to Templeton, the origins lie in annoying and repetitive behavior observed in multiuser dungeons (also know by the acronym MUD, an early term for a real-time, multiperson, shared environment). From there the term "spam" migrated to bulletin boards—where it was used to describe automated, repetitive message content—thence to USENET, where it was applied to messages that were posted to multiple newsgroups.

A history of USENET, and its relationship to the history of spam, is salutary for several reasons. First of all, spam pretty much killed USENET, which was once a great way to meet and communicate with other Internet users who shared common interests, whether those happened to be political humor or HTML coding. Newsgroups got clogged with spam to the point where users sought alternative channels of communication. In other words, a valuable and useful means of communication and an early form of social networking was forever tainted by the bad behavior of a few individuals who were prepared to flaunt the prevailing standards of conduct.

The second spam-USENET connections is that spam migrated from USENET to e-mail through the *harvesting* of e-mail addresses, a technique that spammers—the people who distribute spam—then applied to Web pages and other potential sources of target addresses. Spammers found that software could easily automate the process of reading thousands of newsgroup postings and extracting, or harvesting, any e-mail addresses that appeared in them. It is important to remember that, although it might seem naive today, the practice of including one's e-mail address in a message posted to a newsgroup was common until the mid-1990s. After all, if you posted a message looking for an answer, then including your e-mail address made it easy for people to reply. It may be hard for some computer users to imagine a time when e-mail addresses were so freely shared, but that time is worth remembering because it shows how easily the abuse of a system by a few can erode its value to the many. Harvesting, which resulted in receiving spam at an e-mail address provided in a newsgroup posting for the purposes of legitimate communication, was an enormous "advance" in abuse of the Internet and a notable harbinger of things to come. Elaborate countermeasures had to be developed, all of which impeded the free flow of communication. Much of the role fulfilled by newsgroups migrated to closed forums, where increasingly elaborate measures are used to prevent abuse. A useful historical perspective on spam's depressing impact on e-mail is provided by the reports freely available at the MessageLabs Web site. Its annual reports provide conservative estimates of the growth in spam; for example, the 2007 annual report[6] showed total spam hovering around 85 percent of all e-mails from 2005 through 2007, with new varieties (those previously unidentified by type or source) keeping fairly steady at around 75 percent of all e-mail.

20.3.2 Digging into Spam.   Around 1996, as early adopters of e-mail began experiencing increasing amounts of unsolicited e-mail, efforts were made to define exactly what kind of message constituted spam. This was no academic exercise, and the stakes were surprisingly high. We have already employed one definition: unsolicited commercial e-mail (sometimes referred to as UCE). This definition seems simple enough, capturing as it does two essential points: Spam is e-mail that people did not ask to receive, and spam is somehow commercial in nature.

However, while UCE eventually became the most widely used definition of spam it did not satisfy everyone. Critics point out that it does not address unsolicited messages of a political or noncommercial nature (such as a politician seeking your vote or a charity seeking donations). Furthermore, the term "unsolicited" is open to a lot of interpretation, a fact exploited by early mass e-mailings by mainstream companies whose marketing departments used the slimmest of pretexts to justify sending people e-mail. As the universe of Internet users expanded in the late 1990s, encompassing more and more office workers and consumers, three things about spam became increasingly obvious:

1. People did not like spam.
2. Spammers could make money.
3. Legitimate companies were tempted to send unsolicited e-mail.

20.3.2.1 *"Get Rich Quick" Factor.*

How much money could a spammer make? Consider the business plan of one Arizona company, C.P. Direct, that proved very profitable until it was shut down, in 2002, by the U.S. Customs Service and the Arizona Department of Public Safety. Here are some of the assets that authorities seized:

- Nearly $3 million in cash plus a large amount of expensive jewelry.
- More than $20 million in bank accounts.
- Twelve luxury imported automobiles (including eight Mercedes, plus assorted models from Lamborghini, Rolls-Royce, Ferrari, and Bentley).
- One office building and assorted luxury real estate in Paradise Valley and Scottsdale.

These profits were derived from the sale of $74 million worth of pills that promised to increase the dimensions of various parts of the male and female anatomy. The company had used spam to sell these products, but in fact it was not shuttered for sending spam, the legal status of which remains ambiguous to this day, having been defined differently by different jurisdictions (not least of which was the U.S. Congress, which arguably made a hash of it in 2004).

C.P. Direct crossed several lines, not least of which was the making of false promises about its products (none of which it ever tested and all of which turned out to contain the same ingredients, regardless of which part of the human anatomy they were promised to enhance). The company compounded its problems by refusing to issue refunds when the products did not work as claimed. However, rather than discourage spammers, this case proved that spam can make you rich, quick. Indeed, the hope of getting rich quick remains the main driver of spam. The fact that a handful of people were prosecuted for conducting a dubious enterprise by means of spam was not perceived as a serious deterrent.

20.3.2.2 *Crime and Punishment.*

Spammers keep on spamming because risks are perceived to be small relative to both the potential gains and the other options for getting rich quick. The two people at the center of the C.P. Direct case, Michael Consoli and his nephew and partner, Vincent Passafiume, admitted their guilt in plea agreements signed in August 2003; they but were out of jail before May 2004, and they seemed to have suffered very little in the shame department., Two years after their release, the pair asked the state Court of Appeals to overturn the convictions and give back whatever was left of the seized assets.

Consider what has happened with Jeremy Jaynes, named as one of the world's top 10 spammers in 2003 by Spamhaus, a spam-fighting organization discussed later in Section 20.4.1 of this chapter. When he was prosecuted for spamming, Jaynes was thought to be sending out 10 million e-mails a day. How much did he earn from this? Prosecutors claimed it was about $750,000 a month. In 2004, Jaynes was convicted of sending unsolicited e-mails with forged headers, in violation of Virginia law. He was sentenced to nine years in prison. However, as of the start of 2008, Jaynes had not served any time, remaining free on bail (set at less than two months' worth of his spam earnings). Apparently he is waiting for his case to get to the U.S. Supreme Court.

20.3.2.3 *A Wasteful Game.*

In many ways, spam is heir to the classic sucker's game played out in classified advertisements that promise to teach you how to "get cash in your mailbox." The trick is to get people to send you money to learn how to get cash in their mailbox. If a spammer sends out 25 million e-mail messages touting a product, she *may* sell enough product to make a profit, but there are real production costs associated with a real product. In contrast, if she sends out enough messages touting a list of 25 million proven e-mail addresses for $79.95, she may reel in enough suckers willing to buy that list and make a significant profit because the list costs essentially nothing to generate. The fact that most addresses on such lists turn out to be useless does not seem to stop people from buying or selling them.

One form of spam that does not rely on selling a product is the *pump-and-dump* stock scam. Sending out millions of messages telling people how hot an obscure stock is about to become can create a self-fulfilling prophecy. Here is how it works:

- Buy a lot of shares on margin or a lot of shares in a company that is trading at a few pennies a share.
- Spam millions of people with a message talking up the stock you just bought.
- Wait for the price of the shares to go up, and then sell your shares for a lot more than you paid for them.

Such a scheme breaks a variety of laws but can prove profitable if you are not caught (you can hide your identity as a sender of spam); nevertheless, regulators still can review large buy and sell orders for shares referred to in stock spams.

The underlying reasons for the continuing rise in spam volume can be found in the economics of the medium. Sending out millions of e-mail messages costs the sender very little. An ordinary personal computer (PC) connected to the Internet via a $10-per-month dial-up modem connection can pump out hundreds of thousands of messages a day; a small network of PCs connected via a $50-per-month cable modem or digital subscriber line (DSL) can churn out millions. Obviously, the economic barrier to entry into "get-rich-quick" spam schemes is very low. The risk of running into trouble with the authorities is also very low. The costs of spam are borne downstream, in a number of ways, by several unwilling accomplices:

E-mail Recipient

- Spends time separating junk e-mail from legitimate e-mail. Unlike snail mail, which typically is delivered and sorted once per day, e-mail arrives throughout the day, and night. Every time you check it you face the time-wasting distraction of having to sort out spam.
- Pays to receive e-mail. There are no free Internet connections. When you connect to the Internet, somebody pays. The typical consumer at home pays a flat rate every month, but the level of that rate is determined, in part, by the volume of data that the Internet Service Provider handles, and spam inflates that volume, thus inflating cost.

Enterprise

- Loses productivity because employees, many of whom must check e-mail for business purposes, are spending time weeding spam out of their company e-mail inbox. Companies that allow employees to access personal e-mail at work also pay for time lost to personal spam weeding.
- Wastes resources because spam inflates bandwidth consumption, processing cycles, and storage space.

Internet Service Providers (ISPs) and E-mail Service Providers (ESPs)[7]

- Wastes resources on handling spam that inflates bandwidth consumption, processing cycles, and storage space.
- Have to spend money on spam filtering, block list administration, spam-related customer complaints, and filter/block-related complaints.
- Have to devote resources to policing their users to avoid getting block-listed. (There is more about filters and block lists in the next section.)

Two other economic factors are at work in the rise of spam: hard times and delivery rates. When times are tough, more people are willing to believe that get-rich-schemes like spamming are worth trying, so there are more spammers (tough times affect the receiving end as well, with recipients more willing to believe fraudulent promises of lotteries won and easy money to be made). When delivery rates for spam go down—due to the use of spam filters and other techniques that are discussed in Section 20.4.5—spammers compensate by sending even more spam.

20.3.2.4 *How Big Is the Spam Problem?*   Although most companies and consumers probably will concur that spam has grown from a mere annoyance to a huge burden, some people will say spam is not a big problem. These include:

- Consumers who have not been using e-mail for very long.
- Office users who do not see the spam addressed to them due to some form of antispam device or service deployed by their company.

These perceptions obscure the fact, noted earlier, that spam consumes vast amounts of resources that could be put to better use. The consumer might get cheaper, better Internet service if spam was not consuming so much bandwidth, server capacity, storage, and manpower. In the author's experience working with a regional ISP, growth in spam volume is directly reflected in server costs. The ISP had to keep adding servers to handle e-mail. By the time it got to four servers, 75 percent of all the e-mail was determined to be spam. The ISP had incurred server costs four times greater than needed to handle legitimate e-mail. Furthermore, even with four servers, spikes in spam volumes were causing servers to crash, incurring the added cost of service calls in the middle of the night, not to mention the loss of subscribers annoyed by outages.

In August 2002, three different e-mail service providers, Brightmail, Postini, and MessageLabs, predicted that spam was on track to becoming the majority of message traffic on the Internet by the end of the year. These predictions were met with skepticism in some quarters, discounted as a sales pitch by companies that offered spam-fighting products and services. However, sober analysis indicated that the problem was real.[8] Brightmail's interception exhibits for July 2002 showed that spam made up 36 percent of all e-mail traveling over the Internet, up from 8 percent a year earlier. Postini found that spam made up 33 percent of its customers' e-mail in the same month, up from 21 percent in January. MessageLabs reported that its customers were now classifying from 35 percent to 50 percent of their e-mail traffic as spam. In September 2002, Microsoft let it slip that 80 percent of the e-mail passing through its servers was "junk."

Since that time, spam statistics produced by companies like Postini (now owned by Google) have been validated as genuine and not just marketing hype. According to Postini, 94 percent of all e-mail in December 2007 was spam. According to MessageLabs, spam volume per user was up 57 percent in 2007 over 2006, which implies that the average unprotected user would have received 36,000 spam messages in 2007—nearly 100 per day, seven days a week—compared with 23,000 spam messages in 2006.

As alluded to earlier, these numbers have a direct effect on infrastructure spending. Storage is one of the biggest hardware and maintenance costs incurred by e-mail. If 80 to 90 percent of all e-mail is unsolicited junk, then companies that process e-mail are spending way more on storage than they would if all e-mail was legitimate. The productivity "hit" for companies whose employees waste time weeding spam out of their inboxes is also enormous. Beyond these costs, consider the possibility that spam actually acts as a brake on Internet growth rates, having a negative effective on economies, such as America's, that derive considerable strength from Internet-related goods and services. Although the Internet appears to grow at a healthy clip, it may be a case of doing so well that it is hard to know how badly we are doing. Perhaps the only reason such an effect has not yet been felt is that spam's impact on new users is limited. As noted earlier, when new users first get e-mail addresses, they typically do not get a lot of spam. According to some studies, it can take 6 to 12 months for spammers to find an e-mail address, but when they do, the volume of spam to that address can increase very quickly. This leads some people to cut back on their use of e-mail and the Internet.

20.3.3 Spam's Two-Sided Threat.   When mail servers slow down, falter, and finally crash under an onslaught of spam, the results include lost messages, service interruptions, and unanticipated help desk and tech support costs. Sales are missed. Customers do not get the service they expect. The cost of keeping spam out of your inbox and your enterprise is one thing, the cost of preventing spam from impacting system availability and business operations is another; but there is another side of the spam threat, the temptation to become an abusive mass mailer, otherwise known as a spammer. This is something that spam has in common with competitive intelligence, otherwise known as industrial espionage. When done badly, mass mailings, like competitive intelligence, can tarnish a company's reputation.

Leaving aside the matter of the increasingly nasty payloads delivered with spam, things like Trojans and phishing attacks, even plain old male enhancement spam constitutes a threat to both network infrastructure and productivity. For a start, spam constitutes a theft of network resources. The inflationary effect on server budgets has already been mentioned. The negative impact on bandwidth may be less obvious but is definitely real. In 2002 and 2003, the author was involved in the beta testing of a prototype network-level antispam router. It was not unusual for a company installing this device to discover that spam had been consuming from two-thirds to three-quarters of its network bandwidth. Whether this impact was seen as performance degradation or cost inflation, very few companies were willing to remove this device once it had been installed. In other words, when companies see what their network performance and bandwidth cost is like when spam is taken out of the equation, they realize just what a negative impact spam has. This is something that might otherwise be hard to detect given that spam has risen in volume over time.

An even more dramatic illustration of the damage that spam can cause comes when a network is targeted by a really big "spam cannon" (a purpose-built configuration of MTA devices connected to a really big broadband connection; for example, a six-pack of optimized MTAs can fire off 3.6 million messages an hour). The effect can be to crash the receiving mail servers, with all of the attendant cost and risk that involves. One way to prevent this happening, besides deployment of something like an antispammer router, is to sign up for an antispam service, which intercepts all of your incoming e-mail and screens out the spam. Such a solution addresses a number of e-mail-related problems but at considerable ongoing cost, which still constitutes a theft of resources by spammers.

The company Commtouch.com provides a spam cost calculator that produces some interesting numbers.[9] Consider these input values for a medium-size business:

- Employees: 800
- Average annual salary: $45,000
- Average number of daily e-mails per recipient: 75
- Average percentage of e-mail that is spam: 80%

According to the calculator, total annual cost of spam to this organization, which is assumed to be deploying no antispam measures, is just over $1 million. This is based on certain assumptions, such as the time taken to delete spam messages, but in general, it seems fairly realistic. Of course, the size of the productivity hit caused by the spam that makes it to an employee inbox has been hotly debated over the years, but it is clearly more than negligible and not the only hit. Even if antispam filtering is introduced, there will still be a need to review or adjust the decisions made by the filter to ensure that no important legitimate messages are erroneously quarantined or deleted. In other words, even if the company spends $50,000 per year on antispam filtering, it will not reclaim all of the $1 million wasted by spam.

20.3.3.1   *Threat of Outbound Spam.* Even as organizations like the Coalition Against Unsolicited Commercial E-mail (CAUCE) were trying to persuade companies that spamming was an ill-advised marketing technique that could backfire in the form of very annoyed recipients, and just as various government entities were trying to create rules outlawing spam, some companies were happy to stretch the rules and deluge consumers with e-mail offers, whether those consumers had asked for them or not. This led some antispammers to condemn all companies in the same breath. The author's own experience, working with large companies that have respected brand names, was that none of them actually wanted to offend consumers. Big companies always struggle to rein in maverick marketing activities, and mass e-mailing is very tempting when you are under pressure to produce sales; but upper management is unlikely to condone anything that could be mistaken for spamming.

Not that the motives for corporate responsibility in e-mail are purely altruistic. Smart companies can see that the perpetuation of disreputable e-mail tactics only dilutes the tremendous potential of e-mail as a business tool. Whatever you think of spam, there is no denying that, as a business tool, bulk e-mail is incredibly powerful. It is also very seductive. When you have a story to tell or a product to sell, and a big list of e-mail addresses just sitting there, bulk e-mail can be very tempting. You can find yourself thinking "Where's the harm?" and "Who's going to object?" But unless you have documented permission to send your message to the people on that list, the smart business decision is to resist the temptation. Remember, it only takes one really ticked off recipient of your unsolicited message to ruin your day.

20.3.3.2   *Mass E-mail Precautions.* One of the most basic business e-mail precautions is this: Never send a message unless you are sure you know what it will look like to the person who receives it. This covers the formatting, the language you use, and, above all, the addressing. If you want to address the same message to more than one person at a time, you have three main options, each of which should be handled carefully:

1. Place the e-mail addresses of all recipients in the "To" field or the Copy (Cc) field so all the recipients will be able to see the addresses of the other people to whom you sent the message. This is sometimes appropriate for communications within a small group of people.

2. If the number of people in the group exceeds about 20, or if you do not want everyone to know who is getting the message, move all but one of them to the Blind Copies (Bcc) field. The one address in the "To" field may be your own. If the disclosure of recipients is likely to cause any embarrassment whatsoever, do a test mailing first. Send a copy of the message to yourself and to at least one colleague outside the company, and then have the message looked at to make sure the "Bcc" entries were made correctly.

3. To handle large groups of recipients, or to personalize one message to many recipients, use a specialized application like Group Mail that can reliably build individual, customized messages to each person on a list. This neatly sidesteps errors related to the "To" and "Cc" fields. Group Mail stores e-mail addresses in a database and builds messages on the fly using a merge feature like a word processor. You can insert database fields in the message. For example, a message can refer to the recipient by name. The program also offers extensive testing of messages, so that you can see what recipients will see before you send any messages. And the program has the ability to send messages in small groups, spread over time, according to the capabilities of your Internet connection.

Whether you use a program like Group Mail for your legitimate bulk e-mail, or something even more powerful, depends on several factors, such as the size of your organization, the number of messages you need to send, and your privacy policy. Privacy comes into play because some software used to send e-mail, such as Group Mail, allows the user of the program access to the database containing the addresses to which the mail is being sent. This is generally not a problem in smaller companies, or when the database consists solely of names and addresses without any special context; but it can be an issue when the database contains sensitive information or the context is sensitive. For example, a list of names and addresses can be sensitive if the person handling the list knows, or can infer, that they belong to patients undergoing a certain kind of medical treatment.

You may not want to allow system operators or even programmers to have access to sensitive data simply because they are charged with sending or programming messages. Fortunately, mailing programs can be written that allow an operator to compose mail and send it without seeing the names and addresses of the people to whom it is being sent. Test data can, and should, be used to "proof" the mailing before it is executed.

Another basic e-mail precaution is never to send any message that might offend any of the recipients. In choosing your wording, your design, your message, know your audience. Use particular caution when it comes to humor, politics, religion, sex, or any other sensitive subject. When using e-mail for business e-mail, it is better to stand accused of a lack of humor rather than a lack or judgment.

Respect people's preferences, if you know them, for content. If people have expressed a preference for text-only messages, do not send them HTML and hope they decide to change their minds. Ask first because the "forgiveness later" path is not cost effective when you have to deal with thousands of unhappy recipients calling your switchboard. When you do use HTML content, still try to keep size to a minimum, unless you have recipients who specifically requested large, media-rich messages.

Antispam measures deployed by many ISPs, companies, and consumers sometimes produce "false positives," flagging legitimate e-mail as spam, potentially preventing your e-mail from reaching the intended recipients, even when they have asked to receive your e-mail. If your company's e-mail is deemed to be particularly egregious spam, the server through which it is sent is likely to be blocked. If this is your company's general e-mail server, blocking could affect delivery of a lot more than just the "spam." If the servers through which your large mailing is sent belong to a service provider, and its servers get blocked, that could be a problem for you too. And if you use a service provider to execute the mailing for you but fail to choose wisely, your mail may be branded as spam just because of the bad reputation of the servers through which it passes. Be aware that using spam to advertise your products could place you in a violation of the CAN-SPAM Act of 2003 even if you do not send the spam yourself. (See Section 20.4.9 for more on CAN-SPAM.)

What can be done to prevent messages that are not spam from falling victim to antispam measures? Adherence to responsible e-mail practices is a good first step. Responsible management of the company's e-mail servers will also help, as will selection of reputable service providers. You should also consider tasking someone with tracking antispam measures, to make sure that your e-mail is designed to avoid, as much as possible, any elements of content or presentation that are currently being flagged as spam.

To make sure your company is associated with responsible e-mail practices, become familiar with the "Six Resolutions for Responsible E-Mailers." These were created by the Council for Responsible E-mail (CRE), which was formed under the aegis of the Association for Interactive Marketing (AIM), a subsidiary of the Direct Market Association (DMA). Some of the country's largest companies, and largest legitimate users of e-mail, belong to these organizations, and they have a vested interest in making sure that e-mail is not abused. Here are the six resolutions:

1. Marketers must not falsify the sender's domain name or use a nonresponsive IP address without implied permission from the recipient or transferred permission from the marketer.

2. Marketers must not purposely falsify the content of the subject line or mislead readers from the content of the e-mail message.

3. All bulk e-mail marketing messages must include an option for the recipient to unsubscribe (be removed from the list) from receiving future messages from that sender, list owner, or list manager.

4. Marketers must inform the respondent at the time of online collection of the e-mail address for what marketing purpose the respondent's e-mail address will be used.

5. Marketers must not harvest e-mail addresses with the intent to send bulk unsolicited commercial e-mail without consumers' knowledge or consent. ("Harvest" is defined as compiling or stealing e-mail addresses through anonymous collection procedures such as via a Web spider, through chat rooms, or other publicly displayed areas listing personal or business e-mail addresses.)

6. The CRE opposes sending bulk unsolicited commercial e-mail to an e-mail address without a prior business or personal relationship. ("Business or personal relationship" is defined as any previous recipient-initiated correspondence,

transaction activity, customer service activity, third-party permission use, or proven off-line contact.)

These six resolutions may be considered a reasonable middle ground between antispam extremists and marketing-at-all-costs executives. If everyone abided by these resolutions, there would be no spam, at least according to most people's definition of spam. After all, if nobody received more than one or two messages per week that were unwanted and irrelevant, antispam sentiment would cool significantly.

20.3.3.3 *Appending and Permission Issues.*   Some privacy advocates have objected to the sixth resolution because it permits e-mail appending. This is the practice of finding an e-mail address for a customer who has not yet provided one. Companies such as Yesmail and AcquireNow will do this for a fee. For example, if you are a bank, you probably have physical addresses for all your customers, but you may not have e-mail addresses for all of them. You can hire a firm to find e-mail addresses for customers who have not provided one. However, these customers may not have given explicit permission for the bank to contact them via e-mail, so some people would say that sending e-mail messages to them is spamming.

Whether you agree with that assessment or not, several factors need to be assessed carefully if your company is considering using an e-mail append service. First of all, make sure that nothing in your privacy policy forbids it. Next, think hard about the possible reaction from customers, bearing in mind that e-mail appending is not a perfect science. For more on how appending works, enter "e-mail append" as a search term in Google—you will find a lot of companies offering to explain how they do it, matching data pulled from many different sources using complex algorithms.

Another concern that must be considered is that some messages will go to people who are not customers. For that reason, you probably want to make your first contact a tentative one, such as a polite request to make further contact. Then you can formulate the responses to build a genuine opt-in list. As you might expect, you can outsource this entire process to the append service, which will have its own, often automated, methods of dealing with bounced messages, complaints, and so on.

Do not include any sensitive personal information in the initial contact, since you have no guarantee that bob.jones@majorfree-mail.net is the Robert Jones you have on your customer list. When Citibank did an append mailing in the summer of 2002, encouraging existing customers to use the bank's online account services, it came in for some serious criticism. Although the bank was not providing immediate online access to appended customers, the mere perception of this, combined with a number of mistaken e-mail identities, produced negative publicity. Here is what Citibank said in the message it sent to people it believed to be customers, even though these people had not provided their e-mail address directly to the bank:

> Citibank would like to send you e-mail updates to keep you informed about your Citi Card, as well as special services and benefits . . . With the help of an e-mail service provider, we have located an e-mail address that we believe belongs to you.

Although this message is certainly polite, it clearly raised questions in the minds of recipients. Two questions could undermine appending as a business practice: Where exactly is this service provider looking for these e-mail addresses? Why doesn't the company that wants my e-mail address just write and ask for it? The fact is, conversion rates from e-mail contact are higher than from snail mail, so the argument for append services is that companies that use them move more quickly to the cheaper and better medium of e-mail than those that do not. The counterpoint is that too many people will be offended in the process.

Consider to what lengths you are stretching the "prior business relationship" principle cited in the sixth responsible e-mail resolution. A bank probably has a stronger case for appending e-mail addresses to its account holder list than does a mail order company that wants to append a list of people who requested last year's catalog. The extent to which privacy advocates accept or decry the concept of "prior business relationship" is largely dependent on how reasonable companies are in their interpretation of it.

Marketing to addresses that were not supplied with a clear understanding that they would be used for such purposes is not advisable. Depending on your privacy statement, it could be a violation of your company's privacy policy. Going ahead with such a violation could not only annoy customers, but also draw the attention of industry regulators, such as the Federal Trade Commission (FTC). Of course, you will have to decide for yourself if it is your job or responsibility to point this out to management. And be sure to provide a simple way for recipients to opt out of any further mailings. (A link to a Web form is best for this. Avoid asking the recipient to reply to the message. If the e-mail address to which you mailed the message is no longer their primary address, they may have trouble opting out.)

20.4 FIGHTING SPAM. The fight against incoming spam can be addressed both specifically, as in "What can I do to protect my systems from spam?" and in general, "What can be done to prevent spam in general?" Of course, if the activity of spamming were to be eliminated, everyone would have one less threat to worry about.

20.4.1 Enter the Spam Fighters. In the five-year period from 1997 to 2002, a diverse grouping of interests and organizations fought to make the world aware of the problem of spam, and to encourage counter-measures. The efforts of the Coalition Against Unsolicited Commercial E-mail, which continue to this day, spurred lawmakers into passing antispam legislation and helped bring order to the blacklisting process by which spam-sending servers are identified. In 1998, the Spamhaus Project, a volunteer effort founded by Steve Linford, began tracking spammers and spam-related activity. (The name comes from a pseudo-German expression, coined by Linford, to describe any ISP or other firm that sends spam or willingly provides services to spammers.)

Commercial antispam products started to appear in the late 1990s, starting with spam filters that could be used by individuals. Filtering supplied as a service to enterprises appeared in the form of Brightmail, founded in 1998 and now owned by Symantec, and Postini, founded in 1999 and now owned by Google. A host of other solutions, some free and open source, others commercial, attempted to tackle spam from several different directions. Nevertheless, despite the concerted efforts of volunteers, lawmakers, and entrepreneurs, spam has continued to sap network resources while evolving into part of a subculture of system abuse that includes delivering payloads that do far worse things than spark moral outrage.

20.4.2 A Good Reputation? Since spam is created by humans, it is notoriously difficult, if not impossible, for computers to identify spam with 100 percent reliability. This fact led some spam fighters to consider an alternative approach: reliably identifying legitimate e-mail. If an e-mail recipient or a Mail Transfer Agent could verify that certain incoming messages originated from legitimate sources, all other e-mail could be ignored. One form of this approach is the challenge-response system, perhaps the largest deployment being the one that Earthlink rolled out in 2003. When you send a message to someone at Earthlink who is using this system, and who has not received a message from you before, your message is not immediately delivered. Instead, Earthlink sends an e-mail asking you to confirm your identity, in a way that would be difficult for a machine to fake. The recipient is then informed of your message and decides whether to accept it or not. Unfortunately, this approach can be problematic if the user does a lot of e-commerce involving e-mail coming from many sources that are essentially automated responders (which cannot pass the challenge). Manually building the whitelist of allowed respondents can be tiresome, and failure to do so may mean some messages do not get through (e.g., if the sender is a machine that does not know how to handle the challenge). One solution to this problem is to compile an independent whitelist of legitimate e-mailers whose messages are allowed through without question. This is the reputational approach to spam fighting, and it works like this:

- Bank of America pledges never to spam its customers and only send them e-mail they sign up for (be it online statement notification or occasional news of new bank services).
- Bank of America e-mail is always fast-tracked through ISPs and not blocked as spam.
- Bank of America remains true to its pledge because its reputation as a legitimate mailer enables it to conduct e-mail activities with greater efficiency.

There are considerable financial and logistical obstacles to making such a system work, and it tends to work better with bigger mailers. Adoption also faced skepticism from some privacy and antispam advocates who suspected that the goal of such systems was merely to legitimize mass mailings by companies that still did not understand the need to conduct permission-only mailings. The relentless assault of spam on the world's e-mail systems eventually may lead all legitimate companies to foreswear unsolicited e-mail and thus make a reputational system universally feasible. Tough economic times, though, may tempt formerly "clean" companies to turn to spam in a desperate effort to boost flagging sales.

Another and more universal method of excluding spam would be for ISPs to deliver, and consumers to accept, only those e-mails that were stamped with a verifiable cryptographic seal of some kind. A relatively simple automated system to accomplish this was developed in 2001 by a company called ePrivacy Group, and it proved very successful in real-world trials conducted by MSN and several other companies. If adopted universally, such a system could render spamming obsolete, but that "if" proved to be unattainable. The success of this approach depended on widespread deployment, and the project ultimately was doomed by infighting between the larger ISPs, despite ePrivacy Group's willingness to release the underlying technology to the public domain.

The ultimate in reputation-based approaches to solving the spam problem may well be something that information security experts have urged for years: widespread use of e-mail encryption. If something like Secure/Multipurpose Internal Mail Extensions (S/MIME) was universally implemented, everyone could ignore messages that were not signed by people from whom they were happy to receive e-mail. Of course, the fact that e-mail encryption can be made to work reliably is not proof that it always will, and the encryption approach does not, in itself, solve the fundamental barrier to any universal effort at outlawing spam: the willingness of everyone to participate. One of the qualities that led e-mail to become the most widely used application on the Internet, the lack of central control, is a weakness when it comes to effecting any major change to the way it operates.

20.4.3 Relaying Trouble. When considering the problem of spam in general, the question is why ISPs allow people to send spam. The fact is, many do not. Spamming is a violation of just about every ISP's terms of service. Accounts used for spamming are frequently closed. However, there are some exceptions. As you might imagine, a few ISPs allow spam as a way to get business (albeit business that few others want). Some of these ISPs use facilities in fringe countries to avoid regulatory oversight. Furthermore, some spammers find it easier, and cheaper, to steal service and use unauthorized access to other people's servers to send their messages. A phenomenon of e-mail is mail relaying. According to Janusz Lukasiak of the University of Manchester, mail relaying occurs "when a mail server processes a mail message from an unauthorized external source with neither the sender nor the recipient being a local user. The mail server is an entirely unrelated third party to this transaction and the message should not be passed via the server."[10] The problem with unauthenticated third parties is that they can hide their identity.

In the early days of the Internet, many servers were left *open* so that people could conveniently relay their e-mail through them at any time. It was quite acceptable for individuals to send their e-mail through just about any mail server, since the impact on resources was minimal. Abuses by spammers, whose mass e-mailings *do* impact resources, led to ISPs instituting restrictions. Some ISPs require the use of port 587 for SMTP authentication. Others require logging in to the POP server to collect incoming mail before sending any out. Since that requires a user name and password, it prevents "strangers" from sending e-mail through the server.

Open relays are now frowned on. However, relaying continues to occur, partly because configuring servers to prevent it requires effort. Also, spammers keep finding new ways to exploit resources that are not totally protected. For example, port 25 filtering, instituted to reduce spamming, can be bypassed with tricks like asynchronous routing and proxies. A relatively recent development is the use of botnets, groups of compromised computers, to deliver spam. (For more about botnets see Chapters 15, 16, 17, 30, 32, and 41 in this *Handbook*.)

A war is continually being waged between spammers and ISPs, and that war extends to the ISPs ISP—most Internet Service Providers actually get their service from an even larger service provider, companies like AT&T, MCI, and Sprint, which are the backbone of the Internet. How much trouble do these companies have with spam? As far back as 2002, network abuse (spam) generated 350,000 trouble tickets each month at a single carrier. These companies are working hard to prevent things like mail relaying and to defeat the latest tricks that spammers have devised to get around their preventive measures.

20.4.4 Black Holes and Block Lists. Black hole lists, or block lists, catalog server IP addresses from ISPs whose customers are deemed responsible for spam and from ISPs whose servers are hijacked for spam relaying. ISPs and organizations subscribe to these lists to find out which sending IP addresses should be blocked. The receiving end, such as the consumer recipient's ISP, checks the list for the connecting IP address. If the IP address matches one on the list, then the connection gets dropped before accepting any traffic. Other ISPs choose simply to ignore, or "black hole," IP packets at their routers. Among the better known block lists are RBL, otherwise known as MAPS Realtime Blackhole List, Spamcop, and Spamhaus.[11]

How does an entity's IP address get on these lists? If an ISP openly permits spam, or does not adequately protect its resources against abuse by spammers, it will likely be reported to the list by one or more recipients of such spam. Reports are filed by people who take the time to examine the spam's header, identify the culpable ISP, and make a "nomination" to a block list. Different block lists have different standards for verifying nominations. Some test the nominated server; others take into account the number of nominations. If an ISP, organization, or individual operating a mail server finds itself on the list by mistake, it can request to be removed, which usually involves a test by the organization operating the block-list.

Note that none of this block-list policing of spam is "official." All block lists are self-appointed and self-regulated. They set, and enforce, their own standards. The only recourse for entities that feel they have been unfairly blocked—and there have been plenty of these over the years—is legal action. Some block lists are operated outside of the United States, but if an overseas organization block-lists a server located in the United States, it probably can be sued in a U.S. court. However, it is important to note that the blocking is not done by the operator of the block list, it is done by ISPs that subscribe to, and are guided by, the lists.

20.4.5   Spam Filters.   Block-list systems filter out messages from certain domains or IP addresses, or a range of IP addresses; they do not examine the content of messages. Filtering out spam, based on content, can be done at several levels.

20.4.5.1   End User Filters.   Spam filtering probably began at the client level, and even today many e-mail users perform manual negative filtering for spam, identifying spam by a process of elimination. This is easy to do with any e-mail application that allows user-defined filters or rules to direct messages to different inboxes or folders. Many people have separate mailboxes into which they filter all of the messages they get from their usual correspondents, friends, family, colleagues, subscribed newsletters, and so on. This means that whatever is left in the in basket is likely to be spam, with the notable exception of messages from new correspondents for whom a separate mailbox and filter has not yet been created.

To perform a filter that positively identifies spam, elements common to spam messages need to be identified. Many products do this, and they usually come with a default set of filters that look for things like "From" addresses that contain a lot of numbers and "Subject" text that contains a lot of punctuation characters—spammers often add these in an attempt to defeat filters based on specific text, so the Subject line "You're Approved" might be randomly concatenated with special characters and spaces like this: "**You~re Ap proved!**"

In fact, the tricks and tweaks used by spammers in crafting messages designed to bypass filters are practically endless. Nevertheless, even the spam filtering built into some basic e-mail programs offers a useful line of defense. For example, in Exhibit 20.3 you can see the control panel for spam filtering in the Eudora e-mail application, which places mail in a Junk folder based on a "score" derived from common spam indicators, giving users control over how high they want to set the bar.

Unfortunately, some of the language found in spam also appears in legitimate messages, such as "You are receiving this message because you subscribed to this list" or "To unsubscribe, click here." This means that the default setting in a spam filter is likely to block some messages that you want to get. The answer is to either weaken the filtering or create a whitelist of legitimate "From" addresses so that the spam filter will allow through anything from these addresses. Most personal spam filters, like the one shown in Exhibit 20.3, can read your address book, and add all of the entries to your personal whitelist. New correspondents can be added over time.

Most personal spam filters direct the messages they identify as spam into a special folder or in basket where they can be reviewed by the user, a process sometimes referred to as quarantining. To avoid wasting hard drive space, the filtering software can be programmed to empty the quarantine folder at set intervals or simply to delete suspected spam older than a set number of days. This quarantine approach gives the user time to review and reclaim wrongly suspected spam.

20.4.5.2 ISP Filtering. Faced with customer complaints about increased levels of spam around the turn of the century, ISPs began to institute spam filtering. However, they were hesitant to conduct content-based spam filtering, fearing that it might be construed as reading other people's e-mail and lead to claims of privacy invasion. Yet ISPs must be able to read headers to route e-mail, so filtering on the "From" address and "Subject" field was introduced (hence the increasingly inventive attempts by spammers to randomly vary Subject text). Some ISPs found that distaste for spam reached a level at which some users were prepared to accept revised terms of agreement, to allow machine reading of e-mail content to perform more effective spam filtering. Sticky legal issues still exist for ISPs, however, especially since there is no generally accepted definition of spam and no consensus on the extent to which freedom of speech applies to e-mail. For example, do political candidates have a right to send unsolicited e-mail

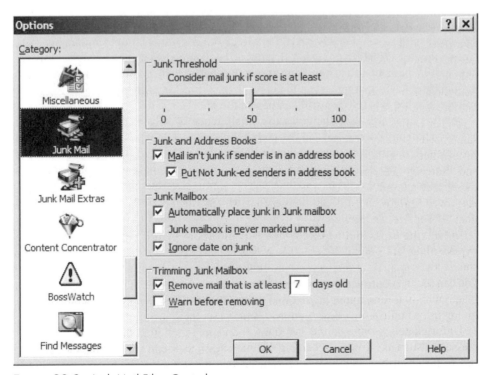

EXHIBIT 20.3 Junk Mail Filter Controls

to constituents? Do ISPs have a right to block it? These are questions on which the courts of law and public opinion have yet to render a conclusive verdict.

One place where content-based spam filters are being deployed with little or no concern for legal challenges is the corporate network. Based on the fact that the company network belongs to the company, the right to control how it is used trumps concerns over privacy. Employees do not have the right to receive, at work, whatever kind of e-mail they want to receive. And most companies would argue that there is virtually no corporate obligation to deliver e-mail to employees.

20.4.5.3 *Filtering Services.* Companies like Brightmail and Postini arose in the late 1990s to offer filtering services at the enterprise level. Brightmail developed filters that sit at the gateway to the enterprise network and filter based on continuously updated rules derived from real-time research about the latest spam outbreaks. Postini actually directs all of a company's incoming e-mail to its servers and filters it before sending it on. With specialization, filtering services can utilize a wide range of spam fighting techniques, including:

- Block lists
- Header analysis
- Content analysis
- Filtering against a database of known spam
- Heuristic filtering for "spamlike" attributes
- Whitelisting through reputational schemes

Because these systems constantly deal with huge amounts of spam, they are able to refine their filters, both positive and negative, quickly and relatively effectively. And they catch a lot of spam that would otherwise reach consumers. For example, by 2008, nine of the top 12 ISPs were using Brightmail, which claims a very low false positive rate and 95 percent catch rate. Unfortunately, that still means that some spam gets through, and when spammers can direct millions of messages an hour at a network, the volume of what gets through still can pose a threat.

Another approach uses the collective intelligence of subscribers to identify spam quickly and spread the word via network connections. Cloudmark, for example, had several million subscribers at the time of writing (April 2008) paying about $40 per year to receive nearly instantaneous updates, from servers that receive and categorize reports from members on any spam that gets through. A member's credibility score rises with every correct identification of spam and sinks with incorrect labeling of legitimate e-mail as spam (e.g., newsletters the member has forgotten subscribing to). The reliability of reporters helps the system screen false information from spammers that might try to game the system by claiming that their own junk e-mail was legitimate.

20.4.5.4 *Collateral Damage.* There are two major drawbacks to spam filters. First, they allow spammers to continue spamming. In other words, because they must decide, on a message-by-message basis, which messages are spam and which are not, filters consume a lot of resources, in some cases more than if all the spam was allowed through. When block lists and whitelists work well, they can substantially reduce the amount of spam that reaches the filtering stage, but eventually all filters are serial, and thus resource constrained and resource intensive.

Second, filters sometimes err, in one of two ways. They sometimes produce a false positive, flagging a legitimate message as spam, preventing a much-needed message from getting to the recipient in a timely manner. And they sometimes produce false negatives, allowing spam messages into the inbox. False negatives and false positives impose a drag on productivity.

20.4.6   Network Devices.   The rapid rise of spam volumes in the late 1990s occurred at a time of massive e-mail-enabled computer virus and worm attacks, arising from the classic malware motivation of bragging rights. Analysis of these problems, according to the classic factors of means, motive, and opportunity, revealed that spammers differed quite significantly from virus writers. Spammers are mostly motivated by money, not bragging rights. This insight opened up a new line of defense against spam, removing that motivation.[12]

All that remained was to understand how spammers make money, that is, the economics of spam, then to find a way to disrupt those economics. The classic spam model is to send out a vast number of e-mails offering a product or service, relying on the fact that at least some of these offers will reach real people, at least some of whom will make a purchase. If enough sales are made to create a profit over and above the cost of doing business, the spammer will continue to operate. Although a good public education and awareness program can reduce the number of people who buy the spammers' offers, it is unlikely to reduce that number enough. Because filtering spam out of the message stream reduces the spammer's return on investment, it tends to make spammers more inventive in their attempts to beat filters and to send even more spam in the hopes that enough will get through. In fact, spammers were able to find companies willing to sell them bandwidth on a massive scale, including dedicated point-to-point T3 digital phone lineconnections.

Another way to attack the economics of spam is by "following the money." Every deal has to be closed, typically via a Web site. Is it possible to shut down the spammer's Web sites? This line of inquiry led the author to an interesting finding: Spam goes stale very quickly. An examination of spam archives showed that most links in old spam were dead, sometimes because the Web site was shut down by the hosting company, sometimes because the spammer did not want to risk being identified. Thus the key to the economics of spam was revealed: time. If you slow spam down, spammers cannot generate enough responses before response sites are taken down.

Shortly after this realization, network security expert David Brussin devised a means of slowing down spam through TCP/IP traffic shaping. This became the technology at the heart of the antispam router. Instead of looking at each message in turn to determine if it is spam, the antispam router samples message traffic in real time and slows that traffic down if the sample suggests the traffic contains spam. To spammers, or rather the spamming software used by spammers, a network protected with an antispam router behaves as if it is on a 300-baud modem. In other words, the connection is too slow to deliver enough messages quickly enough for that one-in-a-million hit that the spam scheme needs in order to make money before the Web site is shut down. The spamming software quickly drops the connection; no messages have been lost and no messages have been falsely labeled as spam. Delivery of legitimate e-mail has not been affected. One or two spam messages have been delivered, but a lot less than are allowed through by the 95 percent catch rate of a typical spam filter.

There are two main tricks to this technology. One is tuning the TCP/IP traffic shaping, the other is tuning the sampling process. The latter needs regular updates about what spam looks like currently, so that it can identify a "spammy connection" as quickly as possible. These updates can be derived from services that constantly identify new spam. An application control panel is used to handle the tuning of the traffic shaping. Network administrators have found that a properly tuned antispam router can reduce bandwidth requirements by as much as 75 percent. Unfortunately, an antispam router works best on a high-volume connection, protecting MTAs at ISPs, larger companies, schools, and government agencies. There is no desktop version. Still, the technology has become a valuable part of the antispam arsenal, although the scourge of spam still continues.

20.4.7   E-mail Authentication.   On a technical level, what allows spam to continue to proliferate is the lack of sender authentication in the SMTP protocol. Several initiatives have sought to change this situation, either by changing the SMTP protocol or by adding another layer to it. One obvious way to authenticate e-mail is via the sender's domain name, and numerous schemes to accomplish this have been proposed:

- **Sender Policy Framework (SFP).** An extension to SMTP that allows software to identify and reject forged addresses in the SMTP MAIL FROM (Return-Path) that are typically indicative of spam. SPF is defined in Experimental RFC 4408.[13]
- **Certified Server Validation (CSV).** A technical method of e-mail authentication that focuses on the SMTP HELO-identity of MTAs.
- **SenderID.** An antispoofing proposal from the former MARID IETF working group that joined Sender Policy Framework and Caller ID. Sender ID is defined primarily in Experimental RFC 4406.[14]
- **DomainKeys.** A method for e-mail authentication that provides end-to-end integrity from a signing MTA to a verifying MTA acting on behalf of the recipient. It uses a signature header verified by retrieving and validating the sender's public key through the Domain Name System (DNS)
- **DomainKeys Identified Mail (DKIM).** A specification that merges DomainKeys and Identified Internet Mail, an e-mail authentication scheme supported by Cisco, to create an enhanced implementation.

When properly implemented, all of these methods can be effective in stopping the kind of forgery that has enabled spam to dominate e-mail. Each has varying pros and cons and requirements. SPF, CSV, and SenderID authenticate just a domain name. SPF and CSV can reject forgeries before message data is transferred. DomainKeys and DKIM use a digital signature to authenticate a domain name and the integrity of message content. In order for SenderID and DomainKeys to work, they must process the headers, and so the message must be transmitted.

Obviously a scheme like DomainKeys makes e-mail more complex than SMTP. Additional data and processing effort are required. DNS records have to be expanded and maintained. However, the effort may be worth it. Although something like DomainKeys does not prevent mail abusive, it does make abuse of e-mail on protected domains easier to detect and track, and this is a deterrent to spamming now that several stiff sentences for spamming have been handed down.[15] Since 2004, the e-mail services of both Yahoo and Google have signed outgoing e-mail with DomainKeys, but it is not yet clear if any one of the described schemes, or some derivative thereof, will become the standard for all e-mail. And therein lies the rub. Spam could be effectively sidelined *if* all legitimate e-mail was reliably authenticated; recipients could simply ignore all unauthenticated messages. However, that is a large *if*.

20.4.8   Industry Initiatives.   Back in 2002, at the urging of consumer advocates, government agencies, and many large corporate users of e-mail, the major e-mail service providers started to hold meetings to discuss a unified approach to improving e-mail and eliminating spam. There were high hopes that the problem of spam would be solved by this group, which was known in the business as AMEY, for AOL, Microsoft, Earthlink, and Yahoo. There was certainly plenty of encouragement. Early in 2003, the FTC, America's main consumer protection agency, convened a conference on spam, and the commissioners made it clear they wanted action. Indeed, by the end of 2003, Congress had passed the first federal antispam legislation (see Section 20.4.9).

In January 2004, then Microsoft chairman and chief executive Bill Gates announced to the World Economic Forum, "Two years from now, spam will be solved." Two months later, the AMEY companies filed lawsuits against persons alleged to be major spammers, claiming that spam cost businesses in North America $10 billion each year in lost productivity, network upgrades, and destroyed or lost data. However, by January 2006, spam constituted more than three-quarters of all e-mail. What went wrong? Repeated efforts to get the AMEY companies to adopt a new, open, royalty-free standard have run aground on concerns over intellectual property rights. Both Microsoft and Yahoo have asserted ownership over parts of the various mechanisms put forward to authenticate e-mail and thus solve the spam problem. Ironically, a lack of trust between the large ISPs has resulted in a lack of trust of the e-mail they deliver.

20.4.9   Legal Remedies.   Laws against spam have been passed by many countries, including the United States. The CAN-SPAM Act of 2003 (Controlling the Assault of Non-Solicited Pornography And Marketing Act, effective January 1, 2004) established certain requirements for anyone sending commercial e-mail. The law also provides penalties for spammers and also for companies whose products are advertised in spam. The law addresses "e-mail whose primary purpose is advertising or promoting a commercial product or service, including content on a Web site."[16]

Enforcement of the CAN-SPAM Act is primarily the job of the FTC, but the act also gives the Department of Justice authority to enforce the act's criminal sanctions. Other federal and state agencies can enforce the law against organizations under their jurisdiction, and ISPs can also sue CAN-SPAM violators. Here are the law's main provisions, as stated by the FTC:

- *Bans false or misleading header information.* The From, To, and routing information of your e-mail—including the originating domain name and e-mail address—must be accurate and identify the person who initiated the e-mail.
- *Prohibits deceptive subject lines.* The subject line cannot mislead the recipient about the contents or subject matter of the message.
- *Requires that your e-mail give recipients an opt-out method.* You must provide a return e-mail address or another Internet-based response mechanism that allows a recipient to ask you not to send future e-mail messages to that e-mail address, and you must honor the requests. You may create a "menu" of choices to allow a recipient to opt out of certain types of messages, but you must include the option to end any commercial messages from the sender.

Any opt-out mechanism you offer must be able to process opt-out requests for at least 30 days after you send your commercial e-mail. When you receive an opt-out request, the law gives you 10 business days to stop sending e-mail to the requestor's e-mail address. You cannot help another entity send e-mail to that address or have another entity send e-mail on your behalf to that address. Finally, it is illegal for you to sell or transfer the e-mail addresses of people who choose not to receive your e-mail, even in the form of a mailing list, unless you transfer the addresses so another entity can comply with the law.

- *Requires that commercial e-mail be identified as an advertisement and include the sender's valid physical postal address.* Your message must contain clear and conspicuous notice that the message is an advertisement or solicitation and that the recipient can opt out of receiving more commercial e-mail from you. It also must include your valid physical postal address.

    Note that messages which are transactional or relationship based—that is, e-mail that "facilitates an agreed-upon transaction or updates a customer in an existing business relationship"—are also covered in the sense that these messages may not contain false or misleading routing information.

Readers will find extensive discussion about whether CAN-SPAM has been—and could ever be—effective by searching the Web with any search engine.

20.5 PHISHING.   Phishing is the use of unsolicited commercial e-mail to obtain—electronically fish for—information about you, information that you would not normally disclose to a stranger, such as your bank account number, personal identification number (PIN), and other personal identifiers such as Social Security number. There was virtually no phishing activity before 2002 and relatively little in 2003, but by 2004 phishing had become an everyday threat and has continued unabated ever since. This is one category of threat that could have been squelched, along with the rest of spam, if industry leaders had chosen to cooperate rather than to compete for customers based on promising "better antispam than the other guys."

20.5.1 What Phish Look Like.   Most of us first became aware of *phishing* when we received an e-mail about a problem with an account, typically a bank account, but possibly an eBay, PayPal, Amazon, or other online account. A typical phishing message is designed to look as if it had been sent by a large enterprise, such as the Bank of America, complete with accurate copies of the company logo, typeface, and terminology. At first glance, such messages can be quite convincing. If you receive a message like this that references an institution at which you *do* have an account, you might be tempted to read it. You might even be tempted to follow the instructions, and these are likely to lead you to a Web site that asks for confidential information. Consider the text of a typical phishing message:

> You are receiving this message, due to you protection, Our Online Technical Security Service Foreign IP Spy recently detected that your online account was recently logged on from am 77.32.11.84 without am International Access Code (I.A.C) and from an unregistered computer, which was not verified by the Our Online Service Department.
>
> If you last logged in you online account on Monday May 5th 2007, by the time 6:45 pm from an Foreign Ip their is no need for you to panic, but if you did log in your account on the above Date and Time, kindly take 2-3 minute of your online banking experience to verify and register your computer now to avoid identity theft, your protection is our future medal.

What looks, at first glance, to be a very official and technical message, turns out to be full of errors. The best thing to do with these messages is delete them. The worst thing to do is respond to them. Until there is a major overhaul of e-mail security, no reputable institution will be using e-mail to request changes or updates to confidential account information.

If you received an e-mail like the one discussed above but did not have a Bank of America account, you might have been confused. The fact is, the people sending these phishing messages usually have no idea whether the recipients have accounts at the institution named in the message. Indeed, this type of mismatch is the easiest way to spot some phishing messages. However, if the phisher, who has likely sent out millions of copies of the same e-mail, gets lucky and you do happen to have an account at the named institution, or if the e-mail is generic, then things get a little trickier. You are more likely to open a message that appears, often quite convincingly, to come from your bank. If you cannot resist looking at e-mail about an account problem, here are some of the clues that the message is bogus. (Note that we are not implying that messages lacking these clues are therefore legitimate.)

- *Deceptive link.* Most phishing messages make an effort to look like they are legitimate, for example, by using logos and graphics stolen from the Web site of the targeted institution. All phishing messages we have seen also include a link to a Web site, where you are asked to provide the data the phisher is trying to steal. However, this link typically is disguised. For example, the link might be long and complicated and include the name of the bank but actually not take you to the bank's Web site. Alternatively, the link may appear to be plain and simple text but in fact it is HTML-coded to go somewhere else. Some e-mail programs, such as Eudora, will warn you of this deception and show you the real link when you place your mouse over the link text prior to clicking.

  The design of the link in a phishing scheme can be critical to its success. An increasing number of users are appropriately wary of long, complex, or merely numerical IP address links in e-mail (e.g., "Click http://123.212.192.68"). By the use of HTML coding, messages typically obscure the destination address. However, the link is also relevant in the next stage of the attack, when the victim clicks the link. If the URL of the phishing site appears as a numerical address in the URL field of the browser, the victim may become suspicious. Various techniques are used to make this address look plausible.

- *Change PIN/Password.* E-mails that ask you to change your account access credentials are highly suspect. Legitimate companies do not make such respects via e-mail precisely because e-mail is so unreliable. No security update to a reputable banking Web site is going to ask that you log in to your account to reset it or to prevent its being suspended. And why would a legitimate message ask you to use a password *that has supposedly been compromised*? No government agency is going to ask for your credentials or personal information via e-mail. And no lottery on earth uses e-mail to notify winners. Ignore these messages, or report them as spam, and move on.

- *Bad spelling, grammar, and logic.* Whoever thought those tedious grammar lessons could be so useful? Bad grammar, spelling, and even faulty logic can be the fastest way to spot bogus e-mail. Consider this example: "Therefore, if you are the rightful holder of the account please fill in the form below so that we can check your identy." There is a telling typo here (*identy* for *identity*), and the logic is hopeless. Think about it: Why would a bank send an e-mail to someone if it was not sure the person was the "rightful holder of the account?" Again, this is not how real companies do business today, so just move on.

- *Generic phish.* Generic account warnings are particularly nasty. They are one way that phishing attacks try to get around the problem of not knowing where the victim (you) has an account. For example, all bank accounts in America are insured by an institution called the Federal Deposit Insurance Corporation. In 2004 someone created a particularly nasty attack that preyed on this fact, potentially snagging anyone with a bank account. This was one of the first phishing attacks to fake the linked URL using a vulnerability in Microsoft Internet Explorer to mask the actual URL. If you clicked the link in the message, the site you went to really looked as if it were www.fdic.org.

20.5.2 Growth and Extent of Phishing.
A snapshot of phishing activity during the last month of 2007 will serve to provide a perspective on this problem. Here are numbers reported by an organization called the Anti-Phishing Working Group (bear in mind that these numbers are for one month).

- Number of unique phishing reports received: 25,683
- Number of unique phishing sites received: 25,328
- Number of brands hijacked by phishing campaigns: 144
- Number of brands comprising the top 80% of phishing campaigns in December: 16
- Country hosting the most phishing Web sites: United States
- Percentage of phish that contain some form of target name in URL: 42.1%
- Percentage of phish that contain no hostname; just IP address: 12%
- Average time online for a phishing site: 3 days
- Longest time online for a phishing site: all month

Any new form of computer abuse can be said to have arrived when a toolkit facilitating the abuse becomes available. Phishing toolkits first appeared in 2006, offering scripts that enable attackers to automatically set up phishing Web sites spoofing the legitimate Web sites of different brands (including the illegal appropriation of images and logos that consumers associate with those brands). These scripts helpfully generate corresponding phishing e-mail messages. Researchers at Symantec found that phishing toolkits tend to create multiple phishing sites at a single IP address. During the first half of 2007, Symantec found that 86 percent of all reported phishing Web sites were hosted on just 30 percent of the phishing IP addresses. Further analysis of the three most widely used phishing toolkits revealed that they were responsible for 42 percent of all phishing attacks detected in the first half of 2007.

20.5.3 Where Is the Threat?
Phishing is clearly a problem, which appears at first to be a personal problem, a matter of consumer computer security rather than enterprise information security. Indeed, the federal agency charged with consumer protection, the FTC, has been active in educating consumers about the problem and the ways to avoid getting scammed by these messages.[17] However, phishing is also a computer-based threat to the information and welfare of companies as well as a threat to e-commerce in general.

Phishing attacks collect usernames and passwords. Many people use the same credentials for work-related systems as they do for personal systems (including the head of a highly secret government facility who was found to be using her bank ATM PIN as her top-secret network password). Criminal hackers are known to have penetrated systems by harvesting personal credentials and applying them to the target's business login. So a company computer security awareness program would do well to include warnings about phishing attacks.

Beyond the penetration threat, phishing can undermine consumer trust in a company. Although it hardly seems fair for consumers to resent Bank of America because a criminal has attempted to defraud them by abusing the bank's identity, such resentments do exist, and they need to be understood in a business context. Automation improves the profitability of banking, which is why banks encourage customers to use online services and offer incentives to drop paper statements and notifications. However, if banks are perceived as providing automation on the cheap, with insufficient safeguards built in to protect customer privacy and account access, some consumers will object, slowing down the pace of automation and jeopardizing productivity increases, potentially impacting the bottom line.

20.5.4 Phish Fighting.   Some clever technological defenses specific to phishing have been put forward, such as methods for enabling browsers to verify URLs, but the best defense is a twofold approach that is entirely obvious. The first step is education, at the consumer and corporate level, teaching people how to spot phishing attacks and avoid falling victim to them. The second step is fixing the fundamentals of e-mail in the ways outlined earlier with respect to spam. From a technical perspective, we already have the technology to do this. All that is missing is a willingness on the part of the leading service providers to take concerted action. Perhaps they could be encouraged to do so by the banks and other institutions that stand to gain a great deal if e-mail is made more secure.

Failure to act on e-mail security has already cost billions of dollars in wasted resources and lost productivity, but the effects go further than that, as evidenced by the emerging relationship among phishing, spamming, criminal hacking, Trojan code, personal data harvesting, and account compromise. The application of skills such as virus and worm writing to commercial ends has been enabled by the willingness of spammers to pay for compromised hosts with which to launch attacks and collect dollars and/or data. Spamming techniques have enabled the growth of phishing, which in turn has solidified the black market in compromised hosts and purloined personal data. New types of attack are constantly emerging from this unholy alliance between coders and criminals. E-mail addresses harvested by spam may be used for "spear phishing" attacks, where a specific company is targeted through e-mails sent to known customers or employees (the Department of Defense faced a rash of spear-phishing attacks in 2006). Trojan code distributed by spam methods has been used to corrupt local Domain Name servers (DNS) and produce the same effect as a phishing message: Users are misdirected to malicious Web sites simply by clicking on an apparently valid URL. (DNS attacks of this type are referred to as "pharming.")

20.6 TROJAN CODE.   Like the original Trojan horse, deployed by the Greeks to defeat the Trojans who were protected by the impregnable walls of the city of Troy, a computer Trojan is a bad thing disguised as a good thing (where Troy is your computer and the Greeks are the people who would like to gain unauthorized access). The technology has come a long way from the "steed of monstrous height" described in Virgil's *Aeneid*, but the goal of Trojan code is the same as that of the original Trojan horse: Fool the defender of a protected place into granting access to outsiders. (See Section 15.3.2.17 for more on the origins of the name.)

Almost as soon as the Internet provided a way to distribute executable code, either as download links or e-mail attachments, some people decided to exploit this ability to distribute their code without explicit permission. In other words, an innocent party might be tempted to download an apparently innocuous executable, which was actually something else. The person doing the downloading does so intentionally but is ignorant of the intentions of the person who crafted the Trojan code within the executable.

20.6.1 Classic Trojans.   Despite the fact that the screens of today's computers do not need saving, screensavers continue to be a source of Trojan code. Some users apparently find the promise of animated waterfalls and fish tanks hard to resist. This leads users to download screensavers that they encounter on Web sites or open screensaver files that they receive in e-mail. In Exhibit 20.4 you can see an example of one screensaver.

The creator of this Trojan screensaver, discovered in February 2007, was apparently unhappy with a file-sharing network popular in Japan and named Winny. When this screensaver is opened, the Trojan displays an image warning the computer operator not to use Winny. This tactic is reminiscent of some of the very earliest viruses, which sought to spread relatively innocuous messages rather than cause damage. In fact, code does not have to have a malicious intent to be considered a Trojan—it merely needs the intent to get installed without permission. Unfortunately, in this particular case, the Trojan does go on to destroy data by overwriting certain files (e.g., those with .txt and .jpg extensions).

Another example of a screensaver Trojan is the one reported to be circulating as an e-mail attachment called bsaver.zip in July 2007. When the file within the ZIP attachment is opened, the system is infected with the Agent-FZB Trojan horse, which then drops two rootkits to evade detection by security software and to make the system

EXHIBIT 20.4 Screensaver Trojan

accessible to unauthorized users. (See Chapter 15 in this *Handbook* for more on root-kits.) This screensaver was distributed by a spam campaign with message subject lines such as *Life is beautiful*, *Life will be better*, *Good summer*, and *help you*. The message text included phrases like "Good morning/evening, man! Really [sic] cool screensaver in your attachment!"

A Trojan tries to look useful or interesting so that users will install it, but buried within is unauthorized, undocumented code for unauthorized functions, just some of which are listed here:

- Deleting files or folders or entire drives
- Changing data, in subtle or dramatic ways
- Encrypting data (possibly for purposes of extortion)
- Copying data to other computers (possibly for purposes of industrial espionage)
- Downloading files without user consent (possibly for purposes of illicit e-commerce, illegal file sharing, pornography site hosting, cheap storage)
- Corrupting browser software and network files to redirect user from legitimate Web sites to fake, bogus, malicious sites
- Enabling remote access to the compromised system (sometimes referred to as a RAT, for Remote Access Trojan), often used to turn computers into "zombies" that can be aggregated into botnets (for the purposes of spamming, phishing, and executing denial-of-service attacks)
- Aiding the spread of viruses using "dropper" code to cause infections
- Disabling antivirus and firewall programs
- Disabling competing forms of malware
- Logging keystrokes to obtain data such as passwords and credit card numbers
- Reporting browsing activity (enabling "spyware")
- Harvesting e-mail addresses for the purpose of spamming and other activities such as phishing

The motives behind Trojan code typically fall into one or more of three categories: malice, bragging rights, and financial gain. The gains can be realized in several ways. Purloined data can be sold. Access to compromised machines can be sold. Encrypted or stolen data can be ransomed. Denial-of-service threats can be used for extortion. Some companies have even used Trojans to try to increase the sales and installed base of their software.

20.6.2 Basic Anti-Trojan Tactics.   Unfortunately, Trojans can be tough to combat. The first line of defense is well-educated users who know better than to execute code of dubious origin. Warnings to this effect should be part of any computer security awareness program, and a computer security awareness program should be part of every enterprise security model. Technical measures can be used to combat Trojans, but because none of these is perfect, it makes no sense to rely on them to the neglect of end user education. In fact, thinking of end users as *computer operators* rather than *computer users* might be a good place to start, given that the role of "user" implies a relatively passive role in maintaining the integrity and health of a computer, whereas "operator" reflects more accurately the level of responsibility required of anyone employing a computer in either work or recreation. (A computer user might be likened to someone who merely drives a car and never checks the oil or the tires; an operator is closer to a commercial driver who knows that getting safely and reliably from A to B takes a lot more than just holding the steering wheel and pressing the correct pedal.)

Technical measures against Trojans start with keeping all operating system and application patches up to date, universal use of memory-resident antivirus software that scans incoming files, and regular scanning of the entire system against a regularly updated virus database. At the same time, it helps to run memory-resident antibot software, such as Norton AntiBot, designed to recognize and thwart activity indicative of botnets. This software does not directly prevent Trojans from getting onto a computer, but it minimizes the damage that a Trojan can cause.

A good antispam solution is also necessary because spam is a major vector for Trojan attacks. If Jim in accounting never gets that message about the cool screensaver, he will not ever be tempted to open the attached file. It is not just screensavers that can be tempting. In April 2007, spam techniques were used to distribute, on a massive scale, messages with subject headings like "Worm Alert!" and "Worm Detected." The messages came with a ZIP file attachment that posed as a patch that would prevent the bogus attack. When recipients, alarmed into action, went to open the ZIP file, they found that it was password protected, and some took that as a sign it was genuine. (The password was included in the message.) Proceeding with installation led to a rootkit, disabling of security software, theft of confidential information from the affected machine, and enrollment in a botnet of compromised computers. In one 24-hour period, Postini counted nearly 5 million copies of this Trojan spam directed at users of its antispam service. The company calculated that this one spam accounted for 87 percent of all malware being spread through e-mail during that time.

20.6.3 Lockdown and Quarantine.   More drastic anti-Trojan measures include preventing unauthorized changes or additions to executables and preventing systems from connecting to networks until they have been vetted. The idea of defeating malicious executables by "freezing" the operating system, and authorized applications in a known good state, goes back a long way, at least to the early days of antivirus efforts. However, the complexity of most operating systems and application code today makes such an approach challenging at best. Consider the emergence of "Patch Tuesday" as a standard means of maintaining the world's most widely used operating system. Indeed, for many years now a lot of software development has been predicated on the assumption that patches and updates can always be pushed out if needed, arguably leading to far less rigor in coding practices than when production code was burned to disk, at considerable expense, and changes required further shipments of disks.

The idea of quarantining computers when they attempt to connect to a network, using some form of network access control, offers a slightly different approach to the idea of locking down machines so that unauthorized code cannot be installed. Some enterprise network security managers have pursued this approach because it is increasingly difficult to control some network "end points," such as the company laptop that travels with the employee to client sites and conferences, hotels, and WiFi hot spots, even spending time in the employee's car and home. Laptops used in this manner face any number of attack vectors. Traditional defense mechanisms can be applied to these end points, including password protection, biometric authentication, disk encryption, and antivirus programs. However, these may not be enough, as many enterprises have discovered to their cost. So why not prevent these machines from

Exhibit 20.5 Table of Prices Paid for Data Traded in the Underground Economy

Rank	Item	Percentage	Range of Prices
1	Credit Cards	22%	$0.50–5
2	Bank Accounts	21%	$30–400
3	E-mail Passwords	8%	$1–350
4	Mailers	8%	$8–10
5	E-mail Addresses	6%	$2/MB–4/MB
6	Proxies	6%	$0.50–3
7	Full Identity	6%	$10–150
8	Scams	6%	$10/week
9	Social Security Numbers	3%	$5–7
10	Compromised UNIX® Shells	2%	$2–10

connecting to the enterprise network until they have been scanned for unauthorized executables, like a routine health check? This approach holds promise but is not easy to implement. Furthermore, it leaves machines open to attack while they are away from the corporate network. A spam-distributed phishing exercise or screensaver Trojan could still lobotomize an end point between checkups and compromise confidential personal or corporate data. As you can see from Exhibit 20.5, a table compiled by Symantec in 2007 to show prices paid for various forms of data in the underground economy, the financial incentives for such activities are real.

20.7 CONCLUDING REMARKS. The threats addressed in this chapter are still evolving, as are the countermeasures discussed here, although some of those mentioned may be rendered obsolete by new developments. If there is one lesson security professionals can learn from studying the threats discussed herein, it is that continued failure to improve the underlying security of Internet e-mail will prolong the onslaught of spam, phishing attacks, and Trojans. The second lesson is that we must continue to educate computer users in order to prevent them falling prey to the deceptions of computer abusers. A third lesson might well be that more effective prosecution of computer criminals is needed, along with stiffer sentences.

20.8 FURTHER READING

Brown, B. C. *The Complete Guide to E-mail Marketing: How to Create Successful, Spam-free Campaigns to Reach Your Target Audience and Increase Sales.* Ocala, FL: Atlantic Publishing Group, 2007.

Goodman, D. *Spam Wars: Our Last Best Chance to Defeat Spammers, Scammers & Hackers.* New York: Select Books, 2004.

Haskins, R., and D. Nielsen. *Slamming Spam: A Guide for System Administrators.* New York: Addison Wesley Professional, 2004.

Jackobsson, M., and S. Myers, eds. *Phishing and Countermeasures: Understanding the Increasing Problem of Electronic Identity Theft.* Hoboken, NJ: John Wiley & Sons, 2006.

James, L. *Phishing Exposed.* Rockland, MA: Syngress, 2005.

Lininger, R., and R. D. Vines. *Phishing: Cutting the Identity Theft Line.* Indianapolis, IN: John Wiley & Sons, 2005.

McWilliams, B. S. *Spam Kings: The Real Story behind the High-Rolling Hucksters Pushing Porn, Pills, and %*@)# Enlargements.* Sebastopol, CA: O'Reilly, 2004.

Schryen, G. *Anti-Spam Measures: Analysis and Design.* Berlin: Springer, 2007.

Silver Lake, Eds. *Scams & Swindles: Phishing, Spoofing, Spyware, Nigerian Prisoner, ID Theft.* Aberdeen, WA: Silver Lake Publishing, 2006.

Spammer-X. *Inside the SPAM Cartel: Trade Secrets from the Dark Side.* Rockland, MA: Syngress, 2004.

Wolfe, P., C. Scott, and M. Erwin. *Anti-Spam Tool Kit.* Emeryville, CA: McGraw-Hill Osborne Media, 2004.

Zdziarski, J. *Ending Spam: Bayesian Content Filtering and the Art of Statistical Language Classification.* San Francisco: No Starch Press, 2005.

20.9   NOTES

1. *Symantec Global Internet Security Threat Report,* Vol. 13 (April 2008), www.symantec.com/business/theme.jsp?themeid=threatreport.

2. Spam constituted approximately 90 percent of all e-mail sent in 2007, according to numbers compiled by a variety of e-mail service providers including Postini, which is owned by Google.

3. The diagram in Exhibit 5.1 and accompanying text originally appeared in *Trusted E-mail Open Standard: A Comprehensive Policy and Technology Proposal for E-mail Reform*, a white paper published in 2003 by a company called ePrivacy Group; contributors to the paper included Vincent Schiavone, David Brussin, James Koenig, and Ray Everett-Church.

4. Several copies of this skit were available on YouTube at the time of writing; one was http://youtube.com/watch?v=anwy2MPT5RE.

5. See online article at www.templetons.com/brad/spamterm.html.

6. See www.messagelabs.com/intelligence.aspx for the list of monthly and annual reports; the 2007 report was available from www.messagelabs.com/mlireport/ MLI_2007_Annual_Security_Report.pdf.

7. The term "E-mail Service Provider" applies to companies that provide e-mail addresses but not necessarily the Internet connection used to access those addresses. Google is a prime example with its Gmail; other examples include AOL, MSN, and Yahoo, although all three of these have at times offered Internet connectivity as well as e-mail and thus operated as Internet Service Providers as well as E-mail Service Providers.

8. At that time the author was the owner of the cobb.com domain. During a 15-month period, starting in 2001 and going into 2002, he monitored spam delivered to cobb.com and recorded a remarkably consistent 10 percent month-on-month spam volume growth rate.

9. Located at www.commtouch.com/site/Resources/calculator.asp.

10. Janusz Lukasiak, "Blocking Spam Relaying and Junk Mail" (October 1999), www.jisc.ac.uk/publications/publications/blockingspamfinalreport.aspx.

11. The exact terminology for block lists and black holes is a subject of ongoing debate involving possible issues of trademark infringement and political correctness.

12. David Brussin, Stephen Cobb, Ray Everett-Church, and Vincent J. Schiavone, "Network Resource Theft Prevention: Destroying the Economics of Spam," http://cobbassociates.com/library/spamsquelcher_wp2.pdf.

13. See www.rfc-archive.org/getrfc.php?rfc=4408.

14. See www.rfc-archive.org/getrfc.php?rfc=4406

15. Sentences for spam convictions have been rising steadily. Although many of those convicted have appealed, at least half a dozen have now served jail time.

16. Federal Trade Commission, "The CAN-SPAM Act: Requirements for Commercial E-mailers," www.ftc.gov/bcp/conline/pubs/buspubs/canspam.shtm.

17. See www.ftc.gov and http://onguardonline.gov/phishing.html.

CHAPTER 21

WEB-BASED VULNERABILITIES

Anup K. Ghosh, Kurt Baumgarten, Jennifer Hadley, and Steven Lovaas

21.1 INTRODUCTION. This chapter systematically reviews the primary software components that make up Web applications, with a primary focus on e-commerce, and provides an overview of the risks to each of these components.[1] The goal of this chapter is to point out that every system will have risks to its security and privacy that need to be systematically analyzed and ultimately addressed.

21.2 BREAKING E-COMMERCE SYSTEMS. To make a system more secure, it may be advisable to break it. Finding the vulnerabilities in a system is necessary in order to strengthen it, but breaking an e-commerce system requires a different mind-set from that of the programmers who developed it. Instead of thinking about developing within a specification, a criminal or hacker looks outside the specifications.

Hackers believe that rules exist only to be broken, and they always use a system in unexpected ways. In doing so, they usually follow the path of least resistance. Those areas perceived to provide the strongest security, or the most resistance to hacking, will likely be ignored. For example, if a system uses Secure Sockets Layer (SSL) to encrypt Web sessions between Web clients and the Web server, a hacker will not try to break the encryption stream but instead will look for an easier way to get at the data after they are decrypted and stored in the clear.

Hackers go where the money is—sometimes literally, sometimes not. They typically try to hack into a site only if there is some reward for their effort. Sometimes hackers are motivated by money, but as often the motivation is the lure of fame, notoriety, or acceptance by a peer group. The level of protection should be commensurate with the value of the resource being protected. For instance, a Web site that publishes the menus for local restaurants may not be seen as a target for a denial of service or any other type attack. Such a Web site simply is not as attractive a target as a bank's online Web site, where a hacker can certainly gain in notoriety and even profit financially. Similarly, most people do not bother encrypting e-mail messages due to lack of security awareness, and because most potential snoopers are not interested in ordinary personal e-mail. Sensitive e-mail from a high-profile organization should be encrypted, however, in order to protect valuable intellectual capital.

It is important to remember that the e-commerce system is a chain that is only as strong as its weakest link.[2] Hackers naturally attempt to attack that point of least resistance. This explains why a site may deliberately set up a honeypot (a sacrificial system) with appealingly vulnerable services in order to track and monitor potential hackers. In e-commerce, or any systems with a Web presence, cryptography often is perceived to provide the strongest level of protection; thus, hackers generally attack host-side services and client-side content.

Maintaining strong host security, both inside and outside of perimeters, is critically important. One unfortunate side effect of corporate perimeters is that system administrators tend to overlook host-based security, which may leave the host completely vulnerable. The result is that once hackers make it through or around perimeter devices and policies (e.g., firewalls, routers, or even receptionists), they can leverage the internal trust relationships to compromise many resources including workstations, servers, and phone systems. The prudent administrator will exercise equal concern both at the entry to systems and within those systems.

21.3 CASE STUDY OF BREAKING AN E-BUSINESS. Consider an online investing e-business application and how a hacker might go about disassembling its security for malicious or financial gain. Online investing is very popular for several reasons. Rather than waiting for quarterly statements in the mail or dealing with a phone menu, customers can quickly view the status, balances, and current value of investment holdings by visiting the Web pages of their portfolio managers. If they wish to buy and sell equity shares on demand, they can establish online Web-enabled brokerage accounts. Exhibit 21.1 shows a simplified workflow diagram of an online investing application that enables users with established accounts to view portfolio holdings and cash balances, to update the stocks tracked, and to conduct online trades.

To see how this application can be broken, it is helpful to look at a sample network architecture that implements the online application. Exhibit 21.2 shows the network architecture of the system that implements the online investing application, along with example exploits. The system consists of the end users' client machines, the Internet, routers, firewall, front-end Web and e-mail servers, application servers, databases, and workstations.

There are many ways a hacker could break this online application. Exhibit 21.2 shows one possible scenario. In step 1 of the attack, the hacker uses the Internet and a Web browser to misuse one of the CGI (Common Gateway Interface) scripts that invoke the application on a server. The CGI script could be a development CGI script

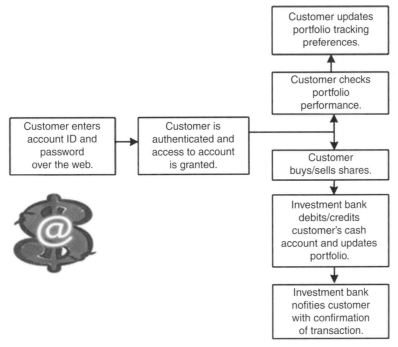

EXHIBIT 21.1 Online Investing Application

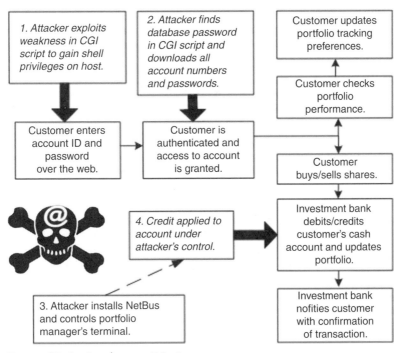

EXHIBIT 21.2 Breaking an E-Business

inadvertently left on the server before going into production, a default CGI script from an application server distribution, or a script that implements flawed logic in the online investment application. Exploiting CGI scripts via cross-site scripting or other common exploit methods allow hackers to gain shell access to Web servers. CGI script vulnerabilities are discussed later in this chapter.

The vulnerability need not be in a CGI script. Application servers can be implemented in Java, C, C++, Perl, or Python in various application server frameworks. The difficulty lies not in which language the business application logic is developed; more important are the vulnerabilities introduced by the complex logic at this middleware layer. One of the key problems in the development of application middleware is poor input sanity checking; that is, the developers fail to impose limits on acceptable input. The hacker can exploit the lack of input sanity checking to feed the application server unexpected input used in system commands. This technique can gain shell privileges on the machine.

Although application server misuse is a common way of breaking into systems, there are many other ways to gain the initial access in step 1 of the attack. For instance, the Web and mail servers may be running any of several network services, such as *FTP* and *BIND/DNS,* which may be misconfigured and thus "poisoned." The Web and mail server software themselves may be vulnerable to attack. Many popular commercial Web and mail servers have been vulnerable to buffer overflow attacks that often permit full system root privileges on the host.[3] Once attackers gain system privileges on an internal host, they can exploit the inherent internal trust often woven among machines through network policies in order to gain access to other systems on the network. This strategy is precisely what the attacker follows in step 2 of the attack illustrated in Exhibit 21.2.

Once attackers have access to the various file systems on the application server, they can view source code of CGI scripts or other application middleware to discover customer account numbers, passwords, and even database administrator passwords for accessing the back-end databases. From there, they can download important and confidential client information stored in the database. In step 3 of the attack, the attacker leverages the internal privileges gained to plant backdoors into the system unnoticed. A suite of software, commonly known as a rootkit and available to hackers, allows them not only to get into a system unnoticed but also to erase their tracks in audit logs. In the example shown, the hacker installs a rogue remote administration program known as Back Orifice, which provides the ability to remotely administer the host and network with the same privileges and power as an authentic system administrator.

At this point in the attack, the hacker has assumed total control of the systems and any Web-facing or commerce-related processes, with many options including:

- Stealing customer or company information for the purpose of financial gain
- Defacing the Web pages for notoriety or to publicize an agenda
- Working in a stealthy manner to uncover proprietary business information and other confidential intellectual capital (espionage)
- Blackmailing the business with threats of discrediting it
- Subverting the application for any other personal gain

Step 4 of the attack illustrates the last case, where the attacker credits a personal cash account. The hacker must move quickly enough to withdraw these funds before traditional back-end auditing discovers the discrepancy. There have been many defaced

Web pages of government agencies, and other important sites, and many reported instances of the other cases. Of course, some companies are understandably reluctant to publicize events that might lessen customer confidence, yet in many cases, legislation now requires the disclosure of a breach.

Unfortunately, it takes only a single flawed, unpatched computer, or overlooked vulnerability, for a hacker to compromise a system as a whole. Although *defense-in-depth* (using multiple forms of security, such as firewalls on the perimeter and intrusion detection inside the network) is a popular strategy, often multiple layers of defense fall like a house of cards when a single hole is exploited. For example, an attacker who gains *root* capability can disable all other security measures. The problem is known as an *asymmetric* attack because it is much more difficult and costly to defend against such an attack than to launch one. Although a committed hacker may be capable of spending as much time as is needed to break into a system, a company cannot spend as much money as needed to defend itself against all possibilities.

The number of flaws that can be exploited is staggering, considering all the different platforms and devices that make up current information technology (IT) infrastructures. Compounding the problem is the fact that a hacker can work in relative anonymity using a $500 computer and modem to launch attacks. Even worse, hackers can work from any number of Internet kiosks available in airports, malls, cafés, and even laundries. As hackers get more sophisticated, and as more easily utilized scripts become available, attacks will be launched from mobile devices that can roam in and out of different geographic zones and then be discarded—making tracking of the attacker next to impossible.

21.4 WEB APPLICATION SYSTEM SECURITY. In spite of the fairly bleak picture painted here, organizations can effectively manage their risk from hackers. As in many other security domains, the security posture or stance assumed by the organization is critical for deterring and thwarting hackers. To use a physical-world analogy, consider burglars who intend to break into homes in a nice neighborhood. As the burglars scope out potential targets, they will notice some houses with burglar alarms—complete with conspicuous signs of the alarm systems—and some without. In all likelihood, the burglars will bypass the houses with the burglar alarms and move on to the other, less well-protected targets. Thus, the security stance assumed by the owner plays an important role.

Every organization must first determine its desired security stance as documented in its security policy. System administrators use the security policy to configure the systems, routers, firewalls, and remote access solutions. Without an explicit security policy, there is no way to determine what the security stance of the organization is, how to configure its systems, or even if a nonobvious security breach has occurred. Once the security policy is developed, the actual security implementation must be assessed. That is, the system must be tested and evaluated to determine how well it meets its security policy. Usually there is a difference between the desired stance and the actual stance. This difference is the security gap between where the organization would like to be (secure against particular threats) and where it actually is in practice.

The process of developing a security policy and evaluating the organization's systems against that policy will identify not only the gaps between the actual security stance and the desired posture but also weaknesses in the security policy itself. It is important to have an independent party, preferably an outside party, evaluate the security stance of the organization. A third party can fairly assess whether the organization's system upholds the security policy. If the group that develops the security policy or the system

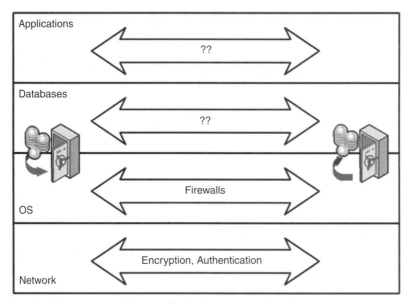

EXHIBIT 21.3   Layered View of an E-Business Application

configuration is also responsible for evaluating it, the evaluation may be biased, and potential vulnerabilities may be overlooked. This may occur not through ill will or dishonesty but rather because of the difficulty of being objective about one's own work.

21.5   PROTECTING WEB APPLICATIONS.   Web application security can be understood from different views. First, consider the view of e-businesses in Exhibit 21.3. The diagram shows two e-businesses communicating over the Internet, perhaps performing business-to-business types of transactions.

In this view, the lowest layer of the e-business is the *networking layer*. At the networking layer, there are concerns about the reliability, integrity, and confidentiality of the data that runs over the communications channel. This layer is of particular concern because the Internet is a public switched network, meaning that any number of third parties may have access to the data that traverses the nodes of the Internet on the way from the data source to its destination. Also, the Internet Protocol (IP) is a connectionless protocol, which means there is no dedicated circuit between source and destination. As a result, packets sent during a given session may take different routes to their destination, depending on traffic congestion and routing algorithms. Because IP is an unreliable datagram protocol (i.e., IP uses independent packets forwarded from node to node, but there is no guarantee of successful transmission), the networking layer includes a connection-oriented reliable transmission layer such as TCP (Transmission Control Protocol) that ensures that dropped or lost packets are retransmitted and that bit flips that may have occurred during transmission (e.g., over wireless networks) are corrected.

Although TCP/IP provides for more reliable delivery of Internet packets, IP version 4 does not provide *secure* connection services. Typically, this means that there is no *guarantee* of confidentiality, identification, or even delivery of packets sent from one Internet host to another. Because packets often traverse several Internet nodes from source to destination, packet contents can be intercepted by third parties, copied, substituted, or even destroyed. This is the risk that most people citing risks of e-commerce have decried; they have overlooked the more substantive risks of e-commerce dealing with server- and client-side security and privacy. IPv6 holds promise to bring many security improvements to the network layer, but it has not been deployed widely in the United States. Fortunately, even in IPv4, we have good solutions to the data confidentiality problem. Cryptographic techniques can provide strong guarantees for data confidentiality, authentication of parties, and integrity of data sent during the transmission. Furthermore, digital signatures can be used to sign received mail in a "return receipt" application that provides guarantees of delivery of e-mail. Thus, as shown in Exhibit 21.3, we can use encryption services to protect data transmitted over the network.

The operating system (OS), or *platform*, that hosts the Web applications lives on the networking layer. In a layered model, the services of one layer use the services of the lower layer and provide services to upper layers. The network layer often is thought of as a core portion of the operating system; however, from a layered services point of view, the OS software runs on top of the network layer.

Operating systems are notoriously rife with software flaws that affect system security. Operating systems are vulnerable because commercial OSs today are immensely complex; for instance, the Windows Vista operating system is purported to have more than 50 million lines of source code. It is impossible to catch all software design and programming errors that may have security consequences in a platform this complex. Even though UNIX operating systems have been in use for the better part of 30 years, new flaws in OS utilities are found on a weekly basis across all the different UNIX platform variants.[4]

Security holes in the platform are critical by nature. That is, if the OS itself is vulnerable to exploitation, security provided by the application can be compromised by holes in the platform. The OS is always the foundation on which applications are built, so cracks in the foundation make for weak security at the application layer. As Exhibit 21.3 suggests, firewalls provide protection against some operating system flaws. One of the key roles of firewalls is their ability to shut down services offered to *logical domain addresses*.

Using Internet domain addresses, the firewall administrator can partition Internet addresses into *trusted* and *untrusted* domain ranges. For instance, any Internet address outside the company's domain can be considered untrusted. As a result, all OS services, such as remote logins, can be shut down to everyone outside of the company's domain. Even within a company, the domains can be partitioned so that certain *subdomains* are trusted for access to certain machines, but others are not. The key benefit then of firewalls is their ability to restrict access to the platform through *offered services* (i.e., specific functions that pass data through the firewall). As a result, firewalls can make it easy to hide OS flaws from untrusted entities.

Even so, firewalls are vulnerable to data- or code-driven attacks through offered services. These are sometimes called "allowed path" vulnerabilities. For instance, an attack through SMTP (mail) or HTTP (Web) will not be stopped by a firewall if the firewall is configured to let e-mail and Web services through, as is necessary for e-commerce. Firewalls also will not stop OS exploits from insiders or from the trusted entities that are granted access to the platform. However, it is important to realize that firewalls, if properly configured, can close down exposure to a significant number of platform vulnerabilities simply by denying untrusted outsiders access to platform utilities and services. Exhibit 21.3 illustrates reasonable protection from network- and platform-based attacks but not from application and database attacks. The database layer is shown separately in the diagram because of the importance of its role in e-commerce; however, database attacks usually can be considered as a type of application attack.

Application-based attacks represent a critical issue that is gaining more attention in recent years. There is no simple solution, but there is a growing sense that the security provided by a firewall, an SSL-enabled Web site, and encryption, together with digital certificates and signatures, is not enough. These measures are necessary but not sufficient. Applications, above all, *are* the online business. The Payment Card Industry Data Security Standards (PCIDSS) puts any organization processing credit card transactions on notice that Web application vulnerability protection was required as of June 2008. The PCIDSS specifies either "having all custom application code reviewed for common vulnerabilities by an organization that specializes in application security" or "installing an application layer firewall in front of Web-facing applications."[5]

Online applications are increasingly sophisticated, and the software that implements the application logic has become highly complex, requiring component-based and object-oriented paradigms such as Enterprise Java Beans, CORBA, and DCOM/COM services. Collectively, these are known as *application servers*. The key point, however, is that because the application logic is custom and complex, it is often rife with errors in implementation or logic that can be and often are exploited by hackers.

Application security must not be confused with marketing claims. A secure online application is one that is resistant to attacks. It is not simply one that authenticates end users, encrypts transaction data, provides nonrepudiation of transactions, and guarantees service. These are all matters of importance that address characteristics of the transaction, not properties of the software. The remainder of this chapter addresses the software problem in some detail. The next section provides a different view of e-commerce systems from the layered view discussed previously. It identifies vulnerabilities in the different software components and strategies for managing the risks.

21.6 COMPONENTS AND VULNERABILITIES IN E-COMMERCE SYSTEMS.
Exhibit 21.4 shows a generic multitier architecture of an e-business, together with a summary of the types of vulnerabilities and risks to each of the major components. Using the Internet, Web clients (running on PCs or handheld devices) interface with a front-end Web server, a middleware layer of business application logic, back-end databases, an ERP system, supply-chain management software, and even some legacy systems that are now brought to the Internet.

21.6.1 Client-Side Risks.
Most e-commerce is performed using standard Web browsers and mail clients. Increasingly, e-commerce is being performed on handheld mobile devices such as personal digital assistants (PDAs) and mobile phones. The security risks particular to wireless devices are covered in Chapter 33 of this *Handbook*. Client-side security risks are mainly from malicious mobile code such as Web scripts, ActiveX controls, and hostile Java applets.[6] Another major risk in client-side software is loss of privacy.[7] Each computer, with its related software, receives and transmits a great deal of personal identifying information (PII). For instance, browsers may convey information about the computers (name, IP address, browser type, version, company name) and sometimes about the users themselves, particularly if automatic form-filling features have been enabled. Browsers also are used to track movements through the Web. For instance, every Web site the browser visits typically gets a record of the previous site from which the user entered. Banner ads in Web pages also track which sites have been visited in order to create a profile of Web usage, and cookies can be

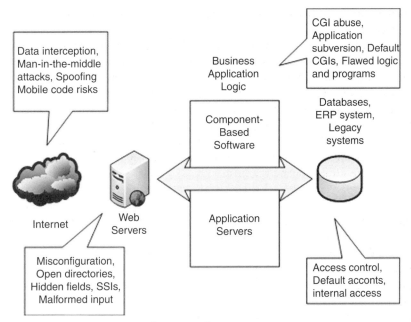

EXHIBIT 21.4 Multitier Architecture of an E-Business

placed on end-user systems for the purpose of tracking and at times re-creating user input.

A class of more insidious programs, known as *spyware*, can send information about computer usage out to specific sites, often without the user's knowledge or approval. One of the key risks with client-side software is that users simply do not know what the programs are revealing about themselves, or to whom. A simple principle is that a program should not be sending out any data that the user does not know about. An audit of the programs on any given machine probably would reveal that quite a few are in violation of that principle. Although most spyware programs are written to provide marketing data for software vendors or to redirect a user to predetermined sites, many manipulate and target users more effectively by spying on usage activity and even installing additional malicious code. For example, SpectorSoft markets a spyware tool known as eBlaster to people who suspect their spouses are engaging in illicit online affairs. This type of spyware program spies on user activity, from keystrokes to screen shots, and sends a log of the activity out over the network to a predetermined logging site. Spyware can be identified using diagnostic programs such as Ad-Aware from Lavasoft (www.lavasoft.com), but because of the dynamic nature of spyware technology, it may be difficult to identify all possibilities of infection.

A final client-side risk that businesses need to be especially concerned about is the risk of malicious executables that run on their user workstations. The desktop machine is like a petri dish for software: It is constantly changing and growing with new software executables—some of an unsavory nature. Malicious software, or *malware* as it is now known, finds many ways of infecting machines. For instance, one common way of disseminating malicious software is via e-mail attachments. Another is by masquerading as legitimate software on a Web page available for download. Users often upload and download software to and from internal network file shares. In addition, USB "thumb drives" and even old-fashioned floppy disks are still a viable way of transmitting malicious software. The Back Orifice "remote administration kit" is a well-known example of malicious software that, when installed, will allow anyone—including a hacker—to administer and control a machine remotely. Some malware products, running on an internal machine, may compromise the entire network because a remote hacker can control a trusted resource, possibly with enterprise administration rights. Data leakage and theft offered by the initial spyware infection can result in incidents that might undermine the integrity, authenticity, availability, or auditability of an entire data infrastructure. It is essential, therefore, that corporations carefully filter and closely monitor the application software that is downloaded and run (with or without the user's knowledge) on all systems from the e-commerce perimeter to the individual internal hosts.

21.6.2   Network Protocol Risks.   Network risks primarily arise from sending confidential data over the Internet—a public, packet-switching network. Many good protocols address the risks of sending confidential data over the Internet.[8] In fact, a few years ago, the list included:

- SET
- SSL
- S/HTTP
- S/MIME
- CyberCash

Although some of these protocols are still around in one form or another, the industry has generally accepted SSL as the protocol of choice for secure Web browser transactions. The objective of most secure network protocols is to layer security properties on top of the TCP/IP network layers. Although TCP/IP provides reliable and robust delivery of datagrams over the Internet, it does not provide confidentiality, authentication, or strong message-integrity services. These are the properties that secure protocols provide. Some go even further. For instance, SET-compliant protocols leave the credit card number encrypted even at the merchant site. Since the merchant does not need to know the consumer's credit card number, by hiding the number from the merchant, a significant portion of credit card fraud can be eliminated. Rather than decrypting the credit card number at the merchant site, it is passed in encrypted form from the merchant to the credit-issuing bank. There it is decrypted, and the merchant's account is credited the amount of the purchase. The protocol details of SET, SSL, and other e-commerce protocols are described in Chapter 30 of this *Handbook*, in *E-Commerce Security: Weak Links, Best Defenses,* and in other books as well.[9]

Depending on the needs of an online business application, there is a requirement for more or less of the security properties afforded by secure protocols. For most Web browsing, a secure protocol is unnecessary; the standard Web protocol, HTTP, suffices. However, when customers send confidential or personal information to a site, a secure protocol that encrypts the data is preferable. The de facto secure protocol standard is SSL, now implemented in every standard Web browser. SSL will not only negotiate a secret session key between the Web site and a client to encrypt the data, but it also will authenticate the Web site. The Web site must have a valid certificate endorsed by a Certificate Authority, which the users implicitly trust. Using a list of trusted Certificate Authorities maintained within the client browser, access can be prevented to other, untrusted sites. Once the connection is established, the user can verify that the Web site is, in fact, the one intended by examining the site certificate. Users rarely do this in practice, but the certificate is available and should be more widely utilized.

These secure properties—that is, encrypted sessions and host site authentication—serve the purpose for most online commerce applications. Some applications, though, may demand even stronger security services. For instance, banking and investment applications often transmit highly confidential information, with the possibility of huge financial losses through inadvertent error or intentional fraud. These types of transactions require not only confidentiality of the data, but also authentication of the client. A financial institution must never give access to account information or permit transactions without authenticating the user.

Common identification schemes on the Internet include simple user name and password authentication. A much more secure solution is to require strong client authentication using client certificates. SSL supports client certificates, although sites rarely use this capability because it involves requiring customers to obtain a certificate from a Certification Authority.

In the future, e-commerce protocols will need to be increasingly sophisticated if they are to meet the stringent security and privacy requirements of new Internet applications. For example, as criminal, medical, patent, and other important databases migrate to the Internet, the protocols developed for accessing them need to consider the security and privacy needs of the database owners and maintainers, as well as those of the client or requester. Today, the progress in genomics is producing much information about the likelihood of developing deadly disease based on a genetic DNA sequence. This knowledge raises moral and ethical questions as to how much information about potential diseases should be revealed to doctors and patients, and also raises the specter of such information getting into the wrong hands once it is accessible on the Internet.

Consider the case of a doctor querying an online genetic disease database with a patient's DNA sequence. The online application attempts to match the DNA sequence with diseases that might develop in the future. If the database were maintained by a commercial entity such as an insurance provider, the patient almost certainly would not want the company to know of any disease that might be returned as the result of a query, because that information could be used to deny both insurance and employment.

Likewise, the database maintainer probably would not want to know of the query or of its result, as such knowledge might put it at risk for lawsuits, should the information be leaked. Furthermore, the database maintainer would want the rest of the database to remain inaccessible except for specific results returned to an approved inquiry. Preventing access to any other information in the database would help to protect the commercial interests of the company, because then the database could not be duplicated easily. Nor could queries be made without a cost-tracking mechanism. To support this dual model of secure and private information access, e-commerce protocols need to be developed and commercialized that not only encrypt data in transmission but also consider the total security and privacy needs of both parties to the transaction.

Another e-commerce application area that will require better security and privacy protocols involves applications that accept e-cash or digital coin payments. Currently, most online payment schemes use either credit or debit cards, with payments made from the buyer's checking account at a bank. Payments are made either with online verification of funds or with off-line batch payments at the end of the day. A number of applications, particularly those involving payments of a few dollars or even pennies, are being created that cannot support the costs of a bank-based transaction.

Many commercial services and products, such as vending machines and parking meters, are coin-activated and do not require customers to have an account or a line of credit. Although efforts are being made to convert such services to computerized devices, with micropayment capabilities, it will be many years before this is actually accomplished. In any case, there will always be customers who want to pay with cash or its electronic equivalent, so that the transaction cannot be tracked by a third party, such as a bank or a creditor.

Newer online applications for micropayments may include collecting fees for downloading music, data, weather reports, stock quotations, articles from magazines, and pages from books. Many of these applications are provided today without charge and supported by banner advertising, but a concern for profits is motivating most Web sites to seek additional sources of income. Whatever the application, there is a need for cash-based alternatives to the current account-based system for making payments. The key security and privacy concerns are with ensuring that e-cash is properly spent and accounted for and that anonymity is preserved throughout. Several protocols have been developed with these goals in mind, but none has reached commercial success or adoption by the vendor community. As mobile e-commerce begins to drive more traditionally cash-based transactions (e.g., parking meters, vending machines, and ticket booths), wireless vendors may adopt these new digital cash-based protocols.

Regardless of the network protocol used in an e-commerce application, the key concern is for those attackers who will attempt to breach the easiest obstacle in their quest to obtain system privileges and unauthorized access to data. If the security provided by the network protocol is perceived to be strong, attackers will look for alternatives that bypass the network security. For instance, these types of standard attacks from the hacker's toolkit will bypass the security provided by most e-commerce protocols:

- **Man-in-the-middle attacks.** Capturing transmissions in transit for eavesdropping or forgery
- **DNS attacks.** Altering records in the worldwide Domain Name System to misdirect connections to the wrong addresses
- **War dialing.** Automated testing of every phone number in a block of numbers
- **Exploiting software vulnerabilities in network services.** Such as FTP, Bind, SMTP, and HTTP servers
- **Internal access.** Improper use of authorized access by an insider (employee, contractor)
- **Leveraging trusted hosts.** Attacking from another system that has a privileged relationship with the target system
- **Brute-force crypto attacks.** Automated testing of all possible decryption keys to decipher a ciphertext

In summary, it is important not only to select the appropriate network protocol for each online application but also to avoid a false sense of security that might arise from use of a "secure" network protocol. Good security engineering will consider vulnerabilities in other components of the system that are more attractive targets to determined hackers.

21.6.3   Business Application Logic.   The business application logic pictured in Exhibit 21.4 represents one of the key areas of vulnerability in e-commerce systems. The program logic encodes what the online business is offering in terms of products, services, and customer convenience. It also defines the look and feel of the Web site and provides all of the interactive features, such as dynamic Web pages, personalized Web pages, and online transaction capabilities. Because each application is unique, the software that implements the logic must be, in many cases, custom-developed for each particular site.

In contrast, most of the other software components of a Web site are commercial off-the-shelf (COTS) software. For instance, the Web server, back-end databases, and supply-chain logistics software are often purchased off the shelf from software vendors. With COTS software, the end user has no control over the code and therefore is not responsible for coding bug fixes. When software bugs in COTS software are discovered, the software vendor usually issues a patch or incorporates a bug fix in the next release version. Software vendors can fix discovered bugs, but they depend on customer sites to actually apply the patches or upgrades to the software. In practice, this occurs less often than desired and is a significant reason why many Internet-based systems are vulnerable.[10] The most important task in securing COTS software systems is to make sure that: (1) they are properly configured for a secure installation according to the site's security policy, (2) the software is properly updated to the current version and patch level, and (3) administrators are aware of the risks associated with bugs in the software.

Because many business applications are custom-developed, either by an in-house staff or by outsourcing to an e-business developer, the programs represent a key risk for several reasons. The dynamic, interactive nature of e-businesses, coupled with increasingly sophisticated online services, requires a significant amount of development to code the logic. As a result, the application programs tend to be very complex pieces of software, likely to contain flaws, and susceptible to the kinds of attacks launched against Web sites. In practice, errors in design and implementation of business application logic often compromise the security of an e-business.

Traditionally, the middle tier of software is implemented on Web servers using the Common Gateway Interface (CGI) and more recently PHP (Hypertext Processing). CGI and PHP scripts are programs that run on the Web server machine as separate processes from the Web server software. The Web server invokes these general-purpose programs in response to user requests. The CGI/PHP script's main function is to process user input and to perform some service, such as retrieving data or dynamically creating a Web page for the end user. Because CGI and PHP scripts process untrusted user input, the security risks associated with them and other forms of middle-tier software are extremely high. Many attacks against Web-based systems are implemented by exploited CGI/PHP scripts. And while CGI and PHP scripts can be written in any general-purpose programming language, they are written most often in Perl, C, Tcl, and Python.

More recently, component-based software (CBS) is making inroads in e-commerce applications as well as in standard Web applications. The purpose of CBS is to develop, purchase, and reuse proven software in order to implement application logic quickly, easily, and with high quality. Two of the more popular component frameworks for e-commerce applications are Enterprise JavaBeans (EJB) using XML and Java 2 Enterprise Edition (J2EE), which supports component-based Java. Other component models include the Object Management Group's (OMG) Common Object Request Broker Architecture (CORBA) and Microsoft's Common Object Model (COM) and Distributed COM (DCOM). These component frameworks are the glue that enables software components to use standard infrastructure services while hiding the details of the implementation by using well-defined interfaces.

Business application logic, when coded in CBS systems, usually runs on application servers with particular component models, such as EJB, CORBA, COM, and DCOM. CBS also provides an interface to back-end services such as database management, enterprise resource planning (ERP), and legacy software systems.

In addition to supporting traditional CGI functions, component-based software is expected to enable distributed, business-to-business applications over the Internet. The component-based software paradigm also supports good software engineering, as described later. The Unified Modeling Language (UML) facilitates object-oriented analysis and design for component-based frameworks. In addition, as the market for component-based software expands, many standard business application components will be available for purchase off the shelf.

Although the benefits of component-based software are numerous, they pose security hazards similar to those of CGI scripts. Component-based software enables development in general-purpose programming languages such as Java, C, and C++, which can execute with all the rights and privileges of server processes. Like CGI, they process untrusted user input, and because component-based software can be used to build sophisticated, large-scale applications, the likelihood for errors may be even greater than for simple CGI scripts. Regardless of the implementation—CGI or application servers—the security risks of server-side software are great, and therefore server-side software must be designed and implemented carefully.

The key risks in the middleware layer of e-commerce sites are:

- Misconfiguration of the CGI
- Default and development CGI scripts being left on the production server
- CGI misuse
- Application subversion
- Flawed logic
- Programming errors

21.6.4   CGI Script Vulnerabilities.   CGI scripts are frequent targets of attackers because they are often misconfigured and vulnerable to misuse.[11] When designing CGI scripts, it is prudent to expect the unexpected, particularly the malicious attack. Although the Web designer has control over the content of CGI scripts, there is no control over what end users are going to send to them. Also, often overlooked are vulnerabilities of CGI scripts that exist on the server as part of the distribution but that are not actually used in the application. Some CGI scripts, included as part of the Web server distribution, have well-known flaws that can be exploited to obtain unauthorized access to the server. Even if the default CGI scripts are not used as part of the Web server pages, anyone can access them by simply knowing the script names.

One of the most common—yet easily preventable—security hazards is misconfiguration of software, especially CGI scripts. One feature supported by many Web servers is the ability of individuals throughout an organization to write CGI scripts and have them execute from their own directories. Although useful for prettying up personal Web pages, this feature also can introduce system security hazards. In Web-based applications, the Web server should be configured to prevent CGI scripts from executing anywhere but in a single CGI directory under control of the system administrator.

The script-aliased CGI mode for Web servers ensures that CGI scripts will execute only from an explicitly named directory in the server configuration file. In addition, the CGI script path is not named in the URL to the CGI. Rather, the server "aliases" the explicit path to the CGI script to a chosen name, such as *cgi-bin*. Thus, running the server in script-aliased CGI mode prevents rogue CGI scripts from executing while it also hides the explicit path to the CGI scripts.

The CGI script directories also should be properly configured using OS access controls. For instance, if CGI scripts are written in a compiled language such as C, the script sources should be excluded from the document root of the Web server, so that they cannot be accessed via the Web. They should be accessible to the system administrator or Web content development group only, and inaccessible to everyone else in the organization. If the script sources fall into the hands of malicious perpetrators, the source code can be inspected for flaws, making the perpetrator's job even easier. Access to the CGI executables directory, frequently called the cgi-bin, should be properly controlled as well. Only the Web server and administrator need access to this directory. Liberal access permissions to the CGI executables directory give those with malicious intent the opportunity to place their own scripts within the site.

Most CGI scripts are written in scripting languages such as Perl, JavaScript, and Python. Scripting languages are useful for rapidly prototyping systems, but they also let the developer write dangerous code very easily. For instance, it is easy to construct system commands with user input, a potentially dangerous situation. Writing the same system functionality requires several lines of programming code and knowledge of system libraries. The easy accessibility of scripting languages makes them appealing, but also threatening to security-critical applications. It is also important to prohibit access to interpreters from the Web server. For instance, system administrators may be tempted to include the Perl interpreter in CGI script directories; however, doing so provides direct Web access to interactively execute Perl commands—an extremely dangerous configuration.

Finally, administrators should account for every CGI program on the server in terms of its purpose, origin, and modifications. Remove CGI scripts that do not serve a business function, and view with suspicion CGI scripts that are distributed with operating systems and Web servers, downloaded from the Internet, or purchased commercially. These steps will eliminate most of the potentially dangerous CGI scripts. Once a stable set of CGI programs is established, make a digital hash of the program executables (e.g., using MD5 or SHA-1) to enable future integrity checks.

21.6.5 Application Subversion.   Application subversion attacks are not discussed often in relation to e-businesses, but they represent a significant threat to most online applications. Application subversion is a form of program misuse. Unlike buffer overflow attacks, application subversion attacks exploit the program logic without violating program integrity, in order to elevate user privileges and gain unauthorized access to data. It is the very complexity of the target program that gives the attacker the means to gain unauthorized access. Application subversion attacks use programs in ways that the program's designers and developers did not anticipate. Typically, these attacks are not scripted, but rather developed from online interactive use and subsequent abuse.

Referring to Exhibit 21.1, an application subversion attack will attempt to discover ways of short-circuiting paths in the workflow. For instance, there may be a hidden path that lets the user gain access to account information without being authenticated to that account. Many such attacks work on the premise that access to confidential information is not properly authenticated.

Another common attack sends malformed input to a program. Many Web pages use forms extensively to drive the application, while the data input on the form is checked using client-side scripting. An attacker can take advantage of the fact that many online application developers assume that the client is going to use the form properly and that the scripts will check all input sent to the site. The attacker can examine the data stream sent by the form and then, rather than using the form, send a modified data stream via URL within the browser or incorporating it into a custom command of the attacker's choosing. An attacker may be able to obtain access to the application by placing system commands in the input stream. If the input stream is subsequently used in a *system()* call by the online application, the end user may force the execution of system commands on the attacker's behalf.

Some application developers rely heavily on hidden fields in the HTML document. Hidden fields allow the Web developer to include information on the page that is not displayed, although the end user can see the hidden field data simply by viewing the HTML source. The mistake application developers make is, first, in believing that the end user cannot see the hidden fields, and, second, in relying on the integrity of the hidden field data for making online decisions. Some online merchants have made the mistake of including pricing information for items in the hidden fields and using those prices to determine the cost of the online transaction. The end user can simply change the pricing in the hidden fields and send lower prices back to the merchants, for a discounted purchase.

Another misuse of hidden fields is to redirect application output. For instance, some Web sites include file system path information in hidden fields on their Web pages. This information is used by a server-side script to determine where to read or write transaction information. Attackers, simply by changing the hidden field, can overwrite files or read files to which they should not have access. In some cases, it may be possible to store a program entered in a form field to be used later as a means of running a privileged shell on the remote system.

In summary, rigorous software quality assurance is necessary throughout the design and development of all Web-enabled and e-business applications, including front-end Web pages, application middleware, and operating systems. Once the software is believed to be immune to application misuse and subversion attacks, the system administrator must perform other activities to ensure the security of the e-business middleware:

- All unnecessary scripts or application server programs must be eliminated from the production server.

- Source code of application middleware must be carefully guarded against download or unauthorized access.

- Proper configuration of the CGI and application middleware is necessary to ensure executable access only to the correct application middleware, with the lowest practical privilege level. Sanity checking of inputs to application middleware must be done to ensure that only well-formed input is accepted.

- Testing of application code with the use of programs such as WebInspect by SPI Dynamics (www.spidynamics.com) that are specifically designed to discover flaws within Web-based applications.

21.6.6   Web Server Exploits.   Web server security has been written about and covered in detail, including in *E-Commerce Security: Weak Links, Best Defenses*[12] and *The Web Security Source Book*,[13] among other titles. Here we highlight some of the common exploits of Web servers used against many e-businesses.

21.6.6.1   Configuration.   The key to Web server security is its configuration. Like other complex pieces of software, Web servers are highly configurable to meet the needs of any given site. By default, most software vendors configure the software application for maximum functionality but minimum security. Thus, by default, when the server is first started, it is likely to be more permissive than any given company's security policy would like. The principal premise for configurability is in the variations that exist among sites.

A correctly configured Web server is the result of a policy that defines what access is allowed, to which individuals, for each resource. This policy, in turn, is used to configure routers, firewalls, and all public servers, such as the Web server. Configuring the Web server, while necessary, is by no means sufficient to secure the system. The discussion of application server exploits in Section 21.6.5 demonstrates this principle.

21.6.6.2 HTML Coding and Server-Side Includes. Once the Web server is configured as securely as possible, it is important to ensure that the Web pages themselves do not open holes in the security. Many Web page developers fall into some common pitfalls that may compromise the site's security. The preceding section mentioned the problem of relying on hidden fields in HTML for security or business-critical data. Users can abuse the hidden field data to subvert an application.

HTML offers other potential vulnerabilities. One that is most often criticized is *Server Side Includes* (SSI). The SSI configuration option, if enabled, allows directives to be embedded in HTML that the server will execute. For instance, if the next statement were embedded in an HTML document, it would direct the server to display the contents of the system password file:

```
<!--#exec /bin/cat /etc/passwd -->
```

Certainly Web pages should not be written with SSIs without a compelling reason. Although access to the HTML code is normally under control of the site, there are many ways an attacker might get an SSI into an HTML page. First, the attacker may have found another way into the system (e.g., by a CGI script exploit) but may want to provide either an easier backdoor or a redundant backdoor in case the CGI script vulnerability is found and closed. Once the CGI script is exploited, the attacker may implant an SSI directive within one of the site's HTML pages. Another way for an attacker to gain access is to have the server generate a Web page with the SSI of choice embedded in the HTML. How can an attacker do this? One approach exploits a server that generates dynamic HTML depending on the end user's data, preferences, or history. If the Web server ends up using some of the attacker's data to generate the HTML page, the attacker may be able to insert an SSI directive in the HTML. In summary, a better solution than continuously monitoring the HTML pages is simply to disable the SSI. In that event, even if SSIs were embedded, the server would not execute them. This is a configuration option, and like all system configuration files, the Web server configuration file should be protected by both file permission protection and file integrity checks, to ensure that it cannot be tampered with.

Although SSIs are often highlighted, a more common risk results from keeping documents or files in a publicly accessible portion of the Web server. The accessible portion of the Web server is called the *document root*. This root specifies the portion of the file system that the Web server can read and display to a Web client if requested. The document root can be a superset of the Web pages that are actually displayed when the user clicks through a Web site. There may be other documents in the document root that are not linked to or from Web pages. This does not mean they are not accessible, however. Simply giving the correct address for any document will result in either displaying or downloading the document to any Web client. Therein lies the problem.

It is worth noting that HTML content is no longer found only in files served by the Web. On the local hard disk, Microsoft Windows applications often install Help documents comprised of CHM ("chum") files and binaries. An attacker could exploit this vulnerability, leading to elevated privileges to the Windows XP "My computer" zone; unfortunately, local files are often overlooked and considered "trusted" during penetration tests.[14] Recognizing these risks, Microsoft Corp. began use of Microsoft Assistance Markup Language with the Windows Vista OS.

21.6.6.3 *Private Documents in Public Directories.* Private documents inadvertently placed in a public directory can result in a compromise of confidential information and loss of privacy. For example, if a database file of credit card numbers (say, *cardnumbers.mdb*) were stored in the document root of the Web server for a fictitious company, *mycompany.com*, this URL address typed in a Web browser could download the file: www.mycompany.com/cardnumbers.mdb

This risk is even greater if *directory browsing,* another configurable feature, is enabled. Directory browsing allows an end user to view the contents of the file system at a given directory level if a Web page does not exist with the same name. Directory browsing is really a way to explore the file system of another site using a Web browser. Users may view this feature if they go back one level from a given Web page by deleting the right-hand section of a page's URL and viewing its higher-level directory (e.g., in http://a.b.com/d/e.htm, one would remove the "e.htm" thus attempting to browse http://a.b.com/d/). Attackers can learn a lot of valuable information from viewing the contents of a directory including private files. Furthermore, the browser itself provides for clicking on a file name in the directory structure, which causes the file to be downloaded. Again, directory browsing, if enabled, is an open vulnerability and an unfortunately easy way to download private or confidential information.

21.6.6.4 *Cookies and Other Client-Side Risks.* Another potential vulnerability for an e-business is the use of *cookies.* Because HTTP is a *stateless protocol*, each new Web page that is visited has no memory of the last Web page that was visited by that user. Cookies are used to "keep state" between different Web pages visited in a given session. Cookies can make an e-business transaction appear to be seamless, sequential, and coordinated.

Most people, when discussing the risks of cookies, focus on the client-side privacy risks. Although these certainly exist, cookies also pose risks to the businesses that employ them. If the information contained in cookies is trusted, much the same way that the content in hidden fields is trusted, then the e-business may be vulnerable to cookie exploits called *cookie poisoning.* Some Web sites use cookies to carry authentication information for a given user who traverses its pages. Once users have authenticated themselves, their token of authentication may be carried with them via cookies from one Web page to all subsequent pages at that site. Using cookies is a fairly weak form of authentication. The cookie can be stolen easily by someone snooping a user's local area network or the Internet and then, with the information gained, to access the user's personal pages on the Web site. Secure protocols such as SSL should be employed to mitigate this risk.

Cookies also are used for other purposes that can introduce new vulnerabilities into critical transactions. Because cookies are under the control of end users, they can be changed in whatever manner a user chooses. If cookies are designed to instruct a Web server where to write a customer-specific file, by changing the cookie data, an end user might overwrite other customer files or even replace critical system files. Similarly, if cookies are used for carrying order information, as is common in electronic shopping carts, then changing the contents of the cookies would corrupt the transaction. This could result in an unauthorized, deep discount to the customer. This example and other cross-site scripting vulnerabilities are quite prevalent on today's Web. Browser exploits, HTTP header injection, cross-site request forgeries (CSRF), and numerous flavors of phishing are all examples of Web client/user attack.

Regardless of the technology used, it is important to examine the features and functions of Web servers from a security-critical viewpoint. Dependence on a specific technology for critical transactions demands that the technology be trustworthy, so that it does not provide vulnerable points of attack.

21.6.7 Database Security.   Databases traditionally have represented an important intellectual property of information-based companies. As a result, they have almost always been company proprietary and unavailable to public access. In the new model of business, however, many of these proprietary databases are made available on the Internet, often without careful consideration of the risks involved. The Web browser becomes the database query interface, often to unknown and untrusted entities.

Although there has been much research in database security over the last two decades, the commercial sector has adopted only two key tenets: authenticating and authorizing principals to certain objects. Access to databases thus is controlled by properly authenticating the credentials of the requesting principal and then verifying which objects the authenticated principal is authorized to access. Any online database application must perform these two functions rigorously to protect the most valuable assets of e-business as well as customer privacy.

Although many vendors claim secure channel access from the Web server to the database, there are many pitfalls. To start with, the fundamental reason why databases are vulnerable is that Web interfaces are commonly appended to what once may have been a closed and proprietary interface, without concern for overall security. Second, unsecured middleware programs such as CGI scripts or application servers usually mediate access from the Web server to the database. Web servers can provide client authentication from simple user name and password entry to strong certificated authentication. The needs of the business and the size of the accessing community will dictate which solution is feasible.

Despite obvious security advantages, most users do not store encrypted information in their databases, primarily for performance reasons. Encrypting and decrypting information on the fly during search, retrieve, and store operations can be too slow for real-time transactions. Also, even encrypting the data in a storage unit would not provide complete protection, as the online application must be able to read from and write to the database in clear text. Application-based attacks would still be able to get at the data while it was in plain, unencrypted text format.

Another key vulnerability of online databases also arises from application-based attacks. As described earlier, attacks that exploit vulnerabilities in the business-application logic often can provide unrestricted access to a database.

Attacks that exploit a buffer-overflow vulnerability in an application server program usually will be able to get command shell access on the remote server. From there, the attacker usually is able to find source code for the application server programs, such as Perl scripts or even C code, that are used to access the database. Because these programs *need* access to the database, they also must know the passwords used to access the various data partitions. If the programmers have foolishly *hard-coded* the passwords, then simply reviewing the source code may be enough to discover these passwords. With passwords in hand, the attacker can use the application server program via the Web interface to gain unauthorized access to the database. More directly, with a password it is possible to query a database from the command shell, using SQL commands or commands from the database language of choice.

Finally, like the other complex programs that run e-businesses, databases must be securely configured. Basic steps that the database administrator (DBA) needs to take include:

- Enforcing Web client authentication to the database
- Enforcing Web client authorization for access to database records
- Eliminating default database and database platform accounts
- Ensuring that passwords are read from encrypted files, not stored in program code
- Changing easily guessed passwords
- Configuring and maintaining internal access controls
- Auditing log files for suspicious activity

Account maintenance can be a key vulnerability in database management. Often the database software vendor will create a DBA account with an easily guessed password. Worse, DBAs may use the default account and password distributed with the database installation. This permits an attacker who has knowledge of the default passwords to gain access to all portions of the database by assuming the identity of the database administrator.

21.6.8 Platform Security.   One area alluded to earlier in this chapter concerns the platforms that host components of an e-business. The platform, or operating system, represents the foundation of the e-business, but it is a potentially weak link in security. If there are cracks in the foundation, there is very little that even strong application software can do to keep the business secure. Therefore, it is imperative that system administrators properly patch platform vulnerabilities and maintain the security of the platform itself. As mentioned earlier, firewalls can go a long way toward blocking access to platform vulnerabilities by unauthorized outsiders. However, authorized but unprivileged users within the firewall can exploit known platform vulnerabilities to yield root privileges on a business-critical machine. Outsiders able to gain user privileges on the platform through any means also may be able to penetrate platform holes into severe security breaches.

Some key steps necessary to maintain platform security include:

- Eliminating default accounts generally installed with the operating system
- Prohibiting easily guessed passwords
- Enforcing password expiration
- Deactivating any unnecessary services that may be running by default
- Regularly applying security patches to the operating system
- Updating the operating system to its most recent release
- Ensuring that file access permissions are properly enforced, so as to prevent unnecessary access to critical files
- Enabling audit logging with intrusion monitoring
- Running system file integrity checks regularly

Some administrators believe that deploying a firewall is an acceptable substitute for configuring their platforms securely. Furthermore, with the plethora of different platforms running their enterprises, many system administrators give up on installing the latest OS patches and on securely configuring their platforms. They mistakenly assume that firewalls will protect them from all threats, even without maintenance. Unfortunately, relaxing host security can make the job of hackers easy. By hopping from machine to machine, they usually can find the valuable information they are looking for, or if that is their goal, they can wreak maximum damage.

21.7 SUMMARY.   This chapter has provided an overview of the weakest links in Web applications, including Web clients, network protocols, front-end Web servers, back-end databases, application servers, and the platforms on which they run. Secure network protocols are necessary but certainly not sufficient for securing e-commerce. The vulnerabilities described here are largely based on software flaws that exist in the application layer of e-commerce transactions.

Perhaps the most common vulnerability in e-commerce systems is misconfiguration of software. Because the responsibility for software configuration lies with the user, a security policy must be implemented and enforced. Once a system is configured, it is important to subject it to third-party validation and testing. A third-party audit can ensure that the configured system, including routers, firewalls, servers, and databases, meets the specifications of the security policy. The system also should be tested periodically against well-known, common attacks as well as against newer threats as they arise.

Like any software system, commercial off-the-shelf software has flaws, many of which are security-critical. It is imperative that system administrators stay current with vendor Web sites, with hacker sites, with newsgroups, and with wherever threats and patches to their software are released. Both the security and hacker communities are constantly at work finding flaws in COTS that software vendors and security firms generally correct quickly. Software consumers—those who buy and use the software—must do their part by applying all relevant patches to their vulnerable software.

For custom-developed software, which includes front-end Web pages, application servers, CGI scripts, and mobile content such as ActiveX or Java, developers must do everything possible to ensure that their software is not vulnerable to attack and that it does not infringe on users' privacy.

21.8 FURTHER READING

Anderson, R. *Security Engineering: A Guide to Building Dependable Distributed Systems.* Hoboken, NJ: John Wiley & Sons, 2001.

Cobb, Stephen. *Privacy for Business: Web Sites and Email.* Saint Augustine, FL: Dreva Hill, 2002.

McGraw, G., and E. Felten. *Securing Java. Hoboken,* NJ: John Wiley & Sons, 2000.

Rubin, A. *White Hat Security Arsenal: Tackling the Threats.* Reading, MA: Addison-Wesley, 2001.

Rubin, A., D. Geer, and M. Ranum. *The Web Security Sourcebook.* Hoboken, NJ: John Wiley & Sons, 1997.

Scambray, J., Shema, M., and C. Sima. *Hacking Exposed Web Applications*, 2nd ed. San Francisco, CA: McGraw-Hill Osborne Media, 2006.

Viega, J., and G. McGraw. *Building Secure Software: How to Avoid Security Problems the Right Way.* Reading, MA: Addison-Wesley, 2001.

21.9   NOTES

1. This original version of this chapter, entitled "E-Commerce Vulnerabilities," was adapted from Anup K. Ghosh, *Security and Privacy for E-Business* (Hoboken, NJ: John Wiley & Sons, 2001), chapter 4; adapted by permission.

2. Anup K. Ghosh, *E-Commerce Security: Weak Links, Best Defenses* (New York: John Wiley & Sons, 1998).

3. C. Cowan, P. Wagle, C. Pu, S. Beattie, and J. Walpole, "Buffer Overflows: Attacks and Defenses for the Vulnerability of the Decade," paper presented at DISCEX 2000, January 25–27, 2000, Hilton Head, S.C. *Proceedings of the DARPA Information Survivability Conference and Exposition* (Los Alamitos, CA: IEEE Computer Society Press, 2000).

4. Cowan, et al. "Buffer Overflows."

5. PCI Security Standards Council, *Payment Card Industry Data Security Standard, v1.1.* (September 2006), retrieved from www.pcisecuritystandards.org/pdfs/pci_dss_v1-1.pdf.

6. G. McGraw and G. Morrisett, "Attacking Malicious Code: A Report to the Infosec Research Council," *IEEE Software* 17, No. 5 (September/October 2000): 33–41.

7. Ghosh, *Security and Privacy for E-Business*, chapter 7.

8. B. Schneier, *Applied Cryptography: Protocols, Algorithms, and Source Code in C*, 2nd ed. (New York: John Wiley & Sons, 1995).

9. Ghosh, *E-Commerce Security*.

10. W. A. Arbaugh, W. L. Fithen, and J. McHugh, "Windows of Vulnerability: A Case Study," *IEEE Computer* 33, No. 12 (December 2000): 52–59.

11. L. Stein, *Web Security: A Step-by-Step Reference Guide* (Reading, MA: Addison-Wesley, 1998).

12. Ghosh, *Security and Privacy for E-Business*.

13. A. Rubin, D. Geer, and M. Ranum, *The Web Security Sourcebook* (New York: John Wiley & Sons, 1997).

14. Michael Howard and David Leblanc. *Writing Secure Code,* 2nd ed. (Redmond, WA: Microsoft Press, 2002).

CHAPTER 22

PHYSICAL THREATS TO THE INFORMATION INFRASTRUCTURE

Franklin Platt

22.1   INTRODUCTION.   This chapter describes the wide array of possible physical threats that can impact information systems (IS) infrastructure. The infrastructure affected can be any component of a computer system or communications network, any of the cables or wiring that transport power or data, or any of the support services or utilities needed to sustain full IS performance. The speed and accuracy of any system is dependent upon the performance of a long chain of physical components as well as upon the productivity of all of the people who utilize or maintain each component. Anything less than full system-wide performance can be very costly.

A physical threat is any event that can degrade the performance of an information system—whether such an event is actually occurring or imminent, or credibly likely or possible, or completely unexpected and without warning. The list of possible threats is a long one beginning with natural and man-made external events that can impact IS performance. Many other possible threats are internal, resulting from accidents or misuse, snooping, vandalism, or deliberate attack. Internal threats also include reliability failures, installation or maintenance issues, or lack of proper testing. Threats can also be caused by situations within the facility, building, or complex, or as a consequence of local or regional events, or, increasingly, events worldwide and even from outer space. Threats happen and can come from almost anywhere, so it is prudent and far less costly to try to anticipate all possible threats.

This chapter begins a threat assessment process, which starts by identifying all possible threat situations. This process must be comprehensive and rigorous and involve all stakeholders. It is not enough simply to assign likelihood and an impact for the usual or the obvious threat situations. There must be a full risk analysis, so that risk, vulnerability, and response and recovery costs can be quantified, as explained in Chapter 23 in this *Handbook*. Otherwise, the whole process is valueless. Absent comprehensive planning, security becomes an irrational selection of vendors and solutions, which can only add cost and increase liability risks. Alternatively, a strategic risk management process can maximize future profits and add value, protect morale and productivity, enhance goodwill, and improve relations with customers and communities.

The events of September 11, 2001, sounded a shattering wake-up call that unexpected threats can actually happen and that even the best security practices, products, and services are of little value without proper planning, implementation, and support. Hurricane Katrina, four years later in 2005, demonstrated again that both business and government are still unprepared, even though such an event was predicted many times.

This chapter suggests a comprehensive perspective on physical security that can add value and help avert disaster. Chapter 23 in this *Handbook* goes on to suggest physical security implementation and management that can protect people and property while optimizing morale, productivity, and profitability.

22.2   BACKGROUND AND PERSPECTIVE.   Historic data and statistics are of limited value in predicting future threats. For a discussion of the unreliability of computer-crime statistics, see Chapter 10 in this *Handbook*. The past is no longer prologue because many new risks are emerging and many types of incidents are increasingly severe, widespread, complex, damaging, and costly. Proliferating and increasingly dispersed infrastructure system components are often vulnerable and hard to protect. And hybrid configurations of new and legacy systems vastly complicate the protection process.

There are few threat statistics that can reliably predict the infrastructure future. Computer crime reports mostly cover logical security, while general crime statistics often do not relate directly to computer security. Historic information is further flawed because many incidents are never detected and far more are not reported for fear of embarrassment, liability, or loss of business. Many security incidents are masked as quality-control problems for the same reasons, or are misdiagnosed because no one had time to determine the true cause(s). Lacking reliable precedents, predicting future threats is especially difficult—yet increasingly necessary. Chapter 10 discusses computer crime statistics in more detail.

Most incidents happen suddenly, without warning, and often where least expected. Many threats, once thought to be unlikely, now occur widely and strike with surprising intensity and devastation. Other contributing factors include poor risk management due to inexperience, denial, or complacency that can quickly turn routine threats into costly incidents. Businesses with good security preparedness can usually survive, while many others will not.

22.2.1 Today's Risks Are Greater. Today's risks are increasingly sophisticated, unpredictable, potentially serious, and increasingly commonplace as well. Disruptive incidents can result from mistakes or accidents, snoopers or hacking, vandalism, disgruntled or disruptive persons, labor disputes, demonstrations, or civil unrest, extremists of many stripes, and, increasingly, both domestic and international terrorism. Although violent crime statistics have decreased in recent years, these data are misleading because they rarely include workplace-related events. Violence in the workplace is now common and often without warning. Incidents can include harassment, bomb scares, robbery, hostage situations, shooting, or arson. And each and every one of these risks can seriously affect IS performance.

The possibility of catastrophic events utilizing weapons of mass destruction is also increasing. Among these, the threat of biological or chemical agents is extremely dangerous, can impact wide areas, and may be contagious as well. An emerging concern is a flu pandemic threat, which can be a natural hazard or a terrorist attack. Flu is highly contagious, spread by many possible vectors that are at best hard to control, and can quickly incapacitate many workers. A 2006 study by the National Governors Association suggests that as many as 40 percent of all workers might stay home for a period up to 14 months if a major pandemic hit.[1] If an anthrax scare, a West Nile outbreak, or a full bird flu pandemic does eventually occur, the affect on unprepared organizations and their information infrastructure could be disastrous.

To make matters worse, today's would-be perpetrators tend to be well trained and funded, determined, persistent, and patient. Many also have the best and latest technology, equipment, and programming skills. And except for a few misguided amateurs, most troublemakers cover their intentions very well. Almost anyone working inside the organization can cause trouble: full-time employees, temporary or contract workers, service personnel, maintenance or construction crews, repair persons, inspectors, meter readers, building personnel, visitors, vendors, consultants, or anyone posing in any of these roles. Externally, there are many local, regional, national, or secular groups sworn to wreak vengeance.

Physical threats can extend beyond direct attacks. Many scares do not result in actual violence, and disruptive incidents can occur outside of the workplace. However and wherever they happen, violence-related incidents are increasingly commonplace, disruptive, and costly.[2]

All too many people with access to the workplace have backgrounds, allegiances, or emotional drives that are entirely unknown. Even previously trustworthy people may be forced to undertake espionage, sabotage, or other criminal activities. Chapter 15 in this *Handbook* discusses such social engineering methods in connection with penetration of computer systems and networks. Some seemingly trustworthy people may be ideologically motivated, while others are simply duped. Still others are drawn by opportunities for personal gain or vengeance. And there is very little risk of detection or apprehension for most well-trained, would-be perpetrators. Government officials can substantiate some of the incidents, but much of this information is not public. Based on consistent conversations among security experts who compare the cases they work on with the cases that are published, what is published is probably only the tip of the iceberg—perhaps a tenth or so of the real rates of attack.

Informed opinion suggests that such crimes are already widespread and rapidly increasing. Yet few incidents are detected and fewer still ever reported. Worse yet, there are scant data on the extent of crimes against information systems, theft of data, espionage, or similar activities that can clearly cause huge business losses.

Those who threaten the IS infrastructure must at least gain access to some physical part of it, but often this can be done inconspicuously, by trickery, deception, or simply forced entry. A physical attack may be the best way to compromise an information system—much more effective and less likely to be detected than a logical attack. Often many vital system components are vulnerable, exposed, or easily accessible. These components include wiring and cable runs, connection and junction points, system and network equipment, and the utilities that support them. Attacks or spying by physical means are often easy, fast, safe, and sure.

22.2.2 Likely Targets.   Businesses and organizations are increasingly likely to be the targets of hackers, disgruntled employees, competitors, disturbed persons, demonstrators, hate groups, extremists, and even terrorists. Motives may include a conspicuous, tempting, or challenging target, rage or revenge, an opportunity to cause reputational damage or at least adverse publicity, to make a political statement, for extortion or blackmail, or for personal gain or profit. Often there are no discernable motives. And beyond being likely targets, most businesses are convenient, easy, and safe targets as well, because most are unaware and unprepared for today's threats, much less for future ones. Although government facilities remain preferred targets, many are now better protected than most businesses, thanks to new procedures that are covered in Chapter 23 in this *Handbook*.

Another likely threat arises from the need of extremists and terrorists to finance their activities. Many groups and all independent, self-directed cells are dependent on crime to finance their operations. Today's crimes can include robbery and holdups, counterfeit currency and credit cards, Internet phishing and scams, theft, extortion, blackmail, and selling pirated software and other knock-offs. In addition, many foreign governments, businesses, and criminal organizations are actively engaged in spying. Although these are mainly corporate security and logical security problems, they also represent potential physical threats that must be deterred.

22.2.3 Productivity Issues.   Good security can be directly correlated with high productivity, which, in turn, can improve performance, customer satisfaction, and goodwill. Good security is measurable and can strategically enhance each of these factors to add both value and profit. Anything less than good security invites wasted time and money.

People who do not feel safe will not be productive. This applies to employees, visitors, vendors, and others on premises, as well as to customers, vendors, stockholders, and other stakeholders at remote locations. Everyone using any information system must be comfortable that physical safety and privacy is assured and that the system is uninterruptible, secure, and operating at full performance. Everyone concerned must be involved in the planning process, generally understand the risks, and support the security procedures. Otherwise, performance inevitably suffers.

Whenever a security incident occurs, morale and productivity are likely to plummet, and can remain low for many weeks, or even months. Whether the infrastructure is actually affected or not, significant disruption of operations is likely. Even when there is no injury or damage, the perception of a potential event can be costly; it can disrupt productivity, lose business and customers, and jeopardize goodwill. Even an unrelated incident, accident, nearby event, or a medical emergency can cause significant and prolonged disruption before productivity eventually climbs back to normal. The costs of recovering from any such event can be enormous.

Some examples of incidents include:

- An outside accountant died from a heart attack during a client meeting with several managers. No one knew enough first aid to be able to help him until an ambulance arrived, too late.
- A construction worker collapsed with a heart attack in a large office building. Many employees saw the man collapse, and word spread almost instantly through hundreds of office workers nearby. Again, no one offered immediate help, and the man died just as an ambulance crew arrived.
- The CFO of a large bank who was in his early 40s choked at a company reception and died in front of over 100 guests and employees.

All three persons died in the workplace, and all three might have been saved had there been proper medical equipment and trained people. In each case, morale and productivity plummeted and remained low for many weeks. The business costs were enormous. There must be thousands of such incidents each year. Good security might have saved lives, money, and reputation.

In another incident, an executive was robbed at gunpoint in a men's rest room that was publicly accessible. Although he managed to flee without injury, the entire office was traumatized, and little work was done for weeks. To make matters worse, there were rumors of similar robberies within the building complex. Here again, morale plummeted and took even longer to restore. Little work was done. Customers who were initially sympathetic soon took their business elsewhere. Again, the cost was high and the damage could have been mitigated or even prevented with effective and honest communications.

None of these incidents related directly to information systems. Yet each incident caused significant and prolonged disruptions that good infrastructure security might have prevented. Prior to each event, senior management had reviewed some security risks but then decided that no special protections were needed. Their premises security people viewed such threats as unlikely, based on assurances from the landlords that the buildings were amply protected. The threat assessments of each tenant were clearly flawed. Furthermore, having downplayed the possibility of some risks, tenants probably ignored many other potential threats.

No one knows how often productivity-related events occur. Businesses generally do not report them, and neither do the media. But these things do happen and probably with considerable frequency. Yet all threats can be mitigated to some extent and many more prevented at far less cost than the consequences by effective technical preparations, adequate employee awareness and training, and well-planned and well-rehearsed responses.

22.2.4 Terrorism and Violence Are Now Serious Threats.

Acts of terrorism and violence are now a reality that can occur anywhere in the world. September 11, 2001, and the events that followed have brought home the stark reality that violence can happen anywhere and can cause massive damage and disruption. And most major disasters can disrupt information systems far removed from the actual incidents.

Workplace violence is also happening with increasing frequency and often at facilities assumed to be safe.[3] Bomb and biological or chemical scares, personal threats, harassment, hostage situations, and shootings are all happening with increasing regularity. Whether actual violence occurs or not, the threats alone, the many rumors generated, and the imagined proximity to danger are all productivity-related events that can seriously disrupt the performance of information systems for a long time. Therefore, these become infrastructure security issues that require special planning and should not be left to premises security personnel to prevent.

There are other serious threats from foreign intelligence, terrorists, and domestic groups generally unknown to the public. Some of these are explained well in the Project Megiddo report published by the Federal Bureau of Investigation (FBI) in 1999 in anticipation of the millennium. The report provides "an FBI strategic assessment of the potential for domestic terrorism in the United States undertaken in anticipation of or response to the arrival of the new millennium."[4] The risks cited then are basically unchanged today, except that more previously unknown threats have since been added. There are consultants with FBI contacts who can offer valuable advice.

Attempted violence is now a serious threat to all IS infrastructures. However, thorough security planning can do much to avoid trouble and needless expenses.

22.2.5 Costs of a Threat Happening.

Direct costs of system downtime can exceed many thousands of dollars per hour. The losses include the slack-time costs of people who cannot use the systems, costs of support and maintenance people diverted to restoring operations, recovery expenses, overtime, and often lodging, food, and travel expenses during recovery. Usually, many outside resources are needed for response and recovery. Everything becomes very expensive, very quickly. Often, to further compound the costs, needed resources are just not available immediately.

Indirect costs can also be significant. Reestablishing and keeping good public relations can be expensive. Often public announcements, news releases, and briefings to the news and financial media and to stockholders are needed to neutralize public embarrassment and control rumors. Key customers must be contacted and reassured, and pending orders rescheduled. Still more costs include lost business or market share and dropping stock prices. Competitors often will take as much advantage as they can, which necessitates further costs defending brands and reputation.

Any number of such costs can devastate an enterprise unless strong security measures are deployed effectively and quickly. Ad-libbed responses are often disastrous. In reality, an infrastructure outage of more than a few hours is often fatal, and the enterprise can never fully recover. Good security usually can prevent disastrous costs.

22.2.6 Who Must Be Involved. Many threats to information systems also involve corporate or premises security personnel, whose role is to protect people and property within and surrounding the workplace. The CEO and the CFO are also involved, because they must now comply with the laws and regulations (covered in Section 23.2.6), in particular the Sarbanes-Oxley Act. This requires that events that might materially affect financial performance must be included within an organization's financial filings and statements. Major security incidents are clearly such events whose impact must now be predicted—as described in this chapter.

Premises security often includes little more than guards, access control, and some surveillance. Their understanding of the IS infrastructure's special security needs is often minimal, lumped in with overall physical security procedures, and rarely extends much beyond the immediate premises. Yet IS security requires additional knowledge, experience, protection, and support. Good security must be strong, fast-acting, focused on specific targets, and closely monitored. Effective early warning systems are necessary in order to prevent threats from happening. In reality, each security function will have its own needs and priorities and use its own resources. During a serious incident, security for the premises, occupants, information systems, and the infrastructure must all coordinate efficiently and effectively. They must also work smoothly with local fire and police departments, with other emergency responders, and with many outside resources.

Who, then, should manage the process of determining the threats to the IS infrastructure? And who are the stakeholders who should be involved in this process?

The best person to manage the physical security of information systems is one who knows a great deal about possible threats and about the IS infrastructure. The office manager, facilities manager, or corporate security director or their staffs are usually ill-equipped to determine or manage IS security. Often, too, the chief information officer (CIO) and IS security officers deal with protecting data and data processing, and are not the best persons to understand IS physical security, especially in a large installation. Therefore, the best person is a trusted individual with the right knowledge and experience and with enough time to manage the process well. Planning and managing infrastructure security, implementing and testing it, training and security awareness, monitoring, and periodic updating of the system and procedures are a full-time job in most organizations, and require a support staff in larger organizations.

Another consideration is that no one person should know all the secrets, which is a rule that has become especially important in dealing with the IS infrastructure. When trouble comes, many experts must mobilize very quickly, efficiently, and effectively. To do this, the responders must be familiar with all the information systems and have fast access to the infrastructure. No matter how well trusted, no one person should know everything about the physical and logical defenses. (If need be, such information should be safely stored with strong access controls.) It is wise to divide the secrets so that no one group knows or has access to them all. Having done this, multiple persons can then share each portion of the secrets and observe each other, so that no one person is indispensable.

But only the security vulnerabilities and defensive implementations should be secrets. There is no point is letting others know about the defenses and where the organization is vulnerable. However, the process of determining the underlying threats should be common knowledge among all the stakeholders involved. By identifying a large number of risks that have been assessed—but keeping the likelihood, vulnerability, and impact information secret—we can discourage would-be troublemakers by at least providing some idea of the *number* of risks that have been considered. With any luck, they will attack less-prepared sites.

22.2.7 Liability Issues.   Aside from the need for efficient emergency response, another issue is becoming increasingly important, is potentially very costly, and is often overlooked. This is the issue of liability. Every organization has a legal and fiduciary duty to protect the people and property within and surrounding its premises. If any injury or damage occurs in or around a workplace—even long afterward—allegations of negligence will likely follow. The motive is often that damages awarded by the courts can be very large and lawyers often take on these cases on speculation, in hopes of receiving very large fees. And whether the organization was actually at fault or not, the resultant legal fees, the time and costs needed to defend the organization, bad publicity and possible loss of business, and the eventual fines and awards can be devastating.

If negligence is alleged, the issue is whether the organization was properly prepared for the emergency and was its response effective. The question is simply: Did management perform its duty to protect the organization? An affirmative answer would require at least:

- Evidence of a thorough threat assessment process
- Good security plans, policies, and procedures that have actually been implemented
- Proper training and current security awareness
- Periodic drills, exercises, security reviews, and feedback from known events
- Periodic updates to assure that security remains effective

If it can be demonstrated that all these measures were not taken, or that there were deviations from generally accepted standards, the result could be punitive as well as compensatory damage awards. Gross negligence will probably be alleged as well, in which case insurance may not defend the accused organization or individuals, who would then be personally liable. Even with insurance in effect, it may not be sufficient to cover the very large penalties that juries commonly award.

Even when all the correct answers are given, the accused often find they are considered to be guilty until they can prove themselves innocent. And this can be a long, painful, and costly process.

However, a nearly iron-clad defense against liability is that federal procedures were followed. And the most comprehensive of these are from the Department of Homeland Security (DHS) and its Federal Emergency Management Agency (FEMA) Directorate.[5] Of all of the other security planning and management procedures, which are many and varied, only the DHS/FEMA methodology is likely to become generally accepted. The procedures are already well known, uniform, and comprehensive, and they consider all threat possibilities and all response resources. It is unlikely that a plaintiff's attorney will ever allege that these procedures are deficient, or ever bring a case once it appears that an organization is compliant. This is not to remove all liability, merely to reduce the scope to situations usually covered by insurance. Chapter 23 in this *Handbook* outlines how to plan, implement, and manage the DHS/FEMA procedures.

22.2.8 Definitions and Terms.   Information infrastructure security is simply a means of IS performance assurance. Good security precludes any IS disruption that might degrade performance in any way. Any slowdown or loss of productivity, loss of data, breach of privacy, or disruption of the systems, networks, and utilities that support any information system diminishes performance. Good security assures that all systems remain fully operational, robust, and accurate, and that all their data remain private and cannot be compromised.

There are three elements of information systems security. Each element must be especially designed and maintained to protect against different threats of varying scope and intensity. The three elements include:

1. **Logical security,** which is also known as information systems security, protects only the integrity of data and of information processing.

2. **Physical security,** which is also called infrastructure security, protects the rest of the information systems and all of the people who use, operate, and maintain the systems. Physical security also must prevent any type of physical access or intrusion that can compromise logical security.

3. **Premises security,** which is also known as corporate or facilities security, protects the people and property within an entire area, facility, or building(s), and is usually required by codes, regulations, and fiduciary obligations. Premises security protects broad areas. It often provides perimeter security, access control, smoke and fire detection, fire suppression, some environmental protection, and usually surveillance systems, alarms, watchmen, and guards. Premises security is often an extension of law enforcement.

Clearly, there is much overlap between each element, and a threat to one is often a threat to the others as well. However, each element is likely to perceive and handle each threat differently. Although the remainder of this chapter deals with physical security, some threats that are usually considered the realm of logical or premises security must also be covered.

Clarification is needed also on what constitutes a "threat." This is any credible situation—whether actual, imminent, predicted, or simply possible—with the potential for causing harm, damage, or disruption. The terms "threat," "hazard," and "risk" are used synonymously and have the same meaning.

22.2.9 Uniform, Comprehensive Planning Process. The threat assessment process can go by a number of names, which are all functionally similar. Among the terms: are emergency, disaster, operations, contingency and crisis-response planning, and damage control. Some processes are proprietary and do not share a common language or standardized procedures that can be understood by everyone involved. Many regulated industries must develop emergency response plans using terms and formats dictated by the regulating agency, which makes these terms and formats proprietary as well. There are many diverse examples of regulated industries that use hazardous or nuclear materials or operate dams.

Many organizations that are involved in emergency response—such as hospitals and emergency medical services, schools, the American Red Cross, and many volunteer agencies, National Guard and military units—may still use other terms and models. Government agencies at the local, state, and federal levels still use a wide variety of security plans and procedures, even though there is now one standard methodology required, as explained in Chapter 23. Most of these procedures are not uniform or comprehensive. And they can be incompatible, present major communications barriers, and cause unnecessary misunderstandings, delays, and wasted resources. In turn, most private organizations are not aware of the government procedures in place or of the many resources that can assist them.

Every organization experiences essentially the same threats and has limited response capabilities and resources. Almost every organization is likely to be overwhelmed in a major emergency, and everyone can benefit enormously from outside resources.

Yet each venue tends to use dissimilar models, terms, and procedures that are often unintelligible to the others. In many cases, their models become file-and-forget plans and procedures that no one understands or accepts.

If only as prudent risk management strategy to avoid liability issues, a single, uniform, and comprehensive standard for processes, procedures, and language is needed. The best way to do this is to adopt the DHS/FEMA methodology, which encompasses all hazards, coordinates all resources efficiently, and is clear, concise, understood, and accepted by everyone involved. Details are given in Chapter 23. This is now required for all federal government departments and agencies, and for state and local jurisdictions as well, if they wish to continue receiving federal grants and assistance.

A useful public/private standard for evaluating disaster/emergency preparedness is published by the Emergency Management Assessment Program[6] (EMAP), which is a nonprofit professional organization. The EMAP standard covers all the current DHS/FEMA methodology and provides a clear and concise method to determine compliance, as well as a self-auditing process. EMAP also provides an independent, outside security audit of any government organization to ascertain that its emergency management program complies with the federal requirements; it may soon be able to audit private organizations also. The audit is done at the applicant's facility by professional, well-trained volunteers. The whole security-audit process is both rigorous and inexpensive. EMAP is therefore a suggested alternative to a CPA-provided security audit as well as to the audit procedures of other professional organizations that generally do not include either infrastructure security or compliance with federal procedures.

Security preparedness that is compliant with these standards may become a requisite for the private sector to obtain insurance, to avoid liability and excessive costs, to establish innocence, or to use capital markets for risk management. Knowing these standards will help the threat assessment process and, later, can provide better protection.

22.3   THREAT ASSESSMENT PROCESS.   Effective security planning begins with a thorough threat assessment. This process begins by establishing an ad hoc organization, obtaining budget approval and the sponsorship of senior management, and formation of a steering committee that represents all the stakeholders.

The first tasks are to:

1. Identify all potential threat situations.
2. Determine the likelihood and estimate the direct and indirect costs of each threat.
3. Evaluate and prioritize each threat.
4. Prepare and present a final report that each committee member signs.

This report becomes evidence of due diligence to avoid liability, and becomes the basis for protecting the infrastructure, which is described in Chapter 23.

The way *not* to go through the planning process is for a few people to decide the risks and then write the security plan. This is the opposite approach to good and effective planning. And it will not work. Very few of the key personnel will accept or even understand the plan, and it will probably be ignored or overlooked when the next emergency arises. Good examples of failed planning are the emergency management plans for New Orleans and Baton Rouge areas that were put in place before Hurricane Katrina in 2005. Apparently, both were good plans. But few officials understood the plans or remembered to use them.

The threat assessment planning process *must* be done thoroughly and completely. For additional perspectives on risk assessment and risk management, see Chapters 62 and 63 of this *Handbook*.

22.3.1 Set Up a Steering Committee. The security planning process is not effective unless all of the stakeholders are represented, and the best way to do this is to establish a steering committee. The committee will help identify and evaluate potential threats, and help develop a comprehensive protection plan.

The committee should represent all stakeholders and include as much experience, knowledge, and perspective as possible. Stakeholders should include users, administrators, management, key partners, customers, vendors, and service providers (such as maintenance, repair, and cleaning personnel). A project manager should participate, as should legal, financial, and human resources representatives. Independent experts and facilitators are recommended as well. The best committee chair is usually an outside facilitator who is immune from political or cultural bias, loyalties, or product preferences. It is also wise to seek input from stockholders, lenders, insurers, and community and government officials.

This can be a virtual committee that rarely needs to meet in full session. Communications by e-mail or phone should be sufficient, and an in-house staff can gather data, issue reports, and work with individual committee members. Confidentiality is not an issue at this point. The committee's purpose is to identify threats and to assist in planning. No member need have full knowledge of the actual vulnerabilities or the resulting security systems and protections. Each member, however, should sign off on the committee's final report.

Once its initial mission is completed, it is best for this committee to convene at least annually to review new and changing threats and to assess how well the security systems have performed. This committee not only represents all concerned stakeholders, but it can provide oversight so that management does not neglect to exercise, review, and update the security plan. In effect, the committee provides due diligence that management has fulfilled its fiduciary responsibilities.

22.3.2 Identify All Possible Threats. The first step is to identify all possible threat situations that might affect the information infrastructure. This is not to say that each threat will someday happen but that, conceivably, it might, nearby or even at a distance. The causal connection could be tenuous at best and the event most unlikely, but it could someday happen. It is far better to think objectively about such things and to plan effectively than to simply write them off as events that could "never happen here" or to claim that, if such a disaster does happen here, "there is nothing we can do to mitigate it." Both statements are patently false and potentially very costly.

The threat list can be very long. The format should tabulate each specific threat with a one-line description to clarify what is meant. For example, "flooding" is too general a term to meaningfully assess its risk. Instead, one might list "riverine flooding," which could be the result of heavy rains, snowmelt, or a breached dam or levee; "local flooding," such as a water-main break, severe storm, or a major fire nearby; "premises flooding" due perhaps to leaking pipes, drains, or leaking windows, roofs, building setbacks, a burst water tank or cooling tower, or fire suppression. The purpose is to have a long list of specific threat situations that can be individually assessed. There can easily be 100 or more threats listed. As the project proceeds, those involved will surely add still more threats and fine-tune the definitions. The threat list should include threats that are direct as well as indirect and threats affecting the general area, the region, or the whole country. It is best to list all threats, including those that are deemed unlikely to occur, as a precaution against inadvertently omitting some that might have more importance than is apparent at first glance.

Unfortunately, threats tend to cascade: One threat situation can create others, and these, in turn, can create more threat situations. For example, severe flooding can close roadways and keep people away from work, impede delivery of supplies necessary to operate (such as food or water or fuel for an emergency generator), disrupt communications, cause mud slides, ignite fires, trigger looting, or cause civil unrest. As another example, during a fire there will likely be loss of electrical power for equipment cooling, ventilation, or communications and released water or chemicals that must be contained. Each of these conditions is a separate risk in itself. In reality, few hazards occur in isolation, and many of the cascading events may be unexpected and unpredictable, and can themselves trigger still more events.

Therefore, the tabulation of each threat should also include two other columns: (1) events that could trigger the threat, and (2) cascading threats that could result from the threat. This is easily done by numbering each threat and referencing the numbers that may interconnect the various threats. The information is needed to evaluate the impact of each threat. It can only be a general indication for planning purposes of what might happen. The actual cascading will probably be different, but the analysis of the threats will still be valid.

Do not rely on force majeure—for example, a major earthquake—as an excuse that a particular threat may be unavoidable. Force majeure does not limit liability because such events can be anticipated and some steps taken to minimize injury and damage. Nor may acts of war serve as an excuse, for the same reasons.

Finally, the threat list should be divided into major categories such as natural events, man-made events, vandalism, attacks, support system failures, and so on. The remainder of this chapter builds on the threat list and establishes categories best suited to particular needs.

22.3.3 Sources of Information and Assistance.

The next step is a compilation of past events: historical records and details as to what happened, when, and how, what injury and damage resulted, was there warning, how fast was the onset? The compilation should include events in both near and distant areas that could possibly cause damage and disruption, either directly or indirectly. Perhaps the 2005 subway and bus bombings in London or the earlier commuter-train bombings in Madrid could affect American workers who commute and become concerned about their own safety.

As the threat list gets bigger, it is necessary for everyone involved to think out of the box and to look for scenarios that past trends suggest could eventually happen. This thinking can be productive when it examines possible scenarios objectively. The author, as a security consultant in New York, worked with tenants in the World Trade Center and tried to suggest disaster planning but was overruled by the landlord who assured everyone that this was "the safest place on earth."

Information sources to investigate include the weather bureau, libraries, local fire and police departments, state and county officials, utility companies, newspaper files, and local knowledge of past events within the region. Power and communications utility companies can provide outage reports, but their terminology must be clearly understood. For example, an electrical "outage" may only include interruptions lasting more than five minutes. Regional and state regulatory authorities, public utility commissions, industry and professional organizations, and business development groups may also provide useful information, once their perspective and terminology are clarified.

All local, regional, and state emergency management agencies should now have an all-hazard mitigation plan that lists all threats that have occurred throughout their jurisdiction. There should also be dates, descriptions, and map locations in their plan; this information may go back historically for a century or more. And each agency should have a local emergency operations plan that lists all potential threat situations within their jurisdiction. Look particularly at the appendices and annexes that discuss particular types of threats. In addition to what is in their plans, each agency should be of considerable assistance describing possible major threats that are man-made, involve hazardous materials, or are major health risks. The threats they identify are probably your threats as well.

Also work with each stakeholder for advice on threats they know about or perceive. Ask each person to reach out to their customers, vendors and suppliers, service providers, business neighbors, and consultants and academics as well. There will be much expertise, perspective, and good advice gleaned from these sources. The time seeking it will be well spent.

At the end of this chapter is a list of some reference books that can be helpful. Although most of the procedures are outdated, there is still much useful source data.

22.3.4 Determine the Likelihood of Each Threat.

The steering committee should consider the likelihood that each risk may happen. The best way to estimate likelihood is as an annual probability on a relative scale (for example) from 0 (none) to 5 (very likely). A perceived likelihood of once every 100 years (which equals a 1 percent annual probability) could be rated a 1. A 5 percent annual probability might be rated a 2, while an annual probability of 20 percent or more had best be rated as a 5. Threats from severe weather should be rated higher than historical data suggests in order to account for the world's changing weather patterns. Threats with a likelihood of 0 should also be included, as this value can be used later to show the relative vulnerability of each and every threat.

The steering committee can adjust each rating as it deliberates so that the final results are useful and meaningful.

22.3.5 Approximate the Impact Costs.

Once all the possible threats are determined and the likelihood of each is estimated, the next step is for the steering committee to deliberate the impact of each threat. Impact considers the potential losses and costs associated with each risk. (Do not consider cascading threats at this point.) Here also, a relative scale of 1 (very low) to 5 (very high) is suggested. A 0 impact rating is probably not relevant, because, in reality, some response and recovery costs will occur.

There may well be individual factors needed to clarify the importance of the overall impact. Such factors might include the likelihood of injury or death, the amount of property damage, the relative response and recovery costs, and, especially for a private organization, the costs of loss of business. The parameters of each factor and the scope of each rating can be adjusted as the planning proceeds, so that the results are realistic and meaningful. The purpose now is to show which threats are potentially the most dangerous or costly if they occur.

Threat assessment planning is best done using a worst-case scenario because this is what tends to happen in reality. Even then, actual costs incurred can be much higher than anticipated. Although the steering committee has only limited knowledge of possible costs, with some discussion the committee should reach consensus as to which rating to apply to each listed threat. Their findings will be reviewed later by others better able to predict potential costs and in a better position to realize that the impact of some threats is much more costly than others.

The impact costs are both direct and consequential. The direct expenses can include costs to locate the trouble(s), stabilize the systems, repair and install replacement infrastructure, reboot, restore databases, and thoroughly test both the data and the systems. Other direct costs that can result from each event include loss of productivity of system users, overtime needed to regain production schedules, temporary contracted services, and interim facilities, or materials and supplies needed immediately.

Add to these potential indirect or consequential costs such as food, sanitation, and lodging; loss of business, customers, or market share, falling stock price, and the costs of public relations efforts to control rumors and adverse news reports. Costs will continue to accumulate during the response phase, throughout the recovery period, and possibly long after. The totals can far exceed expectations.

22.3.6 Costs of Cascading Events.   The possibilities and indeed the likelihood of cascading events have been described. Each event adds to the impact costs, but determining how likely is the cascading, and how much the extra cost, is at best an educated guess. If the causative events for each threat are shown on the threat list and the potential cascading events are there also, the impact costs of each individual event should be estimated. However, cascading may invalidate the likelihood factors. If one threat is already occurring, others may be imminent, regardless of the likelihood shown.

The total impact cost will probably be somewhat less than the sum of the parts. There may be some economies of scale during multiple events, as the response activity for one event can take care of another event for little extra cost. Here is where the experience and perspective of the steering committee, security professionals, and management become valuable. However, the combined costs must still be realistic, or the cost-value analysis described in Chapter 23 will be flawed.

22.3.7 Determine the Vulnerability to Each Threat.   Deciding which threats are the most important can be subjective and controversial and based on unproven assumptions. The approach suggested here yields quantifiable data that are realistic and will clearly indicate which threats are the most important and why. Individual opinions will vary considerably. The steering committee reports can yield approximations that are statistically valid—if the rules are followed and everything is done carefully. The committee's deliberations should be reviewed by experts and senior management, using calculations to be described, followed by the cost-value analyses described in Chapter 23.

One other common alternative is a matrix showing likelihood vertically and impact horizontally, rating both factors as high, medium, or low. This yields nine levels of vulnerability for each threat ranging from high-high to low-low. Such an arrangement is neither useful nor realistic. Since allowance need to be made for those impact factors that are potentially more costly than others.

Once everyone settles on the likelihood and impact of each threat, the current vulnerability of each threat can be calculated. Fundamentally, vulnerability is a calculation combining the likelihood of an event with how much damage it might cause. The method suggested yields six levels of vulnerability, from 0 (none) to 5 (very high). The next two steps are oversimplified but can be adapted to most needs.Simply multiplying the likelihood times the impact will yield vulnerability values from 0 to 25, which would not reflect the relative impact costs of most threats. Neither does simple addition, as some models suggest.

1. It is best to use several impact cost factors, as described earlier, and then combine each factor using constant multipliers for each so the relative importance of each impact cost is preserved. Combination by averaging each cost factor may not yield useful results. Combining the mean value of each factor (or sometimes the highest value) can yield more realistic data.

2. Finally, convert vulnerability calculations to a 0-to-5-point relative scale by choosing a range of results for each scale value.

Working through this procedure for all threats will show that the formulas, multipliers, and ranges of scale values may need to be adjusted slightly to yield meaningful results. As already mentioned, simple multiplication and/or addition or otherwise linear formulae will not yield realistic results.

The importance of calculating vulnerability is that it can be done in real time, and the multipliers can also be adjusted in real time as threat levels change. For example, this can immediately reflect the daily Homeland Security Threat Levels by locale or by possible target types. It can also input warnings from local police and intelligence sources. (Some threat information is probably classified, but the multiplier it can provide is not restricted or even sensitive information.) All the data can be displayed on a spreadsheet, even to the point of color-coding each vulnerability level. Everyone involved in security or emergency management can have real-time access to the same screens, which will update continually as conditions change.

It is well to provide a choice of display screens summarized or in detail by regions and threat categories, or prioritized by vulnerability.

Finally, the complete vulnerability data should be restricted and available only to those with a need to know. This information is highly sensitive; it shows potential wrongdoers where the IS infrastructure is well defended and where it is *not*.

22.3.8 Completing the Threat Assessment Report. Once the detailed threat assessment is completed, a general report should be prepared for circulation to all stakeholders. The report is mostly textual and does not suggest weak spots or what the security defenses may be. Each steering committee member should sign off on this report, and so should the senior management and security staff. The purposes of this report are to develop security awareness, for use in training, and as evidence of due diligence that a thorough threat assessment was indeed performed.

More on how to evaluate and manage the vulnerabilities is described in Chapter 23 of this *Handbook*.

22.4 GENERAL THREATS. A wide array of threat situations can affect the IS infrastructure, degrade productivity, and cause anxiety that will reduce performance and morale. The list suggested earlier begins to identify some of these threats. Some other possible situations that are not generally associated with the IS infrastructure are listed in this section. However, the various threats suggested in this chapter are far from a complete list. Therefore, expert advice, local knowledge, and analysis of current events should all be utilized to customize the threat list to the particular needs of each jurisdiction and then to review and revise the list periodically.

As mentioned before, specific threats are usually divided into broad categories that can easily be summarized to provide situational awareness. Generally, threats are categorized as natural hazards, technical and man-made risks, civil unrest, vandalism, and attacks. Other less likely but potentially more serious possibilities include bombs, hazardous materials release, a pandemic, and threats relating to weapons of mass destruction. A final grouping could be local events that are specific to the sites being protected. The groupings themselves are not important as long as all possible scenarios are covered. Some allocations will be arbitrary, as some threats could be put into any of several categories. (But never list any specific threat more than once.) There is as yet no single, uniform, comprehensive threat list format. As the planning process continues, the best threat groupings will likely evolve.

22.4.1   Natural Hazards.   Natural hazard events are becoming ever more frequent, damaging, and widespread, as their patterns seem to be changing. Increasingly recent events include major flooding, severe thunderstorms; hurricanes and tornadoes; blizzards, heavy snowfall, and ice storms; wildfires and heavy smoke; contamination of air, water, buildings, or soil; and the increasing threats of disease. Although earthquakes tend to occur in cycles, these too seem more prevalent currently. Any of these can disrupt business in any number of direct and consequential ways—many unanticipated—depending on the locations of information systems, networks, terminals, data storage, cables, and utilities. Natural hazard events cannot be prevented, but their impact can be mitigated. A closer look at each category follows.

- **Atmospheric hazards.** These can include severe weather events, such as tropical cyclones and hurricanes; severe thunderstorms with hurricane winds, strong lightning, and large hailstones; tornadoes; windstorms; blizzards, and heavy snows; ice storms; air pollution and high ozone levels; nuclear fallout (which is always occurring, but at low levels); extreme cold weather; and extreme hot weather.

- **Geologic hazards.** These are mainly landslides and mudslides, land subsidence (sinkholes), and expansive soils due to water.

- **Hydrologic hazards.** These hazards include riverine flooding and flooding of low-lying areas due to heavy or prolonged rains; rapid ice or snowmelt; ice jams or debris obstructions in waterways; coastal damage due to storm surge; erosion of streams; and collapse of roadways, bridges, and buildings. Hydrologic events can cascade to disrupt water and sewage systems, cause food and fuel shortages, and even trigger fires or explosions.

  A dam or levee failure is a major hazard that must be carefully considered and then reviewed with experts. Most dams are well maintained and protected from natural hazards but not from vandalism or terrorist attack. Nor are most reservoirs well protected from chemical attack. The consequences of such events can be far more devastating than imagined. The 2005 failure of levees in New Orleans caused by Hurricane Katrina produced catastrophic results over wide areas.

  A prolonged drought can be particularly disruptive. There may be many fires and heavy smoke that require evacuation. Potable and cooling water may be in short supply. Both people and equipment must be protected from dust or smoke that cannot be done effectively within many facilities. Hydroelectric power may be rationed and rolling blackouts imposed.

- **Seismic hazards.** Such hazards include earthquakes and tsunamis. Many areas of the United States are at moderate or even high risk of a large earthquake. There were major events in these areas hundreds of years ago, and it is believed the time is nearing for a recurrence. For example, the Ossipee Fault in central New Hampshire produced a "San Francisco–size" earthquake about 300 years ago and may occur yet again, which would cause significant damage to Boston and its suburbs. At the least it would topple equipment cabinets, break cables and wires, and probably disrupt cooling and ventilation to IS systems.

   Tsunamis, which are caused by undersea earthquakes, could at some time hit U.S. shores, based on historic events. And like Hurricane Katrina, a major seismic event anywhere in North America could impact businesses throughout a wide area.

22.4.2 Other Natural Hazards

- **Major volcanic eruptions.** Volcanic eruptions can spread atmospheric dust worldwide, which can affect weather and cause severe storms, damage cooling systems, disrupt radio and satellite transmissions, and restrict air travel.
- **Wildfire.** Fire can close transportations routes, disrupt utilities and support systems over a wide area, require evacuations, and create heavy smoke that is dangerous to people and equipment.
- **Blight or infestation.** Caused by disease, weather, or insects, blight or infestation can create health problems and disrupt food supplies, which can indirectly impact business.

22.4.3 Health Threats.
Of increasing concern is the possibility of health emergencies, such as a SARS or an anthrax outbreak, or West Nile virus in relatively small areas. Such outbreaks can probably be contained with antiviral medicines and vaccines. However, business disruptions will surely result. Of greater concern is the threat of another pandemic that could quickly spread through large populated areas. As yet, there are no effective means to prevent either the onset or the spread of a pandemic, other than isolation and quarantine, which includes closing businesses and schools and perhaps many municipal offices as well. As mentioned earlier as a possible worst-case scenario, personnel refusing or unable to report to work during a major health emergency might total as much as 40 percent of the workforce, and they might remain away from the workplace for as long as 14 months. Consult local health officials how to access detailed information about these threats.

22.4.4 Man-Made Threats.
Accidents cause most security problems. Accidents, sloppiness, and blunders are the consequences of bad design, poor quality control, improper installation, failure to update, and poor maintenance. Disruption often occurs during maintenance. Deliberate actions such as snooping, pranks, vandalism, and spying are all increasingly prevalent and sophisticated but are still overshadowed by accidental, unintended events.

   Moving furniture or equipment (unless done by trained professionals) can damage wiring, connectors, and other equipment sufficiently to crash systems. And while it rarely happens, substantial "accidental" damage can occur during a labor dispute or when nonunion personnel are brought on site.

Construction work, alterations, repairs, and wiring changes often cause damage to information systems. Crews often drape drop cloths over workstations and equipment to keep off dust and debris. But no one thinks to shut down the equipment first, so it becomes overheated and probably fails either immediately or soon after. Crews also plug in power tools, floor waxing machines, or vacuum cleaners in whatever electrical outlets are handy. If these happen to be dedicated circuits for systems equipment, damage may well result. In like manner, workstation users often plug time stamps, electric staplers, refrigerators, fans, and immersion heaters into outlets intended only for information systems. Such mistakes can cause intermittent problems that are difficult to locate.

Wiring runs and exposed wire can also create threats. Wiring and cabling are vulnerable in many ways—and are becoming increasingly moreso. Data cables tend to be fragile and easily damaged by accident, moving furniture, cleaning and maintenance, improper connections (such as unauthorized equipment), rage, or deliberate attack. Metal wires are also vulnerable to electrical and magnetic interference from nearby light fixtures, motors, transformers, or RF emitters, as will be explained. Lightning is attracted to, and electrical power surges may be induced onto, any metal wires.

Fiber optic wiring, which is fast replacing metal connections, is especially fragile. Any unusual pressure or a sharp bend in any fiber cable can alter its transmission characteristics and may cause failure. However, fiber is not affected by any electrical or RF inference.

Cables, patch panels, cords, and connectors are often exposed to accidental damage during routine premises maintenance and cleaning. Vacuum cleaners and shampooing and waxing machines can easily damage both signal and power wiring. Carpet shampooing can soak connections and flood underfloor wiring. The casters on chairs and equipment or the moving of furniture often damages cables and connectors.

Intrusions are a major threat. There are many ways to gain access to the infrastructure of information systems. Once an intrusion is successful, repeated disruptions may follow due to accidents, mistakes, snooping, hacking, spying, vandalism, extortion, or deliberate attack. Intrusion is not usually prevented by premises access control. The infrastructure's vulnerability points are different, and early detection is necessary to prevent trouble before it happens.

Intrusions via wiring and cabling are covered in the prior section. Here the emphasis is on preventing access to hardware, distribution and termination panels, patch panels, or any of the utilities that support them. Assessing the possible threats first involves inspecting the existing infrastructure and the defenses already in place. It is also necessary to determine what physical threats and vulnerability points are not sufficiently covered by premises and logical security.

Unauthorized persons should not be allowed access to any type of equipment room, rack, or closet. Everyone granted access, including visitors, should be logged in and out. And as a second layer of protection for critical areas, a gatekeeper should be at hand to observe everyone who enters and leaves, to authenticate each person's identity, and to know why access is needed. Gatekeepers may include guards, receptionists, supervisors, or managers. Except where high security is required, the gatekeeping functions can be performed remotely using surveillance and access control systems, and monitored by motion and proximity detectors.

Workstations located outside of equipment rooms are generally protected logically—using login procedures, tokens such as smart cards, and biometric devices—depending on the sensitivity of the data the system handles. Theft of equipment, components, or removable media is possible, especially during nonbusiness hours. Substitution, rather than theft, is a much more serious threat. The only safe defense is that all data must always be fully encrypted. Should a theft occur, spare units should be immediately available from nearby secure storage. To save time, thieves often cut signal cables rather than disconnect them. It is therefore wise to keep spare cables in a nearby secure storage.

There are various theft-deterrent devices to clamp or tether equipment to nearby partitions or furniture. These devices can be cumbersome and intrusive, may hinder maintenance or repairs, and most are quickly defeated with bolt cutters or a pry bar. Intrusion alarms are more effective but only detect an attempted intrusion rather than deter theft. Intrusion alarms are usually silent and triggered whenever a case or cabinet is opened. Software can trigger alarms also when a cable is disconnected or broken, or when equipment is removed or fails. Good, sturdy equipment and cabinet locks are more effective and can dissuade theft, provided the equipment and cabinets themselves are not easily removed.

22.4.5 Wiretaps.   Wiretaps are another means of intrusion whose purpose is to copy data and sometimes also to change it surreptitiously. Most taps can be placed quickly and inconspicuously even in occupied office spaces. And most wiretaps are very hard to detect—if not impossible—except by close visual inspection of all possible entry points, which is time consuming and cumbersome, and must be repeated periodically. Very often, wiretaps are simply not noticed.

Taps are used for surveillance and spying, changing or erasing data, stealing software, theft of service, injecting worms or viruses, or planting decoys to trick responders into thinking they have found the true cause of an incident. Any physical access to the interconnect points, cable runs, servers, clients, or network equipment is a major vulnerability. An experienced person can place a tap within a couple of minutes, unobtrusively, even when under escort and closely watched.

A wiretap is basically a monitoring device. It may be a small box connected directly into a circuit to tap off and record its data. The data can then be retrieved manually or be transmitted by wire or radio signal to a remote location where the information can be permanently stored and analyzed. The monitoring device may be a splitter that can tap off some of the signals traveling through the circuit and reroute them to a remove location or to a small transmitter that is close by and well concealed. The better tapping equipment uses system power, not batteries, so its service life is unlimited. Monitoring the data obtained can occur within the building or outside, via the Internet, from a nearby vehicle, or via a telephone connection to anywhere in the world.

Wiretaps have long been illegal in America without a court order. Years ago, an illicit phone tap in New York City, for example, was patched to a leased telephone line to Mexico where the actual surveillance could take place legally. The patch connection was made by someone at a telephone company central office and was not likely to be discovered. But if it eventually was found, the network could be traced and disconnected. This procedure suggests the lengths and expense that a determined adversary will go to, and it also suggests the high value of the information that could be gleaned. This was years ago, long before today's easy access to the Internet, cheap long-distance calls, Wi-Fi, microwave, satellites, and other broadband systems.

Fiber optic circuits are difficult and expensive to tap and sometimes impossible without breaking the circuit or changing their parameters, which can be detected quickly. There is new high-tech gear available for optical taps. But even with this, good results are problematic.

The first method is to create a sharp bend in the cable and detect some of the light rays that may leak from the outside of the bend. The signal is at best very weak. Cable can be constructed to prevent this. Or cables can be run through metal conduit to make access and then creating a sharp bend very difficult, even at junction boxes. Last, a sharp bend will change the optical impedance of the cable run and will slightly degrade its performance, perhaps enough to effectively crash the circuit. The change in optical impedance can be measured, including the approximate location of the anomaly. The cable-bending method may work, but it is hard to accomplish, detectable, and readily observed by inspection. This method can monitor data, but it cannot inject data.

The only direct method to tap a fiber cable is to open a connection, quickly interpose an interface device, and then reconnect the circuit. Alarms should be triggered immediately when a circuit breaks or otherwise fails, and these may also give some idea where the problem occurred. But with a good interface device and by working quickly, the tap can be inserted and conditions restored to look normal before anyone can respond. If this method succeeds, the intercept quality will be excellent, and data can be injected into the tapped line as well.

Spying on what is carried by fiber circuits may be possible from within equipment rooms or at other points where the optical data are converted to electronic form or to radio waves. The equipment to do this and its capabilities are highly classified and generally unknown to most security experts.

Wireless transmissions do not need to be tapped, but the process still applies. All that is needed is a very sensitive radio and a high-gain antenna, often situated in an outside vehicle.

Metal wires are relatively easy to tap into undetectably. Small, inconspicuous induction coils placed next to a wire can easily pick up the signals without penetrating the insulation. Sometimes the taps are done with tiny probes that reach around the circumference of a wire. Induction taps are generally undetectable, except visually. However, induction taps are difficult when multiconductor, twisted-pair cables are used, especially those where each pair is shielded and the entire cable is metal clad, as are some aerial telephone cables to protect them from radio-frequency interference.

When induction is not practical, bridged taps easily placed within an accessible junction box, cross-connect or patch panel, test box, or termination strip. Bridged taps employ a physical connection. On long cable runs, usually one or more inline terminal strips interconnect two cables. These are good locations for taps, especially where there may be unused wire pairs within the cable itself that can be used to route the tapped data to a safer location. Bridged wiretaps can also be inserted anywhere along a wire by penetrating the insulation with a needle or cutting away a tiny piece of the cladding and insulation in order to splice in a tap wire. Bridged taps are usually very high impedance, so they do not alter the circuit; therefore, like induction taps, they are undetectable, except visually. However, skill is required to place them to avoid damaging the tapped wires. As with fiber wiretaps, there are also high-tech methods of monitoring what metal wires carry, the details of which are classified.

Today, the biggest threat from wiretaps is that they are usually done by foreign intelligence, organized crime, or terrorist groups that are very well equipped, highly trained and experienced, and have almost unlimited funding to carry out their work. It is high likely that most of their surveillance is not detected, located, or removed until long afterward—if ever.

22.4.6   High-Energy Radio-Frequency Threats.   A controversial area of research involves high-energy radio-frequency (HERF) weapons, which some experts claim pose a serious threat to disrupt, damage, or destroy electrical and electronic systems and equipment over a very wide area. There are several scenarios.

A prototype HERF weapon demonstration at security conferences some years ago showed that a bulky apparatus constructed from easily obtained components can cause personal computers to malfunction while the device continues to operate. And it can perhaps cause some system failures as well. There has been no more public information since then as to whether a smaller, portable version could emit a radio-frequency beam of sufficient power to disrupt systems dozens of meters away. Such a device is possible but may not be very practicable, except possibly from a large vehicle.

Along with this is another threat called high-intensity radio-frequency flux, which is simply interference from other electronic devices. These can be nearby transmitters, such as high-powered radio, TV, or radar systems, or transmitters in vehicles. Or there may be interference from close-by RF emitters including cell phones, computers, and devices designed for this purpose. Some of these possibilities are design issues, but when portable RF emitters are involved, the situations become infrastructure threats.

In 2004 another approach was reported that is potentially able to destroy unprotected electric and electronic system nationwide by way of an electromagnetic pulse attack (EMP). This report[7] comes from a commission finding that a low-level nuclear explosion by a missile in the upper atmosphere could cause a massive electromagnetic pulse wave that could wreak catastrophic damage throughout most of the United States. Without extensive shielding, electrical and electronic systems could be destroyed, and power transmission systems as well. However, it appears that such an explosion must be done just right or the damage would be minimal.

The defense against all such RF threats is to shield equipment and wiring effectively. A Faraday cage can envelop and protect everything. This is usually one or more layers of copper screening that are well grounded. There also are Faraday bags to protect and store small items like cell phones or circuit boards.

However, once shielding is installed, it is wise to test that it actually works as expected. The author once toured a large, new data center of a major money-center bank. In touting the huge sums spent on extensive security protections for the new facility, someone mentioned that an impenetrable Faraday shield enveloped the entire room. The only problem was that a transistor radio on top of a cabinet was playing clearly and loudly. Had the room actually been well shielded, no broadcast signal could have penetrated.

Hazardous material incidents can include a release within a building or industrial plant, or from an aircraft, railroad, highway, or waterway accident. Many hazardous substances are routinely transported, stored, and processed throughout the United States. Many of these materials are extremely dangerous when released. They can quickly affect a wide area and may require immediate evacuation. In addition to accidental or deliberate release, these materials may be stolen to become part of an attack elsewhere. And those who attempt to steal, transport, and process the materials into a weapon may accidentally endanger others along the way.

Toxic threats include a buildup of radon within occupied space or in a water supply. Radon is released naturally by many types of rock. It is very prevalent and extremely dangerous if it can enter the body. Radon is an alpha particle that cannot be detected by most traditional measurement devices. Similarly, many toxic substances can accumulate in drinking water or building air. Any of these substances will be disruptive and cause anxiety far beyond the affected areas. Consult local health officials to identify and assess these threats.

Fire and smoke from remote events can be troublesome in several ways. Smoke from events hundreds of miles distant can cause health problems, delay supplies and deliveries, and cause food or fuel shortages. Workers may be unable to get to or from work, and may also be concerned about their families, friends, and homes. Electronic equipment is particularly susceptible to environmental damage from smoke or other airborne particles. And there may be utility problems or loss of cooling caused by a large, distant fire.

Nearby fire or smoke can be particularly troublesome. In addition to the problems just mentioned, an immediate system shutdown and personnel evacuation may be required. Power and data lines may be broken or damaged by heat or water. There may be flooding as well, and hazardous materials released that are potentially injurious to people and equipment. There will also be the need to contain the threats and to clean up the environment before full business can be resumed.

Smoke, dust, or other airborne particles can cause equipment failures, as these block cooling systems, clog filters, and build up inside equipment, constricting ventilation and convection cooling. Although these are mostly maintenance issues, they are also potential threats.

22.5 WORKPLACE VIOLENCE AND TERRORISM.   The use of force, harassment, or physical violence is an increasing reality within the workplace. Drug- and alcohol-related incidents are on the upswing, as are workplace crimes necessary to support and conceal such habits. Adding to the threats is the increasing presence of rage within or upon the workplace. Any of these incidents can cause widespread trauma and disrupt business operations for months. Actual violence or terrorism, or simply the threat or the fear of this, can be extremely costly and disruptive.

Any violence situation—whether threatened, imagined, actual, or peripheral—can seriously disrupt information systems, whether the infrastructure is actually in danger or not. Performance, productivity, and morale will all plummet and remain low for a long time following any perceived or actual threat. Full recovery can take many months—assuming that more incidents do not occur in the meantime. Therefore, a safe working environment, good security planning and implementation, and security training exercises are essential so that everyone feels safe.

The likely tools of choice for inflicting widespread injury and damage may soon be the weapons of mass destruction (WMD) rather than the old-fashioned knives, guns, bombs, or arson that inflict only limited damage. WMD devices are far more dangerous, and many are small and easily concealed in a pocket, package, or briefcase.

A small, common-looking object containing biological toxins, and powered by a flashlight battery, can theoretically kill every person within the largest of office buildings. A vial no larger than a lipstick can contain enough virulent hemolytic viruses to kill every person within a 20- to 50-mile radius, if it is dispersed efficiently. Because few chemical or biological WMD compounds have much odor or color when they are disbursed, occupants, visitors, bystanders, and responders are all likely to be innocent victims. Illness can begin within minutes, hours, or days. Laboratory analysis is needed to identify many of the substances. More time is needed to determine the scope and spread of the damage. Ordinary personal protective gear and breathing apparatus can provide little or no protection.

WMDs can be enormously destructive. A national FEMA, Department of Justice training exercise called TopOff I conducted in May 2000, simulating a biological attack on Denver, Colorado, resulted in an estimated 57,000 fatalities. Since then, similar exercises have not released fatality estimates.

WMD threats can be grouped by the mnemonic B-NICE. They include *biological* agents, such as anthrax, cholera, pneumonic plague, tularemia, Q fever, Ebola, small-pox, botulism, ricin, and some others. These are all living bacteria whose incubation periods (the time of onset following exposure) are measured in hours or days.

Nuclear and radiological releases can cause widespread panic but are not likely to cause mass casualties, except to persons nearby. Radiation levels can easily be monitored, and building structures will often serve as an effective shelter.

Incendiary devices are utilized mainly to cause structural fires. A device can be planted surreptitiously and then triggered remotely or by a timer. Rockets and small missiles are increasingly an incendiary threat, as are 9/11-type incidents: airplanes, vehicles, or boats used as bombs.

Explosive devices are similar. These may be stolen or smuggled ordinance or, increasingly, improvised explosive devices made from commonly available materials.

Combined attacks are possible such as explosive devices used to disburse chemical agents (but not biologicals, which are live bacteria that would be killed by an explosion) or the so-called dirty bombs, which are explosives used to disburse radioactive material.

In a worst-case scenario, all WMD events can be exceedingly dangerous and disruptive, and any of these events may someday happen within the United States. Even the rumor of a WMD event can be damaging and cause widespread hysteria, panic, and create a large army of the walking well. Whether the threat is real or imagined, WMDs are costly to combat.

Most details on WMD and extremist or terrorist threats are classified, but state and federal authorities should be able to provide some insight for an effective threat assessment. The authorities should at least be asked about perceived threats, possible target areas, and regional and local incidents and security concerns.

22.6   OTHER THREAT SITUATIONS

22.6.1   Leaks, Temperature, and Humidity.   Threats involving water and other liquids that may be hazardous should be considered also, as well as temperature and humidly conditions where equipment is located. Sprinkler systems in nearby spaces can cause equipment damage, as can liquid leaks from storage tanks, cooling towers, or pipes near equipment areas. Atmospheric conditions near equipment are threat situations as well. Air temperatures that are either too high or too low can cause equipment failure. High humidity can cause condensation within equipment and, worse, a form of galvanic action that degrades connectors that will then fail eventually. Also, low humidity is a threat because this promotes static electrical discharges that can be deadly to electronic gear and is often undetected until the equipment fails without warning. (See also Chapter 23, Section 23.8.7.)

22.6.2   Off-Hour Visitors.   Cleaning and maintenance personnel usually work off hours and are often hired by a contractor or landlord who rarely provides much, if any, background checking, supervision, or training. Very few of the personnel are aware of security precautions and most know very little about the IS systems their work can damage. Many are poorly paid, forced to rush their work, and may understand little English.

Waxing floors and shampooing carpets are usually done off hours by outside services. Moving furniture and changing workstations are often done after hours, as are repairs, alterations in occupied office space, and other major maintenance. Almost always, these people are unescorted, and many are not even logged into or out of the premises or identified in any way. Worse yet, many of these people prop open doors so they can work faster and sometimes so they can take advantage of air-conditioning in adjacent spaces.

Persons who are unknown often come into the premises without proper authorization. Some work for the landlord or the service organization. Some are delivering food. Some are messengers. And some are snooping, spying, looking to steal, or perhaps bent on violence. Even daytime workers may show up after hours. Therefore, the best security policy is to admit no one after hours until identified positively, logged in, and a need to be there is established. Everyone should be stopped at a reception or delivery desk, with no further access into the workplace until properly cleared. Anyone leaving should be logged out as well, especially if they have been out of sight of where they first entered. Screening visitors at any hour has the added security benefit that outsiders do not see where any IS infrastructure may be located or where money, wallets, or handbags are kept. A night bell or intercom outside an always-locked door should be used to prevent entry to a sensitive facility.

22.6.3 Cleaning and Maintenance Threats.   A floor-waxing machine abrades everything it touches and will very quickly destroy unprotected wiring, connectors, dangling cords, or unseen power extension cords (which, by the way, are illegal according to most electrical codes). The waxing machine operator often cannot see any of these items or may not have time to look carefully at what is plainly visible. Carpet shampooing uses a lot of liquid and can flood floor-level outlet boxes and drain into underfloor ducts and conduits. Electrical plugs, receptacles, and unauthorized extension cords for critical equipment are often unlabeled. The cleaning staff does not know they are critical and can unknowingly unplug servers to power their cleaning equipment. Therefore, the threat assessment must first determine whether premises design invites problems, even though cleaning and maintenance personnel do their work carefully.

Users often compound these threats. Many workstations may be logged off but are left running continuously. No one tells users to shut down and cover their equipment before major cleaning or maintenance.

22.6.4 Storage-Room Threats.   Rooms used to store computer supplies, paper, or forms are especially dangerous if a fire occurs. For example, stored cartons of paper, forms, or stationery expand when they burn, then burst into a conflagration that spreads quickly and burns at a very high temperature. Such a fire occurred in a high-rise office building in Manhattan. Even though the fire department quickly contained the fire, some steel building columns were so weakened by the heat that the building nearly collapsed. The cause of this fire was determined to be a cigarette butt that fell between stacked cartons of paper. This was assumed to have been accidental but could well have been arson.

Any storage room containing sensitive or inflammable materials must have smoke detectors, sprinklers, or other approved fire suppression systems designed to protect both the room and its contents. There must also be fire extinguishers nearby. Storage rooms should be kept locked, and access should be limited to trusted persons, if only to protect the value of the contents. There should be access control systems with admittance limited to authorized persons only, with open-door alarms provided as well. Delivery persons should always be continuously escorted. Loitering, smoking, drinking, drugs, snoozing, or any social activities must be kept out of and away from all storage areas.

22.6.5 Medical Emergencies.   Most medical emergencies will cause business disruptions. People stop work to see what is happening, and if they know the victim may remain demoralized and unproductive for weeks afterward. Many will fixate on the circumstances and increasingly involve others to compound the problems. Even minor medical emergencies can cause large and long disruptions. In many medical emergencies, the first five minutes can decide life or death, and professional medical assistance is very likely unavailable that quickly. Any death that occurs in the workplace will result in long-term, widespread, and lasting trauma and disruption. (See also Chapter 23, Section 23.9.4.)

There must be first aid supplies, oxygen, and automatic electric defibrillators (AED) handy in every workplace. And there must be people nearby who are trained and currently certified in cardiovascular resuscitation and first aid. The costs of a disruption alone are far greater than those for providing ample medical supplies, equipment, and training. In addition, a first aid room and a trained nurse are wise precautions and probably a cost savings as well.

Prompt medical attention is essential for senior executives, visitors, and all workers and visitors. Medical threats will happen and will be very costly if medical assistance is not immediately available.

22.6.6 Illicit Workstation.   A convenient method to set up a logical intrusion or attack is to unplug a desktop terminal or workstation that has limited functionality and substitute a full-featured machine well programmed with spyware and analytic utilities. Anyone with a full-featured notebook computer and physical access to the network may be able to connect easily.

Illicit users may then be able to log onto the network, possibly entering the user's own trusted password. They could then search for restricted information and use the full-featured machine to copy network data. Then the illicit user simply connects to a nearby telephone receptacle to export network data via a dial-up connection. (An Internet connection would likely be blocked by the firewall.) The illicit user may use hacking programs to gain supervisory status and spyware to access more sensitive information, crack passwords, steal software, or infect the network with malicious software. The illicit user may install a backdoor entrance into the network that an accomplice can use to spy, monitor network traffic, and modify or destroy data. An experienced user may then erase all evidence of any intrusion.

The intrusion might be done by an in-house employee, contractor, service technician, vendor, or consultant who could breach the network while ostensibly checking a user's machine or LAN connection. It could also be done within a hot zone using a Wi-Fi connection where there may be few, if any, firewall or security protections. Maintenance personnel working off hours also could substitute a terminal inconspicuously. However it is done, intrusion is a serious physical threat.

Security awareness is the best prevention. No one should be swapping equipment or connections unless a manager, supervisor, or nearby workers know the person's identity and what he or she is doing. If there is any possible doubt, the activity should be reported. The second best prevention is good network security, with alarms when any desktop systems is opened, disconnected, or shut down.

22.6.7 Other Local Threats.   There are many threat situations specific to a group, organization, or community. Usually many of these situations are identified and assessed as planning progresses. For example, for a community, important local threats might include vandalism or actual damage to school buildings, schoolyards, or school buses, a building or bridge collapse, interrupted power or energy transmissions systems, damaged fuel storage facilities, or a communications failure. Many possible specific situations will likely be discussed during the planning process, while review and advice by outside experts and government officials probably will lead to more important situations. Some considerations for local threat situations include:

- **Utility disruptions.** Disruptions happen more frequently than reported. Power outages can last a few minutes, hours, or days, caused by storm damage, equipment failure, tree branches hitting power lines, highway accidents that topple utility poles, digging accidents that break transmissions lines, and vandalism or worse, such as toppling transmission line towers. There are increasing reports of transmission towers and utility poles deliberately toppled, power outages caused by insulators smashed or wires cut by bullets, and outages that occurred when wires and bus bars were stolen for the value of the metal in them. There can be static or RF interference or spikes on a utility line at any time due to atmospheric conditions, lightning, or the utility switching their feeders.

  Communications outages can be even more problematic, and few of these situations are widely known. Communications providers are for-profit enterprises and cannot provide much fail-safe protection, backup, or redundancy when severe weather, vandalism, deliberate attacks, or equipment failure interrupts their services. Although there not many alternate suppliers to choose from, the only security protections are redundancy and alternate suppliers.

- **Civil, political, and economic disruptions.** Such disruptions may be indicated by an elevated Homeland Security Threat Level or by state or regional alerts. Other possible disruptive events include a demonstration, march, disorderly group, or an unruly crowd. Other economic emergencies include a plant closing, a strike or a lockout, a transportation failure, or a shutdown. There are also the threats of violence of any kind; a hostage incident or kidnapping; sabotage of any infrastructure (e.g., power lines); contamination of food, water, air, or soil; a food or fuel shortage, a spike in energy costs or a shortage; and the repercussions of a major evacuation somewhere in the region.

- **Coordinated attacks.** These attacks are also possible, perhaps even by terrorists. Here, many points of the infrastructure are attacked at once, and many forms of attack may be used. There may be diversions in order to plant surveillance devices, place stronger weapons, or simply to distract response teams and stretch their resources more thinly. And whether spying is intended or not, the goal of a coordinated attack is to inflict maximum damage and disruption.

- **High solar activity.** Solar activity can also cause large problems. Sunspots affect electrical distribution systems as well as electronic systems, and they can severely disrupt satellite, microwave, and emergency communications, and radio, TV, and radar transmissions.

22.7   CONFIDENTIAL THREAT INFORMATION.   Many other threat scenarios should not be described publicly because they are easily done by anyone with a grievance, and they tend to incite copycats. Other threats that will not be described utilize simple tools or devices that are readily obtained, are inconspicuous while in use, and can be safely hidden after a crime. Avoiding such threats is difficult, and apprehension is unlikely. Nonetheless, mitigation is possible, and sometimes even deterrence, once these threats are known and understood.

Most vendors, installers, and consultants have long lists of such unmentionable threats and ways they know of to disrupt, snoop into, or destroy specific types of information systems. No threat assessment can be complete without asking all these information sources for whatever attack methods they can suggest as well as for methods of preventing or mitigating each threat.

Many useful sources of information and guidance are not generally public—many sources, indeed, that Internet search engines have not discovered. Some of this material is simply not publicly available, and other sources may be derived from classified documents. But briefings or redacted information may be made available to those who need it. More information may be available from local, state, and federal authorities, regulatory bodies, peer groups, business or vendor associations, professional groups, and security experts and consultants. Each of these sources may be willing to share information not available to the general public.

The Department of Homeland Security announced in July 2006 the establishment of 38 regional fusion centers to facilitate the "two-way flow of timely, accurate, actionable information on all types of hazards." Here, federal, state, and local intelligence analysts can share and evaluate information of common concern.[8]

The FBI is the ultimate source of threat information. But this information is mostly classified, and without the proper security clearance and a need to know, the FBI will not divulge much. A nationwide group of people involved in IS security is sponsored by the FBI and does provide some useful (sensitive but unclassified) information, once each member is vetted and approved. This group is called InfraGard, and there are chapters in most states. Visit www.infragard.net for a list of local chapters, and contact them about membership.

22.8 SUMMARY. A vast array of possible physical threat situations can disrupt the infrastructure of information systems and thereby also disrupt business productivity and performance. The list of specific threats may identify several hundred situations, and each one should be included and considered during a threat assessment process that is well done and thorough.

Some of the threat situations are obvious and well known, while many others are much less so. Many are newly emerging, suggested by recent events worldwide and by reexamination of historic data. There also are issues of apathy, denial, and ignorance, where some persons feel that such things will never affect them or that nothing can be done to prevent a disaster. Both assertions are patently false and potentially very costly if pursued. Most threat situations can and will happen somewhere, someday. But whether they do or not is a matter of statistics and not conjecture.

Every possible threat situation can be mitigated to some extent by careful security planning and concerned management to minimize injury and damage. In fact, good physical security can be affordable, effective, and efficient. The first step is a thorough threat assessment to identify and consider all possible threat situations. The next step is to determine the likelihood that each threat may occur, the potential impact if it does, and the vulnerability of the organization within the context of its current security protections. Each step can be calculated statistically to determine the best possible options.

This chapter begins a threat assessment process that takes all these factors into account. Chapter 23 then suggests some ways to protect the information infrastructure and completes the threat assessment process with a cost-benefit approximation to determine the vulnerability of each threat.

These chapters are based on a uniform and comprehensive methodology recommended by the federal government and now required for all federal, state, and local agencies and departments. Compliance is strongly recommended for the private sector, if only as an effective means of risk management.

The value of this approach is that good security is a wise investment. Anything less than good security is a waste of time and money.

22.9 FURTHER READING

Emergency Response Guidebook (2004). A useful quick reference to the characteristic of hazardous materials, including some WMDs, with a table of isolation and initial-response guides. Free copies may be available from state or local officials or downloaded from http://hazmat.dot/gov/gydebook.htm.

IT-Grundschutz Baseline Protection Manual 2004, published by the (German) Federal Office for Information Security (BSI), available to download in English from www.bsi.de/english/gshb/index.htm. This is a comprehensive reference document in three volumes: *Introduction and Modules, Catalogues of Threats*, and *Catalogues of Safeguards*.

Jane's Chem-Bio Handbook is a good quick reference to chemical and biological weapons. Visit www.janes.com for details and see their *Emergency Response to Terrorism Job Aid* and other handbooks they publish.

Multi-Hazard Identification & Risk Assessment, FEMA Publication 9-0350 released in 1997. This in an excellent reference manual, 355 pages. All types of natural hazards are described in detail, and maps show the likelihood of each threat throughout the country. Printed copies may still be available from FEMA Publications or downloaded from the U.S. Printing Office (www.gpoaccess.gov) or downloaded from www.floodmaps.fema.gov/fhm/ft_mhira.shtm.

State and Local Mitigation Planning, How-to Guide: There are nine manuals, FEMA Publications 386-1 through 386-9. Each is available as a printed book or CD-ROM from FEMA Publications (P.O. Box 2102, Jessup, MD 20794-2012 Tel: 1-800-480-2520) or access and download copies from the U.S. Government Printing Office at www.gpoaccess.gov. Search for "FEMA 386-1" and so on. These guides were published in 2002 and 2003 and provide clear step-by-step instructions how to do a threat assessment. Unfortunately, numbers 5, 6, 8 and 9 were never released.

22.10 NOTES

1. National Governors Association report 07/19/2006, www.nga.org/Files/pdf/0607PANDEMICPRIMER.pdf.

2. See, for example, Duncan Chappell and Vittorio di Martino, *Violence at Work*, 3rd ed. (Geneva: International Labour Organization, 2006). Review available from http://www.workplaceviolence911.com/docs/20060624.htm.

3. The International Labour Organization of the United Nations provides a good view of the rise of workplace violence worldwide. For example, look at the paper at www.ilo.org/public/english/protection/safework/violence/violwk/violwk.htm.

4. www.cesnur.org/testi/FBI_004.htm. Every U.S. police department received a copy of the Project Megiddo report and may provide access.

5. As a result of the FEMA shortcomings following Hurricane Katrina, there are currently many bills before Congress to separate FEMA from DHS or to change its name. Possibly, the Collins-Lieberman Bill will prevail, which will make FEMA independent and elevate it to cabinet status, much as FEMA was during the Clinton administration. The current DHS/FEMA methodology, however, probably will not change.

6. EMAP, P.O. Box 11910, Lexington, KY 40578, Tel: 859-244-8222; www.emaponline.org.

7. "Report of the Commission to Assess the Threat to the United States from Electromagnetic Pulse Attack." Available at www.globalsecurity.org/wmd/library/congress/2004_r/04-07-22emp.pdf.

8. The DHS news release is at www.dhs.gov/dhspublic/display?theme=43&content=5760&print=true.

INTRODUCTION TO PART III

PREVENTION: TECHNICAL DEFENSES

The threats and vulnerabilities described in Part II can be met in part by effective use of technical countermeasures.

The chapter titles and topics in this part include:

23. **Protecting the Information Infrastructure.** Facilities security and emergency management

24. **Operating System Security.** Fundamentals of operating-systems security, including security kernels, privilege levels, access control lists, and memory partitions

25. **Local Area Networks.** Security for local area networks, including principles and platform-specific tools

26. **Gateway Security Devices.** Effective recommendations for implementing firewalls and proxy servers

27. **Intrusion Detection and Intrusion Prevention Devices.** Critical elements of security management for measuring attack frequencies outside and inside the perimeter and for reducing successful penetrations

28. **Identification and Authentication.** What one knows, what one has, what one is, and what one does

29. **Biometric Authentication.** Special focus on who one is and what one does as markers of identity

30. **E-Commerce and Web Server Safeguards.** Technological and legal measures underlying secure e-commerce and a systematic approach to developing and implementing security services

31. **Web Monitoring and Content Filtering.** Tools for security management within the perimeter

32. **Virtual Private Networks and Secure Remote Access.** Encrypted channels (virtual private networks) for secure communication, and approaches for safe remote access

33. **802.11 Wireless LAN Security.** Protecting increasingly pervasive wireless networks

34. Securing VoIP. Security measures for Voice over IP telephony

35. Securing P2P, IM, SMS, and Collaboration Tools. Securing collaboration tools such as peer-to-peer networks, instant messaging, text messaging services, and other mechanisms to reduce physical travel, and to facititate communications

36. Securing Stored Data. Managing encryption and efficient storage of stored data

37. PKI and Certificate Authorities. Concepts, terminology, and applications of the Public Key Infrastructure for asymmetric encryption

38. Writing Secure Code. Guidelines for writing robust program code that includes few bugs, and that can successfully resist deliberate attacks

39. Software Development and Quality Assurance. Using quality assurance and testing to underpin security in the development phase of programs

40. Managing Software Patches and Vulnerabilities. Rational deployment of software patches

41. Antivirus Technology. Methods for fighting malicious code

42. Protecting Digital Rights: Technical Approaches. Methods for safeguarding intellectual property such as programs, music, and video that must by its nature be shared to be useful

CHAPTER 23

PROTECTING THE INFORMATION INFRASTRUCTURE

Franklin Platt

23.1   INTRODUCTION.   There are three steps necessary to protect the information infrastructure properly. The first step is to establish uniform and comprehensive policies and procedures for security planning, implementation, and management. The second step is to review the facilities design factors and security defenses needed to protect the information infrastructure as well as the people who use it. The third step is a cost-benefit analysis to determine which of the security defenses derived from steps 1 and 2 will be the most cost effective. Once all possible threat situations have been identified and assessed as described in Chapter 22, this chapter covers the remaining steps necessary to implement good security protection.

A uniform and comprehensive process for good security planning and management is no longer optional or accidental. Today, anything less than good security is likely to cost any organization dearly. And even more important today is that good security now requires compliance with many new federal laws, regulations, and directives, if only to ensure good risk management and to circumvent unnecessary and potentially costly allegations of negligence. Once insurance was enough to cover most threat situations.

But today, disaster, workplace violence, and terrorism insurance coverage may not be available or affordable without an independent, outside security audit to ascertain a good security program is in place. The security audit will examine all facets of the planning, preparation, policies, training and exercises, management and oversight, and response and recovery plans and procedures. These are all the necessary components of step 1 for protecting the information infrastructure.

Some of the many new federal security requirements apply primarily to government agencies, others are industry specific, and a few others apply only to public companies. Many are confusing and some provisions overlap. In time, more groups may have to comply. But for now, every organization should comply, if only to achieve better risk management and less dependence on insurance.

There is one nearly iron-clad legal defense against negligence allegations, and this is to demonstrate that the organization is following the commonly accepted federal security planning and management procedures. Usually this alone is sufficient that negligence suits are not filed and that any remaining allegations are minor and easily covered by insurance. Conformity to the commonly accepted federal procedures can quickly be ascertained by a recent security audit.

Good protection starts in the boardroom and must involve management and everyone else with access to the information systems. All of the organization's stakeholders should be represented in the planning and preparedness process. The constituents include all information system (IS) users, key customers, suppliers and vendors, lenders and insurers, stockholders, the community, and government officials. Everyone involved must understand and support good security.

Good security results from good strategic planning and management. Simply choosing security products, vendors, or standard solutions is not enough and can easily be ineffective, risky, and wasteful. Protection by comparison shopping among vendors, services, and consultants is neither planning nor strategic. Security is an investment in the future of the enterprise that can be analyzed and implemented like any other investment for the best possible economic return, effectiveness, and efficiency.

23.2 SECURITY PLANNING AND MANAGEMENT. There are many new laws, regulations, and federal directives that should now be incorporated into the security planning and management of any organization. Even when compliance is not yet mandated, it is highly recommended simply to avoid unnecessary and potentially huge costs of defending against allegations of negligence, and establishing in court that the security procedures in place are sufficient (see Section 22.2.7).

Some of the new requirements that may affect almost any organization are explained in the sections that follow.

23.2.1 National Incident Management System Compliance. The National Incident Management System (NIMS) was issued by the Department of Homeland Security (DHS) in March 2004 in accordance with Homeland Security Presidential Directive 5. This was signed by President Bush in February 2003 following the events of 9/11. Implementation activities began in fiscal year 2005, and, for the most part, full implementation was required by the end of fiscal year 2006, which ended on September 30. All departments and agencies of the federal, state, and local governments must implement NIMS. And many are currently far behind.

NIMS is defined as an emergency response template to be used during any threat situation, large or small. It is intended to cover all possible threat situations and utilize all possible response and recovery resources efficiently and effectively. NIMS supplements and unifies the incident command systems long in use by most response agencies. Even though NIMS is basically a response plan, there are security planning and management implications here also.

Currently, every government agency must first declare itself NIMS compliant, implement both NIMS and the National Response Plan (NRP) (see Section 23.2.2) in all its emergency plans and procedures, then train and certify all officials and staff involved in emergency operations or response. Then, during fiscal year 2007, they were required to inventory and categorize response resources and supplies (using a Resource Typing list that is still unclear). Because the DHS and the Federal Emergency Management Agency (FEMA) in particular have been chronically underfunded since 9/11, many of the guidance and instructions required for compliance have been slow in coming. This greatly complicates and delays compliance and also impedes the private sector.

The best source of NIMS guidance and instruction is its home page at www.fema.gov/emergency/nims/index.shtm. This page is kept current, and links to printed materials and downloads explain what activities need to be taken, how, and when. NIMS is still a work in progress, which is why its Web site is the best current information source. There are also many books, white papers, and articles on the new federal requirements, some of which are oversimplified, incomplete, or out of date.

The federal government is beginning to reach out to the private sector to ask them to comply. However, progress is slow at best. An independent study by the Council on Foreign Relations issued in May 2006 reports that the "DHS, state and local governments are failing to mobilize the private sector" and that "security plans and procedures required for the public sector and recommended for the private sector are not being implemented." The report is entitled *Neglected Defense: Mobilizing the Private Sector to Support Homeland Security.*[1] There have been many similar and authoritative reports for decades, reports that events have since proven all too true.

However, in July 2006, DHS also hosted a conference attended by many major corporations that are now endorsing NIMS and the NRP, and urging all private organizations to comply. The goal is to achieve uniform and comprehensive emergency response capabilities nationwide. However, it still appears that most of the failings in the Council on Foreign Relations report still apply.

23.2.2   National Response Plan.   Another new requirement is the National Response Plan (NRP). This replaces the Federal Response Plan and also augments many federal industry-specific plans. The NRP was issued by the Department of Homeland Security in November 2004, also in accordance with Homeland Security Presidential Directive 5 that created NIMS.

As a matter of interest, the previous Federal Response Plan was issued in April 1992 following criticism of FEMA in the aftermath of Hurricane Hugo and the Loma Prieta Earthquake in 1991. A uniform response plan was needed, even though the federal General Accounting Office determined in 1991 that FEMA had fulfilled its statutory obligations. The new plan assigned roles and responsibilities to 27 federal agencies and the American Red Cross in the event of a major disaster. Hurricane Andrew then struck south Florida in August 1992 and FEMA was once again criticized by the press. President George H. W. Bush bypassed FEMA and sent the secretary of transportation, Andrew Card (who was later White House Chief of Staff for the second President Bush), to Florida to head up a recovery task force. Both FEMA and the disaster response planning were greatly improved by James Lee Witt, the head of

FEMA under President Clinton. It is therefore arguable that only a few tweaks were needed following 9/11 and not the time, money, and confusion to reinvent a new NRP.

The NRP was revised by a Notice of Change issued in May 2006. There were many changes—51 pages of them. As of this writing, neither the printed manual nor the online version has been updated, and they may not be for some time as more changes are expected. Therefore, each change must be manually cross-referenced.

As the 27-page *Quick Reference Guide*[2] also issued in May 2006 explains, the

> National Response Plan establishes a single, comprehensive approach to domestic incident management to prevent, prepare for, respond to, and recover from terrorist attacks, major disasters, and other emergencies.... The NRP is always in effect and becomes activated during any Incident of National Importance,

which is where the need for response by one or more federal agencies arises. While NIMS applies to any incident, the NRP is activated only for those deemed to be of national importance.

Despite its title, the NRP is simply an emergency operations plan, which all state and local governments have long been required to have. But the NRP now unifies the content and format for all such plans. Compliance also requires certification of senior officials.

The potential value of the NRP was well illustrated by its absence during Hurricane Katrina in 2005 when federal officials did not think to activate the plan until days after the event. Similarly, New Orleans was said to have a very good response plan in place since 2002 that, among other things, determined that 90 hours would be needed to evacuate the city. The plan itself was largely ignored, and evacuation was not begun until 24 hours before the storm hit. The city, homes, and businesses were devastated; few had preparedness plans, and fewer still remembered to use them.

The lessons learned from Hurricane Pam the year before were also forgotten. This was an exercise conducted in 2004 that simulated a major hurricane hitting New Orleans. The flooding predicted was slightly worse than in Katrina; an estimated 60,000 people would have been killed if Hurricane Pam had actually occurred. The exercise would have used the new NRP, and the lessons learned would have been reviewed and implemented, but the funding that FEMA needed to do this was spent elsewhere within the DHS.

Yet another complication occurred in 2007 when the government revoked the NRP and issued a new National Response Framework. The new 90 page framework was issued as of January 2008. For current information, visit www.fema.gov/nrf.

23.2.3 National Infrastructure Protection Plan. The National Infrastructure Protection Plan (NIPP) was released by the Department of Homeland Security in June 2006 with detailed implementation instructions due within six months. This plan results from Homeland Security Presidential Directive 7, signed in December 2003. (This superseded a similar document issued 10 months earlier that was unintelligible.) The NIPP states that "Protecting critical infrastructure and key recourses of the United States is essential to the Nation's security, public health and safety, economic vitality, and way of life." There is more information at www.dhs.gov/nipp.

This plan is somewhat of a laundry list of good things to do and which agency should do them, but it also confuses and sometimes contradicts both NIMS and NRP responsibilities. Nonetheless, this first installment is an interesting reference for any organization. And it looks now that the DHS intends to enforce compliance.

23.2.4 Other Presidential Directives.

President Bush has issued 14 homeland security presidential directives since 9/11, plus many others that are still unknown or classified. Some of the directives are industry specific or only apply to some federal agencies. Many of the new directives are intended to displace previous ones that are already implemented, understood, and perhaps only in need of tweaking to bring them up to today's needs. For example, President Clinton's PDD/NSC-63, *Critical Infrastructure Protection,* is clear, well written, and contemporary. The problem is that the new directives do not amend the old ones or the existing laws. Collectively, all the new directives impose responsibilities that are vague and often contradictory. It may take many years to achieve a unified, cohesive process.

While government agencies can wrestle with which directives to follow and how, the private sector needs to know whether they must comply and how to do it, if only as a means of risk management. This chapter suggests a uniform, comprehensive approach that is achievable now.

23.2.5 Security-Related Laws and Regulations.

In addition to the presidential directives, there are also security-related laws in effect. The Robert T. Stafford Disaster Relief and Emergency Assistance Act of 1988 (Public Law 100-707) has evolved since the Civil Defense days of World War II. The act was last amended in 2002 to update the Disaster Mitigation Act of 2000 (Public Law 106-390), which was itself enacted to amend the Stafford Act.

Together, these acts require every state and community to have a current and FEMA-approved All-Hazard Mitigation Plan and a current and approved Emergency Operations Plan in place. The latter plan must now comply with the NRP already described. Together, these two plans serve the same purposes, respectively, as the threat assessment covered in Chapter 22 and the response plan suggested in Section 23.11.3.

The reason that private organizations should understand and comply with these two laws is to avoid liability issues. There are numerous state laws as well, where compliance may be necessary. But at least following the federal procedures should be a sufficient protection from litigation.

23.2.6 Some Other Regulatory Requirements.

The next industry-specific regulatory requirements can affect the security planning and management as well.

- **The Sarbanes-Oxley Act of 2002** (SOX) requires a public corporation to report all of its internal financial controls, which may include those relating to security management. The act also requires that any future event that can materially affect future earnings must be reported. Most of the threats identified in Chapter 22 can do this, so that the possible mitigated costs of each threat as determined at the end of this chapter may need to be included in the SOX reporting.

- **The Health Insurance Portability and Accountability Act of 2002** (HIPAA) applies to all organizations that receive personally identifiable individual health information, which must be kept private. Many types of organizations receive and supply such information and are therefore indirectly impacted by HIPAA. Unauthorized disclosure and lost or degraded data are all potential security threats that the information infrastructure must prevent. The fines, damage, and liability of a breach can be significant.

- **The Gramm-Leach-Bliley Act of 1999** imposes similar security responsibilities on financial institutions, lenders, advisors, accountants, and businesses that process or receive financial information.

23.2.7 Security Auditing Standards. The only effective way to ascertain that an organization's security planning, implementation, and management comply with the generally accepted federal security standards is to have a current security-audit report. All that is needed is a brief summary and the auditor's opinion statement that the organization is compliant.

There is now a uniform standard for disaster/emergency preparedness that applies to any organization, public or private. This standard can be utilized as an internal self-auditing process and soon may be available to the private sector using independent outside auditors.

The Emergency Management Assessment Program (EMAP) standard (described in Section 22.2.9) was updated in September 2007, with a document provided to cross-reference the new standard to the current NIMS and NRP requirements. This new standard is endorsed by DHS and by FEMA, includes all of the essential functions that make up a comprehensive emergency management program, and should now have been accepted by ANSI as an approved standard. For information, see note 7 of Chapter 22.

Any organization can conform its emergency management program (or whatever terminology it chooses) to the new standard via an internal self-assessment. However, EMAP may also provide an on-site security audit that is independent, rigorous, and thorough. (Disclosure: The author is an EMAP assessor and has participated in the audit of a large, populous state. Note, however, that all of the EMAP assessors serve as unpaid volunteers and have no commercial interest in any EMAP activities.)

Another common corporate-security audit procedure utilizes Information Security Standard (ISO) 17799. This was last published by the International Standards Organization in June 2005 and can be administered by many independent auditors, accountants, and consultants. This process is lengthy but does not cover much about physical security and does not relate to the federal requirements just listed. Therefore, another audit specifically for protecting the information infrastructure is recommended. For information on ISO 17799, go to www.standardsdirect.org/iso17799.htm.

A good self-audit can be done using the Capability Assessment for Readiness (CAR) Report program jointly developed in 2000 by the National Emergency Management Association and FEMA. This was later revised in 2002 and then discontinued following 9/11, although many communities and regions still use the program. The state CAR Report process is downloadable software. The program presents a long succession of on-screen questions regarding compliance. Each is answerable with a value from 1 to 5. The program can then print a summary of about 35 pages. When states were required to use it, the program submitted a full report to FEMA. The CAR seems to be no longer available from the federal government. However, a search on the full title provides many possible links. Most appear to be only the reports, not the program itself. Anyone interested should ask the state officials for a copy first. The author also can provide a copy.

23.3 STRATEGIC PLANNING PROCESS. The planning process must think ahead strategically to determine the best possible security options to add maximum value and contribute to profits, enhance productivity and performance, and avoid intrusiveness. The process of identifying all possible threat situations and a statistical method to predict the likelihood of injury or damage and the current vulnerability of the enterprise to each individual threat is described in Chapter 22. This chapter builds on the planning process, suggests ways to better protect the infrastructure and thereby reduce its vulnerability, and describes how to implement the security planning and management process.

The planning process should be uniform and comprehensive so that any organization, public or private, understands what others are doing and how organizations can assist one another during an emergency. For the enterprise doing the planning, its response and recovery activities must utilize all possible resources. Its plans should coordinate with any number of outside resources that can assist. Good planning must coordinate everything effectively and efficiently. Otherwise, there will likely be response delays and mistakes, resources may be overwhelmed, and needless injuries, damage, and infrastructure disruptions may occur. The consequences of poor planning will be costly and can be fatal.

Good security planning is an investment in the future of the organization. Good security can be expensive, but the potential benefits of mitigation are predictably far greater. The value added by good planning is approximate, but statistically valid to show how to invest in security as wisely as possible.

Some facets of good physical protection to consider in the planning process are outlined next. These suggest some critical elements and how to protect them, and some possible weak points in the information infrastructure. Section 23.11 completes the planning and mitigation process.

23.3.1 Attractive Targets.   Many types of physical threats are increasingly likely to target information systems. The infrastructure is attractive because it is widely disbursed and often easily accessible, and perpetrators are less likely to be caught. Often a physical attack is easier to inflict and much more costly than a logical attack. Spying, vandalism, and sabotage are becoming increasingly prevalent in the workplace, as is the threat of injury or violence—whether real or imagined—that can disrupt business productivity for extended periods. Systems old and new are becoming increasingly vulnerable to accidents, misuse, snooping, and equipment failures resulting from external events. Utilities and support systems can become undependable, while many types of threats, accidents, or attacks can occur elsewhere and disrupt the infrastructure. All these scenarios require effective defenses.

Much of this chapter deals with what amounts to physical hacking. As with its electronic counterpart, physical attacks cannot be predicted as to when, where, or how they will occur. Electronic hacking from within the organization, over its networks, or from anywhere in the world via the Internet is still the best way to break into most information systems. However, physical intrusion can be harder to detect and locate, and often is more damaging and costly.

All information systems must remain fully operational. To ensure full performance, the best defensive strategies must be in place to detect and identify all threat situations very quickly and also to minimize disruption.

23.3.2 Defensive Strategies.   There are many effective defensive strategies to consider. The planning process must evaluate each approach and how best to combine them strategically to maximize effectiveness and minimize costs. These defensive strategies are common:

- *Prevention* so that specific threats do not affect the enterprise.
- *Deterrence* so that specific threats are not likely to occur.

- *Mitigation* to reduce each threat to tolerable consequences.

- *Redundancies* so there are no critical links in the infrastructure that cannot be bypassed. There are many methods of redundancy, such as multiple data paths; bidirectional data loops; parallel or distributed processing; alternative support systems and utilities; and many more.

- *Early warning* to detect impending trouble and delay onset, so that fast response can prevent or minimize any disruption.

- *Layers of security,* which are like the concentric layers of an onion, so that several layers of security must be penetrated before a target can be reached. This adds reliability, because a failure or breach of one layer does not compromise the other concentric layers.

- *Insurance* that can reimburse some of the recovery costs but usually few of the response costs. Insurance coverage often excludes many threats and can be costly. Insurance may not cover (or even be available for) gross negligence, some acts of God, flooding, terrorism, or acts of war.

- *Capital markets,* which are less costly than insurance and better able to lay off larger and broader risks.

- *Self-insurance* to establish retentions (which are funds accumulated for the purpose) in the hope nothing serious ever happens.

- *Contract security services* that are performed in-house, which basically transfer risks but do not necessarily mitigate threats.

- *Outsourcing,* which is another option that introduces still other and often unrealized threats and vulnerabilities.

23.3.3   Who Is Responsible?   Effective security requires both governance from the boardroom and oversight by senior management. Top management must also actively sponsor it and insist that everyone involved understands, supports, and respects the security plans and procedures. Accountability and oversight are essential, as is insistence on periodic security exercises, review, and updating.

Often the role of protecting the infrastructure is sloughed off to someone with little authority, experience, training, or knowledge of the threats. Many times this person is burdened with many other unrelated responsibilities. Given today's potential for catastrophic losses, the IS security manager must be well trained, highly experienced, and well motivated to create and maintain strong system security. There must also be a clear chain of command laid out in the plan: Who is in charge? And who in the organization has what responsibilities?

If possible, the infrastructure security manager should not also be in charge of IS or corporate or premises security. While managers of these areas face similar threats and their groups must work closely together, their priorities and levels of response to any incident are much different. It is best therefore that two or more specialized security groups report to one senior executive officer with clear lines of authority. Even if the role cannot be full time, an infrastructure security manager is a wise investment.

23.3.4   One Process, One Language.   There are now all too many proprietary programs, best practices, solutions, and systems to measure and manage security risks. These are applied with varying accuracy and the procedures, terminology, and often a myriad of acronyms that very few understand, let along accept or are likely to utilize during an emergency. The names of these procedures vary widely also. Some of the terms used include crisis-, disaster-, or emergency-management or response, disaster recovery, damage control, and contingency planning, yet the intent is basically the same. Instead of promoting good risk management, the many approaches and languages only serve to confuse and hinder people who otherwise might be of considerable assistance in an emergency.

While many of the diverse risk management procedures may indeed provide good security protection, most do not accommodate the many new laws, regulations, and directives that now affect public safety. Therefore, when trouble comes and anyone claims damage or injury, the time and money needed to defend such allegations can be enormous. So can the prolonged disruptions, reputational damage, and loss of business that may result. Like it or not, the organization is usually presumed guilty until it can prove otherwise, and this is usually a costly process.

As mentioned previously, the security planning and management process must be uniform and comprehensive, and applied effectively and efficiently. There should also be a current audit done by an outside, independent group to ascertain both security preparedness and compliance with the pertinent laws, codes, and regulations. The least costly and most effective approach is to follow federal guidelines.

23.3.5 Federal Guidelines.   The Department of Homeland Security and Federal Emergency Management Agency procedures provide a uniform and comprehensive methodology and generally accepted standard practices that are uniform, comprehensive, and most likely to deter liability as well. This process is recommended for any organization, public or private.

Regardless of other risk management precautions taken, few organizations can afford to defer compliance with the federal guidelines. An accredited auditor's report as evidence of compliance is likely to be accepted in court without further proof, whereas most other practices will be expensive to defend whenever negligence is claimed—which is likely to be increasingly often. Nonstandard security practices also invite allegations of gross negligence against officials personally as well as their enterprise, which insurance may not defend or cover and that can result in huge awards. It is well to consider the many benefits from adopting the DHS guidelines as standard procedures, not the least of which is that FEMA has far more experience than any other organization in the world and has no commercial bias.

The FEMA plans and procedures are the products of long years of experience and countless major disasters. They define today's best practices for emergency planning, preparedness, response, and recovery. The FEMA model has been developed by representatives from all government agencies, businesses and organizations, national standards groups, the insurance industry, medical service providers, and the many volunteer agencies, all with many years of disaster experience.

FEMA makes the distinction between an emergency, which is a situation that an organization can handle with its own resources, and a disaster, which is when internal resources are likely to be overwhelmed and outside help is needed. The distinction is not always clear-cut. "Crisis" is not a defined term. FEMA also recommends planning and preparation for worse-case situations, which often turn out to be what happens. Many threats can become disasters to a business, even when outside resources respond quickly. For example, the consequences of an equipment room fire can be disastrous when the local fire department responds with axes and water hoses, cuts off all electrical power to the building, and smashes out windows to vent smoke. Even a major incident that occurs away from the immediate premises can necessitate an evacuation, cutting off building power, and creating serious disruption.

Needless liability is a major issue already mentioned in Section 22.2.7. But how does one protect against liability? Whenever trouble comes—even minor, unimportant events—someone may claim damage or injury, and allegations of negligence will surely follow. Asserting such claims has become a large and very profitable industry, especially since juries are often hostile to business or government defendants. Defense is at best very expensive and disruptive, even when it is successful.

Three simple yes/no questions will likely determine whether a claim is quickly dropped or a lawsuit is filed:

1. Was the organization adequately prepared?
2. Was there a good emergency-response plan that was well implemented?
3. Did everyone follow generally accepted procedures?

Anything less than a clear "yes" to any of the questions can readily result in major damage awards. (See also Section 22.2.7.) Using the DHS/FEMA model is clear evidence of due diligence and also likely to dissuade most plaintiffs from filing suit. Any "yes" answer that has to be qualified, such as the use of a proprietary model, is likely to incur a very costly defense. Anything less than a clear affirmation of every question can trigger allegations of gross negligence that will expose both officers and organizations to large awards that liability insurance may not defend or cover.

23.4   ELEMENTS OF GOOD PROTECTION.   Protecting the infrastructure generally requires different and stronger defenses than premises security or IS logical security can provide. The infrastructure protection must be effective, efficient, and affordable. Yet it must also be nonintrusive and user friendly. Too much protection is unnecessarily costly and often counterproductive. Too little can be even more costly and endanger productivity, morale, and goodwill.

Some of the requisite elements for just the right amount of protection are provided in the sections that follow.

23.4.1   Segmented Secrets.   To maintain good security, no one person should know all the details or inner workings of the security systems and procedures. If total understanding of the security systems is segmented into several parts, there is much less likelihood of misuse, fraud, or error, and less dependency on a few key persons.

However, the more people with knowledge of the security systems and procedures, the more these systems become vulnerable. It is easier to compromise security through coercion or extortion, or by an unwise remark inadvertently disclosing information. The list of those with inside knowledge may include managers, administrators, maintenance personnel, users, partners, suppliers, customers, vendors, and consultants. Although many individuals must know at least some of the security protections, no one needs to know all of the details.

Secrets can be segmented among individuals, so that no one individual knows the entire security system, yet everyone shares the details needed to keep the systems performing efficiently. Usually a manager knows which subordinates understand which segments of the entire security system. The subordinates do not know each other's secrets, and if managed properly, the subordinates are not likely to share their secrets. The managers need know only enough information to be sure the subordinates are well trained and are following proper procedures and practices.

While there are significant benefits to segmenting secrets, the knowledge must be redundant also, so that no one person is indispensable. Redundancy is also needed to facilitate fast response when trouble is widespread or when key people are unavailable. Another benefit is that anyone leaving the organization cannot compromise the whole security system. No individual can be tempted, coerced, or extorted into spying, because the knowledge they possess is too fragmented. There is an intimidation factor also: If all the stakeholders believe that strong security exists, no one is likely to snoop or try to break it. Finally, mounting a successful attack requires collaboration.

Beyond segmenting, there is another precaution needed for good protection. If members of the same group must share sensitive knowledge, a "two-person" rule should apply. This is especially important when anyone is able to modify the security infrastructure, alarms, or event logs. The two-person rule says that any modification to the security system requires two authorized persons working together and that there will always be an audit trail showing who did what and when. This procedure also is used when two or more groups share responsibility for common elements of a security system.

23.4.2   Confidential Design Details.   It is often quite easy for others to locate and identify critical infrastructure components. Many times the information is clearly shown on public documents. The signage on infrastructure locations often clearly describes what is inside, and critical components are often put in spaces easily accessible to outsiders. These are all unsafe design practices.

Many types of documents clearly indicate IS areas, support systems, and other infrastructure. The documents may show the locations of equipment, wiring, utilities, and cable runs. Documents that are likely to reveal sensitive information include building plans that show floor and office layouts, furniture, wiring, and equipment locations. Architectural and engineering documents, drawings, and specifications often show sensitive information. These documents often list the function of each area, and even an occupant's name or title. Other types of documents breach security as well. Examples may be as-built plans, alteration and construction plans, electrical and communications wiring diagrams, patch-panel and cross-connect setups, as well as contract drawings or proposals, shop drawings, installation plans, maintenance diagrams, and, especially, documents filed with code-compliance and regulatory agencies. Good protection requires that all such documents be controlled and kept securely stored. Better yet, sensitive information should be removed and alphanumeric designations that are cross-referenced to sheets than can easily be kept classified should be shown.

All of the listed documents are routinely distributed to a wide range of sources, such as interested contractors and bidders, vendors, suppliers, and maintenance providers. Building managers, landlords, and often real estate offices are likely to keep copies on file, and many other persons can readily access the documents and copy them. Most such documents are publicly available or obtainable via the sunshine laws of each state, by court order, or simply by deception. Moreover, many legitimate persons obtaining or receiving the documents have no internal document control or security provisions.

All room and area designations should always be alphanumerical. Descriptive or functional names should not be used for any area. This caveat pertains to the entire premises, all public areas of the facility, and all building mechanical and core areas. Functional designations or terms such as "treasurer," "marketing director," "security desk," "computer room," "network closet," or "telephone room" should never appear. Nor should the names of any occupants, departments or functional groups, or individual tenants' spaces be given. Use only alphanumeric designations. Never include floor plans, titles, or room numbers in a phone or floor directory, emergency egress plan, or anything accessible to the public.

Lists that correlate area and room numbers, functional areas, or any descriptive names should be kept secure in a locked file, as should equipment room drawings, patch panel connections, and wiring plans. All these must be readily available to system administrators in the event of a system failure or when doing maintenance or upgrades, but only on a need-to-know basis. Ideally, even managers do not have access to this information, except when accompanied by security personnel. As well as controlling access to such documents, it is equally vital that every document be kept current.

Finally, security personnel should review all plans, drawings, and documents for construction, alterations, equipment moves, or any other physical changes before the information is issued. Security personnel should also review the invitations to bid and all the drawings and specifications, review again the quotations received, and continue to review every as-built documents produced throughout a project. Internal security should review all these as a matter of policy. If the security personnel do not have sufficient time or expertise to review everything quickly and thoroughly, outside independent experts can be valuable. When properly chosen, these experts can provide broad experience, perspective, and evidence of due diligence, so that management cannot later be accused of negligence in protecting information, people, or property. Finally, the security leader should sign-off that no project documents violate any internal security policies.

23.4.3 Difficulties in Protecting the Infrastructure.

Not so long ago, most IS equipment was housed inside a single computer room, and most of the external terminals and peripheral equipment were located nearby. Cable runs were short and generally within secure areas, and access controls, alarms, and surveillance could easily cover the critical areas. There were often security guards as well. But in those days, there were fewer threat situations and less cost if trouble did come. Many organizations then were apathetic and security was lax. They were lucky, but a few incidents did occur and often at great cost. There were also likely many undiscovered security breaches and still more that were never reported.

Today, the IS infrastructure is much larger and more complex, and the potential costs of trouble are far greater. Today's infrastructure is much more interdependent, and it now includes many more equipment and network rooms. It extends to many more telephone and utility closets, and interconnects widespread and diverse desktop, peripheral, and remote nodes. Today's infrastructure is increasingly harder to protect, and the future outlook suggests many more threat situations with the potential to cause major business disruption.

To further complicate security, there are now many more and diverse IS interfaces and a complex infrastructure to protect. Interfaces now include direct and switched wiring, wireless topologies, and infrared coupling. Access to the Internet, LAN, and WAN networks may now utilize combinations of metal wiring and fiber optics, wireless, satellite, TV cable, microwave, and telephone dial-up connections. Some of these interfaces will be dedicated, others switched, and still others temporarily patched. It will be difficult to even locate all the interfaces, yet each must be protected, as must be their cable runs and the utilities that support them. Today, the early warnings from the security alarms and defenses must be so effective that most trouble can be prevented before it happens.

23.4.4 Appearance of Good Security.

The appearance of an armed fortress is usually counterproductive. This usually intimidates and obstructs both visitors and staff more than it protects them. The same is often true for too many guards and receptionists stationed to block entry points to internal areas (unless this is deemed absolutely necessary). Such barriers tend to enrage anyone who may be already anxious, and can provoke attacks. Barriers tend to be ineffective as well. Even if the glass is bulletproof and spray-proof, the pass-through holes likely are not. Most barriers can be breached as well, and the person(s) inside injured or at least traumatized. For example, some years ago most banks rushed to put their tellers behind thick glass panels. However, they soon discovered that the glass provoked trouble rather than deterring it. The banks quickly removed both the glass and the pass-throughs, which many businesses then bought and installed, with similar results. Anger and potential violence are best avoided by good facilities design, security systems and access controls, and training in security awareness and violence prevention.

There are also considerations whether security devices should be covert or appear in plain sight for all to see. Defenses that are in plain sight can serve as deterrents and promote a feeling of safety, but they can also be vulnerable themselves. Cameras can be spray-painted, shot out, or knocked aside with a club. Any exposed wiring (which is a security no-no in itself) can be cut or shot through. The alternative is to use concealed devices and/or dummy devices or "honeypots" that are obviously positioned. (Both are discussed later.)

23.4.5 Proper Labeling.   Good security requires quickly locating trouble spots, with certainty that the nomenclature of every cable and connector is clear and current. There must be proper and consistent labeling of all data and power cables, both inside and beyond the secure areas. No label or tagging should reveal confidential information. Many vendors, installers, contract personnel, and in-house staff tend to use their own labeling and tagging systems, some of which are clear and understandable, while others are not. The labeling and tagging must match the documentation, plans, and drawings as well. Sloppy wiring management is often the norm as changes are made but not marked or documented, or wiring abandoned and not removed. The status of in-house personnel, installers, and maintainers is likely to change frequently, creating all the more potential for misinformation and confusion. The inevitable result is poor protection and slow response to a security incident. There are generally accepted wire-management procedures, and a single method should be utilized throughout the information infrastructure. It is especially important that all authorized personnel understand and accept the labeling system.

The Telecommunications Industry Association/Electronic Industry Alliance (TIA/EIA) publishes the generally accepted authority, TIA/EIA Standard 606, *Administration Standard for the Telecommunications Infrastructure of Commercial Buildings*,[3] which describes labeling of cables, connectors, patch panels, cross-connections, and equipment. This standard also requires labeling firestops, grounds, special-ground circuits, and neutral wires. The National Electric Code (NEC), published by the National Fire Protection Association,[4] also includes standards for labeling cables and conduits. Copies may be available from electrical supplies dealers. Many books explain these codes. Local codes probably augment the national codes and may also impose other requirements. Generally, any substantial alterations, moves, or changes and usually all new construction will require full compliance with the current standards throughout the premises—which is probably a wise security investment as well.

23.4.6 Reliability and Redundancy.   The first requisite of reliable system performance is reliable equipment, systems, and infrastructure, properly installed and maintained. But carefulness does not always guarantee reliability or a long service life. Some components may be poorly designed, subject to erratic quality control, damaged in transit, or applied wrong. Much equipment now includes a fail-over mode to maintain full performance when a failure occurs. But good security requires more than good reliability. There must also be redundancy: parallel paths to take the load should one component falter. Effective redundancy also requires alternate sites that are off premises to process and store information. It is best that there be multiple alternate sites, each within a safe environment and well distant so that problems at the primary site will not affect any alternates.

Inside each computer room, storage systems should be Redundant Array of Independent Disks (RAID) compliant with any important data fully mirrored. For critical data, the RAID storage systems should themselves be redundant. Servers should also be redundant. Multiple parallel servers with load balancing are a wise investment, so that one server will automatically take over another's load if it falters or must go off-line for any reason. All critical equipment should have redundant power supplies, fans, and hard drives that can be diagnosed quickly and hot-swapped easily.

Other approaches to reliability and redundancy include outsourcing, hot and cold sites, and contract services, but there must be a thorough security evaluation of any of these options considered. Obviously, data paths to distant points must be secure and reliable. But redundancy, utilizing well-separated data paths, may also be a wise investment, rather than relying on fail-over circuits that often travel within the same cable.

For example, radio and TV stations often order redundant phone lines from their studio to the transmitters, at twice the cost or more of a single (and fairly reliable) phone line. One station did this and lost both lines when a traffic accident wiped out some utility poles in a city many miles distant. It seems that both the primary lines and the fail-over lines were within the same telephone cable where the accident occurred. The chief engineer, however, was cautious; it seems he also had a subcarrier circuit on a microwave link that activated itself immediately when the phone lines both suddenly died. Single redundancy itself may not accomplish much unless the pathways are well separated.

Good system manageability is another vital requirement. This includes hardware that can detect trouble before it happens and, if possible, pinpoint the exact location. It also includes good management software with warning and alert capabilities and good logging systems. Remote management capabilities must also be private and secure to preclude penetration or denial of service attacks. Good security management also requires that any changes or disabling of alarm parameters should require two authorized persons to be physically present inside the equipment room and simultaneously logged on. Good system management adds some cost but is a wise investment in effective security and oversight.

23.4.7   Proper Installation and Maintenance.   Good protection requires that all information systems, equipment, and wiring be installed properly, according to the manufacturer's instructions and the intended usage. All the wiring must conform to, or exceed, local code requirements. Data wiring should be independently tested and certified that it meets specifications, current standards, and, if possible, anticipated future needs.

Out-of-the-box equipment hookups and installations are common and the cause of many system failures. Most security features are disabled when components and software are shipped. Proper installation requires careful setup, customization, and performance testing, for which adequate time and resources must be allocated. Promptly installing the latest modifications, service packs, updates, and security patches is also vital to maintaining performance. Delays of days, weeks, and even months often intervene, while new threats emerge or threat levels escalate until the new defenses are in place. Once installed, the information systems and infrastructure must be periodically reviewed, tested, and kept up to date.

Administrators, installation, and maintenance personnel must be properly trained, experienced, and, in many cases, certified or licensed as well. Each person's credentials should be checked before being permitted on site. Given the limited staff, time, and budgets available, there is often more lip service than actual certainty in the process of reliability assurance. Management must understand that proper installation, upkeep, and maintenance together constitute cheap and effective assurance that IS performance is never compromised.

23.5   OTHER CONSIDERATIONS.   There are many other factors that are sometimes given short shrift that can significantly improve physical security. A few of these are discussed in the next sections.

23.5.1   Threats from Smoke and Fire.   Smoke and fire must be prevented within any equipment room. Otherwise, considerable damage and disruption will occur very quickly. No matter how small the incident, the effects of either smoke or heat are cumulative. Systems will eventually fail and usually without warning. Obviously, smoking must be prohibited—but it often occurs because an equipment room may seem to be a safe, cool place to sneak a smoke. Also, equipment room doors should never be propped open by cleaning, delivery, or maintenance personnel, or others working outside when the air conditioning is off.

The first level of prevention is to keep everything combustible outside of equipment rooms. Paper and supplies not in actual use should be stored outside, never within an equipment room. Any reference materials or documents that must be kept within the room should be stored inside fire-resistant files or cabinets when not in actual use. There should be no trash receptacles within an equipment room, and shredders should be outside, under strict control. There should be a clear and firm policy that nothing combustible can remain inside an equipment room, and frequent inspections should be held to verify compliance.

There should be no unessential furniture within equipment rooms, especially desks that can become cluttered and that are not rated as fire resistant. A metal table with one small drawer and one or two metal chairs with fire-resistant upholstery are usually sufficient. Because plastic accessories, furniture, and upholstery may burn readily and generate large amounts of toxic smoke, they must be excluded from most office areas and especially from equipment rooms. Fire prevention can never be absolute, but the possible heat or smoke damage from electrical fires will likely be minimal.

Equipment and suppliers storage contents rooms should be designed to protect and not to accommodate people. Regardless of the actual furniture or its intended use, any space that accommodates a workstation, or where people can congregate, is considered to be occupied space. Any area labeled as a computer room or data center is also usually considered to be occupied space.

This occupied-space designation is very important because building and occupancy codes, the Occupational Safety and Health Administration (OSHA), and other regulatory agencies require proper heating, ventilation, and air conditioning (HVAC), lighting, and easy means of egress for all occupied spaces. The requirements are many and varied. For example, the room air must be ventilated so that occupants continuously breathe some outside fresh air. HVAC systems are designed to accommodate people and do not necessarily protect equipment very well. HVAC systems can be unreliable in continuous use, inefficient, and unnecessarily costly in an equipment room. Yet HVAC is required by code within any occupied space.

Process-cooling systems, however, are designed specifically to cool equipment, not people. As a result, process cooling is reliable, efficient, and less costly to operate. Process cooling systems recirculate the same air within the room, and there is no need for makeup (outside) ventilation. This keeps out contaminants and cuts operating costs. Outside smoke can be sealed out, maybe sufficiently to avoid having to power-down any equipment. See Sections 23.8.7 and 23.8.8 for environmental considerations and smoke and fire protection within equipment rooms.

Inadequate firestops are a major threat that is often overlooked. A firestop is usually a sleeve and a special material to prevent smoke or heat from penetrating an opening in a partition, floor, or ceiling. It also stops the spread of flame. Many firestops are needed throughout the premises, including the building core and the mechanical, utility, and equipment areas—even within a one-story building. Firestops are rigorously required by most codes, but compliance is often inadequate and the devices often are breached by subsequent alterations or wiring changes.

Partitions, building walls, floors, and ceilings must all be fire-rated in accordance with the national and local building codes and other regulations. Proper construction usually is specified by an architect or engineer, and compliance is inspected or certified as soon as the construction is complete. Inspection often occurs before all of the mechanical systems and wiring installations are finished. Subsequently, if any penetration or opening is made through a wall, floor, or ceiling, its fire rating is thereby invalidated and should be recertified.

The Underwriters Laboratory (UL) or similar recognized authority rates and approves commercial firestops before they can be sold legally. Each manufacturer then specifies the approved applications, installation, and maintenance procedures necessary for compliance. It is therefore wise to utilize specialized vendors with extensive training and experience installing and inspecting firestops and to have them conduct periodic premises inspections and certifications.

Inadequate firestops are particularly common in the core areas of older buildings or where tenants occupy multiple floors. While proper firestops may have been provided during construction, installation of piping, cables, conduit, and subsequent wiring changes often breach them. Wires often poke through large, gaping holes hidden by a hung (suspended) ceiling or behind equipment racks or wire troughs. Proper firestops must be installed and inspected whenever changes occur. Many installers do not understand this, or cut corners hoping no one will notice, or assume others will take care of it.

Without proper firestops throughout, fire and smoke can, and probably will, spread surprisingly quickly. And so will dust. There can be substantial liabilities if any people are harmed or equipment is damaged because of improper firestops or inadequate fire-rated construction. The costs, time lost, and reputational damage will be huge. Periodic and thorough fire inspections by an independent and qualified expert will quickly discover building and firestop violations.

23.5.2   Equipment Cabinets.   Most IS equipment is now open-rack mounted to save floor space, for more reliable performance, and for easier access. Although enclosed equipment cabinets cost more than racks, they offer much better protection. Equipment mounted within a closed cabinet can be better ventilated and cooled, kept freer of contaminates, and may also escape damage from external particulates, water, smoke, or liquids. Should there ever be overheating or smoke generated within an enclosed cabinet, the condition can be detected quickly and usually resolved before equipment or wiring are damaged. Locks keep out those unauthorized, or at least delay access and leave evidence of trouble. Open-door alarms provide another strong layer of protection, and wiring conduits to cabinets can also be protected. Cabinets with redundant fans can better monitor and maintain ventilation and cooling, which, in turn, facilitates more equipment mounted in less floor space. In all, closed cabinets can provide an additional layer of protection against accidental or deliberate damage to the infrastructure.

A fire suppression system within any equipment room is usually required by code and often by equipment vendors as well—and is certainly needed for good infrastructure protection. With all of the IS equipment located inside of closed cabinets, a water system with mist sprinkler heads is an excellent, inexpensive fire suppression system for the room. This eliminates the very high costs of chemical fire suppression systems, and will more than pay for the best equipment cabinets. (See Section 23.8.8.)

23.5.3   Good Housekeeping Practices.   All food and drink must be kept out of equipment rooms, since they can cause considerable damage if spilled on equipment, a monitor keyboard, connectors, and wiring and cable harnesses. Food also attracts insects and rodents (which are found in many buildings), many of which also like to eat wiring. Space for food and drink should be provided outside the equipment room, where routine maintenance personnel can keep the food area clean.

Loose papers, books, supplies, newspapers, and trash are fire hazards and also must be banned from every equipment room.

23.5.4   Overt, Covert, and Deceptive Protections.   Effective protection of the IS infrastructure requires many hidden elements—such as concealed surveillance cameras, sensors, and detectors—and all of the wiring that supports them. But good protection also needs some clearly visible elements. It is important to consider which devices are best hidden to protect them and which should be visible as deterrents.

Overt devices are ones that are evident to workers and visitors, or whose presence is implied by other visible objects, such as warning notices. These visible devices, which suggest that some sort of security exists, are intended to deter troublemakers, so that all but the most determined attackers will go elsewhere. Examples are surveillance cameras, access controls, visible alarm boxes, and visible sensors. Although most overt devices are active and recording data, some may be inexpensive dummy devices that only look real, perhaps with slowly blinking indicator lamps to heighten the effect. Covert protection, however, must not be noticeable to either visitors or insiders. There must be no indication that these protections exist, what they are, how they might function, or where they are located. Most effective security systems operate covertly; examples include stealth and silent alarms, concealed early-warning systems, perimeter and proximity sensors, access monitors, and many other surveillance devices that are not readily seen.

It is important also to conceal the wiring that interconnects all protective systems and the utilities that support them. Whether any part of a system is visible or not, the wiring that connects it should not be. Although overt devices may themselves be vulnerable, they will generally advertise that there is good security here and everyone within the premises can feel safe. However, visible devices can sometimes be covered or spray-painted, knocked aside with a club, or shot to disable them. An expert thief can also defeat many hidden systems, if he or she knows what they are, where they are located, or how they are connected.

Another approach to protection involves deception. Dummy devices that look like surveillance cameras, access control devices, and alarm sensors can be placed to attract troublemakers, who may think they can physically damage, disable, or circumvent the system. These visible devices are intended to distract potential troublemakers and divert them away from vulnerable areas. Some devices are deceptive in that they are not what they appear to be but are actually alarm sensors to measure motion, proximity, sound, or anything that disturbs the device. Deceptive devices often are used to divert troublemakers away from vulnerable people and infrastructure, by offering them a "honeypot": an attractive target to distract them, but often a target equipped with an alarm device, surveillance cameras, or other means of identifying a perpetrator and gathering evidence.

There is a gray area between what management can legitimately do to protect its information systems and what may be unethical or illegal actions. Management has a legal and fiduciary responsibility to protect people and property, and those who support deception say that these techniques are increasingly necessary to protect an organization. Others insist that this amounts to entrapment or violates privacy rights. State and local regulations and interpretations vary widely and are continually changing. It is necessary to check carefully with local officials, legal advisors, and insurers to determine what is acceptable and how to manage such risks. Management must then decide to what extent these techniques may be effective and whether less contentious approaches will suffice.

Whether the protection devices themselves are overt, covert, or deceptive, the security systems behind them must not be obvious. No one seeing or knowing about the elements of a security system should be able to deduce the details of the system, the functionality, or where and how it is monitored. An observer may notice a particular device or product or the suggestion of a vendor's standard security solution, but the particulars of the protection systems must remain obscure, and all the wiring that supports them must be hidden or disguised as well.

Everyone involved must be aware of the security policies and procedures. Conspicuous signs should advise that anyone entering the premises may be monitored, as may all communications. All of the security policies and procedures should be understood and accepted by everyone involved. Employees and other on-site personnel should receive periodic security-awareness training and briefings. And there should be periodic security exercises and drills to test the procedures and reinforce the training.

Finally, protection must not be intrusive. Security cannot limit productivity or IS performance in any way. Instead, the protection must contribute to a feeling of safety and security within the workplace and thereby enhance productivity.

23.6   ACCESS CONTROL.   Access control systems are but one layer of good infrastructure protection. They are usually used in conjunction with surveillance and perimeter control systems in order to provide sufficient early warning to head off trouble before it happens. Effective access control requires three tiers of support that are described next. The strength of each tier and its integration with other security layers determines the security effectiveness.

1. **Privileges.** This tier determines whether a person seeking entry is authorized. It is the initial entry-request process that may use an access or proximity card, radio-frequency identification (RFID), keyed or a combination lock. Since many of these devices can be lost, borrowed, stolen, or copied, and many can be quickly

defeated, there is usually not much effort to ascertain just who is seeking entry. Therefore, privileges alone are not strong security.

2. **Authentication.** It is usually necessary to identify a person seeking entry with some degree of certainty. To do this, the person must possess or know something unique that others cannot readily duplicate. Examples include personal identification numbers (PINs), electronic keys, entry cards, and biometric devices. PINs and passwords may be used, provided they are strong and well implemented. Some of these approaches merely strengthen the privileges process but can still be copied or defeated.

3. **Audit trail.** A log is required for each entry attempt to show the date and time, the identification of the person, and the action taken by the access control system. Access-denied and unable-to-identify events should trigger immediate alarms. Logs must be analyzed in a timely manner for anomalies or unusual patterns. Where better access control is needed, each person's exit also must be authenticated and logged.

See Chapter 28 for more details about identification and authentication access controls.

23.6.1 Locks and Hardware.   Strong protection begins with high-quality locks, door hardware, and access control systems that are nonintrusive yet strong enough to deter most unauthorized entry. Lock types should be hard to pick and should use keys that are hard to duplicate. Examples are Medeco® locks and keys with dimpled sides. Ace® locks with circular keyways require special tools to pick but also tend to signal that there is something important beyond the door. Many types of keys can be created from lock numbers, so keep these numbers stored securely. No lock is completely safe. Someone with equipment, experience, and time can open any lock, often very quickly and without causing attention. Where key mastering is used, an experienced person with a key to any single door can open the lock cylinder and copy the mastering system. Therefore, additional layers of protection are needed.

Interior areas accessed only by a few people usually can be secured with a strong push-button combination lock. Key locks are not appropriate, because the keying cannot be changed periodically or quickly when a key is lost or someone leaves. And misplaced or lost keys may not be reported for days or weeks. However, key locks tend to be stronger and less vulnerable to vandalism, so keys may be the best alternative for outside areas or for doors that remain open during business hours. Wherever keys access critical areas, there should be spare lock cylinders and a new set of keys stored on site that can be utilized quickly when a change is needed. Once a lock cylinder is changed, the old cylinder should be rekeyed and a new set of keys produced.

Locks that use an electronic key are particularly effective. Electronically activated cylinders can replace existing mechanical cylinders, and many do not require any wiring, so the hardware and operating costs are minimal. Most electronic keys have a small cylindrical tip that is touched to the lock for access. Both the lock and the key can log each event, identify the specific lock or key used, the date and time, and whether access was granted. And conveniently, electronic keys are not much larger than mechanical keys. However, both can be defeated with the proper equipment and skill. Often two independent entry locks are utilized to provide stronger, relatively inexpensive protection.

RFID can provide good access control, provided the activating device is not lost or stolen. RFID can be an improvement over card entry systems in that it can activate a lock from several feet away. RFID access cards can include photo ID, name, and perhaps an optical stripe for encrypted identity information. As with other systems, RFID can be breached with the right equipment and skills.

Another inexpensive upgrade of key locks is the card-access lock similar to the ones used by hotels. Many do not require wiring and are battery operated, so the keying of each door remains unchanged and an old key remains valid. Therefore, without central wiring, most card-access locks offer limited security and cannot trigger an alarm although some do at least log events. No matter how strong the access control systems, doors have their limitations. Absent a vault-type door and hardware, a determined attacker with pistol and silencer can gain access readily. A small water cannon that is transported in what looks like a toolbox can breach a standard metal door, or the partition surrounding it, with one shot and very little noise.

23.6.2 Card Entry Systems.   The best means of access control is a card entry system, especially the newer systems that are increasingly capable and less costly as well. A central card entry system often controls the entire premises: all entrances, exits, elevators, rest rooms, and many other interior doors. Access cards are usually similar to a credit card and can be carried concealed or worn as identification badges. Access cards are usually imprinted with a full-face photo, the individual's name, the organization's logo, and often a printed stripe with biometric information. Access cards often show number codes to indicate authorized areas of access, and are usually color-coded to indicate status and whether the person must be escorted.

The means of encoding identification data on the cards include optical bar code, magnetic stripe, smart cards with embedded chips that store biometric data, and cards with embedded bits of metal. Most bar codes are not secure; the cards are easily duplicated. Although the newer, two-dimensional bar codes are nearly tamperproof, they cannot store much information. Magnetic-striped cards also have many drawbacks: They cannot store much data, and they are easily altered, copied, or erased (often by accident). In time, the magnetic data decays and must be reprogrammed. Magnetic card readers are not practical outdoors, because of weather and vandalism. Heavily used magnetic card readers and the cards themselves wear out quickly.

Cards with embedded metal bits are effective. The encoding cannot be seen except by X-ray, and it is durable and permanent. The cards must be held against, or inserted into, a reader that scans the card for the position of each bit. They hold very limited data, the coding is factory installed and cannot be changed, and spare cards must be inventoried. In addition, with the right equipment, these cards can be copied.

The RFID systems will be used increasingly and are a better solution, but most can be compromised or copied. These contain an embedded transmitter or transceiver chip. Smart cards hold more data, and most of the chips will accept new data. Some include miniature batteries to store more data and to increase the operating range, to avoid having to come into close contact with the card reader.

Many states and Canadian provinces now issue drivers' licenses with a photo ID and an optical or magnetic stripe, or a two-dimensional bar code. A few of the new licenses are becoming quite sophisticated, including some with embedded RFID chips. Federal policies now require multiple means of positive identification before issuing the new licenses. But, so far, just as fast as new "foolproof" documents are created, ways of cracking them are announced. For example, the new biometric e-passports being introduced by the United States, United Kingdom, and other countries can reportedly be cloned.[4] Eventually, as drivers' licenses become harder to fake or copy, they can be used to identify retail customers, to verify citizenship and age, as charge or debit cards, and premises for access control.

Methods of using entry cards include proximity, touch, insertion into a slot that returns the card when it is authenticated, or swiping the card through a narrow channel or in and out of a slot. Swiping is fast, but the card must be hand held. Inserting a card has the same shortcoming as swiping and is slower. Wear, weather, or vandalism can damage the card and card reader.

23.6.3   Proximity and Touch Cards.   The best of the new card access control systems use proximity or touch cards. These cards communicate with readers using infrared or microwave transmissions. The reading device powers some types of cards, while others contain miniature batteries. Physically, the cards and card readers are weatherproof, vandal resistant, and do not wear out. Proximity card readers can be surface mounted, recessed flush into a wall, or entirely concealed within a partition so that they do not call attention to a security door.

Touch cards are functionally similar to proximity cards, but they must be held briefly against a reader that is usually visible. Touch cards cost a little less than proximity cards and are good only for entrances with little traffic. The touch-card system is slower, and the cards more easily lost, stolen, or forcefully taken.

Proximity cards (which include RFID cards as well) may be used while concealed inside a pocket, handbag, or wallet. Some are worn concealed or hung on neck lanyards. A proximity card that is also an ID badge that everyone in the workplace wears at all times can access both doors and workstations without being touched. Temporary badges customarily are issued to all visitors, even when escorted, and can be used for access control and to monitor areas entered. Temporary badges are quickly activated with specific privileges and can be revoked automatically and immediately when necessary. Increasingly, the visitor cards are created quickly on site with the visitor's picture and perhaps biometric data as well printed on the card. Longer-term temporary badges can be issued to vendors, contractors, and external employees, although it is best that security personnel store visitor badges safely while the person is off the premises.

The new systems provide many useful functions. They are usually laminated and sealed to prevent wear, damage, or alteration. Individual cards are quickly prepared, activated, and canceled—all on site. The system can restrict entry to specific places, days, and times, and holiday restrictions also can be programmed. Any card can be locked out immediately if lost or stolen, or when the owner leaves.

The newer 13.56 MHz proximity cards function up to three feet away from the card reader; older cards were limited to a range of about four inches. The newer cards are also faster, hold more data, and offer more functionality. Many of the card readers also can write data to the card. There is a trade-off, however, between useful operating range and the amount of data stored. The farther the range, the less the data stored. Most proximity systems are adjustable to optimize distance and speed. For example, on outer perimeter doors, where quick, convenient access is more important than tight security, the systems are set for maximum range. Inner doors that need higher security are adjusted to utilize more information and to function at a shorter distance, which is still far greater than the older systems allowed. It is not easy without very high-tech equipment, but proximity and touch cards can be compromised.

There are also self-expiring visitor badges that noticeably change color or prominently display the word "expired" after an elapsed period. Self-expiring badges are reusable and come with a fixed expiration period that is usually from two to 24 hours following each activation. These badges cannot be reactivated, except with very sophisticated equipment.

Cards are not the only proximity or touch devices. Keys or patches also are used. The keys can be small, rugged, and easily attached to a key ring or to a small handheld wand that a security guard might use. The patches work in place of touch cards, or with separate access control systems, to upgrade existing legacy systems. The patches are about the size and thickness of a quarter and are easily attached to anything a person normally carries, such as an ID card or badge, a pager or cell phone, or the inside of a wallet. The newer RFID devices will be even smaller.

Card access often is used for all equipment rooms containing servers, network components, or telephone gear; for off-hour access to information systems by users, technicians, and administrators, and for any areas where high-value items are stored. Card systems usually are integrated with premises security to control access to and egress from the building, elevators, service areas, parking, and rest rooms, and other parts of the information infrastructure that can also take advantage of the access controls. Plan ahead and consider where additional access control points may someday be needed. Piecemeal additions at a later date can be costly.

Each entry into a controlled area should be logged in a way that cannot be compromised. Logs should provide an accurate audit trail of everyone who sought entry, when, and whether access was denied. Where stronger security is needed, each egress should be logged in the same way. The logging system is best monitored by software that can review all system data in real time, flag trouble quickly, issue periodic summary reports, and quickly search and summarize unusual events. Reviewing logs manually is a cumbersome, time-consuming task. If only manual auditing is possible, there must be a firm policy to do this every few days.

Card entry systems by themselves do not provide strong protection. Therefore, some degree of authentication is required.

23.6.4 Authentication.

Anyone can use an access control card that may be borrowed, lost, copied, altered, stolen, or taken by force. Therefore, authentication is another layer of security that is needed to establish the identity of the person seeking entry with some degree of certainty. Authentication devices commonly include a biometric scanner, a numeric keypad, and visual or voice identification by a computer or by another person. All such devices come in varying security strengths and each can be used in combination.

When an access card is read, the system must verify that the *card* has the requisite privileges for that place, date, and time. If it does, it then becomes necessary to authenticate the identity of the person using the card. For this purpose, a numeric keypad was once the most common device whereby the card user entered a personal identification on a number keypad. Now most use a touch screen where the numbers will appear in random order. If the system validated the PIN, it activated an electric door strike to momentarily unlock the door. This system can be slow, cumbersome, and easily compromised. In some systems, everyone uses the same PIN and is supposed to keep it private. However, PINs can be forgotten, lost, or discovered by others.

Visual authentication is a better approach. This can be done by a computer or by a security guard or receptionist who can see the entrance or monitor it via a surveillance camera or a video intercom. Emergency-type video intercoms work well because they provide the remote authentication with a visual image and can monitor sound continuously, so that the authenticator can speak with and challenge whoever approaches the door. When identify is verified, the system or other person activates the electric door strike to unlock the door. This system offers stronger security and is faster than a keypad. It also facilitates recording and logging all entrances and exits, especially during off-hours. Breaches can happen, if the person seeking entry can deceive the guard or receptionist.

Biometric scanners offer the strongest security. They offer faster, more positive identification of every individual and do away with the need to remember a PIN. Biometric scanners can read any of these personal attributes, which are listed somewhat in order of their current popularity: fingerprint patterns, facial characteristics, voiceprint, handprint, signature, retinal details, or height and weight.

Most biometric systems can be adjusted to be highly sensitive (which is slower and may require repeated entry attempts, but is very hard to breach) or less sensitive (which is still fast but may result in some false authentications). Before choosing a biometric system, it is necessary to determine that the users understand and will accept it. For example, some people balk at having to use a retinal scanner, while others may feel that any biometric device invades their privacy. The latter reason is invalid because most biometric systems cannot be used to identify any person not already known to the system. Increasingly, especially in critical public places, these systems can check every individual against criminal and terrorist databases and quickly alert law enforcement. It is difficult to steal an identity using biometrics because one must also know the encoding algorithms used.

Fingerprint scanners are the most common and are becoming increasingly powerful. Initially, these utilized optical scanning, which could be fooled by photographs, wax impressions, or by a severed digit. The newer capacitive scanners use electronics rather than optics and can provide nearly certain identification. Usually, three of the user's fingers are "enrolled" in the system in case some fingers are later bandaged or dirty. If all the enrolled fingers are incapacitated, single-use passwords can be used to bypass the system.

Most fingerprint scanners cannot identify an individual by name, but only that a person seeking entry matches the person whose biometric identity has been enrolled. Most scanners do not conform to the uniform, automatic fingerprint identification standards used by law enforcement. Instead, they scan a small area of the finger and apply proprietary algorithms and encryption. A template from one system is usually meaningless to another.

Accuracy of fingerprint scanning is affected by the angle and position of the finger and by the pressure applied. Most systems allow sensitivity adjustment to optimize enrollment and verification times and success rates as well as to minimize delays and false negatives that require repeated access attempts. While well suited to most applications, fingerprint scanners may not be appropriate where the user could have dirty or thickly callused hands or must wear gloves (such as healthcare workers).

Facial recognition is the basis of another popular scanning system. It uses graphics technologies and any surveillance camera to measure the size and relationship of prominent facial elements. Most systems are proprietary and cannot be used to identify an individual by name, but some others are compatible with law enforcement standards. Sensitivity and accuracy are dependent on the distance, position, and angle of the head as well as on the background lighting. Cameras at all entry points must be positioned to photograph the subject at the same angle that their faces were "enrolled." Not all facial recognition systems offer strong security; some can be fooled by a face mask or a photograph. Others are best left at their highest sensitivity settings to avoid spoofing, which may require multiple attempts at entry.

Voice-print scanning can be used, but mostly for access to a terminal or workstation. The better systems display random words on the monitor so a prerecorded response cannot be used. Most use the workstation's microphone or, increasingly, a cell phone. Voice scanners can be affected by hoarseness, so there should be a one-time password access provision. These systems can be useful for remote login, especially while traveling, although the low bandwidth of dial-up circuits may lessen the system's usefulness.

Retinal or iris scanners are considered the best security, but authentication can take a few seconds. For access control, the user must generally look closely into an eyepiece, which is traumatic to some people. But for access to a terminal or workstation, a Web camera is generally placed on top of the monitor, 17 to 19 inches from the eye. The user's head must be positioned to align a white dot within a colored circle. The user must hold still, without blinking, while the scan proceeds automatically. The camera can be used for surveillance to see who is near the workstation.

23.6.5 Integrated Card Access Systems.   Biometric scanners are used increasingly by other applications, and most can readily coordinate with an access control system. Applications include network user authorization, and access to terminals and workstations and to software applications and data. Biometric readers can be built into laptops, keyboards, mice, or peripheral readers. They can be used with access cards, badges, and proximity or RFID devices for authentication with some degree of certainty. Scanners that are mostly proprietary are currently integrated with encryption systems (e.g., virtual public networks, public key infrastructure, and smart cards) to authenticate transactions including credit cards, financial, banking, and automatic teller machines. Biometrics are increasingly used to identify hospital patients, welfare recipients, people who frequently enter the United States, and similar applications that involve identifying a diverse or widely dispersed group.

Infrastructure security protection can be independent of, or integrated into, a comprehensive premises security system. Either cards or badges can provide many other functions beyond basic access control. Applications include off-hour access to the building, elevators, and premises; control of building entrances, rest rooms, and parking areas (especially at night); purchases at a cafeteria or company store, or for charging stationery or materials picked up from a supply room. They can also be used to receive classified documents.

For greater protection and efficiency, an integrated enterprise-wide, Web-based system can control access to various premises, locked doors, infrastructure components, networks, workstations, applications, secure data, and Web connections. This arrangement offers comprehensive security by logging every event. Centralized logs can yield much more meaningful security information, because an integrated system provides better early warnings to head off trouble before it happens.

23.6.6 Portal Machines.   Airportlike security checkpoints are perhaps a wise idea in today's environment of increased threats and violence. A portal machine is the archway one must walk through during the airport security process. It detects concealed metal, such as guns and knives, and tools that might be used to cause trouble. A portal and can be used to detect IS components (such as storage media) being smuggled into or out of the premises.

Newer trace-portal machines can detect many explosives as well. The person entering is asked to stand still for a few seconds while the machine releases several puffs of air and captures samples that are then analyzed for a number of hazardous or explosive substances. When a guard is not present, a computerized voice instructs the person to proceed, or a turnstile can hold the person in place. The newer machines were announced in August 2006 for use at Midway International Airport in Chicago.[5]

Such devices might be appropriate for all who enter the premises and at entrances to critical areas or equipment rooms as well.

23.6.7 Bypass Key.

Whatever the systems used, there should be one bypass key that can open every door that uses electronic or electrical controls. The bypass key is for emergency use only. It is a unique key that is not on any mastering system and is available only to a few highly trusted people. The cylinders should be heavy duty and very hard to defeat, with the keys nearly impossible to copy. Careful control and protection of each key is essential. The loss of a key may not be discovered quickly, and the time and costs of rekeying every lock will be substantial. Meanwhile, every door on the access control system is vulnerable.

Bypass passwords for individual users also may be needed. These passwords should trigger a silent alarm whenever used, so that security can respond to the site or verify identity by telephone, surveillance, or intercom. One-time passwords provide the best security.

23.6.8 Intrusion Alarms.

Intrusion alarms are necessary to provide perimeter and early-warning alarms and are usually needed as extra layers of security. There are several methods of intrusion detection. Digital surveillance cameras with motion detection are best because they can monitor visually what is happening and record what they see. Other methods include proximity and pressure sensors mounted within the perimeter walls or floors or inconspicuously within the room. Most of these sensors can detect intrusion and forced entry and can pinpoint the location of trouble, but they provide no details, monitoring, or evidence-recording capabilities. Proximity and pressure sensors can protect long-distance perimeters, cable runs, and utilities inexpensively. Concentric layers of such devices are necessary for sufficient early warning to prevent trouble from happening.

The best motion detectors use digital closed circuit television (CCTV) surveillance cameras that can sense movement while observing and recording the event. Miniature cameras that are inconspicuous or concealed are particularly effective and increasingly inexpensive. Several cameras can record pictures from many angles and often can identify an intruder positively. In a larger area, cameras often use swivel-tilt mounts and zoom lenses, which can be controlled automatically and remotely as well. Color cameras are preferable, as are cameras that automatically adjust to light conditions, including near darkness.

Some CCTV cameras include a military-type night-scope mode, which is relatively inexpensive and functions well in near-total darkness. These cameras also work well in normal light and can switch automatically to night-scope mode when necessary to see clearly and to record evidence. Other types of cameras, such as infrared, work well where there is no (humanly) visible light.

Other intrusion detectors use radar technology or measure changes in capacitance or inductance to sense intrusion. Most cameras and detectors can trigger an alarm as soon as they are disabled or lose power. Detectors may be wall- or ceiling-mounted devices as an overt means of deterrence, but these may then be vulnerable to spray paint, wire cutters, a gun, or a club. Therefore, intrusion detection sensors are usually concealed, or at least inconspicuous.

Perimeter alarms are especially important in building core areas, or public areas within or outside a building, to provide ample early warning of an intrusion that might soon affect a secure area. Digital video cameras are best for this but may be ineffective over large areas or long distances. Therefore, many proximity devices are used to monitor intrusion. Most utilize long sensor wires that are surface-mounted inconspicuously or hidden within partitions, ceilings, and sometimes inside of conduit. These systems detect the presence of a standing adult or a large animal that may come within a few feet of the sensor wire. The sensor wires can be very long, so zoning is often necessary to pinpoint an incident at least within a general location.

A better and cheaper alternative can be fiber optic perimeter alarms. Developed for the military and national security installations, the fiber optic systems are very sensitive and can monitor, evaluate, and record events. The sensor wires can also be embedded inside drywall or masonry partitions, ceilings, floors, or conduit and will detect both pressure changes and ambient sound. Because they do not measure proximity and can monitor and evaluate events, false alarms are less likely. They can warn of an impending accident or efforts at forced entry, and may soon be able to locate the event as well. These systems use software that can discriminate between recognized events and situations that are unknown or potentially dangerous. All the events are recorded and can be replayed and reviewed by a remote operator at any time.

Increasingly, inexpensive monitors are available that connect wirelessly via Wi-Fi, mesh networks, cell phone, satellite, a radio channel or sometimes via microwave. Such devices save the high costs of direct wiring to remote areas and the need to protect and conceal the wiring. But there is also a trade-off with reliability and security, as any radio frequency device can be monitored or jammed and may also be spoofed.

In addition to intrusion alarms, environmental alarms should be provided to measure temperature, humidity, and smoke, fire and flood situations within all critical areas and equipment cabinets as well, as described in Section 23.8.1.

23.6.9 Other Important Alarms.   A duress alarm system is recommended within most critical areas. This is usually a large red button or an emergency intercom conspicuously mounted near the exit. It is used if someone is injured or ill, when trouble occurs that other alarms will not immediately sense, or if violence is threatened. The emergency intercom types are best because each party can talk and listen. Those with a CCTV camera are described here, but many inexpensive emergency intercoms that provide audio only can be useful. Security personnel can constantly monitor all sounds within a secure area, and anyone inside can readily talk with security personnel. Duress alarms are usually silent. And activation devices can be concealed or located inconspicuously in case a potentially violent situation erupts. Duress alarm activators inside of cash drawers, in the knee wells of desks, or under counters have been common for years.

Beyond access control and authentication, it is also important to know whenever a locked door is not fully closed. There should be a sensor that warns whenever an access-controlled door is open or ajar. The sensor is normally built into the door buck (frame) to provide a silent alarm. An open-door alarm system delays for a few seconds in order for one authorized person to enter or exit normally. A short delay prevents leaving a door ajar for someone else to push open, piggybacking when another person enters or leaves, and tends to prevent anything large being taken in or out. The open-door alarm also prevents a door from being propped open at any time. The door-ajar sensors should be concealed at all times so users are unaware of their existence. Otherwise, they may be taped or jammed or otherwise defeated.

A final security protection is to prevent "double-dipping" whereby an authorized person requests multiple entries in order to admit unauthorized persons. The access control system can prevent this; once persons enter a space, they must be logged out before they can try again to enter.

23.7   SURVEILLANCE SYSTEMS.   Today, surveillance systems are designed and laid out to document fully every event, to facilitate positive personal identification, and to provide legal evidence when needed. Today's digital cameras, controllers, and recorders can do all this and more. The old analog or film cameras and recorders are inadequate and should be replaced, especially since the new surveillance systems are much less expensive.

If the protection is designed well, cameras can provide an undisputable, accurate, historical record that is available instantly. Cameras never sleep and are not distracted by repetitive tasks or boredom. More important, cameras can provide early warning, and can document events from many perspectives, concurrently and synchronously. Cameras increasingly incorporate microphones and interface with emergency audio intercoms, better to assess a situation, assist people on the scene, or challenge suspicious persons. The very presence of visible but inaccessible cameras usually deters most troublemakers. Protecting the infrastructure requires both early warning and identifying the nature of trouble before it can happen. The new surveillance systems can do this effectively. And they can be integrated with other alarms and with premises security systems for strong, seamless protection.

23.7.1   Surveillance Cameras.   Surveillance cameras are far more effective and much less expensive than guards, watchmen, or extra receptionists. However, for strong, redundant, and flexible security protection at important locations, both cameras and people will be needed.

Surveillance capabilities are becoming increasingly effective protective devices. They can now see more, detect some dangerous hidden materials, and, increasingly, decide what is important to monitor. For example, General Electric recently announced a smart camera that can detect explosives by recognizing the telltale waves emitted and can also detect erratic or unusual body movements within a crowd to thwart possible terrorism.[6]

Equipment rooms and other sensitive areas once relied on motion detectors for security, but now digital cameras with motion detection work better. Digital cameras also function well indoors and outside, and under most light conditions, from sunlight shining into the lens to near, if not total, darkness. When used outdoors, digital cameras are immune to all but very severe weather conditions. They are, however, affected by heavy smoke, snow, ice, and rain. Wind-blown objects and sometimes birds or small animals can distract their motion-detection systems.

Today's digital systems are far more capable and reliable than the earlier analog or film cameras. Cameras were once the weak link because the details were not clear or too small. Many of the old cameras were needed to cover an area, and even then, necessary details were often out of focus. Now cameras are much smaller, less expensive, and take advantage of auto-focus, tilt, and zoom capabilities to yield much better pictures. Almost all cameras now use color as well for better clarity. Some also incorporate an inexpensive, monochrome, night-scope mode that works well in total darkness. Digital cameras automatically correct electronically and mechanically for varying ambient light conditions. Most can correct for background lighting conditions that would otherwise cause subjects to be underexposed, for sunlight glaring directly into the lens, and for unusual brightness that would otherwise wash out a useful image. All of the images can be viewed in real time, and one or more persons can simultaneously control the views and scroll back to freeze and enlarge frames. All viewers can adjust the brightness, contrast, colors, and zoom, and can apply filters to bring out foggy details. Any viewer can save anything viewed.

All but the smallest indoor cameras now include a microphone so that both video and audio are recorded. Outside the facilities, some installations interface with an emergency intercom so background sound is continuously monitored and dialog recorded. Emergency intercoms are particularly good deterrents because security personnel can confront possible troublemakers and advise them that they are being recorded. Most will back off or flee before trouble occurs. Although many camera control systems provide electronic zoom, the primary zoom function should be mechanical. Electronic zoom systems are inexpensive, but they lose resolution and images can quickly become unidentifiable.

Miniature cameras can be particularly useful and save money as well. Cameras less than one inch in diameter can provide sharp detail. Some units with zoom lenses and pan and tilt mounts can be hidden within any common object.

Opinions vary as to the ethics of using concealed cameras, and some state laws limit their use as invasions of privacy. Generally, the rules of good surveillance practice are the same as monitoring telephone conversations, e-mail, and Internet use. In order to protect itself, the organization has a right to see and hear whatever is going on in and around its premises. But signs should be posted so that workers and the public are advised that all persons entering the premises may be monitored for safety and security purposes. Company policies should explain this, and why surveillance is necessary.

23.7.2 Camera Locations and Mounts.   To serve as a deterrent, some cameras should be readily visible, but this may present some problems. Overt cameras placed too high are not good for identifying people, while cameras placed too low can be spray-painted, covered, or smashed. Any visible camera can be shot out (perhaps unnoticed using a silencer). Older cameras are good for overt use because they are large and may provide backup surveillance. Another option is dummy cameras, some of which have visible indicator lights or automatically pan to attract attention. Some dummy cameras are in fact alarms that will trigger if the unit is disturbed or if its wires are cut.

Surveillance systems should be able to identify troublemakers and must be able to gather evidence admissible in court if needed. The areas monitored, the camera angles, and the lenses selected are all important. Hundreds of millions of facial images are stored in government databases worldwide (including licenses, passports, and other official documents), so a good surveillance system may indeed be useful to identify troublemakers. But the police standard face-recognition technology requires a frontal full-face view, which is possible only when the camera position is not much higher than the person's head.[7] Surveillance of a wider area requires an elevated camera that can see greater distances, zoom in on details (especially faces and vehicle license plates), and closely follow an event. Wide-area views are also necessary to spot multiple troublemakers. Several camera angles will likely be needed to gather good evidence.

Outdoor cameras are usually attached to a swivel, tilt mount, and inside of weatherproof domes or larger enclosures when large zoom lenses are needed. There is usually no attempt at concealment because the cameras are too high to reach, and they provide good deterrence as well. Many may be inconspicuous, however, or even disguised.

When large cameras and enclosures are used, the direction the camera is looking in may be obvious. Often troublemakers will create a distraction to lure the cameras away from the real problems.

23.7.3 Recording Systems.
Once VCRs were the norm, but now most recording is done with hard drives that can store hundreds of hours of audio and video taken from multiple sources. And increasingly, solid state drives are also used.

Once, only one person could review the tapes and then, usually, only after the recording was complete. Now one or more people may access and analyze the information simultaneously. Once, 31 VCR tapes were recommended for each system: one tape for each day of the month, after which the tape was inspected and reused. Now one hard drive can record a month's data, which can then be inexpensively archived on DVDs or at remote storage locations. The VCRs often recorded in a lapse-time mode to save tape until an event occurred to trigger real time recording. Now everything can be recorded continuously in real time to examine fully the happenings before, during, and after an event.

23.7.4 Camera Control Systems.
Camera control systems commonly can direct the swivel (pan), tilt, mechanical zoom, aperture, and background lighting of each camera. Some control systems can automatically pan cameras back and forth across large viewing areas and also provide motion detection. Some control systems can also stop panning and zoom in on any unusual event. This is a valuable feature that must be carefully programmed so the system is not distracted by spurious events or deliberate diversions. Usually each camera can also be controlled manually and often from remote locations.

A major advantage of a digital system is that each camera provides continuous images, usually at about 30 frames per second, which fiber optic and other broadband connections bring to the recording system in real time and high resolution. The control systems usually allow one or more persons to roll back the images without affecting the real-time recording. Each viewer can scroll backward and forward, freeze frames, zoom, crop, or enhance the image electronically, and save any material to another medium or system as evidence.

23.7.5 Broadband Connections.
The advantage of broadband camera connections is that the information is available in real time and with high resolution, and that more camera control functions are possible. Fiber optic cabling does this best, but it should be dedicated and well protected. Remote cameras can also be connected via a LAN, wireless, or broadband Internet connection, if done carefully, so that the data is secure and other traffic is not impeded.

Digital multiplexing is another advantage of broadband connections. Multiplexing over metal wiring once necessitated delays, lower resolution, and fewer frames transmitted per second, even though each camera was providing continuous, high-quality images. Now digital multiplexing over fiber connections allows all data from all cameras to be transmitted simultaneously. Multiplexing is accomplished remotely as signals from several cameras are combined into a single broadband connection to the control system. Connections among control systems are also multiplexed to minimize line charges. The signal interfaces between each camera and the multiplexer can be fiber optic, microwave, a network, or the Internet. This way, hundreds of cameras can be networked economically.

Radio or microwave multiplexing is another option, but it is not very fast and is subject to interference or disruption during severe weather conditions.

23.8   OTHER DESIGN CONSIDERATIONS.   Good protection begins with good facility design that will ensure the safety of the information infrastructure and the people who use it. Protective systems become expensive and inefficient when the premises themselves do not facilitate good security. Proper interior design, facilities layout, engineering, and construction can maximize security effectiveness, minimize costs, enhance productivity and morale, and generally boost profits. The starting point is an inspection of all sites and review of all as-built plans and construction documents.

Premises security inspection and review are best augmented by using independent, outside security experts. Comprehensive and objective architectural, design, engineering, IS infrastructure, and premises security experience are all needed and may not all be available internally or from vendors. The inspection and review process always must be threat-specific and must relate to a thorough threat assessment (which is described in Chapter 22). The premises inspection can then serve to validate the vulnerabilities identified by the threat assessment. Once some of the vulnerabilities are corrected, the premises inspection should be repeated.

For organizations using classified information, or where very strong security is needed, reference should be made to the many publications of the federal National Institute of Standards and Technology (NIST).[8] Begin with FIPS Publication 199, *Standards for Security Categorization of Federal Information and Information Systems*, and FIPS Publication 200, *Minimum Security Requirements for Federal Information and Information Systems*. Also look at the many publications from the Computer Security Resource Center (CSRC) within NIST, beginning with the Automated Security Self-Evaluation Tool.[9] Understanding these standards may require outside expertise to independently certify compliance.

Effective infrastructure protection can prevent trouble from happening. To do this, there must be ample early warning, which, in turn, requires good facilities planning and design, effective premises and infrastructure security in place, and the awareness and vigilance of everyone in the area. All must work together seamlessly, efficiently, and proactively.

Good facilities design can be efficient, nonintrusive, cost effective, and inexpensive—even within existing facilities. Here are some guidelines and suggestions.

23.8.1   Choosing Safe Sites.   Sites for equipment rooms and utility closets should be protected from possible threats. Infrastructure sites should be located far away from all piping, tanks, or equipment that uses any liquid that could possibly leak or spill. Most plumbing tends to leak unexpectedly at some time or can be intentionally breached, so it is well to assume that any pipe, connection, container, or pump will eventually burst or leak. Placing sensitive sites at a distance from such threats is safer and cheaper than any other form of protection. The danger zone where leaks may spread must include an ample vertical distance and horizontal area. Begin the danger zone with a pyramid from any leak source, downward several floors, and outward horizontally well beyond the infrastructure areas.

Most buildings require fire-suppression sprinklers in all areas. Any may activate by accident, vandalism, or an actual fire, and may cause considerable flooding. Also, infrastructure sites should be located away from windows, exterior walls, roofs, skylights, building setbacks, and storm drains, which are all potential sources of flooding. Treated water used in heating, air conditioning, and solar systems presents a worse problem, in that the chemicals can quickly destroy electronic equipment, connectors, and wiring.

If all of the infrastructure cannot be positioned at a safe distance from all liquids and hazardous materials, there must be special protections and alarms. Protections include sealed, waterproof construction, drains, berms or other diversion devices, and proper materials close at hand to control any spill. There should be environmental alarm sensors near where leaks or spills could occur. Floor drains must also protect the equipment areas, especially those that use sprinklers; otherwise, cleanup will be difficult.

Infrastructure sites should not be visible or accessible from any public area. Infrastructure wiring or cables should not run through the building core, public, or mechanical areas, including rest rooms, slop sinks, janitorial closets, and stairwells. Avoid placing equipment or cables where any persons might loiter. All equipment room entrances should be clearly visible from workplaces where employees can readily observe all comings and goings. Choosing inherently safe sites and entrances greatly reduces both risk and costs because less security is needed.

For effective security control, there should only be one access point to each critical area, used for both entry and exiting. However, if local fire or building codes require a secondary means of egress, a delayed-access panic bar is usually acceptable. Such a system delays releasing the exit lock for a few seconds, while an alarm sounds and a surveillance camera is triggered. There should also be surveillance cameras with motion detection throughout all secured areas. All locked doors should look as alike as possible from the outside and be identified only by a room number that looks similar to that of any other premises door. No functional name, person's name or title, or any other means to identify what is inside a locked area should be apparent. No signage or directory should include a functional, personal, or departmental name, but only area or room numbers and directional arrows if needed. Only floor, room, or suite numbers should appear on premises signs, on floors.

23.8.2 Physical Access.
Physical access to all parts of the information infrastructure should be restricted. All information system and network equipment must be inside equipment rooms that are always locked and accessible only to those who need to be there. All utility and wiring closets, power distribution panels, patch panels, wiring blocks, and terminations should be located inside equipment rooms that are always locked. If possible, do not allow unrelated systems, equipment, or utilities inside a restricted area, so that a technician working on an unrelated system cannot access the information infrastructure. If this cannot be avoided, IS personnel should always escort others entering these areas. In high-security areas, all persons entering should be escorted, or use two-trusted-person teams where each person observes the other. Guards and facilities-security personnel are good premises-security escorts but probably do not know the infrastructure and are not the best choice here. IS personnel are better escorts, even though they may not know all the security details. In any event, all persons entering must be positively identified and each visit logged.

It is wise to put critical electrical distribution panels inside an equipment room, so they are quickly accessible and also protected. This is a safety issue as well; someone working on equipment or wiring can readily see that the circuit breaker is off. Otherwise, electrical distribution panels should be located inside a locked area that is unmarked from the outside other than by a coded location number. Panels are often located in public areas in many buildings; they must then be securely locked and alarmed as well. Whenever an electrical panel controls anything critical, access to the area should be restricted and the room alarmed. These precautions reduce any loss of power to critical systems by accident or intentionally.

A mantrap can best control access to critical equipment rooms. A mantrap is a two-door arrangement with an inner door, outer door, and a short corridor in between. Both doors are interlocked; one must be closed before the other can open. The corridor usually is constructed with a shatterproof, full-height glass partition (often one-way glass) on one or both sides for surveillance. Both the doors are usually windowless. And each door must have a strong access control system. But for safety, the outer door can usually be opened from inside the corridor using an alarmed panic bar. Usually one or more surveillance cameras are positioned to identify anyone entering or leaving the mantrap.

Emergency intercoms within the mantrap corridor and at the entrance and exit points are strongly suggested. Conspicuous duress/assistance buttons should activate silently, so security personnel can monitor the area and speak with or challenge anyone who cannot pass through properly. The alarms are best silent so that anyone under duress is not further threatened. Emergency intercoms often include small cameras that are inconspicuous or concealed, so that security personnel can see what is happening, assist if someone is ill or somehow becomes trapped, and avoid public-safety issues. A well-designed mantrap can be valuable for all but heavily traveled entrances.

Mantraps can tighten security in many ways and are usually not intrusive. They can detect "piggybacking," when one or more extra persons closely follow someone who is authorized to enter. Mantraps in themselves do not preclude propped-open doors, but they make removal of objects from the room difficult and risky. The access control log and surveillance recordings can identify troublemakers and provide strong evidence to convict those who might otherwise be suspects or persons unknown.

23.8.3 Protective Construction.

Equipment rooms require sturdy partitions for good security and to support the considerable weight of wiring and equipment. Moreover, the partitions and walls must remain safe and stable during any seismic activity, such as heavy road traffic or a sonic boom, explosion, or earth tremor. Floors may also need to be reinforced. Sturdy partitions deter forced entry, which may be otherwise accomplished with little more than a pocketknife and a fist. Existing walls, partitions, and floors should be inspected and any subsequent alterations approved by a structural engineer. Consider too what might be needed long into the future; changes later may be very costly or simply impractical.

Security doors should be sturdy also. They should be metal, fire-rated, and relatively heavy duty and use heavy-duty hardware. Try not to call attention to controlled doors by any distinctive external appearance. If many occupied areas use wood doors, the security doors should not stand out. Use wood-faced metal doors and hardware that looks similar to all the other doors. Sometimes secure-looking dummy doors that lead to nothing important are used for deception or as an alarmed honeypot to draw troublemakers away from secure areas.

Well-constructed partitions and ceilings will also seal out smoke and contain smoke in the event of an interior fire. Weatherstripping around the perimeter of each door is recommended to keep out dust, contaminants, and humidity and to trap any smoke.

If possible, wiring that must run inside a door should be routed within the hinges so that no wires are visible at any time. Exposed wires can be damaged by accident by cutting, or compromised in many ways. The major hinge manufacturers can supply special hinges to conceal most wiring and match the appearance of other premises hardware.

Masonry partitions are usually unnecessary unless there are special structural or very high security requirements. Drywall partitions with metal studs are usually sufficient but should be extra sturdy. Type-X fire-rated drywall panels at least three-quarters of an inch thick are recommended. Better yet, use double half-inch- or five-eighths-inch-thick panels. Existing drywall partitions can easily be double-paneled for added security and strength. Masonry partitions, especially, and often drywall as well are usually faced with sturdy fire-rated plywood for attaching equipment supports and wiring. Whether the plywood is mounted on stand-offs so that wiring can be run behind it is a matter of preference. Usually it is more efficient to run all wiring exposed inside a secured area.

Do not use a suspended (hung) ceiling in any equipment room. Suspended ceilings just add cost, inconvenience, and diminish the volume of the room. The plenum space above the suspended ceiling is a fire hazard, and everything inside it must be fire rated, including any exposed cables, which adds unnecessary costs. Most building codes require separate fire detection zones and suppression heads within every plenum, which is a major cost. Remove any suspended ceilings and get more useful space for cables, better air circulation, and easier maintenance.

Avoid raised floors for the same reasons. They are very costly, functionally unnecessary for most installations, and take up extra floor space for ramps. Like suspended ceilings, raised floors create a plenum space that needs separate fire detection zones and suppression heads. Raised floors usually restrict the ceiling height because the space was not designed for this, so the room must be enlarged to accommodate everything, and often with little expansion provision for the future. Raised floors soon become dust traps and, in time, usually a clutter of new, old, and abandoned cables that no one can figure out. Many equipment failures have been caused by overheating due to airflow restricted by too shallow a raised floor or by too many obstructing cables. A raised-floor plenum is rarely needed to supply cooling air. Surface-mounted ducts and registers usually can do the job better and much cheaper, and are easily cleaned and modified. All of the wiring can usually be routed efficiently above and between the equipment or by using inexpensive cable troughs mounted on walls and ceilings. If needed, floor outlets can access trench ducts in the floor, which may already exist, unused. Conduit can be installed through the floor slab and along the ceiling below for special needs.

It is important for all wiring outside of equipment rooms to be protected inside of metal conduit. This conduit should not be thin-wall or plastic but rugged, heavy-duty metal. Thick-walled metal conduit is strong, harder to damage or breach, and provides good magnetic and electronic shielding as well. Metal conduits can easily be, and should be, well grounded. Obtain expert advice on where and how to connect the grounds to avoid interference. Metal conduit also may serve as a proximity sensor to warn when something gets too close. Alarm wire concealed within the conduit offers early warning of trouble and often can pinpoint where it is located. Sometimes an inert gas or gel is used to pressurize conduits to protect the wires; a pressure drop indicates a leak or a breach but does not indicate where it may be.

All conduits should look alike whether they carry power or data, or control security systems. Although the diameter of the conduit must vary, the general appearance should be the same. Do not label or mark the outside of any conduit except with an alphanumeric code. Cables inside of a conduit should not be marked either, except alphanumerically. Generally, any wires within conduit should emerge only inside of a secure closet, equipment room, or junction box, where the wires should be labeled.

Data cables and wiring are fragile, whether copper or fiber optic. Any undue pressure, bending, stretching, vibration, or crimping can alter transmissions or cause failure. Fiber optic cables are especially fragile; metal conduit is usually the best and least expensive protection. This avoids special sheathings that are often cumbersome and costly.

Any wiring, whether metal or optical fiber, can be improperly specified, installed, or terminated. Substandard wiring or installations may function well temporarily, but future failure is likely, possibly hard to locate quickly, and will be costly to fix. Therefore, it is important that all cables be acceptance-tested and certified by an independent expert before the installer is fully paid.

Critical cable runs should be alarmed from end to end, whether the conduit carries power, data, or security. There are several ways to alarm a cable run. Outdoor conduits are often pressurized with nitrogen to keep out humidity, or with a special gel to keep out oxygen and humidity and to stabilize the wires inside. Interior conduits can be pressurized and alarmed in the same way. Monitoring the pressure provides an alarm when trouble starts (including failed seals that must be fixed quickly). The system is effective and provides early warning, but breaches cannot be pinpointed, and any future wiring changes may be difficult.

Proximity and pressure-sensitive sensors also can alarm the entire length of critical cables. A monitored run of conduit can be very long and may continue through areas that are difficult to protect or offer no concealment. While surveillance and intrusion detectors can protect most vital areas, there is often much infrastructure that can be protected only by sensor wires running the full length of the conduit. Mechanical pressure sensors will detect unusual vibration, while proximity sensors indicate a change in the magnetic or electronic environment surrounding the cable or conduit. Newer systems utilize fiber-optic sensors that monitor sound pressure. Some of these systems are smart enough to distinguish routine, harmless events from possible trouble, and many can roughly pinpoint the location as well. Sometimes the conduit itself is the sensor, or an external wire is attached to the conduit, but these approaches are often ineffective.

23.8.4 Using Existing Premises Alarms. Various codes require workplaces to have visible and audible fire alarms. And most workplaces have voice paging, emergency intercom, surveillance, and premises security systems as well. All of this equipment can be utilized effectively to augment and support information infrastructure security. Audible alarms are used when persons at the scene must take immediate action, such as to lock down or to evacuate. Conversely, silent alarms provide early warning and allow security to monitor the scene discreetly, gather evidence, and respond and assist as needed. All these alarms can be integrated into infrastructure protection systems to provide better early warning and extra layers of protection.

All alarms and alerts should be transmitted to a central security desk or guard station. The purpose is to document and manage incident response, summon assistance quickly, monitor the scene, accumulate evidence, and support all of the response resources. Central management is especially necessary when threats cascade or multiple events occur, as they often do. Security managers, IS managers, the infrastructure security manager, and key department heads also should be notified immediately. Some of these people may be offsite or at remote locations but will need to communicate effectively with at least the operations center. Notifications and the subsequent communications should be quick, private, secure, and logged to document the events. One or more online backup security control and operations centers provide redundancy, support and assistance, and strong security. (See Sections 23.2.1 and 23.2.2 for the federal incident management requirements.)

An effective method of premises-wide alert uses voice codes broadcast over a paging system. These are usually scripted and often prerecorded so that alerts can be initiated automatically, remotely or manually. Hospitals do this effectively with their color-named codes, which are equivalent to silent alerts, that do not seem unusual to the public. An effective system of alert codes in a large organization also uses the names of fictitious persons. In a smaller setting, such as a school, where the names of all personnel are known, there can be alert messages to an individual to take an innocuous action, which is understood to be an alert code. Additional alphanumeric information in a message can identify the general location of an incident. As in a hospital, it is well to add similar codes for other routine purposes, so the public will generally tune out all the paging. This system is particularly useful when violence is threatened or has erupted.

Although most security personnel now have portable radios, there may be many areas of no reception, and few use earpieces so others cannot readily hear what is happening. However, all security personnel must know immediately when trouble looms, and they must be alerted in a way so as not to excite others. Also, everyone inside the premises needs to know when an emergency threatens. Indeed, everyone has a legal right to know and to promptly receive instructions for their own safety. Anything short of this will result in considerable liability. Therefore, effective procedures, clear simple instructions, good preparation, and periodic training can protect everyone and provide strong security.

23.8.5   Clean Electrical Power.   Protecting electronic equipment requires a source of electrical power that is consistently "clean." Power outages and brownouts can cause obvious trouble, but numerous other disturbances can disrupt or damage the information infrastructure. Some of these include dips and sags, spikes, transients, and magnetic or radio frequency interference. Most of these are intermittent and not necessarily present when the circuit is tested. Understanding each term is not as important as knowing that a wide variety of problems commonly occur in power lines, randomly and without warning.

Brownouts are particularly harmful. These are voltage reductions by the electric utility that can cause air-conditioning equipment, cooling water pumps, and ventilating systems to malfunction or to shut down. The associated equipment may be damaged unless it is quickly shut down or switched over to an uninterruptible power supply or a motor generator.

Few power disturbances will destroy circuits or crash systems immediately, but most can cause cumulative damage. Each incident can weaken electronic circuits that will eventually fail for no apparent reason. Poor equipment quality is often blamed, because the cumulative effect was not recognized. Worse, replacement equipment will probably soon fail also.

Power disturbances can be measured to determine whether a particular circuit seems to be clean. Usually a recording device is left in place continually for at least a week to measure and log the details of every event that occurs. (Avoid any test instrument that merely logs an unnamed event but provides no details.) An independent engineer who is not a vendor may best provide testing that is objective, comprehensive, and covers the entire facility.

Some circuits are likely to show intermittent disturbances caused by something nearby or within the building and sometimes by faulty wiring. Knowing what power problems arrive via the main service helps to determine whether the utility is at fault and to isolate where in the building other disturbances may originate. There may indeed be numerous causes of power disturbances, and all of them may be intermittent, which is why continuous seven-day, 24-hour monitoring is the minimum recommended.

Another major electrical problem is improper grounding that can damage sensitive equipment and cause interference in cables. Electricians must comply with national and local electrical codes, but they do not necessarily understand or provide the special grounding necessary for sensitive IS platforms. Most heavy equipment manufacturers require that each unit have an isolated ground connection with a dedicated wire all the way back to the central building ground bus. A few manufacturers do not provide installation specifications unless asked, and some installers disregard them to remain price competitive.

Opinions vary as to the best building ground configuration for information systems, and as local conditions can vary significantly, no one approach is best. It is wise to consult an independent engineer to inspect the grounding configurations, and to recommend and certify local code compliance. It is also important to provide separate circuits for all IS equipment, and where the equipment plugs into a receptacle, there be no more than a single receptacle. Separate circuit breakers are usually required for all equipment that can draw high current, especially if the load may cycle on and off. This is required by code for large motors, such as pumps, air conditioning, and elevators, whose cycling can cause dirty power on other branch circuits. But copiers and large laser printers (especially older ones) can also create electrical disturbances when starting and when the fuser-heaters cycle. All types of lights can cause a dip or a surge when many fixtures are switched on or off at once. (The newer fluorescent light fixtures with electronic ballasts conserve power and cause much less interference.) A separate circuit connection somewhat isolates the hot and neutral wires from other circuits, but interference may be generated through the grounding connections that often are daisy-chained with many other circuits to cut costs.

Do not share a dedicated circuit with any of this equipment, which can readily disrupt and damage electronic equipment: time stamps, electric staplers, coffeepots, refrigerators, heaters, fans, or any other device with a motor or solenoid. Even if inaccessible, a dedicated outlet should be a single receptacle, not a duplex. It is all too easy for vacuum cleaners, power tools, or maintenance equipment to use the other half of the duplex outlet. This will cause a severe disturbance and may trip the circuit breaker. There must be plenty of convenience outlets that are readily accessible for all noncritical needs.

Yet another cause of power problems is excessive solar activity. These events can be measured only when they occur, which is randomly during an unpredictable interval of several years that peaks about every 11 years. Solar disruptions occur only during daylight hours. High solar activity occurred in 1988, causing major power outages and radio interference in Montreal, Canada. Daily solar activity reports, forecasts, pictures, and historical records are available at www.dxlc.com/solar and other sites. (See also Section 22.6.7.)

There are several remedial options when power disturbances are suspected, encountered, or even possible.

1. Eliminate the problem at the power distribution panel. Better grounding, more separate circuits, suppressors, filters, and isolation transformers may help. But this type of remediation can be difficult, costly, or unreliable.

2. Use a surge suppressor near the equipment it protects. This is inexpensive but useless against brownouts, outages, and severe disturbances.

3. Employ an uninterruptible power supply (UPS), which provides battery backup power, for each piece of critical infrastructure equipment. One type of UPS is activated only when the incoming power fails, although its battery is always being charged. A better type is always online, acting to filter the incoming power, suppress most surges, compensate for minor brownouts, and maintain full system power for five to 10 minutes following an outage—enough time to allow an orderly system shutdown. A third and best type of UPS always powers its load from its batteries, thus isolating the load from the power line and providing optimum protection.

4. For systems that draw high wattage, a motor-generator (MG) set will eliminate most power problems. An MG set is an electric motor driven by the utility power. The motor is coupled to a generator that will always supply clean power to the load. The generator is usually voltage-regulated automatically, although the frequency can vary, which may disrupt some timing circuits. Usually if there is a power outage, mechanical momentum of the unit will provide sufficient power for an orderly equipment shutdown. Motor generators are still used for the ultimate in filtration and regulation, but there must be an electrical bypass to facilitate maintenance.

UPS units should power and protect the servers, network and telephone equipment, computers, and critical monitors. Most UPS units provide outlets with no backup power but with noise suppression for printers, transformer "bricks," fax machines, and peripherals that do not need to be kept running. Most of these devices are somewhat expendable and quickly replaced by spare units if one is damaged.

Individual UPS units, placed near the equipment they protect, cost less and can be powered off by the operator to better protect equipment that may be vulnerable, even when the equipment is already shut down. This can provide an extra layer of protection where lightning might strike. Larger UPS units are used in equipment rooms where they can also monitor and log all power events and trigger remote alarm indications. Most good UPS units can initiate an automatic equipment shutdown when the power fails, the UPS batteries are low, or someone intervenes manually. There can be an issue, however, when some of the protected equipment cannot be restarted until the UPS batteries are fully recharged. Some UPS units are also network devices that can report their condition to a remote location.

Many UPS units also provide telephone and Ethernet line filtering and suppression, and this should be utilized if possible. Lightning transmitted over communications wires can readily damage telephone instruments and modems. Power and communication line spikes can occur asymmetrically, and can devastate equipment that one disturbance alone would not damage. A good UPS unit with communications line suppression is best able to stop both types of spikes.

Another benefit of UPS units is that when an emergency generator is on line, the electrical power would be much dirtier than before. The extra filtration and stabilization provided by the UPS units may be the difference between IS equipment operating or crashing.

23.8.6   Emergency Power.   Most of the critical systems and infrastructure must remain fully operational during any electrical power problem. Filtration and suppressors cannot compensate for power outages, handle most brownouts, or cope with major electrical interference. Disturbances might come from lightning (even when it is too distant to be seen or heard), severe solar activity, or radio-frequency interference corrupting the utility power. UPS units can deal with some of these conditions, but only briefly. Therefore, a backup emergency generator may be the only way to continue operations during sustained power problems.

Although backup generators are often the only alternative, they are not a panacea. Generators are expensive and complex to install, require at least monthly "exercise," and are not always reliable. Their voltage regulation is marginal; during sudden load changes, the output voltage and frequency may fluctuate as well. As the load increases, more current is drawn, and, if the generator is overloaded, the voltage will drop and the frequency may drop below 60 Hertz (which can disrupt IS timing circuits). Because the load current increases to meet the power demand, the amount of heat generated by the equipment being powered will increase as the square of the current. Much of the IS equipment powered is inductive, and there can be a large starting power surge when it is turned on or restarted. Generators, therefore, must have ample reserve capacity beyond the anticipated equipment loads. And given their cost, generators should have ample reserve capacity for the future as well.

Another issue is whether a particular generator can provide sufficiently "clean" electrical power to operate IS equipment as well as power for the other emergency needs of the facility. Be sure, therefore, that the generator specified has ample capacity and that it is intended for use with electronic equipment. Even then, interference from large motors or lighting systems can affect the electronic equipment.

Because backup generators are expensive and complex, planning is often short-sighted, and many installations are not well designed or adequately tested. The inevitable result is that many generators do not perform as expected. Here are a few examples of what can be overlooked.

After considerable discussion at a major money-center bank in Manhattan about what seemed to be the excessive cost of a backup generator, the project was begrudgingly approved. The generator was to power two identical computer systems running in tandem to support a critical securities trading operation. Because the generator would actually cost more than the two computers, cost was an issue until the bank realized that the generator would pay for itself within one day of use. Soon after completion, a sudden citywide blackout erupted and the outage lasted for three days. Despite much inconvenience carrying fuel from the elevator up a flight of stairs to the rooftop generator, the unit performed flawlessly—one of the few systems in Manhattan that did.

Many other generators did not start or cut over properly, despite warm, clear weather conditions. And others did not support the necessary infrastructure. Some installations did not think to include the power requirements of HVAC so the computers had to be shut down within a few minutes to avoid overheating, even though there was ample electrical power for them. Generator power for other necessary support functions was neglected. These included network components and communications systems, lighting for users, an elevator for access by key people and to carry fuel to the generator, security and access control systems, and at least basic electrical provisions for food and rest for those keeping the vital systems running. Very few businesses thought to include all of the necessary support functions on their emergency power systems. This incident happened some years ago when power outages were considered very unlikely in Manhattan. Generators then were somewhat of a status symbol. But today, sudden blackouts anywhere are far more common.

A related example of shortsightedness occurred recently in a large suburban luxury hotel operated by a prestigious hotel chain. Following a severe thunderstorm, the power utility advised the hotel that they must lose power for several hours to repair a damaged substation. Given ample notice, the hotel set out hundreds of candles in the corridors, dining, lounge, reception, and pool areas, and started their emergency generator, which then cut over automatically as soon as the blackout occurred. Emergency exit signs and emergency lights in the corridors and stairs all worked properly. As expected, their batteries soon died but the candles functioned long and well. The generator also powered one elevator, the computer and telephone systems, the access control system, and all the room locks. The generator performed as expected, but the emergency response process did not.

Even with ample warning, no one thought to shut down the other elevators or to post signs to use the stairs. Two very frightened people were trapped in the dark, between floors, proving that a generator can be a liability and not a benefit unless operating procedures are carefully planned, well implemented, and periodically reviewed. There should have been a security checklist used whenever the generator started.

Another recent example involved a state's emergency operations command center, designed to remain safe and fully operational no matter what events might occur. A large generator powered all the critical systems. Everything had been tested many times and had operated smoothly as expected. But then trouble came during a heavy thunderstorm in the vicinity. Electrical power for most of the city flickered several times and then returned to normal. However, the generator tried to start at the first sign of trouble and then faltered as the power returned. A few seconds later when the power again flickered, the generator system had been damaged and was unable to start. The state was lucky that the generator was not needed then, but it was out for several days for repairs.

Most power failures begin with flickering and momentary outages, which can incapacitate a generator system that is not set up properly. Most mission-critical generators are set up to start the engine automatically, and many transfer power automatically as soon as the generator comes up to speed. Manual start-up and transfer are more reliable and cheaper, if trained personnel are always available. The best way to sequence automatic operation follows.

1. After the first start-up signal, the start-up sequence must continue until the engine starts, a failed-start timeout occurs, or the sequence is terminated manually.

2. Power does not transfer until the generator is fully up to speed, at a reliable operating temperature, and the utility power is unusable. All three conditions should occur before transfer, and there can be manual overrides as well.

3. All transfers back to utility power and the generator shutdown should be done manually. It is best also to be able to transfer each circuit individually to utility power.

There are countless examples of critical backup generators failing to operate as expected. Here are some suggestions to determine whether a generator is necessary for protecting information systems and how to utilize a generator efficiently and economically.

- Investigate the outage history of the utility feeders that serve the premises. The electric utility can usually provide this data; if not, the state's Public Utilities Commission usually can. Be sure to ask how the terms are defined, because an "outage" may only include interruptions that continue for more than several minutes. Also ask whether more reliable feeders are available. Loop feeders that are powered from both ends are more reliable and often serve critical equipment.

Ask whether the distribution transformers isolate and filter out power disturbances, whether they can also regulate the incoming voltage, and, if so, the specifications.

- Find out which other customers share the same feeders, and visit them to discuss their experiences and to determine if they use heavy machinery. Although some safeguards are possible and may be at little or no cost to the utility customer, past history is not always a reliable guide to the future. The distribution grid changes as more heavy loads are added. Today, the threat of extended power problems is far greater than in the past and is increasing rapidly. UPS units, motor-generator sets, and backup generators may all be a necessity in mission-critical applications.

- Determine which of the IS infrastructure components need backup power from an emergency generator. Most critical information systems, equipment, networks, and infrastructure must be at peak performance at all times. And so must all the office areas, support systems, utilities, and personnel needed to operate them. Outages can drag on for days or weeks with key people isolated and living inside the facility to keep the systems running. The generator power must serve all of these needs.

- Consider these support systems that may require emergency power:
  - All the IS security systems, protection and monitoring devices; perimeter surveillance, and access control systems, the security stations and consoles.
  - Fire stairs (which may become the primary means of entry and egress), emergency exit doors, fire alarms, and intercoms whose batteries will quickly discharge. Also the need for these batteries to begin recharging immediately as soon as backup power is available.
  - Heating, ventilation, air-conditioning (HVAC), and process-cooling systems, including all the controls, fans, pumps, and valves needed to operate the critical and support systems. In addition to equipment cooling, it is best to provide room comfort for users, operators, and administrators. Area air conditioning may not be possible, but at least supplementary heating in winter and adequate ventilation will be needed.
  - Sufficient lighting for key personnel, equipment rooms, utility closets, corridors, rest rooms, and food service. Many individual light switches can conserve power and generator fuel. Battery-powered lights are suitable only for immediate emergency egress and cannot provide area lighting.
  - Enough live convenience outlets for test equipment, work lights, and any accessories that must be used. Live receptacles may also be needed for portable fans.
  - Sufficient food service equipment and refrigeration, running water and sanitary facilities, and a sleeping area for 24/7 operations that may have to continue for several days.
  - An elevator for critical access to the site, for medical emergencies, delivery of food and supplies, and to carry fuel for the generator.

- Compile a list of all the items a generator must power. Then total the rated power of each item to determine the size of the generator and the number of circuits needed. Power ratings for equipment usually are shown on a nameplate near the power connection and listed in the instructions. Ratings may be given in watts, amperes, or volt-amps. Generally, watts and volt-amps are assumed as equivalent. The latter value is the product of multiplying the rated voltage (e.g., 120 volts) by the rated amperes, while the former multiplies that number by the equipment's power factor. Large generators are rated in kilowatts (1,000 watts) of power. Units intended for short duty cycles cost less and may fail during prolonged, continuous duty. An experienced engineer should review this process.

- Consider the costs per hour of lost productivity, business, and goodwill if any information systems are disrupted. Add to this the recovery costs. In the example of the bank given earlier, the first day that the generator was needed saved the entire cost of the backup power system. The second and third days of that particular outage were sheer delight to the bank as most of their competitors faltered.

Electric codes may require, and good practice dictates, that a generator be sized to handle the sum of the individual start-up loads. This may seem wasteful because not all loads start up at once and average operating load will be somewhat less than the sum of the parts. It is nonetheless a wise practice to provide for the maximum rated load, with additional spare capacity for improved reliability and future additions. There are several reasons for oversizing the generator. When power is first transferred to the generator, the sum of the initial surges can far exceed the anticipated load. All of the UPS units and other battery-operated devices will begin to recharge, and all equipment motors may concurrently draw their maximum surge currents. Extra generator capacity ensures a smoother transfer with better voltage regulation, and enhances the system's reliability.

Most large generators produce three-phase power. And each of the three outputs should be balanced so that each "leg" draws about the same power. To do this, heavy motors, multiple light fixtures controlled by one switch, and other surge-producing equipment may have to be divided among the three legs. Existing wiring at the distribution panels probably will need changing to balance the legs. It is desirable, but not always possible, to reserve one leg for clean power to critical single-phase electronic systems. Balancing each leg is a tricky business best done in consultation with an independent engineer.

As many electronic systems as possible that are powered by a generator should also be protected by UPS units as discussed earlier, even though these add to the generator's load. There will be large voltage surges, dips, sags, and over-voltage conditions as the generator loads are switched and constantly change. Power disturbances will be much greater because electrically noisy motors and lighting cannot be isolated. The UPS units should include noise suppression and voltage regulation as well. And even with all of this, IS equipment will be stressed and may fail.

Locating the generator is the next challenge. The choices are on a roof or setback, inside the premises, or outdoors. Each site has advantages and obstacles. Outdoor generators can be the easiest and cheapest to install but also more expensive to operate. Outdoor generators are noisy, often unsightly, subject to vandalism, and local ordinances may restrict them. When located outside, weatherproof housings are needed to protect the engine, generator, and fuel tank. Most engines used outdoors need to be kept heated, which can become a high overhead expense. Noise is another problem, and persons nearby may object. It is important to use good mufflers and to get written permission from nearby property owners and other tenants. Outdoor units should be fenced with plenty of room for maintenance and fueling. A generator shed is best, if possible, but this does not reduce the need for heating and a good muffler. The whole installation should be securely locked and protected by an open-door alarm and motion detectors, and be in the view of surveillance cameras. Floodlights may deter vandalism and will assist refueling.

Generators on roofs or building setbacks present other problems and these installations too may be restricted by local codes. The first problem is weight. Structural reinforcement probably will be needed. The next problem is getting the unit in place, which may require a crane or a licensed rigger. Very few building elevators come up to the roof level, and they may not be able to handle even a disassembled generator's parts. All the generator components may have to be rigged up outside of the building or manhandled up the fire stairs.

Installations on top of building setbacks will need a special access door, and moving heavy equipment across a finished floor requires heavy planks and floor protection (e.g., sheets of Masonite or plywood) under the casters to avoid considerable floor damage. There must be sufficient space on the roof or setback to fuel and service the generator safely. Noise will usually be a problem and vibration as well.

Indoor installations offer both advantages and challenges. An indoor location that is sometimes feasible is a heated garage-type ground-floor room with a standard garage door to open when the generator operates. This arrangement is good because it is inconspicuous, fireproof, easily protected, and convenient for fueling and maintenance. And, should a generator fail, a trailer-mounted unit can be hooked up easily.

Inside generators may be prohibited by building or fire codes. Large rooms are needed to facilitate fueling and maintenance, and large ventilation systems to dissipate the considerable engine heat. The engine exhaust can be well muffled and piped outside, while engine-intake air is ducted in from outside. Heating and ventilating the room must be designed correctly, for both very hot and very cold weather. The room must be fireproof and soundproof with fire alarms and a suppression system that uses chemicals or dry-head sprinklers that cannot freeze. The floor may need reinforcement and vibration isolators. A floor drain is advisable and must be environmentally approved.

There are advantages to indoor installations. The generator and its fuel can be kept warm easily. Starting is easier and more reliable. Fueling is easier without having to brave the elements. There is less chance of water in the fuel, which can be fatal to diesel engines and maintenance is much easier.

Problems with building installations include building codes that allow only small day tanks for fuel. Every few hours, a lot of fuel must be carried in to keep the generator running. Fuel cannot be stored inside most buildings, and an elevator may not be running or available to help bring in fuel cans.

There are many possible fuels for emergency generators. Diesel fuel is the most efficient, and diesel engines can operate continuously for days but are hard to start, especially in cold weather, and cannot be hand cranked. Home heating oil is basically the same as diesel fuel and can be substituted at any time that diesel fuel is not available, but this requires extra fuel filtering.

If liquid fuel is used, the fuel tank should be full at all times to avoid condensation. Fuel additives can prevent gumming and assist starting. Make sure all diesel fuel is treated for use in a cold climate. Refiners normally do not use this process except in winter, but untreated diesel fuel turns to a gel near freezing temperatures and the fuel will not flow. Never let a dealer "cut" diesel fuel with kerosene, which is corrosive. Diesel fuel also requires additives to avoid bacteria buildup that will clog fuel lines. There should be OSHA-approved cleanup materials ready for any future spills or leaks.

Natural gas or propane are the most convenient fuels. Either one eliminates the day tank and refueling. These engines are the least polluting, and they start much easier, require no preheating, and can be hand cranked. But most are not designed for prolonged continuous duty. Gasoline engines are prohibited by many building codes and are rarely used except for small, portable generators. Gasoline is far more dangerous to handle and store, and gasoline engines do not hold up well under heavy loads.

Continually monitor the engine oil level and be ready to add oil as soon as it is needed. Most generators automatically shut down when the oil level is low. Some also shut down when overheated. Any unexpected generator shutdown will be catastrophic, so monitor closely for early warning signs of trouble.

Once the desired size and type of generator is decided, there are other considerations:

- Automatic engine controls and load transfer switches can be unreliable and may cause damage. Avoid these if possible. However, generators can be monitored and controlled remotely, as well as on site.

- Automatic starting can be unreliable. If the engine does not start quickly, the battery will quickly discharge, especially diesel engines in cold weather, which require glo-plug heaters. If at all possible, someone should be present during the starting process, using a checklist to verify proper operations and then transferring the load manually when the generator is ready. Switches that automatically transfer the load are expensive and sometimes fail. Always transfer back to utility power manually, and do this only after sensitive systems are put into a standby mode. Automatic transfer can cause major damage if the utility power flickers and goes out again or if the voltage or the frequency fluctuates during transfer, as it often does. Do not shut off the engine automatically. This is best done manually, and not until utility power is flowing smoothly.

- The best transfer switches allow each of the major circuits to be transferred individually to minimize the inevitable fluctuations likely to occur when everything is switched over simultaneously.

- An emergency generator must be exercised regularly. The manufacturer will specify when and how the units should be exercised. Usually this must be done monthly and at medium to heavy load. When critical systems are involved, good security practice is to exercise the generator weekly. There should be a written, initialed log entry for each event, including each exercise, inspection, maintenance, oil check, and refueling. Always log operating hours.

Despite the cost and complexity, there is a great feeling of contentment in having a good emergency generator system that functions smoothly, especially when other organizations may be floundering. Once the generator performs well during a real emergency, even skeptics realize the value added.

23.8.7 Environmental Control.   Even though today's information systems do not need as much cooling or the precise environmental controls that legacy systems once demanded, good control of temperature and humidity, good ventilation, and clean air are still important. Information systems can function reliably only when proper environments are maintained in both equipment rooms and user workplaces. But each area requires a different approach.

Air conditioning is basically intended to cool people; equipment should be cooled by a functionally different system, which is best called process cooling. The systems should not be intermixed, nor should either one substitute for the other. Building codes require (HVAC) within all occupied spaces, where people may congregate, or where there are workstations. Building codes also set minimum ventilation requirements for occupied space, including a minimum percentage of makeup (outside) air to be constantly brought into each occupied space so the inside air does not become stale. Most codes do not consider the needs of electronic equipment.

Electronic equipment has many special needs, and many are incompatible with the people comforts required by the codes. Most electronic equipment operates continually, whereas air conditioning operates mostly during business hours. Air-conditioning cooling systems may be shut down for maintenance, during a power brownout, off hours, or in cool weather. By contrast, process cooling must operate continuously and every day, so parallel and redundant systems are often used. The same air should be well filtered and recirculated with no makeup air added to introduce dust or contaminants. This also reduces the cooling capacity needed, so process-cooling equipment can be of smaller capacity and cheaper to operate.

Electrical equipment and wiring also need good humidity control, which process-cooling systems are designed to provide. These systems are designed to be easier, and faster to clean and maintain. Often many components are redundant and hot-swappable. Increasingly, the cooling unit is on the floor or ceiling of the equipment room, so that few ducts, dampers, or registers are needed.

All IS processing, storage, and network equipment should be inside dedicated equipment rooms, which also should be designated as unoccupied spaces to avoid the code-imposed air-conditioning requirements. Avoid using terms such as "computer room" or "data center," which are usually construed to be occupied spaces.

Both the process cooling in equipment rooms and the air conditioning in work areas must provide humidity control. It is important that relative humidity be controlled between 40 and 60 percent at all times, regardless of the climate or season.

When the relative humidity falls below 40 percent, which can easily happen in cold weather, static electricity is generated as people move about. Static charges can quickly accumulate to become many thousand volts, and a spark will jump to any object a person touches that is differently charged. Even though such a spark may not be felt, several thousand volts can annihilate electronic circuits. For example, a static charge jumping from a fingertip to a keyboard can cause serious damage to storage media and circuits. Much of the damage may not be readily apparent. Actual failure may be delayed, so the cause is not identified. Grounded strips can be installed on workstations, and service personnel should wear grounded wrist straps, although these do not completely stop the problem. The only effective solution is always to keep the relatively humidity above 40 percent.

Relative humidity above 60 percent also causes problems that will eventually destroy equipment and wiring. Above 60 percent, condensation and mold will begin to damage some components. Above roughly 80 percent, galvanic action occurs and will eventually cause serious trouble. The process is often called silver migration because most electronic connections are silver-plated. The phenomenon is similar to electrolysis (electroplating), but here the two metals are immersed in high humidity rather than a liquid and there is no external current needed for galvanic action to occur. Molecules of one conductor begin to physically move toward and attach themselves to another less active metal. Even though both surfaces may be gold or silver or copper plated, it is likely that they differ slightly in composition. Therefore, galvanic action will occur whenever the humidity is too high. Connector pins and sockets can disintegrate, fuse together, or fail electrically due to pitting. Printed circuits can also fail. Although this galvanic action happens slowly, it accumulates and is irreversible. The failures are usually without warning, and almost always, poor quality is blamed, rather than high humidity.

The only protection is to control humidity in both equipment rooms and work areas. Process-cooling and air-conditioning systems commonly do this by several methods. Both systems dehumidify naturally when cooling and can use a reheat coil to warm output air if the humidity is too low. Also when the humidity is too low, water is added using a spray, atomizer, or a wet screen through which the supply air is pumped.

There are additional protections, which are wise to install and maintain. In a cold climate, all areas and workplaces with electronic equipment should have low-static floor surfaces. This can be low-static carpeting or floor tile made for this purpose. Do not rely on sprays to control static electricity; they soon dissipate. Be sure that equipment room walls and doors are well sealed so that humidity, dust, and contaminants cannot migrate. Be sure the walls are well sealed from slab to slab and that the slabs themselves are impervious to dust and humidity. See also the need to properly seal firestops in Section 23.5.1.

23.8.8 Smoke and Fire Protection.   Smoke is far more dangerous than flame. And all smoke is toxic! It contains high levels of carbon monoxide, which is invisible, odorless, and quickly fatal. Smoke is the product of the combustion of many materials, and most of these are dangerous to breathe. Some are immediately fatal. Even a little smoke can do considerable harm to humans and much harm to electronic equipment. Smoke is deceptive; even when there does not seem to be very much smoke or heat, and visibility looks good, people within or passing through the area quickly become disabled and some may soon die.

The first priority is the safety of people. Get everyone away from any smoke immediately, and keep everyone away. Only trained responders with proper protective clothing, equipment, and self-contained breathing apparatus should enter any smoky area. Generally, respirators are not enough protection and may leak as well. There must be no heroics; crawling through smoke on the floor or breathing through a wet rag are desperate measures that should be attempted only when unavoidable to escape the area. Everyone should wait in a safe place until firefighters arrive and then follow their instructions.

The best way to prevent an equipment room fire is to keep anything combustible outside the room. Documents, manuals, and supplies should be stored outside the room in closed metal cabinets. Inside furniture should be limited to a metal table and a chair or two. All waste receptacles should be outside. Once combustible materials are eliminated, the only smoke that develops will be from electrical overheating. Electrical fires rarely occur in an equipment room, and those that do occur are likely to be very small, brief, and cease as soon as electrical power is removed. (Note that most computing components now operate on five volts or less, so that a short circuit is no more dangerous than, for example, a shorted flashlight, which presents no smoke hazard.) While sometimes noticeably acrid, there is usually little visible smoke. Therefore, sensitive fire and smoke detectors and an effective means of fire suppression are needed and required by most building and fire codes. Good detectors can provide enough early warning to ward off trouble and injury.

Enough smoke or heat to cause actual equipment damage requires an electrical current higher than most components can draw. Circuit breakers and fuses usually will open before there is much smoke or damage. Perhaps the greatest risk is smoke from the ballasts in low-quality fluorescent light fixtures, which can put out considerable black smoke. Any smoke is corrosive and may condense on connectors and printed circuits, which may then eventually fail.

There should be smoke detectors in every equipment room that are connected to a central alarm system. There should be enough detectors to cover the entire volume of each room. Each detector should include an electric eye to look for haze or smoke, ionization sensors to detect products of combustion well before any are noticed by humans, and rapid-rise-in-temperature detectors in case there is enough heat buildup to cause damage. Even though detected, nothing will stop smoke generated by overheated wiring or components until the electrical power is cut off or other heat source is removed.

There must be a fire suppression system in every equipment room. Both code compliance and good security practice requires this. Fire suppression is best accomplished with sprinkler heads that spray water mist, even though some unprotected equipment may be damaged if the water is not effective quickly. Special waterproof protective covers are often kept near equipment in case of accidents such as ceiling leaks or a damaged sprinkler head. But if an area is already smoky, no one should attempt to place the covers.

Wiring, connections, and most components will dry themselves, even when soaked. The process may be hastened with lint-free towels and careful use of hair dryers. Keyboards, monitors, UPS units, power supplies, some disk or tape drives, and especially printers may be damaged and should be replaced until they can be inspected. Hard drives are usually hermetically sealed and unaffected. A few other components could be damaged by excessive heat, although water mist is very effective in quenching heat sources. Plenty of replacement items should be safely stored nearby. Handling damaged low-voltage components (such as most circuit boards) presents little risk to people—provided there is not too much water and the persons know what they are doing and how to avoid damaging the components. If in doubt, shut down the components temporarily.

Enclosed equipment cabinets offer the best protection regardless of the room's fire suppression system. Enclosed cabinets can monitor temperature and humidity, detect and contain smoke, sound alarms, and often contain systems to suppress a fire before trouble occurs.

Halon 1301 fire suppressant was once widely used in critical areas. But Halon is a fluorocarbon whose manufacture has been banned for many years. Today's chemical systems are designed differently; one example uses the FM200 Suppression Agent made by Siemens. The claimed advantage of the chemical suppressants is that humans can breathe the agent, at least while they are exiting the area. Another fire suppression system uses carbon dioxide, which is effective and less expensive, but can extinguish people as well as fires. The problem with all chemical agents, including carbon dioxide, is that they quickly mix with smoke and become very toxic. The agent itself may be safe to breathe, but the smoke mixed with it is not. These systems are also very expensive.

Regardless of the suppression system, there should be controls and a shutoff near the room's exit, but not accessible to a perpetrator. Generally, an audible, continuous alarm indicates that the suppression system is about to activate. There should be postpone buttons on the control panel, and perhaps remotely as well, that will delay activation for about two minutes while someone intervenes. The postpone mode generally pulses the audible alarm. A silent alarm indication should remain activated whenever a fire suppression system is disabled or the alarms are silenced.

The next level of protection utilizes several fire extinguishers. These are the most useful protections because the suppressant can be aimed where it is needed and not throughout the room. Carbon dioxide is best because it does not leave a residue. Chemical, powder, and foam extinguishers also work well but are hard to clean up. ABC-type extinguishers are best because they are effective for combustible materials, flammable liquids, and electrical fires, respectively. Several handheld extinguishers are better than a few large, heavy units. All fire extinguishers should be conspicuously wall-mounted or placed immediately inside and outside of entrances. An OSHA-approved red patch placed on the wall nearest to every extinguisher highlights its location. Also, check other OSHA, local code, and insurance requirements that may apply.

Supply air from the process-cooling equipment should be shut down quickly and automatically to avoid recirculating the smoke. The IS equipment may have to be shut down soon thereafter before it overheats. It is best to shut down everything promptly and automatically in an orderly sequence—cooling, IS equipment, electrical power, and lighting—and then evacuate. Shut down the lighting, in case it is part of the problem. Shut-down should occur automatically with manual intervention from controls inside the room or remotely. Battery-powered exit and emergency room lighting are advisable so responders do not need flashlights.

A so-called crash cart is a good investment. This is used during a smoke condition, a water leak, and, it is hoped, before a fire suppression system activates. A crash cart is kept outside or nearby major equipment rooms and rolled to where it is needed. The cart usually contains covers to keep smoke and water out of racks and off equipment, large fire extinguishers, and sometimes respirators or self-contained breathing apparatus. The crash cart should include quick-reference procedures, and a checklist for protecting and shutting down the room, as well as safety and notification procedures—usually printed on plastic. The crash cart should be inspected and the procedures reviewed monthly, and there should be periodic training and exercises to practice using the equipment. Before the smoke and water covers are used, be sure the equipment is first powered off. Crash carts were important for yesterday's computer rooms but are increasingly unnecessary in a well-designed equipment room.

Finally, be sure to have smoke-exhaust systems available to quickly purge the areas of smoke. Most fire departments have portable purge fans with long fabric and wire hoses to reach outside. Do not allow anyone to use a respirator or breathing apparatus unless it is approved for this purpose and has been properly fitted to a trained person.

23.9   MITIGATING SPECIFIC THREATS.   Several other threats should be considered before good infrastructure protection is possible. Some of these situations are unlikely but potentially very costly if they should ever occur.

23.9.1   Preventing Wiretaps and Bugs.   Most wiretaps are placed at wiring junction points. Vulnerable spots are within equipment rooms, wiring closets, junction boxes, wiring blocks, or data receptacles. See Section 22.4.5 for methods of tapping into copper or fiber wiring. The tap wire can be fiber or coax or utilize a pair of unused conductors inside an existing cable. It is likely to be a small wire that is hardly noticeable, running to an inconspicuous place where monitoring and recording can occur. Once removed to a safe place, the data can be extracted by phone, wireless, Internet, or manually. Tapped data may even be encoded and stored on the victim's own network. Video and/or audio bugs used for spying are similar to wiretaps in that once the data is monitored, it must then be sent elsewhere for retrieval.

Unless all system data are encrypted—including all data, voice, and video traffic—wiretap protection must be strong because detection is difficult at best. First, determine which cables are critical and inspect the entire cable run. All cables should be inside of metal conduit. Data and power conduits should look similar and with no markings or labels except alphanumeric codes. Keep critical conduits as inconspicuous as possible, and away from places the public might access. There must be strong access controls, intrusion alarms, motion detectors, or surveillance where terminations, connectors, or wires can be accessed. Critical cable runs must be protected over their entire length. See Section 23.8.3 for ways to protect conduit and exposed cables.

Data cables between the desktop and wall or floor outlets are potential wiretap sites. Cables, harnesses, and connectors within office furniture systems may also be compromised. Reasonably good protection is possible with careful design, with devices that harden the data cabling against the possibility of a wiretap, and that detect disconnecting or tampering with any data wires.

For continued protection against wiretaps and bugs, even when all data are fully encrypted, there must be periodic and thorough visual inspections, sweeps for any unusual radio-frequency transmissions, and careful cable testing to determine any anomalies. Everything done must be logged and quickly analyzed. Unfortunately, most spying is never detected and can continue undetected at the will of the perpetrators.

23.9.2 Remote Spying Devices.   There are very sensitive radio receivers that can monitor information system data through walls or from outside the building without the use of an inside bug or wiretap. These devices can simply listen to the data from afar. Such equipment is not available publicly and is well beyond the means of all but the best-financed spies. However, there are many such systems in use today, and many more will be available as prices drop. Any organization whose data are very valuable is a potential target. The best protection is good shielding around equipment rooms and thick-wall metal conduit for data cables, and everything must be properly grounded. There are also interference transmitters that may help; these broadcast white noise that can overwhelm signals radiated from the IS infrastructure.

23.9.3 Bombs, Threats, Violence, and Attacks.   Violent events are unpredictable and potentially devastating. These are not accidents, but deliberate attacks, intended to disrupt, cause damage, and spread fear. The tragic attacks of 9/11, and their aftermath, have proven the vulnerability of people and of their infrastructures. The vulnerabilities remain today, and the risks are even greater.

Protection against violence must be threat-specific, and all possible threats must be addressed as described in Chapter 22. Effective deterrence and mitigation then become a matter of strengthening the protections described throughout this chapter, which need not be very costly considering the response and recovery costs that could otherwise result. Premises or corporate security must deal with most threats of violence, but the infrastructure needs special protections to avoid disruption and to mitigate the downtime and cost consequences of any such event.

Bomb or terrorist threats now happen frequently within the United States. Most are unreported. Many threats are hoaxes or the result of harmless objects discovered. Some threats are prevented before they occur. And many devices fail, but a few do not. The motives to incite violence can now include hate, revenge, a compulsion to eradicate perceived evil, disgruntled and deranged persons (including children), copycat thrill seekers, religious, political, or secular interests, and often extortion or blackmail. Sometimes there are no clear motives. Although such events are statistically unlikely to happen, the potential costs and wide areas of disruptions are too great to be ignored. Protections and preparation will at least reduce the otherwise huge liabilities when any event occurs. The Department of Homeland Security and the Federal Bureau of Investigation both offer considerable information on preparation, protection, and dealing with bomb or other serious threats, including checklists for anyone receiving a warning phone call or a suspicious letter or package.

Powerful can be made with at home materials that are readily available from local stores. Car bombs can destroy whole buildings. Strong explosives may be put into harmless-looking objects, such as sports balls, books, dolls or teddy bears, or concealed as a cell phone, camera, or radio. Devices can be detonated by a fuse, mechanical or electronic timer, radio signal, or trigger mechanism when anyone moves or touches the device. The railroad bombings in Madrid in 2004 were detonated by cell phones used as alarm clocks so they all detonated together. Calls to a cell phone or a digital watch used as a timer are often used as well. A suicide bomber can manually trigger an explosion when it is most effective. A new device showing up in schools is a tennis ball that will explode with considerable force when it is thrown. Other ways to trigger weapons, especially chemical or biological weapons, use a package or a backpack left unattended that will detonate automatically or when touched. For example, consider the threat to an organization from a carton labeled copier paper left unattended near the IS infrastructure.

Reasonably good protection and mitigation measures can be simple and inexpensive. Details cannot be described publicly, but state and regional bomb squads or explosives units can advise and assist in many ways, including current briefings. Weapons of mass destruction (WMDs), other than nuclear weapons, are fast becoming a real threat, especially because many such devices are small and easily concealed. WMDs include chemical and biological agents and incendiary devices, while even small amounts of radioactive materials disbursed by an explosive "dirty bomb" can spread panic. The government considers these devices very serious threats, with businesses and their infrastructures as likely targets.

New federal office space must now be certified as bomb resistant, so that an explosion or the impact of a truck bomb cannot collapse the building. Officials can usually provide a current threat briefing and suggest protective measures. Although small areas may be destroyed, the structure will not collapse.

Small-size bombs are a major concern. A few ounces of a chemical agent can kill hundreds of people, and the victims are usually stricken within minutes or hours, and for no apparent reason. Chemical agents are usually not contagious. Biological agents are even harder to detect quickly. A small vial the size of a lipstick can kill every person within a large metropolitan area. Biological victims usually do not react for several hours or days, and they may be highly contagious. With either agent, death is likely unless the right medical procedures and antidotes are administered quickly.

Should any suspected WMD event occur, call for government help immediately and stay well away from the scene (at least 600 feet upwind, uphill, and upstream) until properly trained and equipped specialists arrive. Make sure the FBI is informed quickly. Advise state and regional emergency officials that mass decontamination may be required before victims can be transported or enter hospitals. Decontamination requires copious amounts of water (fire hoses set on a gentle spray), plenty of detergent, and, possibly, diluted household bleach. Provisions should be made to keep victims comfortable and to protect their modesty. The water runoff may itself be an environmental hazard.

FBI, fire, police, and emergency management officials, trained in WMD and terrorism, should be consulted to better understand the possible threats and how best to deal with them.

23.9.4 Medical Emergencies.
The possibility of a flu epidemic or something like an outbreak of anthrax poisoning can cause enormous disruption to the information infrastructure. People cannot or will not come to work, or will have evacuated the area. This can go on for months, possibly years. The only mitigation is for them to telecommute, work from a safe and remote location, or outsource to organizations that can fill in. (See Section 22.4.3.)

Other medical emergencies can also cause big problems. (See Section 22.6.5.) Although medical emergencies are primarily premises security problems, preventing them is vital to avoid disrupting the performance of information systems. A serious medical emergency is very likely to happen eventually. Any such event can devastate morale and productivity and severely affect IS performance for an extended period. The event can be excessively costly if not promptly treated.

Mitigating medical emergencies requires a first aid room on the premises, first aid and some medical supplies, a registered nurse if possible, and many workers trained in first aid and cardiopulmonary resuscitation (CPR). All security personnel and guards should be certified in first aid and CPR.

Cardiac arrest occurs in the workplace and can hit anyone, visitors, vendors, or staff. Fast response, adequate equipment, and proper training are essential—minutes count. Waiting for a 911 response can result in death or permanent impairment, even when emergency medical technicians arrive quickly. An automated external defibrillator (AED) on site will save lives and can be operated by anybody in an emergency. A portable AED currently costs about $1,000, and the suggested training is inexpensive. An AED is now required in all federally managed buildings. Many shopping malls, places of public assembly, and commercial aircraft are now equipped with one or more units.

Oxygen is often necessary to save lives and prevent permanent impairment. Most sites equipped with an AED also have oxygen units. Good portable units cost $800 or less and can be operated by almost anyone, without training.

23.10 INFORMATION NOT PUBLICLY AVAILABLE.   Many special threat situations cannot be mentioned publicly because the materials and tools are readily obtained, inconspicuous, or easily concealed and disposed of after the crime. It is not possible to describe these threats without explaining how anyone can perpetrate them. Apprehension is difficult, sometimes impossible, so the only protection is deterrence and detection before trouble happens. Chapter 22 excludes these types of threats, and it is equally inappropriate to discuss their specific mitigation in this chapter.

Generally, however, there are effective ways to mitigate these threats as well as some more common ones. It is best to compile a comprehensive list of special threat situations and how to mitigate them by talking with a wide array of experienced consultants, contractors, installers, maintenance personnel, and vendors. Most of these people have long lists of easy and effective ways to disrupt, snoop, or attack the information infrastructures, along with practical countermeasures. No protection can be comprehensive until these resources have been interviewed for their experience and suggestions.

Just like some possible threats, there are also effective protection devices that cannot be mentioned. These are not marketed publicly and therefore are unknown to dealers, resellers, or distributors. The costs can be reasonable because they are only sold direct. Developers may supply classified systems for military or government use and offer declassified versions to other selected users. In this way, developers can restrict knowledge of their products to as few people as possible, so that others cannot discover how to recognize or circumvent them.

Many consultants who have worked with financial, regulated, or very large private companies know some of these specialty vendors. Usually a consultant will approach the vendor and discuss what is needed; the vendor may then contact the customer directly.

Finally, given today's environment of violence, get to know key local, state, and federal law enforcement and investigative officials, and ask their suggestions how best to protect an organization.

23.11   COMPLETING THE SECURITY PLANNING PROCESS.   The last step necessary to protect the information infrastructure has four components. Absent any of these components completed thoroughly, good security is not possible. They include:

1. Develop an all-hazard mitigation plan.
2. Develop all of the mitigation options for each identified threat and perform a cost-benefit analysis to determine which options are best.
3. Develop an overall security response plan to show who is responsible for what.
4. Complete the necessary implementation, accountability, and follow-up procedures.

It is not possible to fully explain each step within the confines of this chapter, but the information that follows at least outlines some of what is needed to complete the security planning process and where to find additional information.

All of the five available FEMA *State and Local Mitigation Planning* How-to Guides referenced in Section 22.9 can be helpful in this final step. Particularly so is FEMA Publication 386-2, *Understanding Your Risks,* that shows a method of cost-estimating potential losses due to flooding using tables rather than by calculation. These tables quickly show that losses can be far greater than expected. In addition to the five available guides, an Internet search for the series title is also suggested as portions of the four unreleased guides (386-5, 386-6, 386-8, and 386-9) may be available from state agencies.

23.11.1   All-Hazard Mitigation Plan.   Once all possible threat situations have been identified and assessed as described in Chapter 22, the next step is to develop as many options as possible to prevent, deter, or mitigate disruption, injury, or damage from each threat. Although some threats cannot be prevented, there are always ways to prepare for and mitigate their impact. Usually there are many mitigation options, so the objective is to determine which options are the most practical and affordable. The only objective way to do this is with cost-benefit analysis (described in Section 23.11.2).

In actuality, the options to protect against many different threats will be similar, but each option should be retained until the best mitigation strategy for each threat is determined. Here also there is likely to be one common mitigation strategy that covers many different threats. All credible threats should be listed in the mitigation plan, but the mitigation projects laid out will be far fewer in number.

When the next step is finished, the All-Hazard Mitigation Plan can be completed. The FEMA 386 how-to manuals listed in Section 22.9 provide the suggested format and content.

The complete mitigation plan should be for official use only, and not released except to those with a need to know this information. The complete plan would be very helpful to a potential troublemaker because it shows where the organization is vulnerable, and to which threats. If disclosure of the complete plan is not well controlled, its contents could be leaked by, extorted from, or sold by an insider. However, the executive summary of the plan and abbreviated findings should be circulated widely, so that all stakeholders know that much is being done to protect them.

23.11.2 Cost-Benefit Analysis.   Security is pointless unless it is cost-effective and also adds value: that is, the cost of mitigating each threat must be less than the potential benefits and savings of the event not occurring, because if the protection is effective. The costs of every option can easily be determined; these are the initial and ongoing costs. Some future benefits, though, will be intangible, and all will have to be approximated. The long-term benefits of something not happening must reflect the approximated costs of:

- Disruptions that would reduce the productivity of the business and the performance of its information systems
- Morale and performance that could plummet, and remain very low because people feel unsafe and unprotected
- Loss of business or customers until operations could be restored to normal
- Response and recovery costs including extra time and overtime, expenses including lodging and meals, temporary facilities, public relations, and legal defense costs that are all likely to be incurred
- Legal, public relations, and other services and expenses to repair reputational damage, and fallen stock price, and to restore goodwill

Not all of these costs will follow every threat. But then again, there may also be additional, unexpected costs as well. In general, the response and recovery costs of any major security event tend to be far greater than expected. Nonetheless, each situation can be studied and some costs determined in order to facilitate a statistically-valid cost-benefit analysis.

Cost and benefit information have no meaning unless each is associated with a common time frame. The likelihood of each threat should be assessed on an annualized basis (see Section 22.3.4), so that both the mitigation costs and the potential benefits can be amortized over the same life cycle.

There are many methods for cost-value analysis, and most are beyond the scope of this chapter. However, for those who are not financially trained, the federal government has a good system, freely available, that is widely required within the government. The government calls this system "BCA," which stands for benefit-cost analysis. It is based on the federal Office of Management and Budget's Circular A-94. Information is available at www.whitehouse.gov/omb/circulars/a094/print/a094.html. But this is best gotten on the *Mitigation BCA Toolkit* CD-ROM, which is available free by telephoning 1-866-222-3580. This CD includes manuals, programs, training documents, and some case studies as well.

One particular advantage of the BCA system is that the OMB publishes current cost-of-funds data needed to project any costs. Some of the private models tend to use wildly optimistic (or grossly out of date) future interest rates, which invalidates meaningful results. Again, it is wise to use a federal government model simply as a matter of risk avoidance. And the BCA model is widely used and required for many grant applications.

FEMA has developed a series of eight *Cost Effectiveness Tools,* which are programs to assist grant applicants with financial analyses, such as net present value. For details go to www.fema.gov and search for the title.

23.11.3 Security Response Plan.   A hazard mitigation plan is needed to document the threat assessment done in Chapter 22 and to list the mitigation options and the predicted costs and benefits associated with each; a security response plan is also needed to direct each stakeholder according to the type of threat experienced. The purpose of the security response plan is to define clearly who is in charge and who will do what, when and how, when any threat occurs. The new and comprehensive NRP format is strongly recommended for uniformity. (See Section 23.2.2.) Begin with this format and table of contents and add more ESFs, annexes, or appendices as needed. Also utilize a current local emergency operations plan (LEOP) and a current state emergency operations plan (SEOP) for guidance and uniformity.

The new NRP format revises and reestablishes the Emergency Support Functions (ESF) concept for each support activity that each organization may need. There are now 16 numbered ESFs, beginning with ESF-1, "Transportation," ESF-2, "Communications & Alerting," and on through ESF-16, "Animal Health." It is recommended that the standard ESF titles be retained, even though many may not be applicable to a nongovernment organization, if only to maintain a uniformity and language that everyone understands. Additional ESFs will be needed to mount an effective response, but number these as "17" and upward. (As mentioned in Section 23.2.2, the NRP may soon be replaced with a new framework, yet to be released. However, the NRP and NIMS [Section 23.2.1] are still instructive.)

The same is true with the NRP's new appendices, support annexes, and incident annexes (which are still confusing as to what information is put where). For uniformity and consistency, it is best to keep the NRP titles and their sequence, edit these to suit the organization's needs, and add more appendices or annexes as needed at the end of each section. Details are beyond the scope of this chapter; look at the actual plan and ask those who are certified in the new processes and know how to implement them.

One useful quick reference in the new response plan format is an Emergency Support Function Assignment Matrix (which is often Figure 1), a one-page graphic that shows which agency or department has primary, secondary, or support responsibility for each ESF. This is a handy quick-reference guide for management and staff when trouble comes.

Once a response plan is ready, "standard operating procedures" should be written by each affected department to outline the procedures it will use to respond. The term is in quotes because these are usually issued as guidelines so that there can be some flexibility to adjust to the actual conditions. The requirement for rigid adherence to a procedure is an invitation that invites litigation.

The complete security response plan should also be for official use only, and released only to those with a need to know. After all, this plan shows troublemakers just how the organization will respond. However, a press release summarizing the plan should be widely circulated so that all stakeholders know the organization is trying to protect them.

23.11.4 Implementation, Accountability, and Follow-Up.   Once all the plans are completed and signed off by management and key officials, the job of implementation begins. Of the How-To Guides mentioned earlier, FEMA 386-4, *Bringing the Plan to Life,* will be helpful here.

This first implementation step is the most critical to the security-protection process. It begins with training so that everyone involved understands and accepts the procedures. There must then be periodic exercises and drills to test the response plan and to validate that the training has been effective. Plans that are not periodically tested are soon forgotten.

Every exercise and drill must be reviewed to determine what went right and, more important, what did not, and how to do better in the future. So too should every emergency response be reviewed. Documentation before, during, and after the event is important. There will be some lessons learned from each event, and these lessons should be used to update and improve the security systems to work better in the future.

It is also critical to establish accountability for the infrastructure security. There should be only one person in charge of each function. Responsibility cannot be spread among management or departments, nor can responsibility be worn as a second hat for someone with many other duties. The senior responsible authority must set up schedules for periodic review and update of the plans and procedures, training, and exercises to make sure that the security program remains current and effective.

Good security management must also include oversight. Good planning must begin in the boardroom, and the directors must also provide continuing oversight to ascertain good security. Outside, independent, auditors who are directed from the boardroom are best able to validate the current condition of the security program. The auditor's written opinion is evidence of whether the organization is fully compliant or not. The best procedure for an infrastructure security audit is suggested in Section 23.2.7.

For management's own peace of mind (and possibly as a requirement for maintaining insurance and obtaining credit), there may be periodic security inspections, testing of defenses, and some penetration tests, including deceptions to gain access done by independent professionals.

23.12   SUMMARY AND CONCLUSIONS.   Here are some parting thoughts and final suggestions how best to protect the information infrastructure.

Looking back on the events since 9/11, the question is often asked: Are we safer now? The only honest answer is mostly no. There are still many gaps in our security processes and procedures, much confusion and inconsistency about what to do, and still many threats not yet identified or addressed.

The question here is therefore: How can any organization best protect itself and still manage its risks most affordably and effectively?

23.12.1   Federal Guidelines and Instructions Are Still Deficient.   This chapter advocates the DHS/FEMA methodology as the best means of risk management for any organization. Compliance with the many new laws, regulations, and directives that can affect security is advocated also. But, as yet, none of these procedures is either uniform or comprehensive. Nearly all of them remain as works in progress that are incomplete, cumbersome, confusing, and misunderstood. Instead of trying to fix, better implement, and follow the systems that worked quite well during the 1990s, the new administration chose to abandon everything and start anew with new directives and procedures, forming new organizational structures with many more layers of bureaucracy. And currently, the administration has even revoked some of its own procedures in favor of new ones yet to be publicly available. Very few of the people involved have much management experience or any background in security or emergency management. The results so far have been to add confusion, impede progress, constrict the channels of communication, and stovepipe (i.e., compartmentalize) information that should be shared among other agencies. In the process, the capacities of FEMA have been stripped, marginalized, and increasingly underfunded.

The system was supposed to be fixed following the events of 9/11 and Hurricane Katrina. Instead, the new regime has gone off in many directions to pursue terrorism, without recognizing that many other serious threats are likely to happen. Is the system better now than it was before? Probably not yet, but it is slowly improving. Will they ever get it right? Yes, probably, eventually. But when big trouble comes, how much help can an organization expect from the government? As of now, any help may be limited, slow in coming, and unrelated to the immediate response needs. So when trouble comes, it may well be very costly to organizations that are not well prepared.

23.12.2   Good Risk Management Is the Answer.   Then why advocate the federal methodology at all? The answers are: (1) better risk management, (2) better able to minimize costs, and (3) by achieving a high level of security planning and management, an organization will be much better able to protect itself and less dependent on help from others. For these reasons, good, effective, and efficient security as described in this chapter is still the best protection.

Good security is an investment that must be carefully planned, analyzed, and implemented, well maintained, and quickly changed when necessary to maximize the investment return. The whole process represents a large investment in time, money, and resources. Management, all who use the infrastructure, and all of the many stakeholders must be involved. Preparedness cannot be relegated to others. Otherwise, security is not a good investment but merely an expense to be tolerated.

The need for security changes and improvements is an ongoing certainty. Threats are always changing and often the information infrastructure is as well. And so too are the many regulations that affect the security process and procedures. Nonetheless, it is possible to maintain good security. Every threat situation can be mitigated to some extent to minimize its potential for injury, damage, and disruption—even though the event itself cannot be prevented. Good security planning and management are required, as is compliance with the many and ever-changing regulations and requirements that directly address indirectly affect security, if only to avoid the high costs of liability. Good risk management seeks to avoid liability. Today, good security is necessarily an integral part of good risk management.

Good security can provide the best possible protection at the least long-term cost for any organization. Anything less than good security is a waste of time and money.

23.13   FURTHER READING

The further readings suggested in Chapter 22 will also be helpful in this chapter.

The Congressional Research Service report to Congress dated June 2006, entitled *Federal Emergency Management and Homeland Security Organization: Historical Development and Legislative Options,* is interesting reading for anyone burdened with security planning and management. This outlines the federal government's struggles since 1947 to get the system right. It also lists legislation before the 109th Congress to fix the problems. The report can be downloaded from http://fpc.state.gov/C4763.htm. The order code is RL33369.

For an interesting discussion of the inner workings of federal response systems and how better security planning and management can be implemented, see Christopher Cooper and Robert Block, *Disaster: Hurricane Katrina and the Future of Homeland Security* by (New York: Times Books, 2006).

23.14   NOTES

1. ISBN 0-87609-358-6 ($10) is available for download at: www.cfr.org/publications/10457/.

2. The Quick Reference Guide of FEMA & NRP is available at www.fema.gov/pdf/emergency/nims/ref_guide_nrp.pdf or search for Quick Guide on FEMA. Gov/nrf.

3. Telephone Communications Industry Association/Electronics Industry Alliance, 2500 Wilson Boulevard, Arlington, VA 22201. Tel: 1-703-907-7700. E-mail at www.wiaonline.org.

4. National Fire Protection Association, 1 Batterymarch Park, Quincy, MA 02169-7471. Tel: 1-800-344-3555. Online catalog at http://catalog.nfpa.org.

5. Cloning e-passports may now be possible because the data cannot be encrypted until all countries implement a common infrastructure. Visit www.vnunet.com/computing/news/2161836/kacers-crack-biometrtic.

6. Trace portal machines deployed at Midway International Airport, www.tsa.gov/press/releases/2006/press_release_0807206.shtm.

7. Announced 08/07/2006 by General Electric's research center in Niskayuna, NY. Visit http://edition.cnn.com/2006/TECH/08/07/terrorism.technology.ap/

8. Electronic Privacy Information Center (EPIC), http://epic.org/privacy/facerecognition/.

9. NIST publications are available free at http://csrc.nist.gov/publications/nistpubs/index.html.

10. NIST's Automated Security Self-Evaluation Tool is available at http://csrc.nist.gov/asset/.

CHAPTER 24

OPERATING SYSTEM SECURITY

William Stallings

24.1 INFORMATION PROTECTION AND SECURITY. This chapter reviews the principles of security in operating systems. Some general-purpose tools can be built into computers and operating systems (OSs) that support a variety of protection and security mechanisms. In general, the concern is with the problem of controlling access to computer systems and the information stored in them. Four types of overall protection policies, of increasing order of difficulty, have been identified:

1. **No sharing.** In this case, processes are completely isolated from each other, and each process has exclusive control over the resources statically or dynamically assigned to it. With this policy, processes often "share" a program or data file by making a copy of it and transferring the copy into their own virtual memory.

2. **Sharing originals of program or data files.** With the use of reentrant code, a single physical realization of a program can appear in multiple virtual address spaces, as can read-only data files. Special locking mechanisms are required for

the sharing of writable data files, to prevent simultaneous users from interfering with each other.

3. **Confined, or memoryless, subsystems.** In this case, processes are grouped into subsystems to enforce a particular protection policy. For example, a "client" process calls a "server" process to perform some task on data. The server is to be protected against the client discovering the algorithm by which it performs the task, while the client is to be protected against the server's retaining any information about the task being performed.

4. **Controlled information dissemination.** In some systems, security classes are defined to enforce a particular dissemination policy. Users and applications are given security clearances of a certain level, while data and other resources (e.g., input/output [I/O] devices) are given security classifications. The security policy enforces restrictions concerning which users have access to which classifications. This model is useful not only in the military context but in commercial applications as well.[1]

Much of the work in security and protection as it relates to OSs can be roughly grouped into three categories.

1. **Access control.** Concerned with regulating user access to the total system, subsystems, and data, and regulating process access to various resources and objects within the system.

2. **Information flow control.** Regulates the flow of data within the system and its delivery to users.

3. **Certification.** Relates to proving that access and flow control mechanisms perform according to their specifications and that they enforce desired protection and security policies.

This chapter looks at some of the key mechanisms for providing OS security and then examines Windows 2000 as a case study.

24.2   REQUIREMENTS FOR OPERATING SYSTEM SECURITY

24.2.1   Requirements.   Understanding the types of threats to OS security that exist requires a definition of security requirements. OS security addresses four requirements:

1. **Confidentiality.** Requires that the information in a computer system be accessible only for reading by authorized parties. This type of access includes printing, displaying, and other forms of disclosure, including simply revealing the existence of an object.

2. **Integrity.** Requires that only authorized parties be able to modify computer system assets. Modification includes writing, changing, changing status, deleting, and creating.

3. **Availability.** Requires that computer system assets are available to authorized parties.

4. **Authenticity.** Requires that a computer system be able to verify the identity of a user.

24.2.2   Computer System Assets.   The assets of a computer system can be categorized as hardware, software, and data.

24.2.2.1   Hardware.   The main threat to computer system hardware is in the area of availability. Hardware is the most vulnerable to attack and the least amenable to automated controls. Threats include accidental and deliberate damage to equipment as well as theft. The proliferation of personal computers and workstations and the increasing use of local area networks (LANs) increase the potential for losses in this area. Physical and administrative security measures are needed to deal with these threats.

24.2.2.2   Software.   The OS, utilities, and application programs are what make computer system hardware useful to businesses and individuals. Several distinct threats need to be considered.

A key threat to software is an attack on availability. Software, especially application software, is surprisingly easy to delete. Software also can be altered or damaged to render it useless. Careful software configuration management, which includes making backups of the most recent version of software, can maintain high availability. A more difficult problem to deal with is software modification that results in a program that still functions but that behaves differently from before. A final problem is software secrecy. Although certain countermeasures are available, by and large the problem of unauthorized copying of software has not been solved.

24.2.2.3   Data.   Hardware and software security typically are concerns of computing center professionals or individual concerns of personal computer users. A much more widespread problem is data security, which involves files and other forms of data controlled by individuals, groups, and business organizations.

Security concerns with respect to data are broad, encompassing availability, secrecy, and integrity. In the case of availability, the concern is with the destruction of data files, which can occur either accidentally or maliciously.

The obvious concern with secrecy, of course, is the unauthorized reading of data files or databases, and this area has been the subject of perhaps more research and effort than any other area of computer security. A less obvious secrecy threat involves the analysis of data and manifests itself in the use of so-called statistical databases, which provide summary or aggregate information. Presumably, the existence of aggregate information does not threaten the privacy of the individuals involved. However, as the use of statistical databases grows, there is an increasing potential for disclosure of personal information. In essence, characteristics of constituent individuals may be identified through careful analysis. To take a simple example, if one table records the aggregate of the incomes of respondents A, B, C, and D and another records the aggregate of the incomes of A, B, C, D, and E, the difference between the two aggregates would be the income of E. This problem is exacerbated by the increasing desire to combine data sets. In many cases, matching several sets of data for consistency at levels of aggregation appropriate to the problem requires a retreat to elemental units in the process of constructing the necessary aggregates. Thus, the elemental units, which are the subject of privacy concerns, are available at various stages in the processing of data sets.

Finally, data integrity is a major concern in most installations. Modifications to data files can have consequences ranging from minor to disastrous.

24.2.3 Design Principles.   Saltzer and Schroeder identify a number of principles for the design of security measures for the various threats to computer systems. These include:

- **Least privilege.** Every program and every user of the system should operate using the least set of privileges necessary to complete the job. Access rights should be acquired by explicit permission only; the default should be "no access."

- **Economy of mechanisms.** Security mechanisms should be as small and simple as possible, aiding in their verification. This usually means that they must be an integral part of the design rather than add-on mechanisms to existing designs.

- **Acceptability.** Security mechanisms should not interfere unduly with the work of users. At the same time, the mechanisms should meet the needs of those who authorize access. If the mechanisms are not easy to use, they are likely to be unused or incorrectly used.

- **Complete mediation.** Every access must be checked against the access-control information, including those accesses occurring outside normal operation, as in recovery or maintenance.

- **Open design.** The security of the system should not depend on keeping the design of its mechanisms secret. Thus, the mechanisms can be reviewed by many experts, and users can have high confidence in them.[2]

24.3 PROTECTION MECHANISMS.   The introduction of multiprogramming brought about the ability to share resources among users. This sharing involves not just the processor but also:

- Memory
- I/O devices, such as disks and printers
- Programs
- Data

The ability to share these resources introduced the need for protection. Pfleeger points out that an OS may offer protection along this spectrum:

- **No protection.** This is appropriate when sensitive procedures are being run at separate times.

- **Isolation.** This approach implies that each process operates separately from other processes, with no sharing or communication. Each process has its own address space, files, and other objects.

- **Share all or share nothing.** The owner of an object (e.g., a file or memory segment) declares it to be public or private. In the former case, any process may access the object; in the latter, only the owner's processes may access the object.

- **Share via access limitation.** The OS checks the permissibility of each access by a specific user to a specific object. The OS therefore acts as a guard, or gatekeeper, between users and objects, ensuring that only authorized accesses occur.

- **Share via dynamic capabilities.** This extends the concept of access control to allow dynamic creation of sharing rights for objects.

- **Limit use of an object.** This form of protection limits not just access to an object but the use to which that object may be put. For example, a user may be allowed to view a sensitive document but not print it. Another example is that a user may be allowed access to a database to derive statistical summaries but not to determine specific data values.[3]

The preceding items are listed roughly in increasing order of difficulty to implement but also in increasing order of fineness of protection that they provide. A given OS may provide different degrees of protection for different objects, users, or applications.

The OS needs to balance the need to allow sharing, which enhances the utility of the computer system, with the need to protect the resources of individual users. This section considers some of the mechanisms by which OSs have enforced protection for these objects.

24.3.1 Protection of Memory.

In a multiprogramming environment, protection of main memory is essential. The concern here is not just security but the correct functioning of the various processes that are active. If one process can inadvertently write into the memory space of another process, then the latter process may not execute properly.

The separation of the memory space of various processes is accomplished easily with a virtual memory scheme. Either segmentation or paging, or the two in combination, provides an effective means of managing main memory. If complete isolation is sought, then the OS simply must ensure that each segment or page is accessible only by the process to which it is assigned. This is accomplished easily by requiring that there be no duplicate entries in page and/or segment tables.

If sharing is to be allowed, then the same segment or page may appear in more than one table. This type of sharing is accomplished most easily in a system that supports segmentation or a combination of segmentation and paging. In this case, the segment structure is visible to the application, and the application can declare individual segments to be sharable or nonsharable. In a pure paging environment, it becomes more difficult to discriminate between the two types of memory, because the memory structure is transparent to the application.

Segmentation, especially, lends itself to the implementation of protection and sharing policies. Because each segment table entry includes a length as well as a base address, a program cannot inadvertently access a main memory location beyond the limits of a segment. To achieve sharing, it is possible for a segment to be referenced in the segment tables of more than one process. The same mechanisms are, of course, available in a paging system. However, in this case the page structure of programs and data is not visible to the programmer, making the specification of protection and sharing requirements more awkward. Exhibit 24.1 illustrates the types of protection relationships that can be enforced in such a system.

An example of the hardware support that can be provided for memory protection is that of the IBM System/370 family of machines, on which OS/390 runs. Associated with each page frame in main memory is a 7-bit storage control key, which may be set by the OS. Two of the bits indicate whether the page occupying this frame has been referenced and changed; these bits are used by the page replacement algorithm. The remaining bits are used by the protection mechanism: a 4-bit access control key and a fetch-protection bit. Processor references to memory and direct memory access (DMA). DMA I/O memory references must use a matching key to gain permission to access that page. The fetch-protection bit indicates whether the access control key applies to writes or to both reads and writes. In the processor, there is a program status word (PSW), which contains control information relating to the process that is currently

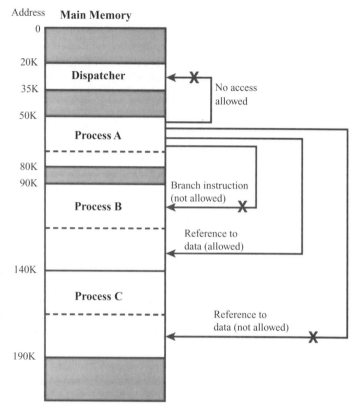

EXHIBIT 24.1   Protection Relationships between Segments

executing. Included in this word is a 4-bit PSW key. When a process attempts to access a page or to initiate a DMA operation on a page, the current PSW key is compared to the access code. A write operation is permitted only if the codes match. If the fetch bit is set, then the PSW key must match the access code for read operations.

24.3.2   User-Oriented Access Control.
The measures taken to control access in a data processing system fall into two categories: those associated with the user and those associated with the data.

User control of access is, unfortunately, sometimes referred to as authentication. Because this term is now widely used in the sense of message authentication, it is not applied here. The reader is warned, however, that this use may be encountered in the literature.

The most common technique for user access control on a shared system or server is the user logon, which requires both a user identifier (ID) and a password. The system will allow a user to log on only if that user's ID is known to the system and if the user knows the password associated by the system with that ID. This ID/password system is a notoriously unreliable method of user access control. Users can forget their passwords and accidentally or intentionally reveal their password. Hackers have become very skillful at guessing IDs for special users, such as system control and system management personnel. Finally, the ID/password file is subject to penetration attempts.

User access control in a distributed environment can be either centralized or decentralized. In a centralized approach, the network provides a logon service, determining who is allowed to use the network and to whom the user is allowed to connect.

Decentralized user access control treats the network as a transparent communication link, and the destination host carries out the usual logon procedure. Of course, the security concerns for transmitting passwords over the network still must be addressed.

In many networks, two levels of access control may be used. Individual hosts may be provided with a logon facility to protect host-specific resources and application. In addition, the network as a whole may provide protection to restrict network access to authorized users. This two-level facility is desirable for the common case, currently, in which the network connects disparate hosts and simply provides a convenient means of terminal-host access. In a more uniform network of hosts, some centralized access policy could be enforced in a network control center.

24.3.3 Data-Oriented Access Control.   Following successful logon, the user is granted access to one or a set of hosts and applications. This is generally not sufficient for a system that includes sensitive data in its database. Through the user access-control procedure, a user can be identified to the system. Associated with each user, there can be a profile that specifies permissible operations and file accesses. The OS can then enforce rules based on the user profile. The database management system, however, must control access to specific records or even portions of records. For example, it may be permissible for anyone in administration to obtain a list of company personnel, but only selected individuals may have access to salary information. The issue is more than just one of level of detail. Whereas the OS may grant a user permission to access a file or use an application, following which there are no further security checks, the database management system must make a decision on each individual access attempt. That decision will depend not only on the user's identity but also on the specific parts of the data being accessed and even on the information already divulged to the user.

A general model of access control as exercised by a file or database management system is that of an *access matrix* (see Exhibit 24.2a). The basic elements of the model are:

- **Subject**. An entity capable of accessing objects. Generally, the concept of subject equates with that of process. Any user or application actually gains access to an object by means of a process that represents that user or application.

- **Object**. Anything to which access is controlled. Examples include files, portions of files, programs, and segments of memory.

- **Access right.** The way in which an object is accessed by a subject. Examples are read, write, and execute.

One dimension of the matrix consists of identified subjects that may attempt data access. Typically, this list will consist of individual users or user groups, although access could be controlled for terminals, hosts, or applications, instead of, or in addition to, users. The other dimension lists the objects that may be accessed. At the greatest level of detail, objects may be individual data fields. More aggregate groupings, such as records, files, or even the entire database, also may be objects in the matrix. Each entry in the matrix indicates the access rights of that subject for that object.

In practice, an access matrix usually is sparse and is implemented by decomposition in one of two ways. The matrix may be decomposed by columns, yielding *access-control lists* (see Exhibit 24.2b). Thus for each object, an access-control list lists users

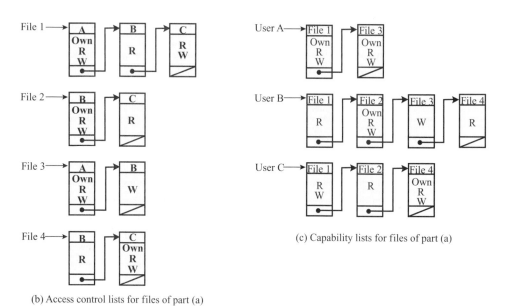

(a) Access matrix

(b) Access control lists for files of part (a)

(c) Capability lists for files of part (a)

EXHIBIT 24.2 Example of Access Control Structures

Source: Based on a figure in Sandhu (1996).

and their permitted access rights. The access-control list may contain a default, or public, entry. This allows users who are not explicitly listed as having special rights to have a default set of rights. Elements of the list may include individual users as well as groups of users.

Decomposition by rows yields *capability tickets* (see Exhibit 24.2c). A capability ticket specifies authorized objects and operations for a user. Each user has a number of tickets and may be authorized to lend or give them to others. Because tickets may be dispersed around the system, they present a greater security problem than access control lists. In particular, the ticket must be unforgeable. One way to accomplish this is to have the OS hold all tickets on behalf of users. These tickets would have to be held in a region of memory inaccessible to users.

Network considerations for data-oriented access control parallel those for user-oriented access control. If only certain users are permitted to access certain items of data, then encryption may be needed to protect those items during transmission to authorized users. Typically, data access control is decentralized, that is, controlled by host-based database management systems. If a network database server exists on a network, then data access control becomes a network function.

24.3.4 Protection Based on an Operating System Mode.

One technique used in all OSs to provide protection is based on the mode of processor execution. Most processors support at least two modes of execution: the mode normally associated with the OS and that normally associated with user programs. Certain instructions can be executed only in the more privileged mode. These would include reading or altering a control register, such as the program status word; primitive I/O instructions; and instructions that relate to memory management. In addition, certain regions of memory can be accessed only in the more privileged mode.

The less privileged mode often is referred to as the *user* mode, because user programs typically would execute in this mode. The more privileged mode is referred to as the *system mode*, *control mode*, or *kernel mode*. This last term refers to the kernel of the OS, which is that portion of the OS that encompasses the important system functions. Exhibit 24.3 lists the functions typically found in the kernel of an OS.

The reason for using two modes should be clear. It is necessary to protect the OS and key OS tables, such as process control blocks, from interference by user programs. In the kernel mode, the software has complete control of the processor and all its instructions, registers, and memory. This level of control is not necessary, and for safety is not desirable, for user programs.

Two questions arise: How does the processor know in which mode it is to be executing, and how is the mode changed? Regarding the first question, typically there is a bit in the program status word that indicates the mode of execution. This bit is changed in response to certain events. For example, when a user makes a call to an OS service, the mode is set to the kernel mode. Typically this is done by executing an instruction that changes the mode. When the user makes a system service call,

EXHIBIT 24.3 Typical Kernel Mode Operating System Functions

Process Management
- Process creation and termination
- Process scheduling and dispatching
- Process switching
- Process synchronization and support for interprocess communication
- Management of process control blocks

Memory Management
- Allocation of address space to processes
- Swapping
- Page and segment management

I/O Management
- Buffer management
- Allocation of I/O channels and devices to processes

Support functions
- Interrupt handling
- Accounting
- Monitoring

or when an interrupt transfers control to a system routine, the routine executes the change-mode instruction to enter a more privileged mode and executes it again to enter a less privileged mode before returning control to the user process. If a user program attempts to execute a change-mode instruction, it will simply result in a call to the OS, which will return an error unless the mode change is to be allowed.

More sophisticated mechanisms also can be provided. A common scheme is to use a ring-protection structure. In this scheme, lower-numbered, or inner, rings enjoy greater privilege than higher-numbered, or outer, rings. Typically, ring 0 is reserved for kernel functions of the OS, with applications at a higher level. Some utilities or OS services may occupy an intermediate ring. Basic principles of the ring system are:

- A program may access only those data that reside on the same ring or a less privileged ring.
- A program may call services residing on the same or a more privileged ring.

An example of the ring protection approach is found on the VAX VMS OS, which uses four modes:

1. **Kernel.** Executes the kernel of the VMS OS, which includes memory management, interrupt handling, and I/O operations.
2. **Executive.** Executes many of the OS service calls, including file and record (disk and tape) management routines.
3. **Supervisor.** Executes other OS services, such as responses to user commands.
4. **User.** Executes user programs, plus utilities such as compilers, editors, linkers, and debuggers.

A process executing in a less privileged mode often needs to call a procedure that executes in a more privileged mode; for example, a user program requires an OS service. This call is achieved by using a change-mode (CHM) instruction, which causes an interrupt that transfers control to a routine at the new access mode. A return is made by executing the REI (return from exception or interrupt) instruction.

24.4 FILE SHARING.   Multiuser systems almost always require that files can be shared among a number of users. Two issues arise: access rights and the management of simultaneous access.

24.4.1 Access Rights.   The file system should provide a flexible tool for allowing extensive file sharing among users. The file system should provide a number of options so that the way in which a particular file is accessed can be controlled. Typically, users or groups of users are granted certain access rights to a file. A wide range of access rights has been used. The next list indicates access rights that can be assigned to a particular user for a particular file.

- **None.** The user may not even learn of the existence of the file, much less access it. To enforce this restriction, the user would not be allowed to read the user directory that includes this file.
- **Knowledge.** The user can determine that the file exists and who its owner is. The user is then able to petition the owner for additional access rights.

- **Execution.** The user can load and execute a program but cannot copy it. Proprietary programs often are made accessible with this restriction.
- **Reading.** The user can read the file for any purpose, including copying and execution. Some systems are able to enforce a distinction between viewing and copying. In the former case, the contents of the file can be displayed to the user, but the user has no means for making a copy.
- **Appending.** The user can add data to the file, often only at the end, but cannot modify or delete any of the file's contents. This right is useful in collecting data from a number of sources.
- **Updating.** The user can modify, delete, and add to the file's data. This normally includes writing the file initially, rewriting it completely or in part, and removing all or a portion of the data. Some systems distinguish among different degrees of updating.
- **Changing protection.** The user can change the access rights granted to other users. Typically only the owner of the file holds this right. In some systems, the owner can extend this right to others. To prevent abuse of this mechanism, the file owner typically is able to specify which rights can be changed by the holder of this extended right.
- **Deletion.** The user can delete the file from the file system.

These rights can be considered to constitute a hierarchy, with each right implying those that precede it. Thus, if a particular user is granted the updating right for a particular file, then that user also is granted these rights: knowledge, execution, reading, and appending.

One user is designated as owner of a given file, usually the person who initially created the file. The owner has all of the access rights listed previously and may grant rights to others. Access can be provided to different classes of users:

- **Specific user.** Individual users who are designated by user ID.
- **User groups.** A set of users who are not individually defined. The system must have some way of keeping track of the membership of user groups.
- **All.** All users who have access to this system. These are public files.

24.4.2 Simultaneous Access.   When access is granted to append or update a file to more than one user, the OS or file management system must enforce discipline. A brute-force approach is to allow a user to lock the entire file when it is to be updated. A finer grain of control is to lock individual records during update. Issues of mutual exclusion and deadlock must be addressed in designing the shared access capability.

24.5 TRUSTED SYSTEMS.   Much of what has been discussed so far has concerned protecting a given message or item from passive or active attack by a given user. A somewhat different but widely applicable requirement is to protect data or resources on the basis of levels of security. This is commonly found in the military, where information is categorized as unclassified (U), confidential (C), secret (S), top secret (TS), or beyond. This concept is equally applicable in other areas, where information can be organized into gross categories and users can be granted clearances to access certain categories of data. For example, the highest level of security might be for strategic corporate planning documents and data, accessible only by corporate officers and their staff; next might come sensitive financial and personnel data, accessible only by administration personnel, corporate officers, and so on.

When multiple categories or levels of data are defined, the requirement is referred to as *multilevel security.* The general statement of the requirement for multilevel security is that a subject at a high level may not convey information to a subject at a lower or incomparable level unless that flow accurately reflects the will of an authorized user. For implementation purposes, this requirement is in two parts and is simply stated. A multilevel secure system must enforce:

1. **No read up.** A subject can only read an object of less or equal security level. This is referred to in the literature as the *simple security property.*

2. **No write down.** A subject can only write into an object of greater or equal security level. This is referred to in the literature as the **-property* (pronounced *star property*).

These two rules, if properly enforced, provide multilevel security. For a data processing system, the approach that has been taken, and has been the object of much research and development, is based on the *reference monitor* concept. This approach is depicted in Exhibit 24.4. The reference monitor is a controlling element in the hardware and OS of a computer that regulates the access of subjects to objects on the basis of security parameters of the subject and object. The reference monitor has access to a file, known as the *security kernel database*, that lists the access privileges (security clearance) of each subject and the protection attributes (classification level) of each object. The reference monitor enforces the security rules (no read up, no write down) and has these properties:

• **Complete mediation.** The security rules are enforced on every access, not just, for example, when a file is opened.

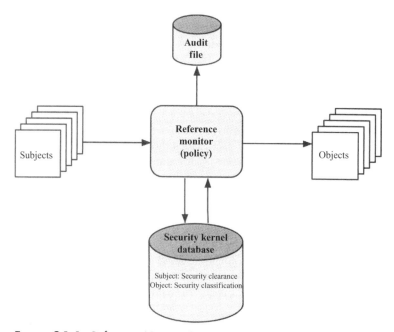

EXHIBIT 24.4 Reference Monitor Concept

- **Isolation.** The reference monitor and database are protected from unauthorized modification.

- **Verifiability**. The reference monitor's correctness must be provable. That is, it must be possible to demonstrate mathematically that the reference monitor enforces the security rules and provides complete mediation and isolation.

These are stiff requirements. The requirement for complete mediation means that every access to data within main memory and on disk and tape must be mediated. Pure software implementations impose too high a performance penalty to be practical; the solution must be at least partly in hardware. The requirement for isolation means that it must not be possible for an attacker, no matter how clever, to change the logic of the reference monitor or the contents of the security kernel database. Finally, the requirement for mathematical proof is formidable for something as complex as a general-purpose computer. A system that can provide such verification is referred to as a *trusted system.*

A final element illustrated in Exhibit 24.4 is an audit file. Important security events, such as detected security violations and authorized changes to the security kernel database, are stored in the audit file.

In an effort to meet its own needs and as a service to the public, the U.S. Department of Defense in 1981 established the Computer Security Center within the National Security Agency (NSA) with the goal of encouraging the widespread availability of trusted computer systems. This goal is realized through the center's Commercial Product Evaluation Program. In essence, the center attempts to evaluate commercially available products as meeting the security requirements just outlined. The center classifies evaluated products according to the range of security features that they provide. These evaluations are needed for Department of Defense procurements but are published and freely available. Hence, they can serve as guidance to commercial customers for the purchase of commercially available, off-the-shelf equipment.

24.5.1   Trojan Horse Defense.   One way to secure against Trojan horse attacks is by the use of a secure, trusted OS. Exhibit 24.5 illustrates an example. In this case, a Trojan horse is used to get around the standard security mechanism used by most file management and OSs: the access-control list. In this example, a user named Bob interacts through a program with a data file containing the critically sensitive character string "CPE170KS". User Bob has created the file with read/write permission provided only to programs executing on his own behalf: that is, only processes that are owned by Bob may access the file.

The Trojan horse attack begins when a hostile user, named Alice, gains legitimate access to the system and installs both a Trojan horse program and a private file to be used in the attack as a "back pocket." Alice gives read/write permission to herself for this file and gives Bob write-only permission (see Exhibit 24.5a). Alice now induces Bob to invoke the Trojan horse program, perhaps by advertising it as a useful utility. When the program detects that it is being executed by Bob, it reads the sensitive character string from Bob's file and copies it into Alice's back-pocket file (see Exhibit 24.5b). Both the read and write operations satisfy the constraints imposed by access-control lists. Alice then has only to access Bob's file at a later time to learn the value of the string.

Now consider the use of a secure OS in this scenario (see Exhibit 24.5c). Security levels are assigned to subjects at logon on the basis of criteria such as the terminal from which the computer is being accessed and the user involved, as identified by

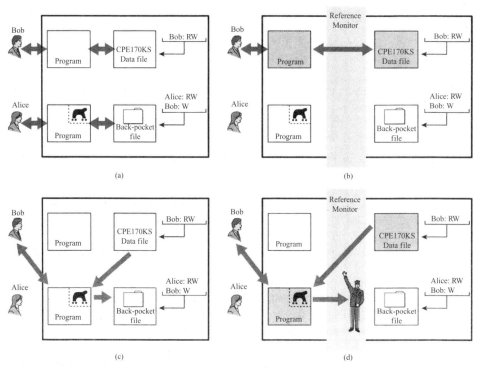

EXHIBIT 24.5 Trojan Horse and Secure Operating Systems

password/ID. In this example, there are two security levels, sensitive (gray) and public (white), ordered so that sensitive is higher than public. Processes owned by Bob and Bob's data file are assigned the security level sensitive. Alice's file and processes are restricted to public. If Bob invokes the Trojan horse program (see Exhibit 24.5d), that program acquires Bob's security level. It is therefore able, under the simple security property, to observe the sensitive character string. When the program attempts to store the string in a public file (the back-pocket file), however, the *-property is violated and the attempt is disallowed by the reference monitor. Thus, the attempt to write into the back-pocket file is denied even though the access-control list permits it: The security policy takes precedence over the access-control list mechanism.

24.6 WINDOWS 2000 SECURITY. A good example of the access control concepts discussed in this chapter is the Windows 2000 (W2K) access-control facility, which exploits object-oriented concepts to provide a powerful and flexible access control capability.

W2K provides a uniform access-control facility that applies to processes, threads, files, semaphores, windows, and other objects. Access control is governed by two entities: an access token associated with each process and a security descriptor associated with each object for which interprocess access is possible.

24.6.1 Access-Control Scheme. When a user logs on to a W2K system, W2K uses a name/password scheme to authenticate the user. If the logon is accepted, a process is created for the user and an access token is associated with that process object. The access token, whose details are described later, include a security ID (SID), which is the identifier by which this user is known to the system for purposes of security. When the initial user process spawns any additional processes, the new process object inherits the same access token.

The access token serves two purposes:

1. It keeps all necessary security information together to speed access validation. When any process associated with a user attempts access, the security subsystem can make use of the token associated with that process to determine the user's access privileges.

2. It allows each process to modify its security characteristics in limited ways without affecting other processes running on behalf of the user.

The chief significance of the second point has to do with privileges that may be associated with a user. The access token indicates which privileges a user may have. Generally the token is initialized with each of these privileges in a disabled state. Subsequently, if one of the user's processes needs to perform a privileged operation, the process may enable the appropriate privilege and attempt access. It would be undesirable to keep all of the security information for a user in one systemwide place, because in that case enabling a privilege for one process enables it for all of them.

A security descriptor is associated with each object for which interprocess access is possible. The chief component of the security descriptor is an access-control list that specifies access rights for various users and user groups for this object. When a process attempts to access this object, the SID of the process is matched against the access-control list of the object to determine if access will be allowed.

When an application opens a reference to a securable object, W2K verifies that the object's security descriptor grants the application's user access. If the check succeeds, W2K caches the resulting granted access rights.

An important aspect of W2K security is the concept of impersonation, which simplifies the use of security in a client/server environment. If client and server talk through a Remote Procedure Call (RPC) connection, the server can temporarily assume the identity of the client so that it can evaluate a request for access relative to that client's rights. After the access, the server reverts to its own identity.

24.6.2 Access Token.   Exhibit 24.6a shows the general structure of an access token, which includes these parameters:

- **Security ID.** Identifies a user uniquely across all of the machines on the network. This generally corresponds to a user's logon name.

- **Group SIDs.** A list of the groups to which this user belongs. A group is simply a set of user IDs that are identified as a group for purposes of access control. Each group has a unique group SID. Access to an object can be defined on the basis of group SIDs, individual SIDs, or a combination.

- **Privileges.** A list of security-sensitive system services that this user may call. An example is create token. Another example is the set backup privilege; users with this privilege are allowed to use a backup tool to back up files that they normally would not be able to read. Most users will have no privileges.

- **Default owner.** If this process creates another object, this field specifies who is the owner of the new object. Generally the owner of the new process is the same as the owner of the spawning process. However, a user may specify that the default

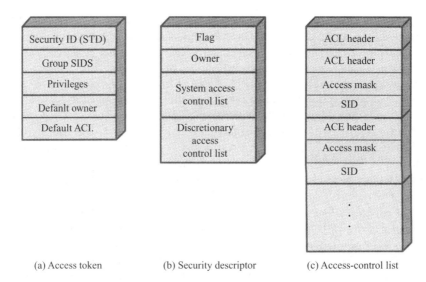

(a) Access token   (b) Security descriptor   (c) Access-control list

Exhibit 24.6   Windows 2000 Security Structures

owner of any processes spawned by this process is a group SID to which this user belongs.

- **Default ACL.** This is an initial list of protections applied to the objects that the user creates. The user may subsequently alter the access-control list (ACL) for any object that it owns or that one of its groups owns.

24.6.3   Security Descriptors.   Exhibit 24.6b shows the general structure of a security descriptor, which includes these parameters:

- **Flags.** Defines the type and contents of a security descriptor. The flags indicate whether the System Access Control List (SACL) and Discretionary Access Control List (DACL) are present, whether they were placed on the object by a defaulting mechanism, and whether the pointers in the descriptor use absolute or relative addressing. Relative descriptors are required for objects that are transmitted over a network, such as information transmitted in an RPC.

- **Owner.** The owner of the object generally can perform any action on the security descriptor. The owner can be an individual or a group SID. The owner has the authority to change the contents of the DACL.

- **System Access Control List (SACL).** Specifies what kinds of operations on the object should generate audit messages. An application must have the corresponding privilege in its access token to read or write the SACL of any object. This is to prevent unauthorized applications from reading SACLs (thereby learning what not to do to avoid generating audits) or writing them (to generate many audits to cause an illicit operation to go unnoticed).

- **Discretionary Access Control List (DACL).** Determines which users and groups can access this object for which operations. It consists of a list of access-control entries (ACEs).

When an object is created, the creating process can assign as owner its own SID or any group SID in its access token. The creating process cannot assign an owner that is not in the current access token. Subsequently, any process that has been granted the right to change the owner of an object may do so, but again with the same restriction. The reason for the restriction is to prevent a user from covering his or her tracks after attempting some unauthorized action.

Let us look in more detail at the structure of access control lists, because these are at the heart of the W2K access control facility (see Exhibit 24.7). Each list consists of an overall header and a variable number of access control entries. Each entry specifies an individual or group SID and an access mask that defines the rights to be granted to this SID. When a process attempts to access an object, the object manager in the W2K executive reads the SID and group SIDs from the access token and then scans down the object's DACL. If a match is found—that is, if an ACE is found with a SID that matches one of the SIDs from the access token—then the process has the access rights specified by the access mask in that ACE.

Exhibit 24.7 shows the contents of the access mask. The least significant 16 bits specify access rights that apply to a particular type of object. For example, bit 0 for a file object is File_Read_Data access, and bit 0 for an event object is Event_Query_Status access.

The most significant 16 bits of the mask contains bits that apply to all types of objects. Five of these are referred to as standard access types:

1. **Synchronize.** Gives permission to synchronize execution with some event associated with this object. In particular, this object can be used in a wait function.

2. **Write_owner.** Allows a program to modify the owner of the object. This is useful because the owner of an object always can change the protection on the object. (The owner may not be denied Write DAC access.)

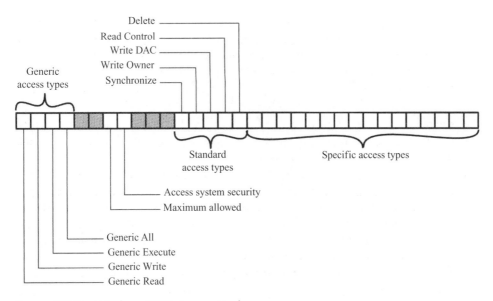

EXHIBIT 24.7 Windows 2000 Access Mask

3. **Write_DAC.** Allows the application to modify the DACL and hence the protection on this object.

4. **Read_control.** Allows the application to query the owner and DACL fields of the security descriptor of this object.

5. **Delete.** Allows the application to delete this object.

The high-order half of the access mask also contains the four generic access types. These bits provide a convenient way to set specific access types in a number of different object types. For example, suppose an application wishes to create several types of objects and ensure that users have read access to the objects, even though read has a somewhat different meaning for each object type. To protect each object of each type without the generic access bits, the application would have to construct a different ACE for each type of object and be careful to pass the correct ACE when creating each object. It is more convenient to create a single ACE that expresses the generic concept *allow read*; simply apply this ACE to each object that is created, and have the right thing happen. That is the purpose of the generic access bits, which are:

- **Generic_all.** Allow all access.
- **Generic_execute.** Allow execution if executable.
- **Generic_write.** Allow write access.
- **Generic_read.** Allow read-only access.

The generic bits also affect the standard access types. For example, for a file object, the Generic_Read bit maps to the standard bits Read_Control and Synchronize and to the object-specific bits File_Read_Data, File_Read_Attributes, and File_Read_EA. Placing an ACE on a file object that grants some SID Generic_Read grants those five access rights as if they had been specified individually in the access mask.

The remaining two bits in the access mask have special meanings. The Access_System_Security bit allows modifying audit and alarm control for this object. However, not only must this bit be set in the ACE for a SID, but the access token for the process with that SID must have the corresponding privilege enabled.

Finally, the Maximum_Allowed bit is not really an access bit but a bit that modifies W2K's algorithm for scanning the DACL for this SID. Normally, W2K will scan through the DACL until it reaches an ACE that specifically grants (bit set) or denies (bit not set) the access requested by the requesting process or until it reaches the end of the DACL, in which latter case access is denied. The Maximum_Allowed bit allows the object's owner to define a set of access rights that is the maximum that will be allowed to a given user. With this in mind, suppose that an application does not know all of the operations that it is going to be asked to perform on an object during a session. There are three options for requesting access:

1. Attempt to open the object for all possible accesses. The disadvantage of this approach is that the access may be denied even though the application may have all of the access rights actually required for this session.

2. Only open the object when a specific access is requested, and open a new handle to the object for each different type of request. This is generally the preferred method because it will not unnecessarily deny access, nor will it allow more access than necessary. However, it imposes additional overhead.

3. Attempt to open the object for as much access as the object will allow this SID. The advantage is that the user will not be artificially denied access, but the

application may have more access than it needs. This latter situation may mask bugs in the application.

An important feature of W2K security is that applications can make use of the W2K security framework for user-defined objects. For example, a database server might create its own security descriptors and attach them to portions of a database. In addition to normal read/write access constraints, the server could secure database-specific operations, such as scrolling within a result set or performing a join. It would be the server's responsibility to define the meaning of special rights and perform access checks. But the checks would occur in a standard context, using systemwide user/group accounts and audit logs. The extensible security model should prove useful to implementers of foreign files systems.

24.7   FURTHER READING

Boebert, W., R. Kain, and W. Young. "Secure Computing: the Secure Ada Target Approach." *Scientific Honeyweller* (July 1985). Reprinted in M. Abrams and H. Podell. *Computer and Network Security.* Los Alamitos, CA: IEEE Computer Society Press, 1987.

Bransted, D. (Ed.). *Computer Security and the Data Encryption Standard.* National Bureau of Standards, Special Publication No. 500-27, February 1978.

Denning, P., and R. Brown. "Operating Systems." *Scientific American* **251** (September 1984): 94–106.

Gasser, M. *Building a Secure Computer System.* Van Nostrand Reinhold, 1988.

Gollmann, D. *Computer Security*, 2nd ed, Hoboken, NJ: John Wiley & Sons, 2006.

Pfleeger, C. P., and S. L. Pfleeger. *Security in Computing*, 4th ed. Prentice-Hall PTR, 2006.

Saltzer, J., and M. Schroeder. "The Protection of Information in Computer Systems." *Proceedings of the IEEE* (September 1975).

Sandhu, R., and P. Samarati, "Access Control: Principles and Practice." *IEEE Communications* (September 1994).

Singhal, M., and N. Shivaratri. *Advanced Concepts in Operating Systems.* New York: McGraw-Hill, 1994.

Sinha, P. K. *Distributed Operating Systems: Concepts and Design.* Wiley-IEEE Press, 1997.

Stallings, W. *Cryptography and Network Security: Principles and Practice*, 4th edition. Prentice-Hall, 2005.

Viega, J., and J. Voas. "The Pros and Cons of Unix and Windows Security Policies." *IT Professional* **2**, no. 5 (September/October 2000): 40–47.

24.8   NOTES

1. P. Denning and R. Brown, "Operating Systems," *Scientific American* (September 1984).

2. J. Saltzer and M. Schroeder, "The Protection of Information in Computer Systems," *Proceedings of the IEEE* (September 1975).

3. C. P. Pfleeger and S. L. Pfleeger, *Security in Computing*, 4th ed. (Prentice-Hall PTR, 2006).

CHAPTER 25

LOCAL AREA NETWORKS

Gary C. Kessler and N. Todd Pritsky

25.1 INTRODUCTION. This chapter discusses generic issues surrounding local area network (LAN) security. Securing the LAN is essential to securing the Internet because LANs are where most of the attackers, victims, clients, servers, firewalls, routers, and other devices reside. Compromised LAN systems on the Internet open other nodes on that local network to attack and put other systems at risk on the Internet as a whole. Many of the general issues mentioned herein are described in more specific terms in other chapters of this *Handbook,* such as Chapters 15, 22, 23, and 47 in particular.

25.2 POLICY AND PROCEDURE ISSUES. Twenty years ago, all users had accounts on a shared mainframe or minicomputer. A single system manager was responsible for security, backup, disaster recovery, account management, policies, and all other related issues. Today all users are system managers, and, in many cases, individuals have responsibility for several systems. Since the vulnerability of a single computer can compromise the entire LAN, it is imperative that there be rules in place so that everyone can work together for mutual efficiency and defense. But where polices and procedures can be centralized, they should be, because most users do not take the security procedures seriously enough.

The next list, modified from the Internet Engineering Task Force (IETF) Request for Comment (RFC) 2196, is a rough outline of LAN-related security policies and procedures that should at least be considered.[1]

1. Administrative Policies Framework

  a. Information Security Issues

    i. Password management procedures

      (1) Are passwords assigned or chosen by user?

      (2) Are password auditing procedures in place?

      (3) Are password policies enforced (e.g., minimum length, allowed and required characters, expiration, blacklisting)?

      (4) How many passwords are required to access all systems?

    ii. Virus protection

      (1) Are servers protected?

      (2) Is there an e-mail "viruswall"?

      (3) Is virus protection a centrally managed activity, or up to each user?

      (4) How do users maintain the current virus signature database?

    iii. Encryption and certificates

    iv. Security event handling

  b. Network Connectivity Issues

    i. Dial-up access

    ii. Hubs versus switches

    iii. Identification and authentication

      (1) Passwords and management

      (2) Authentication systems

      (3) Two-factor authentication?

      (4) Single sign-on?

      (5) Biometrics

  c. Physical site security and disaster recovery

    i. Physical security of systems

    ii. Dial-up access lines and modems

    iii. Scheduling backups

    iv. Access to servers

    v. Storing and limiting access to backup media

    vi. Disaster recovery and contingency plans

  d. Operating system and LAN security

    i. Operating system-specific issues

      (1) Monitoring operating system security vulnerabilities

      (2) Applying security patches

      (3) Securing the OS during installation

      (4) Auditing the systems

    ii. Is Dynamic Host Configuration Protocol (DHCP) employed?

    iii. Log analysis software and procedures

    iv. Vulnerability testing

    v. Intrusion detection tools

2. User Policies Framework

  a. Written, published network security policy

    b. Network/Internet Appropriate Use Policy (AUP)

    c. User training and education

        i. Security (general issues)

        ii. Importance of protecting customer data, client information, and other private information such as medical claim records and patient information

        iii. Policies and AUPs

        iv. Suggestions for how to be safe

    d. Virus protection

        i. Using antivirus software

        ii. Maintaining a current virus signature database

    e. Choosing good passwords

    f. Best practices

        i. E-mail (netiquette and handling attachments)

        ii. Browser (shut off Java, JavaScript, ActiveX, and other auto-execution code)

        iii. Microsoft Office Suite
            (1) Use of macros
            (2) Implications for document management

        iv. Protecting files on the server and your own system
            (1) Use of Windows "shares" and UNIX NFS
            (2) Use of NetWare, New Technology File System, (NTFS), and UNIX access controls
            (i) Spotting a possible compromise (methods for identifying intrusions or other unauthorized activity)
            (ii) What to do and whom to contact if a compromise is suspected

    g. When trouble strikes (computer emergency response procedures)

Not every issue will apply to all networks, but each LAN is an ever-evolving entity, and the policies guiding its operation also must evolve.

25.3 PHYSICAL SITE SECURITY.

25.3 PHYSICAL SITE SECURITY. The physical protection of the site is very important but too often overlooked. One reason that site security is often lacking is that some of the policies and procedures can be perceived as messages to employees that they are not trusted. Nevertheless, physical site security includes many aspects of protecting network servers, communications facilities, individual user's systems, and information.

For more information on facilities security, see Chapters 22 and 23 of this *Handbook.*

25.4 PHYSICAL LAYER ISSUES. The LAN itself has a number of additional vulnerabilities because the systems and media are so widely dispersed. This section discusses securing the LAN infrastructure.

25.4.1 Sniffers and Broadcast LANs. Traditional LAN media access control (MAC) schemes operate assuming a logical, if not physical, broadcast topology. In a broadcast network, every station hears every transmission. When operating in *promiscuous mode*, a LAN station will read every frame that goes by regardless of whether the frame is addressed to the station or not.

When protocol analysis, or *sniffer*, software became available in the 1980s, every station on the LAN became a potential network analysis and management tool—or a surreptitious eavesdropper. Since so many of the network's applications—particularly TCP/IP-based applications—transmit passwords and files in plaintext, this type of software is potentially very dangerous.

A number of sources offer very powerful and very flexible commercial packet-sniffing software, such as Network Associates' SnifferPro and Novell's LANalyzer. These packages usually have additional capabilities, such as network monitoring, performance monitoring, and traffic analysis. Prior to 1990, network protocol analysis required a special piece of hardware with a connection to the network. Today, a large number of software packages that do TCP/IP packet sniffing can help an intruder because they can be installed directly on an individual's laptop or desktop computer. Some of these packages include:

- BUTTsniffer (Windows NT)
- Ethereal (Windows, Unix)
- Network Monitor (free with, and for, Windows NT)
- Sniffit (Linux, SunOS, Solaris, FreeBSD, Irix)
- snort (UNIX)
- Solsniff (Solaris)
- tcpdump (UNIX)
- WinDump (Windows 9x/NT)

Relatively few countermeasures can be taken against these kinds of tools. Fortunately, they are effective only on a broadcast network such as a hubbed LAN. If an Ethernet hub, for example, is replaced with a switch, the only traffic broadcast to all hosts on the network are those frames actually addressed to the LAN's broadcast address. In this case, a station can sniff only that traffic that is going to or coming from the station with the sniffer software. Replacing all hubs with switches may be unreasonable in many environments, but placing all servers on a switch instead of a hub will improve both performance and security.

Other network-based tools that can detect a host with a network interface card (NIC) in promiscuous mode, such as AntiSniff (Windows) and sentinel (UNIX). These tools work by performing a number of tests to detect the promiscuous host; they then check the network host's operating systems, domain name system (DNS) activity, and network and machine latency. An excellent overview of antisniffer tools can be found at www.securitysoftwaretech.com/antisniff/tech-paper.html.

Sniffers can be defeated using cryptography. Use of secure IP (IPsec) and secure shell (SSH) for TCP/IP applications can provide privacy and integrity to all communication and applications. IPsec is available from any of the IPSec Developers Forum members (www.ip-sec.com), and SSH is available from SSH Communications Security (www.ssh.com).

25.4.2   Attacks on the Physical Plant.   The most common medium employed today on LANs is copper-based, unshielded twisted pair (UTP) cable. All copper media, including UTP and coaxial cable, emanate a magnetic field because of the changing current on the wire. Van Eck monitoring devices can pick up these emanations remotely and reproduce the frames on the wire or keystrokes at a machine. As far-fetched as this might sound, the vulnerability is very real. The U.S. Government and military have a set of standards to reduce and limit electromagnetic radiation (EMR) called TEMPEST, and the National Security Agency (NSA) has a list of products that are TEMPEST-compliant. Indeed, this vulnerability may not be a major problem in most organizational networks, but there is some set of networks where this is a concern. An excellent source of TEMPEST information can be found at www.eskimo.com/~joelm/tempest.htm.

An alternative to encasing workstations in Faraday cages (i.e., copper mesh layers surrounding all components) is to generate random electronic noise that masks meaningful radiated data transmissions.[2]

One way to reduce or eliminate EMR is to reduce or eliminate the amount of copper media on the network. Optical fiber, for example, has no EMR because there is no electricity on the line. It does not eliminate the EMR at the desktop itself, but it does prevent its entry into all interconnecting fiber cables.

Users also can be the source of some types of denial-of-service (DoS) attacks, either purposely or accidentally. Consider coaxial cable Ethernet networks (10BASE-5 or 10BASE-2) where nodes are attached to a common LAN medium. In both cases, the coaxial cable has a terminating resistor at the end of the wire to eliminate reflection of the signal. If the resistor is removed, it allows extra noise on the wire that can block all traffic on the network. End-of-cable resistors should be beyond the reach of users if at all possible.

Similar DoS attacks may occur whenever users modify the wiring scheme of the network. Removal of terminating resistors is only one action that can cause problems. Hubs in common areas might be unplugged or have network connectors removed. A token ring hub-to-hub connection can be detached, breaking the integrity of the ring and thus preventing LAN hosts from communicating with other hosts and denying service to users.

It is important that the physical network should be secured to the greatest extent possible. LAN managers should educate users to avoid the accidental problems that might occur and even how to recognize nefarious attacks.

25.4.3 Modems, Dial-up Servers, and Telephone Lines.   Modems anywhere on the LAN are a potential danger, particularly those that are connected directly to a user's system, with or without official sanction. Modems can provide a back door into the LAN, possibly bypassing the firewall, strong authentication, proxy server, and any other network security.

In general, all modems should be concentrated at the network's dial-up server. Individual user systems should, in most cases, be banned from having modems on the network. This is a difficult rule to enforce, however, because laptops and an increasing number of desktop systems include preinstalled modems, and a user can always connect an external modem to the serial port of any system. This is an example of why security managers have to integrate policies into the culture of an organization. Otherwise, users will find a way around what they perceive to be prohibitive and onerous policies, and modems are one way to circumvent the corporate firewall.

Modems in auto-answer mode are particularly dangerous. Although most companies do not advertise their dial-in telephone numbers, these numbers do not remain secret for very long from someone who wants to find them. Anyone with a telephone directory can easily start mapping an organization's block of corporate telephone numbers.

For example, if the main number is 802-555-3700, attackers have a place to start. When attackers call the main number and ask the receptionist for the organization's fax number, they obtain even more information. Using war-dialer software, attackers can scan an entire block of telephone numbers (e.g., 555–3700 through 555–3799) and obtain a list of which numbers are active, which respond with a tone, and what the tone represents (e.g., fax, modem, etc.). If a user has an auto-answer modem on a computer, attackers may gain access to the user's system without so much as a password. Security managers should work with their local telephone companies to obtain telephone numbers for modem lines that are not in the organization's telephone block.

The dial-up server, then, is the place to concentrate the modems and the authentication of dial-up users. There are several strategies for authentication at the dial-up server, the strongest being some form of two-factor authentication, such as a combination of passwords and a token. Another strong protection mechanism is to implement a dial-back mechanism, so that once a bona fide user logs in, the system hangs up and calls back to a preconfigured telephone number. This is a very effective scheme that works well with fixed-location telecommuters but not with roaming employees. In addition, attackers have been known to tamper with the central switch of a telephone company to call-forward from an assigned number to the attacker's own modem.

When a user requires two separate logons, one to the dial-up server and then one to a domain server, security restrictions should control what the caller is allowed to do after passing the first test. One of the authors of this chapter worked with a company that had a shared secret (an oxymoron) telephone number for its modem bank and then a single shared username and password for all the users to authenticate to the dial-up server. To access files and shared network resources, the user then had to authenticate to the domain controller. But after passing the identification and authentication for the first server, an attacker was on the organization's LAN and had complete, unfettered access to the Internet and an identity that implicated the company in any possible malfeasance.

Some guidelines for securing dial-up servers include:

- Maintain and monitor telephone logs
- Configure all software and modems so that a user logout forces the modem to disconnect, and a modem disconnect forces a user logout.
- Configure the modems so that they return to their default configuration after every connection.
- Implement a dial-back mechanism, where possible.
- Use two-factor authentication for roaming users.
- Periodically scan internal telephone numbers for unauthorized modems.
- Prevent the display of any banner message when the user connects to the modem, and certainly do not display any sort of *welcome* message.
- Train the organization help desk in social engineering techniques, and prohibit them from giving out modem telephone numbers, user names, or other sensitive information that could help attackers.

25.4.4   Wireless LAN Issues.   Wireless LANs (WLANs) have vulnerabilities their wired counterparts do not. The most obvious difference between wired and wireless networks is the medium itself. Although copper-based LANs emit a small amount of radiation that can be intercepted, the entire basis of wireless LANs is transmitting data using relatively strong radiation in some form.

There are WLANs based on infrared signals that cannot penetrate building walls and so achieve some degree of security due to the limited propagation of those signals. Such LANs typically are found in networks requiring high levels of security. However, most WLANs today use radio transmission techniques. In these networks, anyone on a nearby street can use a listening device to intercept data and even capture the network identifiers required to connect to the LAN. The practical range of interception is governed by the inverse-square law for the signal strength (it declines as the square of the distance from the source) and by the sensitivity and signal-to-noise characteristics of the receivers.

Fortunately, there is a certain measure of security within the physical layer itself. IEEE 802.11-based LANs employ either Direct-Sequence Spread Spectrum (DSSS) or Frequency-Hopping Spread Spectrum (FHSS) techniques. As always, depending on range and noise levels, it is possible to eavesdrop. However, interpreting the signals is made more difficult by how DSSS and FHSS work.

To make sense of the transmissions, the receiver must know either the *chipping code* used in a DSSS network or the *frequency-hopping pattern* in an FHSS implementation. Without such information, the signal will appear to be nothing more than background noise to the illicit receiver. It is not an insurmountable problem for the would-be eavesdropper, but the work factor is greatly increased when compared to narrowband radio techniques. The spread spectrum approach also offers more reliability in the face of interference from denial of service (i.e., intentional jamming), as the signal is spread over a broad range of frequencies. Some vendor equipment also comes with software components that allow for tuning around interference.

For greater privacy than that provided by the physical layer alone, the 802.11 standard includes an optional encryption method called Wired Equivalent Privacy (WEP). This technique is truly optional so not all vendors support the standard. WEP uses a 40-bit form of the RC4 algorithm by default, although some products support stronger, 128-bit versions. It is a good idea to choose a product that offers more than just the 40-bit version, as a 40-bit keyspace does not provide great security given today's computing power.

Because WEP does not offer strong encryption and does not describe a standard key-exchange mechanism, many vendors have implemented layer three tunneling methods, such as those found in virtual private networks (VPNs), to provide greater privacy. These VPN-based approaches generally employ other encryption processes (e.g., Microsoft Point-to-Point Encryption) as used in the Point-to-Point Tunneling Protocol (PPTP) that use longer keys than WEP and often support Public Key Infrastructure (PKI) or other key-exchange mechanisms. Some implementations also provide authentication through standards such as Remote Access Dial-In User Service (RADIUS) for more flexible client management. The major problem is that these approaches are not all interoperable and are not necessarily multiprotocol capable.

WEP also can be used for authentication to prevent unauthorized access to the WLAN itself. Such authentication adds another layer of protection to the username and password combination employed by typical server software. Before gaining access to information resources on the server, a client first must gain access to the physical medium. Using the shared key scheme, a wireless device must possess the same encryption key as the LAN's access point, the device enabling wireless connectivity to the wired portion of the LAN. Any data transmitted must be encrypted with the key, or the frame will be ignored. Many wireless access products also have the capability to create access control lists based on MAC addresses to filter LAN connections.

In summary, network managers should consider these security items when evaluating wireless network components:

Physical Layer Schemes

- **Infrared.** Cannot penetrate walls and is good for high-security applications
- **Frequency-hopping spread spectrum.** Signal hopping provides good level of security but complexity of technique limits bandwidth
- **Direct-sequence spread spectrum.** Low "spreading ratio" can increase available bandwidth but also the possibility of interception and jamming

Encryption Options

- **Wired equivalent privacy.** Optional default is low-grade encryption, 40-bit strength
- **Alternative encryption methods.** Often more secure than WEP but not always interoperable

Authentication Methods

- **Wired Equivalent Privacy.** Requires clients to have the same encryption key as the LAN access point, which introduces key management issues
- **Access control list.** Allows only certain clients to gain physical access to the LAN, based on the MAC address; this adds complexity to client management
- **Server-based authentication.** Flexible user authentication with RADIUS for an additional layer of protection from illicit connections

25.5   NETWORK OPERATING SYSTEM ISSUES.

In the early 1990s, it was common to find desktop systems running the Windows operating system *and* the Novell NetWare network operating system (NOS). Desktop applications ran over Windows, and NetWare was used only to move files to and from the shared file space, or to print documents.

Today, the distinction among the desktop operating system, server operating system, and NOS is disappearing. Operating systems such as Linux, MacOS, UNIX, and Windows all provide desktop application suites with networking capabilities, including communications protocols such as TCP/IP. There are some general security considerations for all LANs regardless of the specific operating system:

- Use whatever capabilities are provided by the operating system to employ strong passwords.
- Create password policies that force strong passwords. Change passwords periodically and do not allow reuse. Periodically audit passwords using password-cracking tools such as L0phtCrack (Windows NT) or crack (UNIX). Ensure that the administrator and root accounts are given passwords that are not widely distributed or guessed.
- Disable (or uninstall) any services that are not being used.
- Keep the operating system and application software up to date, and with the latest security patches installed.

- Carefully manage access control lists for files and other system/network resources.
- Strictly define users, groups, and network/domain trusts.
- Tightly secure any running applications.
- Log on as administrator or root only when necessary; otherwise log on as a regular user.
- Allow operators and administrators to log on only locally at server systems.
- Limit use of guest, demo, or anonymous accounts.
- Where feasible, put boot and system files as well as application files and data on different partitions, hard drives, or I/O controllers.
- Regularly audit server systems.
- Monitor log files.
- Remove floppy, CD, and DVD drives from servers after the system has a stable configuration.
- Implement best industry practices when securing the operating system.
- Use vulnerability assessment tools on a regular basis to scan servers.
- Use intrusion detection tools to monitor potential attacks on the LAN that are launched from the internal network.
- If using the Simple Network Management Protocol (SNMP) for network administration, carefully choose community names and block external access to the SNMP service. Make Management Information Bases (MIBs) read-only, where possible.
- Avoid use of the Domain Name System (DNS) HINFO (host info) resource record to identify the central processing unit type and the installed operating system.

Specific operating system vulnerabilities are beyond the scope of this chapter; entire books and Web sites are devoted to securing some of these individual operating systems. At a minimum, network managers must monitor their operating system vendor's Web site and all other sites that cover the NOS's security. The sections that follow provide some general observations and comments about the various network operating systems.

25.5.1   Windows 9x.   All of the Windows operating systems (including NT and 2000) support peer-to-peer resource sharing and are vulnerable to exploitation of NetBIOS file and print sharing. In particular, when file and print sharing is enabled, the service is, by default, bound to TCP/IP. Although this does not cause an additional exposure to systems on the local network (since shares can be seen by other nodes on the LAN anyway), it does provide a potential vulnerability for hosts connected to the Internet. File and print sharing can be unbound from TCP/IP using Start, Control Panel, and Network.

Windows 9x (including Windows 95, Windows 98, and Windows ME) systems also have a vulnerability in the way authentication is performed when a user wishes to access a remote share. Windows uses the challenge-handshake authentication protocol (CHAP) for all passwords that need to be sent over the network, so passwords never appear in plaintext on the LAN. However, because Windows 9x uses the *same* challenge during a given 15-minute period, an intruder with a physical access to the LAN and to a sniffer could effect a replay attack by resending a duplicate authentication request and remapping a share on the Windows 9x system. This example illustrates the critical role of physical security in preventing compromise of LANs.

One of the best-known Trojan horse programs for Windows 9x is Back Orifice (BO). Advertised as a remote Win9x administrator tool, it can be used by a nefarious user to take total control of someone else's system, including the capability to modify the registry, reboot the system, transfer files, view cached passwords, spawn processes, and create shares. NetBus is another tool that can be used to take control of a remote Windows system. Some commercial virus scanners can detect these programs on individual systems, and several workstation firewalls exclude communications characteristic of these Trojans.

Windows 9x has no particular logon security mechanism. Although every user might be forced to log on to a system, any user can log in with any username and any password to get at least basic access. Several password-cracking programs are available through the Internet to break Windows' .PWL password files, which are accessible once a user has access to the network. If a password-protected screen saver is preventing an attacker from logging in, there is an easy way around this as well: Simply reboot the computer. However, third-party security programs include nonbreakable secure logins and secure screen savers; many include bootlock functions that prevent any access whatever unless a valid password is entered. Current examples of such software can be located easily using buyers' guides such as the annual listing from the Computer Security Institute.[3]

25.5.2   NT/2000, XP Vista.

From a security perspective, Windows 2000 Millennium Edition (ME) is not significantly stronger than Windows 9x. Network administrators should periodically scan the network's public shares to ensure that they are appropriate. Windows NT Server, NT Workstation, and 2000 Server editions are built for security, and network services and have the software architecture to support these services. However, a security vulnerability announcement related to these operating systems seems to come out almost weekly. Many of the hacking tools available for Win9x also are available for Windows NT and 2000; Back Orifice 2000 (BO2K), for example, is an NT/2000 version of BO and NetBus also can take control of an NT/2000 host.

Scripting holes in Internet Explorer (IE) and Office 2000 make all Windows systems susceptible to a variety of new virus and worm attacks. Although the early viruses, such as Melissa and I LOVE YOU, required users to open e-mail attachments, that is no longer so. Microsoft Outlook and Outlook Express will execute HTML and script code in the body of an e-mail by default. Several ActiveX components also will execute from an e-mail containing HTML and script code; examples of such controls include Scriplet.typlib (ships with IE 4.x and 5.x) and the UA control (Office 2000). The best protection against these types of vulnerabilities are to define Outlook and Outlook Express to read e-mail in the "Restricted Sites Zone" and disable all Active Scripting and ActiveX related settings in that zone. This vulnerability affects all Windows systems with Office 2000 or Internet Explorer 4.x/5.x installed, even if IE is not used.

Securing Windows NT/2000 systems is well beyond the scope of this chapter, but some of the precautions, in addition to those listed already, follow.

- Format the drive using NTFS rather than FAT.
- Use long file names and disable the DOS 8.3 naming format.
- Disable the Everyone group.

- Rename the administrator account.
- Turn auditing on. (It is off by default.)

All NT-based systems have been given the C2 security rating by the National Computer Security Center. At the time of this writing, Windows NT 3.5 and 4.0 and Windows 2000 SQL Server version 8.0 have completed the evaluation process. Windows 2000 Server has been submitted by Microsoft and is expected to be given the C2-level rating. This means that when Windows is installed correctly, it meets evaluation criteria set forth in the NCSC's *Orange Book* of security specifications. C2 certification is not applied to the operating system itself; rather, it is applied to a particular installation. Microsoft provides tools to audit a site so administrator(s) can deploy the correct hardware and software configurations to achieve this level of security in a network.

Windows 2000 introduced a new feature that administrators might want to employ. Windows NT introduced the ability to compress and decompress files on the fly. Windows 2000 introduces the capability to encrypt and decrypt files on the fly. The Encrypting File System (EFS) uses public key cryptography and the Data Encryption Standard (DES) to encrypt files on the hard drive. EFS includes an optional capability for a recovery mechanism in case of key loss. Organizations using EFS on critical systems should consider employing this mechanism to protect against loss or destruction of the private key.

Windows XP, which has sold well over 400 million copies and still enjoys by far the largest installed base of any Microsoft OS, introduced a number of security-oriented features. The major improvement was the inclusion of a firewall capability in both the Home Edition and Professional versions. Professional goes a couple of steps further by offering EFS file encryption, Kerberos,[4] smart card support, and a new software restriction feature allowing administrators to mitigate the impact of viruses and Trojan horses. XP also supports raw sockets, which in itself is not unusual—UNIX and Linux do as well. This feature is intended to increase the functionality of Internet services, but in Microsoft's implementation, it is available to any user, no matter what privilege level. Thus hackers can possibly gain control of a computer running XP and use it to initiate DoS attacks by commanding the OS to generate a flood of traffic.

Although Microsoft's Windows Vista was released with much fanfare—and after a number of delays—it has not been as widely implemented as might have been due to concerns about security and stability of the platform, not to mention a perception that many of the security features create a great deal of inconvenience in the user experience (e.g., User Account Control, to be described, and the Digital Rights Management implementation). Regardless, a prime mover of Vista development was Microsoft's Trustworthy Computing initiative, and as such, a number of new security capabilities were added.

Features include User Account Control (UAC), Bitlocker Drive Encryption, Windows Defender, Data Execution Prevention, Application isolation, Windows Service Hardening, Network Access Protection, and a variety of others. UAC is the most visible from the user perspective, requiring user intervention before allowing any action that requires administrative-level privileges. These include:[5]

- Right-clicking an application's icon and clicking "Run as administrator"
- Changes to files or folders in %SystemRoot% or %ProgramFiles%
- Installing and uninstalling applications

- Installing device drivers
- Installing ActiveX controls
- Changing settings for Windows Firewall
- Changing UAC settings
- Configuring Windows Update
- Adding or removing user accounts
- Changing a user's account type
- Configuring Parental Controls
- Running Task Scheduler
- Restoring backed-up system files
- Viewing or changing another user's folders and files

As an interesting historical aside, the National Security Agency assisted Microsoft in the development of Vista. As reported in the *Washington Post* in January 2007:

> For the first time, the giant software maker is acknowledging the help of the secretive agency, better known for eavesdropping on foreign officials and, more recently, U.S. citizens as part of the Bush administration's effort to combat terrorism. The agency said it has helped in the development of the security of Microsoft's new operating system—the brains of a computer—to protect it from worms, Trojan horses and other insidious computer attackers. . . .

> The NSA declined to comment on its security work with other software firms, but Sager said Microsoft is the only one "with this kind of relationship at this point where there's an acknowledgment publicly."

> The NSA, which provided its service free, said it was Microsoft's idea to acknowledge the spy agency's role. . . .

> "I kind of call it a Good Housekeeping seal" of approval, said Michael Cherry, a former Windows program manager who now analyzes the product for Directions on Microsoft, a firm that tracks the software maker.

> Cherry says the NSA's involvement can help counter the perception that Windows is not entirely secure and help create a perception that Microsoft has solved the security problems that have plagued it in the past. "Microsoft also wants to make the case that [the new Windows] is more secure than its earlier versions," he said. [6]

It is left as an exercise for the reader to decide whether having a spy agency working on a premier OS is a good thing or not.

One of the most important capabilities for the network security manager is to audit the Windows server systems to protect their integrity. These tools are part of the base operating system or the Windows NT Resource Kit:

- *netstat* examines open ports.
- *Event Viewer* examines application, security, and system logs.
- *net start, net user, net group, net local group* display running services, users, groups, and local groups.
- *dumpel* converts Event Viewer logs to ASCII files.
- *NetMon* displays network traffic.
- *netsvc* displays local and remote running services and drivers.
- *addusers* displays users and groups.

- *findgrp* displays local and domain groups for a user.
- *local* and *global* show all members of specific local or global groups.
- *dommon* displays trusted domains.
- *xcacls* examines the file Access Control Lists (ACL).
- *perms* examines the ACLs associated with a user
- *sysdiff* displays changes in the Registry and file system.
- *regdmp* creates an ASCII version of the Registry.
- *ralist* lists a domain's Remote Access Servers (RAS).
- *rasusers* lists users authorized for dial-in access.

25.5.3   UNIX.   UNIX is the oldest operating system still in widespread, growing use today. Readers needing guidance for Novell Netware should refer to Chapter 18 in the fourth edition of this *Handbook*. Originally developed in 1969 at AT&T Bell Laboratories, UNIX became the first operating system to integrate network communications when TCP/IP was bundled into Berkeley Software Development (BSD) 4.2 UNIX in 1984. UNIX had traditionally been reserved for server systems and hardcore computer users. With the development of the X-Windows interface for UNIX and the wide deployment of Linux since the mid-1990s, UNIX and its variants represent the only significant competition to Windows in the desktop and server environment.

Like TCP/IP and the Internet itself, UNIX was developed for functionality and use within a trusted user community. As such, while UNIX has many powerful tools, it does not have a cohesive security architecture, nor is it an inherently secure operating system.

UNIX has most of the basic operating system protections: passwords, access control lists, groups, user privilege levels, and so on. But UNIX also comes with a large variety of services (daemons) enabled by default, including *FTP, Telnet, finger, echo, chargen, daytime, RPC, BIND*, and more. In addition, nearly every UNIX daemon has had some sort of security vulnerability reported at one time or another, with buffer overflows being quite prevalent.

There are many things that an administrator should consider when securing a UNIX/Linux system. In addition to the general steps just listed, the security manager might also:

- Disable (or remove) any unused services, particularly *finger*, the BIND name daemon (*named*), *RPC, sendmail,* Trivial FTP (tftp), POP/IMAP, *sadmind, mountd*, and NFS.
- Install the latest version and security patch of all installed software.
- Take great care when configuring access control lists and other sharing.
- Prevent running *Sendmail* in daemon mode (turn off the -bd switch) on machines that are neither mail servers nor mail relays.
- Limit use of the "r" remote access protocols.
- Use shadow password files.
- Implement TCP Wrappers to control access to services.
- Consider using encrypted communication protocols, such as Secure Shell (SSH) or Secure Sockets Layer (SSL), for remote access. Prevent transmission of cleartext passwords over the Internet.

One of the most important capabilities for the network/security manager is to audit the Windows server systems to protect their integrity. These tools are part of the base operating system or the Windows NT Resource Kit:

- *netstat* examines open ports.
- *lsof* displays hidden file space and network connections.
- *tcpdump* displays network traffic.
- *who* displays users that are logged on and the *utmp* log file.
- *last* displays login history, and the *wtmp* log file.
- *lastb* display a history of bad logins (and the *btmp* log file).
- *syslogd* is a central server facility for managing and logging system messages.
- *TCPWrapper* monitors and manages incoming service requests.

25.5.4   MacOS.   Although the Macintosh operating systems have mostly given way to Windows and UNIX, at least for server systems, they are still worth mentioning. The Macintosh was the first desktop operating system that included networking and resource sharing as integral elements. But like UNIX and TCP/IP before it, the MacOS is designed for convenience and usability but not for security.

Because of its peer-to-peer nature, MacOS has a number of potential exposures. Although Windows and UNIX also can operate in a peer-to-peer mode, a novice user generally will not know how to share resources and thereby may not inadvertently open holes. On the Mac, however, every user is a system administrator and can accidentally open holes to the system. Consider, for example, that a user can share individual files, folders, or disk volumes. Unlike Windows, where a directory is marked as not shared, read, or full, Mac file sharing is more complex and allows the user to establish a set of trusts that require a fair amount of cooperation and knowledge by the users. Network communication is via the proprietary AppleTalk protocol, but this sharing capability is also available over TCP/IP in MacOS.

A nefarious Mac network user can quickly see what servers and shares are available on the network by using the *Chooser* accessory. Network administrators are advised periodically to scan the network in order to ensure that no users have accidentally enabled more "Guest" access than they intended. However, such guest access is a potentially gaping hole if using TCP/IP. Personal file sharing should be disabled, but if file sharing is required, administrators should establish a central file server, with security provisions.

In desktop use, Macs have relatively little security. Password protection is provided by default only with some laptop systems, and not even a password-protected screen saver comes standard with the system. In short, there is very little standing between a determined attacker and a Mac computer. Third-party software is required to provide password protection against access to the system and files, or for data protection with disk encryption.

Mac-based viruses and worms are much less prevalent than their Windows counterparts, but Macs are not totally immune. First, those viruses that depend on Microsoft Office Suite software will work because the Mac versions of Word and Excel employ macros. Second, Internet-based attacks aimed at TCP/IP—such as the Ping-of-Death, Teardrop, and SMURF—can still affect a Mac server. There are a few third-party antivirus packages specific for the Mac, for example, Norton Antivirus.

Increased security can, indeed, be added to individual Mac systems, using such tools as:

- DiskLocker software, which write-protects the hard drive, and FileLock that allows write-protecting individual files
- Empower, which adds strong access control to applications and files
- MacPassword and Sesame, which provide complete password protection for a Mac system, including multiple password levels as for administrators and users

Any system that can employ passwords will also have password crackers, and the Mac is no exception. Password crackers abound for the Mac but they do not target the MacOS itself, since the operating system does not have passwords. Instead, the crackers attack passwords associated with certain MacOS applications. For example:

- FirstClass Thrash! and PassFinder attack FirstClass passwords, an application often used to transform a Mac into an Internet mail and news server
- FMProPeeker, FMP Password Viewer, and MasterKey crack FileMaker passwords.
- Password Killer circumvents PowerBook security.
- Remove Passwords and RemoveIt both break passwords associated with StuffIt archives.

It is just as important to keep the version of MacOS up to date as the other operating systems. Macs running System 7.1 and 7.8, for example, are known to crash if they are subject to a large volume of port scans. Many schools and businesses use FoolProof to limit user access to files and other resources; it also appears to store passwords in memory in plaintext so that any user with a memory editor can access password lists. And the installation of System 8.0 on top of earlier versions of MacOS (on a PowerBook) can disable the Password Control Panel and any password protection. These examples demonstrate the need to stay abreast of security warnings and patches.

A number of Mac administrative tools can be used to improve security. Among these are:

- InterMapper, an SNMP-based network management tool for both AppleTalk and IP
- MacRadius, a Mac version of RADIUS to protect dial-in servers and services
- NetLock, a powerful data security application that employs encryption to protect network sessions, passwords, logins, and other information
- Network Security Guard, software that scans MacOS systems for security vulnerabilities

There are fewer MacOS security incidents reported because the greater popularity of Windows NT and UNIX servers make it easier to learn about them, because there are more potential targets, and because one single attack can affect more systems. Put another way, there are fewer attacks on Macs because the hacker community is not as familiar with them, and there are fewer attractive targets.

25.6 CONCLUSION.   A good administrator can secure almost any NOS, although no NOS is secure initially. The network administrator needs continuous vigilance and monitoring, while recognizing that the operating system is only a part of the overall security plan for the LAN and network services. Most network administrators, due to the nature of their job and training, focus exclusively on the computers attached to the LAN and to the LAN's operating system and software. Unfortunately, this approach is too narrow in its scope. Personal firewall software also might be employed to protect individual systems against attack, but almost all of these products are oriented toward IP-based attacks and miss attacks that employ the NOS's native operating system.

Routers, network firewalls, and proxy servers are essential for protecting LAN systems from attack by an external source. The network administrator also must provide tools to protect servers and workstations from other users on the LAN.

25.7 FURTHER READING

This section lists some books, articles, and Web sites that cover the issues addressed in this chapter. Administrators should monitor vendor, operating system, and security Web sites that will have up-to-date, timely additional information.

Brenton, C. *Mastering Network Security*. San Francisco: SYBEX, 1999.

Edwards, M. J. *Internet Security with Windows NT*. Loveland, CO: Duke Press, 1998.

Fraser, B., ed. "Site Security Handbook." RFC 2196/FYI 8, September 1997; ftp://ftp.isi.edu/in-notes/rfc2196.txt (accessed November 24, 2000).

Garfinkel, S., and G. Spafford. *Practical Unix and Internet Security*. Sebastopol, CA: O'Reilly & Associates, 1996.

IEEE Working Group for WLAN Standards; grouper.ieee.org/groups/802/11/.

Landau, T. *Sad Macs, Bombs, and Other Disasters*, 4th ed. Berkeley, CA: Peachpit Press, 2000.

L0pht. "Overview of AntiSniff," November 24, 2000. www.securitysoftwaretech. com/antisniff/tech-paper.html.

Mann, S., and E. L. Mitchell. *Linux System Security: The Administrator's Guide to Open Source Security Tools*. Englewood Cliffs, NJ: Prentice-Hall, 2000.

Maximum Security, 2nd ed. Indianapolis: SAMS, 1998.

McNamara, J. "The Complete, Unofficial TEMPEST Information Page," October 2, 2000; www.eskimo.com/~joelm/tempest.html (November 21, 2000).

National Computer Security Center. "Commercial Product Evaluations," www. radium.ncsc.mil/tpep.

Payne, W. H., T. Sheldon, and B. Payne. *The Complete Reference to Netware 5*. New York: McGraw-Hill, 1999.

Rizzo, J., and K. D. Clark. *How Macs Work*, Millennium ed. Indianapolis: Que, 2001.

SANS Institute. "How to Eliminate the Ten Most Critical Internet Security Threats: The Experts' Consensus," V1.32, January 18, 2001; www.sans.org/topten.htm (accessed March 6, 2001).

SANS Institute. "Securing Linux Step-by-Step Guide," V1.0. www.sansstore.org (November 23, 2000).

SANS Institute. "Securing Windows NT Step-by-Step Guide," V2.15, July 30, 1999; www.sansstore.org (accessed November 23, 2000).

SANS Institute. "Top 20 List." www.sans.org/top20/.

Scambray, J., S. McClure, and G. Kurtz. *Hacking Exposed*, 2nd ed. Berkeley, CA: Osborne/McGraw-Hill, 2001.

Schmidt, J., T. Hadden, T. Davis, D. Bixler, and A. Kachur. *Microsoft Windows 2000 Security Handbook*. Indianapolis: Que, 2001.

Steen, W., ed. *Netware Security*. Indianapolis: New Riders Publishing, 1996.

University of Toronto. "Local Area Network Security Guidelines," November 21, 2000; www.utoronto.ca/security/LAN.htm.

Wireless Ethernet Compatibility Alliance, www.wirelessethernet.org.

Wireless LAN Association, www.wlana.org

25.8 NOTES

1. See www.ietf.org/rfc/rfc2196.txt.

2. For details of software-based TEMPEST, see Markus G. Kuhn and Ross J. Anderson, "Soft Tempest: Hidden Data Transmission Using Electromagnetic Emanations," 1998; www.cl.cam.ac.uk/~mgk25/ih98-tempest.pdf.

3. See NTP: www.gocsi.com/forms/order/publications.html for the latest CSI Buyers Guide of Computer Security Products and Services CD-ROM.

4. Microsoft came under fire for its original implementation of Kerberos in Windows 2000. Microsoft's version used a piece of proprietary data in the authentication process, making it impossible for third-party Kerberos servers to work with Windows. The company has since released interoperability information.

5. Ed Bott, "What Triggers User Account Control Prompts?" February 2, 2007; www.edbott.com/weblog/?p=1602.

6. Alec Klein and Ellen Nakashima, "For Windows Vista Security, Microsoft Called in Pros," *Washington Post,* January 9, 2007; www.washingtonpost.com/wp-dyn/content/article/2007/01/08/AR2007010801352.html.

CHAPTER **26**

GATEWAY SECURITY DEVICES

David Brussin and Justin Opatrny

26.1 INTRODUCTION.   The firewall has come to represent both the concept and the realization of network and Internet security protections. Due to its rapid acceptance and evolution, the firewall has become the most visible of security technology throughout the enterprise chain of command. In distinct contrast with virtually any other single piece of technology, there is not likely to be a chief executive officer in this country who cannot say a word or two about how firewalls are used to protect enterprise systems and data.

The firewall, as originally devised, was intended to allow certain explicitly authorized communications between networks while denying all others. This approach centralizes much of the responsibility for the security of a protected network at the firewall component while distributing some responsibility to the components handling the authorized communications with outside networks. The centralized responsibility put a lot of attention on the firewall and provided for its rapid maturation as a secure gatekeeper. The maturity and widespread adoption of firewall products led to attention on the responsibility distributed behind those early firewalls: The allowed paths, frequently involving immature software and complex protocols, became the weakest link in the chain. As a result, firewalls have evolved to include features devoted largely to shoring up the allowed paths that pass through them.

The successful use of these devices in contemporary security architecture continues to depend on understanding their specific capabilities and limitations, on managing the security responsibility that rests on nonsecurity devices within protected networks, and on understanding and planning for the failure conditions of security components.

26.1.1 Changing Security Landscape. The changes in enterprise networks, applications, and work patterns have significantly altered the typical enterprise Internet architecture from a few years ago.

Although the perimeter is now much less clearly defined, there has been increased centralization of elements that were previously distributed. Also, many of the protocols that were passed without inspection by early firewalls are now subject to control.

26.1.1.1 Borders Dissolving. The outsourcing of information technology (IT) functions previously contained within the enterprise is one factor redefining the border between internal network and Internet. Hosted applications such as customer relationship management (CRM; e.g., Salesforce.com), e-mail and collaboration (Exchange and SharePoint), storage (Amazon S3), and even custom-built Web applications (Amazon EC2) have created paths across the public Internet for traffic previously contained within enterprise perimeters. Amazon Simple Storage Service (S3) and Elastic Compute Cloud (EC2) are examples of outsourced, Internet-based virtual computing resources.

Enterprise applications are increasingly subject to extension by customers and third parties via mashups (composite applications using various programming tools) and Web service application program interfaces (APIs), and it has become common for employees and customers to use the same systems, with applications handling permissions and security internally.

(For more information on outsourcing and security, see Chapter 68 in this *Handbook*.)

26.1.1.2 Mobility (Physical and Logical). Another major factor in the redefinition of the security perimeter is the mobility of employees. Employees today work from a variety of systems and locations. Employees expect to be able to connect from anywhere, whether within the enterprise or from home or an Internet hot spot. They expect to be able to use kiosks and home systems to access enterprise applications. This mobility, and the impact on trustworthiness of mobile nodes, not only dissolves the network border, but also promotes the class of attack that depends on a compromised client. The challenge is to find a way to control these changes with centralized security devices.

26.1.1.3 Regulatory Compliance. Recent regulatory changes have made companies responsible for a set of requirements for data protection and preservation. The Gramm-Leach-Bliley Act (GLB) and Health Information Portability and Accountability Act (HIPAA) have specific requirements about the protection of personally identifiable information and personal health information. Communications and other corporate data are required to be archived and preserved, and made searchable for legal discovery, by provisions of the Sarbanes-Oxley Act (SOX), SEC rule 17a-4, and the Federal Rules of Civil Procedure as of December 1, 2006. SOX also requires companies to control any transaction path leading to financial data.

Given the rapid, widespread deployment required to meet deadlines associated with emerging regulations, centralized control at the network level has been an attractive architecture, compared to server or desktop agent software deployments.

(See Chapter 64 in this *Handbook* for more details on GLB and Sox; see Chapter 71 for more information about HIPAA.)

26.1.2 Rise of the Gateway Security Device. The firewall first centralized responsibility for authorization of allowed paths and then quickly expanded its role to include additional protections for those allowed paths. These protections have expanded to such an extent that their complexity frequently outweighs that of core firewall function, and it is now more accurate to refer to these expanded firewalls as gateway security devices (GSDs).

Gateway security device capabilities. The processing capacity available per rack unit has increased consistent with Moore's Law, so that many of the security functions that could not be centralized in large organizations are now possible. Previously centralized functions were each implemented on a dedicated, point solution device in the past, but now these functions are being consolidated onto a single platform. Also, the adoption of centralized enterprise assets, such as role-based access control systems and directory services, has made available significant additional context for security decisions.

Enterprise directory integration. Directory integration, such as with an LDAP infrastructure, enables seamless integration of a range of functions from per-user or per-group authorization of host or protocol access to user or group specific rule sets for other GSD functions, such as Web filtering.

Unified threat management. The term "unified threat management" refers to the addition of perimeter-based implementations of antivirus, antispyware, anti-spam, and other malware controls, along with IDS/IPS functions and some elements of content control, to the firewall workload. Providing these capabil-ities at the firewall's location requires significant protocol manipulation, and in many cases these are achieved through full proxy servers for the supported protocols within the device.

Content control and data leakage prevention (DLP). Control of the content of communications, whether for the purpose of filtering offensive Web sites or preventing the disclosure of proprietary information, is in the early stages of consolidation onto GSDs. Ranging from URL and dictionary-based filters for content filtering to content-indexing search engines for DLP, these controls require deep inspection of content within HTTP, SMTP, instant messaging, and other protocols. Content control also includes the implementation of data-handling controls for regulatory compliance and DLP, such as the requirement to use encryption to protect sensitive data sent by e-mail.

Archive and discovery. Regulatory requirements to archive and index corporate data, particularly e-mail communications, have created a product category in messaging security at the perimeter. As with antispam and other functions, this feature will soon be consolidated into GSDs.

26.1.3   Application Firewall: Beyond the Proxy.

The most significant of the allowed paths traversing most firewalls is the Web path, consisting primarily of a combination of HTTP and HTTP over SSL. This path has exploded in complexity with the advent of AJAX and related rich Web application technologies, and with the explosion in the number and importance of internal and external Web applications important to the enterprise. Whereas the early firewall guarded against access to misconfiguration and vulnerability in the protected servers, the Web application firewall guards against misconfiguration and vulnerability within the custom Web applications that run over the HTTP allowed path.

26.2   HISTORY AND BACKGROUND.

The responsibilities and capabilities of traditional security components have been dramatically altered by changing computing paradigms, by changing models for business interaction, and by the global change introduced by the emergence of Internet-centric computing. (For a general introduction to data communication concepts and terminology, see Chapter 5 in this *Handbook*. For a discussion of local area networks, see Chapter 25.)

26.2.1   Changing Network Models.

As connections between systems have changed the way computers are used, security issues have shifted to accommodate the new approaches. The progression from mainframe-centric information processing to increasingly broad networks of systems has changed the idea of the security perimeter. Additionally, as a result of the new connections, the requirements for application security have grown to include new concerns about network and host security.

The mainframe-based information processing approach had well-established security technology and procedures. The transition to client/server computing left these behind to a significant extent, and the continued shift to network-centric computing made clear the need for a new approach.

26.2.1.1   *Mainframe.*

Early information processing systems centered on a glass house approach to networking. Mainframe systems were often solitary, and when multiple systems were present, their connections typically were limited to a single data center. Wide area networks (WANs) were limited to direct leased-line connections between data centers.

Network and physical perimeters were typically the same, with client access provided primarily by green screen terminal services. The need for application security was limited by this single, available, and allowed path. Network security in this environment was the responsibility of the mainframe services connected to network interfaces. For example, these services had security features that controlled access and frequently were located in separate mainframe regions.

Mainframe operating systems predicted the evolution of networks and firewalls to some extent. These operating systems typically ran as instances on a lightweight virtual machine, as in the case of IBM MVS/VM, or were otherwise divided into partitions or regions. The interactions between these virtual systems could be regulated, even to the level of implementing mandatory access control (MAC). (See Chapter 9 in this *Handbook* for more details).

26.2.1.2   *Client/Server.*

As mainframe resources were augmented with midrange servers, running operating systems such as UNIX, NetWare, OS/2, and Windows NT, the number and type of network connections increased rapidly. Also, terminal-based clients were replaced in large part by personal computer (PC)–class client systems with network connections.

This shift represents the initial change in the traditional security perimeter. Network connections reached outside of the data center to the individual desktop, and WANS expanded to connect these systems across the enterprise and beyond. Among the advantages of the midrange server approach was the broad suitability of their operating systems to office productivity, back-end computing, transaction processing, database service, and other tasks. Along with these capabilities came complexity, including default configurations designed to enable maximum functionality out of the box.

As data centers, and even wiring closets, became populated with servers, the network connections and associated available network services became increasingly complex. The security perimeter no longer had any distinct boundaries within the enterprise, as clients and server were connected in increasingly complex ways. Application security was redefined, as application functionality spread across mainframe, server, and PC-class client platforms. The interactions between these platforms within a single application created multiple allowed paths, and the many available network services on a given platform created opportunities to circumvent the intended application flow.

26.2.1.3 Web. The emergence of the commercial Internet in the 1990s was the start of another major shift in enterprise network models. Rapid development of the HTML/HTTP application path led to Web applications that approximate the capabilities of fat client applications. Emerging technologies such as Asynchronous JavaScript and XML (AJAX), which incorporates asynchronous interaction between Web browser and Web server not associated with a page view, have further increased the complexity of communications over the HTTP allowed path. This path now transports countless customized and ad hoc protocols for interaction between rich AJAX client applications and their Web servers.

Although firewalls have increasingly focused attention on inspecting and controlling HTTP-based communications, the growth in complexity has outpaced the abilities of commercial products, putting pressure on Web architects to understand the capabilities of firewall devices and the security context of rich HTTP applications. (For a discussion of Web security, see Chapters 21, 30, and 31 in this *Handbook*.)

26.2.2 Firewall Architectures. As network security mechanisms evolved from functionality added to existing routing devices, to dedicated systems and appliances, the techniques used to implement firewall functionality have evolved as well. Always balancing security requirements against performance and network throughput, vendors have introduced a variety of approaches.

26.2.2.1 Access Control List. The first firewalls were in fact routers, both dedicated routing appliances and UNIX-based bastion hosts. Such devices, routing appliances with access control lists (ACLs), are still widely used as network security mechanisms. Some routing appliances use the stateful inspection architecture discussed later in this section.

Routers using ACLs make authorization decisions for allowed path control based strictly on the packet currently being processed by the router. This decision, without context of previous traffic, is based on such packet data as source and target addresses, and port and packet flags such as the synchronizing field (SYN) present in packets attempting to initiate connections.

This focused view of individual packets has resulted in several vulnerabilities. One such vulnerability exploited combinations of the poorly compliant IP implementation in Windows NT and the strictly compliant implementation in the routers. Attackers crafted fragmented IP packets such that the initial SYN packet contained headers conforming to an ACL on the router. The following packet, however, had a fragment offset that placed new header data into the packet upon reassembly in the Windows NT host behind the firewall. Since this second fragment did not contain a SYN flag, it was not blocked at the router. Windows NT patches and router changes that prevented fragments with offsets within the packet header have addressed this vulnerability. The practice of reassembling fragmented packets at the router also became common as a preventive measure against this type of attack.

Section 26.4, Deployment, shows how existing routing infrastructure, in combination with dedicated network security mechanisms, can be used to enhance security architectures. (For more information about ACLs, see Chapter 24 in this *Handbook*.)

26.2.2.2   Packet Filtering.   Packet-filtering firewalls are appliance, or host-based, firewalls that use the ACL method just described for allowed path authorization but add additional firewall capabilities. These systems typically do formal logging, are capable of user-based authorization, and have intrusion detection and alerting capabilities.

Unfortunately, these firewalls also have suffered from weaknesses due to lack of context information, as described. Additionally, host-based packet-filtering firewalls have suffered from various weaknesses in the network stacks of the underlying operating systems.

Very few firewall vendors currently offer traditional packet-filtering firewalls, but many nonsecurity products now have packet-filtering capabilities. For example, various load balancers, Web caches, and switch products now offer packet-filtering firewall capabilities.

Packet-filtering firewalls are ideally suited to load-balanced and highly available environments, as they can load-balance connections among devices, between each packet, with no additional overhead and can similarly fail-over between devices in the middle of an established connection.

26.2.2.3   Stateful Inspection.   In recognition of the problems with authorizing allowed-path traffic based on the information in a single packet, vendors developed several new technologies. The basic design behind application gateways, discussed in Section 26.2.2.4, was considered by some to be too computationally expensive for real-time processing on firewall devices. A competing technology, stateful inspection, was developed to provide connection context information for allowed-path authorization and still provide for good performance, scalability, load balancing, and fail-over capabilities.

This technique calls for a table of connection information, providing context, to be maintained in memory on the firewall. In order to improve throughput, the information in this table is stored in the form of binary representations of IP packet header information. This information then can be compared to the binary header of an incoming IP packet very efficiently, in many cases using only a few native CPU instructions.

This technique, as it inspects only certain portions of the incoming packet, is effective only against known or predicted classes of IP attack. Attacks that use ignored portions of the packet to attack weak IP implementations on back-end hosts still succeed. As a result, this type of firewall, while it may be configured with a least-privilege rule base, is partially comparable to the packet filter in that it does not do least-privilege data inspection.

Some stateful inspection systems have focused so heavily on performance that they offer a *fast mode* that reduces inspection dramatically once a connection has been opened successfully. This mode, while very efficient, is strongly discouraged by network security experts as sacrificing too much security.

Stateful inspection technology lends itself well to load balancing and highly available solutions, albeit with significant overhead traffic. In order to support load balancing and fail-over between packets and within established connections, the state tables between clustered or paired devices must be synchronized. This operation typically is conducted via in-band network traffic or out-of-band interdevice connectivity, such as through RS-232, a standard that specifies physical connectors, signal voltage characteristics, and an information exchange protocol.

26.2.2.4 Application-Layer Gateway.
A second approach to adding context information to the allowed-path access decision came in the form of application gateway firewalls. These firewalls use protocol-specific proxies on each allowed path port to make access decisions, extract required protocol information, and build internal packets for distribution to the back-end host. Since these firewalls are performing far more complex operations than stateful inspection systems, they have some significant performance challenges to overcome.

Some commentators describe the functional separation of the inspection functions in protocol-specific proxies as analogous to the air gap that physically separates distinct, unconnected networks. The benefit of the so-called *air gap* approach to packet inspection, access decision, data extraction, and packet assembly workflow is that it is effective at protecting not only against known or predicted classes of attack but also against unknown attacks. Since unused packet elements are discarded, they present no danger to internal systems.

Application gateways do not lend themselves easily to load balancing and high-availability solutions. Load balancing typically is accomplished through affinities, where connections will be balanced at their initiation and not change devices thereafter. Fail-over can be accomplished through operating system–level synchronization and fail-over mechanisms, but typically not without disrupting connections in progress.

26.2.2.5 Multifunction/Hybrid.
Hybrid firewalls have emerged as a compromise between the speed and efficiency of the stateful inspection approach and the increased security of the application gateway approach. In fact, most commercial firewalls available today can be classified as hybrids.

Hybrid firewalls, evolved from stateful inspection systems, typically perform their normal inspection for all but a few protocols. These protocols, such as HTTP, are subject to additional application gateway-style inspection and/or proxy.

Application gateways in the hybrid category have always used the proxy approach for known protocols. These systems now implement stateful inspection for unknown or encrypted protocols and offer a fast mode that performs stateful inspection rather than application gateway functionality on established connections.

26.2.2.6 Host Environment Context.
Host-based security—aside from basic network firewalling—has additional complexity and considerations due to the protection requirements of the additional elements (software, services, etc.) running. The

host's ability to better understand its local environment allows for more granular protection and visibility.

Instead of focusing on just allowing or denying port-based access to the network, the environmental context allows the host-based security to define what applications and services can access or receive network information, access or change other services, executing code in a virtual machine to verify if it behaves as expected, and so on.

Firewalls running on, or in special communication with, the hosts they protect can make use of additional context for making security decisions. Whether through native platform information on host-based firewalls, or data and instructions received via a protocol such as Universal Plug and Play (UPnP), information about, for example, the applications running at the time a security decision must be made can be helpful. If a particular application requires inbound connectivity on various ports, the overall risk profile of the protected network is lower if the ports are accessible only when that application is running. Similarly, information from within complex or encrypted protocol exchanges, such as IP addresses of systems expecting access, may provide context for allowed path restrictions.

The host's movement from relying on the network security measures, to context and environmentally aware security measures, will provide more robust and flexible security wherever the host goes.

26.2.3   Firewall Platforms.

The changing problem of perimeter security has produced a succession of network security mechanisms designed to restrict allowed paths and inspect network traffic.

26.2.3.1   *Routing.*

Routers are the heart of TCP/IP networks, directing traffic from segment to segment. Router vendors recognized the need for security controls at the boundaries between different segments and networks, and implemented simple controls that could be activated with negligible performance impact.

ACL. Using explicit *allow* and *deny* statements, router access control lists (ACLs) restrict IP traffic based on source and destination addresses and ports. In addition, these controls can limit traffic based on other parameters, such as whether a packet is in response to an established connection or not. Routers inspect each packet in a vacuum, without any context of previous traffic.

Hardware modules. High-end routers today provide a hardware extensibility platform that permits additional modules (often referred to as blades) to be installed. These modules have access to the full-speed backplane of the parent device, and can be logically inserted into the process for handling traffic. Modules are available for major router platforms that provide each of the firewall architecture types.

26.2.3.2   *Host Based.*

Although routers did an effective job of implementing access control rules, it was clear that they were not suited for more complex requirements. Dedicated server-based firewalls were created to provide for additional capabilities, including protocol traffic inspection, contextual traffic inspection, comprehensive logging and alerting, and air-gap application gateways, which completely rebuild network packets to protect systems on internal networks.

These firewall applications typically are built on top of an existing operating system (OS). Various UNIX variants and Windows platforms are commonly used, often with special hardening or system-monitoring components added to the OS. In some cases, hardening is implemented to the extent that components of the network stack within the underlying OS are completely replaced.

The full OS permits firewalls with significantly greater functionality than is available on routers. Also, development scope and effort can be reduced by using commercial off-the-shelf (COTS) components and scripting languages and building on real-time process scheduling, network input/output (I/O), and file system functionality. Unfortunately, these benefits come at a price: added complexity, unpredictable configurations, third-party component interactions, and uncontrolled changes.

Modern host operating systems frequently include some form of integrated software firewall. In Linux, this firewall has become the foundation of a number of host-based firewall products, and is used for host protection as well as for the protection of additional networks. Windows and Mac OS firewalls are less general in their features, acting more like personal firewalls, and typically are used only to protect the individual host.

26.2.3.3 Appliance. An extension of the host-based firewall concept, the firewall appliance is an effort to realize the benefits of a full OS upon which to build functionality while providing the controlled operating and maintenance characteristics of routers and network appliances. In taking control of the entire host, vendors can closely control software versions and configuration, and can prevent undesired system changes. In order to do so, vendors must increase their expertise to include appliance hardware and operating systems, and they will have to face additional challenges as a hardware vendor as well as possible licensing fees for included software components.

A form of appliance that does not include vendor-supplied hardware has also become popular. So-called *soft appliances* typically require customers to acquire hardware fitting a rigid set of specifications and install the soft appliance by booting from a vendor-supplied disk.

26.2.3.4 Personal and Desktop Agent. As the network perimeter faded, it became increasingly evident that hosts needed to be able to better protect themselves from threats. The most recognizable host protection is antivirus (AV). As security dynamics evolved, the pattern-based protections of AV could not provide adequate protection. The introduction of a software firewall helped reduce the host's footprint on the network. The addition of a Host Intrusion Prevention System (H-IPS) allowed the host greater visibility into finding and stopping different types of malicious packets. (See Section 26.3.2.1 for more details on H-IPS.)

Current-generation agents take advantage of the contextual and environmental awareness of the host's operating capabilities. This allows the agent to integrate deeper into the OS and provide protection where network security products cannot.

To be certain, these agents require as much, if not more, maintenance than its network partners. Pattern/definition files must be constantly updated, and client software must be kept current to remove the potential for exploit. Adding to the support and configuration complexity, the host may be anywhere in the world.

26.2.3.5 Virtual. Virtual firewalls consist of firewall software running on virtual machines under a hypervisor (such as VMware or Xen), protecting physical and virtual networks. As virtualization of networks and applications replaces physical deployments, network security architectures must be translated as well. The simple mapping of physical architectures into virtual environments is not sufficient, since the scope of compromise and consequences of failure of the hypervisor infrastructure must be taken into account.

A special case of the virtual firewall is the virtual appliance: This platform is an extension of the soft appliance concept wherein the vendor supplies a virtual machine image intended to run on a particular hypervisor on customer-specified hardware.

26.2.3.6   Embedded.   GSD functionality is continuing to be more extensible and affordable. This functionality can be fragmented to create Web server-based plug-ins, in order to build customized application firewalls. It can also be used to scale to the level of consumer and small to medium business (SMB) appliances.

Web server plug-ins tightly integrates with the Web server platform. This provides the ability to use predeveloped, downloaded signatures as well as to develop protections specific to custom Web applications and content. Although it increases the administrative overhead of developing and monitoring another security mechanism, it also provides a level of contextual understanding often unavailable to application gateways.

Consumer and SMB appliances typically provide switching, routing, and wireless connectivity. They give smaller operations more flexibility and the ability to incorporate GSD capabilities, such as a stateful inspection firewall, network intrusion prevention systems (N-IPS), antivirus, and beyond. Without such all-in-one devices, it may be infeasible for smaller organizations to get these robust security protections.

26.3   NETWORK SECURITY MECHANISMS.   Recognition of the value of network security mechanisms has changed the way systems are built and managed, from the largest government network to the individual personal workstation. Although IT managers have increased their expertise and recognized the need for these mechanisms, they often have unrealistic expectations about their capabilities. Network security mechanisms are far from the easy answer to Internet security concerns that some believe them to be. An understanding of the capabilities and roles of these components permits the most effective realization of their benefit, both direct and otherwise, without the undesired consequence of insufficient protection in other areas.

26.3.1   Basic Roles.   Network security devices provide for allowed paths, intrusion detection, and intrusion prevention and response.

26.3.1.1   Allowed Paths.   Although network security devices such as firewalls and proxy servers create a distinct physical perimeter between different networks, they also create a logical perimeter that extends to systems within protected networks. Just as the teller windows in a bank branch office restrict customers' interactions with bank personnel to those that are intended, the allowed path protections afforded by a firewall ensure that outside traffic is able to flow only in expected and intended ways.

The perimeter protection and allowed path control roles of the network security mechanism combine to form a least-privilege gateway that comprises the original firewall function. Network security professionals quickly learned that the dangers of external traffic could easily extend to the defined allowed paths. Significant security responsibility still rested with the destination host within the protected network. The many generations of network security mechanisms that followed focused on returning more of this responsibility back to the firewall or proxy server itself.

26.3.1.1.1   Tunneling.   When the security responsibility for allowed path traffic cannot be accepted by a GSD, often for reasons of protocol support or performance, the traffic is tunneled through to an endpoint in the protected network. Tunneling fragments the responsibility for inspection and policy enforcement, and changes the scope of compromise associated with a failure, since that failure may now occur within the protected network. Tunneled traffic can be to and from both endpoints and networks; as discussed further in this chapter situations involving traffic tunneled to networks have additional complexity.

In order to mitigate the risk associated with fragmented inspection and policy enforcement, considerable care must be taken to understand the full inspection and enforcement workflow within the obviated GSD. Those workflow elements that cannot be performed on tunneled traffic must still be handled; responsibility must be assigned to a downstream component. With most endpoint-to-endpoint tunnels, IP-layer policy can still be enforced at the GSD, while application layer and protocol-aware stateful inspection must be performed downstream. In the case of network-to-network tunnels, however, the GSD does not have useful visibility or control. A downstream device with the necessary protocol support, or a separate GSD controlling exploded traffic between the tunnel endpoint and the target network, must enforce IP-layer policy.

26.3.1.1.2 Antispoofing.   Network address spoofing is an ingredient in a variety of attacks aimed at exploiting invalid assumptions about the utility of network addresses for authentication, typically at the application layer. Gateway security devices have an opportunity to inspect traffic with knowledge of the network architecture and thus can recognize and prevent many spoofing attacks.

GSDs with knowledge of which addresses and networks exist on each physical interface are able to prevent spoofing of addresses from one interface by nodes on another interface. This is typically used to prevent external nodes from spoofing internal addresses, since there could be internal systems and applications incorrectly relying on internal source addresses to allow access. Spoofing attacks, which involve spoofing of one external address by another or of one internal address by another, often cannot be detected in this way, even when the spoofed traffic flows through the GSD.

Another form of antispoofing protection is the blocking of traffic claiming to originate in reserved or unallocated address space. Spammers and other attackers are frequently able to publish routes for networks in this address space and use it to dodge filters and other protections. A variety of lists of reserved and unallocated space are available, and some GSDs make automated use of standardized lists.

26.3.1.1.3 Network Address Translation.   Network address translation (NAT) was originally intended to combat the shortage of IPv4 addresses by connecting blocks of privately addressed space using a small number of real IP addresses. Due to a few beneficial side effects, NAT has come to be considered a security tool and a necessary capability of GSDs. These side effects include obfuscation of private network size and topology, a degree of stateful filtering, and endpoint address privacy. Although there is some value to the obfuscation of private networks and endpoint address privacy, the stateful filtering benefit is no substitute for true inspection of allowed path traffic. Use of NAT adds complexity that must be understood in order to express clearly the allowed path policy in the configuration of a GSD.

26.3.1.2 Intrusion Detection.   Another primary role of the network security mechanism is that of intrusion detection: sounding an alarm when all is not well with the network perimeter. Depending on how these mechanisms are deployed, alerts may provide extremely valuable information about real problems or a torrent of information about attempted attacks rather than actual intrusions. Tactics for addressing these issues will be discussed in detail later in this chapter.

When network security mechanisms are working properly, intrusion detection information is really threat-level information, useful in maintaining knowledge of the background levels of hostile activity directed at the protected network. Tests have shown that new Internet hosts are probed and attacked within hours of being placed online and are probed almost continuously thereafter.

Some firewalls incorporate pattern-matching features, such as those found in dedicated intrusion-detection systems, in order to detect hostile traffic along allowed paths. Similar in some ways to virus scanning via pattern matching, this method can detect certain known attacks on specific protocols.

Since multiple firewalls and proxy servers often are used in a given architecture, intrusion-detection data also can report actual security failures. When a network security mechanism observes and rejects traffic that architecturally should never have been present, security failure of an upstream device is possible.

See Chapter 27 of this *Handbook* for more details on intrusion detection and prevention.

26.3.1.3 Intrusion Prevention/Response.

26.3.1.3 Intrusion Prevention/Response. Network administrators, responsible for reacting to the alerts from firewall intrusion-detection components, knew that there had to be a more efficient way to deal with these critical events. Firewall vendors began to integrate various types and levels of intrusion response capability into their products, producing automated responses to intrusion detection alerts.

Connection termination. The simplest of intrusion response capabilities, connection termination involves the firewall terminating a specific allowed path connection from a specific address and port when intrusion-detection components detect traffic that matches known attack patterns. Typically implemented in TCP via an RST, or connection reset command, this functionality also can be implemented on connectionless UDP (User Datagram Protocol) allowed paths through packet dropping.

This intrusion response capability is effective at blocking known attacks on allowed paths but suffers from several drawbacks. Unfortunately, skilled attackers can use this capability to create a denial of service against legitimate clients on specific ports. In many cases the clients rebuild their connections, but a successful attack might deny service completely for some period of time. Also, this technique is not useful for preventing attackers from attempting additional, perhaps unknown, attacks following connection termination of initial attacks.

Dynamic rule modification. The dynamic rule modification technique takes connection termination to the next level, ensuring that attackers are prevented from attempting further attacks from the same address. By dynamically modifying the network security mechanism rule base to block traffic from the offending address, further potential attacks are blocked.

This technique addresses one of the failings of connection termination, namely the exposure to unknown attacks that might follow known attacks, but it is even more exposed to the denial of service issues just discussed. Since dynamic rule modification creates a semipermanent barrier for traffic from a given address, attackers can deny service to broad groups of users for an extended period. Since many enterprises and Internet service providers (ISPs) use only a few proxy server source addresses for all traffic, an attack could quickly deny service for a very large group, such as all AOL users.

System-level actions. Most network security mechanisms perform internal monitoring of component processes and the underlying operating system. In the event of internal problems or evidence of compromise, or certain external intrusion detection events, system-level action can be initiated.

Actions taken can range from firewall interface deactivation to firewall system shutdown. It is important to test firewall shutdown behavior carefully before using this response, as several firewall products have in the past, upon shutdown, permitted open routing of traffic via the underlying operating system.

Application inspection. Within allowed paths such as HTTP, it is now common for firewalls to look for a variety of exploits and vulnerabilities related to the implementation of Web browsers and applications. Attacks such as cross-site scripting (XSS) and SQL query injection can be detected by Web application firewalls and addressed at an application level in addition to more blunt, conservative network-level responses.

Antimalware. Within allowed paths, given sufficient visibility and context by the gateway security device, techniques such as session hijacking and quarantine can be used to respond to malware and other content-related threats. For example, a firewall might hijack a session between a protected browser and an outside Web server in order to prevent the download of malware-infected files, while continuing to download the file into quarantine.

(See Chapter 27 in this *Handbook* for more information about intrusion detection and intrusion prevention.)

26.3.2   Personal and Desktop Agents.   Although firewalls and GSDs play a crucial role in protecting the overall network infrastructure, it is not cost-feasible or infrastructurally sound to deploy these devices at all points in the network. Individual hosts must have a way to protect themselves from threats independent of network security devices. Unlike the network, a host has a contextual understanding of what the system can be, is, or should be doing. This understanding provides the ability to create granular controls around what can access, or leave, the host. Beyond the simple allow and deny functionality, contextual security measures can detect unexpected system configuration changes such as service changes or an application behaving in an unexpected manner.

26.3.2.1   End Point Protection.   When a mobile end point leaves the internal network, it becomes an extension of the network protection profile. By providing adequate local protections at the network and application levels, the mobile end point helps to mitigate potential issues upon reconnecting to the internal network. It is also crucial to determine the level of protection necessary and how each of these additional levels of security affects system performance, management, and end user impact.

- **Network.** Hosts need to be able to determine the types and appropriateness of inbound and outbound traffic. These network restrictions may vary from the internal network to uncontrolled networks. In certain circumstances, all network traffic may be suspect and scrutinized further. For example, when on the internal network, the host allows the inbound ICMP echo request. If the host were on an uncontrolled network, it would not allow any nonestablished packets. Simple host-based network protections are not enough; additional host protection mechanisms such as intrusion prevention can detect and stop network and application-based attacks.

- **Application access.** The host's contextual awareness also helps to dictate the ability for applications to send and receive data. The goal is to ensure that only the appropriate applications or services have access to the network. The host protection policy may allow applications to establish outbound connections but never listen or accept nonestablished inbound packets. For example, an HTTP server uses a daemon to listen for connection attempts. The HTTP client will attempt to make a connection to the HTTP server. By using a host protection mechanism, it would be possible to prevent one or both of these actions.

- **Hybrid protections.** The Host Intrusion Prevention System (H-IPS) functions similarly to Network Intrusion Prevention Systems (N-IPS) by detecting known attack patterns and anomalous behaviors. For example, an ICMP echo request with a payload of 64 bytes of hex $0 \times AA$ does not violate any request for comments (RFCs) or seem menacing, but this single packet was the precursor reconnaissance packet used by the Nachi worm. Hybrid host protections build on the host's contextual awareness and provide the ability to monitor other unusual application-level activity, such as changes to binaries, service manipulation, and spawned listeners.

26.3.3 Additional Roles.
Additional functions carried out by network security devices include encryption, acceleration, content control, and a new version of the Internet Protocol (IP).

26.3.3.1 Encryption.
Security and practical concerns have prompted the inclusion of encryption technology in network security mechanisms. Valid concerns over centralization of responsibility for security decisions, components and perimeter protection, as well as cost and complexity savings have resulted in a variety of hardware and software encryption solutions as part of firewalls and proxy servers.

(See Chapter 7 in this *Handbook* for more details on encryption.)

Inspection. Two approaches are commonly used by gateway security devices to inspect encrypted traffic. The first, termination, requires that the encrypted communication have its endpoint at the firewall so that inspection and control of the plaintext communication can occur. The communication may then be re-encrypted for transit to the intended endpoint. The second approach, passive decryption, involves out-of-band decryption of the communication by a firewall, using escrowed keys. The passive decryption approach can be subject to a variety of issues, and weaknesses, common to intrusion detection technologies, if the decryption and inspection is not synchronous with control of the encrypted channel.

VPN. Virtual private networks (VPNs), which extend the security perimeter of a network to include remote systems as if they were on an internal network, have increased in popularity as a mechanism for allowing remote enterprise access without extensive hardware infrastructure. VPNs over the public Internet are most commonly used in this role.

Savvy network administrators realize that remote VPN clients are very different from true internal hosts and seek a way to mitigate the risk that comes with them.

Using the perimeter protection and allowed path-control capabilities of the firewall, it is possible to create a special rule base specifically for VPN clients. Certain GSD vendors also provide the ability to peer inside the encrypted tunnel.

The P in VPN, which stands for private, is implemented through encryption technology. When the firewall is responsible for allowed path control on traffic from remote VPN clients, it must be able to deal with unencrypted traffic. Rather than place additional servers or appliances outside the firewall, where they might be vulnerable to Internet attacks, vendors chose to integrate the encryption technology directly into the firewall.

(See Chapter 32 in this *Handbook* for more details of VPNs.)

26.3.3.2   Acceleration.   SSL, or Secure Sockets Layer, is the standard encryption protocol for protecting Web-related network traffic. In order to centralize acceleration hardware, enable intrusion detection and allow path inspection, reduce Web server load, and simplify secure Web implementations, vendors have integrated support for SSL, frequently using hardware acceleration, into the network security mechanisms.

The active termination or passive decryption of SSL traffic at a centralized location requires significant processing power, and acceleration is often necessary to permit these activities without impacting the performance of protected traffic.

26.3.3.3   Content Control.   The inspection of content along various allowed paths is performed most easily at a choke point, where all of the traffic flows through one set of components, resulting in the integration of content inspection functionality in network security mechanisms.

26.3.3.3.1   Content Filtering.   Content filtering is not strictly a security capability. In most cases, this technology permits policy enforcement with respect to the actions of internal rather than external users. Business policy regarding the use of enterprise resources, for example, is often enforced through HTTP content inspection and filtering. HTTP (Hypertext Transfer Protocol) and SMTP (Simple Mail Transfer Protocol) filtering are used to isolate users from undesired materials, such as those they might consider offensive.

This technology, which is far from perfect, uses a variety of approaches to filter content. Address-based filtering, which uses IP (Internet Protocol) addresses of destination Web sites, for example, is efficient and easy to implement. This technique requires constant updates to a blocked address list, however, and can easily block sites unintentionally due to virtual hosts sharing IP addresses. Name-based filtering is a slight improvement, using actual domain and resource names, but it still suffers from the list management problem.

In an attempt to address the list management issues, a resource-intensive technique based on real-time content scanning was developed. This technique, which can incorporate anything from keyword scanning to image analysis, also results in significant erroneous filtering.

(See Chapter 31 of this *Handbook* for more details on content filtering.)

26.3.3.3.2   Antimalware.   Virus scanning within network security mechanisms takes various forms, from SMTP message and attachment scanning to HTTP traffic inspection. Typically based on existing pattern recognition, virus scanning systems, this integration sometimes loops traffic through dedicated scanning systems rather than performing the work on the firewall or proxy server itself.

26.3.3.3.3 Active Content.   Active code, such as Flash, QuickTime, ActiveX, VB-Script, and JavaScript, can pose a security threat to internal systems. Many network security mechanisms have been enhanced to support filtering or scanning of these components on certain allowed paths.

On HTTP connections, for example, active code filtering might simply prevent the transfer of certain types of active code. More sophisticated scanning technology can be used to identify hostile code through pattern recognition or sandbox execution.

SMTP connections have seen significant new attention in this area due to active code weaknesses in popular mail clients. The scanning and filtering of active code in SMTP traffic is now being used to address a new breed of e-mail viruses.

(See Chapter 17 of this *Handbook* for more details on mobile code.)

Complex protocols. The complexity of communications over encrypted paths, such as HTTP over SSL, increases the risk of tunneling encrypted traffic beyond perimeter checkpoints. Where this tunneling does occur, application firewalls should be considered to manage the allowed path at its endpoint.

Serialized objects and code. One example of the risk of complex allowed paths is evident in the serialization of code in objects, in languages such as Java, when those objects are then communicated across trust boundaries over protocols such as HTTP. If code is serialized in objects on a trusted server, communicated to an untrusted system and then back to the trusted server, and evaluated on the trusted server, there is potential for compromise. Code should never be evaluated on a trusted system if it has not been continuously in the custody of trusted systems.

26.3.3.3.4 Caching.   Proxy server vendors quickly realized that their devices could dramatically reduce Internet bandwidth consumption and improve internal performance by caching frequently requested items on various protocols. HTTP, FTP (File Transfer Protocol), and streaming media caches are common on enterprise networks.

26.3.3.3.5 Policy Enforcement.   As with the inclusion of content filtering in firewall products, the network gateway is a logical place for deployment of other policy enforcement solutions. In order to protect data assets from loss through allowed paths, and to ensure compliance with the various regulations discussed in Section 3 above, firewall products now implement controls such as requiring encryption of certain communications and scanning communications for sensitive information.

26.3.3.4 IPv6.   Internet Protocol Version 6 (IPv6) is the successor to IPv4, the current standard protocol for Internet communication. IPv6 has many features with security implications, but a few key issues should be considered during the transitional period. (For more information about IPv4 and IPv6, see Chapter 5 in this *Handbook*.)

Support and compatibility. Gateway security devices used to protect IPv6 networks must, at minimum, support inspection and control of a few key protocols: neighbor discovery (ND), router solicitation/advertisement (RS/RA), and multicast listener discovery (MLD).

Stateless address autoconfiguration, which allows IPv6 nodes to automatically address themselves and discover their routers through ND and RS/RA, may break the user/address audit trail in some environments. In these cases, MAC addresses must be used to uniquely identify hardware nodes.

IPv6 resolves the address-space shortage of IPv4; the IPv4 address space is 2^{32} ($\sim 10^9$) compared with the IPv6 address space of 2^{128} ($\sim 10^{38}$). A widely circulated image to describe the difference between these two sizes is that if we were to represent the IPv4 address space as a square about 1 inch on a side, the IPv6 address space would have to be a square roughly the size of our solar system. Although the increased address space of IPv6 does mitigate some of the risks of port scanning and other topology discovery, the introduction of new resource-specific multicast addresses does allow for some discovery. Multicast addresses must be blocked by IPv6 multicast and MLD-aware GSDs at the perimeter to prevent this.

The most important transitional consideration is awareness of IPv6 traffic tunneled over IPv4. Tunneled traffic should not be allowed to transit GSDs unless the GSDs are capable of enforcing the same policies on the tunneled IPv6 traffic as would be enforced on IPv4 traffic. Organizations connecting IPv6 networks via the IPv4 Internet should consider the impact of IPv4 to IPv6 gateways and the possibility of spoofing IPv6 addresses by attackers on the IPv4 Internet; the advantages of IPv6 antispoofing features are negated when IPv4-to-IPv6 gateways are in use.

Specific issues. The address space shortage of IPv4 led to the creation of NAT, and NAT is not intended to persist following the transition. Given the current use of NAT as a security tool, there are some specific risks during the transition. As nodes are deployed with both IPv4 and IPv6 network stacks, the IPv6 network may expose unprotected nodes when the protections were previously implemented via a NAT layer. For example, when the blocking of all externally originated connections is implemented via NAT, the presence of an IPv6 stack will allow external nodes to directly connect to internal nodes on all listening ports.

The introduction in IPv6 of true network mobility, which enables nodes to communicate seamlessly using a single IP address while roaming across multiple networks, challenges the traditional perimeter security model. For example, if a user on an internal network accesses an internal system from a laptop at work and then takes the laptop to lunch at a nearby café with Internet access, the TCP session to the internal system could be uninterrupted despite the fact that the laptop has moved from a local, internal network behind a GSD-protected perimeter to a remote, public network outside the perimeter. Although the remote access seems as though it should be handled as VPN traffic would be on the IPv4 network, the dynamics of movement across the perimeter complicate any stateful aspect of inspection. Significant work will have to be done by GSD vendors during the transition to account for mobility without threatening the integrity of stateful inspection capabilities.

26.4   DEPLOYMENT.   The configuration and topology of network defenses must include consideration of firewall architectures, placement, monitoring, and management.

26.4.1   Screened Subnet Firewall Architectures.   The external router is the architecture's first line of defense against attacks from the outside world. The ACLs on this router should mirror the allowed-path configuration of the external firewall interface, in order to provide the front half of a screened subnet on which the firewall will operate. This screened subnet provides several important benefits.

The firewall is able to operate at maximum efficiency, since traffic rejected based on packet-filtering rules normally would never reach the firewall. This permits the firewall to focus, in terms of load, on protocol inspection. The firewall is able to respond immediately to unexpected conditions. If, for example, the firewall inspects a packet that should never have passed the external router's ACLs, the firewall can assume that the router is not behaving normally. The firewall is then free to respond appropriately, with such actions as terminating all connections from a specific host.

26.4.1.1   Service Networks.   The increasing demands for mobility and accessibility places a heavy burden on Internet-facing systems. Externally available functionality is outpacing the usefulness of the traditional DMZ. As the number of Internet-facing systems grows, so does the administrative overhead of managing external access.

The service network principle breaks down the old DMZ conglomerate into easier-to-manage and protect external networks. Instead of lumping systems such as Web, DNS, and e-mail onto a single network, there may be an advantage by splitting these up. Utility servers such as DNS and e-mail could logically be on the same network. Web servers can demand a great deal of bandwidth, but by using this concept, can protect the entire service network with a simple inbound access rule. Extranet systems create additional complexity since they provide the user interface, while internal systems provide the relevant content. The service network principle provides more flexibility in allowing external connections to reach the extranet servers while providing those same servers access to internal resources.

26.4.1.2   Redirect Back-End Traffic through the Firewall.   Remote access systems such as VPN connection points provide a unique challenge. Even though the front-end traffic arrives encrypted, there is still a heavy risk to providing a back-end link directly into the internal network. Instead, the encrypted traffic should arrive through one firewall interface, and the internal-bound traffic should use a separate unencrypted interface routed back through the firewall to the internal network. This type of deployment provides extra internal network protection in the event of a compromise of the VPN device as well as creating a traffic inspection point that is unimpeded by encryption.

26.4.2   Gateway Protection Device Positioning.   The increased use of encrypted protocols such as SSL and IPSec can create havoc when attempting to provide robust network protections. Although certain GSDs have the ability to terminate encrypted sessions, the increased processing and bandwidth requirements may exceed the limits of the device. Rather, the security architecture should deploy these countermeasures at strategic locations that avoid encrypted traffic. This way, the GSD can focus on its primary role of detecting and preventing malicious activity.

Inline. During packet analysis—whether for troubleshooting or for intrusion detection—the typical procedure is to configure a span port to replicate all data from one or more switch ports to the monitoring port. This approach allows the flexibility to move the passive monitors to different locations without affecting traffic flow, but it has two primary drawbacks. First, there is the potential to overwhelm the monitor's bandwidth. If the monitor connects at 100 Mbps but is monitoring two saturated 100 Mbps ports, there is a high probability that the monitor will miss traffic. Second, these passive devices do not normally provide protection capabilities. Since the passive device does not see the traffic directly, it may be possible for more packets to transmit before closing down a connection.

By placing the GSD inline, there are several specific advantages. This configuration provides a choke point requiring all network traffic to flow through it. If the device handles wire speeds on each interface, then there is little potential to miss network traffic. This method also allows active prevention measures to occur. When a malicious packet enters the GSD, protocol analysis will detect the anomaly and will not allow it to flow out the other interface. Although bandwidth limitations are a typical concern, improperly configured inline devices may also present a denial-of-service condition. With proper infrastructure planning and deployment, it is possible to minimize these risks.

Avoid encrypted traffic. The typical silver bullet for any GSDs is encryption. Encrypted malicious traffic can come and go at will simply because the GSD cannot evaluate the payload. Since mobile devices frequently venture outside of the controlled network, the only logical place to evaluate traffic is on the unencrypted side of the connection. This may be on the backside of a SSL terminator (in some cases on the server itself) or on the unencrypted side of a VPN connection.

26.4.3 Management and Monitoring Strategies. Network security devices are never a plug-and-play endeavor. It is essential to take additional steps to define the security requirements for managing and monitoring GSD components. This approach helps to ensure a well-rounded security posture.

26.4.3.1 *Monitoring.* Firewalls and GSDs provide complex functionality, and monitoring such systems must go beyond just verifying that the system is available. Monitoring mechanisms should cover the areas of device health, availability, and integrity.

- **Health.** Firewalls and GSDs must be solid performers, but these systems require extra administrative attention. Metrics such as processor utilization, available RAM, and number of connections all have an impact on the overall functionality of the system. A centralized management console may provide the ability to monitor these metrics and to issue alerts. If this functionality is unavailable, it may be necessary to use monitoring protocols such as SNMP and/or RMON to gather these statistics. The GSD must tightly restrict the systems able to poll using these methods, because of the inherent insecurities of the monitoring protocols. By observing the trends of these metrics, it may be possible to determine when it is time to increase bandwidth or to purchase systems that are more robust.

- **Availability.** When GSDs are unavailable, the functionality of the network can be dramatically reduced. A simple test of system availability is by using ICMP to Ping the device, so ensuring that the device is responding. This may be for more than one interface depending on the type and functionality of the device. However, this approach can be deceptive; just because the device itself responds does not mean it is properly processing traffic. It is also advisable to send an ICMP or trace route to something on the other side of the interface. Make sure that this other device is actually accepting the packets to ensure valid results. This approach provides a better overall picture of the availability of the GSD.

- **Integrity.** The ability to trust network security systems components is paramount. A rootkit compromising a firewall or GSD is not out of the realm of possibility. These systems should have the ability to protect against modification of system components. This could occur by the device ceasing operation or alerting the change. If this functionality were unavailable, it would be possible to write a script that generates cryptographic hashes of the system components and verifies them against that of a known good version.

26.4.3.2 *Policy.* The GSD policy is the core of providing and protecting allowed paths. These security systems process packets starting at the beginning of the policy

and continuing until there is either a match, or the end of the rule base is reached. As discussed later in this chapter, there are situations in which certain rules process before or after the main rule base.

The ability to manage individual policies on the command line is no longer adequate. Centralized management consoles provide intuitive GUIs to configure and easily manage one or more firewall and GSD policies. Certain platforms also provide the ability to manage policies directly from the device.

Firewall-Allowed Paths. Allowed paths identify specific protocols used to implement communication. In a typical Internet environment, business services require allowed paths, such as HTTP, SSL (HTTPS), SMTP, and DNS. These requirements will vary, but for an environment, each allowed path should directly relate to a required external service.

Starting from an implicit or explicit (depending on the platform) deny-all rule, allowed paths will be added as allow rules, such as PERMIT HTTP, with specifics determined by the following sections.

The systems or groups of systems that send and receive traffic along a specific allowed path are the endpoints of that communication. Although network addressing does not provide effective authentication of systems or users, restrictive endpoints can make it much more difficult for an attacker to exploit an otherwise straightforward vulnerability. It is also important to identify the endpoints carefully, particularly in cases where these endpoints might reside on internal rather than service networks.

The direction of traffic, indicated by the source of the connection initiation, is useful for the rule definitions for several reasons. First, rules can be written so that only responses to internally originated allowed paths are allowed in from the external network, rather than permitting the protocol bidirectionally. In addition, the firewall may process rules at different times based on design or configuration.

Complexity of GSD policies. Standard firewall rules operate on simple Boolean principles: for example, allow network traffic that is going from host X to Y on port Z. The complexities required of GSDs evaluating network traffic are dramatically higher. For example, this evaluation could be a combination of a Boolean test to verify an inbound e-mail address is from a trusted source, to verify message contents are acceptable, and to scan an attachment for viruses. Administrators must understand the higher-level protocols to ensure that the GSD policy matches the types of protections expected and required. As the number and complexity of the rules increases, so do the processing requirements for the GSD.

Change management. Whether managing 1 or 100 policies, the key is to have a process to track policy changes. Change management can be cumbersome but has several advantages. First, it provides back-out information if a change were to cause issues. Second, it provides an audit trail of who requested the change and who changed the policy. Last, it provides a method for streamlining change requests by providing a single method for accepting, reviewing, implementing, and validating policy changes.

Secondary validation. Making changes to a policy tends to be a simple process, such as adding HTTPS access to a new extranet server. However, the more complicated the change, the more likely for mistakes to occur. Having another administrator evaluate the proposed change brings a fresh set of eyes that may catch a small discrepancy that could have negative consequences. This may be another step in the change management process.

26.4.3.3 *Auditing/Testing.*   Is your firewall or GSD working as expected? Would you bet your organization's future on it? Is the firewall truly only letting SMTP

to the e-mail service network? Is the GSD catching the most recent virus-infected attachment? These are simple yet powerful reminders that you must know if the network security devices are working as expected. A proper regimen of auditing and testing will help to answer these questions. Management consoles should provide an audit log that tracks who makes changes to any part of the environment.

Penetration testing and vulnerability assessment are effective ways to determine the validity of policy rules. For example, the firewall should not allow an HTTP connection to a system only with SSL access configured. If this happens, was it a failure of the test rule, is there another rule higher in the rule base erroneously allowing this access, or is something unexpected occurring? The tools and processes must be in place to answer these questions before more serious violations occur.

(For more information on vulnerability assessments, see Chapter 46 in this *Handbook*; for guidance on security audits and inspections, see Chapter 54.)

26.4.3.4 *Maintenance.*

Patching workstations and updating virus definitions are common practice, but this process is even more crucial for systems protecting the network. It is essential to test the validity and stability of an update to ensure that faulty or rogue changes do not interrupt production operations.

Patching. No system is inherently and infinitely secure, and it may be possible to subvert a security device due to some system vulnerability. It is crucial to monitor firewall and GSD Web sites for the most recent operating system and system component patches. By monitoring information sources such as Bugtraq and other message boards, it may be possible to ascertain timely information. This additional research could result in being able to determine and implement a temporary solution until the vendor can provide a permanent fix.

Vendors can take weeks and months to develop and release a patch. In certain cases, third-party patches will become available for unpatched, actively exploited vulnerabilities. While using these patches is an option, it is inadvisable due to the inability to verify the integrity and safety of the patch code. (For more information on patch management, see Chapter 40 in this *Handbook*.)

Pattern updates. Digital threats change constantly. GSDs must be as current as possible to try to protect against these threats. Automatic updates provide the smallest delta of exposure for pattern-based signatures. However, blindly trusting these updates in a production environment may have adverse effects. To avoid issues, there should be a procedure that enables new signatures in monitor-only mode to ensure that they do not cause adverse effects, before implementing full protection. If automatic updates are not a viable option, then testing will require a lab environment or the use of noncritical systems to vet the new patterns.

26.4.3.5 *Logging and Alerting.*

The main purpose of the firewall and GSD is protecting against threats, but it is also necessary to review allowed and denied traffic. In its crudest form, any network security device should provide the ability to log the various functions, from packets allowed and denied, to system changes. In addition, there should be an alerting mechanism that has the ability contact someone (e.g., by e-mail or text message) if something violates a specified threshold.

Whether logs remain local or on a centralized management system, they take up a large amount of disk space, and if ignored, are worthless to keep. There should be a log review process. Instead of trying to determine the anomalies from an entire log set, it is helpful to remove known traffic so as to help expose the unknown or potentially malicious. For example, if you expect outbound SMTP traffic from a single network, you could filter out those known items and then be able to see more easily other nonauthorized hosts or networks originating SMTP traffic.

Logging is a highly subjective but necessary function. Organizations with a large Web-based footprint will generate a large number of HTTP- (and potentially HTTPS-) related events. Each new connection will create an entry in the log. If the firewall is not doing any payload inspection, the logs may be useful only for determining the IP addresses connecting to a Web site. If there are other metrics tracking this, it may be useful to turn off logging on selected rules to reduce the overabundance of logs that are unnecessary to review. Instead, by having a GSD do protocol inspection and logging, there is the potential of gaining a better understanding if packets are expected or malicious. Instead of weeding through many thousands of lines of firewall logs, you now would find immediately actionable information in the GSD log.

Alerting is complementary to and usually depends on the logging mechanism. Once the firewall or GSD generates a log, the administrator can configure alerting options when certain log conditions or thresholds exist. For example, if the administrator wants to know immediately if an internal system process changes state, it may be possible to configure an alerting event that will send an e-mail to notify of the unexpected change. By carefully determining alerting thresholds and notification methods, there is less opportunity to overload the administrator(s) with nuisance alerts.

(For more information on logging, see Chapter 53 in this *Handbook*.)

26.4.3.6 Secure Configurations.
Developing and deploying a firewall or GSD policy is not the only step to protecting the network. Another crucial step is protecting network security devices by creating a secure configuration. In certain cases, the firewall or GSD vendor provides a secured or proprietary version of an operating system. This should not be a green light that the device is secure and ready for production. Rather, this provides even more reason to take the time to evaluate the security posture of the device thoroughly.

Once a secure configuration is set, it can then become the baseline configuration for the remainder of the systems. This provides a standard configuration, helping to ensure that each device functions and is secured in the same manner. There should also be a process to ensure the integrity of the secure configuration as well as to verify and test when valid updates occur.

Default configurations. Default system and policy configuration vary widely. Some policies have an implied deny, while others may allow any. In no case should any network security device deploy with a default configuration. It would also be useful to know if the network security device fails in an open or closed posture. Inline devices may fail open in an attempt to maintain traffic flow. Depending on the network, this may or may not be the optimal response. Although potentially disruptive, a fail-closed posture reduces the likelihood of anomalous or malicious traffic passing undetected.

Implied rules. Implied rules are separate from, but can be a part of, the default configuration. During the processing of the policy, the network security device will process the implied rules prior to packets getting to the policy rules. The implied rules may allow the firewall or GSD to process specific and known administrative traffic without using processing cycles to go through the rule base. It is essential to determine if these rules exist as well as to see if they match the desired security posture. If not, disable or modify the implied rules to fit specific protection needs.

Reduce ancillary exposures. Protecting the network security device is a critical part of the security of the overall infrastructure. The two most common ways to reduce these exposures is through the administrative console and vulnerability assessment.

The management or system console can provide information such as default listening ports, services running, and so on. If a service is not critical to the functioning of the firewall, disable it to remove any threat of its becoming a compromise vector. Only specific administrative hosts should have direct access to the system. As with the firewall and GSD policies, it is useful to test that configuration changes are actually making the device more secure. By conducting a vulnerability assessment, you are able to determine if unexpected services are still available or if other vulnerabilities still exist.

26.4.3.7 Disaster Recovery.   The impact of a firewall or GSD outage can range from an annoyance to a critical event, depending on implementation, necessity, and disaster recovery planning. Since these systems represent part of the backbone of the security infrastructure, it is a necessity to provide continual, protected, network access.

Fail-over/high availability. In situations where reliable access is a necessity, a high-availability (HA) configuration is essential. The HA deployment will typically have an active/standby pair, where the active member is processing live packets and the standby member is ready to take over in the case of a failure of the active member. It is also possible that the standby member is continually synchronizing connection information from the active member. In this scenario, there would be little to no loss of connectivity if the active member fails, because the standby would then become active, already having the connection information to allow continued processing of the current sessions as well as to service new sessions.

Load-balancing. Distributing the load between multiple systems is another way to reduce an availability exposure. If the load equally distributes between two or more systems, the failure of one does not eliminate all access. One caveat is that the load balancer must continue to route each connection to the same system on the back end, to maintain connection information. Otherwise, it may be possible for the load balancer to route traffic to another system that does not know about the established connection. In certain cases, clusters may be able to act as their own load-balancing group.

Backup/restore. Backup and restore functionality is the most rudimentary disaster recover method. If the system crashes or suffers a compromise, there must be a way to recover the system in an efficient manner. By having a reliable backup process, it becomes easier to restore the device configuration in the event of a failure. Depending on the vendor, backups may consist of something as simple as a text file or something more complex like a GZIP file containing the crucial configuration information. The restore process may involve restoring the operating system and the security device configuration. This may be as simple as uploading the backup file, or it may require an out-of-band connection to do prework before uploading a preserved configuration. This process should include a method to move the backup to another system to eliminate a single point of loss.

(For more information on backups, incident response, business continuity planning, and disaster recovery, see Chapters 57, 56, 58, and 59 in this *Handbook* respectively.)

26.5 NETWORK SECURITY DEVICE EVALUATION.   As digital threats continue to evolve, so must network security devices. Internet connectivity costs continue to decline, and the ability to detect complex threats is a necessity. It is a mistake to think the current security systems and infrastructure will be viable for an extended length of time. In essence, the infrastructure is continually under review. One crucial time to revisit these items is when it comes time to replace firewalls and/or GSDs.

Effective security lies at the intersection of protection, functionality, and usability. Every situation will have unique challenges and opportunities to develop a better security solution. The sections that follow provide a framework for evaluating network security devices currently in-service or during a request for information (RFI).

26.5.1   Current Infrastructure Limitations.   It may be technically possible to do a one-for-one replacement of an existing firewall with a GSD, but it is important to review the current infrastructure to ensure maximum effectiveness of the new device(s).

- Are the current network security devices past useful life?
  - This may include devices that are out of warranty, no longer supported by the vendor, and unable to keep up with current needs.
- Is the Internet-facing infrastructure limiting GSD deployment options?
  - A DMZ architecture placing servers between the external router and external interface of the GSD would limit the devices visibility into most of the DMZ network traffic. In addition, placing the GSD in the allowed path of all encrypted traffic relegates the GSD to more of a packet filter than an extensible security solution.

26.5.2   New Infrastructure Requirements.   The dynamics of network and security infrastructures shift constantly. There may already be a known trend of rapidly escalating bandwidth usage or an increased reliance on encrypted communications with business partners and consumers. The prospects of adding the capabilities inherent in GSDs have a dramatic influence on these decisions.

- Are there new demands for more bandwidth, encryption, or traffic inspection?
  - Determining these new demands includes taking into account observed or anticipated growth.
- Is Internet-access redundancy becoming a necessity?
  - For disaster recovery and availability reasons, it may be important to consider a GSD that has built-in redundancy capabilities such as active/passive fail-over or clustering.

26.5.3   Performance.   Technological obsolesce is a common issue throughout the digital world.

- Is the processing power of the current device(s) becoming a bottleneck?
  - Security devices running at high processing or memory usage are good indicators that the system is at, or reaching, its maximum performance threshold.
- Does the device have excess capacity for future needs?
  - Without extra processing capacity, a modest increase in network traffic, or enabling a new feature, could cripple the already resource-starved device.

26.5.3.1   Throughput.   The search for more bandwidth seems endless. Gigabit continues to become obsolete in the core as the price and availability of 10 Gigabit becomes increasingly obtainable. The upcoming 802.11n wireless standard will soon be able to provide speeds over 100 Mbps—at least doubling the current wireless bandwidth maximums. Organizations should take a realistic approach before paying for higher-bandwidth solutions. If an organization is small or has little Web or electronic transactional presence, it is unlikely to produce large amounts of Internet traffic. In this case, there is no reason to purchase a device that guaranties multigigabit performance.

- Does the device meet bandwidth requirements?
    - The GSD should be able to sustain high traffic loads without interruption or service degradation.
- Does the device have excess capacity for future needs?
    - If the device is modular, it may be possible to increase memory, create new network segments, or increase bandwidth by adding or replacing a hardware module.
- Is there sufficient processing power to handle temporary or sustained increases in traffic load?
    - Peaks in network traffic are inevitable. Having additional bandwidth capacity for existing GSD network segments will reduce the impact of these situations.

26.5.3.2 Implications of Added Features.   Many vendors tout near wire speeds—pushing into the multiple gigabits per second. These statistics do not mirror reality, as the standard throughput tests use a 64-byte UDP packet. In actuality, packet types and sizes vary constantly, but the vendors are still able to provide high-bandwidth throughput when using basic security and encryption mechanisms.

- What type of performance impact does activating additional security features create?
    - The greater the number of additional functions and the more detailed the payload inspection, the more impact there will be on the device's processing power and bandwidth.
    - If adding encryption, hardware acceleration, if available, will reduce much of this performance impact.

26.5.4 Management.   GSDs are not set-and-forget or plug-and-play devices. These devices can require substantial planning, configuration, monitoring, and maintenance. Having a robust management platform in a distributed GSD environment is essential to the success of the implementation.

- Does the current environment have the management features needed or required?
    - Self-evaluation of the current management environment is usually fairly easy as the administrator(s) already have likes, dislikes, nice-to-haves, must-haves, and must-goes. This information will provide addition guidance while going through the additional criteria listed here.
- Do you need or want distributed or centralized control of the network security devices?
    - The size and type of GSD deployment is important to consider. It probably does not make sense to use an extensive management platform for a few devices. With larger geographically distributed environments, having centralized control of all devices is necessary for efficient and effective control.

- Do you need redundant management systems?
  - As with GSD redundancy, it may be necessary to have redundant management systems to ensure administrative control and logging of GSD devices. Be sure to review management systems redundancy options as certain instances allow a reduced set of functionality when using the secondary management system.
- Do you want to be able to manage the system from a centralized management console or directly from the device?
  - Certain types of GSDs allow system and policy changes to be made on the device. This feature can be useful during testing but may cause confusion or misconfiguration if not properly understood and managed.
- Do you require encryption to protect management, policy, and logging functions?
  - The need to encrypt sensitive information is second nature to security professionals, but it may be easy to overlook the transmission of GSD management and logging functions. If sent clear-text, it would be possible for someone to monitor these communications and learn a great deal about the network security architecture.
- Do you need a more detailed reporting mechanism?
  - Most logging systems provide the ability to filter data, but it may be useful to do more in-depth reporting. Some example reports include rule-based hit percentages (i.e., what rules receive the highest percentage of hits) or traffic usage statistics (e.g., percent usage by protocol, network segment, or host).
- What amount of granularity do you need for management permissions?
  - If there are only one or a few administrators, this may not be as significant. Larger deployment may have distributed administrators, and the GSD management system should have the ability to restrict access to certain tasks, areas, or logs.
- Do you want drag-and-drop or command-line policy or device management options?
  - Certain GSD brands have the option of configuring devices using a more traditional command line interface and can be useful for quick troubleshooting and scripted changes. A drag-and-drop graphical environment uses the central management systems to create, change, and view policies and logs easily.

26.5.4.1   *Logging and Alerting.*   Although the primary responsibility of the GSD is to stop malicious traffic, logging and alerting play a critical role in the overall security posture. Logging is essential to investigating incidents, viewing trends, and may even be a regulatory requirement. Devices such as Syslog may do text-based logging; others may use a proprietary logging format and database. For more information on logging, see Chapter 53 in this *Handbook*.

- Do you want a graphical interface to view logs?
  - Collecting, searching, and reviewing logs in a text format does have some advantages including consolidation and scripting for log reviews. A graphical interface increases the aesthetic appeal of the logs and can ease viewing by being able to group or filter different types of events as well as add color and graphics that help catch the eyes' attention quicker. These additional features are useful, but the graphical interfaces may be slower to load and may restrict the ability to create complex queries.

- Do you want compressible logs?
  - Even with well-maintained logging standards and grooming processes, many security administrators will attest to the overwhelming volume of logs. Add the additional logs from the remaining GSD functions, and it is possible to create a binary ocean of data. Internal and regulatory requirements may make it necessary to keep this data for long periods of time. Text-based logs lend themselves to high compression ratios and archiving. Some of the proprietary formats may automatically provide some compression but may not be able to match that of nonproprietary formats.

- How do you want to be able to filter logs?
  - Graphical interfaces provide the ability to filter logs based on one or more criteria but can fall short when attempting complex or recursive queries. Text-based logs require scripts to parse through logs, but they have the advantage of being able to use complex queries, and they have the ability to analyze logs virtually anywhere (instead of requiring a specific application or interface).

- How do you want to store logs?
  - Some GSD logging options include storage on the local device, on an integrated logging and management platform, or on a separate storage device. Local storage does create the risk of data loss if the device fails. Sending the logs to other systems increases network traffic, but it allows easier management of the logs.

- What types of alerts do you need?
  - While the logging system provides a location to store and review data, alerting helps to bring information to life without watching logs every minute of the day. It may be possible to create e-mail or SMS alerts if a certain event occurs or goes above or below a configured threshold (e.g., the GSD network throughput is over 85 percent of the maximum possible, or a host is attempting to attack the GSD).

- How granular do you want alerts to be?
  - Simple alerting may be enough, but it may be possible to develop more detailed alerting conditions (e.g., criteria dependencies) to help minimize erroneous alerts.

26.5.4.2 *Auditability.* Having an integrated audit trail of changes made to the GSD environment can be invaluable during an incident. These audit records provide an accounting of what changes occurred, when, by whom, and so on.

- Do you want to be able to audit device changes?
  - Changes to the device itself do not occur nearly as often as changes to policies. Having the ability to collect information about these changes can help uncover system instability, accidental misconfiguration, or malicious intent.

- Do you want to be able to audit policy changes?
  - GSD policies tend to change rapidly as new access requirement develop, new capabilities or requirement appear, and the ever-changing threat landscape progresses. Policy audit trails help to resolve mistakes and to provide archival information of what changes did occur, and when.

- How granularly?
  - Data such as date, time, type of change, to what system(s), and from what administrator are all valuable pieces of information. Increasing auditing granularity also increases the overall number of logs and can increase processing overhead.
- Should the audit logs be independent from the firewall event logs?
  - Having a logging system that automatically separates audit logs from other event logs helps ease viewing and searching. This also creates the ability to provide more granular permissions as to who can see what type of logs.

26.5.4.3 Disaster Recovery. With GSDs providing consolidated security functions, there is a need to incorporate disaster recovery (DR) options into the overall GSD environment to ensure that the new device(s) do not become a single point of failure for the entire organization.

- Do you have any specific disaster recover requirements?
  - As mentioned earlier, different types of redundancy help during DR scenarios. High-availability setups such as active/passive fail-over and clustering will help to increase overall availability.
- Does the device have simple backup and restore mechanisms?
  - The backup mechanism should provide a simple interface to complete backup and restores as well as to move them off the local device for storage and archiving.
- Do you want the ability to do automated restores?
  - Certain GSDs have the ability to do an automated or semiautomated restore using predefined scripts, or through pushable configurations from the management system.
- Should the system fail open or closed?
  - Systems that fail open will allow all network traffic to flow without being evaluated. Systems that fail closed will stop all network traffic. It is important to determine if the uptime advantage of a fail-open system outweighs the problems of network traffic passing uninspected or of downtime associated with a fail-closed system.
- Do you need out-of-band access?
  - During network failure, normal command and control of GSDs can be lost. Having an out-of-band access solution such as a direct serial connection and dial-in solution may provide the ability to monitor and change the system.

26.5.5 Usability. Having a management environment that has every feature imaginable is worthless if it is too complex and convoluted to operate and maintain.

- Is the management console intuitive?
  - The management console should have a consistent and simple interface to interact with the devices and policies. The more intuitive the interface, the less time the administrators will need to spend figuring out how to do necessary tasks.

- Are the primary functions easy to accomplish?
  - Two of the primary functions of administrators are managing policy changes, and changes to log access. The interface should make it easy to follow and edit policies as well as to view and filter logs.

Learning curve. By choosing a GSD vendor that has an intuitive interface and functionality, it should be much easier to learn the environment.

- Is training required to learn the new device(s) and management platform?
  - Even with the best interface and features, it may be necessary for the administrators to get training to use the system more effectively. Check with the vendor to see what training (basic to advanced) is available and at what cost.
- How does the vendor approach security?
  - Every GSD vendor has a different view and different implementation of security features. Some focus primarily on allowing or denying traffic, while others are more concerned with network traffic flows. Moving from one to the other can be confusing, and could slow the conversion.

Features. Although the GSD platform may be able to provide a single source for network security protections, it may not be cost or resource effective to do so, as it must fit the organization's security needs and posture.

- What features do you want the GSD to have?
  - Features may include firewall, IPS, VPN, antivirus, and antispam.
- Are you looking for a device to be an all-in-one solution?
  - The ability to provide a single-solution security platform has merits, but adding each additional feature has an impact on performance, availability, and if implemented improperly, could cause problems.

26.5.6 Price. The cost of a GSD environment varies widely.

- What will be the *true* cost of the upgrade or replacement?
  - Areas for considerations are purchase price for the hardware, price for requested security features, management infrastructure, hardware and software, hardware and software maintenance fees, training costs, direct or third-party support contract, potential downtime during the conversion, and learning curve. Additional features, and elements, if added later, will increase the overall costs.

Initial cost. The initial cost revolves around the entry costs of a GSD deployment.

- How much will the new hardware cost?
  - This includes the price of the GSD and management devices.
- Is there an appliance?
  - The appliance may be a more cost-effective alternative if there are multiple options for deployment.
- How much extra will shipping cost?
  - If this is a distributed deployment, there may be extra shipping costs and tariffs associated with getting the equipment to or from international locations.

- How much will it cost to purchase the features needed?
  - This is highly dependent on the GSD. Certain GSDs come with everything out of the box, while others provide some basic functionality beyond the firewall, VPN, and basic traffic inspection but charge extra to use full functionality of the existing items or add new items.
- Will we need to invest in training to learn the new environment?
  - Training could include attending one or more off-site courses, possibly requiring additional travel, food, and lodging expenses. In some cases, it may be more cost effective to bring a trainer in-house to provide a more tailored, and less expensive, training program.

Ongoing costs.

- How much is the yearly hardware and software maintenance?
  - The maintenance contract is usually negotiable regarding the length of the maintenance term and the costs. These are usually based on a percentage of the purchase price.
- What level of service do you require?
  - GSD vendors normally provide different service levels. Each level corresponds with response times, escalation ability, and access to additional information. The higher the level of service, the more it will cost.
- Can the provider cover you at each location?
  - If necessary, major issues may require a vendor or vendor partner to come on site to complete a repair. If this service is available, specify the total costs, including time and travel expenses, in the maintenance contract
- Is there a requirement for an on site spare or redundant equipment?
  - If the DR plan calls for quick recovery, having spare or redundant equipment on site helps meet this goal. The disadvantage of having a spare, rather than a redundant pair, is that it most likely will become an idle asset. The cost of each of these alternatives, versus a higher-level service contract must be evaluated.
- Are you looking for additional consulting or support time?
  - Vendors and vendor partners may provide blocks of time where a dedicated resource can come on site for additional support or planning needs.

26.5.7 Vendor Considerations.   Being able to trust a vendor's product to protect the organization is crucial. There must be a level of comfort with every aspect of the product and service before turning over the network security reins. In addition to getting the GSD features needed, the vendor providing the solution should have an adequate security foundation, financial stability, and support resources.

- Will this vendor meet the organization's current and future needs?
  - This key question focuses on the vendor's ability to provide a quality product, support that product, and grow with your needs. Be sure to evaluate the vendor's product road map to see how the product (hardware, functionality, cost, etc.) is to evolve and when currently unavailable features will be integrated into the product.

Reputation. Infighting and opinions about the best security platforms abound. The selected vendor should be an active member of the security community.

- Does this vendor have a good reputation in the security community?
  - There is no shortage of product reviews and comparisons to help determine if a product or vendor has a solid reputation for quality and service. These are not the ultimate arbiters of a good product, but they will provide a foundation for additional research.
- What is the vulnerability history of the current and previous systems?
  - Check vulnerability and utilize monitoring sites such as Bugtraq, SecurityFocus, and Milw0rm to see the vulnerability history of current and previous security products.
- What is the mean time to correct vulnerabilities?
  - The optimal time to resolve the vulnerability is immediately (or before it even happens). Check to see how long it takes vendors to respond to and resolve vulnerabilities. This can include verifying that the fix corrected the problem the first time.
- Do they already have deployments similar to yours?
  - If the vendor already has customers with an infrastructure and needs similar to yours, this may provide additional ideas and information to make the deployment more successful.
- Will they provide references?
  - Check with the vendor to see if another company will provide a reference as to their experience with the product and service.

Support options.

- Are there different tiers of initial call support?
  - Determine if all support calls originate through the main support service desk, or if it is possible to have a dedicated resource, possibly one shared among a few other organizations.
- How experienced are the front-line and higher-tier technicians?
  - Ask the vendor to provide information regarding training and experience of the different levels of support technicians.
- Do you have the ability to escalate?
  - Determine if it is possible to escalate an issue immediately, if the local administrators have already gone through standard troubleshooting steps. In addition, find out if there any costs associated with the ability to escalate an issue preemptively.
- Are you willing to work with beta systems?
  - Depending on risk tolerance, being a beta partner with the vendor may provide early access to fixes and enhancements.
- What are current and previous clients' experiences with the quality and availability of support?
  - Again, ask for references to get real-world perspectives on the vendor's support quality and availability.

26.5.8 Managed Security Service Providers.   Organizations now have the ability to transfer varying levels of internal network security responsibilities to a managed security service provider (MSSP). Use of the MSSP may be an opportunity to supplement off-shift log reviews, consolidating, and alerting. In addition, there may be an opportunity to transfer maintenance and change control in order to alleviate resource constraints and knowledge gaps. Choosing to use a service such as this warrants heavy investigation. This brief section gives only a few areas of focus to begin the process.

- What is the MSSP reputation/experience/workload?
  - The MSSP should have trained and experienced personnel to support your GSD infrastructure. Check to see what the number of clients per support resource is, and if other MSSP locations can continue support and operations if a failure occurs at another MSSP location.
- Is it possible to do this securely?
  - This includes transfer of data to the MSSP as well as secure storage, and access to the collected information.
- If necessary, how will the MSSP follow change control?
  - Determine the change control process before turning over the reins to the MSSP. This includes determining change reviews, change windows, change approvals, SLAs regarding time to complete, and so on.
- At what cost?
  - As the number of services and devices increases, so will the cost of doing business with the MSSP. Be sure to investigate the contract to understand all potential fees or additional requirements that may drive up the cost after the signing of the initial contract.

For more about outsourcing security functions, see Chapter 68 in this *Handbook*.

26.6   CONCLUDING REMARKS.   The requirements for network security are changing constantly. Organizations are under continued pressure to meet customer and business partner demands for ready access to information. Technologies such as mobile devices and extranets continue to blur the previously accepted reality of true network borders. Perimeter security is no long as easy as installing a firewall or requiring proxy services for outbound connections. Reliance on a specific technology, or security ideology, is insufficient to protect the information and systems integral to the success of an organization. The frequency and ferocity of both external and internal attacks requires a more robust and flexible mechanism to combat these increasing threats, and the GSD has advanced to provide the current generation of perimeter protection technologies.

The GSD retains all of the previous firewall-based functionality such as allowed path control, VPN services, and network address translation while providing the flexibility to integrate additional services designed to provide visibility into, and protection from, a multitude of threats. The addition of antimalware capabilities provides a new layer of protection by relieving hosts from the responsibility of being the sole providers of full detection, prevention, and remediation services. The integration of proxy services, application and content control, and intrusion prevention allows GSD deployments to simplify the network security architecture as it opens up new inspection and protection opportunities.

Today's threats provide little insight into how protection measures will need to evolve to meet the next generation of attacks and attackers. To remain a viable security option, the GSD security vendors must remain agile. The integration and implementation of new protection measures will need to be simple and seamless. As processing power continues to increase, so will the capabilities of the GSD to take on greater workloads and complexity. Basic content inspection will give way to a greater understanding of, and protection for, data context, value, and flows. The support and protection of worldwide networks will require providing the full existing set of GSD functionality for IPv6 traffic.

No matter the threat, no matter the network, no single device can provide complete security. Each organization must evaluate all avenues of protection to ensure that the technologies deployed meet the security functionality required.

26.7 FURTHER READING

Amon, C., T. W. Shinder, and A. Carasik-Henmi. *Best Damn Firewall Book Period.* Syngress, 2003.

Bishop, M. *Computer Security: Art and Science.* Addison-Wesley, 2003.

Forouzan, B. *TCP/IP Protocol Suite*, 2nd ed. McGraw-Hill, 2002.

McClure, S. *Hacking Exposed: Network Security Secrets & Solutions*, 4th ed. McGraw-Hill Osborne Media, 2003.

Wack, J., K. Cutler, and J. Pole. *Guidelines on Firewalls and Firewall Policy: Recommendations of the National Institute of Standards and Technology.* U.S. Department of Commerce, Special Publication 800-41, 2002; http://csrc.nist.gov/publications/nistpubs/800-41/sp800-41.pdf.

CHAPTER **27**

INTRUSION DETECTION AND INTRUSION PREVENTION DEVICES

Rebecca Gurley Bace

27.1 SECURITY BEHIND THE FIREWALL.   Even today, when asked how they would go about securing a computer or computer network, most people mention firewalls, the first widely accepted network security devices. As network security has become a nonoptional facet of system management, firewall mechanisms of various sorts have become a standard fixture in many networks.

As in any complex protection function, firewalls are necessary but not sufficient to completely protect enterprises from security breaches. Expecting firewalls to provide complete protection is tantamount to expecting guards at the gates of corporate campuses to prevent destructive behavior on the part of those operating vehicles within the facility. A lot can happen as traffic flows between hosts on internal networks; even items that appear benign to gatekeepers can be subverted to carry destructive payloads. Thus, most modern network security architectures include intrusion detection and intrusion prevention systems.

Intrusion detection systems (IDSs) are software or hardware systems that automate the monitoring of events occurring within a computer system or network. IDSs not only collect and synchronize records of these events; they also analyze them for signs of security violations. In strictest terms, vulnerability assessment systems (VASs) are a special class of IDSs in which the system relies on static inspection and attack reenactment to gauge a target system's exposure to specific security vulnerabilities. Intrusion prevention systems (IPSs) are another special class of IDSs in which the system is designed to react to certain detected attacks in a prespecified way.

In recent years, the realm of intrusion detection has broadened and deepened, driven by a number of factors. Security personnel, architectural and operational alike, have gained more experience with IDS technologies, working with commercial product providers to expand product capabilities and management schemes to fit current needs. As operational personnel have become more comfortable in using these systems, they have moved certain IDS capabilities to core network management venues. Finally, threats have evolved, driving needs that IDSs are uniquely qualified to address.

The evolution of IDS has resulted in some changes in nomenclature and tradecraft associated with it. One of these changes is that vulnerability assessment is considered a stand-alone discipline, driven by market needs that are often different from those influencing IDS. Another is that intrusion prevention has evolved as a stand-alone product category, offering the ability to respond automatically to certain classes of attacks. Thus, vulnerability assessment is treated as a separate topic in this *Handbook* (covered in Chapter 46), while both IDS and IPS are discussed in this chapter.

27.1.1 What Is Intrusion Detection?   Intrusion detection is the process of collecting information about events occurring in a computer system or network and analyzing them for signs of *intrusions*. *Intrusions* are defined as violations of security policy, usually characterized as attempts to affect the confidentiality, integrity, or availability of a computer or network. These violations can come from attackers accessing systems from the Internet or from authorized users of the systems who attempt to overstep their legitimate authorization levels or who use their legitimate access to the system to conduct unauthorized activity.

Intrusion detection systems are software or hardware products that automate this monitoring and analysis process.

27.1.2 What Is Intrusion Prevention?   Intrusion prevention is the process of coupling intrusion detection (as defined) with specified responses to certain detected intrusion scenarios. The triggering events can be viewed as a special subset of intrusions, and are often characterized in richer quantitative and qualitative terms than more generic IDS triggers. For example, a specific IPS might focus on monitoring certain types of network traffic. When the rate of a particular traffic type exceeds the anticipated threshold, the IPS would react in a prespecified way (e.g., limiting the rate of subsequent traffic of that type).

27.1.3 Where Do Intrusion Detection and Intrusion Prevention Fit in Security Management?

Intrusion detection is a necessary function in most system security strategies. It (and its offshoot, vulnerability assessment) is the primary security technology that supports the goal of *auditability*. "Auditability" is defined as the ability to independently review and examine system records and activities to:

- Determine the adequacy of system controls
- Ensure compliance with established security policy and operational procedures
- Detect breaches in security
- Recommend any indicated changes[1]

The presence of a strong audit function, in turn, enables and supports several vital security management functions, such as incident handling and system recovery. Intrusion detection also allows security managers a flexible means to accommodate user needs while retaining the ability to protect systems from certain types of threats.

There is some debate over whether IPS will displace IDS in the security management lineup. This displacement is unlikely for the time being, because of the binding between IDS and audit. As security operations become more tightly integrated with traditional system administration and operations, audit functions are necessary to support root cause analysis in diagnosing and addressing system failure. Badly tuned security devices can create problems in operations; it is important to be able to identify and correct such issues quickly and appropriately. Audit functions are also necessary to measure the effectiveness of security measures in mitigating security threats. Although it may appear that transparently detecting and blocking attacks is the optimal security process, such transparency—that is, lack of an audit trail—interferes with demonstrating effectiveness of security measures against real threats. In other words, in order for security management to justify a budget for security measures, it must be able to document and quantify the suitability and effectiveness of such measures. Therefore, regardless of the effectiveness of IPS in blocking attacks, IDS will likely always be necessary to support these audit functions. IDS provides the baseline information on the attack profiles and frequencies that allow managers to demonstrate the effectiveness and return on investment of preventive mechanisms. Without hard evidence of attack frequencies, security managers are left in the position of the man waving a dead chicken around his head while standing on a street corner. Asked why he is doing that, he answers, "To keep the flying elephants away." "But there are no flying elephants," protest the observers. "See? It works!" replies the lunatic. For more information on auditing, see Chapter 54 in this *Handbook.*

Although intrusion detection and intrusion prevention systems are necessary as system security functions, they are not sufficient to protect systems from all security threats. IDS and IPS must be a part of a more comprehensive security strategy that includes vulnerability assessment, security policy and procedural controls, network firewalls, strong identification and authentication mechanisms, access control mechanisms, file and link encryption, file integrity checking, physical security measures, and security training.

27.1.4   Brief History of Intrusion Detection

Intrusion detection is the automation of manual processes that originated in the earliest days of data processing. Joseph Wassermann of the Bell Telephone Company documented the origin of system and security audit as early as the mid-1950s, when the first computerized business system was being designed and implemented.[2]

Auditability was a key security feature from the earliest days of computer security, as proposed in J. P. Anderson's 1973 research study chartered by the U.S. Air Force.[3] Anderson proposed a scheme for automating the review of security audit trails in 1980, in a research report considered by many to be the seminal work in intrusion detection.[4] Dorothy Denning and Peter Neumann led a study of intrusion detection, conducted from 1984 to 1986, producing another seminal work in intrusion detection in 1986, in which Denning proposed a model for intrusion detection.[5]

An instantiation of Denning's intrusion detection model was prototyped as the Intrusion Detection Expert System (IDES) by a team at SRI International. IDES was a hybrid system that constructed statistical profiles of user behaviors as derived from operating system kernel audit logs and other system data sources. IDES also provided a rules-based expert system that allowed users to specify patterns of events to be flagged as intrusions.[6] IDES and the Next Generation IDES (NIDES) system that followed it marked an era in which numerous intrusion detection research projects and prototype systems were developed, including Haystack (Haystack Labs and U.S. Air Force), NADIR (Los Alamos National Laboratory), Wisdom and Sense (Los Alamos National Laboratory and Oak Ridge National Laboratory), ISOA (PRC, Inc), TIM (Digital Equipment Corporation), ComputerWatch (AT&T), and Discovery (TRW, Inc).[7]

In the late 1980s, researchers at the University of California, Davis, designed the first network-based intrusion detection system (initially called the Network Security Monitor, but later renamed NID), which functioned much the same as many current commercial network-based intrusion detection products.[8] A subsequent U.S. Air Force–funded research product, called the Distributed Intrusion Detection System (DIDS), explored coordinating network-based and host-based intrusion detection systems. DIDS was prototyped by teams at the University of California, Davis, Haystack Laboratories, and Lawrence Livermore National Laboratory.[9]

Intrusion prevention was proposed as a logical next step to intrusion detection almost from the start of intrusion detection research. Support for certain models of intrusion prevention grew when concerns regarding attacks on the TCP/IP network infrastructure (e.g., packet flooding and malformed packet attacks) grew in the mid- to late 1990s. Other types of IPS were proposed to deal with kernel-level hacks and information leakage issues.

27.2   MAIN CONCEPTS.

Several strategies used in performing intrusion detection serve to describe and distinguish specific intrusion detection systems. These affect the threats addressed by each system and often prescribe the environments in which specific systems should be used. As noted, intrusion prevention relies first on intrusion detection strategies; thus the differentiators will be highlighted as appropriate.

27.2.1   Process Structure.

Intrusion detection is defined as a monitoring and alarm generation process, and, as such, it can be described using a simple process model. This model is outlined here and will be used to illustrate the fundamental concepts of intrusion detection.

27.2.1.1 *Information Sources.* The first stage of the intrusion detection process comprises one or more information sources, also known as event generators. Information sources for intrusion detection may be categorized by location: network, host, or application.

27.2.1.2 *Analysis Engine.* Once event information is collected, it is passed to the next stage of the intrusion detection process, in which it is analyzed for symptoms of attack or other security problems.

27.2.1.3 *Response.* When the analysis engine diagnoses attacks or security problems, information about these results is revealed via the response stage of the intrusion detection process. Responses span a wide spectrum of possibilities, ranging from simple reports or logs to automated responses that disrupt attacks in progress. The presence of these automated responses defines an intrusion prevention system.

27.2.2 Monitoring Approach. The first major classifier used to distinguish intrusion detection systems is the monitoring approach of the system. Monitoring is the action of collecting event data from an information source and then conveying that data to the analysis engine.

The monitoring approach describes the perspective from which intrusion detection monitoring is performed. The primary monitoring approaches found in intrusion detection systems today are *network based*, *host based*, and *application based*.

27.2.3 Intrusion Detection Architecture. Even in the early days of manual security audit, researchers noted that in order for audit information to be trusted, it should be stored and processed in an environment separate from the one monitored. This requirement has evolved to include most intrusion detection approaches, for three reasons:

1. To keep an intruder from blocking or nullifying the intrusion detection system by deleting information sources
2. To keep an intruder from corrupting the operation of the intrusion detector in order to mask the presence of the intruder
3. To manage the performance and storage load that might result from running intrusion detection tasks on an operational system

In this architecture, the system running the intrusion detection system is called the *host*. The system or network being monitored is called the *target*.

27.2.4 Monitoring Frequency. Another common descriptor for intrusion detection approaches is the timing of the collection and analysis of event data. This is usually divided between *batch-mode* (also known as *interval-based*) and *continuous* (also known as *real-time*) approaches.

In batch-mode analysis, the event data from the information source are conveyed to the analysis engine in a file or other block form. As the name suggests, the events corresponding to a particular interval of time are processed (and results provided to the user) after the intrusion has taken place. This model was the most common for early intrusion detection because system resources did not allow real-time monitoring or analysis.

In real-time analysis, event data from the information source are conveyed to the analysis engine as the information is gathered. The information is analyzed immediately, providing the user with the opportunity to respond to detected problems quickly enough to affect the outcome of the intrusion.

27.2.5 Analysis Strategy.   In intrusion detection, there are two prevalent analysis strategies, *misuse detection* and *anomaly detection.*

In misuse detection, the analysis engine filters event streams, matching patterns of activity that characterize a known attack or security violation. In anomaly detection, the analysis engine uses statistical or other analytical techniques to spot patterns corresponding to abnormal system use. Anomaly detection is based on the premise that intrusions significantly differ from normal system activity. In general, intrusion detection systems rely more heavily on anomaly detection and quantitative measures to detect and block attacks.

27.3 INTRUSION PREVENTION.   As discussed, IPSs are often considered a special case of IDS in which automated responses are specified. However, with the adoption of the first generation of network IPS products, additional specifications for IPSs have evolved in addition to those assigned to IDS.

27.3.1 Intrusion Prevention System Architecture.   As in intrusion detection, most IPSs separate the monitoring and analysis platform from the target platform being monitored. Additional differentiations are drawn between those IPSs that separate the monitoring and analysis platform from the response platform (these are labeled "stand-alone" IPSs) and those that integrate all the functions in a single unit, usually a firewall, network switch, or router (these are labeled "integrated" IPSs.)

27.3.2 Intrusion Prevention Analysis Strategy.   IPSs generally use the same structural approach to data analysis as IDS, but the nomenclature for the analysis strategies differs. IPS analysis schemes fall into two general categories, rate based and content based.

Rate-based IPS analysis makes the decision to block network traffic based on indicators of network load, as measured by statistics such as connect rates and connection counts. This category of analysis is especially useful for detecting packet flood distributed denial-of-service (DDoS) attacks.

Content-based IPS analysis makes the decision to block network traffic based on indicators of anomalous packets and specific content (often represented as IDS signatures.) This approach is useful for detecting malformed packet DDoS and other types of attacks not readily spotted by quantitative measures.[10]

27.4 INFORMATION SOURCES.   Information sources represent the first stage of the intrusion detection process. They provide event information from monitored systems upon which the intrusion detection process bases its decisions. Information sources encompass both *raw* event data (e.g., data collected directly from system audit and logging mechanisms) as well as data output by system management utilities (e.g., file integrity checkers, vulnerability assessment tools, network management systems, and even other intrusion detection systems). In this section, information sources for intrusion detection are classified by location: network, host, or application.

27.4.1 Network Monitoring. The most common monitoring approach utilized in intrusion detection systems is *network based*. In this approach, information is gathered in the form of network packets, often using network interface devices set to promiscuous mode. (Such a device operating in promiscuous mode captures all network traffic accessible to it—usually on the same network segment—not just traffic addressed to it.) Other approaches for performing network-based monitoring include the use of *spanning ports* (specialized monitoring ports that allow capture of network traffic from all ports on a switch) on network switches or specialized Ethernet network taps (e.g., sniffers) to capture network traffic.

27.4.2 Operating System Monitoring. Some monitors collect data from sources internal to a computer. These differ from network-based monitoring in the level of abstraction at which the data is collected. *Host-based* monitoring collects information from the operating system (OS) level of a computer. The most common sources of operating system–level data are operating system audit trails, which are usually generated within the OS kernel, and system logs, which are generated by OS utilities.

27.4.3 Application Monitoring. *Application-based* monitoring collects information from running software applications. Information sources utilized in application-based approaches include application event logs and application configuration information.

Application-based information sources are steadily increasing in importance as systems complexity increases. The advent of object-oriented programming techniques introduces data object naming conventions that nullify much of an analyst's ability to make sense of file access logs. In this situation, the application level is the only place in the system in which one can "see" the data accesses at an appropriate level of abstraction likely to reveal security violations.

One special case of application-based monitoring comprises an entire product category in security. This type of system (sometimes called extrusion detection) monitors data transfers, looking for anomalies associated with data movement across policy boundaries. Such data monitoring is very popular as a compliance mechanism for enterprises dealing with consumer, financial, or other regulated data.

27.4.4 Other Types of Monitoring. As noted, intrusion detection information sources are not limited to raw event data. In fact, allowing intrusion detection systems to operate on results from other systems often optimizes the quality of the intrusion detection system's results. When the data are provided by other parts of the system security infrastructure (e.g., network firewalls, file integrity checkers, virus scanners, or other intrusion detection systems), the sensitivity and reliability of the intrusion detection system's results can increase significantly.

27.4.5 Issues in Information Sources. There are several issues involving information sources for intrusion detection. The major ones that have persisted over the history of intrusion detection include:

- In host-based systems, there must be a balance between collecting enough information to accurately portray security violations and collecting so much information that the collection process cripples the monitored system.

- The fidelity of the intrusion detection process is dependent not only on collecting the appropriate information but on collecting it from appropriate vantage points within the monitored system or network.

- If the IDS is expected to produce event records that will be used to support legal processes, the system must collect and handle event information in a way that complies with legal rules of evidence.

- The information collected by IDSs often includes information of a sensitive nature. This information must be secured and handled in a way that complies with legal and ethical standards.

27.5   ANALYSIS SCHEMES.   Once information sources and sensors are defined and placed, the information so gathered must be analyzed for signs of attack. The *analysis engine* serves this purpose in intrusion detection, accepting event data from the information source and examining it for symptoms of security problems. As mentioned earlier, intrusion detection systems typically provide analysis features that fall into two categories, *misuse detection* and *anomaly detection*.

27.5.1   Misuse Detection.   *Misuse detection* is the filtering of event streams for patterns of activity that reflect known attacks or other violations of security policy. Misuse detectors use various pattern-matching algorithms, operating on large databases of attack patterns or *signatures*. Most current commercial intrusion detection systems support misuse detection.

Misuse detection presumes that there is a clear understanding of the security policy for the system, which can be expressed in patterns corresponding to desirable activity and undesirable activity. Therefore, signatures can be described in terms of "this should never happen" as well as "only this should ever happen." Signatures also can range from simplistic *atomic* (one-part) checks to rather complex *composite* (multipart) checks. An example of an atomic check is a buffer overflow signature, in which one looks for a particular command, followed by a string exceeding a particular length. An example of a composite check is a race condition signature, in which a series of carefully timed commands occur. Signatures are gathered and structured in some way to optimize the filtering of event data against them.

The next requirement for misuse detection is that the event data collected from information sources be encoded in a way that allows it to be matched against the signature data. There are various ways of doing this, ranging from regular expression matching (sometimes called "dirty word" matching) to complex coding schemes involving state diagrams and Colored Petri Nets. State diagrams are a graphical scheme for modeling intrusions. They express intrusions in terms of *states*, represented by nodes or circles, and *transitions*, represented by lines or arcs. Colored Petri Nets are an extension of the state diagram technique that add colored *tokens,* which occupy state nodes, and whose color expresses information about the context of the state.

In some IDSs and content-based IPSs, significant resources are devoted to identifying malformed network packets, especially those in which the format of the content of the packet does not match the format of the service (e.g., SMTP) or of the associated port number of the packet. This malformed packet scheme represents one of the major categories of DDoS attacks, which seek to deny network access to legitimate users.

27.5.2   Anomaly Detection.   *Anomaly detection* is the analysis of system event streams, characterizing them using statistical and other classification techniques in order to find patterns of activity that appear to deviate from normal system operation. This approach is based on the premise that attacks, and other security policy violations, are a subset of abnormal system events.

Several common techniques are used in anomaly detection:

- **Quantitative analysis.** Most modern systems that use anomaly detection provide quantitative analysis, in which rules and attributes are expressed in numeric form. The most common forms of quantitative analysis are triggers and thresholds, in which system attributes are expressed as counts occurring during some time interval, with some level defined as permissible. Triggers and thresholds can be simple, in which the permissible level is constant, or heuristic, in which the permissible level is adapted to observed levels. Network intrusion prevention systems targeting DDoS attacks often use heuristic triggers and thresholds to characterize the normal bandwidth loads, connect rates, and connection counts in network traffic.

- **Statistical analysis.** Most early anomaly detection systems used statistical techniques to identify abnormal data. In statistical analysis, profiles are built for each user and system resource, and statistics are calculated for a variety of user and resource attributes for a particular interval of time (usually a "session," defined as the time elapsed between login and logout).

- **Learning techniques.** There has been a great deal of research interest in using various learning techniques, such as neural networks and fuzzy logic, in performing anomaly detection. Despite encouraging results, there remain many practical impediments to using these techniques in production environments. The practical impediments arise due to the mismatch between those attributes that are suitable for characterization by neural networks and fuzzy logics and those attributes that are actionable by operational personnel and systems. The value of using neural networks (most of them utilizing fuzzy logic) is that they can characterize and recognize very subtle signs of trouble in systems. This is of value in situations where the problems being detected are not subtle. However, in security breaches, the difference between normal behavior and security attack is often influenced by the system context; in these scenarios, few, if any, neural networks can provide insights regarding how they reached their decisions regarding the suspicious events on which they trigger. A security person in an operational context usually requires this sort of insight in order to devise an appropriate reaction to the detected intrusion.

- **Advanced techniques.** Anomaly detection as applied to intrusion detection remains an active research area. Recent research efforts include the application of such advanced analytic techniques as genetic algorithms, data mining, autonomous agents, and immune system approaches to the problem of recognizing new attacks and security violations. Again, these techniques have not yet been widely fielded in commercial IDSs, although they have appeared in special purpose products.

27.5.3 Hybrid Approaches. There are significant issues associated with both misuse detection and anomaly detection approaches to event analysis for intrusion detection; however, combining both approaches provides considerable benefit. The anomaly detection engine can allow the IDS to detect new or unknown attacks or policy violations. This is especially valuable when the target system protected by the IDS is highly visible on the Internet or other high-risk network. In IPS, anomaly detection applied to network traffic attributes allows one of the only means to deal with packet-flood DDoS attacks, a growing concern in today's networks.

The misuse detection engine, in turn, protects the integrity of some anomaly detection engines by assuring that a patient adversary cannot gradually change behavior patterns over time in order to retrain the anomaly detector to accept attack behavior as normal. Thus the misuse detector mitigates a significant deficiency of anomaly detection for security purposes.

27.5.4 Issues in Analysis.   Here are a few of the many issues in intrusion detection analysis:

- Misuse detection systems, although very effective at detecting those scenarios for which detection signatures have been defined, cannot detect new attacks.
- Anomaly detection systems are capable of detecting new attacks but usually have false positive rates so high that users often ignore the alarms they generate.
- Anomaly detection systems that rely on artificial intelligence (AI) techniques often suffer from a lack of adequate training data. (Data are used to define the detector's logic for distinguishing "normal" from "abnormal" events.)
- Malefactors with access privileges to the system, while anomaly-detection systems are being trained, can covertly teach the system to accept specific patterns of unauthorized activities as normal. Later, the anomaly-detection systems will ignore the actual misuse.

27.6 RESPONSE.   The final stage of intrusion detection, response, consists of the actions taken in response to the security violations detected by the IDS. Responses are divided into *passive* and *active* options. The difference between passive and active responses is whether the user of the IDS, or the system itself, is responsible for reacting to the detected violations. As discussed, the former option is associated with classic IDS; the latter is associated with IPS.

27.6.1 Passive Responses.   When passive responses are selected, the IDS simply provides the results of the detection process to the user, who must then act on these results, independent of the IDS. In this option, the user has total control over the response to the detected problem. In some IDSs, the information provided to the user regarding detection results can be divided into *alarms* and *reports*.

27.6.1.1 Alarms.   Alarms are messages that are communicated immediately to users. Commercial IDSs use a variety of channels for conveying these alarms to security personnel. The most common is a message screen or icon written to the IDS control console. Other alarm channels include pagers, e-mail, wireless messaging, and network management system traps.

27.6.1.2 Reports.   Reports are messages or groups of messages that are generated on a periodic basis. They typically document events that have happened in the past and often include aggregate figures and trends information. Many commercial IDS products support extensive reporting features, allowing a user to set up automatic report generation with several versions, each targeting a different level of management.

27.6.2 Active Responses: Man-in-the-Loop and Autonomous. When an IDS provides active response options, these usually fall into two categories. The first requires the IDS to take action, but with the active involvement of an interactive user. This option is sometimes called a man-in-the-loop mechanism. This option is preferred for critical systems, as it allows an operator to track an attacker or intervene in a sensitive situation in a flexible, exacting way.

The other active response option, which usually defines an IPS, provides for preprogrammed actions taken automatically by the system with no human involvement. The automated response option is required when dealing with certain sorts of automated attack tools (viruses or worms) or DDoS attacks. These attacks proceed at machine speed and therefore are outside the reach of a human-controlled manual intervention. As automated and DDoS attacks are the tool of choice for online extortionists, the number of IPSs fielded in commercial networks has grown rapidly over the past few years.

27.6.3 Automated Response Goals. Automated responses support three categories of response goals:

1. Collecting more information about the intrusion or intruder
2. Amending the environment (e.g., changing a switch or router setting to deny access to an intruder)
3. Taking action against the intruder

Although the last of these groups, sometimes labeled *strike back* or *hack back*, occasionally is discussed in security circles, the other options are far more productive in most situations. At this time, taking action against the intruder is considered inappropriate in almost all situations, and should be undertaken only with the advice and counsel of a legal authority.

Amending the environment and collecting more information can occur in either stand-alone or integrated fashions.

27.6.3.1 Stand-alone Responses. Some automated responses are designed to use features that fall entirely within the intrusion detection system. For instance, an intrusion detection system may have special detection rules, more sensitive or detailed than those provided in normal modes of operation. In a stand-alone adaptive response, the IDS would use the more sensitive rules when evidence of the preamble of an attack is detected. This allows the IDS to turn sensitivity levels up only when the additional detection capabilities are needed, so that false alarm rates are reduced.

27.6.3.2 Integrated Responses. The response option often considered the most productive is that of using integrated measures that change the system settings to block the attacker's actions. Such responses can affect the configuration of the target system, the IDS/IPS host, or the network on which both reside. In the first case, the IDS/IPS might change the settings of the logging mechanisms on the target host to increase the amount or type of information collected. The IDS also might change its analysis engine so that more subtle signs of attack are recognized. In another response option reflected in commercial products, the IDS responds to an observed attack signature by querying the target system to determine whether it is vulnerable to that specific attack. Should the vulnerability be present, the IDS directs the target system to correct that vulnerability. In effect, this process provides the target system with an immune function and permits it to "heal" itself, either blocking an attack outright or else interactively repairing any damage done in the course of the attack. Finally, some systems may use special-purpose decoy systems, called *honey pots* or *padded cells,* as diversions for attackers. When these systems are provided, the IDS may be configured to divert attackers into the decoy environments.

In a special case of integrated response seen in many commercial IPS offerings, the IPS is integrated with a switch or router. When an attack is detected, the switch or router is reconfigured on the fly to block the source of the attack. Other IPS offerings that are designed to deal with DDoS attacks use multiple IDS/IPSs to detect the attacks, then manipulate the switching fabric[11] to divert the attacks from the targeted systems. Over time, such IPS features will likely be integrated with network infrastructure devices, as many firewall features already have done.

27.6.4 Investigative Support.   Although the primary design objective of intrusion detection systems is detecting attacks and other possibly problematic system events, information collected and archived by IDSs also can support those charged with investigating security incidents. This functional requirement may levy additional technical requirements on IDSs. For instance, if investigators plan to use IDS monitoring features to perform a targeted surveillance of an attack in progress, it is critical that the information sources be "silent," so that adversaries are not aware that they are being monitored. Furthermore, the IDS monitors must be able to convey information to the investigators through a trustworthy, secure channel. Finally, the IDS itself must be under the control of the investigators or other trusted parties; otherwise, the adversaries may mask their activities by selectively spoofing information sources. Perhaps the most important thing for investigators to remember about IDSs is that the information provided should be corroborated by other information sources (e.g., network infrastructure device logs), not necessarily accepted at face value.

27.6.5 Issues in Responses.   As in information sources and analysis strategies, certain issues associated with IDS response features have endured over the history of intrusion detection. The principal issues are:

- Users' needs for IDS response capabilities are as varied as the users themselves. In some systems environments, the IDS response messages are monitored around the clock, with real-time action taken by system administrators based on IDS alarms. In other environments, users may use IDS responses, in the form of reports, as a metric to indicate the threat environment in which a particular system resides. It is important to consider the specific needs of the user when selecting an IDS.

- Given false-positive error rates for IDSs, response options must be tunable by users. Otherwise, users will simply tune out the IDS responses. This nullifies the value of the IDS.

- When the IDS provides automated responses to detected problems, there is a risk of the IDS itself launching an effective denial-of-service attack against the system it is protecting. For instance, suppose an IDS is configured with rules that tell it "upon detecting an attack from a given IP address, direct the firewall to block subsequent access from that IP address." An attacker, knowing this IDS is so configured, can launch an attack with a forged IP source address that appears to come from a major customer or partner of the organization. The IDS will recognize the attack and then block access from that organization for some period of time, effecting a denial of service.

27.7   NEEDS ASSESSMENT AND PRODUCT SELECTION.   The value of intrusion detection products within an organization's security strategy is optimized by a thorough needs assessment. These needs and security goals can be used to guide the selection of products that will enhance the security stance of the organization.

27.7.1   Matching Needs to Features.   The needs most often addressed by intrusion detection and intrusion prevention systems include:

- Prevention of problem behaviors by increasing the risk of discovery and punishment for system attackers.
- Detection of security violations not prevented (or even, in some cases, not preventable) by other security measures.
- Documentation of the existing level of threat to an organization's computer systems and networks.
- Detection and, where possible, mitigation of attack preambles. (These include activities such as network probes, port scans, and other such "doorknob rattling.")
- Diagnosis of problems in other elements of the security infrastructure (i.e., malfunctions or faulty configurations).
- Granting system security personnel the ability to test the security effects of maintenance and upgrade activities on the organizational networks.
- Providing information about those violations that do take place, enabling investigators to determine and correct the root causes.
- Providing evidence of compliance with a given regulatory requirement for information protection. This represents a significant need for members of various regulated industries, such as banking and health care.

Regardless of which of these specific needs are relevant to the user, it is important to consider the ability of the intrusion detection system to satisfy the needs of the specific environment in which it is installed. A critical part of this determination is considering whether the intrusion detection system has the ability to monitor the specific information sources available in the target environment. What is even more important is whether the organizational security policy translates into a monitoring and detection policy that can be used to configure the IDS (or in the case of an IPS, a monitoring, detection, and response policy.) The structure of the security policy is especially critical to the success of an IPS.

27.7.2   Specific Scenarios.   There is no universally applicable description for computer networks or the IDSs that protect them. There are, however, some common scenarios, given current trends in networking and system usage.

A popular justification for using IDSs early in an organization's security life cycle is to establish the threat level for a given network enclave. Network-based IDSs often are used for this purpose, with monitors placed outside the organizational firewall. Those who are responsible for winning management support for security efforts often find this use of IDSs to be quite helpful.

Many organizations use IDSs to protect Web servers. In this case, the nature of the interactions that the Web server has with users will affect the selection and configuration of the IDS. Most Web servers serve two types of functions: (1) informational (e.g., Web servers that support simple HTTP and FTP queries from users) and (2) transactional (e.g., Web servers that allow user interaction beyond simple HTTP or FTP traffic). Transactional Web servers are usually more difficult to monitor than informational servers, as the range of interactions between users and servers is wider. For critical transactional Web servers, security managers may wish to consider multiple IDSs, monitoring the servers at multiple levels of abstraction (i.e., application, host, and network).

The third scenario involves organizations that wish to use IDSs as additional protection for specific portions of their networked systems. An example of this is the medical organization that wishes to protect the patient record database systems from privacy breaches. In this situation, as in the Web server example just given, it may be advisable to use multiple IDSs, monitoring interactions at multiple levels of abstraction. The output of these multiple systems can be synchronized and inconsistencies noted for a reliable indication of threat levels. Another example that is increasingly common is the organization that is concerned about wireless connectivity. In this case, WiFi monitoring products are commercially available, with information collection and monitoring features that are similar to those of classic IDSs.

In recent years, the expanding use of wireless local area networks (WLANs) in buildings and campuses has stimulated the development of wireless intrusion detection and prevention systems (WIDPSs). The basic principles are the same as for other IDSs and IPSs, with the addition of an interesting wrinkle: The WIDPSs are often used to discover unauthorized access points installed on an organization's WLANs by rogue employees or by intruders. Karen Scarfone and Peter Mell, in their February 2007 edition of NIST SP 800-94, point out that WIDPS sensors should be placed in areas where there should be no wireless network activity. Some security managers walk through and drive around their facilities with WIDPS tools on their laptop computers to identify unauthorized access points. However, completely passive eavesdropping on WLAN traffic cannot be detected.[12]

In extensive networks, should the security architect decide to layer multiple IDSs and IPSs, a security event monitor/security information manager (SIM/SEM) may be required. Such a system would be necessary to consolidate and integrate the results of each IDS/IPS into a coherent set of conclusions.

27.7.3 Integrating IDS Products with Your Security Infrastructure.
As mentioned, an IDS is not a substitute for a firewall, virtual private network, identification and authentication package, or any other security point product. However, an IDS can improve the quality of protection afforded by the other point products by monitoring their operation, noting signs of malfunction or circumvention. Furthermore, an IPS can interact in concert with the rest of the point products to help block an attack in progress.

27.7.4 Deployment of IDS Products.   The first generations of IDS installations have yielded some insights associated with deployment of IDSs. The key points include the location of sensors, scheduling the integration of IDSs, adjusting alarm settings, and outsourcing IDS/IPS services.

27.7.4.1 *Location of Sensors.* There are four general locations for IDS sensors:

1. Outside the main organizational firewall
2. In the network DMZ (inside the main firewall, but outside the internal firewalls)
3. Behind internal firewalls
4. In critical subnets, where critical systems and data reside

As mentioned, IDS sensors placed outside the main organizational firewall are useful for establishing the level of threat for a given network. Sensors placed within the DMZ[13] can monitor for penetration attempts targeting Web servers. IDSs monitors for internal attacks are placed on internal network segments, behind internal firewalls. And for critical subnets, IDS sensors usually are placed at the choke points at which the subnets are connected to the rest of the corporate network. In the case of wireless networking, specialized IPS devices serve to discover and report unauthorized access to networks via WLAN access points or open software access points, through misconfigured WLAN interfaces on laptops and other WLAN devices. These IPS devices are usually placed behind firewalls and distributed across the physical space occupied by the organization and its users.

27.7.4.2 *IDS Integration Scheduling.* Early generations of intrusion detection products proved that integration processes must not be rushed. IDSs still rely on operator interactions to screen out false alarms and to act on legitimate alarms. Hence it is critical that the processes provide adequate time for operational personnel to learn the behavior of the IDS on target systems, developing a sense of how the IDS interoperates with particular system components in different situations. This wisdom applies even more to IPS installation, where a miscue in specifying a response can have disastrous effects on the function of critical networks.

27.7.4.3 *Alarm Settings.* IDSs have significant false alarm rates, with false positive rates as high as 80 percent in some situations. Many knowledgeable IDS integrators advise that alarms be suspended for a period of weeks, even months, as operators gain familiarity with the IDS and target systems. It is especially wise to delay activation of automated responses to attacks until operators and system administrators are familiar with the IDS and have tuned it to the target environment.

27.7.4.4 *Outsourcing of IDS/IPS.* Any discussion of IDS and IPS strategies would be incomplete without mention of outsourcing these security services. There are significant advantages associated with this approach, especially in enterprises too small to afford an extensive security staff. As in other areas of IT outsourcing, one must have an extremely clear idea of the specific security and operational goals desired in order for this approach to be effective. A clearly worded security policy that reflects current concerns is essential. The advantages of outsourcing are many: Managed security service providers usually have considerable experience in dealing with IDS and IPS equipment, their staffs are often well trained and experienced in the use of the equipment, monitoring personnel are usually in attendance around the clock, and contract terms often include specific levels of service agreements.

In the words of a wise CISO, "outsourcing isn't offloading." That means that outsourcing security functions does not relieve you of the responsibility for system security.

It also means that you must exercise due diligence in selecting the service provider, tasking and managing it, and monitoring it to ensure that your policy goals are being well served by the provider.

27.8 CONCLUSION. Intrusion detection and intrusion prevention are valuable additions to system security suites, allowing security managers to spot, and sometimes block, those security violations that inevitably occur despite the placement of preventive security measures. Although current commercial products are imperfect, they serve to recognize many common intrusion types, in many cases quickly enough to allow security personnel and IPSs to block damage to systems and data. Furthermore, as research and development in intrusion detection and prevention continues, the quality and capabilities of available IDSs and IPSs will steadily improve.

27.9 FURTHER READING

Crosbie, M., and E. H. Spafford. "Defending a Computer System Using Autonomous Agents." *Proceedings of the 18th National Information Systems Security Conference.* Baltimore, MD, October 1995.

Jackson, K. A., D. DuBois, and C. Stallings. "An Expert System Application for Network Intrusion Detection." *Proceedings of the 14th National Computer Security Conference.* Washington, DC, October 1991.

Flegel, U. *Privacy-Respecting Intrusion Detection.* New York: Springer, 2007.

Hämmerli, B., and R. Sommer, eds. *Detection of Intrusions and Malware, and Vulnerability Assessment: 4th International Conference*, DIMVA 2007 Lucerne, Switzerland, July 12–13, 2007 Proceedings. New York: Springer, 2007.

Kumar, Sandeep, and E. Spafford. "A Pattern Matching Model for Misuse Intrusion Detection." *Proceedings of the 17th National Computer Security Conference.* Baltimore, MD, October 1994.

Lunt, T., et al. "A Real-Time Intrusion Detection Expert System (IDES)." *Computer Science Lab*, SRI International, Menlo Park, CA, May 1990.

Mukherjee, B., L. T. Heberlein, and K. N. Levitt. "Network Intrusion Detection," *IEEE Network* 8, No. 3 (May–June 1994).

Paxson, V. "Bro: A System for Detecting Network Intruders in Real Time." 7th USENIX Security Symposium, San Antonio, TX, January 1998.

Porras, P., and P. Neumann. "EMERALD: Event Monitoring Enabling Responses to Anomalous Live Disturbances." *Proceedings of 20th National Information System Security Conference.* Baltimore, MD, October 1997.

Scarfone, K. and P. Mell. *Guide to Intrusion Detection and Prevention Systems (IDPS).* NIST Special Publication 800-94. Gaithersburg, MD: National Institute of Standards and Technology, February 2007. Available: http://csrc.nist.gov/publications/nistpubs/800-94/SP800-94.pdf.

Schaefer, M., et al. "Auditing: A Relevant Contribution to Trusted Database Management Systems." *Proceedings of the 5th Annual Computer Security Applications Conference.* Tucson, AZ, December 1989.

Shostack, A., and S. Blake. "Towards a Taxonomy of Network Security Assessment Techniques." *Proceedings of 1999 Black Hat Briefings.* Las Vegas, NV, July 1999.

27.10 NOTES

1. See the Telecom Glossary 2000 from the American National Standards Institute, Inc., www.its.bldrdoc.gov/projects/telecomglossary2000.

2. J. J. Wassermann, "The Vanishing Trail," *Bell Telephone Magazine* 47, No. 4 (July/August 1968).

3. J. P. Anderson, "Computer Security Technology Planning Study Volume II," ESD-TR-73-51, Electronic Systems Division, Air Force Systems Command, Hanscom Field, Bedford, MA 01730 (October 1972).

4. J. P. Anderson, *Computer Security Threat Monitoring and Surveillance* (Fort Washington, PA: James P. Anderson Co. April 1980).

5. D. Denning, "An Intrusion Detection Model," *Proceedings of the 1986 IEEE Symposium on Security and Privacy* (Washington, DC: IEEE Computer Society Press, 1986).

6. T. Lunt et al., "A Real-Time Intrusion Detection Expert System (IDES)," Computer Science Lab, SRI International, May 1990.

7. B. Mukherjee, L. T. Heberlein, and K. N. Levitt, "Network Intrusion Detection," *IEEE Network* 8, No. 3 (May–June 1994).

8. L. T. Heberlein, K. N. Levitt, and B. Mukherjee, "A Network Security Monitor," *Proceedings of the 1990 IEEE Symposium on Research in Security and Privacy,* Oakland, CA, May 1990.

9. S. Snapp et al., "DIDS (Distributed Intrusion Detection System) Motivation, Architecture, and an Early Prototype," *Proceedings of the 14th National Computer Security Conference,* Washington, DC, October 1991.

10. "IPS Quadrant," *Information Security Magazine* (July 2004); http://infosecuritymag.techtarget.com/ss/0,295796,sid6_iss426_art880,00.html.

11. A. Freedman, *Computer Desktop Encyclopedia*, v21.1, 2008 (www.computerlanguage.com) provides this definition: "Switch fabric—(1) The interconnect architecture used by a switching device, which redirects the data coming in on one of its ports out to another of its ports. The word 'fabric' comes from the resulting criss-crossed lines when all the inputs on a switch with hundreds of ports are connected to all possible outputs. (2) The combination of interconnected switches used throughout a campus or large geographic area, which collectively provide a routing infrastructure."

12. K. Scarfone and P. Mell, *Guide to Intrusion Detection and Prevention Systems (IDPS).* NIST Special Publication 800-94 (Gaithersburg, MD: National Institute of Standards and Technology, February 2007); http://csrc.nist.gov/publications/nistpubs/800-94/SP800-94.pdf, pp. 5–12 to 5–13.

13. The DMZ is a reserved area in some network architectures, in which Web servers are often placed, separated from the Internet by one firewall system and separated from the internal corporate network by another firewall.

CHAPTER **28**

IDENTIFICATION AND AUTHENTICATION

Ravi Sandhu, Jennifer Hadley, Steven Lovaas, and Nicholas Takacs

28.1 INTRODUCTION. *Authorization* is the allocation of permissions for specific types of access to restricted information. In the real world, authorization is conferred on real human beings; in contrast, information technology normally confers authorization on *user identifiers* (IDs). Computer systems need to link specific IDs to particular authorized users of those IDs. Even inanimate components, such as network interface cards, firewalls, and printers, need IDs. *Identification* is the process of ascribing an ID to a human being or to another computer or network component. *Authentication* is the process of *binding* an ID to a specific entity. For example, authentication of a user's identity generally involves narrowing the range of possible entities claiming to have authorized use of a specific ID down to a single person.

The focus of this chapter is on person-to-computer authentication. In practice, we also need computer-to-person authentication to prevent spoofing of services on a network. This type of authentication is increasingly important, especially on open networks such as the Internet, where users may be misled about the identity of the Web sites they visit. For example, some criminals send unsolicited e-mail messages in Hypertext Markup Language (HTML) to victims; the messages include links that are labeled to suggest an inoffensive or well-respected Web site, but the underlying HTML actually links to a fraudulent site designed to trick people into revealing personal information, such as credit card numbers or details to support theft of identity. More generally, computer-to-computer mutual authentication, typically in both directions, is essential to safeguard critical transactions such as those of interbank transfers and business-to-business electronic commerce.

In the early decades of computer usage, most computers authenticated users who accessed mainframes from within a single enterprise. User IDs therefore could be assigned in a centralized and controlled manner. Even so, identifiers have never necessarily been unique, for there is no obligatory one-to-one relationship between a user ID and a human being's real-world identity. For example, several people could share an account such as inventory_clerk without interference from the computer; at most, the operating system might be configured to prevent simultaneous sharing of an ID by limiting to one the number of sessions initiated with a specific ID.

Conversely, a single user often has many user IDs. For example, there may be unique identifiers for each of dozens of Web sites for music clubs, book clubs, enterprise e-mail, and so on. Even on the same computer, a given user might have several accounts defined for different purposes; jane_doe and jdoe might be identifiers for two different application packages on a system. These multiple identifiers cause problems for administrators if they do not know that the same user is associated with the different IDs; they also cause practical problems for users who have to use different authentication methods for a range of IDs. One of the critical goals of today's identification and authentication (I&A) research and development is to develop reliable and economical methods for *single signon*, whereby users would not have to reidentify and reauthenticate themselves when accessing different computer systems linked into an Internet. For details of I&A in facilities security, see Chapter 23 in this *Handbook*.

28.2 FOUR PRINCIPLES OF AUTHENTICATION.   Authentication of a claimed identity can be established in four ways:

1. What only you know (passwords and passphrases)
2. What only you have (tokens: physical keys, smart cards)
3. What only you are (static biometrics: fingerprint, face, retina, and iris recognition)
4. What only you do (dynamic biometrics: voice, handwriting, and typing recognition)

In each approach, the assumption is that no one else but the authorized user of an identifier has access to the password or token and that the probability of simulating static or biometric data is acceptably low.

These methods can be combined; for example, passwords often are combined with tokens or biometrics to provide stronger authentication than is possible with either one alone. A familiar example of this *two-factor authentication* occurs with automatic teller machine (ATM) cards. Possession of the card (the token) and knowledge of the personal identification number (the PIN, corresponding to a password) are required to access a user's bank account.

This chapter introduces each of these four authentication methods and provides additional details for each. For discussions of methods of bypassing and subverting identification and authentication techniques, see Chapter 15 in this *Handbook*.

28.2.1   What Only You Know.   Password- or passphrase-based authentication is so widely used that any person who has had any contact with computers and networks probably has had several passwords. Although password technology often is poorly administered and insecure (and frustrating) for users and administrators, passwords can be deployed much more securely and conveniently than they usually are. Many security professionals have felt and hoped for years that passwords would eventually be phased out, to be replaced by tokens or biometrics, but the consensus today is that passwords are not likely to disappear soon and that they will continue to be the dominant authentication technique for years to come.

Demonstrating knowledge of a password does not directly authenticate a human being. It simply authenticates knowledge of the password. Unauthorized knowledge of, or guessing at, a password can lead to impersonation of one user by another; this is called *spoofing*. The theft of a password can be difficult to detect since it is not a tangible asset. Passwords are also very easy to share. It is common for senior executives to give their passwords to their assistants to facilitate their work, even though assigning proxy privileges would be as effective and more secure.

28.2.2   What Only You Have.   Authentication based on possession of a token is used where higher assurance of identity is desired than is possible by passwords alone. As with passwords, possession of a token does not directly authenticate a human being; rather it authenticates possession of the token and ability to use it. Sometimes a password or PIN is required to use the token, thus establishing two-factor authentication; the theory is that the requirement to have both elements decreases the likelihood of successful spoofing.

Tokens can take on a variety of forms. The oldest token is the physical key for a physical lock, but these are not often used for securing computer systems. *Soft tokens* are carried on transportable media or even accessed over a network from a server. Soft tokens contain only data; they typically require a password to access the contents. Modern tokens are usually implemented in self-contained hardware with computing capability. Examples include:

- Credit card–size devices with a liquid crystal display (LCD) that display pseudo-random numbers or other codes.
- LCD devices in the shape of a key fob using the same algorithms as the credit card–shape devices.

- Hardware devices called *dongles* that plug into input-output ports on computers. Examples include dongles for serial ports, parallel ports, Universal Serial Bus (USB) ports, and PC-card interfaces.

All tokens used for computer authentication require software to process information residing in or produced by them. The most significant distinction is whether the tokens require electronic contact with the authentication system. *Contactless* tokens are easier to deploy because they do not require specialized readers. For example, the credit card and key fob pseudorandom number generators simply require the user to enter the visible code in response to a prompt from the authentication software. Contactless tokens are more limited in function than *contact tokens*. For instance, a contact token can be used to create digital signatures whereas a contactless token cannot do so practically.

In cyberspace, a token does not authenticate by means of physical characteristics. Rather the token has some secret, either exclusive to itself or possibly shared with a server on the network. Authentication of the token is really authentication of knowledge of the secret stored on the token. As such, authentication based on possession of a token is tantamount to authentication based on what the token knows. However, this secret can be longer and more random than a secret that a user has to retain in human memory, such as a password. Unfortunately, building cost-effective and secure tokens from which the secret cannot be extracted by tampering or by brute-force guesswork has proven much more difficult than initially anticipated. In the early 1990s, many security professionals believed that tokens would replace passwords; in fact, however, although tokens continue to be an attractive authentication technology, they probably will not become pervasive soon because of the consistent (but highly debatable) belief that passwords are less expensive to implement and manage than other methods of authentication (see Section 28.7).

28.2.3 What Only You Are.

Biometrics takes authentication directly to the human being. This topic is covered more extensively in Chapter 29 in this *Handbook*, but the basics can be mentioned here.

As humans, we recognize each other by a number of characteristics. Biometric authentication seeks to achieve a similar result in cyberspace. A *static biometric* is a characteristic of a person such as fingerprint, hand geometry, or iris pattern; more dramatically, it could be the DNA of an individual. The likelihood of two individuals having identical fingerprints, iris patterns, or DNA is minuscule (with exceptions for genetically identical siblings). Biometrics requires specialized and expensive readers to capture the biometric data, making widespread deployment difficult.

Biometrics also suffers from the problems of replay and tampering. Thus, the biometric reader must itself be trusted and tamper-proof; this reduces the likelihood of an attacker capturing the data input and replaying it at a later time, or creating false biometric profiles to trick the system into accepting an imposter. Moreover, the biometric data themselves must be captured in proximity to the user to reduce the likelihood of substitution, such as the case in stolen blood used to fool a DNA-based biometric system. If the data are transmitted to a distant server for authentication, the transmission requires a secure protocol, with extensive provisions for time-stamping and rapid expiration of the data.

28.2.4 What Only You Do.

Dynamic biometrics captures a dynamic process rather than a static characteristic of a person. A well-known example is that of signature dynamics. Signature dynamics involves recording the speed and acceleration of a person's hand as a signature is written on a special tablet. Rather than merely the shape of the signature, it is the dynamic characteristics of motion while writing the signature that authenticates the person—motions that are extremely hard to simulate. Another possibility is to recognize characteristics of a person's voice as he or she is asked to read aloud some specified text. Keystroke dynamics of a person's typing behavior is another alternative.

As in all other forms of authentication, dynamic biometrics depends on exclusion of capture and playback attacks, in which, for example, a recording of someone's voice might be used to fool a voice-recognition system. Similarly, a signature-dynamics system might be fooled by playback of the data recorded from an authentic signature. Encryption techniques help to make such attacks more difficult.

Security experts agree that biometrics offer a stronger guarantee of authentication, but deployment on a large scale remains to be demonstrated. Whether this technology becomes pervasive ultimately may be determined by its social and political acceptability as much as by improved technology.

28.3 PASSWORD-BASED AUTHENTICATION. Passwords are the pervasive technology for authentication in cyberspace today. At a conservative estimate, there are close to a billion password-based authentications per day. Examples include the vast number of Internet users and the number of passwords each one uses every day. However, the current deployment of password technology needs to be improved in many ways. Today users must remember too many identities and corresponding passwords. Also, the deployed technology is more fragile than it needs to be; for example, many users choose passwords that can be guessed easily. Passwords are never going to be as secure as the strongest biometric systems, so one would not use them as the sole basis for, say, launching nuclear missiles. However, their use can be made strong enough for many less critical transactions.

The next sections review the major risks of password use and their mitigation by technical, social, and procedural means.

28.3.1 Access to User Passwords by System Administrators. One of the most dangerous practices in use today is the storage of unencrypted user passwords accessible to system administrators. In some sites, new users receive passwords that are assigned and written down by system administrators. If these passwords are used only once, for the initial logon, the user can be forced to choose or create a truly secret password that no one else knows. However, in many such sites, administrators keep control of a paper or electronic record, usually for quick access when users forget their own passwords. Such access completely destroys an important element of I&A: *nonrepudiation*. If someone else has access to a password, then authorized users can reasonably *repudiate* transactions by claiming that their identities were spoofed. It is difficult to counter such repudiation, especially in a court of law considering an accusation of malfeasance by the authorized user of that password. In general, passwords that will be used repeatedly should not be written down, and they should not be accessible to system administrators. Critical passwords can be written down, stored in tamper-proof containers, and locked away where at least two signatures will be required for retrieval in case of emergency.

28.3.2 Risk of Undetected Theft. Perhaps the biggest intrinsic risk with passwords is that they can be stolen without knowledge of the user. Observation of someone typing in a password is sufficient to leak it. This can happen surreptitiously without the victim's explicit knowledge. A related risk is disclosure of a password to an attacker who persuades the legitimate user to reveal it by posing as a systems administrator who needs the password to do something beneficial for the user. Loss of a physical token eventually may be discovered, since it is missing, although the possibility of cloning these devices remains. Loss of a password, however, can be discovered only by detecting its misuse or by finding it in the possession of an unauthorized user (e.g., in a list of passwords cracked by using a dictionary-based *password-cracking* program, as described in Section 28.3.6).

There are several mitigations of this risk. First, user education and awareness are critically important. People need to treat important secrets with the care they deserve. In an unsafe environment, a password should be typed in discreetly. Efforts to be discreet should be positively reinforced while negligence in exposing passwords during entry should be considered akin to bad social behavior.

User education and awareness, although extremely important, can never be the whole solution. People will inevitably slip up and make mistakes. Some of us are more negligent than others. Others will be observed surreptitiously. In some cases passwords will be revealed to computers with Trojan horses (see Chapter 16 in this *Handbook*) that capture them. Technologists must pursue technical and human solutions to mitigate these risks.

Since some losses of control over passwords are inevitable, it logically follows that password-based authentication should be used only in situations where misuse detection is not only feasible but actually convenient to do in real time. To make this possible, the system architecture should centralize the information needed for misuse detection in one place. If the required information is dispersed across many servers, it will be difficult to coordinate the different audit trails. Traditionally, users of password systems have not considered the need for misuse detection. However, modern security is firmly based on a mix of prevention and detection techniques. Security professionals should apply similar thinking to authentication systems. Ease of misuse detection should be an important criterion in the design of any authentication system. For password-based systems, misuse detection capability should be considered an essential requirement. (For information on intrusion-detection systems, see Chapter 27 of this *Handbook*.)

What else can system designers do to mitigate this risk? It should be made easy for users to change their passwords themselves. Having a system administrator change a password that will be used more than once is illogical.

If a user feels that a password may have been compromised, changing it should be a simple matter. In particular, the system should never prevent a user's attempt to change a password. Some deployed systems will deny change of a password if the password was changed recently, say in the past 24 hours. Although there are reasons for this kind of restriction, it may create a bigger risk than the one it purports to prevent.

Users should be encouraged to change their passwords fairly often; a typical allowable lifetime for a password is between 30 and 90 days. Without occasional changes, a compromised password could be held until the malicious attacker finds opportunity to use it. Frequent changes to passwords reduce the window of opportunity for such attackers.

28.3.3   Risk of Undetected Sharing.   Another major risk of passwords is the ease with which they can be shared. There are many examples of sharing between executives and their secretaries, between physicians and office staff or nurses, between professors and their secretaries or students, and among coworkers in any activity. User education and strict policies against password and account sharing are obvious first steps to deter this possibility. Strict policies can be effective within an organization, but their deterrent effect may not carry over to large consumer populations. Misuse detection also can be employed to enforce a strict policy.

The root cause of password sharing within an organization is the lack of effective delegation mechanisms whereby selected privileges of one user can be delegated to another. Better authorization mechanisms could eliminate much of the perceived need for password sharing. It should be possible for secretaries to read their boss's e-mail under their own identity and password. In fact, the bosses should be able to segregate the e-mail that the secretaries can read while denying access to more sensitive e-mail. Moreover, reading the boss's e-mail should be possible without allowing the secretary to send e-mail under the boss's identity; a proxy privilege could allow secretaries to answer their boss's e-mail while signing the replies with their own names. In the nonelectronic world, secretaries routinely answer mail for other people without impersonating them, and this should be the practice with computers as well.

Sharing of passwords among consumers is likely to occur when the cost to consumers is minimal. Although consumers are unlikely to share passwords for an online bank or brokerage account with others, they may be willing to share passwords for an online subscription service, possibly with many friends. A dishonest consumer may even make a business of reselling the service. One way to deter such piracy would be to tie exposure of the password to exposure of a sensitive secret of the consumer, such as a credit card number. Few people, criminal or not, would hand over a password that includes their own credit card number.

Another approach that reduces account sharing is one-time passwords that are generated by inexpensive tokens that have recently been distributed to consumers by Web merchants and banks (e.g., Citibank starting in May 2006) as a method for authenticating identity.[1] These tokens generate random passwords that change every minute or so and that can be traced to the specific unit that creates them—and that unit can be tied precisely to the original recipient. Not only does such a system make password sharing virtually impossible, but a shared password can be traced directly to the violator of the terms of use and result in legal action and fines. For more on one-time passwords, see Section 28.4.1.

28.3.4 Risk of Weakest Link. One of the frustrations of passwords is that users have to remember too many. Thus, users tend to repeat selection of the same password at multiple sites. This is a very insidious risk. Exposure of a user password at a poorly maintained site can lead to penetration of the user's account at numerous other sites. It is not easy to deploy technical measures to protect directly against this risk. A particular site can force a user to pick a complex password or can even choose the password for the user. However, it cannot prevent use of the same password elsewhere. This is one area where user education, awareness, and self-interest are paramount. Malicious attackers can set up rogue Web sites easily, to entice users to register for attractive services, whereupon the user's password for other sites may be revealed.

A technical solution to mitigate this problem is to avoid the requirement that a user has to register at multiple sites with user IDs and passwords. Instead, the user should register at a few trusted sites, but the user ID should be usable at multiple sites by secured sharing of assurances that the user has in fact been identified and authenticated sufficiently for business to continue. This is essentially what public key infrastructure (PKI) seeks to do. Once a user has identified him- or herself to a provider of such electronic credentials (client certificates), the certificate becomes a method for authentication, For example, some banks provide a service that allows a user to create a unique number that can substitute for their credit card number in a particular transaction. The user authenticates to the bank site, obtains a unique certificate that substitutes for the credit card number, and gives it to the merchant. The merchant can verify that it generates a valid transaction authorization but never knows the original credit card number. With authentication based on client certificates, it is not necessary to expose a user's password to multiple sites. An effective marriage of passwords and PKI would reduce the exposure to the weakest link. For more details of PKI, see Chapter 37 in this *Handbook.*

A similar approach stores sensitive information in one place and then directs businesses to that place for payment information. For example, today a number of systems (e.g., PayPal) allow a user to register credit card information once, with a trusted service, and then pay online retailers (e-tailers) via that service.

28.3.5   Risk of Online Guessing.   Authentication systems are susceptible to guessing attacks. In *online guessing,* an attacker tries to authenticate using a valid user ID and a guessed password. If the password has been poorly selected, the attacker may get lucky. The attacker also may be able to exploit personal knowledge of the victim to select likely passwords. This approach exploits the documented tendency of naive users to select passwords from lists of obvious words, family, friends, pets, sports, commercial brands, and other easily obtained information. For example, studies of password files consistently show that the most frequently selected password in the world is "password"; the second most frequent is the user ID itself or the user ID backward. An account with the same password as the user ID is often called a *Joe account*, as in User ID: joe; Password: joe.

Another kind of password vulnerable to guessing is a password assigned by default; for example, many software installations create accounts with the same password on all systems. Documentation usually warns users to change those *canonical passwords*, but many people ignore the warning. Canonical passwords are particularly dangerous when they grant access to powerful accounts, such as root accounts or to support functions.

The first line of defense against online attacks is to enforce password complexity rules, in addition to user education and awareness. Many systems today require a minimum of eight-character passwords with a mix of upper- and lower-case letters, numerals, and possibly special characters. Nonetheless, online guessing attacks are still possible, and system logging (see Chapter 53) or application logging (see Chapter 52) can be helpful in identifying successful impersonation. For example, log files may show that a particular user has never logged on to a particular account outside working hours, yet someone has logged on as that user in the middle of the night.

Some systems react to online attacks by a simple rule that locks the account after a certain number of failed attempts. This rule may have been borrowed from a similar rule with ATM cards. The rule actually makes sense in the context of ATMs, with two-factor authentication based on possession of the card and knowledge of the PIN. However, in a password-only scheme, the "three strikes and out" rule can lead to denial of service to legitimate users. An attacker can easily lock up many accounts by entering three wrong passwords repeatedly. A more graceful rule would slow down the rate at which password guessing can be attempted, so that a legitimate user may be perceptibly slowed down in authentication but not denied. For example, locking an account for a couple of minutes after three bad passwords suffices to make brute-force guesswork impractical.

In addition, intrusion-detection systems can be configured to alert system administrators immediately upon repeated entry of bad passwords. Human beings then can intervene to determine the cause of the bad passwords—user error or malfeasance.

28.3.6   Risk of Off-Line Dictionary Attacks.   The paramount technical attack on password-based authentication systems is the *dictionary attack*. Such attacks start with copying the password file for a target system and placing it on a computer under the attacker's control. The password file normally uses *one-way encryption* that allows the system to encrypt an entered password and compare it to the encrypted form of the legitimate password. If the two encrypted strings match, the entered password is presumably correct, and so the system authenticates the user ID.

The dictionary attack is described as off-line because the attacker obtains the necessary information to carry out the attack and then performs computations off-line to discover the password from this information. It is a guessing attack because the attacker tries different likely passwords from an extensive list of possible passwords (the *dictionary*). The list of likely passwords is called a dictionary because it includes words from one or more natural languages, such as English and Spanish; specialized versions used with *password-cracking* programs may sort words by frequency of use rather than alphabetically to speed up successful guesses.

The initial response to dictionary attacks was to stop users from selecting passwords that could be cracked via a dictionary attack. In essence, the system would try a dictionary attack; if it succeeded, it would prohibit the user from selecting this password. This is not a productive approach because attackers' dictionaries are often ahead of the system's dictionaries. The productive approach is to prevent the attacker from collecting the information necessary to carry out the dictionary attack.

Designers of password-based authentication systems were slow to recognize the risk of dictionary attacks. It has long been understood that passwords should not be stored on a server in cleartext because this becomes a single point of catastrophic failure. Time-sharing systems of the early 1970s stored passwords in a "hashed" form. Knowledge of the hashed form of a password did not reveal the actual password. Authentication of passwords was achieved by computing the hash from the presented password and comparing with the stored hash. The UNIX system actually made the hashed form of user passwords easily readable, since reversing the hash was correctly considered computationally infeasible. However, knowledge of the hashed form of a password is sufficient for dictionary attacks. The attacker guesses a password from a list, or dictionary, of likely passwords, computes its hash, and compares it with the stored hash. If they match, the attacker's guess is verified; otherwise the attacker tries another guess. Since the late 1980s, UNIX systems have stopped making the file of hashed passwords easy to read, so this vulnerability has been reduced.

UNIX also introduced the concept of a *salt* to make dictionary attacks more difficult. The user password and a random number called the salt are hashed together and stored on the server. The salt itself is also stored on the server. To authenticate a user, the presented password and the stored salt are hashed and compared with the stored hash value. Use of a salt means that a separate dictionary attack is required for every user, since each password guess must be hashed along with the salt. Otherwise, the same attack could be run simultaneously against multiple presented passwords.

28.3.7   Risk of Password Replay.   If a password is transmitted in cleartext from client to server, it is susceptible to being picked up on the network by an intruder. This is called *password sniffing*. Many systems require the password to be sent to the server in cleartext. Others require transmission of a hash of the password (usually without a salt). Transmitting the hash of a password is risky for two reasons:

1. The hash is sufficient for a dictionary attack unless a salt is used and kept secret.
2. The attacker does not even need to recover the password. Instead, the attacker can replay the hash of the password when needed.

Many existing systems are susceptible to sniffing of passwords on the network in cleartext or hashed form. Fortunately, technical solutions to this problem do exist.

One approach to the replay threat is to use the server's public key to encrypt any transmission of password-related information to the server: Thus, only the server can decrypt the information by using its private key. This is essentially what server-side SSH (Secure Shell) and server-side SSL (Secure Sockets Layer) do. The server-side mode of both SSL and SSH require the server to have a public key certificate. The client-side mode of these protocols requires that the client also have a public key certificate. This approach can be effective but has its own risks.

An alternate approach is to avoid transmitting the password but instead to employ a protocol that requires knowledge of the password to run successfully. One of the earliest and best-known systems to take this approach is Kerberos. In this system, a user's password is converted to a secret key on the client machine and also stored on the Kerberos server. When the user requests authentication, the Kerberos server sends the user's machine a secret session key encrypted using the shared secret key derived from the user's password. The ability to decrypt this message correctly demonstrates knowledge of the password without actually transmitting it, in cleartext, hashed, or encrypted form. Unfortunately, the Kerberos protocol is susceptible to dictionary attacks; any client machine can pretend to be any user and can obtain the necessary information required for a dictionary attack.

Kerberos also does not use a salt, so the same dictionary attack can be applied to multiple users at one time. Kerberos Version 5 provides for a preauthentication option, which makes it somewhat harder to gather the information for a dictionary attack. The data are no longer available by simply asking the Kerberos server for them; instead they must be sniffed on a network. Recent experiments have shown that dictionary attacks on Kerberos are very practical, so this is a serious vulnerability of a widely deployed password-based authentication system.

Since the early 1990s, many password-based authentication protocols have been published that do not suffer from the dictionary attacks to which Kerberos is so vulnerable. In particular, *zero-knowledge password proofs* are based on the idea that two parties (computers and people) can demonstrate that they know a secret password without revealing the password. These methods depend on the ability to establish that the two parties both independently selected the same number—but without knowing what the specific number is.[2] One popular conceptual model of this process is the zero-knowledge password proof, which runs as follows:

1. Two people want to test whether they share a secret number (in this thought experiment, a single digit between 1 and 10). In this example, the shared number is 3.
2. The two people have a deck of 10 blank cards.
3. The first person counts down to the third card and makes a mark on the right edge of that card.

4. The deck of cards is arranged so that the second person can mark the left edge of the cards but cannot see the right edge.

5. The second person also counts down to the third card (in this example) and marks the left edge.

6. The card deck is shuffled so that the sequence order is lost and then displayed to both parties.

7. If a single card has a mark on both the right edge and the left edge, then the two parties share the secret number, but neither had to reveal exactly which number it was.[3]

It will be interesting to see if this approach to authentication can be implemented on actual computers and if it is commercially used on a significant scale in the coming years.

28.3.8 Risk of Server Spoofing. As mentioned earlier, one widely used approach to preventing password exposure in transit on a network is to send passwords from client to server encrypted using the server's public key. The server, which has the corresponding private key, can decrypt the password to recover it. Knowledge of the public key is not sufficient for a spoofer to determine the private key. Naive protocols for protecting the private key can be susceptible to replay attacks. However, there are two well-designed protocols in widespread use today.

Server-side SSL is the protocol that has been used by most Web surfers. In this protocol, the server's public key is used to secure transmission of the user's password from client to server. Like all public key–based schemes, the Achilles' heel of this protocol lies in authentic knowledge of the server's public key. The technology of public key certificates seeks to provide public keys with good assurance of the identity of the server to which they belong. A full discussion of issues with Public Key Infrastructure technology appears in Chapter 37, but it suffices to observe that there are pitfalls with the use of certificates for authentication of servers. A rogue server can collect a user's password by pretending to be something other than what it is. Relying on the look and feel of a Web page for server authentication is hardly sufficient, since it is easy to copy an entire Web page for use as a decoy and to establish confidence before capturing confidential information. An improvement on Web site authentication is to associate a specific image and identifying strings (e.g., a picture of a hippopotamus labeled "Archie's Favorite Critter") with a user ID; the Web site authenticates itself to a specific user (e.g., Archie) by displaying that user's chosen image.[4] Authenticity of the server's certificate can be spoofed in many ways that are hard for the user to detect, and manipulation of the trusted root certificates that are configured in the user's Web browser is possible. Moreover, while trust ultimately chains up to a root certificate, the owner of a single certificate below a trusted root is capable of considerable mischief. Server-side Secure Shell is a similar protocol, typically used to provide secure remote access to UNIX servers. Server-side SSL and server-side SSH share the same fundamental vulnerabilities: Both can be spoofed by certificate manipulation. The use of server-side SSL to protect transmission of passwords from client to server is prevalent on the Internet today, but it is important for customers of authentication products to understand the risks inherent in this approach.

In the client-side mode of these protocols, there is no need for a password to be transmitted from client to server, since client-to-server authentication is based on the client's use of its own private key to generate a digital signature. Hence client-side protocols are not vulnerable to password capture by server spoofing.

28.3.9   Risk of Password Reuse.

The need to change passwords with some reasonable frequency is well recognized, but what is reasonable frequency? And how draconian should the enforcement be? It seems that security administrators have pushed too far on these questions. Forcing users to change passwords every month, and enforcing such rules ruthlessly, actually could lead to less security rather than more because so many frustrated users write down and store their ever-changing passwords in nonsecure places. There is a real risk here, created by well-meaning security administrators who have made the problem worse than it inherently is.

Systems that choose a password for the user have their own set of problems and are generally too user-unfriendly to be viable in the Internet age. This discussion focuses on systems that allow users to select their own passwords.

How does exposure of a password increase with time? Even the strongest password-based system, with immunity to off-line dictionary attacks and password capture by server spoofing, faces increased exposure as time passes. Over a long period of time, a slow, ongoing, online guessing attack could be successful. Also, the likelihood of inadvertent disclosure by surreptitious observation, or exposure on a Trojan horse–infected computer, increases with time. Nevertheless, a good password, carefully chosen by the user to be safe from dictionary attacks and well memorized by the user, should not be changed casually. A change every six months may be appropriate for well-chosen, brute-force–resistant passwords.

Enforcing password changes is a complicated business, and one where the security community has not really done a good job. It is not difficult to keep track of the age of a password and to force a change when an appropriate time has passed. The difficulty is in forcing the new password to be independent of the old one. In fact, the likelihood is that the new password will be a slight variation of the old one. For example, appending the numeral designating a month to a fixed string enables users to have almost the same password, even if they are forced to change it every month. Some systems will keep a history of recently used passwords to prevent their reuse. A system that keeps a history of, say, five passwords can be fooled by rapidly changing the password six times. To prevent this, there are systems that will not allow a user to change password more than once a day. This has the unfortunate effect of actually increasing risk of password exposure, since a user who realizes that the current password may have been inadvertently exposed cannot change it, exactly when the need to do so is greatest.

28.3.10   Authentication Using Recognition of Symbols.

An interesting new approach to user authentication is recognition of particular faces from among a large selection of random photographs. Passfaces software works in this way:

> [A] user sets up an array of photographs and puts some familiar ones into the pool to use as keys—the faces of people the user recognizes; then the software can produce a 3x3 grid of random selections including one of the key pictures. The user picks out the familiar picture and then repeats the exercise twice more with new sets of eight strangers and one friend to authenticate the user.[5]

A white paper explains how human beings are particularly good at recognizing faces; indeed, it seems that we have special circuits that have evolved for rapid and accurate perception of faces. According to the paper, advantages of "using Passfaces over passwords" are that Passfaces:

- Can't be written down or copied
- Can't be given to another person

- Can't be guessed
- Involve cognitive not memory skills
- Can be used as a single or part of a dual form of authentication

The power of the system is enhanced by setting parameters to interfere with misuse of the faces. For example:

> In some high-security applications the grids of faces may be displayed only for a very short time. A half second is long enough for practiced users to recognize their Passfaces. Combined with masking (faces in a grid are overwritten with a common mask face) it is extremely difficult for "shoulder surfers" to learn the Passfaces as the user clicks on them.

28.4 TOKEN-BASED AUTHENTICATION.   Token-based authentication relies on something that the user possesses that no other user of the identifier is supposed to possess or be able to access. This authentication can be achieved in many ways, including:

- One-time password generators
- Smart cards and dongles
- Soft tokens

28.4.1 One-Time Password Generators.   A popular form of token, from vendors such as RSA Data Security Inc. and CryptoCard, displays a *one-time password*, typically a six- or eight-digit numeral, which changes each time an access button is pushed or when a given time has elapsed since the password was last used. The user authenticates by entering the user ID and current value displayed by the token.

The password is called *one-time* because it expires at the end of its allowable period for use. The token is typically contactless, in that it does not need electrical contact with the computer where the user is presenting authentication data. The user transfers the necessary information from the token via a keyboard or other input device. To make this a two-factor authentication, a fixed user password is also required in addition to the changing one-time password displayed by the token. These tokens are based on shared secret keys, so both the token and the server have a shared secret. The server and the token need to be initialized and then kept synchronized for this scheme to work. In the case of RSA's SecurID, if the time discrepancy between a specific token and the authenticating system exceeds a specified limit, the authenticating software adjusts a value in an internal table to compensate for the time slippage. Vendors such as CryptoCard have developed event-based authentication algorithms to solve the "slippage" problem. These tokens use a seed with the algorithm to generate a unique value for each button push or other activating action. After the next login, that value is now "known" to the authenticating system, and a new value must be provided. The token's value increments based on the seed, without requiring synchronization with the authenticating system.

Password generators must be protected against physical tampering. These devices typically include several measures to cause destruction of the electronic circuits if the outer case is opened; for example, in addition to epoxy-resin glue, tokens may include light-sensitive components that are destroyed immediately by exposure to light, rendering the unit unusable. Some password generators and smart cards cannot even be opened to replace batteries, so the entire card must be replaced on a predictable schedule. Tokens of this kind are available that are guaranteed to last one year, two years, or three years, without having the batteries wear out.

28.4.2 Smart Cards and Dongles.

Another form of token is a smart card. These cards can go into a PC card reader or can be read by a specialized reader. *Dongles* are smart cards that fit into input-output ports such as USB. A smart card has its own processing capability and typically stores a private key associated with the user. Often a password or PIN is required to access the card, thereby providing two-factor authentication capability. The smart card enables user authentication by signing some challenge presented to it with the user's private key. The signature is verified by means of the user's public key. A complete discussion of such smart cards involves consideration of public key cryptography, public key certificates or so-called digital certificates, and supporting infrastructure or PKI (see Chapter 37 in this *Handbook*). Suffice it to say that smart cards have long been considered essential for widespread use of public key technology but so far have not been widely deployed.

Hardware tokens offer the potential for stronger authentication than passwords but have seen only limited use due to their perceived costs and their infrastructure requirements. Whether they can be deployed in a scale of millions of users remains to be seen. Authentication by tokens is really authentication by something that the token knows. Since tokens can be programmed to remember and use secrets much more effectively than humans can, they offer the potential of strong cryptographic authentication, but tamper-proof tokens are not easy to produce. In recent years, attacks based on differential power analysis have proven effective in determining the secret keys and PINs stored on smart cards. These attacks require physical access to a card whose loss probably would be known, so, although they may not always be feasible, they certainly call into question the presumed tamper-proof nature of smart cards. As smart cards are more widely deployed, other ingenious attacks are likely to be pursued. Smart cards are more susceptible to secret extraction than tokens because their computations leak such information in the form of electromagnetic radiation.

In comparing tokens with passwords, one can argue that undetected theft is easier with passwords. The token is a physical object whose absence is noticeable. However, tokens create their own problems. Like password generators, they are vulnerable to physical damage and compromise. Smart cards typically are built from thin plastic with a chip embedded in them, making the entire unit susceptible to failure from damage. In addition, users typically may store cards with other credit cards in a wallet or pocket, either of which presents additional environmental hazards. However, for certain industries, the cost of replacing lost or damaged tokens may be worth the reduction in undetected sharing, since a token can be used by only one person at a time.

28.4.3 Soft Tokens.

The idea of *soft tokens,* or *software tokens,* has been proposed as a low-cost alternative to hardware tokens. Early soft tokens consisted of a user's private key encrypted with a password and stored on some transportable medium, such as a floppy disk. Such a scheme is extremely vulnerable to dictionary attacks because a guessed password can be verified easily (by testing a putative private key to see if it decrypts a message encrypted using the user's known public key). Moreover, the physical transport of floppy disks and the possible lack of floppy disk drives have led people to store these soft tokens on network servers so they are accessible as needed. Unfortunately, this location also makes them easily accessible to attackers. Protecting access to soft tokens on a network server by means of a password simply returns to the problems of password-based authentication.

It has been suggested that a user's public key could be kept secret and known only to trusted servers to avoid dictionary attacks on the encrypted private key. This approach comes at the severe cost of a closed PKI rather than an open PKI. Schemes for retrieving the private key by means of a secure password-based protocol have been published and are being implemented by some vendors. These schemes ultimately revert to password-based authentication as their foundation. Schemes based on splitting the private key into two parts have been developed. One part of the private key is computed from the password; the other part is stored on an online server, which functions as a network-based virtual smart card. Both parts of the private key are needed for user authentication but are never brought together in one place.

An alternative scheme would be to store the user's entire private key on an online server and make its use contingent on a secure password-based protocol. This approach allows the server to impersonate any user at will and may not be suitable in all environments. However, in all cases, the security of the token relies on the integrity of the computer that uses it. Newer implementations of soft tokens rely on asymmetric cryptography to eliminate the security concerns with storing private keys in a file or other transportable location. The soft token can generate its own key pair and exchange public keys with the authentication server. Although this increases the security of the soft tokens, the concept is inherently weak and prone to attack.

The U.S. federal government established a standard for the identity cards it has mandated for all federal employees and contractors. The original Homeland Security Presidential Directive 12 (HSPD 12), dated August 27, 2004, was entitled "Policy for a Common Identification Standard for Federal Employees and Contractors." It defined these requirements for

secure and reliable identification that—

- Is issued based on sound criteria for verifying an individual employee's identity
- Is strongly resistant to identity fraud, tampering, counterfeiting, and terrorist exploitation
- Can be rapidly authenticated electronically
- Is issued only by providers whose reliability has been established by an official accreditation process.[6]

28.5   BIOMETRIC AUTHENTICATION.

Biometric authentication looks like an excellent solution to the problem of authentication in cyberspace. However, there are several challenges in implementing biometrics, including drawbacks in accuracy (false positive and false negative results), loss of biometric identifiers, security of templates, and privacy concerns. For a full treatment of biometric authentication, refer to Chapter 29 in this *Handbook*.

28.6   CROSS-DOMAIN AUTHENTICATION.

As more systems and processes become Internet enabled, people come to expect a seamless experience between organizations and applications across the Internet. Furthermore, the ever-increasing risk of identity theft has made individuals and organizations more careful about sending too much identity information across an untrusted network. Over the past several years, efforts have increased to enable easy but secure sharing of authentication and authorization information between organizations. Using the Security Assertion Markup Language (SAML), researchers are developing methods enabling one organization to share just enough information between systems to enable a transaction, without compromising privacy. Shibboleth, a project started in 2000 as an Internet2 middleware initiative, is an open-source project using SAML.[7] Organizations using Shibboleth as a basis for designing new federated authentication and authorization implementations include InCommon[8] and the UK Access Management Federation for Education and Research.[9] To facilitate this kind of information sharing, the participating organizations need to share details about their security policies and procedures, so each may decide in advance whether it will trust the authentication assertions of the other. This kind of information sharing is accomplished most effectively via the policies and practice statements used in a PKI. For details on PKI and certificate requirements for cross-domain authentication, refer to Chapter 37 in this *Handbook*.

28.7   RELATIVE COSTS OF AUTHENTICATION TECHNOLOGIES.   One of the frequent responses from security professionals in discussions of identification and authentication using anything other than passwords is that the expense of buying new equipment is prohibitive. However, passwords are not free. In an analysis of the costs of managing passwords, RSA Data Security, makers of the SecurID token, estimated deployment costs (initializing user accounts) at about $12 per user over three years and management costs (replacing forgotten passwords and resetting locked accounts) at about $660 per user over three years. Worse yet, the well-established failure of most users to select strong passwords (i.e., those resistant to guessing, dictionary attacks, and brute-force attacks) makes passwords a weak authentication mode in practice. In comparison, token-based and biometric authentication are more readily affordable and more effective than passwords.[10]

28.8   CONCLUDING REMARKS.   Identification and authentication are the foundations for almost all other security objectives in cyberspace. In the past, these problems often were viewed as simple ones whose solution was assumed, before the real security issues came into play. Important standards for computer security were published and practiced without much attention to identification and authentication. In cyberspace, the problems associated with I&A are severe, and they have barely begun to be solved effectively. A robust, scalable identification and authentication infrastructure is vital to achieving security. Technologies such as tokens and biometrics hold out considerable promise, but their deployment requires infrastructure costs dominated by the cost of hardware for readers and the like. Meanwhile, passwords continue to be strengthened, as we better understand the real risks in using them and as we develop technical means to mitigate those risks. The fact that modern operating systems continue to provide simple password-based authentication, vulnerable to dictionary attacks, reflects poorly on the pace at which security technology is adopted in the marketplace. Looking to the future, one can predict that we will see a mix of passwords, biometrics, and tokens in use, perhaps in two- or three-factor configurations. Biometrics and tokens are likely to dominate the high-assurance end, while passwords will dominate the lower end.

One of the misconceptions that security specialists should seek to dispel is that identification and authentication are *sufficient* for improving public safety. However, assigning a reliable and nonrepudicable identity to someone is in no way equivalent to asserting the trustworthiness of that individual. In closed populations such as employee pools, employers can check the background of potential employees and monitor the performance of existing employees; under those circumstances, knowing someone's identity at the entrance gate may indeed improve security. However, when dealing with a large number of unscreened people, such as potential air passengers, confidently being able to name them tells us nothing about their trustworthiness. Having a clerk at a government office glance at fuel-oil invoices and a birth certificate before granting someone a photo ID is no basis for assuming that the carrier of the valid ID is an inoffensive traveler. As several writers have noted, unambiguously knowing the name of the suicide bomber sitting next to you in a plane is not a reasonable basis for complacency. Timothy McVeigh, the Oklahoma City bomber, was a perfectly identifiable citizen of the United States, but he committed his atrocity nonetheless.[11]

Since September 11, 2001, the air transport industry has been a very public example of both the difficulty of strong identification and authentication and the use of identification and authentication as a public relations substitute for substantive security involving thorough passenger screening. The inherent difficulties of authentication are becoming evident to the lay public and to political and corporate leaders. It is very difficult, perhaps even impossible, to guarantee foolproof identification and authentication in free societies. As technologists, we realize that absolute guarantees cannot be achieved in cyberspace. Too many security professionals seek absolute goals, and too many security technologies are marketed as being stronger than they really are. Our profession will benefit greatly if we address practical problems with practical cost-effective techniques and develop a sound security discipline that contains, bounds, and mitigates the inevitable residual risk that we must face in any large-scale human situation.

28.9 SUMMARY.   Passwords are widely used in practice and will continue to be a dominant form of user authentication. There are many risks in deploying passwords, and a number of widely used password systems have serious vulnerabilities. Nonetheless, technical measures can mitigate the inherent vulnerabilities of passwords. Although it takes great skill and care, with our current understanding it is technically possible to build and deploy strong password-based authentication systems using commercial products. The truly inherent risks of undetected theft and undetected sharing can be largely mitigated by new technologies, such as intrusion detection systems. Undetected sharing may be deterred further by a system that couples high-value secret data, such as credit card account numbers, with passwords. Tokens are available to generate one-time passwords or to communicate directly with authentication systems. Although costs have been dropping, tokens are still not as widely deployed as early predictions suggested they would be. Biometric authentication has been implemented only infrequently and on a small scale but offers great potential, especially for high-security applications. Interesting new research and applications are extending the use of authentication (and authorization) over untrusted networks between federated organizations.

28.10 FURTHER READING

Anderson, J., and R. Vaughn. *A Guide to Understanding Identification and Authentication in Trusted Systems* (1991). "Light Blue Book" in the Rainbow Series, NCSC-TG-017; www.fas.org/irp/nsa/rainbow/tg017.htm.

Birch, D. G. W., ed. *Digital Identity Management: Technological, Business and Social Implications.* Aldershot, Hampshire: Gower Publishing, 2007.

Integrity Sciences. " Bizcard ZKPP: A Zero-Knowledge Password Proof with Pencil and Paper" (2001); www.integritysciences.com/zkppcard.html

Jablon, D., et al. "Publications on Strong Password Authentication" (2001); www.integritysciences.com/links.html.

Jain, L. C., *et al.*, eds. *Intelligent Biometric Techniques in Fingerprint and Face Recognition*. Boca Raton, FL: CRC Press, 1999.

Kabay, M. E. "Identification, Authentication and Authorization on the World Wide Web," 1998; www2.norwich.edu/mkabay/infosecmgmt/iaawww.pdf.

"One-Time Passwords." FreeBSD Handbook, Chapter 14.5; www.freebsd.org/doc/en_US.ISO8859-l/books/handbook/one-time-passwords.html.

Radhakrishnan, R. *Identity & Security: A Common Architecture & Framework for SOA and Network Convergence*. London: futuretext, 2007.

Smith, R. E. *Authentication: From Passwords to Public Keys*. Reading, MA: Addison-Wesley, 2001.

Todorov, D. *Mechanics of User Identification and Authentication: Fundamentals of Identity Management*. Boca Raton, FL: Auerbach, 2007.

Tung, B. *Kerberos: A Network Authentication System*. Reading, MA: Addison-Wesley, 1999.

Vance, J., "Beyond Passwords: 5 New Ways to Authenticate Users," *Network World*, May 31, 2007; www.networkworld.com/research/2007/060407-multifactor-authentication.html.

Wayman, J. L. "Biometric Technology: Testing, Evaluation, Results" (1999); www.engr.sjsu.edu/biometrics/publications_technology.html.

Windley, P. *Digital Identity*. Sebastopol, CA: O'Reilly, 2005.

Wu, T. "A Real-World Analysis of Kerberos Password Security." Proceedings of the 1999 Network and Distributed System Security Symposium; www.isoc.org/isoc/conferences/ndss/99/proceedings/papers/wu.pdf.

28.11 NOTES

1. "No Token Resistance: Citi rolls out Digipass authentication devices to biz clients," *Bank Systems & Technology,* May 25, 2006; www.banktech.com/features/showArticle.jhtml?articleID=188103117.

2. J.-J. Quisquater, L. Guillou, and T. Berson, "How to Explain Zero-Knowledge Protocols to Your Children," Proceedings of CRYPTO '89, *Advances in Cryptology,* Vol. 435, (1989) pp. 628–631; www.cs.wisc.edu/~mkowalcz/628.pdf.

3. R. Wright, "Secret Communication Using a Deck of Cards." Abstract of presentation from DIMACS Research and Education Institute Cryptography and Network Security, July 28–August 15, 1997 (Abstracts of Talks Presented); ftp://dimacs.rutgers.edu/pub/dimacs/TechnicalReports/TechReports/1997/97-80.ps.gz.

4. M. E. Kabay, "SiteKey Tries to Counter Phishing," *Network World Security Strategies*, April 3, 2007; www.networkworld.com/newsletters/sec/2007/0402sec1.html.

5. M. E. Kabay, "Password Management: Facing the Problem," *Network World Security Strategies,* October 11, 2007; www.networkworld.com/newsletters/sec/2007/1008sec2.html.

6. FIPS 201-1, "Personal Identity Verification (PIV) of Federal Employees and Contractors." Gaithersburg, MD: NIST, 2006; http://csrc.nist.gov/publications/fips/fips201-1/FIPS-201-1-chng1.pdf, p. iv.

7. Shibboleth, http://shibboleth.internet2.edu/.

8. InCommon, www.incommonfederation.org/.

9. UK Access Management Federation for Education and Research, http://ukfederation.org.uk.

10. RSA Data Security, "Are Passwords Really Free? A Closer Look at the Hidden Costs of Password Security," 2006; www.rsa.com/go/wpt/wpindex.asp? WPID=3384.

11. M. E. Kabay, "Airport Safety," 2005; www2.norwich.edu/mkabay/opinion/ airport_safety.pdf.

CHAPTER **29**

BIOMETRIC AUTHENTICATION

David R. Lease, Robert Guess, Steven Lovaas, and Eric Salveggio

29.1   INTRODUCTION.   Once exclusively the purview of law enforcement, intelligence, and national security agencies, biometrics—the automated recognition of people based on their physiological or behavioral characteristics—is entering the business mainstream as a method of identification and authentication for access to physical and logical infrastructure. Biometric authentication technologies promise substantially improved security, convenience, and portability over other commonly used methods of authentication. Falling costs, improvements in technologies, increased security needs, and changing government regulations also encourage the adoption of biometrics. Notwithstanding these factors, to date relatively few organizations have implemented biometric authentication controls.

29.2   IMPORTANCE OF IDENTIFICATION AND VERIFICATION.   Ensuring the identity and authenticity of persons is a prerequisite to security and efficiency in present-day organizational operations. Intruders can damage physical and logical infrastructure, steal proprietary information, compromise competitive assets, and threaten organizational sustainability. Traditional methods of recognition and identification, wherein one individual identifies another based on his or her voice, physical appearance, or gait, are impractical, inefficient, and inaccurate in the scope of contemporary organizational operations. To address the need for rapid, efficient, and cost-effective authentication, organizations today primarily rely on the two methods of "something you know" and "something you have" (either applied individually or in combination) to verify the identity of persons accessing their physical and/or logical infrastructure. The most robust authentication systems use multiple factors of authentication. These forms of authentication are described in Chapter 28 in this *Handbook*.

29.3   FUNDAMENTALS AND APPLICATIONS.   Biometrics are based on the measurement and matching of distinctive physiological and/or behavioral characteristics. The former are based on direct measurement of a physiological characteristic of some part of the human body. Examples of physiological biometrics include finger, hand, retina, and iris scans. The latter indirectly measure characteristics of the human body based on measurements and data derived from an action. Commonly used behavioral biometrics include voice and signature scan and keystroke pattern.

29.3.1   Overview and History.   The use of nonautomated biometrics dates back to the beginning of human civilization, when individuals first began identifying other individuals based on certain physical or behavioral characteristics. The concept of biometrics as a means of authentication dates back more than 2,000 years. As early as 300 BC, Assyrian potters used their thumbprint as an early form of brand identity for their merchandise. The use of handwritten signatures (chops) in classical China is another example of an early biometric. In the first instance of a formal, legal biometric authentication system, fingerprints were used to sign contracts during the Tang dynasty (AD 618–906).

The development of contemporary biometric systems can be viewed as an outgrowth of the efforts of forensic scientists and law enforcement agencies to identify and classify criminals in the late nineteenth and early twentieth centuries. In 1882, Alphonse Bertillon introduced a system of body measurements called *anthropometry* to identify criminals. This system was proven unreliable because the measurements taken were not globally unique. A student of Bertillon, Edmund Locard, later proposed a fingerprint system based on the work of Sir Edmond Galton to identify people by analyzing unique points in fingerprint ridges and pores. Locard's system, which used 12 Galton points, is considered reliable to this day. This methodology underlies fully automated modern biometric including the Integrated Automated Fingerprint Identification Systems (IAFIS) used by law enforcement agencies. Commercial biometric systems (typically relying on hand geometry) designed for use in physical access to buildings, emerged in the 1960s and 1970s.

Biometric methods of identification and identity verification, including automatic fingerprint analysis and facial recognition technologies, have been available and used by some government/public agencies (e.g., law enforcement, intelligence, and national security) and a few private industries (e.g., facial recognition scans in casinos) since the 1960s and 1970s. Notwithstanding the potential benefits and advantages over other authentication methods, biometrics have not been widely applied, particularly in the corporate world. Analysts cite high costs of equipment and implementation, technological problems, vulnerabilities of specific biometrics, lack of standards, and user resistance (notably, concerns over privacy) as reasons for the lack of implementation.

However, in the decades of 1990 and 2000, significant improvements in biometric technologies, a movement toward standardization, changes in regulations requiring organizations to adopt stringent security and privacy controls, and significantly reduced costs have encouraged wider adoption. A number of U.S. Government agencies (e.g., Department of Homeland Security, Department of Transportation, Department of Defense, Customs and Border Protection, Department of Justice, National Library of Medicine) and businesses in certain industries (e.g., healthcare and finance) have significantly increased their use of biometrics during the past few years—a factor that is likely to encourage other organizations to adopt biometrics as well. At least one major computer manufacturer has banked on these rapid developments in biometrics applications. In late 2004, IBM (now Lenovo) began adding fingerprint scanners on its notebook computers, enabling users to increase security by requiring a finger swipe and a password (or just a finger swipe) to access files. Other computer manufacturers and peripheral vendors have added fingerprint scanning to computer keyboards and/or developed standalone fingerprint scanners that connect to computers via a Universal Serial Bus (USB) port.

Some analysts see the 2001 attacks on the World Trade Center and the Pentagon also as a key impetus behind the increased usage of biometrics for authentication and identification. The terrorist attacks have been critical in encouraging adoption not only because they have heightened the security concerns of companies and agencies but also because the impact and implications of the terrorists' attacks seem to have lowered users' resistance to the use of biometrics by employers and government. In other words, in the same way that the threat of global terrorism reduced public objections to possible infringements on civil liberties as a result of implementation of the U.S.A. PATRIOT Act and other security-focused measures, these attacks also appear to have rendered many people less sensitive to the potential privacy-invading implications of biometrics. Boroshok reported that a recent survey sponsored by AuthenTec found that 71 percent of U.S. consumers would pay more for biometric security options in their cell phones and 63 percent of consumers would pay an additional cost for these options to be added to their personal computers.[1]

The changing security environment has prompted forecasts of rapid growth in biometrics. In 2004, the International Biometric Group (IBG) predicted rapid growth for the biometrics industry over the next several years from revenues totaling under $50 million in 2004 to revenues of almost $200 million in 2008.[2] In late 2003, analysts at the San Jose, California–based market research firm Frost and Sullivan predicted that biometric applications from commercial applications (not including the Federal Bureau of Investigation's IAFIS) would jump from $93.4 million in 2001 to $2.05 billion by 2006—up from the $700 million (in 2006) that these analysts predicted prior to the September 11, 2001, attacks. In January 2007, IBG released their most recent projections of market growth for the biometrics industry. They estimate that biometric industry revenues will grow from $3.01 billion in 2007 to over $7.4 billion by 2012.[3]

Despite rosy projections from industry analysts, adoption of biometric authentication systems continues to lag. Some firms continue to cite cost issues and privacy concerns, while others point to problems surrounding biometric implementation in airports and among government agencies. Overall, surveys of companies indicate that forecasts of dramatic and rapid growth in biometrics implementation may be overstated. Hulme reported that "only 9% of 300 business-technology executives surveyed for the *InformationWeek* Research Priorities 1Q2003 study say biometric deployment is a key business priority, down from 12% in the same quarter of 2002."[4] A 2003 Forrester Research survey found that only 1 percent of companies had implemented biometric systems, just 3 percent had a biometric system rollout in progress, only 15 percent were testing biometrics, and 58 percent of those surveyed had *no plans* to try biometrics.

29.3.2 Properties of Biometrics.

The contemporary meaning of biometrics emphasizes its automated aspects, which allow for deployment on a large scale. The most widely cited definition of biometrics is some variation of "the automatic identification of a person based on his or her physiological or behavioral characteristics."[5] The term "biometrics" generally is used as a noun to refer to the automatic recognition of persons based on their physical or behavioral characteristics. The term "biometric" can be used as a noun in reference to a single technology or measure (e.g., finger scan is a commonly used biometric) or as an adjective, as in "a biometric system uses integrated hardware and software to conduct identification or verification."[6]

Biometrics have long been touted as a possible solution to the problems and vulnerabilities of other commonly used methods of authentication and identification. They represent sophisticated versions of the traditional means of identification, such as a guard allowing access to a user whom the guard recognizes by sight. Biometrics commonly are defined as automated methods of recognition/verification/identification of individuals based on some measurable physiological or behavioral characteristics, such as fingerprints, hand geometry, facial shape, iris pattern, voice, signature, and the like.

Whereas identification (ID) badges and keys authenticate the user based on something the user possesses, and passwords/personal identification numbers (PINs) authenticate the user based on what the user knows, biometrics allows authentication and identity verification based on who the user *is*. Because biometric methodologies of authentication actually base identification on physiological or behavioral "pieces" of the user, biometrics represents the only form of authentication that *directly authenticates the user*.

Biometrics have a number of other obvious advantages over other commonly used authentication methods. Unlike an ID badge or a USB key, one cannot easily lose or misplace a fingerprint or other biometric measures. Likewise, unlike the case with passwords and PINs, one does not need to remember and one is not subject to forgetting a physiological or behavioral characteristic. Although biometric measures *can* be compromised, in general, a biometric is much more difficult to manipulate by stealing, forging, sharing, or destroying than other commonly used authentication tools. Biometrics also provide considerable convenience, as opposed to the hassle of memorizing dozens of passwords.

Although the initial costs are quite high, the implementation of biometric systems typically results in much lower administrative costs than other access methodologies due to fewer calls to the help desk for technical support to reset passwords, no need to issue replacement ID badges, and so on. For these and other reasons, biometrics are viewed as providing better security, increased efficiency, and more reliable identity assurance than other commonly used methods of authentication/identification based on what a user possesses or what a user knows.

In theory, almost any human physiological and/or behavioral characteristic can be used as a biometric measure. However, to fit within a viable, potentially accurate, and practical biometric system, the biometric used should also satisfy four other requirements offered by Jain[7] and Bolle, Connell, Pankanti, Ratha, and Senior:[8]

1. **Universality.** Every person should have the biometric characteristic.
2. **Uniqueness.** No two persons should be the same in terms of the biometric characteristic. Jain proposed the somewhat lower standard of distinctiveness, defined as "any two persons would be sufficiently different in terms of the characteristic."[9]
3. **Permanence.** The biometric should be relatively invariant over a significant period of time.
4. **Collectability.** The biometric characteristic should lend itself to quantitative measurement in a practical manner.

Bolle, Connell, Pankanti, Ratha, and Senior argued that the biometric should also have a fifth attribute: acceptability, defined as "the particular user population and the public in general should have no strong objections to the measuring/collection of the biometric."[10] Jain argued that a practical biometric system should consider two other attributes: (1) performance, which is "the achievable recognition accuracy and speed, the resources required to achieve the desired performance, as well as the operational and environmental factors that affect the performance," and (2) circumvention, which "reflects how easily the system can be fooled using fraudulent methods."[11]

29.3.3 Identification, Authentication, and Verification.
In this chapter, we describe the process of providing a user identifier (ID) and data to bind the user of the ID with that ID as *authentication*. However, the process of *establishing* whether the proffered combination of ID and authentication data reliably confirms the identity of the user is called *verification*.

Identification systems answer the question: Whom do you claim to be? and involve establishing a person's claimed identity. Verification systems answer the question: Are you who you claim to be? and involve confirming or denying an individual's claimed identity using knowledge, tokens, biological characteristics, or behavioral patterns that are reliably tied and restricted to the authorized user of the ID.

In verification systems, the user claims an identity (e.g., a Windows username, a given name, an ID number) and provides biometric data (e.g., finger scan), which are compared against the user's enrolled biometric data. The answer returned by the system is that of "match" or "no match."

Biometric verification systems are referred to as 1:1 (one-to-one) systems because, while they may contain thousands or even millions of biometric records, they are "always predicated on a user's biometric data being matched against only his or her own enrolled biometric data."[12] Biometric *verification* systems do not provide "pure" biometric authentication because they rely on a combination of authentication modes—specifically biometric data compared against a unique identifier (e.g., ID number, user name).

Biometric *identification* systems, however, *can* be viewed as pure biometric authentication because identification is based only on biometric measurements. Whereas verification is referred to as a 1:1 system, identification systems often are referred to as *1 : N* (one-to-*N* or one-to-many) systems because an individual's biometric information is compared against multiple (*N*) records. Verification systems return an answer of match or no match; identification systems, however, return an identity (e.g., a name or ID number) as an answer.

Identification systems are further divided into "positive" (designed to find a match for a user's biometric information in a database of biometric information, such as tracking individuals in a prison release program) and "negative" (designed to ensure that a person's biometric information is *not* present in the database, such as preventing people from enrolling more than once in large-scale benefits programs). Although biometric identification systems are generally classified as *1: many* applications, a scaled-back version of identification known as *1 : few*, a system that focuses on identification search against a small number of users is sometimes deployed.

Biometric identification systems are more difficult to design and implement than verification systems because of the extensive biometric database search capabilities needed. Additionally, identification systems are more subject to error than verification systems, because many more matches must be conducted, matches that increase the opportunity for error. Verification systems are overall much faster (often rendering a match/no match decision within less than a second) and more accurate than identification systems. Verification systems, as opposed to identification systems, predominate in private sector applications, particularly for computer and network security applications. Verification systems also predominate in applications designed to authenticate rights-to-access to buildings and rooms, although sometimes identification systems are also deployed in high-security environments. Identification systems are often found in public sector applications, such as law enforcement (e.g., parole and prison administration, forensics, etc.), large-scale public benefits programs, intelligence, and national security applications.

29.3.4 Application Areas.   Although there are many potential applications for biometrics, the primary ones can be divided into four categories: systems security (logical access systems), facilities access (physical access systems), ensuring the uniqueness of individuals, and public identification systems. The common thread among these four applications is that they all rely on individuals enrolled in the systems. The significance of whether individuals are enrolled or not enrolled will be explained in Section 29.3.5.

29.3.4.1 Security (Logical Access Systems).   Logical access systems "monitor, restrict, or grant access to data or information."[13] Examples include accessing a computer or network or accessing an account. In these systems, biometrics replace or complement PINs, passwords, and tokens. The volume and value of electronic commerce plus the value of sensitive and personal information transported and/or stored on networks and computers make the use of biometrics to secure logical access a much more robust industry segment than physical security.

The use of biometric technologies for logical access control is still very much in its infancy. The most common biometric approach is to use fingerprint readers, either with a stand-alone USB reader or with a reader embedded in a laptop. Manufacturers are beginning to incorporate the Trusted Platform Module (TPM) chip in new laptops to support a variety of cryptographic applications. In combination with biometric devices like fingerprint readers, the TPM chip can allow applications like Microsoft's BitLocker to apply biometric access control to encrypted volumes on a hard drive. Such technologies are still new enough to suffer problems with backward compatibility and intervendor support, but they offer the promise of much more secure logical access.

29.3.4.2 *Facilities Access (Physical Access Systems).* Facilities access systems "monitor, restrict, or grant movement of a person or object into or out of a specific area."[14] In these systems, biometrics replace or complement keys, access cards, or security cards, allowing authorized users access to rooms, vaults, and other secure areas. Physical access systems often are deployed in major public infrastructure settings, such as airports, security checkpoints, and border facilities, in order to monitor and restrict movements of unauthorized or suspicious persons. In addition to entry to secure rooms, physical access systems, when applied in business settings, include time-and-attendance systems by combining access to a location with an audit of when the authentication occurred.

Biometric technologies have been in use for physical access control for some time but still represent a range of possible implementations, from stand-alone fingerprint-reading door locks to complete systems with central storage of biometric templates, logging, and power failure protection. Selecting a system from within such a wide product range must fit into the overall security stance of the facility, particularly in regard to the storage of templates. In a simple stand-alone door system, for example, fingerprint templates would be stored in or near the locking device, and the system might not have any logging features. Unless coupled with surveillance and intrusion alarms anticipating physical compromise, these devices are more appropriate for lower security applications, such as storage facilities where physical key access might not be preventing theft. More centrally connected systems, however, offer greater integration into overall monitoring and control of access but suffer from communication and power issues as they push templates across a network. Selecting a product that interacts well with other parts of the overall access control system is crucial.

29.3.4.3 *Ensuring the Uniqueness of Individuals.* Uniqueness biometric identification systems typically focus on preventing double enrollment in programs or applications, such as a social benefits program. The main use of this application occurs in the public sector, although similar systems could be implemented to prevent double enrollment in employee benefits programs.

29.3.4.4 *Public Identification Systems.* A final biometric application of note is its use to identify criminals and/or terrorists. Criminals and terrorists can wear disguises, acquire fake documents, and change their names, but biometric data are fairly difficult to forge. In 2004, the United States Department of Defense started the Automated Biometric Identification System (ABIS), which collects biometric data on Iraqi insurgents in a manner compatible with IAFIS. This allows for identification of known repeat offenders and wanted persons. Soldiers also use the Biometric Automated Toolset (BAT) developed by the Army's Language Technology Office to identify persons on the scene of bombing attacks. Anyone present in the area can be cross-referenced with an existing database of insurgents. The BAT is also used to enroll and identify members of the Iraqi army. Although biometric systems hold much promise, it is also important to understand the limitations of current technology.

29.3.5 Data Acquisition and Presentation.   As Jain explains, "A biometric system is essentially a pattern recognition system that operates by acquiring biometric data from an individual, extracting a feature set from the acquired data, and comparing this feature set against the template set in the database."[15] The starting point for the biometric system is *enrollment*: A user's biometric data are initially collected and processed into a template, the form in which they are then stored for ongoing use. As Woodward, Orlans, and Higgins explain, "Templates are not raw data or the scanned images of a biometric sample, but rather they are an accumulation of the distinctive features extracted by the biometric system."[16] Liu and Silverman describe the template as "a mathematical representation of biometric data. A template can vary in size from 9 bytes for hand geometry to several thousand bytes for facial recognition."[17] Templates are proprietary to each vendor and technology with little or no interoperability between systems. This lack of interoperability is attractive from a privacy perspective but unattractive from the perspective of cost effectiveness and the prospective implementer who is concerned about committing significant investment to a single nonstandardized technology.

The term "presentation" refers to the process by which a user provides biometric data to an acquisition device by looking in the direction of a camera, placing a finger on a pad or sensor, or some other specified physiological exam. For purposes of verification or identification, the user presents biometric data, which are then processed and converted to a template. This template is an extraction of distinctive features and is not adequate for the reconstruction of the original biometric data. The scanned template is then matched against the stored enrollment template(s). Each time a user makes a presentation, a new template is created and matched. It is important to note, especially from the perspective of privacy concerns, that biometric systems do not store raw biometric data; instead they use the data for template creation and, in most cases, discard the biometric data. The biometric system's match/no-match decisions are based on a score, which is "a number indicating the degree of similarity or correlation resulting from the comparison of enrollment and verification templates."[18] Like the templates, the scoring system is based on proprietary algorithms; there is no standard system.

29.4 TYPES OF BIOMETRIC TECHNOLOGIES.   As previously noted, bio-metrics generally can be grouped into two categories: physiological and behavioral. The International Biometric Group provides data on comparative market share of various biometric technologies. The IBG data focus on market share from commercial and government applications. The top four biometric technologies are all from the physiological category (see Exhibit 29.1).

The fifth most widely deployed biometric technology came from the behavioral category: voice scan, with a projected 3.2 percent share in 2007, down from a 6.0 percent share in 2004 and 4.1 percent in 2003.[19] Each of these five biometrics is discussed in detail in the next sections.

29.4.1 Finger Scan.   Finger scan or fingerprint technology is by far the most widely deployed biometric technology. Finger scan's number-one status as a biometric is maintained even if the extensive use of fingerprinting by law enforcement agencies is excluded. The type of fingerprinting employed in commercial biometric systems differs from the one used in law enforcement. In most commercially available biometric applications, the station provides only for the scan of a single finger on one hand, whereas law enforcement agencies often rely on full sets of fingerprints. In addition to

Exhibit 29.1 Comparative Market Share of Biometric Technologies

	Market Share		
Biometric Technology	**2007 (projected)**	**2004**	**2003**
Finger scan	58.9%	48.0%	52.0%
Facial scan	12.9%	12.0%	11.4%
Hand scan	4.7%	11.0%	10.0%
Iris scan	5.1%	9.0%	7.3%

Sources: (1) Market share data from International Biometric Group, *Biometrics Market and Industry Report 2007–2012* (January 2007). Retrieved February 4, 2007, from www.biometricgroup.com/reports/public/market_report.html.
(2) International Biometric Group, *Biometrics Market and Industry Report 2004–2008* (2005). Retrieved June 4, 2005, from www.biometricgroup.com/reports/public/market_report.html.
(3) J. McHale, "Biometrics: The Body's Keys," *Military & Aerospace Electronics* 14, No. 12 (2003): 17–23.

being the most widely used biometric, fingerprinting is also one of the oldest and most well researched biometric technologies. Because it is a widely used, well-documented, and mature technology, costs for the deployment of finger-scan-based technologies are relatively low. Single-quantity pricing for a workstation version with associated software can be as low as $150; server versions are currently priced as low as $50 per unit.

The strengths of finger scan are one of the principal reasons for its popularity and include:

- Wide use.
- Mature technology.
- Low cost.
- High ease of use. (Very little training is required to place a finger on a finger pad.)
- Ergonomic design. (Comfortable to use for most users.)
- Low error incidence. (False match rates are extremely low; crossover error rate is lower than voice scan and facial recognition, higher than hand geometry and iris scan.)
- Fast transaction times. (In most systems, authentication takes less than a second.)
- Capacity to be deployed in a wide range of environments (e.g., on workstations, doorways, indoors/outdoors).
- Ability to increase accuracy levels by enrolling multiple fingers.
- Can provide identification with a high level of accuracy (if properly configured to include multiple enrolled fingers) in addition to verification.

Despite its multiple strengths, finger scan is not without significant weaknesses. As Chirillo and Blaul note, some of this technology's weaknesses stem from the same factors that lend it its strengths. "Because fingerprint technology is one of the oldest and most well-known technologies, a good amount of information is publicly available on how to defeat it."[20] A number of ways exist to foil finger scans and produce a false match (false accept), including the use of a dummy finger constructed of latex or other material, manipulation of the scanner so as to raise the latent print of the person who used the scanner previously, and even use of an actual finger that is no longer attached to a body. (Most finger scanners cannot discriminate between live and dead tissue.) Because of these factors, the security levels of finger scans are not actually as impressive as the low error rates seem to indicate. It should be noted that countermeasures could be taken to overcome the vulnerability of finger scans to fraud. For example, enrolling additional fingers makes fraud more difficult. To reduce the chance that the system will be foiled by synthetic or dismembered fingers, thermal and/or moisture scanners can be added to the sensors to detect finger temperature and moisture levels that would indicate the vitality of the finger.

Other weaknesses include:

- A scanner requires frequent maintenance because screens/sensors tend to retain an obstructing buildup of user skin oil and residue.
- Performance can deteriorate over time, both because of aging of the users (and wearing away of fingertips) and because of the need for system maintenance.
- Finger-scan biometrics are obviously not appropriate for users with missing hands or hand disabilities.
- Performance levels deteriorate among users who have hand tremors because the presentation of biometric data will be distorted.
- Performance levels also deteriorate when users' fingers are either overly dry (a certain amount of normal skin moisture is needed for an accurate reading) or overly moist or oily (as from too much hand lotion).
- There is a small but significant failure to enroll (FTE) rate even among a population with hands and without disabilities. The FTE rate for finger scans is estimated at 2 to 10 percent and is attributed to persons with genetically indistinct prints, scarred fingers, dry skin, and fingerprints worn down by age and/or manual labor.

Perhaps the biggest weakness of finger scan, however, has nothing to do with the accuracy and reliability of the technology. Instead, it relates to user acceptance. Because of the association of finger scans with law enforcement and criminality, often such scans are not readily accepted by users who dislike the technology's "taint" with forensic applications and who may worry that finger-scan biometric data will be used for other purposes.

According to Chirillo and Blaul, "Another reason fingerprint technology is not highly accepted is that it may require individuals to share or touch the same device that others touch."[21]

29.4.2 Facial Scan/Recognition.   Bolle, Connell, Pankanti, Ratha, and Senior note that "face appearance is a particularly compelling biometric because it is one used every day by nearly everyone as the primary means for recognizing other humans. Because of its naturalness, face recognition is more acceptable than other biometrics."[22] However, user acceptance of facial scans drops significantly when users discover that it has been used covertly. As Imparato observes, "Of all the biometric technologies currently in use, face recognition is arguably the most controversial."[23] Like finger scans, face recognition relies on the identification of unknown face images by comparison to a database of (known) face templates. Face recognition is used overtly in access control where it is used for one-to-one identification. This application yields relatively high performance because the environment is highly controlled and input data are predictable. Face recognition may also be used covertly in surveillance where it is used to locate people in crowds (one to many), albeit with mixed results. For example, the city of Virginia Beach, Virginia, has employed a face recognition system to identify known (preenrolled) felons for over five years but has yet to identify a single criminal. A variety of facial recognition technologies, ranging from single image, video sequence, three-dimensional image, near infrared, to facial thermograms, are available.

Facial recognition offers these benefits:

- It has the capacity to leverage existing image acquisition equipment, such as digital cameras, Web, video, and the like.

- Because facial recognition is a software-based technology, it is often unnecessary to purchase new hardware, especially given the number of Closed Circuit Television (CCTV) and surveillance cameras in broad use.

- The lack of need for specialized hardware can help keep the cost of this technology down, assuming that high software costs do not counterbalance the savings from the hardware.

- It is the only biometric capable of identification at a distance without the subject's cooperation or even awareness.

- It is easy to use. All that is required is that the user (or target) look at the camera.

- It does *not* require the user to touch any device (a major objection for some users with finger scans and hand scans).

- When deployed in verification situations, facial scans have extremely low failure-to-enroll rates. (Unlike fingerprints, human faces are almost always distinctive.)

- They are capable of enrolling static images (e.g., photographs on driver's licenses), a factor that makes it possible to implement very large scale enrollments at a relatively low cost and in a brief amount of time.

Facial recognition systems have a number of serious weaknesses too. The predominant weakness (which derives from a combination of the technology's other weaknesses) is the low accuracy and high error rate of this biometric. Whether deployed covertly or overtly, facial recognition has the lowest accuracy rate among all five top biometrics.

Evidence of the technology's low accuracy rate comes from a study at Palm Beach (Florida) International Airport that showed that the system failed more than 50 percent of the time to match the 15 employees who had enrolled in the database for a trial run. Out of 958 pass-throughs, the system matched the employees' faces just 455 times. Some studies suggest that accuracy improvements can be made in facial recognition systems, but these improvements will come at a very high cost. For example, a facial recognition software package from Visionics FaceIt resulted in impressively low error rates, as long as lighting conditions were perfect. The software costs $30,000 for a three-camera system.

Other weaknesses include:

- False matches (false accepts) routinely occur in the case of twins, and most systems are insensitive enough for someone skillful at disguise and impersonation to trick the system into a false match.

- More likely than false matches, however, are false nonmatches (false rejects), which can occur as a result of facial expressions; changes in hairstyle, makeup, facial hair, significant changes in body weight, eyeglasses, and age-related facial changes.

- The acquisition environment can have a dramatic impact on facial recognition system accuracy. In particular, lighting, either too bright or too dim, can dramatically increase the error rate.
- The perceived threat to privacy. Overtly deployed facial recognition technologies (e.g., used for identification and access) are generally judged relatively unobtrusive and meet with a high level of user acceptance. However, covertly deployed systems, such as those used for surveillance, pose significant threats to privacy. This threat is generally viewed as much more serious than that posed by the other top biometrics.

29.4.3   Hand Geometry Scan.   Hand geometry scans refer not to handprints or to any analogy of fingerprints but rather to the geometric structure (or geometric invariants) of the human hand. Nanavati, Thieme, and Nanavati explain that "hand-scan technology utilizes the distinctive aspects of the hand—in particular, the height and width of the back of the hand and fingers—to verify the identity of individuals."[24] The leading hardware maker for this technology, Recognition Systems, Inc. (RSI), has a basic hand scanner that takes upward of 90 measurements from three to four enrollments to create a user template that includes length, width, and thickness, plus surface area of the hand and fingers. Newer systems include temperature-sensing mechanisms to ensure "live" subjects. All the components of a hand scan system (acquisition hardware, matching software, storage components) reside within a stand-alone device. Hand scans are a well-established biometric technology (they have been in widespread use since the 1970s), but compared to other leading biometrics, hand scans tend to be much more limited in their range of applications. Hand scans are used exclusively for verification rather than for identification because the hand measurements are not distinctive or specific enough to allow for identification applications. For this reason, hand scans are used mostly for physical access and time-and-attendance applications. In the latter case, they are used as a way to eliminate the problem of "buddy-punching" whereby one employee punches in or out for a coworker who is not present.

Hand scan technology has changed very little since it was first introduced over 30 years ago, so its strengths and weaknesses are well established. The principal strengths of the hand scan include:

- Operates in very challenging environments. (The equipment is typically unaffected by light, dust, moisture, or temperature.)
- Established and reliable technology.
- Ease of use. (Users simply stick their hand in the unit; placement matters little.)
- Resistance to fraud compared to other biometrics. (It would be difficult and time consuming to substitute a fake sample.)
- Small template size (as low as 9 bytes; much smaller than other biometrics, allowing for storage of thousands of templates in a single unit).
- Based on a relatively stable physiological characteristic.
- High level of user acceptance and lack of attached stigma.

Problems reported in using hand scans include:

- Limited accuracy (which in turn limits its use to verification not identification). The relatively low accuracy of hand scan (higher than facial recognition and behavioral biometrics but lower than finger and iris scans) is a result of the general lack of physical variety expressed in the hand as well as the relatively small number of features measured by hand scan.
- Comparatively large form factor (This limits the technology's deployment in computer-oriented applications that require hardware with a smaller footprint.)
- Some people resent forced contact with possibly unclean surfaces.
- Ergonomic design limits its use by some populations (e.g., the disabled).
- Comparatively high cost. At $1,500 to $2,000 per unit, hand scanners cost significantly more than finger scanners. Nanavati, Thieme, and Nanavati note that the higher price of hand scanners "may be attributable to the lack of competition in the hand scan market."[25]

29.4.4 Iris Scan.   Iris scan technology uses the unique pattern formed by the iris—the colored part of the eye bounded by the pupil and the sclera—to identify or verify the identity of individuals. The iris pattern is unique, for even in the same individual, no two irises are alike. The uniqueness of iris patterns has been likened to that of multilayered snowflakes. The unique aspects of the iris make it an ideal biometric for high-security applications; enrolling both irises from the same individual can enhance the level of security. In addition to high-security physical access applications, iris scan technology has been used in automated teller machines (ATMs) and banking kiosks.

The most important strength of iris biometrics is its accuracy, the most critical weakness of facial scanning. Of all the leading biometrics, iris technology has the lowest error rate and the highest level of overall accuracy. Other strengths of this biometric include:

- Ability to be used both for verification and for identification.
- Stability of its biometric characteristics over a lifetime.
- Relative difficulty to fake or spoof because it is an internal biometric.
- The fact that the iris is minimally subject to outside influences when compared to biometrics like fingerprints and faces.

The major weaknesses of the iris biometric concern user perceptions and problems in the user-technology interface. Other weaknesses include:

- Acquisition of the image requires moderate training and attentiveness: Users must stand still and look straight into the scanner with eyes open and unblinking.
- Users often report some physical discomfort with the use of eye-based technology, although less so than with retina scanning technology.
- Anecdotal reports also suggest a fairly high level of user psychological resistance to iris-scanning technology, with some users believing that the scanner will lead to eye damage.
- Can be adversely affected by lighting and other environmental conditions (although not to the extent of facial scanning).

- In some cases eyewear adversely affects performance (although many iris devices can scan people wearing glasses or contact lenses).
- Although the iris is a relatively stable biometric, it is affected by aging and disease.
- Relies on proprietary hardware and software technologies.
- Costs tend to be high compared to finger scanning, hand scanning, and many facial recognition systems.

On the other hand, the per unit cost of the leading hardware/software combination technology has dropped to as low as $300 per seat, still higher than finger scans but significantly lower than the over $5,000-per-seat price seen a few years ago.

29.4.5 Voice Recognition.   Voice recognition biometrics "utilizes the distinctive aspects of the voice to verify the identity of individuals."[26] Voice recognition generally is classified as a behavioral biometric, although it actually combines elements of behavioral and physiological biometrics: "The shape of the vocal tract determines to a large degree how a voice sounds, a user's behavior determines what is spoken and in what fashion."[27] Stated somewhat differently, "voice is a behavioral biometric but is dependent on underlying physical traits, which govern the type of speech signals we are able and likely to utter."[28] Because of comparatively low levels of accuracy and considerable user variability in voice dynamics, this biometric generally is used only for verification, not identification. Commonly deployed voice recognition systems can be divided into two types: text-dependent systems (the speaker is prompted to say a specific thing) and text-independent systems (the authentication system processes any utterances of the speaker), which provide a higher level of security because they are more difficult to spoof and provide better accuracy than text-dependent systems.
Strengths of voice recognition include:

- Capacity to leverage existing telephony infrastructure (as well as built-in computer microphones).
- Low cost when existing infrastructure is used.
- Ease of use.
- Interface with speech recognition and verbal passwords.
- High level of user acceptance. (This biometric does not suffer from the negative perceptions associated with all of the other leading biometrics.)

Weaknesses of voice recognition include:

- More susceptible to replay attacks than other biometrics.
- Accuracy levels are low compared to iris scanning, finger scans, and hand scans.
- Accuracy levels are negatively affected by ambient noise and low-quality capture devices.
- Accuracy, security, and reliability are challenged by individual variations in voice, such as speaking softly or loudly, hoarseness or nasality because of a cold, and so on.
- The stability of the biometric is affected by illness, aging, and other user behaviors including smoking.

29.4.6   Other Biometric Technologies.   The five major biometric technologies just discussed collectively comprise the vast majority of biometric technology under deployment. The only other biometric technologies that even register on market share breakdowns are two of the behavioral type: signature scan (2.4 percent share in 2003) and keystroke scan (0.3 percent share in 2003). Although both of these behavioral biometrics are well accepted (signature scanning more so than keystroke scanning), their usefulness is limited by their lack of accuracy.

Other behavioral biometrics under investigation include gait and lip motion. One physiological biometric that has received considerable attention because of its high accuracy and security rates is retinal scanning. However, most analysts believe that the problems associated with retinal scanning (lack of user acceptance, high cost, difficult and painful acquisition process) outweigh any advantages to this biometric. The consensus seems to be that iris scanning has replaced retinal scanning as the eye scanning biometric of choice.

The use of DNA as a biometric identifier has also been investigated, although it has significant weaknesses including the fact that DNA in body tissues (e.g., epithelial cells) can be obtained surreptitiously and transferred easily for nefarious purposes whereas the official methods of collection (e.g., taking blood samples) are relatively intrusive.

Other physiological biometrics that may prove useful in the future include body odor, skin reflectance, and ear shape.

29.5   TYPES OF ERRORS AND SYSTEM METRICS.   All types of identification and authentication systems suffer from two types of errors: false accepts and false rejects.

29.5.1   False Accept.   Also known as false match, false positive, or type 1 error, false accept is the likelihood, expressed as a percentage, that an imposter will be matched to a valid user's biometric. In some systems, such as those that attempt to secure entry to a weapons facility, a bank vault, or a high-level system administrator account, the false match/false accept rate is the most important metric to watch. In other systems, such as a facial recognition system deployed by a casino in an effort to spot card counters, a high level of false matches may be tolerated.

29.5.2   False Reject.   Also known as false nonmatch, false negative, or type 2 error, false reject is the probability that "a user's template will be incorrectly judged to *not* match his or her enrollment template."[29] False nonmatches typically result in the user being locked out of the system. These false nonmatches can occur because of changes in a user's biometric data, changes in how the biometric data is presented, and/or changes in the environment. Biometric systems are generally more susceptible to false rejects than they are to false accepts.

29.5.3   Crossover Error Rate.   An important metric in biometric systems is the *crossover error rate* (CER), also known as the equal error rate (EER). This useful metric is the intersection of the false accept and false reject rates. In general, a lower CER indicates the biometric device is more accurate and reliable than another biometric device with a higher CER. Exhibit 29.2 provides a summary of benchmark test-based accuracy/error rates for the five most prevalent biometric technologies. Each biometric technology is rank-ordered from most accurate to least accurate based on CER.

EXHIBIT 29.2   Accuracy/Error Rates of Leading Biometric Technologies

Biometric	False Match Rate	False No-Match Rate
Iris scan	0.0001%	2.0%
Finger scan	0.02%	2.0%
Hand scan	0.3%	3.0%
Voice (text independent)	7.0%	7.0%
Voice (text dependent)	2.0%	0.03%
Face scan	16.0%	16.0%

Source: Based on data contained in L. O'Gorman, "Comparing Passwords, Tokens, and Biometrics for User Authentication," *Proceedings of the IEEE* 91, no. 12 (2003): 2032.

29.5.4   Failure to Enroll.   Another critical metric in biometric systems is the *failure to enroll* (FTE). As Ashbourn explains, FTE refers to "a situation whereupon an individual is unable to enroll their biometric in order to create a template of suitable quality for subsequent automated operation."[30] Common reasons for failure to enroll include physical disability and a user whose physiological/behavioral characteristics are less distinctive than average. Nanavati, Thieme, and Nanavati observe that failure to enroll can be a major problem in "internal, employee-facing deployments" in which "high FTE rates are directly linked to increased security risks and increased system costs."[31] A final important metric is the "transaction time." Transaction time refers to "a theoretical time taken to match the live template against a reference sample."[32]

29.6   DISADVANTAGES AND PROBLEMS

29.6.1   General Considerations.   Despite the many advantages over other commonly used authentication systems, the implementation of biometric authentication controls carries a number of risks and disadvantages. Even the most accurate biometric system is not perfect, and errors will occur. The error rates and the types of errors will vary with specific biometrics deployed and the circumstances of deployment. Certain types of errors, such as false matches, may pose fundamental, critical risks to organizational security. Other types of errors—failure to enroll, false nonmatch—may reduce organizational productivity and efficiency and increase costs. Organizations planning biometrics implementation will need to consider the acceptable error threshold. In any event, organizations deploying biometric authentication systems must not be lulled into a belief that they are invulnerable to errors and/or fraud. Certain biometric systems (e.g., iris scanning) are fairly impervious to fraud, while others (especially behavior-based systems) are much more susceptible to it. Facial scanning systems can be foiled with clothing, makeup, eyeglasses, and/or changes in hairstyle. Even relatively stable physiology-based biometrics like fingerprint scans can be defrauded with the use of rubber or gelatin fingers. Matsumoto outlines a gummy finger approach designed to fool even those countermeasures mentioned in section 29.4.1.[33] The protein used has a similar galvanic response to flesh and, since it is very thin and attached to a live finger, has the correct temperature. In some cases, blowing warm air over the scanner may even raise the latent print of the intruder's predecessor.

The deployment of commonly used authentication systems (i.e., ID badges, passwords, etc.) requires relatively little training, although one could argue that better training on the development and use of passwords would improve security. This limited need for training is not the case with most of the most commonly used biometric systems. Both systems administrators and users need instruction and training to ensure smooth operation of the system. Some biometric systems are exquisitely sensitive to intra- and interuser variation in presentation and performance. Their effectiveness becomes substantially compromised and error rates substantially increase in cases of significant variation and/or irregular presentation. A related problem concerns user acceptance of the biometric system. Some users may object to the deployment of biometrics due to concerns over privacy and intrusiveness. In other instances, users may object to the deployment of biometrics and avoid optimal interface with the system because of safety and/or health concerns, general fears, and/or cultural and religious beliefs. For example, some individuals may be concerned that biometric systems that require them to touch a finger pad or hand pad will unnecessarily expose them to germs and place them at risk for illness. Some users may fear that eye scans will damage their eyes. Other users may object to eye scans on the basis that the eyes are the window to the soul. Anderson notes that some persons may object to the use of biometrics due to a personal interpretation of religious doctrine.[34] Notwithstanding users' beliefs and perceptions about the biometric system, in many cases features or elements related to the users and/or the operating environment will influence the successful implementation and effectiveness of the system.

29.6.2 Health and Disability Considerations.   Individuals with arthritis and/or certain other disabilities and physical limitations may be unable to enroll in systems and subsequently, to align themselves physically in an optimal position with respect to biometric sensors. For example, users with severe hand arthritis may be unable to place their hand firmly as required on the hand geometry sensor, and users with migraines and associated photophobia may find it physically too uncomfortable to look straight into the light sensor for the iris scan. Some disabled people may have to be excluded from biometric systems altogether. Some relatively minor disabilities, such as a slight tremor, may compromise a legitimate user's ability to gain access through certain biometric systems. Variations in physical size can also influence system accuracy. An iris scanner positioned for a standard height range may fail to capture images of either very short or very tall individuals, or in some cases an individual's hands or fingers may be either too large or too small to be read accurately in a hand or finger scanner. Likewise, individuals with neck and back problems may find it difficult to use some biometric devices, depending on the kind of positioning required. Systems that rely on behavioral biometrics such as voice or signature are particularly vulnerable to variations and irregularities in user characteristics. For example, users who speak too softly, too loudly, or too rapidly may cause system errors. Minor changes in users' health can affect some biometric readings. Excessive skin moisture or lack of skin moisture can impact finger scans.

Although one of the ideal properties of a biometric is its universality, in reality not everyone has the characteristic or has it to the same degree. For example, some people are born without distinct fingerprints. In other cases, users may have lost the distinctiveness of their fingerprints because of years of manual labor, use of certain chemicals, scarring, or the aging process. Anderson notes that "people with dark-colored eyes and large pupils give poorer iris codes."[35] Certain eye diseases and metabolic conditions may also reduce or negate the efficacy of eye scan authentication. Age has a significant impact on the user-biometric-system interface. Definite physiological changes are associated with the aging process and can result in poor template matching with the live biometric. In this case, reenrollment may be needed. Fingerprints are affected by the aging process as the skin becomes drier and more brittle; voice patterns change in tonal quality over time; and facial shape or appearance may shift with age. Over-all, the acceptability of a biometric system will be lessened if there is the impression that implementation of the system discriminates against, or has an otherwise adverse impact on, the disabled, the ill, ethnic minorities, the elderly, and other protected or traditionally disadvantaged groups of users. Organizations must ensure compliance with the Americans with Disabilities Act when implementing biometric authentication systems. Compliance may involve providing alternative methods of authentication to those affected.

29.6.3 Environmental and Cultural Considerations.

A broad range of factors in the operating environment can also impact the effectiveness and acceptability of biometric systems. User-related cultural, social, and behavioral factors can influence system performance. For instance, the accuracy of facial scans can be compromised by users' changes in hairstyle, facial hair, and headwear as well as by changes in an individual's physical appearance because of significant weight gain or loss. The accuracy of voice/speech recognition systems is affected by the distance between the scanner and the user as well as by the volume of speech. Fingerprint recognition is impeded in cases when users' skin is too dry, whether the condition arises as a result of aging, skin disease, environmental factors, or occupation-related factors, such as frequent hand washing among healthcare professionals. Factors in the surrounding ambient environment may also affect the accuracy of the biometric system. Ambient lighting will influence accuracy and error rate in facial scans and, to a lesser extent, in iris scans. Noise levels can impede the effectiveness of voice recognition systems. Humidity and air temperature can affect the accuracy of fingerprint and hand scans.

29.6.4 Cost Considerations.

Although the cost of biometric system imple-mentation has fallen dramatically in the past few years, it is still a major barrier for many organizations. Costs vary significantly depending on the type of system. Recent reports suggest that newer fingerprint scanners can be purchased for as little as $50 per unit; voice recognition systems can cost in excess of $50,000. However, even the least expensive biometrics systems are likely to cost more than simpler versions of tra-ditional authentication systems. Experts estimate minimum costs, including hardware and software, at $200 or so per user and upward of $150,000 for corporate-wide pro-tection in a medium-sized business. Compounding the cost issues are problems related to the lack of clear standards and the lack of clear interoperability between various biometric authentication systems.

Many of the problems and difficulties with biometrics systems are likely to be corrected or significantly mitigated with technological improvements, better user and administrator training, and good control of environmental conditions. In other cases, problems can be overcome or ameliorated with the use of countermeasures, such as combining different types of biometrics, combining biometrics with traditional authentication systems, and so on. Two major concerns that will continue to loom large and deserve closer examination are biometric identity theft and user privacy.

29.6.5 Attacks on Biometric Systems.

Although biometrics are much less vulnerable to attack than other authentication controls, they are not immune to fraud. Moreover, when a biometric identity is stolen or spoofed, it creates a much bigger problem than that created by the theft of an ID badge, USB key, or password because a biometric cannot be simply canceled and replaced. One of the principal advantages to using biometrics for authentication is their invariability over time. Consequently, when an imposter or intruder defrauds a biometric authentication system and creates a false match error, the entire biometric security system is defrauded and the individual authorized user's biometric integrity is compromised. Likewise, Prabhakar, Pankanti, and Jain note, "One disadvantage of biometrics is that they cannot be easily revoked. If a biometric is ever compromised, it is compromised forever."[36]

A number of analysts believe that the ultimate solution to the problem of biometric identity theft lies in the development of "cancelable biometrics." Researchers at IBM have developed a prototype for the cancelable biometric that incorporates a repeatable distortion of the biometric. Similar in theory to the use of public and private keys for encryption, a unique distortion of the biometric is introduced at each enrollment. Therefore, if a user's biometric is compromised, only the one system is defrauded, not every system in which the user is enrolled.

29.6.6 Privacy Concerns. The use of biometric authentication controls raises significant privacy concerns, particularly in comparison to conventional authentication methods like passwords and ID badges. User objections to biometrics are often based on privacy concerns, sometimes articulated in terms of the user's sense of the intrusiveness of the biometric system. Anecdotal reports suggest that public perceptions of intrusiveness vary among different biometrics and in how biometrics are implemented. With regard to the latter, Nanavati, Thieme, and Nanavati[37] report that there is a greater risk of privacy invasiveness when:

- Deployment is covert (users are not aware of the system's operation) versus overt.
- The system is mandatory versus opt-in.
- The system is used for identification rather than verification.
- It is deployed for an indefinite duration versus fixed duration.
- It is deployed in the public versus the private sector.
- The user is interfacing with the system as an employee/citizen versus an individual/customer.
- An institution, not the user, owns the biometric information.
- The biometric data are stored in a template database versus the user's personal storage.
- The system stores identifiable biometric data versus templates.

A vivid example of the public's lack of acceptance of the covert use of biometric systems comes from the 2001 Super Bowl and the uproar that ensued after the Tampa Police Department deployed facial scanning technology for the purpose of picking out criminal suspects from the audience. In contrast, in the aftermath of the 2001 attacks on the World Trade Center and the Pentagon, there has been fairly widespread public acceptance of the use of facial scanning at airports in the United States.

Users generally view behavior-based biometrics, such as voice recognition and signature verification, as less intrusive and less privacy-threatening than physiology-based biometrics. Facial scanning is viewed as having a high potential for privacy invasion because of the capacity to deploy it without the user's knowledge and participation. Finger scans may be viewed as intrusive and privacy-invasive because of their association with law enforcement functions. The level of intrusiveness of the scanning technique appears to affect users' perception of privacy invasion, with iris scanning provoking more privacy objections than hand scanning. Civil libertarians and users also raise privacy objections over biometric systems that have the potential to uncover additional information about the user beyond the biometric identity. For example, finger scans, because of their capacity to be linked to large law enforcement databases of fingerprints, could be used to reveal information about the user's criminal background. Iris scans have the capacity to reveal confidential medical/health information about the user. Probably one of the most troubling privacy-related aspects of biometrics is the potential for large-scale linkage between biometric systems and the use of biometric data to facilitate large-scale national ID programs. Even though employers may design a biometric system for purely in-house use in order to facilitate verification of employee identities on corporate networks, federal regulations and laws such as the USA PATRIOT Act may eventually compel employers to surrender employees' private biometric data to government authorities.

In summary, the major privacy concerns associated with biometric deployments include:

- Users' loss of anonymity and autonomy
- Risk of unauthorized use of biometric information and/or unauthorized collection of biometric information
- Unnecessary collection of biometric information
- Unauthorized disclosure of biometric information to others
- Systematic reduction of users' reasonable expectation of privacy
- Potential for misuse on the part of overzealous or corrupt government agents

Many of these concerns can be generally lumped under the heading of "function creep" or "mission creep" wherein biometric systems designed for user authentication may, over time, be used for purposes not originally intended. An example of "mission creep" is the use of Social Security Numbers (SSNs) for identification. The original Social Security cards were stamped "Not for Identification." However, many organizations (including the Internal Revenue Service) use SSNs for identification purposes.

Notwithstanding the privacy risks, supporters of biometric authentication systems argue that, properly deployed and with adequate best practice controls, biometric systems actually can function to enhance and protect privacy. Woodward, Orlans, and Higgins point out that "several newly developed biometric technologies use an individual's physical characteristics to construct a digital code for the individual without storing the actual physical characteristics," thus creating a sort of *biometric encryption* that can be used to protect the privacy of an individual's financial, medical, or other data.[38] Nanavati, Thieme, and Nanavati argue that "privacy-sympathetic" biometric systems can be designed.[39] Such systems would:

- Have limited system scope.
- Eschew use of biometrics as a unique identifier.
- Limit retention of biometric information.
- Limit storage of identifiable biometric data.
- Limit collection and storage of extraneous information, while including "opt-out" provisions for users.
- Enable anonymous enrollment and verification.
- Provide means of correcting and accessing biometric-related information.

- Limit system access.
- Use security tools and access policies to protect biometric information.
- Make provisions for third-party audits.
- Disclose the system purpose and objective.
- Disclose enrollment, verification, and identification processes.
- Disclose policies and protections in place to ensure privacy of biometric information.
- Disclose provisions for system termination.[40]

In contrast to this view, Alterman argues that the deployment of biometric systems and the use of biometric data for identification and verification are ethically questionable because they always entail a violation of privacy and autonomy. Alterman finds "something disturbing about the generalized use of biometric identification apart from the standard data privacy issue."[41] He maintains that biometric data "has inherent moral value"[42] but does not go so far as to argue against *any* deployment of biometric identification or verification systems. Rather, he maintains that they must be judiciously implemented and deployed only with due consideration to users' privacy concerns.

29.7 RECENT TRENDS IN BIOMETRIC AUTHENTICATION

29.7.1 Government Advances in Biometric Authentication.
Although private sector organizations are increasingly adopting biometric technologies for their authentication needs, the government (public) sector has led investment in biometrics. The 2001 terrorist attacks on the World Trade Center and the Pentagon, and the ensuing USA PATRIOT Act, have encouraged increasing government commitment to biometric technologies. The Department of Defense (DoD), the Department of Homeland Security (DHS), the Immigration and Naturalization Service, and the Department of Transportation are the government agencies most involved in the deployment of biometrics technologies. The DoD's Common Access Card program involves putting biometric technology on a smart ID card. The DoD also recently acquired 1,300 U.are.U. fingerprint[43] recognition systems in order to enhance network security at workstations in its offices in the Washington, DC, metropolitan area. The US-VISIT program under the DHS is another government program that incorporates biometrics (including face and fingerprint) into a smart ID card. Another DHS program, the Transportation Worker Identity Credential, incorporates biometric information in an ID card.

29.7.2 Face Scanning at Airports and Casinos.
After the 2001 terrorist attacks on the World Trade Center and the Pentagon, most of the nation's airports moved to incorporate face-scanning technologies into their security systems. Most studies of the effectiveness of these systems, however, have revealed their high error rates and low accuracy rates.

Casinos utilize facial scanning systems to identify professional "advantage players" and cheats. Although this is largely unregulated in the United States, Canadian casinos must notify players regarding the use of such systems. Casinos share data on professionals and cheats. One firm has networked 125 casino surveillance operators in the United States, Canada, Puerto Rico, Aruba, and the Bahamas and provides real-time alerts and other information useful in identifying suspicious players. However, it is unclear as to how such systems may be affected by international law. Article 12 of the

United Nations Universal Declaration of Human Rights guarantees that "[n]o one shall be subjected to arbitrary interference with his privacy, family, home or correspondence, nor to attacks upon his honor and reputation. Everyone has the right to the protection of the law against such interference or attacks."[44] Whether this system amounts to arbitrary interference or an attack on one's honor has not been addressed by the courts, but a case clearly could be made that covert use of such systems does so. A best practice for any surveillance system is informed consent. Organizations should clearly post notifications about the use of surveillance systems in order to protect themselves from legal challenges.

29.7.3 Increased Deployment in the Financial Industry.

Usually slow to embrace new technologies, the financial industry is one of the leaders in the adoption of biometric authentication controls. Current deployments range from fingerprint scanners securing computer networks for brokers, to facial recognition systems at ATMs to iris scanning for high-security access points. International Biometric Group projected that U.S. financial services firms would spend $672 million in 2007 for various biometric deployments. One of the biggest deployments to date has been United Bankers' Bancorporation (UBB) adoption of U.are.U, a fingerprint recognition system that allows UBB customers to automatically log onto UBB's Web site with finger scans versus passwords. UBB also adopted a fingerprint authentication system for its employees. Wells Fargo, Bloomberg Financial, and Janus Capital Management are other well-known financial firms that have adopted biometric authentication systems for employees and/or customers. Although some financial institutions have selected voice, iris, or facial-scan-based systems, most seem to be choosing finger-scan systems.

29.7.4 Biometrics in the Healthcare Industry.

Spurred in part by new regulations that require healthcare institutions to ensure the privacy and security of patient records, healthcare companies have also been at the forefront in the adoption of biometric authentication. Among the major healthcare organizations that have moved to biometric authentication is the Mayo Clinic, which adopted a fingerprint ID system in 2002. The majority of healthcare institutions that have adopted biometric authentication systems have selected finger-scan ID systems. However, deployment of these systems in healthcare organizations has not met with the same success as seen in the financial services industry. Issues involving the potential transmission of illness via physical contact with the fingerprint scanner are not trivial. Additionally, error rates have been higher and accuracy rates much lower than expected. The major reason behind the high incidence of errors appears to be the particulars of the healthcare environment, especially the characteristics of the hands of the doctors, nurses, and other healthcare workers using these systems. Specifically, system performance appears to be undermined by the chronically dry hands of these workers, a condition resulting from frequent hand washing and the use of alcohol-based hand sanitizers. Another problem has been the resistance to using the fingerprint technology by both nurses and doctors, who feel that it involves a privacy intrusion.

29.7.5 Increased Deployment of Time and Attendance Systems.

An increasing number of companies across many different industries are deploying biometric-based time-and-attendance systems. A shift from the past practice is in the increased use of biometric attendance and tracking systems for white-collar workers. Previously the focus was on blue-collar factory workers. Although some employers are

EXHIBIT 29.3 Comparison of Leading Biometric Technologies

	Finger Scan	Facial Scan	Hand Scan	Iris Scan	Voice Recognition
Accuracy	High	Low	Medium	Very high	Low to medium
Ease of Use	High	Medium	High	Low to medium	High
User Acceptance	Medium	High (overt) Low (covert)	High	Low to medium	High
Privacy Concerns	High	Very high (overt)	Medium	High	Very low
Cost	Low to medium	Low to medium	Medium	High	Low
Performance	High	Low	Medium	High	Low
Potential for Circumvention	Medium	High	Low to medium	Very low	High
Distinctiveness	High	Low	Medium	Very high	Low
Barriers to Universality	Worn ridges; hand or finger impairment	None	Hand impairment	Visual impairment	Speech impairment
Susceptibility to Changes in Biometric	Low to medium	Medium to high	Medium	Low	Low to medium
Susceptibility to Changes in the Environment	Low	High	Very low	Low	Medium to high
Error-Causing Factors	Age, trauma, degradation of prints	Lighting, contrast, pose, movement, expression	Hand injury or trauma, inability to place correctly	Positioning, eye angle, glasses, disease	Illness, age, quality of communication system, ambient noise
Mitigations for Potential Errors	Periodic reenrollment, enrollment of multiple fingers	Frequent reenrollment, multiple scans, controlled environment	Periodic reenrollment, enrollment of both hands	Periodic reenrollment, user training, enroll both irises	Periodic reenrollment, control ambient noise

using the traditional hand-scanning systems, there appears to be a shift toward the use of finger-scanning time-and-attendance systems. This shift seems to be related to the more competitive pricing structure for the finger-scanning systems.

29.8   SUMMARY AND RECOMMENDATIONS.   There is no universal "best" biometric authentication system. Each of the five leading biometric technologies carries specific advantages and disadvantages. Some biometric technologies are more appropriate for certain applications and environments than their counterparts. An organization in the midst of evaluating potential biometrics authentication implementation must recognize that there will be trade-offs in any selection, such as cost for accuracy, privacy versus user acceptance, and so on, and there are not yet any universal decision factors for selecting a particular biometric technology for a specific application. There is, however, substantial research into many of the advantages and disadvantages of biometrics. Exhibit 29.3 provides a summary comparison of the features of the five leading biometric technologies discussed in this chapter. The features, shown in the extreme left column, were excerpted from various researcher efforts, and the rankings represent an amalgam of the rankings found in the literature.

Although biometric authentication systems promise cost savings and higher levels of security for organizations, they are not a panacea. Many factors affect how well or poorly biometric authentication controls will perform in a given organizational environment. Included among these factors are the users, the administration, the environment, the infrastructure, the budget, the communication system, and the existing security needs. Although many biometric technologies are capable of operating as stand-alone systems, in reality their accuracy and performance levels would be greatly improved by combining them with more conventional authentication methods, such as passwords and keys. Such multifactor systems offer greater security and reliability.

In selecting a biometric authentication system and preparing for an implementation, organizations should focus on the user-technology interface and the conditions in the operational environment that may influence the technology's performance. For example, the healthcare industry's unreflective embrace of finger scan technology illustrates the dangers of failing to heed environmental realities. It is important that organizations consider not only the practical impediments to effective implementation but also the potential psychological impediments, such as user fears about the technology. Ethically, the organization also has the obligation to consider carefully the extent to which the implementation of biometric authentication compromises the privacy rights of users. In making this assessment, management must take into account the possibility that the organization may be compelled to release employees' biometric-related information to government authorities.

A review of the recent literature (2000–2007) on the adoption of biometric technologies in organizations revealed almost no research regarding the factors influencing the decision to implement biometric access technologies. Research into this area could help explain why organizations are reluctant to implement biometric authentication controls. It could also help information technology and security decision makers to determine what aspects of biometric security technologies are of concern to them and accordingly recommend appropriate security solutions for their organizations. Security technology companies can also benefit from this research by knowing what is important to their customer base while introducing new IT security products and/or technologies.

29.9 FURTHER READING

Kaine, A. K. " The Impact of Facial Recognition Systems on Business Practices within an Operational Setting." *25th International Conference Information Technology Interfaces,* June 16–19, 2003, Cavtat, Croatia, pp. 315–320.

Hamilton, D. P. " Workplace Security; Read My Lips: Are Biometric Systems the Security Solution of the Future?" *Wall Street Journal*, September 29, 2003.

Jain, A. K, P. Flynn, and A. A. Ross, eds. *Handbook of Biometrics*. New York: Springer, 2007.

NIST Biometrics Resource Center Web site. www.itl.nist.gov/div893/biometrics/.

Ratha, N. K., Connell, J. H., & Bolle, R. M. " Enhanced Security and Privacy in Biometrics-Based Authentication Systems." *IBM Systems Journal* **40**, No. 3 (2001): 614–634.

Ratha, N., and R. Bolle, eds. *Automatic Fingerprint Recognition Systems*. New York: Springer, 2003.

Ross, A. A., K. Nandakumar, and A. K. Jain. *Handbook of Multibiometrics*. New York: Springer, 2006.

Vacca, J. R. *Biometric Technologies and Verification Systems*. Boston: Butterworth-Heinemann, 2007.

29.10 NOTES

1. J. Boroshok, "Pointing the Finger at Biometrics." SearchSecurity.com, January 14, 205; retrieved February 4, 2007 from http://searchsecurity.techtarget.com/originalContent/0,289142,sid14_gci1044805,00.html.

2. International Biometric Group, "Biometrics Market and Industry Report 2004–2008" (2005); retrieved June 4, 2005 from www.biometricgroup. com/reports/public/market_report.html.

3. International Biometric Group, "Biometrics Market and Industry Report 2007–2012" (January 2007); retrieved February 4, 2007 from www.biometricgroup. com/reports/public/market_report.html.

4. G. V. Hulme, "Slow Acceptance for Biometrics," *Information Week*, February 10, 2003, p. 57.

5. J. Chirillo and S. Blaul, *Implementing Biometric Security* (Indianapolis, IN: John Wiley & Sons, 2003), p. 2.

6. S. Nanavati, M. Thieme, and R. Nanavati, *Biometrics: Identity Verification in a Networked World* (Hoboken, NJ: John Wiley & Sons, 2002), p. 11.

7. A. K. Jain, "Biometric Recognition: How Do I Know Who You Are," *IEEE Symposia* (2004): 3–5.

8. R. M. Bolle, J. H. Connell, S. Pankanti, N. K. Ratha, & A. W. Senior, *Guide to Biometrics* (New York: Springer-Verlag, 2004).

9. Jain, "Biometric Recognition," p. 3.

10. Bolle et al., *Guide to Biometrics*, p. 6.

11. Jain, "Biometric Recognition," p. 3.

12. Nanavati et al., *Biometrics*, p. 12.

13. Nanavati et al., *Biometrics*, p. 14.

14. Nanavati et al., *Biometrics*, p. 14.

15. Jain, "Biometric Recognition," p. 3.

16. J. D. Woodward, N. M. Orlans, and P. T. Higgins, *Biometrics* (New York: McGraw-Hill/Osborne, 2003), p. 37.

17. S. Liu and M. Silverman, "A Practical Guide to Biometric Security Technology," *IT Pro* (January/February 2001): 20.

18. Nanavati et al., *Biometrics*, p. 20.

19. International Biometric Group, "Biometrics Market and Industry Report 2004–2008." See also International Biometric Group, "Biometrics Market and Industry Report 2007–2012"; J. McHale, "Biometrics: The Body's Keys," *Military & Aerospace Electronics,* 14, No. 12 (December 2003): 17–23.

20. Chirillo and Blaul, *Implementing Biometric Security*, p. 21.

21. Chirillo and Blaul, *Implementing Biometric Security,* p. 24.

22. Bolle et al., *Guide to Biometrics*, p. 36.

23. N. Imparato, "Does Face Recognition Have a Future?" *Intelligent Enterprise* 5, No. 7 (April 2002): 20.

24. Nanavati et al., *Biometrics*, p. 99.

25. Nanavati et al., *Biometrics*, p. 99.

26. Nanavati et al., *Biometrics*, p. 87.

27. Nanavati et al., *Biometrics*, p. 87.

28. Bolle et al., *Guide to Biometrics*. p. 40.

29. Nanavati et al., *Biometrics*, p. 27.

30. J. Ashbourn, *Practical Biometrics: From Aspiration to Implementation* (London: Springer-Verlag, 2003), p. 10.

31. Nanavati et al., *Biometrics*, p. 35.

32. Ashbourn, *Practical Biometrics*, p. 10.

33. T. Matsumoto, "Importance of Open Discussion on Adversarial Analyses for Mobile Security Technologies: A Case Study for User Identification," May 14, 2002; retrieved March 17, 2007 from http://crypto.csail.mit.edu/classes/6.857/papers/gummy-slides.pdf.

34. R. J. Anderson, *Security Engineering: A Guide to Building Dependable Distributed Systems* (Hoboken, NJ: John Wiley & Sons, 2001).

35. Anderson, *Security Engineering*, p. 274.

36. S. Prabhakar, S. Pankanti, and A. K. Jain, "Biometric Recognition: Security and Privacy Concerns," *IEEE Security & Privacy* (March/April 2003): 39.

37. Nanavati et al., *Biometrics*.

38. Woodward et al., *Biometrics*. p. 211.

39. Nanavati et al., *Biometrics*.

40. Nanavati et al., *Biometrics*.

41. A. Alterman, " 'A Piece of Yourself': Ethical Issues in Biometric Identification," *Ethics and Information Technology* 5, No. 3 (2003): 143.

42. Alterman, " 'A Piece of Yourself,' " p. 145.

43. www.digitalpersona.com/products/UPOS.php

44. United Nations, "Universal Declaration of Human Rights," December 10, 1948; retrieved March 17, 2007 from www.un.org/Overview/rights.html.

CHAPTER 30

E-COMMERCE AND WEB SERVER SAFEGUARDS

Robert Gezelter

30.1 INTRODUCTION.   Today, electronic commerce involves the entire enterprise. While the most obvious e-commerce applications involve business transactions with outside customers on the World Wide Web (WWW or Web), they are merely the proverbial tip of the iceberg. The presence of e-commerce has become far more pervasive, often involving the entire logistical and financial supply chains that are the foundations of modern commerce. Even the smallest organizations now rely on the Web for access to services and information.

The pervasive desire to improve efficiency often causes a convergence between the systems supporting conventional operations with those supporting the organization's online business. It is thus common for internal systems at bricks-and-mortar stores to utilize the same back-office systems as are used by Web customers. It is also common for kiosks and cash registers to use wireless networks to establish connections back to internal systems. These interconnections have the potential to provide intruders with access directly into the heart of the enterprise.

The TJX case, which came to public attention in the beginning of 2007, was one of a series of large-scale compromises of electronically stored information on back-office and e-commerce systems. Most notably, the TJX case appears to have started with an insufficiently secured corporate network and the associated back-office systems, not a Web site penetration. This breach escalated into a security breach of corporate data systems. It has been reported that at least 94 million credit cards were compromised.[1] On November 30, 2007, it was reported that TJX, the parent organization of stores including TJ Maxx and Marshall's, agreed to settle bank claims related to VISA cards for US$ 40.9M.[2]

E-commerce has now come of age, giving rise to fiduciary risks that are important to senior management and to the board of directors. The security of data networks, both those used by customers and those used internally, now has reached the level where it significantly affects the bottom line. TJX has suffered both monetarily and in public relations, with stories concerning the details of this case appearing in the *Wall Street Journal*, the *New York Times*, *Business Week*, and many industry trade publications. Data security is no longer an abstract issue of concern only to technology personnel. The legal settlements are far in excess of the costs directly associated with curing the technical problem.

Protecting e-commerce information requires a multifaceted approach, involving business policies and strategies as well as the technical issues more familiar to information security professionals.

Throughout the enterprise, people and information are physically safeguarded. Even the smallest organizations have a locked door and a receptionist to keep outsiders from entering the premises. The larger the organization, the more elaborate the precautions needed. Small businesses have simple locked doors; larger enterprises often have many levels of security, including electronic locks, security guards, and additional levels of receptionists. Companies also jealously guard the privacy of their executive conversations and research projects. Despite these norms, it is not unusual to find that information security practices are weaker than physical security measures. Connection to the Internet (and within the company, to the intranet) worsens the problem by greatly increasing the risk and decreasing the difficulty, of attacks.

30.2 BUSINESS POLICIES AND STRATEGIES. In the complex world of e-commerce security, best practices are constantly evolving. New protocols and products are announced regularly. Before the Internet explosion, most companies rarely shared their data and their propriety applications with any external entities, and information security was not a high priority. Now companies taking advantage of e-commerce need sound security architectures for virtually all applications. Effective information security has become a major business issue. This chapter provides a flexible framework for building secure e-commerce applications and assistance in identifying the appropriate and required security services. The theoretical examples shown are included to facilitate the reader's understanding of the framework in a business-to-customer (B2C) and business-to-business (B2B) environment.

A reasonable framework for e-commerce security is one that:

1. Defines information security concerns specific to the application.
2. Defines the security services needed to address the security concerns.
3. Selects security services based on a cost-benefit analysis and risk versus reward issues.
4. Ensures the ongoing attention to changes in technologies and requirements as both threats and application requirements change.

This four-step approach is recommended to define the security services selection and decision-making processes.

30.2.1 Step 1: Define Information Security Concerns Specific to the Application. The first step is to define or develop the application architecture and the data classification involved in each transaction. This step considers how the application will function. As a general rule, if security issues are defined in terms of the impact on the business, it will be easier to discuss with management and easier to define security requirements.

The recommended approach is to develop a transactional follow-the-flow diagram that tracks transactions and data types through the various servers and networks. This should be a functional and logical view of how the application is going to work—that is, how transactions will occur, what systems will participate in the transaction management, and where these systems will support the business objectives and the organization's product value chain. Data sources and data interfaces need to be identified, and the information processed needs to be classified. In this way a complete transactional flow can be represented. (See Exhibit 30.1.)

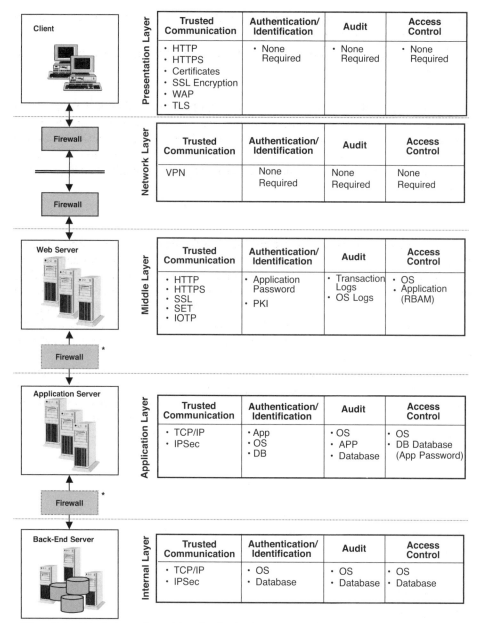

Client	**Presentation Layer**	**Trusted Communication**	**Authentication/ Identification**	**Audit**	**Access Control**
		• HTTP • HTTPS • Certificates • SSL Encryption • WAP • TLS	• None Required	• None Required	• None Required

Firewall / Firewall	**Network Layer**	**Trusted Communication**	**Authentication/ Identification**	**Audit**	**Access Control**
		VPN	None Required	None Required	None Required

Web Server	**Middle Layer**	**Trusted Communication**	**Authentication/ Identification**	**Audit**	**Access Control**
		• HTTP • HTTPS • SSL • SET • IOTP	• Application Password • PKI	• Transaction Logs • OS Logs	• OS • Application (RBAM)

Application Server	**Application Layer**	**Trusted Communication**	**Authentication/ Identification**	**Audit**	**Access Control**
		• TCP/IP • IPSec	• App • OS • DB	• OS • APP • Database	• OS • DB Database (App Password)

Back-End Server	**Internal Layer**	**Trusted Communication**	**Authentication/ Identification**	**Audit**	**Access Control**
		• TCP/IP • IPSec	• OS • Database	• OS • Database	• OS • Database

*Firewall should be between the web layer/application layer or the application/back-end layers depending on the company's architecture.

EXHIBIT 30.1   Trust Levels for B2C Security Services

Common tiered architecture points include:

- **Clients.** These may be PCs, thin clients (devices that use shared applications from a server and have small amounts of memory), personal digital assistants (PDAs), and wireless application protocol (WAP) telephones.
- **Servers.** These may include World Wide Web, application, database, and middleware processors, as well as back-end servers and legacy systems.

- **Network devices.** Switches, routers firewalls, NICs, codecs, modems, and internal and external hosting sites.
- **Network spaces.** Network demilitarized zones (DMZs), intranets, extranets, and the Internet.

It is important at this step of the process to identify the criticality of the application to the business and the overriding security concerns: transactional confidentiality, transactional integrity, or transactional availability. Defining these security issues will help justify the security services selected to protect the system. The more completely the architecture can be described, the more thoroughly the information can be protected via security services.

30.2.2 Step 2: Develop Security Service Options. The second step considers the security services alternatives for each architecture component and the data involved in each transaction. Each architectural component and data point should be analyzed and possible security services defined for each. Cost and feasibility should not be considered to any great degree at this stage. The objective is to form a complete list of security service options with all alternatives considered. The process should be comparable with, or use the same techniques as, brainstorming. All ideas, even if impractical or far-fetched, should be included.

Decisions should not be made during this step; that process is reserved for Step 3.

The information security organization provides services to an enterprise. The services provided by information security organizations vary from company to company. Several factors will determine the required services, but the most significant considerations include:

- Industry factors
- The company's risk appetite
- Maturity of the security function
- Organizational approach (centralized or decentralized)
- Impact of past security incidents
- Internal organizational factors
- Political factors
- Regulatory factors
- Perceived strategic value of information security

Several factors contribute to the services that information security organizations provide. "Security services" are defined as safeguards and control measures to protect the confidentiality, integrity, and accountability of information and computing resources. Security services that are required to secure e-commerce transactions need to be based on the business requirements and on the willingness to assume or reduce the risk of the information being compromised. Information security professionals can be subject-matter experts, but they are rarely equipped to make the business decisions required to select the necessary services. Twelve security services that are critical for successful e-commerce security have been identified:

1. **Policy and procedures** are a security service that defines the amount of information security that the organization requires and how it will be implemented. Effective policy and procedures will dovetail with system strategy, development, implementation, and operation. Each organization will have different policies and procedures; best practice dictates that organizations have policies and procedures based on the risk the organization is willing to take with its information. At a minimum, organizations should have a high-level policy that dictates the proper use of information assets and the ramifications of misuse.

2. **Confidentiality and encryption** are a security service that secures data while they are stored or in transit from one machine to another. A number of encryption schemes and products exist; each organization needs to identify those products that best integrate with the application being deployed. For a discussion of cryptography, see Chapter 7 in this *Handbook*.

3. **Authentication and identification** are a security service that differentiates users and verifies that they are who they claim to be. Typically, passwords are used, but stronger methods include tokens, smart cards, and biometrics. These stronger methods verify what you have (e.g., token) or who you are (e.g., biometrics), not just what you know (password). Two-factor authentication combines two of these three methods and is referred to as strong authentication. For more on this subject, see Chapter 28 in this *Handbook*.

4. **Authorization** determines what access privileges a user requires within the system. Access includes data, operating system, transactional functions, and processes. Access should be approved by management who own or understand the system before access is granted. Authorized users should be able to access only the information they require for their jobs.

5. **Authenticity** is a security service that validates a transaction and binds the transaction to a single accountable person or entity. Also called nonrepudiation, authenticity ensures that a person cannot dispute the details of a transaction. This is especially useful for contract and legal purposes.

6. **Monitoring and audit** provide an electronic trail for a historical record of the transaction. Audit logs consist of operating system logs, application transaction logs, database logs, and network traffic logs. Monitoring these logs for unauthorized events is considered a best practice.

7. **Access controls and intrusion detection** are technical, physical, and administrative services that prevent unauthorized access to hardware, software, or information. Data are protected from alteration, theft, or destruction. Access controls are preventive—stopping unauthorized access from occurring. Intrusion detection catches unauthorized access after it has occurred, so that damage can be minimized and access cut off. These controls are especially necessary when confidential or critical information is being processed.

8. **Trusted communication** is a security service that assures that communication is secure. In most instances involving the Internet, this means that the communication will be encrypted. In the past, communication was trusted because it was contained within an organization's perimeter. Communication is currently ubiquitous and can come from almost anywhere, including extranets and the Internet.

9. **Antivirus** is a security service that prevents, detects, and cleans viruses, Trojan horse programs, and other malware.

10. **System integrity controls** are security services that help to assure that the system has not been altered or tampered with by unauthorized access.

11. **Data retention and disposal** are a security service that keeps required information archived, or deletes data when they are no longer required. Availability of retained data is critical when an emergency exists. This is true whether the problem is a systems outage or a legal process, whether caused by a natural disaster or by a terrorist attack (e.g., September 11, 2001).

12. **Data classification** is a security service that identifies the sensitivity and confidentiality of information. The service provides guides for information labeling, and for protection during the information's life.

Once an e-commerce application has been identified, the team must identify the security issues with that specific application and the necessary security services. Not all of the services will be relevant, but using a complete list and excluding those that are not required will assure a comprehensive assessment of requirements, with appropriate security built into the system's development. In fact, management can reconcile the services accepted with their level of risk acceptance.

30.2.3 Step 3: Select Security Service Options Based on Requirements. The third step uses classical cost-benefit and risk management analysis techniques to make a final selection of security service options. However, we recommend that all options identified in Step 3 be distributed along a continuum, such as shown in Exhibit 30.2, so that they can be viewed together, and compared.

Gauging and comparing the level of security for each security service and the data within the transaction will facilitate the decision process. Feasible alternatives can then be identified and the best solution selected based on the requirements. The most significant element to consider is the relative reduction in risk of each option, compared with the other alternatives. The cost-benefit analysis is based on the risk versus reward issues. The effectiveness information is very useful in a cost-benefit model.

Four additional concepts drive the security service option selection:

1. Implementation risk, or feasibility

2. Cost to implement and support

3. Effectiveness in increasing control, thereby reducing risk

4. Data classification

Implementation risk considers the feasibility of implementing the security service option. Some security systems are difficult to implement due to factors such as product maturity, scalability, complexity, and supportability. Other factors to consider include skills available, legal issues, integration required, capabilities, prior experience, and limitations of the technology.

Cost to implement and support measures the costs of hardware and software implementation, support, and administration. Consideration of administration issues is especially critical because high-level support of the security service is vital to an organization's success.

Effectiveness measures the reduction of risk proposed by a security service option once it is in production. Risk can be defined as the impact and likelihood of a negative event occurring after mitigating strategies have been implemented. An example of a negative event is the theft of credit card numbers from a business's database. Such an

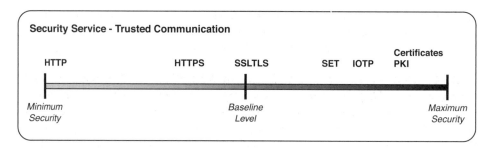

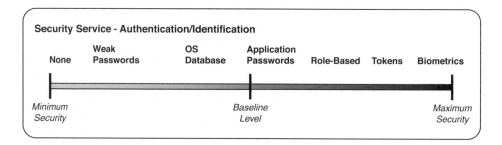

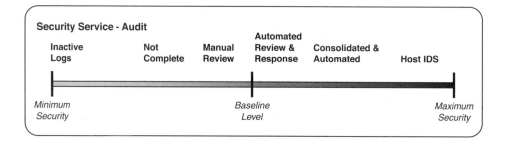

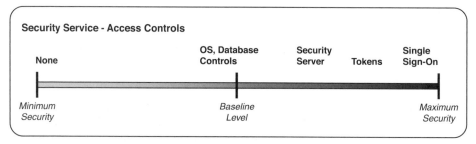

EXHIBIT 30.2   Continuum of Options

event causes not only possible losses to consumers but also negative public relations that may impact future business. Effective security service options reduce the risk of a negative event occurring.

Data classification measures the sensitivity and confidentiality of the information being processed. Data must be classified and protected from misuse, disclosure, theft, or destruction, regardless of storage format, throughout their life (from creation through destruction). Usually the originator of the information is considered to be the owner of the information and is responsible for classification, identification, and labeling. The more sensitive and confidential the information, the more information security measures will be required to safeguard and protect it.

30.2.4 Step 4: Ensures the Ongoing Attention to Changes in Technologies and Requirements. The only constant in this analysis is the need to evolve and to address ever-increasing threats and technologies. Whatever security approaches the preceding steps identify, they must always be considered in the context of the continuing need to update the selected approaches. Changes will be inevitable, whether they arrive from compliance, regulation, technological advances, or new threats.

30.2.5 Using the Security Services Framework. The next two sections are examples to demonstrate the power of the security services methodology. The first example is a B2C model; the business could be any direct-selling application. The second example is a B2B model. Both businesses take advantage of the Internet to improve their product value chain. The examples are a short demonstration of the security services methodology, neither complete nor representative of any particular application or business.

30.2.5.1 *Business-to-Customer Security Services.* The B2C company desires to contact customers directly through the Internet, and allow them to enter their information into the application. These assumptions are made to prepare this B2C system example:

- Internet-facing business
- Major transactions supported
- External customer-based system, specifically excluding support, administration, and operations
- Business-critical application
- Highly sensitive data classification
- Three-tiered architecture
- Untrusted clients, because anyone on the Internet can be a customer

Five layers must be secured:

1. The *presentation layer* is the customer interface, what the client sees or hears using the Web device. The client is the customer's untrusted PC or other device. The security requirements at this level are minimal because the company will normally not dictate the security of the customer. The identification and authentication done at the presentation level are those controls associated with access to the device. The proliferation of appliances in the client space (e.g., traditional PCs, thin desktops, and PDAs) makes it difficult to establish a uniform access control procedure at this level. Although this layer is the terminal endpoint of the secure connection, it is not inherently trustworthy, as has been illustrated by all too many incidents involving public computers in cafes, hotels, and other establishments.

2. The *network layer* is the communication connection between the business and the customer. The client, or customer, uses an Internet connection to access the

B2C Web applications. The security requirements are minimal, but sensitive, and confidential traffic will need to be encrypted.

3. The *middle layer* is the Web server that connects to the client's browser and can forward and receive information. The Web server supports the application by being an intermediary between the business and the customer. The Web server needs to be very secure. Theft, tampering, and fraudulent use of information needs to be prevented. Denial of service and Web site defacement are also common risks that need to be prevented in the middle layer.

4. The *application layer* is where the information is processed. The application serves as an intermediary between the customer requests and the fulfillment systems internal to the business. In some examples, the application server and database server are the same because both the application and database reside on the same server. However, they could reside within the Web server in other cases.

5. The *internal layer* is comprised of the business's legacy systems and databases that support customer servicing. Back-end servers house the supporting application, including order processing, accounts receivable, inventory, distribution, and other systems.

For each of these five levels, we need four security services:

1. Trusted communications
2. Authentication/identification
3. Audit
4. Access controls

Step 1: Define Information Security Concerns Specific to the Application. Defining security issues will be particular to the system being implemented. To understand the risk of the system, the best starting place is with the business risk; then defining risks at each element of the architecture.

Business Risk

• The application needs high availability, because customers will demand contact at off-hours and on weekends.

• The Web pages need to be secure from tampering and cybervandalism, because the business is concerned about the loss of customer confidence as a result of negative publicity.

• Customers must be satisfied with the level of service.

• The system will process customer credit card information and will be subject to the privacy regulations of the Gramm-Leach-Bililey Act, 15 USC §§ 6801–09.

Technology Concerns

Of the five architectural layers in this example, four will need to be secured:

1. The *presentation layer* will not be secured or trusted. Communications between the client and the Web server will be encrypted at the *network layer*.

2. The *network layer* will need to filter unwanted traffic, to prevent denial of service (DoS) attacks and to monitor for possible intrusions.

3. The *middle layer* will need to prevent unauthorized access, be tamper-proof, contain effective monitoring, and support efficient and effective processing.

4. The *application layer* will need to prevent unauthorized access, support timely processing of transactions, provide effective audit trails, and process confidential information.

5. The *internal layer* will need to prevent unauthorized access, especially through Internet connections, and to protect confidential information during transmission, processing, and storage.

Step 2: Develop Security Services Options. The four security services reviewed in this example are the most critical in an e-commerce environment. Other services such as nonrepudiation and data classification are important but not included in order to simplify the example. Services elected are:

- Trusted communication
- Authentication and identification
- Monitoring and auditing
- Access control

Many security services options are available for the B2C case, with more products and protocols on the horizon. There are five architectural layers for each of the services defined in Step 1.

1. **Presentation layer.** Several different options can be selected for trusted communication. Hypertext transfer protocol (HTTP) is the most common, with secure socket layer (SSL) certificates in a PKI, or digital signatures, being even less common, and WAP for wireless communications and transport security layer protocol (TLS) for encrypted Internet communications being the most rare. Because the client is untrusted, the client's authentication, audit, or access control methods cannot be relied on.

2. **Network layer.** Virtual private networks (VPNs) are considered best practice for secure network layer communication. Firewalls are effective devices for securing network communication. The client may have a personal firewall. If the client is in a large corporation, there is a significant likelihood that a firewall will intervene in communications. If the client is using a home or laptop computer, then a personal firewall may protect traffic. There will also be a firewall on the B2C company side of the Internet.

3. **Middle layer.** The Web server and the application server security requirements are significant. Unauthorized access to the Web server can result in Web site defacement by hackers who change the Web data. More important, access to the Web or application server can lead to theft, manipulation, or deletion of customer or proprietary data. Communication between the Web server and the client needs to be secure in e-commerce transactions. HTTP is the most common form of browser communication. In 2000, it was reported that over 33 percent of credit card transactions were using unsecured HTTP.[3] In 2007, VISA reported that compliance with the Payment Card Industry Data Security Standard (PCI DSS) had improved to 77 percent of the largest merchants in the United States,[4] still far from universal. This lack of encryption is a violation of both the merchant's agreement and the PCI, but episodes continue to occur. In the same vein, it is not unusual for organizations to misuse encryption, whether it involves self-signed, expired, or not generally recognized certificates. (See Chapter 37 in this

Handbook.) SSL and HTTPS are the most common secure protocols, but the encryption key length and contents is critical: The larger the key, the more secure the transaction is from brute-force decryption. (See Chapter 7.) Digital certificates in a PKI and digital signatures are not as common, but they are more effective forms of security.

4. **Application layer.** The application server provides the main processing for the Web server. This layer may include transaction processing and database applications; it needs to be secure to prevent erroneous or fraudulent processing. Depending on the sensitivity of the information processed, the data may need to be encrypted. Interception and the unauthorized manipulation of data are the greatest risks in the application layer.

5. **Internal layer.** In a typical example, the internal layer is secured by a firewall protecting the external-facing system. This firewall helps the B2C company protect itself from Internet intrusions. Database and operating system passwords and access control measures are required.

Management can decide which security capability is required and at what level. This format can be repeated to discuss security services at all levels and all systems, not just e-commerce–related systems.

Step 3: Select Security Service Options Based on Requirements. In Step 3 the B2C company can analyze and select the security services that best meet its legal, business, and information security requirements. There are four stages required for this analysis:

1. Implementation risk, or feasibility
2. Cost to implement and support
3. Effectiveness in increasing control, thereby reducing risk
4. Data classification

Implementation risk is a function of the organization's ability to effectively roll out the technology. In this example, we assume that implementation risk is low and resources are readily available to implement the technology.

Costs to implement and support are paramount to the decision making process. Both costs need to be considered together. Unfortunately, the cost to support is difficult to quantify and easily overlooked. In this example, resources are available to both implement and support the technology.

Effectiveness in increasing control is an integral part of the benefit and risk management decisions. Each component needs to be considered in order to determine cross-benefits where controls overlap and supplement other controls. In this case, the control increase is understood and supported by management.

Data classification is the foundation for requirements. It will help drive the cost-benefit discussions because it captures the value of the information to the underlying business. In this example, the data are considered significant enough to warrant additional security measures to safeguard the data against misuse, theft, and loss.

There are many technology decisions required to secure the example environment. Management can use this approach to plot the security levels required by the system. For example, for system audit services, in order of minimal service to maximum:

- The minimal level of security is to have systems with a limited number of system events logged. For example, the default level of logging from the manufacturer is used but does not contain all of the required information. The logs are not reviewed but are available for forensics in the event of a security incident.

- A higher level of security is afforded with a log that records more activities based on requirements and not, for example, the manufacturer's default level. As in the minimal level of security, the activities are logged and available to support forensics but are not reviewed. In this case, more types of information are recorded in the system log, but it still may not contain all that is required.

- A sufficient log is kept on each server and is manually monitored for anomalies and potential security events.

- The log is automatically reviewed by software on each server.

- System logs are consolidated onto a centralized security server. Data from the system logs are transmitted to the centralized security server, and software is then used to scan the logs for specific events that require attention. Events such as attempts to gain escalated privileges to root or administrative access can be flagged for manual review.

- The maximum service level is a host-based intrusion detection system (IDS) used to scan the system logs for anomalies and possible security events. Once detected, action needs to be taken to resolve the intrusion. The procedure should include processes such as notification, escalation, and automated defensive response.

30.2.5.2 Business-to-Business Security Services. The second case study uses the security services framework in a B2B example. Following is a theoretical discussion of how the framework can be applied to B2B e-commerce security. These assumptions may be made in this B2B system example:

- Internet-facing.
- Supports major transactions.
- Descriptions will be external and customer based (excluding support, administration, and operations security services).
- Trusted communication is required.
- Three-tier architecture.
- Untrusted client.
- Business-critical application.
- Data are classified as highly sensitive.

There are five layers in this example that need to be secured:

1. The *presentation layer* is the customer interface and is what the client sees or hears using the Web device. The client is the customer's untrusted PC, but more security constraints can be applied because the business can dictate enhanced security. As noted previously, the security of the presentation layer is complicated by the wide range of potential client devices that may be employed.

2. The *application layer* is where the information is processed. The application serves as an intermediary between the business customer's requests and the

fulfillment systems internal to the business (the back-end server). The application server is the supporting server and database.

3. The *customer internal layer* is the interface between the application server supporting the system at the customer's business location, and the customer's own internal legacy applications and systems.

4. The *network layer* is the communication connection between the business and another business. The Internet is used to connect the two businesses. Sensitive and confidential traffic will need to be encrypted. Best practice is to have the traffic further secured using a firewall.

5. The *internal layer* is the business's legacy systems that support customer servicing. The back-end server houses the supporting systems, including order processing, accounts receivable, inventory, distribution, and other systems.

The four security services are:

1. Trusted communications
2. Authentication/identification
3. Audit
4. Access controls

Step 1: Define Information Security Concerns Specific to the Application. Defining security issues will be particular to the system being implemented. To understand the risk of the system, it is best to start with the business risk, then define risk at each element of the architecture.

Business Risk

- Communication between application servers needs to be very secure. Data must not be tampered with, stolen, or misrouted.
- Availability is critical during normal business hours.
- Cost savings realized by switching from electronic data interchange (EDI) to the Internet is substantial, and will more than cover the costs of the system.

Technology Concerns. There are six architectural layers in this example, five of which need to be secured:

1. The *presentation layer* will not be secured or trusted. The communication between the client and the customer application is trusted because it uses the customer's private network.

2. The *application server* will need to be secure. Traffic between the two application servers will need to be encrypted. The application server is inside the customer's network and demonstrates a potentially high, and perhaps unnecessary degree of trust between the two companies (see § 30.6.5).

3. The *customer's internal layer* will be secured by the customer.

4. The *network layer* needs to filter out traffic that is not required, prevent DoS attacks, and monitor for possible intrusions. Two firewalls are shown: one to protect the client and the other to protect the B2B company.

5. The *application layer* will need to prevent unauthorized access, support timely processing of transactions, provide effective audit trails, and process confidential information.

6. The *internal layer* will need to prevent unauthorized access (especially through Internet connections) and protect confidential information during transmission, processing, and storage.

Step 2: Develop Security Services Options. There are four security services reviewed in this example. Others could have been included, such as authenticity, nonrepudiation, and confidentiality, but they have been excluded to simplify this example. Elected security services include:

1. Trusted communication
2. Authentication/identification
3. Audit
4. Access control

Many security services options are available for B2B environments.

- **Presentation layer.** Several different options can be selected for communication. HTTP is the most common. The communications between the presentation layer residing on the client device and the application server, in this example, are internal to the customer's trusted internal network and will be secured by the customer.

- **Application layer.** Communication between the two application servers needs to be secure. The easiest and most secure method of peer-to-peer communication is via a VPN.

- **Customer internal.** Communications between the customer's application server and the customers back-end server are internal to the customer's trusted internal network and will be secured by the customer.

- **Network layer.** It is common in a B2B environment that a trusted network is created via a VPN. The firewalls will probably participate in these communications, but hardware solutions are also possible.

- **Application layer.** The application server is at both the customer and B2B company sites. VPN is the most secure communication method. The application server also needs to communicate with the internal layer, and this traffic should be encrypted as well.

- **Internal layer.** The internal layer may be secured with another firewall from the external-facing system. This firewall helps the B2B company to protect itself from intrusions and unauthorized access. In this example, a firewall is not assumed so the external firewall and DMZ need to be very secure.

Intrusion detection, log reading, and other devices can easily be added and discussed with management. This format can be repeated to discuss security services at all levels and all systems, not just e-commerce–related systems.

Step 3: Develop Security Service Options. In Step 3, the B2B company can analyze and select the security services that best meet its legal, business, and information security requirements. The biggest difference between B2C and B2B systems is that the B2C system assumes no level of trust. The B2B system assumes trust, but additional coordination and interface with the B2B customer or partner is required. This coordination and interoperability must not be underestimated, because they may prove difficult and expensive to resolve. There are four stages required for this analysis:

1. Implementation risk, or feasibility
2. Cost to implement and support
3. Effectiveness in increasing control, thereby reducing risk
4. Data classification

Implementation risk is a function of the organization's ability to effectively roll out the technology. In this example, we assume that implementation risk is low and resources are readily available to implement the technology.

Cost to implement and support are paramount to the decision-making process. Both businesses' costs need to be considered. Unfortunately, the cost to support is difficult to quantify and easily overlooked. In this example, resources are available both to implement and to support the technology.

Effectiveness in increasing control is an integral part of the benefit and risk management analysis. Each security component needs to be considered in order to determine cross-benefits where controls overlap and supplement others. In this example, increased levels of control are understood and supported by management.

Data classification is the foundation for requirements and will help drive the cost-benefit discussions because it captures the value of the information to the underlying business. In this example, the data are considered significant enough to warrant additional security measures to safeguard the data against misuse, theft, and loss.

Each security service can be defined along a continuum, with implementation risk, cost, and data classification all considered. Management can use this chart to plot the security levels required by the system. This example outlines the effectiveness of security services options relative to other protocols or products. Each organization should develop its own continuums and provide guidance to Web developers and application programmers as to the correct uses and standard settings of the security services. For example, for authentication/identification services, in order of minimal service to maximum:

- The minimal level of security is to have no passwords.
- Weak passwords (e.g., easy to guess, shared, poor construction) are better than no passwords but still provide only a minimal level of security.
- Operating system or database level passwords usually allow too much access to the system but can be effectively managed.
- Application passwords are difficult to manage but can be used to restrict data access to a greater degree.
- Role-based access distinguishes users by their need to know to support their job function. Roles are established and users are grouped by their required function.
- Tokens are given to users and provide for two-part authentication. Passwords and tokens are combined for strong authentication.
- Biometrics are means to validate the person claiming to be the user via fingerprints, retina scans, or other unique body function.

For more information on identification and authentication, see Chapters 28 and 29 in this *Handbook*.

30.2.6   Framework Conclusion.   Internet e-commerce has changed the way corporations conduct business with their customers, vendors, suppliers, and business units. The B2B and B2C sectors will likely continue to grow. Despite security concerns, the acceleration toward increased use of the Internet as a sales, logistics, and marketing channel continues. The challenge for information security professionals' is to keep pace with this change from a security perspective, but not to impede progress. Another equal challenge is that the products that secure the Internet are new and not fully functional or mature. The products will improve, but meanwhile, existing products must be implemented, and later retrofitted, with improved and more secure security services. This changing environment, including the introduction of ever more serious and sophisticated threats, will remain difficult to secure.

The processes described in this section will allow the security practitioner to provide business units with a powerful tool to communicate, select, and implement information security services. Three steps were described and demonstrated with two examples. The process supports decision making. Decisions can be made and readily documented to demonstrate cost effectiveness of the security selections. The risk of specific decisions can be discussed and accepted by management. The trade-offs between cost and benefit can be calculated and discussed. Therefore, it becomes critical that alternatives be reviewed and good decisions made. The processes supporting these decisions need to be efficient and quickly applied. The information security services approach will allow companies to implement security at a practical pace. Services not selected are easily seen. The risk of not selecting specific security services needs to be accepted by management.

30.3   RULES OF ENGAGEMENT.   The Web is a rapidly evolving, complex environment. Dealing with customers electronically is a challenge. Web-related security matters raise many sensitive security issues. Attacks against a Web site always need to be taken seriously. Correctly differentiating "false alarms" from real attacks continues to present a challenge. As an example, the Victoria's Secret online lingerie show, in February 1998, exceeded even the most optimistic expectations of its creators, and the volume of visitors caused severe problems. Obviously, the thousands of people were not attacking the site; they were merely a virtual mob attempting to access the same site at the same time. Similar episodes have occurred when sites were described as interesting on Usenet newsgroups. This effect also occurs with social networking sites such as YouTube, Facebook, and others, where a virtual tidal wave of requests can occur without warning. Physical mobs are limited by transportation, timing, and costs; virtual mobs are solely limited by how many can attempt to access a resource simultaneously, from locations throughout the world.

30.3.1   Web Site–Specific Measures.   Protecting a Web site means ensuring that the site and its functions are available 24 hours a day, seven days a week, and 365 days a year. It also means ensuring that the information exchanged with the site is accurate and secure.

The preceding section focused on protecting Internet-visible systems, predominantly those systems used within the company to interact with the outside world. This section focuses on issues specific to Web interactions with customers as well as to supply and distribution chains. Practically speaking, the Web site is an important, if not the most important, component of an organization's interface with the outside world.

Web site protection lies at the intersection of technology, strategy, operations, customer relations, and business management. Web site availability and integrity directly affect the main streams of cash flow and commerce: an organization's customers, production chains, and supply chains. This is in contrast to the general Internet-related security issues examined in the preceding section, which primarily affect those inside the organization.

Availability is the cornerstone of all Web-related strategies. Idle times have become progressively rarer. Depending on the business and its markets, there may be some periods of lower activity. In the financial trading community, there remain only a few small windows during a 24-hour period when updates and maintenance can be performed. As global business becomes the norm, customers, suppliers, and distributors increasingly expect information, and the ability to effect transactions, at any time of the day or night, even from modest-size enterprises. On the Internet, "nobody knows that you are a dog" also means "nobody knows that you are *not* a large company." The playing field has indeed been leveled, but it was not uniformly raised or lowered, but expectations have increased while capital and operating expenses have dramatically dropped.

Causation is unrelated to impact. The overwhelming majority of Web outages are caused by unglamorous problems. High-profile, deliberate attacks are much less frequent than equipment and personnel failures. The effect on the business organization is indistinguishable. Having a low profile is no defense against random scanning attack.

External events and their repercussions can also wreak havoc, both directly and indirectly. The September 11, 2001, terrorist attacks that destroyed New York City's World Trade Center complex had worldwide impact, not only on systems and firms located in the destroyed complex. Telecommunications infrastructure was damaged or destroyed, severing Internet links for many organizations. Parts supply and all travel was disrupted when North American airspace was shutdown. Manhattan was sealed to exits and entries, while within the city itself, and throughout much of the world, normal operations were suspended. The September 11 attacks were extraordinarily disruptive, but security precautions similar to those described throughout this *Handbook* served to ameliorate damage to Web operations and other infrastructure elements of those concerns that had implemented them. Indeed, the existence of the Web and the resulting ability to organize groups without physical presence proved a means to ameliorate the damage from the attacks, even to firms that had a major presence in the World Trade Center. In the period following the attacks on the World Trade Center, Morgan Stanley and other firms that had offices in the affected area implemented extensive telecommuting and Web-based interactions first to account for their staffs[5] and then to enable work to continue.[6]

Best practices and scale are important. Some practices, issues, and concerns at first glance appear relevant only to very large organizations, such as Fortune 500 companies. In fact, this is not so. Considering issues in the context of a large organization permits them to appear magnified and in full detail. Smaller organizations are subject to the same issues and concerns but may be able to implement less formal solutions. "Formal" does not necessarily imply written procedures. It may mean that certain computer-related practices, such as modifying production facilities in place, are inherently poor ideas and should be avoided. Very large enterprises might address the problems by having a separate group, with separate equipment, responsible for operating the development environment.

30.3.2   Defining Attacks.   Repeated, multiple attempts to connect to a server could be ominous, or they could be nothing more than a customer with a technical problem. Depending on the source, large numbers of failed connects or aborted operations coming from gateway nodes belonging to an organization could represent a problem somewhere in the network, an attack against the server, or anything in between. It could also represent something no more ominous than a group of users within a locality accessing a Web resource through a firewall.

30.3.3 Defining Protection.

There is a difference between protecting Internet-visible assets and protecting Web sites. For the most part, Internet-visible assets are not intended for public use. Thus, it is often far easier to anticipate usage volumes and to account for traffic patterns. With Web sites, activity is subject to the vagaries of the worldwide public. A dramatic surge in traffic could be an attack, or it could be an unexpected display of the site's URL in a television program or in a relatively unrelated news story. Differentiating between belligerence and popularity is difficult.

Self-protective measures that do not impact customers are always permissible. However, care must be exercised to ensure that the measures are truly impact free. As an example, some sites, particularly public FTP servers, often require that the Internet protocol (IP) address of the requesting computer have an entry in the inverse domain name system, which maps IP addresses to host names (e.g., node 192.168.0.1 has a PTR [pointer record] 1.0.168.192.in-addr.arpa) (RFC1034, RFC1035; Mockapetris 1987a, 1987b) as opposed to the more widely known domain name system database, which maps host names into IP addresses. It is true that many machines do have such entries, but it is also true that many sites, including company networks, do not provide inverse DNS information. Whether this entire population should be excluded from the site is a policy and management decision, not a purely technical decision. Even a minuscule incident rate on a popular WWW site can be catastrophic, both for the provider and for the naive end user who has no power to resolve the situation.

30.3.4 Maintaining Privacy.

Logging interactions between customers and the Web site is also a serious issue. A Web site's privacy policy is again a managerial, legal, and customer relations issue with serious overtones. Technical staff needs to be conscious that policies, laws, and other issues may dictate what information may be logged, where it can be stored, and how it may be used. For example, the 1998 Children's Online Privacy Protection Act (COPPA) (15 U.S.C. § 6501 et seq.) makes it illegal to obtain name and address information from children under the age of 13 in the United States. Many firms are party to agreements with third-party organizations such as TRUSTe,[7] governing the use and disclosure of personal information. For more information on legal aspects of protecting privacy, see Chapter 69 in this *Handbook*.

30.3.5 Working with Law Enforcement.

Dealing with legal authorities is similarly complicated. Attempts at fraudulent purchases and other similar issues can be addressed using virtually the same procedures that are used with conventional attempts at mail or phone order fraud. Dealing with attacks and similar misuses is more complicated and depends on the organization's policies and procedures, and the legal environment. The status of the Web site is also a significant issue. If the server is located at a hosting facility, or is owned and operated by a third party, the situation becomes even more legally complicated. Involving law enforcement in a situation will likely require that investigators have access to the Web servers and supporting network, which may be difficult. Last, there is a question of what information is logged, and under what circumstances. For more information on working with law enforcement, see Chapter 61 in this *Handbook*.

30.3.6   Accepting Losses.   No security scheme is foolproof. Incidents will happen. Some reassurance can be taken from the fact that the most common reasons for system compromises in 2001 appear to remain the same as when Clifford Stoll wrote *The Cuckoo's Egg* in 1989. Then and now, poorly secured systems have:

- Obvious passwords into management accounts
- Unprotected system files
- Unpatched known security holes

However, eliminating the simplest and most common ways in which outsiders can compromise Web sites does not resolve all problems. The increasing complexity of site content, and of the applications code supporting dynamic sites, means that there is an ongoing design, implementation, testing, and quality assurance challenge. Server-based and server-distributed software (e.g., dynamic www sites) is subject to the same development hazards as other forms of software. Security hazards will slip into a Web site, despite the best efforts of developers and testers. The acceptance of this reality is an important part of the planning necessary to deal with the inevitable incidents. When it is suspected that a Web site, or an individual component, has been compromised, the reaction plans should be activated. The plans required are much the same as those discussed in Chapter 21 in this *Handbook*. The difference is that the reaction plan for a Web site has to take into consideration that the group primarily impacted by the plan will be the firm's customers. The primary goal of the reaction plan is to contain the damage. For more information on computer security incident response, see Chapter 56.

30.3.7   Avoiding Overreaction.   Severe reactions may create as much, if not more, damage than the actual attack. The reaction plan must identify the decision-making authority and the guidelines to allow effective decisions to be made. This is particularly true of major sites, where attacks are likely to occur on a regular basis. Methods to determine the point at which the Web site must be taken off-line to prevent further damage need to be determined in advance.

In summary, when protecting Web sites and customers, defensive actions are almost always permissible and offensive actions of any kind are almost always impermissible. Defensive actions that are transparent to the customer are best of all.

30.3.8   Appropriate Responses to Attacks.   Long before the advent of the computer, before the development of instant communications, international law recognized that firing upon a naval vessel was an act of war. Captains of naval vessels were given standing orders summarized as *fire if fired upon*. In areas without readily accessible police protection, the right of citizens to defend themselves is generally recognized by most legal authorities. Within the body of international law, such formal standards of conduct for military forces are known as *rules of engagement*, a concept with global utility.

In cyberspace, it is tempting to jettison the standards of the real world. It is easy to imagine oneself master of one's own piece of cyberspace, without connection to real-world laws and limitations on behavior. However, information technology (IT) personnel do not have the standing of ships' captains, with no communications to the outside world. Some argue that fire if fired upon is an acceptable standard for online behavior. Such an approach does not take into account the legal and ethical issues surrounding response strategies and tactics.

Any particular security incident has a range of potential responses. Which response is appropriate depends on the enterprise and its political, legal, and business environment. Acceptability of response is also a management issue as well as potentially a political issue. Determining what responses are acceptable in different situations requires input from management on policy, from legal counsel on legality, from public relations on public perceptions, and from technical staff on technical feasibility. Depending on the organization, it also may be necessary to involve unions and other parties in the negotiation of what constitutes appropriate responses.

What is acceptable or appropriate in one area is not necessarily acceptable or appropriate in another. Often the national security arena has lower standards of proof than would be acceptable in normal business litigation. In U.S. civil courts, cases are decided upon a preponderance of evidence. Standards of proof acceptable in civil litigation are not conclusive when a criminal case is being tried, where guilt must be established beyond a reasonable doubt.

Gambits or responses that are perfectly legal in a national security environment may be completely illegal and recklessly irresponsible in the private sector, exposing the organization to significant legal liability.

Rules of etiquette and behavior are similarly complex. The rights of prison inmates in the United States remain significant, even though they are subject to rules and regulations substantially more restrictive than for the general population. Security measures, as well, must be appropriate for the persons and situations to which they are applied.

30.3.9 Counter-Battery.   Some suggest that the correct response to a perceived attack is to implement the cyberspace equivalent of *counter-battery,* that is, targeting the artillery that has just fired upon you. However, counter-battery tactics, when used as a defensive measure against Internet attacks, will be perceived, technically and legally, as an attack like any other.

Counter-battery tactics may be emotionally satisfying but are prone to both error and collateral damage. Counter-battery can be effective only when the malefactor is correctly identified and the effects of the reciprocal attack are limited to the male-factor. If third parties are harmed in any way, then the retaliatory action becomes an attack in and of itself. One of the more celebrated counter-battery attacks gone awry was the 1994 case when two lawyers from Phoenix, Arizona, spammed over 5,000 Usenet newsgroups to give unsolicited information on a U.S. Immigration and Natu-ralization Service lottery for 55,000 green cards (immigration permits). The resulting retaliation—waves of e-mail protests—against the malefactors flooded their Internet service provider (ISP) and caused at least one server to crash, resulting in a denial of service to all the other, innocent, customers of the ISP.[8]

30.3.10 Hold Harmless.   It is critical that Internet policies adopt a hold harm-less position. Dealing with an Internet crisis often requires fast reactions. That is, if employees act in good faith, in accordance with their responsibilities, and within doc-umented procedures, management should never punish them for such action. If the procedures are wrong, managers should improve the rules and procedures, not blame the employees for following established policies. Disciplinary actions are manifestly inappropriate in such circumstances.

30.4   RISK ANALYSIS.   As noted earlier in this chapter, protecting an organization's Web sites depends on an accurate, rational assessment of the risks. Developing effective strategies and tactics to ensure site availability and integrity requires that all potential risks be examined in turn.

Unrestricted commercial activity has been permitted on the Internet since 1991. Since then, enterprises large and small have increasingly integrated Web access into their second-to-second operations. The risks inherent in a particular configuration and strategy are dependent on many factors, including the scale of the enterprise and the relative importance of the Web-based entity within the enterprise. Virtually all high-visibility Web sites (e.g., Yahoo, America Online, cnn.com, Amazon.com, and eBay) have experienced significant outages at various times.

The more significant the organization's Web component, the more critical is availability and integrity. Large, traditional firms with relatively small Web components can tolerate major interruptions with little damage. Firms large or small that rely on the Web for much of their business must pay greater attention to their Web presences, because a serious outage can quickly escalate into financial or public relations catastrophe.

For more details of risk analysis and management, see Chapters 62 and 63 in this *Handbook*.

30.4.1   Business Loss.   Business losses fall into several categories, any of which can occur in conjunction with an organization's Web presence. In the context of this chapter, customers are both outsiders accessing the Internet presence and insiders accessing intranet applications. In practice, insiders using intranet-hosted applications pose the same challenges as the outside users.

30.4.2   PR Image.   The Web site is the organization's public face 24/7/365. This ongoing presence is a benefit, making the firm visible at all times, but the site's high public profile also makes it a prime target.

Government sites in the United States and abroad have often been the targets of attacks. In January 2000, "Thomas," the Web site of the U.S. Congress, was defaced. Earlier, in 1996, the Web site of the U.S. Department of Justice was vandalized. Sites belonging to the Japanese, U.K., and Mexican governments also have been vandalized.

These incidents have continued, with hackers on both sides of various issues attacking the other side's Web presence. While no conclusive evidence of the involvement of nation states in such activities has become generally known, it is inevitable. Surges of such activity have coincided with major public events, including the 2001 U.S.-China incident involving a aerial collision between military aircraft, the Afghan and Iraqi operations, and the Israeli-Lebanese war of 2006. Such activity has not been limited to the national security arena, however. Many sites were defaced during the incidents following publication of cartoons in a Danish newspaper that some viewed as defaming the prophet Muhammad.

In some cases,[9] companies have suffered collateral damage from hacking contests, where hackers prove their mettle by defacing as many sites as they can. The fact that there is no direct motive or animus toward the company is not relevant; the damage has still been done.

In the corporate world, company Web sites have been the target of attacks intended to defame the corporation for real or imagined slights. Some such episodes have been reported in the news media, whereas others have not been the subjects of extensive reporting. The scale and newsworthiness of the episode is unimportant; the damage done to the targeted organization is the true measure. An unreported incident that is the initiating event in a business failure is more damaging to the affected parties than a seemingly more significant outage with less severe consequences.

Other cybervandals (e.g., sadmind/IIS) have used address scanners to target randomly selected machines. Obscurity is not a defense against address-scanner attacks.

30.4.3 Loss of Customers/Business.

Internet customers are highly mobile. Web site problems quickly translate into permanently lost customers. The reason for the outage is immaterial; the fact that there is a problem is often sufficient to provoke erosion of customer loyalty.

In most areas, there is competitive overlap. Using the overnight shipping business as an example, in most U.S. metropolitan areas there is (in alphabetical order) Airborne Express, Federal Express, United Parcel Service, and the United States Postal Service. All of the firms offer Web-based shipment tracking, a highly popular service. Problems or difficulties with shipment tracking will quickly lead to a loss of business in favor of a different company with easier tracking.

30.4.4 Interruptions.

Increasingly, modern enterprises are being constructed around ubiquitous 24/7/365 information systems, most often with Web sites playing a major role. In this environment, interruptions of any kind are catastrophic.

Production. The past 20 years have seen a streamlining of production processes in all areas of endeavor. Twenty years ago, it was common for facilities to have multiday supplies of components on-hand in inventory. Today, *zero latency* or *just-in-time* (JIT) environments are common, permitting large facilities to have no inventory. Fiscally, zero latency environments may be optimally cost efficient, yet the paradigm leaves little margin for disruptions of the supporting logistical chain. This chain is sometimes fragile, and subject to disruption by any number of hazards.

Supply Chain. Increasingly, it is common for Web-based sites to be an integral part of the supply chain. Firms may encourage their vendors to use a Web-based portal to gain access to the vendor side of the purchasing system. XML[10]-based gateways and *service-oriented architecture* (SOA) approaches, together with other Web technologies, are used to arrange for and manage the flow of raw materials and components required to support production processes. The same streamlining that speeds information between supplier and manufacturer also provides a potential for serious mischief and liability.

Delivery Chain. Web-based sites, both internal and external, also have become the vehicle of choice for tracking the status of orders and shipments, and increasingly as the backbone of many enterprises' delivery chain management and inquiry systems.

Information Delivery. Banks, brokerages, utilities, and municipalities are increasingly turning to the Web as a convenient, low-cost method for managing their relationships with consumers. Firms are also supporting downloading records of transactions and other relationship information in formats required by personal database programs and organizers. These outputs, in turn, are often used as inputs to other processes, which then generate other transactions. Not surprisingly, as time passes, more and more people and businesses depend on the availability of information on demand. Today's Web-based customers presume that information is accessible wherever they can use a personal computer or even a Web-enabled cellular telephone. This is reminiscent of usage patterns of automatic teller machines in an earlier decade, which allowed people to base their plans on access to teller machines, often making multiple $20 withdrawals instead of cashing a $200 check weekly.

30.4.5 Proactive versus Reactive Threats.   Some threats and hazards can be addressed proactively, whereas others are inherently reactive. When strategies and tactics are developed to protect a Web presence, the strategies and tactics themselves can induce availability problems.

As an example, consider the common strategy of having multiple name servers responsible for providing the translation of domain names to IP addresses. It is required before a domain name (properly referred to as a domain name service [DNS] zone) can be entered into the root-level name servers, that at least two name servers be identified to process name resolution requests. Name servers are a prime example of resources that should be geographically diverse.

Updating DNS zones requires care. If an update is performed improperly, then the resources referenced via the symbolic DNS names will become unresolvable, regardless of the actual state of the Web server and related infrastructure. The risk calculus involving DNS names is further complicated by the common, efficient, and appropriate practice of designating ISP name servers as the primary mechanism for the resolution of domain names. In short, name translation provides a good example of the possible risks that can affect a Web presence.

30.4.6 Threat and Hazard Assessment.   Some threats are universal, whereas others are specific to an individual environment. The most devastating and severe threats are those that simultaneously affect large areas or populations, where efforts to repair damage and correct the problem are hampered by the scale of the problem.

On a basic level, threats can be divided into several categories. The first is between deliberate acts and accidents. Deliberate acts comprise actions done with the intent to damage the Web site or its infrastructure. Accidents include natural phenomena (acts of God) and clumsiness, carelessness, and unconsidered consequences (acts of clod).

Broadly put, a deliberate act is one whose goal is to impair the system. Deliberate acts come in a broad spectrum of skill and intent. For the purpose of risk analysis and planning, deliberate acts against infrastructure providers can often appear to be acts of God. To an organization running a Web site, an employee attack against a telephone carrier appears simply as a service interruption of unknown origin.

No enterprise or agency should consider itself an unlikely target. Past high-profile incidents have targeted the FBI (May 26 and 27, 1999), major political parties, and interest groups in the United States. On the consumer level, numerous digital subscriber line (DSL)-connected home systems have been targeted for subversion as preparation for the launching of DDoS attacks. In 2007, several investigations resulted in the arrest of several individuals for running so-called botnets (ensembles of compromised computers). These networks numbered hundreds of thousands of machines.[11] The potential for such networks to be used for mischief cannot be underestimated.

For more details of threats and hazards, see many other chapters in this *Handbook*, including 1, 2, 4, 5, 13, 14, 15, 16, 17, 18, 19, 20, 22, and 23.

30.5 OPERATIONAL REQUIREMENTS.   Internet-visible systems are those with any connection to the worldwide Internet. It is tempting to consider protecting Internet-visible systems as a purely technical issue. However, technical and business issues are inseparable in today's risk management. For example, as noted earlier in this chapter, the degree to which systems should be exposed to the Internet is fundamentally a business risk-management issue. Protection technologies and the policies behind the protection can be discussed only after the business risk questions have been considered and decided, setting the context for the technical discussions. In turn, business risk-management evaluation (see Chapter 62) must include a full awareness of all of the technical risks. Ironically, nontechnical business managers can accurately assess the degree of business risk only after the technical risks have been fully exposed.

Additional business and technical risks result from outsourcing. Today, many enterprises include equipment owned, maintained, and managed by third parties. Some of this equipment resides on the organization's own premises and other equipment resides off site: for example, at application service provider facilities.

Protecting a Web site begins with the initial selection and configuration of the equipment and its supporting elements, and continues throughout its life. In general, care and proactive consideration of the availability and security aspects of the site from the beginning will reduce costs and operational problems. Although virtually impossible to achieve, the goal is to design and implement an automatic system, with a configuration whose architecture and implementation operates even in the face of problems, with minimal customer impact.

That is not to say that a Web site can operate without supervision. Ongoing, proactive monitoring is critical to ensuring the secure operation of the site. Redundancy only reduces the need for real-time response by bypassing a problem temporarily; it does not eliminate the underlying cause. The initial failure must be detected, isolated, and corrected as soon as possible, albeit on a more schedulable basis. Otherwise, the system will operate in its successively degraded redundancy modes until the last redundant component fails, at which time the system will fail completely.

30.5.1   Ubiquitous Internet Protocol Networking.   Business has been dealing with the security of internets (i.e., interconnected networks) since the advent of internetworking in the late 1960s. However, the growing use of Transmission Control Protocol/Internet Protocol (TCP/IP) networks and of the public Internet has exposed much more equipment to attack than in the days of closed corporate networks. In addition, a much wider range of equipment, such as voice telephones based on voice-over IP (VoIP), fax machines, copiers, and even soft drink dispensers, are now network accessible.

IP connectivity has been a great boon to productivity and ease of use, but it has not been without a darker side. Network accessibility also has created unprecedented opportunities for improper, unauthorized access to networked resources and other mischief. It is not uncommon to experience probes and break-in attempts within hours or even minutes of unannounced connection to the global Internet.

Protecting Internet-visible assets is inherently a conflict between ease of access and security. The safest systems are those unconnected to the outside world. Similarly, the easiest to use systems are those that have no perceivable restrictions on use. Adjusting the limits on user activities and access must balance conflicting requirements. As an example, many networks are managed *in-band*, meaning that the switches, routers, firewalls and other elements of the network infrastructure are managed using the actual network as the connection medium. If the management interfaces were not managed over properly encrypted connections, management passwords would be visible on the network. If an outsider, or an unauthorized insider, monitors the network, information sufficient to paralyze the network and, in turn, the organization may be gained.

30.5.2   Internal Partitions.   Complex corporate environments can often be secured effectively by dividing the organization into a variety of interrelated and nested security domains, each with its own legal, technical, and cultural requirements. For example, there are specific legal requirements for medical records (see Chapters 71 in this *Handbook*) and for privacy protection (see Chapter 69 and 70). Partners and suppliers, as well as consultants, contractors, and customers, often need two-way access to corporate data and facilities. These diverse requirements mean that a single corporate firewall is often insufficient. Different domains within the organization will often require their own firewalls and security policies. Keeping track of the multitude of data types, protection and access requirements, and different legal jurisdictions and regulations makes for previously unheard-of degrees of complexity.

Damage control is another property of a network with internal partitions. A system compromised by an undetected malware component will be limited in its ability to spread the contagion beyond its own compartment.

30.5.3   Critical Availability.   Networks are often critical for second-to-second operations; as a result, the side effects of ill-considered countermeasures may be worse than the damage from the actual attack. For example, shutting down the network, or even part of it, for maintenance or repair can wreak more havoc than penetration by a malicious hacker.

30.5.4   Accessibility.   Users must be involved in the evolution of rules and procedures. Today, it is still not unheard of for a university faculty to take the position that any degree of security will undermine the very nature of their community, compromising their ability to perform research and inquiries. This extreme position persists despite the attention of the mass media, the justified beliefs of the technical community, and documented evidence that lack of protection of any Internet-connected system undermines the safety of the entire connected community.

Connecting a previously isolated computer system or network to the global Internet creates a communications pathway to every corner of the world. Customers, partners, and employees can obtain information, send messages, place orders, and otherwise interact 24 hours a day, seven days a week, 365 days a year, from literally anywhere on or near Earth. Even the Space Shuttle and the International Space Station have Internet access. Under these circumstances, the possibilities for attack or inadvertent misuse are limitless.

Despite the vast increase in connectivity, some businesses and individuals do not need extensive access to the global Internet for their day-to-day activities, although they may resent being excluded. The case for universal access is therefore a question of business policy and political considerations.

30.5.5   Applications Design.   Protecting a Web site begins with the most basic steps. First, a site processing confidential information should always support the secure hypertext transfer protocol (HTTPS), typically using TCP port 443. Properly supporting HTTPS requires the presence of an appropriate digital certificate (see Chapter 37).

When the security requirements are uncertain, the site design should err on the side of using HTTPS for communications. Although the available literature on the details of Internet eavesdropping is sparse, the Communications Intelligence and Signals Intelligence (COMINT/SIGINT) historical literature from World War II makes it abundantly clear that encryption of all potentially sensitive traffic is the only way to protect information.

Encryption also should be used within an organization, possibly with a different digital certificate, for sensitive internal communications and transactions. Earlier, it was noted that organizations are not monolithic security domains. This is nowhere more true than when dealing with human resources, employee evaluations, compensation, benefits, and other sensitive employee information. There are positive requirements that this information be safeguarded, but few organizations have truly secured their internal networks against internal monitoring. It is far safer to route all such communications through securely encrypted channels. Such measures also demonstrate a good faith effort to ensure the privacy and confidentiality of sensitive information.

It is also important to avoid providing all of the authentication information on a single page or, for that matter, in a sequence of pages. When parts of information are suppressed, as, for example, portions of a credit card or account number, the division between suppressed and displayed portions should be maintained. Displaying all of the information, even if it is on different screens, is an invitation to a security breach.

30.5.6 Provisioning. Although today's hardware has unprecedented reliability, any failure of hardware between the customer and the data center will impair an enterprise's Web presence. For a highly available, front-line Web site, the effective requirement is a minimum of two diversely located facilities, each with a minimum of two servers. This is not necessarily an expensive proposition. Fairly powerful Web servers can be purchased for less than $5,000, so the total hardware expenditure for four servers is reasonable, substantially less than the annual cost of a single technician. In most cases, the cost of the extra hardware is more than offset by the business cost of downtime, which can sometimes exceed the total cost of the duplicative hardware by a factor as much as 100, in a single episode.[12]

Duplicate hardware and geographic diversity ensure constant customer access to some degree of functionality. The degree of functionality that must be maintained depends on the market and the customers. Financial firms supporting online stock trading have different operational, regulatory, and legal requirements than supermarkets. The key is matching the support level to the activities. Some degree of planned degradation is generally acceptable. Total unavailability is not an option.

30.5.7 Restrictions. All Web servers should be located behind a firewall in a demilitarized zone, as discussed earlier in this chapter). Incoming and outgoing services should be restricted using protocols such as HTTP, HTTPS, and Internet control message protocol (ICMP). For troubleshooting purposes, it is desirable to implement ICMP, which is used by PING, an echo requester, as a way to check connectivity. All unused ports should be disabled. Furthermore, the disabled ports should be blocked by the firewalls separating the DMZ from the outside world.

Customer information should, to the extent possible, be stored on systems separate from the systems actually providing Web serving. Many security episodes appear to exploit file protection errors on the Web server, in order to access the database directly. Segregating customer data on separate machines, and ensuring that the only way to access customer data is through the documented pathways, is likely severely to impede improper attempts to access and modify information.

These safeguards are especially important for high-security information such as credit card numbers. The number of incidents in which malefactors have downloaded credit card numbers directly from Web site is an indication of the importance of such precautions. The systems actually storing the sensitive information should never be accessible from the public Internet.

The TJX case, which came to public attention in the beginning of 2007, was one of a series of large-scale compromises of electronically stored information on back-office and e-commerce systems. Most notably, the TJX case appears to have started with an insufficiently secured corporate network and the associated back-office systems, not a Web site penetration. This breach escalated into a security breach of corporate data systems. It is reported on the TJX Web site that at least 45.7 million credit cards were compromised (original reports in *USA Today* and other publications cite 94 million credit card numbers as being compromised). On November 30, 2007, it was reported that TJX, the parent organization of stores including TJ Maxx and Marshall's, had agreed to settle bank claims related to VISA cards for US\$ 40.9M.[13] Also, as of March 2008, a class action suit on behalf of customers was in process of being settled. It called for fees to be paid to each of the plaintiffs for credit monitoring and identity theft, and for new driver's licenses, as well as \$6.5 million to plaintiff's counsel. In spite of several such high-profile attacks, the lessons appear not to have been learned. As recently as March 2008, Hannaford Bros. Co. reported that 4.2 million credit card numbers had been exposed, with about 1,800 cases of fraudulent usage reported as of that date. Clearly, more stringent controls and safeguards are called for.

30.5.8   Multiple Security Domains.   The front-line Web servers, and the database servers supporting their activities, comprise two different security domains.

The Web servers, as noted previously, need to be globally accessible via HTTP, HTTPS, and ICMP. In turn, they need to access the application or database servers, and *only* those servers. In a production system, it is preferable that application or database servers interact with the Web servers using a dedicated, restricted-use protocol. Properly implemented, such a restriction prevents a hijacked Web server from exploiting its access to the application or database server.

These second-tier servers should be in a security domain separated by restrictive firewalls from the externally accessible front-line Web servers. This seems like a significant expenditure, but it is often less expensive and lower risk than a single significant incident.

30.5.9   What Needs to Be Exposed?   Publicly accessible Web sites need publicly accessible Web servers to perform their functions. The challenge is to provide the desired services to the public without simultaneously providing levers that can be used in unauthorized ways to subvert the site. A penetration incident may lead to significant financial losses, embarrassment, and financial and (in some cases) criminal liability.

No system on the Web site should be directly connected to the public Internet. All connections to the public network should be made through a firewall system, with the firewall configured to pass only Web-related traffic to those hosts.

Many sites will opt to place externally visible Web servers in a security compartment of their own, on a separate port of the firewall (if not a totally separate firewall), using a separate DMZ from other publicly accessible resources. These precautions may seem excessive, but having improperly secured systems can lead to security breaches that are extremely difficult to correct and can lead to extended downtime while the problems are analyzed and remedied. In this case, an ounce of prevention is worth substantially more than a pound of cure.

30.5.9.1   Exposed Systems.   Exposed systems are inherently a security hazard. Systems that are not accessible from the public network cannot be compromised from the public network. Only systems that absolutely need to be publicly accessible should be so configured. Minimizing the number of exposed systems is generally desirable, but this is best considered in terms of machine roles rather than actual counts of systems. Increasing the load on each publicly accessible server by increasing the size of the server, thus increasing the amount of capacity impacted by a single system outage, is not a benefit. However, this must be balanced against the new trend towards server virtualization, which does not increase the size of a server, but which increases its utilization, in order to lower costs and improve reliability.

The introduction of SSL-based VPN implementations and services supporting remote access via secure HTTPS connections (e.g., gotomypc.com) create an entirely new class of security hazard.

30.5.9.2   Hidden Subnets.   The servers directly supporting the Web site need to be accessed by the outside world, and thus must generally have normal Internet addresses. However, in most cases the other systems supporting the Web servers generally have no legitimate need for unrestricted access from or to the public network.

The safest address assignments for supporting, non–outside-visible systems are the IPv4 addresses allocated for use in private Internets[14] and the corresponding IPv6 equivalents. Needless to say, these systems should be in a security compartment separated from the publicly accessible Web servers, and that compartment should be isolated from the publicly accessible compartment with a very restrictive firewall.

30.5.10   Access Controls.   Publicly accessible systems are both the focus of an organization's security efforts and the primary target of attempts to compromise that security. The number of individuals authorized to make changes to the systems and the ways in which changes may be made need to be carefully controlled, reported, and monitored. The cleared individuals should use individual accounts, and the access to sensitive functions through such accounts should be immediately invalidated if the individual's access is no longer authorized or if the employee ceases employment, is under investigation for impropriety, or other reason. For more information on access controls, see Chapters 9, 15, 23, 24, 25, 26, 27 and 28 in this *Handbook*.

30.5.11   Site Maintenance.   Maintaining and updating the Web site requires great care. The immediate nature of the Web makes it possible for a single-character error in a major enterprise-level application to cause hundreds of thousands of dollars of damage within moments. Web servers need to be treated with respect; the entire enterprise is riding on the electronic image projected by the server. Cybervandalism, which most commonly consists of defacing the home page of a well-known site, requires unauthorized updating of the files comprising the site. In 2000 alone, well-known public and private entities including the FBI, OPEC, World Trade Organization, and NASA, as well as educational institutions including the University of Limerick, have been harmed in this way. These attacks continue to be a danger, both in terms of damage to the organization's image and covertly, as using the WWW site as a launching pad for Web-based exploits.

The Web is inherently a highly leveraged environment. Small changes in the content of a single page percolate throughout the Web in a matter of minutes. Information disseminates easily and quickly at low cost. Leverage helps tremendously when things go right; when things go badly, leverage dramatically compounds the damage. For more information on change control, see Chapters 40, 47, and 52 in this *Handbook*.

30.5.12   Maintaining Site Integrity.   Every Web site and its servers is a target. Antagonists can be students, activists, terrorists, disgruntled former employees, or unhappy customers. Because Web sites are an enterprise's most public face, they represent extremely desirable targets.

Maintaining integrity requires that updates and changes to the site be done in a disciplined manner. Write access to the site must be restricted, and those authorized must use secure methods to access the Web servers. The majority of reported incidents appear to be the result of weak security in the update process. For example, unsecured FTP access from the general Internet is a poor practice. Safer mechanisms include:

- Secure FTP
- FTP from a specific node within the inner firewall
- KERMIT on a directly wired port
- Logins and file transfers over secure authenticated connections via SSH
- Physical media transfers

Most of the technologies do not inherently require that an on-site individual perform server updates, which would preclude remote maintenance. It does mean that in order to get to a machine from which an update can be performed, it is necessary to come through a virtual private network with point-to-point tunneling protocol or Layer2 tunneling protocol (VPN PPTP/L2TP) authenticated by at least one of the secure gateways. For more information on VPNs, see Chapters 32, 33, 34, and 35 in this *Handbook.*

30.6 TECHNICAL ISSUES.   There are many technical issues involved in protecting Internet-accessible resources. The technologies used to protect network assets include routers, firewalls, proxy servers, redundancy, and dispersion. When properly designed and implemented, security measures produce a positive feedback loop, where improvements in network security and robustness are self-reinforcing. Each improvement makes other improvements possible and more effective.

30.6.1 Inside/Outside.   Some visions of the future include a utopian world where everything is directly accessible from anywhere without effort, and with only beneficial results. The original Internet operated on this basis, until a number of incidents (including the 1988 Morris worm) caused people to rethink the perceived inherent peacefulness of the networked world. It is a trend that has only accelerated, as the total number of systems grows ever larger.

The architecture and design of protective measures for a network depend on differentiating inside trustable systems from outside untrustworthy systems. This is equally true for intranets, the Internet, or an *extranet,* so called to distinguish private interconnections of networks from the public Internet. Unfortunately, trust is not a black-and-white issue. A system may be trustworthy from one perspective and untrustworthy from another, thus complicating the security design. In addition, the vast majority of inappropriate computer use is thought to be done by those with legitimate access to some aspect of the system and its data. Alternatively, it is not possible to be strong everywhere. There is a significant danger from trusted but compromised systems.

Basic connectivity configuration is one of those few areas that are purely technical, without a business risk element. One of the most obvious elements involves the tables implemented in routers connecting the enterprise to the public carrier–supplied IP connection. The table rules must prevent *IP spoofing*, which is the misrepresentation of IP packet origins. This is also true when originators are within the organization.

There are three basic rules for preventing IP spoofing applicable to all properly configured networks:

1. Packets entering the network from the outside should never have *originator* addresses within the target network.

2. Packets leaving a network and going to the public network must have *originator* addresses within the originating network.

3. Packets leaving a network and going to the public network must not have *destination* addresses within the originating network.

An exception to these rules is in the use of stealth internal networks, those whose internal addresses correspond to legal external addresses.[15]

A corollary to these rules is that packets with originator or destination addresses in the most local intranet addresses range[16] or dynamic IP addresses,[17] should never be permitted to enter or leave an internal network. Nested address spaces may deliberately create aliased address spaces.[18]

30.6.2   Hidden Subnets.   Firewalls funnel network traffic through one or more choke points, concentrating the security task in a small number of systems. The reasoning behind such concentration is that the likelihood of a security breach of the entire network rises rapidly with the number of independent access points.

Firewalls and proxy servers (see Chapter 26 in this *Handbook*) are effective only in topologies where the firewall filters all traffic between the protected systems and the less-trusted world outside its perimeter. If the protected systems can in any way be accessed without going through the firewall, then the firewall itself has been rendered irrelevant. Security audits often uncover systems that violate this policy; relying on administrative sanctions to preclude such holes in the security perimeter generally does not work. The rule of international diplomacy, "Trust but verify," applies.

The simplest solution to this problem is the use of RFC 1918 addresses within protected networks.[19] RFC1918 provides a range of IPv4 addresses guaranteed by the Internet Assigned Numbers Authority (IANA) never to occur in the normal, public Internet. The address ranges used for dynamic IP address assignment have similar properties.[20]

Filtering these addresses on both inbound and outbound data streams is straightforward and highly effective at stopping a wide range of attacks.[21] Requiring the use of such addresses, and prohibiting the internal use of externally valid addresses, goes a long way toward preventing the use of unauthorized protocols and connections.

30.6.3   What Need Be Exposed?   A security implementation starts with an analysis of the enterprise's mission, needs, and requirements. All designs and implementations are a compromise between absolute security, achieved only in a powered-down or disconnected system, and total openness, in which a system is completely open to any and all access from the outside.

Although in most cases communications must be enabled between the enterprise and the outside world for normal business functions, total disconnection, known as an *air gap*, is sometimes both needed and appropriate between specific components. Industrial real-time control systems, life-critical systems, and systems with high requirements for confidentiality remain appropriate candidates for total air gaps.

Often, systems that do not need to receive information from outside sources must publish statistical or other information to less secure systems. This requirement can often be satisfied through the use of limited functionality links such as media exchange, or through tightly controlled one-way transfers. These mechanisms can be implemented with IP-related technologies or with more limited technologies, including KERMIT,[22] UUCP, or vendor-specific solutions.

In other cases, restrictions reflect policies for permitted use and access rather than for protection against outside attack. For example, it is reasonable and appropriate for a public library to limit access to HTTP and related protocols while prohibiting access to such facilities as FTP and TELNET. There is a collateral issue of what provisions should be made to for systems within the perimeter to connect to outside networks using various protocols. PPTP and L2TP are the most well known. Whether these methods of accessing outside networks should be permitted or not is a management question of no small import, equivalent to totally suppressing outside communications.

From a security standpoint, tunnels to the outside world are a perfect storm, potentially permitting unlimited, nonmonitored communications to the outside. From the standpoint of enabling business operations, such access may be a practical necessity. Vendors, contractors, suppliers, and customers all need access to internal systems at their respective organizations, and such access will almost invariably require the use of a tunnel. Perhaps the best solution is to reverse the traditional inside/outside dichotomy, making the LAN an untrusted network. Using the underlying LAN as a universal dial tone. Access to internal corporate systems would be secured separately using VPN technology.

The advent of SSL/HTTP-based tunnels presents another challenge.gotomypc.com offers such a service, and individuals have used it to circumvent firewalls and implemented ad hoc remote access. The cost is nominal, often a small fraction of the monthly out-of-pocket outlay for an individual's daily commute to the office. The solution of blocking connections to the IP addresses assigned to such a provider is a recommended, yet inherently flawed, prophylactic. Blocking one or more such services does nothing to secure the network against an as-yet-unidentified service of this type, such as that hosted on a home server. Limiting the duration of SSL connections is also merely a speed bump to such schemes. These remain a challenge, as does the advent of directly usable SSL/HTTP tunnels communicating using the standard HTTP (TCP Port 80) and HTTPS (TCP Port 443) ports.

In these cases, firewalls are a reasonable solution, so long as their limitations are recognized. For example, firewalls do not prevent mobile code such as Active-X and JAVA from working around prohibited functions. Indeed, several network attacks have been published using code supplied to browsers for local execution within the local network context. Such code, in combination with weak security practices on network infrastructure, can cause severe damage (see Chapter 17 in this *Handbook*).

30.6.4 Multiple Security Domains.   Many networks implement security solely at the point of entry, where the organization's network connects to the public Internet. Such a *monolithic firewall* is a less than effective choice for all but the most simple of small organizations. As a starting point, systems available to the general population should be outside of the internal security domain in a no-man's land between the public Internet and the private internal net; such a barrier is referred to as a *demilitarized zone* (DMZ). These systems should be afforded a degree of protection by sandwiching them between an outer firewall (protecting the DMZ from the public network) and an inner firewall (protecting the internal network from the public network and controlling the communications between the publicly accessible servers located in the DMZ to the internal network). Alternatively, the DMZ may be attached to a

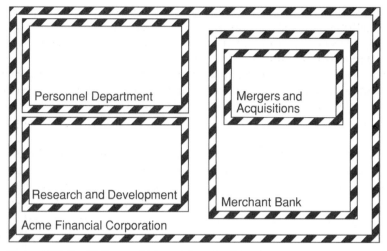

EXHIBIT 30.3 Sibling and Nested Security Domains

separate port on a single firewall, using a different set of traffic management rules. Such a topology permits implementation of the differing security restrictions applicable to the two networks. Systems located within the DMZ should also be suspect, as they are targets for compromise.

Although the industry as a whole agrees on the need for DMZ configurations, it is less appreciated that such restrictions also have a place within organizations. Different groups, departments, and functions within an organization have different security and access requirements. For example, in a financial services firm, the security requirements differ dramatically among departments. Three obvious examples of departments with different requirements are personnel, mergers and acquisitions, and research and development (see Exhibit 30.3).

The personnel department is the custodian of a wide range of sensitive information about the firm, its employees, and often outsiders who are either regularly on company premises or work regularly with the company on projects. Some of this information, such as residence addresses, pay levels, and license plates, is sensitive for personal or cultural reasons. Other information subjects the organization to legal or regulatory sanctions if it is improperly disclosed or used. In the United States, examples of sensitive data include social security numbers, age, sexual orientation, and the presence of human immunodeficiency virus (HIV) or other medical details.

The mergers and acquisitions department handles sensitive information of a different sort. Information about business negotiations or future plans is subject to strict confidentiality requirements. Furthermore, the disclosure of such information is subject to a variety of regulations on governmental and securities industry levels. Within the mergers and acquisitions department, access to information often must be on a need-to-know basis, both to protect the deal and to protect the firm from exposure to civil and criminal liability.

Some information in the research and development department is completely open to the public, whereas other information is restricted to differing degrees.

A full implementation of an adequate security environment will require protections that are not only logically different on a departmental basis but also require that different departments be protected from each other. It is difficult, therefore, if not topologically impossible for a single firewall, located at the connection to the outside world, to implement the required security measures.

Securing systems in isolated logical areas is an example of necessary distrust, merely a matter of ensuring that the interactions between the third-party systems and the outside world are allowed to the extent that they are expected. As an example, consider the straightforward situation at Hypothetical Brokerage. Hypothetical Brokerage uses two trading networks, Omega and Gamma. At first glance, it would seem that that it would be acceptable to place Omega's and Gamma's network gateways on the usual DMZ, together with Hypothetical's Web servers.

However, this grants a high degree of trust to Omega and Gamma and all of their staff, suppliers, and contractors. The most important operative question is whether there is a credible hazard.

Either of the two gateways is well situated to:

- Monitor the communications traffic to and from Hypothetical's Web servers
- Monitor the traffic between Hypothetical and the other, competing network
- Attack the other gateway
- Disrupt communications to and from the other gateway
- Attack Hypothetical's network

Network providers also represent an attractive attack option. A single break-in to a network provider–supplied system component has the effect of compromising large numbers of end user sites. There is ample history of private (PBX) and public (carrier-owned) switches being preferred targets.[23]

The solution (see Exhibit 30.4) is to isolate the third-party systems in separate DMZs, with the traffic between each of the DMZs and the rest of the network scrupulously checked as to transmission control protocol and user datagram protocol (TCP/UDP), port number, and source and destination addresses, to ensure that all traffic is authorized. One method is to use a single firewall, with multiple local area network (LAN) ports, each with different filtering rules, to recast Hypothetical's original single DMZ into disjoint, protected, DMZs.

30.6.5 Compartmentalization.
Breaking the network into separate security compartments reduces the potential for total network meltdown. Limiting the potential damage of an incident is an important step in resolving the problems.

The same rule applies to the DMZs. For example, in a financial trading or manufacturing enterprise, it is not uncommon to have gateways representing access points to trading and partner networks. Where one places these friendly systems is problematic. Many organizations have chosen to place these systems within their regular DMZ.

Sites have belatedly discovered that such gateways have, on occasion, been found to have acted as routers, taking over that function from the intended routers. In other cases, the gateways have experienced malfunctions and impaired the functioning of the rest of the network (or DMZ). As always, the only solutions certain to work are shutdown or isolation.

Compartmentalization also prevents accidents from cascading. A failure in a single gateway is not likely to propagate throughout the network, because the unexpected traffic will be stopped by the firewall isolating the gateway from the network. Such an event can be made to trigger a firewall's attack alarms.

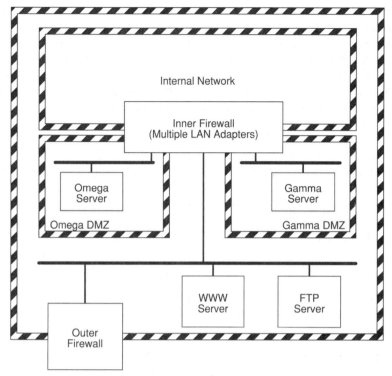

EXHIBIT 30.4   Omega and Gamma Servers in Separate DMZs from Hypothetical's Server

The network problem is not limited to externally provided nodes. An errant system operating within a noncompartmented network, located as it is within the outer security perimeter, can wreak havoc throughout the entire corporation. Constructing the network as a series of nested and peer-related security domains, each protected by appropriate firewalls, localizes the impact of the inevitable incidents, whereas an uncompartmented network permits the contagion to spread throughout the organization, unchecked. The larger the network, the more expensive an incident is. It is quite conceivable that the entire budget for compartmentalizing a corporate network will be less expensive than the single hour of downtime resulting from the first errant system.

The ready availability of portable storage devices, including USB memory devices and external hard drives, makes compartmentalization an even more serious issue.

30.6.6   Need to Access.   Sometimes it is easy to determine who requires access, to which resources, and to which information. However, the question of access control often involves painful choices, with many nuances and subtleties. Legal and contractual responsibilities further complicate the question. For example, lack of access may be a benefit to persons alleged to have misused information.

Physical and logical access controls (see Chapters 27, 28, and 29 in this *Handbook*) need to be implemented for Internet-accessible systems as for any other sensitive and critical system. Controls for such systems must be enforced and respected by all members of the organization. It is important that personnel with restricted access to the network and security infrastructure understand and comprehend the reasons for the security rules and that they not take measures that circumvent those rules. The integrity of an organization's firewalls and network infrastructure is only as good as the physical and logical security of the personnel, equipment, infrastructure, and systems comprising the firewall and network. Regular auditing of both physical and logical access to infrastructure assets is critical and necessary.

The need to maintain information security on communications within the organization argues for the extensive use of security technologies, even when the data packets are never expected to leave the premises. It is sound planning, even within the enterprise, to require applications with privacy or confidentiality requirements to make use of privacy infrastructure such as the secure sockets layer (SSL) for Web-based applications or tunneling such as layer 2 tunneling protocol[24] and point-to-point tunneling protocol.[25] This helps ensure that sensitive information is limited in distribution.

Needless to say, these approaches should employ high-grade encryption and properly signed X.509 certificates from well-accepted Certification Authorities. Self-signed, expired, and not-generally-accepted certificates should not be used.

30.6.7   Accountability.   People often talk about impenetrable systems. However, despite the castle-and-moat analogies used in many discussions of security, no perimeter is likely to be perfect. Given the likelihood of successful attacks, security personnel must use both technical and managerial measures for effective response.

When securing infrastructure, priority should be given to protective measures that ensure accountability for actions. Just as it is desirable to prevent inappropriate activity, it is even more important to ensure that activities can be accounted for.

For example, there are many ways to carry out denial-of-service attacks. The most troublesome are those which are completely legal. Although some of these attacks, such as distributed denial of service, are belligerent or politically and ideologically motivated, involving remote-control *zombie* programs and botnets (described in Chapters 17 and 18), many accidental DoSs can occur without malice in the course of software development. For example, two of the most famous worms that inadvertently led to DoS, the Morris worm and the WANK worm, were detected inadvertently as a result of implementation errors in their replication mechanisms that caused both worms to proliferate extremely quickly, effectively producing unintended DoS attacks and subsequent detection.

When a compromised machine is analyzed forensically, the presence of the attack may remain undetected. This is particularly true when the attack involves designer malware not in general circulation (see Chapter 16 in this *Handbook*).

It is important to analyze security breaches to distinguish among attacks, accidents, and experiments. It is better for weaknesses to be uncovered, even accidentally, within an organization than it is to deal with a truly belligerent security breach. Policies and practices should therefore encourage employees to report accidents rather than try to hide them. As for false alarms caused by overenthusiastic security neophytes, management should avoid punishing those who report illusory breaches or attacks. Accountability provides the raw material to determine what actually happened. The resulting information is the critical underpinning for analysis and education, thus enabling the enterprise to evolve to higher levels of security and integrity.

30.6.8   Read-Only File Security.   Many sites allow downloads, usually via FTP, of large numbers of files. These files may include copies of forms, manuals, instructions, maps, and service guides. If such file serving is provided, then it is critical to ensure that:

- The servers supporting the ftp service are secure.
- The contents of the publicly accessible file store are read-only and subject to change control.
- The entire contents of the public file store can be restored quickly in the event of a possible compromise.
- There is a designated party who is responsible for maintaining and protecting the public file service.

30.6.9   Going Off-Line.   The responsiveness required to a problem with an Internet-connected system is directly related to the out-of-service costs. In some organizations, this may be the cost of lost business; in other organizations, the cost may be that of lost professional time, of damaged public relations, and of lowered morale. In any event, the larger the proportion of the organization (or its customers) affected by the problem, the higher the cost, and the greater the urgency to effect repairs.

Today's interconnected world makes Internet disconnection a truly painful option for a network or security manager. Although the cost of disconnection can run into hundreds of thousands of dollars in lost business and productivity, disconnection in certain situations is both necessary and appropriate. At times, disconnection presents the lowest-cost, most effective way to protect users, systems, and the public. For example, on May 4, 2000, during the epidemic of the Microsoft Outlook–exploiting "I Love You" virus attack, network managers at Ford Motor Company[26] disconnected Ford's network from the outside world to limit the entry of contaminated e-mail into Ford's systems and to prevent Ford's systems from spreading the contagion. The response achieved its goals. It was not painless, but the alternatives were more painful.

The primary issue surrounding disconnection is what can be disconnected, on whose authority. According to well-known corollaries of Murphy's Law, such important incidents require short response times, inevitably on occasions when senior managers are not available. The best way to provide for this contingency is to furnish the personnel with authority to defend the systems within guidelines and a guarantee that actions within the guidelines will be immune from reprisal. If an organization chooses, as some do, not to authorize such actions, they also forswear the benefits.

30.6.10   Auditing.   In any organization, facilities usage should be monitored and analyzed, including network activity. Because people interested in attacking or subverting the enterprise's networks will attack when they wish, such monitoring and analysis must be part of a continuing process. Ongoing observation and review should include:

- Physical communications infrastructure
- Firewalls, router tables, and filtering rules
- Host security
- File security
- Traffic patterns on backbones, DMZ, and other network segments
- Physical security of systems and communications infrastructure

These areas are both synergistic and independent. They are synergistic in that the combination of all of them is mutually reinforcing in promoting a secure computing environment. They are independent because any one of them may represent a weak point in an otherwise secure environment. For more information on auditing, see Chapter 54 in this *Handbook*.

30.6.11   Emerging Technologies.   Emerging technologies continue to recast the challenges in the Internet technology arena. One such challenge is emerging in the use of SSL-based firewalls.

Using HTTPS as a basis for building encrypted tunnels appears at first impression to be a tremendously enabling technology. Most firewalls permit the initiation of connections from within the protected zone on TCP port 443 for the purpose of allowing connection to the wide variety of Web sites that need to secure information, as has been mentioned in other locations throughout this chapter. For privacy and security, such traffic is opaque to monitoring.

The use of HTTPS as the basis for tunneling also provides a tailor-made technique for abuse. For example, such technologies make it possible for a compromised desktop system to monitor the network, extracting data of interest, and to transmit the resulting data securely to an outside location through the firewall. The opaque nature of the SSL-based connection makes it impossible to scan the outgoing data.

This technology may well be the death knell of shared-connectivity LANs. It is ever more important to secure the network infrastructure against attacks that allow a rogue machine to accumulate data by monitoring network traffic.

Intrusion detection systems may also need to be repurposed to identify HTTPS connections that have significant traffic volumes, for signs of compromise or abuse. Approaches that treat the entire network as inherently compromised, with the use of VPN technology from the desktop server, to secure communications infrastructure, may be needed to protect against such attacks and malfeasance.

30.7   ETHICAL AND LEGAL ISSUES.   Managing a Web site poses a variety of ethical and legal issues, mostly surrounding the information that the site accumulates from processing transactions, from performance tracking, problem identification, and auditing. Policies need to be promulgated to ensure that information is not used for unauthorized purposes, and the staff running such systems needs to be aware of, and conform to, the policies. Many of these ethical issues have civil and criminal considerations as well. The topic of information privacy is more completely addressed in Chapter 69 of this *Handbook*. For more information on security policy standards, development and implementation, see Chapters 44, 45, 49, 50, and 51.

30.7.1   Liabilities.   The liability environment surrounding Web servers is too new for litigation to have run its course. However, there is no reason to believe that the myriad laws governing the disclosure of personal information will not be fully enforced in the context of Web sites.

Web sites increasingly handle sensitive information. Financial industry sites routinely handle bank and securities transactions. E-mail services handle large volumes of consumer traffic, and more and more insurance companies, employee benefits departments, and others are using Web sites to deal with extremely sensitive information covered by a variety of regulations.

Part of the rationale for recommending careful attention to the control of Web servers and their supporting systems is the need to create an environment of due diligence, where an organization can show that it took reasonable steps to ensure the integrity, safety, and confidentiality of information.

30.7.2   Customer Monitoring, Privacy, and Disclosure.   Customer monitoring is inherently a sensitive subject. The ability to accumulate detailed information about spending patterns, for example, is subject to abuse. A valid use of this information helps to pinpoint sales offerings that a customer would find relevant while eliminating contacts that would be of no interest. Used unethically or even illegally, such information could be used to assemble a dossier that could be the subject of embarrassing disclosure, of insurance refusal, and even of job termination. The overall problem predates the Web. In fact, more than 20 years ago a major network news segment reconstructed someone's life using nothing more than the information contained in their canceled checks, supplemented with publicly available information. The resulting analysis was surprisingly detailed. A similar experiment was reported in 1999, using the Web.[27]

Organizations sometimes violate the most basic security practices for protecting online information, when all of the information required to access an account improperly is contained on the single page of a billing statement. There have been repeated incidents (e.g., CDUniverse, CreditCard.com) where extremely sensitive information has been stored unencrypted on Web-accessible systems. These incidents recur with regularity and are almost always the result of storing large amounts of sensitive client information on systems that are Internet accessible. There is little question that it is inappropriate to store customer credit card, and similarly sensitive data, on exposed systems.

The security and integrity of systems holding customer order information is critical. The disclosure of customer ordering information is a significant privacy hazard. Failure to protect customer banking information (e.g., credit card numbers and expiration dates) can be extremely costly, both in economic terms and in damaged customer relations. Credit card merchant agreements also may subject the enterprise to additional liabilities and obligations.

A Web site, by its monitoring of customer activity, will accumulate a collection of sensitive material. It may be presumed that the information is useful only for the site, and is inherently valid, but there are a variety of hazards here, most of which are not obvious:

- Information appearing to originate from a single source may indeed be a compilation of data from multiple sources. Shared computers, firewalls, and proxy servers can give rise to this phenomenon.

- Casual correlations may arise between otherwise unrelated items. For example, it is not an uncommon acceptable business practice for one member of a business group to pay for all expenses of a group of traveling colleagues. Failure to correctly interpret such an event could be misconstrued as proof of illicit or inappropriate behavior.

The problem with casual associations is the damage they can cause. In the national security area, the use of casual associations to gather intelligence is a useful tool, albeit one that is recognized to have serious limitations. In other situations, it is an extremely dangerous tool, with significant potential to damage individuals and businesses. An example:

> A California-based married businessman flies to New York City. When he arrives, he checks into a major hotel. A short time later, he makes a telephone call, and shortly a young woman goes up to his room and is greeted warmly. Apparently, a compromising situation. The businessman is old enough to be the woman's father; in fact, he *is* her father. That single fact changes apparently inappropriate behavior into a harmless family get-together. Peter Lewis[28] of *The New York Times* correctly notes that this single fact, easily overlooked, dramatically changes the import of the information.

The danger with correlations and customer monitoring is that there is often no control on the expansive use of the conclusions generated. The information often has some degree of validity, but it is both easy to overstep the bounds of validity, and difficult to correct the damage, once damage has been done.

30.7.3 Litigation.   The increasing pervasiveness of the Web has led to increasing volumes of related litigation. In this chapter, the emphasis is on litigation or regulatory investigation involving commercial or consumer transactions, and the issues surrounding criminal prosecution for criminal activities involving a Web site. More detailed information on this subject appears in Chapter 11 of this *Handbook*

Civil. Web site logs and records can become involved in litigation in many ways. In an increasing number of cases, neither the site owner nor the operator is a party to the action; the records merely document transactions involved in a dispute. The dispute may be a general commercial matter, a personnel matter, or even a domestic relations matter involving divorce.

It is important that records handling and retention policies be developed in concert with counsel. The firm's management and counsel also must determine what the policy is to be with regard to subpoenas and related requests. The counsel also will determine what materials are subject to which procedures and regulations. For example, in a case of an e-mail provider (e.g., hotmail.com), material may be subject to the Electronic Communications Privacy Act of 1986 (18 U.S.C.A. § 2510 et seq.). Other material may be subject to different legal or contractual obligations.

Regulatory. A wide range of rules is enforced (and often promulgated) by various regulatory agencies. In the United States, such agencies exist at the federal, state, regional, and local level. (Outside the United States, many nations have agencies only at the national and provincial levels.) Many of these agencies have the authority to request records and conduct various types of investigations. For many organizations, such investigations are significantly more likely than civil or criminal investigations. Regulatory agencies also may impose record-keeping and retention requirements on companies within their jurisdiction.

Criminal. Criminal prosecutions receive more attention than the preceding two categories of investigation yet are much less frequent. Criminal matters are expensive to investigate and prosecute and must pass a higher standard of proof than regulatory or civil prosecutions. Relatively few computer-related incidents reach the stage of a criminal prosecution, although because of its seriousness, the process is the most visible.

Logs, Evidence, and Recording What Happened. The key to dealing effectively with any legal proceeding relating to a Web site is the maintenance of accurate, complete records in a secure manner. This is a complex topic, some details of which are covered in Chapter 55 of this *Handbook*.

In the context of protecting a Web site, records and logs of activity should be offloaded to external media and preserved for possible later use, as determined by the site's policy and its legal obligations. Once offloaded, these records should be stored using the strict procedures suitable for evidence in a criminal matter. The advent of inexpensive CD-ROM and DVD writers greatly simplifies the physical issues of securely storing such media.

Archival records not intended for evidentiary use also should be stored off-line, either physically, or at least on systems that are not accessible from the public Internet.

The media should be stored in signed, sealed containers in an inventoried, secure storage facility with controlled access. For this reason, the copies archived for records purposes should not be the copies normally used for system recovery. In the event of an investigation or other problem, these records will be carefully examined for possible modification or misuse.

30.7.4   Application Service Providers.   In recent years, it has become increasingly common to outsource entire applications services. External organizations providing such services are known as applications service providers, more commonly referred to as ASPs. Even more recently, this trend has diversified with the emergence of *software as a service*. Both raise similar security and integrity concerns. In both cases, significant applications and data are stored outside of the organization, with the organization retaining responsibility for the integrity and confidentiality of these records.

Conceptually, ASPs are not new. Many organizations have historically outsourced payroll processing and other applications. Theoretically, the ASP is responsible for the entire application. Often, paying a package price for the application seems attractive: no maintenance charges, no depreciation costs, lower personnel costs, latest technology, and moderately priced upgrades. However, just as a ship's captain retains responsibility for the safety of his ship, despite the presence of a harbor pilot, an enterprise must not forget that if something goes wrong, the enterprise, not the ASP, will likely bear the full consequences. In short, the ASP must be required to answer the same questions, and held to the same standards, as an inside IT organization regarding privacy, security, and integrity issues.

The security and integrity issues surrounding the use of ASPs are the same as those surrounding the use of an internal corporate service. Questions of privacy, integrity, and reliability remain relevant, but as with any form of outsourcing, there are additional questions. For example, is stored information commingled with that of other firms, perhaps competitors? Is information stored encrypted? What backup provisions exist? Is there off-site storage of backups? What connectivity does the ASP have? Where are the ASP's servers, and are they dispersed? What are the personnel practices of the ASP? Does the ASP itself own and operate its facilities, or does it in turn contract out to other providers?

The bottom line is that although outsourcing promises speedy implementation, lower personnel costs, and economies of scale, the customer organization will suffer considerable harm if there is a problem with the ASP, with availability, results, or confidentiality.

Finally, in the end analysis, the organization retains liability for its operations and its data. While it is comforting to consider that the legal system will accept "My provider did it." as an excuse for lost, compromised, or untrustable data, it remains an untested theory. Recent experiences with major manufacturers, subcontractors, and tainted products would seem to indicate that outsourcing risk remains a serious potential liability.

Legal process requests, either criminal warrants or civil subpoenas, against ASPs for third-party data represent another hazard. If data belonging to third-parties is commingled on the ASP's system, care is required to prevent the unauthorized and inappropriate disclosure of unrelated data belonging to third parties other than the one that is the subject of the request.

None of the items cited may be reason to justify a negative finding on ASPs as a group. They should, however, serve as reminders that each of the issues related to keeping a Web presence secure, available, and effective apply no less to an ASP than they do to an in-house IT organization.

For information about outsourcing security, see Chapter 68 in this *Handbook*.

30.8   SUMMARY.   Availability is the cornerstone of all Web-related strategies. Throughout this chapter, it has been noted that redundant hosting and routing were necessary to ensure 24/7/365 availability. It was also noted that although some providers of services offer various guarantees, these guarantees almost never provide adequate compensation for consequential damage done to the enterprise. In the end, an enterprise's only protection is to take adequate measures to ensure their own security and integrity.

Operating guidelines and authority are also critical to ensuring the availability of Web resources on a 24/7/365 basis. Systems must be architected and implemented to enhance availability on an overall level. Operating personnel must have the freedom and authority to take actions that they perceive as necessary without fear of reprisal if the procedures do not produce the desired outcome.

Privacy and integrity of information exchanged with the Web site is also important. The implementation and operation of the site and its components must be in compliance with the appropriate laws, regulations, and obligations of the site owner, in addition to being in conformance with the expectations of the user community.

Protecting Internet and Web assets is a multifaceted task encompassing many disciplines. It is an area that requires attention at all levels, beginning at the highest levels of business strategy and descending successively to ever more detailed implementation and technology issues.

It is also an area where the smallest detail can have catastrophic impact. Recent events have shown that the lessons of communications history apply. Even a small error in network architecture, key management, or implementation can snowball until it is an issue that can be felt in the corporate boardroom.

30.9   FURTHER READING

Alderman, E., and C. Kennedy. *The Right to Privacy*. New York: Alfred A. Knopf, 1995. Well-written work concerning legal issues relating to privacy, particularly in the United States.

Ashley, B. K. "The United States Is Vulnerable to Cyberterrorism," *SIGNAL Magazine* (March 2004); retrieved from www.afcea.org/signal/articles/templates/ SIGNAL_Article_Template.asp?articleid=32&zoneid=10 on March 31, 2008.

Barnes, S. "In Ice-Coated Arkansas and Oklahoma, Chaos Rules." *New York Times*, December 28, 2000.

Bernstein, D. "We've Been Hacked." *Inc Technology*, No. 3 (2000).

Bernstein, T., A.B. Bhimani, E. Schultz, and C. A. Siegel. *Internet Security for Business*. New York: John Wiley & Sons, 1996.

Bowman, D., and AFP. "Internet Problems Continue with Fourth Cable Break," *Arabian Business*, February 3, 2008; retrieved from www.arabianbusiness.com/ 510132-internet-problems-continue-with-fourth-cable-break on March 31, 2008.

CERT. "sadmind/IIS Worm." May 8, 2001; retrieved from www.cert.org/advisories/CA-2001-11.html on May 31, 2008.

Cheshire, S., B. Aboba, and E. Gutterman. "RFC 3927—Dynamic Configuration of IPv4 Link-Local Addresses," 2005; retrieved from www.ietf.org/rfc/rfc3927.txt on February 18, 2008.

Children's Online Privacy Protection Act of 1998; 15 U.S.C. § 6501 et seq.

CNN. "Internet Failure Hits Two Continents," January 31, 2008, retrieved from www.cnn.com/2008/WORLD/meast/01/31/dubai.outage on February 19, 2008.

deGroot, G., D. Karrenberg, V. Moskowitz, and Lear E. Rekhter "RFC 1918—Address Allocation for Private Internets" (RFC1597). February 1996; retrieved from www.ietf.org/rfc/rfc1918.txt on May 27, 2008.

Derfler, Frank J., and Jay Munro. "Home Appliances Hit the Net." *PC Magazine*, January 2, 2001; retrieved from www.pcmag.com/article2/0,2817,110893,00.asp on May 28, 2008.

Electronic Communications Privacy Act of 1986; 18 U.S.C.A. § 2510 et seq.

"Employees in the Twin Towers," *New York Times*, September 16, 2001, p. 10.

Ford, W., and M. S. Baum. *Secure Electronic Commerce: Building the Infrastructure for Digital Signatures and Encryption*. Upper Saddle River, NJ: Prentice Hall, 1997.

Fraser, B. "RFC2196—Site Security Handbook," September 1997. Retrieved from www.ietf.org/rfc/rfc2196.txt on May 28, 2008.

Garfinkel, S., and G. Spafford. *Web Security and Commerce*. Sebastopol, CA: O'Reilly & Associates, 1997.

Gezelter, R. "System Security—The Forgotten Issues." Conference Session, US DECUS Symposium, Las Vegas, Nevada, Fall 1990; retrievable via www.rlgsc.com/presentations.html.

Gezelter, R. "Internet Security." In *The Computer Security Handbook*, 3rd ed. New York: John Wiley & Sons, 1995.

Gezelter, Robert. "Plain Talk Management Needs to Hear from Its Technical Support Staff." Commerce in Cyberspace: Expanding Your Enterprise via the Internet, The Conference Board (February 1996); retrieved from www.rlgsc.com/tcb/plaintalk.html on May 28, 2008.

Gezelter, R. "Security Prosecution: Records and Evidence." *DECUS Magazine* (Spring 1996).

Gezelter, R. "Internet Security." In *The Computer Security Handbook*, 3rd ed. supplement. New York: John Wiley & Sons, 1997.

Ghosh, A. K. E-*Commerce Security: Weak Links, Best Defenses*. New York: John Wiley & Sons, 1998.

Glater, J. "Hemming in the World Wide Web," *New York Times*, January 7, 2001.

Guernsey, L. "Keeping the Life Lines Open," *New York Times*, September 20, 2001.

Heyman, K. "A New Virtual Private Network for Today's Mobile World," *IEEE Computer* (December 2007): 17–19.

Internet standards: www.ietf.org

Janofsky, M. "Police Seek Record of Bookstore Patrons in Bid for Drug Charge," *New York Times*, November 24, 2000.

Kahn, D. *Codebreakers*. New York: Macmillan, 1970.

Kahn, D. *Seizing the Enigma*. Boston: Houghton Mifflin, 1991.

Khare, R., ed. *Web Security: A Matter of Trust*. Sebastopol, CA: O'Reilly & Associates, 1998.

Klensin, J., ed. "RFC 2821—Simple Mail Transfer Protocol" (obsoletes RFC 821, RFC

974, and RFC 1869), May 2001; retrieved from www.ietf.org/rfc/rfc2821.txt on May 28, 2008.

Knight, W. "Browser-Based Network Attack Discovered," *New Scientist Tech*, July 31, 2006; retrieved from http://technology.newscientist.com/article.ns?id=dn9645 on February 18, 2008.

Layton, E. *And I Was There—Pearl Harbor and Midway—Breaking the Secrets*. New York: William Morrow, 1985.

Lichtblau, E. "F.B.I. Received Unauthorized E-Mail Access," *New York Times*, February 17, 2008; retrieved from www.nytimes.com/2008/02/17/washington/17fisa.html on February 17, 2008.

Littman, J. *The Fugitive Game—Online with Kevin Mitnick*. Boston: Little, Brown, 1996.

Liu, C., and P. Albitz. *DNS and BIND*, 5th ed. Sebastopol, CA: O'Reilly & Associates, 2006.

Llosa, M. V. "Crossing the Moral Boundary" (op-ed.), *New York Times*, January 7, 2001.

Mockapetris, P. V. "RFC1034—Domain Names: Concepts and Facilities," November 1, 1987; retrieved from www.ietf.org/rfc/rfc1034.txt on May 28, 2008.

Mockapetris, P. V. "RFC1035—Domain Names: Implementation and Specification," November 1, 1987; retrieved from www.ietf.org/rfc/rfc1035.txt on May 28, 2008.

National Computer Network Emergency Response Technical Team/Coordination Center of China, "2006 Annual Report by CNCERT/CC"; retrieved from www.cert.org/cn/english_Web/document/2006AnnualReportByCNCERT.pdf on February 20, 2008.

National Infrastructure Protection Center "Cyber Protests: The Threat to U.S. Information Infrastructure" (October 2001); retrieved from www.au.af.mil/au/awc/awcgate/nipc/cyberprotests.html on February 19, 2008.

Overbye, Dennis. "Engineers Tackle Havoc Underground," *New York Times*, September 18, 2001.

Postel, J., and J.K. Reynolds. " RFC 854—Telnet Protocol Specification" (May 1983); retrieved from http://www.ietf.org/rfc/rfc0854.txt on May 28, 2008.

Postel, J., and J.K. Reynolds. "RFC 959—File Transfer Protocol" (October 1985); retrieved from http://www.ietf.org/rfc/rfc0959.txt on May 28, 2008.

Preatoni, Roberto. "Digital Implication of the Attack to Lebanon: It's Cyberwar," Zone-H.org, August 1, 2006; retrieved from www.zone-h.org/index2.php?option=com_content&task=view&id=13937 on February 19, 2008.

Pummill, T., and B. Manning. "RFC 1878—Variable Length Subnet Table for IPv4" (December 1995); retrieved from http://www.ietf.org/rfc/rfc1878.txt on May 28, 2008.

Schwartau, W. *Information Warfare—Chaos on the Information Superhighway*. New York: Avalon, 1994.

Security-related information: www.cert.org

Shimormura, T., and J. Markoff. *Takedown*. New York: Hyperion, 1996.

Simmons, M. *The Credit Card Catastrophe*. Fort Lee, NJ: Barricade Books, 1995.

Slatalla, M., and J. Quittner. *Masters of Deception*. New York: Harper Collins, 1995.

Stoll, C. *The Cuckoo's Egg*. New York: Bantam Doubleday, 1989.

Talbot, M. "The Devil in the Nursery," *New York Times Magazine*, January 7, 2001.

Tripathy, D. "Internet Chaos Nears Its End," *Arabian Business*, retrieved from www.arabianbusiness.com/510649 on February 19, 2008.

Weinberg, G. *The Psychology of Computer Programming*. New York: Van Nostrand Reinhold, 1971.

Weizenbaum, J. *Computer Power and Human Reason*. San Francisco: W.H. Freeman, 1976.

Wright, B. *The Law of Electronic Commerce: EDI, E-Mail and Internet—Technology, Proof and Liability*, 2nd ed. Boston: Little, Brown, 1996.

Wright, P. *Spycatcher*. Viking Penguin, 1987.

Zoellick, B. "Wide Use of Electronic Signatures Awaits Market Decisions About the Risks and Benefits," *New York State Bar Association Journal* (November/December 2000).

30.10 NOTES

1. J. Swartz, "TJX Data Breach May Involve 94 Million Credit Cards," *USA Today*, October 24, 2007; retrieved from www.usatoday.com/money/industries/technology/2007-10-24-tjx-security-breach_N.htm on March 31, 2008.

2. J. Vijayan, "TJX Agrees to Pay $40.9M to Visa Card Issuers in Breach Case," *Computerworld*, November 30, 2007; retrieved from www.computerworld.com/action/article.do?command=viewArticleBasic&articleId=9050322 on May 29, 2008.

3. E. Murray, "Survey on Information Security," *Information Security Magazine* (October 2000.)

4. VISA, "PCI Compliance Continued to Grow in 2007," Press Release, January 22, 2008.

5. S. Schiesel and R. Atlas, "By-the-Numbers Operation at Morgan Stanley Finds Its Human Side," *New York Times*, September 16, 2001.

6. A. Harmon, "Breaking Up the Central Office; Staffs Make a Virtue of Necessity," *New York Times*, October 29, 2001 (corrected October 30, 2001).

7. www.truste.org.

8. P. G. Neumann, "The Green Card Flap," *RISKS Forum Digest* 15, April 18, 1994.

9. G. Keizer, "Hacker Contest Weekend," *Web Design & Technology News*, July 2, 2003; retrieved from www.webdesignsnow/news/070203.html on February 19, 2008.

10. Extensible Markup Language: A universal standard for structured documents and data on the World Wide Web sponsored by the World Wide Web Consortium (W3C), www.w3c.org.

11. J. Serjeant, "'Botmaster' Admits Infecting 250,000 Computers," Reuters, November 9, 2007; "Computer Security Consultant Charges with Infecting up to a Quarter Million Computers That Were Used to Wiretap, Engage in Identity Theft, Defraud Banks," November 9, 2007; retrieved from www.reuters.com/article/domesticNews/idUSN0823938120071110 on May 31, 2008. Press Release No. 07-143, United States Attorney's Office, Central District of California, retrieved from www.usdoj.gov/usao/cac/pressroom/pr2007/143.html on May 31, 2008. FBI, "BOT ROAST II," Cracking Down on CyberCrime, retrieved from www.fbi.gov/page2/nov07/botnet112907.html on May 31, 2008. FBI, "Bot Roast II Nets 8 [*sic*] Individuals," www.fbi.gov/pressrel/pressrel07/botroast112907.htm on May 31, 2008.

12. TechWise Research, Inc. "Quantifying the Value of Availability" (June 2000).

13. Vijayan, "TJX Agrees to Pay \$40.9M."

14. G. deGroot, D. Karrenberg, V. Moskowitz, and Lear E. Rekhter, "RFC 1597—Address Allocation for Private Internets" (March 1994); retrieved from www.ietf.org/rfc/rfc1597.txt on May 27, 2008.

15. R. Gezelter, "Internet Dial Tones & Firewalls: One Policy Does Not Fit All," IEEE Computer Society, Charleston, SC, June 10, 2003; retrieved from www.rlgsc.com/ieee/charleston/2003-6/internetdial.htmlon May 28, 2008. R. Gezelter, "Safe Computing in the Age of Ubiquitous Connectivity," LISAT 2007 (May 2007); retrieved from www.rlgsc.com/ieee/longisland/2007/ubiquitous.html on February 19, 2007.

16. RFC1597, superseded by RFC1918.

17. RFC 3927.

18. Gezelter, "Internet Dial Tones & Firewalls." Gezelter, "Safe Computing in the Age of Ubiquitous Connectivity."

19. Formerly RFC 1597.

20. RFC 3927.

21. Robert Gezelter, "Stopping Spoofed Addresses Can Cut Down on DDoS Attacks," *Network World Fusion,* August 14, 2000; retrieved from www.networkworld.com/columnists/2000/0814gezelter.html on May 28, 2008.

22. Frank da Cruz, and Christine M. Gianone. *Using C-KERMIT*, 2nd ed. (Boston: Digital Press, 1997).

23. M. Slatalla and J. Quittner, *Masters of Deception* (New York: Harper Collins, 1995).

24. W. Townsley, A. Valencia, A. Rubens, G. Pall, G. Zorn, and B. Palter. "RFC 2661—Layer Two Tunneling Protocol 'L2TP'" (August 1999); retrieved from www.ietf.org/rfc/rfc2661.txt on May 28, 2008.

25. K. Hamzeh, G. Pall, W. Verthein, J. Taarud, W. Little, and G. Zorn "RFC 2637—Point-to-Point Tunneling Protocol" (July 1999); retrieved from www.ietf.org/rfc/rfc2637.txt on May 28, 2008.

26. K. Timms, Telephone interview (Summer 2001); K. Bradsher, "With Its E-mail Infected, Ford Scrambled and Caught Up," *New York Times*, May 8, 2000.

27. T. Kelley, "An Expert in Computer Security Finds His Life Is a Wide Open Book," *New York Times*, December 31. 1999.

28. P. Lewis, "Forget Big Brother," *New York Times,* March 19, 1998.

CHAPTER **31**

WEB MONITORING AND CONTENT FILTERING

Steven Lovaas

31.1 INTRODUCTION.   The Internet has been called a cesspool, sometimes in reference to the number of virus-infected and hacker-controlled machines, but more often in reference to the amount of objectionable content available at a click of the mouse. This chapter deals with efforts to monitor and control access to some of this content. Applications that perform this kind of activity are controversial: Privacy and free-speech advocates regularly refer to "censorware," while the writers of such software tend to use the term "content filtering." This chapter uses "content filtering," without meaning to take a side in the argument by so doing. For more on the policy and legal issues surrounding Web monitoring and content filtering, see Chapters 48 and 72 in this *Handbook*.

This chapter briefly discusses the possible motivations leading to the decision to filter content, without debating the legitimacy of these motives. Given the variety of good and bad reasons to monitor and filter Web content, this chapter reviews the various techniques used in filtering, as well as some ways in which monitoring and filtering can be defeated.

31.2   SOME TERMINOLOGY

Proxy—a computer that intercedes in a communication on behalf of a client. The proxy receives the client request and then regenerates the request with the proxy's own address as the source address. Thus, the server only sees identifying information from the proxy, and the client's identity remains hidden (at least from a network addressing point of view). Proxies are widely used by organizations to control the outward flow of traffic (mostly Web traffic) and to protect users from direct connection with potentially damaging Web sites.

Anonymizing proxy—a proxy that allows users to hide their Web activity. Typically such a proxy is located outside organizational boundaries, and often used to get around filtering rules.

Privacy-enhancing technologies (PET)—a class of technologies that helps users keep their network usage private. These include encryption, anonymizing proxies, mixing networks, and onion routing.

Encryption—reversible garbling of text (plaintext) into random-looking data (ciphertext) that cannot be reversed without using secret information (keys). See Chapter 7 in this *Handbook* for details of cryptography.

Mixing networks—users encrypt their outbound messages with their recipient's (or recipients') public key(s) and then also with the public key of a "Mix server." The encrypted message is sent to the Mix server, which acts as a message broker and decrypts the cryptogram to determine the true recipient's address and to forward the message.[1]

Onion routing—an anonymous and secure routing protocol developed by the Naval Research Laboratory, Center for High Assurance Computer Systems in the 1990s. Messages are sent through a network (cloud) of *onion routers* that communicate with each other using public key cryptography. Once the temporary circuit has been established, the sender encrypts the outbound message with each of the public keys of all the onion routers in the circuit.

> Specifically, the architecture provides for bi-directional communication even though no one but the initiator's proxy server knows anything but previous and next hops in the communication chain. This implies that neither the respondent nor his proxy server nor any external observer need know the identity of the initiator or his proxy server.[2]

A third-generation implementation of onion routing is *Tor* (the onion router).[3]

31.3   MOTIVATION.   As a general concept, an individual or group chooses to monitor network activity and filter content through an authority relationship. The most common relationships leading to monitoring and filtering are:

- Governments controlling their citizenry
- Parents and schools protecting their children
- Organizations enforcing their policies

31.3.1   Prevention of Dissent.   Probably the most common reason for the opposition to content filtering is that many repressive governments filter content to prevent dissent. If citizens (or subjects) cannot access information that either reflects badly on the government or questions the country's philosophical or religious doctrines, then the citizens probably will not realize the degree to which they are being repressed.

In countries such as the United States, where the Constitution guarantees freedoms of speech and the press, many people feel that only those with something to hide would advocate censorship. This notion, combined with objectionable content so readily available on the Internet, may be why efforts to question the use of filtering software in libraries and other public places have met with resistance or indifference. Chapter 72 gives many examples of countries using filtering products to limit the rights of their citizens. These examples should be a cautionary tale to readers in countries that are currently more liberal in information policy.

31.3.2   Protection of Children.   For the same reasons that convenience stores, at least partially, hide adult magazines from view, the government has required that some classes of information on the Internet be off-limits to children in public schools. This stems from the perception of the schools' role as a surrogate parent and government liability involved in possible failure in that role. A variety of regulations have required the use of content monitoring and filtering in schools and libraries, on the theory that such public or publicly supported terminals should not be using taxpayers' money to provide objectionable content to children. The U.S. Supreme Court has ruled several of these efforts unconstitutional after extreme protest from libraries. Most recently, the Child Internet Protection Act (CIPA)[4] required school districts that receive certain kinds of government funding to use filtering technologies. Most schools have implemented Web filtering, aggressively limiting the Web content available to students. Estimates of the amount of blocked content vary widely, but one school district claims to filter about 10 percent of its total Web traffic due to questionable content.[5]

The obvious target of filtering technology in schools is to keep students from viewing material considered *harmful to minors*. Another less-publicized reason to filter Web content is to prevent students from doing things on the Web that they might not do if they knew that someone was watching. The hope is to keep students from getting a criminal record before they even graduate from high school, protecting them from their bad judgment while they are learning to develop good judgment and learning the rules of society. Arguably, this is the job of a parent and not the job of a school, but schools providing Internet access nonetheless must provide this kind of protection.

High school students and kindergarteners generally have differing levels of maturity, and a reasonable filtering policy would include a flexible, gradual degree of filtering depending on age. Schools could use less-intrusive methods of controlling access to Web content as well, such as direct supervision of students using computers. Parents also have the opportunity to filter the content that their children view at home.

31.3.3   Supporting Organizational Human Resources Policy.   Organizations have a variety of reasons for monitoring and filtering the Web content accessed by their employees. The simplest is a desire to keep employees doing work-related activity while at work. Despite studies indicating that the flexibility to conduct limited personal business, such as banking or e-mail, from work produces happier, more productive workers, managers sometimes view personal use of business computers as stealing time from the company.

A more pragmatic reason to filter some Web content is to prevent "hostile workplace" liability under Equal Employment Opportunity laws. The problem with this approach is that many kinds of content would potentially be offensive to coworkers, so it is difficult to use filtering technology to guarantee that no one will be offended while still allowing reasonable work-related use of the Internet.

Some organizations choose to monitor Web traffic with automated systems, rather than blocking anything, and to notify users of the monitoring. The notification could be in general policy documents or in the form of a pop-up window announcing that the user is about to view content that might violate policy. Either way, the notion is that the organization might avoid liability by having warned the user, but might also avoid privacy and freedom-of-speech complaints. The monitor-and-notify approach also sends the message that the organization trusts its employees but wants to maintain a positive and productive work environment.

31.3.4 Enforcement of Laws.   Law enforcement agencies rarely engage in content filtering, but traffic monitoring is an often-utilized tool for investigating computer crime. Investigation involves catching the traffic as it actually arrives at its destination, so filtering would be counterproductive. In this case, proving identity is the key to getting usable evidence, so privacy-enhancing technologies are real problems. In some cases, the logs of Web proxies—which would identify the real source address of the client machine—are available with a subpoena. Investigations of this sort often include child pornography, drug production, or—increasingly—the theft of computer hardware protected by asset-recovery software.

31.4 GENERAL TECHNIQUES.   Filtering methods for Web browsing can focus on targets, sources, the general class of address, and traffic content.

31.4.1 Matching the Request.   The simplest technique used by filtering technologies is the matching of strings against lists of keywords. Every Web request uses a uniform resource locator (URL) in the general form:

```
protocol://server.organization.top-level-domain/path-to-
file.file-format
```

Filtering a request for a URL can examine any portion of the string for a match against prohibited strings:

- Filters can match the *protocol* field to enforce policies about the use of encrypted Web traffic (HTTP versus HTTPS). This is more of a general security concern than it is a Web filtering issue, although an organization worried about the need to analyze all traffic could prevent the use of encrypted Web traffic by blocking all HTTPS requests.

- The *server* and *organization* fields describe who is hosting the content. Filtering based in these strings is a broad approach, as it leads to blocking either an entire Web server or an entire organization's Web traffic. See the discussion of server blocking in Section 32.4.2.

- The *top-level-domain* field can be used to filter content; see Section 31.4.3 for attempts to set up an .xxx domain.

- The *path-to-file* field includes the actual title of the requested Web page, so it varies most between individual requests. Whether it is more likely than other fields to contain information useful in filtering depends on the naming convention of the server. This field (and the *file-format* field) is optional, as shown in the request for www.wiley.com, which directs the server to display its default page.

- The *file-format* field tells the Web browser how to handle the text displayed in the page, whether in straight html format or encoded in some other file format (e.g., doc, pdf), or whether to allow dynamic generation of content (e.g., asp). Few filtering products use this field to filter traditional kinds of objectionable content, although enforcing other policies regarding dynamic code in high-security environments can require matching this field.

31.4.2 Matching the Host.   Some filtering systems attempt to distinguish between acceptable and unacceptable sources on the Web by inspecting the particular servers or general information portals such as search engines.

31.4.2.1 *Block Lists of Servers.*   Objectionable content tends to be concentrated on individual servers. This naturally leads some organizations to block access to those servers. The two methods of blocking servers are by Internet Protocol (IP) address and by name.

Blocking by IP address simply denies all traffic (or all HTTP traffic) to and from certain addresses. This tactic involves several difficulties based on how addresses are used. First, IP addresses are not permanent. While the numeric addresses of most large commercial servers tend to remain the same over time, many smaller servers have dynamically assigned addresses that may change periodically. Thus, blocking an IP address may prevent access to content hosted on a completely different server than intended. Second, commercial servers often host content for many different customers, and blocking the server as a whole will block all of the contents rather than just the objectionable ones. This is a particular problem for very large service providers like AOL, which grants every user the ability to host a Web site. Blocking the AOL servers because of objectionable content would potentially overblock large numbers of personal Web pages. Third, address-based blocking creates the possibility of malicious listing, a practice in which an attacker (or a competitor) spoofs the address of a Web server and provides objectionable content likely to land the server on blocking lists. Some filtering products allow users to submit "bad" sites, which provides another opportunity for malicious listing.

Blocking by name involves the Domain Name System (DNS), in which a human-readable name (e.g., www.wiley.com) maps to a computer-readable IP addresses (in this case, 208.215.179.146). DNS allows an organization to change the physical address of its Web server by updating the DNS listing to point to the new IP address, although this does rely on the system as a whole propagating the change in a reasonable amount of time. A device that monitors or filters traffic based on a domain name needs to be able to periodically refresh its list of name-to-address mappings in order to avoid blocking sites whose addresses periodically change. As with address-based blocking, name-based blocking also risks malicious listing as well as both under- and overblocking. Many organizations register multiple names for their servers, for a variety of reasons. For instance, an organization might register its name in the .net, .com, .org, and .biz top-level domains to prevent the kind of misdirection described in Section 31.4.1 (whitehouse.com). Other reasons for registering a name in multiple domains include preventing competitors from using name registration to steal customers and preventing speculative buying of similar names by individuals hoping to sell them for significant profit. Web hosting companies also provide service to many different organizations, so a variety of URLs would point to the IP address of the same hosting server. Thus, blocking by server name could underblock by not accounting for all the possible registered names pointing to the same server and overblock by matching the server name of a service provider that hosts sites for many different customers who use the provider's server name in the URL of their Web pages.

31.4.2.2   Block/Modify Intermediaries.   The Web has become an enormous repository of information, requiring the development of powerful search tools to find information. Early search engines gave way to more sophisticated information portals like Yahoo!, Google, AOL, and MSN. By allowing advanced searches and customized results, these portals give users easy access to information that would be difficult or impossible to find using manual search techniques. Portals have become wildly popular tools for accessing the Internet as a whole; Google claimed 100 million search queries per day at the end of 2000 and announced in 2004 that its site index contained over 6 billion items.[6] Information access at this scale makes portals natural targets for monitoring and filtering. Few commercial organizations prevent their employees from using popular portals, since they have become so much a part of the way people use the Internet. Some countries, however, have blocked access to certain portals for their citizens, hoping to control access to information that might tend to violate national laws (e.g., access to Nazi memorabilia in France) or inspire citizen resistance to the government (e.g., access to information about the Tiananmen Square massacre in China). For further discussion of these issues, see Chapter 72 in this *Handbook*.

31.4.3   Matching the Domain.   Since 2000, the Internet Corporation for Assigned Names and Numbers (ICANN) has been reviewing requests for a new top-level domain, .xxx, which would allow providers of sexually related content to voluntarily reregister their sites. Such a domain would be easy to filter in the URL of the request, which presumably would appeal to supporters of Web filtering. It would also allow content providers to show that they were complying with laws preventing children from accessing inappropriate material, by enabling more effective parental filtering. Nevertheless, the move has met resistance on both fronts. Conservative religious groups fear that establishing a .xxx domain would legitimize pornography, while not all sexual content providers agree that the perceived benefit would outweigh either the increased filtering of their sites or the easier monitoring of their clients' traffic.

In 2007, ICANN rejected the most recent revision of the .xxx domain proposal, citing the lack of unanimity in the sex content provider community as well as the fear that ICANN might be placed in the position of regulating content, which is outside the organization's charter.[7]

31.4.4   Matching the Content.   String matching is simple to do, but difficult to do without both over- and underblocking. For instance, one of the most common categories for content filtering (particularly in the United States) is sex. Blocking all content exactly matching the word "sex" would fail to match the words "sexy" and "sexual." To avoid this kind of underblocking, word lists need to be very long to account for all permutations. A slightly more effective tactic is to block all works containing the string "sex," but this would overblock the words "Essex," "Sussex," and "asexual." Looking for all strings beginning with the combination "sex" would overblock "sexton," "sextet," and "sextant." Simple string matching also ignores context, so blocking "sex" would match in cases where a survey page asked the respondent to identify gender using the word "sex" or in pages describing inherited sex traits or gender roles or sexual discrimination lawsuits.

Other difficulties in string matching involve the vagaries of language. URLs can be displayed in any language whose character set a computer recognizes, so a filter will underblock requests in a language for which it lacks word lists. More generally, in any language it is possible to obfuscate the contents of a site with a seemingly benign URL to avoid filtering. The classic example of this is the pornography site www.whitehouse.com, presumably set up to catch visitors who mistakenly typed "com" when trying to reach the U.S. White House Web site (www.whitehouse.gov). More recently, spam marketing campaigns have been setting up Web sites linked in e-mail, with meaningless strings of numbers and characters in the URL (e.g., http://2sfh.com/7hioh), making the sites difficult to filter.

In a 2006 study, Veritest compared three of the industry-leading Web filter products (WebSense, SmartFilter, and SurfControl). The winning product underblocked 7 sites, overblocked 8 sites, and miscategorized 10 sites, from a preselected list of 600 URLs. The two competing products fared worse, underblocking 23 and 14 sites, and overblocking 9 and 12 sites out of 600.[8] If this is the performance of the industry's leading edge, then clearly the technology is still developing.

Given the difficulties of accurate matching based on text or address related to the Web page request, a natural alternative is to examine the page content itself. Of course, content matching needs to have access to the unencrypted data in transit, so encrypted Web sessions cause a real problem for this tactic. Some organizations allow (or require) that HTTPS sessions terminate on the organization's own proxy server, potentially allowing the proxy to decrypt the data and perform content analysis.

31.4.4.1   *Text.* It is possible, although resource intensive, to watch the network traffic stream and look for text that matches a list of undesired content. This sort of matching typically does little analysis of context and so is prone to the same kind of false positives (overblocking) and false negatives (underblocking) described in Section 31.4.2. Moreover, as an increasing amount of Web content involves pictures and sounds, text matching becomes less effective.

31.4.4.2   *Graphics.* A promising new technique, with applications in visual searching as well as visual content blocking, breaks a graphic image into smaller objects by color or pattern. The technique then evaluates each object against a database of reference images for matching with desired criteria. In the case of blocking objectionable sex content, objects can be evaluated for skin tone and either blocked outright or referred to administrators for manual review if the match is inconclusive. Although content-based filtering has not yet developed into a commercial product, the tools exist and the technology seems applicable not only to still images, but also to video and even audio content.[9] In 2006, the NASA Inspector General's office used an image-search program called Web ContExt to snare an employee who had been trafficking in child pornography.[10]

31.5   IMPLEMENTATION.   With the exception of content-based matching, which has not yet reached the market in any significant way, most filtering—whether of address, domain, or keyword—involves matching text lists.

31.5.1   Manual "Bad URL" Lists.   Many firewalls provide the capability for administrators to block individual URLs in the firewall configuration. Entered manually, these rules are good for one-time blocking when a security alert or investigation identifies sites hosting viruses or other malware. This approach is also useful for demonstrating the general filtering abilities of the firewall and for testing other Web-blocking technologies. For instance, in an organization using a commercial blocking solution on a Web proxy, a simple URL-blocking rule on the organization's border firewall would provide some easy spot testing of the effectiveness of the commercial solution. Given the extreme size and constant growth of the Web, however, the manual approach does not scale well to protect against all the possible sources of objectionable material.

31.5.2 Third-Party Block Lists.   With the enormous size of the Web, the more typical approach is to use a third-party block list. Most of these are commercial products with proprietary databases, developed through a combination of automated "Web crawlers" and human technicians evaluating Web sites. Some companies have attempted to prevent researchers from trying to learn about blocking lists and strategies, but the U.S. Copyright Office granted a Digital Millennium Copyright Act (DMCA) exemption in 2003 for fair use by researchers studying these lists.[11] Web-filter companies continue to oppose such exemptions. Two open-source filtering alternatives also exist, with publicly viewable (and customizable) block lists that run on caching proxies: SquidGuard[12] and DansGuardian.[13]

31.6   ENFORCEMENT.   Filtering of Web traffic typically occurs either at a network choke point, such as a firewall or Web proxy, or on the individual client machine. Economies of scale lead organizations to filter on a network device, while products designed for parental control of children's Internet use usually reside on individual home computers.

31.6.1   Proxies.   A proxy server is a device that accepts a request from a client computer and then redirects that request to its ultimate destination. Proxies serve a variety of purposes for an organization, including reduction of traffic over expensive wide-area network links and Internet connections, increased performance through caching frequently accessed Web pages, and protection of internal users through hiding their actual IP addresses from the destination Web servers. Proxies also represent a natural locus of control for the organization, enabling authentication and tracking of Web requests that go through this single device. Most browsers support manual configuration of a proxy for all Web traffic as well as automatic discovery of proxies running on the organization's network. Organizations that use Web proxies typically allow outbound Web traffic only from the IP address of the proxy, thus forcing all HTTP traffic to use the proxy. Use of an encrypted Web session (HTTPS) is possible through a proxy, although either at the expense of the ability to monitor content (if the proxy merely passes the traffic through) or at the expense of the end-to-end privacy of the encrypted link (if the proxy decrypts and reencrypts the session).

Individuals also use proxies to maintain the privacy of their activities on the network, as described in Section 31.7.4. Thus, in addition to serving as a natural vehicle for content-filtering applications, proxies also represent a serious threat to those same applications.

31.6.2   Firewalls.   A firewall's job is to analyze information about the traffic passing through it and apply policy rules based on that information. Maintaining acceptable response time and throughput requires that the firewall do its job quickly and efficiently. In order to do so, most firewalls merely look at network-layer information, such as source and destination addresses and ports. More recently, firewall vendors have been adding more features to increase security and product appeal. Many companies now call their more advanced firewalls "service gateways" or "security gateways" as the notion of Unified Threat Management (UTM) becomes more popular. These UTM devices combine many features that formerly required individual devices, such as antivirus, intrusion detection, and filtering of both junk e-mail and Web content.

Sophisticated traffic examination increases the demand on firewall hardware. In order to reduce the performance hit caused by increased packet inspection, many firewalls allow the administrator to define particular rules or protocols for advanced checking. For instance, since viruses are most prevalent in email, Web, and peer-to-peer connections, the firewall administrator might need to configure only antivirus checking on rules applying to these protocols. Similarly, if the firewall needs only to monitor outbound HTTP requests from a single IP address, the Web proxy, then the extra processing load of the monitoring function can be constrained to that traffic profile.

The decision between filtering Web traffic at the proxy server (letting the firewall just pass the traffic from that address) and filtering Web traffic at the firewall (having the firewall do the URL inspection) depends on the amount of Web traffic and the budget (one device or two). The decision also affects the strength of the assertion that the organization is successfully filtering objectionable content. If the organization's border firewall performs the filtering, then this assertion depends on the firewall being the only way for traffic to leave the organization's network. Other traffic vectors, including wireless networking, protocol tunneling, and anonymizing proxies, may come into play. If the organization relies on client computers to use a Web proxy by policy, then the degree to which users can circumvent this policy should also be a consideration.

31.6.3 Parental Tools.   Although client-based Web filtering is not common in large organizations because of the expense and management of such services on a large scale, products enabling parents to block content for their children at home have become a big business. Many large ISPs, such as AOL and MSN, offer parental content-blocking tools as a free feature of their services. Other companies sell stand-alone products that install on a home computer, with password-protected parental administrative access to content-blocking functions. Net Nanny, Cybersitter, and Cyber Patrol are some of the more popular offerings. These products typically reside on individual computers rather than on a network device, although if a home computer is set up as a hub for network connectivity (such as with Microsoft's Internet Connection Sharing), then the controls can filter traffic in the same way as an organizational proxy server. Many of these products also filter other traffic, including e-mail, peer-to-peer file sharing, and instant messaging, as well as offering foreign language filtering, destination-address blocking, and time-of-day access rules.[14]

31.7 VULNERABILITIES.   No security scheme, whether physical or logical, is completely free of vulnerabilities, and Web filtering is certainly no exception to this rule. Users who want to access blocked content have a variety of tactics available to them, although solutions vary in ease of use. IP spoofing, protocol tunneling, and some forms of encryption are not trivial practices, and therefore are the tools of technically adept users in reasonably small number. Other technologies, however, such as anonymizing proxies, translation sites, and caching services, are easy ways for the average user to defeat filtering. Web-filtering vendors are constantly striving to make their products more effective, while privacy and free-speech advocates support ongoing efforts to defeat what they call censorware.

31.7.1   Spoofing.   In an organization that performs Web filtering on a proxy server, the organization's border firewall must allow outbound HTTP requests from the IP address of that proxy. A user who can configure traffic to look as though it is coming from the proxy's IP address might be able to get traffic through the firewall without actually going through the proxy. This tactic, known as address spoofing, takes advantage of lax routing policies on routers that forward all unknown traffic to default gateways without checking to see if that traffic came from a direction consistent with its reported source address. The drawback of spoofing, from the attacker's point of view, is that a large organization with significant amounts of Web traffic traversing the network will notice the temporary unavailability of the proxy caused by the spoofing.

An organization can defeat spoofing by configuring internal routers to check their routing tables, to see if the address of a packet coming into an interface is consistent with the networks available via that interface. The router drops packets with source addresses inconsistent with their actual source. This tactic, called *reverse-path filtering*, requires a more capable (and expensive) router, so it is generally not available for the home user trying to set up network-based protection for parental control.

31.7.2   Tunneling.   A more problematic tactic, because it relies on the behavior of applications rather than on subverting network-layer protections, is protocol or application tunneling. An application can encapsulate any other application's information as a packet of generic data and send it across the network. Virtual private network (VPN) clients use this approach to send traffic through an encrypted tunnel.

Protocol tunneling (sometimes called dynamic application tunneling)[15] relies on applications that send data on commonly allowed ports. For example, a user might tunnel a Web session through the secure shell (SSH) application, which uses TCP port 22. SSH often is allowed through firewalls, and because it uses both authentication and encryption, it can be hard to monitor the difference between a legitimate SSH session and a covert tunnel. In this example, the Web browser issues a request for an HTTP page on TCP port 80, and another application running on the client system captures and redirects the port 80 request into an SSH-encrypted tunnel. The other end of the SSH tunnel could be the destination server or a proxy server somewhere between the client and server. The client application (in this case, the Web browser) is unaware of the traffic diversion and needs no altered configuration. This is similar to the approach used by traditional VPNs.

Application tunneling (also called static application tunneling)[16] requires reconfiguration of the client application to redirect requests through a different port on the client machine. Typically, the user redefines the destination address for the application to a *localhost* address (in the 127.0.0.x range, referring to the local device), and an application then sets up a connection from that local port to the destination on an allowed network port. This approach requires alteration of the client application's configuration. Some Secure Sockets Layer (SSL) VPN products use this approach to tunnel one or more protocols, or all traffic, across an encrypted HTTP tunnel.

Tunneling via protocol or application generally requires access to either configure existing application settings or install extra software. Thus, tunneling is unavailable to users in organizations that give end users limited control over their computers. Tunneling is more of a problem for parents, whose technically adroit children can install tunneling applications to get around parental controls.

31.7.3 Encryption. Security professionals generally encourage the use of encryption, since it protects sensitive information in transit across a network. However, when users encrypt data to hide transactions that violate organizational policy, encryption can become a liability instead of an asset from the organization's perspective.

In an encrypted Web session using HTTPS (which is HTTP over SSL), the contents of the session are encrypted and thus unavailable for monitoring or filtering based on URL or data content. However, the source and destination IP addresses of the session, which are visible to TCP as the session is set up, remain visible on the network. This is necessary for routers to be able to get the encrypted data packets from one end of the transaction to the other. Thus, while an HTTPS session is immune to filtering by URL text matching or content-based filtering, blocking the destination server is still effective.

As mentioned in the previous section, VPN technologies represent another use of encryption to protect the content of a transaction. Again, although the VPN encrypts the contents of the transaction, the IP addresses of the endpoints must remain visible in order to transport the data to their destination.

Another more complicated version of encryption, called *steganography*, actually embeds data inside other information to avoid detection. For instance, a user could embed a text message within the information used to encode a picture. For more details on steganography and other types of encryption, see Chapter 7 in this *Handbook*.

31.7.4 Anonymity. Most Web monitoring and content filtering relies on the identity of the user. Content filtering can happen without identity information, but unless an organization or country chooses to impose draconian broad-based filtering of all Web requests (and some do choose this approach), the organization might like to enforce filtering requirements for only some users. For instance, a school district might wish to impose stricter filtering on elementary school students than on high school students and use a more permissive policy for teachers and administrative employees.

The bane of this approach is anonymity. When privacy concerns by individuals lead to the use of anonymizing technologies on a scale that makes identity of users difficult to determine, then the only way to comply with policies and laws requiring filtering of content for some groups is to filter for all groups at the level of the strictest requirement. In the case of a school district, if the network cannot distinguish between student traffic and teacher traffic, then the district must impose the requirements of student content-filtering on teachers as well. In fact, many school districts have made this choice, due to both the extreme numbers of hard-to-find anonymizing proxies and the technical difficulty of separating student and teacher use of a common school network infrastructure. Even so, external anonymizing proxies bedevil network administrators' attempts to force compliance with filtering regulations.

Other uses of privacy-enhancing technologies (PET) include network-based anonymity schemes, such as mixing networks and onion routing. The project known as TOR (originally an acronym for the onion router) has been gaining popularity in recent years. For more information about anonymity and identity, see Chapter 70 in this *Handbook*. For more about PET, see Chapter 42 in this *Handbook*.

31.7.5 Translation Sites. Language-translation sites, such as Babel Fish (http://babelfish.yahoo.com),[17] also offer the possibility of avoiding content filters. The user enters a URL and clicks a button to request a translation of the text of the site. The user's session is between the client computer and Yahoo!, with the requested URL merely passed as keystroke data within the HTTP session, so the potentially blocked site is made available so long as the user can get to Yahoo! This is a special case of a proxy, in that the request typed into Babel Fish generates a request to the server at the other end but the client does not receive the exact results of that reply; the display, instead, includes all the graphics of the original, but the text is translated into the requested language. So, from the point of view of a monitoring tool, the client is always connected with Yahoo!, and even a content filter looking at text within HTTP packets could be stymied by the foreign language. Recognizing the potential for abuse, Yahoo! published a Terms of Use document for the Babel Fish site prohibiting using the service for "items subject to US embargo, hate materials (e.g. Nazi memorabilia), . . . pornography, prostitution, . . . [or] gambling items,"[18] among many other classes of activities or products.

Translation sites are also annoying to system administrators because translation of a site in a particular language *into* that language usually results in unchanged content. For example, a translation of an English-language Web site from French into English simply passes the content through without alteration.

31.7.6   Caching Services.   One of the primary uses for proxy servers has been to reduce network traffic by saving local copies of frequently requested pages. This behavior can circumvent Web filtering, so long as the user can get to the caching server. Google, for example, caches many pages in an effort to provide very fast response to search requests. Large graphic and video files take up the most bandwidth, so Google's Image Search feature often caches them. Often graphic files are available even for sites that no longer exist. Users wanting to bypass blocks on sexually explicit content often use Google Image Search. Google does provide a feature called Safe Search, with three levels of voluntary filtering. The default (middle) setting filters "explicit images only," while the strict setting filters "both explicit text and explicit images."[19] Google notes, "no filter is 100% accurate, but Safe Search should eliminate most inappropriate material."[20] The Safe Search feature is configurable per user, and offers no password protection, so it is not a Web filtering technology so much as it is a voluntary sex-based search filter.

31.8   THE FUTURE.   As more ways of distributing content emerge, the content-filtering industry will doubtless evolve to cover the new technologies. At present, vendors sell filtering products for e-mail, Web chat, newsgroups, instant messaging, peer-to-peer file sharing, and FTP, as well as filtering of Web requests. New features will appear in "traditional" Web filtering as well. The latest versions of the home filtering products NetNanny and McAfee Parental Controls now offer the ability to force safe search options in the major search engines (like Google Safe Search, described in Section 31.7.6), and provide "object recognition," which recognizes certain versions of Web objects (like visit counters) that are commonly used in pornography sites.[21]

Supporters of content filtering, and those who are required to use it and need a reliable product, will be encouraged by the growth of the industry but perhaps disappointed that the problem never seems to be completely solved. Advances in image recognition could provide much better filtering, but may well spawn new ways to alter content to circumvent these tools. Those who decry these products as censorware will point out that, historically, most attempts to censor speech have failed in the end. Eventually, the two sides will probably work out an uneasy compromise, as has happened regarding sales of "adult" content in print and video. As long as some people insist on their right to distribute information that other people find offensive, this conflict is likely to continue.

31.9 SUMMARY. For a variety of reasons, some better than others, groups of people with power over, or responsibility for, other groups of people want to control the kind of information to which the other groups has access. Web content-filtering products (or censorware) provide this kind of control using computer technology to screen content across the Internet. Free speech and privacy advocates argue that content filtering prevents legitimate, legal access to information. Even should one grant the legitimacy of filtering in some cases, current technologies are prone to error, both failing to block some objectionable content and blocking some sites that contain no such content.

Most filtering techniques involve matching a text string against a database of undesirable content. A Web request filter looks at some portion of the URL, while a content filter looks at the text portion of a returned page. Lists of blocked servers can also be used to block traffic, either by address or by server name. Attempts continue to add top-level domain as a filtering criterion, by the addition of a .xxx domain. Other methods of blocking content examine nontextual parts of a Web page, including graphics. Research into image recognition and flesh-tone matching is progressing, and government agencies have used some image-recognition tools in prosecuting cases, but image recognition has not yet entered the commercial market.

With every protective, or overprotective, strategy comes a group of people dedicated to its defeat. Content filtering has a number of vulnerabilities, chief among which is the use of anonymity via privacy-enhancing technologies such as anonymizing proxies and onion routing. Other ways to defeat Web filtering include the use of protocol and application tunneling, encryption, Web translation sites, and caching services. Filtering technologies have been improving over the years, as has the inventiveness of those dedicated to thwarting them. As information outlets continue to proliferate and new communications media appear, this kind of conflict between protective technologies and privacy-enhancing circumvention is likely to continue.

31.10 FURTHER READING

Barracuda Networks. "CIPA Compliance and the Barracuda Web Filter," www.barracudanetworks.com/ns/downloads/Barracuda_WP_CIPA.pdf (retrieved April 7, 2007).

The Censorware Project, http://censorware.net/ (retrieved April 7, 2007).

Electronic Privacy Information Center. "EPIC Censorware Page," www.epic.org/free_speech/censorware/ (retrieved April 7, 2007).

Kongshem, Lars. "Censorware: How Well Does Internet Filtering Software Protect Students?" Online School, www.electronic-school.com/0198f1.html (retrieved April 7, 2007).

Secure Computing. "Best Practices for Monitoring and Filtering Internet Access in the Workplace," www.securecomputing.com/ webform.cfm? id=92& ref=pdtwp1295 (retrieved April 7, 2007; note: registration required).

"Seth Finkelstein's Anticensorware Investigations—Censorware Exposed," http://sethf.com/anticensorware/ (retrieved April 7, 2007).

31.11 NOTES

1. D. Chaum, "Untraceable Electronic Mail, Return Addresses, and Digital Pseudonyms," *Communications of the ACM* 24, No. 2 (February 1981); Available at: http://world.std.com/~franl/crypto/chaum-acm-1981.html.

2. D. M. Goldschlag, M. G. Reed, and P. F. Syverson, "Hiding Routing Information," Workshop on Information Hiding—*Proceedings*. May 1996, Cambridge, UK.

3. www.onion-router.net/.

4. Codified at 47 U.S.C. § 254(h) and 20 U.S.C. § 9134.

5. Poudre School District (Fort Collins, Colorado), Information Technology Services, www.psdschools.org/services/infotech/index.aspx (retrieved April 7, 2007).

6. "Google Milestones," www.google.com/intl/en/corporate/history.html (retrieved April 7, 2007).

7. Internet Corporation for Assigned Names and Numbers, "Board Rejects .XXX Domain Application," March 30, 2007; www.icann.org/ announcements/ announcement-30mar07.htm (retrieved April 4, 2007).

8. "Websense: Web Filtering Effectiveness Study," January 2006; www.lionbridge. com/NR/rdonlyres/websensecontentfilte7fmspvtsryjhojtsecqomzmiriqoefctif.pdf (retrieved April 7, 2007).

9. "Using eVe for Content Filtering," eVision Visual Search Technology, www.evisionglobal.com/ business/cf.html (retrieved April 4, 2007).

10. "NASA HQ Raided in Kiddie Porn Probe," *The Smoking Gun*, March 31, 2006; www.thesmokinggun.com/archive/0331061nasa1.html (retrieved April 4, 2007).

11. S. Finkelstein, "DMCA 1201 Exemption Transcript," April 11, 2003, http://sethf.com/anticensorware/hearing_dc.php (retrieved April 4, 2007).

12. "Another SquidGuard Website," www.squidguard.org/ (retrieved April 4, 2007).

13. "DansGuardian, True Web Content Filtering for All," http://dansguardian.org/ (retrieved April 4, 2007).

14. Top Ten Reviews, "Internet Filter Review 2007," http://internet-filter-review. toptenreviews.com/ (retrieved April 4, 2007).

15. SSH Communications Security, "Secure Application Connectivity," www.ssh. com/solutions/applications/secure-app-connectivity.html (retrieved April 7, 2007).

16. SSH Communications Security, "Secure Application Connectivity."

17. Named after the tiny Babel fish in Douglas Adams's science-fiction classic *Hitchhiker's Guide to the Galaxy* (New York: Del Rey, 1995). The Babel fish, when inserted in a person's ear, would instantly enable the person to understand any spoken language. The fish name is used for a translation technology developed by AltaVista, now owned by Yahoo!, and is offered as a free service at http:// babelfish.yahoo.com (retrieved April 7, 2007). It is also the name of a commercial translation firm that has registered the trademark, BabelFish.com, www.babelfish.com/ (retrieved April 7, 2007).

18. "Yahoo! Search Builder Terms of Use," http://help.yahoo.com/help/us/ysearch/ ysearch-01.html?fr=bf-home (retrieved April 7, 2007).

19. "Google Preferences," http://images.google.com/preferences?q=we+live+together &um=1&hl=en (retrieved April 7, 2007).

20. "Google Help Center," http://images.google.com/intl/en/help/customize.html#safe (retrieved April 7, 2007).

21. Internet Filter Review, "Internet Filter Terms," http://internet-filter-review. toptenreviews.com/short-definitions.html (retrieved April 7, 2007).

CHAPTER **32**

VIRTUAL PRIVATE NETWORKS AND SECURE REMOTE ACCESS

Justin Opatrny

32.1　INTRODUCTION.　The rise of the Internet created a new chapter in human civilization. People are no longer tied to static information sources such as libraries. The seemingly exponential growth of people looking to access wide varieties of content also spurred the desire for mobility. If a person can search for information residing halfway around the world from home, why not be able to do the same from the local coffee shop or while sitting at an airport during a business trip? This information revolution offered an opportunity to provide information and services to consumers, businesses, and employees at virtually any point on the globe.

32.1.1　Borders Dissolving.　Prolific Internet access redefined the dynamics of network and perimeter protections. Previously, companies needed to focus on protecting the internal network as well as systems exposed to the Internet. A perimeter firewall was sufficient to keep the digital predators at bay. The greater challenge then became how to maintain the security of the internal network when employees use mobile technologies from home or while traveling. Further complicating the issue is how to allow other business partners to access the systems and information that require protection.

Organizations large and small can no longer expect to maintain a competitive advantage by restricting employee network and information access to the confines of the workplace. The days of lost productivity due to these restrictions are long over. Traveling employees can now maintain direct communications with those at the office. Employees stranded at home due to inclement weather can continue to function, with access to necessary information. Organizations now have a viable way to maintain a geographically diverse workforce that allows people to work in closer proximity to customers and partners.

As an organization's network of vendors, suppliers, and partners grows, so does the necessity to share information. No matter the specific reason, the organization must look for methods that allow these outside entities the ability to access relevant information without exposing nonrelevant information. Information sharing is not the limit of partner involvement. Businesses may have situations where in-house staff does not have the necessary experience to develop or support certain information systems. Although having a consultant on staff or on call may be cost prohibitive, the company may opt to allow a vendor to access specific parts of the internal network remotely, to provide the necessary levels of service.

Customers continue to demand increasing levels of convenience. The banking industry is a useful example of how consumer demands increase and how business responds to meet these needs. Instead of having to go to a local bank, the ability to conduct certain inquiries and transactions were possible over the telephone. The limitations of this technology demanded an even greater opportunity, provided by account access and banking services through the Internet. Now the consumer has a visual, point-and-click interface instead of computerized voice and numeric menus. The same convenience requirements are present in the sale of goods and services. Consumers may not want to go to the local mall to make purchases, but by having an online presence, a company can meet this demand by providing an e-commerce Web site that gives the consumer the ability to view and purchase items at the consumer's time and place of choosing.

32.1.2   Secure Remote Access.   While the implications of not meeting consumer demands are obvious, organizations conduct a great deal of planning and review to ensure that meeting these demands does not jeopardize the underlying safety of the information systems that drive the business. The two primary technologies leading to secure remote access are the virtual private network (VPN) and the extranet.

A virtual private network is a secured connection allowing a client the ability to access the internal network through an encrypted tunnel. VPNs also have the ability to extend all or only selected portions of the network to other locations in the organization. Each has dramatic implications on information assurance requirements and goals.

An extranet meets some of the same goals as the VPN with the emphasis being information sharing and e-commerce. Instead of connecting to the internal network, the client establishes an encrypted connection to a web application server sitting on an external service network. Extranets can introduce additional complexity because the external-facing systems normally require access to one or more information assets within the internal network.

32.1.3   Virtual Private Networks.   The theory behind a VPN seems simple: Create an encrypted tunnel into the internal network to protect the transmitted data. In reality, the concepts underlying VPN technologies are complex and require a great deal of planning to ensure the best possible implementation. VPNs normally fall into two categories: secure client VPNs and trusted VPNs. Each VPN type has multiple avenues of implementation, with each having unique requirements.

Allowing people to access internal network resources remotely has major information assurance implications. The main information assurance goals of VPNs are securely extending the internal network, protecting data during transmission, and minimizing the security impact of the process.

The days of focusing on protection at the network perimeter are over and have been for longer than people may realize. Laptops led the initial mobile force charge. Although access to the full processing power of the laptop is useful in some instances, even the lightweight versions are bulky to travel with and have relatively limited battery life. Personal digital assistants (PDAs) and smart phones, fitting in the palm of a hand, now provide the power to access more commonly used applications. These devices may also have the ability to establish a VPN tunnel. No matter the type of mobile device, the organization must meet the requirements for remote access while accomplishing the least amount of additional risk.

When properly architected, managed, monitored, and secured, the internal network can provide a relatively safe environment to transmit data. However, the Internet is an openly hostile environment. The mobile device can no longer count on the internal network protections as a digital comfort zone. Internet access points, such as airports and hotels, can provide even greater challenges to information assurance. These public locations (many configured for open access) create sites for malicious individuals to intercept network traffic with the hopes of gathering information, such as financial information and intellectual property. VPNs and extranets have the ability to thwart this type of monitoring by sending data through encrypted channels.

As the need to increase stricter security measures continues, so does the potential to interfere with the end user experience. It does not take long for a user to figure out that disabling local security measures can have perceived advantages. Without the client firewall running, the connection speed may increase. Worse yet, by disabling another security protection measure, the user is now able to install and run software otherwise blocked from use. The goal must be to maintain a high level of security in a manner transparent to the user. The process of establishing a VPN tunnel or accessing internal resources should be fluid and perceptively uninhibited, while the background security infrastructure provides the necessary levels of protection.

32.1.4   VPN Technology Concepts.   Describing the multitude of conceptual intricacies of VPNs warrants many thousands of pages. This chapter provides only a foundation of information that will allow understanding of the different types, terminologies, and uses for VPNs.

32.2   SECURE CLIENT VPNs.   The most common use of a VPN is for secure, client-remote access. This allows an authorized remote user to connect to a VPN and gain access to internal resources while maintaining the security of the transmission. Secure client VPNs are waging an ongoing battle between traditional Internet Protocol Security (IPSec) and the increasingly popular and powerful Transport Level Security/Secure Sockets Layer (TLS/SSL) VPNs. Each type of VPN has certain distinct advantages, and each warrants thorough investigation prior to selecting the technology that best fits organizational needs.

32.2.1   IPSec.   IPSec is a suite of IP layer protocols, designed to set up and protect VPN transmissions. This traditional VPN implementation uses a client-resident application or embedded service to establish a VPN tunnel into the internal network.

32.2.1.1   Key Exchange and Management.   One of the most complex aspects of IPSec is key exchange and management. IPSec uses Internet Key Exchange (IKE) to facilitate the establishment and management of a Security Association (SA). The NIST "Guide to IPSEC VPNs" provides ample information regarding all aspects of IPSec VPNs; the next two paragraphs paraphrase the key points of IKE Phases 1 and 2 (NIST Special Publication 800-77).

Phase 1 can use main mode or aggressive mode to create the initial IKE Security Association. Main mode—consisting of three pairs of packets—is the most common implementation. The first pair negotiates the four-parameter protection suite: encryption algorithm (e.g., 3DES or AES), integrity protection algorithm (e.g., HMAC-SHA-1), authentication method (e.g., preshared key or PKI certificate), and Diffie-Hellman group. The second pair exchanges encryption keys using Diffie-Hellman. The third pair authenticates each side of the connection to the other. Aggressive mode accomplishes the same task by using only three packets. According to NIST Special Publication 800-77: "The first two messages negotiate the IKE SA parameters and perform a key exchange; the second and third messages authenticate the endpoints to each other."

Phase 2 uses quick mode to establish the IPSec SAs. Each side of the connection will maintain an IPSec SA in its Security Association Database (SAD). The initiating device creates and sends its SA proposal to the VPN device. The VPN device replies with its SA selection and another hash to authenticate the connection. The initiating device then replies with the hash it generates from the previous request. If the hash matches the challenge from the VPN device, the SA goes into the SAD and the connection proceeds.

32.2.1.2   Authentication Header versus Encapsulating Security Payload.   IPSec provides two security protocols for protecting encapsulated data. Authentication Header (AH) protects the integrity of the packet header and payload by using cryptographic hashing to ensure data do not change. Encapsulating Security Payload (ESP) is the more common implementation because it not only provides the integrity protection of AH but also protects the confidentiality by encrypting the entire original packet and creating a new IP header.

32.2.1.3   Transport versus Tunnel Mode.   AH and ESP can transmit data in either transport or tunnel mode. Transport mode preserves the original IP header information while providing payload integrity and confidentiality payload protection. Tunnel mode provides integrity and confidentiality protection for the IP header and payload. Since transport mode uses the original IP header information, this creates incompatibilities with Network Address Translation (NAT) because of TCP integrity checks. NAT causes the IP address of the packet to change during transit and, in turn, will cause the integrity check to fail. Thus, tunnel mode is the primary method for host-to-gateway and gateway-to-gateway VPN connections.

32.2.2   Transport Layer Security.   The Transport Layer Security (TLS) protocol provides a method for protecting client/server communications. One of the most identifiable implementations of TLS is Secure Sockets Layer (SSL), which provides the basis for the HTTPS protocol. Although this chapter uses "TLS" and "SSL" interchangeably, because many products support both, there are some differences. TLS is the next evolution of the Netscape-developed SSL because it is an open standards protocol supported by the Internet Engineering Task Force (IETF) (IETF —Transport Layer Security).

The implementation of TLS/SSL is much less complicated than IPSec. This method provides 128-bit encryption capabilities that already exist on virtually all Internet-connected systems. The host provides SSL-related parameters to negotiate a HTTPS connection with the server. The server then replies with the negotiated SSL-related parameters as well as its digital certificate. The client then uses the certificate to authenticate the server. If authentication is successful, the client and server establish the encryption keys used to protect the session and begin encrypted communications.

32.2.3   User Authentication Methods.   Before allowing unfettered access to internal resources, the client must authenticate to the VPN termination device. The simplest authentication method is the common user name and password combination. Some typical ways for validating user credentials are through RADIUS, LDAP, or Kerberos. To combat the ease of stealing or guessing user names and passwords, most vendors provide alternative or complementary authentication mechanisms. With an existing Public Key Infrastructure (PKI) this opens the possibility for using dual-factor authentication by requiring a user or machine PKI certificate. (See Chapter 37 of this *Handbook* for more information on PKI.) Another multifactor option is to use a cryptographic token such as an RSA SecurID or smartcard.

32.2.4   Infrastructure Requirements.   As described in Chapter 26, VPN networks are an opportunity to use the service network principle. Since the VPN connection device must be Internet facing, the service network principle would call for two different networks connected to the firewall. The external, Internet-facing interface would contain inbound and outbound encrypted traffic only. The second network is for unencrypted traffic moving to and from the internal network. By using this principle, the firewall policy would restrict the external, inbound connections to the VPN connection device using only the few required protocols. The firewall policy would restrict all external connections to the unencrypted network while allowing the appropriate level of access into the internal network. This unencrypted network would also provide a security inspection point.

32.2.5   Network Access Requirements.   IPSec and TLS/SSL Secure Client VPNs provide avenues for secure remote access, but each has unique challenges and opportunities.

32.2.5.1   IPSec.   IPSec VPNs typically provide full network-level access to the internal network upon successful connection and authentication. However, it is possible to restrict access to internal hosts and networks through a RADIUS, VPN connection device, and a firewall policy. One consideration that affects client traffic is split tunneling. With split tunneling enabled, only traffic destined for the internal network flows through the encrypted tunnel. As such, network traffic bound for the Internet takes the most direct route instead of traveling through the tunnel. This can help to reduce bandwidth by not having nonessential traffic flowing through the tunnel. However, the main disadvantage to this is losing the ability to inspect the Internet-bound network traffic.

32.2.5.2 TLS/SSL.   The original implementation of TLS/SSL VPN was far from its IPSec predecessor. These early connections focused on network pass-throughs to specific hosts and protocols as well as a crude, difficult-to-configure dashboard of simple links to internal files shares and Web sites. The dashboard concept for remote access is unique to the TLS/SSL VPN. The current dashboards are more robust and flexible, allowing the administrator to feed specific content and network access depending on a user's classification. The true breakthrough for TLS/SSL VPNs was its match of IPSec's ability to allow full network access, without the necessity for a client-resident VPN application.

32.3   TRUSTED VPNs.   VPNs are not purely for client remote access. Trusted VPNs provide the ability to facilitate internal communications needs. VPN technologies exist that can create meshed, virtual WAN networks, while providing alternatives to traditional WAN implementations.

32.3.1   Multiprotocol Layer Switching.   The increasingly popular multiprotocol layer switching (MPLS) is not a traditional encrypted VPN, but it does provide a similar type of service. This section will not cover most MPLS intricacies because deployment must meet organizational requirements, and because each service provider has different offerings. However, MPLS does have several distinct, advantageous characteristics.

32.3.1.1 Purpose.   A typical WAN environment exists in a star, a hub-and-spoke, a point-to-point topology, or some combination. Instead of hosting the head-end of the WAN network internally, MPLS creates a meshed, routed virtual network at the service provider level. The MPLS network is then free to route packets directly from one WAN endpoint to another within the confines of its virtual network. WAN sites are able to communicate directly, eliminating the hub as a single point of failure. MPLS networks may also provide multiple levels of quality of service (QoS). QoS provides the ability to prioritize network traffic, allowing certain protocols more bandwidth during high utilization periods.

32.3.1.2 Requirements.   As with all WAN routing technologies, the routing hardware and software must support the necessary routing and/or MPLS protocols. In addition, the service provider must already have the technology available. Moving to MPLS may require a significant rearchitecture of the existing routing infrastructure.

32.3.2   Site-to-Site VPNs.   Another common use of an IPSec VPN is for intersite communications through the Internet.

32.3.2.1 Purpose.   Although geographic diversity allows the organization closer proximity to customers and materials, traditional WAN implementations may not be available or practical. Site-to-site (S2S) VPNs provide an avenue for bridging this gap.

32.3.2.2 Alternative WAN.   WAN connections, as with most other technologies, are not cheap. It can be cost prohibitive to run a WAN connection (e.g., Frame Relay, T1, etc.) into a leased office space. In addition, even a lower-bandwidth leased line may be overpriced and underpowered to provide a direct WAN connection to a small branch office. A S2S VPN may provide the necessary level of connectivity without the high cost of a leased line. Since the S2S VPN will travel over an Internet connection, it may be possible to provide a higher bandwidth for the price.

32.3.2.3 *Backup.* An S2S VPN is also an alternative means for WAN backup. The traditional ISDN backup lines have two main disadvantages. ISDN service providers normally charge based on the number of connections and the duration of the call, as well as requiring separate hardware. In addition, ISDN bandwidth is normally limited to 128 Kbps. This may be insufficient if the site requires heavy access to systems and information across the WAN. S2S provides a means for higher bandwidth using existing hardware. The S2S connection provides additional redundancy by providing a standby, routable link. If architected properly, the site should notice little to no outage if the primary WAN link fails.

32.3.2.4 *Requirements.* S2S VPNs require an Internet connection as well as VPN and encryption enabled endpoints. A typical S2S deployment could be between two routers. Some other potential deployments include a router and a VPN-enabled gateway security device (GSD), or GSD to GSD.

32.3.3 Information Assurance Considerations. Although the ability for people and remote sites to connect to internal resources provides mobility and increased productivity, the organization cannot lose sight of the fact that this creates many information assurance caveats. Each implementation will have its own unique requirements, but addressing the main concerns presented in the next sections can make for a more informed decision.

32.3.3.1 *Client-Secure VPN Considerations.* Hosts connecting through client-secure VPNs are at greater risk due to the uncertainty of the network the end user system will be using to connect. All uncontrolled networks deserve to be treated as insecure, thus hostile, computing environments. This understanding will require the security administrators to focus on the necessary precautions to protect all of the company's systems.

32.3.3.2 *Fidelity of the Mobile Device.* Since there is no absolute control when mobile systems leave the confines of the internal network, the fidelity of the mobile device is of concern. The risk of compromise at every level—from physical, to operating system, to applications and beyond—can expose the internal network during a VPN session.

There are several ways to reduce the likelihood of a loss of fidelity. Protections may include any combination of host firewall, antivirus, antimalware, intrusion prevention, and current patch levels. Proper deployment and configuration of these protection measures will help to reduce the possibility of compromise.

Even if the fidelity of the device is acceptable during the initial connection, that does not mean this status cannot change at a later time during the connection. Another more complicated means for ensuring the health of the device is through network access control (NAC). NAC provides the ability to interrogate a connecting device before and during the connection, to determine such information as patch levels, status of security protections, and memory-resident malware. Unfortunately, the NAC option is not just a plug-and-play proposition. There are many other implications and requirements—such as inline versus passive and client-based versus client-less solutions—associated with effectively deploying NAC at any point in the network.

32.3.3.3 *VPN Client Management.* Client administration plays a crucial role in the success of a VPN solution.

IPSec requires the use of a client-side application or embedded operating system mechanism such as the Windows Network Connection Wizard. The primary implications of this include configuring and maintaining the client. The intricacies surrounding a hard-client installation include the necessity of local administrative permissions, potential user interaction, and dealing with a corrupt VPN client application. As with all other applications, there will come a time when the client will require updates due to new enhancements, unsupported versions, and vulnerabilities. In keeping with the goal of minimizing negative user experience, administrators need a way to update client software with little to no user interaction or side effects. One primary question is to determine if the VPN vendor has a mechanism to push configuration and other client software updates upon connection. Without this functionality, it becomes more difficult to change client-side parameters. For example, a VPN using a preshared key for VPN authentication gets hard-coded into the VPN software. This makes changing it difficult without having the end user enter a new key.

TLS/SSL VPN clients do not suffer from the same pitfalls as IPSec regarding client management. Instead of a hard client, the TLS/SSL VPN normally uses a small Java or ActiveX-based dynamic client. In certain VPN systems, the administrator may have the choice to leave the dynamic client resident or remove it upon disconnection. If the client becomes corrupted, the user can delete the control, and it will automatically download upon the next successful connection. Having the dynamic client remain resident has two advantages. First, it may provide the ability to have a local, encrypted workspace to store working documents and other files or to provide access to other resources. Second, it keeps the remote system from having to download the client with each connection. The TLS/SSL client also has an advantage by always checking to see if a resident client is current. If not, the VPN system will force a download of the newest client, helping to minimize client-side management.

32.3.3.4 *Protection of the VPN Device.* The heart of being able to provide VPN services revolves around the existing network security infrastructure. This has direct implications regarding perimeter protection, since the VPN connection devices must be Internet and internal facing. These devices must also follow the service network principle discussed in Chapter 26 of this *Handbook*. The device itself is another part of the overall network security profile.

It is important to remove all ancillary exposures. The primary protection method is to configure the firewall to allow access only to the necessary ports on the VPN device. All unnecessary protocols, services, and configuration options should be shut down. If DES and MD5 are unacceptable cryptographic protocols in the environment, these and all other weaker alternatives must be removed from the negotiable IKE options. If a network management tool uses ICMP and/or SNMP to monitor the VPN device, firewall rules or onboard access control lists (ACLs) should only allow access to these protocols from a specific set of monitoring hosts. Although network reconnaissance and attacks are still possible on these ports, this method drastically reduces the attack profile.

Administrative device access should never use insecure protocols such as Telnet, FTP, or HTTP. Instead, administration should occur using encrypted protocols, such as Secure Shell (SSH) and Hypertext Transfer Protocol Secure (HTTPS). Administrative access should at a minimum be protected with a strong user name and passwords or, better yet, require certificate-based protection. To minimize administrative access, only a specific network or host(s) should be able to access the administrative console directly. To reduce administrative exposures further, it may be possible to use a proxy device for all administrative access. This does carry the potential for a single point of administrative failure if the physical device is not available.

32.3.3.5 Traffic Inspection.
Inspection of network traffic plays a crucial role in keeping the internal network secure. Since the goal of the VPN is to provide secure data transport, this can be a hindrance when attempting to evaluate inbound, encrypted traffic. Network traffic inspection can occur on the VPN connection device or on the unencrypted side leading to the internal network. While the network traffic is one step closer to the internal network, this provides a valid inspection point in which to detect and protect against malicious traffic. Certain VPN devices and GSDs may provide the ability to view data inside the tunnel, evaluate network traffic (providing a troubleshooting point), and inspect data before passing onto the unencrypted network. However, doing all of the inspection on the VPN device can have significant performance implications.

32.3.3.6 Processing Power.
Encryption and decryption of VPN tunnels requires sufficient processing power. This issue escalates as the number of clients increases. For situations where there are only a few remote-access clients, it may be possible to use a GSD to terminate VPN connections and provide security services. The higher the number of remote-access clients, the greater the need for dedicated VPN devices. To ease the processing demands on these units, it is possible to install hardware encryption accelerators. Larger organizations may have thousands of concurrent users that could require multiple VPN devices.

32.3.3.7 Trusted VPN Considerations

32.3.3.7.1 Infrastructure Design.   MPLS can be a wholesale change in how the WAN functions; it also has troubleshooting and security implications.

Since an MPLS network can provide any-to-any functionality, it becomes more difficult to troubleshoot network issues. In a hub-and-spoke configuration, it is possible to deploy probes to monitor and troubleshoot WAN issues. It is unlikely that organizations with many locations would invest the time and money to deploy these types of monitors in all locations. The service provider may be able to provide additional services that assist with this type of troubleshooting.

MPLS networks also add to the overall network security burden by requiring an increase in the number of network security devices. This is largely because the sites can establish direct communications instead of going to the hub first. MPLS places the security of the WAN infrastructure in the service provider's hands. This is a reminder to ensure the MPLS provider has a robust network and strict processes for keeping MPLS networks separate. One added protection against provider-side errors would be to deploy the Border Gateway Protocol (BGP) routing security, where both sides of the connection would authenticate before becoming part of the routing table.

S2S VPNs carry additional risk by placing the Internet directly against the internal network at remote sites. If the Internet connects directly to the site's router, there are several protection options. It is possible to create an access control list (ACL) to restrict communication to this interface only to the other side of the S2S VPN connection. Another option is to enable security features on the router. However, this may require a code upgrade and may increase processing demands on the router. A more secure but expensive option is to deploy a GSD that provides security and VPN services. This puts another level of protection between the Internet and the internal network.

32.3.3.7.2   Cost.   MPLS adds cost on many fronts. These include the cost of new or converted circuits and other services, such as quality of service (QoS), or monitoring capabilities. In addition, the equipment running the network must be able to support the new MPLS and routing architecture. There also may be a significant time investment required to redesign the network routing infrastructure.

S2S VPNs using routing devices require ample processing power (e.g., RAM and encryption modules) and a software revision that supports encryption. In certain cases, it may cost more to get to a level of code supporting encryption. S2S VPN deployments using GSDs will go up in price as the number of security services increase and based on the number of clients that will connect. If deploying GSDs to remote sites, there is not only a monetary cost, but also higher administrative costs for managing this new piece of the routing and security infrastructure.

32.3.3.7.3   Availability.   VPNs are less of a convenience and more of a necessity. There can be disastrous implications for highly mobile workforces when VPN access is unavailable. Even with layers, points of failure do not disappear. If the organization deems VPN as a necessity, high-availability solutions are a requirement. One such solution is to load-balance inbound connections to distribute them across multiple devices. If one device fails, the other devices will continue to service previously connected clients and will provide a place for new clients to connect. Another option is active/standby failover. This may be as simple as if one device fails, the other will be available for new connections. A preferable method would be for the active member to replicate connection information to the standby member. This way, if the active member fails, the standby member can continue servicing the existing VPN tunnels and can provide new connections. This whole strategy also hinges on the main VPN connection points having redundant Internet links, power, and network infrastructure.

32.3.3.7.4   Implications of Illusive VPNs.   Unfortunately, VPNs occur in more places than most people realize. These illusive VPNs range from legitimate VPN services, such as GotoMyPC, to malicious VPNs, such as botnet command-and-control channels or reverse tunnels. Although VPN sites such as GoToMyPC can be useful, it is up to the organization to decide if this is an acceptable means of remote access. Some of the key issues to consider with this type of VPN service are that it bypasses internal security controls such as packet and content inspection, and the third party is creating and managing the VPN connection.

Malicious VPNs are a source of continuing concern. Botnet command-and-control channels can use encryption to evade network defenses and protect information. A reverse tunnel works by redirecting network traffic destined for a listening port to the same port on another host. For example, if a compromised FTP server had an active reverse tunnel, any user attempting to connect to that FTP server would redirect to another FTP server. Beyond the compromised host theory, malicious people already on the internal network may establish an outgoing VPN connection or a legitimate VPN in an effort to hide insidious behavior or network traffic.

The most elusive of all are applications that provide embedded VPN-like services. Peer-to-peer (P2P) networks tunnel file sharing through proprietary and encrypted protocols. Skype not only has the ability to create encrypted voice calls, but also has

VPN-like capabilities that allow encrypted file transfers. Network defenses should be able to detect the setup of these sessions and stop them before the connection is completed.

It is up to the organization to develop the internal network security defenses and policies to protect against all elusive VPNs.

32.3.3.7.5 Impact of IPv6.   Mass migration to IPv6 is still not occurring at the time of writing (2008) even though IPv6 was developed in the late 1990s. The Department of Defense (DoD) is requiring all of its networks to be IPv6 compliant by the end of 2008. Discussion of whether to use IPv6 is beyond the scope of this chapter. However, IPv6 does have some specific implications for VPNs. First, all devices must be able to support the IPv6 protocol. Second, if the entire infrastructure is not IPv6 end to end, devices will need to be able to translate IPv6 traffic into IPv4 and vice versa. Last, IPv6 provides native support for IPSec. The network stack will be able to provide per-packet encryption, potentially eliminating the need for hard clients.

32.4   EXTRANETS.   As the necessity for convenient access to data continues to increase, so do the challenges associated with providing the protections required to secure this type of access.

32.4.1   Information Assurance Goals.   Allowing external entities to access internal data remotely has major information assurance implications. The main information assurance goals of extranets are protecting shared information assets, preventing information exposure, and minimizing ancillary risks.

32.4.1.1 Protecting Shared Information Assets.   Much of the current information security market focuses on protecting hosts and networks from digital threats. Although the loss of a server or portion of the network undoubtedly causes issues, there may be areas of greater concern. Organizations develop and sustain competitive advantage by manipulating data collected or created into valuable and actionable information. By mitigating the risks associated with external access, there is less chance for a breach of information security to occur.

32.4.1.2 Preventing Information Exposure.   The concept of least privilege should be paramount in designing access to systems. One would not expect a financial analyst to have access to proprietary product specifications. The same holds true when apportioning access to external entities. Identity management provides an accountability mechanism for providing rights and monitoring actions of issued accounts. Access management provides the enforcement mechanism that keeps those accounts from viewing or changing data not explicitly necessary. The fusion of these two principles reduces the risk of inappropriate or unexpected access.

32.4.1.3 Minimize Ancillary Risks.   It does not take long for Internet-facing systems to come under attack. Minimizing attack vectors occurs from the network layer to the application layer. The extranet servers are not all-purpose systems. The network protection policies should restrict access to these services, so that the Internet community only has access to the specific service(s) advertised. Extranet services require greater consideration, as network protection devices are rarely suitable for the protocols and customizations routinely occurring at the application layer.

32.4.2   Extranet Concepts

32.4.2.1   *Service Network versus DMZ.* The DMZ architecture places systems on a network between the external router and the external interface of the perimeter firewall. The external router provides packet filtering to reduce access to the DMZ network and hosts, but lacks additional security capabilities. In essence, these systems are accessible from the Internet while not quite trusted to access the internal network. This is hardly a place to put servers requiring robust security at multiple layers.

As described in Chapter 26 in this *Handbook*, extranet networks are another opportunity to use the service network principle. This is largely because extranets make extensive use of resources on the internal network. Instead of residing in the DMZ, the servers move to a separate firewall interface. This segmentation allows administrators to be more granular on the services allowed into the network, as well as providing another place to put additional security mechanisms.

32.4.2.2   N-*Tier Architecture.* If an extranet system provides all aspects of a service, there exists a single point of failure and compromise. *N*-tier architecture provides the ability to distribute different aspects of the service offering to additional systems. The extranet system will provide the front-end user interface, the application server facilitates the logic and processing necessary to access data, and the back-end database server stores and provides the data. Since the extranet server resides on a service network, the firewall policy must allow that server to connect to its next-tier servers on the internal network. When possible, access from the extranet server should be restricted to the internal network or to only necessary systems and services. This architecture helps to create a more robust infrastructure that reduces unnecessary exposures.

32.4.2.3   *SSL Encryption.* The most visible marker of SSL encryption is the little golden padlock that appears in an Internet browser when connecting to a server using HTTPS. When a host attempts to connect to an extranet server, several steps occur before the encrypted session can begin. The connecting host provides SSL-related parameters to negotiate an HTTPS connection with the server. The server then replies with the negotiated SSL-related parameters and a digital certificate. The client then uses the certificate to authenticate the server. If authentication is successful, client and server establish the encryption keys used to protect the session and begin encrypted communications.

32.4.3   Types of Extranet Access. The type of systems and services able to go onto the extranet continues to grow. Providing extranet services is always subject to the needs of the organization. The next sections provide some common examples of extranet systems.

32.4.3.1   *Vendor/Partner Information Sharing.* Business is no longer just about the deal and a handshake. Businesses survive and thrive on competitive advantage, and increasingly need to share information with strategic partners. By providing access to internal information, these partners can better understand and meet the organizational needs. Enterprise resource planning (ERP) systems contain the data that serves as the digital lifeblood of an organization. On the extranet, vendors and business partners could have access to work with information stored in the ERP system.

32.4.3.2 E-Commerce. Conducting business transactions digitally can create efficiencies and reduce costs. E-commerce occurs at the business and consumer level. Businesses can use Electronic Data Interchange (EDI), which allows two entities to exchange standardized, digital versions of documents, such as a purchase order and payments, without human interaction. The extranet provides a means to allow business partners to exchange EDI data without granting access to the internal servers that actually process and store data. Consumers access e-commerce Web sites to view and purchase goods and services.

32.4.3.3 Employee Self-Service. Providing extranet services is not restricted to business partners and consumers. It is possible to enhance employees' access to specific internal services and systems by allowing access without requiring a full VPN connection. E-mail is the universal business tool, and providing webmail services can allow employees to access e-mail from almost anywhere in the world. Employees may find it helpful to be able to access and change benefits information from home. This may also be an opportunity to allow access to Intranet information.

32.4.4   Information Assurance Considerations

32.4.4.1 Technical Security. Securing an extranet is not possible at a single layer or point in the network. Each layer is interdependent and requires specific protections to ensure the security of the extranet network.

32.4.4.2 Infrastructure. Since the extranet sits behind a firewall, network layer security measures are normally the protections encountered first.

32.4.4.3 Traffic Inspection. As reiterated in multiple parts of this and other chapters, security devices have a distinct inability to evaluate encrypted network traffic. Extranets can create additional issues as the encrypted session travels from the client directly to the extranet server. This potentially requires traffic inspection to occur on the extranet server. While possible, this method will increase the processing requirements of the server.

Another option is to terminate the SSL connections on an upstream device. This device would then use unencrypted protocols on the downstream side when communicating with the actual extranet server. This method adds an additional layer of complexity when troubleshooting, but it can relieve the extranet server of the encryption and security inspection processing burdens.

32.4.4.4 Internal Network Exposure. Although the compromise of an extranet server is significant, it should not be a pass to unfettered access to internal resources. The firewall policy allows access to specific extranet services from the Internet; it must also granularly restrict access from the extranet server to internal systems.

32.4.4.5 Server. Server-level protections are the true first line of defense. It is difficult for network layer security mechanisms to protect a server that is advertising a vulnerable service. System hardening is an approach to reducing the overall risk profile of the server. Nonessential protocols and services are shut down. The operating system (OS) may have additional parameters, such as file and account permissions, that further reduce the risk profile. A script can help to ensure these changes occur in a consistent manner. One well-known system-hardening script is Bastille Linux.

Due to the complexities of operating systems and applications, vulnerabilities will occur. The simplest method of remediating vulnerabilities is to update the server with a patch. It is important to test patches for adverse effects before deployment to the production environment. This practice will help to reduce the potential for unexpected results and downtime. Vendors can take weeks and months to develop and release a patch. In certain cases, third-party patches will become available for unpatched, actively exploited vulnerabilities. The ability to use these patches is an option, but it is inadvisable due to the inability to verify the integrity and safety of third-party patch code.

Even though the goal is to minimize the risk profile of the server through all of the aforementioned means, it may also be necessary to provide additional server-level protections. This may include firewall and intrusion detection and prevention software. These protections have the advantage of being contextually aware of operating systems and application functions, unlike those residing at the network layer.

Virtualization is developing rapidly and becoming a viable option for use on the extranet. Virtualization does hold promise for allowing multiple extranet systems to run on a single server, but there are many other security implications. This is another case of a single point of failure if the physical server goes down. There are ongoing concerns of escaping virtual sessions and allowing unauthorized access to another virtual session.

32.4.4.6   *Application.* Some common application layer vulnerabilities include buffer overflows, Structured Query Language (SQL) injection, and cross-site scripting (XSS). Buffer overflows existed decades ago but continue to be a favorite of malicious code developers. This condition exists because the application does not do proper bounds checking on input fields or uses functions that fail to do the same. SQL injection is a malicious attempt to insert a SQL query into server-side requests. By failing to check for and protect against this type of attack, the back-end server may return the information the malicious query requests. XSS is a type of code injection commonly used for phishing. A malicious person may send an unsuspecting person a link that redirects some or all content elsewhere.

Vulnerabilities at the application layer can easily defeat even the most secure network layer configurations. Applications developed by multibillion-dollar organizations can be just as vulnerable as something developed internally in a small facility. Developers must understand and follow secure coding practices to help minimize the number and severity of application vulnerabilities. See Chapters 38, 39, and 52 in this *Handbook* for discussions of programming and application security, and Chapters 25 and 33 for Web-based and wireless network security.

32.4.4.7   *Policies.* Since extranets provide external entities access to internal information and systems, it would be useful to have a policy that governs the use of these systems. The policy may include information about requirements, such as needing a confidentiality agreement before allowing a business partner access to the extranet or mandating the use of TLS/SSL encryption for all extranet communications. Policies do not provide an active protection mechanism but do establish expectations when using extranet systems.

32.4.4.8   *Access and Identity Management.* Access management is crucial to ensuring that only necessary and relevant information gets to the requesting user. The permissions given to this user will dictate the data the user is able to access and should follow the concept of least privilege. Identity management facilitates must ensure that only properly credentialed entities can gain access to the extranet and underlying systems. Typically, an external user will authenticate using a user name and password. Unfortunately, this is a poor way to validate an entity's identity because of the ease of stealing or guessing passwords. A more reliable method for identifying an external entity would be to issue the user a digital certificate. The certificate would then become a part of the connection and authentication process. Although it is not impossible, it is vastly more difficult to spoof or steal a digital certificate. Chapter 28 in this *Handbook* contains detailed information about identification and authentication.

32.4.4.9   Availability.   Extranet systems are an important part of business operations. When extranet access is unavailable, certain transactions do not occur that can cause issues at points throughout the organization. Extranet availability is a function of the network and server infrastructures.

A single Internet connection has an implied single point of failure if that connection goes down. If the network infrastructure leading to the extranet only has a single path to follow, this becomes another single point of failure. By adding redundancy to the network infrastructure, such as a second Internet connection and secondary routing paths, there is less likelihood of downtime.

Server infrastructures have the same potential to be a single point of failure. Instead, using a single server to provide an extranet service, it is possible to deploy a cluster of servers and load balancing. The cluster will protect the availability of the service if one or more servers goes down. In addition, this provides the ability to perform server maintenance with little to no effect on availability. Load balancing helps to optimize the number of connections going to each cluster member.

32.4.4.10   Impact of IPv6.   The largest impact of IPv6 on the extranet is infrastructure and application support. First, the routing infrastructure must be able to communicate using IPv6 natively or though a translation mechanism. Second, operating systems and applications must be able to accept, process, and reply to the IPv6 packets. Last, the security infrastructure must be able to evaluate IPv6 packets. A breakdown in any one of these will render the extranet vulnerable or inaccessible.

32.5   CONCLUSION.   Virtual private networks and extranets have many powerful features that can enhance an organization's ability to conduct and improve employee mobility and business functionality. Support and input must come from all levels of the organization to ensure that the secure remote access systems meet the organization's specific needs and expectations. Most important, these systems must adhere to and enhance, not diminish, the overall security profile.

32.6   FURTHER READING

Carmouche, J. H. *IPsec Virtual Private Network Fundamentals*. Old Tappan, NJ: Cisco Press, 2006.

Edwards, J., R. Bramante, and A. Martin. *Nortel Guide to VPN Routing for Security and VoIP*. Hoboken, NJ: John Wiley & Sons, 2006.

Frankel, S., K. Kent, R. Lewkowski, A. D. Orebaugh, R. W. Ritchey, S. R. Sharma. "Guide to IPSEC VPNs," *NIST Special Publication 800-77*, December 2005. Available: http://csrc.nist.gov/publications/nistpubs/800-77/sp800-77.pdf.

Tan, N.-K. *Building VPNs: with IPSec and MPLS*. Hightstown, NJ: McGraw-Hill, 2003.

Tibbs, R., and E. Oakes. *Firewalls and VPNs: Principles and Practices*. Upper Saddle River, NJ: Prentice-Hall, 2005.

CHAPTER **33**

802.11 WIRELESS LAN SECURITY

Gary L. Tagg

33.1 INTRODUCTION.   Corporations and home users have mass adopted IEEE 802.11 as the protocol for wireless local area networks. These networks have benefits over traditional wired networks, such as mobility, flexibility, rapid deployment, and cost reduction. However, as with any networking technology, it creates new opportunities for unauthorized individuals to access the networks and the information carried over them.

The purpose of this chapter is to introduce wireless LAN technologies, the issues, and ways to address them. Reasons driving the adoption of wireless LANs derive from:

- The 802.11 architecture and product types
- The threats to information presented by wireless LAN technology, and how they compare to other networking threats, such as the Internet
- The security functionality provided by the original 802.11 standard, the security weaknesses, and how to mitigate them
- The security functionality provided by the 802.11i security standard, which was developed to address issues with the original standards

The chapter also provides an overview of the open source and commercial tools that hackers use to break into wireless networks: tools that are useful for people wanting to do their own security auditing.

33.1.1   Scope.   The scope of this chapter is the security of ANSI/IEEE standard 802.11 wireless LANs. This chapter does not consider any other wireless systems, such as mobile telephone networks, or other wireless standards, such as HomeRF, Bluetooth, WiMax, or HiperLAN.

33.1.2   Background and Uses of Wireless LANs.   Business has been using wireless LANs for well over 10 years. However, to begin with, the market was fairly small and the technologies proprietary. In the late 1990s and early 2000s, the groundwork was laid for the mass adoption of wireless LANs (WLANs). The starting point was the publication of ANSI/IEEE standard 802.11, which provided a baseline design enabling manufacturers to develop interoperable products at lower costs. The publication of the 802.11b standard in 1999 increased WLAN bandwidth similar to that of traditional Ethernet LANs, making it a possible technical replacement. Following that were the 802.11a and 802.11g standards, increasing bandwidth to 54Mb/s. Work is currently under way on 802.11n, which will provide a throughput of up to 600Mb/s.

33.1.2.1   Business Uses of Wireless LANs.   The main requirements for implementing wireless networks are mobility and cost reduction. Objectives include to:

- Enable staff to access network information via mobile terminals as they move around the office campus. Two examples are warehouse and hospital staff.
- Enable staff to access the network from meeting rooms for both client-facing and internal meetings.
- Enable external consultants and staff from other offices to connect to the network when on site.
- Enable staff to get away from their desks (e.g., to another office, to a rest area, or to an internal café) and still be able to access the network.
- Enable managers to take a laptop to the desk of a staff member and show what is on the screen.
- Reduce mobile telecommunications costs by implementing Voice over wireless LANS (VoWLANs).

Public wireless networks (known as hot spots) are now available in city centers, hotels, airports, railway stations, pubs, service stations, restaurants, and coffee shops. These hot spots provide a high-speed connection to the Internet, allowing staff to utilize this normally wasted time between meetings or when waiting for airplanes or public transport. Typical uses include access to and other resources on the corporate LAN, along with general research by surfing the Internet.

Matthew Gast says that a major advantage of wireless LANS is flexibility and rapid deployment.[1] A network that runs out of physical LAN connections in a particular area can be a major issue. Running cables is expensive, time consuming, and may require conduits to be fitted within walls, as well as other construction tasks. This can be a big problem for older buildings that have not been designed for today's environment.

Historical buildings often have restrictions on building alterations. It may not be possible to gain authorization for the construction necessary to lay a cable infrastructure. Wireless LANs can overcome this entire issue of having to lay cables. Once the wireless network is built, additional users are easy to add; just plug in a card, install the software, and configure it.

Costs can also be saved by not having to install physical network links between buildings separated by a road, river, railway tracks, or even a city block. With an uninterrupted line of sight between the two buildings, a wireless network link can be set up.

33.1.2.2   *Home Use of Wireless LANs.* In recent years, the use of wireless LAN networks has exploded in the home market. The reasons for this are:

- Households increasingly have access to more than one computer because of work laptops being taken home, and the falling price of computers enables families to upgrade.
- The availability of broadband Internet has encouraged people to network their home computers so that all of them can access the Internet.
- Households often have to locate their computers away from the telephone point, for example, in a bedroom or dining room. This means that a cable has to be run across the floor to access the Internet. Broadband modems with built-in wireless LANs are available, removing the need for the cable.
- WLAN equipment is now affordable. A typical PCMCIA or USB wireless LAN card can now be purchased at a fraction of the original cost. The major advantage of wireless LANs is the ease of installation, because no cables have to be run to the remote computers.

33.2   802.11 ARCHITECTURE AND PRODUCT TYPES.   This section provides a brief overview of 802.11 wireless LAN technologies defined in the 802.11 standard, along with available product types and their architectures. A more detailed overview is available in RFC4118[2] with further information available in additional references.[3]

33.2.1   802.11 Components.   The core components of the architecture as defined in the 802.11 standard are:

- **Stations (Sta).** Any device that contains an 802.11 medium access control (MAC) and physical layer (PHY) interface to the wireless medium (i.e., a PC with a wireless LAN card and software).
- **Access points (AP).** A station that bridges other stations to the distribution system (DS).
- **Basic service sets (BSS).** One or more stations communicating with a single access point. These types of networks are also called infrastructure networks. (See Exhibit 33.1.)
- **Independent basic service set (IBSS).** An ad hoc network where stations communicate directly with one another without an access point. (See Exhibit 33.2.)

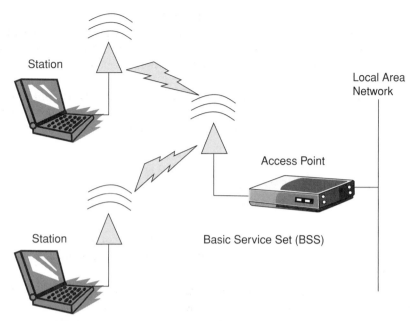

EXHIBIT 33.1   Basic Service Set Network

- **Extended service set (ESS).** A set of one or more interconnected basic service sets (BSSs) and integrated local area networks (LANS) that appears as a single BSS to stations. (See Exhibit 33.3.)
- **Distribution system (DS) and portal.** The distribution system interconnects access points to create an extended service set. The portal is a logical component that integrates the 802.11 architecture with the wired LAN. (See Exhibit 33.3.)

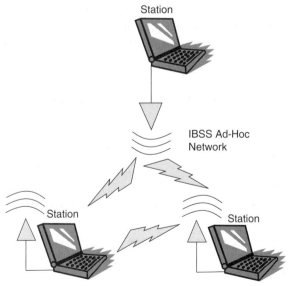

EXHIBIT 33.2   Independent Basic Service Set (Ad Hoc) Network

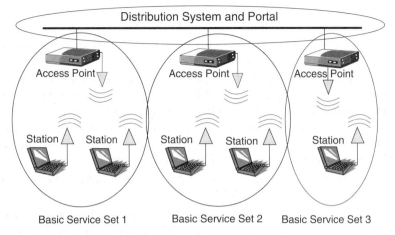

EXHIBIT 33.3 802.11 Architecture—Extended Service Set

33.2.2 802.11 Network Architecture.   In relation to the OSI 7 layer network reference model,[4] 802.11 provide services at the physical layer and the data link layer. Within these two layers, 802.11 is itself structured into three layers:

1. A physical layer (the radio interfaces for transmission and reception)
2. The medium access control (MAC) sublayer, which is a set of services to enable data to be exchanged between devices
3. An 802.2 logical link control (LLC) sublayer

The use of the 802.2 LLC allows the rest of the world to see 802.11 devices as Ethernet devices and use the same Ethernet MAC address range as their hardwired cousins. This architecture is shown in Exhibit 33.4.

33.2.3 802.11 Physical Layer.   The 802.11 standards currently define six different physical interfaces with a seventh in development:

1. **802.11 Infrared.** This is a 2 Mb/s infrared system, but due to line-of-sight limitations, very little development has occurred with this interface.[5]

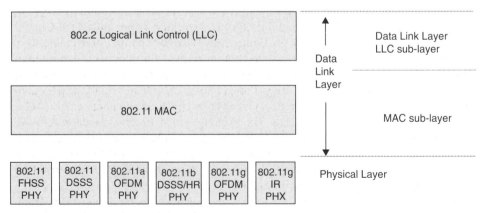

EXHIBIT 33.4 802.11 Network Architecture

2. **802.11 FHSS.** This is a 2 Mb/s radio link using the frequency-hopping spread spectrum (FHSS) algorithm in the 2.4 GHz band. FHSS works by defining 79 1 MHz-wide channels and sending bursts of data over a number of channels, with the system hopping between channels in a defined way.

3. **802.11 DSSS.** This is a 2 Mb/s radio link using the direct sequence spread spectrum (DSSS) technique in the 2.4 GHz band. The standard defines fourteen 5 Mhz-wide DSSS channels. DSSS works by spreading data over a 22 MHz-wide channel. This technique allows for greater transmission rates than FHSS but means that access points need to be five channels apart to avoid interference, reducing the number of effective channels from 14 to 3.[6]

4. **802.11b DSSS.** This is a higher-rate DSSS radio link in the 2.4 GHz band with a maximum throughput of 11 Mb/s.

5. **802.11a OFDM.** 802.11a uses the 5 GHz frequency band and an encoding technique called orthogonal frequency division multiplexing (OFDM) to increase throughput to 54 Mb/s.

6. **802.11g.** This standard implements the OFDM encoding in the 2.4 GHz band to increase throughput to 54 Mb/s and is the standard product available in 2008.

7. **802.11n.** This is a standard under development to increase the throughput up to 600 Mb/s. A number of "pre-n" products are available on the market.

33.2.4   Wireless LAN Product Types.   There are three main types of wireless LAN products available today. The first is where the access point contains all the functionality, including security. These are generally known as fat access points and are used by home and small office and home office (SOHO) users who have a need for a small number of highly functional access points (AP). These "fat" access points were the architecture designed for the original 802.11 standard.

The 802.11 standard is designed primarily for fat access point architecture where all the functionality is in the AP. However, with an extensive WLAN deployment, setting up and managing these access points becomes a major issue. To address this issue, vendors created an alternative architecture based upon light-weight access points (LWAP) and wireless switches. An LWAP is primarily an 802.11 radio that sends all received packets to the wireless switch, which has most of the functionality of traditional fat APs as well as the task of managing the LWAPs. The actual split of functionality between the LWAP and the wireless switch varies depending on the product.

Each wireless switch vendor developed its own proprietary technologies, so the Internet Engineering Task Force (IETF) set up a working group called the Control and Provisioning of Wireless Access Points (CAPWAP).[7] The first deliverable from the group was a problem definition statement, or request for comment, published as RFC3390.[8] It then published an architecture taxonomy as RFC4118[9] that defined the architectures and standard terminology. For example, LWAPs are called "wireless termination points" (WTPs) and wireless switches are called "access controllers" (ACs).

They then extended the scope of the working group to develop the CAPWAP protocol so that different vendors' WTPs and ACs could be interoperable.[10] This protocol is based on the LWAPP with the communications secured by the Datagram Transport Layer Security Protocol (DTLS).[11] DTLS is essentially TLS optimized for user datagram-based protocols such as UDP.

The third classes of WLAN products are known as wireless mesh networks. Traditional fat and LWAPs are all physically connected to the wired network. With wireless mesh networks, the access points connect to each other via the wireless medium and route through each other to get back to services on the wired network. This significantly reduces the cabling required and the deployment costs for wireless networks. In the case of historical buildings, network coverage could be provided without having to install a wired network backbone at all. To establish standards for WLAN meshes, the IEEE has set up the 802.11s working group.

33.2.5   Benefits of Wireless Switch/Access Controller Architecture.
For enterprise use, the LWAP/wireless switch architecture should be the architecture of choice. As well as security benefits that are covered later, it has these general networking benefits:

- **Ease of deployment and management.** The LWAP just needs to know where to find the wireless switch. Once the LWAP is authenticated, all configuration information is downloaded to it. Wireless switch products also include site survey functionality to help you choose where access points should be located before installation. In the event of a denial-of-service attack, the inbuilt wireless intrusion detection system and intrusion prevention system (IDS/IPS) functionality will notify of the attack, reducing the work required to identify the problem.

- **RF management.** A wireless LAN switch is in a position to notice holes in network coverage, or a clash with a neighboring network, and alter LWAP channels, transmitting power dynamically, to avoid these clashes and fill in for lost or failed access points.

- **Load-balancing users.** Wireless clients generally associate with access points having the strongest signal. A wireless switch can direct the user to associate with an alternative access point, if the strongest is already highly loaded.

- **Simplified guest networking.** Guests can be associated with a guest network to provide access to specific services such as Internet access

- **Fast roaming.** Being a central point, the wireless switch is able to coordinate the roaming between LWAPs. This speeds up the roaming process, enabling the use of real-time applications such as voice and video.

- **Layer 3 roaming.** Across a big campus, LWAPs themselves will be connected to many different subnets. However, through tunneling mechanisms, the wireless switch can provide a single subnet across the entire wireless network. This speeds up the roaming process and enables a client to retain a single IP address across the entire campus, further supporting the use of voice and video.

- **Quality of service (QOS).** A wireless LAN switch is able to prioritize traffic centrally, to provide the appropriate QOS for real-time traffic.

- **Unification of wired and wireless.** The use of LWAPs and wireless switches enables the wireless network to be integrated into the wired network, reducing management overheads.

- **AAA accounting.** As all traffic passes through a wireless switch, it is able to collate accurate metrics for usage based charging of the wireless network.[12]

- **Integration with older non–wired equivalent privacy (WPA/WPA2) equipment**. Some vendors provide virtual private network (VPN) functionality in the wireless switch to provide secure connectivity for older equipment that does not have WPA/WPA2 support and integrate it into the enterprise wireless network.

33.2.6 Security Benefits of Wireless Switch/Access Controller Architecture. Wireless switch/access controller architectures have these security benefits:

- **User and device authentication.** Wireless switches are able to authenticate both the user and the device to ensure that only authorized users on approved computers can access the network.

- **Access control.** Based on the user's identity, the wireless switch can assign the user to a specific VLAN that has access to just the resources required. For example, warehouse staff could be given access to only the inventory management and order processing systems. Guests could be given access to the Internet or public product pages.

- **Inbuilt wireless intrusion detection and prevention functionality.** The wireless switches are able to analyze every wireless packet received by all LWAPs, allowing the switches to provide intrusion detection and prevention functionality. This ranges from denial-of-service attacks to active attacks as well as to the detection of rogue access points and clients.

- **Rogue access point detection.** The LWAP can also be used to scan the environment for unauthorized access points. The location of the device can be found by triangulating it from signals received at different access points. Some products can take active measures to remove rogue access points from the network.

33.3 WIRELESS LAN SECURITY THREATS. This section lists the generic security threats to both wired and wireless networks. It then describes the specific threats made possible by wireless LANs.

Hassler,[13] the Dennings,[14] and ISO 7498-2[15] identified these types of threats to networked systems:

- **Eavesdropping.** Intercepting and reading messages intended for other users. Wireless LANs use radio waves to transport the data between wireless stations and the network. These radio waves easily pass through building walls and onto the street. All that is required to eavesdrop on a wireless LAN is a laptop or handheld PC, a wireless LAN card, and some free software available via the Internet.

- **Masquerading.** Sending or receiving messages using another user's identity. An attacker who can eavesdrop on a wireless network may be able to collect enough information to join the network and to masquerade as a legitimate user.

- **Message modification.** The content of messages captured by an attacker could be altered without it being detected and then retransmitted, resulting in an unauthorized effect.

- **Replaying.** Repeating all or part of a message to produce an unauthorized effect. For example, replaying an authentication message to obtain unauthorized access to a network.

- **Denial of service (DoS).** Preventing authorized users of a network from accessing resources. For example, flooding the network with messages to prevent others from using it. See Chapter 18 of this *Handbook* for a full description.

- **Exploiting flaws in design, implementation, or operation.** Using program bugs, poor security system design, and configuration errors to achieve unauthorized access to resources. This topic is covered in depth in Section 33.4.

- **Cracking.** Using brute force or dictionary attacks to guess the values of passwords, or of cryptographic keys. See Chapter 7 for a detailed discussion.

33.3.1   Comparison between Wired and Wireless.

A vulnerability is a weakness that allows a threat to occur to an asset, such as data traveling over a network. For threats to occur on a wired network, the vulnerability is a physical connection to the network. With the mass adoption of the Internet, a physical connection is available to all Internet-connected networks. This allows people from outside the physically controlled areas of an organization's buildings to access the corporate LAN.

Wireless networks also extend the network outside of the physical controls of the building because the network uses radio waves to transport data. People such as Rob Flickenger[16] and Peter Shipley[17] have demonstrated how high-gain aerials, such as parabolic dishes, can enable stations to connect to a wireless LAN over a distance of 25 miles. Several people have modified household satellite television aerials to achieve similar results.[18] But there is no need now to home-build high-gain aerials as they are available commercially for as little as U.S. $69.[19] Because wireless networks and the Internet allow people to connect to the network from outside the physically controlled area of an organization's buildings, it might be of interest to compare the vulnerabilities presented by the two technologies and how they control these vulnerabilities.

Corporate networks are usually protected from the Internet by firewalls and technologies such as virtual private networks. These technologies control access to the resources that are available via the Internet, using tokens and strong cryptography to authenticate users and to encrypt the information while traveling over the Internet. The main reasons for installing wireless LANs are to allow staff to gain access from areas that do not have physical network connections and to access the network's resources while moving about the premises. Wireless LANs are typically connected directly to the LAN, allowing unauthorized people in the street, car park, or even on a hill 20 miles away to access the LAN. A popular pastime for hackers is "war-driving," where people roam the streets searching for wireless networks they can connect to.

Another key difference between Internet connections and wireless networks is the operational management. Internet connections are normally managed by the networking group that has skilled people managing the security of the connection. Wireless LANs, however, are often installed by unqualified nonnetwork staff. This operational vulnerability is a key issue with wireless LANs, because they are consumer items, bought at relatively low cost, that can be easily and improperly attached to the LAN by nonnetworking professionals.

33.3.2   Specific Threats Enabled by Wireless LANs.

Section 33.4 describes in detail the security functionality provided by 802.11 wireless products and the issues; this section provides a brief overview of the technical threats.

There have been two security systems produced for 802.11 WLAN equipment. The first security system was in the original 802.11 standard,[20] which has been completely broken. The security mechanisms in this system are easily overcome obstacles to breaking into a wireless LAN.

The second "enhanced" security system is specified in the 802.11i standard, which specifies a much stronger set of security mechanisms. However, for compatibility with existing equipment, 802.11i includes the original broken security mechanisms. New equipment, when delivered, is usually not configured to use the new security mechanisms. For these reasons, this chapter covers both the previous and new security systems, so that security professionals have full details on WLAN technology issues.

A summary of the security issues found in the original security specification shows that:

- Wireless networks are available outside of the physically controlled areas because the network uses radio waves.
- Networks broadcast their existence, providing all the information required to associate to the network.
- Devices are authenticated rather than users. Stolen devices or keys copied from devices can be used to connect to the network.
- The original authentication protocols can be broken (e.g., by spoofing of shared key authentication).
- Authentication is a one-way protocol. The client does not authenticate the access point, allowing rogue attacks.
- The original privacy protocol (WEP) has been compromised (IV reuse, FMS attack).[21]
- The message integrity check vector (ICV) is a linear algorithm that can be defeated through bit-flipping attacks.
- Messages can be replayed without this being detected.
- Administrators implement wireless products with their default settings, causing the network to be either completely open or open to the use of default keys.
- Wireless LANs use the same set of keys for all users. This allows wireless LAN users to eavesdrop on one another.
- Public wireless LAN services (hot spots) in airports, hotels, and coffee shops are a threat to the confidentiality of business and personal information.

The next sections describe some specific threats enabled by wireless LANs.

33.3.2.1 War-Driving.   It is generally agreed that Peter Shipley invented war-driving in late 2000. It involves people using some form of transport (usually walking or driving), a laptop or handheld PC, a wireless LAN card, and software, to detect and break into wireless networks. When Peter first started war-driving, he found that over 60 percent of wireless networks were installed using the default configuration and that only 15 percent were using encryption (WEP).[22] Additionally, the vast majority of the wireless LANs were installed directly on the network backbone rather than in an untrusted, guarded network segment such as a DMZ. This meant that over 85 percent of wireless LANs were facilitating unauthorized access to the core network.

Since Shipley's original work, there have been a good number of surveys conducted, –all reporting similar findings.[23] The recent U.K. Government DTI survey of information security breaches in 2006 found that:

- 24 percent of U.K. businesses (59 percent of large organizations) have implemented wireless networks; this is a similar adoption from the last survey in 2004.
- The number of wireless networks without any controls has been reduced from 53 percent in 2004 to 20 percent in 2006.

- The number using encryption has increased from 16 percent in 2004 to 58 percent in 2006, with 78 percent of large organizations using encryption.[24]

Although the situation is better than in 2004, even after all the publicity on wireless LAN security, 42 percent of U.K. organizations are still not implementing basic controls such as encryption to protect the confidentiality of information and are still not preventing unauthorized access to the network.

From a consumer perspective, anyone who lives in a built-up area can detect quite a few neighbors' wireless networks, some of which will be unprotected. Of the networks that are protected, WEP still appears to be the protocol used to secure the network, even though a more secure system has been available for several years. As will be covered in detail later, WEP can be easily broken, even in a network with very little traffic.

33.3.2.2 War-Chalking.
Back in 2002, war-drivers began to mark on the pavement or a wall the presence of a wireless network. This activity, known as war-chalking, appears to have died out. Even the home domain www.warchalking.org is no longer active.[25]

33.3.2.3 Dealing with War Drivers.
Most organizations have video surveillance of the outside of their buildings. The physical security department should be briefed to recognize war-drivers and should have procedures for dealing with them. War-drivers only become a real threat when they try to access a network, but to do that they need to be stationary and normally close to the physical premises. War-drivers on foot stand out like sore thumbs because they are usually working on a laptop. Less obvious will be war-drivers in a car because they can be parked unobtrusively. Security procedures should require a review of parked cars, and the appropriate staff should be briefed to recognize war-drivers. The most dangerous war-drivers are those who can sit in a public place, such as a pub or coffee shop, and attack a network. The only defense against these people is a properly designed and secured network.

33.3.2.4 Threats Presented by Laptops with 802.11.
As already covered, wireless networks have been mass-adopted in the consumer market. Low-end laptops now come with wireless as standard. Even if an organization does not have a wireless network, some staff are going to be using it at home, and the laptop's WLAN facility is likely to be active while in the office. The Windows XP WLAN client is constantly monitoring for networks and will often automatically connect to any open access points, or other laptops, to form a peer-to-peer network.

The original 802.11 standard does not authenticate the access point to the client, making it vulnerable to attack from rogue access points. Wireless clients generally are configured to join any network they come across, which makes it very easy for attackers to perform.

Even if the client is tied down to a particular network, the laptop will be regularly sending "probe requests" searching for its home wireless network and providing the name of the network in the probe. An attacker can capture these probes and configure an open source program to emulate the home access point and connect to the client. A typical program for this is the Linux-based driver called *HostAP*, available from http://hostap.epitest.fi/. Once connected, the attacker can scan the laptop. If there are any unprotected file shares or other vulnerable services, then software could be installed onto the laptop, giving access to the corporate network.

An example service that could be exploited is the Microsoft ActiveSync Service for the current generation of Windows Mobile PDAs. The ActiveSync service provides a proxy service for the PDA to access the main network for e-mail and browsing. ActiveSync can be configured to connect over a WLAN,[26] so if any staff have done this, they may be inadvertently providing a wireless proxy server onto the network.

The attack is even simpler if the station belongs to an IBSS network. All the attacker has to do is run Windows XP, which will show the attacker the network and give him or her the option to join it. The attacker can then use Windows networking to search for available file shares. Many people share their C: drive without realizing what they have done. Even with the firewall in Windows XP SP2, people often configure it to provide access to file shares.

33.3.2.5   Threats from Neighbors.
Most businesses do not occupy an entire building; instead they share the premises with other companies and sometimes with residential apartments. Our cities are densely populated, so even if a building is not shared, wireless networks could still be detected in adjacent buildings. In the case of high-rise buildings, there could be a direct line of sight between buildings spanning some distance; this could enable occupants to connect to one another's networks. Hobbyists are using these characteristics of wireless LANs to create wireless community networks and to share Internet connections.[27]

The main risk is to wireless networks that have been installed in their default, insecure state because anyone within range could automatically connect to that network. As a scenario, two businesses occupy the same building and both have WLANs. Business 1 uses WEP and business 2 does not. When an employee of business 1 first powers on a computer, Windows XP networking will display a dialog box showing the available wireless networks, and asking which network the user wants to join. The employee of business 1 unaware that the second network is not his business's network could inadvertently join business 2's network. Windows will then automatically connect the employee to the wrong network. The main impact of this scenario is the improper use of Internet bandwidth, however, should business 1 be a competitor to business 2, the consequences could be much more severe.

This scenario also applies to residents in or near the building; they could have their own wireless network, or bring home their work laptop with inbuilt wireless, and easily join any unprotected network. Residents are likely to be most interested in using a fast Internet connection in the evenings. However, if a neighbor participates in peer-to-peer file sharing networks, the impact could be serious. It might start with a loss of bandwidth, with worst-case scenarios being civil or criminal action if the network appears to be hosting copyrighted or illegal material, such as child pornography. The resident could also have the skills to be more seriously abusive of a network, making it a source of spam, or even directly attacking its systems.

To reduce the cost of broadband, people are using wireless networks to share asymmetric digital subscriber line (ADSL) connections with their neighbors (often in violation of their terms of service). This practice makes ordinary people aware of the value of illegal access to companies' Internet connections and could be an incentive for a resident to connect to an unprotected corporate network. If a network is protected only by WEP, then this attack is easy for someone located within range, and it is undetectable.

33.3.2.6   Threats Presented by Public Wireless LANs (Hot Spots).
A number of organizations are rolling out public 802.11 wireless networks enabling traveling users to access the Internet and through that the corporate network. By

necessity, these networks are completely open and are not encrypted. This allows company information to be captured through the use of unencrypted e-mail, or the PC could be compromised via the Internet connection. An attacker can obtain the PC's IP address by monitoring the wireless network, after which the attacker can then scan the PC for open file shares, or other vulnerable services, from any Internet-connected PC.

This appears to be a real risk. *The Register* reported in July 2003 that at the 802.11 Planet Expo in Boston, security vendor AirDefense monitored the exhibition and found that only 3 percent of e-mail on day 1 and 12 percent on day 2 of the conference was encrypted.[28] AirDefense also detected 149 active scans from war-driving tools, 105 denial-of-service attacks, and 32 attempted man-in-the-middle attacks, 3 of which were successful. This threat is relatively easy to mitigate through the use of VPNs and a personal firewall.

A second attack against hot-spot users takes advantage of 802.11 not authenticating the access point. A program call Airsnarf is a rogue access point utility enabling an attacker to pretend to be a commercial hot spot.[29] Airsnarf was developed to demonstrate how usernames and passwords for public hot spots can be easily captured, enabling the attacker to make use of the user's account. If users happen to be on a metered service, they are likely to get a shock when the next bill comes in.

33.4   ORIGINAL 802.11 SECURITY FUNCTIONALITY.   The IEEE 802.11 group of standards has defined two security systems. The original system is defined in the base 802.11-1999 standard[30] and defines the WEP protocol. The second security system is defined in the 802.11i standard[31] and defines the WPA and WPA2 security systems, which address the issues in the original security system.

Section 33.3 described the high-level threats presented by wireless networks and mentioned that the security functionality provided in the original 802.11 standard has been broken. This section describes in detail the security functionality provided by this standard, along with the issues and how to resolve them.

There are three reasons for covering the original security specification. The first is the amount of legacy equipment still in use that only supports WEP. Second, users still appear to be using WEP in preference to the new 802.11i WPA and WPA2 systems. Third, for backward compatibility, the new security specification includes the original compromised security mechanisms, and the default settings of the new standard are to use these mechanisms.

33.4.1   Security Functionality Overview.   The original 802.11 standard provided this security functionality:

- **Authentication** via two different algorithms called "open authentication" and "shared-key authentication."
- **Confidentiality/privacy** through the "Wired Equivalent Privacy" (WEP) algorithm. This algorithm uses cryptographic keys installed in the station to encrypt the data.
- **Integrity** through use of an encrypted CRC-32 Integrity Check Value (ICV).

These mechanisms are described in this section, along with their security properties and any weaknesses.

33.4.2   Connecting to a Wireless Network and Authentication.   To join a network a station first has to detect the network. There are two ways that wireless

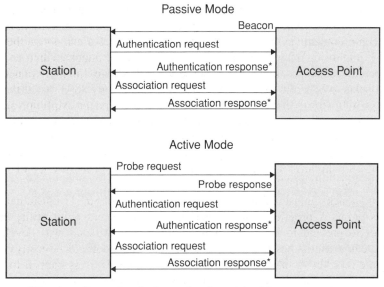

*The shared key authentication protocol consists of 2 message pairs

EXHIBIT 33.5   Connecting to an 802.11 Network

stations detect networks: These are known as passive and active modes. In passive mode, stations listen for "beacon frames" that are regularly transmitted by access points in Infrastructure networks and by stations in ad hoc networks. These beacon frames contain sufficient information to identify the network and what is required to join it. In active mode, a station sends out "probe requests," and network devices reply with a "probe response" that contains similar identification information as the beacon frame. It is common practice for networks to be configured for active mode only and to reply only if the station provides the correct network name. This is done in an attempt to hide the network from unauthorized users.

When a station has detected a network, it first must successfully authenticate to the network and then associate to the network as shown in Exhibit 33.5.

Wired LANs depend largely on physical security to prevent unauthorized access to the network. Anyone who can plug a computer into a LAN port can usually get access to the network. Wireless LANs can circumvent these physical controls, so the 802.11 standard provides an authentication service to compensate. The standard provides two authentication algorithms called "open authentication" and "shared-key authentication" in which the station authenticates itself to the access point. Neither authentication protocol mutually authenticates the two parties, so stations are vulnerable to attacks from rogue access points.

This section describes the open and shared-key authentication algorithms and their security properties and weaknesses.

33.4.2.1 *Open Authentication.*   Open authentication is the default authentication mechanism and is the only required mechanism. The 802.11 standard actually describes the open authentication algorithm as a null algorithm. A station requesting authentication provides its identity (IEEE MAC address) in the authentication request, and the access point sends back a response indicating success or failure. The access point does not attempt to verify the identity of the station, hence the term "null algorithm."

Most products have an access control list (ACL) in the access point that enables the network administrators to specify the MAC addresses of stations that are allowed to connect. If the station's MAC address is not in the list, then an "authentication failure" response is returned. While providing some protection, this mechanism is not very strong because the MAC address in the wireless adaptor can be easily reprogrammed. All an attacker has to do is listen to traffic and collect a list of authorized MAC addresses, then program one of these addresses into an adaptor. MAC filtering also has management issues that make it difficult to implement.

33.4.2.2 *Shared-Key Authentication.*   Shared-key authentication is an optional authentication system that uses the WEP algorithm to authenticate the station. Only stations and access points that support WEP can use this protocol.

The protocol consists of four steps:

1. The station sends a shared-key authentication request to the access point. This request contains its IEEE MAC address.

2. If the access point wishes to continue with the authentication (e.g., it supports WEP and the MAC address is authorized), it uses WEP to generate a random 128-byte authentication challenge string, which is returned in the response to step 1.

3. The station copies the challenge text from step 2 into the authentication data area of the step 3 request message and encrypts the message using the WEP algorithm.

4. The access point decrypts the step 3 request using WEP, checks the integrity check value (ICV), and, if correct, it compares the challenge string against the string sent in step 2. If the ICV and the challenge string are correct, it sends a "success" response to the station, otherwise it sends a "failure" response.

Security Issues with the Shared-key Authentication Protocol. The designers of the shared-key authentication protocol realized there were security issues with it. To quote Section 8.1.2 of the standard, "During the shared key authentication exchange, both the challenge and the encrypted challenge are transmitted. This facilitates unauthorized discovery of the pseudorandom number (PRN) sequence for the key/IV pair used for the exchange. Implementations should therefore avoid using the same key/IV pair for subsequent frames."[32]

Borisov, Goldberg, and Wagner[33] took this flaw one step further to completely defeat the protocol. Because the shared-key authentication exchange enables you to establish a key stream, this key stream can be used to correctly encrypt any challenge sent from the access point and pass the authentication system, without knowledge of the actual WEP key.

Additionally, because the challenge is 128 bytes in length, and the standard does not restrict the repeated use of initialization vectors(IVs), an attacker can correctly encrypt any message 128 bytes or less with the known IV/key stream and inject these messages into the network. These messages can be used to invoke known responses (e.g., Pings) to obtain even more matching IVs and key streams in support of a dictionary attack. This type of attack would not be possible if packets were cryptographically authenticated.

Given these issues, shared-key authentication has been deprecated in 802.11i and should not be used.

33.4.2.3 *Wired Equivalent Privacy.*

Eavesdropping is a threat for wireless technologies so the 802.11 standard specifies the wired equivalent privacy (WEP) option in section 8.2 of the 802.11b standard.[34] WEP is also defined in the 802.11i standard to support transition to the new security systems.

33.4.2.3.1 *Properties of the RC4 Stream Cipher.*

The WEP protocol uses RSA's RC4 stream cipher.[35] Stream ciphers like RC4 operate by generating a stream of key bytes that are exclusive-ORed one byte at a time with the plaintext. Unlike block ciphers, there is no error propagation with stream ciphers. If one bit of the ciphertext is altered, then the plaintext bit is altered in a predictable way, and no other bits are affected. This property is the basis of a number of attacks on the WEP protocol.

Stream ciphers are particular vulnerable to known plaintext attacks. If a known text is encrypted, then the key stream can be easily recovered by exclusive-ORing the plaintext with the ciphertext. This key stream can then be reused to recover other plaintexts encrypted with that particular key stream or to insert new messages into the system. This property is also the basis of a number of attacks on the WEP protocol.

33.4.2.3.2 *WEP Protocol.*

WEP is based on the communicating parties having a shared symmetric key. The 802.11 standard does not specify any key management. As discussed later, this lack of key management is one of the serious problems with WEP.

The WEP encryption protocol consists of:

1. A 32-bit cyclic redundancy check (CRC-32) is calculated from the existing data and appended to it. The purpose is to act as an integrity check value (ICV) and enable a receiving station to check that the data were decrypted correctly.
2. The extended plaintext data were encrypted using the RSA RC4 algorithm. The key is a concatenation of a 24-bit IV and a shared secret key. RC4 is a stream cipher; it produces a stream of bytes that are exclusive-ORed (XOR) with the plaintext bytes to produce the ciphertext.
3. The IV is inserted between the frame header, and the encrypted data and a frame check sequence is calculated (another CRC-32) and appended after the frame body to enable the receiving station to check the integrity of the received frame.

This process is shown in Exhibit 33.6, which is partly based on a figure in Gast.[36]

33.4.2.3.3 *WEP Keys.*

The 802.11 standard specifies that each station have four default 40-bit secret keys numbered 0 to 3. When combined with the 24-bit IV, the key length into RC4 is 64 bits.

Products available today have a nonstandardized option of 104-bit secret keys, which when combined with the IV pass a key length of 128 bits into RC4.

33.4.2.3.4 *Problems with WEP.*

Borisov, Goldberg, and Wagner[37] identified these flaws with WEP:

- **Key length**. The key length defined in the standard is only 40 bits. This is not long enough to prevent brute-force attacks by individuals or corporations. However, this problem is largely overcome with the release of products that support 104-bit secret keys.

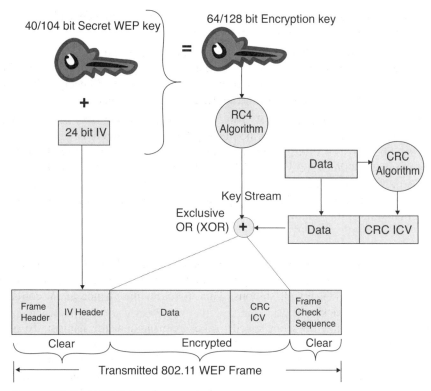

EXHIBIT 33.6   WEP Protocol

- **Key stream reuse**. A well-known weakness with stream ciphers such as RC4, is that if you XOR two ciphertexts encrypted under the same key stream, then the key stream is canceled out. The output is then the two plaintexts XORed together, which is vulnerable to cryptanalysis.

- **Key management**. The 802.11 standard does not specify how keys should be distributed. This has led to vendors relying on manual key management systems that are a weakness in the system. For more details on the key management issues, see Section 33.4.2.3.5.

- **Message modification**. The WEP protocol uses a CRC-32 checksum to detect whether a packet has been modified. The message and the checksum are encrypted, which suggests that it should not be possible to alter a packet without it being detected. However,[38] has demonstrated that an attacker can make calculated changes to an encrypted message that result in the same checksum. This allows an attacker to modify a message and have it accepted by another station. This is possible because WEP uses a linear rather than a cryptographic integrity check function and because of the bitwise XOR property of stream ciphers. A controlled one-bit change in the ciphertext results in a one-bit change in the plaintext bit.

- **Message injection**. If an attacker can obtain the ciphertext equivalent of a plaintext, then she can obtain the key stream by XORing the ciphertext with the plaintext. The attacker can then XOR a new message with the key stream, which will be accepted by a station. This flaw is possible because the CRC-32 integrity check is a linear function and can be calculated by an attacker. If each packet had a keyed cryptographic checksum, such as a SHA-1 HMAC[39] instead, this attack would not be possible. Additionally, the standard allows the reuse of IVs, enabling an attacker to reuse an identified key stream (which depends on the IV) indefinitely to inject messages into the system.

- **IP redirection**. This attack uses the message modification attack already described to alter the destination IP address of a captured encrypted packet to that of a host controlled by the attacker on the Internet. The access point will decrypt the packet for the attacker and then forward it to the Internet for delivery.

- **Reaction attack against TCP**. This attack involves using the message modification technique already described to flip bits in a captured TCP message and resending it to a TCP-based server. If the TCP checksum is incorrect, the message is ignored by the server; if the TCP checksum is correct, then a TCP acknowledgment is sent back. Whether an acknowledgment is sent back leaks one bit of information on the value of the plaintext. This attack can be used to recover virtually all of the plaintext.

33.4.2.3.5 Key Management.   All stations have four default WEP keys and the possibility of a dedicated mapped key with another station. In practice, most installations use just one key for all stations. This increases the chance of IV collisions allowing IV reuse attacks.

The 802.11 standard does not specify a key management mechanism. To quote paragraph 8.1.2: "The required secret, shared key is presumed to have been delivered to participating stations via a secure channel that is independent of IEEE 802.11."

This lack of a defined key management system has meant that the vendors have implemented a manual system, which is a major weakness in the system.

33.4.2.3.6 Problems with a Manual Key Management System.   The main problem with manual key management systems is that the keys need to be physically entered into every user's machine. This creates many points where the keys can become known and many people who have the opportunity to know and compromise the secrecy of the keys. In a number of products, the keys are displayed in clear text for users to easily obtain the key values.

The sharing of keys by many people makes it difficult to change the keys, because it has to be coordinated with all the users. In practice, this is very hard to achieve, and the keys are changed infrequently, if ever. This gives an attacker plenty of time to try breaking into the network. Additionally, ex-staff who have knowledge of the keys may be able to connect to the network from outside the building, undermining the normal physical security controls.

33.4.2.3.7 Default WEP Keys.   To ease the key management burden, many suppliers have default WEP keys programmed into the equipment, and many companies just turn WEP on and use these keys. Unfortunately, knowledge of these keys is widespread, see the frequently asked questions (FAQ) from ISS.[40] Programs such as Netstumbler and Kismet identify the manufacturer of the equipment. This enables attackers to enter the known keys for a particular supplier and quickly break into the network. This problem is the wireless equivalent of the default account/password problem that affects operating systems, databases, and other software.

33.4.2.4 Fluhrer, Mantin, and Shamir (FMS) Attack.   The issues that Borisov, Goldberg, and Wagner described almost pale into insignificance when compared to the FMS attack. In August 2001 Scott Fluhrer, Itsik Mantin, and Adi Shamir

published a paper on weaknesses in the key-scheduling algorithm of RC4 and theorized how this weakness could be used to easily break the WEP protocol.[41] Adam Stubblefield, John Ioannidis, and Ariel Rubin then wrote a paper on a successful implementation of this attack.[42] They found that it took them only a couple of hours to implement the attack and just a few days to gather off-the-shelf hardware and software to recover a WEP key. They concluded that the WEP key can be recovered using the basic FMS attack by passively collecting about 5 million packets; with optimizations, the number of packets required can be reduced to around 1 million. Since then, open source software in the form of Airsnort and WEPCrack has become available that enables relatively unskilled people to implement these attacks.

33.4.2.5 Developments since the FMS Attack.   In response to the FMS attack, vendors took a number of actions including the dropping of "weak" and "interesting" IVs and the development of a new protocol called Dynamic WEP, which is covered in Section 33.4.3.5.

The dropping of weak IVs did make it a little more difficult to break the WEP key with the existing tools, but three developments since then have totally undermined any security that WEP provides.

First, on August 6, 2004, a hacker with the handle Korek posted code for a new tool called chopper, a new statistical attack against WEP that no longer relied on weak or interesting IVs.[43] It also reduced the number of packets required to break WEP from millions to hundreds of thousands. Chopper was very quickly integrated into the Airsnort and Aircrack WEP cracking tools.

Second, Aircrack has been enhanced to simplify the capture and replay of packets. This allows an attacker to capture any encrypted broadcast packets (e.g., ARP requests) and then repeatedly replay them, which the access point dutifully does, creating enough packets to break the WEP key. This means that even a lightly or unused WLAN can still be broken once a suitable broadcast packet is sent.

Third, the Auditor and BackTrack security tool collections at remote-exploit.org. These are bootable Linux ISOs disk images that have all the tools and patched wireless drivers required to break a WEP key. There are also links to movies that show all the commands to type in the correct sequence to achieve this. All that is required is to download the ISO, burn it, boot it up on an existing Windows laptop, and follow the instructions in the movies. This means that script kiddies with very little knowledge can now compromise WEP. Previously, a reasonable knowledge of Linux was required and time had to be spent learning how to do it.

The outcome is that WEP can provide protection for only a very limited time before the network is compromised. For an article covering these developments over the last few years and an overview of wireless hacking tools, refer to the SecurityFocus article written by Michael Mossmann.[44]

33.4.3 Defending against the WEP Vulnerability.   The best way to defend against the WEP vulnerability is to implement the 802.11i WPA or WPA2 systems described in Section 33.5. However, if this is not possible, then an alternative solution is needed. To help design a solution, Exhibit 33.7 briefly reiterates what the problems are with the current architecture and some possible countermeasures.

There are two types of problems listed in the exhibit: technical shortcomings in the 802.11 protocols and implementation and operational problems.

Exhibit 33.8 shows a high-level technical architecture that can overcome the technical shortcomings. Wireless LANs have properties similar to Internet connections, in

EXHIBIT 33.7   802.11 Problems and Countermeasures

Problems with the Current Standard and Products	Possible Countermeasures
The wireless network is available outside of the physically controlled areas because the network uses radio waves.	Locate access points away from outside walls, choose an appropriate aerial, and set transmit power to minimize external radiation Treat the wireless network as untrusted and firewall it from the rest of the network. Monitor it for intrusions. Use strong token-based user authentication. Use strong encryption of data.
Networks broadcast their existence and provide freeware tools, such as Netstumbler, with all the information required to associate to the network.	Configure the access point not to respond to broadcast probe-requests and not to put SSID in Beacons.
Devices are authenticated rather than users. Stolen devices or keys copied from devices can be used to connect to the network.	Authenticate users as well as network devices.
The original authentication protocols can be broken (e.g., spoofing of shared key authentication).	Use strong token-based user authentication via one-time passwords (e.g., RSA's SecurID).
Only wireless clients are authenticated (one-way authentication), allowing rogue access point attacks.	Use mutual authentication protocols such as IPSEC. Use personal firewalls.
The WEP protocol has been compromised (IV reuse, FMS attack).	Use an alternative link-level encryption protocol such as IPSEC ESP or TLS.
The message integrity check vector (ICV) is a linear algorithm that can be defeated.	Use a strong keyed cryptographic function such as the AH header in IPSEC.
Messages can be replayed without this being detected.	Employ replay detection mechanisms, such as those implemented in IPSEC and TLS.
Administrators implement wireless products with their default settings causing the network either to be completely open or to open using default keys and passwords.	Publicized corporate policy on wireless LANs enforced through regular wireless audits. Have an approved wireless LAN architecture and configuration standards.
Wireless LANs use the same set of keys for all users. This allows wireless LAN users to eavesdrop on one another.	Use negotiated session keys specific to a user via mechanisms such as IPSEC or TLS.
Public wireless LAN services in airports, hotels, and coffee shops are a threat to the confidentiality of business and personal information.	Use an alternative link level encryption protocol such as IPSEC ESP or TLS. Use personal firewalls.

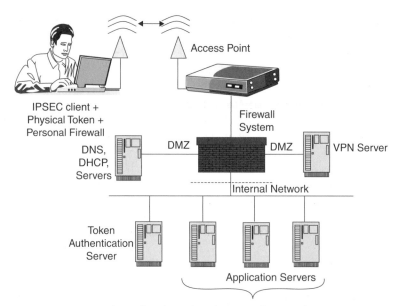

IPSEC client +
Physical Token +
Personal Firewall

Access Point

Firewall
System

DNS,
DHCP,
Servers

DMZ   DMZ   VPN Server

Internal Network

Token
Authentication
Server

Application Servers

EXHIBIT 33.8   High-Level Technical Architecture for Wireless LANs

that they allow individuals outside the physical control of an organization to connect to the network. Therefore, a good solution for securing wireless networks is one based on an IPSEC or SSL VPN to encrypt and authenticate packets and to defeat replay attacks. The VPN terminates in the corporation's untrusted DMZ. Once the VPN is established, the user is authenticated using a physical token, such as RSA's SecurID or PKI credentials on a smartcard. Then and only then is the user granted access to the internal network. This solution works for internal use as well as for connecting via public wireless LANs and the Internet. An organization can usually leverage its existing Internet remote access VPN system.

33.4.3.1 Additional Key Controls.

Three additional key security controls do not in themselves address the WLAN issues but need to be implemented to help maintain a secure environment. These controls are needed even when using the new 802.11i security system.

The first is effective patch management; even with a firewall, the wireless PC can be compromised at the application layer, for example, via browser vulnerabilities. Second, a regularly updated antivirus and antispyware solution is needed to detect and prevent malware from gaining control of a PC. Last, when providing remote access to wireless clients, only systems that are compliant with security policy should be allowed to connect to the network. That is, they must be firewalled, patched, and have up-to-date virus and spyware definitions. If not, there is an increased risk of viruses and Trojan horses accessing the network.

33.4.3.2 VPN and WEP.

One point for a brief discussion is whether to use WEP with a VPN. From a data confidentiality perspective, WEP is not required because the data are protected by the VPN. However, if WEP is not used, then any war-drivers who detect the network will see it as being unprotected and could start trying to break in. The devices at risk are the network infrastructure (access points, routers, switches, etc.) and the DNS and DHCP servers, although they are protected to a certain extent by the firewall and choke routers. The main threat is a denial-of-service attack, which could bring down the wireless network.

By turning on WEP, you will deter the majority of war-drivers and protect your network infrastructure from most attacks.

33.4.3.3 Access Point Configuration.

It is common to configure access points so that they do not publish their SSID in beacons and do not respond to broadcast probe requests. This is done in an attempt to hide the network from unauthorized users.

The effect of these controls is that the Windows XP wireless client and some basic war-driving tools, such as Netstumbler, will not see your network, preventing computers from accidentally joining your network. However, these controls do not provide any protection from a serious war-driver who will locate your network by capturing and processing the data traffic rather than depending on broadcast probe requests. It is possible that these controls just make it harder for authorized users to join the network, without having any real security benefit. Provided you are running a secure system, any attempt to join the network will be rejected.

33.4.3.4 Access Point Location.

Access point location is a simple but effective technique to prevent an outsider detecting your WLAN. If the access point is located in the middle of the room, the signal will be weaker outside. Additionally, if you are on the first or second floor of a building, substantial obstacles between the access point and the street would significantly degrade the signal. If the access point is placed on an outside-facing wall, the signal is likely to be broadcast strongly outside the building onto the street.

I was able to confirm this behavior during an authorized building scan for wireless networks. One building had an access point mounted on a street-facing wall on the fourth floor. This access point could not be detected on the third or fifth floors, even when I was directly below or above it. But I was able to pick up the access point from the street four floors below while sitting on a bench across the road.

33.4.3.5 Dynamic WEP.

One of the responses by vendors to the breaking of WEP was the introduction of dynamic WEP keys, which are established as part of the 802.1x authentication exchange. In this system, every wireless station has its own WEP key that the access point regularly changes, eliminating the use of static WEP keys. This is a standard option in the Windows XP wireless client and is selected via the "This key is provided for me automatically" WEP option.

How good is the dynamic WEP key system? Does it address the security issues with WEP and enable it to be used safely? There is no doubt that it is a massive improvement over static WEP keys and significantly reduces the risk of passive attacks against WEP. However, this system does not address active attacks, which can determine a WEP key in just a few minutes.[45]

If dynamic WEP is the best choice available, it should be used in preference to static WEP, but since it also can be broken, plans should be made to migrate to something stronger. Additionally, equipment supporting 802.1X might be upgradeable to WPA and possibly WPA2, which is highly desirable.

33.4.3.6 Conclusion on WEP.

WEP is fundamentally broken. While tactical solutions have been devised to mitigate specific attacks, new attacks have rapidly followed, taking advantage of the underlying cryptographic flaws and bypassing the mitigating controls. The best thing to do is to use WPA or WPA2, or to encrypt the data using another trusted protocol, such as IPSEC or SSL, before transmission.

33.4.3.7   Resolving the Implementation and Operational Problems.
It is not possible to completely secure a network against intrusion. Through mistakes, carelessness, ignorance, or new types of attack, outsiders at some point will penetrate the network. The first step to resolving these operational issues is an overall security policy that secures each host on an internal network in its own right. Therefore, access to the network would not immediately provide access to business applications or the computers hosting them.

The trend in networking today is to interconnect with partners' networks and with public networks such as the Internet, and to allow staff to connect directly to the LAN via the Internet, using technologies such as the VPNs. A wireless LAN is just another means, with vulnerability that enables authorized and unauthorized individuals to connect to the network.

Wireless LAN products, as they come out of the box, are configured to be insecure, and surveys have shown that a large number of sites install them in this default insecure configuration. Even if WEP is turned on, often the system uses widely known default keys.

This is normal human behavior; operating systems and software in general tend to be delivered and installed in an insecure configuration. System administrators have to take action to secure their systems, such as setting password policy and changing the default account names and passwords. The same techniques that are used to secure computer systems need to be applied to wireless networks:

- Issue a corporate policy on wireless LANs. Without a policy, the organization has no framework to control WLAN usage.
- Publicize and enforce the policy. Unless people are aware that a policy exists and that it is actively enforced via procedures and regular audits, the policy will be ineffective.
- Develop an approved WLAN architecture, configuration standards, and operating procedures that allow the technology to be quickly and securely implemented and used.

33.4.3.8   Remote Access and Public Wireless Access Points (Hot Spots).
WPA and WPA2 are good solutions for connecting to wireless networks, but data sent by remote access via a home wireless network, remote offices, and public access points will not be protected on the wired network or on the Internet. Even WPA/WPA2 only secures wireless transmissions locally. For securing non-WPA equipment, the best practice is to use the same VPN-based solution. Once connected to the access point, the VPN provides a secure tunnel to the organization.

The one threat a VPN cannot mitigate is a rogue hot spot. Upon connection to the access point, the VPN is not yet established and is unable to provide protection. This is a fundamental flaw in the current system, and vendors need to establish an interim solution for this until the 802.11u working group provides a standardized solution.

Going forward, the wireless switch vendors are working to do away completely with the need for VPNs by implementing secure protocols between the LWAPs and the access controllers. Establishing a secure wireless network in a remote branch office will be as simple as shipping an access point to the remote office and plugging it into the network. The story is the same for mobile staff: Given a trusted access point, users connect it to their broadband/cable router at home or to the Ethernet connection in the hotel room, and a secure connection is established.

This could be the beginning of a significant change of paradigm, particularly with the emergence of products that are bringing together wired and wireless networks. In the end, it may not matter where you are or how you are connecting. If you have a trusted device, and individual credentials, it will be easy to connect securely to a corporate network.

Before this can happen, there must be much research to be sure that the loss or theft of an access point, and of the protocols and architecture, will not put the corporate network at risk. Even though users and access points are authenticated, and their credentials are revoked in the event of loss, staff may not return access points when they leave an organization. Knowing who has which particular access point so it can be revoked is another problem.

33.5 IEEE 802.11I.   In June 2004, the IEEE released the 802.11i standard to improve the security of 802.11 networks. This standard can be downloaded free of charge from the IEEE Web site.[46]

The standard is designed for both personal and enterprise users. Enterprise use is based on the 802.1X protocol to provide authentication and to establish a security context. A "personal" profile, using a preshared key (PSK) based on a password, is provided for consumers and SOHO users who do not have the necessary 802.1X authentication infrastructure The PSK option is vulnerable to a dictionary attack; more information is provided in Section 33.5.7.

33.5.1 Structure of the Robust Security Network.   The new security system is called Robust Security Network (RSN) and establishes Robust Security Network Associations (RSNAs). Equipment implementing RSNA algorithms will be called RSNA-capable; earlier equipment is called pre-RSNA. The standard includes the original pre-RSNA algorithms as well as the new RSNA algorithms. A network that supports both RSNA and pre-RSNA equipment is called a transition security network (TSN) and is intended to facilitate migration to the new standard. Use of TSN is not recommended because the network can be compromised via the pre-RSNA equipment.

The core protocol underlying RSNA is IEEE 802.1X. RSNA builds on this protocol to provide these security features:

- Enhanced mutual authentication mechanisms that can authenticate users as well as the network client. The access point is also authenticated to the client station, defeating rogue access point and man-in-the-middle attacks.
- Key management algorithms
- Cryptographic key establishment
- Cryptographic message integrity codes to defeat the bit-flipping attacks possible in the original standard.
- Two data privacy protocols:
  - Temporal key integrity protocol (TKIP), which is an optional protocol specifically designed so that existing WEP-based hardware can be upgraded to use it.
  - Counter mode with CBC-MAC protocol (CCMP), which is mandatory for RSNA compliance. It uses AES in counter mode for confidentiality and CBC-MAC for authentication and integrity. CCMP is a strong protocol that

has been designed for long-term data privacy and the next generation of wireless equipment.

RSNA security is structured into two subsystems:

1. Security association management consisting of:
   - RSNA negotiation procedures to establish a security context
   - IEEE 802.1X authentication, replacing IEEE802.11 authentication
   - IEEE 802.1X key management to establish cryptographic keys
2. Data privacy mechanisms consisting of the two protocols described above.

The sections that follow describe these subsystems.

33.5.2   802.1X Authentication.

RSNA is based on 802.1X, which provides port-based network access controls for IEEE 802 LAN infrastructures. These infrastructures include Ethernet, token ring, and wireless networks. 802.1X authenticates and authorizes devices attached to a LAN port and will not allow a device to access the network if authentication fails.

802.1X defines three roles:

1. **Authenticator.** The device that authenticates a network device before allowing it to access network resources. In an 802.11 BSS network, the access point is the authenticator.
2. **Supplicant.** The device that wants to access network resources and needs to be authenticated
3. **Authentication server (AS).** The AS performs the actual authentication of the supplicant on behalf of the authenticator. The AS can be located with the authenticator but is commonly an external system, such as a RADIUS server.

Additionally, 802.1X defines the object "port access entity" (PAE), which operates the authentication algorithms and protocols in the supplicant and authenticator. An overview of the 802.1X architecture[47] is shown in Exhibit 33.9.

The authenticator has two logical ports; the first is an uncontrolled port that allows access to required functionality, such as the authenticator PAE. The second port is

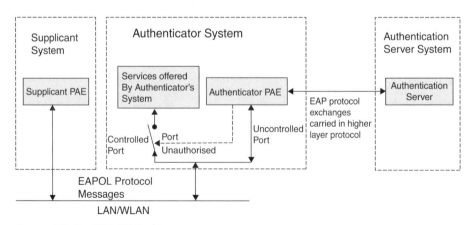

EXHIBIT 33.9   *802.1X Architecture*

the controlled port that allows access to the rest of the network. The status of the controlled port is set by the authenticator PAE and is dependent on the outcome of the authentication between the supplicant and the authentication server.

The messages between the supplicant and authenticator use the Extensible Authentication Protocol (EAP) over LAN (EAPOL) protocol defined in 802.1X. Messages between the authenticator and the AS are encoded using EAP and carried in a higher layer protocol such as RADIUS.

33.5.3 Security Association Management.   Exhibit 33.10 shows the high-level security association management flow. It consists of five stages that:

1. Establish a secure channel between the authenticator and authentication server.
2. Locate the network, negotiate cryptographic algorithms, and associate to it.
3. Authenticate via 802.1X to the authentication server.
4. Mutually authenticate and establish pairwise cryptographic keys.
5. Establish group/multicast cryptographic keys.

The sections that follow describe these stages. Two aspects vary the security association flow. The first is whether the wireless network contains an access point (a BSS) or whether it is an IBSS. The second is whether the master cryptographic key is a global preshared key (PSK) or if it is established during the 802.1X authentication protocol. Any variations caused by BSS/IBSS and 802.1X/PSK are described within the sections.

Stage 1. Establish a secure channel between authenticator and authentication server. In this stage the authenticator and AS mutually authenticate one another and

Stage	Wireless Station (Supplicant)	Access Point/IBSS Station (Authenticator)	Authentication Server
1. Establish secure channel between Authenticator and authentication server		Secure mutual authentication	
2. Locate the network, negotiate cryptographic algorithms and associate	beacons frames containing SSID/IBSS and RSN IE / Probe request and response (includes RSN IE) / Open Authentication request and response / Association request and response		
3. Authenticate to Authentication Server	802.1X Authentication (EAPOL)	EAP over secure protocol (e.g. Radius)	
4. Mutual authentication, establish working pairwise cryptographic keys	4 Way handshake (EAPOL-Key)		
5. Establish Group/Multicast working cryptographic keys	Group Key Handshake		

EXHIBIT 33.10   RSNA Security Association Management

establish a secure channel between them using a protocol such as RADIUS, IPSEC, or TLS. This channel is used to securely carry the authentication exchanges between the supplicant and the AS. This stage is not required if the network uses a PSK.

Stage 2. Locate the network and associate to it. This stage is mostly the original 802.11 functionality for locating, authenticating, and associating to a wireless network as described in Section 33.4.2. Key differences in an RSN are the beacon frames, probe responses, and association requests containing RSN information elements (RSN IE) that indicate RSNA support, along with the available authentication and privacy protocols.

Stage 3. 802.1X authentication to the authentication server. This stage is not required if the network uses a PSK; in this situation, authentication occurs in stage 4.

The purpose of this stage is mutually to authenticate the supplicant and authentication server (AS) to one another and independently to generate the pairwise master key (PMK) for use in stage 4. The EAP used to achieve this has a number of different methods available; RSN requires the use of EAP methods that mutually authenticate the parties, such as EAP-TLS, EAP-PEAP, and EAP-TTLS, to prevent rogue access point and man-in-the-middle attacks. EAP-MD5 is not suitable or secure for RSN. The messages exchanged between the supplicant and the AS are defined by the EAP method. An overview of this stage is given in Exhibit 33.11.

For a BSS network, the wireless station is the 802.1X supplicant and the access point is the authenticator. The access point relays the authentication messages between the supplicant and the authentication server, which can be either a separate service or built in.

For an IBSS, the station wanting to associate to another station is the supplicant, and the target station is the authenticator. This means that stations in an IBSS can simultaneously be supplicants and authenticators, depending on who initiated the association.

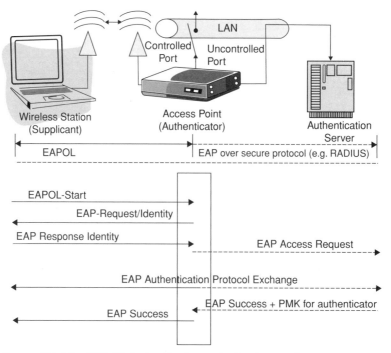

EXHIBIT 33.11   802.1X Authentication to Authentication Server

Additionally, each IBSS station will need an authentication server unless the network uses pre-shared keys.

As covered in stage 1, a secure channel has to be established between the authenticator and the authentication server prior to this exchange. This serves two purposes: to protect the integrity and authenticity of the authentication exchange and to allow the AS to securely send the PMK to the authenticator once authentication is complete.

Stage 4. Mutual authentication and establishment of pairwise working keys. Stage 3 established a PMK in both the supplicant and authenticator. If the network uses a PSK, then the PSK is the PMK. This stage, called the four-way handshake and has three purposes:

1. To authenticate mutually the supplicant and authenticator to one another by confirming that they both have the same valid PMK
2. To generate a pairwise transient key (PTK) from the PMK and fresh temporal keys bound to their MAC addresses
3. To synchronize the installation of the keys in both devices

The four-way handshake is implemented by EAPOL-key messages exchanged between the supplicant and the authenticator, and consists of eight steps, as shown in Exhibit 33.12.

1. The authenticator and the supplicant both generate nonces[48] for use in the authentication protocol. The authenticator's nonce is called ANonce and the supplicant's nonce is called SNonce.

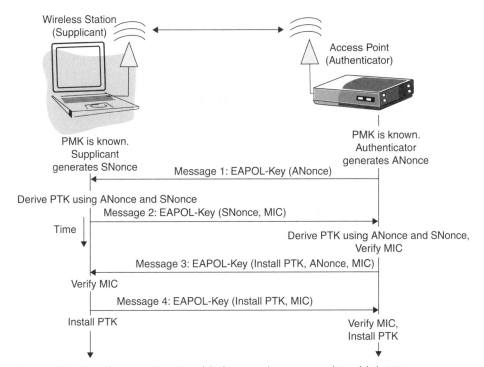

EXHIBIT 33.12   The Four-Way Handshake to Authenticate and Establish PTK

2. The authenticator sends an EAPOL-key message containing the ANonce (Message 1).

3. The supplicant derives the PTK using the ANonce and SNonce and calculates EAPOL-key encrypting key (KEK) and EAPOL-key message integrity key (MIC).

4. The supplicant sends an EAPOL-key message containing the SNonce and a MIC calculated using the EAPOL MIC key (Message 2).

5. The authenticator can now derive the PTK because it has both the ANonce and SNonce. It then calculates the EAPOL-key KEK and EAPOL-key MIC key and verifies the MIC in message 2.

6. The authenticator sends a message containing the ANonce and a flag instructing the supplicant to install the key. The message is also authenticated by a MIC (Message 3).

7. The supplicant verifies the MIC and sends a message to the authenticator confirming the installation of the key. This message is authenticated by a MIC and encrypted using the EAPOL-key KEK (Message 4).

8. The authenticator installs the new keys and starts the last stage to establish the group keys.

Stage 5. Establish group/multicast cryptographic keys. In stage 4 the PTK and temporal keys were established. These keys are used to secure an additional message pair in which the authenticator sends the group temporal key (GTK) in an encrypted form to the station. The group keys are used to secure broadcast messages, such as ARP requests and multicast traffic.

In a BSS network, all stations have the same group/multicast key that is sent to each station by the access point. However, for IBSS networks, there is no access point to set a common key so each station has its own group transmit key that it sends to all stations in the IBSS. This is achieved by executing the four-way handshake and group key handshake in both directions.

33.5.4 RSNA Key Hierarchy and Management.   RSNA defines a key management system that derives working (temporal) keys from a root master key. The exact key hierarchy varies slightly between TKIP and CCMP but broadly follows the same system. This section describes the key management system and notes the differences between TKIP and CCMP.

There are two key hierarchies: The first contains the pairwise keys that are shared between two wireless devices (e.g., between two stations in an IBSS or between a station and an access point in a BSS); the second hierarchy is the group/multicast keys that are used for network broadcasts, such as ARP requests or multicast traffic.

33.5.4.1 Pairwise Key Hierarchy.   There is a maximum of four levels of cryptographic keys in the pairwise key hierarchy.

1. **802.1X authentication keys.** These keys exist only if the supplicant and authentication server mutually authenticate one another using preinstalled keys. An example is EAP-TLS, which requires both the supplicant and authentication servers to have PKI credentials. The 802.1X keys are used to establish the pairwise master key (PMK).

EXHIBIT 33.13   TKIP Temporal Keys

Key Name	Length	Purpose
EAPOL-Key MIC key	128 bits	This key is the first 128 bits of the PTK and authenticates the EAPOL-Key messages that establish the temporal keys. The key is used to calculate a message integrity code (MIC).
EAPOL-Key Encryption key	128 bits	This key is bits 129 to 256 of the PTK and is used to encrypt the contents of EAPOL-Key management messages.
Temporal Encryption Key	128 bits	This key is bits 257 to 384 of the PTK and is used to encrypt a packet using WEP.
Temporal MIC key 1	64 bits	This key is bits 385 to 448 of the PTK and is used to authenticate messages in one direction.
Temporal MIC key 2	64 bits	This key is bits 449 to 512 of the PTK and is used to authenticate messages in the other direction.

2. **Pairwise master key.** The PMK is 256 bits and is either the key established in level 1 or a preshared key (PSK) installed in the devices. The PMK, device MAC addresses, and nonces are fed into a variable-length pseudorandom function (PRF) to generate a pairwise transient key (PTK). The nonces are derived from a 256-bit key counter that is initialized at system start-up from a random number, the time, and the MAC address. The nonce is then incremented every time a key is changed.

3. **Pairwise transient key.** The PTK varies in length from 128 bits to 512 bits and is split up into the required temporal keys. The key lengths and number of keys are dependent on the algorithm. For TKIP, the PTK is 512 bits, and this is split into five temporal keys. For CCMP, the PTK is 384 bits, split into three temporal keys.

4. **Temporal and per-packet keys.** The temporal keys are mixed with variable data such as packet counters, which has the effect of creating a fresh key for every packet. Exhibits 33.13 and 33.14 describe the TKIP and CCMP temporal keys.

Exhibit 33.15 shows the entire key hierarchy for TKIP.

33.5.4.2 Group Key Hierarchy.   The group key hierarchy is similarly structured to the pairwise key hierarchy. The authenticator creates a group master key. This

EXHIBIT 33.14   CCMP Temporal Keys

Key Name	Length	Purpose
EAPOL-Key MIC key	128 bits	This key is the first 128 bits of the PTK and is used to authenticate the EAPOL-Key management messages by calculating a MIC.
EAPOL-Key Encryption key	128 bits	This key is bits 129 to 256 of the PTK and is used to encrypt the contents of EAPOL-Key management messages.
Temporal Key 1	128 bits	This key is bits 257 to 384 of the PTK and is used for message encryption, authentication, and integrity. The nature of the CCM algorithm does not require a separate MIC key.

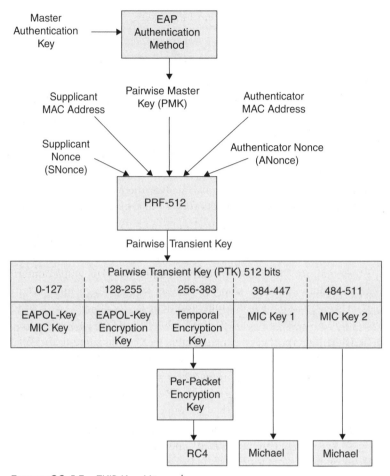

EXHIBIT 33.15   TKIP Key Hierarchy

master key, the authenticator's MAC address, and a group nonce (GNonce) are processed by the PRF to produce a group transient key (GTK), which is then split up into temporal keys.

33.5.5 Temporal Key Integrity Protocol.   The temporal key integrity protocol (TKIP) is a suite of algorithms to resolve the known security issues in WEP for the existing 802.11 equipment already in the field.

To ensure compatibility with the existing base of wireless products, TKIP had to take into account the hardware architecture of the existing wireless products.[49] Wireless products have two CPUs: The first is in the MAC chip that implements the wireless protocol, the second is the host CPU.

For access points, the host CPU is a dedicated CPU that runs the access point. For wireless LAN PC cards, the host CPU is that of the host PC. For performance reasons, most MAC chips have a hardware RC4 encryption engine to perform the encryption. To avoid an unacceptable performance impact by moving encryption to the host CPU, TKIP needed to use this existing MAC encryption engine. This required TKIP to continue to use RC4 and WEP, but in a way to overcome the identified problems.

The designers came up with a solution to the issues, and the result was TKIP with this functionality:

- A MAC service data unit (MSDU) is a message to be sent to another station.
- An MSDU may be fragmented into more than one MAC protocol data unit (MPDU). These data units are packets/frames sent by the physical layer.
- When all the MPDUs have been received, the recipient reconstructs the MSDU and passes it up the protocol stack.
- Each MSDU is authenticated and integrity protected, using a keyed cryptographic message integrity code (MIC).
- The source and destination addresses as well as the MSDU plaintext are included in the MIC calculation. This prevents forgery and masquerading attacks.
- Since the strength of the MIC is limited and can be compromised by trial and error, TKIP provides optional countermeasures that stop communications for a period of time (60 seconds) when an invalid MIC is received and then immediately forces a rekey of all stations. The designers estimated that the MIC with countermeasures would resist attack for about one year before an attacker would correctly guess the MIC. However, any measure that automatically interrupts service in response to probes also provides a mechanism for denial-of-service attacks.
- Each TKIP MPDU (packet) has a sequence number encoded in the WEP initialization vector. Any MPDUs that arrive out of order are dropped.
- TKIP mixes a temporal key, the transmitter's address, and a sequence counter in a two-phase protocol to form the RC4 WEP seed. The mixing is done in a way to defeat weak-key attacks.
- RSNA uses 802.1X EAPOL-key messages to regularly change the temporal keys so that RC4 key streams are not reused. The key change is triggered automatically when the sequence counter is close to exhaustion.

These controls largely address the issues identified in the current standard by introducing cryptographic message authentication, by preventing key stream reuse, and by never using a weak IV. However, TKIP is still not considered a strong solution because of the strength of the MIC. TKIP should be used only as an interim measure until existing equipment can be replaced with CCMP-capable equipment. Exhibit 33.16 and Exhibit 33.17 show the TKIP process in the transmitting and receiving stations. The phrase "using Michael" refers to a particular algorithm for generating a message integrity code (MIC).[50]

33.5.6 Counter Mode/CBC-MAC Protocol (CCMP).
CCMP is the mandatory protocol defined in 802.11i to provide confidentiality, authentication, integrity, and replay protection for the next generation of wireless equipment. It is not possible to upgrade existing equipment to use this protocol.

CCMP uses the Advanced Encryption Standard (AES) encryption in counter mode to provide confidentiality and CBC-MAC (AES-CCM) for message authentication and integrity. The inputs to the algorithm include:

- A 128-bit block cipher encryption key (the temporal key).
- A nonce based on an incrementing packet number that is used only once with the encryption key to encrypt a message. Reusing a nonce to encrypt more than one message destroys its security properties.

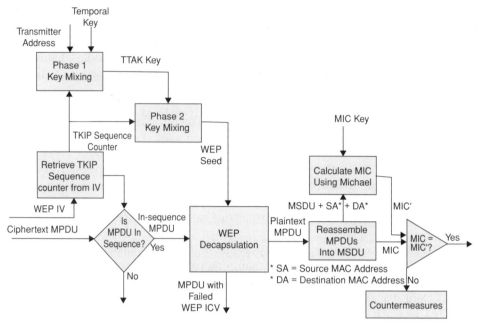

EXHIBIT 33.16 TKIP Algorithm in the Transmitting Station

- The message to be encrypted.
- Additional data to be authenticated but not encrypted, such as the packet header containing the source and destination MAC addresses.

33.5.7 Remaining Implementation Issues. The IEEE 802.11i standard has done a good job addressing the cryptographic flaws in the original standard. However, security is more than good cryptography, and organizations still are likely to be vulnerable if these new wireless networks are not implemented properly.

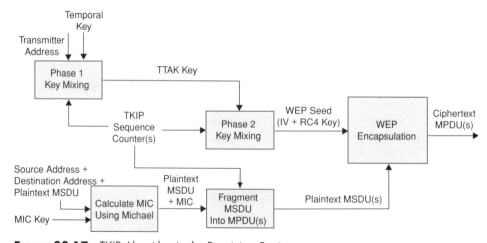

EXHIBIT 33.17 TKIP Algorithm in the Receiving Station

As an example, the standard still supports the original broken protocols to facilitate transition to the new protocols. In addition, the Wi-Fi Alliance says that the new protocols are not enabled by default in new equipment.[51] This means that users who just install the equipment and turn it on will have a completely open network. Additionally, by including the original broken protocols in the new standards, users will still use them, giving attackers the opportunity to compromise the network.

By necessity, the standard supports preshared keys for home use and for smaller organizations that do not have the required authentication server infrastructure. These preshared keys can be entered as a cryptographic key or calculated from a password.

There are three issues with preshared keys. The first is that password based preshared keys are vulnerable to an off-line dictionary attack.[52] This means that the use of poor passwords by users enables the network to be compromised. A number of open source tools, such as Aircrack[53] and coWPAtty,[54] have been developed to automate the attack.

The second issue with preshared keys is that the device is authenticated, rather than the user, and any staff who leave an organization with knowledge of the preshared key may still be able to connect to the network from the outside. The final issue is that the standard states that the installation of preshared keys is outside its scope. This fact suggests that the issue we have today with vendors having poor key management tools, and well-known default keys, could plague the new system too.

The standard focuses heavily on using external authentication servers such as RADIUS to do the authentication and management of the master keys. Unfortunately, home users and smaller organizations are unlikely to have this type of authentication infrastructure. Unless wireless products have built-in user authentication servers, preshared keys will dominate, and the usual avenues of attack, such as default keys and bad passwords, could compromise the system.

33.5.8 Wi-Fi Alliance's WPA and WPA2 Standards.   The Wi-Fi Alliance is a nonprofit organization formed to certify the interoperability of 802.11 products. It is also the organization behind the Wi-Fi labels seen on wireless equipment such as the one shown in Exhibit 33.18.

EXHIBIT 33.18   Wi-Fi Alliance Certification Label

The Wi-Fi Alliance was concerned that the security issues surrounding WEP would hinder the adoption of wireless products, so it worked with the IEEE to quickly bring to market a security standard in advance of 802.11i.

This standard is called Wi-Fi Protected Access (WPA). To maintain compatibility with 802.11i, WPA is just a subset of it. The functionality in WPA consists of TKIP so that existing equipment can be upgraded, 802.1X authentication, and the 802.11i key hierarchy and management system. WPA also includes the preshared key option for home users and for small businesses that do not have a RADIUS infrastructure. This preshared key is based on a password and is vulnerable to an off-line dictionary attack as described.

Wi-Fi Alliance also has a second standard called WPA2. This standard is just another name for the completed 802.11i standard, which includes protocols for stronger data protection based on the AES encryption algorithm. Like WPA, there are two versions of the WPA2: WPA2-Personal, which uses a password to authenticate access to the network, and WPA-Enterprise, which uses an authentication server. Like WPA, WPA2 is designed to secure all 802.11 devices, including 802.11b, 802.11a, and 802.11g.

The Wi-Fi Alliance has many white papers available on its Web site (www.wi-fi.org). One paper to read in particular is "Deploying Wi-Fi Protected Access (WPA™) and WPA2™ in the Enterprise," which provides a good overview of the WPA and WPA2 features along with guidance on how to implement them.

33.6 802.11 SECURITY AUDITING TOOLS. This section looks at the open source and commercial tools available to help audit a wireless environment and to understand the tools that war-drivers have to attack a network. Exhibit 33.19 lists the main programs available and the platform they run under.

33.6.1 Auditor and BackTrack. The first step for anyone wanting to setup a DIY wireless auditing system is to download the Auditor security tool collection from www.remote-exploit.org. Auditor is a live Linux distribution with all the required security tools and patched drivers to do wireless security auditing. All that is necessary is to download the ISO, burn it, and boot it up from the CD-ROM on any PC.

It does access-point emulation, client penetration, LEAP/PPTP cracking, packet injection, scanning, and MAC address changing as well as WEP and WPA PSK cracking. Work is under way to replace Auditor with a new distribution called BackTrack.

33.6.2 Kismet. Kismet is the best open-source wireless auditing tool available, meeting the majority of core requirements. It detects broadcasting and nonbroadcasting access points, and the stations associated to them, as well as stations searching for an access point to connect to. It is a part of the Auditor security distribution and has been well integrated to reduce the configuration issues. Work is in progress on a complete rebuild of the code to improve maintenance and performance.

Being Linux based, Kismet can be cross-compiled for Linux-capable PDAs such as the iPaq and Sharp Zaurus SL-5500.

33.6.3 Netstumbler. Netstumbler[55] is a well-known Windows program used by many war-drivers. The program works by sending out broadcast probe requests (messages searching for wireless networks with which to associate). When an access point receives a probe request, it sends back a probe response containing information that identifies the network. Netstumbler collects this information and displays it in a GUI interface.

Exhibit 33.19 802.11 Security Auditing Software

Tool	Description and Home Page	Operating System
Aircrack	A program that breaks WEP encryption, injects packets (Aireplay) and performs a dictionary attack against WPA PSK. www.aircrack-ng.org	Linux Windows
Auditor	A security collection with all the required drivers and security tools to audit or hack wireless networks. www.remote-exploit.org	Linux
Airmagnet	A commercial wireless LAN analyzer that runs on laptop PCs and pocket PCs. www.airmagnet.com	Windows Pocket PC
Airsnort	Breaks WEP encryption using the RC4 Key Scheduling Vulnerability and Korek optimizations. http://airsnort.shmoo.com/	Linux
Airopeek NX	A commercial wireless LAN analyzer that runs on laptop and tablet PCs. www.wildpackets.com	Windows
BackTrack	A Linux security distribution and is the result of the merging of the Whax and Auditor security collections. www.remote-exploit.org	Linux
CoWPAtty	A WPA PSK cracker. http://sourceforge.net/projects/coWPAtty	Linux
Ethereal	A program that understands the format of packets and dumps out their contents. Can capture packets as well as process a log file created by other programs, such as Airsnort. A skilled person can use Ethereal to ensure that the wireless network is configured properly. www.ethereal.com	Linux Windows
Expert Observer	A commercial wireless analyzer. www.networkinstruments.com	Windows
Kismet	The best open source/freeware wireless auditing tool available, and one that is still being actively developed and improved. http://www.kismetwireless.net/	Linux
Linux-wlan	The Linux drivers for Intersil Prism 2, 2.5, and 3- based cards used by open source software such as Kismet and Wellenreiter. www.linux-wlan.com/linux-wlan/	Linux
NAI Sniffer	Network Associates Sniffer—a commercial network analyzer that runs on laptop PCs and pocket PCs. www.sniffer.com	Windows
Netstumbler	Detects broadcasting 802.11 networks. Netstumbler is not suitable as a network auditing tool because access points can be configured to avoid detection. Netstumbler also does not detect stations. www.netstumbler.com	Windows
Wellenreiter	Provides similar functionality to Netstumbler in that it detects access points. However, Wellenreiter has a major advantage over Netstumbler in that it detects access points that Netstumbler cannot see. www.wellenreiter.net/	Linux
Windows XP wireless client	A built-in wireless subsystem that displays a list of available networks.	Windows XP

To combat the Netstumbler threat, wireless vendors have implemented a "closed network" option that does not respond to broadcast probe requests. This option is effective in avoiding detection by Netstumbler. Additionally, Netstumbler does not detect network stations. Therefore, it will not tell how many stations there are connected to a network, or whether there are any unattached stations that a rogue access point could associate to and use to attack the network.

These limitations make Netstumbler unsuitable for wireless network auditing purposes.

33.6.4   Airsnort.   Airsnort[56] is an open-source Linux program that implements the Fluhrer, Mantin and Shamir,[57] and Korek[58] optimizations to crack a WEP key. It is not a wireless auditing tool, although it does display a list of access points and captures packets, which can be viewed in tools such as Ethereal to help ensure that a network is properly configured.

33.6.5   CoWPAtty and Aircrack.   CoWPAtty is a tool that does a dictionary attack against the WPA PSK algorithm. CoWPAtty must be provided with a libpcap[59] file containing a four-way handshake as well as a dictionary file. The tool then locates the four-way handshake and uses the dictionary to determine the password. The program can be downloaded from http://sourceforge.net/projects/coWPAtty and is included in the Auditor distribution.

Aircrack is a suite of tools that enables the capture of wireless traffic, cracks WEP, injects packets, (aireplay) and performs dictionary attacks against the WPA PSK algorithm. It is being actively developed as aircrack-ng. The program can be downloaded from www.aircrack-ng.org and is included in the Auditor distribution.

33.6.6   Ethereal.   Ethereal is a well-regarded open-source packet capture and analyzer program available on both UNIX and Windows. It is a useful tool to enable a network engineer to check that the wireless network is correctly configured. In particular, it will highlight the presence of clear text traffic (e.g., broadcasts). Ethereal needs to be patched to interface directly with the wireless drivers. To avoid patching, other packet capture tools, such as Airsnort, can be used and then analyzed by Ethereal.

33.6.7   Wellenreiter.   Of all the wireless auditing programs, Wellenreiter is the easiest to get going because it is a Perl program that auto-detects the model of a wireless card and configures itself accordingly.

Wellenreiter has an advantage over Netstumbler in that it detects hidden nonbroadcasting access points. However, it has these shortcomings that limit its usefulness as a wireless auditing tool:

- Wellenreiter only supports 802.11b devices. There is no support for 802.11a or 802.11g.

- It does not list the stations attached to the access points or any unattached stations searching for an access point to connect to.

- It does not provide any signal strength information, so it is hard to track down the source of a signal.

A C++ Opie version is available for running on Linux handhelds such as the iPaq and the Sharp Zaurus. The program can be downloaded from www.wellenreiter.net and is included in the Auditor distribution.

33.6.8 Commercial Wireless Auditing Tools.   Even though Kismet is a respectable tool for wireless auditing, it does not have the functionality of the commercial wireless auditing tools. As well as network management and diagnostic functions, these tools enable an audit of the environment. The available tools include:

- Airmagnet by Airmagnet Inc.
- Airopeek NX by Wildpackets Inc.
- Network Observer by Network Instruments LLC
- Sniffer by Network Associates

33.7 CONCLUSION.   802.11 wireless LAN networks are now a mainstream technology. Approximately a quarter of all businesses have installed them, and consumers have mass-adopted them so they can access their broadband connections from all the PCs at home. Telecommunications companies have rolled out public wireless LAN networks in cities, airports, hotels, railway stations, and coffee shops, enabling broadband access on the move.

Enthusiasts have extended the range of wireless LANs to over 20 miles by modifying old satellite TV dishes and are actively using these to provide broadband access in out-of-the-way places. This technology is here to stay, and its use will become increasingly widespread in homes, businesses, banks, government departments, doctor's offices, and hospitals.

However, wireless technology brings with it risks that need to be managed. The technology, based on radio waves, allows unauthorized individuals outside the physical confines of the home or office to receive these radio signals. It is a hobby for some people to search for wireless networks and to break into them.

Without the proper security controls, unauthorized individuals could connect to the network, compromising sensitive business or personal information such as banking and medical details. The wrong people connecting to a network could inflict huge amounts of damage to the IT systems, even crippling an organization.

The trend in networking today is to interconnect with other partners' networks, and with public networks such as the Internet, and to allow staff to connect directly to the LAN via the Internet, using technologies such as VPNs. A wireless LAN is just another means, with vulnerabilities enabling authorized and unauthorized individuals to connect to the network. These types of risks emphasize the need to secure each host on an internal network from attack.

The 802.11i standard has provided two upgraded security systems to address the security issues with the original system. The first is called TKIP, based on WEP and designed to upgrade existing equipment in the field. This system is also known as WPA.

The second security system is called CCMP. It is based on AES and is designed for new equipment with more powerful processors. It is also known as WPA2. WPA and WPA2 resolve the current identified issues in the original security system. However, they are not panaceas because both systems have a preshared key option, which is vulnerable to an off-line dictionary attack. Additionally, the 802.11i standard still includes the original broken protocols, so organizations could still be vulnerable to attack should administrators or staff install equipment in its default state.

While the 802.11i standard has addressed most of the technical issues in the original standard, there is still a lot of existing equipment installed that cannot be upgraded. For these circumstances, interim measures such as these are needed to secure the existing networks:

- **Treat a wireless network like any other untrusted network** and use well-researched and understood security mechanisms, such as IPSEC or SSL VPNs, to secure the link layer. Additionally, connect the wireless network to an untrusted zone and strongly authenticate the users before allowing access to the internal network.

- **Issue a corporate policy on wireless LANs.** Without a policy, the organization has no framework to control wireless LAN usage.

- **Publicize and enforce the policy.** Unless people are aware that a policy exists and that it is actively enforced via procedures and regular audits, the policy will be ineffective.

- **Develop an approved wireless LAN architecture,** configuration standards, and operating procedures that allow the technology to be quickly and securely implemented and used.

33.8   APPENDIX 33A–802.11 STANDARDS.   This section provides an overview of the 802.11 family of standards and indicates the standards that are relevant to this chapter. Further details can be found on the Internet home page for the IEEE 802.11 group of standards, www.ieee802.org/11/index/shtml. From this page you can get to the rest of the site, two pages in particular should be highlighted:

- The first contains the working group project timelines.[60] As well as the projected dates for each project developing a standard, this page contains links to the approval letters that contain the scope, purpose, and reason for the project, along with additional background information. This page also contains links to the standards for the working groups that have completed their work.

- The second page to highlight is the 802.11 standards download page.[61] The standards become available for free download six months after publication under the Get IEEE 802® program.

33.8.1   802.11 and 802.11b: MAC and Physical Layer Specifications.
ANSI/IEEE Std 802.11-1999 is the base wireless LAN standard that is the subject of this chapter.[62] The 1999 standard is an update to the original 802.11-1997 standard. The 802.11b standard is a higher-speed physical layer extension to 802.11 that does not specify any extra security functionality.[63] Therefore, the security functionality analyzed in this chapter originates from the 802.11-1999 standard.

33.8.2   802.11a: 5GHz High-Speed Physical Layer.   The IEEE/ANSI standard 802.11a-1999 implements a higher-speed physical layer operating in the 5GHz radio band in conjunction with the existing 802.11 MAC. 802.11b operates in the 2.4GHz band and has a maximum speed of 11Mb/s, whereas 802.11a has a maximum speed of 54Mb/s.

802.11a uses the same MAC layer as 802.11b; therefore, it has the same security functionality and vulnerabilities.

Currently, 802.11a does not comply with European requirements so it cannot be freely used in Europe. The 802.11h standard was produced to address these issues.

33.8.3   802.11d: 802.11 Additional Regulatory Domains.   Each country controls the use of the radio spectrum within its jurisdiction, and there are varying levels of conformity between countries. The current 802.11 standard defines operation in only a few regulatory jurisdictions. The purpose of the 802.11d standard is to define the physical layer requirements to allow the use of 802.11 wireless LANs in more countries.

33.8.4   802.11e: MAC Enhancements for Quality of Service.   The IEEE 802.11e standard provides MAC enhancements for quality of service. This enables WLANs to support time-sensitive multimedia applications, such as video and audio on demand, as well as Voice over IP.

33.8.5   802.11F: Inter–Access Point Protocol.   When a user's station roams from one access point to another, there are a series of messages exchanged between the access points so that the station is registered with only one access point at a time and so as to pick up any buffered packets for the station that may not have been delivered while it was moving between locations. The 802.11 standard did not define any standards for these inter–access point communications, resulting in a lack of interoperability between vendors' products.

802.11F specifies the necessary messaging between access points to allow interoperability between products. However, this standard was a trial use recommended practice and has since been withdrawn.

33.8.6   802.11g: Higher-Rate Extension to 802.11b.   The 802.11g standard defined a new physical layer allowing similar data rates as the 802.11a standard (54Mb/s) in the 2.4GHz band but not specifying any extra security functionality.

33.8.7   802.11h: Spectrum Managed 802.11a.   The 802.11h standard enhances the current 802.11 MAC and 802.11a physical specification with spectrum and power management extensions to enable the 802.11a standard to be used in Europe.

33.8.8   802.11i: MAC Security Enhancements.   The 802.11i standard was developed to improve the security of 802.11 wireless networks, in particular to address the issues with WEP. The standard can be downloaded for free from the IEEE Web site,[64] and its contents are covered in depth in Section 33.5.

33.8.9   802.11j: 4.9Ghz–5GHz Operation in Japan.   The 802.11j standard enhances the 802.11 standard, to add channel selection for 4.9 GHz and 5 GHz in Japan to conform to the Japanese rules on operational mode, operational rate, radiated power, spurious emissions, and channel sense.

33.8.10   802.11k: Radio Resource Measurement Enhancements.
The purpose of the 802.11k working group is to define and expose radio and network information to facilitate the management and maintenance of wireless LANs. Currently, wireless clients associate to an access point with the strongest signal. This

can lead to throughput issues if too many clients are using one access point. Through this standard, wireless clients will know when an access point is overloaded, enabling them to choose an underutilized one instead.

This standard will put information requiring security into the measurement frames. The 802.11w working group has been set up to secure this information. The contents of this standard are not further considered in this chapter.[65]

33.8.11   802.11m: Maintenance.   The purpose of the 802.11m working group is to incorporate editorial and technical corrections to the existing standards as well as to provide clarifications and interpretations.[66]

33.8.12   802.11n: Enhancements for Higher Throughput.   The purpose of the 802.11n working group is to define the next-generation physical layer to increase the throughput of wireless LANs up to 600Mbps.[67]

33.8.13   802.11p: Wireless Access for the Vehicular Environment (WAVE).   To quote the working group's status report, "This Task Group will define enhancements to 802.11 required to support Intelligent Transportation Systems (ITS) applications. This includes data exchange between high-speed vehicles and between these vehicles and the roadside infrastructure in the licensed ITS band of 5.9 GHz." Practical applications of this standard include road-toll collection, but other applications include information provision, paying for services, or messaging between vehicles.[68]

33.8.14   802.11r: Fast Roaming/Fast BSS Transition.   The purpose of the 802.11r working group is to develop a standard for fast transitions between access points and to establish the required quality of service before the transition. The primary application for this standard is Voice over Wireless LANs (VoWLAN). It will address the issues with the current standard, where the handover time from one access point to another is measured in hundreds of milliseconds, which could lead to voice degradation and drop-outs.[69]

33.8.15   802.11s: ESS Mesh Networking.   The purpose of the 802.11s working group is to develop a self-configuring multihop wireless distribution system to provide mesh networking. Conventional access points are physically connected to the core network. This can be costly, especially for outdoor municipal wireless networks and for historical buildings with construction restrictions. With wireless mesh networks, the access points connect directly to each other via the wireless medium and can route through the wireless mesh to access services on the wired network. This significantly reduces the cabling required and deployment costs. In the case of historical buildings, network coverage may be provided without any construction activities.

33.8.16   802.11T: Wireless Performance Prediction (WPP).   The purpose of the 802.11T project is to produce a recommended practice for testing, comparison, and deployment planning of 802.11 WLAN devices based on a common and accepted set of performance metrics, measurement methodologies, and test conditions.[70]

33.8.17   802.11u: Interworking with External Networks.   The purpose of this project is to develop a standard specifying interworking with external networks. This objective is to improve the user experience with wireless hot spots, addressing issues such as enrollment, network selection, and authorization for roaming.

33.8.18   802.11v: Wireless Network Management.

The purpose of the 802.11v project is to enable the management of attached wireless stations through a layer 2 mechanism. While the 802.11k project is defining standards for retrieving information from stations, this project will provide the ability to configure the stations. This will be particularly useful for situations where stations need to be configured before they are able to setup an IP connection.[71]

33.8.19   802.11w: Protected Management Frames.

The purpose of the 802.11w project, according to the approval letter, is "to improve the security of some or all 802.11 management frames by defining enhancements such as data integrity, data origin authenticity, replay protection, and data confidentiality."

While 802.11i improved security for WLAN data frames, it did not provide any additional security for the management frames. These frames include the existing deauthentication and disassociation frames that hackers use today to attack WPA/PSK and to launch DoS attacks as well as including the new management frames being created by standards in development, such as 802.11k and 802.11v. These new standards are introducing network management features, which if not protected could be used to attack the network. For an overview on 802.11w, refer to a *Network World* article by Epstein.[72]

33.8.20   802.11y: 3650–3700MHz Operation in the United States.

The 802.11y working group is producing an amendment to the existing 802.11 standard to enable wireless LAN operations in the 3650–3700MHz band for the United States.

33.8.21   802.1x: Port-Based Network Access Control.

802.1X is a published standard to enable the authentication and authorization of network devices before access is provided to the network. 802.1X also enables session keys to be established for the encryption and authentication of frames. This standard is at the heart of the 802.11i security system and is covered in more detail in Section 33.5.2.

33.8.22   Wi-Fi Protected Access (WPA) and WPA2.

WPA is a wireless security standard published by the Wi-Fi Alliance. Its purpose was to address the security issues with current 802.11 wireless products in the interim period until the 802.11i standard was ratified. Strictly speaking, WPA is not an IEEE 802.11 standard; however, WPA is based on stable protocols in a late draft of the 802.11i standard.

WPA2 is the name the Wi-Fi Alliance has given to the strong security mechanisms based on the AES algorithm published in 802.11i. For more information, refer to Section 33.5.8.

33.9   APPENDIX 33B: ABBREVIATIONS, TERMINOLOGY, AND DEFINITIONS.

Most of these abbreviations and definitions originate from the ANSI/IEEE 802.11-1999 standard[73] and the 802.11i standard.[74]

Abbreviation/ Term	Meaning/Definition
802.11	The ANSI/IEEE standard 802.11, 1999 edition. Wireless LAN medium access control (MAC) and physical layer (PHY) specifications.
802.11a	This extension to the 802.11 standard provides an improved throughput of up to 54Mb/S in the 5GHz frequency band.
802.11b	The ANSI/IEEE 802.11b specification is an extension to the 802.11 standard that specifies a higher-speed physical layer (up to 11Mb/s). The rest of the 802.11 standard is unchanged.
802.11d	This standard extends the original 802.11 standard to define physical layers, allowing 802.11 to operate in additional countries.
802.11e	This standard enhances the current 802.11 MAC to provide quality of service support.
802.11F	This withdrawn standard specifies inter–access point messaging to provide multivendor interoperability.
802.11g	This standard provides an improved throughput of up to 54Mb/s in the 2.4GHz band.
802.11h	This standard provides spectrum and transmit-power enhancements to the 802.11a 5GHz standard for Europe.
802.11i	This standard enhanced the 802.11 MAC to provide improvements in security. This standard defined the WPA and WPA2 security systems.
802.11j	This extension to the original 802.11 standard provides operation in the 4.9Ghz and 5GHz bands in Japan.
802.11k	This standard is in development to facilitate the management of wireless LANs.
802.11m	This standard is a maintenance release to incorporate editorial and technical changes into the existing standards.
802.11n	This is a standard in development to provide higher speeds. Current proposals provide a throughput up to 600Mb/s.
802.11p	This is a standard in development to support intelligent transportation applications, such as road-toll collection.
802.11r	This is a standard in development to provide fast roaming and transition in support of real-time applications, such as voice in wireless LANs.
802.11s	This is a standard in development to provide mesh networking.
802.11T	This is the development of a recommended practice to evaluate wireless LAN performance.
802.11u	This is a standard in development to improve the user experience for public wireless networks.
802.11v	This is a standard in development to manage wireless stations.
802.11w	This is a standard in development to improve the security of 802.11 management frames.
802.11y	This is a standard in development to define a wireless service for the 3650–3700MHz band in the United States.
802.1X	IEEE Std 802.1X-2001 defines port-based network access controls. It provides the means to authenticate and authorize a network device before granting access to network resources.[75]
Access controller	The CAPWAP term for a wireless switch that controls and manages light-weight access points (LWAPs).
Access point (AP)	A specialized wireless station that bridges other wireless stations to the physical wired network or distribution system.

(Continued)

Abbreviation/ Term	Meaning/Definition
Authenticator	An 802.1X component that authenticates a network device before allowing it to access network resources
Authentication server (AS)	An 802.1X component that performs the actual authentication of the supplicant on behalf of the authenticator.
BSS	Basic service set. A set of stations controlled by a single coordination function (an access point).
CAPWAP	Control and provisioning of wireless access points. An IETF initiative to establish standards enabling interoperability between different vendors access points and wireless switches.
CBC-MAC	Cipher block chain—message authentication code. A message authentication algorithm based on a symmetric block cipher, where each block chains into the next data block.
CCMP	Counter mode with CBC-MAC protocol. A symmetric block cipher mode providing data privacy using counter mode and data origin authentication using CBC-MAC. This is the protocol required for compliance with the WPA2 standard.
CRC	Cyclic redundancy check.
CRC-32	A 32-bit CRC used in the 802.11 standard.
Distribution system (DS)	A system used to interconnect a set of basic service sets (BSS) to create an extended service set (ESS).
DMZ	Demilitarized zone. Refers to a network segment that separates and protects a trusted network from an untrusted one.
DSSS	Direct sequence spread spectrum. An 802.11 modulation technique that spreads signal power over a wide band of frequencies.
DTLS	Datagram transport layer security. Essentially TLS over UDP.
EAP	Extensible authentication protocol defined in RFC 2284.[76]
EAP-PEAP	Protected EAP. A draft IETF standard by RSA, Microsoft, and CISCO for doing EAP authentication protected by TLS.[77]
EAP-TLS	EAP–transport layer security defined in RFC 2716.[78]
EAP-TTLS	EAP–tunneled TLS authentication protocol. A draft IETF standard that tunnels EAP authentication through TLS.[79]
EAPOL	EAP over LANs. The protocol defined in 802.1X for encapsulating EAP messages exchanged between a wireless station and the access point.
ESS	Extended service set. A set of one or more interconnected basic service sets (BSSs) and integrated LANs that appears as a single BSS to wireless stations.
Exclusive-Or (XOR)	An add-without-carry logical operation. XOR is used in cryptographic algorithms partly because it is reversible by repeating an operation. A XOR B XOR A will result in B; A XOR B XOR B will result in A
FHSS	Frequency-hopping spread spectrum. A transmission method that sends bursts of data over a number of frequencies, with the system hopping between frequencies in a defined way.
IBSS	Independent basic service set. An ad hoc wireless network where stations communication directly with one another rather than via an access point.
ICV	Integrity check value. A CRC-32 value used by the WEP algorithm to detect changes in the ciphertext and to ensure that the packet has been decrypted correctly.

(Continued)

Abbreviation/ Term	Meaning/Definition
IV	Initialization vector. A 24-bit value prepended to the WEP key, which is used as the seed for the RC4 stream cipher as part of the WEP algorithm.
KSA	The key scheduling algorithm of the RC4 stream cipher.
LAN	An IEEE 802 local area network.
LWAP	Light-weight access point. A type of access point that is essentially an 802.11 wireless radio that passes the received packets to a wireless switch for processing.
LWAPP	Light-weight access point protocol. The base protocol chosen for the CAPWAP protocol and used by wireless switches to manage and communicate with access points.
MAC	Medium access control. The data link layer in a wireless LAN that enables stations to share a common transmission medium.
Mb/s	Megabits per second.
MIC	Message integrity code. A cryptographic integrity code to detect changes in a message.
Michael	The message integrity code (MIC) for TKIP.
MITM	Man in the middle. An MITM attack is one where an attacker can sit between two communicating parties and monitor what is being exchanged, without being noticed.
MPDU	MAC protocol data unit. The packets/frames exchanged between stations via the physical layer.
MSDU	MAC service data unit. Information that is to be delivered as a unit between MAC service access points (SAP). If an MSDU is too large to fit into one MPDU, then it will be fragmented into multiple MPDUs and reassembled into one MSDU by the receiver.
OFDM	Orthogonal frequency division multiplexing. A modulation technique used in the 802.11a and 802.11g standards that works by dividing data into several pieces and simultaneously sending the pieces on many different subchannels. This mechanism enables throughput of up to 54 Mb/s.
PAE	Port access entity. An 802.1X object that operates the authentication mechanism in the participants.
PKI	Public key infrastructure.
PMK	Pairwise master key. A master session key derived from the overall master key. For 802.1X authentication mechanisms (e.g., EAP-TLS), the key is generated during authentication. For preshared key authentication, the PMK is the preshared key (PSK).
Port	Network access port.
PRF	Pseudorandom function. An RSNA-defined algorithm that is part of the key generation function.
PSK	Preshared key. A static cryptographic key that is distributed out of band to all stations in the wireless network.
PTK	Pairwise transient key. An RSNA cryptographic key that is the source of working temporal keys that protect wireless messages.
RADIUS	Remote authentication dial-in user service, defined in RFC 2865.[80]
RSN	Robust security network. The name for the new security system implemented in the 802.11i draft standard. An RSN is one that only allows the creation of RSN associations.

(Continued)

Abbreviation/ Term	Meaning/Definition
RSNA	A robust security network association is where two stations have authenticated each other and associated using the four-way handshake protocol.
RSN IE	Robust security network information element. The RSN IE is contained in Beacon and probe frames, and lists the supported authentication mechanisms and cipher suites.
Supplicant	The 802.1X term for the network device that wants to connect to the network.
"The standard"	In this chapter, the term refers to the ANSI/IEEE standard 802.11, 1999 edition.
TKIP	Temporal key integrity protocol. A suite of algorithms enhancing the WEP protocol to provide secure operations for existing 802.11 equipment.
TLS	Transport layer security defined in RFC 2246
TSN	Transient security network. A TSN can form associations with both RSNA-capable and pre-RSNA stations.
UDP	User datagram protocol. An Internet protocol used to send short messages to other systems. UDP does not provide any reliability or ordering guarantees.
WEP	Wired equivalent privacy. The protocol defined in the 802.11-1999 standard to encrypt data on a wireless LAN.
Wireless LAN	In this chapter, the term refers to 802.11 wireless local area networks using a radio physical layer.
WLAN	Wireless local area network.
WTP	Wireless termination point. The CAPWAP term for an access point.
WPA	Wi-Fi protected access. WPA was the first 802.11 wireless security standard from the Wi-Fi Alliance, using the TKIP security mechanism in the 802.11i standard.
WPA2	Wi-Fi protected access V2. WPA2 is the Wi-Fi Alliance's name for the AES-based CCMP wireless security mechanisms in the 802.11i standard.
XOR	Exclusive-OR.

33.10 FURTHER READING

Anjum, F., and P. Mouchtaris. *Security for Wireless Ad Hoc Networks*. Hoboken, NJ: John Wiley & Sons, 2007.

Edney, J., and W. A. Arbaugh. *Real 802.11 Security: Wi-Fi Protected Access and 802.11i*. Boston: Addison-Wesley, 2003.

Gast, M. *802.11 Wireless Networks: The Definitive Guide*, 2nd ed. Sebastopol, CA: O'Reilly & Associates, 2005.

Hassler, V. *Security Fundamentals for E-Commerce*. Norwood, MA: Artech House, 2000.

Laurent-Maknavicius, M., and H. Chaouchi, eds. *Mobile and Wireless Networks Security: Proceedings of the Mwns 2008 Workshop*. Hackensack, NJ: World Scientific Publishing, 2008.

Makki, S., P. Reiher, K. Makki, N. Pissinou, and S. Makki, eds. *Mobile and Wireless Network Security and Privacy*. New York: Springer, 2007.

Vacca, J. R.. *Guide to Wireless Network Security*. New York: Springer, 2006.

Wheat, J., R. Hiser, J. Tucker, A. Neely, and A. McCullough. *Designing a Wireless Network*. Rockland, MA: Syngress Publishing, 2001.

Xiao, Y., X. Shen, and D-Z. Du, eds. *Wireless Network Security*. New York: Springer, 2007.

Zhang, Y., J. Zheng, and H. Hu, eds. *Security in Wireless Mesh Networks*. Boca Raton, FL: Auerbach, 2008.

33.11   NOTES

1. Matthew Gast, *802.11 Wireless Networks: The Definitive Guide,* 2nd ed. (Sebastopol, CA: O'Reilly & Associates, 2005).

2. L. Yang, P. Zerfos, and E. Sadot, RFC4118—Architecture Taxonomy for Control and Provisioning of Wireless Access Points (CAPWAP).

3. J. Wheat, R. Hiser, J. Tucker, A. Neely, and A. McCullough, *Designing a Wireless Network* (Rockland, MA: Syngress Publishing Inc, 2001); ANSI/IEEE Std 802.11, 1999 Edition—Part 11: Wireless LAN Medium Access Control (MAC) and Physical Layer (PHY) Specification.

4. International Organisation for Standardisation, Information Technology, *Open Systems Interconnection, Basic Reference Model, Part 2: Security Architecture,* ISO IS 7498-2, 1989.

5. Wheat et al., Designing a Wireless Network.

6. Gast, 802.11 Wireless Networks.

7. www.ietf.org/html.charters/capwap-charter.html.

8. B. O'Hara, P. Calhoun, and J. Kempf, RFC3990,Configuration and Provisioning for Wireless Access Points (CAPWAP) Problem Statement.

9. Yang, Zerfos, and Sadot, RFC4118.

10. www.ietf.org/Internet-drafts/draft-ietf-capwap-protocol-specification-01.txt.

11. N. Modadugu and E. Rescorla, "The Design and Implementation of Datagram TLS," http://crypto.stanford.edu/~nagendra/papers/dtls.pdf.

12. "AAA is an architectural framework for configuring a set of three independent security functions in a consistent manner. AAA provides a modular way of performing the following services: Authentication . . . Authorization . . . Accounting . . . ." For further details, see the Cisco AAA Overview: www.cisco.com/en/US/docs/ios/12_2/security/configuration/guide/scfaaa.html.

13. Vesna Hassler, *Security Fundamentals for E-Commerce* (Norwood, MA: Artech House, 2000).

14. Dorothy and Peter Denning, *Internet Besieged: Countering Cyberspace Scofflaws* (ACM Press).

15. International Organisation for Standardisation, Information Technology, *Open Systems Interconnection, Basic Reference Model, Part 2.* ISO/IEC 9834-2: 1993.

16. www.oreillynet.com/pub/a/wireless/2001/05/03/longshot.html.

17. Peter Shipley, "Open WLANs—The Early Years of WarDriving," www.dis.org/filez/openlans.pdf.

18. www.trevormarshall.com/biquad.htm.

19. www.radiolabs.com.

20. ANSI/IEEE Standard 802.11, 1999 ed., Part 11: Wireless LAN Medium Access Control (MAC) and Physical Layer (PHY) Specification.

21. S. Fluhrer, I. Mantin, and A. Shamir, "Weaknesses in the Key Scheduling Algorithm of RC4." http://ftp.cs.cornell.edu/people/egs/615/rc4_ksaproc.pdf.

22. Shipley, "Open WLANs."

23. "Out of Thin Air: A Wireless Network Security Survey of London," Orthus Ltd.; The Wireless Security Survey of London—One year on . . . ; www.rsasecurity.com/worldwide/downloads/LondonWirelessSurvey2002.pdf.

24. www.dti.gov.uk/industries/information_security/pdfs/DTI_ISBS_2006_tech_report.pdf.

25. For more background see the Wikipedia article: http://en.wikipedia.org/wiki/Warchalking.

26. http://theillustratednetwork.mvps.org/WM2003/ActiveSync/WM2003Active SyncConfiguration.html.

27. www.wlan.org.uk/ and www.toaster.net/wireless/community.html.

28. www.theregister.co.uk/content/69/31567.html.

29. http://airsnarf.shmoo.com.

30. ANSI/IEEE Standard 802.11, 1999 ed. Part 11.

31. http://standards.ieee.org/getieee802/download/802.11i-2004.pdf.

32. ANSI/IEEE Standard 802.11, 1999 ed., Part 11.

33. N. Borisov, I. Goldberg, and D. Wagner, "Intercepting Mobile Communications: The Insecurity of 802.11." ACM, ISBN: 1-58113-422-3.

34. ANSI/IEEE Standard 802.11, 1999 ed., Part 11.

35. Steven Bellovin, "Problem Areas for the IP Security Protocols." www.cis.upenn.edu/~cis700-2.

36. Gast, 802.11 Wireless Networks papers/probable_plaintext-cryptanalysis-of-ipsec.ps.g2.

37. Borisov, Goldberg, and Wagner, "Intercepting Mobile Communications."

38. Borisov, Goldberg, and Wagner, "Intercepting Mobile Communications."

39. H. Krawczyk, M. Bellare, and R. Canetti, "IETF RFC2104, HMAC: Keying Hash functions for Message Authentication ftp://ftp.crt.dfn.de/pub/docs/crypt/bck2.ps.g2."

40. www.iss.net/wireless/WirelessLAN802_11bSecurityFAQ.htm.

41. Fluhrer, Mantin, and Shamir, "Weaknesses in the Key Scheduling Algorithm of RC4."

42. A. Stubblefield, J. Ioannidis, and A. Rubin, "Using the Fluhrer, Mantin, and Shamir Attack to Break WEP." AT&T Labs technical report TD4ZCPZZ August 6th 2001.

43. www.netstumbler.org/showthread.php?p=89692#post89692.

44. "WEP: Dead Again, Part 1" www.securityfocus.com/infocus/1814, and Part 2 www.securityfocus.com/infocus/1824.

45. "WEP: Dead Again, Part 1" and Part 2.

46. http://standards.ieee.org/getieee802/download/802.11i-2004.pdf.

47. www.networkworld.com/news/tech/2006/040306-80211w-wireless-security.html.

48. An arbitrary number used only once; either the product of a random number generator or a unique number that can exist at only one instant, such as the current date and time.

49. Niels Ferguson, "IEEE 802.11-02/020r0—Michael: An Improved MIC for 802.11 WEP" (January 2002) http://grouper.ieee.org/groups/802/11/documents/documentholder/2-020.zip.

50. Niels Ferguson, "IEEE 802.11-02/020r0—Michael: An Improved MIC for 802.11 WEP".

51. www.wi-fi.org/files/uploaded_files/wp_9_WPA-WPA2%20Implementation_2-27-05.pdf.

52. http://wifinetnews.com/archives/002452.html.

53. www.aircrack-ng.org.

54. http://sourceforge.net/projects/coWPAtty and http://wirelessdefence.org/Contents/coWPAttyMain.htm.

55. www.netstumbler.com.

56. http://airsnort.shmoo.com/.

57. Fluhrer, Mantin, and Shamir, "Weaknesses in the Key Scheduling Algorithm of RC4."

58. "Korek" is the pseudonym of an active hacker who has posted extensively on WEP weaknesses. See, for example, the exchanges at www.netstumbler.org/f49/need-security-pointers-11869/#post89036 and www.netstumbler.org/showthread.php?t=12489.

59. "libpcap is a system-independent interface for user-level packet capture. libpcap provides a portable framework for low-level network monitoring. Applications include network statistics collection, security monitoring, network debugging, etc." See Sourceforge.net for details: http://sourceforge.net/projects/libpcap/.

60. http://grouper.ieee.org/groups/802/11/802.11_Timelines.htm.

61. http://standards.ieee.org/getieee802/802.11.html.

62. ANSI/IEEE Standard 802.11, 1999 ed., Part 11.

63. ANSI/IEEE Standard 802.11, 1999 ed., Part 11.

64. http://standards.ieee.org/getieee802/download/802.11i-2004.pdf

65. http://grouper.ieee.org/groups/802/11/Reports/tgk_update.htm.

66. http://grouper.ieee.org/groups/802/11/Reports/tgm_update.htm.

67. http://grouper.ieee.org/groups/802/11/Reports/tgn_update.htm.

68. http://grouper.ieee.org/groups/802/11/Reports/tgp_update.htm.

69. http://grouper.ieee.org/groups/802/11/Reports/tgr_update.htm.

70. http://grouper.ieee.org/groups/802/11/Reports/tgt_update.htm.

71. http://grouper.ieee.org/groups/802/11/Reports/tgv_update.htm.

72. www.networkworld.com/news/tech/2006/040306-80211w-wireless-security.html.

73. ANSI/IEEE Standard 802.11, 1999 ed., Part 11.

74. http://standards.ieee.org/getieee802/download/802.11i-2004.pdf.

75. IEEE Standard 802.1X-2001, "Port Based Network Access Control."

76. B. Aboba, L. Blunk, J. Vollbrecht, J. Carlson, and H. Levkowetz, "IETF RFC 3748, PPP Extensible Authentication Protocol (EAP)." http://www.ietf.org/rfc/rfc3748.txt.

77. Palekar, Simon, Zorn, Josefsson, "Protected EAP Protocol (PEAP)," in preparation.

78. Aboba and Simon, "IETF RFC 2716 PPP EAP TLS Authentication Protocol," http://www.ietf.org/rfc/rfc2716.txt.

79. Blake-Wilson, "EAP-Tunneled TLS Authentication Protocol Funk," in preparation.

80. C. Rigney, S. Willens, A. Rubens, and W. Simpson, "IETF RFC 2865, Remote Authentication Dial In User Service (RADIUS)" (June 2000). www.faqs.org/rfcs/rfc2865.

CHAPTER **34**

SECURING VOIP

Christopher Dantos and John Mason

34.1 INTRODUCTION. Whether it is referred to as Voice over Internet Protocol (VoIP) or Internet Protocol Telephony (IPT), the digitization of voice messaging has had and will continue to have an impact on society. Voice messaging is part of a shift that some are calling the Unified Messaging System (UMS).[1] The future does not include separate applications for instant messaging, text messaging, voice communications, video conferencing, e-mail, and network presence. These are expected to become one application that will be shared by both the home user and large corporations. New technologies promise to empower users as never before by freeing our communications from geographically stationary limits. For example, users can decide to work from home and have their office telephones ring into their laptops. Aside from convenience and capability, there are also great financial justifications for VoIP/UMS systems. They replace formerly expensive equipment with common microcomputers, resulting in substantial savings.

Just as there are security issues with our current operating systems and applications, the popularity of VoIP will draw the attention of criminals. Most disturbing of all is that many current exploits can be used with deadly effect against VoIP.

34.2 REGULATORY COMPLIANCE AND RISK ANALYSIS.   This section addresses the myriad of regulatory compliance and risk analysis issues that are inherent in VoIP implementations and usage. These issues are categorized into these major areas:

- Federal laws and regulations
- State laws and regulations
- International considerations
- Liability
- Risk analysis: the impact of Sarbanes-Oxley, Health Insurance Portability and Accountability Act, and privacy laws

Each of these areas provides an overview of the key relevant issues and strategies.

34.2.1 Key Federal Laws and Regulations.   The principal federal laws that apply to VoIP include:

- Sarbanes-Oxley Act of 2002 (SOX)[2]
- Health Insurance Portability and Accountability Act of 1996 (HIPAA)[3]
- Gramm-Leach-Bliley Act (GLBA)[4]

Among these laws, and the associated regulations from the Securities and Exchange Commission (SEC), Department of Health and Human Services (HHS), and the Federal Trade Commission (FTC), the principal common denominator is the standard for establishing and maintaining privacy for consumers, for businesses, and for corporate entities. The SEC established the Public Company Accounting Oversight Board (PCAOB) to provide rulemaking concerning SOX.

While HIPAA establishes and defines standards for the protection of patient and consumer information, SOX goes further, as it requires extensive periodic management testing to support management's attestation that the internal controls—including those surrounding privacy—are adequate and functioning effectively. Currently SOX is applicable to most publicly traded and for-profit entities. Although it does not apply to privately or publicly held nonprofits as of this time, many nonprofits have implemented it in advance of upcoming regulations. For example, the National Association of Insurance Commissioners (NAIC) in 2006 extended the application of SOX 404 over the insurance industry; this is to become effective in 2009.[5] In anticipation of this, some health and property casualty insurance companies began implementing the regulation as early as 2004 since the multifaceted SOX review process can be time consuming to implement. Indeed, many organizations have found that SOX is not a one-time compliance effort; multiple calendar years can be required to fine-tune the internal control, monitoring, and assessment processes.

In terms of how this affects VoIP, the implementation process generally includes most, if not all, of these issues:

- Reviewing and enhancing the VoIP and IT-related policies and procedures
- Mapping and verifying major and significant process flows that impact VoIP, or where VoIP can affect significantly the financial condition of the organization
- Creating risk control matrices
- Creating and implementing test plans and matrices
- Testing VoIP controls, both logical and physical
- Reporting the test results, and determining the risk exposure level for exceptions noted
- Effecting the appropriate remediation, as needed
- Follow-up testing to ensure that the remediation was effective, and the proper controls are now in place
- Coordinating and liaising with the external audit firm that files a separate report on management's assessment
- Publicly reporting on management's assessment of the VoIP and other internal controls

Since VoIP affects key areas of an organization, such as systems, applications, privacy, networks, transmissions, and end users, appropriate controls here are part of a well-considered defense in depth strategy. Generally, a SOX review will cover most, if not all, of applicable items for a HIPAA or GLBA audit. It also covers many aspects of an ISO/IEC 27002:2005 audit;[6] however, it should not be considered all-inclusive.

For more information on GLB and SOX, see Chapter 64 in this *Handbook*. For more information about HIPAA, see Chapter 71.

34.2.2   Other U.S. Federal Regulations and Laws

34.2.2.1   Enhanced 911.   Enhanced 911 (E911) mandates a location technology advanced by the Federal Communications Commission (FCC) that enables mobile or cellular phones to process 911 emergency calls and enable emergency services to locate the geographic position of the caller. According to the FCC's Web site:

> The wireless Enhanced 911 (E911) rules seek to improve the effectiveness and reliability of wireless 911 service by providing 911 dispatchers with additional information on wireless 911 calls.[7]

The wireless E911 program is divided into two parts: Phase I and Phase II. Phase I requires carriers, upon valid request by a local Public Safety Answering Point (PSAP), to report the telephone number of a wireless 911 caller and the location of the antenna that received the call. Phase II requires wireless carriers to provide far more precise location information, within 50 to 300 meters in most cases.

The deployment of E911 requires the development of new technologies and upgrades to local 911 PSAPs as well as coordination among public safety agencies, wireless carriers, technology vendors, equipment manufacturers, and local wireline carriers.[8]

In a simple solution, a VoIP provider takes the stored location information, passes that through its own call center, and routes it to the local 911. In a more sophisticated solution, some gateways can map MAC addresses to locations, and the 911 calls then can be passed to a PSAP.

Currently, E911 is not required for companies that are using VoIP for internal purposes only. This law is empowered by the FCC, but the Department of Homeland Security (DHS) and the Federal Bureau of Investigation (FBI) appear to want it for surveillance and location tracking.

34.2.2.2 Communications Assistance for Law Enforcement Act. Electronic surveillance consists of either the interception of call content (commonly referred to as wiretaps) or the interception of call-identifying information (commonly referred to as dialed-number extraction) through the use of pen registers and trap and trace devices.[9]

Although various earlier laws, such as the Omnibus Crime Control and Safe Streets Act (1968),[10] Foreign Intelligence Surveillance Act (FISA; 1978),[11] and Electronic Communications Privacy Act (1986),[12] have provided for the judicial authorization process and the rules surrounding the interception and surveillance of wire, oral, and electronic communications, the purpose of the Communications Assistance for Law Enforcement Act (CALEA) is to preserve law enforcement's ability to conduct electronic surveillance in the face of rapid advances in telecommunications technology. To this end, CALEA

> further defines the existing statutory obligation of telecommunications carriers to assist law enforcement in executing electronic surveillance pursuant to court order or other lawful authorization and requires carriers to design or modify their systems to ensure that lawfully-authorized electronic surveillance can be performed.[13]

The standards for surveillance of VoIP networks have been a joint effort of industry and law enforcement for some time.

The Packet Technologies and Systems Committee (PTSC) has published the Lawfully Authorized Electronic Surveillance (LAES) for Voice over Packet Technologies in Wireline Telecommunications Networks, Version 2 (Revision of T1.678-2004), which is a surveillance standard for basic VoIP.[14] The standard covers basic VoIP and supplementary services and was published in May 2006. The full document is available for a fee from the Alliance for Telecommunications Industry Solutions (ATIS), a U.S. standards organization.[15]

The PTSC published T1.IPNA (IP Network Access) in May 2006. This standard defines the requirements for broadband access.

The Telecommunications Industry Association (TIA) has published J-STD-025-B, which provides a surveillance standard for CDMA2000 broadband access. The Wireless Technology and Systems Committee (WTSC) has created T1.724, which provides a surveillance standard for GPRS/UMTS broadband access.[16]

The FCC's role in implementing CALEA by May 14, 2007, can be summarized in this way:

- **Section 102.** States that the FCC has the authority to establish findings that identify telecommunications services that are subject to the requirements of CALEA, which are not specifically detailed in the law.
- **Section 103.** Requires a telecommunications carrier to ensure that its equipment, facilities, or services that provide a customer or subscriber with the ability to originate, terminate, or direct communications are capable of meeting the assistance capability requirements.

- **Section 105.** Requires the FCC to establish systems security and integrity regulations for carriers to follow.
- **Section 107.** Requires the FCC to establish by rule the technical requirements for CALEA if a party petitions the commission believing that the industry standard is deficient.
- **Section 109.** Requires the FCC, upon petition from a telecommunications carrier, to make determinations of reasonable achievability regarding the assistance capability requirements of Section 103 with respect to any equipment, facility, or service installed or deployed after January 1, 1995. Under CALEA, the surveillance content's call identifying information typically includes the "dialing or signaling information that identifies the origin, direction, destination, or termination of each communication generated or received by a subscriber by means of any equipment, facility, or service of a telecommunications carrier."[17]

A key part of the CALEA enforcement and debate is determining who is really responsible for compliance. According to the law, "all entities engaged in the transmission or switching of wire or electronic communications as a common carrier for hire."[18] However, a question arises when an organization builds its own VoIP solution; that is, does the organization then become a common carrier? It would seem so, according to CALEA:

[A] person or entity engaged in providing wire or electronic communication switching or transmission service to the extent that the Commission finds that such service is a replacement for a substantial portion of the local telephone exchange service and that it is in the public interest to deem such a person or entity to be a telecommunications carrier for purposes of this title.[19]

However, the law specifically excludes "persons or entities insofar as they are engaged in providing information services." Given this possible exclusion, an organization should seek advice from appropriate legal counsel prior to creating its own VoIP network.

34.2.3 State Laws and Regulations.   All states have laws concerning surveillance; 31 states specifically address computers and 14 refer to cell phones. Because a detailed discussion of this diverse environment is beyond the scope of this text, an organization should seek appropriate legal counsel not only concerning the state it is domiciled in, but also the states of any branches, divisions, subsidiaries, or affiliates. The National Conference of State Legislators provides links to the applicable laws of each state and a summary of the coverage (e.g., cell phones, computers, video, photos, etc.).[20]

34.2.4 International Laws and Considerations.   Similar to the diversity in the United States, many countries have laws concerning surveillance and intercepts. As such, appropriate legal guidance and advice should be sought before installing or using VoIP networks in international locations. In particular, standards such as ISO/IEC 27002:2005 and privacy laws may be applicable, and may affect VoIP implementation and usage.

34.2.5 Liability.   Because both laws and standards apply to VoIP, violations may result in criminal penalties as well as civil penalties in the United States; this may vary by state and by the nature of the violation, since federal violations may take precedence over the state jurisdiction and prosecution. At the federal level, violations concerning surveillance often involve the Communications Act and 18 U.S.C. 2511 and 2520.[21] These penalties can include:

- Injunctive relief and fines of more than $500 for each violation[22]
- Statutory damages of whichever is the greater of $100 a day for each day of violation or $10,000[23]
- Fines of $500 per day of violation[24]
- Civil liability

Additional penalties can be incurred if the violations involve SOX, GLBA, or HIPAA. These can include:

- Fines of up to $250,000 (HIPAA, under certain circumstances)[25]
- Imprisonment
- Adverse review or audit findings that possibly can affect an organization's SOX annual control assessment
- Stock delisting (SOX)
- Additional regulatory reviews (SOX)
- Additional SOX-related attestations (SOX)

34.2.6   Risk Analysis

34.2.6.1   SOX.   In estimating the impact of SOX, the primary measure is whether a weakness or deficiency in management's controls relative to VoIP could result in a material impact to the organization's financial statements. This need not result from a single failure of a single control, but can result from a single failure of multiple controls that may have a compounding effect on each other, or multiple failures of a single control. The control can be manual, automated, or a combination of both.

The materiality will vary by organization; if management is unsure of the materiality threshold (e.g., 5 percent of net income), then the external auditors who attest to management's assessment of its (management's) internal control over financial reporting usually can provide this information. Using this threshold, the "in-scope" systems and applications are identified, given their potential effect on the financial statements. If there is a disagreement between management and the external auditors as to whether a system or application is deemed in scope, then this difference of opinion should be resolved as quickly as possible, so that sufficient time and sample size are available for testing. If there is insufficient time or sample size available, then generally the testing will fail and could result in at least a significant deficiency, even though the tests performed were acceptable and encountered no errors.

Among the key tools that commonly are used in identifying and assessing the risk are a management-created risk control matrix and a segregation of duties (SoD) matrix. The former identifies and describes the key or primary controls that management relies on. The SoD matrix identifies which employee activities, roles, and functions are or are not acceptable; for example, a software developer may not be permitted to edit code on the production system at all, or, if permitted to do so, will require subsequent verification. Depending on the extent of implementation and the number of staff involved, the SoD matrix can impact any VoIP risk significantly, particularly in a small organization or area, since there may be challenges in restricting or segmenting access in the various job activities or roles. For example, an organization might have a single person who creates, reviews, and effects the changes in the VoIP-related systems and applications; the SoD matrix likely would prohibit this. Management's challenge then is to determine how much risk is acceptable in this type of situation and how to mitigate it to an acceptable level; methods might include detailed auditing, logging, and reviews.

Monitoring of the VoIP-related controls and deficiency status are effected within the overall SOX framework. For example, spreadsheets and simple databases can be used to record and monitor these key controls:

- Level of financial risk associated with the control or area
- Control objectives
- Control or business application owner(s)
- Related tests
- Testing status
- Test results
- Deficiency and remediation status and follow-up
- Compensating controls
- Executive-level "dashboard" for status
- Other related information

Often organizations will use third-party tools to assist them in this process. Doing so can help streamline and facilitate intraorganizational communications and ultimately help reduce the VoIP risk by helping ensure that all appropriate areas are addressed. However, it is beyond the scope of this text to provide a general SOX discussion or specific recommendations regarding these tools.

In determining the risk for VoIP-related systems and applications, there is a key difference among internal audits, external audits, and SOX reviews; in both internal and external audits, when errors are encountered, the test may still receive a "pass" because the errors are not material or significant enough to impede the normal operations or the reliability of the financial statements. In SOX testing, the results are interpreted in more of a black-or-white or yes-or-no manner. If there are any errors in VoIP testing, then the test fails, unless the testing allows for a very minimal number of errors, and provided that an expanded test sample does not identify any additional errors. Multiple minor control deficiencies may have a compounding or magnifying effect on each other, or on the reliability of minor controls used to detect if a major control is not working properly.

34.2.6.2   *HIPAA.* The applicability of and risks related to HIPAA generally go much farther than might be presumed initially. It might appear that HIPAA applies solely to healthcare-related organizations, but any organization that offers and retains information on employee benefits must comply with the law. Generally, if an organization is considered SOX-applicable, then the appropriate privacy controls should be in place, or under review; this includes both the documentation and the periodic security testing that is to be performed. However, neither the IT control objectives nor SOX itself specifically mandate compliance with HIPAA.

Still, there is overlap between SOX and HIPAA regarding the VoIP security testing and documentation (e.g., periodic vulnerability assessments, information and document protection, and policies and procedures) that can help reduce some of the duplicated review areas. Some of this can be affected by measures utilized to reduce risk exposure concerning privacy laws (see the next section), particularly as they concern encryption and data protection. Therefore, in evaluating and measuring the risks addressed by HIPAA, a more integrated, holistic risk evaluation approach should be used.

34.2.6.3   Privacy Laws.   GLBA is among the best-known federal laws and California's Senate Bill 1386 (SB1386) is among the best-known state laws concerning privacy and protection of information. GLBA's reach specifically extends to financial institutions and to financially related information. It was enacted in early 2002 and became effective in July 2003. It is one of the best-known state-initiated privacy laws; many other states have subsequently followed California's lead with similar legislation. The common emphasis of these laws is on the unauthorized access to or disclosure of consumer-protected information; the type of information protected may vary slightly from state to state. Also, rather than apply only to events that occur within its borders, often these laws apply to and protect the state's residents, irrespective of the state in which the breach or unauthorized access occurred. For example, if a California resident's personal identifying information, as defined by the law, is breached because of business transacted in another state (perhaps while vacationing), the law applies.

Given this type of situation, appropriate VoIP security should be provided at all times, varying by state as required. Some states, such as California, provide a "safe harbor" if the protected information is encrypted within the system; however, no level of encryption strength is mandated, nor is transmission encryption required. Because other states with similar laws may vary in security requirements, the VoIP security that management is considering may need to reflect the laws and consumer information protection requirements of other states. Appropriate legal counsel may, therefore, be needed to provide advice and to help management assess the level of risk.

34.3   TECHNICAL ASPECTS OF VOIP SECURITY.   The next section is designed to provide a technical overview of VoIP and related security issues. It starts with an introduction to the protocols used and then progresses to associated threats. Following that is a discussion of best practices and then encryption.

34.3.1   Protocol Basics

34.3.1.1   Audio Stream Protocols: RTP and UDP.   Real-time Transport Protocol (RTP) is the packet-based communication protocol that provides the base for virtually all VoIP architectures. Part of RTP is timing and packet sequence information that can be used to reconstruct audio streams. Like TCP, User Datagram Protocol (UDP) is a layer 4 network communication protocol. Both of these protocols provide the basic packet addressing needed to get from one network address to another. When dealing with VoIP, packet delivery time is of the essence. Both TCP and UDP add overhead to the organization's network communication. This overhead results in greater time delays to the communication. UDP adds less overhead as it provides comparatively little packet error checking. The compromise is that UDP will help deliver packets quicker but will also result in more lost packets. It has been observed that a packet loss of 10 percent spread over a VoIP call may be virtually undetectable to most users. However, all of the features that can make VoIP secure also add latency. Added latency means more lost or discarded packets, which then results in an unpleasant or unacceptable user experience. In the end, a slow packet is a lost packet.

34.3.1.2 *Signaling Protocols: SIP and H.323.* Session Initiation Protocol (SIP) is a protocol that is used to establish interactive multimedia sessions between users. In addition to VoIP, it is also used for video conferencing and online gaming. SIP appears to be the most commonly accepted form of establishing VoIP calls. Secure SIP (SSIP) is discussed in Section 34.5.1. Like SIP, H.323 can be used for video conferencing or VoIP call setup. While SIP appears to be the standard for new installations. One may find H.323 in use at enterprise scale installations that have large investments in older, analog communication equipment.

Briefly, the basics of a VoIP call include these details. A VoIP client application, whether on a personal computer or a dedicated handset, uses SIP or H.323 to set up the call. This call setup is an exchange of control parameters that may include encryption and compression algorithms to be used. This is called "signaling." Once the call is set up, the VoIP client uses RTP to start packetizing the voice data. The RTP packets are incorporated into a UDP packet that adds addressing and sequencing information. The UDP packets are collected and sorted by sequence number at the receiving station. Some systems use a "jitter buffer" to assemble and store the packets. The endpoint VoIP client then reads the jitter buffer and turns the RTP packets back into voice.

34.3.2 VoIP Threats. Although not an exhaustive list, these hacks represent some of the vulnerabilities likely to be encountered when using VoIP:

- SPIT
- Eavesdropping
- Theft of service
- Man-in-the-middle attacks

34.3.2.1 *SPIT.* Most users have become accustomed to finding 10 or 20 (or 100 or 200) spam e-mail messages in an inbox on daily basis. The thought of receiving an equal number of voicemails on a daily basis leads to the unappetizing acronym SPam over Internet Telephony (SPIT). Even the most ambitious devotees of fear, uncertainty, and doubt (FUD) will admit that SPIT has yet to become a major issue. This is because there appears to be no current method of sending one voicemail to a number of telephones (i.e., SPIT messages must be sent one at a time, which is not an efficient use of resources). However, would-be SPIT spammers may have been both encouraged and then disheartened when, in 2004, Qovia,

> a company that sells enterprise tools for VoIP monitoring and management, ... applied for a patent on technology to broadcast messages via VoIP—and another one for a method of blocking such broadcasts. The broadcast methodology only works on a pure VoIP network, while most of today's services are hybrids of IP and traditional telephone lines.[26]

The author explains that Qovia realized that broadcasting VoIP messages could be useful for agencies such as Homeland Security but could also be abused by spammers. Therefore, Qovia pledged to "incorporate its SPIT-blocking technology in future releases of its security products, while enforcement of its patent on broadcasting, if granted, could be used to shut down VoIP spammers."

Filter:	rtp.payload			▼	Expression...	Clear	Apply	

No. ▾	Time	Source	Destination	Protocol	Info
624	1444.509099	192.168.1.2	212.242.33.36	RTP	Payload type=ITU-T G.711 PCMA, SSRC=932629361, Seq=28590, Time=1240
625	1444.579046	192.168.1.2	212.242.33.36	RTP	Payload type=ITU-T G.711 PCMA, SSRC=932629361, Seq=28591, Time=1400
626	1444.582579	192.168.1.2	212.242.33.36	RTP	Payload type=ITU-T G.711 PCMA, SSRC=932629361, Seq=28592, Time=1560
627	1444.588245	192.168.1.2	212.242.33.36	RTP	Payload type=ITU-T G.711 PCMA, SSRC=932629361, Seq=28593, Time=1720
628	1444.590352	192.168.1.2	212.242.33.36	RTP	Payload type=ITU-T G.711 PCMA, SSRC=932629361, Seq=28594, Time=1880
629	1444.625165	192.168.1.2	212.242.33.36	RTP	Payload type=ITU-T G.711 PCMA, SSRC=932629361, Seq=28595, Time=2040
630	1444.627060	192.168.1.2	212.242.33.36	RTP	Payload type=ITU-T G.711 PCMA, SSRC=932629361, Seq=28596, Time=2200
631	1444.664688	192.168.1.2	212.242.33.36	RTP	Payload type=ITU-T G.711 PCMA, SSRC=932629361, Seq=28597, Time=2360
632	1444.671724	192.168.1.2	212.242.33.36	RTP	Payload type=ITU-T G.711 PCMA, SSRC=932629361, Seq=28598, Time=2520

EXHIBIT 34.1 Packet Capture Showing RTP Packets

34.3.2.2 *Eavesdropping.* In an unsecured VoIP environment, eavesdropping is reduced to a task that is quite straightforward. Earlier, it was mentioned that RTP is the de facto protocol for VoIP communication. RTP adds unique sequencing information to its packets. Because of this, one could collect a number of RTP packets and then assemble them in a consecutive order, as a receiving station would collect these packets in a jitter buffer.

Knowing this, the first step in eavesdropping is be to obtain a packet-sniffing tool such as Ethereal from www.ethereal.com. One may then use Ethereal to perform a packet capture, or one may obtain sample capture files from the Ethereal Web site. If the user chooses to perform packet capture, care must be exercised not to violate any privacy laws applicable to the user's network. Once obtained, Ethereal is used to sort out any RTP packets. Exhibit 34.1 depicts a packet capture filtered to show RTP packets. Notice that the first column at the left contains a list of sequential numbers. These numbers indicate the packet placement within the capture. However, farther to the right is the actual conversation sequence number. Once the RTP packets are assembled by sequence number, they can be saved as an ".au" file, which can be played on most computers. As shown with this example, eavesdropping on unencrypted VoIP traffic is not a complicated or expensive process.

34.3.2.3 *Theft of Service.* One of the classic theft-of-service attacks that has occurred was reported in June 2006. In this case, a brute-force attack yielded special access codes allowing attackers entry into the provider network. Once in, the attackers obtained router passwords and login credentials; they then programmed the network transport devices to implicitly accept and route VoIP messages from the attackers' server. The attackers then sold VoIP access to public providers, who then sold it to the public. In the end, 15 exploited companies were left to pay the bill for the calls that were routed out of their network.[27]

An organization's own employees could exploit its VoIP infrastructure as these attackers did.

34.3.2.4 *Man-in-the-Middle Attacks.* As with any technology that digitizes communications, VoIP that sends data without encryption is inherently open to manipulation if an attacker can intercept traffic, alter its content, and send it on its way to the recipient in a classic man-in-the-middle (MITM) attack.[28] Once an attacker has control of VoIP traffic, the attacker can not only eavesdrop but can also:

- Initiate calls to a third party and impersonate a caller by sending data that appear to come from a legitimate phone belonging to someone else

- Deflect calls to the wrong destination
- Intercept traffic in real time and generate simulated voice content to create misleading impressions or cause operational errors

This last point warrants expansion. An eavesdropper could collect the digital patterns corresponding to words or phonemes generated by a particular user during normal conversation. Using simple programs, it would be possible to generate data streams corresponding to any spoken sequence including those words or phonemes in real time, allowing the MITM to feed the recipient (or even both sides of a conversation) with distorted or invented information and responses. The potential for mayhem is enormous, especially if the conversation involved, say, emergency response.

34.4   PROTECTING THE INFRASTRUCTURE.   This section focuses entirely on VoIP networks. For general information on infrastructure protection, see Chapters 22 and 23 in this *Handbook*.

34.4.1   Real-Time Antivirus Scanning.   Protecting the VoIP infrastructure would appear to be a routine decision. Remember that as with VoIP, a slow packet is a lost packet. Many of the routine measures used to protect a typical server will introduce latency into the voice system, leading to jitter and sporadic communication. One of the first routine measures to be sacrificed is real-time antivirus protection of the VoIP server. Some vendors will suggest that real-time scanning of the organization's entire VoIP server is next to impossible, and unsupportable. This is an unacceptable myth. The VoIP server must be scanned in a fashion that is at least consistent with other production servers. Requests from system administrators asking to disable real-time scanning is a common first step in creating issues with the VoIP system.

34.4.2   Application Layer Gateways and Firewalls.   An organization's VoIP infrastructure is much more than a series of systems that are digitizing voice and forwarding packets. Its servers will have real-time contact with e-mail servers and central authentication systems using Remote Authentication Dial-in User Service (RADIUS) or perhaps Active Directory. It may also have database systems devoted to logging call information or even recording the calls themselves. An attacker who gains access to part of the organization's VoIP infrastructure may be able to access the most sensitive parts of its network. Consider the use of application layer gateways (ALGs) or SIP/VoIP-aware firewalls to segregate the VoIP systems.

34.4.3   Logical Separation of Voice and Data.   It would be ideal to have a separate network for the organization's VoIP system. Bandwidth issues would be minimized and troubleshooting simplified. In most instances, it may not be possible to make a business case justifying the installation of a separate set of cables and network gear. The VoIP handset on the user's desk or the VoIP softphone in the user's PC will share the same wire as the workstation. The logical separation of voice and data begins with assigning the organization's VoIP devices to a network subnet separate from the data devices. This is initiated by a Dynamic Host Configuration Protocol (DHCP) request from the user's handset. Part of this request allows the DHCP servers to distribute addresses based on hardware identification parameters. For example, connecting a laptop to the organization's network will result in the assignment of an address that is on a subnet different from the Cisco handset that is plugged into the same connection. This logical separation of voice and data allows the organization's

firewalls to protect its VoIP infrastructure by screening out protocols and requests that are not voice related.

34.4.4 Quality of Service.

The term "quality of service" (QOS) refers to a set of configurable parameters that can be used to control and/or prioritize communication through the network. Again, with respect to VoIP, a slow packet is a lost packet. QOS can be used to prioritize the VoIP packets so they can be delivered in a timely fashion. Most vendors will provide a choice of default QOS configurations to be used according to the organization's needs. Some even provide VoIP firewalls that are capable of buffering VoIP messages and retransmitting packets. Regarding QOS, it is not just one parameter that can be turned on to make the VoIP installation work properly; it is a series of parameters that may need to be tuned to fit the organization's exact needs. For more technical detail, see IEEE standards 802.1p and 802.1q.

34.4.5 Network Monitoring Tools.

Best practices require a dedicated security operation center (SOC) watching the organization's networks for attacks. Whether it is a 7×24 SOC or just one network administrator who does everything, it is absolutely critical to provide the tools and training necessary to detect attacks and to troubleshoot performance issues. With VoIP, the staff will be facing attacks using a new set of attack vectors and protocols. If the network administration is outsourced, review of existing service-level agreements to guarantee that the provider is capable of supporting VoIP is strongly recommended.

34.4.6 Device Authentication.

Device authentication can be accomplished in a variety of ways. The simplest is to store a list of device MAC addresses on the organization's VoIP server and to authenticate all SIP requests through that list of addresses. The standard is to deploy devices to desktops without configuration. Upon connection, a technician enters a setup utility that connects to the VoIP server and then downloads a preconfigured image.

34.4.7 User Authentication.

The organization's finance people likely will demand some type of call tracking and usage so departments can be charged or reviewed appropriately. Users can also be placed into different groups that the organization can configure. This group-level access can be used to limit services, such as long distance or international calling. It is common for a VoIP infrastructure to have ties to a central authentication server, such as Lightweight Directory Access Protocol (LDAP) or Active Directory. This central authentication will ease functions such as forwarding voicemail to a personal computer or cell phone. There are two common problems to watch for:

1. The *authentication interval* will be set by user. The organization can configure a demand for authentication to be hours, days, or months; 24 hours is suggested. Some users complain, and demand that their central credentials be stored in the handset for months so they only need to log in infrequently; this practice is generally undesirable.

2. Most handsets will come with *default accounts and passwords*. These accounts must be disabled or, at the least, strong password discipline must be maintained over them.

34.4.8 Network Address Translation and NAT-Traversal.

Network address translation (NAT) is a technique commonly used by firewalls and routers to allow multiple devices on an internal network to share one IP address on the Internet. A user's internal address should be known only to systems on that user's own network. When connecting to an external network, the organization's router or firewall forwards the user's communication to an external address but replaces the user's private address with its public address. When the communication is returned, the firewall routes the message back to the correct private address. Similarly, consider the broadband router in a home. The user may connect a series of systems to this device, each with a unique internal address distributed by the router, but the ISP sees it as only one address. These internal or private addresses are stored in what is commonly called a "translation table." At a higher level, the process of getting a packet through a NAT device is called NAT-Traversal (NAT-T). Understanding how NAT-T issues affect VoIP is vital to understanding the danger of sending a voice call to the Internet.

Section 34.3.1.2 outlined how SIP is commonly used to set up a call. Once the call is set up, the actual audio stream typically is relayed via RTP/UDP. This is where the issues start. The firewall does not have a problem with passing SIP traffic back and forth to the Internet, as the internal address of the VoIP device is stored in the translation table. However, the SIP signaling has passed on the private address of the user's VoIP device. This means that a device outside of the local network is trying to send the RTP/UDP audio stream to a fictional IP address. Essentially, NAT prevents VoIP from functioning.

Several work-arounds are commonly used. Sometimes the NAT device can be configured to provide VoIP support. Sometimes VoIP devices can be configured to work over otherwise open ports, overloading a common protocol such as HTTP, unfortunately, often with unintended side effects. Or VoIP proxy servers can be used on either side of the NAT in order to facilitate the traversal. Each of these solutions opens up its own security concerns, which should be carefully addressed; these concerns include the consequences of external proxy servers or creating anomalous traffic over other protocols, as in the overloading example.

34.5   ENCRYPTION.   Encryption plays a critical role in communications security. For a general introduction to encryption, see Chapter 7 in this *Handbook*; for more details of public key encryption, see Chapter 37.

34.5.1   Secure SIP.   Transport Layer Security (TLS) was sponsored by the Internet Engineering Task Force (IETF) to secure and encrypt data communications crossing public networks. It is intended to replace Secure Sockets Layer (SSL) as a widely accepted form of securing data communication. This protocol consists of a "handshake" and a "record." TLS was designed to be application independent so developers could choose their own way of initiating a TLS session.

Secure SIP is a mechanism designed to send SIP signaling messages over an encrypted TLS channel. A SSIP session is initiated by a SIP client contacting a SIP proxy and requesting a TLS session. The proxy returns a certificate that the SIP client then authenticates. The client and proxy then exchange encryption keys for the session. If the call is destined for another network segment, the SIP proxy will contact that segment and negotiate a sequential TLS session, so the SIP message is protected by TLS the entire time.

34.5.2   Secure Real-Time Protocol.   Secure Real-Time Protocol (SRTP) is an enhancement of RTP that provides encryption, authentication, and integrity to the VoIP audio stream. The Advanced Encryption Standard (AES) originally was a block cipher;

SRTP incorporates AES into the data stream with an implementation that utilizes it as a stream cipher.

Encryption is good but it does not protect the user or organization against replay attacks. SRTP uses a Hashed Message Authentication Code (HMAC-SHA1) algorithm to provide authentication and integrity checks. The MAC is calculated using a cryptographic hashing function in conjunction with a private key. SRTP uses one of the five Secure Hash Algorithms (SHA) designed by the National Security Agency. All five of these algorithms are compliant with requirements set in the Federal Information Processing Standards (FIPS).

34.5.3 Session Border Control.

To this point, a number of issues affecting a VoIP deployment have been identified. Session border control (SBC) is a set of services that address VoIP issues related to security, QOS, NAT traversal, and network interoperability. SBC collects real-time bandwidth statistics that can be used to allocate the network resources necessary to maintain the QOS desired. SBC will also support a number of NAT-T algorithms that will allow calls to be routed to public networks while maintaining the anonymity of internal resources. At the same time, SBC can accommodate both SIP and H.323. This allows the signaling protocol translation necessary to connect both types of networks.

34.6 CONCLUDING REMARKS.

VoIP provides expanded functionality and lower costs for corporate users, but managers must integrate security considerations into the architecture and implementation of all such systems to prevent interception, deception, and denial-of-service attacks. In addition, technologists must monitor developments in this rapidly changing field to keep abreast of new attack methodologies and countermeasures.

34.7 FURTHER READING

Boyter, B. "Voice-over-IP Sniffing Attack," 2003, www.giac.org/certified_professio nals/practicals/gcih/0442.php.

Davidson, J., J. Peters, and B. Gracely. *Voice over IP Fundamentals*. Indianapolis, IN: Cisco Press, 2000.

Endler, D., and M. Collier. *Hacking Exposed—VoIP: Voice Over IP Security Secrets & Solutions*. New York: McGraw-Hill Osborne Media, 2007. See also the associated Web site, www.hackingVoIP.com.

Kuhn, D. R., T. J. Walsh, and S. Fries. "Security Considerations for VoIP Systems." NIST Special Publication 800-58, 2005, http://csrc.nist.gov/publications/ nistpubs/800-58/SP800-58-final.pdf.

Long, T. "Eavesdropping an IP Telephony Call." GIAC Security Essentials Certification Practical Assignment, 2002, www.sans.org/reading_room/whitepapers/ telephone/318.php.

Molitor, A. "Deploying a Dynamic Voice over IP Firewall with IP Telephony Applications," 2000, http://cnscenter.future.co.kr/resource/rsc-center/vendor-wp/aravox/ aravox_deploying_dynamic.pdf.

Molitor, A. "Securing VoIP Networks with Specific Techniques, Comprehensive Policies and VoIP-Capable Firewalls," 2000, http://cnscenter.future.co.kr/resource/ rsc-center/vendor-wp/aravox/aravox_specifictechniques.pdf.

Porter, T., B. Baskin, L. Chaffin, M. Cross, J. Kanclirz, A. Rosela, C. Shim, and A. Zmolek. *Practical VoIP Security*. Rockland, MA: Syngress, 2006.

Thalhammer, J. "Security in VoIP Telephony Systems." Master's thesis, Institute for Applied Information Processing and Communications at the Graz University of Technology, Graz, Austria, 2002; www.iaik.tugraz.at/teaching/11_diplomarbeiten/archive/thalhammer.pdf.

Thermos, P., and A. Takanen. *Securing VoIP Networks: Threats, Vulnerabilities, and Countermeasures*. Boston, MA: Addison-Wesley, 2007.

VOIP Security Alliance White Papers: www.voipsa.org/Resources/whitepapers.php.

34.8 NOTES

1. Unified Messaging System Project, www.cs.vu.nl/~jms/ums/.

2. Sarbanes-Oxley Act, www.sec.gov/about/laws/soa2002.pdf.

3. Health Insurance Portability and Accountability Act of 1996, http://aspe.hhs.gov/admnsimp/pl104191.htm.

4. Gramm-Leach-Bliley Act, www.ftc.gov/privacy/glbact/glbsub1.htm.

5. W. Boyd, "NAIC Alternate SOX Proposal Remains Problematic," *NAMIC* (National Association of Mutual Insurance Companies) *Issue Brief* (2006), www.namic.org/insbriefs/060130NAICAltSOX.pdf.

6. ISO 27002, the Information Security Standard (formerly ISO 17799), www.standardsdirect.org/iso17799.htm.

7. Federal Communications Commission Enhanced 911—Wireless Services, www.fcc.gov/pshs/services/911-services/enhanced911/Welcome.html.

8. Federal Communications Commission 9-1-1 Services, www.fcc.gov/pshs/services/911-services/.

9. Communications Assistance for Law Enforcement Act, "Frequently Asked Questions," www.askcalea.net/faqs.html.

10. Omnibus Crime Control and Safe Streets Act of 1968, www.usdoj.gov/crt/split/42usc3789d.htm.

11. Foreign Intelligence Surveillance Act (FISA), www4.law.cornell.edu/uscode/50/ch36.html

12. Computer Professionals for Social Responsibility, "Electronic Communications Privacy Act of 1986," www.cpsr.org/issues/privacy/ecpa86.

13. Communications Assistance for Law Enforcement Act, "Frequently Asked Questions."

14. IHS Electronics, "ATIS Releases LAES Standard for Internet Access, Services—ATIS PP-1000013," March 30, 2007, http://electronics.ihs.com/news/atis-laes-internet.htm.

15. Alliance for Telecommunications Industry Solutions, "Lawfully Authorized Electronic Surveillance (LAES) for Voice over Packet Technologies in Wireline Telecommunications Networks, Version 2 (Revision of T1.678-2004)" (May 2006). $367 for download; www.atis.org/docstore/product.aspx?id=21221.

16. Communications Assistance for Law Enforcement Act, "Frequently Asked Questions."

17. Communications Assistance for Law Enforcement Act, Home page, www.askcalea.net.

18. Alliance for Telecommunications Industry Solutions, "Lawfully Authorized Electronic Surveillance (LAES) for Voice over Packet Technologies in Wireline Telecommunications Networks, Version 2 (Revision of T1.678-2004)."

19. Communications Assistance for Law Enforcement Act, Definitions, www.askcalea.net/calea/102.html.

20. National Conference of State Legislatures, "Electronic Surveillance Laws," www.ncsl.org/programs/lis/CIP/surveillance.htm.

21. Federal Trade Commission, Notice of Proposed Rulemaking: Communications Assistance for Law Enforcement Act, October 2, 1997, www.fcc.gov/Bureaus/Common_Carrier/Notices/1997/fcc97356.txt.

22. Wire and Electronic Communications Interception and Interception of Oral Communications, www.usdoj.gov/criminal/cybercrime/18usc2511.htm.

23. Crimes and Criminal Procedure, 18 U.S.C. Section 2520: Recovery of Civil Damages Authorized, http://law.onecle.com/uscode/18/2520.html.

24. Communications Act of 1934, www.fcc.gov/Reports/1934new.pdf.

25. UC Davis Health System, "Penalties Under HIPAA," www.ucdmc.ucdavis.edu/compliance/guidance/privacy/penalties.html.

26. S. Kuchinskas, "Don't SPIT on VoIP," *Small Business Computing,* August 24, 2004, www.smallbusinesscomputing.com/news/article.php/3399011

27. "VoIP Hacker Arrested on Fraud Charges," *Technology News Daily,* 2006, www.technologynewsdaily.com/node/3252.

28. See, for example, P. Thermos, "Two Attacks against VoIP," *SecurityFocus,* 2006, www.securityfocus.com/infocus/1862/1.

CHAPTER 35

SECURING P2P, IM, SMS, AND COLLABORATION TOOLS

Carl Ness

35.1 INTRODUCTION.   Peer-to-peer (P2P) communications, instant messaging (IM), short message services (SMS), and collaboration tools must be directly addressed in any comprehensive security plan. The dangers are very real, as is the probability that at least one of these technologies is in use on almost every information system.

35.2 GENERAL CONCEPTS AND DEFINITIONS.   This chapter is designed to present enough information and resources to aid in integrating the defense of each function into the organization's security plan. A list of resources is provided at the end of the chapter to aid in further research.

35.2.1   Peer to Peer.   Peer-to-peer networking, also referred to as P2P, is not a new concept or technology. The term was contained in some of the original designs and proposals for the Internet as an efficient and logical way to exchange information from one resource, or peer, to another, on a large interconnected network. Today, the term is most associated with applications that transfer multimedia files across the Internet.

Peer-to-peer networks generally consist of different computers, or nodes, that communicate directly with each other, often with very little, if any, need for a central computer to control the activity. Often utilizing an application with a client-server appearance, the two computers set up a direct connection between each other for file transfer. A central indexing computer may or may not be needed to help these computers "find" each other, to index and publish their contents, or to facilitate the connection. However, what is most important, the two computers must have a direct, logical connection to transfer the file or files. File transport may take place over a local network (LAN), a wide area network (WAN), a value-added network (VAN), or via the Internet.

Peer-to-peer technologies and applications were much more common in the early days of networking when it was not financially possible for many organizations to have expensive servers and complicated network topologies. This is especially true of personal computer networks that performed simple file sharing from computer to computer in a one-to-one model instead of today's much more common one-to-many server-to-client setup. However, there are legitimate uses for peer-to-peer technologies. One common example is the sharing of Linux distribution software images. Peer-to-peer sharing of these often very large ISO disk images requires much fewer resources for the distributor because there may be thousands of computers distributing the software among themselves, instead of every user trying to download the file from a single server.

35.2.2   Instant Messaging.   Instant messaging, or IM, has become one of the most widely used communication mediums. This technology allows users to communicate with each other in a real-time, live, instantaneous fashion via computer. Today's IM applications are not the first generation of IM. The concept of communicating, or chatting, in real time made its appearance on multiuser computer systems, when users could initiate a text-based conversation with each other. The most common example of this type of communication was a host-based system such as a mainframe environment or UNIX system using programs like *talk* or *ytalk*. Initially, users may have been restricted to messaging each other when logged into the same machine; eventually users were able to communicate with each other, either via peer-to-peer or over the Internet. The first widespread uses of IM were made possible with the advent of the PC and were used mainly for informal, personal conversations.

With time, IM has become a business tool and, in some organizations, a necessity. The need to communicate with coworkers, colleagues, salespeople, clients, customers, and the like has transformed a gimmick technology into ubiquity. With this change, it is necessary for security management to change and adapt accordingly. Users are able to send messages, files, real-time streaming video and audio, and just about anything else developers can think of, almost instantly. Essential to the organization or not, IM can become a very dangerous medium for security breaches.

35.2.3   Short Message Service.   Short message service, or more commonly SMS, is another previously minor technology that has become ubiquitous and a large part of everyday life for many people. Although some mobile phone standards and companies had different ideas for the uses of SMS, a common early use was to notify customers of information one way, from the mobile phone provider to the user. A popular example was alerting the user of a missed call or voicemail message. Many carriers never dreamed customers would actually be able to send text messages from one mobile phone to another, nor did the carriers think users would ever *want* to do such a thing. The name, short message service, also implied a limited amount of text a message could contain. Originally, users were limited to 160 characters or less.

SMS has morphed into something much larger. The commonality of mobile phones has pushed the original concept far beyond its original meaning and function. Today, two-way communication between mobile phone customers, often on different mobile phone carrier networks, between customers and mobile phone providers, and between customers and other information systems has become a way of life. Customers expect instant, always-on, reliable SMS services. Many mobile phones are capable of SMS text messages, taking and sending pictures, instant alerts, and a number of other services that utilize or expand on the original concept of short message service.

35.2.4   Collaboration Tools.   People working together have created a need for even more technology to aid them in completing their tasks. There are many products in today's market to facilitate sharing, collaboration, and organization of data. As some information security professionals joke, "Computers and technology are generally safe and secure, until you let a human near them." Humans are inevitable when it comes to collaboration tools and systems. Many collaboration tools and systems are designed to aid workgroups that are physically far apart. Once a system has requirements that contain the words "open," "via the Internet," or "access from anywhere," information security managers are alerted. Securing collaboration tools can be very difficult, especially when it comes to balancing functionality versus security. Google has begun offering free, highly functional, Web-based tools intended to aid users in online productivity. These include many powerful, and potentially dangerous, tools to share information and to collaborate with other online users. A recent example is the feature for Google calendar users to make events or calendars public. However, if the user is not careful, private data may be readily available to any user via Google's calendar search feature.[1]

35.3   PEER-TO-PEER NETWORKS.   One of the earliest mass applications of P2P was for free file-sharing of music through Napster, LLC. Despite difficulties over copyrights, and a subsequent bankruptcy, Napster's technology, in substantially the same form, is still in widespread use. Practical applications have expanded beyond music downloads into the business world, such as allowing small groups of users to share files without the interaction of a systems administrator and distribution of open source software. Likewise, it may be possible that employees are utilizing the organization's high-speed Internet connection to supplement their at-home movie collection via P2P downloads.

35.3.1   Dangers to the Business.   Using P2P technology without proper care and controls, an organization may face serious consequences. There are many threats to an organization that does not properly control P2P networking, as for any other network configuration or protocol. Many problems are discussed in Chapters 21, 25, and 26 in this *Handbook*. However, this section contains several important issues that information security management should consider while performing risk analysis and policy implementation for P2P networking.

35.3.1.1 *Abusing Company Resources and Illegal Content.* Organizations must have an acceptable usage policy in place, one that limits what employees can do with the technology resources provided to them. The policy should clearly state the kinds of technology and applications that are prohibited or restricted in specific ways. In most cases, P2P technology used to download music or videos for personal use will violate the policy.

P2P technology is a specific danger to company technology resources because the inherent nature of P2P technology is to use every resource to the maximum extent possible. For example, a single P2P application, configured properly, will use every bit of bandwidth that is made available to it. This would include local area network bandwidth, wide area network bandwidth, and Internet bandwidth. One of the most popular uses for P2P technology still remains the sharing of extremely large files, especially multimedia files including full-length movies. These large files can take hours to download in full. This fact can have an extremely negative impact on an organization's network infrastructure—including expensive Internet bandwidth.

In practice, a single P2P application has been demonstrated to completely saturate a 10-megabit Internet connection, virtually denying, or severely limiting, access to all other computers. In this case, these dangers to the business are common to many areas of information security management:

- Threat to **availability.** If an organization's resources, including network resources, are not available, the business cannot properly function.

- Threat to **integrity.** If the organization's resources are crippled or misused by employees utilizing P2P technology, data may suffer from a breakdown of integrity and usability.

- Threat to the **organization's image.** If the organization's information systems and infrastructure cannot be relied on because of interruptions from P2P abuses, there is a risk of financial or public image degradation. Some organizations are not able to overcome a substantial loss of image, credibility, or both.

- Threat from **litigation.** It is very common to see illegal content being shared via P2P technology; illegal music and video sharing is often credited with having made P2P technology popular. An organization may suffer legal troubles, including copyright and intellectual property suits, if its resources are involved with the sharing of illegal materials. Some antipiracy groups have become extremely aggressive in combating illegal sharing of copyrighted content.

35.3.1.2 *Loss of Confidentiality.* There are many ways an organization may suffer a loss of confidentiality from P2P technology. One common mistake is a misconfigured P2P application. The case study in Section 35.3.4 describes one situation. However, the dangers of a misconfigured P2P application are very real—it is quite easy for data to be shared inadvertently. When users are in a hurry or do not understand what they are doing, a P2P application may allow for unauthorized access to information because its restrictions are too lax or missing altogether. A common mistake in a Microsoft Windows environment may be to share the entire "My Documents" folder when a user intended to share only photos. It is also possible for a P2P application to be hijacked or altered by malware. An attacker may be able to alter the configuration or operation of a P2P application to reveal data that were not intended for sharing, distribution, or transmission. A misconfigured or compromised P2P application may

also become a conduit or access point for an attacker to enter an otherwise secure network environment.

Another, less well known and often overlooked threat involves the amount of data a P2P application can reveal to unauthorized persons. For example, a P2P application may offer detailed information about its host, including:

- Operating system, version, and configuration
- Corporate IP address scheme, host naming convention, DNS information
- Detail about the P2P application version or build (useful for attackers to exploit known vulnerabilities in a "buggy" release or version)
- Network routes
- Open network ports in the organization's firewall

Although many of these examples may seem rather benign by themselves, the P2P application may be revealing information that an attacker can use as part of a bigger attack. Chapter 19 of this *Handbook* details how small pieces of information can be gathered and used together in an information security breach. The very nature and functionality of P2P applications leaks sensitive information that otherwise would not be revealed.

All P2P applications are not created equal; a P2P application may be very different from the user's expectations. Can the P2P application actually be a reliable, malware-free, secure application—especially when the application is a free download from the Internet? It is possible that a backdoor exploit, malware, spyware, or the like may be built into the P2P application, or introduced later. This was especially true in the days of Napster; many applications included unwanted malware that ranged from innocent to downright dangerous.[2] Similar exploits are still possible.

35.3.1.3 Consequences.   Any organization that does not protect against data loss via P2P networking is at great risk of public disclosure and scrutiny, financial penalties, regulatory penalties, and so on. The functionality and nature of P2P applications may provide an investigator or, worse yet, the press with definitive evidence of the use of P2P technology within an organization. A majority of the public may only understand P2P technologies to be used in conjunction with illegal music sharing; even this simple, negative perception can greatly influence public opinion on the organization. It would be very difficult to refute packet analysis or screen shots containing an organization's IP address in which the computer was compromised, used for illegal software or media sharing, or the computer was used by an unauthorized entity to extract data. In the age of P2P applications commonly used to illegally share and distribute the intellectual property of unwilling participants, organizations are taking aggressive steps to find and prosecute offenders. See Chapter 55 in this *Handbook* for a discussion of cyber investigations; see Chapter 61 for guidance on working with law enforcement.

35.3.2 Prevention and Mitigation.   Protecting the organization from information security breaches via P2P technologies is one of many important parts to an overall security plan. Depending on an organization's structure, leadership, function, and similar factors, methods for preventing and mitigating P2P threats can range from simple to very complicated. Obviously, each organization must perform a risk analysis and determine its threat threshold when it comes to P2P technology. Chapter 62 provides means for risk assessment. The guidelines that follow can help an organization defend against the threat of P2P technology causing security breaches.

35.3.2.1   Policy.   It is important for every organization to address the use of P2P technology in a policy, such as an acceptable use policy, a personnel guideline policy, or security policies. The relevant policy, along with all other security-related policies, should be clearly stated, clearly communicated to the entire organization, uniformly and equally enforced, and updated as necessary.

35.3.2.2   Complete Ban on Peer-to-Peer Technology.   In *most* cases, the organization can ban the use of P2P completely, especially through enforceable policy. Care should be taken to ensure all employees and computers are in compliance with the ban. It should be forbidden or, even better, impossible to install P2P applications on personal computers, servers, and all other information systems that could be used to send and receive P2P-related traffic. If employees are allowed to install software on their workstations, regular inventories and audits of the computers should take place. Removal should be immediate, and appropriate corrective actions taken. Several technologies may also aid in disallowing P2P traffic, although no technological solution is completely foolproof. These measures are additional safeguards, not complete solutions. Firewalls should be configured to block those ports common to P2P applications, and although many P2P applications are able to tunnel through TCP/IP ports such as those used by HTTP or other common protocols, this is a necessary first defense. Packet-shaping technologies can also be useful to identify P2P-related traffic and block its communications. Packet-shaping and traffic management devices are often able to detect the signature of P2P traffic, no matter what TCP/IP port the application may be using. Some intrusion-detection and intrusion-prevention systems may also be able to identify and block P2P traffic, as would many Internet filtering devices. Logs and reports should be examined daily and infractions should be quickly remedied.

35.3.2.3   Information Security and Information System Audits.   All information systems and components should be audited regularly to ensure that they are not configured, intentionally or unintentionally, to participate in P2P file sharing. This task should be part of every organization's regular information system and information security audit processes. If possible, external and neutral resources are most useful to ensure all systems are audited in a uniform, exact, repeatable, and objective fashion.

35.3.2.4   Legitimate Business Use Must Be Managed.   There are times when an organization does not wish to completely ban or block the use of P2P technologies. One increasingly common and legitimate use for P2P involves open source software distribution via BitTorrent. BitTorrent is a P2P-based protocol for the distribution of data—often very large amounts of data. A widespread use includes the distribution of the Linux open source operating system. Software distribution of Linux often involves obtaining CD-ROM or DVD images to create install discs. By utilizing BitTorrent technology, software vendors and distributors are able to provide large amounts of data to their clients without carrying the entire burden of distribution, bandwidth, and computing resources. However, the organization must manage how this technology is used to ensure resources are not abused and that the P2P applications are used for only allowed, legal ends.

This can be accomplished through policy, auditing, and various network access and control technologies. Each organization must define its own level of acceptable risk for legitimate P2P technology usage and must find solutions that will match the acceptable level. Some examples include:

- Use of encryption
- "Anonymous" P2P routing technologies such an ONION routing (see Chapter 31 in this *Handbook*)
- Network isolation for computers used to obtain software with P2P applications
- Company-acquired DSL or cable modem connections to the Internet, avoiding the use of corporate network resources

35.3.3   Response.   It is necessary for all organizations to define exactly how to respond to security breaches and policy violations, including situations where P2P technology is involved. Not only should the process be included in the overall security plan, but also technological processes should be in place to remove offending systems from the network. In some cases, the rebuilding of a compromised resource may be necessary, but some organizations may choose to completely remove the compromised machine from the organization or to archive the machine for legal, forensic, or investigative processes.

35.3.4   Case Study.   Misconfiguration, unintentional use, curiosity, and experimentation with P2P in the workplace do happen, with consequences. Although this case is only one type of specific security incident involving P2P technology, it should serve as an example of how such a situation can occur.

An employee of one organization reported a very slow-running computer to the help desk. All of the usual help desk suggestions and tricks were exhausted with little effect on the performance of the computer. The usual symptoms of a very slow computer were present—massive wait times to accomplish simple tasks, random errors and shutdowns, lockups, and other operational problems. However, there was one difference: After a reboot, it would take several minutes for the computer to slow down and become unresponsive. After some time, an employee commented, "I did try installing a music sharing program last week, but I didn't like it and uninstalled it." This led the engineer to examine each and every process that was running on the computer.

Although it appeared that the P2P application had been uninstalled, it actually had not been; it was still installed and running in a stealth mode. The uninstaller only masked the P2P application. Not only was the P2P application still running, but it was misconfigured to share the entire contents of the C: drive. There were literally thousands of other P2P users attached to the machine actively searching, uploading, downloading, and altering the contents of the computer's hard drive. The computer was not only giving away all of its data, it was being used for a server to host thousands of media files. Since the computer was on a network segment that had full TCP/IP 1-to-1 network address translation, it was effectively completely open to the outside world—and the outside world was taking full advantage of the opportunity. The hard drive was virtually full, and files were being added and deleted at will by remote users.

It is unknown if the user's personal data was actually accessed, downloaded, or used for any malicious activity, but the capability was certainly there. Because of a user's unauthorized downloads, inadequate network security, and other policy violations, the organization could not be sure of the confidentiality or integrity of the computer or its data. Necessary steps were taken to prevent this incident from occurring again, but this scenario has played out at other organizations, and will continue to do so as long as the P2P risk exists.

35.4   SECURING INSTANT MESSAGING.   Instant messaging has become an integral part of communications—both business and personal—for many people. Although personal usage in a business environment usually carries with it a waste of time and resources, IM does have legitimate uses in the business world, from sales contacts to interoffice real-time communications, with rapid response. From executives to interns, IM may be found on many desktops, but it must be managed and secured on all.

35.4.1   Dangers to the Business.   With any technology, especially those that make connections to the Internet, there is a risk to the organization. Instant messaging is not a petty annoyance that should be taken lightly; if the technology is not controlled by the organization, a serious breach of security could occur. Instant messaging technology has come a long way since its inception. IM applications are capable of transmitting much more than just interpersonal text banter.

35.4.1.1   Loss of Information.   Information loss and loss of confidentiality, intentionally or unintentionally, is most likely the biggest threat of IM to the business. There are several ways information can be harmfully conveyed via IM:[3]

- Revealing secrets via text chat, especially given the instant transmission when compared with e-mail, which usually allows a configurable delay between hitting *send* and actually having the message sent.
- Copy-and-paste functions used to transmit confidential or secret information.
- File transfers.
- Screen sharing and real-time collaboration functions such as shared whiteboards.
- Relaying voice, video, or both to another party (unintentional or intentional).
- Use of Webcam technology to relay visual information within a secure facility.
- Downloading malware to collect and steal data.
- Impersonation. (This tactic usually involves stealing a known IM account or creating a fake account to impersonate someone the victim knows.)
- Subpoenas or search warrants executed to collect IM logs, conversations, and so on may be harmful to the organization, or to certain employees, but of benefit to others.

Although this is not a complete list, it should serve to aid in security planning. There are many good resources on the Internet to further explain similar threats and consequences, but the preceding list should encourage thoughtful brainstorming about the ways in which an organization may lose control of data, including a complete loss of the data altogether. Some of the listed methods would be extremely difficult to detect and remedy. With high-speed networks and high-speed Internet links at most organizations, a massive amount of data can be conveyed within a very small amount of time.

35.4.1.2   Consequences.   Like other security threats, the consequences of not securing IM technology can be serious. Many organizations have experienced a security breach that involved IM, and there are probably more to come. Instant messaging security breaches can be deadly to an organization by themselves or as part of a much larger attack on the business. Stealing or transmitting information through IM is no less risky than any other form of information theft. One single file, whether sent through an IM file transfer or meticulously cut and pasted, bit by bit over a great period of time, can destroy a company's reputation and standing in the public eye. A breach from a single IM conversation has the potential to depress a corporation's stock price in a matter of hours or days. There have even been cases where a chief executive officer's confidential information was captured and posted on the Internet for all to see.[4]

35.4.1.3 Denial of Service.   IM cannot be written off as a tiny application with no real footprint on network resources. Instant messaging can be a tool used to create a denial of service attack on an organization, resulting in a loss of availability. IM technology can be a very powerful and useful tool for an attacker, including the use of IM clients with a direct connection to the Internet. With the right combination of malware and access, an attacker may be able to exploit one of many vulnerabilities discovered in IM applications, including the ever-popular buffer overflow. The National Vulnerability Database listed 12 vulnerabilities in instant messaging software as of March 2008.[5]

35.4.2 Prevention and Mitigation.   Every organization must guard against the threats caused by IM technology. Proper review and analysis of the risks associated with IM must be carried out within the organization, and the organization must determine the amount of risk it is willing to take. It is also necessary to evaluate the costs and efforts associated with the prevention and mitigation of this threat. Different organizations will judge the risks and rewards of using IM differently. There is no set standard for every organization or business; there is no universal set of rules that can be applied in all situations. (For a discussion of risk assessment and management, see Chapter 62 in this *Handbook*.) The next sections provide strategies, tactics, and considerations for securing IM.

35.4.2.1 Policy.   Before all else, policy should come first, especially with the popularity and widespread use of IM. Without adequate policies, the organization has no chance of actually protecting itself. Policy must be the foundation that all other considerations rest upon. Clearly defined, well-communicated, and equally enforced policy is one of the most important fundamentals information security relies on. No matter what the organization decides when it comes to IM rules, it must be stated in a policy.

Instant messaging, while risky, is one of the most visible policy decisions a business will make. While it might be best, and preferred for best security, to completely disallow IM, which could lead to frustrated employees, unable to use the facility for personal use, business use, or both. Every management team should be conscious of the potential ramifications of an overly strict policy. Conversely, allowing unfettered IM is certainly not the best solution.

Compliance and governmental regulations must be taken into consideration. If IM communications are to be allowed, they become part of the organization's digital information, and therefore may be subject to subpoena, search warrant, and document retention requirements. New regulations and legal rules may greatly affect policy decisions. It is important to remember that instant messaging logs and conversations *may* be subject to legal discovery, search, and seizure. Consult counsel for proper legal advice.

35.4.2.2 Complete Ban.   A ban on all IM technology would be the best way to ensure better enterprise security. However, this will only produce dissatisfied users, without being effective. Users can become technology-savvy in a hurry if they are determined to circumvent a policy. A block on IM communications often causes users to do just about anything they can to accomplish their goal of unobstructed IM. Many IM clients will help users avoid technology put in place to block communications. The software may be configured to bypass firewall rules, detect and avert packet-shaping technology, and tunnel its way to the Internet. Many IM services also provide Web-only interfaces that do not require software to be installed while communicating via HTTP. Unfortunately, this technology can be a very difficult and frustrating one to ban within the organization; a complete ban is probably not a practical solution.

35.4.2.3 Prevent Installation of Instant Messaging Software.   Although a complete ban may not be possible, or even desirable, one step that a more secure organization can take is to prevent users from installing IM software. This tactic is not going to solve the whole problem, but it certainly will help. Controlling the installation of IM software should be part of the organization's overall software installation policy. In general, installing software without permission should be denied. If it is feasible, local workstation administrator rights should be denied for most employees. In many user or system management solutions, it is also possible to block software installation through individual, group, or workstation policy templates and procedures. Universal software installation prevention is much easier than trying to define policies or templates for every possible IM peer, application, group, or tool.

35.4.2.4 Fight Technology with Technology.   This suggestion on its own will not provide the organization with an all-in-one solution for securing IM. However, there are a number of network devices, appliances, traffic monitoring software, and other technologies to help an organization minimize IM use. Do not believe marketing claims that any device or technology can guarantee IM blocking; very few can deliver on this promise. The only *true* way to guarantee an IM-free company is to block access to the Internet completely—which is not very realistic.

35.4.2.5 Limit Risk and Exposure.   For most organizations, *limiting* IM through policy and technology is the solution to the threats that IM introduces. Combining those two approaches will help to reduce the possibility of data loss. Security managers and administrators should agree on what can and what cannot be allowed within the organization. An organization may choose to block file transfers, Webcam functions, or screen-sharing functions for IM communications. These types of actions will not prevent IM security breaches, but they could limit data loss. As with any policy and risk management, proper audit, reporting, and compliance controls must be in place.

35.4.2.6 Providing Secure Instant Messaging.   In environments where IM is needed to run the business, the best strategy is to provide secure, managed IM services to the employees. Of course, the needs will vary among different organizations for different levels of IM connectivity, functions, and software. Many of today's popular corporate e-mail and collaboration systems have built-in or optional IM services.

When properly deployed, these IM systems can meet many of these secure IM best practices:

- Encrypt IM communications wherever possible: client to server, server to Internet, and so on.
- Encrypt logs and chat conversations at the workstation and server.
- Ensure that all logs, chat conversations, file transfers, and archives meet data transmission, retention, and destruction policies.
- Ensure that "presence awareness" features (software features that allow the user to communicate his or her presence or availability, such as "online," "away" or "out to lunch" to all users) comply with corporate personnel policies.
- Administratively disable features that cannot be encrypted or properly managed (screen sharing, file transfer, whiteboard, etc.).
- Where possible, lock or force configuration settings to ensure policy compliance.
- Establish procedures for periodic monitoring and auditing of IM systems; do not ignore logs.
- Enforce prudent password policies for IM systems.
- Properly secure IM communication systems with Internet connectivity; consider placing systems in demilitarized zones (DMZ); ensure appropriate server lockdown policies and procedures.

Corporate-owned and managed IM systems may not be possible in all situations. In those cases, the organization must form policies and procedures to limit risk and exposure with commercial IM systems. Some systems do provide "secure" IM, but be skeptical of exactly how much protection they provide. Consider limiting commercial IM needs to nonessential computers with limited network access, limiting or restricting users to specific IM applications or services, and monitoring instant message network traffic and usage. Some commercial IM services also provide "corporate" or "business" IM services, often for a fee. These premium offerings may provide the organization with the necessary or acceptable level of functionality and security.

35.4.3   Response.   Instant messaging breaches and compromised systems generally do not require special handling after a security incident. In general, normal policies and procedures can be followed to properly investigate, clean, and document security breaches. There are many commercial tools, including forensic software, to aid in incident response. Infected or compromised systems, if no longer needed for investigation should be reimaged before redeployment to an employee or, if allowed by policy, destroyed. There is no guarantee that a machine has been cleaned up or that all malware has been removed. Format the storage elements, and start clean—it is just better practice to do so.

35.4.4   Safe Messaging.   Although most users at the organization are generally satisfied with mainstream IM systems, clients, and services, there are dangers to be considered. There seems to be almost an unlimited number of open source IM clients, Web-based IM and chat providers, social networking Web sites providing IM, and the like. When considering policy and management of IM within the organization, it is important to judge the source and intentions of all of the possible services. All IM software and services are not created equal; some may originate from untrusted sources and may contain malware and other security risks. Instant messaging software or providers may be logging information without the user's knowledge or consent.

Also, if the organization will utilize commercial IM software and services, it is critical to carefully examine the provider's terms of use and license agreements. The responsibilities and liabilities of both parties should be carefully weighed by information security managers, company executives, and legal counsel before allowing use of the software and associated services.

35.5   SECURING SMS.   Few technologies are more ubiquitous than short message services. Virtually all mobile phones are capable of sending and receiving SMS communications. Since mobile phones are virtually everywhere, security considerations must be in place to guard against the threats that they present. A technology with a relatively minor footprint can cause a world of destruction when used as a weapon. Today, SMS technology, and its associated complementary services, has grown exponentially. Securing, and defending against SMS must be included in every organization's comprehensive security plan.

To understand SMS security, it is important to look at the underlying devices most associated with SMS. SMS does not require a cell phone to utilize the technology. Many phone carriers allow SMS messages to be generated and sent from an unsecured, public Web site. SMS messages may also originate from e-mail messages, instant messaging services, and the like. Today's mobile phones, including smart phones, are more powerful and contain many more features than prior years' phones. Phones are increasingly gaining processing power, memory, complex operating systems, and other features that essentially could redefine the device as a personal computer. Phones are able to access the Internet, install applications, communicate from phone to phone, and even access corporate data networks. Information security managers and professionals should never underestimate the power or versatility of a mobile phone. They are a threat to all of an organization's information security.

35.5.1   Dangers to the Business.   SMS can introduce many types of security threats into an organization. SMS can cause a data breach by innocent mistakes or by deliberate attacks. This technology can be used as a criminal tool to deliberately steal information, to extract data, to extort information, and to deceive. It may also be a conduit for inadvertent data loss. The consequences of data lost via SMS are relatively the same as any other data breach: loss of confidence in the organization, loss of image, bad public relations, financial penalties, and so on. A serious or even minor data breach may appear to communicate to the world that the organization does not have a comprehensive security plan in effect, or the company does not abide by such a plan— whether true or not. Some investors, customers, or people in the general community may look at a breach of such a simple technology and ask, "How could the company not have proper security for something as simple as a cell phone?" A missing laptop with confidential data is a serious security breach, but a mobile phone, with all its capabilities, must be treated as nearly the same type of critical infraction.

35.5.1.1   SMS as a Tool for Deliberate Data Loss.   One danger an organization may face involves an individual or group of people utilizing SMS technology to ferry critical data to unauthorized persons, usually outside the organization. This action would replicate an age-old tactic of stealing information piece by piece from within the organization to someone who should not possess the information. Consider classic tricks of criminals, such as copying information in tiny pieces over great amounts of time to avoid causing suspicion. Any number of technologies can be used to move data, including flash or thumb drives, iPods, scraps of paper, photographs, screen printouts, embedded code, or even memorization. Disgruntled employees may use SMS to send confidential information to an accomplice or even to themselves for later use, such as selling the data, extortion, and the like. It would be virtually impossible to know that an employee is slowly leaking data outside the business from a mobile phone. What may appear to coworkers as a serious text-messaging addiction may actually be a serious data breach.

Another fact information security management must consider is that SMS service, whether exactly true to the original definition or not, has expanded well beyond messages of only 160 characters. Mobile phone users are able to send real-time video streams, recorded video, photographs, substantially longer text messages beyond 160 characters, Web page links, and just about anything else the phone carriers can implement. If the mobile phone industry considers all of these features to be synonymous with SMS, the organization's security plan should as well. Business risk has increased greatly with every new technology addition.

35.5.1.2 Inadvertent Data Loss via SMS.   Data loss can occur by mistake, badluck, stupidity, misinformed user, or misunderstanding of features as well as by theft of the data device itself. Both deliberate data theft and inadvertent data losses are extremely dangerous, with potentially serious consequences. Search engines reveal many different tactics and war stories of data loss from a mobile phone as well as other SMS-specific security issues. These are scenarios and techniques to consider:

- SMS via e-mail or the Internet
- SMS snooping or sniffing
- Recovery of improperly deleted data
- Stolen, mixed up, or lost phones
- Misdialed numbers
- Wi-Fi connectivity
- Unattended phone with no password
- Malware installed on phone (keyloggers)
- Recipient's phone is lost, stolen, or borrowed
- Impersonation

35.5.2 Prevention and Mitigation.   SMS technology is not going to disappear anytime soon, so every organization must come up with a plan to prevent data loss and protect itself from this risk. Once again, the organization's leadership, security management, and security professionals must evaluate the risk of SMS versus the need to operate the business and maintain an amiable group of employees. Every organization must decide for itself exactly what kind of practices to put into place for SMS security and the cost/benefit of each practice. Everything must be considered, from policy and procedures, to deployment of security technologies and mobile phone company-provided services. With today's varying needs, newly emerging technologies and an array of mobile phones, it is very difficult for any two organizations to adopt the same prevention and mitigation strategies. However, the next suggestions can be used to begin, update, or enhance the organization's security plan when addressing SMS technology.

35.5.2.1   Policy.   It is impossible for information security managers to provide any security whatsoever if there is limited or no SMS policy. Human resources also will have difficulty dealing with an employee, current or separated, who is perceived as having broken a policy that does not exist in writing. Vague acceptable use policy will not be enough. A clearly stated position must be written, adopted, and communicated to all employees. The policy should apply to every employee, new or old, executive or trainee, with no exceptions. The policy should regularly be reviewed, updated, and redistributed, with recurrent training as necessary, especially in a rapidly changing world such as SMS.

A good policy must also address an important distinction common to mobile phone use in the organization: personal phones versus company-provided phones. The policy must address: what is acceptable for employee conduct on the job; whether personal phones are allowed on the premises; what type of phone is allowed (usually refers to whether employees are allowed to have camera phones); where, when, and for what purposes can they use personal mobile phones; what is allowed on business-provided phones; and the like.

35.5.2.2   Mobile Phone Ban.   In some cases, security needs may necessitate prohibiting the use or even possession of mobile phones on company grounds or in certain areas. This type of action should be included in company policy and should be clearly communicated. It may be necessary to remind employees with signs and repeated communication as well. This is a common practice to prevent data loss from any mobile phone function, including SMS. The organization should be sure to make distinctions for employee-owned phones and emergencies. If an area requires a very high amount of security, err on the side of caution, and forbid mobile phones completely. The policy must extend to visitors, vendors, contractors, and other outside entities as well as to every employee—regardless of rank.

35.5.2.3   Providing Secure SMS.   Providing "secure" SMS can prove to be difficult, and it can be easy to fall into a false sense of security. Information security managers must know exactly how their mobile phone infrastructure works before declaring the system secure. Although one component of a phone's connection may be secure—for example, from the phone to its messaging server—the entire path of a SMS message may not be secure. Some devices, such as the BlackBerry from Research in Motion (RIM), provide encrypted transport for messaging. However, e-mail or messages to users on different phone networks or other messaging servers may not be encrypted. Information security professionals must clearly understand the technology they are deploying, and they must test for proper installation and configuration. If a solution is to be encrypted end to end, it is prudent to double check to prove the solution really is as secure as it is believed to be. Organizations may also need to work closely with the solution providers and mobile phone carrier to properly implement necessary security solutions. However, it is important to remember that if a solution is not as secure as the organization's policies and needs require, SMS, mobile phones, or both should be banned. Some phones or smart phone solutions allow administrators to "block out" services such as SMS or to install secure communications software. Carefully consider and evaluate all options and solutions.

35.5.2.4   Ubiquitous BlackBerry.   There are many smart phones on the market, but probably none is as popular as the BlackBerry. A device so ubiquitous and addictive to users that it earned the nickname "crackberry" surely is a concern for security managers. The device is meant for business users, and more and more organizations have adopted it. Its services, however, go well beyond SMS, so that security measures must cover anything of which the device is capable. As of this writing, several devices, including the BlackBerry, have been introduced with the capability to connect with both cellular wireless technology (such as Enhanced Data rate for GSM Evalution (EDGE) and Collision Detection Multiple Access Evalution Data Only (CDMA EVDO) etc.) and 802.x Wi-Fi communications. Now security managers have twice the communication pathways to secure.

As far as information security is concerned, the BlackBerry is a mobile computer with wireless communications. Security features and software included with enterprise-wide deployment of the BlackBerry should be utilized, upgraded when necessary, and extraordinarily well managed. The BlackBerry, and all of its communications, applications, features, and the like, must be secured exactly as well as a laptop with the same features.

35.5.2.5 Other Considerations. The next list provides points to consider when planning for SMS security, many of which are from NIST Special Publication 800-48, "Wireless Network Security."[6]

1. Create policies and procedures to deal with lost mobile phones. The phone may contain sensitive data, including stored and deleted SMS messages.

2. If cell phones are banned from the organization's premises, ensure that physical security has procedures and rules for checking visitors and employees for mobile phones.

3. Many mobile phones have the capability to back up and synchronize their contents to the desktop. Ensure proper procedures to secure data and data leakage.

4. Policies and procedures should be in place to limit and manage the acquisition of mobile phones by employees—information security may not be aware of the existence of new phones in the environment.

5. Mobile phones are not easily audited, nor is there much software to aid in the auditing process.

6. Despite proper labeling of a company-owned device, if lost it will rarely be returned to the organization. Plan to mitigate damage caused by a lost mobile phone; utilize security features such as remote wiping the device after loss via "poison pill" features or "auto-destruct" features after several invalid password attempts.

7. If a mobile device supports screen-lock and power-on passwords, use these simple protections wherever possible.

8. Through policy and education, prevent as much sensitive and private information on the organization's mobile phones as possible, including SMS messages.

9. Utilize Public Key Infrastructure (PKI) technology where possible.

10. Install antivirus software where possible.

11. Utilize VPN and firewall technology for safer data communications.

12. If a phone is to be carried on international travel, SMS messaging should be prohibited if it all possible. The risks associated with taking a mobile phone to international destinations increase exponentially.

35.5.3   Reaction and Response.   When a security incident involving a mobile phone and SMS does happen, it may be best to work with the mobile phone provider, possibly also the manufacturer. Procedures and correct processes associated with data retrieval, preservation, investigation, and so on are best handled by those most qualified. Most of the large mobile phone companies have special divisions with specially trained personnel who can assist the organization. If necessary, involve law enforcement. This is an area where a long-standing good relationship with local, state, or federal law enforcement is extremely beneficial—even if the investigation would not necessarily require law enforcement investigation. For more information on this subject, see Chapter 61 of this *Handbook*.

Investigating SMS issues, including tracking messages, tracking phone location, and tracking the path an SMS message took, can often be accomplished with the help of the mobile phone carrier. Law enforcement and court-ordered subpoenas may be necessary, depending on the situation.

Compromised devices should be carefully reviewed before returning them to regular use. Mobile phone providers can assist in "wiping" the device clean of all software, including malware. Specific practices and procedures vary by phone and provider, but some organizations may choose to archive or destroy devices involved with a security breach of any kind.

35.6   SECURING COLLABORATION TOOLS.   Information systems that provide online facilities for collaboration are increasingly valuable business tools. Although these tools provide excellent conduits for increased information sharing, they also have the potential to increase security threats. Even the Internet itself, with many Web sites dedicated to information sharing, groupware, shared tools, and data storage, has become a collaboration workspace. New features and movements such as Google Apps, "Web 2.0," and even conference calling services must be taken into account in any organization's security plan. The nature of collaboration and the need to get critical business done efficiently is critical to most of today's organizations. Many companies and organizations are trying to get more work done with less people. Technology has become an important partner to allow employees to work together and to accomplish more in less time. Collaboration tools have become even more critical as businesses expand to include people working together from very different geographical locations.

35.6.1   Security versus Openness.   One of the longtime battles for security managers is security versus openness or functionality. The nature of collaboration requires uninhibited data and information sharing, which can be very difficult to secure. Organizations have to find the right balance between allowing users free and open information exchange and providing the required level of security. Finding this balance takes cooperation and respect between the two groups: those who use the tools and those charged with securing the organization. The two groups must fully understand each other's position; without this understanding, finding a middle ground and negotiating compromise cannot take place. The goal of the organization surely must be efficient, uninterrupted business, but not at the expense of good security. The only way to work through this complication is with good-natured, open, goal-oriented communication. This is *not* an information technology–only a problem or process. Finding that optimum balance of security and functionality will require all types of management and staff to work together. Although this may be true of all information security domains, it is especially true of collaboration tools security. Without this important balance, the tools are essentially worthless: too secure and they will not be used, too open and the business could suffer catastrophic data and integrity loss. Some businesses are not able to recover from such a loss.

35.6.2   Dangers of Collaboration Tools.   Collaboration tools are very powerful, and they must be given full security considerations. These tools should not be installed or integrated into the business without the proper planning, risk analysis, security configurations, and testing; ad hoc, unmanaged systems, installed without the knowledge of security personnel, must be prohibited, and violators punished. Collaboration tools can easily become a nightmare for security management, especially if securing these tools is not a primary consideration from the beginning. Designing and implementing security measures on an already-deployed production system is invariably a frustrating exercise in futility for both the users and the information security personnel.

Some of the features and general dangers associated with many of these systems include loss of confidentiality, integrity, or availability. These dangers can occur due to any of these problems:

- **Lack of authentication requirements, rules, or procedures.** A wide-open system or one with poor authentication would allow for unauthorized persons to gain access.

- **Data snooping or capture.** Transmission of data to and from the system could be intercepted by unknown persons.

- **Impersonation.** Proving exactly who the user is may be difficult if not well managed, especially with weak authentication and authorization methods.

- **Unauthorized posting** of confidential information in unsecure or public areas.

- **Misconfiguration.** A simple mistake in setup could reveal private information. (See Google calendar example from this chapter's introduction.)

- **Search engines.** Documents or other information may be subject to search engine crawlers/agents/spiders if proper security is not established.

- **Rogue collaboration systems.** If a department or group deploys its own tools, privately or publicly, without the knowledge of the security group, proper security cannot be guaranteed.

- **Internal threats.** One cannot be concerned only with external threats. One department's collaboration system may be another department's limitless temptation.

- **Users.** Users may not always have security in mind. Small mistakes or shortcuts could lead to major security breaches.

When deploying or evaluating collaboration tools, risk analysis must be performed to determine if the organization is able and willing to accept the associated risks. Security groups should thoroughly brainstorm and research as many possible security threats to the collaboration system as possible. It may be very beneficial to work with the solution provider's support group to minimize or eliminate as many security risks as possible.

Workgroups utilizing collaboration tools place a great amount of trust in the application and the tools. Many of the applications available today are light on security and heavy on marketable features. Although many online companies have become much more serious about data security, they are not the owners or protectors of the organization's data; that is still up to the organization.

35.6.3   Prevention and Mitigation.   Collaboration tools and systems should receive the same security care as any other information system. Although the nature of collaboration may be somewhat open, the same policies, procedures, and careful controls should apply. The goal must still be the confidentiality, integrity, and availability of the data and the information system. Collaboration tools must still benefit the business while ensuring the business will not be harmed by a security incident. By taking the necessary steps to prevent and mitigate security issues, collaboration tools can be invaluable to the organization.

The next suggestions can be utilized to aid an organization in securing collaboration tools and systems.

35.6.3.1   Policy.   It is debatable whether collaboration tools necessitate specific, separate policies. What is more important is that a complete, well-written, and well-communicated policy exists, one that includes provisions for collaboration tools, systems, and associated technology. Clear understanding and communication of collaboration tool security must be well researched, well written, concise, well communicated, and updated regularly. It is critical that the policy remain valid as new and more complex collaboration tools are developed and deployed.

Policies should also include security options that may otherwise be out of the control of the organization. For example, if a company forbids using public file-sharing services, the policy should cover users attempting to use the service from outside the organization as well as within it. Employees should not be able to use services or systems that do not comply with the policy, no matter where or how the service is to be used.

A good policy should be inclusive, especially when defining exactly what the organization considers a collaboration tool. It would be easy to forget applications such as e-mail, IM, online meetings, blogs, social networking, shared network resources, remote access software, peer-to-peer file sharing, and the like. Many technologies have collaboration components that must be considered to ensure security.

35.6.3.2   Prevent Access or Use.   Another option, in conjunction with policy, is to block the use of collaboration tools, depending on the organization's needs. This may involve deploying technology to accomplish this goal, including content blocking, firewalls, or both. This should disallow installation or use of rogue collaboration tools. Periodic review of networked systems and network traffic should be conducted to ensure compliance with prevention or limitation of collaboration tools.

35.6.3.3   Limit Access.   Many collaboration tools can be deployed as an internal-only system, external-only system, or both. Organizations will want to choose how users will access these systems. For example, disallowing unsecured communications from the Internet may help increase security. Likewise, it may be necessary to block access to public services from within the organization's network. Or technical solutions, such as VPN connections from outside the organization's network, may be used to meet communication needs.

35.6.3.4   Deploy or Enhance Security Frameworks and Technologies.
Wherever possible, install solutions that will increase collaboration tool security and that can be integrated into existing security frameworks. If the organization has a high-security, single sign-on solution, integrate the collaboration systems into it. Another example would be to integrate the collaboration systems into a new or existing PKI infrastructure. Utilize well-known and reliable solutions such as Secure Sockets Layer

(SSL) and encryption for the host and all participants. This greatly reduces the risk of security breaches during data transmission.

35.6.3.5   *Audit.*   No matter what level of policy, procedures, or preventions are put into place, every organization *must* audit for compliance. Procedures for auditing collaboration tools and their use should be included in the organization's regular, structured, information security auditing functions. Any deviations from the policies and procedures mandated for collaboration tools must be acted on in a timely manner.

35.6.3.6   *Monitoring.*   Any organization that deploys collaboration tools must monitor and report on the system's usage, audit results, and data contents. (The organization must examine the actual data contents to ensure compliance with protections such as Protected Health Information (PHI) or Social Security Number (SSN). Many new products have rules written for this very reason.) Monitoring and reporting work to ensure that collaboration tools and systems are being used for their intended purposes. Monitoring and reporting of active projects should look for unusual patterns of use, policy violations, inactive users, inactive or outdated systems, and the like. Proper system management should already be in place, but it is important to check the systems periodically. For example, if a group is utilizing a collaboration system for a project, once the project has been completed, all project materials and users should be removed from the system. Reports from system monitoring and auditing should be acted on at once.

35.6.3.7   *Consider Outsourcing Carefully.*   Some organizations are tempted to use commercial online-only collaboration systems or hosted solutions. This decision should not be made lightly; consider the risks versus the returns. The organization should carefully review all terms of service, license agreements, service-level agreements, and legal responsibilities carefully. Legal counsel must be involved to ensure the organization is protected, especially in the area of data ownership, possession, legal discovery, and subpoena power.[7]

35.6.3.8   *Penetration Testing.*   As with most information systems, providing necessary security should involve regular, external, third-party penetration testing. Collaboration tools and associated systems should be tested and evaluated for their security fitness. Any problems discovered should be documented and swiftly remedied. Allowing a neutral, external entity to test the system independently is superior to internal testing, so that bias can be ruled out.

35.6.3.9   *Keep Collaboration Tools Current.*   Keeping collaboration tools and their associated information systems up to date is critically important. Applying patches for vulnerabilities is good information technology and information security best practice. After thoroughly testing patches in a test environment, they should be applied to production environments as soon as possible. Do not ignore software vendor patches, especially those for known vulnerabilities.

35.6.4   Reaction and Response.   Once a security breach has been discovered involving collaboration tools, the organization's usual policies and procedures should be followed. Procedures for compromised information systems should be well-formed, repeatable processes to preserve evidence, provide for rapid discovery and investigation, and meet necessary regulatory guidelines. When necessary, law enforcement, legal advisors, or both should be utilized to ensure proper evidence collection and documentation. Policies should also dictate the procedures for postinvestigation tasks as well, such as requiring compromised systems to be copied, archived, destroyed, reimaged, or reinstalled. It is generally not advisable to try simply to "clean up" a compromised system. It can be very difficult to guarantee that a compromised system once again has integrity.

35.7 CONCLUDING REMARKS. This chapter introduces security managers and professionals to securing peer-to-peer technologies, instant messaging, short messaging services, and collaboration tools. The suggestions and information in this chapter are meant to aid in making decisions regarding these tools within the organization's overall security plan. Many of the examples and concepts are meant to aid in the planning, policy development, and review of the organization's exposure to these technologies and their dangers. This chapter should serve as only a starting point for the organization's research on each topic and to ensure that information security managers at least have a brief understanding of each concept, its risks, prevention and mitigation strategies, and suggestions for response. It is very difficult to recommend solutions for every type of business, so each organization must make its own judgment for securing these technologies. The popularity and ubiquity of P2P, IM, SMS, and collaboration tools ensures that they will be part of every security plan for many years to come.

35.8 FURTHER READING

Kunz, T., and S. S. Ravi, eds. "Ad-Hoc, Mobile, and Wireless Networks." 5th International Conference, ADHOC-NOW 2006, Ottawa, Canada, August 17–19; *2006 Proceedings*. New York: Springer, 2007.

Piccard, P., B. Baskin, G. Spillman, and M. Sachs. *Securing IM and P2P Applications for the Enterprise*. Norwell, MA: Syngress, 2005.

Rittinghouse, J., and J. F. Ransome. *IM Instant Messaging Security*. Burlington, MA: Elsevier/Digital Press, 2005.

Taylor, I. J., and A. Harrison. *From P2P to Web Services and Grids: Peers in a Client/Server World*. New York: Springer, 2004.

35.9 NOTES

1. R. McMillan, "Google Corporate Calendar Leaks Corporate Data," *CSO Online*, April 17, 2007. Available: http://www2.csoonline.com/article/216451/ Google_Corporate_Calendar_Leaks_Corporate_Data?page=2&.

2. J. Borland, " 'Spyware' Piggybacks on Napster Rivals," *CNET News.com*, May 14, 2001. Available: http://news.com.com/2100-1023-257592.html.

3. N. Hindocha, "Instant Insecurity: Security Issues of Instant Messaging," *Security Focus*, January 14, 2003. Available: www.securityfocus.com/infocus/1657.

4. P. Festa, "ICQ logs spark corporate nightmare," *CNET News.com*, March 15, 2001. Available: http://news.com.com/2100-1023-254173.html?legacy=cnet.

5. National Vulnerability Database, http://nvd.nist.gov/nvd.cfm.

6. K. Scarfone and D. Dicoi, *Wireless Network Security for IEEE 802.11a/b/g and Bluetooth (DRAFT)*, NIST Special Publication 800-48 Revision 1 (Draft), 2007. Available: http://csrc.nist.gov/publications/drafts/800-48-rev1/Draft-SP800-48r1.pdf.

7. M. Rasch, "Don't Be Evil," *SecurityFocus*, 2007. Available: www.securityfocus.com/print/columnists/447.

CHAPTER 36

SECURING STORED DATA

David J. Johnson, Nicholas Takacs, and Jennifer Hadley

36.1 INTRODUCTION TO SECURING STORED DATA. This chapter reviews methods of securing data stored on nonvolatile media. Nonvolatile media include magnetic disks and their (hard) drives, compact discs (CDs), and digital video disks (DVDs) with their optical drives, and flash drives (also known as USB drives, flash disks, and memory keys). Volatile storage devices, which are not covered in this chapter, include random access memory (RAM) and other storage that loses its contents with a power loss.

36.1.1 Security Basics for Storage Administrators.

Storage systems have developed outside the security umbrella of other organizational assets. Because the storage arena is one of the most strategic parts of the infrastructure, professionals should take the same care in developing comprehensive security controls as those that are addressed for the remainder of the network. A number of vendors have focused on the development of secure storage environments that are scalable yet flexible; most address both the logical and physical aspects of security. However, any appropriate strategy for data storage protection includes a balance between protecting the confidentiality and integrity of the information while also ensuring its availability and utility to the system and to authorized users. Ultimately, those with a responsibility for data storage will also be tasked with maintaining this balance at a reasonable cost.

Knowing how and where data will be stored on a network, and addressing the identified risks to the data, is often a better and more efficient option in terms of resource usage (time and money) than applying the highest level of protection to all data. For example, unreleased earnings statements may have a higher impact to a company if disclosed than a job posting that ran in newspapers months before. An organization need not be a high-profile entity to suffer from a compromised pool of data. A single backup tape can contain enough concentrated personal or sensitive corporate information to experience a loss of credibility, lost revenue, and might even bring the organization to its knees. Worse, a backup that is copied illicitly may show no signs of having led to loss of control over confidential data.

36.1.2 Best Practices.

Every organization must keep its applications, servers, and end user systems up and running to make use of information and to maintain the highest degree of information availability and integrity. A tiered data protection model works best; it includes a layered defense, due diligence, and restricted management. Implemented correctly, security should be transparent. Best practices for providing a secure data storage environment include:

- Performing an audit and risk assessment on the storage infrastructure, looking for risks and vulnerabilities.
- Implementing authentication across the storage network that could coordinate authorization, password maintenance, and encryption.
- Implementing strong role-based access controls and assigning access rights to parties on a need-to-know basis.
- Adopting and enforcing data encryption and data classification policies. Based on the classification level assigned to the data, the organization's policy may require the encryption of the data at rest throughout the life cycle of the data. There may also be requirements to encrypt the data "in flight" (across the network) as well.
- Requiring strong security features and practices from storage system vendors and off-site storage providers.
- Remembering to secure the storage area network (SAN) at the switch (or fabric) level. Carving up the fabric by zones is one technique that limits access to various parts of the SAN.

- Creating a policy for discarding old devices and media, to include routinely performing tasks such as scrubbing and destroying all data storage devices and media.

- Evaluating retention policies and organizational or government regulatory issues.

- Isolating the storage management network from the organization's primary network. By not isolating the network, every employee potentially has access to the stored data.

- Establishing access log monitoring.

- Performing employee and contractor background checks as part of the human resources (HR) hiring procedures.

- Investigating physical controls in the organization to restricted access to data centers, locking storage cabinets and server racks, using locks built into some servers, and ensuring the reliability of the perimeter and building(s).

- Treating backups as an "orange alert" or heightened alarm process. Adopting secure media management tracking and handling policies that include backup requirements for financial information, employee data, and intellectual property.[1] Chapter 57 in this *Handbook* contains much information about data backup.

36.1.3 DAS, NAS, and SAN.   There are three primary methods for storing data: direct attached storage (DAS), network attached storage (NAS), and storage area networks (SANs).

Direct attached storage drives are those that are connected directly to the computer. DAS can either be internal, contained within the computer's case, or external and attached via a Peripheral Component Interconnect (PCI), or other bus channel. The risks to DAS devices are either their physical theft or access through the computer system that they service.

Network attached storage devices are specialized servers that run minimized operating systems and file systems designed specifically to support input/output (I/O) from other servers. The servers that attach to the NAS devices have DAS that contains their operating systems, applications, and other components but, normally, write all data to the NAS device via Transmission Control Protocol/Internet Protocol (TCP/IP) over Ethernet connections. NAS is utilized via file sharing protocol such as Network File System (NFS) for UNIX systems and Server Message Block (SMB) or Common Internet File System (CIFS) for Microsoft systems. (As CIFS grew out of SMB, the two are often listed as SMB/CIFS or CIFS/SMB.) As with any Ethernet connection, connections between a system and the NAS server that it uses are subject to being sniffed, to eavesdropping, and to packet capture. NFS and CIFS threats are discussed later in this chapter.

Storage area networks are collections of centralized disks that can be accessed by numerous servers. Using SANs can facilitate company growth, as most SANs options allow additional disks to be added to the pool as data storage needs increase, without having to take the attached systems off-line, as would need to occur if new DAS were being added to individual systems. Data backups can also be easier to control, as a single storage resource could potentially be backed up instead of each individual system. With the implementation of Redundant Array of Inexpensive (or Independant) Drive (RAID) or other disk redundancy techniques, writing data to multiple disks can be accomplished without impacting the application servers' performance. Such redundancy techniques can help to assure the availability of data stored on disks in the event that a disk crashes or otherwise becomes unusable. Systems can be attached to the SAN by various methods including TCP/IP and fiber channels. Fiber channels are discussed later in this chapter. Using IP for SANs connections enables servers to connect over the Internet—but this option must be used with caution, due to the security concerns of transferring data over the Internet.

36.1.4 Out-of-Band and In-Band Storage Management.   Managers may have to control storage locations remotely, that is, from a location other than a directly attached console. There are two approaches to such control communications, each with its own particular security issues:

1. **In-band management** uses the same network as the data transfers.
2. **Out-of-band management** uses a separate network.[2]

While in-band storage management uses the same channels as the data itself traverses for storage, out-of-band management uses alternative methods. For example, an out-of-band solution might have a storage administrator working from a desk and connecting to the storage system over the primary network used by all employees, while the data traverses a dedicated channel between the application server and the storage system.

With out-of-band management, consideration must be given to how to ensure that only authorized systems, such as the administrator's, are connecting to the storage system. This is especially necessary if the storage system does not require authenticated connections being established before a command is accepted. Without authentication, any system able to communicate with the storage system could issue commands that would negatively impact the storage system. Another risk is due to the interface used by management communications and the commands being sent across the wire without being encryption. For storage systems that are managed by HTTP interfaces by default, it may be possible to use HTTPS instead, in order to mitigate the risk of commands and logins being exposed and/or compromised due to network packet capture.

In-band management also has concerns. Commands sent in-band are normally sent in clear-text. Other threats of in-band storage management include:[3]

- Management interfaces being subjected to denial-of-service (DoS) attacks
- Commands providing information on other devices and controllers
- Set and reset commands being issued inappropriately

36.1.5 File System Access Controls.   File systems provide access control to data. UNIX file systems provide controls based on the user owner, the group owner, and "other," or those that are not the user or a member of the group that owns the data. Microsoft Windows systems allow for data owners to be specified and access granted by either individual usernames or group accounts. Access control lists (ACLs) can also be used to provide access exceptions to the normal access permissions of the data files.

When correctly applied, these access controls can be effective in preventing unauthorized access to data through normal usage. However, the file system trusts that the computer's operating system access controls have correctly authenticated and authorized the user. If the access controls for the operating system are circumvented, then file system access controls lose their effectiveness.

For more details of operating system and local area network access controls, see Chapters 24 and 25 in this *Handbook*.

36.1.6 Backup and Restore System Controls.   Systems used for the backup and restoration of data need extra security consideration because the data

contained on them are often critical to disaster recovery and business continuity. There are several threats to backup data that are not faced by attacks against other data stores. Although most systems only have their data stored on disk (DAS, NAS, or SAN), backup systems often write data to tapes or other removable media specifically intended for off-site storage. Another option is to back up data electronically to a remote system, either at another of the organization's data centers or with an off-site backup vendor. As with any transmission of data to remote facilities, the data must be protected during transit and at the destination facility.

Regardless of the media used, all data backups need to be stored at a secure, environmentally protected facility sufficiently distant from the originating location to mitigate the risk of losing both primary and backup data from a single major event, such as an earthquake, flood, or volcanic eruption. Additionally, the backup media storage needs to be secured by restricting access to authorized personnel only. Media used for backups needs to be evaluated to ensure that they meet or exceed the longevity needs of the data, as defined by the organization's backup policies and standards.

Additional risk from system imitation also needs to be considered. If an attacker is able to insert a system that impersonates a backup system, all of the data intended to be backed up may instead be written directly to the attacker's system. Conversely, if an attacker is able to insert a system that can masquerade as one or more data storage systems, then the attacker could request a restoration of data from existing backups, gaining unauthorized access to the information.

To mitigate such risks, interactions between data storage systems and backup systems should be authenticated. For manually controlled backups, systems could have backup accounts created that require an interactive login to authenticate the backup request. For automated backups, other options may be available, including the use of client and server certificates to authenticate both systems involved in the backup connection.

Off-site storage of data, whether written directly to a storage vendor's server or to removable media such as tape, deserves its own security considerations. For example, how does the vendor secure physical access to its site? How does it vet its employees? Most risks such as these can be mitigated by performing due diligence of the vendor prior to entering a contract and by eliminating prospective vendors that do not meet the organization's security needs.

Another mitigation strategy is to encrypt data backups before they are sent off-site. Many backup applications offer encryption methods. The use of encryption for files and other data storage systems is discussed later in Section 36.5 of this chapter. Similar techniques can be applied to backup data by encrypting it as it is written to the backup media.

For more details of backup strategies and security, see Chapter 57 in this *Handbook*.

36.1.7 Protecting Management Interfaces. Management interfaces pose one of the greatest threats to the security of stored data. These interfaces provide administrative access to the data stores, allowing individuals with appropriate access the ability to manipulate data elements, update account security, and perform other housekeeping activities. Therefore, care is required when implementing a storage solution to ensure that a well-defined defense in depth exists. Although two-factor authentication is more secure, it is not always practical. At a bare minimum, each administrative user should have a set of credentials, and complex password requirements, with a regular password change frequency. In addition, the individuals responsible for administering security should not be the same individuals responsible for managing the storage environment. This separation of duties limits the ability of any one individual to circumvent security controls, without some type of conspiracy between the storage and security administrators.

Another important component of the defense-in-depth strategy involves the use of audit logs. Logging should be enabled to detect violations of policy and of prescribed procedures. However, logs are valueless unless subjected to regular and random review, with follow-up if anomalies are detected. It is unrealistic to expect an individual to pore over voluminous log files on a daily basis. However, log aggregation and correlation technology can be employed to provide an additional layer of confidence as anomalous activity across systems can be related—potentially identifying an attack pattern or other irregular activity that would not be apparent from a single log. Regardless of the final implementation, the use of audit logs, and restrictions on the ability to access and modify those logs, plays an important part in guaranteeing that no data corruption occurred.

Mitigating these risks to the management interface requires careful monitoring and control of who can access and install these interfaces. With the movement to Web-based interfaces, this discussion comes down to strict user access control and authentication. In any case, it is imperative that only trusted users with a need to know be allowed access to the management interface. Once inside, individuals can manipulate the environment as needed to support their goals, whether to further organizational objectives or to perform malicious actions.

36.2   FIBER CHANNEL WEAKNESS AND EXPLOITS.   Fiber channels, while very economical, present unique challenges to the storage environment. The term "fiber channel" refers to more than just a fiber-based communication pathway, but rather a complex communication protocol. There are a number of inherent weaknesses in the technology, some of which are fairly straightforward and manageable, while others introduce questions of the viability of the technology in larger storage environments.

One of the most serious security weaknesses with a fiber channel is that all communications occur in clear-text. Fortunately, when fiber channel implementations occur completely within a data center or other secured area, this is not a major concern, as the ability of unauthorized individuals to intercept traffic on the "wire" is limited. However, fiber channel does not natively support authentication or data integrity checking, leaving the potential for unauthorized tampering.

From a vulnerability perspective, attackers can use the Internet Protocol (IP) to craft exploits against fiber channel, since both protocols use a frame-based communication scheme. Unfortunately, based on the clear-text issue just discussed, an attacker could sniff frames off the fiber channel connection and gain information needed to craft an attack. This section focuses on three types of common attacks: man in the middle, session hijacking, and name server corruption. It is important to note that most attacks on a storage network require physical access to that environment or access to the appropriate sniffing hardware, which increases the overall complexity of the attack.

36.2.1   Man-in-the-Middle Attacks.   Man-in-the-middle attacks take advantage of weaknesses in the frame-based communications that fiber channel employs. Similar to IP-based attacks, man-in-the-middle attacks involve an attacker intercepting communications, stealing or changing data, and passing that frame on to the intended destination. Fiber channel includes a sequence ID and sequence count, both intended to ensure consistent communication from sender to receiver. Much like IP, the sequence count is a very predictable, sequential number, allowing an attacker to anticipate the next sequence number and forward a packet ahead of the sending system. This allows the attacker to intercept the stream without the authorization of either party. Mitigating this issue requires data integrity checking to guarantee reception of the correct information.

36.2.2   Session Hijacking.   Session hijacking presents the same type of problem as man-in-the-middle attacks and occurs in much the same way. However, this type of attack focuses on the lack of authentication in fiber channel environments. Instead of the attacker manipulating data in each frame and passing it on, knowledge of the sequence ID and sequence count is used to intercept and control the session, making the recipient believe that the attacker is really the original sender. The newly controlled session can then be used to extract whatever data or other information the attacker wishes. Mitigating this issue requires strong authentication to provide a guarantee that the original sender is still the same system throughout the length of the connection.

36.2.3   Name Server Corruption.   The last type of attack in this section involves address spoofing, similar to DNS spoofing in the IP world. Each fiber channel connection registers its name with World Wide Name (WWN) service, through two processes, a Fabric Login (FLOGI) and a Port Login (PLOGI). Typically, name server corruption occurs during the PLOGI process, by allowing an incorrect host to register itself with the fiber channel switch (which contains the WWN service) using a spoofed address. The switch would register that host under that address as if it were valid, due to the lack of any host authentication. When the real host tries to connect, the switch would deny that connection, because the incorrect host is already connected. This type of attack requires some timing on the attacker's part but can be easy to accomplish due to the weaknesses previously discussed.

36.2.4   Fiber Channel Security.   This short examination of fiber channels has pointed out that many weaknesses exist. However, this does not mean that fiber channel should be dismissed as a suitable technology. When implementing fiber channel into an environment, care must be taken to address these vulnerabilities, taking into consideration location, distance, and availability of the implementation to individuals, systems, and other devices on the network. Taking this one step further, consideration must also be given to the physical placement of the devices and wiring to mitigate the risks associated with using fiber channels. Vendors are also answering the call by offering technology to help secure fiber channel. Although that discussion is outside the scope of this section, zoning and LUN masking are two options for securing fiber channel implementations.[4]

36.3   NFS WEAKNESS AND EXPLOITS.   Network file systems (NFS) provide a service allowing a user on a client machine to access network-based resources as if they were local to that user. This service is built upon the remote procedure call (RPC) service. While very useful in a networked computing environment, NFS presents a number of security issues that must be addressed prior to implementation. NFS is typically geared toward high-bandwidth environments, such as a LAN, or networks sharing nonsensitive information. Since NFS does not provide encryption between hosts, using this technology for other networks, especially those exposed to the Internet, introduces additional risk. This section describes three of the most common weaknesses and exploits for NFS: user and file permissions, trusted hosts, and buffer overflows.

36.3.1   User and File Permissions.   Although a full treatment of NFS weaknesses is outside the scope of this chapter, it is important to call out the major issues. Aside from the aforementioned lack of encryption, NFS allows user access based on the particular host connected to the NFS share. This means that any user connected to that host can access the network resources. Restricting users to read-only access eliminates the potential to use NFS as a collaborative technology, because users can no longer create or update information on the shares. This leads to another issue when mounting shares as read-write. Any user connected to the host can access another user's files, as the only protection the file has is its permissions. Administrators attempt to mitigate this risk by forcing all users to access the share under a group or common set of read-only credentials, but this approach eliminates some of the benefits that a network share provides. The read-only share then requires administrators to update or edit files providing a library-style approach, rather than a collaborative file management environment.

36.3.2   Trusted Hosts.   Problems with the trusted host technology specifically concern the authentication of hosts to the NFS environment. Because NFS controls mount requests based on the host connecting, and not a particular user, a rogue host could request an NFS mount and make changes to resources. Additionally, an attacker could compromise a DNS server used by the system exporting the NFS and then modify the DNS entry to point to an unauthorized machine, thus allowing an unauthorized system to mount the file share. Because there are no login credentials shared prior to mounting NFS shares, if the hosts are not trusted, there are no additional checks to validate the integrity of the host.

36.3.3   Buffer Overflows.   In many implementations of NFS, data input checking does not occur before processing a request. This presents an opportunity for a buffer overflow attack. Where a directory removal request comes to an NFS server from a user with read-write privileges, the server does not check the length of the path name, and the user can include additional instructions beyond what the server should normally receive. Those instructions, probably malicious, could then be executed by the server as an administrative account, such as "root" or "administrator." As a result, unintended or unauthorized data manipulation can occur.

36.3.4   NFS Security.   NFS provides benefits to network-connected users by its ability to share files, directories, and other resources, but there are inherent security weaknesses in the technology. Recent implementations of NFS have included Kerberos authentication to help validate the users and what they are able to do. In addition, the same validation can be used to validate hosts before they connect to the NFS server. However, these improvements are only partial solutions. Buffer overflows continue to be discovered, and it would be unwise to assume that NFS, or any other network technology, can be completely secured.

36.4   CIFS EXPLOITS.   The Common Internet File System (CIFS), an Internet-enabled Server Message Block (SMB) protocol, builds on that protocol by including encryption and secure authentication to the existing resource sharing capabilities of SMB. Unfortunately, from a security perspective, CIFS blends some of the new with some of the old, and the result includes a number of security issues.

36.4.1 Authentication. CIFS implementations provide either a straight password-based authentication scheme or a challenge-response scheme. Both of these approaches occur in clear-text, allowing anyone with wire access to intercept and capture authentication credentials to the network share. Even with the challenge-response approach, attackers could spoof a transaction and gain access to the share. Recent implementations of CIFS rely on Kerberos for authentication and, much like NFS, while providing additional security, introduce Kerberos-based vulnerabilities, which are outside the scope of this section. Some CIFS implementations also provide a "share-level" security model rather than a "user-level" security model. In essence, rather than each user maintaining individual credentials, the share has only one set of credentials, which all users share. The weaknesses inherent to a share-level model are similar to those found with the use of group or shared accounts on any other system.

In addition to the authentication issues, CIFS is also vulnerable to dictionary and brute-force attacks against a user's credentials. These generally involve a chosen plaintext attack, helped by intercepting challenge-response pairs during the authentication process. However, both online and off-line dictionary attacks are available to the attacker depending on the amount of time available to watch the connection attempts.

36.4.2 Rogue or Counterfeit Hosts. It is important to identify the differences between the attack surface of CIFS and that of NFS. Man-in-the-middle and the trusted host issue both apply to CIFS, with some different concerns. Improperly configured CIFS clients can be fooled into thinking that they should supply a password instead of interacting with a challenge-response scenario, thus supporting man-in-the-middle attacks. Additionally, if a CIFS environment does not enable session or message authentication, it removes security controls designed specifically to protect against these types of attacks.

CIFS shares many of the same security issues with NFS. However, most of the issues can be avoided by enabling security features included with the protocol. Man-in-the-middle and session-hijacking attacks, in addition to replay and spoofing attacks, can be avoided by message and session authentication. This does not suggest that CIFS can be completely secured; rather, care must be taken during the configuration step of implementation to make use of all available security controls.

36.5 ENCRYPTION. Many individuals and organizations focus on encrypting data while it is in motion and transiting networks, especially the Internet. The use of encryption for data while at rest, or stored, is equally important. As previously mentioned, stored data are compromised by security breaches more often than data in transit. With the use of a sufficiently strong algorithm and sufficiently sized key, data that are stored encrypted can be made unusable for those without the ability to decrypt them. Even if an attack is successful at gaining full control of the data for brute-force attempts at decryption, a proper algorithm and key can prevent the data from being decrypted for a reasonably sufficient period—long enough that any personally identifiable information (PII) or other sensitive, confidential, or proprietary information would be of no value except to historians.

See Chapter 7 in this *Handbook* for more details of cryptography; see Chapter 37 for details of the public key cryptosystem.

36.5.1 Recoverability. Key principles of information assurance (IA) include protecting the availability and utility of data. By its nature, encryption can take away these protections in exchange for protecting the authenticity, confidentiality, and integrity of the data while it mitigates the risk of losing possession of the data. When using data encryption, it is important to consider the possible need to recover the data in the event that the user or primary key is unable to be located. There are several ways to accomplish this.

Key escrow is one method to facilitate the recovery of encrypted data. By storing the key with a trusted party, a lost key can be removed from escrow and used to decrypt the data. With public key encryption, additional decryption keys (ADKs) can be used with some encryption tools. Corporate ADKs are keys that can be used during the encryption process to encrypt the data automatically with a key that is tightly controlled and used only by designated individuals for the recovery of encrypted data.

36.5.2   File Encryption.   The use of encryption on a file-by-file basis is a good method for securing data. With file encryption, a user can pick and choose which files to encrypt. Files containing sensitive data can be encrypted while nonsensitive files are stored without encryption. This method has the least impact on a system, but it puts most responsibility on a user, who must determine which files should be encrypted.

Operating system files cannot be encrypted, so configuration files that may contain information on the organization's systems are left as risk—as are application code files. These code files may be for the organization's proprietary application that provides a significant competitive advantage. However, such files are rarely encrypted, as doing so can provide a hindrance for users, who must remember to decrypt each and every file when required.

36.5.3   Volume Encryption and Encrypted File Systems.   Both volume encryption and encrypted file systems offer protection to data and can be easier for users than per-file encryption. The ease of use comes from the single operation required to access multiple files. Depending on its configuration, a location can remain decrypted and accessible for a few minutes or several hours.

A critical difference between file encryption and volume encryption is that decryption is carried out at the driver level as data are moved from disk into RAM. The entire volume is *not* decrypted in its totality. For example, an entire 4 GB partition encrypted by PGP Desktop would take several minutes to decrypt, whereas access to the PGP container for the volume is granted within a second when the encrypted volume or folder is mounted. In addition, dynamic decryption ensures that there is no large decrypted copy of the original materials stored on the hard disk for reverse cryptanalysis in case of an aborted shutdown.

With partial encryption of a disk, only a portion of the data stored on the disk and specifically written to the encrypted partition is protected. Usually operating system and application files are not encrypted, so a stolen or otherwise compromised disk is vulnerable to attackers who would gain access to any file not saved into the encrypted volume or file system. If a user forgets to encrypt a file containing sensitive data, then the data are accessible to anyone who can activate the operating system or read the disk drive.

36.5.4   Full Disk Encryption.   Author Ryan Groom lists cogent reasons for using full disk encryption on laptops.[5] These can be restated for any system. The primary reasons to use full disk encryption are that it protects data if a drive is lost or stolen, it is safer and more effective than volume encryption or encrypted file systems, it can be transparent to users, and it helps comply with legal and regulatory issues.

Full disk encryption secures the file system and operating system files but leaves a small boot portion of the drive unencrypted. The unencrypted region allows the encryption software to load; to request the password, passphrase, or token needed to initiate dynamic decryption of the drive contents on demand; and to continue loading the operating system.

Depending on the solution chosen, users can see relatively little difference between a system using full disk encryption and a system that does not. The primary visibility to users is that on a system boot, the user will be prompted to decrypt the drive. System performance is somewhat reduced, primarily during the boot of the system while significant data from the disk are decrypted, and again on shutdown as unencrypted data are cleaned up to prevent readability without authorization. This minimal impact on users is greatly outweighed by the protection afforded by full disk encryption.

As with volume encryption, full disk encryption involves dynamic decryption of ciphertext as it flows from disk to memory buffers. With modern data-transfer speeds and processor capabilities, there is no significant performance delay due to on-the-fly decryption once the operating system has been loaded.

When a system is lost or stolen, an attacker has, essentially, an unlimited amount of time to gain access to the data. If the data are not encrypted, they can simply be read. With encrypted file systems or volume encryption, only a portion of the data is stored encrypted. Data that are not in one of these encrypted locations are vulnerable—including swap spaces and temporary file locations used by the operating system. With full disk encryption, the entire contents of the drive are protected. Even with full physical access to the disk (e.g., by installing it into another computer under the attacker's control) or with a copy of the encrypted disk, an attacker must break the encryption in order to gain any information—an almost impossible task with the key sizes currently in use, except perhaps by government cryptanalysis labs using massively parallel architectures for brute-force cracking. With strong encryption, management may be able to satisfy the concerns of clients if an organization has to disclose the loss of equipment and must provide an assurance that, even though the disk was lost, the client and organization's data cannot be accessed.

36.5.5 Vulnerability of Volume, File System, and Full Disk Encryption.
As strong as the protection provided by volume, file system, and full disk encryption, there is one significant weakness. Once a user is authorized to access the data, and the operating system dynamically decrypts data as required, the system is vulnerable to attacks by any interloper who has physical access to the unlocked, unprotected session. For example, if a system contains sensitive data and is connected to a network, any attack over the network can potentially compromise the data when the authorized user's session allows access to the decrypted data. Additionally, some researchers have identified attacks against keys while they are stored in RAM by freezing the RAM using substances such as liquid nitrogen and putting the RAM in another machine to read it. The practicality of this attack is limited as RAM is volatile memory and the period during which an attack could occur is limited.

This vulnerability must be stressed to users who may misunderstand the implications of encryption, especially those who insist on storing sensitive data on their laptops. Although full disk encryption protects the data when the system is not booted, once the user decrypts the disk at boot, the data are available not just to them but to anyone else who gains access to the system. Systems must use defense-in-depth strategies with personal firewalls to prevent unauthorized network access to the system; users must maintain physical possession of the system, especially once they have entered their decryption key. If a user with a Windows operating system on a laptop locks the screen and then walks away, the data are protected only by the strength of the system password.

Especially sensitive data should be encrypted at the file level. Alternatively, volume and file system encryption can be used with reasonable timeouts applied. Both of these options provide increased protection of data while a system is booted. Combined with full disk encryption, the risks to data are greatly reduced. Moreover, what could be worse for an attacker who broke the full disk encryption only to find that the information is encrypted another time, or two if file encryption, volume encryption, and full disk encryption are all in use?

36.5.6   Database Encryption.   For many organizations, the databases that are the primary location for storing data are also an excellent target for attackers. By employing database encryption, the time an attacker needs to gain access can be greatly increased.

Databases can be protected by placing them on a system that can be accessed only via a secured connection and one that employs volume or full disk encryption. In addition, there are database encryption tools designed to protect the data held within these stores even without disk encryption. These tools employ encryption at the field (individual data element), column (a collection of fields that align in a column when seen in a tabular view), and full database encryption. One of the advantages of database-specific encryption is that it can support stricter control around access, as users would need different keys, passwords, or passphrases in order to access the different databases instead of all users being able to use a single credential to access multiple databases.

In an article for SearchSecurity.com, James C. Foster points out that applying database encryption as a tactical way to address compliance with laws, regulations, or company policy is not without risk, as application speed and performance can be negatively impacted if the encryption is not implemented correctly.[6] Foster recommends considering these factors to help mitigate this risk:

- **Encryption of foreign or super keys** should *not* be done as the keys are used to provide relational connections between tables, schema, and/or databases. Since these values are not encrypted, they should not contain information that is personally identifiable or needs to be encrypted, such as a customer's credit card or Social Security Number.

- **Encryption key protection** needs to be addressed as if a single key is used for all data. The database is vulnerable to being fully compromised if control of the key is lost.

- **Full versus partial database encryption** needs to be determined as performance is impacted due to the need to encrypt and decrypt data as it is written to or read from the database. Consider only encrypting columns that contain sensitive data; often this is all that is required or suggested to be protected by regulations or laws.

36.5.6.1   Improving Vendor Provided Options.   Database vendors such as Oracle Corporation and Microsoft have encryption options that are specifically designed to protect the information in their databases. These options have improved over time and are becoming more robust and mature.

Microsoft SQL Server 2005 offers enhancements to column encryption. Also introduced was "an integrated and hierarchical infrastructure for managing encryption keys." The product documentation continues: "Built-in encryption functions and application programming interfaces (APIs) make it easier for an organization to create an encryption security framework."[7]

Oracle Database 10*g* Release 2 improves on existing encryption options within Oracle databases by introducing Transparent Data Encryption (TDE). When using TDE, a database administrator is able to specify that a column needs to be encrypted, and the database automatically encrypts data during insert operations and decrypts the data during selects. This can be achieved "without writing a single line of code."[8] Arup Nanda provides a good overview of this feature in the September/October 2005 issue of *Oracle Magazine*.[9]

36.5.6.2 *Implementation Considerations.* As with any implementation of encryption, careful consideration must be given to determining the method and process for implementing the solution as well as to the data that are being encrypted. Encrypting a key field needs to be avoided. If sensitive data are in the key field, significant work may be required to create new key fields and re-create table linkages, or the organization may decide to accept the performance degradation that could occur with encrypting the key field. That is, of course, assuming that encrypting the key field does not cause the database to become unusable.

The costs associated with implementing an encrypted database solution must also be weighed against the business risk. For companies that have little data needing encryption, database encryption may be inappropriate. Legal and regulatory requirements also need to be considered; database encryption may be mandated in order to protect data and to avoid criminal or civil liabilities. The attendant loss of public and customer confidence, in the event of a data breach, is also a powerful incentive.

36.6 DATA DISPOSAL. A final consideration for securing stored data is the disposal of the media that contains the data.

For sanitizing electronic media, United States Department of Defense 5220.22-M can provide guidance.[10] Essentially, the media should be sanitized such that the data originally written to it cannot be recovered. One method for achieving this can include these four steps:

1. Erase the data.
2. Write random or meaningless data to the media.
3. Erase the data.
4. Repeat until the desired level of sanitization is met.

For information stored on paper, the paper should, at a minimum, be shredded before being discarded. Use of a cross-cut shredder is preferable as it increases the difficulty of piecing the documents back together. Additional steps can that can be taken if needed, and facilities are available that burn the shredded paper and mix it with water to speed its deterioration. Over the past several years, vendors specializing in on-site paper destruction have become commonplace. These vendors bring trucks to a client's site and collect paper that is then shredded on-site before being taken to a facility that recycles, burns, or otherwise disposes of the waste in a secure manner.

For more information about data disposal, see Chapter 57 in this *Handbook*.

36.7   CONCLUDING REMARKS.   The security of stored data is of critical importance. More data breaches occur against data in unsecured storage locations than is compromised during transit. With proper data storage security, there is less risk to data from all kinds of threats, internal and external. Using secure channels for writing data to disk and protecting the disks themselves is of increasing importance as attackers usually have one of two goals: causing systems or data to be made unavailable, or compromising the confidentiality and integrity of data. By combining secure communication channels, data encryption, and physical protection of data storage devices, the security of information can be better assured.

36.8   FURTHER READING

Barker, E. B., W. C. Barker, and A. Lee. " Guideline for Implementing Cryptography in the Federal Government," NIST Special Publication 800-21. National Institute for Standards and Technology, Technology Administration, United States Department of Commerce. Accessed online at: http://csrc.nist.gov/publications/nistpubs/800-21-1/sp800-21-1_Dec2005.pdf.

Barker, W. C. " Recommendation for the Triple Data Encryption Algorithm (TDEA) Block Cipher," NIST Special Publication 800-67. National Institute for Standards and Technology, Technology Administration, United States Department of Commerce. Accessed online at: http://csrc.nist.gov/publications/nistpubs/800-67/SP800-67.pdf

Chudnow, C.. "Storage Area Network Security: The Human Factor," *Computer Technology Review* (Fall 2006). Accessed online at: www.wwpi.com/index.php?option=com_content&task=view&id=1580&Itemid=44.

Curtis, W. C. *Backup & Recovery*. Sebastopol, CA: O'Reilly, 2007.

Curtis, W. C. *Using SANs and NAS*. Sebastopol, CA: O'Reilly, 2002.

Dwivedi, H.. *Securing Storage: A Practical Guide to SAN and NAS Security*. Chapter 2: "SANs: Fibre Channel Security". Boston: Addison-Wesley: 2006. Accessed online at: www.awprofessional.com/content/images/0321349954/samplechapter/Dwivedi_ch02.pdf.

FalconStor Software and Ologic. "Fibre Channel Security White Paper," White Papers, ITtoolbox, October 11, 2005. Accessed online at: http://storage.ittoolbox.com/white-papers/fibre-channel-security-white-paper-3422.

Foster, J. C. "Look before Leaping into Database Encryption." Compliance Counselor, SearchSecurity.com, September 29, 2006. Accessed online at: http://searchsecurity.techtarget.com/tip/0,289483,sid14_gci1219561,00.html.

Harris, S. *All-in-One CISSP Certification Exam Guide*, 2nd ed. New York: McGraw/Hill/Osborne, 2003.

Polk, W. T., D. F. Dodson, and W. E. Burr. "Cryptographic Algorithms and Key Sizes for Personal Identity Verification," NIST Special Publication 800-78. National Institute for Standards and Technology, Technology Administration, United States Department of Commerce. Accessed online at: http://csrc.nist.gov/publications/nistpubs/800-78/sp800-78-final.pdf.

Regan, K. "Mounting Data Spurs Corporate Storage Spending," *E-Commerce Times*, March 13, 2007. Accessed online at: www.ecommercetimes.com/story/56270.html.

Shepler, S., *et al.*, Network Working Group. "RFC 3530 Network File System Version 4 Protocol" (April 2003). Proposed Standard Requests for Comment, Internet Engineering Task Force. Accessed at: http://tools.ietf.org/html/rfc3530.

Troppens, U., R. Erkens, and W. Müller. *Storage Networks Explained: Basics and Application of Fibre Channel SAN, NAS iSCSI and InfiniBand.* Hoboken, NJ: John Wiley & Sons, 2004.

United States National Security Agency. " Fact Sheet NSA Suite B Cryptography." Accessed online at: www.nsa.gov/ia/industry/crypto_suite_b.cfm.

Verhelst, W. "Securing NFS," Free Software Magazine, Wouter Verhelst's Blog, November 26, 2006. Accessed online at: www.freesoftwaremagazine.com/blogs/securing_nfs.

36.9 NOTES

1. M. Kincora, "Strategic Storage: Storage Security—Change Old Habits and Stop Data Theft," SearchStorage.com (November 2005). Accessed online at: http://searchstorage.techtarget.com.au/topics/article.asp?DocID=1115249&NodeID=298728.

2. W. C. Preston, H. Dwivedi, M. E. Kabay, and S. Gordon, *Storage Security Handbook* (Neoscale Systems, 2002). Accessed online at: www.neoscale.com/English/Downloads/Storage_Security_Handbook/.

3. Preston et al., *Storage Security Handbook.*

4. A. Loftus and C. Kerner, "SAN Lessons Learned," 2003. Accessed online at: http://dims.ncsa.uiuc.edu/set/san/src/San_Lessons_Learned.pdf.

5. R. Groom, "8 Reasons for Full Disk Encryption," "Business Security," About.com. Accessed online at: http://bizsecurity.about.com/od/windowsdesktopsecurity/a/top8fulldisk.htm.

6. James C. Foster, "Look before Leaping into Database Encryption," SearchSecurity.com, September 29, 2006. Accessed online at: http://searchsecurity.techtarget.com/tip/0,289483,sid14_gci1219561,00.html.

7. "Improving Data Security by Using SQL Server 2005," Microsoft® TechNet. Accessed online at http://technet.microsoft.com/en-us/library/bb735261.aspx.

8. A. Nanda, "Transparent Data Encryption," TECHNOLOGY:Security, ORACLE® Technology Network. Accessed online at: www.oracle.com/technology/oramag/oracle/05-sep/o55security.html.

9. Nanda, "Transparent Data Encryption."

10. "DoD 5220.22-M National Industrial Security Program Operating Manual (NISPOM)," 1997. Available from www.usaid.gov/policy/ads/500/d522022m.pdf; also J. Vacca, "The Basics of SAN Security, Part I"; www.enterprisestorageforum.com/sans/features/article.php/11188_1431341_2.

CHAPTER 37

PKI AND CERTIFICATE AUTHORITIES

Santosh Chokhani, Padgett Peterson, and Steven Lovaas

37.1 INTRODUCTION.   Where at one time the use of encryption across the Internet consisted mainly of individuals with Pretty Good Privacy (PGP) exchanging secure e-mail and each maintaining a private "web of trust," today's use of encryption encompasses a much wider range of elements including proofing, issuance, revocation, identification, federation, bridging, encryption, digital signing and a myriad of ancillary processes. In fact, what the user experiences is just the tip of the required support structure. Proper management of information involved in an encryption infrastructure (or cryptosystem) is about trust, what is required to establish that trust, and how much to grant.

Originally, the prime use of encryption was outside the network perimeter, where unprotected data sent and received by the organization over public networks were perceived as most vulnerable to disclosure, modification, insertion, deletion, and replay attacks. To protect the data being transported over untrusted networks, the only practical and cost-effective technology is cryptography. Cryptography is at the heart of both virtual private networks (VPNs) and public key infrastructures. For further information on encryption, see Chapter 7. For a review of cryptography, see Chapter 7 in this *Handbook* and *Applied Cryptography* by Bruce Schneier.[1]

37.1.1 Symmetric Key Cryptography.   Symmetrical cryptography (aka single key or secret key) uses the same key to encrypt cleartext into ciphertext and to decrypt ciphertext back into cleartext. This process is illustrated in Exhibit 37.1.

Although symmetric cryptography (e.g., Advanced Encryption Standard (AES), Data Encryption Standard (DES), Rivest Cipher 4 (RC4) has specific advantages in that it has a dense keyspace (any integer) and is computationally very fast, it has a fundamental weakness: Both the originator and each recipient must have the key. Key sharing has two issues:

1. Key exchange must be performed: Somehow each user must have the same key.
2. There is weak accountability: Anyone with the symmetric key could have produced the document.

37.1.2 Public Key Cryptosystem.   In contrast to secret key cryptosystems, public key cryptosystems (PKCs) use pairs of related keys that are generated together. The ciphertext produced by one key can be decrypted only with the other member of the same key pair. One of these keys is kept secret (the *private* key) and the other is published for all to use (the *public* key). It does not matter which is designated as which, but once designated, the key cannot be changed. In practice, encryption with one key is often faster than with the other. This one is generally selected as the public key.

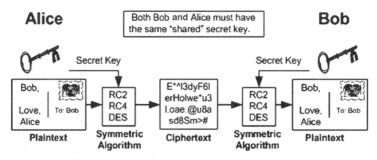

EXHIBIT 37.1 Symmetric (Secret) Key Encryption

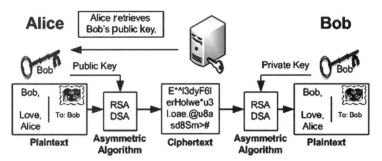

EXHIBIT 37.2   Asymmetric or Public Key Encryption

In the simplest form, to conceal a message in transit so that only the desired recipient may read it, the cleartext is encrypted using the recipient's public key, as shown in Exhibit 37.2. Only the recipient's secret key can decrypt the transmitted ciphertext. Similarly, to verify message integrity and authenticity, it is possible to encrypt information with a sender's private key. This allows anyone with access to that sender's public key to validate the message by decrypting the ciphertext successfully.

37.1.3 Advantages of Public Key Cryptosystem over Secret Key Cryptosystem.   For securing data transmissions, public key cryptosystems are preferred over secret key cryptosystems for these reasons:

- Public key cryptosystems require fewer keys to manage: Each party (n) has a key pair, so the total number of keys is $2n$, instead of being proportional to n^2 as for secret key cryptosystems.

- Because private keys need not be distributed or otherwise managed, public key cryptosystems require only demonstrated integrity and authenticity of the public keys themselves. Users (the *relying parties*) must have assurance that their public keys truly belong to the publishers. This requires signing by a trusted third party or by a mutually trusted source.

- Because no secret keys are transmitted over any network, PKCs are not susceptible to compromise even when public keys have to be changed. PKCs can be used to encrypt temporary keys (*session keys*) that can be used one time for secret key cryptography to obviate the heavier computational load of the PKC.

- To encrypt a message so that multiple PKC users can receive and decipher the ciphertext securely, PKC software can create a session key. This secret key is then encrypted with each recipient's public key and sent with the ciphertext to all recipients without compromising confidentiality.

PKC-based digital signatures can also provide the basis for nonrepudiation in the event of a dispute. Only the possessor of a private key could have sent a message decrypted by its public key. In contrast, because of the use of shared secrets, symmetric secret key cryptosystems alone cannot reasonably support nonrepudiation.

37.1.4 Combination of the Two.   At this point, it may be easiest to consider the elements of the different types of cryptography, as shown in Exhibit 37.3.

The difference is similar to that between electronic data interchange and e-commerce. Symmetric encryption is good for a very few exchanges with people you

Exhibit 37.3   Symmetric versus Asymmetric Encryption

Type	Keyspace	Speed
Asymmetric	Sparse	Slow
Symmetric	Dense	Fast

trust; asymmetric encryption is good for many, many small exchanges with people or devices you may have never met.

Today, the most common use is to combine both types: For a document to be e-mailed securely, a symmetric algorithm is selected and a random key generated. The document is encrypted using the symmetric algorithm and key. The symmetric key is then encrypted with the asymmetric public key of each recipient and is then added as a header to the document.

For digital signing, a similar mechanism is used except that a hashing algorithm (e.g., Secure Hash Algorithm (SHA), Message Digest 5 (MD5)) is used to create a hash value of the document, and the hash is then encrypted (signed) with the private key of the originator and accompanies the document. The originator's public key can be used to decrypt (verify) the hash, and the hash is used to verify the document.

37.2   NEED FOR PUBLIC KEY INFRASTRUCTURE.   The PKC depends on the integrity of each public key and of that public key's binding to a specific entity, such as a person, an institution, or a network component. Without mechanisms for ensuring integrity and authenticity, a relying party is vulnerable to masquerading attacks through public key substitution.

To illustrate, suppose that ABC Company wants to send a confidential message to XYZ Corp. that no one else can read. ABC could use XYZ's public key to encrypt the message, although, for the sake of efficiency, ABC probably would use a symmetric algorithm to encrypt the message and the public key algorithm to encrypt the symmetric key. However, if ABC can be tricked into using an attacker's public key as if it were XYZ's public key, then the attacker would be able to decrypt the message. This technique is known as public key *spoofing*.

Such public key spoofing by the attacker would, however, make it impossible for XYZ to read the message from ABC, as was originally intended. Therefore, such an attack probably would continue with the attacker reencrypting ABC's message, using XYZ's real public key, and sending it on to XYZ. Such interception and reencryption is an example of a *man-in-the-middle* attack. However, if the sender also signed the original message, this is something that the attacker could not duplicate, so the message could not be changed but only intercepted.

Another example of breaching the connection between a public key and its owner involves digital signature verification. Suppose ABC wants to verify XYZ's signature. If the attacker could trick ABC into using the attacker's public key as if it were XYZ's public key, then the attacker would be able to sign messages masquerading as XYZ using the attacker's private key. ABC would unknowingly use the replaced public key and be spoofed into thinking that the message actually was signed by XYZ.

This same problem exists with the core of Internet commerce today, Secure Sockets Layer v2 (SSLv2). SSLv3 and Transport Layer Security (TLS) can prevent this, but then every participant must have a certificate trusted by the other party. This is where the concept of a *trust chain* comes in. If a trusted third party has signed XYZ's public key, then the attacker would also have to have a key signed by the same authority as well. Otherwise, a warning would appear that the key was not recognized.

A serious issue is the sheer number of certificate authorities (over 100) built into most browsers, from a variety of countries. The browser trusts all certificates issued by any of these by default, and not all are necessarily worthy of trust.

In summary, both for digital signature and encryption services, the relying party must use the public key of the correct party in order to maintain security. There are various manual, electronic, and hybrid mechanisms for the distribution of public keys in a trusted manner, so that the relying party can be sure to have the correct public keys of the subscribers. These mechanisms for distribution and binding of public keys are known as a Public Key Infrastructure (PKI)).

The beauty of a signed public key is that the trust is inherent with the signature provided the signer is trusted. Unlike a *web of trust,* such as that used by the original PGP which requires all keys be accepted individually by each user, with a *chain of trust* a single signer (the root certificate authority) can provide trust to millions of certificates. Trust need not be absolute; it may be contextual. For example, a certificate signed by an employer can be trusted for elements relating to employment but not for credit cards. See the discussion of trust levels in Section 37.6.1.

37.3   PUBLIC KEY CERTIFICATE.   The technique that is most scalable uses a public key certificate issued by a trusted party called the certification authority (CA). A CA issues public key certificates to the various subscribers by putting together subscriber information and signing the information using the CA's private key. The generally accepted standard for public key certificates is the X.509 version 3,[2] as defined in RFC 5280 and subsequent text.

X.509 certificates are expressed in Abstract Syntax Notation 1 (ASN.1), which is a complex binary notation. In order to be passed through e-mail, certificates are usually MIME (aka Base 64) encoded, expressing the binary syntax in ASCII characters.[3]

The advantage to using a CA and a chain of trust is that by trusting the root, the user automatically trusts all keys that it has issued whether or not the user has ever seen them.

Each CA's certificate may contain this key information:

- Version number of certificate standard
- Certificate serial number (unique for every certificate issued by the CA)
- Algorithm and associated parameters used by CA to sign the certificate
- CA name
- Validity period for the certificate
- Subscriber name
- Subscriber public key, public key algorithm, and associated parameters
- CA unique identifier (optional)
- Subscriber unique identifier (optional)
- Extensions (optional)
- CA's digital signature

The relying parties require the CA's public key so that they can verify the digital signatures on the certificates issued by the CA. The relying party must trust the CA's public key, most likely obtained during the registration process. Once the signatures are verified, relying parties can use the subscriber name and subscriber public key in the certificate with as much confidence in the accuracy of the information as they have in the trustability of the CA.

In some situations, a CA may need to revoke the binding between a subscriber and that subscriber's public key. For example, the subscriber private key may be compromised (i.e., there may be reason to believe that the secret key has fallen into the hands of someone else). Since a public key certificate is an electronic object and can reside in several places at the same time, it is neither practical nor possible to recall, delete, or erase all the copies of the subscriber certificate in a distributed environment. Thus, to invalidate a public key certificate by severing the binding between the subscriber and the subscriber public key, the CA creates a list of invalid certificates. This list is called a certificate revocation list (CRL). The relying parties must check that a certificate is not on the CRL prior to using the public key in the certificate. If the certificate is on the CRL, the relying party must not use it. The CA signs the CRL to allow the relying parties to verify the CRL's integrity and authenticity. The key information in the X.509 version 2 CRL is:

- Version number of CRL standard
- Algorithm and associated parameters used by CA to sign the certificate
- CA name
- This CRL issuance time
- Next CRL issuance time (optional)
- List of revoked certificates (listing these items for each certificate):
  ○ Certificate serial number
  ○ Time CA was notified of revocation
  ○ Extensions related to the revoked certificate (optional)
- Extensions related to CRL (optional)
- A's digital signature

It is important that a certificate contain only those elements specifically required for operation and that these be used properly otherwise confusion and improper/unexpected use may result.

Probably the most misused element is the *Key Usage* extension. (It is used so badly that often a second extension, the *Extended Key Usage*, is used to clarify the first.) The most common error is to have the *Non-Repudiation Bit* set on a key intended for identity only. Non-repudiation should be asserted only on a key intended as a legal signature, not for identity alone.

A dangerous extension (and one that really does not belong in a user certificate) is the *SMIME Capabilities* extension. This only has meaning in the context of specific e-mail clients but can cripple the use of encryption. Although it may have had some use in early mail applications, today it only establishes a maximum allowed symmetric encryption strength, which may be less than desired. If this extension is not present, RFC 5280 requires a default to triple-DES.

In the case of certificates, less is more. The minimum number of fields and extensions that is required for the assertions the certificate is intended to make is best. PKI systems in the past have failed when too many, and sometimes mission-conflicting extensions, were added.

Particular care needs to be taken that the CA server vendor chosen does not add anything not specified by the certificate template in the Certificate Policy.

37.4   ENTERPRISE PUBLIC KEY INFRASTRUCTURE.

The *use* of a certificate is relatively simple, but establishing trust that the certificate is valid and appropriate for use requires a complex set of back-office elements, illustrated in Exhibit 37.4. Each group of users covered by a CA is called a domain. Subscribers in a domain receive public key certificates from the appropriate CA. The CA is responsible for generation of subscriber certificates and for CRL generation. The CA posts these signed objects to the repository where the relying parties can obtain them. The CA also archives the certificates and CRLs in case they are required in the future to resolve disputes among the subscribers and the relying parties.

The registration authority (RA) is the trusted representative of the CA and is responsible for authenticating the subscriber identity. The RA typically performs these functions:

- Authenticates (proofs) the subscriber's claimed identity. For example, the RA could require the subscriber to provide a valid photo ID, such as a driver's license or a passport for minimum assurance. Both I-9 authentication, as required by the Immigration Reform and Control Act (IRCA), and a Local Agency Check or a National Agency Check (LAC/NAC) plus "Need to Know" may be required for a higher level.[4]

- Obtains the subscriber public key from the subscriber.

- Provides the CA public key to the subscriber. A trust anchor is a CA's public key that the relying party trusts. This trust generally is established by obtaining the public key from a trusted source using trusted means, such as physical hand-off or via Secure Sockets Layer (SSL) from a trusted or known Web site. The CA public key becomes a subscriber trust anchor.

- Sends the certificate creation request to the CA. Typically, the RA creates an electronic mail message containing the subscriber name and the subscriber public

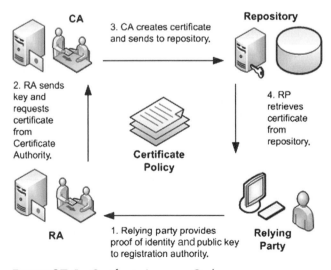

EXHIBIT 37.4   Certificate Issuance Cycle

key, digitally signs the message, and sends the message to the CA. Other transport means, such as manual or on the Web, also are appropriate as long as there is assurance that the subscriber identity and the public key are not changed. X.509 standard does not specify a protocol for certificate generation requests. The Public Key Infrastructure for X.509 Certificate (PKIX) working group of the Internet Engineering Task Force (IETF) has developed Internet standards in this area.[5]

37.5 CERTIFICATE POLICY. To ensure the security of the PKI, the PKI components need to operate with a high degree of security. To assure this:

- Private keys must be kept confidential.
- Private keys must be used only by the owners of the keys.
- Trust anchors' public key integrity must be assured.
- Initial authentication of the subscriber (private key holder and the subject of the public key certificate) must be strong so that identity theft does not occur at the point of certificate creation.
- CA and RA computer systems and applications must be protected from tampering.
- Requirements for level of trust must be clearly defined

The Certificate Policy (CP) must specifically enumerate the certificate contents, both fields and extensions. Anything absent from the CP should not be found in the certificate.

In addition to the security requirements and in order to facilitate electronic commerce, the PKI must address obligations of all parties and their liabilities in case of dispute. These issues of security, liability, level of trust, and obligations are articulated in a CP.

According to the X.509 standard, a CP is "a named set of rules that indicates the applicability of a certificate to a particular community and/or class of application with common security requirements."[6] A certificate user may use a CP to decide whether a certificate, and the binding implied between the certificate and its owner, is sufficiently trustworthy for a particular application. The CP addresses security and obligations of all PKI components, not just the CA; this includes the CA, RA, repository, subscriber, and relying party.

A more detailed description of the practices followed by a CA in issuing and managing certificates is contained in a certification practice statement (CPS) published by or referenced by the CA. According to the American Bar Association's *Digital Signature Guidelines* (hereinafter referred to as ABA *Guidelines*), "a CPS is a statement of the practices which a certification authority employs in issuing certificates."[7]

Although a CP and a CPS both address the same topics, the CP defines the security requirements and obligations for an enterprise PKI, and the CPS describes how these requirements are satisfied by the enterprise PKI.

The CP and CPS also are used differently. The CP forms the basis for cross-certification across enterprise boundaries to facilitate secure, interenterprise electronic commerce. An object identifier (OID) pointing to the CP (which may be a Universal Resource Locator [URL]) is used to create a certificate that can be put into the "Certificate Policies" extension of X.509 certificates. The OID thus enables relying parties to learn the care taken during the generation of certificates, recommended usage, and obligations of the various parties.

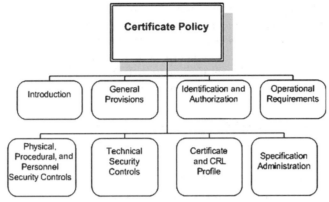

Exhibit 37.5   Elements of a Comprehensive Certification Practice Statement

Since certificates can be created with different levels of trust and can be either based in software or hardware (more secure), often the "Certificate Policies" extension is the only indicator of the level of trust that should be placed in a certificate.

The CPS enables PKI personnel to use and administer the PKI components. The CPS also forms the basis for compliance audits in order to ensure that the PKI components are operating in accordance with the stipulations of the CPS. Exhibit 37.5 illustrates the components of a comprehensive CPS. Components are divided further into subcomponents, which in turn are divided into elements. Components may be appropriate for various PKI entities but may be applied in the same way or differently. For example, technical security controls may apply to CA, RA, subscribers, and relying parties. These controls may be different for each of these entities, being most stringent for the CA, then the RA, and then the subscribers and relying parties.[8]

Sample policies may be found at www.certipath.com/library/library.htm and www.verisign.com/repository/vtnCp.html.

37.6   GLOBAL PUBLIC KEY INFRASTRUCTURE.   The principles of an enterprise PKI with a single CA can be extended to support global, secure, electronic commerce by relying on multiple CAs and/or CAs to certify other CAs and each other. How the CAs cross-certify each other is also called trust model, trust graph, or PKI architecture. For one person to communicate securely with another, there must be a trust path from the trust anchor(s) of the relying party to the subscriber whose signature needs to be verified or to whom an encrypted message is to be sent.

37.6.1   Levels of Trust.   As referenced in Office of Manpower and Budget Memorandum OMB M04-04, Section 2.1, there are four basic levels of trust:[9]

Level 1. Little or no confidence in the asserted identity's validity

Level 2. Some confidence in the asserted identity's validity

Level 3. High confidence in the asserted identity's validity

Level 4. Very high confidence in the asserted identity's validity

Each level requires a different initial authentication of identity, and higher levels (or those used for classified information) require background investigations. Level

EXHIBIT 37.6   Trust Level Determination

Category	Required Trust Level			
	1	**2**	**3**	**4**
Inconvenience or distress	Low	Med	High	High
Financial loss	Low	Med	Med	High
Harm to agency programs or public interests	N/A	Low	Med	High
Personal safety	N/A	N/A	Low	Med/high
Civil or criminal violations	N/A	Low	Med	High
Information classification				
Confidentiality	Low	Med	High	High
Integrity	Low	Med	High	High

3 is also known as Medium Assurance and is divided into two forms: (1) software (certificates and keys can be exported and moved between devices) and (2) hardware (certificates may be exported but keys and cryptographic functions are performed on a specific hardware device [e.g., a smart card, USB token, or PC-Card device]). Most commercial PKI uses the equivalent of the Medium level of assurance.

Exhibit 37.6 shows one way to determine the required trust level as a function of threat of misuse.[10]

37.6.2 Proofing.   Each assurance level has a proofing (also known as vetting) requirement that increases with the trust level involved, as shown in Exhibit 37.7. Essentially none is required for level 1 (Basic) while extensive in-person requirements exist for level 4 (High).

37.6.3 Trusted Paths.   The trust model can be viewed as a chain, with its tail a certificate-issuing CA and its head the subscriber (i.e., the subject of the certificate). The subscriber can be another CA or an end entity. To ascertain the trustworthiness of a certificate, it is necessary to start with the relying party trust anchor and to follow in the

EXHIBIT 37.7   Trust Levels and Proofing

Level	Title	Proofing	Authentication
1	Default	Anonymous allowed.	None
2	Basic	Simple assertion — may be online.	Password
3	Medium (software)	I-9 employment eligibility verification and authorization. Must be in person.	Software certificate
3	Medium (hardware)	I-9 employment eligibility verification and authorization. Must be in person. Biometrics may be captured.	Hardware certificate
4	High	National agency check or local agency check, background investigation, and authorization required. Final proofing must be in person.	Hardware certificate

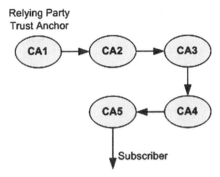

EXHIBIT 37.8   Trust Path through
Multiple Trusting Certificate Authorities

direction of the chain until the subscriber (of interest to the relying party) is reached. Global secure communications require that there be a trust path from every subscriber to every other subscriber.

The relying party can start with its trust anchor and verify the certificates issued by the trust anchor. Once that happens, the public keys can be trusted and used to verify the certificates issued by these CAs. This can be done recursively by the relying party until the public key certificate of the subscriber of interest is verified. Then the subscriber public key can be used to verify digital signatures and to perform encryption. Exhibit 37.8 illustrates this pathway. The arrows represent certificates. This is called a *certification path*.

37.6.4   Trust Models.   Examples of trust models within PKI that relate to the trust in a certificate and are different from proofing (trust of an identity) include:

- Strict hierarchy
- Hierarchy
- Bridge
- Multiple trust anchors
- Mesh (aka anarchy or web)
- Combination

37.6.4.1   *Strict Hierarchy.*   Exhibit 37.9 illustrates a strict hierarchy. It is a tree structure with a single root. In a strict hierarchy, for two parties to communicate with each other securely, they require the public key of their common ancestor as the trust anchor. Verifiable certificate chains require that the parties have a common ancestor. For all parties to communicate securely with each other, they require the single root as the trust anchor, since it is the only common trust anchor.

37.6.4.2   *Hierarchy.*   In a (nonstrict) hierarchy, the subordinate CAs certify their parents. Since the directed graph is bidirectional, any CA can be the trust anchor for the relying parties. But from practical, operational, and performance (i.e., certificate path length) viewpoints, the local CA should be the trust anchor. The local CA is the CA that issued a certificate to the relying party.

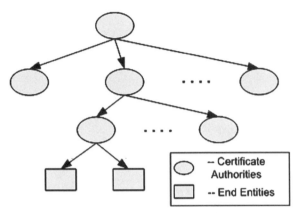

EXHIBIT 37.9   *Strict Hierarchical Trust Chain*

37.6.4.3 *Bridge.*   Another trust model is the bridge. Under this model, one CA cross-certifies with each CA from various domains. The domains can be organizations or vertical segments, such as banking or healthcare. Exhibit 37.10 illustrates the bridge CA. The bridge CA is not the trust anchor for any relying party. A CA in the domain of the relying party is the trust anchor.

Within a domain, there are no constraints on the trust model. The domain PKI itself could be organized as any of the trusted models, including bridge, leading to possible layers of bridge CAs.

37.6.4.4 *Multiple Trust Anchors.*   Another alternative is for the relying party to obtain the public keys of the various CAs in a trusted manner and then use those public keys as trust anchors. This approach is attractive when the CAs cannot, or are not willing to, cross-certify, and the relying party needs to communicate securely with the subscribers in the domains of the originating CAs. This approach is called *multiple trust anchors*. Each trust anchor representing a domain could be a single CA or a PKI with a collection of CAs in a trust model.

37.6.4.5 *Mesh.*   The final example of trust model is a mesh (aka web or anarchy). The term "mesh" describes any depiction representing trust among CAs or certificates without any particular rules or patterns. This model sometimes is known as a *web of*

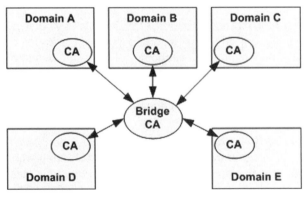

EXHIBIT 37.10   Bridge CA

trust and is particularly associated with the original design of Pretty Good Privacy, one of the first popular systems implementing public key certificates. Within this structure, each recipient must explicitly trust each other participant. The major problem is that it does not scale very well beyond a few hundred users.

37.6.5   Choosing a Public Key Infrastructure Architecture.   Whether a domain (enterprise) chooses a single CA or multiple CAs for its intradomain operation should be determined from a variety of factors, including:

- Management culture
- Organization politics
- Certification path size
- Subscriber population size
- Subscriber population distribution
- Revocation information

In many situations, the politics or management structure may dictate that there be multiple CAs within the domain. In other words, organizations at business-unit level, regional office level, corporate level, or national level may want to create a CA in order to provide them with a certain degree of control, independence, autonomy, and prestige. How these CAs are organized (bilateral cross-certification, hierarchy, etc.) also will depend on the management and political landscape of the domain. The trust model should be such that it keeps the certification path size manageable; otherwise, end users will see unacceptable performance degradation in obtaining certificates and CRLs and in verifying digital signatures on the certificates and the CRLs.

Similarly, large subscriber populations may require more than a single CA in order to ensure that the CA can manage the subscribers and to keep the CRL size small. If CA products that issue partitioned CRLs are selected, the CRL sizes can be kept manageable even for a very large subscriber population. For further discussion of the CRL issue, see Section 37.7 on revocation alternatives.

When considering interdomain cross-certification, similar issues should be considered.

37.6.6   Cross-Certification.   In the simplest form, cross-certification consists of two CAs that certify each other by issuing each other a certificate. The certificates can be stored in specific attributes of the directory entry in a certificate; examples include the cross-certificate attribute pair or the CA certificate.

There are two practical problems with cross-certification. One deals with the commercial products. If the two domains use different products, their CAs may not be able to exchange information to cross-certify, and their directories may not be able to chain to permit the relying parties to retrieve certificates.

The other problem is operational. Before certifying another CA, the certificate-issuing CA needs to make sure that the subject CA is operating in accordance with the acceptable controls, articulated in a CP. The issuing CA asserts the appropriate CP in the "certificate policies" extension of the X.509 version 3 certificate of the subject CA.

In practice, the two CAs cross-certify each other after reviewing each other's CP and after ensuring that the CPs can be claimed to be equivalent. This does not mean that all the security controls and obligations are identical, but they need to offer roughly similar amounts of trust and of obligations and similar liability and financial relief.

When two CAs cross-certify each other, the trust generally is for a limited set of policies, through assertions in "certificate policies" extensions, and trust is only bilateral. In other words, trust will not commute; it will remain between the two CAs. The CAs ensure this by inhibiting policy mapping through the "policy constraints" extension. Policy constraint extensions permit differing policy-mapping inhibitions down the certificate chain. In most direct cross-certifications, policy mapping should be inhibited immediately. In the case of cross-certification using the bridge CA model, in order to take advantage of the policy-mapping services of the bridge CA, the policy-mapping inhibition should be different for one certificate (namely the bridge CA certificate).

In addition, the two CAs should use the "name constraints" extension in the X.509 version 3 certificates to ensure that they trust the other domain for the names over which the other has control. The use of this extension also minimizes the chances of name collision.

Exhibits 37.11 and 37.12 illustrate cross-certification examples. These examples are for illustrative purposes only and do not represent real-world entities.

In the case of bilateral cross-certification, policy mapping should be inhibited immediately by using a value of "0" in the "inhibit policy mapping" field of the policy constraints extension in X.509 certificates. When bridge CA is used for interdomain interoperability, a value of "1" should be used in this field. This will permit the issuing CA domain to map its policies to the bridge CA policies and then permit the bridge CA to map its policies to the subject CA domain, in effect mapping from the issuing CA domain to the subject CA domain.

As long as the issuing CA uses its control on inhibit policy mapping, the bridge CA need not use inhibit policy mapping to control the mapping inhibition.

37.6.7 Public Key Infrastructure Interoperability.   The complexity of the technology, standards, and products of PKI technology from one domain to another

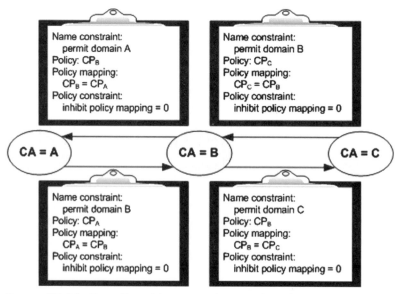

EXHIBIT 37.11   Trust Chain Mapping with Dissimilar Policies

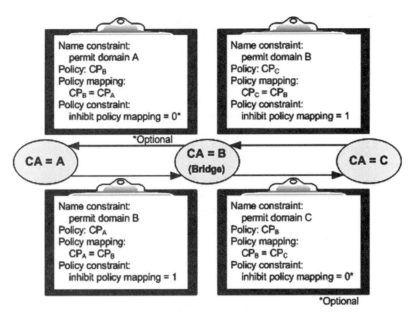

EXHIBIT 37.12   Policy Mapping with a Bridge

and from one place to another sometimes creates interoperability problems. Yet without interdomain interoperability there can be no global trust, only individual trust.

These factors play a critical role in ensuring PKI interoperability:

- Trust path
- Cryptographic algorithms
- Certificate and CRL formats
- Certificate and CRL dissemination
- Certificate policies
- Names

37.6.7.1 *Trust Path.* The communicating parties must be able to form trust paths from their trust anchors to their subscribers. This can be achieved through multiple trust anchors, cross-certification, and other trust models described earlier.

37.6.7.2 *Cryptographic Algorithms.* The communicating parties must implement the cryptographic algorithms, such as hashing, digital signatures, key encryption, and data encryption, used by each other.

In addition, the parties should be able to communicate to each other the algorithms they use. In X.509 certificates and CRL, this information may be contained in the objects themselves, as in the *algorithm* field. In X.509 certificates, for the information being communicated, algorithms such as the digital signature and key encryption algorithm may be carried in the end-entity certificate. The hashing algorithm and the data encryption algorithm can be part of the implicit agreement between the parties or can be carried with the information being communicated. The information also can be obtained from the *supported algorithms* attribute of the X.500 directory entry of the user, although this option is not widely used.

Although the expected public key algorithms used by the CA to create the certificate must be discernible by the recipient (in order to understand the certificate contents), it is important that the certificate not make any assertions as to the symmetric algorithms that may be used. The certificate should be application-agnostic and not impose any rules on applications when not necessary.

In all these situations, the algorithm is identified using the object identifiers. Different organizations may register the same algorithm under their OID arc. Thus, it is important that either the two domains use the same OID for the algorithms, or that their software interpret the multiple OIDs as the same algorithm. For this reason, OID proliferation for algorithms in not recommended.

Variants of the same base algorithm further exacerbate the problems of algorithm interoperability. For example, subtle padding and other differences exist between definitions of the RSA algorithm in the Public Key Cryptography Standards (PKCS) and in the American National Standards Institute (ANSI) X9 committee. Similarly, the Diffie-Hellman algorithm has various modes and various ways to reduce the calculated secret to symmetric key size (i.e., ways to make session keys smaller). Any of these differences in algorithms must be documented through different OIDs so that the OID invokes the appropriate implementation.

It is important that extensions be chosen carefully. Those pertaining to algorithms often have meaning within the context of a particular application. As mentioned earlier, a good example of an extension that should not be placed in a certificate is the *SMIME Capabilities* extension, since it does not set minimum expectations and instead may limit the symmetric key length that can be used by applications.

Such application-specific extensions should be avoided in user/subscriber certificates. The algorithms and key lengths used by the public key (asymmetric) elements are specified in the *Field* values such as *Subject Public Key Information.*

37.6.7.3 Certificate and Certificate Revocation List Format.   The communicating parties must share, or must be able to understand, each other's certificate and CRL formats. The most common way to achieve this is to use a common standard, such as X.509. Many times this has not been sufficient due to the ambiguity in the standard and associated encoding schemes, although, over time, those bugs have been worked out. The primary reason today why certificates and CRLs issued by one product may not be understood by another is that either one or both are not compliant with the standard, or one product does not implement all the features of the standard used by the other product.

37.6.7.4 Certificate and Certificate Revocation List Dissemination.
The communicating parties must obtain the certificates and CRLs issued by the various CAs in each other's domain. These certificates and CRLs may be obtained from a repository such as an X.500 and Lightweight Directory Access Protocol (LDAP) server. Alternatively, the certificates and CRLs can be carried as part of the communication protocol between the parties, for example, as defined in S/MIME (Secure/Multipurpose Internet Mail Extension) version 3.

The X.500 and LDAP repositories are based on hierarchical databases. Each node in the hierarchical tree structure belongs to an object class. The node's object class determines the attributes that are stored for that node. Examples of attributes are job title, phone number, fax number, and the like. Certificates and CRLs are also attributes.[11]

X.500 and LDAP have defined a standard schema for PKI certificates and CRLs. For certificates, these attributes are *userCertificate*, *cACertificate*, and *crossCertificatePair*.

The end-entity certificates should be stored in *userCertificate* attribute. All CA certificates should be stored in the forward element of the *crossCertificatePair* attribute of the subject CA. In addition, all certificates issued to the CAs in the same domain should be stored in the *cACertificate* attribute of the subject CA.

Various revocation lists should be stored in the *cRL*, *aRL*, and *deltaCRL* attributes of the issuing CA as applicable.

If the certificates and CRLs are not stored in these standardized attributes, the relying-party software may not be able to obtain these objects. Furthermore, X.500 directory products still may not always interoperate due to additional complexity of the X.500 standard and to product differences. When implementing X.500 directories and connecting X.500 directory products from different vendors, implementers should allow time to make the products and directories interoperate.

37.6.7.5 Certificate Policies.
In order to trust and cross-certify each other, the CAs in two domains need to operate under similar policies. Users in the two domains should be able to accept or reject certificates of each other's domains based on the security requirements of the application, and on the policy under which the certificates were issued.

In order to determine the similarity, or equivalence, of the policies of the two domains, the CP should be written using the IETF standard RFC-2527 framework. The CP is represented using an OID in the certificate. To ensure that the user software accepts and rejects certificates based on the application requirements and on the CP, PKI products should be selected and configured so that the CA asserts the certificate policies, policy mapping, and policy constraints extensions appropriately. The user's PKI-enabling software must process these extensions appropriately and fully in compliance with the requirements of X.509 certificate-path validation rules.

37.6.7.6 Names.
The communicating domains must not assign the same name to two different entities. X.500 distinguished names (DN) are steps in that direction but not sufficient to achieve this.

To illustrate the point, consider, for example, CygnaCom, is a company incorporated in the Commonwealth of Virginia. While it is highly unlikely that there is another CygnaCom in Virginia, there is no assurance that there is no CygnaCom incorporated in other U.S. states. Thus, it would be possible that c=US, O=CygnaCom could be asserted by the CAs for several different domains.

In order to avoid this name collision and ambiguity, the *name constraints* extension in X.509 should be used. The CA for one domain can prevent any other entity from using a name registered in that domain. The issuing CA (CA "Y" in this example) uses the *name constraints* extension to assert priority and control over the specified identifier. For example, the first CA that certifies a company called CygnaCom in its domain should set the *name constraint* attribute in its certificate for its CygnaCom stating that only its CygnaCom is allowed to issue certificates under the name space c=US, O=CygnaCom. If another CygnaCom were to come along, CA "Y" would ask the second CygnaCom to choose another name in order to avoid name collision. Although this example focuses on the DN, the *name constraint* can be used for any hierarchical name forms, including DN, RFC 822-compliant names, and others.

PKI products should be selected and configured so that the CA asserts the *name constraints* extension appropriately. The user's PKI-enabling software must process this extension appropriately and fully in compliance with the requirements of X.509 certificate-path validation rules.

37.7   FORMS OF REVOCATION.

As discussed earlier, a PKI includes mechanisms for key revocation. It is necessary to make provisions for the revocation of compromised keys in order to maintain the trust relationships of any PKI employed in a real-world environment.

The first form of revocation designed was the CRL. It seems the most appropriate form of revocation, given the distributed authentication framework of PKI. The CRL mechanism allows the CA to generate the objects and the relying parties to process them securely without worrying about the security of the servers or system that supply the CRL, and without concerns about the network(s) over which the CRL has traveled.

37.7.1   Types of Revocation-Notification Mechanisms.

However, there have been several concerns about the CRL, and these concerns have led to other forms of revocation-notification mechanisms. Many of these mechanisms are variations on the CRL in the sense that these are revocation lists, but they are not complete. The second category of revocation mechanisms defers the processing of revocation information to a server e.g. through the Online Certificate Status Protocol (OCSP.), See RFC 2560. A third category of mechanisms lets the users check the status of a single certificate from the directory and allows the CA to update the status of that certificate in the directory. A final category lets a CA or another trusted server organize the revocation information in a B-tree.

Which mechanism(s) to choose depends on a variety of factors, such as:

- The communication model (i.e., which class of users is communicating with which other class). For example, if a user communicates with several users who are subscribers to the same CA, a single CRL from that CA will provide relevant information about all those targeted users. If a user is communicating with users who belong to different CAs, each CRL provides information about only one user.
- The directory architecture: Where they are located and what portions of the directory information is replicated or shadowed?
- The communication bandwidth available.
- The bind time (i.e., the time to set a connection with the repository in order to perform retrievals and updates) to access the repository.
- The size of the revocation response from the repository (e.g., the CRL size).
- The processing load on the repository, especially for digital signature *generation* on the revocation information.
- The processing load on the user workstation, especially for digital signature *verification* on the revocation information.

37.7.2   Certificate Revocation Lists and Their Variants.

The first set of mechanisms, CRL and its various forms, is the most versatile, effective, and recommended approach for revocation notification. Like X.509 certificates, CRLs are expressed in ASN.1 format. There are several basic types of CRL, and they should be carefully considered, based on the user communication model and anticipated revocation rate:

- Full and complete CRL
- Authority revocation list (ARL)
- Distribution-point CRL
- Delta CRL

37.7.2.1   Full and Complete CRL.   The full and complete CRL is a CRL that contains the revocation information for all certificates issued by a CA. This type of CRL is rarely seen; instead a normal CRL includes only information about revoked certificates and not currently valid ones. Expired certificates are not included, and revoked certificates will drop off the CRL when they expire.

37.7.2.2   Authority Revocation List.   The ARL is a CRL that contains the revocation information for all the CA certificates issued by a CA; that is, the ARL is a subset of CRL for certificates issued to the CAs only. The ARL is a very desirable mechanism for these reasons:

- It is likely to be short. A CA is likely to certify fewer CAs than other types of subscribers. Also, given that CAs are expected to operate with a great deal of vigilance, and given that CAs are not going to be revoked for reasons such as name change or organizational affiliation change, CAs will be revoked far less often than the end entities. These factors will contribute to making the ARL very small.
- For all of the certificates except one, only the ARL needs to be checked, since in a certificate path all but the last certificate is issued to a CA.

Due to a security flaw in X.509 version 1, a CA should never issue ARLs defined using that version. In X.509 version 1, there is no difference between the CRL format and the ARL format. Since both CRLs and ARLs are signed by the same CA, if an adversary (directory or network adversary) were to supply an ARL to the relying party in lieu of a full CRL, the relying party would have no way of knowing that it had received an ARL instead of the requested CRL. The ARL would not have end-entity revocation information and therefore could mislead the relying party into using the revoked certificate of an end entity.

The X.509 version 2 ARL fixes this security flaw using an *issuing distribution point* extension. An ARL must use this extension and assert a field that states that the list contains only CA certificates. The presence of this field in the signed ARL tells the relying party that it is not a full CRL. Now, if an adversary were to supply an ARL in lieu of a CRL, the relying party would detect this substitution by using the *issuing distribution point* field.

This is one of the several security reasons that PKI-enabling software must be able to process the various extensions properly in accordance with the requirements stated in X.509 standard.

37.7.2.3   Distribution-Point CRL.   Distribution-point CRL is a mechanism that has several useful functions:

- To replicate a CRL
- To consolidate revocation information from the various CAs so that the relying parties need to obtain only one CRL
- To partition the revocation information for the subscribers of a CA into multiple smaller pieces

This latter function, partition, is achieved by asserting the *CRL Distribution Point* extension in the certificate that points to the name entry under which revocation information for the certificate will appear. The partitioned CRL will assert the same name in the *Distribution Point* field of the *issuing distribution point* extension in the CRL.

Since all the partitioned (distribution point) CRLs are signed by the same CA, it is not sufficient for the relying party simply to validate the CA's signature on the Distribution Point CRL. The relying party must match the Distribution Point name in the *issuing distribution point* extension of the CRL with the Distribution Point name in the *distribution point* extension in the certificate.

37.7.2.4 *Delta Certificate Revocation List.*   Yet another way to reduce the size of the CRL is to publish changes to the revocation information since the last CRL. The CRL that contains changes only is called the delta CRL, and the CRL to which changes are published is called the base CRL. The delta CRL can be applied to any of these CRLs: CRL, ARL, and Distribution Point CRL. In order to construct current revocation information, the latest delta CRL and its base must be used. There is an algorithm that could be used to allow a subset of changes to be applied to an earlier CRL that would still match the digital signature of the new CRL.

37.7.3 **Server-Based Revocation Protocols.**   Server-based revocation uses protocols, such as On-Line Certificate Status Protocol (OCSP) and Simple Certificate Validation Protocol (SCVP). In general, these protocols suffer from several flaws, including these:

- Since the revocation information is produced at the server, the communication channel between the relying party and the server must be secured, most likely by using digital signatures.
- Signed operations will limit server scalability since digital signature generation is computationally intensive.
- Since the revocation information is produced at the server, the scheme requires a trusted server as opposed to an untrusted repository.
- Revocation of a server public key requires a method for checking the server public key status. This method is likely to use the server public key as an additional trust anchor or to rely on a CRL mechanism.
- There needs to be a nonsuppressible mechanism for the CA to provide revocation information to the trusted server; that is, the CA should know whether the revocation information has or has not reached the trusted server. Although a CA itself can act as a trusted server, this is not recommended for security reasons; in addition, we do not want to impose the high-performance requirement on the CA architecture. The trusted server must be a high-performance system.
- There are no standards in the area of CA to provide nonsuppressible mechanisms for transmitting the revocation information to the trusted server.

These mechanisms may be desirable under one of four situations:

1. Need to have thinnest possible PKI client
2. Need to generate revenue for CA services
3. Need to check changing credentials, such as available credit
4. Need to update dynamic credentials, such as the remaining credit line

The last two situations permit the trusted server to provide the revocation information and to check or change the credentials of the subscriber.

Delta CRLs and server-based revocation/authentication protocols such as OCSP (RFC 2560) are standards-compliant and can provide the same information as in the CRL for a single certificate in a significantly smaller bandwidth. They do require some form of acceptable authentication since the original CA will not be available for signing.

37.7.4   Summary of Recommendations for Revocation Notification.
The most scalable and versatile revocation-notification mechanism can be achieved by using a combination of:

- CRLs.
- Replication of the CA directory entry, at locations determined by the enterprise network topology, for fast access to CRL.
- Use of ARLs.
- Consolidation of ARLs for all CAs in a domain through the use of distribution points. Consolidation is achieved by placing the name of a CA that can revoke a certificate in the certificate's CRL *Distribution Point* extension.
- Consolidation of all the reason-codes of key compromise for all certificates in a domain through the use of the *Distribution Point* extension. This CRL can be issued very frequently to meet the freshness requirements of the domain. This mechanism makes the CRL mechanism as current as the OCSP.
- Partitioning routine revocation information using Distribution Point CRLs if CRLs become too large.

Several other techniques can help improve CRL retrieval efficiency:

- Repositories may store both enciphered CRLs to send to the relying parties and also deciphered (plaintext) CRLs to perform fast searches. Storing both forms reduces the overhead that would result from using encryption or decryption at the time of each request.
- If the repository does not store any private information, bind operations for retrieval can be configured to require no authentication, thus eliminating another potential performance bottleneck.
- CRL size can be reduced by having a short validity period for the certificates, by using a coarse domain name so that reorganization does not invalidate a name, and by allowing some changes (e.g., name change or transfer) without forcing revocation.

37.8   REKEY.
The public key certificates for the subscribers have a defined validity period. Once the validity period expires, subscribers require new public key certificates. There are two primary reasons why public key certificates have a limited life. One relates to the life of a private key based on the potential cryptanalysis threat. Another reason is to help control CRL size since no certificate gets off a CRL until it expires.

No public key should be used longer than the estimated time for brute-force cryptanalysis using current technology (its *cryptanalysis threat period*). At that point, the certificate should be assigned a new public key (i.e., it should be *rekeyed*). However, before the cryptanalysis threat period expires, the same key can be renewed or *recertified*. Certificates can be renewed easily by having subscribers send a digitally signed request to the CA or by having the CA perform automatic renewal. During renewal, any information (other than the subscriber public key) may be changed.

For the foreseeable future, the life of a 1024-bit RSA key can be expected to be 25 years. By reusing the same key with new certificates for as long as possible, the number of past keys required to be escrowed in order to retrieve or validate older files is reduced. The level of trust should also be considered when rekeying, but keys stored in tamper-resistant hardware can be expected to achieve their full lifetime.

Elements using soft keys are inherently at risk to a determined attack and should be used only for lower levels of trust.

Certificates also can be rekeyed easily by having the subscriber send a digitally signed *rekey request message* that also contains the new public key. The message is signed using the current private key so that it can be verified using the current public key. If the subscriber being rekeyed is a CA, these requirements also come into play:

- The relying parties should be able to verify certificate chains after the CA is rekeyed.
- The relying parties should be able to verify CRLs issued by the CA.
- The rekey should not have a ripple effect on the PKI. Just because one CA rekeys, other CAs or end entities should not have to rekey.
- The length of certificate paths should be minimized.
- The operational impact on the PKI entities should be minimal.

A good way to meet these requirements is for the CA to:

- Issue all current valid certificates when it rekeys, without changing the validity periods in the subscriber certificates.
- Continue to sign CRLs with all current valid private keys. This will result in multiple CRLs, all with the same information. A CA private key is considered valid until all certificates signed using that key have expired.

If the CA is a trust anchor, it can use one of two approaches to rekey itself in-band, over the untrusted network:

1. The CA can send out a rekey message that contains its new public key and is signed using the current key. The CA needs to ensure that all the subscribers receive and process the rekey message prior to expiration of the current key.

2. The CA can provide the hash of the next public key and parameters (if the cryptographic algorithm has parameters; RSA does not have parameters, but Digital Signature Standard [DSS] does) with the current key. When it is time to publish the new public key, the CA can publish a new self-signed public key certificate that contains the new public key and parameters as well as the hash of the next public key and parameters.

37.9   KEY RECOVERY.   Subscriber public keys can be used to encrypt data-encryption keys (for symmetric-key encryption). Such data-encryption keys are used to encrypt data quickly with the lower overhead of symmetric-key encryption. Subscribers require their private keys to decrypt the data-encryption keys and thus allow decryption of the data.

It is critically important to distinguish between *signing* keys and *data-encryption* keys. The former may *never* be subjected to key recovery; the latter *may* be protected using key-recovery techniques.

High levels of trust keys may require a separate identification key that may not be used to sign a document; this login key should have only the signing bit and not the nonrepudiation bit set in the Key Usage extension.

Sometimes a subscriber's private-key token (e.g., a diskette, hard drive, smart card, etc.) may be corrupted or the subscriber may forget the password associated with the token. Similarly, sometimes a subscriber may not be available yet the subscriber's employer may need to decrypt corporate information encrypted by the missing subscriber. Key-recovery techniques are designed to meet these emergency needs for access to encrypted information. Inherently, they provide a form of back door to the keys, but they also impose additional overhead costs. Thus, the need to provide key recovery should be balanced carefully against potential costs and complexity.

The two most popular forms of key-recovery mechanisms are:

1. **Key escrow.** Under this form, the subscriber's long-term private decryption key is provided to a trusted third party called a *key recovery agent* (KRA)

2. **Key encapsulation.** Under this form, the subscriber encrypts the data-encrypting key using the public key of the KRA so that the KRA can decrypt the data.

Of these two schemes, key escrow is becoming more widely available in the PKI products because it is simpler to implement at the infrastructure level. It is also independent of organization boundaries between the sender and receiver of encrypted communications. If a party's private date-encryption key is escrowed, than communications to the party can be decrypted.

Subscribers may always recover their own data-encryption key from the key-recovery system. Authorized third parties, such as a subscriber's employer, also may request keys. Such an authorized party is called a *key recovery requester* (KRR). All of the components are governed by a *key recovery policy* (KRP) and associated *key recovery practices statement* (KRPS). The KRP and KRPS are akin to the *Certificate Policy* and *Certification Practice Statement* but have some differences. One of the main differences is in the technical security-controls sections. There are several requirements to check the communication protocols among the components to ensure confidentiality, integrity, and authorization. Exhibit 37.13 illustrates the components of a key-recovery system, as would be expressed in the KPRS.

A general criticism of key recovery is that it provides secrets to a single party, namely a KRA. One way to mitigate that concern is to share the secret among multiple recipients in a way that requires cooperation (if it is authorized) or collusion (if it is not) among two or more holders of the escrowed secret. For example, superencryption (encryption of ciphertext) can make unauthorized discovery of a key more difficult. The secret key S is encrypted with one recipient's public key (say, K_1), producing a ciphertext, represented as $E(S, K_1)$, and then that ciphertext is super-encrypted using a second recipient's public key, K_2, to produce the ciphertext $E(E(S, K_1), K_2)$. Unlike encryption of the same message for two recipients, where each recipient can decrypt the ciphertext independently, superencryption requires decryption by each recipient in the reverse order of priority. Thus, if a user encrypts a secret key using A's public key and then superencrypts the ciphertext using B's public key, key recovery requires decryption by B using the corresponding private key and then decryption of the resulting ciphertext by A with that user's private key.

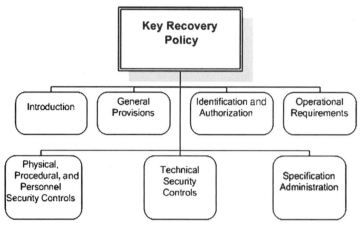

EXHIBIT 37.13   Elements of a Key Recovery Policy

To use superencryption so that fewer than all recipients may decrypt the key, the sender encrypts to a first group of recipients and then superencrypts to a second group of recipients. Thus, any one of the members of the first group and any member of the second group of recipients can cooperate to decrypt the secret key.

This technique allows key escrow even in the absence of a formal PKI, such as in informal webs of trust using PGP.

Another solution to making collusion more difficult in key escrow is to split the key using Shamir's n out of m rule.[12] In a properly implemented key-splitting scheme, parts of a secret key are distributed to m destinations and at least n recipients are required to reconstitute the secret key. Thus, $n-1$ or fewer persons colluding together cannot determine even a single bit of the escrowed key. Successful collusion requires at least n individuals. The split-key approach can be applied to key escrow, in which case the private key can be split and different splits can be provided to different KRAs. Alternatively, the split-key approach may be applied to encapsulation, where the session key can be split, and different splits can be encrypted using public keys of different KRAs.

This strategy also theoretically allows full reconstitution of the secret key to be performed by the authorized recipient of the partial keys, instead of by any of the escrow agents.

37.10 PRIVILEGE MANAGEMENT.   The primary purpose of PKI is to provide entity authentication in a global, distributed environment. In most systems and applications, authentication becomes the basis for access control. There are three fundamental ways to implement access control:

1. The systems and applications can perform access control on their own. The PKI continues to provide the authentication framework.
2. The privileges, attributes, roles, rights, and authorizations can be carried in a public key certificate in the *subject directory attribute* extension.
3. The privileges, attributes, roles, rights, and authorizations can be carried in an *attribute certificate*. The X.509 standard is being revised to include the concept of attribute certificates. The attribute certificates carry privileges and authorizations instead of the public key, and thus provide a distributed authorization framework.

EXHIBIT 37.14 Privilege Management

Alternative	Pros	Cons
Application-based access control	Easy to implement. Does not require additional infrastructure, so saves cost.	Need to manage privileges on an application-by-application basis. Synchronization of privileges may be hard as applications increase and as they are distributed. Security may be compromised if privileges are not removed from all applications. Higher operational costs.
Public Key Certificate	Easy to add to PKI. Privileges can be managed easily by revoking certificate.	Changes in privileges require revocation of identity certificate. Sometimes this is a small price to pay for savings that result from not having to deploy and operate a separate privilege management infrastructure (PMI). Parties issuing identity certificate may not have authority to bestow privileges.
Attribute Certificate	Privileges can be managed easily by revoking attribute certificates. Change in privilege does not require revocation of public key certificate.	Cost of privilege management infrastructure (PMI).

User login, signing, and encryption certificates should never be used to carry authorizations or application information. Where needed, separate certificates can be issued for those tasks. Such authorization certificates can be issued daily, or even for shorter periods, eliminating the need for a CRL since the certificate would expire before one would be issued. These authorization certificates could be used in place of Kerberos (the Greek mythological three-headed dog that guards the entrance to Hades) Tickets. Exhibit 37.14 summarizes the pros and cons of each of the three approaches.

These factors should be considered when architecting an access infrastructure. Although the attribute certificate seems to be the latest fad in the PKI world, users should carefully study putting privileges in public key certificates to save the cost of implementing a Privilege Management Infrastructure (PMI) over and above the cost of PKI.

37.11 TRUSTED ARCHIVAL SERVICES AND TRUSTED TIME STAMPS.

PKI technology supports global electronic commerce through the use of digital signature technology. Digital signature technology is a detection or passive mechanism. In other words, the technology does not *prevent* someone from modifying data in storage or in transit, nor from impersonating someone else. The technology merely detects that an attempt had been made to modify the data or that someone had tried to impersonate someone else.

In a court of law, digital signatures may be disputed long after they were applied, if, for example, the cryptanalysis threat period for the keys has expired. In those circumstances, producing a document with a verified digital signature may not prevent repudiation. A party could claim that the cryptanalysis threat period has passed and the private key might have been discovered or broken by an adversary.

To mitigate both of these threats—data corruption and expiry of the cryptanalysis threat period—trusted archival services are required for transactions with a potential for this kind of dispute. Such an archival service also would be able to safeguard associated certificates and CRLs. Trusted archival services should depend on controls such as physical security, stable media (e.g., write-once read-many (WORM) devices), and appropriate techniques to maintain readability despite changing technologies. Such services should be capable of error-free transcription of data on older media and of translating outdated encoding into more modern media, and into current encoding schemes. For example, Extended Binary Coded Decimal Interchange Code (EBCDIC)-encoded data on nine-track magnetic tapes could be copied onto optical disks using ASCII encoding.

A related technology is the trusted time stamp, where a trusted third party attaches the current valid time to a document and signs it to prove the existence of the document at a given time. If the document owner does not want to reveal the contents of the document to the time stamp server, then a hash of the document may be stamped and signed instead.

In most applications, a trusted archival service may obviate the need for trusted time stamp service because, for the long term, the trusted archival service can attest to the time of the transaction. For the short term, both parties can date and digitally sign the transaction when it is consummated, rendering it valid as a contract. If the date is not acceptable to any party—it is either too far in the future or in the past—that party can either reject the transaction or invoke some dispute-resolution procedure immediately.

37.12 COST OF PUBLIC KEY INFRASTRUCTURE.   One of the misconceptions about Public Key Infrastructure technology is that it is too costly, but these costs should be compared to the alternatives.

Short of taking a major risk, there is no practical technology other than cryptography to protect data in transit over untrusted network. The only choice, then, is between symmetric key cryptography and public key cryptography. Aside from the difficulties of distributing and supporting symmetric, secret keys, such cryptosystems require approximately n^2 keys for a group of n individuals who must communicate with each other.

A secret key cryptosystem requires n^2 keys to be kept confidential, with their integrity maintained; PKI requires managing only n keys. Clearly, it should be cheaper to maintain the integrity of n keys than to manage n^2 keys and their confidentiality and integrity. PKI is needed to manage the public keys.

PKI costs seem large when they must provide global trust and interoperability, something not asked of most systems or infrastructures. Currently no other technology works as well or is as cost effective as PKI to achieve global, secure, trusted communication and electronic commerce. The alternative is to assume the risk without PKI, or to continue with the last century's approach of paper-based trust.

37.13 FURTHER READING

Adams, C., S. Lloyd, and S. Kent. *Understanding the Public-Key Infrastructure*, 2nd edition. Upper Saddle River, NJ: Addison-Wesley Professional, 2002.

Atzeni, A. S., and A. Lioy, eds. *Public Key Infrastructure, Third European PKI Workshop: Theory and Practice, EuroPKI 2006, Turin, Italy, June 19–20, 2006. Proceedings*. New York: Springer, 2006.

Austin, T. *PKI: A Wiley Technical Brief*. New York: John Wiley & Sons, 2000.

Australian Government Public Key Infrastructure; see: www.govonline.gov.au/projects/publickey/index.asp.

Baltimore Technologies Learning Center. *Introduction to PKI*; see: www.baltimore.com/library/pki.

Certipath Certificate Policies: www.certipath.com/library/downloads/CertiPath%20CP.pdf.

Chadwick, D., and G. Zhao, eds. *Public Key Infrastructure. Second European PKI Workshop: Research and Applications, EuroPKI 2005, Canterbury, UK, June 30–July 1, 2005. Revised Selected Papers*. New York: Springer, 2005.

Desmedt, Y. G., ed. *Secure Public Key Infrastructure: Standards, PGP and Beyond*. New York: Springer, 2008.

ECA Certificate Policies: http://iase.disa.mil/pki/eca/documents.html.

Ford, W., and M. S. Baum. *Secure Electronic Commerce: Building the Infrastructure for Digital Signatures and Encryption*. Upper Saddle River, NJ: Prentice-Hall, 1997.

Housley, R., and T. Polk. *Planning for PKI: Best Practices Guide for Deploying Public Key Infrastructure*. New York: John Wiley & Sons, 2001.

Howes, T., *et al. Understanding and Deploying LDAP Directory Services*. New York: Macmillan, 2002.

IETF Public Key Infrastructure (X.509) charter; see: www.ietf.org/html. charters/pkixcharter.html.

Lopez, J., P. Samarati, and J. L. Ferrer, eds. *Public Key Infrastructure: Fourth European PKI Workshop: Theory and Practice, EuroPKI 2007, Palma de Mallorca, Spain, June 28–30, 2007. Proceedings*. New York: Springer, 2007.

Menezes, A., P. van Oorschot, and S. Vanstone. *Handbook of Applied Cryptography*. Boca Raton, FL: CRC Press, 1996.

Level of Trust in E-Authentication Guide OMB M-04-04: www.whitehouse.gov/omb/memoranda/fy04/m04-04.pdf

Sabo, J. T., and Y. A. Dzambasow. " PKI Policy in the Business Environment," *SC Magazine Asia* (June 2002), http://scmagazine.com/asia/news/article/419807/pkipolicy-business-environment/.

Vacca, J. R. *Public Key Infrastructure: Building Trusted Applications and Web Services*. Boca Raton, FL: Auerbach, 2004.

37.14 NOTES

1. B. Schneier, *Applied Cryptography: Protocols, Algorithms, and Source Code in C*, 2nd ed. (New York: John Wiley & Sons, 1995).

2. Additional details on X.509 certificates can be obtained from X.509 standard ISO/IEC 9594-8.

3. For more information on ASN.1, see http://asn1.elibel.tm.fr/.

4. The I-9 "Employment Eligibility Verification" form, properly known as OMB No. 1615-0047, can be found at: www.uscis.gov/files/form/i-9.pdf.

5. These standards can be obtained from www.ietf.org.

6. RFC 2527, Internet X.509 Public Key Infrastructure Certificate Policy and Certification Practices Framework: www.ietf.org/rfc/rfc2527.txt.

7. American Bar Association, "Digital Signatures Guidelines: Legal Infrastructure for Certification Authorities and Electronic Commerce." Draft, 1995. http://www.abanet.org/scitech/ec/isc/dsgfree.html

8. Further details on CP and CPS format and contents can be found in S. Chokhani and W. Ford, *Certificate Policy and Certification Practices Framework*, RFC 2527 (April 1998) www.ietf.org/rfc/rfc2527.txt.

9. www.whitehouse.gov/omb/memoranda/fy04/m04-04.pdf

10. New York Office for Technology, "Potential Impacts of Authentication Errors," www.oft.state.ny.us/policy/G07-001/table1.htm.

11. For further discussion on repositories, see T. Howes et al., *Understanding and Deploying LDAP Directory Services* (New York: Macmillan, 1998).

12. A. Shamir, "How to Share a Secret," *Communications of ACM* 22, No. 11 (1979): 612–613.

CHAPTER 38

WRITING SECURE CODE

Lester E. Nichols, M. E. Kabay, and Timothy Braithwaite

38.1 INTRODUCTION. The topic of secure coding cannot be adequately addressed in a single chapter. Unfortunately, programs are inherently difficult to secure because of the large number of ways that execution can traverse the code as a result of different input sequences and data values.

This chapter provides a starting point and additional resources for security professionals, system architects, and developers to build a successful and secure development methodology. Writing secure code takes coordination and cooperation of various functional areas within an organization, and may require fundamental changes in the way software development currently is designed, written, tested, and implemented.

38.2 POLICY AND MANAGEMENT ISSUES. There are countless security hurdles facing those writing code and developing software. Today dependence on the reliability and security of the automated system is nearly total. For an increasing number of organizations, distributed information processes, implemented via networked environments, have become the critical operating element of their business. Not only must the processing system work when needed, but the information processed must retain its integrity so that it can be trusted in use. Because of a general lack of basic IT organizational discipline, and of adherence to fundamental software and systems development and maintenance principles, most software development efforts have been significantly lacking at best. If the same inadequate practices are left unchanged in the face of increasing cyberthreats, they will continue contributing to the insecure systems of tomorrow, just as they have contributed to the insecure systems of today.

The fundamental problem underlying this kind of assertion is the difficulty of justifying what are often perceived as non–revenue-generating activities. The difficulty also stems from the infeasibility of proving a negative. For example, one cannot prove to the uninvolved or unimpressed observer that the time, money, and human resources spent on prevention are well spent simply because a disaster was averted. Such an observer will take the fact that a disaster did not occur as evidence that the possibility of disaster never really existed, or that the problem was exaggerated. In the same way, a skeptical observer may take the absence of security breaches as evidence that no such threat existed, or that it was never as bad as claimed. The problem is exacerbated after spending time and effort on establishing security policies, security controls, and enforcement mechanisms.

In both cases, the money, time, and effort expended to prevent adverse computing consequences from harming an organization are viewed with suspicion. However, such suspicions are not new in the world of information processing. Throughout the history of IT, this attitude has existed regarding problem-prevention activities such as quality assurance, quality control testing, documentation, configuration management, change management, and other system-management controls designed to improve quality, reliability, and system maintainability.

Problems with security are management problems. Management dictates how much time and money can be spent on security activities such as risk management and software testing. How much time and energy are invested in designing, building, testing, and fixing software is in the end a management call. Thus, the primary concern of those striving to improve software security must be the correction of these same basic and fundamental IT management defects; otherwise effective security can never be attained or maintained.

38.2.1 Software Total Quality Management.
The nature of the computer security challenge is that of dynamically changing vulnerabilities and threats, based on rapidly changing technologies, used in increasingly complex business applications. Organizations need to build software around the idea of a continuous improvement model, as popularized by the total quality management (TQM) articulated in the ISO 9000 family of standards. For purposes of quality improvement, this model was viewed as a continuing cycle of plan-do-check-and-act. For software security, it can be thought of as a cycle of plan-fix-monitor-and-assess. A security management process to execute this model must be established and integrated into the day-to-day operations of the business. Integration means that the security initiative does not stand alone as a watchdog or act merely as an audit function, and it must move away from a policing function. Security must be considered an essential part of all other systems development and management activities, including requirements definition, systems design, programming, package integration, testing, systems documentation, training, configuration management, operations, and maintenance. Security must be viewed as good architecture.

A security management process must be designed in such a way that the activities of planning, fixing, monitoring, and assessing are accomplished in an iterative fashion for systems being defined, designed, and implemented and for systems that are currently executing the day-to-day business operations.

For many organizations, it has not been uncommon for software to be built with little or no attention to security concerns. Consequently, many business-critical applications have made their way into full production with inadequate or nonexistent security controls in place. For example, a quickly built application to resolve an initial need for tracking information within a database through a Web interface may not get all the access control configurations designed into the application that are needed for proper security. It serves a quick purpose but becomes a long-term tool because of its success. Because of the nature of business (moving from one task to the next), nothing is really done to develop it into the function it now fills. As a result, users or hackers may be unintentionally or intentionally capable of accessing and modifying critical information within the database or within the system itself. Fortunately, this trend has started to change, but it is still in need of significant attention. Because such systems are already operating, the only way realistically to identify and assess their security risks is to begin aggressively monitoring for intrusions and then to design and implement corrective security policies and controls based on what is discovered. The effective sequence of security activities for systems already in operational status will be to monitor current operations, assess suspicious activity, plan a corrective policy and technology control, implement the control on the system, and then monitor for continuing effectiveness.

38.2.2   Due Diligence.   To address the software and code security effectively, it must become an issue for management, just as other security concerns have began to demand management attention. Business executives and IT managers are now all too familiar with the concept of due diligence as applied to the uses of information technology. Because of the potential for legal fallout, it has become necessary to view IT-related actions through the definitions of due diligence and reasonable care.

The significance of the concepts of due diligence and reasonable care is that they allow for an evolving metric against which an organization's application security deliberations, decisions, and actions can be compared. The comparison is usually against a similar organization, in like circumstances of vulnerability and threat, and with similar predictable adverse impacts on customers, partners, shareholders, employees, and the public.

For example, if one company employs a security control and does not experience any security breaches that the technique was supposed to prevent, that fact could be used to establish a baseline against which other similar organizations could be compared. If enough similar organizations employ the same technique, the security control may become categorized as a best practice for that industry.

If, however, another company in the same industry did not employ the security control and did experience security breaches of the type the technique was suppose to prevent, it might clearly indicate a lack of due diligence or reasonable care. Software security decisions and implementations are not a one-time event, but need to be under a continuous process of risk evaluation, management, and improvement.

It is therefore imperative, in order to demonstrate an ability to exercise continual due diligence to management, to establish a documented computer security risk management program and to integrate it into the overall management processes of the software development process. Nothing less will demonstrate that a company, and its board, is capable of assessing computer security threats and of acting in a reasonable manner.

For software developers working on commercial software for sale to a specific client under contract, or even to a wide range of customers governed by end-user license agreements, the exercise of due diligence and improved security may reduce the risk of lawsuits claiming damages for negligence. Whether successful or not, such lawsuits are never positive publicity for makers of software products.

38.2.3   Regulatory and Compliance Considerations.   If an organization is subject to specific regulations (e.g., those dictated by Sarbanes-Oxley legislation), then documentation of the errors encountered, and the resulting internal reporting and remediation efforts, is critical. The error should clearly indicate how it was identified, who identified it, how it was reported to management, what the remediation will be, and when it is anticipated to be completed. Without these details, management may encounter significant difficulties in confirming that adequate internal control mechanisms exist, together with the appropriate and adequate involvement of management. In addition, an error could result in a control weakness being identified by the external auditors or, even worse, as a material weakness (a material weakness would be the use of a programming language that has a known inherent flaw rather than another more appropriate and without the flaw, similar to using aluminum instead of steel for a bridge), depending on its nature and severity.

Additionally, when errors are noted that affect multilocation systems or applications, the significance and materiality—that is to say the extent to which the errors impact or may impact the system or any other system to which the application interfaces—must be considered from the aspect of both the subsidiary and the headquarters locales. Since laws differ among states and countries, what might be considered legally acceptable standards of privacy or accounting in one locale might not be acceptable elsewhere.

38.3   TECHNICAL AND PROCEDURAL ISSUES.   Security should be integrated into every stage of the application life cycle. This includes the requirements analysis, the design stage for software, and the operating system security kernel, in corporate policy development, and in human awareness, training, and education programs.

Writing secure code can be a daunting and technically challenging undertaking. That is not to say that it cannot be done, but it requires the developer to work in conjunction with the rest of the project team to meet the challenges that must be defined, reconciled, and overcome prior to the release of the software or system. The additional push to market that can drive the rapid development process can also have a negative impact on the security of the application. The problem must be dealt with in two ways, technical and procedural. Technically, the programmers must be aware of the pitfalls associated with application development and avoid them. Procedurally, the development team and organization need to adhere to a consistent methodology of development. This consistency also needs to include the identification of security risks at every stage of the process, including the requirements analysis.

38.3.1   Requirements Analysis.   Security must be a part of the requirements analysis within any development project. Most application developers know that adding security after the fact increases cost and time, and becomes more complicated. Requirements can be derived from different sources:

- Functional needs of the system (this includes the operating system the application will run on)

- National, international, or organizational standards or guidelines
- Regulatory restrictions
- Sensitivity level of data
- Existing security policies
- Cost/benefit analysis
- Risk rating

The purpose of analysis is to determine what information and processes are needed to support the desired objectives and functions of the software and the business model.

38.3.2 Design.   The informational data gathered during the analysis gathering goes into the software design as requirements. What comes out of the analysis are the data, logic, and procedural design.

Developers take the data and the informational model data and transform them into the data structures that will be required to implement the software. The logic design defines the relationships between the major structures and components of the application. The procedural design transforms structural components into descriptive procedures. Access control mechanisms are chosen, rights and permissions are defined, any other security specifications are appraised, and solutions are determined. A work breakdown structure includes the development and implementation stages. The structure includes a timeline and detailed activities for testing, development, staging, integration testing, and product delivery.

The decisions made during the design phase are pivotal to application development. The design is the only way the requirements are translated into software components. It is in this way that software design is the foundation of the development process, and it greatly affects software quality and maintenance. If good product design is not put in place in the beginning, the rest of the development process will be that much more challenging.

38.3.3 Operating System.   The operating system security kernel is responsible for enforcing the security policy within the operating system and the application. As such, the architecture of the kernel operating system is typically layered, with the kernel at the most privileged layer. This is a small portion of the operating system, but all references to information and changes to authorization pass through the kernel.

To be secure the kernel must meet three basic criteria:

1. **Completeness.** All access to information must go through the kernel.
2. **Isolation.** The kernel must be protected from unauthorized access.
3. **Verifiability.** The kernel must be proven to meet design specifications.

As mentioned, the kernel runs in the most privileged layer. Most operating systems have two processor access modes, user and kernel. General application code runs in user mode, while the operating system runs in kernel mode. Kernel mode allows the processor full access to all system memory and CPU instructions. When applications are not written securely, this separation of modes can become compromised, enabling exploitation of vulnerabilities through arbitrary code, buffer overflows, and other techniques.

38.3.4   Best Practices and Guidelines.
"Best practices" is a term that can cause vigorous debate, especially with regard to security. Best practices in general, and particularly with regard to security, often fall prey to a dogmatic, and sometimes blind, devotion to nonsensical practices that have little to do with security and more to do with faith or tradition. Regardless, best practices help provide a set of guidelines that help provide structure. In addition, best practices can be adapted to help meet the needs of a particular situation. An example would be the National Institute of Standards and Technology (NIST) Special Publication Series 800. This series provides best practices and recommendations that can be adapted or integrated into other practices to assist in improving and eliminating the tradition to a particular practice that may no longer have a legitimate use. Considering this, most general security textbooks contain recommendations on security-related aspects of programming—see, for example, Stallings—that do in fact have a very real benefit in creating more secure software.

In addition to designing security into a system from the start, there are also some obvious guidelines that will help in developing secure software:

- Impose strong identification and authentication for critical and sensitive systems in addition to the I&A available from the operating system; ideally, use token-based or biometric authentication as part of the initialization phase of your application.

- Document your code thoroughly, including using data dictionaries for full definition of allowable input and output to functions and allowable range and type of values for all variables.

- Use local variables, not global variables, when storing sensitive data that should be used only within a specific routine (i.e., use the architecture of the process stack to limit inadvertent or unauthorized access to data in the stack).

- Reinitialize temporary storage immediately after the last legitimate use for the variable, thus making scavenging harder for malefactors.

- Limit functionality in a specific module to what is required for a specific job (e.g., do not use the same module for supervisory functions and for routine functions carried out by clerical staff).

- Define views of data in databases that conform to functional requirements and limit access to sensitive data (e.g., the view of data from a medical records database should exclude patient identifiers when a worker in the finance department is using the database for statistical aggregation).

- Use strong encryption (*not* homegrown encryption) that has industry-standard routines to safeguard sensitive and critical data on disk. Locally developed, homegrown encryption is generally not as safe.

- Disallow access by programmers to production databases.

- Randomize or otherwise mask sensitive data when generating test subsets from production data.

- Use test-coverage monitors to verify that all sections of source code are in fact exercised during quality assurance tests; investigate the functions of code that never is executed.

- Integrate logging capability into all applications for debugging work, for data recovery after crashes in the middle of a transaction, and for security purposes such as forensic analysis.

- Create log-file records that include a cryptographically sound message authentication code (MAC) that itself includes the MAC of the preceding record as input for the algorithm; this technique ensures that forging a log file or modifying it will be more difficult for a malefactor.

- Log all process initiations for a program and log process termination; include full details of who loaded the program or module.

- Log all modifications to records and optionally provide logging for read access as well.

- Use record-level locking to prevent inadvertent overwriting of data on records that are accessed concurrently. Be sure to unlock a sequence of locks in the inverse order of the lock sequence to prevent deadlocks. (Thus if you lock resource A, B, and C in that order, unlock C, then B, then A.)

- Sign your source code using digital signatures.

- Use checksums in production executables to make unauthorized modifications more difficult to conceal.

Mike Gerdes, former manager at AtomicTangerine, contributed these suggestions in the course of a discussion:

- Recommend the readers adopt a practice of designing code in a more holistic fashion. A common practice is to write and test routines in a way that verifies the code processes the data in the way intended. To avoid the effects of malicious code and data input attacks, the programmer must also write code that deals with what is *not* supposed to be processed. A more complete design methodology would also include testing of all inbound information to ensure exclusion of any data which did not fit the requirements for acceptable data. This method should be applied to high-risk applications and those with an extremely arduous test cycle and will eliminate many of the common attack methods used today.

- Establish the criteria for determining the sensitivity level of information contained in, or processed by, the application and subroutines.

- If they are not already present, consider implementing formal control procedures in the software programming methodology to ensure that all data is reviewed during QA processes and to be sure it is classified and handled appropriately for the level assigned.

- Identify and include any mandatory operating system, and network security characteristics for the production system in the specifications of the software. In addition to providing the development and QA teams some definition of the environment the software is designed to run in, giving the administrator and end users an idea of what your expectations were, when you created the code, can be extremely useful in determining where software can, or cannot, be used.

- Where appropriate, verify the digital signatures of routines that process sensitive data when the code is being loaded for execution.

- If you include checksums on executables for production code, include routines that verify the checksums at every system restart.

38.3.5   Languages.   To date, no common computer languages have security specific features built-in. Java does include provisions for limiting access to resources outside the "sandbox" reserved for a process, as described in the books by Falten and McGraw. PASCAL uses strong typing and requires full definition of data structures, thus making it harder to access data and code outside the virtual machine defined for a given process. In contrast, C and C++ allow programmers to access any region of memory at any time the operating system permits it.

Computer languages allow developers to write code as well as they can. Strongly typed languages may offer better constraints on programmers, but the essential requirement is that the programmers continue to think about security as they design and build code.

There are several sets of security utilities and resources available for programmers; for example, RSA has a number of cryptographic toolkits. Some textbooks (e.g., Schneier's *Applied Cryptography*) include CD-ROMs with sample code. In addition, the Computer Emergency Response Team Coordination Center (CERT/CC) was started in December 1988 by the Defense Advanced Research Projects Agency, which was part of the U.S. Department of Defense. CERT/CC is located at the Software Engineering Institute, a federally funded research center operated by Carnegie Mellon University.

CERT/CC studies Internet security vulnerabilities, provides services to Web sites that have been attacked, and publishes security alerts. CERT/CC's research activities include the area of WAN computing and developing improved Internet security.

38.4   TYPES OF SOFTWARE ERRORS.   New programmers should review the range of root causes for software errors. Such review is particularly useful for students who have completed training that did not include discussions of systematic quality assurance methodology. The next sections can serve as a basis for creating effective sets of test data and test procedures for unit tests of new or modified routines.

38.4.1   Internal Design or Implementation Errors.   A general definition of a software error is a mismatch between a program and its specifications; a more specific definition is the failure of a program to do what the end user reasonably expects. There are many types of software errors. Some of the most important include:

- Initialization
- Logic flow
- Calculation
- Boundary condition violations
- Parameter passing
- Race condition
- Load condition
- Resource exhaustion
- Resource, address, or program conflict with the operating system or application(s)
- Regulatory compliance considerations
- Other errors

38.4.1.1   Initialization.   Initialization errors are insidious and difficult to find. The most insidious programs save initialization information to disk and fail only the first time used—that is, before they create the initialization file. The second time a given user activates the program, there are no further initialization errors. Thus, the bugs appear only to employees and customers when they activate a fresh copy of the defective program. Other programs with initialization errors may show odd calculations or other flaws the first time they are used or initialized; because they do not store their initialization values, these initialization errors will continue to reappear each time the program is used.

38.4.1.2 Logic Flow. Modules pass control to each other or to other programs. If execution passes to the wrong module, a logic-flow error has occurred. Examples include calling the wrong function, or branching to a subroutine that lacks a RETURN instruction, so that execution falls through the logical end of a module and begins executing some other code module.

38.4.1.3 Calculation. When a program misinterprets complicated formulas and loses precision as it calculates, it is likely that a calculation error has occurred; for example, an intermediate value may be stored in an array with 16 bits of precision when it needs 32 bits. This category of errors also includes computational errors due to incorrect algorithms.

38.4.1.4 Boundary Condition Violations. Boundaries refer to the largest and smallest values with which a program can cope; for example, an array may be dimensioned with 365 values to account for days of the year, and then fail in a leap year when the program increments the day-counter to 366 and thereby attempts to store a value in an illegal address. Programs that set variable ranges and memory allocation may work correctly within the boundaries but, if incorrectly designed, may crash at or outside the boundaries. The first use of a program also can be considered a boundary condition.

One of the most important types of boundary violations is the buffer overflow. In this error, data placed into storage exceed the defined maximum size and overflow into a section of memory identified as belonging to one or more different variables. The consequences can include data corruption (e.g., if the overflow overwrites data that are interpreted as numerical or literal values) or changes in the flow of execution (e.g., if the altered data include logical flags that are tested in branch instructions).

Buffer overflows have been exploited by writers of malicious code who insert data that overflows into memory areas of interpreted programs and thus become executed as code.

All programs should verify that the data being stored in an array or in any memory location do not exceed the expected size of the input. Data exceeding the expected size should be rejected or, at least, truncated to prevent buffer overflow.

38.4.1.5 Parameter Passing. Sometimes there are errors in passing data back and forth among modules. For instance, a call to a function accidentally might pass the wrong variable name so that the function acts on the wrong values. When these parameter-passing errors occur, data may be corrupted, and the execution path may be affected because of incorrect results of calculations or comparisons. As a result, the latest changes to the data might be lost, or execution might fall into error-handling routines even though the intended data were correct.

38.4.1.6 Race Condition. When a race occurs between event A and event B, a specific sequence of events is required for correct operation, but the program does not ensure this sequence. For example, if process A locks resource 1 and waits for resource 2 to be unlocked while process B locks resource 2 and waits for resource 1 to be unlocked, there may be a deadly embrace that freezes the operations if the processes overlap in execution. If they do not happen to overlap, there is no problem at that time.

Race conditions can be expected in multiprocessing systems and interactive systems, but they can be difficult to replicate; for example, the deadly embrace just described might happen only once in 1,000 transactions if the average transaction time is very short. Consequently, race conditions are among the most difficult to detect during quality assurance testing and are best identified in code reviews. Programmers should establish and comply with standards on sequential operations that require exclusive access to more than one resource. For example, if all processes exclusive-lock resources in a given sequence and unlock them in the reverse order, there can be no deadly embrace.

38.4.1.7 Load Condition.
All programs and systems have limits to storage capacity, numbers of users, transactions, and throughput. Load errors are caused by exceeding the volume limitations of storage, transactions, users, and networks can occur due to high volume, which includes a great deal of work over a long period, or high stress, which includes the maximum load all at one time. For example, if the total theoretical number of transactions causes a demand on the disk I/O system that exceeds the throughput of the disk controller, processes will necessarily begin piling up in a queue waiting for completion of disk I/Os. Although theoretical calculations can help to identify where possible bottlenecks can occur in CPU, memory, disk, and network resources, a useful adjunct is automated testing that permits simulation of maximum loads defined by service-level agreements.

38.4.1.8 Resource Exhaustion.
The program running out of high-speed memory (RAM), mass storage (disk), central processing unit (CPU) cycles, operating system table entries, semaphores, network bandwidth, or other resources can cause failure of the program. For example, inadequate main memory may cause excessive swapping of data to disk (thrashing), typically causing drastic reductions in throughput, because disk I/O is typically 1,000 times slower than memory access.

38.4.1.9 Interapplication Conflicts.
With operating systems (OS) as complex as they are, OS manufacturers routinely distribute the code requirements and certain parameters to the application software manufacturers, so that the likelihood of program conflicts or unexpected stoppages are minimized. While this certainly helps reduce the number of problems and improves the forward and backward compatibility with previous OS versions, even the OS vendors on occasion experience or cause difficulties when they do not conform to the parameters established for their own programs.

38.4.1.10 Other Sources of Error.
It is not unusual for errors to occur where programs send bad data to devices, ignore error codes coming back, and even try to use devices that are busy or missing. The hardware might well be broken, but the software also is considered to be in error when it does not recover from such hardware conditions.

Additional errors can occur through improper builds of the executable; for example, if an old version of a module is linked to the latest version of the rest of the program, the wrong sign-on screens may pop up, the wrong copyright messages may be displayed, the wrong version numbers may appear, and various other inaccuracies may occur.

38.4.1.11 *User Interface.* Generally speaking, the term "user interface" denotes all aspects of a system that are relevant to a user. It can be broadly described as the user virtual machine (UVM). This would include all screens, the mouse and keyboard, printed outputs, and all other elements with which the user interacts. A major problem arises when system designers cannot put themselves in the user's place and cannot foresee the problems that technologically challenged users will have with an interface designed by a technologically knowledgeable person.

Documentation is a crucial part of every system. Each phase of development—requirements, analysis, development, coding, testing, errors, error solutions and modifications, implementation, and maintenance—needs to be documented. All documents and their various versions need to be retained for both future reference and auditing purposes. Additionally, it is important to document the correct use of the system and to provide adequate instructional and reference materials to the user. Security policies and related enforcement and penalties also need to be documented. Ideally, the documentation should enable any technically qualified person to repair or modify any element, as long as the system remains operational.

38.4.1.12 *Functionality.* A program has a functionality error if performance that can reasonably be expected is confusing, awkward, difficult, or impossible. Functionality errors often involve key features or functions that have never been implemented. Additional functionality errors exist when:

- Features are not documented.
- Required information is missing.
- A program fails to acknowledge legitimate input.
- There are factual errors or conflicting names for features.
- There is information overload.
- The material is written to an inappropriate reading level.
- The cursor disappears, or is in the wrong place.
- Screen displays are wrong.
- Instructions are obscured.
- Identical functions require different operations in different screens.
- Improperly formatted input screens exist.
- Passwords or other confidential information are not obscured or protected adequately.
- Tracing the user data entry or changes is unavailable or incomplete.
- Segregation of duties is not enforced. (This can be particularly critical for organizations subject to legal and regulatory requirements.)

38.4.1.13 *Control (Command) Structure.* Control structure errors can cause serious problems because they can result in:

- Users getting lost in a program.
- Users wasting time because they must deal with confusing commands.
- Loss of data or the unwanted exposure of data.
- Work delay.

- Financial cost.
- Unanticipated exposure to data leakage or compromise; this can result in significant liability if consumers' personal identifying information (PII) is compromised.
- Data not being encrypted as intended or being visible to unauthorized users.

Some common errors include:

- Inability to move between menus.
- Confusing and repetitive menus.
- Failure to allow adequate command-line entries.
- Requiring command-line entries that are neither intuitive nor clearly defined on screen.
- Failure of the application program to follow the operating system's conventions.
- Failure to distinguish between source and parameter files, resulting in the wrong values being made available to the user through the interface, or failure to identify the source of the error
- Inappropriate use of the keyboard, when new programs do not meet the standard of a keyboard that has labeled function keys tied to standard meanings.
- Missing commands from the code and screens resulting in the user being unable to access information, to utilize programs, or to provide for the system to be backed up and recoverable. There are a host of other commands that can leave the system in a state of less-than-optimum operability.
- Inadequate privacy or security that can result in confidential information being divulged, in the complete change or loss of data without recoverability, in poor reporting, and even in undesired access by outside parties.

38.4.1.14   Performance.   Speed is important in interactive software. If a user feels that the program is working slowly, that can be an immediate problem. Performance errors include slow response, unannounced case sensitivity, uncontrollable and excessively frequent automatic saves, inability to save, and limited scrolling speed. Slow operation can depend on (but is not limited to) the OS, the other applications running, memory saturation and thrashing (excessive swapping of memory contents to virtual memory on disk or on other, relatively slow, memory resources such as flash drives), memory leakage (the failure to deallocate memory that is no longer needed), disk I/O inefficiencies (e.g., reading single records from very large blocks), and program conflicts (e.g., locking errors). For more information on program performance, see Chapter 52 in this *Handbook*.

At another level, performance suffers when program designs make it difficult to change their functionality in response to changing requirements. In a database design, defining a primary index field that determines the sequence in which records are stored on disk can greatly speed access to records during sequential reads on key values for that index—but it can be counterproductive if the predominant method for accessing the records is sequential reads on a completely different index.

38.4.1.15   Output Format.   Output format errors can be frustrating and time consuming. An error is considered to have occurred when the user cannot change fonts, underlining, boldface, and spacing that influence the final look of the output; alternatively, delays or errors when printing or saving document may occur. Errors occur when the user cannot control the content, scaling, and look of tables, figures, and graphs. Additionally, there are output errors that involve expression of the data to an inappropriate level of precision.

38.5   ASSURANCE TOOLS AND TECHNIQUES.   Buffer overflow vulnerabilities, as an example, have been known to the security community for the past 25 or 30 years, yet the vulnerabilities are still increasing. Clearly greater efforts are neccessary to teach and to enforce awareness and implementation of source code requirements.

38.5.1   Education Resources.   Build Security In (BSI) is a project of the Software Assurance program of the Strategic Initiatives Branch of the National Cyber Security Division (NCSD) of the U.S. Department of Homeland Security. BSI (http://buildsecurityin.us-cert.gov/portal) contains and links to best practices, tools, guidelines, rules, principles, and other resources that software developers, architects, and security practitioners can use to build security into software in every phase of its development. BSI content is based on the principle that software security is fundamentally a software engineering problem and must be addressed in a systematic way throughout the software development life cycle.

In addition to BSI, and out of the multitudes of sites on the Web that address some facet of secure coding, some sites are listed next to assist in secure application development:

- AusCERT Secure Programming Checklist: ftp://ftp.auscert.org.au/pub/auscert/papers/secure_programming_checklist
- FreeBSD Security Information: www.freebsd.org/security/security.html
- International Systems Security Engineering Association (ISSEA): www.issea.org/
- Open Web Application Security Project: www.owasp.org/
- Secure, Efficient, and Easy C Programming: http://irccrew.org/~cras/security/c-guide.html
- Secure Programming for Linux and UNIX HOWTO: www.dwheeler.com/secure-programs/
- Secure UNIX Programming FAQ: www.whitefang.com/sup/secure-faq.html
- Systems Security Engineering—Capability Maturity Model: www.sse-cmm.org/
- Windows Security: www.windowsecurity.com/
- World Wide Web Security FAQ: www.w3.org/Security/Faq/www-security-faq.html

38.5.2   Code Examination and Application Penetration Testing. Scanning once is not enough; ongoing application assessment is essential to implementing effective secure development practices and, in turn, a secure application.

38.5.2.1   *White Box.* White box testing strategy deals with the internal logic and structure of the code. White box testing is also known as glass, structural, open box, or clear box testing. In order to implement white box testing, the tester has to deal with the code, and therefore needs to possess knowledge of coding and logic (i.e., internal working of the code). White box tests also need the tester to look into the code and to find out which unit/statement/chunk of the code is malfunctioning.

Advantages of white box testing are:

- It becomes very easy to find out which type of input/data can help in testing the application effectively.
- It helps in optimizing the code.
- It helps in removing the extra lines of code, which can bring in hidden defects.

Disadvantages of white box testing are:

- A skilled tester is needed to carry out this type of testing, which increases the cost.
- It is nearly impossible to look into every bit of code to find hidden errors that may create problems, resulting in failure of the application.

38.5.2.2   Black Box.   Black box testing is testing without knowledge of the internal workings of the item being tested. Black box testing is also known as behavioral, functional, opaque box, and closed box. For this reason, the tester and the programmer can be independent of one another, avoiding programmer bias toward his own work. Test groups are often used. Due to the nature of black box testing, the test planning can begin as soon as the specifications are written.

Advantages of black box testing are:

- It is more effective on larger units of code than glass box testing.
- The tester needs no knowledge of implementation, including specific programming languages.
- Tester and programmer are independent of each other.
- Tests are done from a user's point of view.
- It will help to expose any ambiguities or inconsistencies in the specifications.
- Test cases can be designed as soon as the specifications are complete.

Disadvantages of black box testing are:

- Only a small number of possible inputs can actually be tested; to test every possible input stream on a complex system would take nearly forever.
- Without clear and concise specifications, test cases are hard to design.
- There may be unnecessary repetition of test inputs if the tester is not informed of test cases the programmer has already tried. It is always critical to validate any testing claims through reports or result output to help avoid duplication. Likewise it is always important to rerun tests that may have ambiguous results.
- It may leave many program paths untested.
- It cannot be directed toward specific segments of code that may be very complex.

38.5.2.3   Gray Box—Blended Approach.   Gray box testing is a software testing technique that uses a combination of black box testing and white box testing. Gray box testing is not black box testing, because the tester does know some of the internal workings of the software under test. In gray box testing, the tester applies a limited number of test cases to the internal workings of the software under test. In the remaining part of the gray box testing, the tester takes a black box approach in applying inputs to the software under test and observing the outputs.

38.5.3 Standards and Best Practices.   Testing is a complete software engineering discipline in its own right. Volumes have been written about the various techniques that software engineers use to test and validate their applications. Some basic best practices can be employed regardless of the testing methodology selected. These are:

- Perform automated testing.
- Make a test plan.
- Follow a specific methodology.
- Test at every stage.
- Test all system components.

In addition to these best practices, use of these standards can provide additional resources:

- ISO 17799, Information Technology: Code of Practice for Information Security Management
- ISO/IEC 15408, Evaluation Criteria for IT Security (the Common Criteria)
- SSE-CMM, System Security Engineering Capability Maturity Model
- ISO/IEC WD 15443, Information Technology: Security Techniques

38.6 CONCLUDING REMARKS.   Computer security practitioners and top-level managers must understand that IT management deficiencies, left unchanged, will sabotage efforts to establish and sustain effective computer security programs. The costs of neglecting security at the start will continue to be a serious issue until software security is fully integrated into every aspect of the development life cycle. Security must be built in, and building security into systems starts with the software development practices and techniques used to build those systems.

38.7 FURTHER READING

Campanella, J. (1999), ed. *Principles of Quality Costs: Implementation and Use*, 3rd ed. Milwaukee, Wisconsin: ASQ Quality Press.

Felten, E., & G. McGraw (1999). *Securing Java: Getting Down to Business with Mobile Code*. New York: John Wiley & Sons. Also free and unlimited Web access from www.securingjava.com.

Fox, C., and P. Zonneveld (2006). *IT Control Objectives for Sarbanes-Oxley: The Role of IT in the Design and Implementation of Internal Control Over Financial Reporting*, 2nd ed. IT Governance Institute.

Institute of Electrical and Electronics Engineers. *IEEE Standard for Software Test Documentation*. ANSI/IEEE Std. 829-1983. 1983.

Institute of Electrical and Electronics Engineers. *IEEE Standard for Software Quality Assurance Plans. ANSI/IEEE Std. 730-1981*. 1981.

McGraw, G., and E. W. Felten *Java Security: Hostile Applets, Holes and Antidotes—What Every Netscape and Internet Explorer User Needs to Know*. New York: John Wiley & Sons, 1997.

McGraw, G., and E. W. Felten. " Understanding the Keys to Java Security—the Sandbox and Authentication," 1997; www.javaworld.com/javaworld/jw-05-1997/jw-05-security.html.

NASA Software Assurance Technology Center, http://satc.gsfc.nasa.gov/.

Ould, M.A. *Strategies for Software Engineering: The Management of Risk and Quality.* New York: John Wiley & Sons, 1990.

RSA Data Security, www.rsasecurity.com/products/.

Schneier, B. *Applied Cryptography: Protocols, Algorithms, and Source Code in C*, 2nd ed. New York: John Wiley & Sons, 1995.

Stallings, W. *Network and Internetwork Security: Principles and Practice.* Englewood Cliffs, NJ: Prentice Hall, 1995.

Tipton, H. F., and K. Henry. *Official (ISC) Guide to the CISSP CBK.* Boca Raton, FL: Auerbach Publications, 2006.

CHAPTER **39**

SOFTWARE DEVELOPMENT AND QUALITY ASSURANCE

Diane E. Levine, John Mason, and Jennifer Hadley

39.1   INTRODUCTION.   Software development can affect all of the six fundamental principles of information security as described in Chapter 6 in this *Handbook*, but the most frequent problems caused by poor software involve integrity, availability, and utility.

Despite the ready availability of packaged software on the open market, such software frequently has to be customized to meet its users' particular needs. Where this is not possible, programs must be developed from scratch. Unfortunately, during any software development project, despite careful planning, unforeseen problems inevitably arise. Custom software and customized packages frequently are delivered late, are faulty, and do not meet specifications. Generally, software project managers tend to underestimate the impact of technical as well as nontechnical difficulties. Because of this experience, the field of software engineering has developed; its purpose is to find reasonable answers to questions that occur during software development projects.

39.2   GOALS OF SOFTWARE QUALITY ASSURANCE.   In the IEEE *Glossary of Software Engineering Terminology*, quality is defined as "the degree to which a system, component, or process meets customer or user needs or expectations." In accordance with this definition, software should be measured primarily by the degree to which user needs are met. Because software frequently needs to be adapted to changing requirements, it should be adaptable at reasonable cost. Therefore, in addition to being concerned with correctness, reliability, and usability, the customer also is concerned with testability, maintainability, portability, and compliance with the established standards and procedures for the software and development process. Software quality assurance (SQA) is an element of software engineering that tries to ensure that software meets acceptable standards of completeness and quality. SQA acts as a watchdog overseeing all quality-related activities involved in software development.

The principal goals of SQA are:

- Uncover all of a program's problems.
- Reduce the likelihood that defective programs will enter production.
- Safeguard the interests of users.
- Safeguard the interests of the software producer.

39.2.1   Uncover All of a Program's Problems.   Quality must be built into a product. Testing can only reveal the presence of defects in the product. To ensure quality, SQA monitors both the development process and the behavior of software. The goal is not to pass or certify the software; the goal is to identify all the inadequacies and problems in the software so that they can be corrected.

39.2.2   Reduce the Likelihood that Defective Programs Will Enter Production.   All software development must comply with the standards and policies established within the organization to identify and eliminate errors before defective programs enter production.

39.2.3 Safeguard the Interests of Users.

The ultimate goal is to achieve software that meets the users' requirements and provides them with needed functionality. To meet these goals, SQA must review and audit the software development process and provide the results of those reviews and audits to management. SQA, as a functioning department, can be successful only if it has the support of management and if it reports to management at the same level as software development. Likewise, each SQA project will possess specific attributes, and the SQA program should be tailored to accommodate project needs. Characteristics to be considered include: mission criticality, schedule and budget, size and complexity of project, and size and competence of project staff organization.

39.2.4 Safeguard the Interests of Software Producers.

By ensuring that software meets requirements, SQA can help prevent legal conflicts that may arise if purchased software fails to meet contractual obligations. When software is developed in-house, SQA can prevent the finger-pointing that otherwise would damage relations between software developers and corporate users.

39.3 SOFTWARE DEVELOPMENT LIFE CYCLE.

Good software, whether developed in-house or bought from an external vendor, needs to be constructed using sound principles. Because software development projects often are large and have many people working on them for long periods of time, the development process needs to be monitored and controlled.

Although progress of such projects is difficult to measure, using a phased approach can control the projects. In a phased approach, a number of clearly identifiable milestones are established between the start and the finish of the project. A common analogy that is used is that of constructing a house, where the foundation is laid initially and each phase of construction is achieved in an orderly and controlled manner. Frequently, with both house construction and software development, payments for phases are dependent on reaching the designated milestones.

When developing systems, we refer to the phased process as the system development life cycle (SDLC). The SDLC is the process of developing information systems through investigation, analysis, design, coding and debugging, testing, implementation, and maintenance. These seven phases are common, although different models and techniques may contain more or fewer phases.

Generally, milestones identified in the SDLC correspond to the points in time when specified documents become available. Frequently the documents explain and reinforce the actions taken during the just-completed phase of the SDLC. We therefore say that traditional models for the phased development are document driven to a large extent.

There are problems and drawbacks inherent in the document-driven process. The method of viewing the development process via the SDLC is not totally realistic to the actual projects. In reality, errors found in earlier phases are noted, and fixes are developed, prototyping is introduced, and solutions are implemented. This, in effect, is more than what is assumed will be necessary in the debugging and maintenance phases. Also, often the problems are solved before those later phases are reached. Because of the recognition that much of what in traditional models is referred to as maintenance is really evolution, other models of the SDLC, known as evolutionary models, have been developed.

In traditional models, the initial development of a system is kept strictly separate from the maintenance phase. The major goal of the SDLC is to deliver a first production version of the software system to the user. It is not unusual for this approach to result in excessive maintenance costs to make the functioning or final system fit the needs of the real user. There are other models available, and it is necessary, for each project, to choose a specific systems development life cycle model. To do this, it is necessary to identify the need for a new system and to follow this by identifying the individual steps and phases, possible interaction of the phases, the necessary deliverables, and all related materials.

There are four major system development techniques:

1. Traditional systems development life cycle (SDLC)
2. Waterfall model (a variant of the traditional SDLC)
3. Rapid application development (RAD)
4. Joint application development (JAD)

Although these four development techniques frequently are seen as mutually exclusive, in truth they represent solutions that place different emphasis on common elements of systems design. Defined at different times, each methodology's strengths demonstrate the technology, economics, and organizational issues that were current at the time the methodology was first defined.

Software generally is constructed in phases, and tests should be conducted at the end of each phase before development continues in the next phase. Four major phases that are always present in software construction are:

1. The analysis phase, where software requirements are defined
2. The design phase, based on the previously described requirements
3. The construction, programming, or coding phase
4. The implementation phase, where software is actually installed on production hardware and finally tested before release to production

The programming phase always includes unit testing of individual modules and system testing of overall functions. Sometimes, in addition to testing during programming and implementation, a fifth phase, solely devoted to functional testing, is established. Review and modification generally follow all phases, where weaknesses and inadequacies are corrected.

39.3.1 Phases of the Traditional Software Development Life Cycle.
The seven phases discussed here comprise the most common traditional SDLC:

1. Investigation
2. Analysis
3. Design
4. Decoding and debugging
5. Testing
6. Implementation
7. Maintenance

From this traditional model, other models with fewer or more phases have been developed.

39.3.1.1 *Investigation.*   This phase involves the determination of the need for the system. It involves determining whether a business problem or opportunity exists and conducting a feasibility study to determine the cost effectiveness of the proposed solution.

39.3.1.2 *Analysis.*   Requirements analysis is the process of analyzing the end users' information needs, the environment of the organization and the current system, and developing functional requirements for a system to meet users' needs. This phase includes recording all of the requirements. The documentation must be referred to continually during the remainder of the system development process.

39.3.1.3 *Design.*   The architectural design phase lists and describes all of the necessary specifications for the hardware, software, people and data resources, and information products that will satisfy the proposed system's functional requirements. The design can best be described as a blueprint for the system. It is a crucial tool in detecting and eliminating problems and errors before they are built into the system.

39.3.1.4 *Coding and Debugging.*   This phase involves the actual creation of the system. It is done by information technology professionals, sometimes on staff within a company and sometimes from an external company that specializes in this type of work. The system is coded, and attempts are made to catch and eliminate all coding errors before the system is implemented.

39.3.1.5 *Testing.*   Once the system is created, testing is absolutely essential.
   Testing proves the functionality and reliability of the system and acts as another milestone for finding problems and errors before implementation. This phase is instrumental in determining whether the system will meet users' needs.

39.3.1.6 *Implementation.*   Once the previous five phases have been completed and accepted, with substantiating documentation, the system is implemented and users are permitted to utilize it.

39.3.1.7 *Maintenance.*   This phase is ongoing and takes place after the system is implemented. Because systems are subject to variances, flaws, and breakdowns, as well as difficulties when integrating with other systems and hardware, maintenance continues for as long as the system is in use.

39.3.2 Classic Waterfall Model.   Although phased approaches to software development appeared in the 1960s, the waterfall model, attributed to Roy Royce, appeared in the 1970s. The waterfall model demands a sequential approach to software development and contains only five phases:

1. Requirements analysis phase
2. Design
3. Implementation
4. Testing
5. Maintenance

39.3.2.1 *Analysis or Requirements Analysis.* The waterfall model emphasizes analysis as part of the requirements analysis phase. Since software is always part of a larger system, requirements are first established for all system elements, and then some subset of these requirements is allocated to software. Identified requirements, for both the system and the software, are then documented in the requirements specification. A series of validation tests is required to ensure that, as the system is developed, it continues to meet these specifications.

The waterfall model includes validation and verification in each of its five phases. This means that in each phase of the software development process, it is necessary to compare the obtained results against the required results. Testing is done within every phase to answer this question and does not occur strictly in the testing phase that follows the implementation phase.

39.3.2.2 *Design.* The design phase is actually a multistep process focusing on data structure, software architecture, procedural detail, and interface characterization. During the design phase, requirements are translated into a representation of the software that then can be assessed for quality before actual coding begins. Once again, documentation plays an important role because the documented design becomes a part of the software configuration. Coding is incorporated into the design phase instead of being a separate phase. During coding, the design is translated into machine-readable form.

39.3.2.3 *Implementation.* During the implementation phase, the system is given to the user. Many developers feel that a large problem with this model is that the system is implemented before it actually is ready to be given to the user. However, waterfall model advocates claim that the consistent testing throughout the development process permits the system to be ready by the time this phase is reached. Note that in the waterfall model, the implementation phase precedes the testing phase.

39.3.2.4 *Testing.* Although testing has been going on during the entire development process, the testing phase begins after code has been generated and the implementation phase has occurred. This phase focuses on both the logical internals of the software and the functional externals. Ideally, the end users and the process/business owners should be enlisted to assist in this phase, since they usually:

- Are familiar with the business requirements
- Know how the current software and hardware operates
- Know what types of activity are anticipated and planned
- Provide the ultimate acceptance approval of the software and hardware

Although not directly required by many of the regulatory reviews, involving the end users and process owners provides the IT area with additional resources, not only from a human resource perspective but also from a business knowledge and regulatory compliance perspective.

39.3.2.5 *Maintenance.* The maintenance phase reapplies each of the preceding life cycle steps to existing programs. Maintenance is necessary because of errors that are detected, necessary adaptation to the external environment, and functional and performance enhancements required and requested by the customer.

The waterfall model is considered to be unreliable, partly due to failure to obey the strict sequence of phases advocated by the traditional model. In addition, the waterfall model often fails because it delivers products whose usefulness is limited when requirements have changed during the development process.

39.3.3 Rapid Application Development and Joint Application Design.

Rapid application development (RAD) supports the iteration and flexibility necessary for building robust business process support. RAD emphasizes user involvement and small development teams, prototyping of software, software reuse, and automated tools. Activities must be carried out within a specified time frame known as a time box. This approach differs from other development models where the requirements are fixed first and the time frame is decided later. RAD, in an effort to keep within the time box and its immovable deadline, may sacrifice some functionality.

RAD has four phases within its cycle:

1. Requirements planning
2. User design
3. Construction
4. Cutover

The main techniques used in RAD are joint requirements planning (JRP) and joint application design (JAD). The word "joint" refers to developers and users working together through the heavy use of workshops. JAD enables the identification, definition, and implementation of information infrastructures. The JAD technique is discussed with RAD because it enhances RAD.

39.3.4 Importance of Integrating Security at Every Phase.

Security should never be something added to software at the end of a project. Security must be considered continuously during an entire project in order to safeguard both the software and the entire system within which it functions. Regardless of which software development model is used, it is essential to integrate security within each phase of development and to include security in the testing at each phase. Rough estimates indicate that the cost of correcting an error rises tenfold with every additional phase. For example, catching an error at the analysis phase might require only several minutes—time for a user to correct the analyst—and therefore cost only a few dollars. Catching the same error once it has been incorporated into the specifications document might cost 10 times more; after implementation, 1,000 times more.

39.4 TYPES OF SOFTWARE ERRORS

39.4.1 Internal Design or Implementation Errors.

A general definition of a software error is a mismatch between a program and its specifications; a more specific definition is "the failure of a program to do what the end user reasonably expects." There are many types of software errors. Some of the most important include:

- Initialization
- Logic flow
- Calculation
- Boundary condition violations

- Parameter passing
- Race condition
- Load condition
- Resource exhaustion
- Resource, address, or program conflict with the operating system or application(s)
- Regulatory compliance considerations
- Other errors

39.4.1.1   Initialization.   Initialization errors are insidious and difficult to find. The most insidious programs save initialization information to disk and fail only the first time they are used—that is, before they create the initialization file. The second time a given user activates the program, there are no further initialization errors. Thus the bugs appear only to employees and customers when they activate a fresh copy or installation of the defective program. Other programs with initialization errors may show odd calculations or other flaws the first time they are used or initialized; because they do not store their initialization values, these initialization errors will continue to reappear each time the program is used.

39.4.1.2   Logic Flow.   Modules pass control to each other or to other programs. If execution passes to the wrong module, a logic-flow error has occurred. Examples include calling the wrong function, or branching to a subroutine that lacks a RETURN instruction, so that execution falls through the logical end of a module and begins executing some other code module.

39.4.1.3   Calculation.   When a program misinterprets complicated formulas and loses precision as it calculates, it is likely that a calculation error has occurred; for example, an intermediate value may be stored in an array with 16 bits of precision when it needs 32 bits. This category of errors also includes computational errors due to incorrect algorithms.

39.4.1.4   Boundary Condition Violations.   The term "boundaries" refers to the largest and smallest values with which a program can cope; for example, an array may be dimensioned with 365 values to account for days of the year and then fail in a leap year when the program increments the day-counter to 366 and thereby attempts to store a value in an illegal address. Programs that set variable ranges and memory allocation may work within the boundaries but, if incorrectly designed, may crash at or outside the boundaries. The first use of a program also can be considered a boundary condition.

39.4.1.5   Parameter Passing.   Sometimes there are errors in passing data back and forth among modules. For instance, a call to a function accidentally might pass the wrong variable name so that the function acts on the wrong values. When these parameter-passing errors occur, data may be corrupted and the execution path may be affected because of incorrect results of calculations or comparisons. As a result, the latest changes to the data might be lost or execution might fall into error-handling routines even though the intended data were correct.

39.4.1.6 *Race Condition.* When a race occurs between event A and event B, a specific sequence of events is required for correct operation, but this sequence is not ensured by the program. For example, if process A locks resource 1 and waits for resource 2 to be unlocked while process B locks resource 2 and waits for resource 1 to be unlocked, there will be a deadly embrace that freezes the operations.

Race conditions can be expected in multiprocessing systems and interactive systems, but they can be difficult to replicate; for example, the deadly embrace just described might happen only once in 1,000 transactions if the average transaction time is very short. Consequently, race conditions are among the least tested.

39.4.1.7 *Load Condition.* All programs and systems have limits to storage capacity, numbers of users, transactions, and throughput. Load errors can occur due to high volume, which includes a great deal of work over a long period of time, or high stress, which includes the maximum load all at one time.

39.4.1.8 *Resource Exhaustion.* The program's running out of high-speed memory (RAM), mass storage (disk), central processing unit (CPU) cycles, operating system table entries, semaphores, or other resources can cause failure of the program. For example, inadequate main memory may cause swapping of data to disk, typically causing drastic reductions in throughput.

39.4.1.9 *Interapplication Conflicts.* With operating systems (OS) as complex as they are, OS manufacturers routinely distribute the code requirements and certain parameters to the application software manufacturers, so that the likelihood of program conflicts or unexpected stoppages are minimized. Although this certainly helps reduce the number of problems and improves the forward and backward compatibility with previous OS versions, on occasion even the OS vendors experience or cause difficulties when they do not conform to the parameters established for their own programs.

39.4.1.10 *Other Sources of Error.* It is not unusual for errors to occur where programs send bad data to devices, ignore error codes coming back, and even try to use devices that are busy or missing. The hardware might well be broken, but the software also is considered to be in error when it does not recover from such hardware conditions.

Additional errors can occur through improper builds of the executable; for example, if an old version of a module is linked to the latest version of the rest of the program, the wrong sign-on screens may pop up, the wrong copyright messages may be displayed, the wrong version numbers may appear, and various other inaccuracies may occur.

39.4.1.11 *Regulatory Compliance Considerations.* If an organization is subject to Sarbanes-Oxley (SOX), then documentation of the errors encountered and the resulting internal reporting and remediation efforts is critical. The error should clearly indicate how it was identified, who identified it, how it was reported to management, what the remediation will be, and when it is anticipated to be completed. Without these details, management may encounter significant difficulties in confirming that adequate internal control mechanisms exist and that it is informed and involved appropriately and adequately. Also, an error could result in a control weakness being identified by the external auditors or, even worse, as a material weakness, depending on its nature and severity.

Additionally, if and when errors are noted that affect multilocation systems or applications, the significance and materiality must be considered from the aspect of both the subsidiary and the headquarters locales. Since laws differ among states and countries, what might be considered legally acceptable standards of privacy or accounting in one locale might not be acceptable elsewhere.

39.4.2   User Interface.   Generally speaking, the term "user interface" denotes all aspects of a system that are relevant to a user. It can be broadly described as the user virtual machine (UVM). This would include all screens, the mouse and keyboard, printed outputs, and all other elements with which the user interacts. A major problem arises when system designers cannot put themselves in the user's place and cannot foresee the problems that a technologically challenged user will have with an interface designed by a technologically knowledgeable person.

Documentation is a crucial part of every system. Each phase of development—requirements, analysis, development, coding, testing, errors, error solutions and modifications, implementation, and maintenance—needs to be documented. All documents and their various versions need to be retained for both future reference and auditing purposes. Additionally, it is important to document the correct use of the system and provide adequate instructional and reference materials to the user. Security policies and related enforcement and penalties also need to be documented. Ideally, the documentation should enable any technically qualified person to repair or modify any element, as long as the system remains operational.

39.4.2.1   Functionality.   A program has a functionality error if performance that can reasonably be expected is confusing, awkward, difficult, or impossible. Functionality errors often involve key features or functions that have never been implemented. Additional functionality errors exist when:

- Features are not documented.
- Required information is missing.
- A program fails to acknowledge legitimate input.
- There are factual errors or conflicting names for features.
- There is information overload.
- The material is written to an inappropriate reading level.
- The cursor disappears or is in the wrong place.
- Screen displays are wrong.
- Instructions are obscured.
- Identical functions require different operations in different screens.
- Improperly formatted input screens exist.
- Passwords or other confidential information are not obscured or protected adequately.
- Tracing the user data entry or changes is unavailable or incomplete.
- Segregation of duties is not enforced. (This can be particularly critical for organizations subject to HIPAA, SOX, ISO 17799, and/or GLBA.)

39.4.2.2 Control (Command) Structure. Control structure errors can cause serious problems because they can result in:

- Users getting lost in a program
- Users wasting time because they must deal with confusing commands
- Loss of data or the unwanted exposure of data
- Work delay
- Financial cost
- Unanticipated exposure to data leakage or compromise; this can result in significant liability if consumers' personal identifying information (PII) is compromised
- Data not being encrypted as intended or being visible to unauthorized users

Some common errors include:

- Inability to move between menus
- Confusing and repetitive menus
- Failure to allow adequate command-line entries
- Requiring command-line entries that are neither intuitive nor clearly defined on screen
- Failure of the application program to follow the operating system's conventions
- Failure to distinguish between source and parameter files, resulting in the wrong values being made available to the user through the interface, or failure to identify the source of the error
- Inappropriate use of the keyboard when new programs do not meet the standard of a keyboard that has labeled function keys tied to standard meanings
- Missing commands from the code and screens resulting in the user being unable to access information, to utilize programs, or to provide for the system to be backed up and recoverable, as well as a host of other commands that leave the system in a state of less-than-optimum operability
- Inadequate privacy or security that can result in confidential information being divulged, the complete change or loss of data without recoverability, poor reporting, and even undesired access by outside parties

39.4.2.3 Performance. Speed is important in interactive software. If a user feels that the program is working slowly, that can be an immediate problem. Slow operation can depend on (but is not limited to) the OS, the other applications running, memory allocation, memory leakage, and program conflicts. At another level, performance suffers when program designs make it difficult to change their functionality in response to changing requirements. Performance errors include slow response, unannounced case sensitivity, uncontrollable and excessively frequent automatic saves, inability to save, and limited scrolling speed.

39.4.2.4 Output Format. Output format errors can be frustrating and time consuming. An error is considered to have occurred when the user cannot change fonts, underlining, boldface, and spacing that influence the final look of the output; alternatively, delays or errors when printing or saving document may occur. Errors occur when the user cannot control the content, scaling, and look of tables, figures, and graphs. Additionally, there are output errors that involve expression of the data to an inappropriate level of precision.

39.5   DESIGNING SOFTWARE TEST CASES

39.5.1   Good Tests.   No software program can ever be tested completely, since it would not be cost effective or efficient to test the validity, parameters, syntax, and boundaries of every line of code. Even if all valid inputs are defined and tested, there is no way to test all invalid inputs and all the variations on input timing. It is also difficult, if not impossible, to test every path the program might take, find every design error, and prove programs to be logically correct. Nevertheless, a good test procedure will find most of the problems that would occur, allowing the designers and developers to correct those problems and ensure that the software works properly. Generally, OS and application manufacturers classify the severity level of errors encountered, and many (as evidenced by the frequency and content of program patches) correct only the most serious ones that either they or the users notice.

Over the past several years, there has been an increasing debate on whether software vulnerabilities should be publicized immediately by researchers, or if the researchers should automatically notify and give the manufacturer time to correct the flaw. Generally, from a casual review of the vulnerabilities discovered concerning Microsoft's Internet Explorer version 6 over the past few years, the trend appears to have been that the researcher notifies Microsoft and allows Microsoft a varying period of time to create and distribute the patch (e.g., three to six months) before the researcher publicly announces the weakness. This trend is based on published reports in the technical news media.

Whenever you expect the same results from two tests, you consider the tests equivalent. A group of tests forms an equivalence class if the tester believes that the tests all test the same thing, and if one test catches or does not catch a bug, the others probably will do the same. Classical boundary tests check a program's response to input and output data; equivalence tests, however, teach a way of thinking about analyzing programs that enhances and strengthens test planning.

Finding equivalence classes is a subjective process. Different people analyzing the same program will come up with different lists of equivalence classes because of what the programs appear to achieve. Test cases often are lumped into the same equivalence class when they involve the same input variables, result in similar operations, affect the same output variables, or handle errors in the same manner.

Equivalence classes can be groups of tests dealing with ranges or multiple ranges of numbers, members of a group, and even time determined. Equivalence classes are generally the most extreme values, such as the biggest, smallest, fastest, and slowest. When testing, it is important to test each edge of an equivalence class, on all sides of each edge. Testers should use only one or two test cases from each equivalence class because a program that passes the tests generally will pass any test drawn from that class. Invalid input equivalence classes often allow program bugs to be overlooked during debugging.

39.5.2   Emphasize Boundary Conditions.   Boundaries are crucial for checking each program's response to input and output data. Equivalence class boundaries are the most extreme values of the class; for example, boundary conditions may consist of the biggest and smallest, soonest and latest, shortest and longest, or slowest and fastest members of an equivalence class.

Tests should include values below, at, and above boundary values. Additionally, they should be tested at various user levels (e.g., administrator, root or super user, data entry, and read-only access). This must ensure that there are no conditions at any level that permit unintended access or unauthorized escalation of privileges. When programs fail with nonboundary values, they generally fail at the boundaries too. Programs passing these tests probably also will pass any other test drawn from that class. Tests should also be able to generate the largest and smallest legitimate output values, remembering that input-boundary values may not generate output-boundary values.

Today, the most prevalent security breaches involve buffer overflows in active code (ActiveX and Java), in which inadequate bounds checking on input strings allows overflowing text to be interpreted as code that then can carry out improper operations. Restrictions on input length and type would prevent these exploits. Such overflows can result in the exposure of consumers' PII and incurring unwanted liability for the exposure; currently, the liability exists principally at the state level and may include criminal sanctions, depending on the state in which the consumers reside.

39.5.3   Check All State Transitions.   All interactive programs move from one state to another. A program's state is changed whenever something causes the program to alter output (e.g., to display something different on the screen) or to change the range of available choices (e.g., displaying a new menu of user options).

To test state transitions, the test designer should lay out a transition probability matrix to show all the paths people are likely to follow. State transitions can be very complex and often depend not on the simple choices provided but on the numbers the user enters. Testers often find it useful to construct menu maps that show exactly where to go from each choice available.

Menu maps also can show when and where users go when menu or keyboard commands take them to different states or dialogs. Maps are particularly handy when working with spaghetti code (code that has been poorly designed or badly maintained so that logical relationships are difficult to see); maps allow the designer or user to reach a dialog box in several ways and then proceed from the dialog box to several places. For spaghetti code, the menu maps afford a simpler method of spotting relationships between states than trying to work exclusively from the program itself because the map shows transition between states on paper or on screen. After mapping the relationships, the designer or user can check the program against the map for correctness.

Full testing theoretically requires that all possible paths are tested. However, in practice, complete testing may be unattainable for complex programs. Therefore, it makes sense to test the most frequently used paths first.

39.5.3.1   *Test Every Limit.*   It is necessary to test every limit on a program's behavior that is specified by any of the program's documents. Limits include the size of files, the number of terminals, the memory size the program can manage, the maximum size it requires, and the number of printers the program can drive. It is important to check on the ability of the program to handle large numbers of open files on an immediate basis and on a long-term, continuing basis as well. Load testing is actually boundary condition testing and should include running tests the program ought to pass and tests the program should not pass.

For Web applications, tools exist to simplify this task, as some will check the boundaries and limits of fields at varying depths of data entry to test the protections against buffer overflow, invalid data, and incorrect data syntax; such tools include but are not limited to WebInspect by Spi Dynamics.

39.5.3.2 *Test for Race Conditions.*   After testing the system under "normal" load, it should be tested for race conditions. A "race condition" is usually defined as anomalous behavior due to unexpected critical dependence on the relative timing of events. Race conditions generally involve one or more processes accessing a shared resource such as a file or variable, where this multiple access has not been properly controlled. Systems that are vulnerable to races, especially multiuser systems with concurrent access to resources, should undergo a full cycle of testing under load. Race conditions sometimes can be identified through testing under heavy load, light load, fast speed, slow speed, multiprocessors running concurrent programs, enhanced and more numerous input/output devices, frequent interrupts, less memory, slower memory, and related variables.

39.5.4 Use Test-Coverage Monitors.   For complex programs, path testing usually cannot or would not test every possible path throughout a program for practical as well as cost-effectiveness reasons. A more practical glass box approach (i.e., with knowledge of the internal design of a program) is to use the source code listing to force the program down every branch visible in the code. When programmers add special debugging code during development, a unique message will print out or be added to a log file whenever the program reaches a specified point. Typically such messages can be generated by calling a print routine with a unique parameter for each block of code. When source code is compiled, many languages permit a switch to be set to allow conditional compilation, so that a test version of the code contains active debugging statements whereas a production version does not. For interpreted code, such as most fourth-generation languages, similar switches allow for inclusion or activation of debugging instructions.

Since distinct messages are planted, it is possible to know exactly what point in the program the test has reached. Programmers specifically insert these messages at significant parts of the program. Once these messages have been added, anyone can run the program and conclude whether the different parts actually have run and been tested.

Special devices or tools also can be used to add these messages to the code automatically. Once source code is fed to such a coverage monitor, it analyzes the control structures in the code and adds probes for each branch of the program. Adding these probes or lines of code is called instrumenting the program. It is possible to tell that the program has been pushed down every branch when all the probes have been printed. Besides instrumenting code, a good coverage monitor can capture probe outputs, perform analyses, and summarize them. Some coverage monitors also log the time used for each routine, thus supporting performance analysis and optimization.

A coverage monitor is designed for glass box testing, but knowledge of the internals of the program under test is not needed in order to use the monitor. The coverage monitor counts the number of probe messages, reports on the number of probes triggered, and even reports on the thoroughness of the testing. Because it is possible for the coverage monitor to report on untriggered branches, the monitor can find and identify code that does not belong, such as routines included by default but never used or deliberately inserted undocumented code (a Trojan horse). Some commercially available coverage monitors are, unfortunately, themselves full of bugs. It is important to obtain a full list of the known bugs and patches from the developer. In addition, such tools should themselves be tested with programs that contain known errors, in the process known as seeding, to verify their correctness.

39.5.5   Seeding.   Quality assurance procedures themselves benefit from testing. One productive method, known as seeding, is to add known bugs to a program and measure how many of them are discovered through normal testing procedures. The success rate in identifying such known bugs can help estimate the proportion of unknown bugs left in a program. Such seeding is particularly important when establishing automated testing procedures and test-coverage monitors; also, it is useful for SOX or other compliance-related testing.

39.5.6   Building Test Data Sets.   One of the most serious errors in quality assurance is to allow programmers to use production data sets for testing. Production data may include confidential information that should not be accessible to programming staff, so access should be forbidden not only to production data but even to copies of production data, or even to copies of subsets or samples from production data. However, *anonymizing* processes applied to copies of production data (e.g., scrambling names and addresses of patients in a medical records database) may produce test data sets suitable for use in quality assurance.

Alternatively, if the organization has a test system that is completely (logically and physically) segregated from the production system, using historical data may be appropriate. In doing so, particular care and appropriate documentation must be maintained to ensure that there is no chance of the test system interfacing with the production system. A side benefit of such testing is that it may help the organization's SOX or HIPAA periodic testing and documentation regarding the availability, utility, and integrity of backup media and systems.

39.6   BEFORE GOING INTO PRODUCTION

39.6.1   Regression Testing.   Regression testing is fundamental work done by glass box and black box testers. The term is used in two different ways. The first definition involves those tests where an error is found and fixed and the test that exposed the problem is performed again. The second definition involves finding and fixing an error and then performing a standard series of tests to make certain the changes or fix made did not disturb anything else.

The first type of regression testing serves to test that a fix does what it is intended to do. The second type tests the fix and also tests the overall integrity of the program. It is not unusual for people who mention regression testing to be referring to both definitions, since both involve fixing and then retesting. It is recommended that both types of testing be done whenever errors are fixed. If an organization is subject to SOX or HIPAA, appropriate documentation should be maintained that details the test methodology, the sample selection, the frequency, the results, and the remediation (if any).

39.6.2   Automated Testing.   In some enterprises, every time a bug is fixed, every time a program is modified, and every time a new version is produced, a tester runs a regression test. All of this testing takes a considerable amount of time and consumes both personnel and machine resources. In addition, repetitive work can become mind-numbing, so testers may accidentally omit test cases or overlook erroneous results.

To cut down on the time consumption of personnel and the repetitive nature of the task, it is possible to program the computer to run acceptance and regression tests. This type of automation results in execution of the tests, collection of the results, comparison of the results with known good results, and a report of the results to the tester.

Early test automation consisted essentially of keyboard macros or scripts, with limited capacity for responding to errors; typically, an error would produce invalid results that would be fed into the next step of processing and lead to long chains of meaningless results. Slightly more advanced test harnesses would halt the test process at each error and require human intervention to resume. Both methods were of only modest help to the test team. However, today's test-automation software can include test databases that allow orderly configuration of tests, specific instructions for restarting test sequences after errors, and full documentation of inputs and results. For realistic load testing, some systems can be configured to simulate users on workstations, with scripts that define a range of randomly generated values, specific parameter limits, and even variable response times. Large-scale load testing can connect computers together through networks to simulate thousands of concurrent users and thus speed identification of resource exhaustion or race conditions.

Test automation can be well worth the expenditures required. Automated testing is usually more precise, more complete, faster, and less expensive than the tests done by human personnel. Typically, automated tests can accomplish tenfold or hundredfold increases in the number of tests achievable through manual methods. In addition to freeing personnel to do more rewarding work, such methods greatly reduce overall maintenance costs due to detection of errors before systems reach production. Additionally, for regulatory purposes, the automated testing requires significantly less sampling, documentation, and testing. Appropriate management review and reporting of results still are required, as is documentation of remediation follow-up.

39.6.3 Tracking Bugs from Discovery to Removal.   Finding a bug is not enough. Even eliminating a bug is insufficient. A system also must allow the causes of each bug to be identified, documented, and rectified. For these reasons, it is important to track and document all problems from the time of their discovery to their removal, to be certain that the problems have been resolved and will not affect the system. Too, this provides important historical records in diagnosing and remediating incidents and provides appropriate documentation for audit and regulatory purposes.

Problem-tracking systems must be used to report bugs, track solutions, and write summary reports about them. An organized system is essential to ensure accountability and communication regarding the bugs. Typical reports include: where bugs originate (e.g., which programmers and which teams are responsible for the greatest number of bugs); types of problems encountered (e.g., typographical errors, logic errors, boundary violations); and time to repair. However, problem-tracking systems can raise political issues, such as project accountability, personal monitoring, control issues, and issue remediation regarding the data in the database and who owns them.

Once a tracking system is established, a bug report is entered into the database system and a copy goes to the project manager, who either prioritizes it and passes it along or responds to it personally. Eventually the programmers will be brought into the loop, will fix the problem, and will mark the problem as fixed. The fixed problem then is tested and a status report is issued. If a fix proves not to work, that becomes a new problem that needs to be addressed.

39.7 MANAGING CHANGE.   Many people may be involved in creating and managing systems; whenever changes are made to the system, those changes need to be managed and monitored in an organized fashion to avoid chaos.

39.7.1 Change Request.   The change request is an important document that requests either a fix or some other change to a program or system. Information contained on the change request form generally includes who is requesting the change, the date the request is being made, the program and area affected, the date by which the change is needed, and authorization to go ahead and make the change.

Most companies have paper forms that are retained for monitoring and auditing purposes. As the popularity of digital signatures grows and society continues to move toward a paperless office, it seems logical that some of these change requests eventually will become totally automated.

39.7.2 Tracking System.   The tracking system may be manual, automated, or a combination of methods; for regulatory and control purposes, a system that incorporates automated tracking is best, since it reduces the chance for error, and it can enhance follow-up and remediation. Regardless of how it is kept, the original change form generally is logged into a system, either manually filed or entered into an automated database by some identifying aspect, such as date, type of change, or requesting department.

The system is used to track what happens to the change. When an action is taken, information must be entered into the system to show who worked on the request, what was done, when action was taken, what the result of the action was, who was notified of the actions taken, whether the change was accepted, and related information. This information is crucial in ensuring that issues are managed appropriately, escalated as needed to senior management, and tracked until remediated.

39.7.3 Regression Testing.   When a change or fix has been made, regression testing verifies that the change has indeed been made and that the program now works in the fashion desired, including all other functions. The successful completion of the testing should be documented in writing; this can be through the tracking system or in documentation appended to the tracking system entry.

39.7.4 Documentation.   Documentation is crucial when considering, approving, and implementing changes. If information is retained strictly in an individual's head, what happens when the individual goes on vacation, is out sick, or leaves the enterprise permanently? What if the individual simply does not remember what changes were made, or when; how does an organization know who was involved, what actually was done, and who signed off that the changes were made and accepted?

Undocumented changes can result in:

- System crashes
- Inconsistent data entry
- Inappropriate segregation of duties
- Data theft or corruption
- Embezzlement
- Other serious crimes

Lack of documentation can mean that unauthorized changes were made and likely can result in regulatory and audit violations. Undocumented changes may violate segregation of duties (e.g., a person might be informally approving changes to his or her own account, approving changes carried out by a supervisor, or authorizing changes by a person who is not under the responsibility of the approver).

Lack of documentation is often a violation of corporate policy and is often cited in audits; it often will cause significant difficulties regarding SOX, GLBA, and HIPAA compliance efforts and reviews, since management's assertions might not be supported adequately. Because constructing adequate documentation after the fact is almost impossible (and frequently can be considered to be falsification of records in sectors such as financial services), documentation must proceed in step with every phase of a system's development and operation. Thereafter, documentation must be retained according to company policy and legal requirements.

39.8   SOURCES OF BUGS AND PROBLEMS.   Locating and fixing bugs is an important task, but it is also essential to try to determine where and why the bugs and related problems originated. By finding and studying the source, often it is possible to prevent a recurrence of the same or similar type of problem.

39.8.1   Design Flaws.   Design flaws often occur because of poor communication between users and designers. Users are not always clear about what they want and need, while designers misunderstand, misinterpret, or simply ignore what the users relate to them. Within the design process, even when users' feelings and requirements are known and understood, design flaws can occur. However, they are easier to identify and remedy if the appropriate documentation is effected. Without the proper documentation, it may not be possible to identify the source of an error; this can result in patches or remedies that need to be patched. Often flaws result from attempts to comply with unrealistic delivery schedules. Managers should support their staff in resisting the pressure to rush through any of the design, development, and implementation stages.

39.8.2   Implementation Flaws.   Whenever a program is developed and implemented, there are time limits and deliverable dates. Most problems during development cause delay, so developers and testers often are rushed to get the job done. Sometimes they sacrifice the documentation, the review portion of the project, or even cut short testing, leaving unrecognized design and implementation flaws in place. Managers should emphasize the value of thorough review and testing, and allocate enough time to avoid such blunders.

39.8.3   Unauthorized Changes to Production Code.   If problems are traced to unauthorized changes, project managers should examine their policies. If the policies are clear, perhaps employee training and awareness programs need improvement. Managers also should examine their own behavior to ensure that they are not putting such pressure on their staff that cutting corners is perceived to be acceptable.

39.8.4   Insufficient or Substandard Programming Quality.   A programmer can make or break a program and a project. Programmers play essential roles in software development. Therefore, it is important that all programmers on a project be capable and reliable. Project programmers should be carefully screened before being placed on a software development project to ensure that their skills meet project requirements. Sometimes holes in programmers' skills can be filled with appropriate training and coaching. However, if problems appear to be consistent, management may want to check a programmer's background to verify that he or she did not falsify information when applying for the job. Truly incompetent programmers need to be removed from the project. Additionally, if management suspects that the programming quality is inadequate, then it should consider having an independent programmer review the code, performing particularly rigorous quality assurance (QA) testing.

39.8.5 Data Corruption. Data corruption can occur because of poor programming, invalid data entry, inadequate locking during concurrent data access and modification, illegal access by one process to another process data stack, and hardware failures. Data corruption can occur even when a program is automatically tested or run without human intervention. In any event, when searching for the sources of bugs and other problems, it is important to do a careful review of the data after each round of testing, in order to identify deviations from the correct end state. The review should be documented appropriately and escalated to management; it then will assist the regulatory compliance efforts.

39.8.6 Hacking. When bugs and problems do occur, hacking—both internal and external—should be considered a possibility and searched for by reviewing the logs of who worked on the software and when that work was done. Managers should be able to spot the use of legitimate IDs when the individuals involved were on vacation, out sick, or not available to log on for other reasons.

Archiving logs and retrieving them is an increasingly critical capability, aside from the regulatory requirements of SOX, HIPAA, GLBA, and so on. Logs are often used for:

- Incident response activities, particularly in determining:
  - If an incident occurred
  - When an incident occurred
  - What happened prior to and subsequent to when an incident is suspected to have occurred
- Research; this can be to review performance capabilities or issues of hardware or software or networking

To ensure that the logs are available when needed, the organization needs a sound strategy that preserves and archives logs periodically, so that an attacker or a system anomaly does not wipe them from the system's hard drive. Although there are many means to accomplish this, a frequently used inexpensive method involves establishing a log server. For example, an organization might identify a discarded desktop computer, outfit it with a new, high-speed, high-capacity optical read-only memory (ROM) drive, and increase memory capacity (if needed). By routing the logs to the optical drive frequently and recording them throughout the day (perhaps multiple times during an hour) and changing the optical disk at least daily, the organization will create a forensically sound archive that can be duplicated easily for research, law enforcement, or legal use. Often the daily logs volume will not fill a DVD or a CD. However, having the regular routine of changing the media daily helps ensure that the media does not reach its capacity at an inopportune time—indeed, if a worm such as Blaster or Nimda infects the organization, then the logs likely will swell rapidly. Too, if an attacker within the system stops the logging, the organization should encounter less difficulty determining the date, time (or time period), and extent of the intrusion because ROM cannot be overwritten, in contrast with read-write (RW) media.

Unauthorized changes to code and data sometimes can be identified even if the perpetrator stops the logging and deletes or modifies log files. One method is to create checksums for production or other official versions of software and to protect the checksums against unauthorized access and modification using encryption and digital signatures. Similarly, unauthorized data modifications sometimes can be made more difficult by creating checksums for records and linking the checksums to time and data stamps and to the checksums for authorized programs. Under those conditions, unauthorized personnel and intruders find it difficult to create valid checksums for modified records. Other products, such as intrusion detection systems (IDS) or intrusion prevention systems (IPS), may be useful in an organization's protection and risk management strategy.

39.9   CONCLUSION.   This chapter has presented a comprehensive overview of the software development and quality assurance processes that must be utilized when developing, implementing, and modifying software. Software development involves more than simply selecting and utilizing an approach such as the traditional, waterfall, or RAD methodology. It means working as a team to develop, review, refine, and implement a viable working product. Many good techniques and products can be applied to both the SDLC and the quality assurance portions of producing software; some of the key elements are good documentation, allowing sufficient time for testing in the development and maintenance processes, building good tests, establishing test data, automating testing, and keeping track of change requests.

39.10   FURTHER READING

Campanella, J., ed. *Principles of Quality Costs: Implementation and Use*, 3rd ed. Milwaukee, WI: ASQC, Quality Press, 1998.

Institute of Electrical and Electronics Engineers. *IEEE Standard for Software Quality Assurance Plans*. ANSI/IEEE Std. 730-1998. New York: IEEE, 1998.

Institute of Electrical and Electronics Engineers. *An American National Standard: IEEE Standard for Software Test Documentation*. ANSI/IEEE Std. 829-1998. New York: IEEE 1998.

Fox, C., and P. Zonneveld. *IT Control Objectives for Sarbanes-Oxley: The Role of IT in the Design and Implementation of Internal Control Over Financial Reporting*, 2nd ed. IT Governance Institute, 2006.

NASA Software Assurance Technology Center: http://satc.gsfc.nasa.gov/.

Horton, W. K. *Designing and Writing Online Documentation: Help Files to Hypertext*. New York: John Wiley & Sons, 1990.

King, D. *Current Practices in Software Development*. New York: Yourdon Press, 1984.

Ould, M. A. *Strategies for Software Engineering: The Management of Risk and Quality*. New York: John Wiley & Sons, 1990.

Schwarz, D. "Some Words about Software Engineering," in *Spectral Envelopes in Sound Analysis and Synthesis*, part 8.1, 1998, www.ircam.fr/anasyn/schwarz/da/specenv/8_1Some_Words_about_Softwar.html.

Whitten, N. *Managing Software Development Projects*, 2nd ed. New York: John Wiley & Sons, 1995.

CHAPTER 40

MANAGING SOFTWARE PATCHES AND VULNERABILITIES

Peter Mell and Karen Kent

40.1 INTRODUCTION. *Vulnerabilities* are flaws that can be exploited by a malicious entity to gain greater access or privileges than it is authorized to have on a computer system. *Patches* are additional pieces of code developed to address problems (commonly called "bugs") in software. Patches enable additional functionality, or they address security flaws such as vulnerabilities within a program. Not all vulnerabilities have related patches, especially when new vulnerabilities are first announced, so system administrators must be aware not only of applicable vulnerabilities and available patches, but also of other methods of remediation (e.g., device or network configuration changes, or employee training) that limit the exposure of systems to vulnerabilities.

Patch and vulnerability management is a security practice designed to proactively prevent the exploitation of IT vulnerabilities that exist within an organization. The expected result is to reduce the time and money spent dealing with vulnerabilities and the exploitation of those vulnerabilities. Proactively managing system vulnerabilities will reduce or eliminate the potential for exploitation and involve considerably less time and effort than responding after an exploitation has occurred.

This chapter is designed to assist organizations in implementing patch and vulnerability remediation programs. It first explains the impact that vulnerability exploitation can have and then illustrates how automated patching solutions can reduce that impact. Next, the chapter discusses in detail how to create an organizational process, and how to test the effectiveness of the process. It also seeks to inform the reader about the technical solutions that are available for vulnerability remediation.[1]

For more general information about related topics, see selected chapters in this *Handbook:*

- Writing secure code—Chapter 38
- Vulnerability assessments—Chapter 46
- Operations security—Chapter 47
- Application controls—Chapter 52
- Monitoring and control systems—Chapter 53

40.2   MOTIVATION FOR USING AUTOMATED PATCHING SOLUTIONS.

From January through December 2007, the total number of published computer vulnerabilities recorded in the U.S. National Vulnerability Database was 6,691, or 557 per month and 18 per day.[2] Even a small organization with a single server can expect to spend time reviewing a handful of critical patches each month. This stream of vulnerabilities has resulted in systems constantly being threatened by new attacks.

The level of damage caused by an attack can be quite severe. A number of Internet worms (self-propagating code that exploits vulnerabilities over the Internet), such as Code Red, Nimda, Blaster, and MyDoom, have been released in recent years. There are some common data points for these worm outbreaks. First, as the authors of worm code have gotten more sophisticated, the worms have been able to spread faster than their predecessors. Second, they each hit hundreds of thousands of computers worldwide. Most important, each one of them attacked a known vulnerability for which a patch or other mitigation steps had already been released. Each major outbreak has been preventable.

Benjamin Franklin once said that "an ounce of prevention equals a pound of cure." Patch and vulnerability management is the "ounce of prevention" compared to the "pound of cure" that is incident response. The decision on how and when to mitigate via patching or other remediation methods should come from a comparison of time, resources, and money to be spent. For example, assume that a new computer worm is released that can spread rapidly and damage any workstation in the organization unless it is stopped. The potential cost to not mitigate is described by this equation:

Cost not to mitigate $= W^*T^*R$

Where:

W $=$ Number of workstations

T $=$ Time spent fixing systems or lost in productivity

R $=$ Hourly rate of the time spent

In addition to the costs identified through this formula, a security incident could also cause damage to an organization's reputation. This is most significant for organizations that are entrusted with sensitive information or operations. When determining the potential cost of not mitigating, an organization should consider the possible impact to its reputation, its stock price, and even to its marketing.

For an organization where there are 1,000 computers to be fixed, each taking an average of 8 hours of downtime (4 hours for one worker to rebuild a system, plus 4 hours during which the computer owner is without a computer to do work) at a rate of $70/hour for wages and benefits:

1, 000 computers $*$ 8 hours $*$ $70/hour $=$ $560,000 to respond after an attack

Compare this to the cost of manual monitoring and prevention. Assume the vulnerability exploited by the worm and the corresponding patch are announced in advance of the worm being created. This has been true for most past exploits, as true zero-day attacks (those with no advance knowledge) are not frequent. Manually monitoring for new patches for a single workstation type takes as little as 10 minutes each day, or 60.8 hours/year. Applying a workstation patch generally takes no more than 10 minutes. This makes the cost equation:

60.8 hours monitoring $*$ $70/hour $=$ $4,256 monitoring cost per year

0.16 hours patching $*$ 1, 000 computers @$70/hour $=$ $11,200 to manually apply each patch

Total cost to maintain the systems $=$ $4,256 + $11,200/patch

For any single vulnerability for which a widespread worm will be created, manual monitoring and patching is much more cost effective than responding to a worm infection. However, because patches are constantly released, manual patching becomes prohibitively expensive unless the operating environment consists of only a few software packages (thus decreasing the total number of patches needed) or the organization relies on end users to patch their systems (thus distributing the patching workload, but also introducing a need for patch installation oversight). Since few organizations use a small number of software packages or can rely on end users to effectively patch systems, widespread manual patching is not a cost-effective organizational approach.[3]

A third option is to invest in an automated patching solution. These solutions automatically check for required patches and deploy them. Both free and commercial solutions are available. Assume that a commercial solution costs $15,000 and charges $20 per computer for annual maintenance. This approach will be much cheaper than the manual solution, even though it will be necessary to dedicate possibly an entire person to maintaining, updating, and patching with the automated solution.

40 hours/week*52 weeks/year*$70/hour = $145,600/year for the
administrator to run the patching solution

$145,600 + 1,000 computers*$20/computer = $165,600 annual patching
cost for the automated solution

It is not possible to save money by neglecting patch installation. It is extremely expensive to employ manual patching efforts, and it is difficult to do it effectively. Therefore, it is strongly recommended that all organizations make effective use of automated patching solutions.

40.3   PATCH AND VULNERABILITY MANAGEMENT PROCESS.   This section discusses a systematic approach to patch and vulnerability management. The approach is provided as a model that an organization should adapt to its environment as appropriate. Implementing such an approach is necessary to respond cost effectively to the ever-growing number of vulnerabilities in IT systems.

40.3.1   Recommended Process.   Organizations should create a group of individuals, called the patch and vulnerability group (PVG), who are specially tasked to implement the patch and vulnerability management program. The PVG is the central point for vulnerability remediation efforts (e.g., patching and configuration changes). Since the PVG must actively work with local administrators, large organizations may need to have several PVGs. These PVGs could work together in a confederation or could be structured hierarchically with an authoritative top-level PVG. The remainder of this chapter is based on the assumption that there is only one PVG per organization.

As much as possible, the burden of implementing and testing remediations should be shifted from local administrators to the PVG. This should save money by eliminating duplication of effort (e.g., multiple system administrators testing the same patch on similar computers) and by enabling automated solutions, thereby avoiding costly manual installations. The easiest way to accomplish this is by implementing enterprise patching solutions that allow the PVG, or a group they work closely with, to automatically push patches out to many computers quickly. If automated patch management tools are not available, the PVG should coordinate local administrator efforts.

For the PVG to be able to test automatically deployed patches adequately, organizations should use standardized configurations for IT devices (e.g., desktop computers, routers, firewalls, and servers) as much as possible. Enterprise patch management tools will be ineffective if deployed in an environment where every IT device is configured uniquely, because the side effects of the various patches will be unknown.

To implement a cost-effective PVG, the scope of the PVG must be well defined. The PVG will monitor for and address only vulnerabilities and remediations applicable to IT technologies that are widely used within the organization. Some organizations might choose to have their PVG monitor for vulnerabilities and remediations for all IT technologies used within them. This is most feasible when the organization has a relatively small variety of IT technologies in use, or when the PVG uses an external vulnerability monitoring service (as described in Appendix C of NIST SP800-40v2)[1] that can monitor for all the necessary IT technologies on behalf of the PVG.

The list of IT technologies will be carefully formulated and made available to all local administrators. The local administrators will be responsible for securing IT technologies that are not within the PVG scope. The PVG will provide assistance and training to local administrators in how to perform this function. The remainder of this section provides details on the roles and responsibilities of the PVG and system administrators.

40.3.1.1 Patch and Vulnerability Group. The PVG should be a formal group that incorporates representatives from information security and operations. These representatives should include individuals with knowledge of vulnerability and patch management as well as of system administration, intrusion detection, and firewall management. In addition, it is helpful to have specialists in the operating systems and applications most used within the organization. Personnel who already provide system or network administration functions, perform vulnerability scanning, or operate intrusion detection systems are also likely candidates for the PVG.

The size of the group and the amount of time devoted to PVG duties will vary broadly across various organizations. Much depends on the size and complexity of the organization, the size and complexity of its network, and its budget. The PVG of smaller organizations may be comprised of only one or two members, with a focus on critical vulnerabilities and systems. Regardless of the organization's size or resources, patch and vulnerability management can be accomplished with proper planning and process.

The duties of the PVG are outlined next. Subsequent sections discuss certain duties in more detail.

1. **Create a system inventory.** The PVG should use existing inventories of the organization's IT resources to determine which hardware equipment, operating systems, and software applications are used within the organization. The PVG should also maintain a manual inventory of IT resources not captured in the existing inventories.

2. **Monitor for vulnerabilities, remediations, and threats.** The PVG is responsible for monitoring security sources for vulnerability announcements, patch and nonpatch remediations, and emerging threats that correspond to the software within the PVG's system inventory.

3. **Prioritize vulnerability remediation.** The PVG should prioritize the order in which the organization addresses vulnerability remediation.

4. **Create an organization-specific remediation database.** The PVG should create a database of remediations that need to be applied to the organization.

5. **Conduct generic testing of remediations.** The PVG should be able to test patches and nonpatch remediations on IT devices that use standardized configurations. This will avoid the need for local administrators to perform redundant testing. The PVG should also work closely with local administrators to test patches and configuration changes on important systems.

6. **Deploy vulnerability remediations.** The PVG should oversee vulnerability remediation.

7. **Distribute vulnerability and remediation information to local administrators.** The PVG is responsible for informing local administrators about vulnerabilities and remediations that correspond to software packages included within the PVG scope and that are in the organizational software inventory.

8. **Perform automated deployment of patches.** The PVG should deploy patches automatically to IT devices using enterprise patch management tools. Alternatively, the PVG could work closely with the group actually running the patch

management tools. Automated patching tools allow an administrator to update hundreds or even thousands of systems from a single console. Deployment is fairly simple when there are homogeneous computing platforms, with standardized desktop systems and similarly configured servers. Multiplatform environments, nonstandard desktop systems, legacy computers, and computers with unusual configurations may also be integrated, although not as easily.

9. **Configure automatic update of applications whenever possible and appropriate.** Many newer applications provide a feature that checks the vendor's Web site for updates. This feature can be very useful in minimizing the level of effort required to identify, distribute, and install patches. However, some organizations may not wish to implement this feature because it might interfere with their configuration management process. A recommended option would be a locally distributed automated update process, where the patches are made available from the organization's network. Applications can then be updated from the local network instead of from the Internet.

10. **Verify vulnerability remediation through network and host vulnerability scanning**. The PVG should verify that vulnerabilities have been successfully remediated.

11. **Vulnerability remediation training.** The PVG should train administrators on how to apply vulnerability remediations. In organizations that rely on end users to patch computers, the PVG must also train users in this function.

40.3.1.2 System Administrators.   System administrators are responsible for making sure that applicable IT resources follow the organization's standard configuration and that those resources are participating in the organization's automated patching system. If the organization is not using an automated patching system, system administrators must use the PVG as a primary resource for vulnerability remediation and work with the PVG on time frames for remediation application. For IT resources that are outside of the PVG scope, system administrators are responsible for monitoring for vulnerabilities and remediations, for applying remediations, and for testing those remediations

40.3.2 Creating a System Inventory.   The PVG should use existing inventories of the organization's IT resources to determine which hardware equipment, operating systems, and software applications are used within the organization and then to group and prioritize those resources. The PVG should also maintain a manual inventory of IT resources not captured in the existing inventories. Having a system inventory and priority listing will enable the PVG to determine which hardware and software applications they will support by monitoring for vulnerabilities, patches, and threats, and will enable them to respond quickly and effectively.

40.3.2.1 IT Inventory.   An inventory of all IT resources contained within the system should be created. This inventory should be updated regularly as part of the system's configuration management process. All IT resources within an organization must be assigned to a particular system such that the set of all systems covers all IT resources.

Creating and maintaining a separate inventory for each system may not be cost effective. Therefore, organizations may prefer to maintain an organization-wide inventory containing all IT resources. This is perfectly acceptable (and in many cases recommended) as long as each IT resource is labeled so that it is associated with one and only one system. The capability to output the list of IT resources associated with each system must exist. Organizations often have multiple inventories of IT resources. For example, some organizations use automated asset management software that inventories devices and the software each device runs. Organizations might also have inventories performed as part of business continuity planning and other efforts.

Each organization must determine the proper level of abstraction for its inventory. For example, one organization may track what software is installed on each computer, while another organization may also track software version numbers. Organizations should carefully and deliberately choose their level of abstraction because sometimes collecting too much information is just as bad (or worse) than collecting too little. Organizations should determine what uses they will make of their inventory, in addition to patch management, and collect only the information needed for those uses.

A sample list of items that an organization could include within its inventory follows (not all items will apply to all IT resources).

1. Associated system name
2. Property number
3. Owner of the IT resource (i.e., main user)
4. System administrator
5. Physical location
6. Connected network port(s)
7. Software configuration
   a. Operating system and version number
   b. Software packages and version numbers
   c. Network services
   d. Internet Protocol (IP) address, if it is static
8. Hardware configuration
   a. Central processing unit
   b. Memory
   c. Disk space
   d. Ethernet addresses (i.e., network cards)
   e. Wireless capability
   f. Input/output capability (e.g., Universal Serial Bus, Firewire)
   g. Firmware versions

It is usually impractical to require people to enter this information manually for each IT resource. Organizations that try this approach may end up with inventories that contain large sets of IT resources that are inaccurate and updated infrequently. A more effective approach is to use commercially available automated inventory management tools whenever possible. These tools typically require organizations to install an agent on each computer. The agent then actively monitors changes in the computer's configuration and reports to a central database, thereby providing the PVG and management an accurate picture of a system's IT resources. Unfortunately, as good as the automated tools are, some information will always need to be manually keyed (e.g., physical location). An automated tool should provide the option to gather this information periodically by presenting users with forms to fill out.

40.3.2.2 Grouping and Prioritizing Information Technology Resources.
The resources within the inventory should be grouped and assigned priority levels to facilitate remediation efforts. These prioritizations can be stored in the inventory itself. Resource grouping and prioritization is helpful in assessing risk to systems, and should be used to help identify which systems may require the special attention of the patch and vulnerability management program. The primary grouping should be by system name and by the level of impact that a compromise of each system could have on the organization. An example of impact categorization for systems is FIPS PUB 199, *Standards for Security Categorization of Federal Information and Information Systems*. It defines low-, moderate-, and high-impact categories that are based on the potential impact of a loss of confidentiality, integrity, or availability of a system. The categories should be used to prioritize multisystem vulnerability remediation efforts.[4] For example, systems used as servers or for security management, and systems containing information of higher importance, typically have a higher impact category than standard users' systems. It may also be useful to group resources by network location. This is particularly important for those resources that are directly exposed to the Internet and those that reside within internal high-security areas.

If this grouping and prioritization is not performed, organizations may embark on unnecessarily costly remediation strategies. For example, when a new vulnerability is discovered within an organization that does not do remediation prioritization, system administrators might be instructed to patch all vulnerable computers immediately. This could result in a major disruption as system administrators stop all other work so they can patch computers. Even worse, the patch may be applied quickly without thorough testing, resulting in actual damage to the organization's systems. With prioritization, the organization may realize that a majority of the vulnerable computers could be patched over a period of time using the organization's standard configuration management process and patch-testing procedures. The organization could then focus its immediate patching efforts on the vulnerable computers that are most at risk, possibly those directly exposed to the Internet.

40.3.2.3 Use of the IT Inventory and Scope of Related Duties.
The inventory is the foundation on which the PVG will conduct its operations, since it is the PVG's window into understanding the organization's IT configuration. The inventory will be used primarily to create a list of PVG-supported hardware equipment, operating systems, and software applications. It will also help the PVG and administrators to respond quickly to threats, and provide system personnel information to help them secure their systems.

The PVG should define a set of hardware equipment, operating systems, and software applications that will be supported. The PVG will then be responsible for monitoring information regarding vulnerabilities, patches, and threats corresponding to the supported hardware, operating systems, and applications. The PVG should clearly communicate the supported resources to system administrators so that the administrators know which hardware, operating systems, and applications the PVG will be checking for new patches, vulnerabilities, and threats. The list of supported resources should be created by analyzing the inventory and identifying those resources that are used. Hardware equipment, operating systems, and software applications used on high-priority or sensitive systems, or on a large number of systems, should be included on the list. By publishing this list, the PVG will enable system administrators to know when, or if, they have an unsupported resource. System administrators should be taught how to monitor independently and how to remediate unsupported hardware equipment, operating systems, and software applications.

The PVG should also give system owners, system security officers, and system administrators access to the inventory information. Typically, these parties already have access to existing inventories, but the PVG inventory might contain additional inventory information that is otherwise unavailable. This will help them better to secure the organization's systems. However, system personnel should have access only to their own system inventory, since system inventory information is sensitive in nature. Giving system personnel access to their own inventory is also important because maintaining the inventory will require the PVG to work closely with system personnel.

40.3.3 Monitoring for Vulnerabilities, Remediations, and Threats.
The PVG is responsible for monitoring security sources for vulnerability announcements, patch and nonpatch remediations, and threats that correspond to the software within the organizational software inventory. A variety of sources should be monitored to ensure that the PVG is aware of all newly discovered vulnerabilities.

40.3.3.1 *Types of Security Concerns.* The PVG is responsible for monitoring for vulnerabilities, remediations, and threats.

- **Vulnerabilities.** Vulnerabilities are software flaws or misconfigurations that cause a weakness in the security of a system. Vulnerabilities can be exploited by a malicious entity to violate policies—for example, to gain greater access or permission than is authorized.
- **Remediations.** There are three primary methods of remediation: installation of a software patch, adjustment of a configuration setting, and removal of affected software. Refer to Section 40.3.7 of this chapter for further details regarding methods of remediation.
- **Threats.** Threats are capabilities or methods of attack developed by malicious entities to exploit vulnerabilities and potentially to cause harm to a computer system or network. Threats usually take the form of exploit scripts, worms, viruses, rootkits, and Trojan horses.

System administrators should also monitor for vulnerabilities, remediations, and threats to systems under their control but running software not contained in the organizational inventory.

40.3.3.2 *Monitoring Vulnerabilities, Remediations, and Threats.*
There are several types of resources available for monitoring the status of vulnerabilities, remediations, and threats. Each type of resource has its own strengths and weaknesses. We recommend using more than one type of resource to ensure accurate and timely knowledge. The most common types of resources are:

- Vendor Web sites and mailing lists
- Third-party Web sites
- Third-party mailing lists and newsgroups
- Vulnerability scanners
- Vulnerability databases

- Enterprise patch management tools
- Other notification tools

Vendors are the authoritative source of information for patches related to their products. However, many vendors will not announce vulnerabilities in their products until patches are available; accordingly, monitoring third-party vulnerability resources, as well, is recommended. Enterprise patching tools usually provide lists of all patches available from supported vendors, which relieves the PVG from constantly having to monitor a large number of vendor security Web sites and mailing lists.

Organizations should monitor for vulnerabilities, remediation, and threats using these resource types at a minimum:

- Enterprise patch management tools, to obtain all available patches from supported vendors.

- Vendor security mailing lists and Web sites, to obtain all available patches from vendors not supported by the enterprise patch management tool.

- Vulnerability database or mailing lists, to obtain immediate information on all known vulnerabilities and suggested remediations (e.g., the National Vulnerability Database).

- Third-party vulnerability mailing lists that highlight the most critical vulnerabilities (e.g., the US-CERT Cyber Security Alerts). Such lists will help organizations focus on the most important vulnerabilities that may be overlooked among the myriad of published vulnerabilities.

After initial assessment of a new vulnerability, remediation, or threat, the PVG should continue to monitor it for updates and new information. For example, a software vendor might release a new patch in place of a software reconfiguration it originally recommended as a temporary remediation measure. By ongoing monitoring for new information, the PVG would be aware of the new patch and could determine if it would provide a better solution than the software reconfiguration. Ongoing monitoring is also important because additional analysis of vulnerabilities might determine that they are more or less severe than previously thought.

40.3.4 Prioritizing Vulnerability Remediation. The PVG should consider each threat and its potential impact on the organization when setting priorities for vulnerability remediation. This evaluation would include these steps:

- **Determine the significance of the threat or vulnerability.** Establish which systems are vulnerable or exposed, with a focus on those systems that are essential for operation, as well as other high-priority systems. Evaluate the impact on the systems, the organization, and the network if the vulnerability is not removed and it is exploited. The organization's security architecture may automatically mitigate certain threats, thus reducing the urgency to apply relevant patches. For example, if the organization disables certain functionality within its browsers (e.g., scripting languages), then applying patches that fix vulnerabilities within those scripting languages is not a priority.

- **Determine the existence, extent, and spread of related worms, viruses, or exploits.** Ascertain whether malicious code has been published, and the level of distribution. Determine the damage caused, such as system access, information disclosure, arbitrary code execution, or denial of service. Organizations should assume that malicious individuals are in possession of exploit code for any vulnerability for which there is a patch, since patches are often reverse engineered quickly.

- **Determine the risks involved with applying the patch or nonpatch remediation.** Identify, through research and testing, whether the fix will affect the functionality of other software applications or services. Establish what degree of risk is acceptable.

The PVG is not expected to perform this evaluation on its own. System and network security officers and administrators might assist the PVG by assessing the impact of threats to individual systems, based on vulnerability, remediation, and threat information provided by the PVG.

The PVG should be aware of the resource constraints of local administrators and should attempt to avoid overwhelming them with a large number of patches or other remediations for identified vulnerabilities. With the exception of small IT deployments, it is a complex and difficult endeavor for local administrators to perform all remediations in a timely manner. This is attributed not only to time and resource constraints, but also to the greater complexity and heterogeneity of systems in larger environments. Thus, setting priorities for which systems, to patch in what order, is essential for an effective patch process.

40.3.5   Creating an Organization-Specific Remediation Database.
The PVG should create a database of remediations that need to be applied within the organization. Enterprise patch management tools usually supply such a database, but the PVG may need to manually maintain a separate one for IT technologies not supported by the patch management tool. Manually maintained databases should contain instructions on removing vulnerabilities by installing patches or performing workarounds as well as the actual patches when applicable.

Organizations might also find it helpful to have the PVG write a threat assessment summary for the most significant vulnerabilities and patches, then distribute the summary to local administrators and management, or make it available through the remediation database. The summary should be helpful in ensuring that people understand the importance of performing the remediation and the possible consequences of not doing so.

Whether automated or manual, databases should contain a copy of each patch for situations when the Internet may not be accessible or when the vendor's Web site may have been compromised. In addition, it is likely easier for local administrators to apply a patch using the PVG database as opposed to a vendor site that might overwhelm administrators with a large array of available patches. Although the creation of a database is recommended, resource constraints may limit an organization to listing only Web sites or specific Uniform Resource Locators (URLs) for each patch. Such a solution should be feasible when each hyperlink to a patch is associated with documented advice and time frames from the PVG. Manually maintaining databases may be possible, but purchasing automated patching products that inherently contain such databases is strongly recommended.

40.3.6   Testing Remediations.   If an organization uses standardized host configurations, the PVG will be able to test patches and nonpatch remediations on those configurations. This will avoid the need for redundant testing by each local system

administrator. System administrators are responsible for testing patches and nonpatch remediations to mitigate vulnerabilities and threats identified for software not monitored by the PVG.

Precautions should be taken before applying the identified patch or nonpatch remediation. Remediation testing guidelines may include these points:

- Most vendors provide some type of authentication mechanism. The downloaded patch should be checked against any of the authenticity methods the vendor provides, including cryptographic checksums, Pretty Good Privacy (PGP) signatures, and digital certificates. Some of these methods, such as verifying digital signatures, are highly automated, requiring little user interaction. Others, such as SHA-1 or MD5 checksums, require the user to visit the vendor's Web site to compare the checksum listed there against the checksum for the downloaded patch. Although these methods add another level of authentication, they are not foolproof.

- A virus scan should also be run on all patches before installation. Before running the scan, the PVG or system administrator should ensure that the virus signature database in the antivirus program is up to date. Again, this system is not foolproof. For example, if an attacker has created an entirely new Trojan horse and included it with the patch, it might not be detected by the virus scan.

- Patches and configuration modifications should be tested on nonproduction systems since remediation can easily produce unintended consequences. Organizations should use existing change management procedures when possible for testing patches and configuration modifications. Also, using images of standard configurations on test systems, or within virtual machines on test systems, can expedite the testing process. Many patches are extremely complicated and can affect many portions of a system, since they often replace system files and alter security settings. Examples include enabling default user accounts that had been disabled, resetting the passwords for default user accounts, and enabling services and functions that had been disabled.

- Patches may also include fixes for multiple vulnerabilities or contain nonsecurity changes, such as new functionality. In addition, patches and configuration changes are often released in haste to repair a vulnerability quickly, and therefore they often receive less testing than the original software. Installing patches, modifying configurations, and uninstalling software may change the system behavior so that it causes other programs to crash or otherwise fail.

- Installing one patch might also inadvertently uninstall or disable another patch. If there is a dependency, there is the need to ensure that patches are installed in a certain sequence. Also, it is important to determine whether other patches are uninstalled when a particular patch is installed.

- Testing should be performed on a selection of systems that accurately represent the configuration of the systems in deployment. So many possible system configurations exist that the vendor cannot possibly test against all of them. Thus, the remediation may have unintended consequences only on one particular configuration. After the remediation is performed, the PVG should check that all related software is operating correctly.

- Before performing the remediation, and especially if there is a lack of time or resources to perform a test on the patch before employing it on a production system, the PVG may wish to learn what experiences others have had in installing or using the patch. For instance, others' experiences could indicate whether the patch or configuration adjustment corrects the vulnerability, opens an old vulnerability, creates a new vulnerability, degrades performance, or is incompatible with other required applications. It is important to remember that others' experiences might vary due to environment-specific factors, implementation differences, and other reasons.

- If one or more of the described problems apply, the PVG will need to consider whether the disadvantages of installing the patch outweigh the benefits. If the remediation is not critical, it may be better to wait until the vendor releases a newer patch that corrects the major issues. (This is a common occurrence.) Also, the ability to "undo" or uninstall a patch should be considered; however, even when this option is provided, the uninstall process does not always return the system to its previous state.

40.3.7 Deploying Vulnerability Remediations. Organizations should deploy vulnerability remediations to all systems that have the vulnerability, even for systems that are not at immediate risk of exploitation. For example, if a system has a vulnerable service disabled, the service is not immediately exploitable, but it could be enabled inadvertently or intentionally at any time, which would cause the system to be vulnerable. Vulnerability remediations should also be incorporated into the organization's standard builds and configurations for hosts. Three primary methods of remediation can be applied to an affected system:

1. **Applying a security patch** (also called a "fix" or "hotfix") repairs the vulnerability, since patches contain code that modifies the software application to address and eliminate the problem. Patches downloaded from vendor Web sites are typically the most up to date and are likely free of malicious code.
2. **Configuration adjustment.** Adjusting how an application or security control is configured can effectively block attack vectors (the paths by which an exploit can penetrate a computer) and reduce the threat of exploitation. Common configuration adjustments include disabling services and modifying privileges as well as changing firewall rules and modifying router access controls. Vulnerable software applications can be modified by adjusting file attributes or registry settings.
3. **Software removal.** Removing or uninstalling the affected software, or vulnerable service, eliminates the vulnerability and any associated threat. This is a practical solution when an application is not needed on a system. Determining how the system is used, removing unnecessary software and services, and running only what is essential for the system's purpose is a recommended security practice.

The mitigation of vulnerabilities and threats may be as simple as modifying a configuration setting or as involved as the installation of a completely new version of the software. No simple patch application methodology applies to all software and operating systems. Before performing the remediation, the administrator may want to conduct a full backup of the system to be patched. This will allow for a timely restoration of the system to a previous state if the patch has an unintended or unexpected impact on the host.

Applying patches to multiple systems is a constant administrative challenge that may seem especially daunting when implementing patches on hundreds or thousands of servers and desktop systems. This task can be made less burdensome with the use of applications that automatically distribute updates to end user computers. These enterprise patch management tools are included with network operating system software and distributed by third-party vendors. The capabilities of these tools vary greatly. Some focus on the distribution of patches, relying on the system administrator to identify a necessary patch and to arrange for the tool to deliver and install the patch. Other tools actively search for necessary patches and automatically notify the system administrator of the available ones; the administrator can then approve the tool's installation of the patches on the appropriate hosts. Enterprise management tools can vary greatly in their support of different operating systems and applications. Those that are bundled with an operating system tend to support the fewest operating systems and applications. Those from third-party vendors are generally compatible with the widest range of systems. Automated patch distribution tends to work best for organizations with a relatively homogenous environment and standardized configurations. Refer to Section 40.4.1 for further information on enterprise patching solutions.

Organizations need to apply patches manually for operating systems and applications that their enterprise patch management tools do not support. Also, many appliance-based devices cannot be updated by patch management tools, even if the appliances use operating systems and applications that the patch management tools support. This is because appliances often use customized limited-functionality versions of operating systems and applications, which are not intended for administrators to access directly. Because the appliances' customized operating systems and applications are based on the same code as the standard programs, they are typically susceptible to many of the same vulnerabilities. However, often the appliances cannot be patched as quickly as standard devices, because patches for appliances typically can be applied only through updates provided by the device's manufacturer. In many organizations, substantial effort is needed to apply patches manually for appliances, and for operating systems and applications, not supported by patch management tools.

Regardless of whether remediation involves automated patching or manual updates, system administrators may believe that the disadvantages of a suggested remediation outweigh its benefits. They may not wish to install the patches or perform the configuration modifications at all. The reasons behind these decisions should be documented and communicated back to the PVG and then to the appropriate management for approval.

The risk of delaying remediation must be weighed carefully. Consider these issues:

- **Threat level.** Does the organization or system requiring remediation face numerous or significant threats? For example, public Web servers often face high threat levels. In general, timely remediation is critical for these systems. In contrast, for an intranet site that is inaccessible from the Internet, remediation can often be delayed because such a site usually faces a lower threat level.

- **Risk of compromise.** What is the likelihood that a compromise will occur? If the vulnerability is easy to exploit, then remediation should be applied swiftly.

- **Consequences of compromise.** What are the consequences of compromise? If the system is critical or contains sensitive data, then the remediation should be performed immediately. This holds true even for noncritical systems if a successful exploitation would lead to an attacker gaining full control of the system.

Unfortunately, neither decision—to apply or not to apply a remediation—is risk free. The correct decision is not always clear. The PVG, system administrators, and management must work together to create a systematic process for evaluating risks and determining the appropriate decision within the context of their organization.

It is desirable to integrate the remediation process with the existing configuration management procedures, in order to secure IT devices without causing unintended damage.

40.3.8   Distributing Vulnerability and Remediation Information to Administrators.   The primary way in which the PVG should distribute patches is through enterprise patch management software. However, it is sometimes necessary for the PVG to communicate remediations directly to local administrators. E-mail lists provide an effective method for distributing information regarding the priority of vulnerabilities, particulars about corresponding patches, configuration modifications, and other details. However, to decrease the chance of a spoofed e-mail containing a Trojan horse patch, actual patches should be distributed by the PVG to administrators from an internal secured Web site. (Ideally patches are distributed using automated patching tools.) Additional controls, such as using digital signatures, may be used to support the integrity of the patches and of the e-mail lists themselves. Several e-mail lists may be maintained for administrators who are responsible for various types of systems (e.g., UNIX administrators and Windows administrators). Alternative methods of patch and information distribution, such as on removable media, should be considered if the network or the secured Web site is unstable or unusable.

40.3.9   Verifying Remediation.   The PVG and system administrators should verify that they have remediated or mitigated vulnerabilities as intended. There are understandable benefits in confirming that the remediations have been conducted appropriately, possibly avoiding the experience of a security incident or unplanned downtime. This can be accomplished by several methods:

- Verify that the files or configuration settings the remediation was intended to correct have been changed, as stated in the vendor's documentation.
- Scan the host with a vulnerability scanner that is capable of detecting known vulnerabilities.
- Verify whether the recommended patches were installed properly by reviewing patch logs.
- Employ exploit procedures or code, and attempt to exploit the vulnerability (i.e., perform a penetration test).
- Organizations should consider having the PVG verify remediations on new servers before they are deployed to production, if the PVG has sufficient resources.

Only an experienced administrator or security officer should perform exploit tests, since they involve launching actual attacks within a network or on a host. Generally, this type of testing should be performed only on nonproduction equipment and only for certain vulnerabilities. The tests should be conducted only by qualified personnel who are thoroughly aware of the risk.

The next sections provide more details on using vulnerability scanners, reviewing patch logs, and checking patch levels when computers attempt to join an organization's network.

40.3.9.1   *Performing Vulnerability Scanning.*   Vulnerability scanners are commonly used in many organizations to identify vulnerabilities on their hosts and networks. A vulnerability scanner identifies not only hosts and open ports on those hosts, but also associated vulnerabilities. Running vulnerability scanners frequently can be helpful in identifying new hosts on a network as well as their vulnerabilities. A host's operating system and active applications are identified and then compared with a database of known vulnerabilities. Vulnerability scanners can be of two types: network and host.

Network scanners are used to map an organization's network and identify open ports, vulnerable software, and misconfigured services. They can be installed on a single system on the network and can quickly locate and test numerous hosts. Network scanners are generally ineffective at gathering accurate information on hosts using personal firewalls, unless the personal firewalls are configured to permit the network scanning activity.

Host scanners must be installed on each host to be tested. These scanners are used primarily to identify specific host operating system and application misconfigurations and vulnerabilities. Host scanners have high detection granularity and usually require not only local host access but also a root or administrative account. Some host scanners offer the capability of repairing misconfigurations.

Vulnerability scanners vary widely in capability and performance. Some perform optimized searching and can scan a host or network much faster than other systems. Some provide detailed reports and information about the remediation of each discovered vulnerability, while others provide only the most basic information about which vulnerabilities were found.

Vulnerability scanners employ large databases of vulnerabilities to identify those associated with commonly used operating systems and applications. The vulnerability database must be updated frequently, so that the scanners can identify the newest vulnerabilities. When a match is found, the scanner will alert the operator to a possible vulnerability. Most vulnerability scanners also generate reports to help system administrators fix the discovered vulnerabilities. Unfortunately, vulnerability scanners are not completely accurate; some vulnerabilities may be missed, and others that do not exist may be identified. Organizations should consider using multiple vulnerability scanning products so that false positives generated by one scanner could be validated by another.[5]

Vulnerability scanners provide these capabilities:

- Identify active hosts on networks.
- Identify active and vulnerable services on hosts.
- Identify vulnerabilities associated with operating systems and applications.
- Test compliance with host application usage and security policies.

Vulnerability scanners can help identify out-of-date software versions and applicable patches or system upgrades. Generally, host-based scanners are more effective at doing this than network-based scanners. Although scanners can be helpful at finding outdated software, scanners may identify deliberately deployed settings as vulnerabilities. The person assessing the vulnerability scanner reports needs to know how to interpret them and should compare them to the organization's business requirements. In addition, certain vulnerability scanners are able to make corrections and fix certain discovered vulnerabilities automatically.

40.3.9.2 *Reviewing Patch Logs.*   Log files keep track of the history of a system. Patch logs can assist the PVG and system administrators with tracking and verifying installed patches. Using patch logs to monitor an organization's systems can help to achieve consistency and compliance with the remediation plan. Patch logs can provide these capabilities:

- Identify which patches are installed on a system, allowing easy confirmation that the appropriate set of patches has been applied.
- Ensure that patches are applied in a consistent manner across the organization, through a comparison of log files.
- Verify that each patch has been installed properly.
- Determine whether the patch, or a subsequent update, improperly removed or damaged a previous patch.

40.3.9.3   *Checking Patch Levels.*   An organization might wish to verify the patch levels of hosts before allowing them to join its networks. This can be done through the use of separate virtual local area networks (VLANs) for unverified hosts. In most deployments, each host runs an agent that monitors various characteristics, such as OS and application patches and antivirus updates. When the host attempts to connect to the network, a network device such as a router requests information from the host's agent. If the host does not respond to the request, or the response indicates that the host is not fully patched, the network device causes the host to be placed onto a separate VLAN. This allows the organization to update the unpatched hosts while severely restricting what they can do. Once a host on the VLAN has been fully updated, it is moved automatically from the VLAN to the organization's regular network. The VLAN strategy can be particularly helpful for ensuring that mobile hosts are fully patched.

40.3.10   Vulnerability Remediation Training.   Although the PVG will monitor for new patches and vulnerabilities found within the software listed in the organizational software inventory, local administrators may use software not listed in the inventory. This situation may result from a management decision that the PVG only has resources to focus on the more popular software packages. In this situation, it is essential that local administrators have some knowledge of how to identify new patches and vulnerabilities. By providing them with such knowledge, a second line of defense is created in the patching process. Local administrators should be trained by the PVG on the various vulnerability and patching resources described in Section 40.4. Organizations may choose to train their administrators with only a few tools that are known to be comprehensive.

In addition, all end users who will be expected to implement recommended remediations on their own systems should be educated about the organization's vulnerability management process. These end users should also be provided with instructions on installing patches and performing other types of remedial actions. This education must be applied to the organization's remote workers.

40.4   PATCH AND VULNERABILITY MANAGEMENT ISSUES.   This section provides an overview of common issues in patch and vulnerability management. First, it explains the major types of patch management tools and discusses the advantages and disadvantages of each type. It also examines the security risks inherent in the use of the tools and provides guidance on effective deployment strategies for patch management tools. Next, this section explains how including patch management considerations in the

purchase of IT products can reduce the need to patch the acquired products in the future. Finally, this section endorses the use of standardized configurations for IT resources and briefly provides recommendations for patching after a security compromise has occurred.

40.4.1 Enterprise Patching Solutions.   All moderate- to large-size organizations should be using enterprise patch management tools for the majority of their computers. Even small organizations should be migrating to some form of automated patching tool. Widespread manual patching of computers is becoming ineffective, as the number of patches that need to be installed grows and as attackers continue to develop exploit code more rapidly. Only uniquely configured computers, and other computers that cannot be updated effectively through automated means, such as many appliance-based devices, should continue to be patched manually.

40.4.1.1 *Types of Patching Solutions.*   There are two primary categories of enterprise patch management tools: those that use agents and those that do not. Some products support both approaches and allow the administrator to choose the approach that is most efficient for the environment. With both approaches, there usually is a central computer that holds all of the patches that should be, or could be, installed on computers participating in the patching solution. The central computer often contains a console that allows the patching administrator to control which computers get which patches. Some implementations use multiple central computers to provide redundancy and to divide the patching load across multiple devices and networks.

Both approaches utilize a centralized model with a single computer (or cluster of computers) controlling the patching process for all computers participating in the patching solution. This is in contrast to the standard Microsoft Windows Update service, which uses a completely decentralized model in which each computer (or the administrator of that computer) decides which patches to install and when to install them. Some products have features that combine the centralized and decentralized models. Such solutions usually follow the centralized model but give the end user some control over the process, such as the ability to choose not to install a patch.

Although the two primary categories of enterprise patch management tools have similarities, they also have important differences that should be considered when purchasing a particular solution.

40.4.1.1.1 Nonagent Patching Solutions.   Nonagent patching solutions are similar to network-based vulnerability scanners. There is usually a single computer that scans computers through the network. However, unlike many vulnerability scanners, the nonagent patching solution is usually given administrator access to the computers participating in the automated patching program. This gives the patching program access to much more information than is available through simple network scanning. It also gives the patching program the ability to install patches on participating computers. Given the similarity between nonagent patching solutions and vulnerability scanners, it is not surprising that some commercial nonagent patching solutions also detect vulnerabilities, and can do so with greater accuracy than a vulnerability scanning program that does not have administrator access to the computer.

Since nonagent patching solutions rely on network scanning, they may consume a large amount of network bandwidth. Most products resolve this problem by enabling the patch administrator to throttle the amount of network bandwidth that is used by the product. However, limiting the network bandwidth that can be used by the product may increase the total amount of time needed to complete the network scan. In large networks, it may not be possible to scan all computers as quickly as needed, and agent-based solutions may be preferable. Additionally, computers for employees that telecommute might not be included in the scan. Another problem with nonagent patching solutions is that personal firewalls on computers will typically block the scanning activity, unless they are specifically configured to permit it. Since the prevalence of personal firewalls is increasing, this is becoming a more significant problem.

40.4.1.1.2 Agent-Based Patching Solutions.   Agent-based patching solutions, as mentioned previously, usually use a centralized computer, or a cluster of computers, that manage the patching process for all participating computers. However, with this model a software program (agent) is installed on each participating computer. As discussed in Section 40.3.8, many appliance-based devices do not permit direct administrator access to the operating system, which typically prevents the installation of patching agents. Although each product works differently, the overall agent patching process generally works in this way:

1. The agent communicates with the central computer to learn about new patches. Depending on the implementation, the agent may poll the central computer periodically, or it may be contacted directly by the central computer, which is more efficient.

2. The agent has administrator or root access to the computer, and it uses that privilege to determine which patches are missing. This status is usually transmitted to the central computer, so that the overall patching administrator (e.g., the PVG representative) can view the status of all participating computers. This also enables the central administrator to produce patching reports regarding the patch security level for each system.

3. The agent receives instructions from the central computer on which patches to install and how to install them. In cases where a reboot is required, the central computer may instruct the agent to patch and automatically reboot the computer. Alternatively, the central computer may instruct the agent to patch and then notify the user that the computer needs rebooting (with the option of an automated reboot within a specified time frame).

The architecture of the agent-based solution eliminates the excessive network bandwidth usage that may occur with the nonagent-based solution. The primary drawback is that the agents must be installed on each computer and must run with administrator or root privileges. Second, computers already taxed by running with high processing or memory loads may suffer further performance degradation due to the agent process. Another possible drawback is that agents may not be available for all platforms, but platform support can also be an issue with nonagent approaches.

40.4.1.1.3 Advantages and Disadvantages.   Each approach has advantages and disadvantages that should be considered.

Nonagent Solution Advantages

- Does not need to install software agents on all participating computers.

Nonagent Solution Disadvantages

- Utilizes a significant amount of network bandwidth while scanning computers. (Both nonagent and agent solutions are likely to use approximately the same bandwidth for delivering patches to computers.)

- May require the use of ports and services that would otherwise be turned off as part of locking down the system (e.g., Remote Procedure Call [RPC] for UNIX, NetBIOS for Windows).
- May take a long time to scan large networks.
- May not produce accurate results for hosts that use personal firewalls.
- May require that the central computer be given administrator access to participating computers. (Managing the credentials that the central computer needs to log on to the individual hosts can be very challenging if there are many individual accounts, particularly if passwords are changed very frequently—e.g., monthly.)

Agent-Based Solution Advantages

- Can scan large networks quickly.
- Minimizes use of network bandwidth while scanning computers.

Agent-Based Solution Disadvantages

- Requires that software agents be installed, running, and managed on all participating computers. If an agent is not running due to failure or misconfiguration, the computer will not be patched.
- Must run agents with administrator or root privileges, which creates the possibility of remote attacks against such agents.

Deploying enterprise patch management tools within an enterprise can create additional security risks for an organization; however, organizations that do not effectively patch their systems face a much greater risk. Patching tools usually increase security far more than they decrease security, especially when the tools contain built-in security measures to protect against security risks and threats. Some risks with using these tools are listed next.

- A software vendor might distribute a patch to the enterprise patch management vendor that was corrupted with malicious code.
- The enterprise patch management vendor may provide a patch that has been maliciously altered by an employee or attacker.
- An attacker could break into the central patch computer and use the enterprise patch management tool as an efficient distribution tool for malicious code, potentially providing remote access to every participating computer.
- An attacker could break into the central patch computer on nonagent systems and steal the administrator passwords for all computers participating in the patch management program.
- An attacker could discover a locally exploitable vulnerability with the patch management agent software. This could enable the attacker to elevate access to a participating computer from user-level access to administrator access. This assumes that the attacker has already broken into the computer and gained access.
- An attacker could discover a remotely exploitable vulnerability with the patch management agent software. This could enable an attacker to remotely penetrate a participating computer and gain administrator access. It could also enable an attacker to launch a denial-of-service attack on the participating computer.
- An attacker could sniff enterprise patch management tool network communications to determine which patches have not been installed on particular computers.

These risks can be partially mitigated through the application of standard security techniques that should be used when deploying any enterprise-wide application. Examples of countermeasures include:

- Encrypting network connections
- Performing IP address authentication for network communications
- Disabling unneeded ports and services on the central patch management server
- Testing patches before deployment
- Performing timely application of patches
- Conducting timely mitigation of vulnerabilities for which there are no patches
- Using firewalls properly

40.4.1.2 Integrated Software Inventory Capabilities.

Enterprise patch management tools require administrator access to each participating computer and must inventory the software packages on each computer to determine which patches are needed. Therefore, it is natural for such programs to make this information available to the administrators and to incorporate a software inventory management capability. An increasing number of products provide this capability, and it appears that this is the natural way for the market to move. Such inventory products can be purchased separately but often require a separate agent to be installed on each computer. Since it is costly from an IT management point of view to install and manage multiple agents on each computer, it would be ideal if both functions (patching and inventorying) could be performed by the same product.

Some patch management systems can only recognize software, or versions of software, that have known vulnerabilities. This would preclude the use of such a patch management system as the sole source of software inventory information for an organization.

40.4.1.3 Integrated Vulnerability Scanning Capabilities.

Enterprise patch management tools are also beginning to incorporate vulnerability scanning functionality. This enables the administrator not just to see which patches are missing, but also to understand what vulnerabilities are associated with those patches and thus understand what real risks exist to the unpatched computers. This capability also allows administrators to see vulnerabilities within computers before the patches are even available. This is very important, given the speed at which attack tools are developed whenever a new vulnerability is announced.

Not only do some of these tools have the capability to scan for vulnerabilities, but they may also be able to scan for vulnerabilities with greater accuracy than network-based vulnerability scanners. Many network-based vulnerability scanners do not have administrator access to the computers that they scan, so they are forced to identify vulnerabilities by relying on imprecise guesses based on how different network ports respond to different inputs. Enterprise patch management tools do not have any such advantage over host-based vulnerability scanners. However, as with inventory management tools, it would be better to have patch management and vulnerability scanning capabilities integrated within one agent, instead of having to install and manage two separate agents on each computer. Readers should note the contrast between network-based vulnerability scanners that use banner grabbing to identify vulnerabilities versus software that actually has root access on a box. The industry has evolved, and most network-based scanners currently do have the ability to log in remotely as root to do scanning.

40.4.1.4 *Deployment Strategies.* Although all moderate- to large-size organizations should be using enterprise patch management tools, deploying those tools universally within an organization can be difficult. Organizations should deploy enterprise patch management tools using a phased approach. This allows process and user communication issues to be addressed with a small group before deploying the patch application universally.

Most organizations deploy patch management tools first to standardized desktop systems and single-platform server farms of similarly configured servers. Once this has been accomplished, organizations should address the more difficult issue of integrating multiplatform environments, nonstandard desktop systems, legacy computers, and computers with unusual configurations. Manual methods may need to be used for operating systems and applications not supported by automated patching tools as well as for computers with unusual configurations; examples include embedded systems, industrial control systems, medical devices, and experimental systems. For such computers, there should be a written and implemented procedure for manual patching.

Nonstandard systems and legacy computers can hamper widespread deployment, but personnel issues can be an even greater challenge. System owners (and computer users) may have some initial qualms about giving administrator access to their computers to another group and having that group regularly install and update software. Their concerns include these issues:

- The agent software may decrease computer performance or stability.
- The patches being installed may cause unexpected problems with existing software.
- A user may lose data when the enterprise patching application reboots the computer to install a patch.
- The enterprise patching application itself may present a new security risk.
- A mobile user may become frustrated and confused when the enterprise patching application attempts to install a large set of patches as soon as the mobile user connects to the network.

These concerns should be discussed with system owners and computer users. All of them can be addressed by good communication, a careful phased rollout, and the selection of a robust and secure enterprise patch management tool.

40.4.2 Reducing the Need to Patch through Smart Purchasing.
Some software products have more vulnerabilities than other products with equivalent purpose and functionality. By considering several factors during the purchasing process, organizations may be able to reduce the number of future vulnerabilities experienced and thus reduce the need to patch the software. The future likelihood of vulnerabilities should not be the only factor in purchasing a product, but it should be an element in the decision-making process. A list of considerations in choosing products that are less likely to experience vulnerabilities in the future follows.

- Consider a product for which there is a detailed checklist specifying how to secure the product. NIST manages the Security Configuration Checklists Program for IT Products (http://checklists.nist.gov/), which collects reviewed checklists for a variety of operating systems and applications.

- Search a vulnerability database (such as the National Vulnerability Database at http://nvd.nist.gov/) for known vulnerabilities of products under consideration. Examine the type, severity, and quantity of vulnerabilities in the product under consideration. This is not foolproof because it often takes longer for vulnerabilities to be discovered (and patches released) for less popular software products.

- Consider a more mature product. Recently released products usually have more unknown vulnerabilities that will require future patches and possibly lead to increased exposure to risk.

- Consider less complicated products. More code, features, and services can mean more bugs, vulnerabilities, and patches. Consider not purchasing a product that has more features than needed. To the extent possible, delay implementing recently released major operating systems or applications until the experiences of others can be included in the decision-making process.

- Purchase products that conform to appropriate national or international security design standards (e.g., NIST FIPS PUB 140-2 for encryption modules).

- Consider software validated by independent testing. For the greatest assurance, the software's source code should be evaluated. (However, despite the benefit, software source code evaluations are generally not performed due to the cost of such analyses.)

- Use only versions of software that are currently supported. Obsolete software beyond its life cycle often has flaws that are addressed only in the newer, supported versions.

- Evaluate the speed with which the vendor responds to new vulnerabilities with a patch.

40.4.3   Using Standardized Configurations.   Using standardized configurations for IT resources reduces the labor involved in identifying, testing, and applying patches, and ensures a higher level of consistency, which leads to improved security. Organizations that use standard configurations for their IT resources will find it much easier and less costly to implement a patch and vulnerability management program. Comprehensive patch and vulnerability management is almost impossible (or at least very costly) within large organizations that do not deploy standard configurations.

A standard configuration should be defined for each major group of IT resources (e.g., routers, user workstations, file servers). Organizations should focus standardization efforts on types of IT resources that make up a significant portion of their entire IT inventory. Likely candidates for standardization include end user workstations, file servers, and network infrastructure components (e.g., routers and switches). The standard configuration description will likely include these items:

- Hardware type and model
- Operating system version and patch level
- Major installed applications, version, and patch level
- Security settings for the operating system and applications

In many cases, these standardized configurations can be maintained centrally, and changes can be propagated to all participating IT resources. An organization that relies on a hardware supplier to place a standard configuration on new computers should coordinate closely with that supplier to ensure that changes, including new patches, are implemented quickly. NIST SP 800-70, *Security Configuration Checklists Program for IT Products—Guidance for Checklists Users and Developers,* provides guidance on creating and using security configuration checklists, which are helpful tools for documenting standard security settings.[6]

40.4.4 Patching after a Security Compromise.

Patching after a security compromise is significantly more complicated than merely applying the appropriate patch. Although applying a patch after a security compromise will generally correct the vulnerability that was exploited, it will not eliminate rootkits, backdoors (secret avenues of access placed on a compromised computer system by an attack that allows future unauthorized access), or most other changes that might have been introduced by the intruder. For example, the Code Red II worm placed backdoors on compromised systems, and later the Nimda worm exploited those backdoors. In most cases a compromised system should be reformatted and reinstalled or restored from a known safe and trusted backup. If that is not possible, significant expertise will be required to manage the possible dangers inherent in compromised systems. Organizations may find it helpful to maintain fully patched images of their standard configurations. A current, known good image can replace a compromised system, and then data can safely be restored from backups. NIST SP 800-61, *Computer Security Incident Handling Guide*, is an extensive resource for handling security incidents and recovering compromised computers.[7]

40.5 CONCLUSION AND SUMMARY OF MAJOR RECOMMENDATIONS.

When designing a process for handling patches, consider the principles that make up the PVG patching concept. The core concepts should be found within the chosen patching methodology, although other patching variations may be acceptable. These concepts include using organizational inventories, patch and vulnerability monitoring, patch prioritization techniques, organizational patch databases, patch testing, patch distribution, patch application verification, patch training, automated patch deployment, and automatic updating of applications.

Except for the smallest organizations and selected areas of large organizations, the move to automated patching methods should be swift. Implementation of automated patch methods should parallel organizational plans to centralize services and to standardize desktop configurations. For this reason, computer security personnel must be actively involved in designing centralized services and standardized desktop models.

Although patching and vulnerability monitoring can often appear to be overwhelming tasks, consistent mitigation of organizational vulnerabilities can be achieved through a tested and integrated patching process. Having a mature patch and vulnerability management program will make the organization more proactive than reactive with regard to maintaining appropriate levels of security. Efficient patch automation, combined with effective preventive maintenance, should result in spending less time, resources, and money on incident response.

This chapter contains a variety of recommendations to assist organizations in implementing an effective patch and vulnerability management program. The primary recommendations are:

1. Create a patch and vulnerability group.
2. Continuously monitor for vulnerabilities, remediations, and threats.
3. Prioritize patch application and use phased deployments as appropriate.

4. Test patches prior to deployment.

5. Deploy enterprise-wide automated patching solutions.

6. Use automatically updating applications as appropriate.

7. Create an inventory of all information technology assets.

8. Use standardized configurations for IT resources as much as possible.

9. Verify that vulnerabilities have been remediated.

10. Consistently measure the effectiveness of the organization's patch and vulnerability management program, and apply corrective actions as necessary.

11. Train applicable staff on vulnerability monitoring and remediation techniques.

12. Periodically test the effectiveness of the organization's patch and vulnerability management program.

40.6 FURTHER READING

Nicastro, F. M. *Curing the Patch Management Headache*. Boca Raton, FL: Auerbach Publications, 2005.

CRC IIA *Change and Patch Management Controls: Critical for Organizational Success*. (Global Technology Audit Guide 2). Institute of Internal Auditors, 2005.

Jang, M. *Linux® Patch Management: Keeping Linux® Systems Up To Date*. Bruce Perens' Open Source Series. Prentice Hall PTR, 2006.

40.7 NOTES

1. This chapter is based on the National Institute of Standards and Technology (NIST) Special Publication 800-40 Version 2.0, *Creating a Patch and Vulnerability Management Program,* which is available at http://csrc.nist.gov/publications/nistpubs/.

2. The source for this information is the National Vulnerability Database, which is available at http://nvd.nist.gov/.

3. Manual patching is still useful and necessary for many legacy and specialized systems.

4. FIPS PUB 199 is available for download at http://csrc.nist.gov/publications/fips/fips199/FIPS-PUB-199-final.pdf.

5. NIST SP 800-42, *Guidelines on Network Security Testing*, contains detailed advice on the use of vulnerability scanners. It is available at http://csrc.nist.gov/publications/nistpubs/800-42/NIST-SP800-42.pdf.

6. NIST SP 800-70 is available from the Security Configuration Checklists Web site at http://checklists.nist.gov/.

7. NIST SP 800-61 is available at http://csrc.nist.gov/publications/nistpubs/800-61/sp800-61.pdf.

CHAPTER 41

ANTIVIRUS TECHNOLOGY

Chey Cobb and Allysa Myers

41.1 INTRODUCTION. For over two decades, computer viruses have been a persistent, annoying, and costly threat, and there is no end in sight to the problem. There are many vendors offering to provide a cure for viruses and malware, but the mere existence of these software pests is understandably vexing to those charged with system security.

Initially, most viruses were not designed to cause harm but were created more to gain notoriety for the creator or as a prank. Because these early viruses were designed to subvert legitimate program operations across multiple systems, they were more likely to cause unexpected problems. These viruses, and later some Trojans, often damaged data and caused system downtime. The cleanup required to recover from even a minor virus infection was expensive in terms of lost productivity and unbudgeted labor costs.

Viruses and Trojan behavior have merged, and now both are considered as part of the larger family referred to as malware. No longer is malware just written for a virus writer's 15 minutes of fame; today, malware is created primarily for financial gain. Malware can still cause damage, but now it is more likely to have been created to steal valuable information or the resources of an infected computer. Malware can steal passwords, send spam from a compromised machine, or install software designed to display ads (with programs known as adware), to name a few examples. Some malware programs can give full access to a hacker to control infected machines, and a new trend has been the creation of "zombie nets." These hijack the computers of unsuspecting users, in order to launch an attack. A zombie net makes use of the increased power of networked computers, while making it more difficult to trace a suspected attacker. For more information about malware, see Chapter 16 in this *Handbook.*

Because of this shift to a financial motivation for malware writing, something of an open source community has sprung up to develop new malware. There have been two major areas where development has been most notable: evasion of traditional antivirus defenses and distribution by exploiting vulnerabilities in common software. In their efforts to evade traditional antivirus defenses, viruses are often slightly modified and compressed with "packers," which frequently use sophisticated obfuscation or anti–reverse-engineering techniques. The primary focus of malware writers is to avoid the newsworthy outbreaks of the past, staying under the radar to accomplish targeted attacks. Some of the most common malware families now have as many as tens of thousands of variants with hundreds of variants being released each day. Once they are in a system, they often employ stealthing techniques such as kernel-mode rootkits to hide themselves from the operating system and from many antivirus (AV) products.

New malware programs are being developed every day because vulnerabilities in software programs are so numerous, and it is often months between the time a vulnerability is discovered and the time that the vendor issues a security patch. Even more often, patches are announced but not implemented. Malware writers take advantage of these vulnerabilities and time lags, so research into vulnerabilities is imperative in order to create effective defenses with antivirus programs. A layered defense against malware infection is essential and should employ a traditional string-based antivirus scanner as well as a firewall and behavioral scanners.

Although the threat of new malware remains, and its growth has become exponential, the technology deployed to defend computers against viruses and malware is one of the least understood aspects of security architecture. As a result, antivirus defenses are often set up improperly. This chapter describes available antivirus technologies and how they work. Their effective application within a comprehensive program of computer security is outlined.

41.1.1   Antivirus Terminology.

The acronym "AV" is widely used to describe the industry, the products, and the programs that have been developed to defeat computer viruses. Early AV programs used simple hard drive scans to search for a specific text string hidden within a specific file. This is the origin of the term "AV scanner," which is now widely used as a generic term for all AV programs. That is how the term is used in this chapter, although it should be pointed out that many of today's AV scanners do much more than merely scan, and detection now includes Trojans and unwanted programs such as adware and malware.

When exploring AV product literature, it is common to see statements about the number of viruses and Trojans that exist. It is not unusual to see six-digit estimates of the total number of malware variants and four-digit estimates of the number of new malware added every month. However, it is important to bear in mind that not all numbers are created equal. For a start, there is a difference between threats that exist only in a research setting (*in the zoo*) and those that are actively infecting users' computers (*in the wild*). Viruses held *in the zoo* are used to help create new AV technology, and they are well secured against inadvertent release. These viruses and malware come from samples that are sometimes sent directly to virus researchers by virus writers, while others are sent by researchers who have created a proof-of-concept virus.

The term "in the wild" is applied to viruses that are active, as tracked by virus researchers. In the early 1990s, Joe Wells developed a coordinated reporting procedure that synchronized the work of responsible AV researchers around the world, resulting in a reliable and consistent monthly accounting of virus activity. This pioneering move was called the WildList.[1]

41.1.2 Antivirus Issues. In the early days of viruses, aside from having the ability to spread to other machines, there was little benefit in keeping a virus on a machine for any length of time. During the early days, viruses were relatively easy to find, because a virus usually caused noticeable damage that made users aware that their systems were infected. At other times, an unmistakable message or image appeared on the screen, alerting users to the infection. As virus writers discovered a monetary benefit to remaining on a system as long as possible, the number of infected machines increased tremendously. Viruses and malware have become complex, are adept at disguising themselves, and are not as easy to find and eradicate. To counter this problem, AV scanners have become sophisticated logic machines. This new level of complexity, of both the problem and the solution, has made it even more confusing for users. Too many people fail to understand the importance of having up-to-date AV products. Users do not know what to look for, and do not understand that viruses and malware do not necessarily announce their existence. This is probably why reports of Netsky virus variants are still appearing years after they were initially released and why Robot Network (botnet) infections number more than 2,000 a day.

Most AV software has an automatic update capability, which has made updating a less labor-intensive process. Updates are the key to keeping systems virus and malware free because updates give the AV program the information necessary to find the newest viruses and malware. Unfortunately, because viruses and Trojans are released at such a prodigious pace, even daily updates of a traditional string-based scanner may not be enough to keep systems totally clear of viruses. Most AV scanners look at what has happened before (i.e., known behavior of known viruses), in order to detect infections. Although AV products now attempt to anticipate new viruses, that is not their strong point. Additionally, many consumers who buy a new computer receive a working AV product with their purchase, but they do not choose to buy a subscription for AV updates once their free use period expires. They do not understand why they have to pay for something that seems to be working, and they are lulled into a false sense of security by thinking that their AV product is doing its job. The vendors have not done a good job educating the public that an AV scanner without current updates is useless. Consumers who bring work from home into the office can quickly infect an entire network.

Security products historically have suffered from a lack of upper management support because they are often viewed as high-cost/low-return items, and they are given a low priority in the security budget. The information technology (IT) team of an organization needs resources for things like identifying and patching vulnerable systems, monitoring and managing machines entering their network, monitoring suspicious behavior identified by firewalls, AV products, and security scanners. Considering the plethora of AV products from which to choose, and the large number of patches introduced each day, many system administrators despair. They will install and patch just what they have time for, and consider it good enough.

41.2   HISTORY OF VIRAL CHANGES.   Early viruses were usually distributed via floppy disks in the 1980s because PCs were not normally networked, and the Internet was not yet widely used. However, shortly after the first viruses began appearing on PCs, AV scanners made their debut. The first scanners only detected the presence of a virus but did nothing to disinfect the system. Users often had to search message boards to find information for the removal of a particular virus or to obtain specific removal programs from vendors. The virus problem was not considered a priority at that time because there were a limited number of viruses, and most were only a nuisance.

Changes in the computing environment are responsible for both the type of viruses and the rate at which they infect. For example, until 1992, the number of boot sector viruses and file-infecting viruses was roughly equivalent. In 1992, the number of file-infecting viruses began to decrease and boot sector viruses began to increase. This trend continued through 1995, when the change from DOS-based computing to Windows-based computing tipped the scales in favor of boot-sector viruses. Most PCs were still diskette based, and boot disks were standard equipment. Users frequently swapped information between computers via floppies on the "sneaker net" because interconnected computers were rare. Infected floppies that were left in the drive during the boot process allowed the virus to take up residence in the computer's memory, and would subsequently infect every disk used on that machine. Because boot sector viruses did not cause Windows to crash, many users did not realize that they had been infected until the virus caused problems on the system or until someone decided to check the system on suspicion that it might be infected.

Another factor favoring boot sector viruses for a time was the complexity of Windows 3.1 relative to earlier operating systems. When Windows was first introduced, virus writers did not have much experience in writing viruses for Windows systems. Because most file-infecting viruses of that period caused Windows to crash, and because Windows 3.1 was itself notoriously unstable, users frequently reformatted hard drives and reinstalled the operating system as a matter of course. As a result, whether the users were aware of the fact that a virus was resident or not, reformatting and reinstalling the hard drive quickly eliminated the file-infecting viruses.

The introduction of Windows 95 again changed the course of viruses. Once more, the virus writers had a new operating system with which to contend, and they quickly discovered that Windows 95 included an enhancement that warned users when changes were made to the boot sectors. These warnings would alert users that a virus might be present. Boot sector viruses stalled at this point, and the rate of file infections slowed to a near halt. Eventually, it was the power of sharing data files between applications that led to the next stage in virus evolution: the macro virus.

Microsoft's dominance of the office suite market through its MS Office products (Word, Excel, PowerPoint, and Access) provided a uniform platform for the spread of macro viruses, based on its proprietary Visual BASIC (VB) programming language. Because VB macros are easy to develop and can be quickly exchanged among users through file sharing, it is natural that macro viruses quickly became the most prevalent type of virus. These facts, combined with increased connectivity between systems and networks, made macro viruses able to spread faster than the traditional boot sector or file-infecting viruses.

Early viruses also required the interaction of a human being to assist it in spreading. The user had to (unknowingly) execute the infected program, copy it from a hard disk to a floppy, and physically move it to another machine. However, with code and application sharing in browser, media, and operating system software, viruses no longer require human interaction to execute. They spread as executables or data files, from one vulnerable system to the next, without a user ever being aware that code had been run. Many people sitting at home, connected to the Internet, did not realize that, by simply going to an infected Web site or viewing an infected ad on an otherwise benign site, a program had been silently executed and had installed a virus or malware on their system.

In recent years, instant messaging (IM) and peer-to-peer (P2P) file-sharing clients have gained a great deal of popularity, and viruses have changed to take advantage of the ease of sharing. In the case of IM, this is accomplished primarily through links sent to people on an infected user's contact list. In the case of P2P clients, this is accomplished by copying the malicious files to "shared" directories with enticing names. Both methods rely heavily on social engineering to get people to click on a file that will then install infected files.

41.3   ANTIVIRUS BASICS.   AV scanners are a bit like police officers walking the beat. They try to watch everything that is going on around them, look out for suspicious behavior, and attempt to intercede when they think something bad is happening or about to happen. Both the police and AV scanners look for certain patterns and behaviors, and they leap into action when a suspect crosses a predetermined threshold of acceptability. Like the police, however, AV scanners sometimes reach the wrong conclusions. This is usually caused by insufficient data or by new and unexpected behavioral patterns.

Virus detection is an inexact science, and it is impossible to create an AV scanner with a 100 percent success rate. It is simply not possible to know the intent of every bit of code that enters a computer, and it is not feasible to test every bit of code before it executes. To do so would require that the AV scanner demand so much of the processing power of the CPU that valid programs would not be able to execute. Viral behaviors are subject to broad variations, and many use stealthing or cloaking techniques to hide from the operating system and even from the AV scanner itself. There are no longer hard-and-fast rules that a user can apply to determine if a system harbors a virus.

41.3.1   Early Days of AV Scanners.   When viruses first started appearing with regularity in the late 1980s, their detection and eradication was relatively straightforward, but not necessarily easy. The viruses were quite simple and normally did not spread very quickly. The AV community quickly researched them, determined what made them work, and published effective fixes in short order. These fixes tended to be written for a specific virus and could not disinfect other viruses, even if they were of similar types. Most of the work fell on users to identify which virus (or type of virus) they thought they had and then search for a program that would fix it. Because Internet connectivity was not as prevalent as it is now, users frequently spent much time calling friends and associates in the hope that they could forward a disk copy of the necessary AV program. Additionally, there were no naming conventions for viruses, and it was difficult to determine with any conviction that the fix obtained would actually work.

Viruses of that period generally inserted their code in predictable sections of a program. The early scanners ran a search for a specific string of characters. If they found it, they would delete the virus code and attempt to restore the host program to its original uninfected form. Failing that, the scanner would usually advise the user that disinfection was incomplete and that they should delete the infected application and reinstall it.

As the number of viruses began to climb, software companies that had ventured into the AV market began to realize that creating and distributing individual fixes was no longer feasible. Instead, they began to develop more comprehensive scanners that could look for more viruses, both old and new. The new generations of scanners were comprised of two components: the scanning engine and the signature files. Each component was entirely dependent on the other to work. The engine consisted of the user interface and the application that scanned the system for viruses. The signature files were a database of the *fingerprints* (unique segments of code) of known viruses. Although some of these early scanners did a good job, many did not. None of the early AV scanners was able to catch all known viruses.

41.3.2 Validity of Scanners.   The vendors of software scanners in the late 1980s and early 1990s faced a number of obstacles. It seemed there was a new AV vendor appearing every month, and the market became highly competitive as user awareness of the virus problem grew. Given this competitive state, there was vast dissension among the AV community as to how viruses for research should be stored and tested. Many AV vendors kept a library of viruses for their own use, and this fact was used in their marketing. Claims that one program worked better than another because it checked for more viruses were misleading because no one knew how many viruses existed. There was simply no method of commercial or independent testing to check the validity of claims made by the AV product vendors. Additionally, there was a problem of naming the viruses. Each vendor created its own names for viruses, and it was not uncommon for one virus to be known by several names.

The AV vendors also disagreed on how AV scanners should operate in principle. Some vendors felt that AV scanners should only look for new viruses, and others felt that a good product should search for both old and new viruses. While this argument raged, viruses looked as though they would eventually gain the upper hand, especially as virus writers began to use underground bulletin boards, and later the Internet, to share and distribute virus code.

With no standards for the AV products, the public had little to go by other than the vendors' marketing copy and the advice of other users. However, if a recommendation was made by a friend for Brand X Antivirus because no viruses were found on the friend's system, it was possible that no viruses had ever been introduced in the friend's system at all, and Brand X could not find old viruses, new viruses, or any viruses at all.

Two things happened that revolutionized the AV scanner market. In 1993, Joe Wells, a research editor with a business magazine, began collecting viruses and virus reports from experts around the world and began assembling a library of these viruses. As was noted earlier, he named this library of viruses the "WildList" and made it available to legitimate AV researchers. His list divided viruses into those known to have infected systems (in the wild) and those that had been written but were not actively infecting (in the zoo). A naming convention of viruses also began to emerge in order to maintain an efficient and searchable database. The other notable event was the development of commercial AV testing and certification by a company known as the National Computer Security Association (NCSA), which is now known as ICSA Labs. The NCSA started a consortium of AV vendors that, for a fee, submitted their products to be tested. NCSA and Joe Wells began collaboration for the use of his WildList, and Dr. Richard Ford, a noted virus expert, created a virus testing laboratory for NCSA. Dr. Ford fashioned an environment in which AV scanners were put through their paces to see if they could detect all of the viruses in the WildList. AV vendors submitted their products every time a new version of their product was about to be released. Although the original test results were dismal (many scanners could not detect more than 80 percent of the viruses in the list), an environment had been created in which measurable improvements in the effectiveness of AV technology could be achieved. Naturally, the public and the press began to look for AV products that had been certified by NCSA. Eventually other commercial and independent test laboratories independently developed their own certification schemes to help users find reliable AV products.

41.3.3 Scanner Internals.   As was noted earlier, an AV scanner cannot simply put each program into a computer's RAM and test it for viruses before the program is allowed to execute. To do that would require almost all the resources of the CPU, and users would have a system that operated at a snail's pace.

In order to operate efficiently, and in harmony with the other programs on a computer, AV scanners have had to resort to numerous tricks to prevent virus infections, find infections, disinfect programs, and still operate at a reasonably high speed, without bringing the entire system to a halt. They can use some or all of these four basic methods of operation:

1. **Specific detection.** Looking for infections by known viruses
2. **Generic detection.** Looking for infections by variants of known viruses
3. **Heuristics.** Scanning for previously unknown viruses by noting suspicious behavior or file structures, as described more fully in Section 41.4.3
4. **Intrusion prevention.** Monitoring known-suspicious system changes and behaviors to prevent unknown infections

41.3.4 Antivirus Engines and Antivirus Databases.   The AV engine and its signature database work in concert to prevent and detect viruses entering a system. The engine generally provides a library of commonly used functions. It consists of dozens of complex searching algorithms, CPU emulators, and various forms of programming logic. The engine determines which files to scan, which functions to run, and how to react when a suspected virus is found. However, the engine knows absolutely nothing about the viruses themselves and is almost useless without the signature database.

The signature database (also known as the *dat* file by some vendors) contains the fingerprints (snippets of distinctive code) of hundreds of thousands of viruses. As new viruses and variants appear at an accelerating rate, it is imperative that the signature database be updated often. In 1995, the experts advised updating the database files at least once a month, but with so many viruses appearing each day, users today are advised to update daily. AV manufacturers now provide products that check for updates automatically and download changes whenever a user is connected to the Internet.

The database also contains the rule sets used in the heuristic scans. These types of scans can be slower and more intrusive than simple signature scans, and their design and implementation vary greatly between products. Most products now give users configurable options to lessen or increase heuristics as desired. Although signature scans can be considered a heuristic in themselves, the term is more commonly used to identify the more complex AV functions that attempt to locate viruses by identifying suspicious behavior and/or file structure.

Because the distinction between a scanning engine and a signature database is not obvious to many system administrators, many religiously update the database but are unaware that the engine also may need updating. This is a poor strategy that can result in many viruses slipping by the scanner undetected.

41.4   SCANNING METHODOLOGIES.   AV products are configurable by the user or the system administrator to scan upon startup, constantly, or on demand. They can also be host-based scans or individual workstation scans. To be at its most effective, a scanner should be set to a continuous or "on access" scan, with a periodic, scheduled scan set to occur when the system is on but not in use. Users running older, slower AV programs will find that this degrades the system performance. Some scanners need to use much of the system's memory on continuous scans in order to be able to test sections of code, which may make the applications noticeably slower when they first run. Therefore, a happy medium must be found—the AV scanner must be able to protect the system, while the user must be able to have full use of the system.

There is no one scanning method that is superior to the others. All of the scanning methods have their advantages and disadvantages, but none is able to detect viruses with unfailing accuracy. A scan is looking for code and behaviors that have been noticed in other viruses, and if a new virus exhibits new, previously unknown behaviors, it can pass by undetected. Therefore, most AV scanners do not rely on only one scanning method to detect viruses, but have several included in their design.

41.4.1   Specific Detection.   Each virus uses different code to perform its functions, such as copying itself from one executable file or host system to another. The sequence of code that is specific to each virus is referred to as the fingerprint, or signature of that virus. To detect the presence of a virus, the scanner looks for the signature, removes its code from the host file or system, and attempts to restore the infected program or system to an uninfected state. In early viruses, it was discovered that the signatures were usually found within specific areas of a program, specific to each virus. The scanners set out to inspect only those areas of a file rather than scanning an entire program from top to bottom. This saved vast amounts of time and processing power.

Every vendor's AV product has a different implementation of scanner and database, although the signature scanning technique is the most common. Signature scans can identify whether a program contains one of the many signatures contained in the database, but it cannot say for certain whether a system has actually been infected by a virus (e.g., the virus may be present but not yet executed). Users can only trust the guess of the AV scanner, because the odds are in the scanner's favor. It is possible, however, that a program that is suspected of being infected actually contains random data that only coincidentally looks like a virus signature. The legitimate program could contain instructions that by sheer chance matched the search string in the virus database. However, when there is a possibility that the code is actually from a virus, the scanner reports it as a positive hit.

False-positive reports are a possible problem of signature scanners. If users notice that their scanner falsely reports the presence of viruses too often, they view this as an annoyance, and will likely seek to disable the software or find ways of circumventing the scans.

41.4.2   Generic Detection.   As was discussed earlier, malware is now often created for financial purposes, and it makes fiscal sense for its authors to get as much use as possible out of successful creations. They often make open-source code that is shared widely in the malware-author's community, so that it is often updated with new functionality such as exploit-code or password-stealing capabilities, to target new games, applications, or online banking sites.

Likewise, it makes sense for AV scanners to look for common properties of popular virus and Trojan families, in order to proactively detect variants based on those codebases. These generic detections can vary from being more heuristic in nature, to being fairly specific, depending on the complexity of the codebase or on the number of variants that have been distributed.

Generic detection is one of the newer techniques used by AV scanners, and it caused a great deal of controversy in the early days of AV products. There was concern, when most viruses spread by infecting clean files parasitically, that generic detection would require generic cleaning, which could leave host files mangled beyond repair or usability. As the vast majority of malware now infects systems rather than host files, simple deletion of malicious files and cleaning of registry entries are often all that is required to return a system to its original state. Generic cleaning routines are now quite common and are very effectively used to repair infected machines.

41.4.3 Heuristics.

By adding heuristics to their AV scanners, vendors looked to increase the efficacy of their products. The scanners could now look for viruses that were new and unknown and not contained within the signature database.

The word "heuristic" comes from a Greek word meaning "to discover." The term is used today in computer science to describe algorithms that are effective in solving complex questions quickly. A heuristic algorithm makes certain assumptions about the problem it is trying to solve. In the case of an AV scanner, it analyzes a program's structure, its attributes, and its behavior to see if these meet the rules that have been established for identifying a virus, even without its specific signature being known. Basically, a heuristic algorithm works on the assumption that if it "looks like a duck, walks like a duck, and sounds like a duck, it must be a duck."

The drawback to heuristic scanning is that it makes intelligent assumptions but is nevertheless bound to make mistakes. Another problem with heuristic scanning is that, on slower systems, it may take longer to run and may require user interaction. Some users consider this intrusive and may turn off the feature. By combining both signature scanning and heuristic scanning in their products, AV vendors have increased their effectiveness and speed.

Heuristic scanners use a rule-based system to verify the existence of a virus. It applies all the rules to a given program and gives the program an overall score. If the score is high, there is a good likelihood that a virus is present. Generally, the scanner looks for the most likely location for a virus to attach itself to a program. This is a crucial step because program files can be tens of megabytes in size. A well-designed heuristic scanner will limit the regions of the program to be examined in order to scan the highest number of suspects in the shortest possible time. The scanner then examines the logic of the suspected program to determine if it might be a virus. This is considered to be a *static* scan. The static method applies the rules and gives a pass/fail score to the program—whether the program has actually executed or not.

The other type of heuristic scanning is called the *dynamic method*. This method applies basically the same rules as the static method, and if the score is high, it attempts to emulate the program. Rather than examining the logic of the suspected code, the dynamic scanner runs a simulation of the virus in a virtual environment. This technique has come to be known as *sandbox* emulation, and is effective for attempting to identify new viruses that do not appear in the signature database.

Neither of these heuristic scanning methods is necessarily better than the other, but in concert they give fairly good results. Although a static heuristic scan may miss some viruses because they have not yet executed and started an infection, the dynamic heuristic scan can catch previously unknown viruses before they execute. Between heuristic and generic detections, it is becoming increasingly frequent for at least one AV vendor to identify any new virus as soon as it is released.

41.4.4 Intrusion Detection and Prevention.   As more complex viruses appear at an increasingly prodigious pace, scanning programs solely for signatures has become less effective at finding viruses. Virus authors use encryption or obfuscation techniques, or release a large number of individual variants in the hopes that the AV scanner will not find them. Today's operating systems and legitimate programs have bloated to millions of lines of code, so that finding a virus signature may be resource intensive. Because viruses and Trojans are malicious and may steal valuable data or damage systems, it is not a good strategy to let them infect and then attempt to clean up the mess. A better strategy is to try to find malware before it has had a chance to infect a system and to prevent it from doing harm.

The use of a cyclical redundancy check (CRC), or checksums, was added to some security products, including AV suites, to aid in the detection and prevention of virus infections. This method tracks unauthorized file and system changes, as when a virus or a hacker enters and alters a system. To track those changes, a fingerprint of each executable program and data file is computed and stored in a database when the AV product is first installed. These fingerprints are quite small, usually consisting of less than 100 bytes of information—this is the "sum" or checksum. Because viruses must add or change files on the system in order to infect them, the checksums of the fingerprints are compared with any newer version. If the checksums vary, then the AV scanner runs other routines to investigate further. If the change in the size of the program cannot be attributed to a known virus in the signature files or to a legitimate operation, then a generic disinfection routine is run to see if it can restore the program to its original state.

In the case of intrusion prevention systems, a behavior-based scan is executed on each new file when it is run. If certain suspicious behaviors are observed, a user may be asked whether the behavior should be allowed to continue. If a sequence of behaviors is observed that is sufficiently malicious, the program may be halted entirely. This technique has been found to be remarkably effective in preventing execution of new, unknown viruses, although it shares the same sort of difficulties found with using heuristic scans. Again, as part of a complete security arsenal, it can be a valuable tool. For more information on intrusion detection and intrusion prevention, see Chapter 27 in this *Handbook*.

41.5 CONTENT FILTERING.   In the early days of virus infections, computer security experts often allayed the fears of computer users by telling them that they could never catch a computer virus from e-mail. This assurance was based on the fact that e-mail was almost exclusively composed of ASCII text documents, with no ability to execute program code. At the same time, the skeptics were saying "never say never." The skeptics won. First, there were several waves of macro virus–infected documents sent as file attachments to e-mail. This led to the modified assurance from security experts that no one could ever catch a computer virus from an e-mail message attachment, if the attachment was not opened. Then virus writers started embedding commands that use HTML and the scripting capability of e-mail programs. This led to the further modified assurance from experts that a computer virus could not be caught from unopened e-mail. This assurance in turn proved unwarranted, because e-mail preview capabilities were exploited to trigger malicious code even without user intervention. At one point, merely highlighting a message subject in MS Outlook was enough to execute an attachment, although this default was later changed.

Virus writers also began to exploit the user's e-mail facility by forwarding copies of the virus to entries in the user's e-mail address book. The Melissa virus was the first virus that really leveraged e-mail to spread rapidly. Since the Melissa virus, users have be advised to suspect just about any unsolicited e-mail. Virus writers are always looking for new delivery methods, and they were richly rewarded when e-mail programs began to allow executable code within the e-mail. Although users enjoy the point-and-click convenience of this feature, it is allowing new viruses to proliferate at a rate not seen before.

The Web also has seen an explosion in malicious code distribution, particularly since the advent of "Web 2.0"— social networking and collaboration sites. Through JavaScript and ActiveX controls that exploit vulnerabilities in Internet browsers or media-viewer software, malware and adware can be automatically downloaded and installed on users' machine without their being aware. This is commonly referred to as a drive-by download. Most recently, comments on forum or journal sites frequently try to entice users into going to those sites that contain malicious scripts for drive-by downloads.

Content filtering is an effective way of controlling Web and e-mail threats. It consists of a server-based application that interrogates all incoming and outgoing traffic, according to its configuration and rule sets. Early versions were cumbersome to configure, due to a text-based interface that required all rules to be composed in a laborious text editor. Misconfigurations were commonplace because administrators often were not sure which of the text files was causing a failure.

The new generation of content filters has increased user friendliness, using interactive graphic user interfaces to set and adjust policies. Administrators are able to fine-tune policies so that they meet the specific needs of their organizations. For example, all e-mail containing executable attachments may be blocked, quarantined, or simply deleted. This may be established as a rule, for some users or all users. The policy also may be set to strip macros out of all incoming e-mail, thus preventing any macro viruses from entering the system via this route.

Content filters have been used effectively in preventing infections of e-mail–borne viruses, even before the specific virus signature was even released. For example, when the security officer of one government office heard of the Love Bug virus on the morning news, that person set the content filters to block all e-mail attachments containing the extension ".vbs," thus averting infection of a large network. No user interaction was required, and most users were not aware that the block had been placed. The costs and downtime of a virus attack were prevented.

41.5.1 How Content Filters Work.   These applications work in the same general manner that AV scanners do. They scan all incoming data on specific ports on the server, and they compare the traffic to rules and strings in the database. Because content filters are capable of blocking more than one type of file or program, they have the ability to scan text files, graphics, zipped files, self-extractors, and various executables. At this point many content filters contain AV scanners in the program, so if an e-mail does contain a virus, it can be intercepted and disinfected before it is sent to the recipient.

The standards for formatting e-mail for transmission using standard protocols have long been in place and detail the type of information in every section. It is easy for a program to look for particular information within these sections to determine what is included in the message—attachments, for example. Content filters first begin by disassembling a message to look at its various parts before scanning the message for the items to be allowed or denied into the system. Before sending the message onward, it is reassembled and checked for the conditions specified in the configurations. For example, a condition may state that any attachments be stripped and deleted, that the message body be sent to the recipient, and that an outward e-mail be sent to the sender stating that attachments are not allowed in e-mail.

In terms of computer security, a content filter adds several elements that are beyond the traditional AV scanner. For example, message and attachment content can be scanned for inappropriate material. This might be proprietary company information that employees should not be sending out via e-mail, or it could be offensive material, such as pornography, that should not be coming into the company's e-mail system. Content filtering also can stop the spread of common forms of spam mail, such as chain letters and get-rich-quick schemes.

41.5.2 Efficiency and Efficacy.

Speed of operations is a concern with content-filtering mechanisms, given the large volume of e-mail traffic in some organizations. However, because the operations are all contained within the *server*, the users will not notice any change in performance of their desktop systems; that is, the e-mail processing will be completed before the messages are received by the client systems. When the filters are examining large attachments, waiting mail will queue up, and delivery of mail may suffer for a period. Putting a limit on the size of attachments is one method of reducing these lags.

Content filters are also subject to the same failures as traditional AV scanners. New viruses can be missed if the data are not present in the scanning database. Additionally, the configuration of the product and the application of patches and updates are crucial to its successful operation. False positives are also a problem, where a legitimate message inadvertently includes content that triggers a block. It is possible to quarantine questionable messages and have a system administrator follow up with the sender. This can lead to refinement of the filters or to the detection of serious offenses. Before a content-filtering system is deployed, it is important to put in place the response mechanisms, so that abuses of e-mail policy can be addressed appropriately. This may well involve several departments besides security, including legal and human resources.

41.6 ANTIVIRUS DEPLOYMENT.

AV scanners can be installed on the desktop or on servers. Each strategy has its advantages and disadvantages. For example, if the system is server based, viruses on USB thumb drives, floppy disks, DVDs, and CDs on the desktop will not be scanned. The consensus of most experts, however, is to use both. With the advances in AV products and network management systems, it is entirely possible to install scanners on both the desktop and on servers while still maintaining an acceptable level of control and performance.

41.6.1 Desktops Alone.

If an organization's computer security policy allows unrestricted use of thumb drives, floppies, DVDs, and CDs, it imperative that AV scanners be deployed to the desktop. Unless these drives are locked or disabled, there is no way, other than scanning, to prevent users from accidentally introducing viruses. The preferences of a desktop AV scanner can be set to automatically scan external media.

Updates to desktop AV scanners can now be distributed via a central server. This is particularly effective when new signature files are needed to prevent infection by a newly discovered virus. The updates can be pushed to the desktop, and the users need not be present at the workstation, although the desktop system must be on and connected to the network at the time. If the updates are scheduled after working hours, it is important to verify that systems have updates pushed to them as soon as they log back into the network. Some AV products have management consoles that will allow this to occur automatically, rather than having someone check each system individually.

In order to prevent unauthorized AV-setup changes, it is possible to prevent the users from changing the configuration of their desktop AV scanners. Since that may not be the default installation, it must be checked. Again, with the use of a management console, it is possible to enforce security-software policies remotely.

41.6.2 Server-Based Antivirus. Many companies have sought to bolster the defenses at the perimeter of their network by installing AV products on the server where downloads are frequently stored and traffic is high. A server-based AV scanner can be configured to send alerts to administrators when a suspected virus is detected. Like the desktop-based scanners, the response to a virus detection can be predetermined. Many system administrators set the program to erase all infected files rather than to send them to quarantine. This strategy works to lessen the possibility that a quarantined virus can be "released" by mistake.

41.7 POLICIES AND STRATEGIES. In the battle against viruses, the promulgation of appropriate policies and the implementation of realistic plans of action are equally as important as the installation of an AV scanner. The policies should spell out in detail what actions are allowed or denied, and they should also be specific about the users' responsibilities. The policies and responsibilities should be updated whenever major changes occur in the organization or in the pattern of virus infections.

End user AV awareness training should be high on the list of priorities in every organization. Users are more likely to cooperate in preventing and quarantining infections if they are aware of the types of viruses that may infect the system and of the damage they can cause. A simple security-incident bulletin board in a central location is an easy and effective way to communicate with users. E-mail is probably not an effective method of distributing virus awareness because users become confused between the education effort, actual and legitimate virus alerts, and bogus virus alerts.

The roles and responsibilities of each person within an organization should be clearly defined and communicated to the general populace. For example, the responsibilities of an average user will be different from those of a system administrator, and the responsibilities should be reflected in their roles. An individual user's role may describe the actions required of the user if a virus is detected on a workstation, while the system administrator's role may describe how to handle the report from the user and prepare for disinfection.

Problems and catastrophes will usually occur when they are least expected, so every organization should have an emergency response plan in its policies. The emergency plan should detail the list of persons to be called in an emergency and the priority order in which they should be called.

For every major virus infection event within an organization, care must be taken that a "lessons learned" session be undertaken as soon after the event as possible. No matter how well written a policy may be, it cannot be proven effective until it is put into use. An actual infection will highlight the failures of a policy in action, which should be rectified before the next attack. For more on security policy guidelines see Chapter 4 in this *Handbook*.

For more details of computer security incident response team management, see Chapter 56 in this *Handbook*.

Management's support for such policies is vital. Support is required not only to approve the AV budget and the policies, but also to ensure that everyone abides by the policies. It is highly unlikely that users will follow a policy that upper management routinely flouts.

41.8 CONCLUDING REMARKS.   Both AV technology and malware technology have progressed rapidly over time, and AV technology largely remains in step with malware technology. The success of malware is now primarily due to financial motivation, but a large part of the reason it is such a lucrative business is that people continue to dismiss the threat of malware. However good AV technology gets, it will not make a serious dent in the malware problem unless it is appropriately implemented by organizations and properly employed by users who act responsibly. As AV technology continues to improve and becomes better understood, we hope that it will continue to be used more widely and more wisely.

41.9 FURTHER READING

Antiviral Software Evaluation: www.claws-and-paws.com/virus/faqs/evaluation.html.

Aycock, J. D. *Computer Viruses and Malware*. New York: Springer, 2006.

Grimes, R. A. *Malicious Mobile Code: Virus Protection for Windows*. Sebastopol, CA: O'Reilly, 2001.

IBM Research—Antivirus Research Papers: www.research.ibm.com/antivirus/ SciPapers.htm.

Johnston, J. R. *Technological Turf Wars: A Case Study of the Antivirus Industry*. Philadelphia: Temple University Press, 2008.

Nazario, J. *Defense and Detection Strategies against Internet Worms*. Artech House, 2003.

Skoudis, E., and L. Zeltser *Malware: Fighting Malicious Code*. Prentice Hall, 2003.

Spyware/AdWare/Malware FAQ: www.io.com/~cwagner/spyware/.

Szor, P. *The Art of Computer Virus Research and Defense*. Addison-Wesley, 2005.

Virus Bulletin: www.virusbtn.com/index.

41.10 NOTE

1. WildList Organization: www.wildlist.org/faq.htm.

CHAPTER 42

PROTECTING DIGITAL RIGHTS: TECHNICAL APPROACHES

Robert Guess, Jennifer Hadley, Steven Lovaas, and Diane E. Levine

42.1 INTRODUCTION. Ever since publishing and commerce were introduced to the digital world, the risks to intellectual property and to personal privacy in cyberspace have steadily escalated on comparable but separate paths. These paths have now converged. Unfortunately, many times, antipiracy efforts lead to possible breaches in personal privacy.

Efforts to stem the flow of pirated software worldwide remain mediocre in efficacy; piracy is still proving to be big business in the new millennium. According to the Business Software Alliance (BSA), a 2006 study shows that "thirty-five percent of the packaged software installed on personal computers (PC) worldwide in 2005 was illegal, amounting to $34 billion in global losses due to software piracy."[1] This single-year loss equals 57 percent of the total for years 1995 to 2000 combined. Although the methods the BSA used to make this estimate have been criticized,[2] the problem is nevertheless significant for the software industry. Continuing piracy means lost jobs, wages, tax revenues, and a potential barrier to success for software start-ups around the globe.

At the same time, freedoms inherent in the Internet have made maintaining privacy of personal information a true challenge. Identity theft keeps rising, as more and more companies actively engage in the accumulation of customer data through e-commerce. By paying bills, checking medical insurance accounts, or completing taxes online, people are making their personal information available to be stockpiled, shared, and regurgitated to the point that simply "Googling" one's identity can be a real eye opener. Technologies that aim to prevent piracy have the potential to use this wealth of available personal information in a way that significantly erodes personal privacy. In particular, some of these technologies send personally identifiable information to servers on a routine basis (see, e.g., Section 42.4.2). The idea that a corporation—or a government—could be scanning what a specific person reads, listens to, or views is grounds for concern to civil libertarians.

42.1.1   Digital Rights.   In this environment of rapid change in both piracy and privacy, even the term "digital rights" is ambiguous. When software companies and music producers talk about digital rights, they mean the kinds of rights long protected by copyright, trademark, and patent law. When privacy advocates argue about digital rights, however, they may be talking about a completely different thing: that an individual does not forfeit personal rights, including the right to privacy, merely by turning on a computer. This chapter's primary focus is on technologies designed to protect traditional rights of content producers, but it also enumerates areas where those technologies threaten personal privacy.

42.1.2   Patent, Copyright, and Trademark Laws.   There are differences among the applicable laws and the materials they protect.

Patents give owners exclusive rights to use and license their ideas and materials; patents generally protect nonobvious inventions in mechanical and electrical fields, as well as those that can be embodied in computer software and hardware.

Copyrights give owners the exclusive rights to create derivative works, to reproduce original works, and to display, distribute, and conduct their works. Copyrights apply to original works of authorship including paintings, photographs, drawings, writings, music, videos, computer software, and any other works that are fixed in a tangible medium. Copyrights, their infringement, and remedies are described in the Copyright Act of 1976.

Trademarks give owners the right to restrict the use of distinctive marks in certain contexts. These rights may apply to words, sounds, distinctive colors, symbols, and designs.

For an extensive discussion of intellectual property law, see Chapter 11 in this *Handbook*.

42.1.3   Piracy.   Once thought of as a mere copyright infringement of printed matter or production of a counterfeit audiotape, piracy has grown with technology and has expanded to encompass intellectual property, digital data, DVDs, CDs, VHS, analog and high-definition TV, and streaming media.

There are several types of piracy. End user piracy occurs when end users use a single copy of software to run on several different systems, or when they distribute copies of software to others without permission of the software manufacturer. Reseller piracy occurs when unscrupulous resellers distribute multiple copies of a single software package to multiple customers, preload the same software on multiple systems, or knowingly sell counterfeit software to customers. Internet and bulletin board (BBS) piracy occurs when users download and upload copyrighted materials and use it or make it available for use by others without proper licenses.

To understand why and how piracy occurs and the enormous impact on society worldwide, we need to have a clear understanding of what we mean by the word "piracy." Whenever information is created and published in print, on the Internet, or incorporated into software, that information may be protected by copyright, patent, or trademark law. This principle applies to a broad spectrum of material that includes, for example, the Wright Brothers' specifications for their "Flying Machine"; Microsoft Windows software; the icon Mickey Mouse and all related materials; television shows, plays, movies, and music created and performed live and on recordings. Making unauthorized copies of such material in any medium is referred to as piracy.

In 2000, the Software & Information Industry Association (www.siia.net) found that 91 percent of software for sale on Internet auction sites like Yahoo!, eBay, Excite, and ZDNet is pirated. SIIA initiated action against a total of 1,016 companies during that year. Enforcement efforts have grown more effective recently; in 2006, two major data pirates were given record jail terms and fines. One was given 7 years 3 months in jail and was ordered to pay $5.4 million in restitution for illegally selling over $20 million in copyrighted software via text ads on Google.[3]

42.1.4 Privacy.   As in many aspects of security, end users are now being called on to protect their online (and off-line) identities through diligent monitoring of financial activities and through awareness programs focused on personal rights, laws, and obligations of Internet use. The average Web user today can create and publish a blog or personal video to the Web faster than that same user can apply software patches to a desktop PC. So widespread is this new facility that the law has yet to catch up with the needs and expectations of the users in online society. It is difficult to keep data private when—with a mouse click—it is easy to share personal information with the whole world.

Beyond bad personal habits that reduce privacy, however, a whole new class of applications termed "Digital Rights Management" (DRM) collects more personal information than ever before in an effort to reduce improper use of copyrighted material. DRM products may record and report on an individual's Web-browsing habits, types of files created and accessed by a particular program, number of uses of a particular file or program, source IP address of the user's system, and presence (or absence) of a license for a program. In the name of protecting digital rights for content producers, the consumers of this content are being cataloged and tracked in a way that the framers of copyright laws would have been hard-pressed to imagine.

For extensive coverage of privacy issues on the Internet, see Chapter 69 in this *Handbook*.

For a glossary of terminology used in discussing digital rights management, see Section 42.8.

42.2 SOFTWARE-BASED ANTIPIRACY TECHNIQUES.   A variety of software-based technical approaches are used to prevent inappropriate use of copyrighted and otherwise protected material in an organization's networks and on the public Internet. Current methods include ensuring proper configuration of operating systems, monitoring of installed software, encryption of content, and insertion of some sort of key or identifier in the digital product itself.

42.2.1   Organizational Policy.   Controls in free-standing commercial applications represent only one of the technical means to protect digital content. Existing system controls are also useful in this regard. Operating system access controls can specify who can access particular content, while encryption supported by the OS and other applications can limit access to users who possess the appropriate key. More generally, organizational policy should specify good practices in configuring operating systems and applications in order to help protect content. Such policy includes:

- Allow users to install only software that is necessary.
- Encrypt information that should not be publicly viewable.
- Install software with the lowest possible privilege consistent with the ability to do its job.
- Disable active content (Java, JavaScript, ActiveX, cookies, etc.) wherever feasible.
- Use network operating system access controls to limit access to shared, copyrighted media to members of the organization for whom licenses are purchased.

42.2.2   Software Usage Counters.   Software metering has been popular for several years. Special software monitors system usage and inventories the software on the system or network. This type of software also can be used to block or limit the use of specific software, such as browsers and games. In addition to fighting piracy, it can reduce the load on IT personnel by reducing complications due to use of unauthorized software.

42.2.2.1   *Controlling Concurrent Installations.*   Software metering products can monitor concurrent installations even on networks used by people in different geographic areas who have different requirements and different software installed. The metering software permits an administrator to maintain a live and updated inventory of the software installed at different locations on the network. The logs show where installation has taken place, when the licenses expire, and when updates are necessary. Alerts can be set to notify system administrators when a license is about to expire or when an update has been accomplished.

42.2.2.2   *Controlling Concurrent Usage.*   Software metering allows network administrators to identify and resolve cases of illegal installation of unauthorized copies of authorized software and also to catch people who install unauthorized software on the organization's computers. Metering software also allows a company to report and analyze logon and logout times, track software usage, and meter software licenses to keep those in the company legal. In addition to avoiding legal entanglements, monitoring can reduce the demand on system resources, network bandwidth, and technical support staff.

42.2.2.3   *Examples and Implementation.*   Microsoft announced in 2000 that to combat piracy, new releases of the Office 2000 program would include a counting feature making the programs malfunction if the owner had not registered the software after launching it 50 times.[4] Prior to this announcement, Microsoft published antipiracy literature and provided a great deal of consumer education regarding the effects of software piracy on society; it established, as well, a piracy hotline (1-800-RU-LEGIT). Novell (1-800-PIRATES), Adobe, and Xerox are other companies that have vigorous antipiracy programs in place, although they have not yet announced that they are building metering into their products.

Metering software requires a bona fide license in order for it to be implemented. Typically, companies establish CD-ROM keys that are printed on legitimate copies of their product installation discs or jewel cases. The keys include checksums or message authentication codes that can be checked by the installation routines. The algorithms for the checksums are intended to cause difficulty for people trying to create counterfeit keys. The security of such measures depends on the cryptographic strength of the validation keys.

Software counters for controlling concurrent usage need to store information securely so that each load operation increments a counter and each unload operation decrements it. However, the security problem is to store this information in such a way that unauthorized people cannot modify it easily. Encrypting the data in a complex sequence of operations can stop most abuses of the system by making the effort required for circumventing the mechanisms more costly than buying a license.

More recently, copies of the Windows Vista operating system must be registered (Microsoft calls this "activating" a copy) soon after installation, or they will go into "reduced functionality mode," in which basic functions are available for only an hour of operation before logging on again.[5] For single-copy home use, Vista relies on a license key encoded on the installation medium. For enterprise deployments of Vista, an organization needs to run key servers to allow the registration to occur.[6]

42.3 HARDWARE-BASED ANTIPIRACY TECHNIQUES.   Working on the theory that software is prone to misconfiguration and compromise, antipiracy groups and researchers have experimented with a variety of hardware-based approaches to preventing inappropriate use of protected content. These techniques include dongles and specialized readers attached to the reading hardware, evanescent media designed for viewing or playing only a limited number of times, and software keys incorporated into the media and the reading hardware.

42.3.1 Dongles.   Dongles are hardware lock devices or modules that connect to a computer and communicate with software running on the computer. Without a dongle in place, the external device or regulated software does not work fully, or at all.

Initially, dongles controlled printing. With a dongle installed on the computer, no one could print data from the computer without authorization. However, there is now a necessity for protecting all types of devices. Now dongles are used to protect scanners; external drives (e.g., ZIP drives); CD-ROMs and rewritable CD-ROMs; DVDs and DVD-Rs; VHS recorders; Playstation, Nintendo, and Sega video gaming systems; and even personal digital assistants (PDAs).

The most common type of dongle provides a pass-through port to connect a device cable. Generally a dongle incorporates some type of algorithmic encryption in its onboard microelectronic circuitry. The sophistication of the encryption varies depending on the manufacturer and the device. Many dongles provide additional onboard nonvolatile memory for the software to access. Some models even have real-time checks that keep track of date and time information, including when an application's license (temporary or leased) is set to expire.

Dongles provide some definite advantages:

- Because a dongle is an external device, it is fairly simple to install and uninstall. Early dongles used serial or parallel ports, but USB has become the norm in recent years. In most cases, since manufacturers support their devices, an ordinary user can install and use a dongle without help from an IT department.

- Dongles also require registration, which provides adequate control over the use of the dongle and thus provides legitimacy to both the device and the users. Registration (dependent on the contract in place) may provide support for both the software and the hardware.

- Dongles that support encryption provide an extra layer of protection by making transmitted data indecipherable until it reaches its destination, unless the hardware is in place.

There are also disadvantages to using dongles:

- Consumers resist the requirement for installation, maintenance, and additional cost. Most large corporations do not use dongles for their products.

- Dongles can be lost or stolen, and they also may fail.

- Sometimes a dongle will work well with a slow computer but cause errors when installed on a faster computer.

- Since not every manufacturer automatically replaces lost or stolen dongles without charge, there may be additional costs involved in getting replacements.

- Dongles can present a serious risk-management problem for critical applications where delays in obtaining replacements or registering them may be unacceptable.

- As with any device, there can be a serious problem if the dongle manufacturer ceases to support the model of dongle a company has installed or if the manufacturer goes out of business entirely.

- Laws regarding encryption usage differ in various countries. Specialized dongles that may be legal to use in the United States may be illegal in another country.

42.3.2   Specialized Readers.   One of the impediments to illegal copying used to be the difficulty and cost of obtaining specialized hardware and software for reading and copying proprietary materials with fidelity. However, today such copying equipment is inexpensive and easy to find. In addition, the media for distributing illegal copies are less expensive than ever.

42.3.2.1   Audio.   According to the Recording Industry Association of America (RIAA), the global audio industry loses in excess of $4 billion every year to piracy worldwide.[7] RIAA says that $1 million a day, in just physical product, is lost in the United States alone. The loss of ancillary revenues drives the figures higher. But the RIAA claims that these figures are low, since it estimates that in some countries up to 98 percent of the music in use comes from illegal copies.

As part of an industry-wide, organized approach to highlighting and reducing the music piracy problem, the RIAA has taken a very active role in pursuing legal action against suspected pirates. Through the 1990s and continuing into the current decade, the biggest problem with audio piracy was illegally copied CDs. In 1998, for example, the RIAA confiscated 23,858 illegal CDs in the first half of the year. In that same year,

Operation Copycat—a joint investigation by RIAA, the Motion Picture Association of America (MPAA), and the New York Police Department—saw the arrest of 43 CD pirates and the shutdown of 15 illegal manufacturing locations. Many of the CDs seized in these types of operations apparently came from Asia and Eastern Europe, financed by organized crime operations with ties to drugs and prostitution.[8] By 2002, even corner convenience stores were contributing to the problem, providing coin-operated CD copying machines akin to photocopiers, along with the familiar posted warning transferring liability to the user.[9] Given the enormous profits involved, the problem has been simply too large and widespread for law enforcement to control. In 2005, the RIAA seized approximately 5 million illegal CDs.[10]

More recently, the RIAA has focused on the problem of music files illegally shared across the Internet. Using free software, sometimes already bundled into commercial operating systems, anyone can download music tracks and burn CDs. The MP3 music file format has become a ubiquitous way to share music with others. The RIAA originally protested against MP3 players, but the phenomenal success of personal digital music players, particularly the Apple iPod, has rendered such efforts futile. Some musicians and independent record labels have adopted the MP3 format to promote their records, showing that the technology itself has no inherent ties to piracy. These musicians and recording studios claim that they are happy with consumers downloading the music, and they are at odds with the RIAA.

Some musical groups have even experimented with severing ties with the traditional music industry altogether, using Web sites and social networking services to advertise and distribute digital music files directly to their listeners.[11] As more musicians begin to use the Internet either in addition to or in lieu of traditional distribution models, the very model of music distribution is in flux.

Meanwhile, the music industry continues to face serious financial loss due to illegal downloading. The industry, through the RIAA, has been pursuing legal remedies. Some major lawsuits have achieved significant press coverage and have been instrumental in enforcing or changing existing laws or in helping develop new laws. For instance, deliberate copyright violations resulted in an award of $50 million in statutory damages and $3.4 million in legal fees to Universal Studios in a suit against the MyMP3.com music service. MyMP3 created a database of over 80,000 albums, which, when combined with the MyMP3 software, let users access and store music digitally, without paying a fee.

Perhaps the most recognizable name in the music field in regard to piracy at one time was Napster, a site that enabled individuals to share tracks of music via the Internet. The site provided free downloadable software for downloading and playing MP3 files. Essentially, Napster software turned a user's PC into part of a distributed server network that published available music files. It did not take long for the site to acquire a user group of millions of people who after "sampling" the music might then go to a store and buy the entire CD.

However, since the Napster site did not limit the length of the download, many users simply downloaded the entire track. Most never bought the commercial version of the music. Adding to successful piracy attempts was the development and ready availability of rewritable CD drives. More and more Napster users decided to download the music tracks they wanted and then burn their own CDs without ever purchasing the CDs made by the recording artists and music companies.

Creating a stir in the industry and ultimately a landmark judicial case, Napster was forced to radically alter operations in March 2000 after protracted court proceedings. Upon the verdict, Jack Valenti, president and chief executive officer of MPAA, commented that the consumer would benefit most from the court's decision because "You cannot take for free what belongs to someone else."[12] But the subject of Napster and audio piracy remains highly controversial. Although some people argued that little-known artists received exposure that they may never have gotten without the free file-sharing service, others, especially large music companies and recording artists, argue that they were being denied the royalties they deserve.

Napster attempted to re-create itself as a pay-for-subscription music download service but found record labels unwilling to work with it. In 2002, Napster folded; the name was eventually purchased by Roxio, Inc. to rebrand its own subscription service. In the meantime, other peer-to-peer (P2P) file-sharing protocols and applications appeared to fill the void left by Napster. By the time the iTunes Music Store emerged as a powerful contender with music company backing and with copyright protection, the world of free file sharing was reinvigorated by names such as Gnutella, FastTrack, Grokster, Limewire, and Kazaa.

Over the last few years, the music industry has identified universities as fertile ground for pursuing illegal downloading activities. In 2007, the RIAA launched a new round of attempts to bring music pirates to justice, sending letters offering to settle with students identified as probably sharing copyrighted files, in advance of any trial.[13] The RIAA's tactics have been raising hackles in the higher education community, with opponents criticizing the letters as bordering on extortion. Some universities are refusing to forward the letters to students; one university agreed to forward the letters, but promised to bill the RIAA $11 for every letter to pay for its staff time.[14]

42.3.2.2 Video. On the video side, Scour, Inc., provided free downloads of digital movies as well as software allowing users to share the downloaded files among themselves without the use of a central server. With an easy-to-use interface and quick response time, Scour.com became quite popular in a short period of time. Launched in 1997, with a Web search feature added in 1998 and a subsequent P2P tool, Scour eventually attracted negative attention from the movie and music industries. In July 2000, MPAA, RIAA, and the National Music Publishers Association (NMPA) sued Scour, accusing it of large-scale theft of copyrighted material and of trafficking in stolen works. By November 2000, the company was out of business.[15]

This case did not stop the counterfeiting of video media. Despite increasingly steep fines, judicial rulings, and even raids by various law enforcement agencies, counterfeit video is readily available. Along Fifth Avenue in New York City, for $5 to $10 anyone can buy the latest films and DVDs; in markets in Hong Kong, Southeast Asia, and India, the copies are even cheaper. It is true that some of the copies available may have been "legally produced," but it is more than likely that the counterfeit or bootleg copies were made illegally from a master copy that was either borrowed or stolen.

Advances in consumer electronics help the trend, as many PCs now come with a recordable/rewritable DVD player as a standard component. Arguments about legality of time-shifting and space-shifting that once defended the practice of making personal mixes on audiocassette have now moved to the realm of digital video.

42.3.2.3 Television (Analog). Broadcast television has been one of the most successful technologies in history, and financial interests are still huge, despite the growth of cable and satellite services. In January 2000, major television companies, the National Football League, and the National Basketball League all filed complaints against iCraveTV, a Canadian company that had been in existence for only a year.

According to the complaints, iCraveTV was illegally using broadcast television signals without authorization or payment and streaming the signals to the iCrave Internet site for viewing free of charge. Although this practice apparently did not violate Canadian copyright laws at the time, U.S. judges ruled in February 2000 that the unauthorized transmissions of broadcast signals into the United States via the Internet were a direct violation of U.S. copyright law, and iCraveTV was ordered to stop the practice. Shortly after iCraveTV agreed to an out-of-court settlement, the Web site was shut down and iCraveTV went out of business.[16]

Hacking cable decoders is another technique for obtaining services without paying for them. Although it is not illegal to buy, install, or modify equipment for converting encoded cable TV signals from pay-per-view or other commercial suppliers, it is illegal to use such set-top decoders to obtain services without paying for them.

In the United States, Congress has mandated that after February 17th 2008 all TV stations must transmit in digital format (DTV) only.

42.3.2.4 Television (HDTV).
The first television image was created in 1884 when Paul Nipkow created a mechanical scanning disk. With only 18 lines of resolution, the picture was poor. Current National Television System Committee (NTSC) standard TV transmissions are done with bandwidth that does not exceed 6 MHz. The current analog system broadcasts 30 frames per second and 525 lines per frame.

High-definition television (HDTV) is a digital television system that offers twice the horizontal and vertical resolution of the current TV system. HDTV has the ability to deliver a video composed of approximately 1,125 lines per frames and 60 frames per second. Viewers then see a picture quality close to that of 35mm film. Obviously, transmitting images containing that large amount of audio and video information requires wide bandwidth, actually about 18 MHz. Such bandwidth would permit the transmission of 1,050 lines of 600 pixels per line. However, the Federal Communications Commission (FCC) decided to limit HDTV to a 6-MHz maximum bandwidth. In order to meet that requirement, MPEG compression would be used.

MPEG compression applies algorithms to pixel groups and records information that changes within a frame, rather than all of the information in all of the frames. Audio is synchronized to the video. Using MPEG saves storage space and transmission requirements while retaining high image and sound quality. According to the Advanced Television Committee Standard (ASTC), the FCC will require that audio and video compression as well as the transmission of HDTV terrestrial signals follow this standard.

As with all other transmissions and media, there are serious concerns about piracy of HDTV transmissions and programs. At the present time, even though many TV transmissions are scrambled in order to thwart reception, it is fairly simple, although illegal, to purchase a descrambler and unscramble the transmissions. It is, however, legal for home viewers to record programs for their own personal use.

The HDTV market space has been evolving, and consumer demand for HD-capable devices has exploded over the past several years. Attempts by U.S. television producers to protect themselves and their content using a variety of scrambling and encryption schemes, including content scrambling systems (CSSs), have been made difficult by the frequent changes in hardware and signal formatting that have accompanied this rapid market expansion.

Encrypting terrestrial broadcast television programming would secure the transmissions, but according to the Home Recording Rights Coalition (HRRC), such encryption will threaten established home recording rights. The HRRC contends that Section 1202

(k) of the Digital Millennium Copyright Act provides a carefully balanced approach to analog home recording rights and stipulates that mandated technology may not be applied to interfere with consumer recording of free, over-the-air terrestrial broadcasts.

Furthermore, the HRRC contends that encrypting the free television broadcast content will create very little incentive for consumers to switch from regular analog to digital television. Instead of thwarting digital pirates, the HRRC contends that strong encryption will impose unfair and even illegal restrictions on consumers.

42.3.2.5 *Consumer Acceptance of Specialized Readers.*

Illegal sharing of copyrighted content is common across the Internet. When the Software Publishing Association (SPA) was first formed, the group, together with law enforcement agencies, raided the physical premises of companies believed to be using pirated software. As a result of finding quantities of the pirated software, SPA won many legal actions and related settlements.

Some people see encryption as a challenge and work at breaking the algorithms so they can pirate the data—digital, video, or audio. In addition, the lack of standardization of laws throughout industries and countries has led to controversy and ongoing piracy.

Although average consumers do not think of themselves as intellectual property pirates, many otherwise honest citizens do get and use illegal programs, applications, games, audio tracks, CDs, DVDs VHS, and television signals. This situation might be attributed to a lack of ethical education, but many people like to save money and simply do not believe they will be caught and punished for such pilfering. A 2001 study by the Pew Internet & American Life Project, based on phone interviews with 4,205 adults 18 and over, some 2,299 of whom were Internet users, suggested that around 30 million U.S. residents had downloaded music from the Internet.[17] At that time, the phrase "had downloaded music from the Internet" was basically equivalent to "had *illegally* downloaded music from the Internet," since legal means of doing so had yet to evolve.

Since that report, Apple's 2001 announcement of its iTunes and iPod products, and the 2003 launch of the iTunes Music Store, began a movement to provide consumer-friendly ways of downloading music that also give compensation to copyright owners. iTunes uses device authentication and proprietary encoding formats to limit redistribution of downloaded songs and videos. Despite—or perhaps because of—Apple's attempts to comply with copyright laws, it is clear that Apple filled a perceived need in the market, as it has generated both a host of competitors and substantial sales. Consumers downloaded the first million songs from the iTunes Store in five days, and the overall market for digital music has grown to at least $790 million per year. At $0.99 per song, downloads from the iTunes Music Store passed the $1 billion mark on January 23, 2006.[18]

42.3.3 Evanescent Media.

There are many interpretations of the term "evanescent media." The broad interpretation includes digital imaging, optics, multimedia and other electronic art, and data that are short-lived or transitory. When such media are original, creative works, society has an interest in protecting them against piracy.

Since most evanescent media involve some visual aspects as well as text, antipiracy techniques now being used or considered for other types of data may be applicable. Such techniques include previously discussed dongles, software keys, watermarks, encryption, and digital rights management. Part of the problem in electing and implementing a solution is the lack of existing standards that specifically deal with this new area of art and science.

42.3.4 Software Keys.   Software keys of various kinds are used to secure data and equipment. A software key is generally a string of numbers that is used for identification purposes, either to allow access to the use of equipment or to permit authorized printing, processing, or copying of data. As described earlier in the discussion of dongles, most anticopying hardware devices are accompanied by software that works in tandem with the hardware. A software key activates or deactivates the hardware lock. When the software is working perfectly, there are generally no difficulties. However, all software can malfunction, and when that happens, there can be serious problems in getting equipment to work. Additional problems occur when the computer containing the software key malfunctions, and the software key cannot be made to work on a replacement machine.

42.3.4.1 Videocassettes versus Copy Machines.   Watermarking is one of the techniques being seriously considered for protecting videocassettes and DVDs. In 1995, the ASTC formed a Copyright Protection Technical Working Group, which spun off a special Watermarking and Embedded Data Encoding subgroup. The group has broad representation including representatives from the PC market, the Macintosh market, the MPAA, the Consumer Electronics Manufacturers Association (CEMA) and related manufacturers, technicians, and users. Their task is to look for technologies and services that might use hidden data clues as a means of inhibiting or barring digital piracy. Using a hidden watermark that can be embedded in the content would then prevent machines from making copies or would alert the operator that the videocassette is marked and that unauthorized copies would be considered pirated.

42.3.4.2 DVD Area Encoding.   Digital video requires very large storage space—too large for a single CD to hold. However, by applying compression techniques, the digital video can be compressed to fit into the digital videodisc's maximum capacity of 17 gigabytes. Two different types of compression are used for encoding audio and video content for DVD: constant bit rate (CBR) and variable bit rate (VBR) compression.

   In order to prevent piracy of the content of the DVD, many companies are turning to encryption. The compressed data are encapsulated through a mathematical algorithm that can be decrypted only through the use of a decryption key.

42.3.4.3 Implementation.   For shorter programs, CBR is ideal. Based on MPEG-2 encoding, CBR compresses each frame of audio and video by a user-selected amount. This degree of compression is then applied to the entire program. Using VBR, it is possible to create a database of video content based on the amount of change in each frame or scene. This is particularly useful in programs with a long format. To construct the database, the encoding software does several analytical passes of the master footage and then makes a final digitizing pass. From the created database, the computer can encode the video with a variable data rate allowing a higher bit rate for scenes with pans, zooms, and fast motion and giving scenes with little or no motion low data rates. By greatly compressing the areas of lower detail, areas of higher details can be allocated more space and use less compression.

42.3.4.4 Watermarks.   Watermarking involves embedding one set of data inside a larger set of data. The embedded set of data identifies the origins or ownership of a specific work, just as a watermark does on paper.

Using digital watermarks can help copyright owners track the use of anything digital, including music, movies, photographs, and clip art. Digital watermarking is widely used for protecting images. For instance, photographers often post low-resolution (low-res) versions of their photos on public Web sites and use visible digital watermarks to clearly label the low-res images as copyrighted. Upon payment of the appropriate fee, the customer receives the high-resolution version of the photo, presumably with at least any visible watermarks removed. The use of invisible watermarks to prevent undetected sharing after purchase of digital content is more controversial and more prone to questions about reliability of detection; for instance, how many false positives and false negatives will occur? Additionally, there is the question of survivability of the mark itself as it is run through various transformations.

The music industry flirted with digital watermarking to protect music files beginning in 1998 with the formation of the Secure Digital Media Initiative (SDMI), a consortium of technology, security, and music organizations. The SDMI developed several watermarking schemes, and in 2000, it offered a reward to anyone who could crack the code and remove the watermark from a song protected by SDMI's technologies. The Electronic Frontier Foundation asked the Internet community to boycott the contest, stressing that the use of DMAT (Digital Music Access Technology) would mean that manufacturers and users would be forced to adopt the DMAT format in equipment and would create additional costs for manufacturers and consumers. A team of researchers, led by Princeton professor Ed Felten, was able to remove the invisible watermarks. When Felten attempted to publish the results of his process, attorneys for SDMI threatened to sue him under the Digital Millennium Copyright Act (DMCA). SDMI never filed suit, but Felten himself sued for a declaratory judgment to clarify the matter. Felten's suit was dismissed by a federal judge, but not before the government and the RIAA agreed that researchers should not be punished under the DMCA for testing technologies to protect copyright.[19] The SDMI has been inactive since 2001.[20]

42.3.4.5 *Resistance to Reverse Engineering.*

42.3.4.5 Resistance to Reverse Engineering. Reverse engineering allows a programmer to work backward from the finished program or product. Encryption keys can be extracted by reverse engineering playback software. Reverse engineering can circumvent most antipiracy solutions. As a result, manufacturers of antipiracy software and hardware are strongly opposed to permitting reverse engineering. The DMCA does allow reverse engineering, but the provisions of DMCA were not intended to enable the circumvention of technical protection measures (TMPs) in order to gain unauthorized access to or to make unauthorized copies of copyrighted works.

42.3.4.6 Published Attacks. The most notable attack on a software key took place when a licensee of CSS neglected to encrypt a decryption key. Obtaining a key by reverse engineering the XingDVD from Xing Technologies, the hackers were then able to guess many other keys. This left the hackers with a collection of decryption keys; even if the XingDVD key was removed, they could still copy DVDs by using the other keys. Using the results of this compromise, a group of people including the Norwegian teenager Jon Lech Johansen developed a program called DeCSS to decrypt CSS-encrypted DVDs and play them on Linux machines.

A variety of groups, including the DVD CCA, sued Johansen for publishing tools to subvert copyright protection. Johansen was acquitted twice in Norwegian courts. As of 2007, all remaining lawsuits against him have been dropped,[21] and a number of programs like DeCSS are freely available across the Internet.

42.4   DIGITAL RIGHTS MANAGEMENT.   Recognizing that piracy is a huge moral and financial problem, software developers have adopted and modified another type of system that can be applied to print, audio, video, and streaming media. Called Digital Rights Management (DRM), the system was originally devised to protect proprietary information and military information. The idea behind the system is to protect all types of intellectual digital content from anyone who would take it without the consent of the developer(s) or owners. Major companies like Microsoft, Adobe, and IBM are developing and marketing DRM systems, and dozens of smaller companies are springing up.

42.4.1   Purpose.   The purpose of DRM is to protect all digital content that originators or owners want protected. DRM permits distributors of electronic content to control viewing access to that content. The content can be text, print, music, or images. Basically, DRM systems use a form of customized encryption. When an end user purchases viewing, listening, or printing rights, an individual "key" is provided. The system works on rules, meaning that although a key is provided, it generally comes with limitations regarding the copying, printing, and redistribution.

Unfortunately, there is no agreement on a DRM solution. Lack of standards is hampering businesses from moving forward with online business initiatives. Because there are so many companies promoting their own incompatible forms of DRM, customers will have to download megabytes of code for each version. Maintaining, upgrading, and managing all of those different versions are major headaches for customers. There does not appear to be a simple solution; rather than being a technology issue, it is really a matter of business and politics.

42.4.2   Application.   Typically, when users become prospective owners of digital rights, they download a content file. The DRM software does an identity check of users, contacts a financial clearinghouse to arrange for the payment to be made, and then decrypts the requested file and assigns users a key. The key is used for future access to the content.

Because the system works on rules, it is possible to impose restrictions. One user might pay just to view material, while another user might want to have printing privileges. A third user might want to download the content to his or her own machine, and, finally, a fourth user might want to have viewing privileges for a specified time. The four different authorized users would thus use the same content, and each would pay according to a rate scale established by the content distributor. Throughout all of the transactions, each user would need a mechanism that allows secure transmissions and identifies that user and the associated level of access privileges.

Although this approach to publishing may sound fairly simple, it is really quite complex. In addition to arranging for different users to access material according to the set rules and to pay according to a rate schedule, it is also necessary for content distributors to handle the back end of the application. Everyone involved in the creation, production, and distribution of the content has to be paid fairly for the use of the content.

Payment is especially important as more and more content providers digitize materials that they can show or print on demand. Many users will read books online, but some physical printing on paper will continue. However, publishers will be able to print precisely those volumes that are requested. This approach will provide customized printing (e.g., large-print editions) as well as saving paper and physical warehouse storage space.

42.4.3 Examples.   Several different types of DRM systems exist. Experts agree that the best DRM systems combine both hardware and software access mechanisms. With the advent of the eBook, the digital pad, PDA modems, Internet access devices, and increasingly smaller laptop computers, tying access rights directly to storage media gives publishers and distributors control of where the content is being used as well as by whom.

With the passage of the Electronic Signatures in Global and National Commerce Act, referred to as the E-Sign Bill and the increasing use of digital signatures, original documents (e.g., legal, medical, or financial) will be stored digitally. President Clinton signed the E-Sign Bill on June 30, 2000, in Philadelphia's Congress Hall using a ceremonial pen and a digital smart card. The bill went into effect on October 1, 2000. The E-Sign Bill gives an online signature (a John Hancock) the same legal status as a signature etched on paper and makes the digital document the original. Any printout will be considered a copy so the ability to view documents and videos (e.g., living wills) digitally will actually give the viewer access to the original. Eventually, records for medical treatment and documents for trials may be totally digital and may require submission and viewing digitally. When this becomes the norm rather than the exception, strict adherence to DRM in order to maintain privacy, as well as to provide restitution, will be paramount. In addition, such content-protection schemes will prevent unauthorized modifications of the digital data that would otherwise contribute to fraud.

For example, IBM has released antipiracy technology called the Electronic Media Management System that allows for downloading music tracks but puts controls on how many copies can be made or allows for a copy length limitation to be inserted. Thus, a minute of music could be downloaded to give a listener a taste, but not a chance to pirate the entire music track. To obtain the entire track, the user would be required to pay a fee.

Microsoft distributes free software that embeds metatags in each audio file. The metatags refer back to a central server in which the business rules are stored. This approach requires that material be tagged as it is created; otherwise, if it is released without the embedded tags, it can be illegally copied.

Major companies like Xerox, Microsoft, IBM, and Adobe got heavily involved producing and using this software in the 1990s, and many smaller firms opened shop. As with other new technology launches, eventually many of the small entrants went out of business or were bought by larger firms. Some of the small companies, such as ContentGuard (www.contentguard.com) and Pay2See (www.pay2see.com), continue to exist independently, as of this writing.

42.5 PRIVACY-ENHANCING TECHNOLOGIES.   Although DRM may seem to be a valid solution for the piracy problem, dissenters feel that DRM and other antipiracy measures give producers and distributors too much control. The rationale is that excessively restrictive rights management may undermine the fair use rights of consumers and academics. Partly as a result of these conflicting viewpoints, many consumers are making increasing use of privacy-enhancing technologies (PET), a broad term for a range of technologies designed to hide the identity and activities of individual users and computers as their traffic traverses the Internet.

42.5.1 Network Proxy.   One broad class of tactics and tools used to enhance privacy is based on the concept of a network proxy. In its most general form, a proxy takes a network connection request from a client and redirects it to the ultimate destination, changing the address headers to make it look like the original request came from the proxy itself. When the destination server responds, the proxy returns the results to the requesting client. Proxies have long been used within organizations, both to protect internal users as they make requests to untrusted networks and to track and sometimes block access to undesirable content. For more details on the use of proxies in Web content filtering and monitoring, see Chapter 31 in this *Handbook*.

More recently, proxies have been employed outside the bounds of corporate networks to allow anonymous connections across the Internet. These so-called anonymizing proxies sometimes use encryption to hide the traffic in transit and so also provide protection from traffic analysis. Anonymizing proxies are a serious threat to organizations that desire (or are required by law) to monitor and block users from accessing certain kinds of information. More advanced versions of this concept use multiple routers to hide the path that a request takes through the public network. As a general class, these are known as mixing networks. One example described as early as 1981 is the Chaum Mix.[22] Recently, a concept known as onion routing has become popular in its incarnation as TOR (The Onion Router), which uses nested layers of traffic encryption as a session travels from one router to the next.[23] See Chapter 70 in this *Handbook* for further information about anonymity on the Internet.

42.5.2 Hidden Operating Systems.   Rather than relying on network technologies, some users are choosing to make their actions on the network private by using hidden operating systems. Two basic approaches are common: the virtual machine and the bootable system.

A virtual machine is a system that runs within another operating system. Long used for cross-platform compatibility and the ability to run multiple systems on a single hardware platform, virtual machines, such as Java Virtual Machine, VirtualPC, and VMware, are also used to hide activity from those who would disapprove of it (system administrators, parents, law enforcement, etc.), since the activities of the virtual machine can be made invisible to the host machine.

The bootable system approach, however, stores an entire operating system on some sort of bootable medium, such as a CD or USB device. If a computer can boot from such media and store downloaded content to a peripheral device rather than the host operating system's hard drive, then no record of the usage will remain when the host is next booted up.[24]

42.6 FUNDAMENTAL PROBLEMS.   A number of experts have pointed out that there are fundamental flaws in all the methods for preventing illegal copying of digital materials as described in this chapter. Bruce Schneier, a respected cryptographer, has repeatedly explained that all digital information must be converted to a cleartext (unencrypted) form before it is displayed or otherwise used. Schneier calls this "the Achilles' heel of all content protection schemes based on encryption."[25] Because the cleartext version has to reside somewhere in volatile or nonvolatile memory for at least some period of time to be usable, it is theoretically possible to obtain a copy of the cleartext version regardless of the complexity of the methods that originally concealed or otherwise limited access to the data. For example, if a DVD movie using complex regional encoding is to be seen on a monitor, at some point the hardware and software that decoded the DVD have to send that data stream to a monitor driver. The decoded data stream is vulnerable to interception. By modifying the low-level routines in the monitor driver, it is possible to divert a copy of the raw data stream to a storage device for unauthorized replay or reconstruction. Similarly, a system may be devised to prevent more than one copy of a document from being printed directly on a printer; however, unless the system prevents screen snapshots, a user can circumvent the restrictions by copying the screen as a bit image and storing that image for later, unauthorized use. Although hardware devices such as dedicated DVD or CD players may successfully interfere with piracy for some time, the problem is exacerbated under the current popular operating systems that have no security kernel and thus allow any processes to access any region of memory without regard to security levels.

42.7   SUMMARY.   Piracy is a rapidly growing societal problem affecting a multitude of people and industries. Although producers may suffer the greatest financial losses, there is a substantial impact on consumers. Pirated copies are generally inferior in quality and are sometimes defective. If anything goes wrong, pirated copies, being illegal, are unsupported. Additionally, producers' financial losses due to pirated copies may push the cost of legitimate copies up. Retailers and distributors also suffer due to the loss of sales to pirates. Illegal copies generally are sold more inexpensively than legitimate copies, so retailers and distributors cannot compete on price.

Creative talent, whether software developers, writers, musicians, artists, or performers, plus all the people who helped create the book, magazine, record, performance, painting, concert, or other media, are cheated out of their royalties by pirates. Frequently, because of the amount of time and effort needed to create the end product, the creators depend on the royalties for their livelihood. In addition, poor quality of stolen concepts can irreparably damage the reputation of the creative talent.

Publishers, record companies, art dealers, and other individuals and companies that invest artistic and technical skill along with money and effort to create an original work also lose revenues when that work is pirated. Because of the expenses already laid out to create the original product, companies frequently have to recoup their losses by raising prices for the consumer.

Due to the sophistication of systems and the increased use of the Internet, piracy has become more widespread and has an even greater financial impact worldwide. Many different types of antipiracy systems and techniques have been developed and implemented in an effort to cut down on the ever-increasing instances of piracy. One drawback to all of the systems is the lack of standards applied to software, audio, video, and other media. One of the most promising antipiracy systems is digital rights management. However, even DRM systems are not yet standardized, thus creating even more confusion regarding which is best and what to use.

The media industry is still working out which DRM solution it likes best, or whether it likes DRM at all. As this book was going to print, Apple's Steve Jobs was announcing that a large portion of EMI's song catalog will be available for DRM-free download from the iTunes Music Store, at a price per song just $0.30 higher than the standard $0.99. Previously downloaded songs, with DRM, will be upgradeable to a DRM-free version for the difference in the two prices.[26] This move echoes Jobs's recent comments encouraging the music industry to move away from DRM. Apple's actions notwithstanding, some consumers and privacy organizations continue fighting what they see as serious threats to individual privacy in nascent DRM efforts. The use of network proxies and hidden operating systems is adding to the difficulty of discovering inappropriate use of content, much less preventing or prosecuting it. As the balance between content producers and consumers works itself out, it seems likely that many more technologies will come and go, and DRM may be the harbinger of things to come or an unfortunate choice on the way to a bold, new business model for the media industry.

42.8 GLOSSARY.   Discussions of piracy and privacy often are riddled with a confusing array of terms and acronyms. Some of the most commonly used terms, organizations, and acronyms are listed in this glossary.

AAC—Advanced Audio Coding. A standardized, lossy compression and encoding scheme for digital audio. Most commonly used format for compressing audio CDs for Apple's iPod and iTunes.

ACATS. Advisory Committee on Advanced Television Service.

Anti-Bootleg Statute (Section 2319A). A U.S. federal statute that criminalizes the unauthorized manufacture, distribution, or trafficking in sound recordings and music videos of "live" musical performances.

ATSC. Advanced Television Systems Committee.

ATV. Advanced Television.

Bootleg recordings. The unauthorized recording of a musical broadcast on radio or television, or at a live concert or performance. These recordings are also known as underground recordings.

BSA—Business Software Alliance. A consortium of major software developers, including IBM, Microsoft, Novell, Apple, Dell, and Sun Microsystems, that is attempting to stem lost revenues from pirated computer software. BSA educates computer users on software copyrights and fights software piracy. Individual members, such as Microsoft and Adobe, have their own antipiracy programs in addition to belonging to the BSA.

CEA. Consumer Electronics Association.

CEMA. Consumer Electronics Manufacturers Association.

CSS—Content Scrambling System. A form of data encryption used to discourage reading media files directly from the disc, without a decryption key. Descrambling the video and audio requires a 5-byte, 40-bit key.

DeCSS—Descrambling Content Scrambling System. A utility developed by Norwegian programmers via reverse engineering and posted on the Web. This utility decrypts CSS and allows individuals to make illegal copies of DVD movies.

DFAST. Dynamic Feedback Arrangement Scrambling Technique.

DMAT. Digital Music Access Technology.

DMCA. The Digital Millennium Copyright Act signed into law October 28, 1998. Designed to implement World Intellectual Property Organization (WIPO) treaties (signed in Geneva in December 1996); the DMCA strengthens the protection of copyrighted materials in digital formats.

DivX. A brand name of products created by DivX, Inc. (formerly DivXNetworks, Inc.), including the DivX Codec. Known for its ability to compress lengthy video segments into small sizes, it has been the center of controversy because of its use in the replication and distribution of copyrighted DVDs. Many newer DVD players are able to play DivX movies.

DRM—Digital Rights Management. Refers to any of several technologies used by publishers or copyright owners to control access to, and usage of, digital data or hardware and to restrictions associated with a specific instance of a digital work or device.

DVD CCA—DVD Copy Control Association. A not-for-profit corporation that owns and licenses CSS. DVD CCA has filed numerous lawsuits against companies and individuals that make pirated copies of films.

EFF—Electronic Frontier Foundation. A nonprofit organization working in the public interest to protect fundamental civil liberties, including privacy where computers and the Internet are concerned. The organization frequently disagrees with the steps that other organizations and corporations want to take to protect copyrighted materials.

EPIC—Electronic Privacy Information Center. A public interest research group established in 1994 to focus public attention on emerging civil liberties issues and to protect privacy, the First Amendment, and constitutional values.

FairPlay. A digital rights management (DRM) technology created by Apple Inc. (formerly known as Apple Computer), built in to the QuickTime multimedia technology, and used by the iPod, iTunes, and the iTunes Store. Every file bought from the iTunes Store with iTunes is encoded with FairPlay. It digitally encrypts AAC audio files and prevents users from playing these files on unauthorized computers.

FAST—Federation Against Software Theft. A group headquartered in Great Britain represents software manufacturers and works with law enforcement agencies in finding and stopping software pirates in Europe.

FCC. Federal Communications Commission.

grpff. A 7-line, 526-character program of Perl code developed by two students at the Massachusetts Institute of Technology. More compact than DeCSS, the program descrambles DVDs but does not contain a decryption key. The code is readily available on the MIT campus via hats, T-shirts, business cards, and bumper stickers.

Hard disk loading. PCs with unlicensed software preinstalled. Use of a single copy of a software program but installed illegally on many machines. The original disks and the documents that should come with the PC are often missing or incomplete.

HDTV—High-Definition Television. Digital television transmissions are mandated in the U.S. to be the standard.

HRRC—Home Recording Rights Coalition. A coalition representing consumers, retailers, and manufacturers of audio and audiovisual recording products and media. The HRRC dedicates itself to keeping products free of government-imposed charges or restraints on the products' distribution or operation.

IFPI—International Federation of the Phonographic Industry. An organization that promotes the interests of the international recording industry worldwide. Its mission is to fight music piracy; promote fair market access and good copyright laws; help develop the legal conditions and the technologies for the recording industry to prosper in the digital era; and promote the value of music.

IIPA—International Intellectual Property Alliance. A private-sector coalition formed in 1984. The organization represents the U.S. copyright–based industries in efforts to improve international protection of copyrighted materials.

MP3. A technology for downloading music files using the MPEG format via the Internet.

MPAA—Motion Picture Association of America. Composed of member companies that produce and distribute legitimate films and videos. This organization serves as the official voice and advocate of the American motion picture industry. MPAA also assists law enforcement in raids and seizure of pirated videocassettes and DVDs.

MPEG—Moving Pictures Experts Group. A generic means of compactly representing digital video and audio signals for consumer distribution. MPEG video syntax provides an efficient way to represent image sequences in the form of more compact coded data.

NMPA—National Music Publishers Association. A trade association that represents 700 U.S. businesses that own, protect, and administer copyrights in musical works.

NTSC. National Television System Committee.

PET—Privacy-Enhancing Technologies. The general term for a variety of new technologies and Internet protocols designed to enhance online privacy; includes anonymizing proxies, mixing networks, and onion routing.

Pirated recordings. Unauthorized duplicates of the sounds of one or more legitimate recordings.

RIAA—Recording Industry Association of America. The group has an antipiracy unit that handles initial examination of product on behalf of the recording industry. Pirates can be turned in by calling RIAA at 1-800-BAD-BEAT.

SAG—Screen Actors Guild. The union for screen actors. Members do not get residuals from pirated films, as they do from authorized copies.

SDMI—Secure Digital Music Initiative. A forum of 200 companies from the electronics, music, telecommunications, and information technology industries and the RIAA. The group was active from 1998 to 2001.

SIIA—Software & Information Industry Association. A trade organization of the software and information content industries representing over 800 high-tech companies that develop and market software and electronic content. The organization provides policies and procedures for dealing with software and Internet use within businesses. SIIA also provides guidelines for telling if software is pirated or counterfeited. The SIIA Anti-Piracy Hotline is 1-800-388-7478.

SPA—Software Publishers Association. This association, a division of SIIA, assists in enforcement in dealing with software piracy and also provides education about software piracy. SPAudit Software is one of the first software audit and inventory tools made available for use by companies (in the 1980s). Improved versions of the software are now available.

Trademark Counterfeiting—Title 18 U.S.C. Section 2320. A federal statute that deals with sound recordings that contain the counterfeit trademark of the legitimate manufacturer or artists.

Trafficking in Counterfeit Labels—Title 18 U.S.C., Section 2318. A federal statute that covers counterfeit labels printed for use on a sound recording.

U.S. Copyright Law (Title 17 U.S.C.). A federal law that protects copyright owners from the unauthorized reproduction or distribution of their work.

WGA—Writers Guild of America. The union for writers of television, video, and film scripts.

WMA—Windows Media Audio. A proprietary compressed audio file format developed by Microsoft Corporation.

42.9 FURTHER READING

Business Software Alliance-USA Homepage. *Anti-Piracy Information*, 2007, www.bsa.org/usa/.

Cohen, Julie E. "DRM and Privacy." *Berkeley Technology Law Journal*, 2003, www.law.berkeley.edu/institutes/bclt/drm/papers/cohen-drmandprivacy-btlj2003.html.

Copyright Act of 1976 (Public Law 94-553); Title 17 U.S.C. Sections 101–120, www4.law.cornell.edu/uscode/html/uscode17/usc_sec_17_00000101—000-.html.

Electronic Freedom Foundation home page: www.eff.org.

Electronic Privacy Information Center (EPIC) home page: www.epic.org.

Gross, T. "The Music Industry, Adapting to a Digital Future: Terry Gross interviews Eliot Van Buskirk." *Fresh Air* podcast, March 13, 2008, www.npr.org/templates/story/story.php?storyId=88145070.

Harte, L. *Introduction to Digital Rights Management (DRM); Identifying, Tracking, Authorizing and Restricting Access to Digital Media*. Fuquay Varina, NC: Althos, 2006.

May, C. *Digital Rights Management: The Problem of Expanding Ownership Rights*. Oxford, UK: Chandos Publishing, 2006.

Recording Industry Association of America: www.riaa.com/default.asp.

Schneier.com: www.schneier.com/index.html.

Zeng, W., H. Yu, and C-Y. Lin, eds. *Multimedia Security Technologies for Digital Rights Management*. New York: Academic Press, 2006.

42.10 NOTES

1. BSA/IDC Global Piracy Study, 2006, www.bsa.org/globalstudy/upload/2005%20Piracy%20Study%20-%20Official%20Version.pdf.

2. J. Schultz, "The Economist Rails on Flawed BSA Piracy Study," May 5, 2005, http://copyfight.corante.com/archives/2005/05/25/the_economist_rails_on_flawed_bsa_piracy_study.php.

3. S. Musil, "Man Gets 7 Years for Software Piracy," CNET News.com, September 10, 2006, http://news.com.com/Man+gets+7+years+for+software+piracy/2100-1014_3-6114012.html (retrieved April 1, 2007).

4. Microsoft, "Microsoft Incorporates New Anti-Piracy Technologies in Windows 2000, Office 2000," www.microsoft.com/Presspass/press/2000/feb00/apfeaturespr.mspx (retrieved March 15, 2008).

5. Microsoft, "The Behavior of Reduced Functionality Mode in Windows Vista," http://support.microsoft.com/kb/925582 (retrieved March 15, 2008).

6. Microsoft, "Microsoft Product Activation," www.microsoft.com/licensing/resources/vol/default.mspx (retrieved March 16, 2008).

7. RIAA, "Anti-Piracy," www.riaa.com/issues/piracy/default.asp (retrieved April 1, 2007).

8. GrayZone Digest, "Worldwide Update," October 1997, www.grayzone.com/1097.htm (retrieved March 15, 2008).

9. P. Mercer, "Copycat CDs in an Instant," BBC News, April 16, 2002, http://news.bbc.co.uk/2/hi/entertainment/1930923.stm (retrieved March 15, 2008).

10. Recording Industry Association of America, "2005 Commercial Piracy Report," http://76.74.24.142/6BE200AF-5DDA-1C2B-D8BA-4174680FCE66.pdf (retrieved March 16, 2008).

11. E. VanBuskirk, "Fans Pay Whatever They Want for Radiohead's Upcoming Album," Underwire Blog from Wired.com, October 1, 2007, http://blog.wired.com/underwire/2007/10/fans-to-determi.html (retrieved March 15, 2008).

12. J. Valenti, Napster Statement, February 12, 2001, www.mpaa.org/Napster_2-12-2001.asp.

13. S. Butler, "RIAA Sends Another Wave of Settlement Letters," Billboard.biz, September 20, 2007, www.billboard.biz/bbbiz/content_display/industry/e3i39f76c017d89e0747eaafd53d458f14b (retrieved March 15, 2008).

14. University of Nebraska—Lincoln, "The Recording Industry and UNL," ASUN Student Government, http://asun.unl.edu/index.php?option=com_content&task=view&id=85&Itemid=78 (retrieved March 15, 2008).

15. S. Musil, "Scour to End File-Swapping Service," CNET News.com, November 14, 2000, http://news.com.com/2100-1023-248631.html (retrieved April 1, 2007).

16. J. Borland, "Broadcasters Win Battle Against iCraveTV.com," CNET News.com, January 28, 2000, http://news.com.com/2100-1033-236255.html (retrieved April 1, 2007).

17. M. Graziano and Lee Rainie, "The Music Downloading Deluge: 37 million American adults and youths have retrieved music files on the Internet," www.pewinternet.org/reports/toc.asp?Report=33.

18. J. Silverstein, "iTunes: 1 Billion Served," http://abcnews.go.com/Technology/story?id=1653881 (retrieved April 1, 2007).

19. C. Cohn, "Security Researchers Drop Scientific Censorship Case," www.eff.org/IP/DMCA/Felten_v_RIAA/20020206_eff_felten_pr.html.

20. www.sdmi.org/whats_new.htm.

21. C. Cohn, "DVD Descrambling Code Not a Trade Secret," http://www.eff.org/IP/Video/DVDCCA_case/20040122_eff_pr.php (retrieved April 1, 2007).

22. D. Chaum, "Untraceable Electronic Mail, Return Addresses, and Digital Pseudonyms," *Communications of the ACM* 24, No. 2 (February 1981); available online at http://freehaven.net/anonbib/cache/chaum-mix.pdf (retrieved April 1, 2007).

23. Tor: Anonymity Online, http://tor.eff.org/.

24. B. Schneier, "Anonym.OS," www.schneier.com/blog/archives/2006/01/anonymos.html (retrieved April 1, 2007).

25. B. Schneier, "The Futility of Digital Copy Prevention," www.schneier.com/crypto-gram-0105.html (retrieved March 15, 2008).

26. American Public Radio, *Marketplace,* April 2, 2007, http://marketplace.publicradio.org/shows/2007/04/02/PM200704024.html.